CIVIL
AIRCRAFT
MARKINGS
2000

Alan J. Wright

D1143531

Ian Allan
PUBLISHING

Contents

This fifty first edition published 2000

ISBN 0 7110 2707 2

Published by Ian Allan Publishing

an imprint of Ian Allan Publishing Ltd,
Terminal House, Shepperton, Surrey TW17 8AS.
Printed by Ian Allan Printing Ltd, Riverdene Business Park, Hersham, Surrey KT12 4RG.

Code: 0003/L2

Front cover: D-ABEK-Boeing 737 of Lufthansa. *Austin J. Brown / Aviation Picture Library*

All photographs by Alan J. Wright unless otherwise indicated.

Introduction

The 'G' prefixed four letter registration system was adopted in 1919 after a short-lived spell of about three months with serial numbers beginning at K-100. Until July 1928 the UK allocations were in the G-Exxx range, but as a result of further International agreements, this series was ended at G-EBZZ, the replacement being G-Axxx. From this point the registrations were issued in a reasonably orderly manner through to G-AZZZ, reached in July 1972. There were two exceptions. To avoid possible confusion with signal codes, the G-AQxx sequence was omitted, while G-AUxx was reserved for Australian use originally. In recent years however, an individual request for a mark in the latter range has been granted by the Authorities.

Although the next logical sequence was started at G-Bxxx, it was not long before the strictly applied rules relating to aircraft registration began to be relaxed. Permission was readily given for personalised marks to be issued incorporating virtually any four-letter combination, while re-registration has also become a common feature, a practice almost unheard of in the past. In this book, where this has taken place at some time, all previous UK civil identities appear in parenthesis after the owner's/operator's name. An example of this is BAe 146-200 G-MANS which originally carried G-CHSR.

Some aircraft have also been allowed to wear military markings without displaying their civil identity. In this case the serial number actually carried is shown in parenthesis after the type's name. For example EE Canberra TT.18 G-BURM flies in RAF colours as WJ680. As an aid to the identification of these machines, a military conversion list is provided.

Other factors caused a sudden acceleration in the number of registrations allocated by the Civil Aviation Authority in the early 1980s. The first surge came with the discovery that it was possible to register plastic bags and other items even less likely to fly, on payment of the standard fee. This erosion of the main register was checked in early 1982 by the issue of a special sequence for such devices commencing at G-FYAA. Powered hang-gliders provided the second glut of allocations as a result of the decision that these types should be officially registered. Although a few of the early examples penetrated the normal in-sequence register, the vast majority were given marks in other special ranges, this time G-MBxx, G-MGxx, G-MJxx, G-MMxx, G-MNxx, G-MTxx, G-MVxx, G-MWxx, G-MYxx and G-MZxx. At first it was common practice for microlights to ignore the requirement to display their official identity. However the vast majority now display their registration somewhere on the structure, the size and position depending on the dimensions of the component to which it is applied.

There was news of a further change in mid-1998 when the CAA announced that with immediate effect microlights would be issued with registrations in the normal sequence alongside aircraft in other classes. In addition, it meant that microlight owners could also apply for an out-of-sequence mark upon payment of the current fee of £170 from April 1999, a low price for those wishing to display their status symbol. These various changes have played their part in exhausting the G-Bxxx range after some 26 years, with G-BZxx coming into use before the end of 1999.

Throughout the UK section of this book, there are many instances where the probable base of the aircraft has been included. This is positioned at the end of the owner/operator details preceded by an oblique stroke. It must of course be borne in mind that changes do take place and that no attempt has been made to record the residents at the many private strips. The base of airline equipment has been given as the company's headquarter's airport, although frequently aircraft are outstationed for long periods.

Non-airworthy and preserved aircraft are shown with a star ★ after the type.

The three-letter codes used by airlines to prefix flight numbers are included for those carriers appearing in the book. Radio frequencies for the larger airfields/airports are also listed.

The air transport scene has changed considerably through the years with many airlines now leasing aircraft as required. It has therefore become increasingly difficult to record all of the frequent changes, especially since the companies often do not finalise their plans for the coming summer season until the early months of the year. However, every effort is made to produce an accurate source of reference, but it must be borne in mind that it is inevitable that discrepancies will occur.

Acknowledgments

Once again thanks are extended to the Registration Department of the Civil Aviation Authority for its assistance and allowing access to its files. As usual the comments and amendments flowing from the indefatigable Wal Gandy have proved of considerable value, while Richard Cawsey, Bob Elliot, Kenny Nimbley and George Pennick also contributed useful facts. The help given by numerous airlines or their information agencies has been much appreciated. Both A. S. Wright and C. P. Wright provided valuable assistance during the update of this edition which enabled the multitude of facts to be assembled to meet the press deadline. AJW

International Civil Aircraft Markings

A2-	Botswana	OB-	Peru
A3-	Tonga	OD-	Lebanon
A4O-	Oman	OE-	Austria
A5-	Bhutan	OH-	Finland
A6-	United Arab Emirates	OK-	Czech Republic
A7-	Qatar	OM-	Slovakia
A9C-	Bahrain	OO-	Belgium
AP-	Pakistan	OY-	Denmark
B-	China/Taiwan/Hong Kong	P-	Korea (North)
C-/CF-	Canada	P2-	Papua New Guinea
C2-	Nauru	P4-	Aruba
C3	Andora	PH-	Netherlands
C5-	Gambia	PJ-	Netherlands Antilles
C6-	Bahamas	PK-	Indonesia and West Irian
C9-	Mozambique	PP-,PT-	Brazil
CC-	Chile	PZ-	Surinam
CN-	Morocco	RA-	Russia
CP-	Bolivia	RDPL-	Laos
CS-	Portugal	RP-	Philippines
CU-	Cuba	S2-	Bangladesh
CX-	Uruguay	S5-	Slovenia
D-	Germany	S7-	Seychelles
D2-	Angola	S9-	São Tomé
D4-	Cape Verde Islands	SE-	Sweden
D6-	Comores Islands	SP-	Poland
DQ-	Fiji	ST-	Sudan
E3-	Eritrea	SU-	Egypt
EC-	Spain	SX-	Greece
EI-	Republic of Ireland	T2-	Tuvalu
EK-	Armenia	T3-	Kiribati
EL-	Liberia	T7-	San Marino
EP-	Iran	T9-	Bosnia-Herzegovina
ER-	Moldova	TC-	Turkey
ES-	Estonia	TF-	Iceland
ET-	Ethiopia	TG-	Guatemala
EW-	Belarus	TI-	Costa Rica
EX-	Kyrgyzstan	TJ-	United Republic of Cameroon
EY-	Tajikistan	TL-	Central African Republic
EZ-	Turkmenistan	TN-	Republic of Congo (Brazzaville)
F-	France, Colonies and Protectorates	TR-	Gabon
G-	United Kingdom	TS-	Tunisia
H4-	Solomon Islands	TT-	Tchad
HA-	Hungary	TU-	Ivory Coast
HB-	Switzerland and Liechtenstein	TY-	Benin
HC-	Ecuador	TZ-	Mali
HH-	Haiti	UK-	Uzbekistan
HI-	Dominican Republic	UN-	Kazakhstan
HK-	Colombia	UR-	Ukraine
HL-	Korea (South)	V2-	Antigua
HP-	Panama	V3-	Belize
HR-	Honduras	V4	St Kitts & Nevis
HS-	Thailand	V5-	Namibia
HV-	The Vatican	V6	Micronesia
HZ-	Saudi Arabia	V7-	Marshall Islands
I-	Italy	V8-	Brunei
J2-	Djibouti	VH-	Australia
J3-	Grenada	VN-	Vietnam
J5-	Guinea Bissau	VP-B	Bermuda
J6-	St Lucia	VP-C	Cayman Islands
J7-	Dominica	VP-F	Falkland Islands
J8-	St Vincent	VP-G	Gibraltar
JA-	Japan	VP-LA	Anguilla
JY-	Jordan	VP-LM	Montserrat
LN-	Norway	VP-LV	Virgin Islands
LV-	Argentina	VQ-T	Turks & Caicos Islands
LX-	Luxembourg	VT-	India
LY-	Lithuania	XA-,XB-,XC-	Mexico
LZ-	Bulgaria	XT-	Burkina Faso
MT-	Mongolia	XU-	Cambodia
N-	United States of America	XY-	Myanmar

YA-	Afghanistan	5U-	Niger
YI-	Iraq	5V-	Togo
YJ-	Vanuatu	5W-	Western Samoa (Polynesia)
YK-	Syria	5X-	Uganda
YL-	Latvia	5Y-	Kenya
YN-	Nicaragua	6O-	Somalia
YR-	Romania	6V-	Senegal
YS-	El Salvador	6Y-	Jamaica
YU-	Yugoslavia	7O-	Yemen
YV-	Venezuela	7P-	Lesotho
Z-	Zimbabwe	7Q-	Malawi
Z3-	Macedonia	7T-	Algeria
ZA-	Albania	8P-	Barbados
ZK-	New Zealand	8Q-	Maldives
ZP-	Paraguay	8R-	Guyana
ZS-	South Africa	9A-	Croatia
3A-	Monaco	9G-	Ghana
3B-	Mauritius	9H-	Malta
3C-	Equatorial Guinea	9J-	Zambia
3D-	Swaziland	9K-	Kuwait
3X-	Guinea	9L-	Sierra Leone
4K-	Azerbaijan	9M-	Malaysia
4L-	Georgia	9N-	Nepal
4R-	Sri Lanka	9Q-	Congo (Democratic Republic)
4X-	Israel	9U-	Burundi
5A-	Libya	9V-	Singapore
5B-	Cyprus	9XR-	Rwanda
5H-	Tanzania	9Y-	Trinidad and Tobago
5N-	Nigeria		
5R-	Malagasy Republic (Madagascar)		
5T-	Mauritania		

Aircraft Type Designations & Abbreviations

(eg PA-28 Piper Type 28)

A.	Beagle, Auster, Airbus	CUAS	Cambridge University Air Squadron
AA-	American Aviation, Grumman American	Cycl	Cyclone
		D.	Druine
AB	Agusta-Bell	DC-	Douglas Commercial
AG	American General	D.H.	de Havilland
AS	Aérospatiale	D.H.A.	de Havilland Australia
A.S.	Airspeed	D.H.C.	de Havilland Canada
A.W.	Armstrong Whitworth	DR.	Jodel (Robin-built)
B.	Blackburn, Bristol, Boeing, Beagle	EE	English Electric
BA	British Airways	EAA	Experimental Aircraft Association
BAC	British Aircraft Corporation	EMB	Embraer
BAe	British Aerospace	EoN	Elliotts of Newbury
BAPC	British Aviation Preservation Council	EP	Edgar Percival
BAT	British Aerial Transport	F.	Fairchild, Fokker
B.K.	British Klemm	F.A.A.	Fleet Air Arm
BN	Britten-Norman	FFA	Flug und Fahrzeugwerke AG
Bo	Bolkow	FH	Fairchild-Hiller
Bu	Bücker	FrAF	French Air Force
CAARP	Co-operative des Ateliers Aer de la Région Parisienne	FRED	Flying Runabout Experimental Design
		Fw	Focke-Wulf
CAC	Commonwealth Aircraft Corporation	G.	Grumman
CAF	Canadian Air Force	GA	Gulfstream American
C.A.S.A.	Construcciones Aeronautics SA	G.A.L.	General Aircraft
CCF	Canadian Car & Foundry Co	G.C.	Globe
CEA	Centre-Est Aeronautique	GECAS	General Electric Capital Aviation Services
C.H.	Chrislea		
CHABA	Cambridge Hot-Air Ballooning Association	GY	Gardan
		H	Helio
CLA	Comper	HM.	Henri Mignet
CP.	Piel	HP.	Handley Page

HPR	Handley Page Reading	RF	Fournier
HR.	Robin	R.N.	Royal Navy
H.S.	Hawker Siddeley	S.	Short, Sikorsky
IHM	International Helicopter Museum	SA, SE, SO	Sud-Aviation, Aérospatiale, Scottish Aviation
III	Iniziative Industriali Italiane		
IL	Ilyushin	SAAB	Svenska Aeroplan Aktieboleg
ILFC	International Lease Finance Corporation	SC	Short
		SCD	Side Cargo Door
IMCO	Intermountain Manufacturing Co	SNCAN	Societe Nationale de Constructions Aeronautiques du Nord
J.	Auster		
JT	John Taylor	SOCATA	Societe de Construction d'Avions de Tourisme et d'Affaires
L.	Lockheed		
L.A.	Luton, Lake	Soc	Society
M.	Miles, Mooney	S.R.	Saunders-Roe, Stinson
MBB	Messerschmitt-Bölkow-Blohm	SS	Special Shape
McD	McDonnell	ST	SOCATA
MDH	McDonnell Douglas Helicopters	SW	Solar Wings
MH	Max Holste	T.	Tipsy
MHCA	Manhole Cover	TB	SOCATA
MJ	Jurca	Tu	Tupolev
M.S.	Morane-Saulnier	UH.	United Helicopters (Hiller)
NA	North American	UK	United Kingdom
NC	Nord	USAF	United States Air Force
NE	North East	USAAC	United States Army Air Corps
P.	Hunting (formerly Percival), Piaggio	USN	United States Navy
PA-	Piper	V.	Vickers-Armstrongs
PC.	Pilatus	V.L.M.	Vlaamse Luchttransportmaatschappij
QAC	Quickie Aircraft Co	V.S.	Vickers-Supermarine
R.	Rockwell	WA	Wassmer
RAF	Rotary Air Force	WAR	War Aircraft Replicas
RAAF	Royal Australian Air Force	WHE	W.H.Ekin
RAFGSA	Royal Air Force Gliding & Soaring Association	W.S.	Westland
		Z.	Zlin
RCAF	Royal Canadian Air Force		

British Civil Aircraft Registrations

Reg.	Type (†False registration)	Owner or Operator	Notes
G-EAGA	Sopwith Dove (replica)	A. Wood/O. Warden	
G-EAOU†	Vickers Vimy (replica)(NX71MY)	Greenco (UK) Ltd	
G-EASD	Avro 504L	AJD Engineering Ltd	
G-EASQ†	Bristol Babe (replica) (BAPC87)★	Bristol Aero Collection (stored)/Kemble	
G-EAVX	Sopwith Pup (B1807)	K. A. M. Baker	
G-EBED†	Vickers 60 Viking (replica) (BAPC114)	Brooklands Museum of Aviation/ Weybridge	
G-EBHX	D.H.53 Humming Bird	The Shuttleworth Collection/O. Warden	
G-EBIA	RAF SE-5A (F904)	The Shuttleworth Collection/O. Warden	
G-EBIB	RAF SE-5A ★	Science Museum/S. Kensington	
G-EBIC	RAF SE-5A (F938) ★	RAF Museum	
G-EBIR	D.H.51	The Shuttleworth Collection/O. Warden	
G-EBJE	Avro 504K (E449) ★	RAF Museum	
G-EBJG	Parnall Pixie III ★	Midland Aircraft Preservation Soc	
G-EBJO	ANEC II ★	The Shuttleworth Collection/O. Warden	
G-EBKY	Sopwith Pup (N6181)	The Shuttleworth Collection/O. Warden	
G-EBLV	D.H.60 Cirrus Moth	British Aerospace PLC/Woodford	
G-EBMB	Hawker Cygnet I ★	RAF Museum	
G-EBNV	English Electric Wren	The Shuttleworth Collection/O. Warden	
G-EBQP	D.H.53 Humming Bird (J7326) ★	Russavia Collection	
G-EBWD	D.H.60X Hermes Moth	The Shuttleworth Collection/O. Warden	
G-EBXU	D.H.60X Moth Seaplane	D. E. Cooper-Maguire	
G-EBZM	Avro 594 Avian IIIA ★	Manchester Museum of Science & Industry	
G-EBZN	D.H.60X Moth	J. Hodgkinson (G-UAAP)	

Other G-E registrations are listed in the Out-of-Sequence section

G-AAAH†	D.H.60G Moth (replica) (BAPC 168) ★	Hilton Hotel/Gatwick	
G-AAAH	D.H.60G Moth ★	Science Museum Jason/S. Kensington	
G-AACA†	Avro 504K (BAPC 177) ★	Brooklands Museum of Aviation/ Weybridge	
G-AACN	H.P.39 Gugnunc ★	Science Museum/Wroughton	
G-AADR	D.H.60GM Moth	H. F. Moffatt	
G-AAEG	D.H.60G Moth	J. Dixon	
G-AAHI	D.H.60G Moth	N. J. W. Reid	
G-AAHY	D.H.60M Moth	D. J. Elliott	
G-AAIN	Parnall Elf II	The Shuttleworth Collection/O. Warden	
G-AALY	D.H.60G Gipsy Moth	K. M. Fresson	
G-AAMX	D.H.60GM Moth ★	Aerospace Museum/Cosford	
G-AAMY	D.H.60GMW Moth	Totalsure Ltd	
G-AANG	Blériot XI	The Shuttleworth Collection/O. Warden	
G-AANH	Deperdussin Monoplane	The Shuttleworth Collection/O. Warden	
G-AANI	Blackburn Monoplane	The Shuttleworth Collection/O. Warden	
G-AANJ	L.V.G.-C VI (7198/18)	The Shuttleworth Collection/O. Warden	
G-AANL	D.H.60M Moth	P. L. Allwork	
G-AANM	Bristol 96A F.2B (D7889) (BAPC166)	Aero Vintage Ltd	
G-AANO	D.H.60GMW Moth ★	A. W. & M. E. Jenkins	
G-AANV	D.H.60G Moth	R. A. Seeley	
G-AAOK	Curtiss Wright Travel Air 12Q	Shipping & Airlines Ltd/Biggin Hill	
G-AAOR	D.H.60G Moth	V. S. E. Norman/Rendcomb	
G-AAPZ	Desoutter I (mod.)	The Shuttleworth Collection/O. Warden	
G-AAUP	Klemm L.25-1A	J. I. Cooper	✓
G-AAWO	D.H.60G Moth	N. J. W. Reid & L. A. Fenwick	
G-AAXK	Klemm L.25-1A ★	C. C. Russell-Vick (stored)	
G-AAYX	Southern Martlet	The Shuttleworth Collection/O. Warden	
G-AAZP	D.H.80A Puss Moth	R. P. Williams	
G-ABAA	Avro 504K ★	Manchester Museum of Science & Industry	
G-ABAG	D.H.60G Moth	The Shuttleworth Collection/O. Warden	
G-ABBB	B.105A Bulldog IIA (K2227) ★	RAF Museum/Hendon	
G-ABDW	D.H.80A Puss Moth (VH-UQB) ★	Museum of Flight/E. Fortune	
G-ABDX	D.H.60G Moth	M. D. Souch	
G-ABEV	D.H.60G Moth	Wessex Aviation & Transport Ltd	

Notes	Reg.	Type	Owner or Operator
	G-ABLM	Cierva C.24 ★	Mosquito Aircraft Museum
	G-ABLS	D.H.80A Puss Moth	R. C. F. Bailey
	G-ABMR	Hart 2 (J9941) ★	RAF Museum
	G-ABNT	Civilian C.A.C.1 Coupe	Shipping & Airlines Ltd/Biggin Hill
	G-ABNX	Redwing 2	J. A. Pothecary (stored)/Shoreham
	G-ABOI	Wheeler Slymph ★	Midland Air Museum/Coventry
	G-ABOX	Sopwith Pup (N5195)	C. M. D. & A. P. St. Cyrien/Middle Wallop
	G-ABSD	D.H.A.60G Moth ★	M. E. Vaisey
	G-ABTC	CLA.7 Swift	P. Channon (stored)
	G-ABUL†	D.H.82A Tiger Moth ★	F.A.A. Museum (G-AOXG)/Yeovilton
	G-ABUS	CLA.7 Swift	R. C. F. Bailey
	G-ABVE	Arrow Active 2	J. D. Penrose
	G-ABWP	Spartan Arrow	R. E. Blain/Barton
	G-ABXL	Granger Archaeopteryx ★	The Shuttleworth Collection/O. Warden
	G-ABZB	D.H.60G-III Moth Major	R. Earl & B. Morris
	G-ACAA	Bristol 96A F.2B (D8084†)	Patina Ltd/Duxford
	G-ACBH	Blackburn B.2 ★	–/West Hanningfield, Essex
	G-ACCB	D.H.83 Fox Moth	E. A. Gautrey
	G-ACDA	D.H.82A Tiger Moth	B. D. Hughes
	G-ACDC	D.H.82A Tiger Moth	Tiger Club Ltd/Headcorn
	G-ACDI	D.H.82A Tiger Moth	J. A. Pothecary/Shoreham
	G-ACDJ	D.H.82A Tiger Moth	P. Henley
	G-ACEJ	D.H.83 Fox Moth	Newbury Aeroplane Co
	G-ACET	D.H.84 Dragon ★	M. D. Souch
	G-ACGT	Avro 594 Avian IIIA ★	Yorkshire Light Aircraft Ltd/Leeds
	G-ACGZ	D.H.60G-III Moth Major	N. H. Lemon
	G-ACIT	D.H.84 Dragon ★	Science Museum/Wroughton
	G-ACLL	D.H.85 Leopard Moth	D. C. M. & V. M. Stiles
	G-ACMA	D.H.85 Leopard Moth	S. J. Filhol/Sherburn
	G-ACMD	D.H.82A Tiger Moth	M. J. Bonnick
	G-ACMN	D.H.85 Leopard Moth	C. S. Grace
	G-ACOJ	D.H.85 Leopard Moth	Norman Aeroplane Trust/Rendcomb
	G-ACSP	D.H.88 Comet ★	K. Fern
	G-ACSS	D.H.88 Comet ★	The Shuttleworth Collection Grosvenor House/O. Warden
	G-ACSS†	D.H.88 Comet (replica) (BAPC216) ★	G. Gayward
	G-ACSS†	D.H.88 Comet (replica) (BAPC257) ★	The Galleria/Hatfield
	G-ACTF	CLA.7 Swift ★	The Shuttleworth Collection/O. Warden
	G-ACUS	D.H.85 Leopard Moth	Norman Aeroplane Trust/Rendcomb
	G-ACUU	Cierva C.30A (HM580) ★	G. S. Baker/Duxford
	G-ACUX	S.16 Scion (VH-UUP) ★	Ulster Folk & Transport Museum
	G-ACVA	Kay Gyroplane ★	Glasgow Museum of Transport
	G-ACWM	Cierva C.30A (AP506) ★	IHM/Weston-s-Mare
	G-ACWP	Cierva C.30A (AP507) ★	Science Museum/S. Kensington
	G-ACXB	D.H.60G-III Moth Major ★	D. F. Hodgkinson
	G-ACXE	B.K. L-25C Swallow ★	J. G. Wakeford
	G-ACYK	Spartan Cruiser III ★	Museum of Flight (front fuselage)/ E. Fortune
	G-ACZE	D.H.89A Dragon Rapide	Wessex Aviation & Transport Ltd (G-AJGS)/Henstridge
	G-ADAH	D.H.89A Dragon Rapide ★	Manchester Museum of Science & Industry Pioneer
	G-ADEV	Avro 504K (H5199)	The Shuttleworth Collection (G-ACNB)/ O. Warden
	G-ADFV	Blackburn B-2 ★	Lincolnshire Aviation Heritage Centre
	G-ADGP	M.2L Hawk Speed Six	R. A. Mills
	G-ADGT	D.H.82A Tiger Moth	D. R. & Mrs M. Wood
	G-ADGV	D.H.82A Tiger Moth	K. J. Whitehead
	G-ADHD	D.H.60G-III Moth Major ★	M. E. Vaisey
	G-ADIA	D.H.82A Tiger Moth	S. J. Beaty
	G-ADJJ	D.H.82A Tiger Moth ★	J. M. Preston
	G-ADKC	D.H.87B Hornet Moth	A. J. Davy/Carlisle
	G-ADKK	D.H.87B Hornet Moth	R. G. Anniss
	G-ADKL	D.H.87B Hornet Moth	A. de Cadenet
	G-ADKM	D.H.87B Hornet Moth	L. V. Mayhead
	G-ADLY	D.H.87B Hornet Moth	Totalsure Ltd
	G-ADMT	D.H.87B Hornet Moth	P. A. de Courcy Swaffer
	G-ADMW	M.2H Hawk Major (DG590) ★	Museum of Army Flying/Middle Wallop
	G-ADND	D.H.87B Hornet Moth (W9385)	The Shuttleworth Collection/O. Warden

Reg.	Type	Owner or Operator	Notes
G-ADNE	D.H.87B Hornet Moth	G-ADNE Ltd	
G-ADNL	M.5 Sparrowhawk ★	A. G. Dunkerley	
G-ADNZ	D.H.82A Tiger Moth (DE673)	D. C. Wall	
G-ADOT	D.H.87B Hornet Moth ★	Mosquito Aircraft Museum	
G-ADPC	D.H.82A Tiger Moth	N. J. Baker & J. Beattie	
G-ADPJ	B.A.C. Drone ★	N. H. Ponsford/Breighton	
G-ADPS	B.A. Swallow 2	J. F. Hopkins	
G-ADRA	Pietenpol Air Camper	A. J. Mason	
G-ADRG†	Mignet HM.14 (replica) (BAPC77) ★	G. Lewis	
G-ADRH	D.H.87B Hornet Moth	R. G. Grocott/Switzerland	
G-ADRR	Aeronca C.3 ★	S. J. Rudkin	
G-ADRX †	Mignet HM.14 (replica) (BAPC231)	S. Copeland Aviation Group	
G-ADRY†	Mignet HM.14 (replica) (BAPC29) ★	Brooklands Museum of Aviation/ Weybridge	
G-ADSK	D.H.87B Hornet Moth	R. G. Grocott	
G-ADUR	D.H.87B Hornet Moth	Wessex Aviation & Transport Ltd	
G-ADVU	Mignet HM.14 (replica) (BAPC211) ★	N.E. Aircraft Museum/Usworth	
G-ADWJ	D.H.82A Tiger Moth ★	C. Adams	
G-ADWO	D.H.82A Tiger Moth (BB807) ★	Southampton Hall of Aviation	
G-ADXS	Mignet HM.14 ★	Thameside Aviation Museum/Shoreham	
G-ADXT	D.H. 82A Tiger Moth	R. G. Hanauer/Goodwood	
G-ADYS	Aeronca C.3	B. C. Cooper	
G-ADYV †	Mignet HM.14 (replica) (BAPC243)	P. Ward	
G-ADZW †	Mignet HM.14 (replica) (BAPC253)	H. Shore/Sandown	
G-AEBB	Mignet HM.14 ★	The Shuttleworth Collection/O. Warden	
G-AEBJ	Blackburn B-2	British Aerospace (Operations) Ltd/Brough	
G-AEDB	B.A.C. Drone 2 ★	R. E. Nerou & P. L. Kirk	
G-AEDU	D.H.90 Dragonfly	Norman Aeroplane Trust/Rendcomb	
G-AEEG	M.3A Falcon	Skysport Engineering Ltd	
G-AEEH	Mignet HM.14 ★	Aerospace Museum/Cosford	
G-AEFG	Mignet HM.14 (BAPC75) ★	N. H. Ponsford/Breighton	
G-AEFT	Aeronca C.3	N. S. Chittenden	
G-AEGV	Mignet HM.14 ★	Midland Air Museum/Coventry	
G-AEHM	Mignet HM.14 ★	Science Museum/Wroughton	
G-AEJZ	Mignet HM.14 (BAPC120) ★	Bomber County Museum/Hemswell	
G-AEKR	Mignet HM.14 (BAPC121) ★	S. Yorks Aviation Soc	
G-AEKV	Kronfeld Drone ★	Brooklands Museum of Aviation/ Weybridge	
G-AELO	D.H.87B Hornet Moth	M. J. Miller	
G-AEML	D.H.89 Dragon Rapide	Amanda Investments Ltd	
G-AENP	Hawker Hind (K5414) (BAPC78)	The Shuttleworth Collection/O. Warden	
G-AEOA	D.H.80A Puss Moth	P. & A. Wood/O. Warden	
G-AEOF†	Mignet HM.14 (BAPC22) ★	Aviodome/Schiphol, Netherlands	
G-AEOF	Rearwin 8500	Shipping & Airlines Ltd/Biggin Hill	
G-AEOH	Mignet HM.14 ★	Midland Air Museum	
G-AEPH	Bristol F.2B (D8096)	The Shuttleworth Collection/O. Warden	
G-AERV	M.11A Whitney Straight ★	Ulster Folk & Transport Museum	
G-AESB	Aeronca C.3 ★	R. J. M. Turnbull	
G-AESE	D.H.87B Hornet Moth	J. G. Green/Redhill	
G-AESZ	Chilton D.W.1 ★	R. E. Nerou	
G-AETA	Caudron G.3 (3066) ★	RAF Museum/Hendon	
G-AEUJ	M.11A Whitney Straight	R. E. Mitchell	
G-AEVS	Aeronca 100	A. M. Lindsay & N. H. Ponsford/Breighton	
G-AEVZ	B. A. Swallow 2	B. R. Cox	
G-AEXD	Aeronca 100	Mrs M. A. & R. W. Mills	
G-AEXF	P.6 Mew Gull	J. D. Penrose/Old Warden	
G-AEXT	Dart Kitten II	A. J. Hartfield	
G-AEXZ	Piper J-2 Cub	Mrs M. & J. R. Dowson/Leicester	
G-AEZF	S.16 Scion 2 ★	Acebell Aviation/Redhill	
G-AEZJ	P.10 Vega Gull	R. A. J. Spurrell/White Waltham	
G-AEZX	Bücker Bü133C Jungmeister (LG+03)	A. J. E. Ditheridge	
G-AFAP†	C.A.S.A. C.352L ★	Aerospace Museum/Cosford	
G-AFAX	B. A. Eagle 2	J. G. Green	

Notes	Reg.	Type	Owner or Operator
	G-AFBS	M.14A Hawk Trainer 3 ★	G. D. Durbridge-Freeman (G-AKKU)/ Duxford
	G-AFCL	B. A. Swallow 2	A. M. Dowson/O. Warden
	G-AFDO	Piper J-3F-60 Cub	R. Wald
	G-AFDX	Hanriot HD.1 (HD-75) ★	RAF Museum/Hendon
	G-AFEL	Monocoupe 90A	M. Rieser
	G-AFFD	Percival Q-6 ★	B. D. Greenwood
	G-AFFH	Piper J-2 Cub	M. J. Honeychurch
	G-AFFI	Mignet HM.14 (replica) (BAPC76) ★	Yorkshire Air Museum/Elvington
	G-AFGC	B. A. Swallow 2 ★	G. E. Arden
	G-AFGD	B. A. Swallow 2	A. T. Williams & ptnrs/Shobdon
	G-AFGE	B. A. Swallow 2	G. R. French
	G-AFGH	Chilton D.W.1.	M. L. & G. L. Joseph
	G-AFGI	Chilton D.W.1.	J. E. & K. A. A. McDonald
	G-AFGM	Piper J-4A Cub Coupé	A. J. P. Marshall/Carlisle
	G-AFGZ	D.H.82A Tiger Moth	M. R. Paul & P. A. Shaw (G-AMHI)
	G-AFHA	Mosscraft MA.1. ★	C. V. Butler
	G-AFIN	Chrislea LC.1 Airguard	N. Wright ★
	G-AFIR	Luton LA-4 Minor	A. J. Mason
	G-AFJA	Watkinson Dingbat ★	K. Woolley
	G-AFJB	Foster-Wikner G.M.1. Wicko (DR613) ★	J. Dibble
	G-AFJR	Tipsy Trainer 1	M. E. Vaisey (stored)
	G-AFJU	M.17 Monarch ★	Museum of Flight/E. Fortune
	G-AFJV	Mosscraft MA.2 ★	C. V. Butler
	G-AFLW	M.17 Monarch	N. I. Dalziel/Biggin Hill
	G-AFNG	D.H.94 Moth Minor	The Gullwing Trust
	G-AFNI	D.H.94 Moth Minor	B. N. C. & C. M. Mogg
	G-AFOB	D.H.94 Moth Minor	Wessex Aviation & Transport Ltd
	G-AFOJ	D.H.94 Moth Minor ★	Mosquito Aircraft Museum
	G-AFPN	D.H.94 Moth Minor	J. W. & A. R. Davy/Carlisle
	G-AFRZ	M.17 Monarch	R. E. Mitchell (G-AIDE)
	G-AFSC	Tipsy Trainer 1	G. A. Cull
	G-AFSV	Chilton D.W.1A	R. E. Nerou
	G-AFSW	Chilton D.W.2 ★	R. I. Souch
	G-AFTA	Hawker Tomtit (K1786)	The Shuttleworth Collection/O. Warden
	G-AFTN	Taylorcraft Plus C2 ★	Leicestershire County Council Museums
	G-AFUP	Luscombe 8A Silvaire	R. Dispain
	G-AFVE	D.H.82A Tiger Moth (T7230)	P. A. Shaw & M. R. Paul
	G-AFVN	Tipsy Trainer 1	D. F. Lingard
	G-AFWH	Piper J-4A Cub Coupé	O. T. Taylor
	G-AFWI	D.H.82A Tiger Moth	E. Newbigin
	G-AFWT	Tipsy Trainer 1	C. C. & J. M. Lovell
	G-AFYD	Luscombe 8F Silvaire	J. D. Iliffe
	G-AFYO	Stinson H.W.75	R. N. Wright
	G-AFZA	Piper J-4A Cub Coupe	G-AFZA Group
	G-AFZK	Luscombe 8A Silvaire	M. G. Byrnes
	G-AFZL	Porterfield CP.50	P. G. Lucas & S. H. Sharpe/ White Waltham
	G-AFZN	Luscombe 8A Silvaire	A. L. Young/Henstridge
	G-AGAT	Piper J-3F-50 Cub	G. S. Williams
	G-AGBN	G.A.L.42 Cygnet 2 ★	Museum of Flight/E. Fortune
	G-AGEG	D.H.82A Tiger Moth	Norman Aeroplane Trust/Rendcomb
	G-AGFT	Avia FL.3 (W7)	P. A. Smith/Leicester
	G-AGHY	D.H.82A Tiger Moth ★	P. Groves
	G-AGIV	Piper J-3C-65 Cub	P. C. & F. M. Gill
	G-AGJG	D.H.89A Dragon Rapide	M. J. & D. J. T. Miller/Duxford
	G-AGLK	Auster 5D	C. R. Harris/Biggin Hill
	G-AGMI	Luscombe 8A Silvaire	P. R. Bush
	G-AGNJ	D.H.82A Tiger Moth ★	B. P. Borsberry & Ptnrs
	G-AGNV	Avro 685 York 1 (TS798) ★	Aerospace Museum/Cosford
	G-AGOH	J/1 Autocrat ★	Newark Air Museum
	G-AGOS	R.S.4 Desford Trainer (VZ728) ★	Museum of Flight/E. Fortune
	G-AGOY	M.48 Messenger 3 (U-0247) ★	P. A. Brook
	G-AGPG	Avro 19 Srs 2 ★	Avro Heritage Soc/Woodford
	G-AGPK	D.H.82A Tiger Moth	Delta Aviation Ltd
	G-AGRU	V.498 Viking 1A ★	Brooklands Museum of Aviation/Weybridge
	G-AGSH	D.H.89A Dragon Rapide 6	Venom Jet Promotions Ltd/Bournemouth
	G-AGTM	D.H.89A Dragon Rapide 6	Aviation Heritage Ltd/Kemble
	G-AGTO	J/1 Autocrat	M. J. Barnett & D. J. T. Miller/Duxford

Reg.	Type	Owner or Operator	Notes
G-AGTT	J/1 Autocrat	R. Farrer	
G-AGVG	J/1 Autocrat	S. J. Riddington/Leicester	
G-AGVN	J/1 Autocrat	G. H. Farrar	
G-AGVV	Piper J-3C-65 Cub	M. Molina-Ruano/Spain	
G-AGXN	J/1N Alpha	Gentleman's Aerial Touring Carriage Syndicate Ltd	
G-AGXT	J/1N Alpha ★	Nene Valley Aircraft Museum	
G-AGXU	J/1N Alpha	A. J. Tuttle	
G-AGXV	J/1 Autocrat	B. S. Dowsett	
G-AGYD	J/1N Alpha	P. D. Hodson	
G-AGYH	J/1N Alpha	W. R. V. Marklew	
G-AGYK	J/1 Autocrat	Autocrat Syndicate	
G-AGYL	J/1 Autocrat ★	Military Vehicle Conservation Group	
G-AGYT	J/1N Alpha	P. J. Barrett	
G-AGYU	D.H.82A Tiger Moth (DE208)	P. L. Jones	
G-AGYY	Ryan ST.3KR (27)	Nostalgic Flying/Netherlands	
G-AGZZ	D.H.82A Tiger Moth	G. C. P. Shea-Simonds/Netheravon	
G-AHAL	J/1N Alpha	Wickenby Flying Club Ltd	
G-AHAM	J/1 Autocrat	A. J. Twemlow	
G-AHAN	D.H.82A Tiger Moth	Tiger Associates Ltd	
G-AHAP	J/1 Autocrat	F.J. Bellamy	
G-AHAT	J/1N Alpha ★	Dumfries & Galloway Aviation Museum	
G-AHAU	J/1 Autocrat	A. C. Webber & ptnrs	
G-AHBL	D.H.87B Hornet Moth	H. D. Labouchere	
G-AHBM	D.H.87B Hornet Moth	P. A. & E. P. Gliddon	
G-AHCK	J/1N Alpha	Skegness Air Taxi Service Ltd	
G-AHCL	J/1N Alpha	Electronic Precision Ltd (G-OJVC)	
G-AHCR	Gould-Taylorcraft Plus D Special	D. E. H. Balmford & D. R. Shepherd/ Dunkeswell	
G-AHEC	Luscombe 8A Silvaire	S. P. Parsons/Rush Green	
G-AHED	D.H.89A Dragon Rapide (RL962) ★	RAF Museum Storage & Restoration Centre/Cardington	
G-AHGD	D.H.89A Dragon Rapide	R. Jones	
G-AHGW	Taylorcraft Plus D (LB375)	C. V. Butler/Coventry	
G-AHGZ	Taylorcraft Plus D	M. Pocock	
G-AHHH	J/1 Autocrat	H. A. Jones/Norwich	
G-AHHT	J/1N Alpha	A. C. Barber & N. J. Hudson	
G-AHHU	J/1N Alpha ★	L. A. Groves & I. R. F. Hammond	
G-AHIP	Piper J-3C-65 Cub	V. L. Tanner	
G-AHIZ	D.H.82A Tiger Moth	C.F.G. Flying Ltd/Cambridge	
G-AHKX	Avro 19 Srs 2	BAe PLC/Avro Heritage Soc/Woodford	
G-AHKY	Miles M.18 Series 2 ★	Museum of Flight/E. Fortune	
G-AHLK	Auster 3	E. T. Brackenbury/Leicester	
G-AHLT	D.H.82A Tiger Moth	K. J. Jarvis	
G-AHMN	D.H.82A Tiger Moth (N6985)	Museum of Army Flying/Middle Wallop	
G-AHNR	Taylorcraft BC-12D	P. E. Hinkley/Redhill	
G-AHOO	D.H.82A Tiger Moth	J. T. & A. D. Milsom	
G-AHPZ	D.H.82A Tiger Moth	N. J. Wareing	
G-AHRI	D.H.104 Dove 1 ★	Newark Air Museum	
G-AHRO	Cessna 140	R. H. Screen/Kidlington	
G-AHSA	Avro 621 Tutor (K3215)	The Shuttleworth Collection/O. Warden	
G-AHSD	Taylorcraft Plus D	A. L. Hall-Carpenter	
G-AHSO	J/1N Alpha	W. P. Miller	
G-AHSP	J/1 Autocrat	R. M. Weeks	
G-AHSS	J/1N Alpha	A. M. Roche	
G-AHST	J/1N Alpha	A. C. Frost	
G-AHTE	P.44 Proctor V	D. K. Tregilgas	
G-AHTW	A.S.40 Oxford (V3388) ★	Skyfame Collection/Duxford	
G-AHUF	D.H.82A Tiger Moth (T7997)	First County Finance (UK) Ltd	
G-AHUG	Taylorcraft Plus D	D. Nieman	
G-AHUI	M.38 Messenger 2A ★	Museum of Berkshire Aviation/Woodley	
G-AHUJ	M.14A Hawk Trainer 3 (R1914) ★	Strathallan Aircraft Collection	
G-AHUN	Globe GC-1B Swift	R. J. Hamlett	
G-AHUV	D.H.82A Tiger Moth	J. D. Gordon	
G-AHVU	D.H.82A Tiger Moth (T6313)	Foley Farm Flying Group	
G-AHVV	D.H.82A Tiger Moth	R. Jones	
G-AHWJ	Taylorcraft Plus D (LB294)	M. D. Pitcher	
G-AHXE	Taylorcraft Plus D (LB312)	J. M. C. Pothecary/Shoreham	
G-AIBE	Fulmar II (N1854) ★	F.A.A. Museum/Yeovilton	
G-AIBH	J/1N Alpha	M. J. Bonnick	
G-AIBM	J/1 Autocrat	D. G. Greatrex	

Notes	Reg.	Type	Owner or Operator
	G-AIBR	J/1 Autocrat	K. L. Clarke
	G-AIBW	J/1N Alpha	W. E. Bateson/Blackpool
	G-AIBX	J/1 Autocrat	Wasp Flying Group
	G-AIBY	J/1 Autocrat	D. Morris/Sherburn
	G-AICX	Luscombe 8A Silvaire	R. V. Smith/Henstridge
	G-AIDL	D.H.89A Dragon Rapide 6	Atlantic Air Transport Ltd/Coventry
	G-AIDS	D.H.82A Tiger Moth	K. D. Pogmore & T. Dann
	G-AIEK	M.38 Messenger 2A (RG333)	J. Buckingham
	G-AIFZ	J/1N Alpha	M. D. Ansley
	G-AIGD	J/1 Autocrat	R. B. Webber
	G-AIGF	J/1N Alpha	A. R. C. Mathie
	G-AIGU	J/1N Alpha	N. K. Geddes
	G-AIIH	Piper J-3C-65 Cub	J. A. de Salis
	G-AIJI	J/1N Alpha ★	C. J. Baker
	G-AIJM	Auster J/4	N. Huxtable
	G-AIJS	Auster J/4 ★	(stored)
	G-AIJT	Auster J/4 Srs 100	Aberdeen Auster Flying Group
	G-AIJZ	J/1 Autocrat	A. A. Marshall (stored)
	G-AIKE	Auster 5	C. J. Baker
	G-AIPR	Auster J/4	MPM Flying Group/Booker
	G-AIPV	J/1 Autocrat	W. P. Miller
	G-AIRC	J/1 Autocrat	R. C. Tebbett/Shobdon
	G-AIRI	D.H.82A Tiger Moth	E. R. Goodwin (stored)
	G-AIRK	D.H.82A Tiger Moth	R. C. Teverson & ptnrs
	G-AISA	Tipsy B Srs 1	G. A. Cull
	G-AISC	Tipsy B Srs 1	Wagtail Flying Group
	G-AISS	Piper J-3C-65 Cub	K. W. Wood & F. Watson/Insch
	G-AIST	V.S.300 Spitfire 1A (AR213)	Sheringham Aviation UK Ltd
	G-AISX	Piper J-3C-65 Cub	Cubfly
	G-AITB	A.S.10 Oxford (MP425) ★	RAF Museum Store/Cardington
	G-AIUA	M.14A Hawk Trainer 3	P. A. Brook
	G-AIUL	D.H.89A Dragon Rapide 6	I. Jones/Chirk
	G-AIXA	Taylorcraft Plus D	C. W. Udale
	G-AIXJ	D.H.82A Tiger Moth	D. Green/Goodwood
	G-AIXN	Benes-Mraz M.1C Sokol	A. J. Wood
	G-AIYG	SNCAN Stampe SV-4B	L. Casteleyn/Belgium
	G-AIYR	D.H.89A Dragon Rapide	Fairmont Investments Ltd/Duxford
	G-AIYS	D.H.85 Leopard Moth	Wessex Aviation & Transport Ltd
	G-AIZE	F.24W Argus 2 ★	Aerospace Museum/Coventry
	G-AIZF	D.H.82A Tiger Moth ★	(stored)
	G-AIZG	V.S. Walrus 1 (L2301) ★	F.A.A. Museum/Yeovilton
	G-AIZU	J/1 Autocrat	C. J. & J. G. B. Morley
	G-AJAD	Piper J-3C-65 Cub	N. A. Rooney
	G-AJAE	J/1N Alpha	A. C. Ladd
	G-AJAJ	J/1N Alpha	R. B. Lawrence
	G-AJAM	J/2 Arrow	D. A. Porter
	G-AJAO	Piper J-3C-65 Cub	M. Stow
	G-AJAP	Luscombe 8A Silvaire	R. J. Thomas
	G-AJAS	J/1N Alpha	C. J. Baker
	G-AJCP	D.31 Turbulent	B. R. Pearson
	G-AJDW	J/1 Autocrat	D. R. Hunt
	G-AJEB	J/1N Alpha ★	Manchester Museum of Science & Industry
	G-AJEE	J/1 Autocrat	A. R. C. De Albanoz/Bournemouth
	G-AJEH	J/1N Alpha	J. T. Powell-Tuck
	G-AJEI	J/1N Alpha	W. P. Miller
	G-AJEM	J/1 Autocrat ★	K. A. Jones
	G-AJES	Piper J-3C-65 Cub (330485)	P. A. Crawford
	G-AJGJ	Auster 5 (RT486)	British Classic Aircraft Restoration Flying Group
	G-AJHJ	Auster 5 ★	(stored)
	G-AJHS	D.H.82A Tiger Moth	Vliegend Museum/Netherlands
	G-AJHU	D.H.82A Tiger Moth (T7471)	G. Valentini/Italy
	G-AJIH	J/1 Autocrat	A. H. Diver
	G-AJIS	J/1N Alpha	Husthwaite Auster Group
	G-AJIT	J/1 Kingsland Autocrat	A. J. Kay
	G-AJIU	J/1 Autocrat	M. D. Greenhalgh/Netherthorpe
	G-AJIW	J/1N Alpha	Truman Aviation Ltd/Tollerton
	G-AJJP	Jet Gyrodyne (XJ389) ★	Museum of Berkshire Aviation/Woodley
	G-AJJS	Cessna 120	Robhurst Flying Group
	G-AJJT	Cessna 120	J. S. Robson
	G-AJJU	Luscombe 8E Silvaire	L. C. Moon

Reg.	Type	Owner or Operator	Notes
G-AJKB	Luscombe 8E Silvaire	A. F. Hall & P. S. Hatwell	
G-AJOA	D.H.82A Tiger Moth (T5424)	F. P. Le Coyte	
G-AJOC	M.38 Messenger 2A ★	Ulster Folk & Transport Museum	
G-AJOE	M.38 Messenger 2A	Cotswold Aircraft Restoration Group	
G-AJON	Aeronca 7AC Champion	A. Biggs & J. L. Broad/Booker	
G-AJOV†	Sikorsky S-51 ★	Aerospace Museum/Cosford	
G-AJOZ	F.24W Argus 2 ★	Thorpe Camp Preservation Group	
G-AJPI	F.24R-41a Argus 3 (314887)	T. H. Bishop	
G-AJPZ	J/1 Autocrat ★	Wessex Aviation Soc	
G-AJRB	J/1 Autocrat	N. Ravine/Sywell	
G-AJRC	J/1 Autocrat	M. Baker	
G-AJRE	J/1 Autocrat (Lycoming)	C. W. & A. A. M. Huke	
G-AJRH	J/1N Alpha ★	Charnwood Museum/Loughborough	
G-AJRS	M.14A Hawk Trainer 3 (P6382)	The Shuttleworth Collection/O. Warden	
G-AJTW	D.H.82A Tiger Moth (N6965)	J. A. Barker/Tibenham	
G-AJUE	J/1 Autocrat	P. H. B. Cole	
G-AJUL	J/1N Alpha ★	M. J. Crees	
G-AJVE	D.H.82A Tiger Moth	R. A. Gammons	
G-AJWB	M.38 Messenger 2A	G. E. J. Spooner	
G-AJXC	Auster 5 ★	J. E. Graves	
G-AJXV	Auster 4 (NJ695)	B. A. Farries/Leicester	
G-AJXY	Auster 4 ★	P. D. Lowdon	
G-AJYB	J/1N Alpha	P. J. Shotbolt	
G-AKAT	M.14A Hawk Trainer 3 (T9738)	J. D. Haslam/Breighton	
G-AKAZ	Piper J-3C-65 Cub (57-H)	J. R. Frazer/Duxford	
G-AKBM	M.38 Messenger 2A ★	Bristol Plane Preservation Unit	
G-AKBO	M.38 Messenger 2A	B. du Cros	
G-AKDN	D.H.C. 1A Chipmunk 10	D. S. Backhouse	
G-AKDW	D.H.89A Dragon Rapide	De Havilland Aircraft Museum Trust Ltd	
G-AKEL	M.65 Gemini 1A ★	Ulster Folk & Transport Museum	
G-AKER	M.65 Gemini 1A ★	Berkshire Aviation Group/Woodley	
G-AKEZ	M.38 Messenger 2A (RG333)	P. G. Lee	
G-AKGD	M.65 Gemini 1A ★	Berkshire Aviation Group/Woodley	
G-AKGE	M.65 Gemini 3C ★	Ulster Folk & Transport Museum	
G-AKHP	M.65 Gemini 1A	P. G. Lee	
G-AKHZ	M.65 Gemini 7 ★	Museum of Berkshire Aviation/Woodley	
G-AKIB	Piper J-3C-90 Cub (480015)	M. C. Bennett	
G-AKIF	D.H.89A Dragon Rapide	Airborne Taxi Services Ltd/Booker	
G-AKIN	M.38 Messenger 2A	R. Spiller & Sons/Sywell	
G-AKIU	P.44 Proctor V	Air Atlantique Ltd/Coventry	
G-AKKB	M.65 Gemini 1A	J. Buckingham	
G-AKKH	M.65 Gemini 1A	M. C. Russell	
G-AKKR	M.14A Magister (T9707) ★	Manchester Museum of Science & Industry	
G-AKKY	M.14A Hawk Trainer 3 (L6906) ★ (BAPC44) ★	Museum of Berkshire Aviation/Woodley	
G-AKLW	SA.6 Sealand 1 ★	Ulster Folk & Transport Museum	
G-AKOE	D.H.89A Dragon Rapide 4	H. J. E. Pierce/Chirk	
G-AKOT	Auster 5 ★	C. J. Baker	
G-AKOW	Auster 5 (TJ569) ★	Museum of Army Flying/Middle Wallop	
G-AKPF	M.14A Hawk Trainer 3 (V1075)	P. A. Brook/Sandown	
G-AKPI	Auster 5 (NJ703)	B. H. Hargrave/Doncaster	
G-AKRA	Piper J-3C-65 Cub	W. R. Savin	
G-AKRP	D.H.89A Dragon Rapide 4	Fordaire Aviation Ltd/Sywell	
G-AKSY	Auster 5	Aerofab Flying Group	
G-AKSZ	Auster 5	A. R. C. Mathie	
G-AKTH	Piper J-3C-65 Cub	G. H. Harry & Viscount Goschen	
G-AKTI	Luscombe 8A Silvaire	M. W. Olliver	
G-AKTK	Aeronca 11AC Chief	R. W. Marshall & ptnrs	
G-AKTN	Luscombe 8A Silvaire	D. Taylor	
G-AKTO	Aeronca 7BCM Champion	D. C. Murray	
G-AKTP	PA-17 Vagabond	G-AKTP Flying Group	
G-AKTR	Aeronca 7AC Champion	C. Fielder/Dunkeswell	
G-AKTS	Cessna 120	J. J. Boon/Popham	
G-AKTT	Luscombe 8A Silvaire	S. J. Charters	
G-AKUE	D.H.82A Tiger Moth	D. F. Hodgkinson	
G-AKUF	Luscombe 8F Silvaire	A. G. Palmer	
G-AKUG	Luscombe 8A Silvaire	G-AKUG Group	
G-AKUH	Luscombe 8E Silvaire	I. M. Bower	
G-AKUI	Luscombe 8E Silvaire	D. A. Sims	
G-AKUJ	Luscombe 8E Silvaire	R. Fraser & R. C. Green	
G-AKUK	Luscombe 8A Silvaire	Leckhampstead Flying Group	

Notes	Reg.	Type	Owner or Operator
	G-AKUL	Luscombe 8A Silvaire	E. A. Taylor
	G-AKUM	Luscombe 8F Silvaire	D. A. Young
	G-AKUN	Piper J-3F-65 Cub	W. R. Savin
	G-AKUO	Aeronca 11AC Chief	KUO Flying Group/White Waltham
	G-AKUP	Luscombe 8E Silvaire	R. J. Willies
	G-AKUR	Cessna 140	J. Greenaway & C. A. Davies/Popham
	G-AKUW	Chrislea C.H.3 Super Ace 2	D. R. Bean
	G-AKVF	Chrislea C.H.3 Super Ace 2	T. Pate
	G-AKVM	Cessna 120	N. Wise & S. Walker
	G-AKVN	Aeronca 11AC Chief	Breckland Aeronca Group
	G-AKVO	Taylorcraft BC-12D	Albion Flyers
	G-AKVP	Luscombe 8A Silvaire	J. M. Edis
	G-AKVR	Chrislea C.H.3 Skyjeep 4	D. R. Bean
	G-AKVZ	M.38 Messenger 4B	Shipping & Airlines Ltd/Biggin Hill
	G-AKWS	Auster 5A-160	G. R. Lacey
	G-AKWT	Auster 5 ★	Loughborough & Leicester Aircraft Preservation Soc
	G-AKXP	Auster 5	M. Pocock
	G-AKXS	D.H.82A Tiger Moth	P. A. Colman
	G-AKZN	P.34A Proctor 3 (Z7197) ★	RAF Museum/Hendon
	G-ALAH	M.38 Messenger 4A (RH377) ★	RAF Museum/Henlow
	G-ALAX	D.H.89A Dragon Rapide ★	Durney Aeronautical Collection/Andover
	G-ALBJ	Auster 5	P. N. Elkington
	G-ALBK	Auster 5	S. J. Wright & Co (Farmers) Ltd
	G-ALBN	Bristol 173 (XF785) ★	RAF Museum Storage & Restoration Centre/Cardington
	G-ALCK	P.34A Proctor 3 (LZ766) ★	Skyfame Collection/Duxford
	G-ALCS	M.65 Gemini 3C ★	(stored)
	G-ALCU	D.H.104 Dove 2 ★	Midland Air Museum/Coventry
	G-ALDG	HP.81 Hermes 4 ★	Duxford Aviation Soc (fuselage only)
	G-ALEH	PA-17 Vagabond	A. D. Pearce/White Waltham
	G-ALFA	Auster 5	S. P. Barrett
	G-ALFT	D.H.104 Dove 6 ★	Caernarfon Air World
	G-ALFU	D.H.104 Dove 6 ★	Duxford Aviation Soc
	G-ALGA	PA-15 Vagabond	D. A. Lord
	G-ALIJ	PA-17 Vagabond	Popham Flying Group/Popham
	G-ALIW	D.H.82A Tiger Moth	D. I. M. Geddes & F. Curry/Booker
	G-ALJF	P.34A Proctor 3	J. F. Moore/Biggin Hill
	G-ALJL	D.H.82A Tiger Moth★	C. G. Clarke
	G-ALLF	Slingsby T.30A Prefect (ARK)	J. F. Hopkins & K. M. Fresson
	G-ALNA	D.H.82A Tiger Moth	R. J. Doughton
	G-ALNV	D.H.82A Tiger Moth (N9191)	J. T. Powell-Tuck
	G-ALNV	Auster 5 ★	C. J. Baker (stored)
	G-ALOD	Cessna 140	J. R. Stainer
	G-ALRH	EoN Type 8 Baby	P. D. Moran/Chipping
	G-ALRI	D.H.82A Tiger Moth (T5672)	Wessex Aviation & Transport Ltd
	G-ALSP	Bristol 171 Sycamore (WV783)★	R.N. Fleetlands Museum
	G-ALSS	Bristol 171 Sycamore (WA576)★	Dumfries & Galloway Aviation Museum
	G-ALST	Bristol 171 Sycamore (WA577)★	N.E. Aircraft Museum/Usworth
	G-ALSW	Bristol 171 Sycamore (WT933)★	Newark Air Museum
	G-ALSX	Bristol 171 Sycamore (G-48-1)★	IHM/Weston-s-Mare
	G-ALTO	Cessna 140	J. P. Bell
	G-ALTW	D.H.82A Tiger Moth ★	A. Mangham
	G-ALUC	D.H.82A Tiger Moth	D. R. & M. Wood
	G-ALVP	D.H.82A Tiger Moth ★	V. & R. Wheele (stored)
	G-ALWB	D.H.C.1 Chipmunk 22A	M. L. & J. M. Soper/Perth
	G-ALWF	V.701 Viscount ★	Viscount Preservation Trust RMA Sir John Franklin/Duxford
	G-ALWS	D.H.82A Tiger Moth ★	A. P. Benyon/Welshpool
	G-ALWW	D.H.82A Tiger Moth	D. E. Findon
	G-ALXT	D.H.89A Dragon Rapide ★	Science Museum/Wroughton
	G-ALXZ	Auster 5-150	M. F. Cuming
	G-ALYB	Auster 5 (RT520) ★	S. Yorks Aircraft Preservation Soc
	G-ALYG	Auster 5D	A. L. Young/Henstridge
	G-ALYW	D.H.106 Comet 1 ★	RAF Exhibition Flight (fuselage converted to Nimrod)
	G-ALZE	BN-1F ★	M. R. Short/Southampton Hall of Aviation
	G-ALZO	A.S.57 Ambassador ★	Duxford Aviation Soc
	G-AMAW	Luton LA-4 Minor	R. H. Coates
	G-AMBB	D.H.82A Tiger Moth ★	J. Eagles
	G-AMCA	Douglas C-47B	Air Atlantique Ltd/Coventry

Reg.	Type	Owner or Operator	Notes
G-AMCK	D.H.82A Tiger Moth	D. L. Frankel	
G-AMCM	D.H.82A Tiger Moth ★	B. C. Cooper & ptnrs	
G-AMDA	Avro 652A Anson 1 (N4877) ★	Skyfame Collection/Duxford	
G-AMEN	PA-18 Super Cub 95	A. Lovejoy & W. Cook	
G-AMHF	D.H.82A Tiger Moth	Wavendon Social Housing Ltd	
G-AMHJ	Douglas C-47A	Air Atlantique Ltd/Coventry	
G-AMIU	D.H.82A Tiger Moth	R. & Mrs J. L. Jones	
G-AMKU	J/1B Aiglet	P. G. Lipman	
G-AMLZ	P.50 Prince 6E ★	Caernarfon Air World Museum	
G-AMMS	J/5K Aiglet Trainer	A. J. Large	
G-AMNN	D.H.82A Tiger Moth	M. Thrower Spirit of Pashley/Shoreham	
G-AMOG	V.701 Viscount ★	Aerospace Museum/Cosford	
G-AMPG	PA-12 Super Cruiser	R. Simpson	
G-AMPI	SNCAN Stampe SV-4C ★	T. W. Harris	
G-AMPO	Douglas C-47B	Air Atlantique Ltd/Coventry	
G-AMPY	Douglas C-47B	Air Atlantique Ltd/Coventry	
G-AMPZ	Douglas C-47B	Air Atlantique Ltd/Coventry	
G-AMRA	Douglas C-47B	Air Atlantique Ltd (stored)/Coventry	
G-AMRF	J/5F Aiglet Trainer	A. I. Topps/E. Midlands	
G-AMRK	G.37 Gladiator I (427)	The Shuttleworth Collection/O. Warden	
G-AMSG	SIPA 903	S. W. Markham	
G-AMSN	Douglas C-47B ★	Aces High Ltd/North Weald	
G-AMSV	Douglas C-47B	Air Atlantique Ltd/Coventry	
G-AMTA	J/5F Aiglet Trainer	N. H. T. Cottrell	
G-AMTF	D.H.82A Tiger Moth (T7842)	M. W. Zipfell/Marham	
G-AMTK	D.H.82A Tiger Moth	S. W. McKay & M. E. Vaisey	
G-AMTM	J/1 Autocrat	R. J. Stobo & D. Clewley (G-AJUJ)	
G-AMTV	D.H.82A Tiger Moth	Medalbest Ltd	
G-AMUF	D.H.C.1 Chipmunk 21	Redhill Tailwheel Flying Club Ltd	
G-AMUI	J/5F Aiglet Trainer	D. Hatelie	
G-AMVD	Auster 5	M.Hammond	
G-AMVP	Tipsy Junior	A. R. Wershat	
G-AMVS	D.H.82A Tiger Moth ★	J. T. Powell-Tuck	
G-AMXA	D.H.106 Comet 2 (nose only) ★	Spectators' Terrace/Gatwick	
G-AMYA	Zlin Z.381	D. M. Fenton	
G-AMYD	J/5L Aiglet Trainer	G. H. Maskell	
G-AMYJ	Douglas C-47B	Air Atlantique Ltd/Coventry	
G-AMYL	PA-17 Vagabond	P. J. Penn-Sayers/Shoreham	
G-AMZI	J/5F Aiglet Trainer	J. F. Moore/Biggin Hill	
G-AMZT	J/5F Aiglet Trainer	D. Hyde & ptnrs/Cranfield	
G-AMZU	J/5F Aiglet Trainer	J. A. Longworth & ptnrs	
G-ANAP	D.H.104 Dove 6 ★	Brunel Technical College/Lulsgate	
G-ANCF	B.175 Britannia 308 ★	Bristol Aero Collection (stored)/Kemble	
G-ANCS	D.H.82A Tiger Moth	M. A. B. Mitchell	
G-ANCX	D.H.82A Tiger Moth	D. R. Wood/Biggin Hill	
G-ANDE	D.H.82A Tiger Moth	Montrose Aviation Ltd/Duxford	
G-ANDM	D.H.82A Tiger Moth	N. J. Stagg	
G-ANDP	D.H.82A Tiger Moth	A. H. Diver	
G-ANEC	D.H.82A Tiger Moth ★	(stored)	
G-ANEH	D.H.82A Tiger Moth (N6797)	G. J. Wells/Goodwood	
G-ANEL	D.H.82A Tiger Moth	Chauffair Ltd	
G-ANEM	D.H.82A Tiger Moth	P. J. Benest	
G-ANEN	D.H.82A Tiger Moth	R. J. Jackson	
G-ANEW	D.H.82A Tiger Moth	A. L. Young	
G-ANEZ	D.H.82A Tiger Moth	C. D. J. Bland/Sandown	
G-ANFC	D.H.82A Tiger Moth	H. J. E. Pierce/Chirk	
G-ANFH	Westland S-55 ★	IHM/Weston-s-Mare	
G-ANFI	D.H.82A Tiger Moth (DE623)	G. P. Graham	
G-ANFL	D.H.82A Tiger Moth	IDA Flying Group	
G-ANFM	D.H.82A Tiger Moth	S. A. Brook & ptnrs/Booker	
G-ANFP	D.H.82A Tiger Moth	D. R. Taylor	
G-ANFU	Auster 5 (NJ719) ★	N.E. Aircraft Museum/Usworth	
G-ANFV	D.H.82A Tiger Moth (DF155)	R. A. L. Falconer	
G-ANFW	D.H.82A Tiger Moth	G. M. Fraser/Denham	
G-ANGK	Cessna 140A	D. W. Munday	
G-ANHK	D.H.82A Tiger Moth	J. D. Iliffe	
G-ANHR	Auster 5	C. G. Winch	
G-ANHS	Auster 4	Tango Uniform Group	
G-ANHU	Auster 4	D. J. Baker (stored)	
G-ANHX	Auster 5D	D. J. Baker	
G-ANIE	Auster 5 (TW467)	S. J. Partridge	
G-ANIJ	Auster 5D (TJ672)	M. Pocock	

Notes	Reg.	Type	Owner or Operator
	G-ANIS	Auster 5	J. Clarke-Cockburn
	G-ANIX	D.H.82A Tiger Moth	J. M. Koch
	G-ANJA	D.H.82A Tiger Moth (N9389)	P. Auckland
	G-ANJD	D.H.82A Tiger Moth	A. C. Ladd
	G-ANKK	D.H.82A Tiger Moth (T5854)	Halfpenny Green Tiger Group
	G-ANKT	D.H.82A Tiger Moth (T6818)	The Shuttleworth Collection/O. Warden
	G-ANKV	D.H.82A Tiger Moth (T7793) ★	Westmead Business Group/Croydon Airport
	G-ANKZ	D.H.82A Tiger Moth (N6466)	D. W. Graham
	G-ANLD	D.H.82A Tiger Moth	K. Peters
	G-ANLH	D.H.82A Tiger Moth	T. S. Warren & J. J. Woodhouse/Sandown
	G-ANLS	D.H.82A Tiger Moth	P. A. Gliddon
	G-ANLU	Auster 5	B. H. Hargrave
	G-ANLW	W.B.1. Widgeon (MD497) ★	Sloane Helicopters Ltd/Sywell
	G-ANLX	D.H.82A Tiger Moth	B. J. Borsberry & ptnrs
	G-ANMO	D.H.82A Tiger Moth (K4259)	E. & K. M. Lay
	G-ANMV	D.H.82A Tiger Moth (T7404)	J. W. Davy/Cardiff
	G-ANMY	D.H.82A Tiger Moth (DE470)	R. Earl & B. Morris
	G-ANNB	D.H.82A Tiger Moth ★	G. M. Bradley
	G-ANNE	D.H.82A Tiger Moth ★	C. R. Hardiman
	G-ANNG	D.H.82A Tiger Moth	P. F. Walter
	G-ANNI	D.H.82A Tiger Moth	A. R. Brett
	G-ANNK	D.H.82A Tiger Moth ★	P. J. Wilcox/Cranfield
	G-ANNN	D.H.82A Tiger Moth ★	H. C. Cox
	G-ANOA	Hiller UH-12A ★	Redhill Technical College
	G-ANOD	D.H.82A Tiger Moth	P. G. Grafton
	G-ANOH	D.H.82A Tiger Moth	N. Parkhouse/White Waltham
	G-ANOK	SAAB S.91C Safir ★	A. F. Galt & Co (stored)
	G-ANOM	D.H.82A Tiger Moth	A. L. Creer
	G-ANON	D.H.82A Tiger Moth (T7909)	A. C. Mercer/Sherburn
	G-ANOO	D.H.82A Tiger Moth	R. K. Packman/Shoreham
	G-ANOR	D.H.82A Tiger Moth (T6991)	R. Clifford
	G-ANOV	D.H.104 Dove 6 ★	Museum of Flight/E. Fortune
	G-ANPE	D.H.82A Tiger Moth	I. E. S. Huddleston (G-IESH)/Clacton
	G-ANPK	D.H.82A Tiger Moth	The D. & P. Group
	G-ANPP	P.34A Proctor 3	C. P. A. & J. Jeffrey
	G-ANRF	D.H.82A Tiger Moth	C. D. Cyster
	G-ANRM	D.H.82A Tiger Moth	Fairmont Investments Ltd/Clacton
	G-ANRN	D.H.82A Tiger Moth	J. J. V. Elwes/Rush Green
	G-ANRP	Auster 5 (TW439)	A. Brier/Breighton
	G-ANRX	D.H.82A Tiger Moth ★	Mosquito Aircraft Museum
	G-ANSM	D.H.82A Tiger Moth	J. L. Bond
	G-ANTE	D.H.82A Tiger Moth (T6562)	M. R. Keen/Liverpool
	G-ANTK	Avro 685 York ★	Duxford Aviation Soc
	G-ANTS	D.H.82A Tiger Moth (N6532)	J. G. Green
	G-ANUO	D.H.114 Heron 2D (G-AOXL) ★	Westmead Business Group/Croydon Airport
	G-ANUW	D.H.104 Dove 6 ★	Aces High Ltd/North Weald
	G-ANWB	D.H.C.1 Chipmunk 21	G. Briggs (stored)/Blackpool
	G-ANWO	M.14A Hawk Trainer 3 ★	A. G. Dunkerley
	G-ANXB	D.H.114 Heron 1B ★	Newark Air Museum
	G-ANXC	J/5R Alpine	Alpine Group
	G-ANXR	P.31C Proctor 4 (RM221)	L. H. Oakins/Biggin Hill
	G-ANZJ	P.31C Proctor 4 (NP303) ★	A. Hillyard
	G-ANZT	Thruxton Jackaroo	D. J. Neville & P. A. Dear
	G-ANZU	D.H.82A Tiger Moth	P. A. Jackson
	G-ANZZ	D.H.82A Tiger Moth	J. I. B. Bennett & P. P. Amershi
	G-AOAA	D.H.82A Tiger Moth	R. C. P. Brookhouse
	G-AOBG	Somers-Kendall SK.1 ★	(stored)/Breighton
	G-AOBH	D.H.82A Tiger Moth (NL750)	P. Nutley/Thruxton
	G-AOBO	D.H.82A Tiger Moth	J. S. & S. V. Shaw
	G-AOBU	P.84 Jet Provost T.1 (XD693)	T. J. Manna/Cranfield
	G-AOBV	J/5P Autocar	P. E. Champney (stored)
	G-AOBX	D.H.82A Tiger Moth	D. G. Ross
	G-AOCP	Auster 5 ★	C. J. Baker (stored)
	G-AOCR	Auster 5D (NJ673)	G. J. McDill
	G-AOCU	Auster 5	S. J. Ball/Leicester
	G-AODA	Westland S-55 Srs 3 ★	IHM/Weston-s-Mare
	G-AODT	D.H.82A Tiger Moth (R5250)	R. A. Harrowven
	G-AOEH	Aeronca 7AC Champion	R. A & S. P. Smith
	G-AOEI	D.H.82A Tiger Moth	C.F.G. Flying Ltd/Cambridge

Reg.	Type	Owner or Operator	Notes
G-AOEL	D.H.82A Tiger Moth ★	Museum of Flight/E. Fortune	
G-AOES	D.H.82A Tiger Moth	A. Twemlow & G. A. Cordery	
G-AOET	D.H.82A Tiger Moth	Venom Jet Promotions Ltd/Bournemouth	
G-AOEX	Thruxton Jackaroo	A. T. Christian	
G-AOFE	D.H.C.1 Chipmunk 22A (WB702)	E. J. F. McEntee	
G-AOFM	J/5P Autocar	W. H. Dyozinski	
G-AOFS	J/5L Aiglet Trainer	P. N. A. Whitehead	
G-AOGA	M.75 Aries ★	Irish Aeroplane Club	
G-AOGE	P.34A Proctor 3 ★	N. I. Dalziel (stored)/Biggin Hill	
G-AOGI	D.H.82A Tiger Moth ★	W. J. Taylor	
G-AOGR	D.H.82A Tiger Moth (XL714)	M. I. Edwards	
G-AOGV	J/5R Alpine	R. E. Heading	
G-AOHY	D.H.82A Tiger Moth	Historic Aircraft Flight/Middle Wallop	
G-AOHZ	J/5P Autocar	A. D. Hodgkinson	
G-AOIL	D.H.82A Tiger Moth	T. C. Lawless	
G-AOIM	D.H.82A Tiger Moth	D. A. Hardiman/Shobdon	
G-AOIR	Thruxton Jackaroo	L. H. Smith & I. M. Oliver	
G-AOIS	D.H.82A Tiger Moth	J. K. Ellwood	
G-AOIY	J/5G Autocar	J. B. Nicholson	
G-AOJH	D.H.83C Fox Moth	Norman Aeroplane Trust/Rendcomb	
G-AOJJ	D.H.82A Tiger Moth (DF128)	JJ Flying Group	
G-AOJK	D.H.82A Tiger Moth	D. E. Guck & P. W. Crispe	
G-AOJR	D.H.C.1 Chipmunk 22	G. J-H. Caubergs & N. Marien/Belgium	
G-AOJT	D.H.106 Comet 1 (F-BGNX) ★	Mosquito Aircraft Museum (fuselage only)	
G-AOKH	P.40 Prentice 1	J. F. Moore/Biggin Hill	
G-AOKL	P.40 Prentice 1 (VS610)	The Shuttleworth Collection/O. Warden	
G-AOKO	P.40 Prentice 1 ★	Airport Fire Section/Coventry	
G-AOKZ	P.40 Prentice 1 (VS623) ★	Midland Air Museum/Coventry	
G-AOLK	P.40 Prentice 1	Hilton Aviation Ltd/Southend	
G-AOLU	P.40 Prentice 1 (VS356)	N. J. Butler	
G-AORB	Cessna 170B	Eaglescott Parachute Centre	
G-AORG	D.H.114 Heron 2	Duchess of Brittany (Jersey) Ltd	
G-AORW	D.H.C.1 Chipmunk 22A	Bushfire Investments Ltd/North Weald	
G-AOSF	D.H.C.1 Chipmunk 22 (WB571)	D. Mercer/Germany	
G-AOSK	D.H.C.1 Chipmunk 22 (WB726)	E. J. Leigh/Audley End	
G-AOSO	D.H.C.1 Chipmunk 22 (WD288)	Earl of Suffolk & Berkshire & J. Hoerner	
G-AOSU	D.H.C.1 Chipmunk 22 (Lycoming)	RAFGSA/Kinloss	
G-AOSY	D.H.C.1 Chipmunk 22 (WB585)	Propshop Ltd/Duxford	
G-AOTD	D.H.C.1 Chipmunk 22 (WB588)	S. Piech	
G-AOTF	D.H.C.1 Chipmunk 23 (Lycoming)	RAFGSA/Dishforth	
G-AOTI	D.H.114 Heron 2D ★	Mosquito Aircraft Museum	
G-AOTK	D.53 Turbi	The T. K. Flying Group	
G-AOTR	D.H.C.1 Chipmunk 22	M. R. Woodgate/Aldergrove	
G-AOTY	D.H.C.1 Chipmunk 22A (WG472)	A. A. Hodgson	
G-AOUJ	Fairey Ultra-Light ★	IHM/Weston-s-Mare	
G-AOUO	D.H.C.1 Chipmunk 22 (Lycoming)	RAFGSA/Bicester	
G-AOUP	D.H.C.1 Chipmunk 22	A. R. Harding	
G-AOUR	D.H.82A Tiger Moth ★	Ulster Folk & Transport Museum	
G-AOVF	B.175 Britannia 312F ★	Aerospace Museum/Cosford	
G-AOVS	B.175 Britannia 312F ★	Airport Fire Section/Luton	
G-AOVT	B.175 Britannia 312F ★	Duxford Aviation Soc	
G-AOVW	Auster 5	B. Marriott/Cranwell	
G-AOXL†	See G-ANUO		
G-AOXN	D.H.82A Tiger Moth	S. L. G. Darch	
G-AOZH	D.H.82A Tiger Moth (K2572)	G. J. & S. Wheele/Shoreham	
G-AOZL	J/5Q Alpine	R. M. Weeks/Stapleford	
G-AOZP	D.H.C.1 Chipmunk 22	H. Darlington	
G-APAA	J/5R Alpine ★	L. A. Groves (stored)	
G-APAF	Auster 5 (TW511)	J. E. Allen (G-CMAL)	
G-APAH	Auster 5 (TJ324)	T. J. Goodwin	
G-APAL	D.H.82A Tiger Moth (N6847)	P. S. & R. A. Chapman	
G-APAM	D.H.82A Tiger Moth	R. P. Williams	
G-APAO	D.H.82A Tiger Moth	Fairmont Investments Ltd/Clacton	
G-APAP	D.H.82A Tiger Moth	J. Romain/Duxford	
G-APAS	D.H.106 Comet 1XB ★	Aerospace Museum/Cosford	
G-APBE	Auster 5	A. M. Edwards	
G-APBI	D.H.82A Tiger Moth	A. Wood	
G-APBO	D.53 Turbi	R. C. Hibberd	
G-APBW	Auster 5	N. Huxtable	
G-APCB	J/5Q Alpine	A. A. Beswick & I. A. Freeman	
G-APCC	D.H.82A Tiger Moth	L. J. Rice/Henstridge	
G-APDB	D.H.106 Comet 4 ★	Duxford Aviation Soc	

G-APEP – G-APWA

Notes	Reg.	Type	Owner or Operator
	G-APEP	V.953C Merchantman ★	Brooklands Museum of Aviation/Weybridge
	G-APFA	D.54 Turbi	F. J. Keitch
	G-APFG	Boeing 707-436 ★	Cabin water spray tests/Cardington
	G-APFJ	Boeing 707-436 ★	Aerospace Museum/Cosford
	G-APFU	D.H.82A Tiger Moth	Mithril Racing Ltd/Goodwood
	G-APGL	D.H.82A Tiger Moth ★	K. A. Broomfield
	G-APHV	Avro 19 Srs 2 (VM360) ★	Museum of Flight/E. Fortune
	G-APIE	Tipsy Belfair B	D. Beale
	G-APIH	D.H.82A Tiger Moth	K. Stewering
	G-APIK	J/1N Alpha	G-APIK Flying Group
	G-APIM	V.806 Viscount ★	Brooklands Museum of Aviation/Weybridge
	G-APIT	P.40 Prentice 1 (VR192) ★	WWII Aircraft Preservation Soc/Lasham
	G-APIY	P.40 Prentice 1 (VR249) ★	Newark Air Museum
	G-APIZ	D.31 Turbulent	E. J. I. Musty/White Waltham
	G-APJB	P.40 Prentice 1 (VR259)	Atlantic Air Transport Ltd/Coventry
	G-APJJ	Fairey Ultra-light ★	Midland Aircraft Preservation Soc
	G-APJO	D.H.82A Tiger Moth ★	D. R. & M. Wood
	G-APJZ	J/1N Alpha ★	P. G. Lipman
	G-APKH	D.H.85 Leopard Moth	R. G. Grocott (G-ACGS)
	G-APKM	J/1N Alpha	D. E. A. Huggins (stored)
	G-APKN	J/1N Alpha	P. R. Hodson Ltd
	G-APKY	Hiller UH-12B	D. A. George (stored)
	G-APLG	J/5L Aiglet Trainer ★	Solway Aviation Soc
	G-APLO	D.H.C.1 Chipmunk 22A (WD379)	Lindholme Aircraft Ltd/Jersey
	G-APLU	D.H.82A Tiger Moth	R. A. Bishop & M. E. Vaisey
	G-APMB	D.H.106 Comet 4B ★	Gatwick Handling Ltd (ground trainer)
	G-APMH	J/1U Workmaster	J. L. Thorogood
	G-APMX	D.H.82A Tiger Moth	G. A. Broughton
	G-APMY	PA-23 Apache 160 ★	South Yorkshire Aviation Museum
	G-APNJ	Cessna 310 ★	Chelsea College/Shoreham
	G-APNS	Garland-Bianchi Linnet	Paul Penn-Sayers Model Services Ltd
	G-APNT	Currie Wot	J. W. Salter
	G-APNZ	D.31 Turbulent	J. Knight
	G-APOD	Tipsy Belfair ★	L. F. Potts
	G-APOI	Saro Skeeter Srs 8	Skeeter Heritage Trust
	G-APOL	D.31 Turbulent	A. Gregori & S. Tinker
	G-APPA	D.H.C.1 Chipmunk 22	D. M. Squires
	G-APPL	P.40 Prentice 1	S. J. Saggers/Biggin Hill
	G-APPM	D.H.C.1 Chipmunk 22 (WB711)	Freston Aviation Ltd
	G-APPN	D.H.82A Tiger Moth	E. C. Waite-Roberts
	G-APRF	Auster 5	W. B. Bateson/Blackpool
	G-APRJ	Avro 694 Lincoln B.2 ★	Aces High Ltd/North Weald
	G-APRL	AW.650 Argosy 101 ★	Midland Air Museum/Coventry
	G-APRR	Super Aero 45	R. H. Jowett
	G-APRS	SA Twin Pioneer Srs 3	Bravo Aviation Ltd (G-BCWF)/Coventry
	G-APRT	Taylor JT.1 Monoplane	D. A. Slater
	G-APSA	Douglas DC-6A	Atlantic Air Transport Ltd/Coventry
	G-APSO	D.H.104 Dove 5 ★	Cormack (Aircraft Services) Ltd/Cumbernauld
	G-APSR	J/1U Workmaster	D. & K. Aero Services Ltd/Shobdon
	G-APTP	PA-22 Tri-Pacer 150 (tailwheel)	Contest (Ralph & Susan Chesters) Ltd
	G-APTR	J/1N Alpha	C. J. & D. J. Baker
	G-APTU	Auster 5	G-APTU Flying Group
	G-APTW	W.B.1 Widgeon ★	N.E. Aircraft Museum/Usworth
	G-APTY	Beech G.35 Bonanza	G. E. Brennand
	G-APTZ	D.31 Turbulent	The Tiger Club (1990) Ltd/Headcorn
	G-APUD	Bensen B.7M (modified) ★	Manchester Museum of Science & Industry
	G-APUE	L.40 Meta Sokol	S. E. & M. J. Aherne
	G-APUP	Sopwith Pup (replica) (N5182) ★	RAF Museum/Hendon
	G-APUR	PA-22 Tri-Pacer 160	L. F. Miller
	G-APUW	J/5V-160 Autocar	Anglia Auster Syndicate
	G-APUY	D.31 Turbulent	C. Jones/Barton
	G-APUZ	PA-24 Comanche 250	R. R. & A. L. Stadle
	G-APVF	Putzer Elster B (97+04)	A. J. Robinson
	G-APVG	J/5L Aiglet Trainer	R. Farrer/Cranfield
	G-APVN	D.31 Turbulent	R. Sherwin/Shoreham
	G-APVS	Cessna 170B	N. Simpson Stormin ' Norman
	G-APVU	L.40 Meta Sokol	S. E. & M. J. Aherne
	G-APVZ	D.31 Turbulent	I. D. Daniels
	G-APWA	HPR-7 Herald 101 ★	Museum of Berkshire Aviation/Woodley

Reg.	Type	Owner or Operator	Notes
G-APWJ	HPR-7 Herald 201 ★	Duxford Aviation Soc	
G-APWL	EoN 460 Srs 1A	D. G. Andrew/Eaglescott	
G-APWN	WS-55 Whirlwind 3 ★	Midland Air Museum/Coventry	
G-APWY	Piaggio P.166 ★	Science Museum/Wroughton	
G-APWZ	EP.9 Prospector	Prospector Flying Group	
G-APXJ	PA-24 Comanche 250	T. Wildsmith/Netherthorpe	
G-APXR	PA-22 Tri-Pacer 160	A. Troughton	
G-APXT	PA-22 Tri-Pacer 150 (modified)	J. W. & I. Daniels	
G-APXU	PA-22 Tri-Pacer 125 ★	K. Hassell	
G-APXW	EP.9 Prospector (XM819) ★	Museum of Army Flying/Middle Wallop	
G-APXX	D.H.A.3 Drover 2 (VH-FDT) ★	WWII Aircraft Preservation Soc/Lasham	
G-APXY	Cessna 150	Merlin Flying Club Ltd/Hucknall	
G-APYB	Tipsy T.66 Nipper 3	B. O. Smith	
G-APYD	D.H.106 Comet 4B ★	Science Museum/Wroughton	
G-APYG	D.H.C.1 Chipmunk 22	E. J. I. Musty & P. A. Colman	
G-APYI	PA-22 Tri-Pacer 135	B. T. & J. Cullen	
G-APYN	PA-22 Tri-Pacer 160	S. J. Raw	
G-APYT	Champion 7FC Tri-Traveller	B. J. Anning	
G-APZJ	PA-18 Super Cub 150	Southern Sailplanes Ltd/Membury	
G-APZL	PA-22 Tri-Pacer 160	R. T. Evans	
G-APZR	Cessna 150 ★	Engine test-bed/Biggin Hill	
G-APZS	Cessna 175A	G. A. Nash/Booker	
G-APZX	PA-22 Tri-Pacer 150	Applied Signs Ltd	
G-ARAD	Luton LA-5A Major ★	D. J. Bone & P. L. Jobes	
G-ARAI	PA-22 Tri-Pacer 160	T. Richards & G. C. Winters	
G-ARAM	PA-18 Super Cub 150	Fairmont Investments Ltd/Clacton	
G-ARAN	PA-18 Super Cub 150	A. P. Docherty/Redhill	
G-ARAO	PA-18 Super Cub 95 (607327)	R. G. Manton	
G-ARAS	Champion 7FC Tri-Traveller	Alpha Sierra Flying Group	
G-ARAT	Cessna 180C	S. Peck	
G-ARAW	Cessna 182C Skylane	M. & E. N. Ford	
G-ARAX	PA-22 Tri-Pacer 150	P. J. Fahie	
G-ARAZ	D.H.82A Tiger Moth	D. A. Porter	
G-ARBE	D.H.104 Dove 8	M. Whale & M. W. A. Lunn/Old Sarum	
G-ARBG	Tipsy T.66 Nipper 2 ★	J. Horovitz & J. McLeod	
G-ARBM	J/1B Aiglet	B. V. Nabbs & C. Chaddock	
G-ARBO	PA-24 Comanche 250 ★	C. Matthews	
G-ARBP	Tipsy T.66 Nipper 2	F. W. Kirk	
G-ARBS	PA-22 Tri-Pacer 160 (tailwheel)	S. D. Rowell	
G-ARBV	PA-22 Tri-Pacer 160	G-ARBV Oaksey Pacers Group	
G-ARBZ	D.31 Turbulent	J. Mickleburgh	
G-ARCC	PA-22 Tri-Pacer 150	Popham Flying Group/Popham	
G-ARCF	PA-22 Tri-Pacer 150	B. Southerland	
G-ARCS	Auster D6/180	E. A. Matty/Shobdon	
G-ARCT	PA-18 Super Cub 95 ★	K. A. Kirk & C. M. Goodwin	
G-ARCV	Cessna 175A	R. Francis & C. Campbell	
G-ARCW	PA-23 Apache 160	D. R. C. Reeves	
G-ARCX	A.W. Meteor 14 ★★	Museum of Flight/E. Fortune	
G-ARDB	PA-24 Comanche 250	Delta Bravo Aircraft Associates/Booker	
G-ARDD	CP.301C1 Emeraude	R. M. Shipp/Breighton	
G-ARDE	D.H.104 Dove 6	T. E. Evans	
G-ARDG	EP.9 Prospector ★	Museum of Army Flying/Middle Wallop	
G-ARDJ	Auster D.6/180	RN Aviation (Leicester Airport) Ltd	
G-ARDO	Jodel D.112	W. R. Prescott	
G-ARDS	PA-22 Caribbean 150	A. C. Donaldson & C. I. Lavery	
G-ARDT	PA-22 Tri-Pacer 160	M. Henderson	
G-ARDV	PA-22 Tri-Pacer 160	R. W. Christie	
G-ARDY	Tipsy T.66 Nipper 2	M. J. A. Trudgill	
G-ARDZ	Jodel D.140A	M. J. Wright	
G-AREA	D.H.104 Dove 8 ★	Mosquito Aircraft Museum	
G-AREF	PA-23 Aztec 250 ★	Southall College of Technology	
G-AREH	D.H.82A Tiger Moth	N. K. Geddes	
G-AREI	Auster 3 (MT438)	P. J. Stock	
G-AREL	PA-22 Caribbean 150	H. H. Cousins/Fenland	
G-AREO	PA-18 Super Cub 150	DRA (Farnborough) Gliding Club Ltd	
G-ARET	PA-22 Tri-Pacer 160 ★	I. S. Runnalls	
G-AREV	PA-22 Tri-Pacer 160	D. J. Ash	
G-AREX	Aeronca 15AC Sedan	R. J. Middleton-Turnbull & P. Lowndes	
G-AREZ	D.31 Turbulent	J. St. Clair-Quentin/Shobdon	
G-ARFB	PA-22 Caribbean 150	C. T. Woodward & ptnrs	
G-ARFD	PA-22 Tri-Pacer 160	J. R. Dunnett	
G-ARFG	Cessna 175A Skylark	Foxtrot Golf Group	

Notes	Reg.	Type	Owner or Operator
	G-ARFH	PA-24 Comanche 250	A. B. W. Taylor
	G-ARFI	Cessna 150A	J. H. Fisher
	G-ARFL	Cessna 175B Skylark	D. J. Mason
	G-ARFO	Cessna 150A	M. A. Artherton
	G-ARFT	Jodel DR. 1050 ★	R. Shaw
	G-ARFV	Tipsy T.66 Nipper 2	W. Buchan
	G-ARGB	Auster 6A ★	C. J. Baker (stored)
	G-ARGG	D.H.C.1 Chipmunk 22 (WD305)	B. Hook
	G-ARGO	PA-22 Colt 108	M. J. Speakman
	G-ARGV	PA-18 Super Cub 180 ★	Deeside Gliding Club (Aberdeenshire) Ltd/Aboyne
	G-ARGY	PA-22 Tri-Pacer 160	G. K. Hare (G-JEST)
	G-ARGZ	D.31 Turbulent	The Tiger Club (1990) Ltd/Headcorn
	G-ARHB	Forney F-1A Aircoupe	A. V. Rash & D. R. Wickes
	G-ARHC	Forney F-1A Aircoupe	A. P. Gardner/Elstree
	G-ARHI	PA-24 Comanche 180	D. D. Smith
	G-ARHL	PA-23 Aztec 250	C. J. Freeman/Headcorn
	G-ARHM	Auster 6A	D. Hollowell & ptnrs/Finmere
	G-ARHN	PA-22 Caribbean 150	D. B. Furniss & A. Munro/Doncaster
	G-ARHP	PA-22 Tri-Pacer 160	R. N. Morgan
	G-ARHR	PA-22 Caribbean 150	A. R. Wyatt
	G-ARHT	PA-22 Caribbean 150 ★	Moston Technical College
	G-ARHW	D.H.104 Dove 8	Pacelink Ltd
	G-ARHX	D.H.104 Dove 8 ★	N.E. Aircraft Museum/Usworth
	G-ARHZ	D.62 Condor	T. J. Goodwin/Andrewsfield
	G-ARID	Cessna 172B	L. M. Edwards
	G-ARIE	PA-24 Comanche 250	The Com Group
	G-ARIF	Ord-Hume O-H.7 Minor Coupé ★	N. H. Ponsford (stored)
	G-ARIH	Auster 6A (TW591)	India Hotel Group
	G-ARIK	PA-22 Caribbean 150	C. J. Berry
	G-ARIL	PA-22 Caribbean 150 ★	K. Knight
	G-ARIM	D.31 Turbulent ★	R. M. White
	G-ARJB	D.H.104 Dove 8 ★	Cormack (Aircraft Services) Ltd/Cumbernauld
	G-ARJC	PA-22 Colt 108 ★	F. W. H. Dulles
	G-ARJE	PA-22 Colt 108 ★	Touchdown Aviation Ltd
	G-ARJF	PA-22 Colt 108	M. J. Collins
	G-ARJH	PA-22 Colt 108	A. Vine
	G-ARJR	PA-23 Apache 160G ★	Instructional airframe/Kidlington
	G-ARJS	PA-23 Apache 160G	Bencray Ltd/Blackpool
	G-ARJT	PA-23 Apache 160G	Hiveland Ltd
	G-ARJU	PA-23 Apache 160G	G. R. Manley
	G-ARJV	PA-23 Apache 160G	Metham Aviation Ltd
	G-ARJW	PA-23 Apache 160G	(stored)/Bristol
	G-ARJZ	D.31 Turbulent	C. J. Tilson
	G-ARKG	J/5G Autocar	C. M. Milborrow
	G-ARKJ	Beech N35 Bonanza	T. Cust
	G-ARKK	PA-22 Colt 108	Rochford Hundred Flying Group/Southend
	G-ARKM	PA-22 Colt 108	B. J. Thorogood/Earls Colne
	G-ARKN	PA-22 Colt 108	N. Rawlinson & J. M. Lilley
	G-ARKP	PA-22 Colt 108	C. J. & J. Freeman/Headcorn
	G-ARKR	PA-22 Colt 108	B. J. M. Montegut
	G-ARKS	PA-22 Colt 108	R. A. Nesbitt-Dufort
	G-ARLG	Auster D.4/108	Auster D4 Group
	G-ARLK	PA-24 Comanche 250	Gibad Aviation Ltd
	G-ARLO	A.61 Terrier 1 ★	(stored)
	G-ARLP	A.61 Terrier 1 ★	Gemini Flying Group
	G-ARLR	A.61 Terrier 2	M. Palfreman
	G-ARLU	Cessna 172B Skyhawk ★	Instructional airframe/Irish AC
	G-ARLW	Cessna 172B Skyhawk ★	(spares' source)/Barton
	G-ARLX	Jodel D.140B	Shipping & Airlines Ltd/Biggin Hill
	G-ARLZ	D.31A Turbulent	Turb Group
	G-ARMA	PA-23 Apache 160G	C. J. Hopewell
	G-ARMB	D.H.C.1 Chipmunk 22A (WB660)	P. A. Layzell
	G-ARMC	D.H.C.1 Chipmunk 22A (WB703)	John Henderson Children's Trust
	G-ARMD	D.H.C.1 Chipmunk 22A	D. M. Squires
	G-ARMF	D.H.C.1 Chipmunk 22A (WZ868)	D. M. Squires
	G-ARMG	D.H.C.1 Chipmunk 22A	MG Group/Wellesbourne
	G-ARML	Cessna 175B Skylark	R. W. Boote
	G-ARMN	Cessna 175B Skylark	G. A. Nash
	G-ARMO	Cessna 172B Skyhawk	G. M. Jones
	G-ARMR	Cessna 172B Skyhawk	Sunsaver Ltd/Barton

Reg.	Type	Owner or Operator	Notes
G-ARMZ	D.31 Turbulent ★	J. Mickleburgh & D. Clark	
G-ARNB	J/5G Autocar ★	R. F. Tolhurst	
G-ARND	PA-22 Colt 108	E. J. Clarke	
G-ARNE	PA-22 Colt 108	T. D. L. Bowden/Shipdham	
G-ARNG	PA-22 Colt 108	S. S. Delwarte/Shoreham	
G-ARNH	PA-22 Colt 108 ★	Fenland Aircraft Preservation Soc	
G-ARNI	PA-22 Colt 108	B. A. Drury	
G-ARNJ	PA-22 Colt 108	R. A. Keech	
G-ARNK	PA-22 Colt 108 (tailwheel)	N. G. & A-L. N. M. McDonald	
G-ARNL	PA-22 Colt 108	J. A. Dodsworth/White Waltham	
G-ARNO	A.61 Terrier 1 ★	–/Sywell	
G-ARNP	A.109 Airedale	S. W. & M. Isbister	
G-ARNY	Jodel D.117	D. P. Jenkins	
G-ARNZ	D.31 Turbulent	The Tiger Club (1990) Ltd/Headcorn	
G-AROA	Cessna 172B Skyhawk	D. E. Partridge	
G-AROC	Cessna 175B	A. J. Symes (G-OTOW)	
G-AROJ	A.109 Airedale ★	D. J. Shaw *(stored)*	
G-ARON	PA-22 Colt 108	R. W. Curtis	
G-AROO	Forney F-1A Aircoupe	W. J. McMeekan/Newtownards	
G-AROW	Jodel D.140B	Cubair Ltd/Redhill	
G-AROY	Boeing Stearman A.75N.1	W. A. Jordan	
G-ARPH	H.S.121 Trident 1C ★	Aerospace Museum/Cosford	
G-ARPK	H.S.121 Trident 1C ★	Manchester Airport Authority	
G-ARPO	H.S.121 Trident 1C ★	CAA Fire School/Teesside	
G-ARPP	H.S.121 Trident 1C ★	BAA Airport Fire Service/Glasgow	
G-ARPZ	H.S.121 Trident 1C ★	RFD Ltd/Dunsfold	
G-ARRD	Jodel DR.1050	C. M. Fitton	
G-ARRE	Jodel DR.1050	A. Luty & M. P. Edwards/Barton	
G-ARRF	Cessna 150A ★	Electrical Engineering Services	
G-ARRL	J/1N Alpha	G. N. Smith & C. Webb	
G-ARRM	Beagle B.206-X ★	Bristol Aero Collection *(stored)*	
G-ARRS	CP.301A Emeraude	Arssy Aviation	
G-ARRT	Wallis WA-116-1	K. H. Wallis	
G-ARRU	D.31 Turbulent	N. A. Morgan & J. Paget	
G-ARRX	Auster 6A (VF512)	J. E. D. Mackie	
G-ARRY	Jodel D.140B	Fictionview Ltd	
G-ARRZ	D.31 Turbulent	C. I. Jefferson	
G-ARSG	Roe Triplane Type IV (replica)	The Shuttleworth Collection/O. Warden	
G-ARSJ	CP.301-C2 Emeraude	R. J. Lewis	
G-ARSL	A.61 Terrier 1 ★	D. J. Colclough	
G-ARSU	PA-22 Colt 108	D. P. Owen	
G-ARSW	PA-22 Colt 108	M. J. Kirk	
G-ARSX	PA-22 Tri-Pacer 160	S. Hutchinson	
G-ARTH	PA-12 Super Cruiser	R. I. Souch & B. J. Dunford	
G-ARTJ	Bensen B.8M ★	Museum of Flight/E. Fortune	
G-ARTL	D.H.82A Tiger Moth (T7281)	F. G. Clacherty	
G-ARTT	MS.880B Rallye Club	R. N. Scott	
G-ARTZ	McCandless M.4 gyroplane	W. R. Partridge	
G-ARUG	J/5G Autocar	D. P. H. Hulme/Biggin Hill	
G-ARUH	Jodel DR.1050	PFA Group/Denham	
G-ARUI	A.61 Terrier	T. W. J. Dann	
G-ARUL	LeVier Cosmic Wind	P. G. Kynsey/Headcorn	
G-ARUO	PA-24 Comanche 180	Uniform Oscar Group	
G-ARUV	CP.301A Emeraude	S. T. & J. A. Smoothy	
G-ARUY	J/1N Alpha	K. B. Mace & R. M. Chaplin	
G-ARUZ	Cessna 175C	Cardiff Skylark Group	
G-ARVM	V.1101 VC10 ★	Aerospace Museum/Cosford	
G-ARVO	PA-18 Super Cub 95	Northamptonshire School of Flying Ltd/Sywell	
G-ARVT	PA-28 Cherokee 160	Red Rose Aviation Ltd/Liverpool	
G-ARVU	PA-28 Cherokee 160	G-ARVU Flying Group	
G-ARVV	PA-28 Cherokee 160	G. E. Hopkins/Shobdon	
G-ARVZ	D.62B Condor	J. D. Jewitt	
G-ARWB	D.H.C.1 Chipmunk 22 (WK611)	Thruxton Chipmunk Flying Club	
G-ARWH	Cessna 172C ★	*(stored)*	
G-ARWO	Cessna 172C	J. P. Stafford	
G-ARWR	Cessna 172C	Devanha Flying Group	
G-ARWS	Cessna 175C	B. A. I. Torrington	
G-ARXD	A.109 Airedale ★	D. Howden	
G-ARXG	PA-24 Comanche 250	Fairoaks Comanche	
G-ARXH	Bell 47G	A. B. Searle	
G-ARXP	Luton LA-4 Minor	E. Evans	
G-ARXT	Jodel DR.1050	CJM Flying Group	

Notes	Reg.	Type	Owner or Operator
	G-ARXU	Auster AOP.6A (VF526)	E. C. Tait & M. Pocock
	G-ARXW	M.S.885 Super Rallye	A. F. Danton & A. Kennedy
	G-ARYB	H.S.125 Srs 1 ★	Midland Air Museum/Coventry
	G-ARYC	H.S.125 Srs 1 ★	The Mosquito Aircraft Museum
	G-ARYD	Auster AOP.6 (WJ358) ★	Museum of Army Flying/Middle Wallop
	G-ARYF	PA-23 Aztec 250B	I. J. T. Branson/Biggin Hill
	G-ARYH	PA-22 Tri-Pacer 160	C. Watt
	G-ARYI	Cessna 172C	J. Rhodes
	G-ARYK	Cessna 172C	G. W. Goodban
	G-ARYR	PA-28 Cherokee 180	G-ARYR Flying Group
	G-ARYS	Cessna 172C	D. J. Squires & ptnrs
	G-ARYV	PA-24 Comanche 250	A. G. Wintle & D. C. Hanss
	G-ARYZ	A.109 Airedale	Rutland Aviation
	G-ARZB	Wallis WA-116 Srs 1	K. H. Wallis
	G-ARZE	Cessna 172C ★	*Parachute jump trainer*/Cockerham
	G-ARZM	D.31 Turbulent ★	The Tiger Club (1990) Ltd/Headcorn
	G-ARZN	Beech N35 Bonanza	D. W. Mickleburgh/Leicester
	G-ARZW	Currie Wot	B. R. Pearson/Eaglescott
	G-ASAA	Luton LA-4 Minor	J. W. Cudby
	G-ASAI	A.109 Airedale ★	K. R. Howden & ptnrs
	G-ASAJ	A.61 Terrier 2 (WE569)	G-ASAJ Flying Group
	G-ASAK	A.61 Terrier 2	J. H. Oakins/Biggin Hill
	G-ASAL	SA Bulldog Srs 120/124 ★	Pioneer Flying Co. Ltd/Prestwick
	G-ASAM	D.31 Turbulent ★	The Tiger Club (1990) Ltd/Headcorn
	G-ASAN	A.61 Terrier 2	R. J. Bentley
	G-ASAT	M.S.880B Rallye Club	M. Cutovic
	G-ASAU	M.S.880B Rallye Club	T. C. & R. Edwards
	G-ASAX	A.61 Terrier 2	P. G. & F. M. Morris
	G-ASAZ	Hiller UH-12E4 (XS165)	Pan-Air Ltd/North Weald
	G-ASBA	Currie Wot	M. A. Kaye
	G-ASBB	Beech 23 Musketeer	Five Musketeers Flying Group/Bourn
	G-ASBH	A.109 Airedale	D. T. Smollett
	G-ASBY	A.109 Airedale ★	R. K. Wilson
	G-ASCC	Beagle E3 Mk 11 (XP254)	K. R. Harris
	G-ASCD	A.61 Terrier 2 (TJ704) ★	Yorkshire Air Museum/Elvington
	G-ASCM	Isaacs Fury II (K2050)	M. M. Ward
	G-ASCU	PA-18A Super Cub 150	Farm Aviation Services Ltd
	G-ASCZ	CP.301A Emeraude	I. Denham-Brown
	G-ASDF	Edwards Gyrocopter ★	B. King
	G-ASDK	A.61 Terrier 2	M. L. Rose (G-ARLM)
	G-ASDL	A.61 Terrier 2	C. E. Mason (G-ARLN)
	G-ASDY	Wallis WA-116/F	K. H. Wallis
	G-ASEA	Luton LA-4A Minor ★	J. Bradstock
	G-ASEB	Luton LA-4A Minor	S. R. P. Harper
	G-ASEG	A.61 Terrier (VF548)	M. J. Kirk
	G-ASEO	PA-24 Comanche 250	Planetalk Ltd
	G-ASEP	PA-23 Apache 235	Arrowstate Ltd/Denham
	G-ASEU	D.62A Condor	W. M. Grant
	G-ASFA	Cessna 172D	D. Halfpenny
	G-ASFD	L-200A Morava	M. Emery/Bournemouth
	G-ASFK	J/5G Autocar	T. D. G. Lancaster
	G-ASFL	PA-28 Cherokee 180	J. Simpson & D. Kennedy
	G-ASFR	Bo 208A1 Junior	S. T. Dauncey
	G-ASFX	D.31 Turbulent	E. F. Clapham & W. B. S. Dobie
	G-ASGC	V.1151 Super VC10 ★	Duxford Aviation Soc
	G-ASHD	Brantly B-2A ★	IHM/Weston-s-Mare
	G-ASHS	SNCAN Stampe SV-4C	Three Point Flying Ltd
	G-ASHT	D.31 Turbulent	C. W. N. Huke
	G-ASHU	PA-15 Vagabond	G. J. Romanes & T. J. Ventham/ Henstridge
	G-ASHV	PA-23 Aztec 250B ★	Alderney Airport Fire Service
	G-ASHX	PA-28 Cherokee 180	Powertheme Ltd/Barton
	G-ASIB	Cessna F.172D	G-ASIB Flying Group
	G-ASII	PA-28 Cherokee 180	T. R. Hart & Natocars Ltd
	G-ASIJ	PA-28 Cherokee 180	G-ASIJ Group
	G-ASIL	PA-28 Cherokee 180	J. Dickenson & C. D. Powell
	G-ASIT	Cessna 180	A. & P. A. Wood
	G-ASIY	PA-25 Pawnee 235	RAFGSA/Bicester
	G-ASJL	Beech H.35 Bonanza	R. H. B. Malim/Shobdon
	G-ASJM	PA-30 Twin Comanche 160 ★	Via Nova Ltd *(stored)*
	G-ASJO	Beech B.23 Musketeer	G-ASJO Group/Sandown
	G-ASJV	V.S.361 Spitfire IX (MH434)	Merlin Aviation Ltd/Duxford

Reg.	Type	Owner or Operator	Notes
G-ASJY	GY-80 Horizon 160	P. D. Bradbury & S. M. Derbyshire	
G-ASJZ	Jodel D.117A	W. J. Siertsema	
G-ASKC	D.H.98 Mosquito 35 (TA719) ★	Skyfame Collection/Duxford	
G-ASKJ	A.61 Terrier 1 (VX926) ★	C. C. Irvine	
G-ASKK	HPR-7 Herald 211 ★	Norwich Aviation Museum	
G-ASKL	Jodel 150	J. M. Graty	
G-ASKP	D.H.82A Tiger Moth	Tiger Club (1990) Ltd/Headcorn	
G-ASKT	PA-28 Cherokee 180	A. A. Mattacks	
G-ASKV	PA-25 Pawnee 235	Southdown Gliding Club Ltd/Parham Park	
G-ASLH	Cessna 182F	J. M. Powell & J. A. Horton	
G-ASLK	PA-25 Pawnee 235	Bristol Gliding Club (Pty) Ltd/Nympsfield	
G-ASLL	Cessna 336 ★	*(stored)*/Bournemouth	
G-ASLR	Agusta-Bell 47J-2 ★	N. M. G. Pearson	
G-ASLV	PA-28 Cherokee 235	Sackville Flying Group/Riseley	
G-ASLX	CP.301A Emeraude	D. Wallace	
G-ASMA	PA-30 Twin Comanche 160 C/R	Mike Alpha Group	
G-ASME	Bensen B.8M	R. M. Harris & R. T. Bennett	
G-ASMF	Beech D.95A Travel Air	M. J. A. Hornblower	
G-ASMJ	Cessna F.172E	A. J. G. Crawshaw	
G-ASML	Luton LA-4A Minor	Fenland Strut Flying Group	
G-ASMM	D.31 Tubulent	W. J. Browning	
G-ASMO	PA-23 Apache 160G ★	Aviation Enterprises/Fairoaks	
G-ASMS	Cessna 150A	P. P. Conner/Barton	
G-ASMT	Fairtravel Linnet 2	A. F. Cashin	
G-ASMV	CP.1310-C3 Super Emeraude	P. F. D. Waltham/Leicester	
G-ASMW	Cessna 150D	Yorkshire Light Aircraft Ltd/Leeds	
G-ASMY	PA-23 Apache 160 ★	R. D. & E. Forster	
G-ASMZ	A.61 Terrier 2 (VF516)	R. C. Burden	
G-ASNB	Auster 6A (VX118)	S. Alexander	
G-ASNC	Beagle D.5/180 Husky	Peterborough & Spalding Gliding Club/Crowland	
G-ASND	PA-23 Aztec 250	J. R. Grange/Shoreham	
G-ASNF	Ercoupe 415CD ★	C. R. Weldon	
G-ASNI	CP.1310-C3 Super Emeraude	D. Chapman	
G-ASNK	Cessna 205	Justgold Ltd	
G-ASNN	Cessna 182F ★	*Parachute jump trainer*/Tilstock	
G-ASNW	Cessna F.172E	G-ASNW Group	
G-ASNY	Campbell-Bensen B.8M gyroplane ★	R. Light & T. Smith	
G-ASOC	Auster 6A	Auster 6 Group	
G-ASOH	Beech 95-B55A Baron	GMD Group	
G-ASOI	A.61 Terrier 2	N. K. & C. M. Geddes	
G-ASOK	Cessna F.172E	D. W. Disney	
G-ASOM	A.61 Terrier 2	S. J. Tootell (G-JETS)	
G-ASOX	Cessna 205A ★	A. Turnbull	
G-ASPF	Jodel D.120	T. J. Bates	
G-ASPI	Cessna F.172E	Icarus Flying Group/Rochester	
G-ASPK	PA-28 Cherokee 140	Westward Airways (Lands End) Ltd/St Just	
G-ASPP	Bristol Boxkite (replica)	The Shuttleworth Collection/O. Warden	
G-ASPS	Piper J-3C-90 Cub	A. J. Chalkley/Blackbushe	
G-ASPU	D.31 Turbulent	M. W. Bodger	
G-ASPV	D.H.82A Tiger Moth	B. S. Charters/Shipdham	
G-ASRB	D.62B Condor	T. J. McRae & H. C. Palmer/Shoreham	
G-ASRC	D.62C Condor	O. R. Pluck	
G-ASRH	PA-30 Twin Comanche 160	Island Aviation & Travel Ltd	
G-ASRI	PA-23 Aztec 250B ★	Graham Collins Associates Ltd	
G-ASRK	A.109 Airedale	R. K. Wilson & M. R. H. Wheatley	
G-ASRO	PA-30 Twin Comanche 160	D. W. Blake	
G-ASRR	Cessna 182G	P. Ragg/Austria	
G-ASRT	Jodel 150	P. Turton	
G-ASRW	PA-28 Cherokee 180	MK Aero Sport Ltd	
G-ASSE	PA-22 Colt 108	G-ASSE Flying Group	
G-ASSF	Cessna 182G Skylane	B. W. Wells	
G-ASSM	H.S.125 Srs 1/522 ★	Science Museum/S. Kensington	
G-ASSP	PA-30 Twin Comanche 160	P. H. Tavener	
G-ASSS	Cessna 172E	D. H. N. Squires & P. R. March/Filton	
G-ASST	Cessna 150D	F. R. H. Parker	
G-ASSU	CP.301A Emeraude ★	R. W. Millward *(stored)*/Redhill	
G-ASSV	Kensinger KF ★	C. I. Jefferson	
G-ASSW	PA-28 Cherokee 140	W. G. R. Wunderlich/Biggin Hill	
G-ASSY	D.31 Turbulent	D. Silsbury	
G-ASTA	D.31 Turbulent	P. A. Cooke	

Notes	Reg.	Type	Owner or Operator
	G-ASTH	Mooney M.20C ★	E. L. Martin *(stored)*/Guernsey
	G-ASTI	Auster 6A	R. B. Webber
	G-ASTL	Fairey Firefly I (Z2033) ★	Skyfame Collection/Duxford
	G-ASTP	Hiller UH-12C ★	IHM/Weston-s-Mare
	G-ASUB	Mooney M.20E Super 21	S. C. Coulbeck
	G-ASUD	PA-28 Cherokee 180	S. J. Rogers & M. N. Petchey
	G-ASUE	Cessna 150D	D. Huckle/Panshanger
	G-ASUG	Beech E18S ★	Museum of Flight/E. Fortune
	G-ASUI	A.61 Terrier 2	K. W. Chigwell & D. R. Lee
	G-ASUL	Cessna 182G Skylane	Blackpool & Fylde Aero Club Ltd
	G-ASUP	Cessna F.172E	GASUP Air/Cardiff
	G-ASUR	Dornier Do 28A-1	Sheffair Ltd
	G-ASUS	Jurca MJ.2B Tempete	D. G. Jones/Coventry
	G-ASVG	CP.301B Emeraude	K. S. Woodard
	G-ASVM	Cessna F.172E	Golf Victor Mike Flying Group
	G-ASVN	Cessna U.206 Super Skywagon	L. Rawson
	G-ASVP	PA-25 Pawnee 235	Aquila Gliding Club Ltd/ Hinton-in-the-Hedges
	G-ASVZ	PA-28 Cherokee 140	J. S. Garvey
	G-ASWH	Luton LA-5A Major ★	J. T. Powell-Tuck
	G-ASWJ	Beagle 206 Srs 1 (8449M) ★	Brunel Technical College/Bristol
	G-ASWL	Cessna F.172F	J. A. Clegg
	G-ASWN	Bensen B.8M ★	D. R. Shepherd
	G-ASWP	Beech A.23 Musketeer	J. Holdon & G. Benet
	G-ASWW	PA-30 Twin Comanche 160	R. J. Motors
	G-ASWX	PA-28 Cherokee 180	A. F. Dadds
	G-ASXC	SIPA 901	M. K. Dartford & M. Cookson
	G-ASXD	Brantly B.2B	Lousada PLC
	G-ASXI	Tipsy T.66 Nipper 3	B. Dixon
	G-ASXJ	Luton LA-4A Minor	M. R. Sallows
	G-ASXR	Cessna 210	A. Schofield
	G-ASXS	Jodel DR.1050	R. A. Hunter
	G-ASXU	Jodel D.120A	The Jodel Group/Defford
	G-ASXX	Avro 683 Lancaster 7 (NX611) ★	Lincolnshire Aviation Heritage Centre/ E. Kirkby
	G-ASXY	Jodel D.117A	P. A. Davies & ptnrs/Cardiff
	G-ASXZ	Cessna 182G Skylane	Last Refuge Ltd
	G-ASYD	BAC One-Eleven 475 ★	Brooklands Museum of Aviation/ Weybridge
	G-ASYG	A.61 Terrier 2 ★	G. Rea
	G-ASYJ	Beech D.95A Travel Air	Crosby Aviation (Jersey) Ltd
	G-ASYP	Cessna 150E	Henlow Flying Group
	G-ASYZ	Victa Airtourer 100	N. C. Grayson
	G-ASZB	Cessna 150E	R. J. Scott
	G-ASZD	Bo 208A2 Junior	M. J. Ayers
	G-ASZE	A.61 Terrier 2	P. J. Moore
	G-ASZR	Fairtravel Linnet 2	R. Palmer & D. Scott
	G-ASZS	GY.80 Horizon 160	ZS Group
	G-ASZU	Cessna 150E	T. H. Milburn
	G-ASZV	Tipsy T.66 Nipper 2	R. L. Mitcham/Elstree
	G-ASZX	A.61 Terrier 1	R. B. Webber
	G-ATAF	Cessna F.172F	P. J. Thirtle
	G-ATAG	Jodel DR. 1050	T. M. Dawes-Gamble
	G-ATAS	PA-28 Cherokee 180	S. D. Turner
	G-ATAT	Cessna 150E ★	The Derek Pointon Group *(stored)*
	G-ATAU	D.62B Condor	M. A. Peare/Redhill
	G-ATAV	D.62C Condor	R. W. H. Watson
	G-ATBG	Nord 1002 (NJ+C11)	T. W. Harris/Little Snoring
	G-ATBH	Aero 145 ★	P. D. Aberbach
	G-ATBI	Beech A.23 Musketeer	Three Musketeers Flying Group
	G-ATBJ	Sikorsky S-61N	Brintel Helicopters
	G-ATBL	D.H.60G Moth	J. M. Greenland
	G-ATBP	Fournier RF-3	D. McNicholl
	G-ATBS	D.31 Turbulent	D. R. Keene & J. A. Lear
	G-ATBU	A.61 Terrier 2	K9 Flying Group
	G-ATBW	Tipsy T.66 Nipper 2	Stapleford Nipper Group
	G-ATBX	PA-20 Pacer 135	G. D. & P. M. Thomson
	G-ATBZ	W.S.58 Wessex 60 ★	IHM/Weston-s-Mare
	G-ATCC	A.109 Airedale	J. R. Bowden
	G-ATCD	Beagle D.5/180 Husky	T. C. O'Gorman
	G-ATCE	Cessna U.206	British Parachute Schools/Langar
	G-ATCJ	Luton LA-4A Minor	P. R. Diffey

Reg.	Type	Owner or Operator	Notes
G-ATCL	Victa Airtourer 100	A. D. Goodall	
G-ATCN	Luton LA-4A Minor	J. C. Gates & C. Neilson	
G-ATCR	Cessna 310 ★	ITD Aviation Ltd/Denham	
G-ATCU	Cessna 337	University of Cambridge	
G-ATCX	Cessna 182H	K. J. Fisher/Bodmin	
G-ATDA	PA-28 Cherokee 160	Portway Aviation	
G-ATDB	Nord 1101 Noralpha ★	J. W. Hardie	
G-ATDN	A.61 Terrier 2 (TW641)	S. J. Saggers/Biggin Hill	
G-ATDO	Bo 208C1 Junior	H. Swift	
G-ATEF	Cessna 150E	Swans Aviation	
G-ATEM	PA-28 Cherokee 180	Chiltern Valley Aviation Ltd	
G-ATEP	EAA Biplane ★	E. L. Martin (stored)/Guernsey	
G-ATES	PA-32 Cherokee Six 260 ★	Parachute jump trainer/Stirling	
G-ATET	PA-30 Twin Comanche 160	S. J. Gaveston	
G-ATEV	Jodel DR. 1050 ★	R. A. Smith	
G-ATEW	PA-30 Twin Comanche 160	Air Northumbria Group/Newcastle	
G-ATEX	Victa Airtourer 100	Medway Victa Group	
G-ATEZ	PA-28 Cherokee 140	EFI Aviation Ltd	
G-ATFD	Jodel DR. 1050	V. Usher	
G-ATFF	PA-23 Aztec 250C	Neatspin Ltd	
G-ATFG	Brantly B.2B ★	Museum of Flight/E. Fortune	
G-ATFK	PA-30 Twin Comanche 160	D. J. Crinnon/White Waltham	
G-ATFM	Sikorsky S-61N	Brintel Helicopters	
G-ATFR	PA-25 Pawnee 150	Borders (Milfield) Gliding Club Ltd	
G-ATFV	Agusta-Bell 47J-2A ★	Caernarfon Air World	
G-ATFW	Luton LA-4A Minor	P. A. Rose	
G-ATFY	Cessna F.172G	H. Cowan	
G-ATGE	Jodel DR.1050	L. S. & K. L. Johnson	
G-ATGN	Thorn Coal Gas balloon ★	British Balloon Museum/Newbury	
G-ATGO	Cessna F.172G	W. J. Baker	
G-ATGP	Jodel DR.1050	Madley Flying Group/Shobdon	
G-ATGY	GY.80 Horizon	P. W. Gibberson/Birmingham	
G-ATGZ	Griffiths GH-4 Gyroplane ★	R. W. J. Cripps	
G-ATHA	PA-23 Apache 235 ★	Brunel Technical College/Bristol	
G-ATHD	D.H.C.1 Chipmunk 22 (WP971)	Spartan Flying Group Ltd/Denham	
G-ATHF	Cessna 150F ★	Lincolnshire Aviation Heritage Centre/ E. Kirkby	
G-ATHK	Aeronca 7AC Champion	T. P. McDonald & ptnrs/Liverpool	
G-ATHM	Wallis WA-116 Srs 1	Wallis Autogyros Ltd	
G-ATHN	Nord 1101 Noralpha ★	E. L. Martin (stored)/Guernsey	
G-ATHR	PA-28 Cherokee 180	Britannia Airways Ltd/Luton	
G-ATHT	Victa Airtourer 115	D. A. Breeze	
G-ATHU	A.61 Terrier 1	J. A. L. Irwin	
G-ATHV	Cessna 150F	Cessna Hotel Victor Group	
G-ATHX	Jodel DR. 100A	Mourne Flying Club	
G-ATHZ	Cessna 150F	E. & R. D. Forster	
G-ATIA	PA-24 Comanche 260	L. A. Brown	
G-ATIC	Jodel DR.1050	R. J. Major	
G-ATIE	Cessna 150F ★	Parachute jump trainer/Chetwynd	
G-ATIN	Jodel D.117	G. G. Simpson	
G-ATIR	AIA Stampe SV-4C	N. M. Bloom	
G-ATIS	PA-28 Cherokee 160	R. M. Jenner & J. H. Peploe	
G-ATIZ	Jodel D.117	D. K. Shipton/Leicester	
G-ATJA	Jodel DR.1050	Bicester Flying Group	
G-ATJC	Victa Airtourer 100	Aviation West Ltd/Cumbernauld	
G-ATJG	PA-28 Cherokee 140	H. M. Wittman	
G-ATJL	PA-24 Comanche 260	M. J. Berry & T. R. Quinn/Blackbushe	
G-ATJM	Fokker Dr.1 (replica) (152/17)	R. Lamplough/Duxford	
G-ATJN	Jodel D.119	R. F. Bradshaw	
G-ATJT	GY.80 Horizon 160	N. Huxtable	
G-ATJV	PA-32 Cherokee Six 260	Wingglider Ltd	
G-ATKF	Cessna 150F	C. J. Freeman/Headcorn	
G-ATKH	Luton LA-4A Minor	H. E. Jenner	
G-ATKI	Piper J-3C-65 Cub	P. H. Wilmot-Allistone	
G-ATKT	Cessna F.172G	P. J. Megson	
G-ATKU	Cessna F.172G	Holdcroft Aviation Services Ltd	
G-ATKX	Jodel D.140C	A. J. White & G. A. Piper/Biggin Hill	
G-ATKZ	Tipsy T.66 Nipper 2	M. W. Knights	
G-ATLA	Cessna 182J Skylane	Shefford Transport Engineers Ltd/Luton	
G-ATLB	Jodel DR.1050/M1	La Petite Oiseau Syndicate/Breighton	
G-ATLC	PA-23 Aztec 250C ★	Alderney Air Charter Ltd (stored)	
G-ATLM	Cessna F.172G	Air Fotos Aviation Ltd/Newcastle	
G-ATLP	Bensen B.8M	R. F. G. Moyle	

Notes	Reg.	Type	Owner or Operator
	G-ATLT	Cessna U.206A	A. I. M. & A. J. Guest
	G-ATLV	Jodel D.120	L. S. Thorne
	G-ATLW	PA-28 Cherokee 180	R. D. Masters
	G-ATMC	Cessna F.150F	C. J. & E. J. Leigh
	G-ATMG	M.S.893 Rallye Commodore 180	D. R. Wilkinson & T. Coldwell
	G-ATMH	Beagle D.5/180 Husky	Dorset Gliding Club Ltd
	G-ATMI	H.S.748 Srs 2A	Emerald Airways Ltd *Old Ben*/Liverpool
	G-ATMJ	H.S.748 Srs 2A	Emerald Airways Ltd/Liverpool
	G-ATML	Cessna F.150F	G. I. Smith
	G-ATMM	Cessna F.150F	B. Powell
	G-ATMT	PA-30 Twin Comanche 160	Montagu-Smith & Co Ltd
	G-ATMU	PA-23 Apache 160G	P. K. Martin & R. W. Harris
	G-ATMW	PA-28 Cherokee 140	Bencray Ltd/Blackpool
	G-ATMX	Cessna F.150F	N. E. Binner
	G-ATMY	Cessna 150F	J. A. Starbuck/Crosland Moor
	G-ATNB	PA-28 Cherokee 180	G. Taylor/Woodford
	G-ATNE	Cessna F.150F	N. H. Scott
	G-ATNL	Cessna F.150F	G. A. Lauf
	G-ATNV	PA-24 Comanche 260	B. S. Reynolds/Bourn
	G-ATOA	PA-23 Apache 160G	K. A. Passmore
	G-ATOD	Cessna F.150F	E. Watson & ptnrs/St Just
	G-ATOE	Cessna F.150F	J. A. Richardson
	G-ATOH	D.62B Condor	Three Spires Flying Group
	G-ATOI	PA-28 Cherokee 140	R. W. Nash
	G-ATOJ	PA-28 Cherokee 140	A Flight Aviation Ltd
	G-ATOK	PA-28 Cherokee 140	ILC Flying Group
	G-ATOL	PA-28 Cherokee 140	L. J. Nation & G. Alford
	G-ATOM	PA-28 Cherokee 140	A. Flight Aviation Ltd
	G-ATON	PA-28 Cherokee 140	R. G. Walters/Shobdon
	G-ATOO	PA-28 Cherokee 140	I. Wilson
	G-ATOP	PA-28 Cherokee 140	P. R. Coombs/Blackbushe
	G-ATOR	PA-28 Cherokee 140	Aligator Group
	G-ATOT	PA-28 Cherokee 180	Totair Ltd
	G-ATOU	Mooney M.20E Super 21	M20 Flying Group/Sherburn
	G-ATOY	PA-24 Comanche 260 ★	Museum of Flight/E. Fortune
	G-ATOZ	Bensen B.8M	N. C. White & W. Stark
	G-ATPD	H.S.125 Srs 1B	Wessex Air (Holdings) Ltd
	G-ATPN	PA-28 Cherokee 140	M. F. Hatt & ptnrs/Southend
	G-ATPT	Cessna 182J Skylane	G. B. Scholes
	G-ATPV	JB.01 Minicab ★	C. F. O'Neill
	G-ATRG	PA-18 Super Cub 150	Lasham Gliding Soc Ltd
	G-ATRI	Bo 208C1 Junior	Chertwood Ltd
	G-ATRK	Cessna F.150F	Armstrong Aviation
	G-ATRL	Cessna F.150F	A. A. W. Stevens
	G-ATRM	Cessna F.150F	J. Redfearn
	G-ATRO	PA-28 Cherokee 140	390th Flying Group
	G-ATRR	PA-28 Cherokee 140	Marnham Investments Ltd
	G-ATRW	PA-32 Cherokee Six 260	Pringle Brandon Architects
	G-ATRX	PA-32 Cherokee Six 260	J. W. Stow
	G-ATSI	Bo 208C1 Junior	G-ATSI Group
	G-ATSL	Cessna F.172G	L. McMullin
	G-ATSM	Cessna 337A	Landscape & Ground Maintenance
	G-ATSR	Beech M.35 Bonanza	D. G. Lewendon
	G-ATSX	Bo 208C1 Junior	M. H. Jeffries
	G-ATSY	Wassmer WA41 Super Baladou IV	Baladou Flying Group
	G-ATSZ	PA-30 Twin Comanche 160B	Richardson Aviation Consultamts Ltd
	G-ATTB	Wallis WA-116-1 (XR944)	D. A. Wallis
	G-ATTD	Cessna 182J Skylane	K. M. Brennan & ptnrs
	G-ATTF	PA-28 Cherokee 140	D. H. Fear
	G-ATTG	PA-28 Cherokee 140	D. E. Spells
	G-ATTI	PA-28 Cherokee 140	G-ATTI Flying Group/Lulsgate
	G-ATTK	PA-28 Cherokee 140	G-ATTK Flying Group/Southend
	G-ATTM	Jodel DR.250-160	R. W. Tomkinson
	G-ATTN	Piccard balloon ★	Science Museum/S. Kensington
	G-ATTR	Bo 208C1 Junior	S. Luck
	G-ATTV	PA-28 Cherokee 140	D. B. & M. E. Meeks
	G-ATTX	PA-28 Cherokee 180	IPAC Aviation Ltd
	G-ATUB	PA-28 Cherokee 140	R. H. Partington & M. J. Porter
	G-ATUD	PA-28 Cherokee 140	J. J. Ferguson
	G-ATUF	Cessna F.150F	D. P. Williams
	G-ATUG	D.62B Condor	R. Crosby
	G-ATUH	Tipsy T.66 Nipper 1	D. G. Spruce

Reg.	Type	Owner or Operator	Notes
G-ATUI	Bo 208C1 Junior	A. W. Wakefield	
G-ATUL	PA-28 Cherokee 180	Kirkland Ltd	
G-ATVF	D.H.C.1 Chipmunk 22 (Lycoming)	RAFGSA/Syerston	
G-ATVK	PA-28 Cherokee 140	Franchi Aviation Ltd	
G-ATVL	PA-28 Cherokee 140	White Waltham Airfield Ltd	
G-ATVO	PA-28 Cherokee 140	G. R. Bright	
G-ATVP	F.B.5 Gunbus (2345) ★	RAF Museum/Hendon	
G-ATVS	PA-28 Cherokee 180	S. M. Patterson	
G-ATVW	D.62B Condor	J. P. Coulter & J. Chidley/Panshanger	
G-ATVX	Bo 208C1 Junior	D. & G. Aviation	
G-ATWA	Jodel DR.1050	Jodel Syndicate	
G-ATWB	Jodel D.117	Andrewsfield Whiskey Bravo Group	
G-ATWJ	Cessna F.172F	C. J. & J. Freeman/Headcorn	
G-ATWR	PA-30 Twin Comanche 160B	Lubair (Transport Services) Ltd/ E. Midlands	
G-ATXA	PA-22 Tri-Pacer 150	S. Hildrop	
G-ATXD	PA-30 Twin Comanche 160B	Jet Heritage Ltd/Bournemouth	
G-ATXJ	H.P.137 Jetstream 300 ★	Fire Service Training Airframe/Cardiff	
G-ATXM	PA-28 Cherokee 180	G-ATXM Flying Group	
G-ATXN	Mitchell-Proctor Kittiwake 1	P. A. Dawson	
G-ATXO	SIPA 903	S. A. & D. C. Whitehead	
G-ATXZ	Bo 208C1 Junior	Bradbury & ptnrs	
G-ATYM	Cessna F.150G	J. F. Perry & Co	
G-ATYN	Cessna F.150G	J. S. Grant	
G-ATYS	PA-28 Cherokee 180	G-ATYS Flying Group	
G-ATZK	PA-28 Cherokee 180	Austen Associates Partnership	
G-ATZM	Piper J-3C-90 Cub	R. W. Davison	
G-ATZS	Wassmer WA41 Super Baladou IV	Temporal Songs Ltd & Anti Climb Guards/Biggin Hill	
G-ATZY	Cessna F.150G	Fraggle Leasing Ltd/Edinburgh	
G-AVAK	M.S.893A Rallye Commodore 180	W. K. Anderson *(stored)*/Perth	
G-AVAR	Cessna F.150G	J. A. Rees	
G-AVAU	PA-30 Twin Comanche 160B	Enrico Ermano Ltd	
G-AVAW	D.62B Condor	Condor Aircraft Group	
G-AVAX	PA-28 Cherokee 180	J. J. Parkes	
G-AVBG	PA-28 Cherokee 180	G-AVBG Flying Group/White Waltham	
G-AVBH	PA-28 Cherokee 180	T. R. Smith (Agricultural Machinery) Ltd	
G-AVBS	PA-28 Cherokee 180	A. G. Arthur	
G-AVBT	PA-28 Cherokee 180	J. F. Mitchell	
G-AVBZ	Cessna F.172H	M. Byl/Crosland Moor	
G-AVCM	PA-24 Comanche 260	F. Smith & Sons Ltd/Stapleford	
G-AVCV	Cessna 182J Skylane	University of Manchester Institute of Science & Technology/Woodford	
G-AVCX	PA-30 Twin Comanche 160B	T. Barge	
G-AVDA	Cessna 182K Skylane	F. W. Ellis & M. C. Burnett	
G-AVDF	Beagle Pup 100 ★	Beagle Owners Club	
G-AVDG	Wallis WA-116 Srs 1	K. H. Wallis	
G-AVDT	Aeronca 7AC Champion	D. Cheney & G. Moore	
G-AVDY	PA-22 Tri-Pacer 150 (tailwheel)	S. C. Brooks/Slinfold	
G-AVDY	Luton LA-4A Minor	M. Stoney	
G-AVEC	Cessna F.172H	W. H. Ekin (Engineering) Co Ltd	
G-AVEF	Jodel 150	Heavy Install Ltd	
G-AVEH	SIAI-Marchetti S.205	EH Aviation	
G-AVEM	Cessna F.150G	T. D. & J. A. Warren	
G-AVEN	Cessna F.150G	150 Flying Group	
G-AVER	Cessna F.150G	E. Atherden	
G-AVEU	Wassmer WA.41 Baladou IV	G. J. Richardson	
G-AVEX	D.62B Condor	J. Riley & M. Mordue	
G-AVEY	Currie Super Wot	B. J. Anning	
G-AVEZ	HPR-7 Herald 210 ★	*Rescue trainer*/Norwich	
G-AVFB	H.S.121 Trident 2E ★	Duxford Aviation Soc	
G-AVFE	H.S.121 Trident 2E ★	Belfast Airport Authority	
G-AVFG	H.S.121 Trident 2E ★	*Ground handling trainer*/Heathrow	
G-AVFH	H.S.121 Trident 2E ★	Mosquito Aircraft Museum *(fuselage only)*	
G-AVFM	H.S.121 Trident 2E ★	Brunel Technical College/Bristol	
G-AVFP	PA-28 Cherokee 140	R. L. Howells/Barton	
G-AVFR	PA-28 Cherokee 140	VFR Flying Group/Newtownards	
G-AVFS	PA-32 Cherokee Six 300	Comed Aviation Ltd	
G-AVFU	PA-32 Cherokee Six 300	M. J. Hoodless	
G-AVFX	PA-28 Cherokee 140	Wessex Flyers Group/Thruxton	
G-AVFZ	PA-28 Cherokee 140	G-AVFZ Flying Group	
G-AVGA	PA-24 Comanche 260	Conram Aviation/Biggin Hill	

Notes	Reg.	Type	Owner or Operator
	G-AVGC	PA-28 Cherokee 140	P. A. Hill
	G-AVGD	PA-28 Cherokee 140	S. & G. W. Jacobs
	G-AVGE	PA-28 Cherokee 140	A. J. Cutler
	G-AVGI	PA-28 Cherokee 140	D. G. Smith & C. D. Barden
	G-AVGK	PA-28 Cherokee 180	Golf Kilo Flying Group
	G-AVGY	Cessna 182K Skylane	R. M. C. Sears & R. N. Howgego
	G-AVGZ	Jodel DR.1050	D. C. Webb
	G-AVHH	Cessna F.172H	The Bristol & Wessex Aeroplane Club
	G-AVHL	Jodel DR.105A	V. D. Long
	G-AVHM	Cessna F.150G	Airbase Aircraft Ltd
	G-AVHT	Auster AOP.9 (WZ711)	M. Somerton-Rayner/Middle Wallop
	G-AVHY	Fournier RF.4D	J. Connelly
	G-AVIA	Cessna F.150G	Cheshire Air Training Services Ltd/ Liverpool
	G-AVIB	Cessna F.150G	Edinburgh Air Centre Ltd
	G-AVIC	Cessna F.172H	Leeside Flying Ltd
	G-AVID	Cessna 182K	Jaguar Aviation Ltd
	G-AVII	AB-206A JetRanger	Bristow Helicopters Ltd
	G-AVIL	Alon A.2 Aircoupe (VX147)	M. J. Close
	G-AVIN	M.S.880B Rallye Club	P. Bradley
	G-AVIP	Brantly B.2B	N. J. R. Minchin
	G-AVIS	Cessna F.172H	C. J. Freeman
	G-AVIT	Cessna F.150G	Invicta Flyers
	G-AVIZ	Scheibe SF.25A Motorfalke	Spilsby Gliding Trust
	G-AVJE	Cessna F.150G	G-AVJE Syndicate
	G-AVJF	Cessna F.172H	J. A. & G. M. Rees
	G-AVJI	Cessna F.172H ★	Northbrook College/Shoreham
	G-AVJJ	PA-30 Twin Comanche 160B	A. H. Manser
	G-AVJK	Jodel DR.1050/M1	M. H. Wylde
	G-AVJO	Fokker E.III (replica) (422-15)	Bianchi Aviation Film Services Ltd/Booker
	G-AVJV	Wallis WA-117 Srs 1	K. H. Wallis (G-ATCV)
	G-AVJW	Wallis WA-118 Srs 2	K. H. Wallis (G-ATPW)
	G-AVKB	MB.50 Pipistrelle	Aerogroup 98 Ltd
	G-AVKD	Fournier RF-4D	Lasham RF4 Group
	G-AVKE	Gadfly HDW.1 ★	IHM/Weston-s-Mare
	G-AVKG	Cessna F.172H	P. E. P. Sheppard/Breighton
	G-AVKI	Slingsby T.66 Nipper 3	J. M. Greenway
	G-AVKJ	Slingsby T.66 Nipper 3	G-AVKJ Group
	G-AVKK	Slingsby T.66 Nipper 3	C. Watson
	G-AVKL	PA-30 Twin Comanche 160B	Bravo Aviation Ltd
	G-AVKN	Cessna 401	Law Leasing Ltd
	G-AVKP	A.109 Airedale	D. R. Williams
	G-AVKR	Bo 208C1 Junior	C. W. Grant
	G-AVLB	PA-28 Cherokee 140	M. Wilson
	G-AVLC	PA-28 Cherokee 140	NE Wales Institute of Higher Education/Welshpool
	G-AVLD	PA-28 Cherokee 140	WLS Flying Group/Blackbushe
	G-AVLE	PA-28 Cherokee 140	Video Security Services/Tollerton
	G-AVLF	PA-28 Cherokee 140	G. H. Hughesdon
	G-AVLG	PA-28 Cherokee 140	R. Friedlander & D. C. Raymond
	G-AVLH	PA-28 Cherokee 140	M. B. Rothschild
	G-AVLI	PA-28 Cherokee 140	Lima India Aviation Club
	G-AVLJ	PA-28 Cherokee 140	Demeter Aviation Ltd
	G-AVLM	B.121 Pup 3	T. M. & D. A. Jones/Egginton
	G-AVLN	B.121 Pup 2	C. A. Thorpe
	G-AVLO	Bo 208C1 Junior	P. J. Swain
	G-AVLR	PA-28 Cherokee 140	Group 140/Panshanger
	G-AVLW	Fournier RF-4D	J. W. Scott
	G-AVLY	Jodel D.120A	N. V. de Candole
	G-AVMA	GY-80 Horizon 180	B. R. Hildick
	G-AVMB	D.62B Condor	L. J. Dray
	G-AVMD	Cessna 150G	Bagby Aviation Flying Group
	G-AVMF	Cessna F. 150G	J. F. Marsh
	G-AVMI	BAC One-Eleven 510ED	European Aircharter Ltd
	G-AVMJ	BAC One-Eleven 510ED ★	European Aviation Ltd *(cabin trainer)*
	G-AVML	BAC One-Eleven 510ED	European Aviation Ltd
	G-AVMM	BAC One-Eleven 510ED	European Aviation Ltd
	G-AVMN	BAC One-Eleven 510ED	European Aviation Ltd
	G-AVMO	BAC One-Eleven 510ED ★	Aerospace Museum/Cosford
	G-AVMP	BAC One-Eleven 510ED	European Aviation Ltd
	G-AVMR	BAC One-Eleven 510ED	European Aviation Ltd
	G-AVMS	BAC One-Eleven 510ED	European Aviation Ltd
	G-AVMT	BAC One-Eleven 510ED	European Aviation Ltd

Reg.	Type	Owner or Operator	Notes
G-AVMU	BAC One-Eleven 510ED ★	Duxford Aviation Soc	
G-AVMV	BAC One-Eleven 510ED	European Aviation Ltd	
G-AVMW	BAC One-Eleven 510ED	European Aviation Ltd	
G-AVMX	BAC One-Eleven 510ED	European Aviation Ltd	
G-AVMY	BAC One-Eleven 510ED	European Aviation Ltd	
G-AVMZ	BAC One-Eleven 510ED	European Aviation Ltd	
G-AVNC	Cessna F.150G	J. Turner	
G-AVNE	W.S.58 Wessex Mk 60 Srs 1 ★	IHM/Weston-s-Mare	
G-AVNN	PA-28 Cherokee 180	B. Andrews & C. S. Mitchell	
G-AVNO	PA-28 Cherokee 180	Allister Flight Ltd	
G-AVNP	PA-28 Cherokee 180	R. W. Harris & ptnrs	
G-AVNR	PA-28 Cherokee 180	R. R. Livingstone	
G-AVNS	PA-28 Cherokee 180	E. Alexander/Earls Colne	
G-AVNU	PA-28 Cherokee 180	D. Durrant	
G-AVNW	PA-28 Cherokee 180	Len Smith's School of Sports Ltd	
G-AVNX	Fournier RF-4D	W. G. Woollard	
G-AVNZ	Fournier RF-4D	V. S. E. Norman/Rendcomb	
G-AVOA	Jodel DR.1050	D. A. Willies/Cranwell	
G-AVOC	CEA Jodel DR.221	J. M. Graty	
G-AVOH	D.62B Condor	Rankhart Ltd	
G-AVOM	CEA Jodel DR.221	M. A. Mountford/Headcorn	
G-AVOO	PA-18 Super Cub 150	London Gliding Club (Pty) Ltd/Dunstable	
G-AVOZ	PA-28 Cherokee 180	Oscar Zulu Flying Group	
G-AVPC	D.31 Turbulent	S. A. Sharp	
G-AVPD	Jodel D.9 Bebe	S. W. McKay (stored)	
G-AVPH	Cessna F.150G	Zero 9 Flight Academy/Norwich	
G-AVPI	Cessna F.172H	R. W. Cope	
G-AVPJ	D.H.82A Tiger Moth	C. C. Silk	
G-AVPM	Jodel D.117	J. C. Haynes/Breighton	
G-AVPN	HPR-7 Herald 213 ★	Yorkshire Air Museum/Elvington	
G-AVPO	Hindustan HAL-26 Pushpak	J. A. Rimell	
G-AVPR	PA-30 Twin Comanche 160B	J. O. Coundley	
G-AVPS	PA-30 Twin Comanche 160B	J. M. Bisco/Staverton	
G-AVPV	PA-18 Cherokee 180	S. Moore	
G-AVRK	PA-28 Cherokee 180	J. Gama	
G-AVRP	PA-28 Cherokee 180	Trent-199	
G-AVRS	GY-80 Horizon 180	Air Venturas Ltd	
G-AVRT	PA-28 Cherokee 140	C. Hawkins/Stapleford	
G-AVRU	PA-28 Cherokee 180	G-AVRU Partnership/Clacton	
G-AVRW	GY-20 Minicab	Kestrel Flying Group/Tollerton	
G-AVRY	PA-28 Cherokee 180	Brigfast Ltd/Blackbushe	
G-AVRZ	PA-28 Cherokee 180	Mantavia Group Ltd	
G-AVSA	PA-28 Cherokee 180	G-AVSA Flying Group	
G-AVSB	PA-28 Cherokee 180	T. H. Lloyd	
G-AVSC	PA-28 Cherokee 180	Medidata Ltd	
G-AVSD	PA-28 Cherokee 180	Landmate Ltd	
G-AVSF	PA-28 Cherokee 180	Monday Club	
G-AVSI	PA-28 Cherokee 140	G-AVSI Flying Group	
G-AVSP	PA-28 Cherokee 180	L. J. Jones	
G-AVSR	Beagle D.5/180 Husky	A. L. Young	
G-AVSZ	AB-206B JetRanger	Burman Aviation Ltd/Cranfield	
G-AVTJ	PA-32 Cherokee Six 260	J. A. Carr	
G-AVTP	Cessna F.172H	Tango Papa Group/White Waltham	
G-AVTT	Ercoupe 415D	Wright's Farm Eggs Ltd/Andrewsfield	
G-AVTV	M.S.893A Rallye Commodore	D. B. & M. E. Meeks	
G-AVUD	PA-30 Twin Comanche 160B	F.M.Aviation/Biggin Hill	
G-AVUG	Cessna F.150H	Skyways Flying Group	
G-AVUH	Cessna F.150H	C. M. Chinn	
G-AVUS	PA-28 Cherokee 140	D. J. Hunter	
G-AVUT	PA-28 Cherokee 140	Bencray Ltd/Blackpool	
G-AVUU	PA-28 Cherokee 140	A. Jahanfar & ptnrs/Southend	
G-AVUZ	PA-32 Cherokee Six 300	Ceesix Ltd/Jersey	
G-AVVC	Cessna F.172H	A. Turnbull	
G-AVVE	Cessna F.150H ★	R. Windley (stored)	
G-AVVF	D.H.104 Dove ★	Airport Fire Service/Staverton	
G-AVVJ	M.S.893A Rallye Commodore	AVVJ Group	
G-AVVL	Cessna F.150H	N. E. Sams/Cranfield	
G-AVVO	Avro 652A Anson 19 (VL348) ★	Newark Air Museum	
G-AVWA	PA-28 Cherokee 140	SFG Ltd	
G-AVWD	PA-28 Cherokee 140	Evelyn Air	
G-AVWI	PA-28 Cherokee 140	L. M. Veitch	
G-AVWJ	PA-28 Cherokee 140	F. E. Telling	
G-AVWL	PA-28 Cherokee 140	Bobev Aviation	

Notes	Reg.	Type	Owner or Operator
	G-AVWM	PA-28 Cherokee 140	P. E. Preston & ptnrs/Southend
	G-AVWN	PA-28R Cherokee Arrow 180	Vawn Air Ltd/Jersey
	G-AVWO	PA-28R Cherokee Arrow 180	R. G. Tweddle
	G-AVWR	PA-28R Cherokee Arrow 180	S. J. French & ptnrs/Exeter
	G-AVWT	PA-28R Cherokee Arrow 180	Cloudbase Aviation Ltd
	G-AVWU	PA-28R Cherokee Arrow 180	Arrow Flyers Ltd
	G-AVWV	PA-28R Cherokee Arrow 180	Strathtay Flying Group
	G-AVWY	Fournier RF-4D	B. Houghton
	G-AVXA	PA-25 Pawnee 235	S. Wales Gliding Club Ltd
	G-AVXC	Slingsby T.66 Nipper 3	D. S. T. Eggleton
	G-AVXD	Slingsby T.66 Nipper 3	D. A. Davidson
	G-AVXF	PA-28R Cherokee Arrow 180	JDR Arrow Group
	G-AVXI	H.S.748 Srs 2A	Emerald Airways Ltd/Liverpool
	G-AVXJ	H.S.748 Srs 2A	Emerald Airways Ltd/Liverpool
	G-AVXW	D.62B Condor	A. J. Cooper/Rochester
	G-AVXY	Auster AOP.9 (XK417)	Auster Nine Group
	G-AVXZ	PA-28 Cherokee 140 ★	ATC Hayle *(instructional airframe)*
	G-AVYB	H.S.121 Trident 1E-140 ★	*SAS training airframe*/Hereford
	G-AVYE	H.S.121 Trident 1E-140 ★	–
	G-AVYK	A.61 Terrier 3	J. P. Roland
	G-AVYL	PA-28 Cherokee 180	Cherokee G-AVYL Flying Group
	G-AVYM	PA-28 Cherokee 180	Carlisle Aviation (1985) Ltd/Crosby
	G-AVYP	PA-28 Cherokee 140	Aldergrove Flight Training Centre
	G-AVYR	PA-28 Cherokee 140	D.R. Flying Club Ltd/Staverton
	G-AVYS	PA-28R Cherokee Arrow 180	A. M. Playford
	G-AVYT	PA-28R Cherokee Arrow 180	E. J. Booth & B. D. Tipler
	G-AVYV	Jodel D.120	A. J. Sephton
	G-AVZB	Aero Z-37 Cmelak ★	Science Museum/Wroughton
	G-AVZI	Bo 208C1 Junior	C. F. Rogers
	G-AVZN	B.121 Pup 1	Shipdham Aviators Flying Group
	G-AVZO	B.121 Pup 1 ★	Thamesside Aviation Museum/ E. Tilbury
	G-AVZP	B.121 Pup 1	T. A. White
	G-AVZR	PA-28 Cherokee 180	Lincoln Aero Club Ltd/Sturgate
	G-AVZU	Cessna F.150H	R. D. & E. Forster/Swanton Morley
	G-AVZV	Cessna F.172H	E. M. & D. S. Lightbown/ Crosland Moor
	G-AVZW	EAA Biplane Model P	R. G. Maidment & G. R. Edmundson/Goodwood
	G-AVZX	M.S.880B Rallye Club	T. C. Bayes/Shobdon
	G-AWAA	M.S.880B Rallye Club	P. A. Cairns *(stored)*/St Just
	G-AWAC	GY-80 Horizon 180	Gardan Party Ltd
	G-AWAH	Beech 95-D55 Baron	B. J. S. Grey/Duxford
	G-AWAJ	Beech 95-D55 Baron	Standard Hose Ltd/Leeds
	G-AWAT	D.62B Condor	Tarwood Ltd/Redhill
	G-AWAU	Vickers F.B.27A Vimy (replica) (F8614) ★	Bomber Command Museum/ Hendon
	G-AWAW	Cessna F.150F ★	Science Museum/S. Kensington
	G-AWAX	Cessna 150D	H. H. Cousins
	G-AWAZ	PA-28R Cherokee Arrow 180	R. Staniszewski
	G-AWBA	PA-28R Cherokee Arrow 180	March Flying Group/Stapleford
	G-AWBB	PA-28R Cherokee Arrow 180	M. D. Parker & J. Lowe
	G-AWBC	PA-28R Cherokee Arrow 180	Anglo Aviation (UK) Ltd
	G-AWBE	PA-28 Cherokee 140	B. E. Boyle
	G-AWBH	PA-28 Cherokee 140	G-AWBH Group
	G-AWBJ	Fournier RF-4D	J. M. Adams
	G-AWBM	D.31 Turbulent	A. D. Pratt
	G-AWBN	PA-30 Twin Comanche 160B	Stourfield Investments Ltd/Jersey
	G-AWBS	PA-28 Cherokee 140	M. A. English & T. M. Brown
	G-AWBT	PA-30 Twin Comanche 160B ★	*Instructional airframe*/Cranfield
	G-AWBU	Morane-Saulnier N (replica) (MS.824)	Personal Plane Services Ltd/Booker
	G-AWBW	Cessna F.172H ★	Brunel Technical College/Bristol
	G-AWBX	Cessna F.150H	J. Meddings
	G-AWCM	Cessna F.150H	R. Garbett
	G-AWCN	Cessna FR.172E	Y. F. Herdman
	G-AWCP	Cessna F.150H (tailwheel)	C. E. Mason/Shobdon
	G-AWDA	Slingsby T.66 Nipper 3	J. A. Cheesebrough
	G-AWDI	PA-23 Aztec 250C ★	Queens Head/Willington, Beds
	G-AWDO	D.31 Turbulent	R. N. Crosland
	G-AWDP	PA-28 Cherokee 180	B. H. & P. M. Illston/Shipdham
	G-AWDR	Cessna FR.172E	B. A. Wallace

Reg.	Type	Owner or Operator	Notes
G-AWDU	Brantly B.2B	B. M. Freeman	
G-AWEF	SNCAN Stampe SV-4B	The Tiger Club (1990) Ltd/Headcorn	
G-AWEI	D.62B Condor	M. J. Steer	
G-AWEK	Fournier RF-4D	P. Barrett	
G-AWEL	Fournier RF-4D	A. B. Clymo/Halfpenny Green	
G-AWEM	Fournier RF-4D	B. J. Griffin/Wickenby	
G-AWEP	Barritault JB-01 Minicab	J. A. Stewart & J. Taylor	
G-AWET	PA-28 Cherokee 180D	Broadland Flying Group Ltd/Shipdham	
G-AWEV	PA-28 Cherokee 140	Norflight Ltd	
G-AWEX	PA-28 Cherokee 140	Sir W. G. Armstrong Whitworth Flying Group	
G-AWFB	PA-28R Cherokee Arrow 180	T. R. Leighton & ptnrs	
G-AWFB	PA-28R Cherokee Arrow 180	Luke Aviation Ltd/Bristol	
G-AWFC	PA-28R Cherokee Arrow 180	B. J. Hines	
G-AWFD	PA-28R Cherokee Arrow 180	D. J. Hill	
G-AWFF	Cessna F.150H	J. A. Hardiman/Shobdon	
G-AWFJ	PA-28R Cherokee Arrow 180	Parplon Ltd	
G-AWFN	D.62B Condor	R. James	
G-AWFO	D.62B Condor	T. A. Major	
G-AWFP	D.62B Condor	Blackbushe Flying Club	
G-AWFR	D.31 Turbulent	J. R. Froud	
G-AWFT	Jodel D.9 Bebe	W. H. Cole	
G-AWFW	Jodel D.117	F. H. Greenwell	
G-AWFZ	Beech A23 Musketeer	R. Sweet & B. D. Corbett	
G-AWGA	A.109 Airedale ★	stored/Sevenoaks	
G-AWGD	Cessna F.172H	D. Whitton & P. Storey	
G-AWGJ	Cessna F.172H	J. & C. J. Freeman/Headcorn	
G-AWGK	Cessna F.150H	G. E. Allen	
G-AWGN	Fournier RF-4D	R. H. Ashforth/Staverton	
G-AWGR	Cessna F.172H	P. A. Hallam	
G-AWGZ	Taylor JT.1 Monoplane	R. L. Sambell	
G-AWHB	C.A.S.A. 2-111D (6J+PR) ★	Aces High Ltd/North Weald	
G-AWHX	Rollason Beta B.2	S. G. Jones	
G-AWHY	Falconar F.11-3	B. E. Smith (G-BDPB)	
G-AWIF	Brookland Mosquito 2	–/Husbands Bosworth	
G-AWII	V.S.349 Spitfire VC (AR501)	The Shuttleworth Collection/O. Warden	
G-AWIP	Luton LA-4A Minor	J. Houghton	
G-AWIR	Midget Mustang	K. E. Sword/Leicester	
G-AWIT	PA-28 Cherokee 180	Cherry Orchard Aparthotel Ltd	
G-AWIV	Airmark TSR.3	D. J. & F. M. Nunn	
G-AWIW	SNCAN Stampe SV-4B	R. E. Mitchell	
G-AWJE	Slingsby T.66 Nipper 3	T. Mosedale	
G-AWJV	D.H.98 Mosquito TT Mk 35 (TA634) ★	Mosquito Aircraft Museum	
G-AWJX	Zlin Z.526 Trener Master	Aerobatics International Ltd	
G-AWJY	Zlin Z.526 Trener Master	M. Gainza	
G-AWKD	PA-17 Vagabond	A. T. & M. R. Dowie/ White Waltham	
G-AWKM	B.121 Pup 1	D. M. G. Jenkins/Swansea	
G-AWKO	B.121 Pup 1	E. C. Felix	
G-AWKP	Jodel DR.253	G-AWKP Group	
G-AWKT	M.S.880B Rallye Club	D. G. Cochrane	
G-AWKX	Beech A65 Queen Air ★	(Instructional airframe)/Shoreham	
G-AWLA	Cessna F.150H	Bagby Aviation	
G-AWLF	Cessna F.172H	Gannet Aviation Ltd/Aldergrove	
G-AWLG	SIPA 903	S. W. Markham	
G-AWLI	PA-22 Tri-Pacer 150	J. S. Lewery/Shoreham	
G-AWLO	Boeing Stearman E.75	N. D. Pickard/Shoreham	
G-AWLP	Mooney M.20F	I. C. Lomax	
G-AWLR	Slingsby T.66 Nipper 3	T. D. Reid	
G-AWLS	Slingsby T.66 Nipper 3	G. A. Dunster & B. Gallagher	
G-AWLZ	Fournier RF-4D	Nympsfield RF-4 Group	
G-AWMD	Jodel D.11	D. A. Barr-Hamilton	
G-AWMF	PA-18 Super Cub 150 (modified)	Booker Gliding Club Ltd	
G-AWMI	Glos-Airtourer 115	W. G. Jones	
G-AWMK	AB-206B JetRanger	M. D. Souster	
G-AWMN	Luton LA-4A Minor	B. J. Douglas	
G-AWMP	Cessna F.172H	R. J. D. Blois	
G-AWMR	D.31 Turbulent	M. J. Bond	
G-AWMT	Cessna F.150H	Oilfield Expertise Ltd/Tilstock	
G-AWMZ	Cessna F.172H ★	Parachute jump trainer/Cark	
G-AWNT	BN-2A Islander	Aerofilms Ltd/Elstree	
G-AWOA	M.S.880B Rallye Club	J. A. Rimmer	
G-AWOE	Aero Commander 680E	J. M. Houlder/Elstree	

Notes	Reg.	Type	Owner or Operator
	G-AWOF	PA-15 Vagabond	C. M. Hicks
	G-AWOH	PA-17 Vagabond	The High Flatts Flying Group
	G-AWOT	Cessna F.150H	J. M. Montgomerie & J. Ferguson
	G-AWOU	Cessna 170B	S. Billington/Denham
	G-AWOX	W.S.58 Wessex 60 (150225) ★	IHM/Weston-s-Mare
	G-AWPH	P.56 Provost T.1	J. A. D. Bradshaw
	G-AWPJ	Cessna F.150H	W. J. Greenfield
	G-AWPN	Shield Xyla	K. R. Snell
	G-AWPP	Cessna F.150H	K2 Aviation Ltd & R. S. Willcock
	G-AWPS	PA-28 Cherokee 140	A. R. Matthews
	G-AWPU	Cessna F.150J	LAC (Enterprises) Ltd/Barton
	G-AWPW	PA-12 Super Cruiser	AK Leasing (Jersey) Ltd
	G-AWPY	Bensen B.8M	J. Jordan
	G-AWPZ	Andreasson BA-4B	J. M. Vening
	G-AWRK	Cessna F.150H	Systemroute Ltd/Shoreham
	G-AWRP	Cierva Rotorcraft ★	IHM/Weston-s-Mare
	G-AWRS	Avro 19 Srs. 2 ★	N. E. Aircraft Museum/Usworth
	G-AWRY	P.56 Provost T.1 (XF836)	Slymar Aviation & Services Ltd
	G-AWSA	Avro 652A Anson 19 (VL349) ★	Norfolk & Suffolk Aviation Museum
	G-AWSH	Zlin Z.526 Trener Master	Aerobatics International Ltd
	G-AWSL	PA-28 Cherokee 180D	Fascia Services Ltd/Southend
	G-AWSM	PA-28 Cherokee 235	Aviation Projects
	G-AWSN	D.62B Condor	M. K. A. Blyth
	G-AWSP	D.62B Condor	R. Q. & A. S. Bond/Wellesbourne
	G-AWSS	D.62A Condor	N. J. & D. Butler
	G-AWST	D.62B Condor	P. L. Clements
	G-AWSV	Skeeter 12 (XM553)	Maj. M. Somerton-Rayner/Middle Wallop
	G-AWSW	D.5/180 Husky (XW635)	Windmill Aviation/Spanhoe
	G-AWTJ	Cessna F.150J	D. G. Williams
	G-AWTL	PA-28 Cherokee 180D	E. Alexander
	G-AWTS	Beech A.23 Musketeer	J. Holden & G. Benet
	G-AWTV	Beech A.23 Musketeer	L. Mariscotti
	G-AWTX	Cessna F.150J	Norfolk & Norwich Aero Club
	G-AWUB	GY-201 Minicab	H. P. Burrill
	G-AWUE	Jodel DR.1050	K. W. Wood & F. M. Watson
	G-AWUG	Cessna F.150H	Fraggle Leasing Ltd/Edinburgh
	G-AWUJ	Cessna F.150H	S. R. Hughes
	G-AWUL	Cessna F.150H	C. A. & L. P. Green
	G-AWUN	Cessna F.150H	D. S. Paton
	G-AWUO	Cessna F.150H	SAS Flying Group
	G-AWUT	Cessna F.150J	S. J. Black/Leeds
	G-AWUU	Cessna F.150J	A. L. Grey
	G-AWUX	Cessna F.172H	D. K. Brian & ptrs
	G-AWUZ	Cessna F.172H	G. F. Burling
	G-AWVA	Cessna F.172H	Barton Air Ltd
	G-AWVB	Jodel D.117	H. Davies
	G-AWVC	B.121 Pup 1	J. H. Marshall & J. J. West
	G-AWVE	Jodel DR.1050/M1	E. A. Taylor/Southend
	G-AWVF	P.56 Provost T.1 (XF877)	Hunter Wing Ltd/Bournemouth
	G-AWVG	AESL Airtourer T.2	C. J. Schofield
	G-AWVN	Aeronca 7AC Champion	Champ Flying Group
	G-AWVZ	Jodel D.112	D. C. Stokes
	G-AWWE	B.121 Pup 2	J. M. Randle/Coventry
	G-AWWI	Jodel D.117	W. J. Evans
	G-AWWM	GY-201 Minicab	J. S. Brayshaw
	G-AWWN	Jodel DR.1051	R. A. J. Hurst
	G-AWWO	Jodel DR.1050	Whiskey Oscar Group/Barton
	G-AWWP	Aerosport Woody Pusher III	M. S. Bird & R. D. Bird
	G-AWWT	D.31 Turbulent	E. L. Phillips
	G-AWWU	Cessna FR.172F	Westward Airways (Lands End) Ltd
	G-AWWW	Cessna 401	Treble Whisky Aviation Ltd
	G-AWXR	PA-28 Cherokee 180D	Aero Club de Portugal
	G-AWXS	PA-28 Cherokee 180D	J. A. Hardiman/Shobdon
	G-AWXY	M.S.885 Super Rallye	K. Henderson
	G-AWXZ	SNCAN Stampe SV-4C	Personal Plane Services Ltd/Booker
	G-AWYB	Cessna FR.172F	C. W. Larkin/Southend
	G-AWYJ	B.121 Pup 2	H. C. Taylor
	G-AWYL	Jodel DR.253B	I. R. Elms
	G-AWYO	B.121 Pup 1	B. R. C. Wild/Popham
	G-AWYV	BAC One-Eleven 501EX	European Aviation Ltd
	G-AWYX	M.S.880B Rallye Club	M. J. Edwards/Hendstridge
	G-AWYY	T.57 Camel replica (B6401) ★	F.A.A. Museum/Yeovilton

Reg.	Type	Owner or Operator	Notes
G-AWZI	H.S.121 Trident 3B ★	Surrey Fire Brigade (instructional airframe)/Reigate	
G-AWZJ	H.S.121 Trident 3B ★	Prestwick Fire Department	
G-AWZK	H.S.121 Trident 3B ★	Ground trainer/Heathrow	
G-AWZM	H.S.121 Trident 3B ★	Science Museum/Wroughton	
G-AWZO	H.S.121 Trident 3B ★	Mosquito Aircraft Museum/Hatfield	
G-AWZP	H.S.121 Trident 3B ★	Manchester Museum of Science & Industry (nose only)	
G-AWZU	H.S.121 Trident 3B ★	BAA Airport Fire Service/Stansted	
G-AWZX	H.S.121 Trident 3B ★	BAA Airport Fire Services/Gatwick	
G-AWZZ	H.S.121 Trident 3B ★	Airport Fire Services/Birmingham	
G-AXAB	PA-28 Cherokee 140	D. M. Loughlin	
G-AXAK	M.S.880B Rallye Club	A. G. Foster	
G-AXAN	D.H.82A Tiger Moth (EM720)	M. E. Carrell	
G-AXAS	Wallis WA-116T	K. H. Wallis (G-AVDH)	
G-AXAT	Jodel D.117A	P. S. Wilkinson	
G-AXAU	PA-30 Twin Comanche 160C	Bartcourt Ltd/Bournemouth	
G-AXBF	Beagle D.5/180 Husky	C. H. Barnes	
G-AXBH	Cessna F.172H	D. F. Ranger	
G-AXBJ	Cessna F.172H	Bravo Juliet Group/Leicester	
G-AXBW	D.H.82A Tiger Moth (T5879)	Hunter Wing Ltd/Bournemouth	
G-AXBZ	D.H.82A Tiger Moth	D. H. McWhir	
G-AXCA	PA-28R Cherokee Arrow 200	R. A. Symmonds	
G-AXCG	Jodel D.117	Charlie Golf Group/Andrewsfield	
G-AXCI	Bensen B.8M	N. Martin (stored)	
G-AXCL	M.S.880B Rallye Club	P. P. Loucas/Andrewsfield	
G-AXCM	M.S.880B Rallye Club	D. C. Manifold	
G-AXCX	B.121 Pup 2	L. A. Pink	
G-AXCY	Jodel D.117	R. D. P. Cadle	
G-AXDC	PA-23 Aztec 250D	N. J. Lilley/Bodmin	
G-AXDI	Cessna F.172H	M. F. & J. R. Leusby/Conington	
G-AXDK	Jodel DR.315	Delta Kilo Flying Group/Sywell	
G-AXDM	H.S.125 Srs 400B	GEC Ferranti Defence Systems Ltd/ Edinburgh	
G-AXDN	BAC-Sud Concorde 01 ★	Duxford Aviation Soc	
G-AXDV	B.121 Pup 1	T. A. White	
G-AXDW	B.121 Pup 1	Cranfield Delta Whiskey Group	
G-AXDY	Falconar F-11	J. Nunn	
G-AXDZ	Cassutt Racer IIIM	A. Chadwick/Little Staughton	
G-AXED	PA-25 Pawnee 235	Wolds Gliding Club Ltd/Pocklington	
G-AXEH	B.125 Bulldog 1 ★	Museum of Flight/E. Fortune	
G-AXEI	Ward Gnome ★	Real Aeroplane Club/Breighton	
G-AXEO	Scheibe SF.25B Falke	The Borders (Milfield) Gliding Club Ltd	
G-AXEV	B.121 Pup 2	D. S. Russell & J. Powell-Tuck	
G-AXFG	Cessna 337D	Helitechnique Ltd	
G-AXFH	D.H.114 Heron 1B/C	(stored)/Southend	
G-AXFN	Jodel D.119	Fox November Group	
G-AXGC	M.S.880B Rallye Club	P. A. Crawford & M. C. Bennett	
G-AXGE	M.S.880B Rallye Club	R. P. Loxton	
G-AXGG	Cessna F.150J	U. Schluter	
G-AXGP	Piper J-3C-65 Cub	W. K. Butler	
G-AXGR	Luton LA-4A Minor	B. A. Schlussler	
G-AXGS	D.62B Condor	L. D. Johnston	
G-AXGV	D.62B Condor	R. J. Wrixon	
G-AXGZ	D.62B Condor	J. Evans	
G-AXHA	Cessna 337A	G. Evans	
G-AXHC	SNCAN Stampe SV-4C	D. L. Webley	
G-AXHE	BN-2A Islander ★	Airport Fire Service/Cumbernauld	
G-AXHO	B.121 Pup 2	L. W. Grundy/Stapleford	
G-AXHP	Piper J-3C-65 Cub (480636)	Witham (Specialist) Vehicles Ltd	
G-AXHR	Piper J-3C-65 Cub (329601)	G-AXHR Cub Group	
G-AXHS	M.S.880B Rallye Club	B. & A. Swales	
G-AXHT	M.S.880B Rallye Club	D. E. Guck	
G-AXHV	Jodel D.117A	Derwent Flying Group/Hucknall	
G-AXIA	B.121 Pup 1	M. R. J. Hill & S. W. Goodswen	
G-AXIE	B.121 Pup 2	G. A. Ponsford/Goodwood	
G-AXIF	B.121 Pup 2	J. A. Holmes & S. A. Self	
G-AXIG	B.125 Bulldog 104	A. A. A. Hamilton	
G-AXIO	PA-28 Cherokee 140B	White Waltham Airfield Ltd	
G-AXIR	PA-28 Cherokee 140B	A. G. Birch	
G-AXIT	M.S.893A Rallye Commodore 180	T. J. Price	
G-AXIW	Scheibe SF.25B Falke	M. B. Hill	

Notes	Reg.	Type	Owner or Operator
	G-AXIX	Glos-Airtourer 150	J. C. Wood
	G-AXJB	Omega 84 balloon	Southern Balloon Group
	G-AXJH	B.121 Pup 2	J. S. Chillingworth
	G-AXJI	B.121 Pup 2	D. R. Vale
	G-AXJJ	B.121 Pup 2	M. L. Jones & ptnrs
	G-AXJO	B.121 Pup 2	J. A. D. Bradshaw
	G-AXJR	Scheibe SF.25B Falke	Falke Syndicate
	G-AXJV	PA-28 Cherokee 140B	N. J. Atherton
	G-AXJX	PA-28 Cherokee 140B	Patrolwatch Ltd/Sleap
	G-AXKH	Luton LA-4A Minor	M. E. Vaisey
	G-AXKJ	Jodel D.9 Bebe	C. C. Gordon & N. Mowbray
	G-AXKO	Westland-Bell 47G-4A	G. P. Hinkley
	G-AXKS	Westland Bell 47G-4A ★	Museum of Army Flying/Middle Wallop
	G-AXKW	Westland-Bell 47G-4A	Eyre Spier Associates Ltd
	G-AXKX	Westland Bell 47G-4A	Copley Farms Ltd
	G-AXKY	Westland Bell 47G-4A	G. A. Knight & G. M. Vowles
	G-AXLG	Cessna 310K	Smiths (Outdrives) Ltd
	G-AXLI	Slingsby T.66 Nipper 3	K. R. H. Wingate
	G-AXLL	BAC One-Eleven 523FJ	European Aircharter Ltd
	G-AXLS	Jodel DR.105A	Axle Flying Club
	G-AXLZ	PA-18 Super Cub 95	R. J. Quantrell
	G-AXMA	PA-24 Comanche 180	J. D. Bingham
	G-AXMD	Omega O-56 balloon ★	British Balloon Museum/Newbury
	G-AXMN	J/5B Autocar	A. Phillips
	G-AXMP	PA-28 Cherokee 180	B. Stewart
	G-AXMT	Bücker Bü133 Jungmeister (U-99)	W. R. M. Beesley/Breighton
	G-AXMW	B.121 Pup 1	DJP Engineering (Knebworth) Ltd
	G-AXMX	B.121 Pup 2	Susan A. Jones/Cannes
	G-AXNJ	Wassmer Jodel D.120	Clive Flying Group/Sleap
	G-AXNL	B.121 Pup 1	J. Coleman
	G-AXNM	B.121 Pup 1	F. E. Green
	G-AXNN	B.121 Pup 2	Gabrielle Aviation Ltd/Shoreham
	G-AXNP	B.121 Pup 2	J. W. Ellis
	G-AXNR	B.121 Pup 2	The November Romeo Group
	G-AXNS	B.121 Pup 2	Derwent Aero Group/Netherthorpe
	G-AXNW	SNCAN Stampe SV-4C	C. S. Grace
	G-AXNX	Cessna 182M	D. B. Harper
	G-AXNZ	Pitts S.1C Special	W. A. Jordan
	G-AXOG	PA-E23 Aztec 250D	G. H. Nolan
	G-AXOH	M.S.894 Rallye Minerva	Bristol Cars Ltd/White Waltham
	G-AXOJ	B.121 Pup 2	Pup Flying Group
	G-AXOR	PA-28 Cherokee 180D	Oscar Romeo Aviation Ltd
	G-AXOS	M.S.894A Rallye Minerva	P. Mather
	G-AXOT	M.S.893 Rallye Commodore 180	P. Evans & J. C. Graves
	G-AXOZ	B.121 Pup 1	R. J. Ogborn/Liverpool
	G-AXPA	B.121 Pup 1	D. G. Lewendon
	G-AXPB	B.121 Pup 1	M. J. K. Seary & R. T. Austin
	G-AXPC	B.121 Pup 2	T. A. White
	G-AXPF	Cessna F.150K	D. R. Marks/Denham
	G-AXPG	Mignet HM-293	W. H. Cole (stored)
	G-AXPM	B.121 Pup 1	R. G. Hayes/Elstree
	G-AXPN	B.121 Pup 2	The Pup Club
	G-AXPZ	Campbell Cricket	W. R. Partridge
	G-AXRC	Campbell Cricket	E. N. Simmons
	G-AXRK	Practavia Pilot Sprite 115 ★	M. Oliver
	G-AXRO	PA-30 Twin Comanche 160C	Comanche Hire Ltd/Staverton
	G-AXRP	SNCAN Stampe SV-4C	C. C. Manning (G-BLOL)
	G-AXRR	Auster AOP.9 (XR241)	R. J. Burgess
	G-AXRT	Cessna FA.150K (tailwheel)	C. C. Walley
	G-AXSC	B.121 Pup 1	R. J. MacCarthy
	G-AXSD	B.121 Pup 1	A. C. Townend
	G-AXSF	Nash Petrel	Nash Aircraft Ltd/Lasham
	G-AXSG	PA-28 Cherokee 180	Admiral Property Ltd
	G-AXSI	Cessna F.172H	St. Mary's Flying Club (G-SNIP)
	G-AXSM	Jodel DR.1051	K. D. Doyle
	G-AXSR	Brantly B.2B	A. Murzyn (G-ROOF)
	G-AXSW	Cessna FA.150K	R. Mitchell
	G-AXSZ	PA-28 Cherokee 140B	The White Wings Flying Group/ White Waltham
	G-AXTA	PA-28 Cherokee 140B	G-AXTA Aircraft Group
	G-AXTC	PA-28 Cherokee 140B	G-AXTC Group
	G-AXTJ	PA-28 Cherokee 140B	K. Patel/Elstree
	G-AXTL	PA-28 Cherokee 140B	Pegasus Aviation (Midlands) Ltd

Reg.	Type	Owner or Operator	Notes
G-AXTO	PA-24 Comanche 260	J. L. Wright	
G-AXTP	PA-28 Cherokee 180	C. W. R. Moore/Elstree	
G-AXTX	Jodel D.112	C. Sawford	
G-AXTZ	B.121 Pup 1★	Shoreham Aviation Heritage Trust	
G-AXUA	B.121 Pup 1	D. S. Sweet	
G-AXUB	BN-2A Islander	Headcorn Parachute Club Ltd	
G-AXUC	PA-12 Super Cruiser	J. J. Bunton	
G-AXUF	Cessna FA.150K	A. D. McLeod	
G-AXUK	Jodel DR.1050	Ambassadeurs Flying Group	
G-AXUM	H.P.137 Jetstream 1	Cranfield University	
G-AXVB	Cessna F.172H	R. & J. Turner	
G-AXVM	Campbell Cricket	D. M. Organ	
G-AXVN	McCandless M.4	W. R. Partridge	
G-AXWA	Auster AOP.9 (XN437)	M. L. & C. M. Edwards/Biggin Hill	
G-AXWT	Jodel D.11	R. C. Owen	
G-AXWV	Jodel DR.253	J. R. D. Bygraves/O. Warden	
G-AXWZ	PA-28R Cherokee Arrow 200	P. Walkley	
G-AXXC	CP.301B Emeraude	J. A. Sykes	
G-AXXV	D.H.82A Tiger Moth (DE992)	C. N. Wookey	
G-AXXW	Jodel D.117	M. Ward/Sandtoft	
G-AXYK	Taylor JT.1 Monoplane	D. J. Hulks & R. W. Davies	
G-AXYU	Jodel D.9 Bebe	D. J. Laughlin	
G-AXYZ	WHE Airbuggy	B. Gunn	
G-AXZA	WHE Airbuggy	C. Verlaan/Holland	
G-AXZD	PA-28 Cherokee 180E	G. M. Whitmore	
G-AXZF	PA-28 Cherokee 180E	E. P. C. & W. R. Rabson/Southampton	
G-AXZK	BN-2A-26 Islander	Headcorn Parachute Club Ltd	
G-AXZM	Slingsby T.66 Nipper 3	G. R. Harlow	
G-AXZO	Cessna 180	Golf Centres Group Ltd	
G-AXZP	PA-E23 Aztec 250D	Aztec Flying Group	
G-AXZT	Jodel D.117	N. Batty	
G-AXZU	Cessna 182N	S. E. Bradney	
G-AYAA	PA-28 Cherokee 180E	Alpha-Alpha Ltd/Liverpool	
G-AYAB	PA-28 Cherokee 180E	Films Ltd	
G-AYAC	PA-28R Cherokee Arrow 200	Fersfield Flying Group	
G-AYAJ	Cameron O-84 balloon	E. T. Hall	
G-AYAL	Omega 56 balloon ★	British Balloon Museum/Newbury	
G-AYAN	Slingsby Motor Cadet III	N. C. Stone	
G-AYAR	PA-28 Cherokee 180E	D. M. Markscheffel/Stapleford	
G-AYAT	PA-28 Cherokee 180E	AYAT Flying Group	
G-AYAW	PA-28 Cherokee 180E	R. C. Pendle & M. J. Rose	
G-AYBD	Cessna F.150K	Evendy Holdings	
G-AYBG	Scheibe SF.25B Falke	D. J. Rickman	
G-AYBO	PA-23 Aztec 250D	Twinguard Aviation Ltd/Elstree	
G-AYBP	Jodel D.112	G. J. Langston	
G-AYBR	Jodel D.112	R. T. Mosforth	
G-AYCC	Campbell Cricket	D. J. M. Charity	
G-AYCE	CP.301C Emeraude	S. D. Glover	
G-AYCF	Cessna FA.150K	E. J. Atkins/Popham	
G-AYCG	SNCAN Stampe SV-4C	N. Bignall/Booker	
G-AYCJ	Cessna TP.206D	White Knuckle Airways Ltd	
G-AYCK	AIA Stampe SV-4C	J. F. Graham (G-BUNT)	
G-AYCN	Piper J-3C-65 Cub	W. R. & B. M. Young	
G-AYCO	CEA DR.360	B. N. Stevens	
G-AYCP	Jodel D.112	D. J. Nunn	
G-AYCT	Cessna F.172H	Haimoss Ltd & D. C. Scouller	
G-AYDG	M.S.894A Rallye Minerva	Hunt & Ptnrs Ltd	
G-AYDI	D.H.82A Tiger Moth	R. B. Woods & ptnrs	
G-AYDR	SNCAN Stampe SV-4C	A. J. McLuskie	
G-AYDV	Coates SA.II-1 Swalesong	J. R. Coates	
G-AYDW	A.61 Terrier 2	A. S. Topen	
G-AYDX	A.61 Terrier 2	R. A. Kirby	
G-AYDY	Luton LA-4A Minor	T. Littlefair & N. Clark	
G-AYDZ	Jodel DR.200	L. J. Cudd & C. A. Bailey	
G-AYEB	Jodel D.112	C. H. G. Baulf	
G-AYEC	CP.301A Emeraude	Redwing Flying Group	
G-AYED	PA-24 Comanche 260	J. V. Hutchinson	
G-AYEE	PA-28 Cherokee 180E	Rankart Ltd	
G-AYEF	PA-28 Cherokee 180E	G-AYEF Group	
G-AYEG	Falconar F-9	T. J. Wilkinson/Riseley	
G-AYEH	Jodel DR.1050	John Scott Jodel Group	
G-AYEJ	Jodel DR.1050	J. M. Newbold	

Notes	Reg.	Type	Owner or Operator
	G-AYEN	Piper J-3C-65 Cub	P. Warde & C. F. Morris
	G-AYET	M.S.892A Rallye Commodore 150	A. T. R. Bingley
	G-AYEV	Jodel DR.1050	L. G. Evans/Headcorn
	G-AYEW	Jodel DR.1051	Taildragger Group/Halfpenny Green
	G-AYFA	SA Twin Pioneer Srs 3 ★	Solway Aviation Soc/Carlisle
	G-AYFC	D.62B Condor	A. G. Stevens
	G-AYFD	D.62B Condor	B. G. Manning
	G-AYFE	D.62C Condor	D. I. H. Johnstone & W. T. Barnard
	G-AYFF	D.62B Condor	Condor Syndicate
	G-AYFG	D.62C Condor	W. A. Braim
	G-AYFJ	M.S.880B Rallye Club	Rallye FJ Group
	G-AYFP	Jodel D.140	F. L. Rivett
	G-AYFV	Crosby BA-4B	A. R. C. Mathie/Norwich
	G-AYGA	Jodel D.117	R. L. E. Horrell
	G-AYGB	Cessna 310Q ★	*Instructional airframe*/Perth
	G-AYGC	Cessna F.150K	Alpha Aviation Group/Barton
	G-AYGD	Jodel DR.1051	G-AYGD Flying Group
	G-AYGE	SNCAN Stampe SV-4C	L. J. Proudfoot & ptnrs/Booker
	G-AYGG	Jodel D.120	J. M. Dean
	G-AYGX	Cessna FR.172G	A. Douglas & J. K. Brockley
	G-AYHA	AA-1 Yankee	K. & A. D. Ambrose-Hunt
	G-AYHX	Jodel D.117A	L. J. E. Goldfinch
	G-AYHY	Fournier RF-4D	P. M. & S. M. Wells
	G-AYIA	Hughes 369HS ★	G. D. E. Bilton/Sywell
	G-AYIF	PA-28 Cherokee 140C	The Hare Flying Group
	G-AYIG	PA-28 Cherokee 140C	Biggles Ltd
	G-AYII	PA-28R Cherokee Arrow 200	P. W. J. & P. A. S. Gove/Exeter
	G-AYIJ	SNCAN Stampe SV-4B	E. A. Stevenson-Rouse & T. C. Beadle/Headcorn
	G-AYIM	H.S.748 Srs 2A	Emerald Airways Ltd/Liverpool
	G-AYIT	D.H.82A Tiger Moth	Ulster Tiger Group/Newtownards
	G-AYJA	Jodel DR.1050	G. Connell
	G-AYJB	SNCAN Stampe SV-4C	F. J. M. & J. P. Esson/Middle Wallop
	G-AYJD	Alpavia-Fournier RF-3	E. Shouler
	G-AYJP	PA-28 Cherokee 140C	RAF Brize Norton Flying Club Ltd
	G-AYJR	PA-28 Cherokee 140C	RAF Brize Norton Flying Club Ltd
	G-AYJW	Cessna FR.172G	J. D. Kelsall & ptnrs
	G-AYJY	Isaacs Fury II	M. G. Jeffries/Little Gransden
	G-AYKA	Beech 95-B55A Baron	Walsh Bros (Tunnelling) Ltd/Elstree
	G-AYKD	Jodel DR.1050	S. D. Morris
	G-AYKJ	Jodel D.117A	J. M. Alexander
	G-AYKK	Jodel D.117	D. M. Whitham
	G-AYKL	Cessna F.150L	M. A. Judge
	G-AYKS	Leopoldoff L-7	W. B. Cooper
	G-AYKT	Jodel D.117	D. I. Walker & S. A. Chambers
	G-AYKW	PA-28 Cherokee 140C	B. A. Mills
	G-AYKX	PA-28 Cherokee 140C	Robin Flying Group/Woodford
	G-AYKZ	SAI KZ-8	R. E. Mitchell/Cosford
	G-AYLA	Glos-Airtourer 115	D. S. P. Disney
	G-AYLB	PA-39 Twin Comanche 160 C/R	G. N. Snell
	G-AYLC	Jodel DR.1051	E. W. B. Trollope
	G-AYLF	Jodel DR.1051	Sicile Group
	G-AYLL	Jodel DR.1050	C. Joly
	G-AYLP	AA-1 Yankee	D. Nairn & E. Y. Hawkins
	G-AYLV	Jodel D.120	M. R. Henham
	G-AYLZ	SPP Super Aero 45 Srs 04	M. Emery
	G-AYME	Fournier RF-5	R. D. Goodger/Biggin Hill
	G-AYMK	PA-28 Cherokee 140C	The Piper Flying Group/Newcastle
	G-AYMO	PA-23 Aztec 250C	R. W. Hinton
	G-AYMP	Currie Wot Special	H. F. Moffatt
	G-AYMR	Lederlin 380L Ladybug	J. S. Brayshaw
	G-AYMU	Jodel D.112	M. R. Baker
	G-AYMV	Western 20 balloon	G. F. Turnbull
	G-AYMW	Bell 206A JetRanger 2	PLM Dollar Group Ltd
	G-AYNA	Currie Wot	J. Evans
	G-AYND	Cessna 310Q	Source Ltd/Thruxton
	G-AYNF	PA-28 Cherokee 140C	BW Aviation
	G-AYNJ	PA-28 Cherokee 140C	R. H. Ribbons
	G-AYNN	Cessna 185B Skywagon	Bencray Ltd/Blackpool
	G-AYNP	W.S.55 Whirlwifind Srs 3 ★	IHM/Weston-s-Mare
	G-AYOP	BAC One-Eleven 530FX	European Aircharter Ltd
	G-AYOW	Cessna 182N Skylane	D. W. Parfrey
	G-AYOY	Sikorsky S-61N Mk 2	British International Helicopters

Reg.	Type	Owner or Operator	Notes
G-AYOZ	Cessna FA.150L	I. J. Black	
G-AYPE	MBB Bo 209 Monsun	Papa Echo Ltd/Biggin Hill	
G-AYPG	Cessna F.177RG	D. P. McDermott	
G-AYPH	Cessna F.177RG	M. R. & K. E. Slack	
G-AYPI	Cessna F.177RG	Cardinal Aviation Ltd/Guernsey	
G-AYPJ	PA-28 Cherokee 180	Mona Aviation Ltd	
G-AYPM	PA-18 Super Cub 95	R. Horner	
G-AYPO	PA-18 Super Cub 95	A. W. Knowles	
G-AYPR	PA-18 Super Cub 95	D. G. Holman & J. E. Burrell	
G-AYPS	PA-18 Super Cub 95	R. J. Hamlett & ptnrs	
G-AYPT	PA-18 Super Cub 95	B. L. Proctor & T. F. Lyddon	
G-AYPU	PA-28R Cherokee Arrow 200	Alpine Ltd/Jersey	
G-AYPV	PA-28 Cherokee 140D	Ashley Gardner Flying Club Ltd	
G-AYPZ	Campbell Cricket	A. Melody	
G-AYRF	Cessna F.150L	D. T. A. Rees	
G-AYRG	Cessna F.172K	Comed Aviation Ltd	
G-AYRH	M.S.892A Rallye Commodore 150	J. D. Watt	
G-AYRI	PA-28R Cherokee Arrow 200	A. E. Thompson & Delta Motor Co (Windsor) Sales Ltd/White Waltham	
G-AYRM	PA-28 Cherokee 140D	M. J. Saggers/Biggin Hill	
G-AYRO	Cessna FA.150L Aerobat	Flying Services	
G-AYRS	Jodel D.120A	L. R. H. D'Eath	
G-AYRT	Cessna F.172K	P. E. Crees	
G-AYRU	BN-2A-6 Islander	Joint Service Parachute Centre/ Netheravon	
G-AYSA	PA-23 Aztec 250C	N. Parkinson & W. Smith	
G-AYSB	PA-30 Twin Comanche 160C	C. P. Heptonstall	
G-AYSD	Slingsby T.61A Falke	P. W. Hextall	
G-AYSH	Taylor JT.1 Monoplane	C. J. Lodge	
G-AYSJ	Bücker Bü133C Jungmeister (LG+01)	Patina Ltd/Duxford	
G-AYSK	Luton LA-4A Minor	Luton Minor Group	
G-AYSX	Cessna F.177RG	C. P. Heptonstall	
G-AYSY	Cessna F.177RG	Horizon Flyers Ltd/Denham	
G-AYTA	SOCATA M.S.880B Rallye Club ★	Manchester Museum of Science & Industry	
G-AYTR	CP.301A Emeraude	G. N. Hopcraft	
G-AYTT	Phoenix PM-3 Duet	H. E. Jenner	
G-AYTV	MJ.2A Tempete	Shoestring Flying Group/Shoreham	
G-AYUA	Auster AOP.9 (XK416)	P. T. Bolton	
G-AYUB	CEA DR.253B	D. J. Brook	
G-AYUH	PA-28 Cherokee 180F	C. S. Sidle	
G-AYUJ	Evans VP-1	T. N. Howard	
G-AYUM	Slingsby T.61A Falke	Hereward Flying Group/Crowland	
G-AYUN	Slingsby T.61A Falke	C. W. Vigar & R. J. Watts	
G-AYUP	Slingsby T.61A Falke	P. R. Williams	
G-AYUR	Slingsby T.61A Falke	R. Hanningan & R. Lingard	
G-AYUS	Taylor JT.1 Monoplane	R. R. McKinnon	
G-AYUT	Jodel DR.1050	R. Norris	
G-AYUV	Cessna F.172H	Justgold Ltd	
G-AYVO	Wallis WA-120 Srs 1	K. H. Wallis	
G-AYVP	Woody Pusher	J. R. Wraight	
G-AYVT	Brochet MB.84 ★	Dunelm Flying Group (stored)	
G-AYWA	Avro 19 Srs 2 ★	N. K. Geddes	
G-AYWD	Cessna 182N	Wild Dreams Group	
G-AYWE	PA-28 Cherokee 140	N. Roberson	
G-AYWH	Jodel D.117A	D. Kynaston & J. Deakin	
G-AYWM	Glos-Airtourer Super 150	The Star Flying Group/Staverton	
G-AYWT	AIA Stampe SV-4C	B. K. Lecomber/Denham	
G-AYXP	Jodel D.117A	G. N. Davies	
G-AYXS	SIAI-Marchetti S205-18R	M. D. Friend	
G-AYXT	W.S. 55 Whirlwind Srs 2 (XK940)	G. P. Hinkley	
G-AYXU	Champion 7KCAB Citabria	Norfolk Gliding Club Ltd/Tibenham	
G-AYXW	Evans VP-1	J. S. Penny	
G-AYYK	Slingsby T.61A Falke	Cornish Gliding & Flying Club Ltd/ Perranporth	
G-AYYL	Slingsby T.61A Falke	C. Wood	
G-AYYO	Jodel DR.1050/M1	Bustard Flying Club Ltd	
G-AYYT	Jodel DR.1050/M1	Echo November Flight	
G-AYYU	Beech C23 Musketeer	Sundowner Aviation/Sturgate	
G-AYYW	BN-2A Islander	RN & R. Marines Sport Parachute Association/Dunkeswell	
G-AYYX	M.S.880B Ralle Club	J. G. MacDonald	

Notes	Reg.	Type	Owner or Operator
	G-AYZE	PA-39 Twin Comanche 160 C/R	J. E. Palmer/Staverton
	G-AYZI	SNCAN Stampe SV-4C	W. H. Smout
	G-AYZJ	W.S.55 Whirlwind Srs 2 (XM685) ★	Newark Air Museum
	G-AYZK	Jodel DR.1050/M1	D. G. Hesketh & R. L. Sambell
	G-AYZS	D.62B Condor	P. E. J. Huntley & M. N. Thrush
	G-AYZU	Slingsby T.61A Falke	The Falcon Gliding Group/Elstree
	G-AYZW	Slingsby T.61A Falke	Portmoak Falke Syndicate
	G-AZAB	PA-30 Twin Comanche 160B	Bickertons Aerodromes Ltd
	G-AZAJ	PA-28R Cherokee Arrow 200B	J. McHugh & P. Woulfe/Stapleford
	G-AZAW	GY-80 Horizon 160	T. Brown
	G-AZAZ	Bensen B.8M ★	F.A.A. Museum/Yeovilton
	G-AZBA	T.66 Nipper 3	L. A. Brown
	G-AZBB	MBB Bo 209 Monsun 160FV	G. N. Richardson/Staverton
	G-AZBC	PA-39 Twin Comanche 160 C/R	R. G. James & P. E. Mitchell
	G-AZBE	Glos-Airtourer Super 150	BE Flying Group/Staverton
	G-AZBI	Jodel 150	F. M. Ward
	G-AZBL	Jodel D.9 Bebe	J. Hill
	G-AZBN	AT-16 Harvard IIB (FT391)	Swaygate Ltd/Shoreham
	G-AZBU	Auster AOP.9 (XR246)	Auster Nine Group
	G-AZBY	W.S.58 Wessex 60 Srs 1 ★	IHM/Weston-s-Mare
	G-AZBZ	W.S.58 Wessex 60 Srs 1 ★	IHM/Weston-s-Mare
	G-AZCB	SNCAN Stampe SV-4C	M. L. Martin
	G-AZCK	B.121 Pup 2	D. R. Newell
	G-AZCL	B.121 Pup 2	J. J. Watts & D. Fletcher
	G-AZCN	B.121 Pup 2	R. C. Antonini/Biggin Hill
	G-AZCP	B.121 Pup 1	T. J. Watson/Elstree
	G-AZCT	B.121 Pup 1	J. Coleman
	G-AZCU	B.121 Pup 1	A. A. Harris/Shobdon
	G-AZCV	B.121 Pup 2	N. R. W. Long/Elstree
	G-AZCY	B.121 Pup 2	D. J. Deas
	G-AZCZ	B.121 Pup 2	L. & J. M. Northover
	G-AZDA	B.121 Pup 1	B. D. Deubelbeiss
	G-AZDD	MBB Bo 209 Monsun 150FF	Double Delta Flying Group/Biggin Hill
	G-AZDE	PA-28R Cherokee Arrow 200B	Paul James Knitwear Ltd
	G-AZDG	B.121 Pup 2	D. J. Sage & J. R. Heaps
	G-AZDJ	PA-32 Cherokee Six 300	K. J. Mansbridge & D. C. Gibbs
	G-AZDK	Beech 95-B55 Baron	C. C. Forrester
	G-AZDX	PA-28 Cherokee 180F	M. Cowan
	G-AZDY	D.H.82A Tiger Moth	J. B. Mills
	G-AZEE	M.S.880B Rallye Club	J. Shelton
	G-AZEF	Jodel D.120	J. R. Legge
	G-AZEG	PA-28 Cherokee 140D	Ashley Gardner Flying Club Ltd
	G-AZEU	B.121 Pup 2	G. M. Moir
	G-AZEV	B.121 Pup 2	G. P. Martin
	G-AZEW	B.121 Pup 2	K. Cameron
	G-AZEY	B.121 Pup 2	M. E. Reynolds
	G-AZFA	B.121 Pup 2	K. F. Plummer
	G-AZFC	PA-28 Cherokee 140D	M. L. Hannah/Blackbushe
	G-AZFF	Jodel D.112	R. Pidcock
	G-AZFI	PA-28R Cherokee Arrow 200B	G-AZFI Ltd/Sherburn
	G-AZFM	PA-28R Cherokee Arrow 200B	T. N. Jenness
	G-AZFR	Cessna 401B	Westair Flying Services Ltd/Blackpool
	G-AZGA	Jodel D.120	A. F. Vizoso
	G-AZGC	SNCAN Stampe SV-4C (No 120)	V. Lindsay
	G-AZGE	SNCAN Stampe SV-4A	M. R. L. Astor/Booker
	G-AZGF	B.121 Pup 2	K. Singh
	G-AZGI	M.S.880B Rallye Club	B. McIntyre
	G-AZGL	M.S.894A Rallye Minerva	The Cambridge Aero Club Ltd
	G-AZGY	CP.301B Emeraude	C. J. R. Gray
	G-AZGZ	D.H.82A Tiger Moth (NM181)	R. J. King
	G-AZHB	Robin HR.100-200	C. & P. P. Scarlett/Sywell
	G-AZHC	Jodel D.112	Aerodel Flying Group
	G-AZHD	Slingsby T.61A Falke	N. J. Orchard-Armitage
	G-AZHE	Slingsby T.61B Falke	M. R. Shelton/Tatenhill
	G-AZHH	SA 102.5 Cavalier	D. W. Buckle
	G-AZHI	Glos-Airtourer Super 150	H. J. Douglas/Biggin Hill
	G-AZHJ	SA Twin Pioneer Srs 3 ★	Air Atlantique Ltd/Coventry
	G-AZHK	Robin HR.100/200B	A. Bendkowski & T. A. Houghton (G-ILEG)
	G-AZHR	Piccard Ax6 balloon	C. Fisher
	G-AZHT	Glos-Airtourer T.3	Aviation West Ltd/Glasgow

Reg.	Type	Owner or Operator	Notes
G-AZHU	Luton LA-4A Minor	W. Cawrey/Netherthorpe	
G-AZIB	ST-10 Diplomate	W. B. Bateson/Blackpool	
G-AZID	Cessna FA.150L	Aerobat Ltd	
G-AZII	Jodel D.117A	J. S. Brayshaw	
G-AZIJ	Jodel DR.360	K. J. Fleming & T. W. Conlan	
G-AZIK	PA-34-200 Seneca II	Walkbury Aviation Ltd	
G-AZIL	Slingsby T.61A Falke	D. W. Savage/Portmoak	
G-AZIO	SNCAN Stampe SV-4C (Lycoming) ★	—/Booker	
G-AZIP	Cameron O-65 balloon	Dante Balloon Group Dante	
G-AZJC	Fournier RF-5	W. St. G. V. Stoney/Italy	
G-AZJE	Ord-Hume JB-01 Minicab	J. B. Evans/Sandown	
G-AZJN	Robin DR.300/140	Wright Farm Eggs Ltd	
G-AZJV	Cessna F.172L	R. P. Smith	
G-AZJY	Cessna FRA.150L	G. Firbank/Manchester	
G-AZKC	M.S.880B Rallye Club	L. J. Martin/Redhill	
G-AZKE	M.S.880B Rallye Club	B. S. Rowden & W. L. Rogers	
G-AZKK	Cameron O-56 balloon	Gemini Balloon Group Gemini	
G-AZKO	Cessna F.337F	P. W. Crispe	
G-AZKP	Jodel D.117	J. Lowe	
G-AZKR	PA-24 Comanche 180	T. E. Groves	
G-AZKS	AA-1A Trainer	M. D. Henson	
G-AZKW	Cessna F.172L	J. C. C. Wright	
G-AZKZ	Cessna F.172L	R. D. & E. Forster/Swanton Morley	
G-AZLE	Boeing N2S-5 Kaydet (2)	Air Farm Flyers	
G-AZLF	Jodel D.120	M. S. C. Ball	
G-AZLH	Cessna F.150L	Coulson Flying Services Ltd	
G-AZLJ	BN-2A Mk.III-1 Trislander	Keenair Charter (G-OREG/G-OAVW)/Liverpool	
G-AZLN	PA-28 Cherokee 180F	Liteflite Ltd/Kidlington	
G-AZLV	Cessna 172K	B. L. F. Karthaus/Newcastle	
G-AZLY	Cessna F.150L	Cleveland Flying School Ltd/Teesside	
G-AZLZ	Cessna F.150L	A. G. Martlew	
G-AZMC	Slingsby T.61A Falke	Essex Gliding Club Ltd	
G-AZMD	Slingsby T.61C Falke	R. A. Rice/Wellesbourne	
G-AZMF	BAC One-Eleven 530FX	European Aircharter Ltd	
G-AZMJ	AA-5 Traveler	R. T. Love/Bodmin	
G-AZMN	Glos-Airtourer T.5	W. Crozier & I. Young	
G-AZMX	PA-28 Cherokee 140 ★	NE Wales Institute of Higher Education (Instructional airframe)/Flintshire	
G-AZMZ	M.S.893A Rallye Commodore 150	P. J. Wilcox/Cranfield	
G-AZNK	SNCAN Stampe SV-4A	P. D. Jackson & R. A. G. Lucas	
G-AZNL	PA-28R Cherokee Arrow 200D	B. P. Liversidge	
G-AZNO	Cessna 182P	T. & K. Andrews	
G-AZOA	MBB Bo 209 Monsun 150FF	M. W. Hurst	
G-AZOB	MBB Bo 209 Monsun 150FF	G. N. Richardson/Staverton	
G-AZOE	Glos-Airtourer 115	G-AZOE 607 Group/Newcastle	
G-AZOF	Glos-Airtourer Super 150	Cirrus Flying Group/Denham	
G-AZOG	PA-28R Cherokee Arrow 200D	J. G. Collins/Cambridge	
G-AZOL	PA-34-200 Seneca II	D. I. Barnes	
G-AZOR	MBB Bo 105D	Bond Air Services/Aberdeen	
G-AZOS	Jurca MJ.5-F1 Sirocco	M. K. Field	
G-AZOT	PA-34-200 Seneca II	MK Aero Support Ltd	
G-AZOU	Jodel DR.1050	Horsham Flying Group/Slinfold	
G-AZOZ	Cessna FRA.150L	Seawing Flying Club Ltd/Southend	
G-AZPA	PA-25 Pawnee 235	Black Mountains Gliding Club Ltd	
G-AZPC	Slingsby T.61C Falke	A. M. Parker	
G-AZPF	Fournier RF-5	R. Pye/Blackpool	
G-AZPH	Craft-Pitts S-1S Special ★	Science Museum/S. Kensington	
G-AZPV	Luton LA-4A Minor	J. R. Faulkner	
G-AZRA	MBB Bo 209 Monsun 150FF	Alpha Flying Ltd/Denham	
G-AZRD	Cessna 401B	Romeo Delta Group	
G-AZRH	PA-28 Cherokee 140D	Trust Flying Group	
G-AZRK	Fournier RF-5	P. M. Brocklington & J. F. Rogers	
G-AZRL	PA-18 Super Cub 95	B. J. Stead	
G-AZRM	Fournier RF-5	A. R. Dearden & R. Speer/Shoreham	
G-AZRN	Cameron O-84 balloon	C. A. Butter & J. J. T. Cooke	
G-AZRP	Glos-Airtourer 115	B. F. Strawford/Shobdon	
G-AZRR	Cessna 310Q	Routarrow Ltd/Norwich	
G-AZRS	PA-22 Tri-Pacer 150	Sandpiper Group	
G-AZRV	PA-28R Cherokee Arrow 200B	General Airline Ltd	
G-AZRZ	Cessna U.206F	Hinton Skydiving Centre	
G-AZSA	Stampe et Renard SV-4B	J. K. Faulkner/Biggin Hill	

Notes	Reg.	Type	Owner or Operator
	G-AZSC	AT-16 Harvard IIB (43)	Machine Music Ltd/Duxford
	G-AZSD	Slingsby T.29B Motor Tutor	Essex Aviation
	G-AZSF	PA-28R Cherokee Arrow 200D	Flight Simulation/Coventry
	G-AZSW	B.121 Pup 1	I. T. Dall/Sywell
	G-AZSZ	PA-23 Aztec 250D	International Cladding Systems Ltd
	G-AZTA	MBB Bo 209 Monsun 150FF	A. I. D. Rich/Elstree
	G-AZTD	PA-32 Cherokee Six 300D	Presshouse Publications Ltd/Enstone
	G-AZTF	Cessna F.177RG	D. A. Wiggins
	G-AZTK	Cessna F.172F	Vascas Ltd
	G-AZTR	SNCAN Stampe SV-4C	P. G. Palumbo/Booker
	G-AZTS	Cessna F.172L	C. E. Stringer
	G-AZTV	Stolp SA.500 Starlet	G. R. Rowland
	G-AZTW	Cessna F.177RG	R. M. Clarke/Leicester
	G-AZUM	Cessna F.172L	Fowlmere Fliers
	G-AZUP	Cameron O-65 balloon	R. S. Bailey & A. B. Simpson
	G-AZUT	M.S.893A Rallye Commodore 180	J. Palethorpe
	G-AZUV	Cameron O-65 balloon ★	British Balloon Museum/Newbury
	G-AZUX	Western O-56 balloon	D. M. & K. R. Sandford
	G-AZUY	Cessna E.310L	George Moss & Sons Ltd/Liverpool
	G-AZUZ	Cessna FRA.150L	D. J. Parker/Netherthorpe
	G-AZVA	MBB Bo 209 Monsun 150FF	J. Nivison
	G-AZVB	MBB Bo 209 Monsun 150FF	P. C. Logsdon/Dunkeswell
	G-AZVF	M.S.894A Rallye Minerva	Minerva Flying Group
	G-AZVG	AA-5 Traveler	Grumair Flying Group
	G-AZVH	M.S.894A Rallye Minerva	P. L. Jubb
	G-AZVI	M.S.892A Rallye Commodore	Shobdon Flying Group
	G-AZVJ	PA-34-200 Seneca II	Skyfotos Ltd/Lydd
	G-AZVL	Jodel D.119	Forest Flying Group/Stapleford
	G-AZVM	Hughes 369HS	Diagnostic Reagents Ltd
	G-AZVP	Cessna F.177RG	Cardinal Flyers Ltd
	G-AZWB	PA-28 Cherokee 140	B. N. Rides & L. Connor
	G-AZWD	PA-28 Cherokee 140	BM Aviation (Winchester)
	G-AZWE	PA-28 Cherokee 140	G-AZWE Flying Group
	G-AZWF	SAN Jodel DR.1050	G-AZWF Jodel Syndicate
	G-AZWS	PA-28R Cherokee Arrow 180	Arrow 88 Flying Group/Newcastle
	G-AZWT	Westland Lysander IIIA (V9441)	The Shuttleworth Collection/O. Warden
	G-AZWY	PA-24 Comanche 260	Keymer Son & Co Ltd/Biggin Hill
	G-AZXA	Beech 95-C55 Baron	F.R. Aviation Ltd/Bournemouth
	G-AZXB	Cameron O-65 balloon	R. J. Mitchener & P. F. Smart
	G-AZXC	Cessna F.150L	D. C. Bonsall
	G-AZXD	Cessna F.172L	Birdlake Ltd/Wellesbourne
	G-AZXG	PA-23 Aztec 250D ★	Instructional airframe/Cranfield
	G-AZYA	GY-80 Horizon 160	M. L. Moore & T. Twelvetree
	G-AZYB	Bell 47H-1 ★	IHM/Weston-s-Mare
	G-AZYD	M.S.893A Rallye Commodore	Storey Aviation Services
	G-AZYM	Cessna E.310Q	Offshore Marine Consultants Ltd
	G-AZYS	CP.301C-1 Emeraude	F. P. L. Clauson
	G-AZYU	PA-23 Aztec 250E	L. J. Martin/Biggin Hill
	G-AZYY	Slingsby T.61A Falke	J. A. Towers
	G-AZYZ	WA.51A Pacific	J. Ward
	G-AZZG	Cessna 188 Agwagon	N. C. Kensington
	G-AZZH	Practavia Pilot Sprite 115	A. Moore
	G-AZZO	PA-28 Cherokee 140	R. J. Hind/Elstree
	G-AZZR	Cessna F.150L	G-AZZR Flying Group
	G-AZZT	PA-28 Cherokee 180 ★	Ground instruction airframe/Cranfield
	G-AZZV	Cessna F.172L	D. J. Hockings
	G-AZZX	Cessna FRA.150L	M. Hewison
	G-AZZZ	D.H.82A Tiger Moth	S. W. McKay
	G-BAAD	Evans Super VP-1	K. McNaughton/Breighton
	G-BAAF	Manning-Flanders MF1 (replica)	Aviation Film Services Ltd/Booker
	G-BAAI	M.S.893A Rallye Commodore	R. D. Taylor/Thruxton
	G-BAAL	Cessna 172A	Rochester Aviation Ltd
	G-BAAT	Cessna 182P	Melrose Pigs Ltd
	G-BAAU	Enstrom F-28A-UK	G. Firbank
	G-BAAW	Jodel D.119	Alpha Whiskey Flying Group
	G-BAAZ	PA-28R Cherokee Arrow 200D	A. W. Rix/Guernsey
	G-BABB	Cessna F.150L	Seawing Flying Club Ltd/Southend
	G-BABC	Cessna F.150L	Fordaire Ltd/Sywell
	G-BABD	Cessna FRA.150L (modified)	R, C, Boyall
	G-BABE	Taylor JT.2 Titch	P. D. G. Grist/Sibson
	G-BABG	PA-28 Cherokee 180	Mendip Flying Group/Bristol
	G-BABH	Cessna F.150L	Sherburn Aero Club Ltd

Reg.	Type	Owner or Operator	Notes
G-BABK	PA-34-200 Seneca II	D. F. J. Flashman/Biggin Hill	
G-BABY	Taylor JT.2 Titch	R. E. Finlay	
G-BACB	PA-34-200 Seneca II	Rankart Ltd	
G-BACC	Cessna FRA.150L	C. M. & J. H. Cooper/Cranfield	
G-BACE	Fournier RF-5	R. W. K. Stead/Perranporth	
G-BACJ	Jodel D.120	Wearside Flying Association/Newcastle	
G-BACL	Jodel 150	M. L. Sargeant/Biggin Hill	
G-BACN	Cessna FRA.150L	Cornwall Flying Club Ltd/Bodmin	
G-BACO	Cessna FRA.150L	M. M. Pepper/Sibson	
G-BACP	Cessna FRA.150L	Vectair Aviation 1995 Ltd	
G-BADC	Rollason Beta B.2A	J. C. Mead	
G-BADH	Slingsby T.61A Falke	Falke Flying Group	
G-BADI	PA-23 Aztec 250D ★	Aces High Ltd/North Weald	
G-BADJ	PA-E23 Aztec 250E	C. Papadakis/Kidlington	
G-BADL	PA-34-200 Seneca II	K. Smith & M. Corbett	
G-BADM	D.62B Condor	M. Harris & J. St. J. Mehta	
G-BADO	PA-32 Cherokee Six 300E	G-BADO Ltd	
G-BADW	Pitts S-2A Special	R. E. Mitchell/Cosford	
G-BADZ	Pitts S-2A Special	A. F. D. Kingdon	
G-BAEB	Robin DR.400/160	P. D. W. King	
G-BAEC	Robin HR.100/210	Robin Travel & Designways (Interior Design) Ltd	
G-BAED	PA-23 Aztec 250C	K. G. Manktelow & N. Brewitt/Ronaldsway	
G-BAEE	Jodel DR.1050/M1	R. Little	
G-BAEM	Robin DR.400/125	M. A. Webb/Booker	
G-BAEN	Robin DR.400/180	European Soaring Club Ltd	
G-BAEO	Cessna F.172M	L. W. Scattergood	
G-BAEP	Cessna FRA.150L (modified)	A. M. Lynn	
G-BAER	Cosmic Wind	R. S. Voice/Redhill	
G-BAET	Piper J-3C-65 Cub	C. J. Rees	
G-BAEU	Cessna F.150L	L. W. Scattergood	
G-BAEV	Cessna FRA.L150L	S. C. Griffin	
G-BAEW	Cessna F.172M ★	Westley Aircraft/Cranfield	
G-BAEY	Cessna F.172M	R. Fursman/Southampton	
G-BAEZ	Cessna FRA.150L	Donair Flying Club Ltd/E. Midlands	
G-BAFA	AA-5 Traveler	C. F. Mackley/Stapleford	
G-BAFG	D.H.82A Tiger Moth	J. E. & P. J. Shaw	
G-BAFH	Evans VP-1	C. M. Gibson	
G-BAFI	Cessna F.177RG	Gloucestershire Flying Club	
G-BAFL	Cessna 182P	Farm Aviation Services Ltd	
G-BAFP	Robin DR.400/160	A. S. Langdale & J. Bevis-Lawson	
G-BAFS	PA-18 Super Cub 150	G-BAFS Group/Sandown	
G-BAFT	PA-18 Super Cub 150	T. J. Wilkinson/Riseley	
G-BAFU	PA-28 Cherokee 140	M. Kostiuk	
G-BAFV	PA-18 Super Cub 95	T. F. & S. J. Thorpe	
G-BAFX	Robin DR.400/140	K. R. Gough	
G-BAGB	SIAI-Marchetti SF.260	British Midland Airways Ltd/E. Midlands	
G-BAGC	Robin DR.400/140	W. P. Nutt	
G-BAGE	Cessna T.210L ★	Aeroplane Collection Ltd	
G-BAGF	Jodel D.92 Bebe	E. Evans	
G-BAGG	PA-32 Cherokee Six 300E	D. Anthill	
G-BAGI	Cameron O-31 balloon	Red Section Balloon Group	
G-BAGL	SA.341G Gazelle Srs 1	Triangle Computer Services Ltd	
G-BAGN	Cessna F.177RG	R. W. J. Andrews	
G-BAGO	Cessna 421B	M. S. Choksey	
G-BAGR	Robin DR.400/140	F. C. Aris & J. D. Last/Mona	
G-BAGS	Robin DR.400/180 2+2	Flying Services	
G-BAGT	Helio H.295 Courier	B. J. C. Woodall Ltd	
G-BAGV	Cessna U.206F	Scottish Parachute Club/Strathallan	
G-BAGX	PA-28 Cherokee 140	Golf X-Ray Group	
G-BAGY	Cameron O-84 balloon	P. G. Dunnington	
G-BAHD	Cessna 182P Skylane	G. G. Ferriman	
G-BAHE	PA-28 Cherokee 140	A. H. Evans & A. O. Jones	
G-BAHF	PA-28 Cherokee 140	BJ Services (Midlands) Ltd	
G-BAHG	PA-24 Comanche 260	B. Walker & Co (Dursley) Ltd	
G-BAHH	Wallis WA-121	K. H. Wallis	
G-BAHI	Cessna F.150H	P. Wagstaff/Elstree	
G-BAHJ	PA-24 Comanche 250	K. Cooper	
G-BAHL	Robin DR.400/160	M. D. Hinge & L. A. Maynard	
G-BAHO	Beech C.23 Sundowner	P. H. White & J. A. L. Staig	
G-BAHP	Volmer VJ.22 Sportsman	Seaplane Group	
G-BAHS	PA-28R Cherokee Arrow 200-II	J. T. Mirley	
G-BAHX	Cessna 182P	PP Dupost Group	

Notes	Reg.	Type	Owner or Operator
	G-BAIG	PA-34-200-2 Seneca	Mid-Anglia School of Flying
	G-BAIH	PA-28R Cherokee Arrow 200-II	M. G. West
	G-BAII	Cessna FRA.150L	Cornwall Flying Club Ltd/Bodmin
	G-BAIK	Cessna F.150L	Wickenby Aviation Ltd
	G-BAIN	Cessna FRA.150L	Cornwall Flying Club Ltd/Bodmin
	G-BAIP	Cessna F.150L	G. & S. A. Jones
	G-BAIS	Cessna F.177RG	Cardinal Syndicate
	G-BAIW	Cessna F.172M	W. J. Greenfield/Humberside
	G-BAIX	Cessna F.172M	R. A. Nichols/Elstree
	G-BAIZ	Slingsby T.61A Falke	Falke Syndicate/Hinton-in-the-Hedges
	G-BAJA	Cessna F.177RG	Don Ward Productions Ltd/Biggin Hill
	G-BAJB	Cessna F.177RG	C. M. Bain
	G-BAJC	Evans VP-1	S. J. Greer
	G-BAJE	Cessna 177 Cardinal	T. Barge
	G-BAJN	AA-5 Traveler	H. Snelson
	G-BAJO	AA-5 Traveler	G-BAJO Group
	G-BAJR	PA-28 Cherokee 180	Chosen Few Flying Group/Newtownards
	G-BAJY	Robin DR.400/180	Rolines Aviation
	G-BAJZ	Robin DR.400/125	Weald Air Services/Headcorn
	G-BAKD	PA-34-200 Seneca II	Andrews Professional Colour Laboratories/Elstree
	G-BAKH	PA-28 Cherokee 140	Marnham Investments Ltd
	G-BAKJ	PA-30 Twin Comanche 160B	M. F. Fisher & ptnrs
	G-BAKK	Cessna F.172H ★	*Parachute jump trainer*/Hinton-in-the-Hedges
	G-BAKM	Robin DR.400/140	D. V. Pieri
	G-BAKN	SNCAN Stampe SV-4C	M. Holloway
	G-BAKR	Jodel D.117	R. W. Brown
	G-BAKV	PA-18 Super Cub 150	A. J. B. Shaw & ptnrs/Thruxton
	G-BAKW	B.121 Pup 2	H. Beavan
	G-BAKY	Slingsby T.61C Falke	T. J. Wiltshire
	G-BALF	Robin DR.400/140	N. A. Smith
	G-BALG	Robin DR.400/180	R. Jones
	G-BALH	Robin DR.400/140B	G-BALH Flying Group
	G-BALI	Robin DR.400 2+2	A. Brinkley
	G-BALJ	Robin DR.400/180	D. A. Bett & D. de Lacey-Rowe
	G-BALN	Cessna T.310Q	O'Brien Properties Ltd/Shoreham
	G-BALZ	Bell 212	Bristow Helicopters Ltd
	G-BAMB	Slingsby T.61C Falke	G-BAMB Syndicate
	G-BAMC	Cessna F.150L	Billy Pickles Ltd
	G-BAMF	MBB Bo 105D	Bond Air Services/Aberdeen
	G-BAMJ	Cessna 182P	A. E. Kedros
	G-BAMK	Cameron D-96 airship	D. W. Liddiard
	G-BAML	Bell 206B JetRanger 2	Heliscott Ltd
	G-BAMM	PA-28 Cherokee 235	T. A. Astell
	G-BAMR	PA-16 Clipper	H. Royce
	G-BAMS	Robin DR.400/160	G-BAMS Ltd/Headcorn
	G-BAMU	Robin DR.400/160	The Alternative Flying Group
	G-BAMV	Robin DR.400/180	K. Jones & E. A. Anderson/Booker
	G-BAMY	PA-28R Cherokee Arrow 200-II	G-BAMY Group/Birmingham
	G-BANA	Robin DR.221	G. T. Pryor
	G-BANB	Robin DR.400/180	D. R. L. Jones
	G-BANC	GY-201 Minicab	J. T. S. Lewis & J. E. Williams
	G-BANK	PA-34-200 Seneca II	S. Eastwood
	G-BANU	Wassmer Jodel D.120	W. M. & C. H. Kilner
	G-BANV	Phoenix Currie Wot	K. Knight
	G-BANW	CP.1330 Super Emeraude	P. S. Milner
	G-BANX	Cessna F.172M	Oakfleet Ltd
	G-BAOB	Cessna F.172M	Rentair Ltd & ptnrs
	G-BAOG	M.S.880B Rallye Club	J. Luck
	G-BAOH	M.S.880B Rallye Club	M. Lally
	G-BAOJ	M.S.880B Rallye Club	R. E. Jones
	G-BAOM	M.S.880B Rallye Club	D. H. Tonkin
	G-BAOP	Cessna FRA.150L	M. P. Guckian
	G-BAOS	Cessna F.172M	Wingtask 1995 Ltd
	G-BAOU	AA-5 Traveler	R. C. Mark
	G-BAOW	Cameron O-65 balloon	I. Chadwick
	G-BAPB	D.H.C.1 Chipmunk 22	G. V. Bunyan
	G-BAPI	Cessna FRA.150L	Industrial Supplies (Peterborough) Ltd/Sibson
	G-BAPJ	Cessna FRA.150L	M. D. Page/Manston
	G-BAPL	PA-23 Turbo Aztec 250E	Donington Aviation Ltd/E. Midlands
	G-BAPP	Evans VP-1	V. Mitchell

Reg.	Type	Owner or Operator	Notes
G-BAPR	Jodel D.11	J. B. Liber & J. F. M. Bartlett	
G-BAPS	Campbell Cougar ★	IHM/Weston-s-Mare	
G-BAPV	Robin DR.400/160	J. D. & M. Millne/Newcastle	
G-BAPW	PA-28R Cherokee Arrow 180	I. W. Lindsey & P. S. Ferren/Elstree	
G-BAPX	Robin DR.400/160	M. A. Musselwhite	
G-BAPY	Robin HR.100/210	D. M. Hansell	
G-BARC	Cessna FR.172J	Severn Valley Aviation Group	
G-BARD	Cessna 337C	D. W. Horton	
G-BARF	Jodel D.112 Club	J. J. Penney	
G-BARG	Cessna E.310Q	Anglo American Airmotive Ltd/ Bournemouth	
G-BARH	Beech C.23 Sundowner	J. R. Pybus	
G-BARN	Taylor JT.2 Titch	R. G. W. Newton	
G-BARP	Bell 206B JetRanger 2	S.W. Electricity Board/Bristol	
G-BARS	D.H.C.1 Chipmunk 22 (1377)	J. Beattie/Yeovilton	
G-BARV	Cessna 310Q	Old England Watches Ltd/Elstree	
G-BARZ	Scheibe SF.28A Tandem Falke	K. Kiely	
G-BASG	AA-5 Traveler	ASG Aviation Group/Glenrothes	
G-BASH	AA-5 Traveler	BASH Flying Group	
G-BASJ	PA-28 Cherokee 180	Challenger Flying Group	
G-BASL	PA-28 Cherokee 140	Air Navigation & Trading Ltd/Blackpool	
G-BASM	PA-34-200 Seneca II	M. Gipps & J. R. Whetlor	
G-BASN	Beech C.23 Sundowner	M. F. Fisher	
G-BASO	Lake LA-4 Amphibian	C. J. A. Macauley	
G-BASP	B.121 Pup 1	B. J. Coutts/Sywell	
G-BASX	PA-34-200 Seneca II	London Executive Aviation Ltd	
G-BATC	MBB Bo 105D	Bond Air Services/Aberdeen	
G-BATJ	Jodel D.119	D. J. & K. S. Thomas	
G-BATN	PA-23 Aztec 250E	Marshall of Cambridge Ltd	
G-BATR	PA-34-200 Seneca II	Falcon Flying Services/Biggin Hill	
G-BATT	Hughes 269C	Calderbrook Estates Ltd	
G-BATV	PA-28 Cherokee 180D	J. N. Rudsdale	
G-BATW	PA-28 Cherokee 140	Tango Whiskey Flying Partnership	
G-BATX	PA-23 Aztec 250E	Aviation Services (Southern) Ltd/ Shoreham	
G-BAUA	PA-23 Aztec 250D	David Parr & Associates Ltd	
G-BAUC	PA-25 Pawnee 235	Southdown Gliding Club Ltd/Parham Park	
G-BAUH	Jodel D.112	G. A. & D. Shepherd	
G-BAUJ	PA-23 Aztec 250E ★	S. J. & C. J. Westley/Cranfield	
G-BAUN	Bell 206B JetRanger	Bristow Helicopters Ltd	
G-BAUV	Cessna F.150L	Skyviews & General Ltd	
G-BAUW	PA-23 Aztec 250E	R. E. Myson	
G-BAUY	Cessna FRA.150L	P. A. Layzell/Old Buckenham	
G-BAUZ	SNCAN NC.854S	W. A. Ashley & D. Horne	
G-BAVB	Cessna F.172M	C. P. Course	
G-BAVH	D.H.C.1 Chipmunk 22	Portsmouth Naval Gliding Club/ Lee-on-Solent	
G-BAVL	PA-23 Aztec 250E	S. P. & A. V. Chillott	
G-BAVO	Boeing Stearman N2S (26)	Vallingstone Aviation Ltd	
G-BAVR	AA-5 Traveler	G. E. Murray	
G-BAVS	AA-5 Traveler	V. J. Peake/Headcorn	
G-BAVU	Cameron A-105 balloon	J. D. Michaelis	
G-BAVZ	PA-23 Aztec 250E	Ravenair/Manchester	
G-BAWG	PA-28R Cherokee Arrow 200-II	Solent Air Ltd	
G-BAWK	PA-28 Cherokee 140	Newcastle-upon-Tyne Aero Club Ltd	
G-BAWR	Robin HR.100/210	T. Taylor	
G-BAWU	PA-30 Twin Comanche 160B	Syndicate Clerical Services Ltd	
G-BAXE	Hughes 269A	Reethorpe Engineering Ltd	
G-BAXJ	PA-32 Cherokee Six 300B	UK Parachute Services/Stirling	
G-BAXK	Thunder Ax7-77 balloon	A. R. Snook	
G-BAXP	PA-23 Aztec 250E	(stored)/Shoreham	
G-BAXS	Bell 47G-5	RK Helicopters	
G-BAXU	Cessna F.150L	M. A. Wilson/Liverpool	
G-BAXV	Cessna F.150L	G. & S. A. Jones	
G-BAXY	Cessna F.172M	R. J. W. Wood	
G-BAXZ	PA-28 Cherokee 140	H. Martin & D. Norris/Halton	
G-BAYL	SNCAN Nord 1101 Norecrin ★	(stored)/Chirk	
G-BAYO	Cessna 150L	W. J. Barnes & A. J. Fisher	
G-BAYP	Cessna 150L	Yankee Papa Flying Group	
G-BAYR	Robin HR.100/210	L. A. Christie/Stapleford	
G-BAYV	SNCAN 1101 Noralpha (3) ★	Macclesfield Historical Aviation Soc/Barton	
G-BAYZ	Bellanca 7GCBC Citabria	Rodger Aircraft Ltd	

Notes	Reg.	Type	Owner or Operator
	G-BAZC	Robin DR.400/160	Southern Sailplanes Ltd/Membury
	G-BAZJ	HPR-7 Herald 209 ★	Guernsey Airport Fire Services
	G-BAZM	Jodel D.11	A. F. Simpson
	G-BAZS	Cessna F.150L	L. W. Scattergood
	G-BAZT	Cessna F.172M	Exeter Flying Club Ltd
	G-BAZU	PA-28R Cherokee Arrow 200	S. C. Simmons/White Waltham0
	G-BBAK	M.S.894A Rallye Minerva	R. B. Hemsworth & C. L. Hill
	G-BBAW	Robin HR.100/210	J. R. Williams
	G-BBAX	Robin DR.400/140	G. J. Bissex & P. H. Garbutt
	G-BBAY	Robin DR.400/140	Rothwell Group
	G-BBBC	Cessna F.150L	W. J. Greenfield
	G-BBBI	AA-5 Traveler	M. E. J. & S. A. Smith
	G-BBBK	PA-28 Cherokee 140	Bencray Ltd/Blackpool
	G-BBBM	Bell 206B JetRanger 2	Express Newspapers PLC
	G-BBBN	PA-28 Cherokee 180	Estuary Aviation Ltd
	G-BBBO	SIPA 903	Mersey SIPA Group
	G-BBBW	FRED Srs 2	M. Palfreman
	G-BBBX	Cessna E310L	Atlantic Air Transport Ltd/Coventry
	G-BBBY	PA-28 Cherokee 140	J. M. Scott
	G-BBCA	Bell 206B JetRanger 2	Stonewell Services Ltd
	G-BBCC	PA-23 Aztec 250D	Richard Nash Cars Ltd
	G-BBCH	Robin DR.400/2+2	A. J. & S. P. Smith
	G-BBCI	Cessna 150H	Domeastral Ltd
	G-BBCK	Cameron O-77 balloon	W. R. Teasdale
	G-BBCN	Robin HR.100/210	Gloucestershire Flying Club
	G-BBCP	Thunder Ax6-56 balloon	J. M. Robinson
	G-BBCS	Robin DR.400/140	Westfield Flying Group
	G-BBCW	PA-23 Aztec 250E	JDT Holdings Ltd/Sturgate
	G-BBCY	Luton LA-4A Minor	T. G. Solomon
	G-BBCZ	AA-5 Traveler	Golf Charlie Zulu Ltd
	G-BBDC	PA-28 Cherokee 140	P. Doggett & P. A. Gray
	G-BBDE	PA-28R Cherokee Arrow 200-II	R. L. Coleman & A. E. Stevens/ Panshanger
	G-BBDG	Concorde 100 ★	British Aerospace PLC/Filton
	G-BBDH	Cessna F.172M	J. C. Holland
	G-BBDL	AA-5 Traveler	Delta Lima Flying Group
	G-BBDM	AA-5 Traveler	P. J. Marchant
	G-BBDO	PA-23 Turbo Aztec 250E	Anstee & Ware Ltd/Bristol
	G-BBDP	Robin DR.400/160	Robin Lance Aviation Associates Ltd
	G-BBDT	Cessna 150H	Delta Tango Group
	G-BBDV	SIPA S.903	W. McAndrew
	G-BBEA	Luton LA-4A Minor	Luton Minor Group
	G-BBEB	PA-28R Cherokee Arrow 200-II	R. D. Rippingale/Thruxton
	G-BBEC	PA-28 Cherokee 180	A. A. Gardner
	G-BBED	M.S.894A Rallye Minerva 220	Vista Products
	G-BBEF	PA-28 Cherokee 140	Comed Aviation Ltd/Blackpool
	G-BBEL	PA-28R Cherokee Arrow 180	J. Paulson/Liverpool
	G-BBEN	Bellanca 7GCBC Citabria	C. A. G. Schofield
	G-BBEO	Cessna FRA.150L	Moray Flying Club (1990) Ltd/Kinloss
	G-BBEV	PA-28 Cherokee 140	Comed Aviation Ltd/Blackpool
	G-BBEX	Cessna 185A	V. M. McCarthy
	G-BBEY	PA-23 Aztec 250E	M. Hall
	G-BBFC	AA-1B Trainer	I. J. Hiatt
	G-BBFD	PA-28R Cherokee Arrow 200-II	CR Aviation Ltd
	G-BBFL	GY-201 Minicab	D. Silsbury
	G-BBFS	Van Den Bemden gas balloon	A. J. F. Smith
	G-BBFV	PA-32 Cherokee Six 260	Airlaunch
	G-BBGB	PA-E23 Aztec 250E	Ravenair/Manchester
	G-BBGC	M.S.893E Rallye 180GT	Seahawk Glding Club/Culdrose
	G-BBGH	AA-5 Traveler	L. W. Mitchell & D. Abbiss
	G-BBGI	Fuji FA.200-160	G. C. B. Weir
	G-BBGL	Baby Great Lakes	F. Ball
	G-BBGR	Cameron O-65 balloon	M. L. & L. P. Willoughby
	G-BBGX	Cessna 182P Skylane	GX Group
	G-BBGZ	CHABA 42 balloon	G. Laslett & ptnrs
	G-BBHF	PA-23 Aztec 250E	G. J. Williams/Sherburn
	G-BBHI	Cessna 177RG	T. G. W. Bunce
	G-BBHJ	Piper J-3C-65 Cub	R. V. Miller & J. Stanbridge
	G-BBHK	AT-16 Harvard IIB (FH153)	Bob Warner Aviation/Exeter
	G-BBHL	Sikorsky S-61N Mk II	Bristow Helicopters Ltd *Glamis*
	G-BBHM	Sikorsky S-61N	Bristow Helicopters Ltd
	G-BBHY	PA-28 Cherokee 180	Air Operations Ltd/Guernsey
	G-BBIA	PA-28R Cherokee Arrow 200-II	G. H. Kilby/Stapleford

Reg.	Type	Owner or Operator	Notes
G-BBIF	PA-23 Aztec 250E	Home Doors (GB) Ltd	
G-BBIH	Enstrom F-28A-UK	Stephenson Marine Co Ltd	
G-BBII	Fiat G-46-3B (14+)	Bianchi Aviation Film Services Ltd	
G-BBIL	PA-28 Cherokee 140	India Lima Flying Group	
G-BBIO	Robin HR.100/210	R. A. King/Headcorn	
G-BBIX	PA-28 Cherokee 140	Sterling Aviation Ltd	
G-BBJB	Thunder Ax7-77 balloon	St Crispin Balloon Group	
G-BBJI	Isaacs Spitfire (RN218)	T. E. W. Terrell	
G-BBJU	Robin DR.400/140	J. C. Lister	
G-BBJV	Cessna F.177RG	Pilot Magazine/Biggin Hill	
G-BBJX	Cessna F.150L	Yorkshire Flying Services Ltd	
G-BBJY	Cessna F.172M	J. Lucketti/Barton	
G-BBJZ	Cessna F.172M	Burks, Green & ptnrs	
G-BBKA	Cessna F.150L	R. Hall	
G-BBKB	Cessna F.150L	Justgold Ltd/Blackpool	
G-BBKE	Cessna F.150L	J. D. Woodward	
G-BBKF	Cessna FRA.150L	D. W. Mickleburgh	
G-BBKG	Cessna FR.172J	R. Wright	
G-BBKI	Cessna F.172M	C. W. & S. A. Burman	
G-BBKL	CP.301A Emeraude	P. J. Griggs	
G-BBKR	Scheibe SF.24A Motorspatz	P. I. Morgans	
G-BBKU	Cessna FRA.150L	Penguin Group	
G-BBKX	PA-28 Cherokee 180	DRA Flying Club Ltd/Farnborough	
G-BBKY	Cessna F.150L	Telesonic Ltd/Barton	
G-BBKZ	Cessna 172M	KZ Flying Group/Exeter	
G-BBLH	Piper J-3C-65 Cub (31145)	Shipping & Airlines Ltd/Biggin Hill	
G-BBLL	Cameron O-84 balloon ★	British Balloon Museum/Newbury	
G-BBLM	SOCATA Rallye 100S	Skillcomps Ltd	
G-BBLP	PA-23 Aztec 250D	Donington Aviation Ltd/E. Midlands	
G-BBLS	AA-5 Traveler	A. D. Grant	
G-BBLU	PA-34-200 Seneca II	Falcon Flying Services/Biggin Hill	
G-BBMB	Robin DR.400/180	Regent Flying Group/Biggin Hill	
G-BBMH	EAA. Sports Biplane Model P.1	K. Dawson	
G-BBMJ	PA-23 Aztec 250E	Tindon Ltd/Little Snoring	
G-BBMN	D.H.C.1 Chipmunk 22	R. Steiner/Rush Green	
G-BBMO	D.H.C.1 Chipmunk 22	D. M. Squires/Wellesbourn	
G-BBMR	D.H.C.1 Chipmunk 22 (WB763)	A. J. Parkhouse	
G-BBMT	D.H.C.1 Chipmunk 22	J. Evans & D. Withers	
G-BBMV	D.H.C.1 Chipmunk 22 (WG348)	P. J. Morgan (Aviation) Ltd	
G-BBMW	D.H.C.1 Chipmunk 22 (WK628)	Mike Whisky Group/Shoreham	
G-BBMX	D.H.C.1 Chipmunk 22	Chipmunk 4 Ever Foundation/Holland	
G-BBMZ	D.H.C.1 Chipmunk 22	Wycombe Gliding School Syndicate/ Booker	
G-BBNA	D.H.C.1 Chipmunk 22 (Lycoming)	Coventry Gliding Club Ltd/ Husbands Bosworth	
G-BBNC	D.H.C.1 Chipmunk T.10 (WP790) ★	Mosquito Aircraft Museum	
G-BBND	D.H.C.1 Chipmunk 22 (WD286)	Chipmunk G-BCIW Syndicate 1984	
G-BBNG	Bell 206B JetRanger 2	Helicopter Crop Spraying Ltd	
G-BBNH	PA-34-200 Seneca II	M. G. D. Baverstock/Bournemouth	
G-BBNI	PA-34-200 Seneca II	Channel Aviation Holdings Ltd	
G-BBNJ	Cessna F.150L	Sherburn Aero Club Ltd	
G-BBNO	PA-23 Aztec 250E ★	stored/Biggin Hill	
G-BBNV	Fuji FA.200-160	Caseright Ltd	
G-BBNX	Cessna FRA.150L	General Airline Ltd/Blackbushe	
G-BBNZ	Cessna F.172M	R. J. Nunn	
G-BBOA	Cessna F.172M	J. D & A. M. Black	
G-BBOC	Cameron O-77 balloon	J. A. B. Gray	
G-BBOD	Thunder O-45 balloon	B. R. & M. Boyle	
G-BBOE	Robin HR.200/100	T. D. Saveker	
G-BBOH	Pitts S-1S Special	Venom Jet Promotions Ltd/Bournemouth	
G-BBOJ	PA-23 Aztec 250E ★	Instructional airframe/Cranfield	
G-BBOL	PA-18 Super Cub 150	Lakes Gliding Club Ltd/Walney Island	
G-BBOO	Thunder Ax6-56 balloon	K. Meehan Tigerjack	
G-BBOR	Bell 206B JetRanger 2	M. J. Easey	
G-BBOX	Thunder Ax7-77 balloon	R. C. Weyda	
G-BBPK	Evans VP-1	G. D. E. MacDonald	
G-BBPM	Enstrom F-28A	R. Brennan & ptnrs	
G-BBPN	Enstrom F-28A	J. R. Jeffers	
G-BBPO	Enstrom F-28A	Southern Air Ltd & Jewelhaven Ltd	
G-BBPS	Jodel D.117	A. Appleby/Redhill	
G-BBPW	Robin HR.100/210	S. D. Cole	
G-BBPX	PA-34-200 Seneca II	Richel Investments Ltd/Guernsey	

Notes	Reg.	Type	Owner or Operator
	G-BBPY	PA-28 Cherokee 180	Sunsaver Ltd
	G-BBRA	PA-23 Aztec 250D	FK Global Aviation
	G-BBRB	D.H.82A Tiger Moth (DF198)	R. Barham/Biggin Hill
	G-BBRC	Fuji FA.200-180	BBRC Ltd
	G-BBRH	Bell 47G-5A	Helicopter Supplies & Engineering Ltd
	G-BBRI	Bell 47G-5A	Alan Mann Helicopters Ltd/Fairoaks
	G-BBRJ	PA-23 Aztec 250E	Millennium Air Ltd
	G-BBRN	Procter Kittiwake 1 (XW784)	R. de H. Dobree-Carey
	G-BBRV	D.H.C.1 Chipmunk 22	ABC Advertising Ltd/Biggin Hill
	G-BBRX	SIAI-Marchetti S.205-18F	R. C. & A. K. West
	G-BBRZ	AA-5 Traveler	C. P. Osbourne
	G-BBSA	AA-5 Traveler	Usworth 84 Flying Associates Ltd
	G-BBSB	Beech C23 Sundowner	Sundowner Group/Woodford
	G-BBSC	Beech B24R Sierra	Beechcombers Flying Group
	G-BBSM	PA-32 Cherokee Six 300E	MT Management Ltd
	G-BBSS	D.H.C.1A Chipmunk 22	Coventry Gliding Club Ltd/ Husbands Bosworth
	G-BBSW	Pietenpol Air Camper	J. K. S. Wills
	G-BBTB	Cessna FRA.150L	Griffin Marston Ltd/Compton Abbas
	G-BBTG	Cessna F.172M	R. W. & V. P. J. Simpson/Redhill
	G-BBTH	Cessna F.172M	K. Kwok-Kin Lee
	G-BBTJ	PA-23 Aztec 250E	Cooper Aerial Surveys Ltd/Sandtoft
	G-BBTK	Cessna FRA.150L	Cleveland Flying School Ltd/Teesside
	G-BBTL	PA-23 Aztec 250C	Air Navigation & Trading Co Ltd/ Blackpool
	G-BBTS	Beech V35B Bonanza	Eastern Air
	G-BBTU	ST-10 Diplomate	D. Hayden-Wright
	G-BBTX	Beech C23 Sundowner	K. Harding/Blackbushe
	G-BBTY	Beech C23 Sundowner	A. W. Roderick & W. Price
	G-BBTZ	Cessna F.150L	Marnham Investments Ltd
	G-BBUE	AA-5 Traveler	Hebog (Mon) Cyfyngedig/Mona
	G-BBUF	AA-5 Traveler	W. McLaren
	G-BBUG	PA-16 Clipper	J. Dolan
	G-BBUJ	Cessna 421B	Coolflourish Ltd
	G-BBUT	Western O-65 balloon	G. F. Turnbull
	G-BBUU	Piper J-3C-65 Cub	O. J. J. Rogers
	G-BBUW	SA.102.5 Cavalier ★	Aeroplane Collection Ltd
	G-BBVA	Sikorsky S-61N Mk II	Bristow Helicopters Ltd Vega
	G-BBVF	SA Twin Pioneer Srs 3 ★	Museum of Flight/E. Fortune
	G-BBVG	PA-23 Aztec 250C ★	(stored)/Little Staughton
	G-BBVI	Enstrom F-28A ★	Ground trainer/Kidlington
	G-BBVJ	Beech B24R Sierra	T. Keely
	G-BBVO	Isaacs Fury II (S1579)	C. M. Barnes & D. A. Wirdnam
	G-BBVP	Westland-Bell 47G-3B1	CKS Air Ltd/Southend
	G-BBWZ	AA-1B Trainer	D. K. Barrett & ptnrs
	G-BBXB	Cessna FRA.150L	D. M. Fenton
	G-BBXH	Cessna FR.172F	D. Ridley
	G-BBXK	PA-34-200 Seneca	Poyston Aviation
	G-BBXL	Cessna 310Q	Thornhill Aviation Ltd
	G-BBXO	Enstrom F-28A	Stephenson Marine Ltd
	G-BBXS	Piper J-3C-65 Cub	M. J. Butler (G-ALMA)/Langham
	G-BBXU	Beech B24R Sierra	B. M. Russell/Coventry
	G-BBXY	Bellanca 7GCBC Citabria	R. R. L. Windus
	G-BBXZ	Evans VP-1	R. W. Burrows
	G-BBYB	PA-18 Super Cub 95	Tiger Club (1990) Ltd/Headcorn
	G-BBYH	Cessna 182P	Croftmarsh Ltd
	G-BBYM	H.P.137 Jetstream 200	British Aerospace (Operations) Ltd (G-AYWR)/Warton
	G-BBYP	PA-28 Cherokee 140	Jersey Aircraft Maintenance Ltd
	G-BBYS	Cessna 182P Skylane	I. M. Jones
	G-BBZF	PA-28 Cherokee 140	Winchester 95 Associates Ltd
	G-BBZH	PA-28R Cherokee Arrow 200-II	Zulu Hotel Club
	G-BBZJ	PA-34-200 Seneca II	Eurofly Share Ltd
	G-BBZN	Fuji FA.200-180	J. Westwood & P. D. Wedd
	G-BBZO	Fuji FA.200-160	G-BBZO Group
	G-BBZV	PA-28R Cherokee Arrow 200-II	P. B. Mellor/Kidlington
	G-BCAH	D.H.C.1 Chipmunk 22 (WG316)	Southern Air Ltd/Shoreham
	G-BCAN	Thunder Ax7-77 balloon	D. D. Owen
	G-BCAP	Cameron O-56 balloon	S. R. Seager
	G-BCAR	Thunder Ax7-77 balloon ★	British Balloon Museum/Newbury
	G-BCAS	Thunder Ax7-77 balloon	D. P. Busby
	G-BCAZ	PA-12 Super Cruiser	A. D. Williams

Reg.	Type	Owner or Operator	Notes
G-BCBG	PA-23 Aztec 250E	M. J. L. Batt	
G-BCBH	Fairchild 24R-46A Argus III	Ebork Ltd	
G-BCBJ	PA-25 Pawnee 235	Deeside Gliding Club (Aberdeenshire) Ltd/Aboyne	
G-BCBL	Fairchild 24R-46A Argus III (HB751)	F. J. Cox	
G-BCBM	PA-23 Aztec 250C	Hatton & Westerman Trawlers	
G-BCBR	AJEP/Wittman W.8 Tailwind	R. J. Willies	
G-BCBX	Cessna F.150L	J. Kelly/Newtownards	
G-BCBZ	Cessna 337C	J. J. Zwetsloot	
G-BCCC	Cessna F.150L	Airtime Maintenance Ltd	
G-BCCD	Cessna F.172M	Austin Aviation Ltd	
G-BCCE	PA-23 Aztec 250E	Falcon Flying Services/Biggin Hill	
G-BCCF	PA-28 Cherokee 180	Topcat Aviation Ltd	
G-BCCG	Thunder Ax7-65 balloon	N. H. Ponsford	
G-BCCJ	AA-5 Traveler	T. Needham/Woodford	
G-BCCK	AA-5 Traveler	Prospect Air Ltd/Barton	
G-BCCR	CP.301A Emeraude (modified)	J. H. & C. J. Waterman	
G-BCCU	BN-2A Mk.III-1 Trislander	Keenair Charter	
G-BCCX	D.H.C.1 Chipmunk 22 (Lycoming)	RAFGSA/Dishforth	
G-BCCY	Robin HR.200/100	Charlie Yankee Ltd	
G-BCDB	PA-34-200 Seneca II	P. A. S. Dyke	
G-BCDJ	PA-28 Cherokee 140	Bristol Aero Club/Filton	
G-BCDK	Partenavia P.68B	Flyteam Aviation Ltd/Elstree	
G-BCDL	Cameron O-42 balloon	D. P. & Mrs B. O. Turner Chums	
G-BCDN	F.27 Friendship Mk 200 ★	*Instructional airframe*/Norwich	
G-BCDY	Cessna FRA.150L	Mid-Anglia Flying School Ltd/Cambridge	
G-BCEA	Sikorsky S-61N Mk II	Brintel Helicopters	
G-BCEB	Sikorsky S-61N Mk II	Brintel Helicopters/Penzance	
G-BCEC	Cessna F.172M	A. R. & S. D. Bamber	
G-BCEE	AA-5 Traveler	Echo Echo Ltd/Bournemouth	
G-BCEF	AA-5 Traveler	K. W. Longden/France	
G-BCEN	BN-2A-26 Islander	Atlantic Air Transport Ltd/Coventry	
G-BCEO	AA-5 Traveler	Echo Oscar Flying Group	
G-BCEP	AA-5 Traveler	Golf Echo Papa Flying Group	
G-BCER	GY-201 Minicab	D. Beaumont/Sherburn	
G-BCEU	Cameron O-42 balloon	Entertainment Services Ltd	
G-BCEX	PA-23 Aztec 250E	Western Air (Thruxton) Ltd	
G-BCEY	D.H.C.1 Chipmunk 22 (WG465)	Gopher Flying Group	
G-BCEZ	Cameron O-84 balloon	Balloon Collection	
G-BCFC	Cameron O-65 balloon	B. H. Mead Candy Twist	
G-BCFD	West balloon ★	British Balloon Museum Hellfire/Newbury	
G-BCFF	Fuji FA-200-160	G. W. Brown & M. R. Gibbons	
G-BCFO	PA-18 Super Cub 150	Portsmouth Naval Gliding Club/ Lee-on-Solent	
G-BCFR	Cessna FRA.150L	Rentair Ltd	
G-BCFW	SAAB 91D Safir	D. R. Williams	
G-BCFY	Luton LA-4A Minor	G. Capes	
G-BCGB	Bensen B.8	J. W. Birkett	
G-BCGC	D.H.C.1 Chipmunk 22 (WP903)	Transport Command Ltd/Shoreham	
G-BCGG	Jodel DR.250 Srs 160	C. G. Gray (G-ATZL)	
G-BCGH	SNCAN NC.854S	Nord Flying Group	
G-BCGI	PA-28 Cherokee 140	A. Dodd/Redhill	
G-BCGJ	PA-28 Cherokee 140	BCT Aircraft Leasing Ltd	
G-BCGM	Jodel D.120	M. H. D. Soltau	
G-BCGN	PA-28 Cherokee 140	Golf November Ltd/Kidlington	
G-BCGS	PA-28R Cherokee Arrow 200	Arrow Aviation Group	
G-BCGT	PA-28 Cherokee 140	EFS Flying Group/Earls Colne	
G-BCGW	Jodel D.11	G. H. & M. D. Chittenden	
G-BCHK	Cessna F.172H	E. C. & A. K. Shimmin	
G-BCHL	D.H.C.1 Chipmunk 22A (WP788)	Shropshire Soaring Ltd/Sleap	
G-BCHM	SA.341G Gazelle 1	The Auster Aircraft Co Ltd	
G-BCHP	CP.1310-C3 Super Emeraude	G. Hughes & A. G. Just (G-JOSI)	
G-BCHT	Schleicher ASK.16	Dunstable K16 Group	
G-BCHX	SF.23A Sperling	*(stored)*/Rufforth	
G-BCID	PA-34-200 Seneca II	C. J. Freeman/Headcorn	
G-BCIH	D.H.C.1 Chipmunk 22 (WD363)	J. M. Hosey/Stansted	
G-BCIJ	AA-5 Traveler	R. J. Warne	
G-BCIK	AA-5 Traveler	Trent Aviation Ltd	
G-BCIN	Thunder Ax7-77 balloon	P. G & R. A. Vale	
G-BCIR	PA-28-151 Warrior	P. J. Brennan	
G-BCJH	Mooney M.20F	P. B. Bossard	
G-BCJM	PA-28 Cherokee 140	Topcat Aviation Ltd	

Notes	Reg.	Type	Owner or Operator
	G-BCJN	PA-28 Cherokee 140	Topcat Aviation Ltd
	G-BCJO	PA-28R Cherokee Arrow 200	R. Ross
	G-BCJP	PA-28 Cherokee 140	Omletair Flying Group
	G-BCKN	D.H.C.1A Chipmunk 22 (Lycoming)	RAFGSA/Cranwell
	G-BCKP	Luton LA-5A Major	D. & W. H. Gough
	G-BCKS	Fuji FA.200-180	Kestrel Aviation Ltd
	G-BCKT	Fuji FA.200-180	M. A. Petrie
	G-BCKU	Cessna FRA.150L	Stapleford Flying Club Ltd
	G-BCKV	Cessna FRA.150L	Cleveland Flying School Ltd/Teesside
	G-BCLC	Sikorsky S-61N	Bristow Helicopters/HM Coastguard
	G-BCLD	Sikorsky S-61N	Bristow Helicopters Ltd
	G-BCLI	AA-5 Traveler	Pioneer Aviation Ltd/Cranfield
	G-BCLL	PA-28 Cherokee 180	S. R. & J. Nash
	G-BCLS	Cessna 170B	Teesside Flight Centre Ltd
	G-BCLT	M.S.894A Rallye Minerva 220	Rallye Group
	G-BCLU	Jodel D.117	N. A. Wallace
	G-BCLW	AA-1B Trainer	A. F. Duncan & B. Hepburn
	G-BCMD	PA-18 Super Cub 95	J. G. Brooks/Dunkeswell
	G-BCMT	Isaacs Fury II	M. H. Turner
	G-BCNC	GY-201 Minicab	J. R. Wraight
	G-BCNP	Cameron O-77 balloon	P. Spellward
	G-BCNX	Piper J-3C-65 Cub (540)	K. J. Lord
	G-BCNZ	Fuji FA.200-160	J. Bruton & A. Lincoln/Manchester
	G-BCOB	Piper J-3C-65 Cub (329405)	R. W. & Mrs J. W. Marjoram
	G-BCOI	D.H.C.1 Chipmunk 22	D. S. McGregor
	G-BCOJ	Cameron O-56 balloon	T. J. Knott & M. J. Webber
	G-BCOL	Cessna F.172M	A. H. Creaser
	G-BCOM	Piper J-3C-65 Cub	Dougal Flying Group/Shoreham
	G-BCOO	D.H.C.1 Chipmunk 22	T. G. Fielding & M. S. Morton/Blackpool
	G-BCOP	PA-28R Cherokee Arrow 200-II	Oscar Papa Ltd
	G-BCOR	SOCATA Rallye 100ST	P. R. W. Goslin & ptnrs
	G-BCOU	D.H.C.1 Chipmunk 22 (WK522)	P. J. Loweth
	G-BCOX	Bede BD-5A	H. J. Cox & B. L. Robinson
	G-BCOY	D.H.C.1 Chipmunk 22 (Lycoming)	Coventry Gliding Club Ltd/Husbands Bosworth
	G-BCPB	Howes radio-controlled model free balloon	R. B. & Mrs C. Howes
	G-BCPD	GY-201 Minicab	A. H. K. Denniss/Halfpenny Green
	G-BCPG	PA-28R Cherokee Arrow 200-II	Roses Flying Group/Liverpool
	G-BCPH	Piper J-3C-65 Cub (329934)	M. J. Janaway
	G-BCPJ	Piper J-3C-65 Cub	Piper Cub Group
	G-BCPK	Cessna F.172M	Tilbrook Industries Ltd
	G-BCPN	AA-5 Traveler	A. Butterfield
	G-BCPO	Partenavia P.68B	J. Bowles & ptnrs
	G-BCPU	D.H.C.1 Chipmunk 22	P. Waller/Booker
	G-BCPX	Szep HFC.125	A. Szep/Netherthorpe
	G-BCRB	Cessna F.172M	D. E. Lamb
	G-BCRE	Cameron O-77 balloon	A. R. Langton
	G-BCRH	Alaparma Baldo B.75 ★	A. L. Scadding (stored)
	G-BCRI	Cameron O-65 balloon	V. J. Thorne
	G-BCRK	SA.102.5 Cavalier	M. F. Newman
	G-BCRL	PA-28-151 Warrior	BCRL Ltd
	G-BCRP	PA-E23 Aztec 250E	Airlong Charter Ltd
	G-BCRR	AA-5B Tiger	N. A. Whatling
	G-BCRT	Cessna F.150M	Blue Max Flying Group
	G-BCRX	D.H.C.1 Chipmunk 22 (WD292)	Tuplin Ltd/Denham
	G-BCSA	D.H.C.1 Chipmunk 22 (Lycoming)	RAFGSA/Bicester
	G-BCSB	D.H.C.1 Chipmunk 22 (Lycoming)	RAFGSA/Cosford
	G-BCSL	D.H.C.1 Chipmunk 22	Jalawain Ltd/Barton
	G-BCSM	Bellanca 8GCBC Scout	B. T. Spreckley/France
	G-BCST	M.S.893A Rallye Commodore 180	P. J. Wilcox/Cranfield
	G-BCSX	Thunder Ax7-77 balloon	C. Wolstenholm
	G-BCSY	Taylor JT.2 Titch	I. L. Harding
	G-BCTF	PA-28-151 Warrior	The St. George Flying Club/Teesside
	G-BCTI	Schleicher ASK.16	Tango India Syndicate/Cranfield
	G-BCTJ	Cessna 310Q	TJ Flying Group
	G-BCTK	Cessna FR.172J	R. T. Love
	G-BCTT	Evans VP-1	B. J. Boughton
	G-BCTU	Cessna FRA.150M	Haverfordwest School of Flying
	G-BCUB	Piper J-3C-65 Cub	A. L. Brown & G. Attwell/Bourn
	G-BCUF	Cessna F.172M	John L. R. James & Co Ltd
	G-BCUH	Cessna F.150M	M. G. Montgomerie

Reg.	Type	Owner or Operator	Notes
G-BCUJ	Cessna F.150M	N. E. Binner	
G-BCUL	SOCATA Rallye 100ST	C. A. Ussher & Fountain Estates Ltd	
G-BCUO	SA Bulldog Srs 120/122	Cranfield University	
G-BCUS	SA Bulldog Srs 120/122	S. J. & J. J. Oliver	
G-BCUV	SA Bulldog Srs 120/122	Dolphin Property (Management) Ltd	
G-BCUW	Cessna F.177RG	S. J. Westley	
G-BCUY	Cessna FRA.150M	J. C. Carpenter	
G-BCVA	Cameron O-65 balloon	J. C. Bass & ptnrs	
G-BCVB	PA-17 Vagabond	A. T. Nowak/Popham	
G-BCVC	SOCATA Rallye 100ST	N. R. Vine	
G-BCVE	Evans VP-2	D. Masterson & D. B. Winstanley/Barton	
G-BCVF	Practavia Pilot Sprite	D. G. Hammersley	
G-BCVG	Cessna FRA.150L	G-BCVG Flying Group	
G-BCVH	Cessna FRA.150L	Yorkshire Light Aircraft Ltd/Leeds	
G-BCVJ	Cessna F.172M	Rothland Ltd	
G-BCVW	GY-80 Horizon 180	P. M. A. Parrett/Dunkeswell	
G-BCVY	PA-34-200T Seneca II	Oxford Aviation Services Ltd/Kidlington	
G-BCWB	Cessna 182P	Whisky Bravo Ltd	
G-BCWH	Practavia Pilot Sprite	R. Tasker/Blackpool	
G-BCWK	Alpavia Fournier RF-3	T. J. Hartwell & D. R. Wilkinson	
G-BCXB	SOCATA Rallye 100ST	A. Smails	
G-BCXE	Robin DR.400/2+2	C. J. Freeman	
G-BCXJ	Piper L-4J Cub (480752)	Major W. F. Stockdale MBE/Old Sarum	
G-BCXN	D.H.C.1 Chipmunk 22 (WP800)	G. M. Turner/Halton	
G-BCYH	DAW Privateer Mk. 3	D. B. Limbert/Crosland Moor	
G-BCYJ	D.H.C.1 Chipmunk 22 (WG307)	R. A. L. Falconer	
G-BCYK	Avro CF.100 Mk 4 Canuck (18393) ★	Imperial War Museum/Duxford	
G-BCYM	D.H.C.1 Chipmunk 22	G-BCYM Group	
G-BCYR	Cessna F.172M	Donne Enterprise/Edinburgh	
G-BCZH	D.H.C.1 Chipmunk 22 (WK622)	A. C. Byrne/Norwich	
G-BCZI	Thunder Ax7-77 balloon	R. G. Griffin & R. Blackwell	
G-BCZM	Cessna F.172M	Cornwall Flying Club Ltd/Bodmin	
G-BCZN	Cessna F.150M	Mona Aviation Ltd	
G-BCZO	Cameron O-77 balloon	W. O. T. Holmes Leo	
G-BDAD	Taylor JT.1 Monoplane	G-BDAD Group	
G-BDAG	Taylor JT.1 Monoplane	T. K. Gough	
G-BDAH	Evans VP-1	G. H. J. Geurts	
G-BDAI	Cessna FRA.150M	A. Sharma	
G-BDAK	R. Commander 112A	R. W. Fairless	
G-BDAL	R. 500S Shrike Commander	Quantel Ltd	
G-BDAM	AT-16 Harvard IIB (FE992)	N. A. Lees & K. D. English/North Weald	
G-BDAO	SIPA S.91	J. E. Mead	
G-BDAP	AJEP Tailwind	J. Whiting	
G-BDAR	Evans VP-1	R. B. Valler	
G-BDAY	Thunder Ax5-42A balloon	T. M. Donnelly Meconium	
G-BDBD	Wittman W.8 Tailwind	Tailwind Taildragger Group	
G-BDBF	FRED Srs 2	J. M. Brightwell & A. J. Wright	
G-BDBH	Bellanca 7GCBC Citabria	R. Dixon	
G-BDBI	Cameron O-77 balloon	C. A. Butter & J. J. Cook	
G-BDBJ	Cessna 182P	H. C. Wilson	
G-BDBP	D.H.C.1 Chipmunk 22 (WP843)	F. A. de Munck/Netherlands	
G-BDBS	Short SD3-30 ★	Ulster Aviation Soc	
G-BDBU	Cessna F.150M	R. Edgar	
G-BDBV	Jodel D.11A	Seething Jodel Group	
G-BDBZ	W.S.55 Whirlwind Srs 2 ★	Ground instruction airframe/Kidlington	
G-BDCC	D.H.C.1 Chipmunk 22 (Lycoming)	Coventry Gliding Club Ltd/ Husbands Bosworth	
G-BDCD	Piper J-3C-85 Cub (480133)	Suzanne C. Brooks/Slinfold	
G-BDCE	Cessna F.172H	Copperplane Ltd	
G-BDCI	CP.301A Emeraude	D. L. Sentance	
G-BDCK	AA-5 Traveler	Northfield Garage Ltd	
G-BDCL	AA-5 Traveler	J. Crowe	
G-BDCO	B.121 Pup 1	Shipdham Aviators Flying Group	
G-BDCS	Cessna 421B	British Aerospace (Operations) Ltd/Warton	
G-BDDD	D.H.C.1 Chipmunk 22	DRA Aero Club Ltd	
G-BDDF	Jodel D.120	Sywell Skyriders Flying Group	
G-BDDG	Jodel D.112	Wandering Imp Group	
G-BDDS	PA-25 Pawnee 235	Vale of Neath Gliding Club/Rhigos	
G-BDDT	PA-25 Pawnee 235	Pawnee Aviation	
G-BDDX	Whittaker MW.2B Excalibur ★	Cornwall Aero Park/Helston	

Notes	Reg.	Type	Owner or Operator
	G-BDDZ	CP.301A Emeraude	V. W. Smith & E. C. Mort/Barton
	G-BDEC	SOCATA Rallye 100ST	M. Mulhall
	G-BDEF	PA-34-200T Seneca II	L. R. Chiswell
	G-BDEH	Jodel D.120A	EH Flying Group
	G-BDEI	Jodel D.9 Bebe	The Noddy Group/Booker
	G-BDET	D.H.C.1 Chipmunk 22 (WP851)	C. Zoeteman/Holland
	G-BDEU	D.H.C.1 Chipmunk 22 (WP808)	A. Taylor
	G-BDEW	Cessna FRA.150M	Griffin Marston Ltd/Compton Abbas
	G-BDEX	Cessna FRA.150M	Griffin Marston Ltd
	G-BDEY	Piper J-3C-65 Cub	Ducksworth Flying Club
	G-BDEZ	Piper J-3C-65 Cub	R. J. M. Turnbull
	G-BDFB	Currie Wot	J. Jennings
	G-BDFC	R. Commander 112A	R. Fletcher
	G-BDFG	Cameron O-65 balloon	N. A. Robertson *Golly II*
	G-BDFH	Auster AOP.9 (XR240)	R. O. Holden/Booker
	G-BDFJ	Cessna F.150M	C. J. Hopewell
	G-BDFR	Fuji FA.200-160	A. G. Brindle & A. Houghton
	G-BDFS	Fuji FA.200-160	B. Lawrence
	G-BDFU	Dragonfly MPA Mk 1 ★	Museum of Flight/E. Fortune
	G-BDFW	R. Commander 112A	M. E. & E. G. Reynolds
	G-BDFX	Auster 5 (TW517)	J. Eagles
	G-BDFY	AA-5 Traveler	Grumman Group
	G-BDFZ	Cessna F.150M	L. W. Scattergood
	G-BDGA	Bushby-Long Midget Mustang	J. R. Owen
	G-BDGB	GY-20 Minicab	D. G. Burden
	G-BDGH	Thunder Ax7-77 balloon	R. J. Mitchener & P. F. Smart
	G-BDGM	PA-28-151 Warrior	B. Whiting
	G-BDGO	Thunder Ax7-77 balloon	Justerini & Brooks Ltd
	G-BDGP	Cameron V-65 balloon	A. Mayers & V. Lawton
	G-BDGY	PA-28 Cherokee 140	S. J. Willcox
	G-BDHJ	Pazmany PL.1	L. J. Greenhough
	G-BDHK	Piper J-3C-65 Cub (329417)	A. Liddiard
	G-BDIE	R. Commander 112A	R. J. Adams
	G-BDIG	Cessna 182P	Air Group 6/Gamston
	G-BDIH	Jodel D.117	N. D. H. Stokes
	G-BDIJ	Sikorsky S-61N	Bristow Helicopters Ltd
	G-BDIX	D.H.106 Comet 4C ★	Museum of Flight/E. Fortune
	G-BDJC	AJEP W.8 Tailwind	J. H. Medforth
	G-BDJD	Jodel D.112	J. E. Preston
	G-BDJF	Bensen B.8MV	R. P. White
	G-BDJG	Luton LA-4A Minor	Very Slow Flying Club
	G-BDJN	Robin HR.200/100	E. C. Huggett
	G-BDJP	Piper J-3C-90 Cub	Holdcroft Aviation Services Ltd
	G-BDKC	Cessna A185F	Bridge of Tilt Co Ltd
	G-BDKD	Enstrom F-28A	Normans (Burton-on-Trent) Ltd
	G-BDKH	CP.301A Emeraude	P. N. Marshall
	G-BDKJ	K. & S. SA.102.5 Cavalier	D. A. Garner
	G-BDKM	SIPA 903	S. W. Markham
	G-BDKU	Taylor JT.1 Monoplane	B. N. Stevens & A. J. L. Eves
	G-BDKW	R. Commander 112A	R. W. Denny
	G-BDLO	AA-5A Cheetah	S. & J. Dolan/Denham
	G-BDLS	AA-1B Trainer	A. L. Hall-Carpenter
	G-BDLT	R. Commander 112A	D. L. Churchward
	G-BDLY	SA.102.5 Cavalier	P. R. Stevens/Southampton
	G-BDMS	Piper J-3C-65 Cub (FR886)	A. T. H. Martin
	G-BDMW	Jodel DR.100A	R. O. F. Harper
	G-BDNC	Taylor JT.1 Monoplane	A. W. Wright & P. Gaskell
	G-BDNG	Taylor JT.1 Monoplane	S. B. Churchill
	G-BDNO	Taylor JT.1 Monoplane	S. D. Glover
	G-BDNP	BN-2A Islander ★	*Ground parachute trainer*/Headcorn
	G-BDNR	Cessna FRA.150M	Cheshire Air Training School Ltd/ Liverpool
	G-BDNT	Jodel D.92 Bebe	R. F. Morton
	G-BDNU	Cessna F.172M	J. & K. G. McVicar
	G-BDNW	AA-1B Trainer	P. Mitchell
	G-BDNX	AA-1B Trainer	R. M. North
	G-BDNZ	Cameron O-77 balloon	I. L. McHale
	G-BDOC	Sikorsky S-61N Mk II	Bristow Helicopters Ltd
	G-BDOD	Cessna F.150M	D. M. Moreau
	G-BDOE	Cessna FR.172J	P. E. Ward & ptnrs
	G-BDOF	Cameron O-56 balloon	The New Holker Estates Co Ltd
	G-BDOG	SA Bulldog Srs 200	D. C. Bonsall/Netherthorpe
	G-BDOL	Piper J-3C-65 Cub	L. R. Balthazor

Reg.	Type	Owner or Operator	Notes
G-BDON	Thunder Ax7-77A balloon	M. J. Smith	
G-BDOT	BN-2A Mk.III-2 Trislander	Atlantic Bridge Aviation Ltd/Lydd	
G-BDOW	Cessna FRA.150	A. Brinkley	
G-BDPA	PA-28-151 Warrior	G-BDPA Flying Group/Staverton	
G-BDPJ	PA-25 Pawnee 235B	W. J. Taylor	
G-BDPK	Cameron O-56 balloon	Rango Balloon & Kite Co	
G-BDRD	Cessna FRA.150M	I. P. Diment/Edinburgh	
G-BDRF	Taylor JT.1 Monoplane	B. R. Ratcliffe	
G-BDRG	Taylor JT.2 Titch	D. R. Gray	
G-BDRJ	D.H.C.1 Chipmunk 22 (WP857)	J. C. Schooling	
G-BDRK	Cameron O-65 balloon	D. L. Smith Smirk	
G-BDRL	Stitts SA-3A Playboy	O. C. Bradley	
G-BDSA	FRED Srs 2	W. D. M. Turtle	
G-BDSB	PA-28-181 Archer II	Testair Ltd/Blackbushe	
G-BDSE	Cameron O-77 balloon	British Airways *Concorde*	
G-BDSF	Cameron O-56 balloon	J. H. Greensides	
G-BDSH	PA-28 Cherokee 140	The Wright Brothers Flying Group	
G-BDSK	Cameron O-65 balloon	Southern Balloon Group *Carousel II*	
G-BDSL	Cessna F.150M	D, C, Bonsall	
G-BDSM	Slingsby T.31B Cadet III	N. F. James	
G-BDTB	Evans VP-1	T. F. Crossman	
G-BDTL	Evans VP-1	A. K. Lang	
G-BDTN	BN-2A Mk III-2 Trislander	Aurigny Air Services Ltd	
G-BDTO	BN-2A Mk III-2 Trislander	Aurigny Air Services Ltd (G-RBSI/G-OTSB)	
G-BDTU	Omega III gas balloon	R. G. Turnbull	
G-BDTV	Mooney M.20F	S. Redfearn	
G-BDTW	Cassutt Racer IIIM	R. Mohlenkamp/Germany	
G-BDTX	Cessna F.150M	S. L. Lefley & F. W. Ellis	
G-BDUI	Cameron V-56 balloon	D. C. Johnson	
G-BDUL	Evans VP-1	C. K. Brown	
G-BDUM	Cessna F.150M	Techair Aviation Ltd	
G-BDUN	PA-34-200T Seneca II	Air Medical Ltd	
G-BDUO	Cessna F.150M	BM Aviation	
G-BDUX	Slingsby T.31B Cadet III	J. C. Anderson/Cranfield	
G-BDUY	Robin DR.400/140B	J. G. Anderson	
G-BDUZ	Cameron V-56 balloon	Zebedee Balloon Service	
G-BDVA	PA-17 Vagabond	I. M. Callier	
G-BDVB	PA-15 (PA-17) Vagabond	B. P. Gardner	
G-BDVC	PA-17 Vagabond	A. R. Caveen	
G-BDVU	Mooney M.20F	D. H. G. Penney/Biggin Hill	
G-BDWA	SOCATA Rallye 150ST	J. Thompson-Wilson	
G-BDWE	Flaglor Scooter	Flaglor Flyers	
G-BDWH	SOCATA Rallye 150ST	M. A. Jones	
G-BDWJ	SE-5A (replica) (F8010)	D. W. Linney	
G-BDWL	PA-25 Pawnee 235	Peterborough & Spalding Gliding Club/Crowland	
G-BDWM	Mustang scale replica (FB226)	D. C. Bonsall	
G-BDWO	Howes Ax6 balloon	R. B. & C. Howes	
G-BDWP	PA-32R Cherokee Lance 300	W. M. Brown & B. J. Wood/Birmingham	
G-BDWV	BN-2A Mk III-2 Trislander	Aurigny Air Services Ltd/Guernsey	
G-BDWX	Jodel D.120A	R. P. Rochester	
G-BDWY	PA-28 Cherokee 140	Comed Aviation Ltd/Blackpool	
G-BDXA	Boeing 747-236B	British Airways	
G-BDXB	Boeing 747-236B	British Airways/Nigeria Airways	
G-BDXC	Boeing 747-236B	British Airways	
G-BDXE	Boeing 747-236B	British Airways	
G-BDXF	Boeing 747-236B	British Airways	
G-BDXG	Boeing 747-236B	British Airways	
G-BDXH	Boeing 747-236B	British Airways	
G-BDXI	Boeing 747-236B	British Airways	
G-BDXJ	Boeing 747-236B	British Airways	
G-BDXK	Boeing 747-236B	British Airways	
G-BDXL	Boeing 747-236B	British Airways	
G-BDXM	Boeing 747-236B (SCD)	British Airways	
G-BDXN	Boeing 747-236B (SCD)	British Airways	
G-BDXO	Boeing 747-236B	British Airways	
G-BDXP	Boeing 747-236B (SCD)	British Airways	
G-BDXX	SNCAN NC.858S	M. Gaffney & K. Davis	
G-BDYD	R. Commander 114	L. A. & A. A. Buckley	
G-BDYF	Cessna 421C	Hawkair	
G-BDYG	P.56 Provost T.1 (WV493) ★	Museum of Flight/E. Fortune	
G-BDYH	Cameron V-56 balloon	B. J. Godding	

G-BDZA – G-BEJD

Notes	Reg.	Type	Owner or Operator
	G-BDZA	Scheibe SF.25E Super Falke	Norfolk Gliding Club Ltd/Tibenham
	G-BDZB	Cameron S-31 balloon	Kenning Motor Group Ltd
	G-BDZC	Cessna F.150M	A. M. Lynn/Sibson
	G-BDZD	Cessna F.172M	Northamptonshire School of Flying Ltd/Sywell
	G-BDZU	Cessna 421C	Eagle Flying Group/E. Midlands
	G-BEAB	Jodel DR.1051	R. C. Hibberd
	G-BEAC	PA-28 Cherokee 140	Clipwing Flying Group/Humberside
	G-BEAD	WG.13 Lynx ★	*Instructional airframe*/Middle Wallop
	G-BEAG	PA-34-200T Seneca II	Oxford Aviation Services Ltd/Kidlington
	G-BEAH	J/2 Arrow	W. J. & Mrs M. D. Horler
	G-BEBC	W.S.55 Whirlwind 3 (XP355) ★	Norwich Aviation Museum
	G-BEBE	AA-5A Cheetah	Bills Aviation Ltd
	G-BEBG	WSK-PZL SDZ-45A Ogar	The Ogar Syndicate
	G-BEBI	Cessna F.172M	Hatfield Flying Club
	G-BEBN	Cessna 177B	A. J. Franchi & D. J. French
	G-BEBO	Turner TSW-2 Wot	The Turner Special Flying Group
	G-BEBR	GY-201 Minicab	A. S. Jones & D. R. Upton
	G-BEBS	Andreasson BA-4B	N. J. W. Reid
	G-BEBT	Andreasson BA-4B	A. Horsfall/Breighton
	G-BEBU	R. Commander 112A	R. Hodgkinson
	G-BEBZ	PA-28-151 Warrior	Goodwood Terrena Ltd/Goodwood
	G-BECA	SOCATA Rallye 100ST	Bredon Flying Group/Defford
	G-BECB	SOCATA Rallye 100ST	A. J. Trible
	G-BECC	SOCATA Rallye 150ST	D. T. Price
	G-BECF	Scheibe SF.25A Falke	North County Ltd
	G-BECK	Cameron V-56 balloon	H. & D. J. Farrar
	G-BECN	Piper J-3C-65 Cub (480480)	R. C. Partridge & M. Oliver
	G-BECT	C.A.S.A.1.131E Jungmann 2000 (A-57)	Alpha 57 Group
	G-BECW	C.A.S.A.1.131E Jungmann 2000 (A-10)	R. G. Meredith
	G-BECZ	CAARP CAP.10B	Aerobatic Associates Ltd
	G-BEDA	C.A.S.A.1.131E Jungmann 2000	M. G. Kates & D. J. Berry
	G-BEDB	Nord 1203 Norecrin ★	B. F. G. Lister *(stored)*/Chirk
	G-BEDD	Jodel D.117A	P. B. Duhig
	G-BEDF	Boeing B-17G-105-VE (124485)	B-17 Preservation Ltd/Duxford
	G-BEDG	R. Commander 112A	L. E. Blackburn
	G-BEDJ	Piper J-3C-65 Cub (44-80594)	R. Earl
	G-BEDL	Cessna T.337D	T. J. Brammer & D. T. Colley
	G-BEDP	BN-2A Mk.III-2 Trislander	Atlantic Bridge Aviation Ltd/Lydd
	G-BEDV	V.668 Varsity T.1 (WJ945) ★	Duxford Aviation Soc
	G-BEEE	Thunder Ax6-56A balloon	I. R. M. Jacobs Avia
	G-BEEG	BN-2A-26 Islander	NW Parachute Centre Ltd/Cark
	G-BEEH	Cameron V-56 balloon	Sade Balloons Ltd
	G-BEEP	Thunder Ax5-42 balloon	B. C. Faithfull/Holland
	G-BEER	Isaacs Fury II (K2075)	N. Davis
	G-BEEU	PA-28 Cherokee 140F	J. Maffia & H. Merkado
	G-BEEW	Taylor JT.1 Monoplane (Boeing P-26) ★	P. A. Boyden
	G-BEFA	PA-28-151 Warrior	Firmbeam Ltd/Booker
	G-BEFF	PA-28 Cherokee 140F	J. JH. Howard
	G-BEFO	BN-2A Mk.III-2 Trislander	Keen Leasing Ltd (G-SARN)/Belfast
	G-BEFV	Evans VP-2	D. A. Cotton
	G-BEGA	Westland-Bell 47G-3B1	Reel-Time Entertainments Ltd
	G-BEGG	Scheibe SF.25E Super Falke	G-BEGG Flying Group
	G-BEHH	PA-32R Cherokee Lance 300	SMK Engineering Ltd/Leeds
	G-BEHS	PA-25 Pawnee 260C	Southern Sailplanes Ltd/Membury
	G-BEHU	PA-34-200T Seneca II	Pirin Aeronautical Ltd/Stapleford
	G-BEHV	Cessna F.172N	Fraggle Leasing Ltd/Edinburgh
	G-BEHX	Evans VP-2	G. S. Adams
	G-BEIA	Cessna FRA.150M	Rankart Ltd
	G-BEIB	Cessna F.172N	J. Shelton
	G-BEIC	Sikorsky S-61N	Brintel Helicopters
	G-BEIF	Cameron O-65 balloon	C. Vening
	G-BEIG	Cessna F.150M	D. A. Hardiman Ltd/Shobdon
	G-BEII	PA-25 Pawnee 235D	Burn Gliding Club Ltd
	G-BEIL	SOCATA Rallye 150T	The Rallye Flying Group
	G-BEIP	PA-28-181 Archer II	S. W. & J. K. Stevens
	G-BEIS	Evans VP-1	P. J. Hunt
	G-BEJB	Thunder Ax6-56A balloon	Justerini & Brooks Ltd
	G-BEJD	Avro 748 Srs 1	Emerald Airways Ltd *John Case*/Liverpool

Reg.	Type	Owner or Operator	Notes
G-BEJK	Cameron S-31 balloon	Rango Balloon & Kite Co	
G-BEJL	Sikorsky S-61N	Brintel Helicopters	
G-BEJV	PA-34-200T Seneca II	Oxford Aviation Services Ltd/Kidlington	
G-BEKL	Bede BD-4E-150	A. J. Harpley	
G-BEKM	Evans VP-1	G. J. McDill/Glenrothes	
G-BEKN	Cessna FRA.150M ★	RFC (Bourn) Ltd/Sibson	
G-BEKO	Cessna F.182Q	G. J. & F. J. Leese	
G-BEKR	Rand KR-2	A. N. Purchase	
G-BELF	BN-2A-26 Islander	The Black Knights Parachute Centre Ltd	
G-BELP	PA-28-151 Warrior	R. J. Doughton	
G-BELT	Cessna F.150J	Yorkshire Light Aircraft Ltd (G-AWUV)/ Leeds	
G-BELX	Cameron V-56 balloon	V. & A. M. Dyer	
G-BEMB	Cessna F.172M	Stocklaunch Ltd	
G-BEMM	Slingsby T.31B Motor Cadet	J. Beirne	
G-BEMU	Thunder Ax5-42 balloon	I. J. Liddiard	
G-BEMW	PA-28-181 Archer II	Touch and Go Ltd	
G-BEMY	Cessna FRA.150M	Euroair Flying Club Ltd	
G-BEND	Cameron V-56 balloon	Dante Balloon Group Le Billet	
G-BENJ	R. Commander 112B	E. J. Percival/Blackbushe	
G-BENK	Cessna F.172M	Graham Churchill Plant Ltd	
G-BENN	Cameron V-56 balloon	S. H. Budd	
G-BEOD	Cessna 180 ★	Avionics Research Ltd/Cranfield	
G-BEOE	Cessna FRA.150M	W. J. Henderson	
G-BEOH	PA-28R-201T Turbo Arrow III	G-BEOH Group	
G-BEOI	PA-18 Super Cub 150	Southdown Gliding Club Ltd/Parham Park	
G-BEOK	Cessna F.150M	D. C. Bonsall	
G-BEOX	L-414 Hudson IV (A16-199) ★	RAF Museum/Hendon	
G-BEOY	Cessna FRA.150L	R. W. Denny	
G-BEOZ	A.W.650 Argosy 101 ★	Aeropark/E. Midlands	
G-BEPC	SNCAN Stampe SV-4C	Dawn Patrol Flight Training Ltd	
G-BEPF	SNCAN Stampe SV-4A	L. J. Rice	
G-BEPH	BN-2A Mk III-2 Trislander	Aurigny Air Services Ltd/Guernsey	
G-BEPI	BN-2A Mk III-2 Trislander	Aurigny Air Services Ltd/Guernsey	
G-BEPS	SC.5 Belfast	HeavyLift Cargo Airlines Ltd/Stansted	
G-BEPV	Fokker S.11-1 Instructor	L. C. MacKnight	
G-BEPY	R. Commander 112B	G-BEPY Group/Blackbushe	
G-BERA	SOCATA Rallye 150ST	C. S. Randall	
G-BERC	SOCATA Rallye 150ST	Severn Valley Aero Group/Welshpool	
G-BERD	Thunder Ax6-56A balloon	P. M. Gaines	
G-BERI	R. Commander 114	K. B. Harper/Blackbushe	
G-BERN	Saffrey S-330 balloon	B. Martin Beeze	
G-BERT	Cameron V-56 balloon	Southern Balloon Group Bert	
G-BERW	R. Commander 114	Malvern Holdings Ltd	
G-BERY	AA-1B Trainer	R. H. J. Levi	
G-BETD	Robin HR.200/100	W. A. Stewart	
G-BETE	Rollason B.2A Beta	T. M. Jones/Tatenhill	
G-BETF	Cameron 'Champion' SS balloon ★	British Balloon Museum/Newbury	
G-BETG	Cessna 180K Skywagon	Norman Aeroplane Trust/Rendcomb	
G-BETI	Pitts S-1D Special	P. Metcalfe/Teesside	
G-BETL	PA-25 Pawnee 235D	Cambridge University Gliding Trust Ltd/Gransden Lodge	
G-BETM	PA-25 Pawnee 235D	Yorkshire Gliding Club (Pty) Ltd/ Sutton Bank	
G-BETO	MS.885 Super Rallye	G-BETO Group	
G-BETP	Cameron O-65 balloon	J. R. Rix & Sons Ltd	
G-BETT	PA-34-200 Seneca II	D. F. J. Flashman	
G-BEUA	PA-18 Super Cub 150	London Gliding Club (Pty) Ltd/Dunstable	
G-BEUD	Robin HR.100/285R	E. A. & L. M. C. Payton/Cranfield	
G-BEUI	Piper J-3C-65 Cub	C. P. L. Jenkins	
G-BEUK	Fuji FA.200-160	BM Aviation	
G-BEUM	Taylor JT.1 Monoplane	J. M. Burgess	
G-BEUN	Cassutt Racer IIIM	R. McNulty	
G-BEUP	Robin DR.400/180	A. V. Pound & Co Ltd	
G-BEUU	PA-18 Super Cub 95	F. Sharples/Sandown	
G-BEUV	Thunder Ax6-56A balloon	Silhouette Balloon Group	
G-BEUX	Cessna F.172N	Multiflight Ltd/Leeds-Bradford	
G-BEUY	Cameron N-31 balloon	A. C. Beaumont	
G-BEVA	SOCATA Rallye 150ST	The Rallye Group	
G-BEVB	SOCATA Rallye 150ST	N. R. Haines	
G-BEVC	SOCATA Rallye 150ST	B. W. Walpole	
G-BEVG	PA-34-200T-2 Seneca	C. Deith	

Notes	Reg.	Type	Owner or Operator
	G-BEVO	Sportavia-Pützer RF-5 ★	T. Barlow/Barton
	G-BEVP	Evans VP-2	G. Moscrop & R. C. Crowley
	G-BEVR	BN-2A Mk III-2 Trislander	Cormack (Aircraft Services) Ltd
	G-BEVS	Taylor JT.1 Monoplane	D. Hunter
	G-BEVT	BN-2A Mk III-2 Trislander	Aurigny Air Services Ltd/Guernsey
	G-BEVV	BN-2A Mk III-2 Trislander	Cormack (Aircraft Services) Ltd (G-BEND)
	G-BEVW	SOCATA Rallye 150ST	P. C. Goodwin
	G-BEWN	D.H.82A Tiger Moth	H. D. Labouchere
	G-BEWO	Zlin Z.326 Trener Master	Nimrod Group Ltd/Staverton
	G-BEWR	Cessna F.172N	Cheshire Air Training Services Ltd/ Liverpool
	G-BEWX	PA-28R-201 Arrow III	A. Vickers
	G-BEWY	Bell 206B JetRanger 3	PLM Dollar Group Ltd (G-CULL)
	G-BEXK	PA-25 Pawnee 235D	Howard Avis (Aviation) Ltd
	G-BEXN	AA-1C Lynx	Lynx Flying Group
	G-BEXO	PA-23 Apache 160	G. R. Moore & A. A. K. Hulme
	G-BEXW	PA-28-181 Archer II	T. R. Kingsley
	G-BEXZ	Cameron N-56 balloon	D. C. Eager & G. C. Clark
	G-BEYA	Enstrom 280C	Hovercam Ltd
	G-BEYB	Fairey Flycatcher (replica) (S1287) ★	F.A.A. Museum/Yeovilton
	G-BEYF	HPR-7 Herald 401 ★	Channel Express (Air Services) Ltd
	G-BEYL	PA-28 Cherokee 180	Yankee Lima Group
	G-BEYO	PA-28 Cherokee 140	W. B. Bateson/Blackpool
	G-BEYT	PA-28 Cherokee 140	B. A. Mills
	G-BEYV	Cessna T.210M	Austen Aviation/Edinburgh
	G-BEYW	Taylor JT.1 Monoplane	R. A. Abrahams/Barton
	G-BEYZ	Jodel DR.1051/M1	M. L. Balding
	G-BEZA	Zlin Z.226T Trener	L. Bezak
	G-BEZC	AA-5 Traveler	P. N. & S. E. Field
	G-BEZE	Rutan Vari-Eze	H. C. Mackinnon
	G-BEZF	AA-5 Traveler	RAF College Flying Club Ltd/Cranwell
	G-BEZG	AA-5 Traveler	M. D. R. Harling & T. W. Cubbin
	G-BEZH	AA-5 Traveler	L. & S. M. Sims
	G-BEZI	AA-5 Traveler	G-BEZI Flying Group/Elstree
	G-BEZK	Cessna F.172H	Zulu Kilo Flying Group/Earls Colne
	G-BEZL	PA-31-310 Turbo Navajo C	London Flight Centre (Stansted) Ltd
	G-BEZO	Cessna F.172M	Staverton Flying Services Ltd
	G-BEZP	PA-32 Cherokee Six 300D	Falcon Styles Ltd/Booker
	G-BEZR	Cessna F.172M	Kirmington Aviation Ltd
	G-BEZV	Cessna F.172M	Insch Flying Group
	G-BEZY	Rutan Vari-Eze	R. J. Jones/Cranfield
	G-BEZZ	Jodel D.112	G-BEZZ Jodel Group
	G-BFAA	GY-80 Horizon 160	Mary Poppins Ltd
	G-BFAF	Aeronca 7BCM (7797)	D. C. W. Harper/Finmere
	G-BFAH	Phoenix Currie Wot	R. W. Clarke
	G-BFAI	R. Commander 114	Aeronautical & Marine Investments Ltd
	G-BFAK	M.S.892A Rallye Commodore 150	Draycott Rallye Group
	G-BFAO	PA-20 Pacer 135	E. A. M. Austin
	G-BFAP	SIAI-Marchetti S.205-20R	A. O. Broin
	G-BFAS	Evans VP-1	A. I. Sutherland
	G-BFAW	D.H.C.1 Chipmunk 22	R. V. Bowles/Husbands Bosworth
	G-BFAX	D.H.C.1 Chipmunk 22 (WG422)	A. C. Kerr
	G-BFBA	Jodel DR.100A	W. H. Sherlock
	G-BFBB	PA-23 Aztec 250E	Air Training Services Ltd/Booker
	G-BFBC	Taylor JT.1 Monoplane	R. Trickett
	G-BFBE	Robin HR.200/100	A. C. Pearson
	G-BFBF	PA-28 Cherokee 140	Marnham Investments Ltd
	G-BFBM	Saffery S.330 balloon	B. Martin Beeze II
	G-BFBR	PA-28-161 Warrior II	Lowery Holdings Ltd/Fairoaks
	G-BFBU	Partenavia P.68B	Premiair Charter Ltd
	G-BFBY	Piper J-3C-65 Cub	U. Schuhmacher
	G-BFCT	Cessna TU.206F	Cecil Aviation Ltd/Cambridge
	G-BFCZ	Sopwith Camel (B7270) ★	Brooklands Museum Trust Ltd/Weybridge
	G-BFDC	D.H.C.1 Chipmunk 22	N. F. O'Neill/Newtownards
	G-BFDE	Sopwith Tabloid (replica) (168) ★	RAF Museum Storage & Restoration Centre/Cardington
	G-BFDF	SOCATA Rallye 235E	D. J. Lindsay Wood
	G-BFDI	PA-28-181 Archer II	Truman Aviation Ltd/Tollerton
	G-BFDK	PA-28-161 Warrior II	Priory Garage
	G-BFDL	Piper J-3C-65 Cub (454537)	S. Beresford & G. S. Claybourn/Sandtoft

Reg.	Type	Owner or Operator	Notes
G-BFDO	PA-28R-201T Turbo Arrow III	A. J. Gow	
G-BFDZ	Taylor JT.1 Monoplane	G. J. Clare	
G-BFEB	Jodel 150	S. Russell	
G-BFEF	Agusta-Bell 47G-3B1	R. C. Hields	
G-BFEH	Jodel D.117A	C. V. & S. J. Philpott	
G-BFEK	Cessna F.152	Staverton Flying Services Ltd	
G-BFER	Bell 212	Bristow Helicopters Ltd	
G-BFEV	PA-25 Pawnee 235	Trent Valley Aerotowing Club Ltd	
G-BFEW	PA-25 Pawnee 235	Cornish Gliding & Flying Club Ltd	
G-BFFB	Evans VP-2 ★	(stored)/Eaton Bray	
G-BFFC	Cessna F.152-II	Yorkshire Flying Services Ltd/ Leeds-Bradford	
G-BFFE	Cessna F.152-II	J. Easson/Edinburgh	
G-BFFJ	Sikorsky S-61N Mk II	British International Helicopters	
G-BFFP	PA-18 Super Cub 150 (modified)	Booker Gliding Club Ltd	
G-BFFT	Cameron V-56 balloon	R. I. M. Kerr & D. C. Boxall	
G-BFFW	Cessna F.152	Tayside Aviation Ltd/Dundee	
G-BFFY	Cessna F.150M	G. & S. A. Jones	
G-BFFZ	Cessna FR.172 Hawk XP	Bravo Aviation Ltd/Caernarfon	
G-BFGD	Cessna F.172N-II	J. T. Armstrong	
G-BFGF	Cessna F.177RG	J. E. Searson	
G-BFGG	Cessna FRA.150M	Cornwall Flying Club Ltd/Bodmin	
G-BFGH	Cessna F.337G	T. Perkins/Sherburn	
G-BFGK	Jodel D.117	B. F. J. Hope	
G-BFGL	Cessna FA.152	Yorkshire Flying Services Ltd/ Leeds-Bradford	
G-BFGO	Fuji FA.200-160	Butane Buzzard Aviation Corporation Ltd	
G-BFGS	M.S.893E Rallye 180GT	Chiltern Flyers Ltd	
G-BFGW	Cessna F.150H	C. E. Stringer	
G-BFGX	Cessna FRA.150M	-/Edinburgh	
G-BFGZ	Cessna FRA.150M	W. J. D. Tollett	
G-BFHH	D.H.82A Tiger Moth	P. Harrison & M. J. Gambrell/Redhill	
G-BFHI	Piper J-3C-65 Cub	N. Glass & A. J. Richardson	
G-BFHP	Champion 7GCAA Citabria	Griffin Marston Ltd	
G-BFHR	Jodel DR.220/2+2	J. E. Sweetman	
G-BFHT	Cessna F.152-II	Westward Airways (Lands End) Ltd	
G-BFHU	Cessna F.152-II	Deltair Ltd/Liverpool	
G-BFHV	Cessna F.152-II	Falcon Flying Services/Biggin Hill	
G-BFHX	Evans VP-1	A. D. Bohanna & D. I. Trussler	
G-BFIB	PA-31 Turbo Navajo	Richard Hannon Ltd	
G-BFID	Taylor JT.2 Titch Mk III	N. A. Scully	
G-BFIE	Cessna FRA.150M	Solo Services Ltd/Shoreham	
G-BFIG	Cessna FR.172K XPII	Tenair Ltd	
G-BFIJ	AA-5A Cheetah	T. H. & M. G. Weetman	
G-BFIN	AA-5A Cheetah	G-BFIN Group	
G-BFIP	Wallbro Monoplane 1909 (replica) ★	Norfolk & Suffolk Aviation Museum/ Flixton, Suffolk	
G-BFIU	Cessna FR.172K XP	B. M. Jobling	
G-BFIV	Cessna F.177RG	Kingfishair Ltd/Blackbushe	
G-BFIX	Thunder Ax7-77A balloon	R. Owen	
G-BFIY	Cessna F.150M	Yorkshire Aeroplane Club/Leeds-Bradford	
G-BFJJ	Evans VP-1	M. J. Collins	
G-BFJK	PA-23 Aztec 250F	H. G. Keighley	
G-BFJR	Cessna F.337G	Mannix Aviation/E. Midlands	
G-BFJZ	Robin DR.400/140B	Rochester Aviation Ltd	
G-BFKB	Cessna F.172N	R. M. Collins	
G-BFKC	Rand KR-2	L. H. S. Stephens & I. S. Hewitt	
G-BFKF	Cessna FA.152	Klingair Ltd/Conington	
G-BFKH	Cessna F.152	TG Aviation Ltd/Manston	
G-BFKL	Cameron N-56 balloon	Merrythought Toys Ltd Merrythought	
G-BFKY	PA-34-200 Seneca II	S.L.H. Construction Ltd/Biggin Hill	
G-BFLH	PA-34-200T Seneca II	Air Medical Ltd	
G-BFLI	PA-28R-201T Turbo Arrow III	J. K. Chudzicki	
G-BFLP	Amethyst Ax6 balloon	K. J. Hendry Amethyst	
G-BFLU	Cessna F.152	Bravo Aviation Ltd	
G-BFLX	AA-5A Cheetah	G-Force Aviation Ltd	
G-BFLZ	Beech 95-A55 Baron	Caterite Food Service	
G-BFME	Cameron V-56 balloon	Warwick Balloons	
G-BFMG	PA-28-161 Warrior II	Stardial Ltd	
G-BFMH	Cessna 177B	Span Aviation Ltd/Newcastle	
G-BFMK	Cessna FA.152	RAF Halton Aeroplane Club Ltd	
G-BFMM	PA-28-181 Archer II	Aldergrove Flight Training Centre	
G-BFMR	PA-20 Pacer 125	J. Knight	

Notes	Reg.	Type	Owner or Operator
	G-BFMX	Cessna F.172N	Broomco (406) Ltd
	G-BFMY	Sikorsky S-61N	Bristow Helicopters Ltd
	G-BFMZ	Payne Ax6 balloon	E. G. Woolnough
	G-BFNG	Jodel D.112	M. T. Taylor
	G-BFNI	PA-28-161 Warrior II	P. Elliott/Biggin Hill
	G-BFNJ	PA-28-161 Warrior II	Fleetlands Flying Association Ltd
	G-BFNK	PA-28-161 Warrior II	Oxford Aviation Services Ltd/Kidlington
	G-BFOD	Cessna F.182Q	G. N. Clarke
	G-BFOE	Cessna F.152	Redhill Air Services Ltd
	G-BFOF	Cessna F.152	Staverton Flying School Ltd
	G-BFOG	Cessna 150M	Griffin Marston Ltd
	G-BFOJ	AA-1 Yankee	A. J. Morton/Bournemouth
	G-BFOM	PA-31 Turbo Navajo C	Deer Hill Aviation Ltd
	G-BFOP	Jodel D.120	R. J. Wesley & G. D. Western
	G-BFOS	Thunder Ax6-56A balloon	N. T. Petty
	G-BFOU	Taylor JT.1 Monoplane	G. Bee
	G-BFOV	Cessna F.172N	D. J. Walker
	G-BFPA	Scheibe SF.25B Falke	N. Meiklejohn & J. Steel
	G-BFPB	AA-5B Tiger	Stesco Ltd/Guernsey
	G-BFPH	Cessna F.172K	Linc-Air Flying Group
	G-BFPM	Cessna F.172M	Sigma Corporation Ltd
	G-BFPO	R. Commander 112B	J. G. Hale Ltd
	G-BFPP	Bell 47J-2	M. R. Masters
	G-BFPS	PA-25 Pawnee 235D	Kent Gliding Club Ltd/Challock
	G-BFRA	R. Commander 114	Ischia Investments Ltd
	G-BFRD	Bowers Fly-Baby 1A	R. A. Phillips
	G-BFRF	Taylor JT.1 Monoplane	E. R. Bailey
	G-BFRI	Sikorsky S-61N	Bristow Helicopters Ltd *Braerich*
	G-BFRM	Cessna 550 Citation II	Marshall of Cambridge (Engineering) Ltd
	G-BFRR	Cessna FRA.150M	J. R. Duller
	G-BFRS	Cessna F.172N	Poplar Toys Ltd
	G-BFRV	Cessna FA.152	Solo Services Ltd
	G-BFRY	PA-25 Pawnee 260	Yorkshire Gliding Club (Pty) Ltd/ Sutton Bank
	G-BFSA	Cessna F.182Q	Clark Masts Ltd/Sandown
	G-BFSB	Cessna F.152	Tatenhill Aviation
	G-BFSC	PA-25 Pawnee 235D	M. A. Pruden
	G-BFSD	PA-25 Pawnee 235D	Deeside Gliding Club (Aberdeenshire) Ltd/Aboyne
	G-BFSK	PA-23 Apache 160 ★	*Sub-aqua instructional airframe/ Croughton*
	G-BFSR	Cessna F.150J	S. Jayyousi
	G-BFSS	Cessna FR.172G	Minerva Services
	G-BFSY	PA-28-181 Archer II	Downland Aviation
	G-BFTC	PA-28R-201T Turbo Arrow III	M. J. Milns/Sherburn
	G-BFTF	AA-5B Tiger	F. C. Burrow Ltd/Leeds
	G-BFTG	AA-5B Tiger	D. Hepburn & G. R. Montgomery
	G-BFTH	Cessna F.172N	J. Birkett
	G-BFTT	Cessna 421C	P&B Metal Components Ltd/Manston
	G-BFTX	Cessna F.172N	E. Kent Flying Group
	G-BFTY	Cameron V-77 balloon	Regal Motors (Bilston) Ltd
	G-BFUB	PA-32RT-300 Lance II	Jolida Holdings Ltd
	G-BFUD	Scheibe SF.25E Super Falke	Lakes Libelle Syndicate/Walney Island
	G-BFUG	Cameron N-77 balloon	Headland Services Ltd
	G-BFUZ	Cameron V-77 balloon	Skysales Ltd
	G-BFVF	PA-38-112 Tomahawk	Goodair Leasing Ltd
	G-BFVG	PA-28-181 Archer II	G-BFVG Flying Group/Blackpool
	G-BFVH	D.H.2 Replica (5894)	M. J. Kirk
	G-BFVM	Westland-Bell 47G-3B1	K. R. Dossett
	G-BFVP	PA-23 Aztec 250F	Litton Aviation Services Ltd
	G-BFVS	AA-5B Tiger	S. W. Biroth & T. Chapman/Denham
	G-BFVU	Cessna 150L	Deer Hill Aviation Ltd/Exeter
	G-BFWB	PA-28-161 Warrior II	Mid-Anglia School of Flying
	G-BFWD	Currie Wot	F. R. Donaldson
	G-BFWE	PA-23 Aztec 250E	Air Navigation & Trading Co Ltd/ Blackpool
	G-BFWL	Cessna F.150L	G-BFWL Flying Group/Barton
	G-BFXD	PA-28-161 Warrior II	Oxford Aviation Services Ltd/Kidlington
	G-BFXE	PA-28-161 Warrior II	Oxford Aviation Services Ltd/Kidlington
	G-BFXF	Andreasson BA.4B	A. Brown/Sherburn
	G-BFXG	D.31 Turbulent	E. J. I. Musty & M. J. Whatley
	G-BFXK	PA-28 Cherokee 140	G. S. & M. T. Pritchard/Southend
	G-BFXL	Albatross D.5A (D5397/17) ★	F.A.A. Museum/Yeovilton

Reg.	Type	Owner or Operator	Notes
G-BFXR	Jodel D.112	Jodel Group	
G-BFXS	R. Commander 114	Cashmore Associates	
G-BFXW	AA-5B Tiger	Campsol Ltd	
G-BFXX	AA-5B Tiger	W. R. Gibson	
G-BFYA	MBB Bo 105DB	Sterling Helicopters Ltd/Norwich	
G-BFYB	PA-28-161 Warrior II	Oxford Aviation ServicesLtd/Kidlington	
G-BFYC	PA-32RT-300 Lance II	A. A. Barnes	
G-BFYE	Robin HR.100/285 ★	(stored)/Sywell	
G-BFYI	Westland-Bell 47G-3B1	B. Walker & Co (Dursley) Ltd	
G-BFYK	Cameron V-77 balloon	L. E. Jones	
G-BFYL	Evans VP-2	W. C. Brown	
G-BFYM	PA-28-161 Warrior II	Oxford Aviation Services Ltd/Kidlington	
G-BFYO	SPAD XIII (replica) (1/4513) ★	American Air Museum/Duxford	
G-BFZB	Piper J-3C-85 Cub	Zebedee Flying Group/Shoreham	
G-BFZD	Cessna FR.182RG	R. B. Lewis & Co/Sleap	
G-BFZG	PA-28-161 Warrior II	Oxford Aviation Services Ltd/Kidlington	
G-BFZH	PA-28R Cherokee Arrow 200	W. E. Lowe/Shobdon	
G-BFZM	R. Commander 112TC	R. J. Lamplough/North Weald	
G-BFZN	Cessna FA.152	Falcon Flying Services/Biggin Hill	
G-BFZO	AA-5A Cheetah	J. McCloskey	
G-BFZT	Cessna FA.152	N. Grantham/Conington	
G-BFZU	Cessna FA.152	Redhill Aviation Services Ltd	
G-BFZV	Cessna F.172M	R. Thomas	
G-BGAA	Cessna 152 II	PJC Leasing Ltd	
G-BGAB	Cessna F.152 II	TG Aviation Ltd/Manston	
G-BGAD	Cessna F.152 II	Keen Leasing (IOM) Ltd	
G-BGAE	Cessna F.152 II	Klingair Ltd/Conington	
G-BGAF	Cessna FA.152	M. F. Hatt & ptnrs/Southend	
G-BGAG	Cessna F.172N	Aerohire Ltd/Halfpenny Green	
G-BGAJ	Cessna F.182Q II	Ground Airport Services Ltd/Guernsey	
G-BGAX	PA-28 Cherokee 140	C. D. Brack/Breighton	
G-BGAZ	Cameron V-77 balloon	C. J. Madigan & D. H. McGibbon	
G-BGBA	Robin R.2100A	D. Faulkner/Redhill	
G-BGBE	Jodel DR.1050	J. A. & B. Mawby	
G-BGBF	D.31A Turbulent	S. M. Cryer	
G-BGBG	PA-28-181 Archer II	Harlow Printing Ltd/Newcastle	
G-BGBI	Cessna F.150L	Falcon Flying Services/Biggin Hill	
G-BGBK	PA-38-112 Tomahawk	F. Marshall & R. C. Priest/Netherthorpe	
G-BGBN	PA-38-112 Tomahawk	Bonus Aviation Ltd/Cranfield	
G-BGBP	Cessna F.152	Stapleford Flying Club Ltd	
G-BGBR	Cessna F.172N	Falcon Flying Services/Biggin Hill	
G-BGBU	Auster AOP.9 (XN435)	P. Neilson	
G-BGBW	PA-38-112 Tomahawk	Truman Aviation Ltd/Tollerton	
G-BGBY	PA-38-112 Tomahawk	Ravenair/Liverpool	
G-BGBZ	R. Commander 114	R. S. Fenwick/Biggin Hill	
G-BGCG	Douglas C-47A	(stored)	
G-BGCM	AA-5A Cheetah	G. & S. A. Jones	
G-BGCO	PA-44-180 Seminole	J. R. Henderson	
G-BGCY	Taylor JT.1 Monoplane	M. T. Taylor	
G-BGDA	Boeing 737-236	British Airways	
G-BGDE	Boeing 737-236	British Airways	
G-BGDF	Boeing 737-236	British Airways	
G-BGDJ	Boeing 737-236	British Airways	
G-BGDL	Boeing 737-236	British Airways	
G-BGDO	Boeing 737-236	British Airways	
G-BGDR	Boeing 737-236	British Airways	
G-BGDT	Boeing 737-236	British Airways	
G-BGEA	Cessna F.150M	C. J. Hopewell	
G-BGED	Cessna U.206F	Chapman Aviation Ltd	
G-BGEE	Evans VP-1	R. Wheeler & B. E. Holmes	
G-BGEF	Jodel D.112	G. G. Johnson & S. J. Davies	
G-BGEH	Monnett Sonerai II	P. C. Dowbor-Musnicki	
G-BGEI	Baby Great Lakes	A. R. Robinson	
G-BGEK	PA-38-112 Tomahawk	Ravenair/Liverpool	
G-BGEP	Cameron D-38 balloon	Aeronord SAS/Italy	
G-BGEW	SNCAN NC.854S	Tavair Ltd	
G-BGFC	Evans VP-2	S. W. C. Hollins	
G-BGFF	FRED Srs 2	I. Daniels	
G-BGFG	AA-5A Cheetah	Plane Talking Ltd/Elstree	
G-BGFH	Cessna F.182Q	Ray Thompson Engineering Ltd	
G-BGFI	AA-5A Cheetah	I. J. Hay & A. Nayyar/Biggin Hill	
G-BGFJ	Jodel D.9 Bebe	M. D. Mold	

Notes	Reg.	Type	Owner or Operator
	G-BGFT	PA-34-200T Seneca II	Oxford Aviation Services Ltd/Kidlington
	G-BGFX	Cessna F.152	Falcon Flying Services/Biggin Hill
	G-BGGA	Bellanca 7GCBC Citabria	L. A. King
	G-BGGB	Bellanca 7GCBC Citabria	G. H. N. Chamberlain
	G-BGGC	Bellanca 7GCBC Citabria	R. P. Ashfield & J. P. Stone
	G-BGGD	Bellanca 8GCBC Scout	Bristol & Gloucestershire Gliding Club/ Nympsfield
	G-BGGE	PA-38-112 Tomahawk	Truman Aviation Ltd/Tollerton
	G-BGGF	PA-38-112 Tomahawk	Truman Aviation Ltd/Tollerton
	G-BGGG	PA-38-112 Tomahawk	Teesside Flight Centre Ltd
	G-BGGI	PA-38-112 Tomahawk	Truman Aviation Ltd/Tollerton
	G-BGGL	PA-38-112 Tomahawk	Grunwick Processing Laboratories Ltd/ Elstree
	G-BGGM	PA-38-112 Tomahawk	Grunwick Processing Laboratories Ltd/ Elstree
	G-BGGN	PA-38-112 Tomahawk	Domeastral Ltd/Elstree
	G-BGGO	Cessna F.152	E. Midlands Flying School Ltd
	G-BGGP	Cessna F.152	E. Midlands Flying School Ltd
	G-BGGU	Wallis WA-116/RR	K. H. Wallis
	G-BGGW	Wallis WA-112	K. H. Wallis
	G-BGGY	AB-206B Jet Ranger ★	*Instructional airframe*/Cranfield
	G-BGHE	Convair L-13A	J. M. Davis/Wichita
	G-BGHF	Westland WG.30 ★	IHM/Weston-s-Mare
	G-BGHI	Cessna F.152	Taxon Ltd/Shoreham
	G-BGHM	Robin R.1180T	H. Price
	G-BGHP	Beech 76 Duchess	Magneta Ltd
	G-BGHS	Cameron N-31 balloon	W. R. Teasdale
	G-BGHT	Falconar F-12	C. R. Coates
	G-BGHU	NA T-6G Texan (115042)	C. E. Bellhouse
	G-BGHV	Cameron V-77 balloon	E. Davies
	G-BGHW	Thunder Ax8-90 balloon	Edinburgh University Balloon Group
	G-BGHY	Taylor JT.1 Monoplane	R. A. Hand
	G-BGHZ	FRED Srs 2	A. Smith
	G-BGIB	Cessna 152 II	Redhill Air Services Ltd
	G-BGID	Westland-Bell 47G-3B1	M. J. Cuttell
	G-BGIG	PA-38-112 Tomahawk	Air Claire Ltd
	G-BGIO	Bensen B.8M	R. M. Savage & F. G. Shepherd/Carlisle
	G-BGIP	Colt 56A balloon	R. D. Allen & M. Walker
	G-BGIU	Cessna F.172H	Skyhawk Flying Group
	G-BGIX	H.295 Super Courier	C. M. Lee
	G-BGIY	Cessna F.172N	Glasgow 172 Group
	G-BGJU	Cameron V-65 Balloon	J. A. Folkes
	G-BGKC	SOCATA Rallye 110ST	J. H. Cranmer & T. A. Timms
	G-BGKD	SOCATA Rallye 110ST	P. A. Cairns
	G-BGKJ	MBB Bo 105D ★	*Instructional airframe*/Bourn
	G-BGKO	GY-20 Minicab	R. B. Webber
	G-BGKS	PA-28-161 Warrior II	Marnham Investments Ltd
	G-BGKT	Auster AOP.9 (XN441)	Auster Nine Group
	G-BGKU	PA-28R-201 Arrow III	Aerolease Ltd
	G-BGKV	PA-28R-201 Arrow III	R. Haverson & R. G. Watson
	G-BGKY	PA-38-112 Tomahawk	Prospect Air Ltd
	G-BGKZ	J/5F Aiglet Trainer	D. Hatelie
	G-BGLA	PA-38-112 Tomahawk	Norwich School of Flying
	G-BGLB	Bede BD-5B ★	Science Museum/Wroughton
	G-BGLF	Evans VP-1 Srs 2	J. B. McNab
	G-BGLG	Cessna 152	A. T. Wright
	G-BGLI	Cessna 152	Luton Flying Club *(stored)*
	G-BGLN	Cessna FA.152	Bournemouth Flying Club Ltd
	G-BGLO	Cessna F.172N	A. H. Slaughter/Southend
	G-BGLS	Oldfield Super Baby Lakes	J. F. Dowe
	G-BGLW	PA-34-200 Seneca II	London Executive Aviation Ltd
	G-BGLZ	Stits SA-3A Playboy	Stitts Playboy Flying Group
	G-BGME	SIPA S.903	M. Emery & C. A. Suckling (G-BCML)/ Redhill
	G-BGMJ	GY-201 Minicab	S. L. Wakefield & ptnrs
	G-BGMN	H.S.748 Srs 2A	Emerald Airways Ltd/Liverpool
	G-BGMO	H.S.748 Srs 2A	Emerald Airways Ltd/Liverpool
	G-BGMP	Cessna F.172G	R. W. Collings
	G-BGMR	GY-201 Minicab	Mike Romeo Flying Group
	G-BGMS	Taylor JT.2 Titch	M. A. J. Spice
	G-BGMT	SOCATA Rallye 235E	C. G. Wheeler
	G-BGMU	Westland-Bell 47G-3B1	V. L. J. & V. English
	G-BGMV	Scheibe SF.25B Falke	Mendip Falke Flying Group

Reg.	Type	Owner or Operator	Notes
G-BGND	Cessna F.172N	A. J. M. Freeman	
G-BGNT	Cessna F.152	Klingair Ltd/Conington	
G-BGNV	GA-7 Cougar	G. J. Bissex	
G-BGOD	Colt 77A balloon	C. Allen & M. D. Steuer	
G-BGOG	PA-28-161 Warrior II	W. D. Moore	
G-BGOI	Cameron O-56 balloon	S. H. Budd	
G-BGOL	PA-28R-201T Turbo Arrow III	Valley Flying Co Ltd	
G-BGON	GA-7 Cougar	Walsh Aviation	
G-BGOO	Colt 56 SS balloon	British Gas Corporation	
G-BGOP	Dassault Falcon 20F	Nissan (UK) Ltd/Heathrow	
G-BGOR	AT-6D Harvard III (14863)	M. L. Sargeant	
G-BGPA	Cessna 182Q	Papa Alpha Group	
G-BGPB	CCF T-6J Texan (1747)	J. Romain/Duxford	
G-BGPD	Piper J-3C-65 Cub (479744)	P. D. Whiteman	
G-BGPH	AA-5B Tiger	Shipping & Airlines Ltd/Biggin Hill	
G-BGPI	Plumb BGP-1	B. G. Plumb	
G-BGPJ	PA-28-161 Warrior II	W. Lancs Warrior Co Ltd/Woodvale	
G-BGPK	AA-5B Tiger	A. Green/Elstree	
G-BGPL	PA-28-161 Warrior II	TG Aviation Ltd/Manston	
G-BGPM	Evans VP-2	M. G. Reilly	
G-BGPN	PA-18 Super Cub 150	Clacton Aero Club (1988) Ltd	
G-BGPU	PA-28 Cherokee 140	Air Navigation & Trading Ltd/Blackpool	
G-BGPZ	M.S.890A Rallye Commodore	Popham Flying Group	
G-BGRC	PA-28 Cherokee 140	Tecair Aviation Ltd/Swanton Morley	
G-BGRE	Beech A200 Super King Air	Martin-Baker (Engineering) Ltd/Chalgrove	
G-BGRG	Beech 76 Duchess	Liddell Aircraft Ltd/Bournemouth	
G-BGRH	Robin DR.400/22	Bagby Aviation	
G-BGRI	Jodel DR.1051	R. T. Gunn & J. R. Redhead	
G-BGRK	PA-38-112 Tomahawk	Goodwood Terrena Ltd/Goodwood	
G-BGRL	PA-38-112 Tomahawk	G. G. Mepham/Goodwood	
G-BGRM	PA-38-112 Tomahawk	Goodwood Terrena Ltd/Goodwood	
G-BGRN	PA-38-112 Tomahawk	Goodwood Terrena Ltd/Goodwood	
G-BGRO	Cessna F.172M	Turnhouse Flying Club	
G-BGRR	PA-38-112 Tomahawk	Goodair Leasing Ltd/Cardiff	
G-BGRS	Thunder Ax7-77Z balloon	P. M. Gaines & P. B. Fountain	
G-BGRT	Steen Skybolt	J. H. Kimber & O. Meier	
G-BGRX	PA-38-112 Tomahawk	Bonus Aviation Ltd	
G-BGSA	M.S.892E Rallye 150GT	D. H. Tonkin	
G-BGSG	PA-44-180 Seminole	D. J. McSorley	
G-BGSH	PA-38-112 Tomahawk	Scotia Safari Ltd/Prestwick	
G-BGSI	PA-38-112 Tomahawk	Ravenair/Liverpool	
G-BGSJ	Piper J-3C-65 Cub	A. J. Higgins	
G-BGST	Thunder Ax7-65 balloon	J. L. Bond	
G-BGSV	Cessna F.172N	Southwell Air Services Ltd	
G-BGSW	Beech F33 Debonair	Marketprior Ltd/Swansea	
G-BGSX	Cessna F.152	Denham Aircraft Maintenance Ltd	
G-BGSY	GA-7 Cougar	Plane Talking Ltd/Elstree	
G-BGTB	SOCATA TB.10 Tobago ★	D. Pope (stored)	
G-BGTC	Auster AOP.9 (XP282)	P. T. Bolton	
G-BGTF	PA-44-180 Seminole	NG Trustees & Nominees Ltd	
G-BGTG	PA-23 Aztec 250F	Keen Leasing (IOM) Ltd	
G-BGTI	Piper J-3C-65 Cub	A. P. Broad	
G-BGTJ	PA-28 Cherokee 180	Serendipity Aviation/Staverton	
G-BGTP	Robin HR.100/210	J. C. Parker	
G-BGTT	Cessna 310R	Aviation Beauport Ltd/Jersey	
G-BGTX	Jodel D.117	Madley Flying Group/Shobdon	
G-BGUA	PA-38-112 Tomahawk	Rhodair Maintenance Ltd/Cardiff	
G-BGUB	PA-32 Cherokee Six 300E	A. P. Diplock	
G-BGUY	Cameron V-56 balloon	J. L. Guy	
G-BGVB	Robin DR.315	Victor Bravo Group	
G-BGVE	CP.1310-C3 Super Emeraude	Victor Echo Group	
G-BGVH	Beech 76 Duchess	Velco Marketing	
G-BGVK	PA-28-161 Warrior II	D. S. Wells	
G-BGVN	PA-28RT-201 Arrow IV	H. S. Davies	
G-BGVS	Cessna F.172M	Kirkwall Flying Club	
G-BGVT	Cessna R.182RG	Bain Transport	
G-BGVV	AA-5A Cheetah	A. H. McVicar/Prestwick	
G-BGVW	AA-5A Cheetah	Computech Aviation Ltd	
G-BGVY	AA-5B Tiger	R. J. C. Neal-Smith	
G-BGVZ	PA-28-181 Archer II	W. Walsh & S. R. Mitchell	
G-BGWC	Robin DR.400/180	D. C. Shepherd/Rochester	
G-BGWH	PA-18 Super Cub 150	V. D. Speck/Clacton	
G-BGWI	Cameron V-65 balloon	Army Balloon Club/Germany	

Notes	Reg.	Type	Owner or Operator
	G-BGWJ	Sikorsky S-61N	British Executive Air Services Ltd
	G-BGWK	Sikorsky S-61N	Bristow Helicopters Ltd
	G-BGWM	PA-28-181 Archer II	Thames Valley Flying Club Ltd
	G-BGWN	PA-38-112 Tomahawk	Teesside Flight Centre Ltd
	G-BGWO	Jodel D.112	G-BGWO Group/Sandtoft
	G-BGWR	Cessna U.206A	C. M. J. Parton (G-DISC)/Tilstock
	G-BGWS	Enstrom 280C Shark	JHS Consultants Ltd
	G-BGWU	PA-38-112 Tomahawk	J. S. & L. M. Markey
	G-BGWV	Aeronca 7AC Champion	RFC Flying Group/Popham
	G-BGWW	PA-23 Turbo Aztec 250E	Aldergrove Flight Training Centre
	G-BGWY	Thunder Ax6-56Z balloon	P. J. Eley
	G-BGWZ	Eclipse Super Eagle ★	F.A.A. Museum/Yeovilton
	G-BGXA	Piper J-3C-65 Cub (329471)	K. Nicholls
	G-BGXB	PA-38-112 Tomahawk	Sightest Ltd/Biggin Hill
	G-BGXC	SOCATA TB.10 Tobago	D. H. Courtley
	G-BGXD	SOCATA TB.10 Tobago	P. N. Atkin & ptnrs
	G-BGXJ	Partenavia P.68B	Cecil Aviation Ltd/Cambridge
	G-BGXK	Cessna 310R	Turnhouse Flying Club
	G-BGXL	Bensen B.8MV	B. P. Triefus
	G-BGXN	PA-38-112 Tomahawk	Panshanger School of Flying Ltd
	G-BGXO	PA-38-112 Tomahawk	Goodwood Terrena Ltd
	G-BGXR	Robin HR.200/100	E. G. Cleobury
	G-BGXS	PA-28-236 Dakota	Bawtry Road Service Station Ltd
	G-BGXT	SOCATA TB.10 Tobago	D. A. H. Morris
	G-BGYG	PA-28-161 Warrior II	Oxford Aviation Services Ltd/Kidlington
	G-BGYH	PA-28-161 Warrior II	Oxford Aviation Services Ltd/Kidlington
	G-BGYN	PA-18 Super Cub 150	B. J. Dunford
	G-BGYR	H.S.125 Srs 600B	British Aerospace (Operations) Ltd/ Warton
	G-BGYT	EMB-110P1 Bandeirante	Keenair Charter/Liverpool
	G-BGZF	PA-38-112 Tomahawk	Aerohire Ltd/Halfpenny Green
	G-BGZJ	PA-38-112 Tomahawk	W. R. C. M. Foyle
	G-BGZL	Eiri PIK-20E	F. Casolari/Italy
	G-BGZN	WMB.2 Windtracker balloon	S. R. Woolfries
	G-BGZW	PA-38-112 Tomahawk	Ravenair/Liverpool
	G-BGZY	Jodel D.120	M. Hale
	G-BGZZ	Thunder Ax6-56 balloon	J. M. Robinson
	G-BHAA	Cessna 152 II	Herefordshire Aero Club Ltd/Shobdon
	G-BHAC	Cessna A.152	Herefordshire Aero Club Ltd/Shobdon
	G-BHAD	Cessna A.152	Shropshire Aero Club Ltd/Sleap
	G-BHAI	Cessna F.152	Fraggle Leasing Ltd/Edinburgh
	G-BHAJ	Robin DR.400/160	Rowantask Ltd
	G-BHAL	Rango Saffery S.200 SS balloon	A. M. Lindsay *Anneky Panky*
	G-BHAM	Thunder Ax6-56 balloon	D. M. & K. R. Sandford
	G-BHAR	Westland-Bell 47G-3B1	J. Bird & R. Cove
	G-BHAT	Thunder Ax7-77 balloon	C. P. Witter Ltd *Witter*
	G-BHAV	Cessna F.152	T. M. & M. L. Jones/Egginton
	G-BHAW	Cessna F.172N	E. Alexander
	G-BHAX	Enstrom F-28C-UK-2	PVS (Barnsley) Ltd
	G-BHAY	PA-28RT-201 Arrow IV	Alpha Yankee Ltd
	G-BHBA	Campbell Cricket	G. J. Layzell
	G-BHBB	Colt 77A balloon	S. D. Bellew
	G-BHBE	Westland-Bell 47G-3B1 (Soloy)	T. R. Smith (Agricultural Machinery) Ltd
	G-BHBF	Sikorsky S-76A	Bristow Helicopters Ltd
	G-BHBG	PA-32R Cherokee Lance 300	L. T. Halpin
	G-BHBI	Mooney M.20J	G-BHBI Group
	G-BHBT	Marquart MA.5 Charger	R. G. & C. J. Maidment/Shoreham
	G-BHBZ	Partenavia P.68B	Philip Hamer & Co
	G-BHCC	Cessna 172M	Langtry Flying Group Ltd
	G-BHCE	Jodel D.112	D. M. Parsons
	G-BHCM	Cessna F.172H	J. Dominic
	G-BHCP	Cessna F.152	D. Copley
	G-BHCT	PA-23 Aztec 250F	Falcon Flying Services (G-OLBC)/ Biggin Hill
	G-BHCW	PA-22 Tri-Pacer 150	V. F. Kemp
	G-BHCZ	PA-38-112 Tomahawk	J. E. Abbott
	G-BHDD	V.668 Varsity T.1 (WL626) ★	Aeropark/E. Midlands
	G-BHDE	SOCATA TB.10 Tobago	A. E. Allsop
	G-BHDK	Boeing B-29A-BN (461748) ★	Imperial War Museum/Duxford
	G-BHDM	Cessna F.152 II	Tayside Aviation Ltd/Dundee
	G-BHDP	Cessna F.182Q II	Zone Travel Ltd/White Waltham
	G-BHDR	Cessna F.152 II	Tayside Aviation Ltd/Dundee

Reg.	Type	Owner or Operator	Notes
G-BHDS	Cessna F.152 II	Tayside Aviation Ltd/Dundee	
G-BHDU	Cessna F.152 II	Falcon Flying Services/Biggin Hill	
G-BHDV	Cameron V-77 balloon	P. Glydon	
G-BHDW	Cessna F.152 II	Tayside Aviation Ltd/Dundee	
G-BHDX	Cessna F.172N	Skyhawk Group	
G-BHDZ	Cessna F.172N	Arrow Flying Ltd	
G-BHEC	Cessna F.152 II	Stapleford Flying Club Ltd	
G-BHED	Cessna FA.152	TG Aviation Ltd/Manston	
G-BHEG	Jodel 150	D. M. Griffiths	
G-BHEH	Cessna 310G	F. J. Shevill	
G-BHEK	CP.1315-C3 Super Emeraude	D. B. Winstanley/Barton	
G-BHEL	Jodel D.117	N. Wright & C. M. Kettlewell	
G-BHEM	Bensen B.8M	G. C. Kerr	
G-BHEN	Cessna FA.152	Leicestershire Aero Club Ltd	
G-BHEO	Cessna FR.182RG	J. G. Hogg	
G-BHER	SOCATA TB.10 Tobago	Vale Aviation Ltd	
G-BHEU	Thunder Ax7-65 balloon	D. G. Such	
G-BHEV	PA-28R Cherokee Arrow 200	7-Up Group	
G-BHEX	Colt 56A balloon	A. S. Dear & ptnrs *Super Wasp*	
G-BHEZ	Jodel 150	Air Yorkshire Group	
G-BHFC	Cessna F.152	TG Aviation Ltd/Manston	
G-BHFE	PA-44-180 Seminole	Grunwick Ltd/Elstree	
G-BHFF	Jodel D.112	P. A. Dowell	
G-BHFG	SNCAN Stampe SV-4C	Stormswift Ltd	
G-BHFH	PA-34-200T Seneca II	Aerohire Ltd/Halfpenny Green	
G-BHFI	Cessna F.152	BAe (Warton) Flying Group/Blackpool	
G-BHFJ	PA-28RT-201T Turbo Arrow IV	T. L. P. Delaney	
G-BHFK	PA-28-151 Warrior	Ilkeston Car Sales Ltd	
G-BHFR	Eiri PIK-20E-1	J. T. Morgan	
G-BHFS	Robin DR.400/180	D. S. Chandler	
G-BHGA	PA-31-310 Turbo Navajo	Heltor Ltd	
G-BHGC	PA-18 Super Cub 150	M. R. & P. A. Dawson	
G-BHGF	Cameron V-56 balloon	P. Smallward	
G-BHGJ	Jodel D.120	Q. M. B. Oswell	
G-BHGK	Sikorsky S-76A	Bond Helicopters Ltd	
G-BHGO	PA-32 Cherokee Six 260	DOCS Ltd/Newcastle	
G-BHGP	SOCATA TB.10 Tobago	Inter Textiles Ltd	
G-BHGX	Colt 56B balloon	M. N. Dixon	
G-BHGY	PA-28R Cherokee Arrow 200	V. Humphries/Gamston	
G-BHHB	Cameron V-77 balloon	R. Powell	
G-BHHE	Jodel DR.1051/M1	P. Bridges	
G-BHHG	Cessna F.152 II	TG Aviation Ltd/Manston	
G-BHHH	Thunder Ax7-65 balloon	C. A. Hendley (Essex) Ltd	
G-BHHK	Cameron N-77 balloon	I. S. Bridge	
G-BHHN	Cameron V-77 balloon	Itchen Valley Balloon Group	
G-BHHX	Jodel D.112	P. J. Errd & D. M. Gale	
G-BHHZ	Rotorway Scorpion 133	L. W. & O. Usherwood	
G-BHIB	Cessna F.182Q	S. N. Chater & B. Payne	
G-BHIC	Cessna F.182Q	W. F. Alton & Son	
G-BHIG	Colt 31A Arm Chair SS balloon	P. A. Lindstrand	
G-BHIH	Cessna F.172N	M. A. Wilkinson	
G-BHII	Cameron V-77 balloon	R. V. Brown	
G-BHIJ	Eiri PIK-20E-1 (898)	I. W. Paterson/Portmoak	
G-BHIK	Adam RA-14 Loisirs	L. Lewis	
G-BHIR	PA-28R Cherokee Arrow 200	Factorcore Ltd/Barton	
G-BHIS	Thunder Ax7-65 balloon	Hedgehoppers Balloon Group	
G-BHIT	SOCATA TB.9 Tampico	ABC Advertising Ltd	
G-BHIY	Cessna F.150K	G. J. Ball	
G-BHJA	Cessna A.152	Cornwall Flying Club Ltd/Bodmin	
G-BHJB	Cessna A.152	Sky Pro Ltd	
G-BHJF	SOCATA TB.10 Tobago	Flying Fox Group	
G-BHJI	Mooney M.20J	S. F. Lister	
G-BHJK	Maule M5-235C Lunar Rocket	S. Sampson	
G-BHJN	Fournier RF-4D	RF-4 Flying Group	
G-BHJO	PA-28-161 Warrior II	The Brackla Flying Group/Inverness	
G-BHJS	Partenavia P.68B	J. J. Watts & D. Fletcher	
G-BHJU	Robin DR.400/2+2	T. J. Harlow	
G-BHKE	Bensen B.8MS	C. Baldwin	
G-BHKH	Cameron O-65 balloon	D. G. Body	
G-BHKJ	Cessna 421C	Totaljet Ltd	
G-BHKR	Colt 12A balloon ★	British Balloon Museum/Newbury	
G-BHKT	Jodel D.112	The Evans Flying Group	
G-BHKV	AA-5A Cheetah	Alouette Flying Club Ltd/Biggin Hill	

Notes	Reg.	Type	Owner or Operator
	G-BHKY	Cessna 310R II	ILS Air Ltd
	G-BHLE	Robin DR.400/180	B. D. Greenwood
	G-BHLH	Robin DR.400/180	P. E. Davis
	G-BHLJ	Saffery-Rigg S.200 balloon	I. A. Rigg
	G-BHLT	D.H.82A Tiger Moth	P. J. & A. J. Borsberry
	G-BHLU	Fournier RF-3	M. C. Roper
	G-BHLW	Cessna 120	L. W. Scattergood
	G-BHLX	AA-5B Tiger	C. B. Dew
	G-BHMA	SIPA 903	H. J. Taggart
	G-BHMG	Cessna FA.152	R. D. Smith
	G-BHMI	Cessna F.172N	GMI Aviation Ltd (G-WADE)
	G-BHMJ	Avenger T.200-2112 balloon	R. Light *Lord Anthony 1*
	G-BHMK	Avenger T.200-2112 balloon	P. Kinder *Lord Anthony 2*
	G-BHMR	Stinson 108-3	D. G. French/Sandown
	G-BHMT	Evans VP-1	P. E. J. Sturgeon
	G-BHNA	Cessna F.152	Sheffield Aero Club Ltd/Netherthorpe
	G-BHNC	Cameron O-65 balloon	D. & C. Bareford
	G-BHND	Cameron N-65 balloon	S. M. Wellband
	G-BHNK	Jodel D.120A	G-BHNK Flying Group
	G-BHNL	Jodel D.112	J. C. Mansell
	G-BHNO	PA-28-181 Archer II	Airfluid Hydraulics & Pneumatics (Wolverhampton) Ltd
	G-BHNP	Eiri PIK-20E-1	D. A. Sutton/Riseley
	G-BHNV	Westlan-Bell 47G-3B1	Leyline Helicopters Ltd
	G-BHNX	Jodel D.117	A. J. Chalkley
	G-BHOA	Robin DR.400/160	M. L. Sargeant
	G-BHOH	Sikorsky S-61N Mk.II	Bristow Helicopters Ltd
	G-BHOL	Jodel DR.1050	D. G. Hart
	G-BHOM	PA-18 Super Cub 95	C. H. A. Bott
	G-BHOO	Thunder Ax7-65 balloon	D. Livesey & J. M. Purves *Scraps*
	G-BHOR	PA-28-161 Warrior II	Oscar Romeo Flying Group/Biggin Hill
	G-BHOT	Cameron V-65 balloon	Dante Balloon Group
	G-BHOU	Cameron V-65 balloon	F. W. Barnes
	G-BHOZ	SOCATA TB.9 Tampico	M. Brown
	G-BHPK	Piper J-3C-65 Cub (236800)	L-4 Group
	G-BHPL	C.A.S.A. 1.131E Jungmann 1000 (E3B-350)	R. G. Gray/North Weald
	G-BHPM	PA-18 Super Cub 95	P. I. Morgans
	G-BHPN	Colt 14A balloon	Lindstrand Balloons Ltd
	G-BHPS	Jodel D.120A	T. J. Price
	G-BHPT	Piper J-3C-65 Cub	Rolfe Air Services
	G-BHPX	Cessna 152 II	Southern Air Ltd/Shoreham
	G-BHPY	Cessna 152 II	Rankart Ltd
	G-BHPZ	Cessna 172N	O'Brien Properties Ltd/Redhill
	G-BHRB	Cessna F.152 II	LAC (Enterprises) Ltd/Barton
	G-BHRC	PA-28-161 Warrior II	Sherwood Flying Club Ltd/Tollerton
	G-BHRH	Cessna FA.150K	Merlin Flying Club Ltd/Hucknall
	G-BHRI	Saffery S.200 balloon	N. J. & H. L. Dunnington
	G-BHRM	Cessna F.152	Aerohire Ltd/Halfpenny Green
	G-BHRN	Cessna F.152	Fraggle Leasing Ltd/Edinburgh
	G-BHRO	R. Commander 112A	John Raymond Transport Ltd/Cardiff
	G-BHRP	PA-44-180 Seminole	M. S. Farmers
	G-BHRR	CP.301A Emeraude	T. W. Offen
	G-BHRW	Jodel DR.221	Dauphin Flying Group
	G-BHRY	Colt 56A balloon	A. S. Davidson
	G-BHSA	Cessna 152 II	D. Copley
	G-BHSB	Cessna 172N	ABK Aviation Services Ltd
	G-BHSD	Scheibe SF.25E Super Falke	Lasham Gliding Soc Ltd
	G-BHSE	R. Commander 114	604 Sqdn Flying Soc Ltd
	G-BHSL	C.A.S.A. 1.131E Jungmann	H. I. Taylor
	G-BHSN	Cameron N-56 balloon	I. Bentley
	G-BHSP	Thunder Ax7-77Z balloon	Out-Of-The-Blue
	G-BHSS	Pitts S-1C Special	Bottoms Up Syndicate
	G-BHSY	Jodel DR.1050	T. R. Allebone
	G-BHTA	PA-28-236 Dakota	Dakota Ltd
	G-BHTC	Jodel DR.1050/M1	G. Clark
	G-BHTG	Thunder Ax6-56 balloon	F. R. & Mrs S. H. MacDonald
	G-BHTH	NA T-6G Texan (2807)	J. J. Woodhouse
	G-BHUB	Douglas C-47A (315509) ★	Imperial War Museum/Duxford
	G-BHUE	Jodel DR.1050	M. J. Harris
	G-BHUG	Cessna 172N	FGT Aircraft Hire
	G-BHUI	Cessna 152	Galair International Ltd
	G-BHUJ	Cessna 172N	Small World Aviation

Reg.	Type	Owner or Operator	Notes
G-BHUM	D.H.82A Tiger Moth	S. G. Towers	
G-BHUO	Evans VP-2	D. A. Wood	
G-BHUR	Thunder Ax3 balloon	B. F. G. Ribbans	
G-BHUU	PA-25 Pawnee 235	Booker Gliding Club Ltd	
G-BHVB	PA-28-161 Warrior II	Bobbington Air Training School Ltd	
G-BHVF	Jodel 150A	J. D. Walton	
G-BHVP	Cessna 182Q	J. Kettles & C. Stevenson	
G-BHVR	Cessna 172N	G-BHVR Group	
G-BHVV	Piper J-3C-65 Cub	P. R. Wright/Barton	
G-BHWA	Cessna F.152	Lincoln Aviation/Wickenby	
G-BHWB	Cessna F.152	Lincoln Aviation/Wickenby	
G-BHWH	Weedhopper JC-24A	G. A. Clephane	
G-BHWK	M.S.880B Rallye Club	L. L. Gayther	
G-BHWS	Cessna F.152 II	Turnhouse Flying Club	
G-BHWY	PA-28R Cherokee Arrow 200-II	Kilo Foxtrot Flying Group/Sandown	
G-BHWZ	PA-28-181 Archer II	I. R. McCue	
G-BHXA	SA Bulldog Srs 120/1210	D. A. Williams/Liverpool	
G-BHXD	Jodel D.120	P. H. C. Hall	
G-BHXK	PA-28 Cherokee 140	GXK Flying Group	
G-BHXL	Evans VP-2	R. S. Wharton	
G-BHXS	Jodel D.120	I. R. Willis	
G-BHXT	Thunder Ax6-56Z balloon	Ocean Traffic Services Ltd	
G-BHXY	Piper J-3C-65 Cub (44-79609)	F. W. Rogers/Aldergrove	
G-BHYA	Cessna R.182RG II	Card Tech Ltd	
G-BHYC	Cessna 172RG II	IB Aeroplanes Ltd	
G-BHYD	Cessna R.172K XP II	Sylmar Aviation Services Ltd	
G-BHYE	PA-34-200T Seneca II	Oxford Aviation Services Ltd/Kidlington	
G-BHYF	PA-34-200T Seneca II	Oxford Aviation Services Ltd/Kidlington	
G-BHYG	PA-34-200T Seneca II	Oxford Aviation Services Ltd/Kidlington	
G-BHYI	SNCAN Stampe SV-4A	P. A. Irwin	
G-BHYO	Cameron N-77 balloon	Adventure Balloon Co Ltd	
G-BHYP	Cessna F.172M	Avior Ltd/Biggin Hill	
G-BHYR	Cessna F.172M	G-BHYR Group	
G-BHYV	Evans VP-1	L. Chiappi/Blackpool	
G-BHYX	Cessna 152 II	Stapleford Flying Club Ltd	
G-BHZE	PA-28-181 Archer II	Wild Blue Aviation Ltd	
G-BHZF	Evans VP-2	W. J. Evans	
G-BHZH	Cessna F.152	Plymouth School of Flying Ltd	
G-BHZK	AA-5B Tiger	ZK Group/Elstree	
G-BHZO	AA-5A Cheetah	A. H. McVicar	
G-BHZR	SA Bulldog Srs 120/1210	M. A. Elobeid	
G-BHZS	SA Bulldog Srs 120/1210	D. A. Williams/Liverpool	
G-BHZT	SA Bulldog Srs 120/1210	W. M. Bax	
G-BHZU	Piper J-3C-65 Cub	J. K. Tomkinson	
G-BHZV	Jodel D.120A	K. J. Scott	
G-BHZX	Thunder Ax7-65A balloon	R. J. & H. M. Beattie	
G-BIAB	SOCATA TB.9 Tampico	H. W. A. Thirlway	
G-BIAC	SOCATA Rallye 235E	Aerobatic Displays Ltd & A. G. Kay	
G-BIAH	Jodel D.112	D. Mitchell	
G-BIAI	WMB.2 Windtracker balloon	I. Chadwick	
G-BIAK	SOCATA TB.10 Tobago	Westmead Business Group Ltd	
G-BIAL	Rango NA.8 balloon	A. M. Lindsay	
G-BIAP	PA-16 Clipper	P. J. Bish/White Waltham	
G-BIAR	Rigg Skyliner II balloon	I. A. Rigg	
G-BIAU	Sopwith Pup (replica) (N6452) ★	F.A.A. Museum/Yeovilton	
G-BIAX	Taylor JT.2 Titch	J. T. Everest	
G-BIAY	AA-5 Traveler	M. D. Dupay & ptnrs	
G-BIBA	SOCATA TB.9 Tampico	TB Aviation Ltd	
G-BIBB	Mooney M.20C	P. M. Breton	
G-BIBG	Sikorksy S-76A	Bristow Helicopters Ltd	
G-BIBJ	Enstrom 280C-UK-2	Kempspray Ltd	
G-BIBN	Cessna FA.150K	B. V. Mayo	
G-BIBO	Cameron V-65 balloon	I. Harris	
G-BIBS	Cameron P-20 balloon	Cameron Balloons Ltd	
G-BIBT	AA-5B Tiger	Vizor Tempered Glass Ltd	
G-BIBW	Cessna F.172N	Farley Aviation	
G-BIBX	WMB.2 Windtracker balloon	I. A. Rigg	
G-BICD	Auster 5	R. T. Parsons	
G-BICE	AT-6C Harvard IIA (41-33275)	C. M. L. Edwards	
G-BICG	Cessna F.152 II	Falcon Flying Services/Biggin Hill	
G-BICJ	Monnett Sonerai II	I. Parr	
G-BICM	Colt 56A balloon	Avon Advertiser Balloon Club	

Notes	Reg.	Type	Owner or Operator
	G-BICP	Robin DR.360	Bravo India Flying Group/Liverpool
	G-BICR	Jodel D.120A	Beehive Flying Group/White Waltham
	G-BICS	Robin R.2100A	I. Young/Sandown
	G-BICT	Evans VP-1	A. S. Coombe & D. L. Tribe
	G-BICU	Cameron V-56 balloon	S. D. Bather
	G-BICW	PA-28-161 Warrior II	D. Gellhorn
	G-BICX	Maule M5-5C Lunar Rocket	A. T. Jeans & J. F. Clarkson/Old Sarum
	G-BICY	PA-23 Apache 160	A. M. Lynn/Sibson
	G-BIDD	Evans VP-1	J. Hodgkinson
	G-BIDF	Cessna F.172P	E. Alexander
	G-BIDG	Jodel 150A	D. R. Gray/Barton
	G-BIDH	Cessna 152 II	Cumbria Aero Club (G-DONA)/Carlisle
	G-BIDI	PA-28R-201 Arrow III	Ambrit Ltd
	G-BIDJ	PA-18A Super Cub 150	Flight Solutions Ltd
	G-BIDK	PA-18 Super Cub 150	J. McCullough
	G-BIDO	CP.301A Emeraude	A. R. Plumb
	G-BIDU	Cameron V-77 balloon	E. Eleazor
	G-BIDV	Colt 14A balloon	International Distillers & Vintners (House Trade) Ltd
	G-BIDW	Sopwith 1 1/2 Strutter (replica) (A8226) ★	RAF Museum/Hendon
	G-BIDX	Jodel D.112	H. N. Nuttall & P. Turton
	G-BIEF	Cameron V-77 balloon	D. S. Bush
	G-BIEJ	Sikorsky S-76A	Bristow Helicopters Ltd
	G-BIEN	Jodel D.120A	Tonbridge Autos
	G-BIEO	Jodel D.112	Clipgate Flyers
	G-BIES	Maule M5-5C Lunar Rocker	William Proctor Farms
	G-BIET	Cameron O-77 balloon	G. M. Westley
	G-BIEY	PA-28-151 Warrior	Falcon Flying Services/Biggin Hill
	G-BIFA	Cessna 310R II	J. S. Lee
	G-BIFB	PA-28 Cherokee 150C	N. A. Ayub
	G-BIFN	Bensen B.8MR	B. Gunn
	G-BIFO	Evans VP-1	R. Broadhead
	G-BIFP	Colt 56C balloon	J. Philp
	G-BIFY	Cessna F.150L	Astra Associates/Elstree
	G-BIFZ	Partenavia P.68C	Jet Airmotive Ltd
	G-BIGD	Cameron V-77 balloon	D. L. Clark
	G-BIGF	Thunder Ax7-77 balloon	M. D. Stever & C. A. Allen
	G-BIGJ	Cessna F.172M	V. D. Speck/Clacton
	G-BIGK	Taylorcraft BC-12D	N. P. S. Ramsay
	G-BIGL	Cameron O-65 balloon	P. L. Mossman
	G-BIGP	Bensen B.8M	R. H. S. Cooper
	G-BIGR	Avenger T.200-2112 balloon	R. Light
	G-BIGX	Bensen B.8M	W. C. Turner
	G-BIGZ	Scheibe SF.25B Falke	G-BIGZ Syndicate/Saltby
	G-BIHD	Robin DR.400/160	K. B. Mainstone
	G-BIHF	SE-5A (replica) (F943)	K. J. Garrett/Booker
	G-BIHG	PA-28 Cherokee 140	Parham Flying Group
	G-BIHI	Cessna 172M	Fenland Flying School
	G-BIHO	D.H.C.6 Twin Otter 310	Isles of Scilly Skybus Ltd/St. Just
	G-BIHP	Van Den Bemden gas balloon	J. J. Harris
	G-BIHT	PA-17 Vagabond	G. H. Cork
	G-BIHU	Saffrey S.200 balloon	B. L. King
	G-BIHW	Aeronca A65TAC Defender	T. J. Ingrouille
	G-BIHX	Bensen B.8M	P. P. Willmott
	G-BIIA	Fournier RF-3	T. M. W. Webster
	G-BIIB	Cessna F.172M	Civil Service Flying Club (Biggin Hill) Ltd
	G-BIID	PA-18 Super Cub 95	D. A. Lacey
	G-BIIE	Cessna F.172P	Sterling Helicopters Ltd
	G-BIIG	Thunder Ax6-56Z balloon	Chiltern Flyers Ltd
	G-BIIK	M.S.883 Rallye 115	H. & K. M. Bowen
	G-BIIL	Thunder Ax6-56 balloon	G. W. Reader
	G-BIIP	BN-2B-27 Islander	Hebridean Air Services Ltd
	G-BIIT	PA-28-161 Warrior II	Tayside Aviation Ltd/Dundee
	G-BIIV	PA-28-181 Archer II	Stratton Motor Co Ltd
	G-BIIX	Rango NA.12 balloon	Rango Kite Co
	G-BIIZ	Great Lakes 2T-1A Sport Trainer	C. D. Baird
	G-BIJB	PA-18 Super Cub 150	Essex Gliding Club Ltd/North Weald
	G-BIJD	Bo 208C Junior	C. G. Stone
	G-BIJE	Piper J-3C-65 Cub	R. L. Hayward & A. G. Scott
	G-BIJS	Luton LA-4A Minor	I. J. Smith
	G-BIJU	CP-301A Emeraude	Eastern Taildraggers Flying Group (G-BHTX)

Reg.	Type	Owner or Operator	Notes
G-BIJV	Cessna F.152 II	Falcon Flying Services/Biggin Hill	
G-BIJW	Cessna F.152 II	Falcon Flying Services/Biggin Hill	
G-BIJX	Cessna F.152 II	Falcon Flying Services/Biggin Hill	
G-BIKA	Boeing 757-236	British Airways	
G-BIKB	Boeing 757-236	British Airways	
G-BIKC	Boeing 757-236	British Airways	
G-BIKD	Boeing 757-236	British Airways	
G-BIKE	PA-28R Cherokee Arrow 200	R. V. Webb Ltd/Elstree	
G-BIKF	Boeing 757-236	British Airways	
G-BIKG	Boeing 757-236	British Airways	
G-BIKH	Boeing 757-236	British Airways	
G-BIKI	Boeing 757-236	British Airways	
G-BIKJ	Boeing 757-236	British Airways	
G-BIKK	Boeing 757-236	British Airways	
G-BIKL	Boeing 757-236	British Airways	
G-BIKM	Boeing 757-236	British Airways	
G-BIKN	Boeing 757-236	British Airways	
G-BIKO	Boeing 757-236	British Airways	
G-BIKP	Boeing 757-236	British Airways	
G-BIKR	Boeing 757-236	British Airways	
G-BIKS	Boeing 757-236	British Airways	
G-BIKT	Boeing 757-236	British Airways	
G-BIKU	Boeing 757-236	British Airways	
G-BIKV	Boeing 757-236	British Airways	
G-BIKW	Boeing 757-236	British Airways	
G-BIKX	Boeing 757-236	British Airways	
G-BIKY	Boeing 757-236	British Airways	
G-BIKZ	Boeing 757-236	British Airways	
G-BILA	Daletol DM.165L Viking	R. Lamplough (stored)	
G-BILB	WMB.2 Windtracker balloon	B. L. King	
G-BILE	Scruggs BL.2B balloon	P. D. Ridout	
G-BILG	Scruggs BL.2B balloon	P. D. Ridout	
G-BILI	Piper J-3C-65 Cub (454467)	G-BILI Flying Group	
G-BILJ	Cessna FA.152	Bournemouth Flying Club Ltd	
G-BILK	Cessna FA.152	Exeter Flying Club Ltd	
G-BILL	PA-25 Pawnee 235	Pawnee Aviation	
G-BILR	Cessna 152 II	Shropshire Aero Club Ltd/Sleap	
G-BILS	Cessna 152 II	Keen Leasing (IOM) Ltd	
G-BILU	Cessna 172RG	Full Sutton Flying Centre Ltd	
G-BILZ	Taylor JT.1 Monoplane	A. Petherbridge	
G-BIMK	Tiger T.200 Srs 1 balloon	M. K. Baron	
G-BIMM	PA-18 Super Cub 150	Fairmont Investments Ltd/Clacton	
G-BIMN	Steen Skybolt	G. P. Gregg	
G-BIMO	SNCAN Stampe SV-4C	R. A. Roberts	
G-BIMT	Cessna FA.152	Staverton Flying Services Ltd	
G-BIMU	Sikorsky S-61N	Bristow Helicopters Ltd	
G-BIMX	Rutan Vari-Eze	D. G. Crow/Biggin Hill	
G-BIMZ	Beech 76 Duchess	A. J. Nurse	
G-BINF	Saffery S.200 balloon	T. Lewis	
G-BING	Cessna F.172P	M. P. Dolan	
G-BINI	Scruggs BL.2C balloon	S. R. Woolfries	
G-BINL	Scruggs BL.2B balloon	P. D. Ridout	
G-BINM	Scruggs BL.2B balloon	P. D. Ridout	
G-BINO	Evans VP-1	G. Ravichandran	
G-BINR	Unicorn UE.1A balloon	Unicorn Group	
G-BINS	Unicorn UE.2A balloon	Unicorn Group	
G-BINT	Unicorn UE.1A balloon	Unicorn Group	
G-BINU	Saffery S.200 balloon	T. Lewis	
G-BINX	Scruggs BL.2B balloon	P. D. Ridout	
G-BINY	Oriental balloon	J. L. Morton	
G-BIOB	Cessna F.172P	Aerofilms Ltd/Elstree	
G-BIOC	Cessna F.150L	Southside Flyers	
G-BIOI	Jodel DR.1051/M	H. F. Hambling	
G-BIOJ	R. Commander 112TCA	A. T. Dalby	
G-BIOK	Cessna F.152	Tayside Aviation Ltd/Dundee	
G-BIOM	Cessna F.152	Falcon Flying Services/Luton	
G-BION	Cameron V-77 balloon	Flying Doctors Balloon Syndicate	
G-BIOR	M.S.880B Rallye Club	R. L. & K. P. McLean/Rufforth	
G-BIOU	Jodel D.117A	Dubious Group/Booker	
G-BIOW	Slingsby T.67A	A. B. Slinger/Sherburn	
G-BIPA	AA-5B Tiger	J. Campbell/Walney Island	
G-BIPH	Scruggs BL.2B balloon	C. M. Dewsnap	
G-BIPI	Everett gyroplane	C. A. Reeves	

Notes	Reg.	Type	Owner or Operator
	G-BIPN	Fournier RF-3	J. C. R. Rogers & I. F. Fairhead
	G-BIPO	Mudry/CAARP CAP.20LS-200M.	C. Sandford
	G-BIPS	SOCATA Rallye 100ST	McAully Flying Group/Little Snoring
	G-BIPT	Jodel D.112	C. R. Davies
	G-BIPV	AA-5B Tiger	Airtime Aviation Ltd
	G-BIPW	Avenger T.200-2112 balloon	B. L. King
	G-BIPY	Montgomerie-Bensen B.8MR	C. G. Ponsford
	G-BIRD	Pitts S-1C Special	Pitts Artists Flying Group
	G-BIRE	Colt 56 Bottle SS balloon	K. R. Gafney
	G-BIRH	PA-18 Super Cub 135 (R-163)	Aquila Gliding Club Ltd
	G-BIRI	C.A.S.A. 1.131E Jungmann 1000	M. G. & J. R. Jeffries
	G-BIRK	Avenger T.200-2112 balloon	D. Harland
	G-BIRL	Avenger T.200-2112 balloon	R. Light
	G-BIRM	Avenger T.200-2112 balloon	P. Higgins
	G-BIRP	Arena Mk 17 Skyship balloon	A. S. Viel
	G-BIRS	Cessna 182P	Air Nova PLC (G-BBBS)/Liverpool
	G-BIRT	Robin R.1180TD	W. D'A. Hall/Booker
	G-BIRW	M.S.505 Criquet (F+IS) ★	Museum of Flight/E. Fortune
	G-BIRY	Cameron V-77 balloon	P. & H. Mann
	G-BIRZ	Zenair CH.250	T. N. Fox & I. R. Nash
	G-BISG	FRED Srs 3	R. A. Coombe
	G-BISH	Cameron O-42 balloon	Zebedee Balloon Service
	G-BISJ	Cessna 340A	Billair
	G-BISK	R. Commander 112B ★	P. A. Warner
	G-BISL	Scruggs BL.2B balloon	P. D. Ridout
	G-BISM	Scruggs BL.2B balloon	P. D. Ridout
	G-BISS	Scruggs BL.2C balloon	P. D. Ridout
	G-BIST	Scruggs BL.2C balloon	P. D. Ridout
	G-BISV	Cameron O-65 balloon	Hylyne Rabbits Ltd
	G-BISX	Colt 56A balloon	Colt G-BISX Ltd
	G-BISZ	Sikorsky S-76A	Bristow Helicopters Ltd
	G-BITA	PA-18 Super Cub 150	Intrepid Aviation Co/North Weald
	G-BITE	SOCATA TB.10 Tobago	M. A. Smith & R. J. Bristow/Fairoaks
	G-BITF	Cessna F.152 II	Tayside Aviation Ltd/Dundee
	G-BITH	Cessna F.152 II	Tayside Aviation Ltd/Dundee
	G-BITK	FRED Srs 2	D. J. Wood
	G-BITM	Cessna F.172P	D. G. Crabtree/Liverpool
	G-BITO	Jodel D.112D	A. Dunbar/Barton
	G-BITR	Sikorsky S-76A	Bristow Helicopters Ltd
	G-BITS	Drayton B-56 balloon	M. J. Betts
	G-BITY	FD.31T balloon	A. J. Bell
	G-BIUM	Cessna F.152	Sheffield Aero Club Ltd/Netherthorpe
	G-BIUP	SNCAN NC.854S	BIUP Flying Group
	G-BIUU	PA-23 Aztec 250D ★	G. Cormack/Glasgow
	G-BIUV	H.S.748 Srs 2A	Emerald Airways Ltd City of Liverpool (G-AYYH)/Liverpool
	G-BIUW	PA-28-161 Warrior II	D. R. Staley
	G-BIUY	PA-28-181 Archer II	J. S. Devlin & Z. Islam
	G-BIVA	Robin R.2112	P. A. Richardson
	G-BIVB	Jodel D.112	D. Silsbury
	G-BIVC	Jodel D.112	M. J. Barmby/Cardiff
	G-BIVF	CP.301C-3 Emeraude	R. J. Moore
	G-BIVK	Bensen B.8M	K. Balch
	G-BIVT	Saffery S.80 balloon	L. F. Guyot
	G-BIVV	AA-5A Cheetah	Plane Talking Ltd/Elstree
	G-BIWB	Scruggs RS.5000 balloon	P. D. Ridout
	G-BIWC	Scruggs RS.5000 balloon	P. D. Ridout
	G-BIWD	Scruggs RS.5000 balloon	D. Eaves
	G-BIWF	Warren balloon	P. D. Ridout
	G-BIWG	Zelenski Mk 2 balloon	P. D. Ridout
	G-BIWJ	Unicorn UE.1A balloon	B. L. King
	G-BIWK	Cameron V-65 balloon	I. R. Williams & R. G. Bickerdike
	G-BIWL	PA-32-301 Saratoga	A. R. Ward
	G-BIWN	Jodel D.112	C. R. Coates
	G-BIWR	Mooney M.20F	A. C. Brink
	G-BIWU	Cameron V-65 balloon	L. P. Hooper
	G-BIWW	AA-5 Traveler	B & K Aviation/Cranfield
	G-BIWY	Westland WG.30 ★	Instructional airframe
	G-BIXA	SOCATA TB.9 Tampico	Lord deSaumarez
	G-BIXB	SOCATA TB.9 Tampico	L. B. W. & F. H. Hancock
	G-BIXH	Cessna F.152	Cambridge Aero Club Ltd
	G-BIXI	Cessna 172RG Cutlass	J. F. P. Lewis/Sandown
	G-BIXL	P-51D Mustang (472216)	R. Lamplough/North Weald

Reg.	Type	Owner or Operator	Notes
G-BIXN	Boeing Stearman A.75N1	R. R. White	
G-BIXR	Cameron A-140 balloon	Skysales Ltd	
G-BIXS	Avenger T.200-2112 balloon	M. Stuart	
G-BIXV	Bell 212	Bristow Helicopters Ltd	
G-BIXW	Colt 56B balloon	N. A. P. Bates	
G-BIXX	Pearson Srs 2 balloon	D. Pearson	
G-BIXZ	Grob G-109	D. L. Nind & I. Allum/Booker	
G-BIYI	Cameron V-65 balloon	Sarnia Balloon Group	
G-BIYJ	PA-18 Super Cub 95	S. Russell	
G-BIYK	Isaacs Fury	D. Silsbury	
G-BIYO	PA-31-310 Turbo Navajo	Executive Jet Leasing Ltd	
G-BIYP	PA-20 Pacer 125	R. J. Whitcombe	
G-BIYR	PA-18 Super Cub 150 (R-151)	Delta Foxtrot Flying Group	
G-BIYT	Colt 17A balloon	J. M. Francois/France	
G-BIYU	Fokker S.11.1 Instructor (E-15)	C. Briggs	
G-BIYW	Jodel D.112	Pollard/Balaam/Bye Flying Group	
G-BIYX	PA-28 Cherokee 140	Comed Aviation Ltd/Blackpool	
G-BIYY	PA-18 Super Cub 95	A. E. & W. J. Taylor/Ingoldmells	
G-BIZE	SOCATA TB.9 Tampico		
G-BIZF	Cessna F.172P	R. S. Bentley/Bourn	
G-BIZG	Cessna F.152	M. A. Judge	
G-BIZI	Robin DR.400/120	BIZI Club Ltd	
G-BIZK	Nord 3202	A. I. Milne/Swanton Morley	
G-BIZM	Nord 3202	Magnificent Obsessions Ltd	
G-BIZN	Slingsby T.67A	Sport to Business	
G-BIZO	PA-28R Cherokee Arrow 200	Bizo Air Ltd	
G-BIZR	SOCATA TB.9 Tampico	R. C. Walker (G-BSEC)	
G-BIZU	Thunder Ax6-56Z balloon	M. J. Loades	
G-BIZV	PA-18 Super Cub 95 (18-2001)	S. J. Pugh & R. L. Wademan	
G-BIZW	Champion 7GCBC Citabria	G. Read & Sons	
G-BIZY	Jodel D.112	Wayland Tunley & Associates/Cranfield	
G-BJAE	Lavadoux Starck AS.80	D. J. & S. A. E. Phillips/Coventry	
G-BJAF	Piper J-3C-65 Cub	P. J. Cottle	
G-BJAG	PA-28-181 Archer II	J. F. Clark	
G-BJAJ	AA-5B Tiger	A. H. McVicar/Prestwick	
G-BJAL	C.A.S.A. 1.131E Jungmann 1000	I. C. Underwood & S. B. J. Chandler/Brighton	
G-BJAO	Bensen B.8M	A. P. Lay	
G-BJAP	D.H.82A Tiger Moth (K2587)	K. Knight	
G-BJAS	Rango NA.9 balloon	A. Lindsay	
G-BJAV	GY-80 Horizon 160	A. J. Martlew	
G-BJAW	Cameron V-65 balloon	G. W. McCarthy	
G-BJAX	Pilatus P2-05 (U-108) ★	(stored)	
G-BJAY	Piper J-3C-65 Cub	K. L. Clarke/Ingoldmells	
G-BJBK	PA-18 Super Cub 95	M. S. Bird/Old Sarum	
G-BJBM	Monnett Sonerai II	G. J. Townsend	
G-BJBO	Jodel DR.250/160	Wiltshire Flying Group	
G-BJBW	PA-28-161 Warrior II	J. C. Lucas	
G-BJBX	PA-28-161 Warrior II	Haimoss Ltd	
G-BJCA	PA-28-161 Warrior II	QBS Trading Co Ltd	
G-BJCF	CP.1310-C3 Super Emeraude	K. M. Hodson & C. G. H. Gurney	
G-BJCI	PA-18 Super Cub 150 (modified)	The Borders (Milfield) Aero-Tour Club Ltd	
G-BJCW	PA-32R-301 Saratoga SP	G. R. Patrick & Co Ltd	
G-BJDE	Cessna F.172M	H. P. K. Ferdinand/Denham	
G-BJDF	M.S.880B Rallye 100T	G-BJDF Group	
G-BJDI	Cessna FR.182RG	P. R. Piggin	
G-BJDJ	H.S.125 Srs 700B	Falcon Jet Centre Ltd (G-RCDI)	
G-BJDK	European E.14 balloon	Aeroprint Tours	
G-BJDO	AA-5A Cheetah	Flying Services	
G-BJDT	SOCATA TB.9 Tampico	C. P. Bignell	
G-BJDW	Cessna F.172M	J. Rae	
G-BJEI	PA-18 Super Cub 95	H. J. Cox	
G-BJEL	SNCAN NC.854	N. F. & S. G. Hunter	
G-BJEN	Scruggs RS.5000 balloon	N. J. Richardson	
G-BJEV	Aeronca 11AC Chief (897)	R. F. Willcox	
G-BJEX	Bo 208C Junior	G. D. H. Crawford/Thruxton	
G-BJFB	Mk 1A balloon	Aeroprint Tours	
G-BJFC	European E.8 balloon	P. D. Ridout	
G-BJFE	PA-18 Super Cub 95	P. H. Wilmot-Allistone	
G-BJFL	Sikorsky S-76A	Bristow Helicopters Ltd	
G-BJFM	Jodel D.120	J. V. George & P. A. Smith/Popham	
G-BJGF	Mk 1 balloon	D. & D. Eaves	

Notes	Reg.	Type	Owner or Operator
	G-BJGG	Mk 2 balloon	D. & D. Eaves
	G-BJGK	Cameron V-77 balloon	T. J. Orchard & ptnrs
	G-BJGL	Cremer balloon	G. Lowther
	G-BJGM	Unicorn UE.1A balloon	D. Eaves & P. D. Ridout
	G-BJGX	Sikorsky S-76A	Bristow Helicopters Ltd
	G-BJGY	Cessna F.172P	Lucca Wines Ltd
	G-BJHA	Cremer balloon	G. Cope
	G-BJHB	Mooney M.20J	Zitair Flying Club Ltd/Redhill
	G-BJHK	EAA Acro Sport	M. R. Holden
	G-BJHP	Osprey 1C balloon	N. J. Richardson
	G-BJHT	Thunder Ax7-65 balloon	A. H. & L. Symonds
	G-BJHV	Voisin Replica ★	Brooklands Museum of Aviation/Weybridge
	G-BJHW	Osprey 1C balloon	N. J. Richardson
	G-BJIA	Allport balloon	D. J. Allport
	G-BJIC	Dodo 1A balloon	P. D. Ridout
	G-BJID	Osprey 1B balloon	P. D. Ridout
	G-BJIG	Slingsby T.67A	G-BJIG Slingsby Syndicate
	G-BJIR	Cessna 550 Citation II	Gator Aviation Ltd
	G-BJIV	PA-18 Super Cub 180	Yorkshire Gliding Club (Pty) Ltd/ Sutton Bank
	G-BJJE	Dodo Mk 3 balloon	D. Eaves
	G-BJJN	Cessna F.172M	Ospreystar Ltd *(stored)*/Stapleford
	G-BJKF	SOCATA TB.9 Tampico	Venue Solutions
	G-BJKW	Wills Aera II	J. K. S. Wills
	G-BJKY	Cessna F.152	Air Charter & Travel Ltd/Ronaldsway
	G-BJLB	SNCAN NC.854S	M. J. Barnaby
	G-BJLC	Monnett Sonerai IIL	A. R. Ansell
	G-BJLE	Osprey 1B balloon	I. Chadwick
	G-BJLF	Unicorn UE.1C balloon	I. Chadwick
	G-BJLG	Unicorn UE.1B balloon	I. Chadwick
	G-BJLH	PA-18 Super Cub 95 (44)	Felthorpe Flying Group Ltd
	G-BJLO	PA-31-310 Turbo Navajo	RJ Aviation Ltd
	G-BJLX	Cremer balloon	P. W. May
	G-BJLY	Cremer balloon	P. Cannon
	G-BJMI	European E.84 balloon	D. Eaves
	G-BJMJ	Bensen B.8V	J. I. Hewlett
	G-BJML	Cessna 120	D. F. Lawlor/Inverness
	G-BJMO	Taylor JT.1 Monoplane	R. C. Mark
	G-BJMR	Cessna 310R	J. McL. Robinson/Sherburn
	G-BJMW	Thunder Ax8-105 balloon	G. M. Westley
	G-BJMX	Jarre JR.3 balloon	P. D. Ridout
	G-BJMZ	European EA.8A balloon	P. D. Ridout
	G-BJNA	Arena Mk 117P balloon	P. D. Ridout
	G-BJND	Osprey Mk 1E balloon	A. Billington & D. Whitmore
	G-BJNF	Cessna F.152	Exeter Flying Club Ltd
	G-BJNG	Slingsby T.67A	D. F. Hodgkinson
	G-BJNN	PA-38-112 Tomahawk	Scotia Safari Ltd/Prestwick
	G-BJNP	Rango NA.32 balloon	N. H. Ponsford
	G-BJNX	Cameron O-65 balloon	B. J. Petteford
	G-BJNY	Aeronca 11CC Super Chief	P. I. & D. M. Morgans
	G-BJNZ	PA-23 Aztec 250F	Bonus Aviation Ltd (G-FANZ) Cranfield
	G-BJOA	PA-28-181 Archer II	Channel Islands Aero Services Ltd
	G-BJOB	Jodel D.140C	T. W. M. Beck & M. J. Smith
	G-BJOE	Jodel D.120A	Forth Flying Group
	G-BJOP	BN-2B-26 Islander	Loganair Ltd/BA Express
	G-BJOT	Jodel D.117	R. Meares-Davies & ptnrs
	G-BJOV	Cessna F.150K	J. A. Boyd
	G-BJPI	Bede BD-5G	M. D. McQueen
	G-BJRA	Osprey Mk 4B balloon	E. Osborn
	G-BJRB	European E.254 balloon	D. Eaves
	G-BJRC	European E.84R balloon	D. Eaves
	G-BJRD	European E.84R balloon	D. Eaves
	G-BJRG	Osprey Mk 4B balloon	A. E. de Gruchy
	G-BJRH	Rango NA.36 balloon	N. H. Ponsford
	G-BJRP	Cremer balloon	M. D. Williams
	G-BJRR	Cremer balloon	M. D. Williams
	G-BJRV	Cremer balloon	M. D. Williams
	G-BJRW	Cessna U.206G	SPD Ltd
	G-BJSA	BN-2A-26 Islander	Police Aviation Services Ltd/Staverton
	G-BJSC	Osprey Mk 4D balloon	N. J. Richardson
	G-BJSD	Osprey Mk 4D balloon	N. J. Richardson
	G-BJSF	Osprey Mk 4B balloon	N. J. Richardson

Reg.	Type	Owner or Operator
G-BJSG	V.S.361 Spitfire LF.IXE (ML417)	Patina Ltd/Duxford
G-BJSI	Osprey Mk 1E balloon	N. J. Richardson
G-BJSP	Guido 1A Srs 61 balloon	G. A. Newsome
G-BJSS	Allport balloon	D. J. Allport
G-BJST	CCF T-6J Harvard IV	A. Winter/Germany
G-BJSU	Bensen B.8M	J. D. Newlyn
G-BJSV	PA-28-161 Warrior II	Airways Flight Training (Exeter) Ltd
G-BJSW	Thunder Ax7-65 balloon	Sandicliffe Garage Ltd
G-BJSX	Unicorn UE-1C balloon	N. J. Richardson
G-BJSZ	Piper J-3C-65 Cub	H. Gilbert
G-BJTB	Cessna A.150M	V. D. Speck/Clacton
G-BJTK	Taylor JT.1 Monoplane	E. N. Simmons
G-BJTO	Piper J-3C-65 Cub	K. R. Nunn
G-BJTP	PA-18 Super Cub 95 (115302)	J. T. Parkins
G-BJTW	European E.107 balloon	C. J. Brealey
G-BJTY	Osprey Mk 4B balloon	A. E. de Gruchy
G-BJUB	BVS Special 01 balloon	P. G. Wild
G-BJUC	Robinson R-22HP	Heli Services
G-BJUD	Robin DR.400/180R	Lasham Gliding Soc Ltd
G-BJUI	Osprey Mk 4B balloon	B. A. de Gruchy
G-BJUR	PA-38-112 Tomahawk	Truman Aviation Ltd/Tollerton
G-BJUS	PA-38-112 Tomahawk	Panshanger School of Flying
G-BJUV	Cameron V-20 balloon	P. Spellward
G-BJUY	Colt Ax7-77 Golf Ball SS balloon	Balloon Sports HB/Sweden
G-BJVC	Evans VP-2	C. J. Morris
G-BJVF	Thunder Ax3 balloon	A. G. R. Calder/California
G-BJVH	Cessna F.182Q	R. J. de Courcy Cuming/Wellesbourne
G-BJVJ	Cessna F.152	Cambridge Aero Club Ltd
G-BJVK	Grob G-109	B. Kimberley/Enstone
G-BJVM	Cessna 172N	I. C. MacLennan
G-BJVS	CP.1310-C3 Super Emeraude	A. E. Futter/Norwich
G-BJVT	Cessna F.152	Cambridge Aero Club Ltd
G-BJVU	Thunder Ax6-56 Bolt SS balloon	G. V. Beckwith
G-BJVV	Robin R.1180	Medway Flying Group Ltd/Rochester
G-BJVX	Sikorsky S-76A	Bristow Helicopters Ltd
G-BJWC	Saro Skeeter AOP.12 (XK 482)★	Sloane Helicopters Ltd/Sywell
G-BJWH	Cessna F.152 II	Plane Talking Ltd/Elstree
G-BJWI	Cessna F.172P	Bournemouth Flying Club Ltd
G-BJWJ	Cameron V-65 balloon	R. G. Turnbull & S. G. Forse
G-BJWO	BN-2A-26 Islander	Peterborough Parachute Centre Ltd (G-BAXC)/Sibson
G-BJWT	Wittman W.10 Tailwind	Tailwind Group
G-BJWV	Colt 17A balloon	D. T. Meyes
G-BJWW	Cessna F.172N	Air Charter & Travel Ltd/Blackpool
G-BJWX	PA-18 Super Cub 95	Acebell JWX Syndicate
G-BJWY	S-55 Whirlwind HAR.21 (WV198) ★	Solway Aviation Museum/Carlisle
G-BJWZ	PA-18 Super Cub 95	G-BJWZ Syndicate
G-BJXA	Slingsby T.67A	Comed Aviation Ltd/Blackpool
G-BJXB	Slingsby T.67A	A. K. Halvorsen/Barton
G-BJXK	Fournier RF-5	G-BJXK Syndicate/Cardiff
G-BJXP	Colt 56B balloon	H. J. Anderson
G-BJXX	PA-23 Aztec 250E	V. Bojovic
G-BJXZ	Cessna 172N	T. M. Jones/Egginton
G-BJYD	Cessna F.152 II	Cleveland Flying School Ltd/Teesside
G-BJYF	Colt 56A balloon	A. Van Wyk
G-BJYG	PA-28-161 Warrior II	S. R. Mitchell/Liverpool
G-BJYK	Jodel D.120A	T. Fox & D. A. Thorpe
G-BJYN	PA-38-112 Tomahawk	Panshanger School of Flying Ltd (G-BJTE)
G-BJZA	Cameron N-65 balloon	A. D. Pinner
G-BJZB	Evans VP-2	J. A. MacLeod
G-BJZF	D.H.82A Tiger Moth	R. Blast
G-BJZN	Slingsby T.67A	A. R. T. Marsland
G-BJZR	Colt 42A balloon	Selfish Balloon Group
G-BJZT	Cessna FA.152	E. Blanche/Biggin Hill
G-BJZX	Grob G.109	Oxfordshire Sport Flying Ltd/Enstone
G-BJZY	Bensen B.8MV	P. J. Dockerill
G-BKAC	Cessna F.150L	Motioncraft Ltd
G-BKAE	Jodel D.120	M. P. Wakem
G-BKAF	FRED Srs 2	J. Mc. D. Robinson
G-BKAM	Slingsby T.67M Firefly	A. J. Daley

Notes	Reg.	Type	Owner or Operator
	G-BKAO	Jodel D.112	R. Broadhead
	G-BKAR	PA-38-112 Tomahawk	Deltair/Liverpool
	G-BKAS	PA-38-112 Tomahawk	Deltair/Liverpool
	G-BKAY	R. Commander 114	The Rockwell Group
	G-BKAZ	Cessna 152	A. T. Wright
	G-BKBB	Hawker Fury Mk I (replica)	R. Landuyt/Belgium
	G-BKBD	Thunder Ax3 balloon	M. J. Casson
	G-BKBF	M.S.894A Rallye Minerva 220	J. A. Gibbs
	G-BKBN	SOCATA TB.10 Tobago	David Newby Associates
	G-BKBO	Colt 17A balloon	J. Armstrong & ptnrs
	G-BKBP	Bellanca 7GCBC Scout	H. G. Jefferies & Son/Little Gransden
	G-BKBR	Cameron Chateau 84 SS balloon	Forbes Europe Ltd/France
	G-BKBV	SOCATA TB.10 Tobago	N. R. Batey
	G-BKBW	SOCATA TB.10 Tobago	Merlin Aviation
	G-BKCB	PA-28R Cherokee Arrow 200	Western Air (Thruxton) Ltd
	G-BKCC	PA-28 Cherokee 180	Archer Aviation Ltd
	G-BKCE	Cessna F.172P II	Far North Flight Training/Wick
	G-BKCH	Thompson Cassutt	S. Alexander
	G-BKCI	Brügger MB.2 Colibri	E. R. Newall
	G-BKCJ	Oldfield Baby Great Lakes	S. V. Roberts/Sleap
	G-BKCL	PA-30 Twin Comanche 160C	Yorkair Ltd/Leeds
	G-BKCN	Currie Wot	N. A. A. Podmore
	G-BKCR	SOCATA TB.9 Tampico	A. Whitehouse
	G-BKCT	Cameron V-77 balloon	Quality Products General Engineering (Wickwar) Ltd
	G-BKCV	EAA Acro Sport II	T. N. Jinks
	G-BKCW	Jodel D.120A	A. Greene & G. Kerr/Dundee
	G-BKCX	Mudry CAARP CAP.10	Mahon & Associates/Booker
	G-BKCY	PA-38-112 Tomahawk II ★	Pool Aviation Ltd/Welshpool
	G-BKCZ	Jodel D.120A	M. R. Baker/Shoreham
	G-BKDC	Monnett Sonerai II	K. J. Towell
	G-BKDH	Robin DR.400/120	Airbase Aircraft Ltd
	G-BKDI	Robin DR.400/120	Cotswold Aero Club Ltd/Staverton
	G-BKDJ	Robin DR.400/120	M. D. Joyce & R. R. Wills
	G-BKDK	Thunder Ax7-77Z balloon	A. J. Byrne
	G-BKDP	FRED Srs 3	M. Whittaker
	G-BKDR	Pitts S-1S Special	T. J. Reeve
	G-BKDT	SE-5A (replica) (F943) ★	Yorkshire Air Museum/Elvington
	G-BKDX	Jodel DR.1050	DX Group
	G-BKEK	PA-32 Cherokee Six 300	S. W. Turley
	G-BKEP	Cessna F.172M	G-BKEP Group
	G-BKER	SE-5A (replica) (F5447)	N. K. Geddes
	G-BKET	PA-18 Super Cub 95	H. M. MacKenzie
	G-BKEU	Taylor JT.1 Monoplane	R. J. Whybrow & J. M. Springham
	G-BKEV	Cessna F.172M	J. W. Finlayson
	G-BKEW	Bell 206B JetRanger 3	N. R. Foster
	G-BKEX	Rich Prototype glider	D. B. Rich
	G-BKEY	FRED Srs 3	G. S. Taylor
	G-BKFC	Cessna F.152 II	Sulby Aerial Surveys Ltd
	G-BKFI	Evans VP-1	Foxtrot India Flying Group
	G-BKFK	Isaacs Fury II	G. G. C. Jones
	G-BKFL	Aerosport Scamp	J. Sherwood
	G-BKFM	QAC Quickie	F. Rothers
	G-BKFN	Bell 214ST	Bristow Helicopters Ltd
	G-BKFP	Bell 214ST	Bristow Helicopters Ltd
	G-BKFR	CP.301C Emeraude	C. R. Beard
	G-BKFW	P.56 Provost T.1 (XF597)	Sylmar Aviation & Services Ltd
	G-BKFZ	PA-28R Cherokee Arrow 200	Shacklewell Flying Group
	G-BKGA	M.S.892E Rallye 150GT	BJJ Aviation
	G-BKGB	Jodel D.120	B. A. Ridgway
	G-BKGC	Maule M.6-235	M. C. Woodhouse
	G-BKGD	Westland WG.30 Srs.100 ★	IHM/Weston-s-Mare
	G-BKGL	Beech D.18S (1164)	Propshop Ltd & T. Darrah/Duxford
	G-BKGM	Beech D.18S (HB275)	A. E. Hutton/North Weald
	G-BKGR	Cameron O-65 balloon	K. Kidner & L. E. More
	G-BKGT	SOCATA Rallye 110ST	Long Marston Flying Group
	G-BKGW	Cessna F.152-II	Leicestershire Aero Club Ltd
	G-BKHA	W.S.55 Whirlwind HAR.10 (XJ763) ★	C. J. Evans
	G-BKHD	Oldfield Baby Great Lakes	P. J. Tanulak/Sleap
	G-BKHG	Piper J-3C-65 Cub (479766)	K. G. Wakefield
	G-BKHJ	Cessna 182P	Augur Films Ltd
	G-BKHL	Thunder Ax9-140 balloon	R. Carr/France

Reg.	Type	Owner or Operator	Notes
G-BKHR	Luton LA-4 Minor	C. B. Buscombe & R. Goldsworthy	
G-BKHW	Stoddard-Hamilton Glasair IIRG	G. R. W. Monksfield & ptnrs	
G-BKHY	Taylor JT.1 Monoplane	B. C. J. O'Neill	
G-BKHZ	Cessna F.172P	L. R. Leader	
G-BKIA	SOCATA TB.10 Tobago	M. F. McGinn	
G-BKIB	SOCATA TB.9 Tampico	G. A. Vickers	
G-BKIC	Cameron V-77 balloon	C. A. Butler	
G-BKIF	Fournier RF-6B	G. G. Milton	
G-BKII	Cessna F.172M	M. S. Knight/Goodwood	
G-BKIJ	Cessna F.172M	V. Speck	
G-BKIK	Cameron DG-10 airship	Airspace Outdoor Advertising Ltd	
G-BKIN	Alon A.2A Aircoupe	D. W. Vernon	
G-BKIR	Jodel D.117	R. Shaw & D. M. Hardaker/Sherburn	
G-BKIS	SOCATA TB.10 Tobago	Wessex Flyers Group	
G-BKIT	SOCATA TB.9 Tampico	D. N. Garlick & ptnrs	
G-BKIY	Thunder Ax3 balloon	A. Hornak	
G-BKIZ	Cameron V-31 balloon	A. P. S. Cox	
G-BKJB	PA-18 Super Cub 135	Haimoss Ltd/O. Sarum	
G-BKJF	M.S.880B Rallye 100T	Journeyman Aviation Ltd	
G-BKJG	BN-2B-21 Islander	Pilatus BN Ltd/Bembridge	
G-BKJR	Hughes 269C	March Helicopters Ltd/Sywell	
G-BKJS	Jodel D.120A	Clipgate Flying Group	
G-BKJW	PA-23 Aztec 250E	Alan Williams Entertainments Ltd	
G-BKKN	Cessna 182R	R. A. Marven/Elstree	
G-BKKO	Cessna 182R	B. & G. Jebson Ltd/Crosland Moor	
G-BKKR	Rand KR-2	D. Beale & S. P. Gardner	
G-BKKZ	Pitts S-1D Special	J. A. Coutts	
G-BKLC	Cameron V-56 balloon	M. A. & J. R. H. Ashworth	
G-BKLJ	Westland Scout AH.1 ★	N. R. Windley	
G-BKLO	Cessna F.172M	Stapleford Flying Club Ltd	
G-BKLP	Cessna F.172N	Euroair Flying Club Ltd	
G-BKMA	Mooney M.20J Srs 201	Foxtrot Whisky Aviation	
G-BKMB	Mooney M.20J Srs 201	W. A. Cook & ptnrs	
G-BKMD	SC.7 Skyvan Srs 3	Army Parachute Association/Netheravon	
G-BKMG	Handley Page O/400 (replica)	Paralyser Group	
G-BKMI	V.S.359 Spitfire HF.VIIIc (MT928)	Aerial Museum (North Weald) Ltd	
G-BKMT	PA-32R-301 Saratoga SP	Severn Valley Aviation Group	
G-BKMX	Short SD3-60 Variant 100	Jersey European Airways (UK) Ltd	
G-BKNB	Cameron V-42 balloon	D. N. Close	
G-BKNI	GY-80 Horizon 160D	A. Hartigan & ptnrs/Fenland	
G-BKNL	Cameron D-96 airship	Sport Promotion SRL/Italy	
G-BKNO	Monnett Sonerai IIL	M. D. Hughes	
G-BKNP	Cameron V-77 balloon	E. K. K. & C. E. Odman	
G-BKNZ	CP.301A Emeraude	R. N. Crosland & P. R. Teager	
G-BKOA	SOCATA M.S.893E Rallye 180GT	N. F. Nowell	
G-BKOB	Z.326 Trener Master	W. G. V. Hall	
G-BKOT	Wassmer WA.81 Piranha	B. N. Rolfe	
G-BKOU	P.84 Jet Provost T.3 (XN637)	A. Haig-Thomas/North Weald	
G-BKPA	Hoffmann H-36 Dimona	A. Mayhew	
G-BKPB	Aerosport Scamp	E. D. Burke	
G-BKPC	Cessna A.185F	Black Knights Parachute Centre	
G-BKPD	Viking Dragonfly	E. P. Browne & G. J. Sargent	
G-BKPE	Jodel DR.250/160	J. S. & J. D. Lewer	
G-BKPK	Everett gyroplane	J. C. McHugh	
G-BKPN	Cameron N-77 balloon	R. H. Sanderson	
G-BKPS	AA-5B Tiger	A. E. T. Clarke	
G-BKPX	Jodel D.120A	N. H. Martin	
G-BKPY	SAAB 91B/2 Safir (56321) ★	Newark Air Museum	
G-BKPZ	Pitts S-1T Special	M. A. Frost	
G-BKRA	NA T-6G Texan (51-15227)	Pulsegrove Ltd/Shoreham	
G-BKRB	Cessna 172N	Saunders Caravans Ltd	
G-BKRF	PA-18 Super Cub 95	K. M. Bishop	
G-BKRH	Brügger MB.2 Colibri	M. R. Benwell	
G-BKRI	Cameron V-77 balloon	D. W. & J. M. Westlake	
G-BKRK	SNCAN Stampe SV-4C	Strathgadie Stampe Group	
G-BKRL	Chichester-Miles Leopard ★	(stored)/Cranfield	
G-BKRN	Beechcraft D.18S	A. A. Marshall & P. L. Turland	
G-BKRS	Cameron V-56 balloon	D. N. & L. J. Close	
G-BKRZ	Dragon G-77 balloon	J. R. Barber	
G-BKSB	Cessna T.310Q II	G. H. Smith & Son	
G-BKSC	Saro Skeeter AOP.12 (XN351)	R. A. L. Falconer	
G-BKSD	Colt 56A balloon	M. J. Casson	
G-BKSE	QAC Quickie Q.1	M. D. Burns	

Notes	Reg.	Type	Owner or Operator
	G-BKSP	Schleicher ASK.14	J. H. Bryson/Bellarena
	G-BKSS	Jodel D.150	D. H. Wilson-Spratt/Ronaldsway
	G-BKST	Rutan Vari-Eze	R. Towle
	G-BKSX	SNCAN Stampe SV-4C	C. A. Bailey & J. A. Carr
	G-BKTA	PA-18 Super Cub 95	M. J. Dyson & M. T. Clark
	G-BKTH	CCF Hawker Sea Hurricane IB (Z7015)	The Shuttleworth Collection/Duxford
	G-BKTM	PZL SZD-45A Ogar	Repclif Chemical Services Ltd
	G-BKTR	Cameron V-77 balloon	A. Palmer
	G-BKTV	Cessna F.152	Seawing Flying Club Ltd/Southend
	G-BKTY	SOCATA TB.10 Tobago	B. M. & G. M. McClelland
	G-BKTZ	Slingsby T.67M Firefly	D. C. Mayle & M. V. Pettifer (G-SFTV)
	G-BKUE	SOCATA TB.9 Tampico	W. J. Moore/Kirkbride
	G-BKUJ	Thunder Ax6-56 balloon	R. J. Bent
	G-BKUR	CP.301A Emeraude	R. Wells
	G-BKUS	Bensen B.8M	A. Charles
	G-BKUU	Thunder Ax7-77-1 balloon	D. A. Kozuba-Kozubska
	G-BKVA	SOCATA Rallye 180T	Buckminster Gliding Club Syndicate
	G-BKVB	SOCATA Rallye 110ST	C. Tilley
	G-BKVC	SOCATA TB.9 Tampico	H. P. Aubin-Parvu
	G-BKVE	Rutan Vari-Eze	Vanguard ACG Ltd & Temporal Songs Ltd (G-EZLT)
	G-BKVF	FRED Srs 3	J. M. Brightwell & A. J. Wright
	G-BKVG	Scheibe SF.25E Super Falke	G-BKVG Ltd
	G-BKVK	Auster AOP.9 (WZ662)	J. D. Butcher
	G-BKVL	Robin DR.400/160	Tatenhill Aviation
	G-BKVM	PA-18 Super Cub 150 (115684)	D. G. Caffrey
	G-BKVO	Pietenpol Air Camper	B. P. Waites
	G-BKVP	Pitts S-1D Special	P. J. Leggo
	G-BKVS	Bensen B.8M	A. J. Unwin
	G-BKVT	PA-23 Aztec 250E	BKS Surveys Ltd (G-HARV)
	G-BKVW	Airtour 56 balloon	L. D. & H. Vaughan
	G-BKVX	Airtour 56 balloon	P. Aldridge
	G-BKVY	Airtour 31 balloon	M. Davies
	G-BKWD	Taylor JT.2 Titch	E. H. Booker
	G-BKWE	Colt 17A balloon	Flying Pictures Ltd
	G-BKWG	PZL-104 Wilga 35	H. & C. Balfour Paul
	G-BKWR	Cameron V-65 balloon	K. J. Foster
	G-BKWW	Cameron O-77 balloon	A. M. Marten
	G-BKWY	Cessna F.152	Cambridge Aero Club
	G-BKXA	Robin R.2100	G-BKXA Group
	G-BKXD	SA.365N Dauphin 2	Bond Helicopters Ltd
	G-BKXF	PA-28R Cherokee Arrow 200	P. L. Brunton/Caernarfon
	G-BKXG	Cessna T.303	W. M. Ewington & Co Ltd
	G-BKXM	Colt 17A balloon	R. G. Turnbull
	G-BKXN	ICA IS-28M2A	T. J. Mills/Shobdon
	G-BKXO	Rutan LongEz	D. F. P. Finan
	G-BKXP	Auster AOP.6	B. J. & W. J. Ellis
	G-BKXR	D.31A Turbulent	M. B. Hill
	G-BKXX	Cameron V-65 balloon	L. J. H. Decabooter & L. P. Neirynck/Belgium
	G-BKZB	Cameron V-77 balloon	G. W. G. C. Sudlow
	G-BKZE	AS.332L Super Puma	British International Helicopters
	G-BKZF	Cameron V-56 balloon	A. D. Brice
	G-BKZG	AS.332L Super Puma	British International Helicopters
	G-BKZH	AS.332L Super Puma	British International Helicopters
	G-BKZI	Bell 206B JetRanger 2	Dolphin Property (Management) Ltd
	G-BKZM	Isaacs Fury II (K2060)	B. Jones
	G-BKZT	FRED Srs 2	D. C. Mayle & ptnrs
	G-BKZV	Bede BD-4A	G. I. J. Thomson
	G-BLAA	Fournier RF-5	A. D. Wren/Southend
	G-BLAC	Cessna FA.152	Tilbrook Industries Ltd
	G-BLAD	Thunder Ax7-77-1 balloon	P. J. Bish
	G-BLAF	Stolp SA.900 V-Star	P. R. Skeels
	G-BLAG	Pitts S-1D Special	P. M. Ambrose
	G-BLAH	Thunder Ax7-77-1 balloon	T. M. Donnelly
	G-BLAI	Monnett Sonerai IIL	T. Simpon
	G-BLAM	Jodel DR.360	D. J. Durell
	G-BLAT	Jodel 150	D. J. Dulborough & A. J. Court
	G-BLAX	Cessna FA.152	Bournemouth Flying Club Ltd
	G-BLAY	Robin HR.100/200B	B. A. Mills
	G-BLCA	Bell 206B JetRanger 3	R.M.H. Stainless Ltd

Reg.	Type	Owner or Operator
G-BLCG	SOCATA TB.10 Tobago	Charlie Golf Flying Group (G-BHES)/ Shoreham
G-BLCH	Colt 65D balloon	Balloon Flights Club Ltd
G-BLCI	EAA Acro Sport	M. R. Holden
G-BLCM	SOCATA TB.9 Tampico	Repclif Aviation Ltd/Liverpool
G-BLCP	Short SD3-60 Variant 100	Aer Arann
G-BLCT	Jodel DR.220 2+2	Christopher Robin Flying Group
G-BLCU	Scheibe SF.25B Falke	C. F. Sellers
G-BLCV	Hoffmann H-36 Dimona	R. L. Braithwaite
G-BLCW	Evans VP-1	K. D. Pearce
G-BLCY	Thunder Ax7-65Z balloon	C. M. George
G-BLDB	Taylor JT.1 Monoplane	C. J. Bush
G-BLDG	PA-25 Pawnee 260C	Ouse Gliding Club Ltd/Rufforth
G-BLDK	Robinson R-22	Warrenform Ltd
G-BLDV	BN-2B-26 Islander	Loganair Ltd/BA Express
G-BLEB	Colt 69A balloon	I. R. M. Jacobs
G-BLEJ	PA-28-161 Warrior II	Eglinton Flying Club Ltd
G-BLEP	Cameron V-65 balloon	D. Chapman
G-BLES	Stolp SA.750 Acroduster Too	G. N. Davies
G-BLET	Thunder Ax7-77-1 balloon	Servatruc Ltd
G-BLEW	Cessna F.182Q	D. J. Cross
G-BLEZ	SA.365N Dauphin 2	Bond Air Services/Aberdeen
G-BLFI	PA-28-181 Archer II	Bonus Aviation Ltd
G-BLFW	AA-5 Traveler	Grumman Club
G-BLFY	Cameron V-77 balloon	A. N. F. Pertwee
G-BLFZ	PA-31-310 Turbo Navajo C	London Executive Aviation Ltd
G-BLGH	Robin DR.300/180R	Booker Gliding Club Ltd
G-BLGO	Bensen B.8MV	F. Vernon
G-BLGR	Bell 47G-4A	Courteenhall Farms
G-BLGS	SOCATA Rallye 180T	Lasham Gliding Society Ltd
G-BLGT	PA-18 Super Cub 95	T. A. Reed/Dunkeswell
G-BLGV	Bell 206B JetRanger 3	Heliflight (UK) Ltd
G-BLGX	Thunder Ax7-65 balloon	The 45
G-BLHH	Jodel DR.315	Central Certification Service Ltd
G-BLHI	Colt 17A balloon	J. A. Folkes
G-BLHJ	Cessna F.172P	J. Easson/Edinburgh
G-BLHK	Colt 105A balloon	Hale Hot-Air Balloon Club
G-BLHM	PA-18 Super Cub 95	B. N. C. Mogg
G-BLHN	Robin HR.100/285	N. A. Onions
G-BLHR	GA-7 Cougar	T. E. Westley
G-BLHS	Bellanca 7ECA Citabria	N. J. F. Campbell
G-BLHW	Varga 2150A Kachina	Kachina Hotel Whiskey Group
G-BLID	D.H.112 Venom FB.50 (J-1605) ★	P. G. Vallance Ltd/Charlwood
G-BLIH	PA-18 Super Cub 135	I. R. F. Hammond
G-BLIK	Wallis WA-116/F/S	K. H. Wallis
G-BLIT	Thorp T-18 CW	K. B. Hallam
G-BLIW	P.56 Provost T.51 (177)	Provost Flying Group/Shoreham
G-BLIX	Saro Skeeter Mk 12 (XL809)	K. M. Scholes
G-BLIY	M.S.892A Rallye Commodore	A. J. Brasher & K. R. Haynes
G-BLJD	Glaser-Dirks DG.400	M. I. Gee
G-BLJF	Cameron O-65 balloon	M. D. Mitchell
G-BLJH	Cameron N-77 balloon	Phillair
G-BLJJ	Cessna 305 Bird Dog	P. Dawe
G-BLJM	Beech 95-B55 Baron	R. A. Perrot
G-BLJO	Cessna F.152	Redhill School of Flying Ltd
G-BLKA	D.H.112 Venom FB.54 (WR410)	De Havilland Aviation Ltd/Swansea
G-BLKK	Evans VP-1	D. J. Hunter
G-BLKL	D.31 Turbulent	D. L. Ripley
G-BLKM	Jodel DR.1051	T. C. Humphreys
G-BLKP	BAe Jetstream 3102	British Aerospace (Operations) Ltd/ Warton
G-BLKY	Beech 95-58 Baron	J. C. Hall
G-BLKZ	Pilatus P2-05	R. W. Hinton
G-BLLA	Bensen B.8M	K. T. Donaghey
G-BLLB	Bensen B.8M	D. H. Moss
G-BLLD	Cameron O-77 balloon	G. Birchall
G-BLLH	Jodel DR.220A 2+2	P. Chamberlain & D. E. Starkey
G-BLLM	PA-23 Aztec 250E	C. & M. Thomas (G-BBNM)/Cardiff
G-BLLN	PA-18 Super Cub 95	P. A. Layzell
G-BLLO	PA-18 Super Cub 95	D. G. & M. G. Margetts
G-BLLP	Slingsby T.67B	Cleveland Flying School Ltd/Teesside
G-BLLR	Slingsby T.67B	R. L. Brinklow/Biggin Hill
G-BLLS	Slingsby T.67B	Western Air (Thruxton) Ltd

Notes	Reg.	Type	Owner or Operator
	G-BLLV	Slingsby T.67B	R. L. Brinklow
	G-BLLW	Colt 56B balloon	G. Fordyce & ptnrs
	G-BLLZ	Rutan LongEz	R. S. Stoddart-Stones
	G-BLMA	Zlin 326 Trener Master	G. P. Northcott/Redhill
	G-BLMC	Avro 698 Vulcan B.2A (XM575) ★	Aeropark/E. Midlands
	G-BLME	Robinson R-22HP	Heli Air Ltd/Wellesbourne
	G-BLMG	Grob G.109B	Mike Golf Syndicate
	G-BLMI	PA-18 Super Cub 95	G-BLMI Flying Group
	G-BLMN	Rutan LongEz	G-BLMN Flying Group
	G-BLMP	PA-17 Vagabond	M. Austin/Popham
	G-BLMR	PA-18 Super Cub 150	Flying Services
	G-BLMT	PA-18 Super Cub 135	I. S. Runnalls
	G-BLMW	T.66 Nipper 3	S. L. Millar
	G-BLMX	Cessna FR.172H	C. J. W. Littler/Felthorpe
	G-BLMZ	Colt 105A balloon	M. D. Dickinson
	G-BLNJ	BN-2B-26 Islander	Loganair Ltd/BA Express
	G-BLNO	FRED Srs 3	L. W. Smith
	G-BLNW	BN-2B-26 Islander	Loganair Ltd/BA Express
	G-BLOB	Colt 31A balloon	Jacques W. Soukup Enterprises Ltd/USA
	G-BLOL	SNCAN Stampe SV-4A	Skysport Engineering (G-AXRP)
	G-BLOR	PA-30 Twin Comanche 160	R. L. C. Appleton
	G-BLOS	Cessna 185A (also flown with floats)	E. Brun
	G-BLOT	Colt Ax6-56B balloon	H. J. Anderson
	G-BLPA	Piper J-3C-65 Cub	C. J. Gray
	G-BLPB	Turner TSW Hot Two Wot	I. R. Hannah
	G-BLPE	PA-18 Super Cub 95	A. Haig-Thomas
	G-BLPF	Cessna FR.172G	W. A. F. Cuninghame
	G-BLPG	J/1N Alpha (16693)	R. Knowles (G-AZIH)
	G-BLPH	Cessna FRA.150L	New Aerobat Group/Shoreham
	G-BLPI	Slingsby T.67B	RAF Wyton Flying Group Ltd
	G-BLPP	Cameron V-77 balloon	L. P. Purfield
	G-BLRA	BAe 146-100	British Aerospace (Operations) Ltd
	G-BLRC	PA-18 Super Cub 135	A. J. McBurnie
	G-BLRD	MBB Bo.209 Monsun 150FV	M. D. Ward
	G-BLRF	Slingsby T.67C	Bristow Helicopters Ltd/Redhill
	G-BLRG	Slingsby T.67B	R. L. Brinklow
	G-BLRJ	Jodel DR.1051	M. P. Hallam
	G-BLRL	CP.301C-1 Emeraude	B. C. Davis
	G-BLRM	Glaser-Dirks DG.400	D. J. Barke/Tatenhill
	G-BLRN	D.H.104 Dove 8 (WB531) ★	Pionier Hangaar Collection/Lelystad
	G-BLRW	Cameron 77 Elephant SS balloon	Forbes Europe Inc/France
	G-BLSD	D.H.112 Venom FB.54 (J-1758) ★	R. Lamplough/North Weald
	G-BLSF	AA-5A Cheetah	J. P. E. Walsh (G-BGCK)
	G-BLSK	Colt 77A balloon	R. D. MacKenzie
	G-BLSM	H.S.125 Srs 700B	Dravidian Air Services Ltd/Heathrow
	G-BLST	Cessna 421C	Cecil Aviation Ltd/Cambridge
	G-BLSU	Cameron A-210 balloon	A. C. Elson
	G-BLSX	Cameron O-105 balloon	B. J. Petteford
	G-BLTA	Thunder Ax7-77A	K. A. Schlussler
	G-BLTC	D.31A Turbulent	G. P. Smith & A. W. Burton
	G-BLTF	Robinson R-22A	Stuart Taylor International
	G-BLTK	R. Commander 112TC	B. Rogalewski/Denham
	G-BLTM	Robin HR.200/100	B. D. Balcanquall
	G-BLTN	Thunder Ax7-65 balloon	J. A. Liddle
	G-BLTP	H.S.125 Srs 700B	Dravidian Air Services Ltd/Heathrow
	G-BLTR	Scheibe SF.25B Falke	V. Mallon/Germany
	G-BLTS	Rutan LongEz	R. W. Cutler
	G-BLTT	Slingsby T.67B	S. E. Marples/Newcastle
	G-BLTU	Slingsby T.67B	RAF Wyton Flying Club Ltd
	G-BLTV	Slingsby T.67B	R. L. Brinklow
	G-BLTW	Slingsby T.67B	Cheshire Air Training Services Ltd/ Liverpool
	G-BLTZ	SOCATA TB.10 Tobago	Martin Ltd/Biggin Hill
	G-BLUE	Colt Ax7-77A balloon	D. P. Busby
	G-BLUI	Thunder Ax7-65 balloon	S. Johnson
	G-BLUL	CEA Jodel DR.1051/M1	J. Owen
	G-BLUM	SA.365N Dauphin 2	Bond Helicopters Ltd
	G-BLUN	SA.365N Dauphin 2	Bond Helicopters Ltd
	G-BLUV	Grob G.109B	The 109 Flying Group/North Weald
	G-BLUX	Slingsby T.67M	R. L. Brinklow
	G-BLUZ	D.H.82 Queen Bee (LF858)	The Bee Keepers Group
	G-BLVA	Airtour AH-56 balloon	A. Van Wyk

Reg.	Type	Owner or Operator	Notes
G-BLVB	Airtour AH-56 balloon	T. C. Hinton	
G-BLVI	Slingsby T.67M	Hunting Aviation Ltd/Barkston Heath	
G-BLVK	CAARP CAP-10B	E. K. Coventry/Earls Colne	
G-BLVL	PA-28-161 Warrior II	Marair (Jersey) Ltd	
G-BLVN	Cameron N-77 balloon	Servo & Electronic Sales Ltd	
G-BLVS	Cessna 150M	Tindon Ltd	
G-BLVW	Cessna F.172H	R. & D. Holloway Ltd	
G-BLWB	Thunder Ax6-56 balloon	G. J. Bell	
G-BLWD	PA-34-200T Seneca	Acre 123 Ltd	
G-BLWE	Colt 90A balloon	Huntair Ltd/Germany	
G-BLWF	Robin HR.100/210	Starguide Ltd	
G-BLWH	Fournier RF-6B-100	I. R. March	
G-BLWM	Bristol M.1C (replica) (C4994) ★	RAF Museum/Hendon	
G-BLWP	PA-38-112 Tomahawk	A. Dodd/Booker	
G-BLWT	Evans VP-1	C. J. Bellworthy	
G-BLWV	Cessna F.152	Redhill Flying Club	
G-BLWW	Taylor Mini Imp Model C	M. K. Field	
G-BLWY	Robin 2161D	K. D. Boardman	
G-BLXA	SOCATA TB.20 Trinidad	Tango Bravo Aviation Ltd	
G-BLXF	Cameron V-77 balloon	P. Lawman	
G-BLXG	Colt 21A balloon	A. Walker	
G-BLXH	Fournier RF-3	A. Rawicz-Szczerbo	
G-BLXI	CP.1310-C3 Super Emeraude	R. Howard	
G-BLXO	Jodel 150	P. R. Powell	
G-BLXP	PA-28R Cherokee Arrow 200	M. B. Hamlett	
G-BLXR	AS.332L Super Puma	Bristow Helicopters Ltd	
G-BLXT	RAF SE-5A (B4863) ★	Museum of Army Flying/Middle Wallop	
G-BLXY	Cameron V-65 balloon	Gone With The Wind Ltd/Tanzania	
G-BLYD	SOCATA TB.20 Trinidad	Gourmet Trotters	
G-BLYE	SOCATA TB.10 Tobago	G. Hatton	
G-BLYK	PA-34-220T Seneca III	Oxford Aviation Services Ltd/Kidlington	
G-BLYP	Robin 3000/120	Weald Air Services/Headcorn	
G-BLYT	Airtour AH-77 balloon	I. J. & B. A. Taylor	
G-BLZA	Scheibe SF.25B Falke	Chiltern Gliding Club	
G-BLZB	Cameron N-65 balloon	D. Bareford	
G-BLZE	Cessna F.152 II	Flairhire Ltd (G-CSSC)/Redhill	
G-BLZF	Thunder Ax7-77 balloon	H. M. Savage	
G-BLZH	Cessna F.152 II	Plane Talking Ltd/Elstree	
G-BLZM	Rutan LongEz	Zulu Mike Group/Shoreham	
G-BLZN	Bell 206B JetRanger	Capital Helicopter Group Ltd	
G-BLZP	Cessna F.152	E. Midlands Flying School Ltd	
G-BLZS	Cameron O-77 balloon	M. M. Cobbold	
G-BLZT	Short SD3-60 Variant 100	Gill Airways Ltd/Newcastle	
G-BMAD	Cameron V-77 balloon	M. A. Stelling	
G-BMAL	Sikorsky S-76A	Bond Helicopters Ltd	
G-BMAO	Taylor JT.1 Monoplane	V. A. Wordsworth	
G-BMAV	AS.350B Ecureuil	Heli-Trans Ltd	
G-BMAX	FRED Srs 2	D. A. Arkley	
G-BMAY	PA-18 Super Cub 135	R. W. Davies	
G-BMBB	Cessna F.150L	Dacebow Aviation	
G-BMBC	PA-31-350 Navajo Chieftain	Air Navigation & Trading Ltd/Blackpool	
G-BMBE	PA-46-310P Malibu	Barfax Distributing Co Ltd & Glasdon Group Ltd/Blackpool	
G-BMBJ	Schempp-Hirth Janus CM	RAFGSA/Dishforth	
G-BMBS	Colt 105A balloon	H. G. Davies	
G-BMBW	Bensen B.8MR	M. E. Vahdat	
G-BMBZ	Scheibe SF.25E Super Falke	Cornish Gliding & Flying Club Ltd/ Perranporth	
G-BMCC	Thunder Ax7-77 balloon	A. K. & C. M. Russell	
G-BMCD	Cameron V-65 balloon	M. C. Drye	
G-BMCG	Grob G.109B	Lagerholm Finnimport Ltd/Booker	
G-BMCI	Cessna F.172H	A. B. Davis/Edinburgh	
G-BMCK	Cameron O-77 balloon	D. L. Smith	
G-BMCN	Cessna F.152	Lincoln Aero Club Ltd/Sturgate	
G-BMCS	PA-22 Tri-Pacer 135	Rickard Lazenby & Co. Ltd & T. A. Hodges	
G-BMCV	Cessna F.152	Leicestershire Aero Club Ltd	
G-BMCW	AS.332L Super Puma	Bristow Helicopters Ltd	
G-BMCX	AS.332L Super Puma	Bristow Helicopters Ltd	
G-BMDB	SE-5A (replica) (F235)	D. Biggs	
G-BMDC	PA-32-301 Saratoga	MacLaren Aviation/Newcastle	
G-BMDD	Slingsby T.29	A. R. Worters	

Notes	Reg.	Type	Owner or Operator
	G-BMDE	Pietenpol Air Camper	P. B. Childs
	G-BMDJ	Price Ax7-77S balloon	D. A. Kozuba-Kozubska
	G-BMDK	PA-34-220T Seneca III	Air Medical Ltd/Kidlington
	G-BMDO	ARV Super 2	R. M. Roullier
	G-BMDP	Partenavia P.64B Oscar 200	B. A. Parker
	G-BMDS	Jodel D.120	J. V. Thompson
	G-BMEA	PA-18 Super Cub 95	C. L. Towell
	G-BMEB	Rotorway Scorpion 145	L. S. Elliott
	G-BMEE	Cameron O-105 balloon	A. G. R. Calder/Los Angeles
	G-BMEG	SOCATA TB.10 Tobago	G. H. N. & R. V. Chamberlain
	G-BMEH	Jodel 150 Special Super Mascaret	Wm. Coupar Ltd
	G-BMET	Taylor JT.1 Monoplane	M. K. A. Blyth
	G-BMEU	Isaacs Fury II	G. R. G. Smith
	G-BMEV	PA-32RT-300T Turbo Lance II	Arrow Aviation Ltd
	G-BMEX	Cessna A.150K	N. A. M. Brain & C. Butler
	G-BMFD	PA-23 Aztec 250F	Gold Air International Ltd (G-BGYY)
	G-BMFG	Dornier Do.27A-4	R. F. Warner
	G-BMFI	PZL SZD-45A Ogar	S. L. Morrey
	G-BMFL	Rand KR-2	E. W. B. Comber & M. F. Leusby
	G-BMFN	QAC Quickie Tri-Q.200	A. H. Hartog
	G-BMFP	PA-28-161 Warrior II	Bravo-Mike-Fox-Papa Group
	G-BMFU	Cameron N-90 balloon	J. J. Rudoni
	G-BMFY	Grob G.109B	P. J. Shearer
	G-BMFZ	Cessna F.152 II	Cornwall Flying Club Ltd/Bodmin
	G-BMGB	PA-28R Cherokee Arrow 200	Malmesbury Specialist Cars
	G-BMGC	Fairey Swordfish Mk II (W5856)	F.A.A. Museum/Yeovilton
	G-BMGG	Cessna 152 II	Falcon Flying Services/Biggin Hill
	G-BMGR	Grob G.109B	M. Clarke & D. S. Hawes
	G-BMHA	Rutan LongEz	S. F. Elvins
	G-BMHC	Cessna U.206F	Fairmont Investments Ltd/Clacton
	G-BMHJ	Thunder Ax7-65 balloon	M. G. Robinson
	G-BMHL	Wittman W.8 Tailwind	T. G. Hoult
	G-BMHS	Cessna F.172M	Tango X-Ray Flying Group
	G-BMHT	PA-28RT-201T Turbo Arrow IV	Scalpay Ltd
	G-BMHZ	PA-28RT-201T Turbo Arrow IV	Arrow Association/Elstree
	G-BMID	Jodel D.120	G-BMID Flying Group
	G-BMIG	Cessna 172N	J. R. Nicholls/Sibson
	G-BMIH	H.S.125 Srs 700B	Surewings Ltd
	G-BMIM	Rutan LongEz	R. M. Smith
	G-BMIO	Stoddard-Hamilton Glasair RG	J. W. E. de Frayssinet & J. M. Ayres
	G-BMIP	Jodel D.112	M. T. Kinch
	G-BMIR	Westland Wasp HAS.1 (XT788) ★	Park Aviation Supply
	G-BMIS	Monnett Sonerai II	B. A. Bower/Thruxton
	G-BMIV	PA-28R-201T Turbo Arrow III	Maurice Mason Ltd
	G-BMIW	PA-28-181 Archer II	Oldbus Ltd
	G-BMIY	Oldfield Baby Great Lakes	J. B. Scott (G-NOME)
	G-BMJA	PA-32R-301 Saratoga SP	European Flyers/Blackbushe
	G-BMJB	Cessna 152 II	Bobbington Air Training School Ltd/ Halfpenny Green
	G-BMJC	Cessna 152 II	Cambridge Aero Club Ltd
	G-BMJD	Cessna 152 II	Donair Flying Club Ltd/E. Midlands
	G-BMJL	R. Commander 114	Wardair Ltd
	G-BMJM	Evans VP-1	M. J. Veary
	G-BMJN	Cameron O-65 balloon	P. M. Traviss
	G-BMJO	PA-34-220T Seneca III	Oxford Aviation Services Ltd/Kidlington
	G-BMJR	Cessna T.337H	John Roberts Services Ltd (G-NOVA)
	G-BMJS	Thunder Ax7-77 balloon	S. E. Burton
	G-BMJT	Beech 76 Duchess	Mike Osborne Properties Ltd
	G-BMJX	Wallis WA-116X	K. H. Wallis
	G-BMJY	Yakovlev C18M (07)	R. J. Lamplough/North Weald
	G-BMJZ	Cameron N-90 balloon	Bristol University Hot Air Ballooning Soc
	G-BMKB	PA-18 Super Cub 135	Cubair Flight Training Ltd/Redhill
	G-BMKC	Piper J-3C-65 Cub (329854)	R. J. H. Springall
	G-BMKD	Beech C90A King Air	A. E. Bristow
	G-BMKF	Jodel DR.221	L. Gilbert & ptnrs
	G-BMKG	PA-38-112 Tomahawk II	APB Leasing Ltd/Welshpool
	G-BMKI	Colt 21A balloon	A. C. Booth
	G-BMKJ	Cameron V-77 balloon	R. C. Thursby
	G-BMKK	PA-28R Cherokee Arrow 200	Colony Aviation
	G-BMKP	Cameron V-77 balloon	R. Bayly
	G-BMKR	PA-28-161 Warrior II	Field Flying Group (G-BGKR)/Goodwood
	G-BMKV	Thunder Ax7-77 balloon	A. Hornak & M. J. Nadel

Reg.	Type	Owner or Operator	Notes
G-BMKW	Cameron V-77 balloon	A. C. Garnett	
G-BMKY	Cameron O-65 balloon	A. R. Rich	
G-BMLB	Jodel D.120A	W. O. Brown	
G-BMLJ	Cameron N-77 balloon	C. J. Dunkley	
G-BMLK	Grob G.109B	Brams Syndicate/Rufforth	
G-BMLL	Grob G.109B	P. C. Broome	
G-BMLM	Beech 95-58 Baron	N. J. Webb	
G-BMLS	PA-28R-201 Arrow III	R. M. Shorter	
G-BMLT	Pietenpol Air Camper	W. E. R. Jenkins	
G-BMLU	Colt 90A balloon	L. J. Goldsmith	
G-BMLW	Cameron O-77 balloon	M. L. & L. P. Willoughby	
G-BMLX	Cessna F.150L	C. J. Freeman	
G-BMLZ	Cessna 421C	Hadagain Investments Ltd (G-OTAD/ G-BEVL)	
G-BMMC	Cessna T310Q	Cooper Clegg Ltd	
G-BMMD	Rand KR-2	D. J. Howell	
G-BMMF	FRED Srs 2	J. M. Jones	
G-BMMI	Pazmany PL.4A	M. K. Field/Sleap	
G-BMMJ	Siren PIK-30	J. R. Greig	
G-BMMK	Cessna 182P	G. G. Weston	
G-BMML	PA-38-112 Tomahawk	Western Air (Thruxton) Ltd	
G-BMMM	Cessna 152 II	Luton Flight Training Ltd	
G-BMMP	Grob G.109B	E. W. Reynolds	
G-BMMU	Thunder Ax8-105 balloon	N. Metcalfe	
G-BMMV	ICA-Brasov IS-28M2A	F. R. Temple-Brown	
G-BMMW	Thunder Ax7-77 balloon	P. A. George	
G-BMMY	Thunder Ax7-77 balloon	S. W. Wade & S. E. Hadley	
G-BMNL	PA-28R Cherokee Arrow 200	Arrow Flying Group	
G-BMNT	PA-34-220T Seneca III	Channel Airways Ltd	
G-BMNV	SNCAN Stampe SV-4D	Wessex Aviation & Transport Ltd	
G-BMNX	Colt 56A balloon	C. N. Marshall	
G-BMOE	PA-28R Cherokee Arrow 200	E. P. C. Robson	
G-BMOF	Cessna U206G	Wild Geese Skydiving Centre	
G-BMOG	Thunder Ax7-77A balloon	R. M. Boswell	
G-BMOH	Cameron N-77 balloon	P. J. Marshall & M. A. Clarke	
G-BMOI	Partenavia P.68B	Simmette Ltd	
G-BMOJ	Cameron V-56 balloon	S. R. Bridge	
G-BMOK	ARV Super 2	J. C. F. Dalton	
G-BMOL	PA-23 Aztec 250D	LDL Enterprises (G-BBSR)/Elstree	
G-BMOM	ICA-Brasov IS-28M2A	Brasov Flying Group	
G-BMOP	PA-28R-201T Turbo Arrow III	P. Murer	
G-BMOT	Bensen B.8M	Performance Associates Ltd	
G-BMOV	Cameron O-105 balloon	C. Gillott	
G-BMPC	PA-28-181 Archer II	C. J. & R. J. Barnes	
G-BMPD	Cameron V-65 balloon	D. E. & J. M. Hartland	
G-BMPL	Optica Industries OA.7 Optica	Sunhawk Ltd/North Weald	
G-BMPP	Cameron N-77 balloon	I. B. Lumsden	
G-BMPR	PA-28R-201 Arrow III	AH Flight Services Ltd	
G-BMPS	Strojnik S-2A	G. J. Green	
G-BMPY	D.H.82A Tiger Moth	S. M. F. Eisenstein	
G-BMRA	Boeing 757-236	British Airways	
G-BMRB	Boeing 757-236	British Airways	
G-BMRC	Boeing 757-236	British Airways	
G-BMRD	Boeing 757-236	British Airways	
G-BMRE	Boeing 757-236	British Airways	
G-BMRF	Boeing 757-236	British Airways	
G-BMRG	Boeing 757-236	British Airways	
G-BMRH	Boeing 757-236	British Airways	
G-BMRI	Boeing 757-236	British Airways	
G-BMRJ	Boeing 757-236	British Airways	
G-BMSA	Stinson HW.75 Voyager	M. A. Thomas (G-BCUM)/Barton	
G-BMSB	V.S.509 Spitfire IX (MJ627)	M. S. Bayliss (G-ASOZ)/Coventry	
G-BMSC	Evans VP-2	J. Holme	
G-BMSD	PA-28-181 Archer II	General Airline Ltd	
G-BMSE	Valentin Taifun 17E	A. J. Nurse	
G-BMSF	PA-38-112 Tomahawk	B. Catlow	
G-BMSG	SAAB 32A Lansen ★	J. E. Wilkie/Cranfield	
G-BMSL	FRED Srs 3	A. C. Coombe	
G-BMSU	Cessna 152 II	G-BMSU Group	
G-BMTA	Cessna 152 II	Turnhouse Flying Club	
G-BMTB	Cessna 152 II	Sky Leisure Aviation (Charters) Ltd	
G-BMTJ	Cessna 152 II	The Pilot Centre Ltd/Denham	
G-BMTL	Cessna F.152 II	Bournemouth Flying Club Ltd	

Notes	Reg.	Type	Owner or Operator
	G-BMTN	Cameron O-77 balloon	Industrial Services (MH) Ltd
	G-BMTO	PA-38-112 Tomahawk	Falcon Flying Services/Biggin Hill
	G-BMTR	PA-28-161 Warrior II	Aeroshow Ltd
	G-BMTS	Cessna 172N	Falcon Flying Services/Biggin Hill
	G-BMTU	Pitts S-1E Special	D. E. Hickson
	G-BMTX	Cameron V-77 balloon	J. A. Langley
	G-BMUD	Cessna 182P	M. E. Taylor
	G-BMUG	Rutan LongEz	P. Richardson & J. Shanley
	G-BMUJ	Colt Drachenfisch balloon	Virgin Airship & Balloon Co Ltd
	G-BMUK	Colt UFO balloon	Virgin Airship & Balloon Co Ltd
	G-BMUL	Colt Kindermond balloon	Virgin Airship & Balloon Co Ltd
	G-BMUN	Cameron 78 Harley SS balloon	Forbes Europe Inc/France
	G-BMUO	Cessna A.152	Sky Leisure Aviation (Charters) Ltd
	G-BMUT	PA-34-200T Seneca II	Newcastle Aeroplane Co Ltd
	G-BMUU	Thunder Ax7-77 balloon	G. Anorewartha
	G-BMUZ	PA-28-161 Warrior II	Newcastle-upon-Tyne Aero Club Ltd
	G-BMVA	Scheibe SF.25B Falke	M. L. Jackson
	G-BMVB	Cessna F.152 II	LAC (Enterprises) Ltd/Barton
	G-BMVG	QAC Quickie Q.1	P. M. Wright
	G-BMVI	Cameron O-105 balloon	Heart of England Balloons
	G-BMVJ	Cessna 172N	Green Aviation Associates Ltd
	G-BMVL	PA-38-112 Tomahawk	Airways Aero Associations Ltd/Booker
	G-BMVM	PA-38-112 Tomahawk	Airways Aero Associations Ltd/Booker
	G-BMVO	Cameron O-77 balloon	Warners Motors (Leasing) Ltd
	G-BMVT	Thunder Ax7-77A balloon	M. L. & L. P. Willoughby
	G-BMVU	Monnett Moni	J. Holme
	G-BMVW	Cameron O-65 balloon	S. P. Richards
	G-BMWA	Hughes 269C	P. J. Brown
	G-BMWE	ARV Super 2	R. J. A. Noble
	G-BMWF	ARV Super 2	N. R. Beale
	G-BMWM	ARV Super 2	P. G. Hayward
	G-BMWN	Cameron 80 SS Temple balloon	Forbes Europe Inc/France
	G-BMWR	R. Commander 112A	M. & J. Edwards
	G-BMWU	Cameron N-42 balloon	Balloon Preservation Flying Group
	G-BMWV	Putzer Elster B	E. A. J. Hibbard
	G-BMXA	Cessna 152 II	E. Alexander
	G-BMXB	Cessna 152 II	H. Daines Electronics Ltd
	G-BMXC	Cessna 152 II	European Flyers/Blackbushe
	G-BMXD	F.27 Friendship Mk 500	BAC Express Airlines Ltd
	G-BMXJ	Cessna F.150L	Arrow Aircraft Group
	G-BMXL	PA-38-112 Tomahawk	Airways Aero Associations Ltd/Booker
	G-BMXX	Cessna 152 II	Aerohire Ltd/Halfpenny Green
	G-BMYC	SOCATA TB.10 Tobago	E. A. Grady
	G-BMYD	Beech A36 Bonanza	Seabeam Partners Ltd
	G-BMYF	Bensen B.8M	G. Callaghan
	G-BMYG	Cessna FA.152	Edinburgh Air Centre Ltd
	G-BMYI	AA-5 Traveler	W. C. & S. C. Westran
	G-BMYJ	Cameron V-65 balloon	A. Lutz
	G-BMYN	Colt 77A balloon	Spectacles Balloon Group
	G-BMYP	Fairey Gannet AEW.3 (XL502)	D. Copley
	G-BMYS	Thunder Ax7-77Z balloon	J. E. Weidema/Netherlands
	G-BMYU	Jodel D.120	P. M. Standen & A. J. Roxburgh
	G-BMZA	Air Command 503 Commander	R. W. Husband
	G-BMZB	Cameron N-77 balloon	D. C. Eager
	G-BMZE	SOCATA TB.9 Tampico	R. F. Keene
	G-BMZF	WSK-Mielec LiM-2 (MiG-15bis) (01420) ★	F.A.A. Museum/Yeovilton
	G-BMZG	QAC Quickie Q.2	R. Dann
	G-BMZN	Everett gyroplane	K. Ashford
	G-BMZP	Everett gyroplane	M. N. Morris-Jones
	G-BMZS	Everett gyroplane	L. W. Cload
	G-BMZW	Bensen B.8MR	P. D. Widdicombe
	G-BMZX	Wolf W-II Boredom Fighter (146-11042)	A. R. Meakin & S. W. Watkins
	G-BMZZ	Stephens Akro Z	F. Actis/Switzerland
	G-BNAD	Rand KR-2	P. J. Brookman
	G-BNAG	Colt 105A balloon	R. W. Batchelor
	G-BNAI	Wolf W-II Boredom Fighter (146-11083)	P. J. D. Gronow
	G-BNAJ	Cessna 152 II	Galair Ltd/Biggin Hill
	G-BNAN	Cameron V-65 balloon	A. M. Lindsay
	G-BNAO	Colt AS-105 airship	Heather Flight Ltd

Reg.	Type	Owner or Operator	Notes
G-BNAR	Taylor JT.1 Monoplane	C. J. Smith	
G-BNAU	Cameron V-65 balloon	C. L. E. Lewis	
G-BNAW	Cameron V-65 balloon	A. Walker	
G-BNBL	Thunder Ax7-77 balloon	E. Stivala	
G-BNBR	Cameron N-90 balloon	Airborne Promotions Ltd	
G-BNBU	Bensen B.8MV	B. A. Lyford	
G-BNBV	Thunder Ax7-77 balloon	J. M. Robinson	
G-BNBW	Thunder Ax7-77 balloon	I. S. & S. W. Watthews	
G-BNBY	Beech 95-B55A Baron	Earthline Aviation Ltd (G-AXXR)	
G-BNBZ	LET L-200D Morava	C. A. Suckling/Redhill	
G-BNCB	Cameron V-77 balloon	Tyred & Battered Balloon Group	
G-BNCC	Thunder Ax7-77 balloon	C. J. Burnhope	
G-BNCE	G.159 Gulfstream 1 ★	(stored)/Aberdeen	
G-BNCH	Cameron V-77 balloon	Royal Engineers Balloon Club	
G-BNCJ	Cameron V-77 balloon	I. S. Bridge	
G-BNCK	Cameron V-77 balloon	G. Randall/Germany	
G-BNCL	WG.13 Lynx HAS.2 (XX469) ★	Lancashire Fire Brigade HQ/Lancaster	
G-BNCM	Cameron N-77 balloon	C. A. Stone	
G-BNCN	Glaser-Dirks DG.400 (421)	M. C. Costin/Husbands Bosworth	
G-BNCO	PA-38-112 Tomahawk	D. K. Walker	
G-BNCR	PA-28-161 Warrior II	Airways Aero Associations Ltd/Booker	
G-BNCS	Cessna 180	C. Elwell Transport Ltd	
G-BNCU	Thunder Ax7-77 balloon	P. Mann	
G-BNCV	Bensen B.8	J. M. Benson	
G-BNCX	Hawker Hunter T.7 (XL621) ★	Brooklands Museum of Aviation/ Weybridge	
G-BNCZ	Rutan LongEz	P. A. Ellway	
G-BNDG	Wallis WA-201/R Srs1	K. H. Wallis	
G-BNDN	Cameron V-77 balloon	J. A. Smith	
G-BNDO	Cessna 152 II	Simair Ltd	
G-BNDP	Brügger MB.2 Colibri	J. P. Kynaston	
G-BNDR	SOCATA TB.10 Tobago	A. N. Reardon/Woodvale	
G-BNDT	Brügger MB.2 Colibri	Colibri Flying Group/Waddington	
G-BNDV	Cameron N-77 balloon	R. E. Jones	
G-BNDW	D.H.82A Tiger Moth	N. D. Welch	
G-BNDY	Cessna 425-1	Standard Aviation Ltd/Newcastle	
G-BNED	PA-22 Tri-Pacer 135	P. Storey	
G-BNEE	PA-28R-201 Arrow III	Britannic Management (Aviation) Ltd	
G-BNEI	PA-34-200T Seneca II	P. J. Morrison	
G-BNEJ	PA-38-112 Tomahawk II	V. C. & S. G. Swindell	
G-BNEK	PA-38-112 Tomahawk II	APB Leasing Ltd/Welshpool	
G-BNEL	PA-28-161 Warrior II	S. C. Westran	
G-BNEN	PA-34-200T Seneca II	Warwickshire Aerocentre Ltd	
G-BNEO	Cameron V-77 balloon	J. G. O'Connell	
G-BNES	Cameron V-77 balloon	G. Wells	
G-BNET	Cameron O-84 balloon	C. & A. I. Gibson	
G-BNEV	Viking Dragonfly	N. W. Eyre	
G-BNEX	Cameron O-120 balloon	The Balloon Club Ltd	
G-BNFG	Cameron O-77 balloon	Capital Balloon Club Ltd	
G-BNFI	Cessna 150J	T. D. Aitken	
G-BNFK	Cameron 89 Egg SS balloon	Forbes Europe Inc/France	
G-BNFM	Colt 21A balloon	M. E. Dworski/France	
G-BNFN	Cameron N-105 balloon	P. Glydon	
G-BNFO	Cameron V-77 balloon	D. Newton & M. Sherbourn	
G-BNFP	Cameron O-84 balloon	B. F. G. Ribbans	
G-BNFR	Cessna 152 II	Eastern Executive Air Charter Ltd/ Southend	
G-BNFS	Cessna 152 II	C & S Aviation Ltd/Halfpenny Green	
G-BNFV	Robin DR.400/120	J. P. A. Freeman	
G-BNGE	Auster AOP.6 (TW536)	M. Pocock	
G-BNGJ	Cameron V-77 balloon	Latham Timber Centres (Holdings) Ltd	
G-BNGN	Cameron V-77 balloon	C. B. Leeder	
G-BNGO	Thunder Ax7-77 balloon	J. S. Finlan	
G-BNGP	Colt 77A balloon	Headland Services Ltd	
G-BNGR	PA-38-112 Tomahawk	Teesside Flight Centre Ltd	
G-BNGS	PA-38-112 Tomahawk	Frontline Aviation Ltd/Teesside	
G-BNGT	PA-28-181 Archer II	Berry Air/Edinburgh	
G-BNGV	ARV Super 2	N. A. Onions	
G-BNGW	ARV Super 2	Southern Gas Turbines Ltd	
G-BNGX	ARV Super 2	Southern Gas Turbines Ltd	
G-BNGY	ARV Super 2	M. T. Manwaring(G-BMWL)	
G-BNHB	ARV Super 2	I. M. Godfrey-Davies	
G-BNHE	ARV Super 2	L. J. Joyce/Liverpool	

Notes	Reg.	Type	Owner or Operator
	G-BNHG	PA-38-112 Tomahawk II	D. A. Whitmore
	G-BNHI	Cameron V-77 balloon	C. J. Nicholls
	G-BNHJ	Cessna 152 II	The Pilot Centre Ltd/Denham
	G-BNHK	Cessna 152 II	General Airline Ltd
	G-BNHN	Colt Ariel Bottle SS balloon ★	British Balloon Museum/Newbury
	G-BNHO	Thunder Ax7-77 balloon	M. J. Forster
	G-BNHP	Saffrey S.330 balloon	N. H. Ponsford *Alpha II*
	G-BNHT	Fournier RF-3	G-BNHT Group
	G-BNID	Cessna 152 II	Mercia Aircraft Leasing & Sales Ltd/ Coventry
	G-BNIE	Cameron O-160 balloon	D. K. Fish
	G-BNIF	Cameron O-56 balloon	D. V. Fowler
	G-BNII	Cameron N-90 balloon	Topless Balloon Group
	G-BNIJ	SOCATA TB.10 Tobago	Flying Start Aviation
	G-BNIK	Robin HR.200/120	A. W. Eldridge
	G-BNIM	PA-38-112 Tomahawk	Aurs Aviation Ltd
	G-BNIN	Cameron V-77 balloon	Cloud Nine Balloon Group
	G-BNIO	Luscombe 8A Silvaire	G. G. Pugh
	G-BNIP	Luscombe 8A Silvaire	D. R. C. Hunter & S. Maric
	G-BNIU	Cameron O-77 balloon	ASTP SRL/Belgium
	G-BNIV	Cessna 152 II	Aerohire Ltd/Halfpenny Green
	G-BNIW	Boeing Stearman PT-17	R. C. Goold
	G-BNIZ	F.27 Friendship Mk.600	Channel Express (Air Services) Ltd/Bournemouth
	G-BNJA	WAG-Aero Wag-a-Bond	B. E. Maggs
	G-BNJB	Cessna 152 II	Klingair Ltd/Conington
	G-BNJC	Cessna 152 II	Stapleford Flying Club Ltd
	G-BNJD	Cessna 152 II	Southern Air Ltd/Shoreham
	G-BNJF	PA-32RT-300 Lance II	PFB Aviation Ltd
	G-BNJG	Cameron O-77 balloon	A. M. Figiel
	G-BNJH	Cessna 152 II	Turnhouse Flying Club
	G-BNJL	Bensen B.8	C. G. Ponsford
	G-BNJM	PA-28-161 Warrior II	Teesside Flight Centre Ltd
	G-BNJO	QAC Quickie Q.2	J. D. McKay
	G-BNJR	PA-28RT-201T Turbo Arrow IV	Intelligent Micro Software Ltd
	G-BNJT	PA-28-161 Warrior II	Hawarden Flying Group
	G-BNJU	Cameron 80 Bust SS balloon	Ballon Team Bonn GmbH & Co Kg/ Germany
	G-BNJX	Cameron N-90 balloon	Mars UK Ltd
	G-BNJZ	Cassutt Racer IIIM	A. P. Meredith & J. R. Burry
	G-BNKC	Cessna 152 II	Herefordshire Aero Club Ltd/Shobdon
	G-BNKD	Cessna 172N	Bristol Flying Centre Ltd
	G-BNKE	Cessna 172N	Kilo Echo Flying Group
	G-BNKF	Colt AS-56 airship	Formtrack Ltd/USA
	G-BNKH	PA-38-112 Tomahawk	Goodwood Terrena Ltd
	G-BNKI	Cessna 152 II	RAF Halton Aeroplane Club Ltd
	G-BNKP	Cessna 152 II	Fairmont Investments Ltd/Clacton
	G-BNKR	Cessna 152 II	Keen Leasing (IOM) Ltd
	G-BNKS	Cessna 152 II	Shropshire Aero Club Ltd/Sleap
	G-BNKT	Cameron O-77 balloon	British Airways PLC
	G-BNKV	Cessna 152 II	Premiair Flying Club Ltd/Shoreham
	G-BNLA	Boeing 747-436	British Airways
	G-BNLB	Boeing 747-436	British Airways
	G-BNLC	Boeing 747-436	British Airways
	G-BNLD	Boeing 747-436	British Airways
	G-BNLE	Boeing 747-436	British Airways
	G-BNLF	Boeing 747-436	British Airways
	G-BNLG	Boeing 747-436	British Airways
	G-BNLH	Boeing 747-436	British Airways
	G-BNLI	Boeing 747-436	British Airways
	G-BNLJ	Boeing 747-436	British Airways
	G-BNLK	Boeing 747-436	British Airways
	G-BNLL	Boeing 747-436	British Airways
	G-BNLM	Boeing 747-436	British Airways
	G-BNLN	Boeing 747-436	British Airways
	G-BNLO	Boeing 747-436	British Airways
	G-BNLP	Boeing 747-436	British Airways
	G-BNLR	Boeing 747-436	British Airways
	G-BNLS	Boeing 747-436	British Airways
	G-BNLT	Boeing 747-436	British Airways
	G-BNLU	Boeing 747-436	British Airways
	G-BNLV	Boeing 747-436	British Airways
	G-BNLW	Boeing 747-436	British Airways

Reg.	Type	Owner or Operator	Notes
G-BNLX	Boeing 747-436	British Airways	
G-BNLY	Boeing 747-436	British Airways	
G-BNLZ	Boeing 747-436	British Airways	
G-BNMA	Cameron O-77 balloon	A. Wilkes & N. Woodham	
G-BNMB	PA-28-151 Warrior	Britannia Airways Ltd/Luton	
G-BNMC	Cessna 152 II	M. L. Jones/Egginton	
G-BNMD	Cessna 152 II	T. M. Jones/Egginton	
G-BNME	Cessna 152 II	Northamptonshire School of Flying Ltd/ Sywell	
G-BNMF	Cessna 152 II	Aerohire Ltd	
G-BNMG	Cameron O-77 balloon	J. H. Turner	
G-BNMH	Pietenpol Air Camper	N. M. Hitchman	
G-BNMI	Colt Flying Fantasy SS balloon	Air 2 Air Ltd	
G-BnmK	Dornier Do.27A-1	G. Mackie	
G-BNML	Rand KR-2	R. F. Cresswell	
G-BNMO	Cessna TR.182RG	Kenrye Developments Ltd	
G-BNMT	Short SD3-60 Variant 100	Loganair Ltd	
G-BNMU	Short SD3-60 Variant 100	Loganair Ltd	
G-BNMW	Short SD3-60 Variant 100	Loganair Ltd	
G-BNMX	Thunder Ax7-77 balloon	S. A. D. Beard	
G-BNNA	Stolp SA.300 Starduster Too	D. F. Simpson	
G-BNNE	Cameron N-77 balloon	Balloon Flights International Ltd	
G-BNNG	Cessna T.337D	Somet Ltd (G-COLD)	
G-BNNI	Boeing 727-276	Sabre Airways Ltd/Gatwick	
G-BNNK	Boeing 737-4Q8	GB Airways Ltd	
G-BNNL	Boeing 737-4Q8	GB Airways Ltd	
G-BNNO	PA-28-161 Warrior II	Tindon Ltd/Little Snoring	
G-BNNR	Cessna 152	Sussex Flying Club Ltd/Shoreham	
G-BNNS	PA-28-161 Warrior II	Warrior Aircraft Syndicate	
G-BNNT	PA-28-151 Warrior	S. T. Gilbert & D. J. Kirkwood	
G-BNNU	PA-38-112 Tomahawk	Edinburgh Flying Club Ltd	
G-BNNX	PA-28R-201T Turbo Arrow III	P. J. Lague	
G-BNNY	PA-28-161 Warrior II	Falcon Flying Services/Biggin Hill	
G-BNNZ	PA-28-161 Warrior II	European Flyers	
G-BNOB	Wittman W.8 Tailwind	M. Robson-Robinson	
G-BNOE	PA-28-161 Warrior II	Sherburn Aero Club Ltd	
G-BNOF	PA-28-161 Warrior II	Tayside Aviation Ltd/Dundee	
G-BNOG	PA-28-161 Warrior II	BAe Flying College/Prestwick	
G-BNOH	PA-28-161 Warrior II	Sherburn Aero Club Ltd	
G-BNOI	PA-28-161 Warrior II	BAe Flying College/Prestwick	
G-BNOJ	PA-28-161 Warrior II	BAe (Warton) Flying Club	
G-BNOK	PA-28-161 Warrior II	BAe Flying College/Prestwick	
G-BNOL	PA-28-161 Warrior II	BAe Flying College/Prestwick	
G-BNOM	PA-28-161 Warrior II	Sherburn Aero Club Ltd	
G-BNON	PA-28-161 Warrior II	Tayside Aviation Ltd/Dundee	
G-BNOO	PA-28-161 Warrior II	BAe Flying College/Prestwick	
G-BNOP	PA-28-161 Warrior II	BAe (Warton) Flying Club	
G-BNOR	PA-28-161 Warrior II	BAe Flying College/Prestwick	
G-BNOS	PA-28-161 Warrior II	BAe Flying College/Prestwick	
G-BNOT	PA-28-161 Warrior II	BAe Flying College/Prestwick	
G-BNOU	PA-28-161 Warrior II	BAe Flying College/Prestwick	
G-BNOV	PA-28-161 Warrior II	BAe Flying College/Prestwick	
G-BNOW	PA-28-161 Warrior II	BAe Flying College/Prestwick	
G-BNOX	Cessna R.182RG II	D. C. Sherhered	
G-BNOZ	Cessna 152 II	Bobbington Air Training School Ltd	
G-BNPE	Cameron N-77 balloon	Kent Garden Centres Ltd	
G-BNPF	Slingsby T.31M	S. Luck & ptnrs	
G-BNPH	P.66 Pembroke C.1 (WV740)	M. J. Willing/Jersey	
G-BNPI	Colt 21A balloon	Virgin Airship & Balloon Co Ltd	
G-BNPL	PA-38-112 Tomahawk	Modern Air (UK) Ltd/Fowlmere	
G-BNPM	PA-38-112 Tomahawk	Papa Mike Aviation Ltd	
G-BNPN	PA-28-181 Archer II	Z. Mahmood/Elstree	
G-BNPO	PA-28-181 Archer II	Bonus Aviation Ltd	
G-BNPU	P.66 Pembroke (XL929) ★	D-Day Museum/Shoreham	
G-BNPV	Bowers Fly-Baby 1B	J. G. Day & R. Gauld-Galliers	
G-BNPY	Cessna 152 II	Traffic Management Services/Gamston	
G-BNPZ	Cessna 152 II	C & S Aviation Ltd/Halfpenny Green	
G-BNRA	SOCATA TB.10 Tobago	Double D Airgroup	
G-BNRG	PA-28-161 Warrior II	RAF Brize Norton Flying Club Ltd	
G-BNRI	Cessna U.206G	Target Technology Ltd	
G-BNRK	Cessna 152 II	Redhill Flying Club	
G-BNRL	Cessna 152 II	J. R. Nicholls/Sibson	
G-BNRP	PA-28-181 Archer II	Bonua Aviation Ltd/Cranfield	

Notes	Reg.	Type	Owner or Operator
	G-BNRR	Cessna 172P	Cornwall Flying Club Ltd/Bodmin
	G-BNRX	PA-34-200T Seneca II	Truman Aviation Ltd/Tollerton
	G-BNRY	Cessna 182Q	Reefly Ltd
	G-BNRZ	Robinson R-22B	R. D. Jordan/Cranfield
	G-BNSG	PA-28R-201 Arrow III	Armada Aviation Ltd/Redhill
	G-BNSI	Cessna 152 II	Sky Leisure Aviation (Charters) Ltd
	G-BNSL	PA-38-112 Tomahawk II	APB Leasing Ltd/Welshpool
	G-BNSM	Cessna 152 II	Cornwall Flying Club Ltd/Bodmin
	G-BNSN	Cessna 152 II	M. K. Barnes & G. N. Olson/Bristol
	G-BNSO	Slingsby T.67M Mk II	Hunting Aviation Ltd/Barkston Heath
	G-BNSP	Slingsby T.67M Mk II	Hunting Aviation Ltd/Barkston Heath
	G-BNSR	Slingsby T.67M Mk II	Hunting Aviation Ltd/Barkston Heath
	G-BNST	Cessna 172N	Martin Aviation
	G-BNSU	Cessna 152 II	Channel Aviation Ltd
	G-BNSV	Cessna 152 II	Channel Aviation Ltd
	G-BNSY	PA-28-161 Warrior II	Carill Aviation Ltd/Southampton
	G-BNSZ	PA-28-161 Warrior II	Carill Aviation Ltd/Southampton
	G-BNTC	PA-28RT-201T Turbo Arrow IV	M. F. Lassan
	G-BNTD	PA-28-161 Warrior II	A. M. Patel & ptnrs
	G-BNTE	FFA AS.202/18A4 Bravo	BAe Flying College Ltd/Prestwick
	G-BNTF	FFA AS.202/18A4 Bravo	BAe Flying College Ltd/Prestwick
	G-BNTH	FFA AS.202/18A4 Bravo	BAe Flying College Ltd/Prestwick
	G-BNTI	FFA AS.202/18A4 Bravo	BAe Flying College Ltd/Prestwick
	G-BNTJ	FFA AS.202/18A4 Bravo	BAe Flying College Ltd/Prestwick
	G-BNTK	FFA AS.202/18A4 Bravo	BAe Flying College Ltd/Prestwick
	G-BNTL	FFA AS.202/18A4 Bravo	BAe Flying College Ltd/Prestwick
	G-BNTM	FFA AS.202/18A4 Bravo	BAe Flying College Ltd/Prestwick
	G-BNTN	FFA AS.202/18A4 Bravo	BAe Flying College Ltd/Prestwick
	G-BNTO	FFA AS.202/18A4 Bravo	BAe Flying College Ltd/Prestwick
	G-BNTP	Cessna 172N	Westnet Ltd
	G-BNTS	PA-28RT-201T Turbo Arrow IV	Nasaire Ltd/Liverpool
	G-BNTT	Beech 76 Duchess	Airtime Maintenance Ltd
	G-BNTW	Cameron V-77 balloon	P. Goss
	G-BNTZ	Cameron N-77 balloon	Balloon Team
	G-BNUC	Cameron O-77 balloon	T. J. Bucknall
	G-BNUI	Rutan Vari-Eze	I. T. Kennedy & K. H. McConnell
	G-BNUL	Cessna 152 II	Exeter Air Training School Ltd
	G-BNUN	Beech 95-58PA Baron	British Midland Airways Ltd/E. Midlands
	G-BNUO	Beech 76 Duchess	G. A. F. Tilley
	G-BNUR	Cessna 172E	Cardiff Aeronautical Services Ltd
	G-BNUS	Cessna 152 II	Stapleford Flying Club Ltd
	G-BNUT	Cessna 152 Turbo	Stapleford Flying Club Ltd
	G-BNUV	PA-23 Aztec 250F	L. J. Martin
	G-BNUX	Hoffmann H-36 Dimona	Buckminster Dimona Syndicate
	G-BNUY	PA-38-112 Tomahawk II	Aerohire Ltd/Halfpenny Green
	G-BNUZ	Robinson R-22B	J. C. Reid
	G-BNVB	AA-5A Cheetah	A. M. Glazer
	G-BNVD	PA-38-112 Tomahawk	Channel Aviation Ltd/Guernsey
	G-BNVE	PA-28-181 Archer II	Steve Parrish Racing
	G-BNVT	PA-28R-201T Turbo Arrow III	Victor Tango Group
	G-BNVZ	Beech 95-B55 Baron	W. J. Forrest & P. Schon
	G-BNWA	Boeing 767-336ER	British Airways
	G-BNWB	Boeing 767-336ER	British Airways
	G-BNWC	Boeing 767-336ER	British Airways
	G-BNWD	Boeing 767-336ER	British Airways
	G-BNWE	Boeing 767-336ER	British Airways
	G-BNWF	Boeing 767-336ER	British Airways
	G-BNWH	Boeing 767-336ER	British Airways
	G-BNWI	Boeing 767-336ER	British Airways
	G-BNWJ	Boeing 767-336ER	British Airways
	G-BNWL	Boeing 767-336ER	British Airways
	G-BNWM	Boeing 767-336ER	British Airways
	G-BNWN	Boeing 767-336ER	British Airways
	G-BNWO	Boeing 767-336ER	British Airways
	G-BNWP	Boeing 767-336ER	British Airways
	G-BNWR	Boeing 767-336ER	British Airways
	G-BNWS	Boeing 767-336ER	British Airways
	G-BNWT	Boeing 767-336ER	British Airways
	G-BNWU	Boeing 767-336ER	British Airways
	G-BNWV	Boeing 767-336ER	British Airways
	G-BNWW	Boeing 767-336ER	British Airways
	G-BNWX	Boeing 767-336ER	British Airways
	G-BNWY	Boeing 767-336ER	British Airways

Reg.	Type	Owner or Operator	Notes
G-BNWZ	Boeing 767-336ER	British Airways	
G-BNXA	BN-2A-26 Islander	Cormack (Aircraft Services) Ltd/ Cumbernauld	
G-BNXC	Cessna 152 II	Sir W. G. Armstrong Whitworth Flying Group/Coventry	
G-BNXD	Cessna 172N	A. Jahanfar	
G-BNXE	PA-28-161 Warrior II	Rugby Autobody Repairs/Coventry	
G-BNXI	Robin DR.400/180R	London Gliding Club (Pty) Ltd/Dunstable	
G-BNXK	Nott-Cameron ULD-3 balloon	J. R. P. Nott (G-BLJN)	
G-BNXL	Glaser-Dirks DG.400	G-BNXL Group	
G-BNXM	PA-18 Super Cub 95	G-BNXM Group	
G-BNXR	Cameron O-84 balloon	J. A. B. Gray	
G-BNXT	PA-28-161 Warrior II	Falcon Flying Services/Manston	
G-BNXU	PA-28-161 Warrior II	Friendly Warrior Group	
G-BNXV	PA-38-112 Tomahawk	St George Flying Club/Teesside	
G-BNXX	SOCATA TB.20 Trinidad	D. M. Carr	
G-BNXZ	Thunder Ax7-77 balloon	Hale Hot Air Balloon Group	
G-BNYB	PA-28-201T Turbo Dakota	A. G. E. Camisa & C. J. Freeman	
G-BNYD	Bell 206B JetRanger 3	Sterling Helicopters Ltd/Norwich	
G-BNYI	Short SD3-60 Variant 100	Gill Airways Ltd	
G-BNYK	PA-38-112 Tomahawk	APB Leasing Ltd/Welshpool	
G-BNYL	Cessna 152 II	APB Leasing Ltd/Welshpool	
G-BNYM	Cessna 172N	N. B. Lindley	
G-BNYN	Cessna 152 II	Redhill Flying Club	
G-BNYO	Beech 76 Duchess	Sub Marine Services Ltd	
G-BNYP	PA-28-181 Archer II	R. D. Cooper/Cranfield	
G-BNYS	Boeing 767-204ER	Britannia Airways Ltd/Luton	
G-BNYV	PA-38-112 Tomahawk	Channel Aviation Ltd/Guernsey	
G-BNYX	Denney Kitfox Mk 1	R. W. Husband	
G-BNYZ	SNCAN Stampe SV-4E	Tapestry Colour Ltd	
G-BNZB	PA-28-161 Warrior II	EFG Flying Services Ltd/Biggin Hill	
G-BNZC	D.H.C.1 Chipmunk 22 (18671)	D. A. Horsley	
G-BNZG	PA-28RT-201T Turbo Arrow IV	Brightday Ltd	
G-BNZJ	Colt 21A balloon	N. Charbonnier/Italy	
G-BNZK	Thunder Ax7-77 balloon	T. D. Marsden	
G-BNZL	Rotorway Scorpion 133	J. R. Wraight	
G-BNZM	Cessna T.210N	A. J. M. Freeman	
G-BNZO	Rotorway Executive	M. G. Wiltshire	
G-BNZR	FRED Srs 2	R. M. Waugh/Newtownards	
G-BNZV	PA-25 Pawnee 235	Northumbria Gliding Club Ltd	
G-BNZZ	PA-28-161 Warrior II	Zoom Aviation Ltd	
G-BOAA	Concorde 102	British Airways (G-N94AA)	
G-BOAB	Concorde 102	British Airways (G-N94AB)	
G-BOAC	Concorde 102	British Airways (G-N81AC)	
G-BOAD	Concorde 102	British Airways (G-N94AD)	
G-BOAE	Concorde 102	British Airways (G-N94AE)	
G-BOAF	Concorde 102	British Airways (G-N94AF/G-BFKX)	
G-BOAG	Concorde 102	British Airways (G-BFKW)	
G-BOAH	PA-28-161 Warrior II	Keen Leasing (IOM) Ltd	
G-BOAI	Cessna 152 II	Galair Ltd/Biggin Hill	
G-BOAK	PA-22 Tri-Pacer 150	A. M. Noble	
G-BOAL	Cameron V-65 balloon	A. M. Lindsay	
G-BOAM	Robinson R-22B	Burman Aviation Ltd/Cranfield	
G-BOAO	Thunder Ax7-77 balloon	D. V. Fowler	
G-BOAS	Air Command 503 Commander	R. Robinson	
G-BOAU	Cameron V-77 balloon	G. T. Barstow	
G-BOBA	PA-28R-201 Arrow III	Small World Aviation	
G-BOBB	Cameron O-120 balloon	S. E. & V. D. Hurst	
G-BOBD	Cameron O-160 balloon	J. Spindler	
G-BOBH	Airtour AH-77 balloon	J. & K. Francis	
G-BOBJ	PA-38-112 Tomahawk	Pearl Technology Ltd	
G-BOBK	PA-38-112 Tomahawk	Pearl Technology Ltd	
G-BOBL	PA-38-112 Tomahawk	Aerohire Ltd/Halfpenny Green	
G-BOBR	Cameron N-77 balloon	C. Bradley & M. Morris	
G-BOBT	Stolp SA.300 Starduster Too	G-BOBT Group	
G-BOBU	Colt 90A balloon	Prescott Hot Air Balloons Ltd	
G-BOBV	Cessna F.150M	Sheffield Aero Club Ltd/Netherthorpe	
G-BOBY	Monnett Sonerai II	R. G. Hallam *(stored)*/Sleap	
G-BOBZ	PA-28-181 Archer II	Trustcomms International Ltd	
G-BOCC	PA-38-112 Tomahawk	J. M. Green	
G-BOCF	Colt 77A balloon	Lindstrand Balloons Ltd	
G-BOCG	PA-34-200T Seneca II	Oxford Aviation Services Ltd/Kidlington	

Notes	Reg.	Type	Owner or Operator
	G-BOCI	Cessna 140A	J. B. Bonnell
	G-BOCK	Sopwith Triplane (replica) (N6290)	The Shuttleworth Collection/O. Warden
	G-BOCL	Slingsby T.67C	Richard Brinklow Aviation Ltd
	G-BOCM	Slingsby T.67C	Richard Brinklow Aviation Ltd
	G-BOCN	Robinson R-22B	Sloane Helicopters Ltd/Sywell
	G-BOCP	PA-34-220T Seneca III	BAe Flying College Ltd/Prestwick
	G-BOCR	PA-34-220T Seneca III	BAe Flying College Ltd/Prestwick
	G-BOCS	PA-34-220T Seneca III	BAe Flying College Ltd/Prestwick
	G-BOCT	PA-34-220T Seneca III	BAe Flying College Ltd/Prestwick
	G-BOCU	PA-34-220T Seneca III	BAe Flying College Ltd/Prestwick
	G-BOCV	PA-34-220T Seneca III	BAe Flying College Ltd/Prestwick
	G-BOCW	PA-34-220T Seneca III	BAe Flying College Ltd/Prestwick
	G-BOCX	PA-34-220T Seneca III	BAe Flying College Ltd/Prestwick
	G-BOCY	PA-34-220T Seneca III	BAe Flying College Ltd/Prestwick
	G-BODA	PA-28-161 Warrior II	Oxford Aviation Services Ltd/Kidlington
	G-BODB	PA-28-161 Warrior II	Oxford Aviation Services Ltd/Kidlington
	G-BODC	PA-28-161 Warrior II	Oxford Aviation Services Ltd/Kidlington
	G-BODD	PA-28-161 Warrior II	Oxford Aviation Services Ltd/Kidlington
	G-BODE	PA-28-161 Warrior II	Oxford Aviation Services Ltd/Kidlington
	G-BODF	PA-28-161 Warrior II	Oxford Aviation Services Ltd/Kidlington
	G-BODH	Slingsby T.31 Motor Cadet III	H. P. Vox (G-ALNK)
	G-BODI	Stoddard-Hamilton SH-3R Glasair III	C. A. C. Tilney
	G-BODM	PA-28 Cherokee 180	R. Emery
	G-BODO	Cessna 152	A. R. Sarson
	G-BODP	PA-38-112 Tomahawk	D. A. Whitmore
	G-BODR	PA-28-161 Warrior II	Airways Aero Associations Ltd/Booker
	G-BODS	PA-38-112 Tomahawk	P. J. Houlton
	G-BODT	Jodel D.18	L. D. McPhillips
	G-BODU	Scheibe SF.25C Falke	Monica English Memorial Trust/Rufforth
	G-BODX	Beech 76 Duchess	Liddell Aircraft Ltd
	G-BODY	Cessna 310R	Atlantic Air Transport Ltd/Coventry
	G-BODZ	Robinson R-22B	Langley Construction Ltd
	G-BOEE	PA-28-181 Archer II	T. B. Parmenter
	G-BOEH	Jodel DR.340	Piper Flyers Group
	G-BOEK	Cameron V-77 balloon	A. J. E. Jones
	G-BOEM	Aerotek-Pitts S-2A	M. Murphy
	G-BOEN	Cessna 172M	G-BOEN Group
	G-BOER	PA-28-161 Warrior II	M. & W. Fraser-Urquhart
	G-BOET	PA-28RT-201 Arrow IV	B. C. Chambers (G-IBEC)
	G-BOEW	Robinson R-22B	Plane Talking Ltd/Elstree
	G-BOEX	Robinson R-22B	Plane Talking Ltd/Elstree
	G-BOEZ	Robinson R-22B	Plane Talking Ltd/Elstree
	G-BOFC	Beech 76 Duchess	Magenta Ltd/Kidlington
	G-BOFD	Cessna U.206G	D. M. Penny
	G-BOFE	PA-34-200T Seneca II	Alstons Upholstery Ltd
	G-BOFF	Cameron N-77 balloon	R. C. Corcoran
	G-BOFL	Cessna 152 II	GEM Rewinds Ltd/Coventry
	G-BOFM	Cessna 152 II	GEM Rewinds Ltd/Coventry
	G-BOFO	Ultimate Aircraft 10-200	M. Werdmuller
	G-BOFW	Cessna A.150M	Vectair Aviation 1995 Ltd
	G-BOFX	Cessna A.150M	Aldergrove Flight Training Centre
	G-BOFY	PA-28 Cherokee 140	BCT Aircraft Leasing Ltd
	G-BOFZ	PA-28-161 Warrior II	R. W. Harris
	G-BOGC	Cessna 152 II	Keen Leasing (IOM) Ltd
	G-BOGG	Cessna 152 II	The Royal Artillery Aero Club Ltd/ Middle Wallop
	G-BOGI	Robin DR.400/180	A. L. M. Shepherd
	G-BOGK	ARV Super 2	D. R. Trouse
	G-BOGM	PA-28RT-201T Turbo Arrow IV	RJP Aviation
	G-BOGO	PA-32R-301T Saratoga SP	A. S. Doman/Biggin Hill
	G-BOGP	Cameron V-77 balloon	Wealden Balloon Group
	G-BOGV	Air Command 532 Elite	G. M. Hobman
	G-BOGW	Air Command 532 Elite	A. Gault
	G-BOGY	Cameron V-77 balloon	R. A. Preston
	G-BOHA	PA-28-161 Warrior II	M. Clark
	G-BOHD	Colt 77A balloon	D. B. Court
	G-BOHF	Thunder Ax8-84 balloon	J. A. Harris
	G-BOHG	Air Command 532 Elite	T. E. McDonald
	G-BOHH	Cessna 172N	T. Scott
	G-BOHI	Cessna 152 II	V. D. Speck/Clacton
	G-BOHJ	Cessna 152 II	Airlaunch/Old Buckenham

Reg.	Type	Owner or Operator	Notes
G-BOHL	Cameron A-120 balloon	J. M. Holmes	
G-BOHM	PA-28 Cherokee 180	M. J. Anthony & B. Keogh	
G-BOHO	PA-28-161 Warrior II	Egressus Flying Group	
G-BOHR	PA-28-151 Warrior	G. Cockerton/Coventry	
G-BOHS	PA-38-112 Tomahawk	Falcon Flying Services/Biggin Hill	
G-BOHT	PA-38-112 Tomahawk	St George Flying Club/Teesside	
G-BOHU	PA-38-112 Tomahawk	Avon Aircraft Leasing Ltd	
G-BOHV	Wittman W.8 Tailwind	R. A. Povall	
G-BOHW	Van's RV-4	P. J. Robins	
G-BOHX	PA-44-180 Seminole	Airpart Supply Ltd/Booker	
G-BOIA	Cessna 180K	R. E. Styles & ptnrs	
G-BOIB	Wittman W.10 Tailwind	L. Fairs	
G-BOIC	PA-28R-201T Turbo Arrow III	M. J. Pearson	
G-BOID	Bellanca 7ECA Citabria	D. Mallinson	
G-BOIG	PA-28-161 Warrior II	D. Vallence-Pell/Jersey	
G-BOIJ	Thunder Ax7-77 balloon	R. A. Hughes	
G-BOIK	Air Command 503 Commander	F. G. Shepherd	
G-BOIL	Cessna 172N	Upperstack Ltd	
G-BOIN	Bellanca 7ECA Citabria	LAC (Enterprises) Ltd/Barton	
G-BOIO	Cessna 152	AV Aviation Ltd	
G-BOIP	Cessna 152	Stapleford Flying Club Ltd	
G-BOIR	Cessna 152	Shropshire Aero Club Ltd/Sleap	
G-BOIT	SOCATA TB.10 Tobago	Buckland Newton Hire Ltd	
G-BOIU	SOCATA TB.10 Tobago	R & B Aviation Ltd	
G-BOIV	Cessna 150M	J. B. Green	
G-BOIW	Cessna 152	EFG Flying Services Ltd/Biggin Hill	
G-BOIX	Cessna 172N	JR Flying Ltd	
G-BOIY	Cessna 172N	Aviation Aces Ltd	
G-BOIZ	PA-34-200T Seneca II	S. F. Tebby & Son	
G-BOJB	Cameron V-77 balloon	K. L. Heron & R. M. Trotter	
G-BOJD	Cameron V-77 balloon	L. H. Ellis	
G-BOJF	Air Command 532 Elite	C. Verlaan/Netherlands	
G-BOJH	PA-28R Cherokee Arrow 200	Piper-Air (Glasgow) Ltd	
G-BOJI	PA-28RT-201 Arrow IV	B. A. Mintowt-Czyz & T. A. Stoate	
G-BOJK	PA-34-220T Seneca III	Redhill Flying Club (G-BRUF)	
G-BOJM	PA-28-181 Archer II	Fernborough Ltd	
G-BOJR	Cessna 172P	Exeter Flying Club Ltd	
G-BOJS	Cessna 172P	I. S. H. Paul	
G-BOJU	Cameron N-77 balloon	M. A. Scholes	
G-BOJW	PA-28-161 Warrior II	G-BOJW Flying Group	
G-BOJZ	PA-28-161 Warrior II	Southern Air Ltd/Shoreham	
G-BOKA	PA-28-201T Turbo Dakota	CBG Aviation Ltd/Biggin Hill	
G-BOKB	PA-28-161 Warrior II	Southern Air Ltd/Shoreham	
G-BOKF	Air Command 532 Elite	D. Beevers	
G-BOKH	Whittaker MW.7	I. D. Evans	
G-BOKI	Whittaker MW.7	R. K. Willcox	
G-BOKJ	Whittaker MW.7	M. R. Payne	
G-BOKL	PA-28-161 Warrior II	BAe Flying College Ltd/Prestwick	
G-BOKM	PA-28-161 Warrior II	BAe Flying College Ltd/Prestwick	
G-BOKN	PA-28-161 Warrior II	BAe Flying College Ltd/Prestwick	
G-BOKO	PA-28-161 Warrior II	BAe Flying College Ltd/Prestwick	
G-BOKP	PA-28-161 Warrior II	BAe Flying College Ltd/Prestwick	
G-BOKR	PA-28-161 Warrior II	BAe Flying College Ltd/Prestwick	
G-BOKS	PA-28-161 Warrior II	BAe Flying College Ltd/Prestwick	
G-BOKT	PA-28-161 Warrior II	BAe Flying College Ltd/Prestwick	
G-BOKU	PA-28-161 Warrior II	BAe Flying College Ltd/Prestwick	
G-BOKX	PA-28-161 Warrior II	W. P. J. Jackson	
G-BOKY	Cessna 152 II	D. F. F. & J. E. Poore	
G-BOLB	Taylorcraft BC-12-65	A. T. E. Pacewicz & R. J. Rhys-Williams	
G-BOLC	Fournier RF-6B-100	W. H. Hendy/Dunkeswell	
G-BOLD	PA-38-112 Tomahawk	B. R. Pearson & B. F. Fraser-Smith/Eaglescott	
G-BOLE	PA-38-112 Tomahawk	M. W. Kibble & E. A. Minard	
G-BOLF	PA-38-112 Tomahawk	Teesside Flight Centre Ltd	
G-BOLG	Bellanca 7KCAB Citabria	B. R. Pearson/Eaglescott	
G-BOLI	Cessna 172P	Boli Flying Club	
G-BOLL	Lake LA-4 Skimmer	S. Armstrong	
G-BOLN	Colt 21A balloon	Virgin Airship & Balloon Co Ltd	
G-BOLO	Bell 206B JetRanger	Hargreaves Construction Co Ltd/Shoreham	
G-BOLP	Colt 21A balloon	Virgin Airship & Balloon Co Ltd	
G-BOLR	Colt 21A balloon	Virgin Airship & Balloon Co Ltd	
G-BOLS	FRED Srs 2	I. F. Vaughan	

Notes	Reg.	Type	Owner or Operator
	G-BOLT	R. Commander 114	H. J. D. S. Baices
	G-BOLU	Robin R.3000/120	Classair/Biggin Hill
	G-BOLV	Cessna 152 II	Falcon Flying Services/Biggin Hill
	G-BOLW	Cessna 152 II	JRB Aviation Ltd/Southend
	G-BOLX	Cessna 172N	R. J. Burrough/Headcorn
	G-BOLY	Cessna 172N	D. A. T. Skidmore
	G-BOLZ	Rand KR-2	B. Normington
	G-BOMB	Cassutt Racer IIIM	S. Adams
	G-BOMK	BAe 146-200QT	GD Express Worldwide NV
	G-BOMN	Cessna 150F	D. G. Williams
	G-BOMO	PA-38-112 Tomahawk II	APB Leasing Ltd/Welshpool
	G-BOMP	PA-28-181 Archer II	SRC Contractors Ltd & D. Carter
	G-BOMS	Cessna 172N	Aerohire Ltd/Halfpenny Green
	G-BOMT	Cessna 172N	C. E. Derbyshire
	G-BOMU	PA-28-181 Archer II	RJ Aviation/Blackbushe
	G-BOMY	PA-28-161 Warrior II	Carill Aviation Ltd/Southampton
	G-BOMZ	PA-38-112 Tomahawk	BOMZ Aviation/White Waltham
	G-BONC	PA-28RT-201 Arrow IV	Finglow Ltd
	G-BOND	Sikorsky S-76A	Manchester Helicopter Centre/Barton
	G-BONE	Pilatus P2-06 (U-142)	R. H. Cooper & S. Swallow
	G-BONG	Enstrom F-28A-UK	TR Bitz
	G-BONK	Colt 180A balloon	Wye Valley Aviation Ltd
	G-BONO	Cessna 172N	Mer-Air Aviation Ltd
	G-BONP	CFM Streak Shadow	T. J. Palmer
	G-BONR	Cessna 172N	D. I. Craik/Biggin Hill
	G-BONS	Cessna 172N	BONS Group/Elstree
	G-BONT	Slingsby T.67M Mk II	Hunting Aviation Ltd/Barkston Heath
	G-BONU	Slingsby T.67B	R. L. Brinklow
	G-BONV	Colt 17A balloon	Bryant Group PLC
	G-BONW	Cessna 152 II	Lincoln Aero Club Ltd/Sturgate
	G-BONY	Denney Kitfox Mk 1	M. J. Walker
	G-BONZ	Beech V35B Bonanza	P. M. Coulten
	G-BOOB	Cameron N-65 balloon	J. Rumming
	G-BOOC	PA-18 Super Cub 150	R. R. & S. A. Marriott
	G-BOOD	Slingsby T.31M Motor Tutor	G. F. M. Garner
	G-BOOE	GA-7 Cougar	N. Gardner
	G-BOOF	PA-28-181 Archer II	European Flyers/Blackbushe
	G-BOOG	PA-28RT-201T Turbo Arrow IV	Simair Ltd
	G-BOOH	Jodel D.112	J. A. Crabb
	G-BOOI	Cessna 152	Stapleford Flying Club Ltd
	G-BOOJ	Air Command 532 Elite	Roger Savage (Gyroplanes) Ltd
	G-BOOL	Cessna 172N	Surrey & Kent Flying Club Ltd/Biggin Hill
	G-BOOV	AS.355F-2 Twin Squirrel	Merseyside Police Authority/Liverpool
	G-BOOW	Aerosport Scamp	I. E. Bloys
	G-BOOX	Rutan LongEz	I. R. Thomas & I. R. Wilde
	G-BOOZ	Cameron N-77 balloon	J. E. F. Kettlety
	G-BOPA	PA-28-181 Archer II	J. H. & L. F. Strutt
	G-BOPB	Boeing 767-204ER	Britannia Airways Ltd *Captain Sir Ross Smith*
	G-BOPC	PA-28-161 Warrior II	Channel Aviation Ltd
	G-BOPD	Bede BD-4	S. T. Dauncey
	G-BOPG	Cessna 182Q	G. Wimlett
	G-BOPH	Cessna TR.182RG	E. A. L. Sturmer
	G-BOPO	Brooklands OA.7 Optica	Sunhawk Ltd
	G-BOPR	Brooklands OA.7 Optica	Sunhawk Ltd
	G-BOPT	Grob G.115	LAC (Enterprises) Ltd/Barton
	G-BOPU	Grob G.115	LAC (Enterprises) Ltd/Barton
	G-BOPV	PA-34-200T Seneca II	G. J. Powell
	G-BOPX	Cessna A.152	Aerohire Ltd/Halfpenny Green
	G-BORB	Cameron V-77 balloon	M. H. Wolff
	G-BORD	Thunder Ax7-77 balloon	D. D. Owen
	G-BORE	Colt 77A balloon	Little Secret Hot-Air Balloon Group
	G-BORG	Campbell Cricket	N. G. Bailey
	G-BORH	PA-34-200T Seneca II	Aerolease Ltd
	G-BORI	Cessna 152 II	Staryear Ltd
	G-BORJ	Cessna 152 II	Cumbria Aero Club/Carlisle
	G-BORK	PA-28-161 Warrior II	A. W. Collett
	G-BORL	PA-28-161 Warrior II	Westair Flying School Ltd/Blackpool
	G-BORM	H.S.748 Srs 2B ★	Airport Fire Service/Exeter
	G-BORN	Cameron N-77 balloon	I. Chadwick
	G-BORO	Cessna 152 II	Tatenhill Aviation
	G-BORR	Thunder Ax8-90 balloon	W. J. Harris
	G-BORS	PA-28-181 Archer II	Ambrose Air

Reg.	Type	Owner or Operator	Notes
G-BORT	Colt 77A balloon	I. E. A. Joslyn/Germany	
G-BORV	Bell 206B JetRanger 3	C. A. Rosenberg/Redhill	
G-BORW	Cessna 172P	Briter Aviation Ltd/Coventry	
G-BORY	Cessna 150L	Harrison Aviation Ltd	
G-BOSB	Thunder Ax7-77 balloon	M. Gallagher	
G-BOSD	PA-34-200T Seneca II	Barnes Olson Aeroleasing Ltd	
G-BOSE	PA-28-181 Archer II	C. Hudson & A. Thomas	
G-BOSF	Colt 69A balloon	Virgin Airship & Balloon Co Ltd	
G-BOSG	Colt 17A balloon	Virgin Airship & Balloon Co Ltd	
G-BOSJ	Nord 3400 (124)	A. I. Milne	
G-BOSM	Jodel DR.253B	Sierra Mike (Ware) Group	
G-BOSO	Cessna A.152	Redhill Flying Club	
G-BOSR	PA-28 Cherokee 140	Sierra Romeo Group	
G-BOSU	PA-28 Cherokee 140	R. A. Sands	
G-BOSV	Cameron V-77 balloon	K. H. Greenaway	
G-BOTB	Cessna 152 II	Stapleford Flying Club Ltd	
G-BOTD	Cameron O-105 balloon	P. J. Beglan/France	
G-BOTF	PA-28-151 Warrior	G-BOTF Group/Southend	
G-BOTG	Cessna 152 II	Donington Aviation Ltd/E. Midlands	
G-BOTH	Cessna 182Q	G-BOTH Group	
G-BOTI	PA-28-151 Warrior	Falcon Flying Services/Biggin Hill	
G-BOTK	Cameron O-105 balloon	F. R. & V. L. Higgins	
G-BOTM	Bell 206B JetRanger 3	David McLean Homes Ltd	
G-BOTN	PA-28-161 Warrior II	A. Watson	
G-BOTO	Bellanca 7ECA Citabria	G-BOTO Group	
G-BOTP	Cessna 150J	M. Colson	
G-BOTU	Piper J-3C-65 Cub	T. L. Giles	
G-BOTV	PA-32RT-300 Lance II	Robin Lance Aviation Association Ltd	
G-BOTW	Cameron V-77 balloon	M. R. Jeynes	
G-BOTZ	Bensen B.8MR	C. Jones	
G-BOUD	PA-38-112 Tomahawk	A. J. Wiggins	
G-BOUE	Cessna 172N	Aviation Access Ltd	
G-BOUF	Cessna 172N	Amber Valley Aviation	
G-BOUJ	Cessna 150M	R. D. Billins	
G-BOUK	PA-34-200T Seneca II	C. J. & R. J. Barnes	
G-BOUL	PA-34-200T Seneca II	Oxford Aviation Services Ltd/Kidlington	
G-BOUM	PA-34-200T Seneca II	Oxford Aviation Services Ltd/Kidlington	
G-BOUN	Rand KR-2	W. J. Allan	
G-BOUP	PA-28-161 Warrior II	Oxford Aviation Services Ltd/Kidlington	
G-BOUR	PA-28-161 Warrior II	Oxford Aviation Services Ltd/Kidlington	
G-BOUS	PA-28RT-201 Arrow IV	Hamilton Compass Aviation Ltd/Liverpool	
G-BOUT	Colomban MC.12 Cri-Cri	C. K. Farley	
G-BOUV	Bensen B.8R	A. J. Dickson	
G-BOUZ	Cessna 150G	Atlantic Bridge Aviation Ltd/Lydd	
G-BOVB	PA-15 Vagabond	Oscar Flying Group/Shoreham	
G-BOVC	Everett gyroplane	J. W. Highton	
G-BOVH	PA-28-161 Warrior II	R. W. Tebby	
G-BOVK	PA-28-161 Warrior II	Air Nova PLC/Liverpool	
G-BOVR	Robinson R-22	P. J. Homan	
G-BOVS	Cessna 150M	Blue Skies Aviation Ltd	
G-BOVT	Cessna 150M	C. J. Hopewell	
G-BOVU	Stoddard-Hamilton Glasair III	B. R. Chaplin	
G-BOVW	Colt 69A balloon	V. Hyland	
G-BOVX	Hughes 269C	Autohaus Ltd	
G-BOVY	Hughes 269C	P. J. Brown	
G-BOWB	Cameron V-77 balloon	R. C. Stone	
G-BOWD	Cessna F.337G	Badgehurst Ltd (G-BLSB)	
G-BOWE	PA-34-200T Seneca II	Oxford Aviation Services Ltd/Kidlington	
G-BOWK	Cameron N-90 balloon	S. R. Bridge	
G-BOWL	Cameron V-77 balloon	P. G. & G. R. Hall	
G-BOWM	Cameron V-56 balloon	C. G. Caldecott & G. Pitt	
G-BOWN	PA-12 Super Cruiser	R. W. Bucknell	
G-BOWO	Cessna R.182	D. P. Bennett (G-BOTR)	
G-BOWP	Jodel D.120A	A. R. Gedney & ptnrs/Sibson	
G-BOWU	Cameron O-84 balloon	St Elmos Fire Syndicate	
G-BOWV	Cameron V-65 balloon	R. A. Harris	
G-BOWY	PA-28RT-201T Turbo Arrow IV	A. Davies	
G-BOWZ	Bensen B.80V	W. M. Day	
G-BOXA	PA-28-161 Warrior II	Channel Islands Aero Services Ltd	
G-BOXB	PA-28-161 Warrior II	Channel Islands Aero Services Ltd	
G-BOXC	PA-28-161 Warrior II	Channel Islands Aero Services Ltd	
G-BOXG	Cameron O-77 balloon	R. A. Wicks	
G-BOXH	Pitts S-1S Special	D. Medrek & M. Turkington	

Notes	Reg.	Type	Owner or Operator
	G-BOXJ	Piper J-3C-65 Cub	J. D. Tseliki/Shoreham
	G-BOXR	GA-7 Cougar	Plane Talking Ltd/Elstree
	G-BOXT	Hughes 269C	Goldenfly Ltd
	G-BOXU	AA-5B Tiger	Marcher Aviation Group
	G-BOXV	Pitts S-1S Special	G. R. Clark
	G-BOXW	Cassutt Racer Srs IIIM	D. I. Johnson
	G-BOXX	Robinson R-22B	Plane Talking Ltd/Elstree
	G-BOXY	PA-28-181 Archer II	Sheffield Aero Club Ltd/Netherthorpe
	G-BOYB	Cessna A.152	Northamptonshire School of Flying Ltd/Sywell
	G-BOYC	Robinson R-22B	Yorkshire Helicopters/Leeds Bradford
	G-BOYF	Sikorsky S-76B	Darley Stud Management Co Ltd/Blackbushe
	G-BOYH	PA-28-151 Warrior	Superpause Ltd/Booker
	G-BOYI	PA-28-161 Warrior II	S. J. Harris
	G-BOYL	Cessna 152 II	Aerohire Ltd/Halfpenny Green
	G-BOYM	Cameron O-84 balloon	Frontline Distribution Ltd
	G-BOYO	Cameron V-20 balloon	J. M. Willard
	G-BOYP	Cessna 172N	Guildtons Ltd
	G-BOYU	Cessna A.150L	Upperstack Ltd/Liverpool
	G-BOYV	PA-28R-201T Turbo Arrow III	Arrow Air Ltd
	G-BOYX	Robinson R-22B	R. Towle
	G-BOYY	Cameron A-105 balloon	Hoyers (UK) Ltd
	G-BOZI	PA-28-161 Warrior II	Klingair Ltd/Conington
	G-BOZK	AS.332L Super Puma	British International Helicopters
	G-BOZM	PA-38-112 Tomahawk	Falcon Flying Services/Biggin Hill
	G-BOZN	Cameron N-77 balloon	Calarel Developments Ltd
	G-BOZO	AA-5B Tiger	Caslon Ltd
	G-BOZP	Beech 76 Duchess	Newcastle upon Tyne Aero Club Ltd
	G-BOZR	Cessna 152 II	GEM Rewinds Ltd/Coventry
	G-BOZS	Pitts S-1C Special	R. J. & M. B. Trickey
	G-BOZU	Sparrow Hawk Mk II	R. V. Phillimore
	G-BOZV	CEA DR.340 Major	Datamax Computer Consultants Ltd
	G-BOZW	Bensen B.8M	M. E. Wills
	G-BOZY	Cameron RTW-120 balloon	L. V. Mastis
	G-BOZZ	AA-5B Tiger	Solent Tiger Group/Southampton
	G-BPAA	Acro Advanced	Acro Engines & Airframes Ltd
	G-BPAB	Cessna 150M	Alpha Bravo Group/Earls Colne
	G-BPAC	PA-28-161 Warror II	G. G. Pratt
	G-BPAF	PA-28-161 Warrior II	RAF Brize Norton Flying Club Ltd
	G-BPAH	Colt 69A balloon	Justerini & Brooks Ltd
	G-BPAI	Bell 47G-3B-1 (modified)	LRC Leisure Ltd
	G-BPAJ	D.H.82A Tiger Moth	P. A. Jackson (G-AOIX)
	G-BPAL	D.H.C.1 Chipmunk 22 (WG350)	K. F. & P. Tomsett (G-BCYE)
	G-BPAS	SOCATA TB.20 Trinidad	Syndicate Clerical Services Ltd
	G-BPAU	PA-28-161 Warrior II	Lapwing Flying Group Ltd/Denham
	G-BPAV	FRED Srs 2	P. A. Valentine
	G-BPAW	Cessna 150M	A. Phillips
	G-BPAX	Cessna 150M	The Dirty Dozen
	G-BPAY	PA-28-181 Archer II	Leicestershire Aero Club Ltd
	G-BPBB	Evans VP-2	P. J. Manifold
	G-BPBG	Cessna 152 II	Atlantic Air Transport Ltd/Coventry
	G-BPBI	Cessna 152 II	B. W. Wells & Burbage Farms Ltd
	G-BPBJ	Cessna 152 II	W. Shaw & P. G. Haines
	G-BPBK	Cessna 152 II	Burbage Farms Ltd
	G-BPBM	PA-28-161 Warrior II	Halfpenny Green Flight Centre Ltd
	G-BPBO	PA-28RT-201T Turbo Arrow IV	S. C. May
	G-BPBP	Brügger MB.2 Colibri	D. A. Preston
	G-BPBR	PA-38-112 Tomahawk	Cardiff Wales Flying Club Ltd
	G-BPBU	Cameron V-77 balloon	M. C. Gibbons & J. E. Kite
	G-BPBV	Cameron V-77 balloon	W. E. & L. A. Newman
	G-BPBW	Cameron O-105 balloon	R. J. Mansfield
	G-BPBY	Cameron V-77 balloon	L. Hutley (G-BPCS)
	G-BPBZ	Thunder Ax7-77 balloon	A. W. J. Weston
	G-BPCA	BN-2B-26 Islander	Loganair Ltd/BA Express (G-BLNX)
	G-BPCF	Piper J-3C-65 Cub	T. I. Williams
	G-BPCG	Colt AS-80 airship	N. Charbonnier/Italy
	G-BPCI	Cessna R.172K	P. A. Warner
	G-BPCK	PA-28-161 Warrior II	W. G. Booth
	G-BPCL	SA Bulldog Srs 120/128	Isohigh Ltd/Denham
	G-BPCM	Rotorway Executive	Aircare Group
	G-BPCR	Mooney M.20K	T. & R. Harris

Reg.	Type	Owner or Operator	Notes
G-BPCV	Montgomerie-Bensen B.8MR	O. J. Blackbourn	
G-BPCX	PA-28-236 Dakota	G. E. J. Spooner	
G-BPDE	Colt 56A balloon	J. E. Weidema/Netherlands	
G-BPDF	Cameron V-77 balloon	The Ballooning Business Ltd	
G-BPDG	Cameron V-77 balloon	D. F. H. Smith	
G-BPDJ	Christena Mini Coupe	J. J. Morrissey/Popham	
G-BPDK	Sorrell SNS-7 Hyperbipe ★	A. J. Cable *(stored)*/Barton	
G-BPDM	C.A.S.A. 1.131E Jungmann 2000 (781-32)	J. D. Haslam	
G-BPDT	PA-28-161 Warrior II	Channel Islands Aero Services Ltd	
G-BPDU	PA-28-161 Warrior II	Southern Air Ltd/Shoreham	
G-BPDV	Pitts S-1S Special	J. Vize/Sywell	
G-BPDY	Westland-Bell 47G-3B1	Howden Helicopters/Spaldington	
G-BPEA	Boeing 757-236	British Airways	
G-BPEB	Boeing 757-236	British Airways	
G-BPEC	Boeing 757-236	British Airways	
G-BPED	Boeing 757-236	British Airways	
G-BPEE	Boeing 757-236	British Airways	
G-BPEF	Boeing 757-236	British Airways (G-BOHC)	
G-BPEI	Boeing 757-236	British Airways (G-BMRK)	
G-BPEJ	Boeing 757-236	British Airways (G-BMRL)	
G-BPEK	Boeing 757-236	British Airways (G-BMRM)	
G-BPEL	PA-28-151 Warrior	R. W. Harris & A. J. Jahanfar	
G-BPEM	Cessna 150K	R. G. Lindsey & R. Strong	
G-BPEO	Cessna 152 II	Seawing Flying Club Ltd & Eastern Executive Air Charter Ltd/Southend	
G-BPES	PA-38-112 Tomahawk II	Sherwood Flying Club Ltd/Tollerton	
G-BPEZ	Colt 77A balloon	J. E. F. Kettlety & W. J. Honey	
G-BPFB	Colt 77A balloon	S. Ingram	
G-BPFC	Mooney M.20C	D. P. Tinsley	
G-BPFD	Jodel D.112	K. Manley	
G-BPFF	Cameron DP-70 airship	E. F. H. Wothe/Germany	
G-BPFH	PA-28-161 Warrior II	M. H. Kleiser	
G-BPFI	PA-28-181 Archer II	F. Teagle	
G-BPFK	Montgomerie-Bensen B.8MR	J. W. Birkett	
G-BPFL	Davis DA-2	B. W. Griffiths	
G-BPFM	Aeronca 7AC Champion	L. A. Borrill	
G-BPFN	Short SD3-60 Variant 100	Loganair Ltd	
G-BPFV	Boeing 767-204ER	Britannia Airways Ltd *Bobby Moore OBE*	
G-BPFZ	Cessna 152 II	C. J. Ward	
G-BPGB	Cessna 150J	Magnificent Obsessions Ltd	
G-BPGC	Air Command 532 Elite	E. C. E. Brown	
G-BPGD	Cameron V-65 balloon	Gone With The Wind Ltd	
G-BPGE	Cessna U.206C	Scottish Parachute Club/Strathallan	
G-BPGF	Thunder Ax7-77 balloon	M. Schiavo	
G-BPGH	EAA Acro Sport II	G. M. Bradley	
G-BPGK	Aeronca 7AC Champion	T. M. Williams	
G-BPGM	Cessna 152 II	Fraggle Leasing Ltd/Edinburgh	
G-BPGT	Colt AS-80 Mk II airship	P. Porati/Italy	
G-BPGU	PA-28-181 Archer II	G. Underwood	
G-BPGV	Robinson R-22B	Polo Aviation Ltd	
G-BPGX	SOCATA TB.9 Tampico	D. A. Lee	
G-BPGY	Cessna 150H	R. A. Watson	
G-BPGZ	Cessna 150G	P. G. Gardner	
G-BPHB	PA-28-161 Warrior II	Channel Islands Aero Services Ltd	
G-BPHD	Cameron N-42 balloon	P. J. Marshall & M. A. Clarke	
G-BPHE	PA-28-161 Warrior II	APB Leasing Ltd/Welshpool	
G-BPHG	Robin DR.400/180	K. J. & M. B. White/Redhill	
G-BPHH	Cameron V-77 balloon	C. D. Aindow	
G-BPHI	PA-38-112 Tomahawk	J. S. Devlin & Z. Islam/Redhill	
G-BPHJ	Cameron V-77 balloon	C. W. Brown	
G-BPHL	PA-28-161 Warrior II	Teesside Flight Centre Ltd	
G-BPHO	Taylorcraft BC-12	A. A. Alderdice	
G-BPHP	Taylorcraft BC-12-65	D. C. Stephens	
G-BPHR	D.H.82A Tiger Moth (A17-48)	N. Parry	
G-BPHT	Cessna 152	Bobbington Air Training School Ltd/ Halfpenny Green	
G-BPHU	Thunder Ax7-77 balloon	R. P. Waite	
G-BPHW	Cessna 140	M. Day	
G-BPHX	Cessna 140	M. McChesney	
G-BPHZ	M.S.505 Criquet (TA+RC)	The Aircraft Restoration Co/Duxford	
G-BPID	PA-28-161 Warrior II	K. J. Newman	
G-BPIE	Bell 206B JetRanger 3	Frey Aviation Ltd	

Notes	Reg.	Type	Owner or Operator
	G-BPIH	Rand KR-2	J. R. Rowley
	G-BPII	Denney Kitfox	G. A. Davidson
	G-BPIJ	Brantly B.2B	R. B. Payne
	G-BPIK	PA-38-112 Tomahawk	A. P. Daines/Earls Colne
	G-BPIL	Cessna 310B	A. L. Brown & R. A. Parsons
	G-BPIM	Cameron N-77 balloon	Thermalite Ltd
	G-BPIN	Glaser-Dirks DG.400	J. N. Stevenson
	G-BPIO	Cessna F.152 II	I. D. McClelland
	G-BPIP	Slingsby T.31 Motor Cadet III	J. H. Beard
	G-BPIR	Scheibe SF.25E Super Falke	Coventry Gliding Club Ltd/ Husbands Bosworth
	G-BPIT	Robinson R-22B	NA Air Ltd
	G-BPIU	PA-28-161 Warrior II	P. G. Doble & P. G. Stewart
	G-BPIV	B.149 Bolingbroke Mk IVT (L8841)	The Aircraft Restoration Co/Duxford
	G-BPIY	Cessna 152 II	Falcon Flying Services/Biggin Hill
	G-BPIZ	AA-5B Tiger	D. A. Horsley
	G-BPJB	Schweizer 269C	Elborne Holdings Ltd/Portugal
	G-BPJD	SOCATA Rallye 110ST	G-BPJD Rallye Group
	G-BPJE	Cameron A-105 balloon	J. S. Eckersley
	G-BPJG	PA-18 Super Cub 150	M. W. Stein
	G-BPJH	PA-18 Super Cub 95	P. J. Heron
	G-BPJK	Colt 77A balloon	Saran UK Ltd
	G-BPJL	Cessna 152 II	Eastern Executive Air Charter Ltd
	G-BPJN	Jodel D.18	W. J. Evans
	G-BPJO	PA-28-161 Cadet	Plane Talking Ltd/Elstree
	G-BPJP	PA-28-161 Cadet	Oxford Aviation Services Ltd/Kidlington
	G-BPJR	PA-28-161 Cadet	Walsh Aviation
	G-BPJS	PA-28-161 Cadet	Oxford Aviation Services Ltd/Kidlington
	G-BPJU	PA-28-161 Cadet	Oxford Aviation Services Ltd/Kidlington
	G-BPJV	Taylorcraft F-21	TC Flying Group
	G-BPJW	Cessna A.150K	G. & S. A. Jones
	G-BPJZ	Cameron O-160 balloon	M. L. Gabb
	G-BPKF	Grob G.115	Steventon Morgan Aviation
	G-BPKK	Denney Kitfox Mk 1	D. Moffat
	G-BPKL	Mooney M.20J	London Link Flying Ltd
	G-BPKM	PA-28-161 Warrior II	M. J. Greasby
	G-BPKO	Cessna 140	G. R. Pitchfork
	G-BPKR	PA-28-151 Warrior	Aeroshow Ltd
	G-BPLF	Cameron V-77 balloon	I. R. Warrington & R. A. MacMillan
	G-BPLH	Jodel DR.1051	D. W. Tovey
	G-BPLM	AIA Stampe SV-4C	C. J. Jesson/Redhill
	G-BPLV	Cameron V-77 balloon	MC VH SA/Belgium
	G-BPLY	Pitts S-2B Special	M. Mountstephen
	G-BPLZ	Hughes 369HS	Pyramid Precision Engineering Ltd
	G-BPMB	Maule M5-235C Lunar Rocket	Earth Products Ltd/Crosland Moor
	G-BPME	Cessna 152 II	Eastern Executive Air Charter Ltd
	G-BPMF	PA-28-151 Warrior	L. & A. Hill
	G-BPMH	Schempp-Hirth Nimbus 3DM	Southern Sailplanes/Membury
	G-BPML	Cessna 172M	J. Birnie/Sandown
	G-BPMM	Champion 7ECA Citabria	J. Murray
	G-BPMR	PA-28-161 Warrior II	B. McIntyre
	G-BPMU	Nord 3202B	A. I. Milne (G-BIZJ)
	G-BPMV	PA-28-161 Warrior II	Oxford Aviation Services Ltd
	G-BPMW	QAC Quickie Q.2	P. M. Wright (G-OICI/G-OGKN)
	G-BPMX	ARV Super 2	T. P. Toth
	G-BPNA	Cessna 150L	Griffin Marston Ltd
	G-BPNC	Rotorway Executive	S. J. Hanson
	G-BPND	Boeing 727-2D3	Sabre Airways Ltd Katie/Gatwick
	G-BPNF	Robinson R-22B	Heli Air Lta
	G-BPNI	Robinson R-22B	Heliflight (UK) Ltd
	G-BPNL	QAC Quickie Q.2	J. Catley
	G-BPNN	Montgomerie-Bensen B.8MR	M. E. Vahdat
	G-BPNO	Zlin Z.326 Trener Master	J. A. S. Bailey & S. T. Logan
	G-BPNT	BAe 146-300	Flightline Ltd
	G-BPNU	Thunder Ax7-77 balloon	M. J. Barnes
	G-BPOA	Gloster Meteor T.7 (WF877) ★	39 Restoration Group/North Weald
	G-BPOB	Sopwith Camel F.1 (replica) (B2458)	Bianchi Aviation Film Services Ltd/ Booker
	G-BPOL	Pietenpol Air Camper	G. W. Postance
	G-BPOM	PA-28-161 Warrior II	APB Leasing Ltd/Welshpool
	G-BPON	PA-34-200T Seneca II	Aeroshare Ltd/Staverton
	G-BPOO	Montgomerie-Bensen B.8MR	M. E. Vahdat

Reg.	Type	Owner or Operator	Notes
G-BPOS	Cessna 150M	K. J. Goggins	
G-BPOT	PA-28-181 Archer II	P. Fraser	
G-BPOU	Luscombe 8A Silvaire	M. J. Negus & R. Hardley	
G-BPOV	Cameron 90 Magazine SS balloon	Forbes Europe Inc/France	
G-BPPA	Cameron O-65 balloon	Rix Petroleum Ltd	
G-BPPD	PA-38-112 Tomahawk	Belting Products/Cardiff	
G-BPPE	PA-38-112 Tomahawk	M. R. Tingle	
G-BPPF	PA-38-112 Tomahawk	Bristol Strut Flying Group	
G-BPPJ	Cameron A-180 balloon	H. R. Evans	
G-BPPK	PA-28-151 Warrior	UK Technical Consultants Ltd	
G-BPPL	Enstrom F-28A	M. & P. Food Products Ltd	
G-BPPM	Beech B200 Super King Air	Gama Aviation Ltd/Fairoaks	
G-BPPO	Luscombe 8A Silvaire	I. K. Ratcliffe	
G-BPPP	Cameron V-77 balloon	Sarnia Balloon Group	
G-BPPS	Mudry CAARP CAP.21	J. E. Davies	
G-BPPU	Air Command 532 Elite	J. Hough	
G-BPPW	Schweizer 269C	Browns Distribution Services Ltd	
G-BPPY	Hughes 269B	N. J. Edmonds	
G-BPPZ	Taylorcraft BC-12D	Zulu Warriors Flying Group	
G-BPRA	Aeronca 11AC Chief	R. M. C. Hunter	
G-BPRC	Cameron 77 Elephant SS balloon	G. V. Beckwith/Germany	
G-BPRD	Pitts S-1C Special	S. M. Trickey	
G-BPRI	AS.355F-1 Twin Squirrel	Skyhopper Ltd (G-TVPA)	
G-BPRJ	AS.355F-1 Twin Squirrel	PLM Dollar Group Ltd/Inverness	
G-BPRL	AS.355F-1 Twin Squirrel	Gas & Air Ltd	
G-BPRM	Cessna F.172L	D. Rychlik (G-AZKG)	
G-BPRN	PA-28-161 Warrior II	Air Navigation & Trading Co Ltd/Blackpool	
G-BPRO	Cessna A.150K	Armphase Ltd	
G-BPRR	Rand KR-2	R. Trickett	
G-BPRS	Air Command 532 Elite	B. K. Snoxall	
G-BPRX	Aeronca 11AC Chief	D. J. Dumolo & C. R. Barnes/Breighton	
G-BPRY	PA-28-161 Warrior II	White Wings Aviation	
G-BPSA	Luscombe 8A Silvaire	K. P. Gorman/Staverton	
G-BPSH	Cameron V-77 balloon	P. G. Hossack	
G-BPSI	Thunder Ax10-160 balloon	Airborne Adventures Ltd	
G-BPSJ	Thunder Ax6-56 balloon	Capricorn Balloons Ltd	
G-BPSK	Montgomerie-Bensen B.8M	G. C. Kerr	
G-BPSL	Cessna 177	G-BPSL Group	
G-BPSO	Cameron N-90 balloon	J. Oberprieler/Germany	
G-BPSP	Cameron 90 Ship SS balloon	Forbes Europe Inc/France	
G-BPSR	Cameron V-77 balloon	K. J. A. Maxwell	
G-BPSS	Cameron A-120 balloon	Anglian Countryside Balloons	
G-BPSZ	Cameron N-180 balloon	A. Bolger	
G-BPTA	Stinson 108-2	M. L. Ryan	
G-BPTB	Boeing Stearman A.75N1 (FJ992)	Aero Vintage Ltd	
G-BPTD	Cameron V-77 balloon	J. Lippett	
G-BPTE	PA-28-181 Archer II	I. Chaplin	
G-BPTF	Cessna 152 II	Falcon Flying Services/Biggin Hill	
G-BPTG	R. Commander 112TC	M. A. Watteau	
G-BPTI	SOCATA TB.20 Trinidad	N. Davis	
G-BPTL	Cessna 172N	Cleveland Flying School Ltd/Teesside	
G-BPTO	Zenith CH.200-AA	B. Philips	
G-BPTP	Robinson R-22	Thorneygrove Ltd	
G-BPTS	C.A.S.A. 1.131E Jungmann 1000 (E3B-153)	Aerobatic Displays Ltd/Duxford	
G-BPTT	Robin DR.400/120	The Cotswold Aero Club Ltd/Staverton	
G-BPTU	Cessna 152	A. M. Alam/Panshanger	
G-BPTV	Bensen B.8	C. Munro	
G-BPTX	Cameron O-120 balloon	Skybus Ballooning	
G-BPTZ	Robinson R-22B	J. Lucketti	
G-BPUA	EAA Sport Biplane	V. Millard	
G-BPUB	Cameron V-31 balloon	M. T. Evans	
G-BPUC	QAC Quickie Q.200	S. R. Harvey	
G-BPUE	Air Command 532 Elite	A. H. Brent	
G-BPUF	Thunder Ax6-56Z balloon	R. C. & M. A. Trimble (G-BHRL)	
G-BPUG	Air Command 532 Elite	T. A. Holmes	
G-BPUJ	Cameron N-90 balloon	D. Grimshaw	
G-BPUL	PA-18 Super Cub 150	C. D. Duthy-James	
G-BPUM	Cessna R.182RG	R. C. Chapman	
G-BPUP	Whittaker MW-7	J. H. Beard	
G-BPUR	Piper J-3L-65 Cub★	A. D. Monro	
G-BPUS	Rans S.9	T. A. Wright	

Notes	Reg.	Type	Owner or Operator
	G-BPUU	Cessna 140	Sherburn Aero Club Ltd
	G-BPUW	Colt 90A balloon	Huntair Ltd
	G-BPUX	Cessna 150J	BCT Aircraft Leasing Ltd
	G-BPVA	Cessna 172F	S. Lancashire Flyers Group Ltd
	G-BPVC	Cameron V-77 balloon	J. B. R. Elliot
	G-BPVE	Bleriot IX (replica) (1197) ★	Bianchi Aviation Film Services Ltd/Booker
	G-BPVH	Cub Aircraft J-3C-65 Prospector	D. E. Cooper-Maguire
	G-BPVI	PA-32R-301 Saratoga SP	M. T. Coppen/Booker
	G-BPVJ	Cessna 152 II	Multiflight Ltd
	G-BPVK	Varga 2150A Kachina	H. W. Hall
	G-BPVM	Cameron V-77 balloon	Royal Engineers Balloon Club
	G-BPVN	PA-32R-301T Turbo Saratoga SP	Y. Leysen
	G-BPVO	Cassutt Racer IIIM	R. J. Adams & D. R. Puleston
	G-BPVP	Pitts S-2B Special	J. A. Harris
	G-BPVU	Thunder Ax7-77 balloon	B. J. Hammond
	G-BPVW	C.A.S.A. 1.131E Jungmann 2000	C. & J-W. Labeij/Netherlands
	G-BPVY	Cessna 172D	Unitek Aviation Ltd/Eaton Bray
	G-BPVZ	Luscombe 8E Silvaire	W. E. Gillham & P. Ryman
	G-BPWA	PA-28-161 Warrior II	Leisure Park Management Ltd
	G-BPWB	Sikorsky S-61N	Bristow Helicopters Ltd
	G-BPWC	Cameron V-77 balloon	H. B. Roberts
	G-BPWD	Cessna 120	Peregrine Flying Group
	G-BPWE	PA-28-161 Warrior II	RPR Associates Ltd/Swansea
	G-BPWF	PA-28 Cherokee 140 ★	(static display)/1244 Sqdn ATC/Swindon
	G-BPWG	Cessna 150M	W. R. Spicer & I. D. Carling
	G-BPWI	Bell 206B JetRanger 3	S. & J. M. Taylor
	G-BPWK	Sportavia Fournier RF-5B	S. L. Reed
	G-BPWL	PA-25 Pawnee 235	Marchington Gliding Club Ltd
	G-BPWM	Cessna 150L	M. E. Creasey
	G-BPWN	Cessna 150L	International Aerospace Engineering Ltd
	G-BPWP	Rutan LongEz (modified)	D. A. Field
	G-BPWR	Cessna R.172K	A. M. Skelton
	G-BPWS	Cessna 172P	Chartstone Ltd
	G-BPWT	Cameron DG-19 airship	Airspace Outdoor Advertising Ltd
	G-BPXA	PA-28-181 Archer II	Cherokee Flying Group/Netherthorpe
	G-BPXB	Glaser-Dirks DG.400	K. M. Fresson & G. C. Westgate
	G-BPXE	Enstrom 280C Shark	A. Healy
	G-BPXF	Cameron V-65 balloon	D. Pascall
	G-BPXH	Colt 17A balloon	Sport Promotion SRL/Italy
	G-BPXJ	PA-28RT-201T Turbo Arrow IV	K. M. Hollamby/Biggin Hill
	G-BPXX	PA-34-200T Seneca II	Laden Project Management Services
	G-BPXY	Aeronca 11AC Chief	S. Hawksworth
	G-BPYI	Cameron O-77 balloon	Fly by Night Balloon Group
	G-BPYJ	Wittman W.8 Tailwind	J. Dixon
	G-BPYK	Thunder Ax7-77 balloon	A. R. Swinnerton
	G-BPYL	Hughes 369D	Morcorp (BVI) Ltd
	G-BPYN	Piper J-3C-65 Cub	The Aquila Group/White Waltham
	G-BPYO	PA-28-181 Archer II	Sherburn Aero Club Ltd
	G-BPYR	PA-31-310 Turbo Navajo	Multi Ltd (G-ECMA)
	G-BPYS	Cameron O-77 balloon	D. J. Goldsmith
	G-BPYT	Cameron V-77 balloon	M. H. Redman
	G-BPYV	Cameron V-77 balloon	Zebedee Balloon Service Ltd
	G-BPYY	Cameron A-180 balloon	G. D. Fitzpatrick
	G-BPYZ	Thunder Ax7-77 balloon	J. E. Astall
	G-BPZA	Luscombe 8A Silvaire	T. P. W. Hyde
	G-BPZB	Cessna 120	C. & M. A. Grime
	G-BPZC	Luscombe 8A Silvaire	C. C. & J. M. Lovell
	G-BPZD	SNCAN NC.858S	G. Richards
	G-BPZE	Luscombe 8E Silvaire	WFG Luscombe Associates
	G-BPZI	Christen Eagle II	S. D. Quigley/Breighton
	G-BPZK	Cameron O-120 balloon	D. L. Smith
	G-BPZM	PA-28RT-201 Arrow IV	R. Taylor (G-ROYW/G-CRTI)
	G-BPZO	Cameron N-90 balloon	Seaward Homes (South) Ltd
	G-BPZP	Robin DR.400/180R	Lasham Gliding Soc. Ltd
	G-BPZS	Colt 105A balloon	L. V. Mastis
	G-BPZU	Scheibe SF.25C Falke	G-BPZU Group/Parham Park
	G-BPZY	Pitts S-1C Special	J. S. Mitchell
	G-BPZZ	Thunder Ax8-105 balloon	Capricorn Balloons Ltd
	G-BRAA	Pitts S-1C Special	C. Davidson
	G-BRAF	V.S.394 Spitfire FR.XVIII (SM969)	Wizard Investments Ltd
	G-BRAJ	Cameron V-77 balloon	A. W. J. & C. Weston
	G-BRAK	Cessna 172N	T. I. Mason & C. J. Mewis

Reg.	Type	Owner or Operator	Notes
G-BRAM	Mikoyan MiG-21PF (503)	Jet Heritage/Bournemouth	
G-BRAP	Thermal Aircraft 104	Thermal Aircraft	
G-BRAR	Aeronca 7AC Champion	C. D. Ward	
G-BRAW	Pitts S-1C Special	P. G. Bond & P. B. Hunter	
G-BRAX	Payne Knight Twister 85B	R. Earl	
G-BRBA	PA-28-161 Warrior II	Halfpenny Green Flight Centre Ltd	
G-BRBB	PA-28-161 Warrior II	Aeroshow Ltd	
G-BRBC	NA T-6G Texan	A. P. Murphy	
G-BRBD	PA-28-151 Warrior	Bravo Delta Group/Bournemouth	
G-BRBE	PA-28-161 Warrior II	Solo Services Ltd/Shoreham	
G-BRBF	Cessna 152 II	Jackson's Tool & Plant Hire	
G-BRBG	PA-28 Cherokee 180	Ken MacDonald & Co	
G-BRBH	Cessna 150H	Professional Flight Management Ltd & S. J. Reeves	
G-BRBI	Cessna 172N	G-BRBI Flying Group	
G-BRBJ	Cessna 172M	I. R. March	
G-BRBK	Robin DR.400/180	R. Kemp	
G-BRBL	Robin DR.400/180	C. A. Merren	
G-BRBM	Robin DR.400/180	R. W. Davies/Headcorn	
G-BRBN	Pitts S-1S Special	D. R. Evans	
G-BRBO	Cameron V-77 balloon	M. B. Murby	
G-BRBP	Cessna 152	Staverton Flying Services Ltd	
G-BRBS	Bensen B.8M	K. T. MacFarlane	
G-BRBT	Trotter Ax3-20 balloon	R. M. Trotter	
G-BRBU	Colt 17A balloon	Virgin Airship & Balloon Co Ltd	
G-BRBV	Piper J-4A Cub Coupé	M. Yeo & J. Schonburg	
G-BRBW	PA-28 Cherokee 140	Cherokee Cruiser Aircraft Group/ Shoreham	
G-BRBX	PA-28-181 Archer II	M. J. Ireland	
G-BRBY	Robinson R-22B	Plane Talking Ltd/Elstree	
G-BRCA	Jodel D.112	R. C. Jordan	
G-BRCD	Cessna A.152	D. E. Simmons/Shoreham	
G-BRCE	Pitts S-1C Special	R. O. Rogers	
G-BRCF	Montgomerie-Bensen B.8MR	J. S. Walton	
G-BRCG	Grob G.109	Oxfordshire Sportflying Ltd/Enstone	
G-BRCI	Pitts S-1C Special	G. L. A. Vandormael/Belgium	
G-BRCJ	Cameron NS-20 balloon	P. de Cock/Belgium	
G-BRCM	Cessna 172L	S. G. E. Plessis & D. C. C. Handley	
G-BRCO	Cameron NS-20 balloon	M. Davies	
G-BRCT	Denney Kitfox Mk 2	L. A. James	
G-BRCV	Aeronca 7AC Champion	J. M. Gale	
G-BRCW	Aeronca 11AC Chief	R. B. McComish	
G-BRDB	Zenair CH.701 STOL	D. L. Bowtell	
G-BRDC	Thunder Ax7-77 balloon	Zebedee Balloon Service	
G-BRDD	Avions Mudry CAP.10B	R. D. Dickson/Gamston	
G-BRDE	Thunder Ax7-77 balloon	C. C. Brash	
G-BRDF	PA-28-161 Warrior II	White Waltham Airfield Ltd	
G-BRDG	PA-28-161 Warrior II	White Waltham Airfield Ltd	
G-BRDJ	Luscombe 8A Silvaire	J. D. Parker	
G-BRDM	PA-28-161 Warrior II	White Waltham Airfield Ltd	
G-BRDN	M.S.880B Rallye Club	B. J. D. Peatfield	
G-BRDO	Cessna 177B	Cardinal Aviation	
G-BRDP	Colt Jumbo SS balloon	Virgin Airship & Balloon Co Ltd	
G-BRDT	Cameron DP-70 airship	M. M. Cobbold	
G-BRDV	Viking Wood Products Spitfire Prototype replica (K5054)	Replica Spitfire Ltd	
G-BRDW	PA-24 Comanche 180	I. P. Gibson/Switzerland	
G-BREA	Bensen B.8MR	T. J. Deane	
G-BREB	Piper J-3C-65 Cub	L. W. & O. Usherwood	
G-BREE	Whittaker MW.7	G. Hawkins	
G-BREH	Cameron V-65 balloon	S. E. & V. D. Hurst	
G-BREL	Cameron O-77 balloon	R. A. Patey	
G-BREM	Air Command 532 Elite	T. W. Freeman	
G-BREP	PA-28RT-201 Arrow IV	TDR Aviation Ltd	
G-BRER	Aeronca 7AC Champion	Rabbit Flight	
G-BREU	Montgomerie-Bensen B.8MR	M. A. Hayward	
G-BREX	Cameron O-84 balloon	Ovolo Ltd	
G-BREY	Taylorcraft BC-12D	BREY Group	
G-BRFB	Rutan LongEz	R. A. Gardiner	
G-BRFE	Cameron V-77 balloon	Ezmeralda Balloon Syndicate	
G-BRFF	Colt 90A balloon	Amber Valley Aviation	
G-BRFH	Colt 90A balloon	Polydron UK Ltd	
G-BRFI	Aeronca 7DC Champion	A. C. Lines	

Notes	Reg.	Type	Owner or Operator
	G-BRFJ	Aeronca 11AC Chief	A. Gault
	G-BRFL	PA-38-112 Tomahawk	Teesside Flight Centre Ltd
	G-BRFM	PA-28-161 Warrior II	Air Caernarfon Ltd
	G-BRFN	PA-38-112 Tomahawk	Light Aircraft Leasing (UK) Ltd
	G-BRFO	Cameron V-77 balloon	Hedge Hoppers Balloon Group
	G-BRFP	Schweizer 269C	Heli Hopper Ltd
	G-BRFW	Montgomerie-Bensen B.8 2-seat	J. M. Montgomerie
	G-BRFX	Pazmany PL.4A	D. E. Hills
	G-BRGD	Cameron O-84 balloon	J. R. H. & M. A. Ashworth
	G-BRGE	Cameron N-90 balloon	Oakfield Farm Products Ltd
	G-BRGF	Luscombe 8E Silvaire	Luscombe Flying Group
	G-BRGG	Luscombe 8A Silvaire	M. A. Lamprell
	G-BRGI	PA-28 Cherokee 180	Golf India Aviation Ltd/Redhill
	G-BRGN	BAe Jetstream 3102	BAe (Operations) Ltd (G-BLHC)/Warton
	G-BRGO	Air Command 532 Elite	A. McCredie
	G-BRGT	PA-32 Cherokee Six 260	P. Cowley
	G-BRGW	GY-201 Minicab	R. G. White
	G-BRGX	Rotorway Executive	D. W. J. Lee
	G-BRHA	PA-32RT-300 Lance II	Lance G-BRHA Group
	G-BRHB	Boeing Stearman B.75N1	D. Calabritto
	G-BRHC	Cameron V-77 balloon	Golf Centres Balloons Ltd/Italy
	G-BRHG	Colt 90A balloon	Bath University Students' Union
	G-BRHL	Montgomerie-Bensen B.8MR	A. McCredie/Carlisle
	G-BRHM	Bensen B.8M	H. P. Latham
	G-BRHN	Robinson R-22B	Plane Talking Ltd/Elstree
	G-BRHO	PA-34-200 Seneca	D. A. Lewis/Luton
	G-BRHP	Aeronca O-58B Grasshopper (31923)	J. G. Townsend
	G-BRHR	PA-38-112 Tomahawk	Air Nova PLC/Liverpool
	G-BRHT	PA-38-112 Tomahawk	Air Nova PLC/Liverpool
	G-BRHU	Montgomerie-Bensen B.8MR	G. L. & S. R. Moon
	G-BRHW	D.H.82A Tiger Moth	P. J. & A. J. Borsberry
	G-BRHX	Luscombe 8E Silvaire	J. Lakin
	G-BRHY	Luscombe 8E Silvaire	D. Lofts & A. R. W. Taylor/Sleap
	G-BRHZ	Stephens Akro Astro 235	T. A. Shears
	G-BRIA	Cessna 310L	B. J. Tucker & R. C. Pugsley
	G-BRIB	Cameron N-77 balloon	D. Stitt
	G-BRIE	Cameron N-77 balloon	S. J. Bettin
	G-BRIF	Boeing 767-204ER	Britannia Airways Ltd *Horatio Nelson*
	G-BRIG	Boeing 767-204ER	Britannia Airways Ltd *Eglantyne Jebb*
	G-BRIH	Taylorcraft BC-12D	A. D. Duke
	G-BRII	Zenair CH.600 Zodiac	A. C. Bowdrey
	G-BRIJ	Taylorcraft F-19	K. E. Ballington
	G-BRIK	T.66 Nipper 3	C. W. R. Piper
	G-BRIL	Piper J-5A Cub Cruiser	P. L. Jobes
	G-BRIM	Cameron O-160 balloon	Golf Centres Balloons Ltd/Italy
	G-BRIO	Turner Super T-40A	G-BRIO Flyers
	G-BRIR	Cameron V-56 balloon	H. G. Davies & C. Dowd
	G-BRIS	Steen Skybolt	P. D. Harrison
	G-BRIV	SOCATA TB.9 Tampico Club	Gowad Aviation Ltd
	G-BRIY	Taylorcraft DF-65 (42-58678)	J. D. Tseliki
	G-BRJA	Luscombe 8A Silvaire	A. D. Keen
	G-BRJB	Zenair CH.600 Zodiac	D. J. Hunter
	G-BRJC	Cessna 120	One Twenty Group
	G-BRJK	Luscombe 8A Silvaire	C. J. L. Peat & M. Richardson
	G-BRJL	PA-15 Vagabond	C. P. Ware & C. R. Leech
	G-BRJN	Pitts S-1C Special	W. Chapel
	G-BRJR	PA-38-112 Tomahawk	Chester Aviation Ltd
	G-BRJT	Cessna 150H	J. Eagles
	G-BRJV	PA-28-161 Cadet	Newcastle-upon-Tyne Aero Club Ltd
	G-BRJW	Bellanca 7GCBC Citabria	F. A. L. Castleden & A. J. Sillis
	G-BRJX	Rand KR-2	D. H. Evans
	G-BRJY	Rand KR-2	R. E. Taylor
	G-BRKC	J/1 Autocrat	J. W. Conlon
	G-BRKD	Piaggio FWP.149D	P. E. H. Scott
	G-BRKH	PA-28-236 Dakota	P. A. Wright & P. W. Lever
	G-BRKL	Cameron H-34 balloon	B. J. Newman
	G-BRKN	Robinson R-22 Mariner	P. M. Webber/Greece
	G-BRKR	Cessna 182R	A. R. D. Brooker
	G-BRKW	Cameron V-77 balloon	T. J. Parker
	G-BRKX	Air Command 532 Elite	K. Davis
	G-BRKY	Viking Dragonfly Mk II	G. D. Price
	G-BRLB	Air Command 532 Elite	F. G. Shepherd

Reg.	Type	Owner or Operator	Notes
G-BRLF	Campbell Cricket (replica)	D. Wood	
G-BRLG	PA-28RT-201T Turbo Arrow IV	C. G. Westwood	
G-BRLI	Piper J-5A Cub Cruiser	Little Bear Ltd	
G-BRLJ	Evans VP-2	R. L. Jones	
G-BRLL	Cameron A-105 balloon	Adventure Flights Ltd	
G-BRLO	PA-38-112 Tomahawk	Scotia Safari Ltd/Prestwick	
G-BRLP	PA-38-112 Tomahawk	D. A. Whitmore	
G-BRLR	Cessna 150G	D. C. Maxwell	
G-BRLS	Thunder Ax7-77 balloon	E. C. Meek	
G-BRLT	Colt 77A balloon	D. Bareford	
G-BRLV	CCF Harvard IV (93542)	B. C. Abela	
G-BRLX	Cameron N-77 balloon	National Power	
G-BRLY	BAe ATP	Trident Leasing Services Ltd	
G-BRMA	W.S.51 Dragonfly HR.5 (WG719) ★	IHM/Weston-s-Mare	
G-BRMB	B.192 Belvedere HC.1 (XG452) ★	IHM/Weston-s-Mare	
G-BRME	PA-28-181 Archer II	Keen Leasing Ltd	
G-BRMG	V.S.384 Seafire XVII (SX336)	P. J. Wood	
G-BRMI	Cameron V-65 balloon	M. Davies	
G-BRMJ	PA-38-112 Tomahawk	Aerohire Ltd/Halfpenny Green	
G-BRML	PA-38-112 Tomahawk	P. H. Rogers/Coventry	
G-BRMS	PA-28RT-201 Arrow IV	Fleetbridge Ltd	
G-BRMT	Cameron V-31 balloon	T. C. Hinton	
G-BRMU	Cameron V-77 balloon	K. J. & G. R. Ibbotson	
G-BRMV	Cameron O-77 balloon	P. D. Griffiths	
G-BRMW	Whittaker MW.7	N. Crisp	
G-BRNC	Cessna 150M	D. C. Bonsall	
G-BRND	Cessna 152 II	T. M. & M. L. Jones/Egginton	
G-BRNE	Cessna 152 II	Aerohire Ltd/Halfpenny Green	
G-BRNJ	PA-38-112 Tomahawk	Aerohire Ltd/Halfpenny Green	
G-BRNK	Cessna 152 II	Sheffield Aero Club Ltd/Netherthorpe	
G-BRNM	Chichester-Miles Leopard	Chichester-Miles Consultants Ltd	
G-BRNN	Cessna 152 II	Sheffield Aero Club Ltd/Netherthorpe	
G-BRNP	Rotorway Executive	R. Turner	
G-BRNT	Robin DR.400/180	M. J. Cowham	
G-BRNU	Robin DR.400/180	November Uniform Travel Syndicate Ltd/ Booker	
G-BRNV	PA-28-181 Archer II	B. S. Hobbs	
G-BRNW	Cameron V-77 balloon	N. Robertson & G. Smith	
G-BRNX	PA-22 Tri-Pacer 150	R. S. Tomlinson & B. Yager	
G-BRNZ	PA-32 Cherokee Six 300B	IML Aviation Ltd	
G-BROB	Cameron V-77 balloon	R. W. Richardson	
G-BROE	Cameron N-65 balloon	R. H. Sanderson	
G-BROG	Cameron V-65 balloon	R. Kunert	
G-BROH	Cameron O-90 balloon	P. A. Wenlock	
G-BROI	CFM Streak Shadow Srs SA	G. W. Rowbotham	
G-BROJ	Colt 31A balloon	Virgin Airship & Balloon Co Ltd	
G-BROL	Colt AS-80 Mk II airship	G. Gratius/Germany	
G-BROP	Vans RV-4	K. E. Armstrong	
G-BROR	Piper J-3C-65 Cub	White Hart Flying Group	
G-BROX	Robinson R-22B	Defence Products Ltd	
G-BROY	Cameron V-77 balloon	T. G. S. Dixon	
G-BROZ	PA-18 Super Cub 150	P. G. Kynsey	
G-BRPE	Cessna 120	J. M. Fowler	
G-BRPF	Cessna 120	D. Sharp/Breighton	
G-BRPG	Cessna 120	I. C. Lomax	
G-BRPH	Cessna 120	J. A. Cook	
G-BRPJ	Cameron N-90 balloon	Cloud Nine Balloon Co	
G-BRPK	PA-28 Cherokee 140	J. P. A. Gomes	
G-BRPL	PA-28 Cherokee 140	Comed Aviation Ltd/Blackpool	
G-BRPM	T.66 Nipper 3	T. C. Horner	
G-BRPO	Enstrom 280C Shark	C. M. Evans & J. W. Blaylock	
G-BRPP	Brookland Hornet (modified)	B. J. L. P. & W. J. A. L. de Saar	
G-BRPR	Aeronca O-58B Grasshopper (31952)	C. S. Tolchard	
G-BRPS	Cessna 177B	R. C. Tebbett	
G-BRPT	Rans S.10 Sakota	B. G. Morris	
G-BRPU	Beech 76 Duchess	Hamilton Compass Aviation Ltd/Liverpool	
G-BRPV	Cessna 152	GEM Rewinds Ltd/Coventry	
G-BRPX	Taylorcraft BC-12D	M. J. Brett	
G-BRPY	PA-15 Vagabond	J. P. Esson	
G-BRPZ	Luscombe 8A Silvaire	S. L. & J. P. Waring	
G-BRRA	V.S.361 Spitfire LF.IXe (MK912)	Historic Flying Ltd/Audley End	

Notes	Reg.	Type	Owner or Operator
	G-BRRB	Luscombe 8E Silvaire	C. G. Ferguson & D. W. Gladwin
	G-BRRD	Scheibe SF.25B Falke	Richard Collings Ltd
	G-BRRF	Cameron O-77 balloon	Mid-Bucks Farmers Balloon Group
	G-BRRG	Glaser-Dirks DG.500M	Glider Syndicate/Sutton Bank
	G-BRRJ	PA-28RT-201T Turbo Arrow IV	M. Stower
	G-BRRK	Cessna 182Q	M. G. Mitchell
	G-BRRL	PA-18 Super Cub 95	Acebell G-BRRL Syndicate/Redhill
	G-BRRM	PA-28-161 Cadet	R. H. Sellier
	G-BRRN	PA-28-161 Warrior II	Spinseal Ltd
	G-BRRO	Cameron N-77 balloon	P. W. Limpus & I. J. Liddiard
	G-BRRR	Cameron V-77 balloon	L. M. Heal & A. P. Wilcox
	G-BRRS	Pitts S-1C Special	R. C. Atkinson
	G-BRRU	Colt 90A balloon	Reach For The Sky Ltd
	G-BRRW	Cameron O-77 balloon	D. V. Fowler
	G-BRRY	Robinson R-22B	P. W. Vellacott
	G-BRSA	Cameron N-56 balloon	C. Wilkinson
	G-BRSC	Rans S.10 Sakota	M. A. C. Stephenson
	G-BRSD	Cameron V-77 balloon	T. J. Porter & J. E. Kelly
	G-BRSE	PA-28-161 Warrior II	Startown Ltd
	G-BRSG	PA-28-161 Cadet	Holmes Rentals/Denham
	G-BRSH	C.A.S.A. 1.131E Jungmann 2000 (781-25)	L. Ness/Norway
	G-BRSJ	PA-38-112 Tomahawk II	APB Leasing Ltd/Welshpool
	G-BRSK	Boeing Stearman N2S-3 (1180)	Wymondham Engineering
	G-BRSL	Cameron N-56 balloon	S. Budd
	G-BRSN	Rand-Robinson KR-2	K. W. Darby
	G-BRSO	CFM Streak Shadow Srs SA	D. J. Smith
	G-BRSP	Air Command 532 Elite	G. M. Hobman
	G-BRSW	Luscombe 8A Silvaire	Bloody Mary Aviation
	G-BRSX	PA-15 Vagabond	C. Milne-Fowler
	G-BRSY	Hatz CB-1	G. A. Barrett & Son/Breighton
	G-BRTA	PA-38-112 Tomahawk	Cardiff-Wales Flying Club Ltd
	G-BRTD	Cessna 152 II	152 Group
	G-BRTH	Cameron A-180 balloon	The Ballooning Business Ltd
	G-BRTI	Robinson R-22B	Morhire
	G-BRTJ	Cessna 150F	Avon Aviation Ltd
	G-BRTK	Boeing Stearman E.75 (FJ777)	Eastern Stearman Ltd/Swanton Morley
	G-BRTL	Hughes 369E	Crewhall Ltd
	G-BRTM	PA-28-161 Warrior II	Oxford Aviation Services Ltd/Kidlington
	G-BRTN	Beech 95-B58 Baron	Colneway Ltd/Guernsey
	G-BRTP	Cessna 152 II	Tatenhill Aviation
	G-BRTT	Schweizer 269C	Fairthorpe Ltd/Denham
	G-BRTV	Cameron O-77 balloon	C. Vening
	G-BRTW	Glaser-Dirks DG.400	I. J. Carruthers
	G-BRTX	PA-28-151 Warrior	Spectrum Flying Group
	G-BRTZ	Slingsby T.31 Motor Cadet III	R. R. Walters/Belgium
	G-BRUA	Cessna 152 II	Griffin Marston Ltd/Compton Abbas
	G-BRUB	PA-28-161 Warrior II	Flytrek Ltd/Bournemouth
	G-BRUD	PA-28-181 Archer II	Wilkins & Wilkins Special Auctions Ltd
	G-BRUE	Cameron V-77 balloon	B. J. Newman & P. L. Harrison
	G-BRUG	Luscombe 8E Silvaire	P. A. Cain & N. W. Barratt
	G-BRUH	Colt 105A balloon	D. C. Chipping/Portugal
	G-BRUI	PA-44-180 Seminole	Tatenhill Aviation
	G-BRUJ	Boeing Stearman A.75N1 (6136)	M. Walker/Liverpool
	G-BRUM	Cessna A.152	Aerohire Ltd/Halfpenny Green
	G-BRUN	Cessna 120	O. C. Brun (G-BRDH)
	G-BRUO	Taylor JT.1 Monoplane	G. Verity
	G-BRUT	Thunder Ax8-90 balloon	Moet & Chandon (London) Ltd
	G-BRUU	EAA Biplane Model P.1	R. D. Harper
	G-BRUV	Cameron V-77 balloon	T. W. & R. F. Benbrook
	G-BRUX	PA-44-180 Seminole	Hambrair Ltd/Tollerton
	G-BRVB	Stolp SA.300 Starduster Too	M. N. Petchey & S. Turner
	G-BRVC	Cameron N-180 balloon	A. J. Street
	G-BRVE	Beech D.17S	Intrepid Aviation Co/North Weald
	G-BRVF	Colt 77A balloon	The Ballooning Business Ltd
	G-BRVG	NA SNJ-7 Texan (27)	Intrepid Aviation Co/North Weald
	G-BRVH	Smyth Model S Sidewinder	I. S. Bellamy
	G-BRVI	Robinson R-22B	P. M. Whitaker
	G-BRVJ	Slingsby T.31 Motor Cadet III	B. Outhwaite
	G-BRVL	Pitts S-1C Special	M. F. Pocock
	G-BRVN	Thunder Ax7-77 balloon	D. L. Beckwith
	G-BRVO	AS.350B Ecureuil	Malcolm Wilson (Motorsport) Ltd
	G-BRVR	Barnett J4B-2 Rotorcraft	Ilkeston Contractors

Reg.	Type	Owner or Operator	Notes
G-BRVS	Barnett J4B-2 Rotorcraft	Ilkeston Contractors	
G-BRVT	Pitts S-2B Special	C. J. & M. D. Green	
G-BRVU	Colt 77A balloon	J. K. Woods	
G-BRVV	Colt 56B balloon	S. J. Hollingsworth	
G-BRVY	Thunder Ax8-90 balloon	G. E. Morris	
G-BRVZ	Jodel D.117	J. G. Patton	
G-BRWA	Aeronca 7AC Champion	D. D. Smith & J. R. Edwards	
G-BRWB	NA T-6G Texan (51-14526)	R. Clifford	
G-BRWD	Robinson R22B	Matrix Aviation Ltd	
G-BRWF	Thunder Ax7-77 balloon	D. J. Greaves	
G-BRWH	Cameron N-77 balloon	C. P. G. Edmond	
G-BRWO	PA-28 Cherokee 140	Fergair Ltd/Bournemouth	
G-BRWP	CFM Streak Shadow	M. M. Bain	
G-BRWR	Aeronca 11AC Chief	R. M. Lee	
G-BRWT	Scheibe SF.25C Falke	Booker Gliding Club Ltd	
G-BRWU	Luton LA-4A Minor	R. B. Webber & P. K. Pike	
G-BRWV	Brügger MB.2 Colibri	S. J. McCollum	
G-BRWX	Cessna 172P	D. A. Abels	
G-BRWY	Cameron H-34 balloon	E. Kraft/Belgium	
G-BRWZ	Cameron 90 Macaw SS balloon	Forbes Europe Inc/France	
G-BRXA	Cameron O-120 balloon	Gone With The Wind Ltd & R. J. Mansfield	
G-BRXB	Thunder Ax7-77 balloon	H. Peel	
G-BRXC	PA-28-161 Warrior II	Oxford Aviation Services Ltd/Kidlington	
G-BRXD	PA-28-181 Archer II	D. D. Stone	
G-BRXE	Taylorcraft BC-12D	W. J. Durrad	
G-BRXF	Aeronca 11AC Chief	A. B. Newman	
G-BRXG	Aeronca 7AC Champion	X-Ray Golf Flying Group	
G-BRXH	Cessna 120	BRXH Group	
G-BRXL	Aeronca 11AC Chief (42-78044)	G-BRXL Group	
G-BRXN	Montgomerie-Bensen B.8MR	G. Robertson	
G-BRXO	PA-34-200T Seneca II	Aviation Services Ltd	
G-BRXP	SNCAN Stampe SV-4C (modified)	P. G. Kavanagh & D. T. Kaberry/Barton	
G-BRXS	Howard Special T Minus	A. Shuttleworth	
G-BRXU	AS.332L Super Puma	Bristow Helicopters Ltd	
G-BRXV	Robinson R-22B	Tukair Aircraft Charter	
G-BRXW	PA-24 Comanche 260	Oak Group	
G-BRXY	Pietenpol Air Camper	P. S. Ganczakowski	
G-BRYA	D.H.C.7-110 Dash Seven	Brymon Off Shore Charter	
G-BRYD	D.H.C.7-110 Dash Seven	Brymon Off Shore Charter	
G-BRYI	D.H.C.8-311 Dash Eight	Brymon Airways Ltd/British Airways	
G-BRYJ	D.H.C.8-311 Dash Eight	Brymon Airways Ltd/British Airways	
G-BRYN	SOCATA TB.20 Trinidad	Anglo American Airmotive Ltd	
G-BRYO	D.H.C.8-311 Dash Eight	Brymon Airways Ltd/British Airways	
G-BRYP	D.H.C.8-311 Dash Eight	Brymon Airways Ltd/British Airways	
G-BRYR	D.H.C.8-311 Dash Eight	Brymon Airways Ltd/British Airways	
G-BRYS	D.H.C.8-311 Dash Eight	Brymon Airways Ltd/British Airways	
G-BRYT	D.H.C.8-311 Dash Eight	Brymon Airways Ltd/British Airways	
G-BRYU	D.H.C.8Q-311 Dash Eight	Brymon Airways Ltd/British Airways	
G-BRYV	D.H.C.8Q-311 Dash Eight	Brymon Airways Ltd/British Airways	
G-BRYW	D.H.C.8Q-311 Dash Eight	Brymon Airways Ltd/British Airways	
G-BRYX	D.H.C.8Q-311 Dash Eight	Brymon Airways Ltd/British Airways	
G-BRYY	D.H.C.8Q-311 Dash Eight	Brymon Airways Ltd/British Airways	
G-BRYZ	D.H.C.8Q-311 Dash Eight	Brymon Airways Ltd/British Airways	
G-BRZA	Cameron O-77 balloon	L. & R. J. Mold	
G-BRZB	Cameron A-105 balloon	Headland Services Ltd	
G-BRZD	Hapi Cygnet SF-2A	L. G. Millen	
G-BRZE	Thunder Ax7-77 balloon	G. V. Beckwith & F. Schoeder/Germany	
G-BRZG	Enstrom F-28A	S. M. Bell/Barton	
G-BRZI	Cameron N-180 balloon	Eastern Balloon Rides	
G-BRZK	Stinson 108-2	Voyager G-BRZK Syndicate	
G-BRZL	Pitts S-1D Special	R. T. Cardwell/Elstree	
G-BRZO	Jodel D.18	J. D. Anson	
G-BRZP	PA-28-161 Warrior II	Keen Leasing (IOM) Ltd	
G-BRZS	Cessna 172P	YP Flying Group/Blackpool	
G-BRZT	Cameron V-77 balloon	B. Drawbridge	
G-BRZU	Colt Flying Cheese SS balloon	N. Charbonnier/Italy	
G-BRZV	Colt Flying Apple SS balloon	Thrust Drive Ltd/Austria	
G-BRZW	Rans S.10 Sakota	D. L. Davies	
G-BRZX	Pitts S-1S Special	J. H. Milne & T. H. Bishop	
G-BRZZ	CFM Streak Shadow	Shetland Flying Group	

Notes	Reg.	Type	Owner or Operator
	G-BSAI	Stoddard-Hamilton Glasair III	K. J. & P. J. Whitehead
	G-BSAJ	C.A.S.A. 1.131E Jungmann 2000	P. G. Kynsey/Redhill
	G-BSAK	Colt 21A balloon	Northern Flights
	G-BSAS	Cameron V-65 balloon	J. R. Barber
	G-BSAV	Thunder Ax7-77 balloon	E. A. Evans & ptnrs
	G-BSAW	PA-28-161 Warrior II	Carill Aviation Ltd/Southampton
	G-BSAX	Piper J-3C-65 Cub	K. & J. I. Harness
	G-BSAZ	Denney Kitfox Mk 2	A. J. Lloyd & ptnrs
	G-BSBA	PA-28-161 Warrior II	Doughton Aviation Services
	G-BSBG	CCF Harvard IV (20310)	A. P. St John/Liverpool
	G-BSBH	Short SD3-30 ★	Ulster Aviation Soc Museum *(stored)*
	G-BSBI	Cameron O-77 balloon	D. M. Billing
	G-BSBK	Colt 105A balloon	Zebra Ballooning Ltd
	G-BSBN	Thunder Ax7-77 balloon	B. Pawson
	G-BSBP	Jodel D.18	R. T. Pratt
	G-BSBR	Cameron V-77 balloon	R. P. Wade
	G-BSBT	Piper J-3C-65 Cub	R. W. H. Watson
	G-BSBV	Rans S.10 Sakota	R. V. Cameron
	G-BSBW	Bell 206B JetRanger 3	D. T. Sharpe
	G-BSBX	Montgomerie-Bensen B.8MR	B. Ibbott
	G-BSBZ	Cessna 150M	DTG Aviation
	G-BSCA	Cameron N-90 balloon	P. J. Marshall & M. A. Clarke
	G-BSCB	Air Command 532 Elite	P. H. Smith
	G-BSCC	Colt 105A balloon	Capricorn Balloons Ltd
	G-BSCE	Robinson R-22B	S. Thompson
	G-BSCF	Thunder Ax7-77 balloon	V. P. Gardiner
	G-BSCG	Denney Kitfox Mk 2	N. L. Beever/Breighton
	G-BSCH	Denney Kitfox Mk 2	M. P. M. Read
	G-BSCI	Colt 77A balloon	J. L. & S. Wrigglesworth
	G-BSCK	Cameron H-24 balloon	J. D. Shapland
	G-BSCL	Robinson R-22B	Skyhopper Ltd
	G-BSCM	Denney Kitfox Mk 2	S. A. Hewitt
	G-BSCN	SOCATA TB.20 Trinidad	B. W. Dye
	G-BSCO	Thunder Ax7-77 balloon	F. J. Whalley
	G-BSCP	Cessna 152 II	Moray Flying Club (1990) Ltd/Kinloss
	G-BSCS	PA-28-181 Archer II	Wing Task Ltd
	G-BSCV	PA-28-161 Warrior II	Southwood Flying Group/Southend
	G-BSCW	Taylorcraft BC-65	S. Leach
	G-BSCX	Thunder Ax8-105 balloon	Balloon Flights Club Ltd
	G-BSCY	PA-28-151 Warrior	Falcon Flying Services/Biggin Hill
	G-BSCZ	Cessna 152 II	Eastern Executive Air Charter Ltd
	G-BSDA	Taylorcraft BC-12D	D. G. Edwards
	G-BSDB	Pitts S-1C Special	S. Adams
	G-BSDD	Denney Kitfox Mk 2	J. Windmill
	G-BSDG	Robin DR.400/180	P. A. Stephens
	G-BSDH	Robin DR.400/180	R. L. Brucciani
	G-BSDI	Corben Junior Ace Model E	T. K. Pullen & A. J. Staplehurst
	G-BSDJ	Piper J-4E Cub Coupé	B. M. Jackson
	G-BSDK	Piper J-5A Cub Cruiser	S. Haughton & I. S. Hodge
	G-BSDL	SOCATA TB.10 Tobago	Delta Lima Group/Sherburn
	G-BSDN	PA-34-200T Seneca II	McCormick Consulting Ltd
	G-BSDO	Cessna 152 II	L. W. Scattergood
	G-BSDP	Cessna 152 II	I. S. H. Paul
	G-BSDS	Boeing Stearman E.75 (118)	E. Hopper
	G-BSDU	Bell 206B JetRanger 3	Eaglecray Ltd
	G-BSDV	Colt 31A balloon	Virgin Airship & Balloon Co Ltd
	G-BSDW	Cessna 182P	Delta Whiskey Ltd
	G-BSDZ	Enstrom 280FX	Avalon Group Ltd (G-ODSC)
	G-BSED	PA-22 Tri-Pacer 160 (modified)	M. Henderson
	G-BSEE	Rans S.9	P. M. Semler
	G-BSEF	PA-28 Cherokee 180	B. Mills
	G-BSEG	Ken Brock KB-2 gyroplane	S. J. M. Ledingham
	G-BSEJ	Cessna 150M	Halfpenny Green Flight Centre Ltd
	G-BSEK	Robinson R-22	Heli Air Ltd/Booker
	G-BSEL	Slingsby T.61G Super Falke	RAFGSA/Hullavington
	G-BSEP	Cessna 172	R. J. Tyson & Ptnrs/Redhill
	G-BSER	PA-28 Cherokee 160	Yorkair Ltd
	G-BSET	B.206 Srs 1 Basset (XS765)	Lawgra (No.386) Ltd/Cranfield
	G-BSEU	PA-28-181 Archer II	Euro Aviation 91 Ltd
	G-BSEV	Cameron O-77 balloon	The Ballooning Business Ltd
	G-BSEX	Cameron A-180 balloon	Heart of England Balloons
	G-BSEY	Beech A36 Bonanza	K. Phillips Ltd
	G-BSFA	Aero Designs Pulsar	S. A. Gill

Reg.	Type	Owner or Operator	Notes
G-BSFB	C.A.S.A. 1.131E Jungmann 2000 (S5-B06)	C. D. Beal	
G-BSFD	Piper J-3C-65 Cub	E. G. & N. S. C. English	
G-BSFE	PA-38-112 Tomahawk II	Chubbs Aviation Services (UK) Ltd	
G-BSFF	Robin DR.400/180R	Lasham Gliding Soc Ltd	
G-BSFJ	Thunder Ax8-105 balloon	C. Gibson & ptnrs	
G-BSFK	PA-28-161 Warrior II	Oxford Aviation Services Ltd/Kidlington	
G-BSFN	SE.313B Alouette II	A. C. Watson	
G-BSFP	Cessna 152T	J. R. Nicholls/Sibson	
G-BSFR	Cessna 152 II	Galair Ltd/Biggin Hill	
G-BSFS	SE.313B Alouette II	S. Lee/Coventry	
G-BSFV	Woods Woody Pusher	M. J. Wells	
G-BSFW	PA-15 Vagabond	J. R. Kimberley	
G-BSFX	Denney Kitfox Mk 2	T. A. Crone	
G-BSFY	Denney Kitfox Mk 2	A. R. Hawes	
G-BSGB	Gaertner Ax4 Skyranger balloon	B. Gaertner	
G-BSGD	PA-28 Cherokee 180	R. J. Cleverley	
G-BSGF	Robinson R-22B	Direct Helicopters (Southend) Ltd	
G-BSGG	Denney Kitfox Mk 2	C. G. Richardson	
G-BSGH	Airtour AH-56B balloon	G. Luck	
G-BSGJ	Monnett Sonerai II	G. A. Brady	
G-BSGK	PA-34-200T Seneca II	GK Aviation	
G-BSGL	PA-28-161 Warrior II	Keywest Air Charter Ltd/Liverpool	
G-BSGP	Cameron N-65 balloon	Mid-Sussex Flying School	
G-BSGS	Rans S.10 Sakota	M. R. Parr	
G-BSGT	Cessna T.210N	B. J. Sharpe/Booker	
G-BSGY	Thunder Ax7-77 balloon	P. B. Kenington	
G-BSHA	PA-34-200T Seneca II	Justgold Ltd/Blackpool	
G-BSHC	Colt 69A balloon	L. V. Mastis	
G-BSHD	Colt 69A balloon	D. B. Court	
G-BSHE	Cessna 152 II	J. A. Pothecary/Shoreham	
G-BSHH	Luscombe 8E Silvaire	G. M. Whiteman	
G-BSHI	Luscombe 8F Silvaire	G-BSHI Group	
G-BSHK	Denney Kitfox Mk 2	D. Doyle & C. Aherne	
G-BSHO	Cameron V-77 balloon	D. J. Duckworth & J. C. Stewart	
G-BSHP	PA-28-161 Warrior II	Keen Leasing (IOM) Ltd	
G-BSHR	Cessna F.172N	A. Simmers Ltd (G-BFGE)	
G-BSHT	Cameron V-77 balloon	ECM Construction Ltd	
G-BSHV	PA-18 Super Cub 135	Fen Tigers Flying Group	
G-BSHW	Hawker Tempest II (MW800)	P. Y. C. Denis/France	
G-BSHX	Enstrom F-28A	Stephenson Aviation Ltd/Goodwood	
G-BSHY	EAA Acro Sport I	R. J. Hodder	
G-BSHZ	Enstrom F-28F	S. G. Oliphant-Hope	
G-BSIC	Cameron V-77 balloon	C. Wilcock	
G-BSIE	Enstrom 280FX	S. G. Oliphant-Hope	
G-BSIF	Denney Kitfox Mk 2	J. C. W. & J. Smith	
G-BSIG	Colt 21A balloon	E. C. & A. J. Moore	
G-BSIH	Rutan LongEz	W. S. Allen	
G-BSII	PA-34-200T Seneca II	N. H. N. Gardner	
G-BSIJ	Cameron V-77 balloon	A. S. Jones	
G-BSIK	Denney Kitfox Mk 1	G. J.Sargent	
G-BSIM	PA-28-181 Archer II	E. Midlands Aircraft Hire Ltd	
G-BSIN	Robinson R-22B	PDM Aviation	
G-BSIO	Cameron 80 Shed SS balloon	R. E. Jones	
G-BSIR	Cessna 340	Walterston Holdings/Cardiff	
G-BSIT	Robinson R-22B	Helicentre Ltd/Blackpool	
G-BSIU	Colt 90A balloon	S. Travaglia/Italy	
G-BSIY	Schleicher ASK.14	Winwick Flying Group	
G-BSIZ	PA-28-181 Archer II	A. M. L. Maxwell	
G-BSJB	Bensen B.8	J. W. Limbrick	
G-BSJU	Cessna 150M	A. C. Williamson	
G-BSJW	Everett Srs 2 gyroplane	R. Sarwan	
G-BSJX	PA-28-161 Warrior II	D. A. Shields & L. C. Brekkeflat	
G-BSJZ	Cessna 150J	BCT Aircraft Leasing Ltd	
G-BSKA	Cessna 150M	P. R. Edwards	
G-BSKC	PA-38-112 Tomahawk	J. Marioni/Panshanger	
G-BSKD	Cameron V-77 balloon	M. J. Gunston	
G-BSKE	Cameron O-84 balloon	The Blunt Arrows Balloon Team	
G-BSKG	Maule MX-7-180	J. R. Surbey	
G-BSKI	Thunder Ax8-90 balloon	G-BSKI Balloon Group	
G-BSKK	PA-38-112 Tomahawk	Falcon Flying Services/Biggin Hill	
G-BSKL	PA-38-112 Tomahawk	Falcon Flying Services/Biggin Hill	
G-BSKO	Maule MXT-7-180	M. A. Ashmole	

Notes	Reg.	Type	Owner or Operator
	G-BSKP	V.S.379 Spitfire F.XIV (SG-3)	Historic Flying Ltd/Audley End
	G-BSKT	Maule MX-7-180	Maule Flying Group
	G-BSKU	Cameron O-84 balloon	Alfred Bagnall & Sons (West) Ltd
	G-BSKW	PA-28-181 Archer II	Shropshire Aero Club Ltd/Sleap
	G-BSLA	Robin DR.400/180	A. B. McCoig/Biggin Hill
	G-BSLD	PA-28RT-201 Arrow IV	S. Gawronek
	G-BSLE	PA-28-161 Warrior II	Oxford Aviation Services Ltd/Kidlington
	G-BSLG	Cameron A-180 balloon	B. J. Newman
	G-BSLH	C.A.S.A. 1.131E Jungmann 2000	P. Warden/France
	G-BSLI	Cameron V-77 balloon	J. D. C. & F. E. Bevan
	G-BSLK	PA-28-161 Warrior II	R. A. Rose
	G-BSLM	PA-28 Cherokee 160	Old Sarum Cherokee Group
	G-BSLT	PA-28-161 Warrior II	APB Leasing Ltd/Welshpool
	G-BSLU	PA-28 Cherokee 140	D. J. Budden/Shobdon
	G-BSLV	Enstrom 280FX	Beaufort Securities Ltd
	G-BSLW	Bellanca 7ECA Citabria	Shoreham Citabria Group
	G-BSLX	WAR Focke-Wulf Fw.190 (replica) (4+)	E. C. Murgatroyd
	G-BSMB	Cessna U.206E	Army Parachute Association/Netheravon
	G-BSMD	Nord 1101 Noralpha (+114)	R. J. Lamplough
	G-BSME	Bo 208C1 Junior	D. J. Hampson
	G-BSMF	Avro 652A Anson C.19 (TX183)	G. M. K. Fraser
	G-BSMG	Montgomerie-Bensen B.8M	A. C. Timperley
	G-BSMK	Cameron O-84 balloon	G-BSMK Shareholders
	G-BSML	Schweizer 269C	Triangle Computer Services Ltd
	G-BSMM	Colt 31A balloon	D. V. Fowler
	G-BSMN	CFM Streak Shadow	K. Daniels
	G-BSMO	Denney Kitfox	Kitfox Group
	G-BSMS	Cameron V-77 balloon	Sade Balloons Ltd
	G-BSMT	Rans S.10 Sakota	I. M. Ashpole & Wye Valley Aviation Ltd
	G-BSMU	Rans S.6 Coyote II	J. S. M. Cattle (G-MWJE)
	G-BSMV	PA-17 Vagabond (modified)	A. Cheriton
	G-BSMX	Bensen B.8MR	J. S. E. McGregor
	G-BSND	Air Command 532 Elite	K. Brogden & W. B. Lumb
	G-BSNE	Luscombe 8E Silvaire	Aerolite Luscombe Group
	G-BSNF	Piper J-3C-65 Cub	D. A. Hammant
	G-BSNG	Cessna 172N	A. J. & P. C. MacDonald/Edinburgh
	G-BSNJ	Cameron N-90 balloon	D. P. H. Smith/France
	G-BSNL	Bensen B.8MR	A. C. Breane
	G-BSNN	Rans S.10 Sakota	O. & S. D. Barnard
	G-BSNP	PA-28-201T Turbo Arrow III	D. F. K. Singleton/Germany
	G-BSNR	BAe 146-300A	K.L.M. uk/Buzz/Stansted
	G-BSNS	BAe 146-300A	K.L.M. uk/Stansted
	G-BSNT	Luscombe 8A Silvaire	A. L. Nightingale
	G-BSNU	Colt 105A balloon	Sun Life Assurance Soc PLC
	G-BSNV	Boeing 737-4Q8	British Airways
	G-BSNW	Boeing 737-4Q8	British Airways
	G-BSNX	PA-28-181 Archer II	Cavcok Aviation Ltd
	G-BSNY	Bensen B.8M	H. McCartney
	G-BSNZ	Cameron O-105 balloon	W. O. Hawkins
	G-BSOF	Colt 25A balloon	H. C. J. Williams
	G-BSOG	Cessna 172M	B. Chapman & A. R. Budden/Goodwood
	G-BSOI	AS.332L Super Puma	Brintel Helicopters Ltd
	G-BSOJ	Thunder Ax7-77 balloon	R. J. S. Jones
	G-BSOK	PA-28-161 Warrior II	Archer Aviation Ltd
	G-BSOM	Glaser-Dirks DG.400	G-BSOM Group/Tibenham
	G-BSON	Green S.25 balloon	J. J. Green
	G-BSOO	Cessna 172F	Double Oscar Flying Group
	G-BSOR	CFM Streak Shadow Srs SA	J. P. Sorenson
	G-BSOT	PA-38-112 Tomahawk II	APB Leasing Ltd/Welshpool
	G-BSOU	PA-38-112 Tomahawk II	Chubbs Aviation Services (UK) Ltd
	G-BSOV	PA-38-112 Tomahawk II	A. Dodd/Panshanger
	G-BSOX	Luscombe 8AE Silvaire	D. Gill
	G-BSOY	PA-34-220T Seneca III	BAe Flying College Ltd/Prestwick
	G-BSOZ	PA-28-161 Warrior II	Moray Flying Club Ltd/Kinloss
	G-BSPA	QAC Quickie Q.2	G. V. McKirdy & B. K. Glover
	G-BSPB	Thunder Ax8-84 balloon	Nigs Pertwee Ltd
	G-BSPE	Cessna F.172P	A. M. J. Clark
	G-BSPG	PA-34-200T Seneca II	D. P. Hughes
	G-BSPI	PA-28-161 Warrior II	Oxford Aviation Services Ltd/Kidlington
	G-BSPJ	Bensen B.8	C. M. Jones
	G-BSPK	Cessna 195A	A. G. & D. L. Bompas
	G-BSPL	CFM Streak Shadow Srs SA	MEL (Aviation Oxygen) Ltd

Reg.	Type	Owner or Operator	Notes
G-BSPM	PA-28-161 Warrior II	White Waltham Airfield Ltd	
G-BSPN	PA-28R-201T Turbo Arrow III	R. G. & W. Allison	
G-BSPW	Light Aero Avid Flyer C	M. J. Sewell	
G-BSPX	Lancair 320	C. H. Skelt	
G-BSPY	BN-2A Islander	G-WATS Aviation Ltd (G-AXYM)/ Halfpenny Green	
G-BSRH	Pitts S-1C Special	M. R. Janney	
G-BSRI	Lancair 235	G. Lewis/Liverpool	
G-BSRJ	Colt AA-1050 gas balloon	Trezpark Ltd	
G-BSRK	ARV Super 2	D. M. Blair	
G-BSRL	Everett Srs 2 gyroplane	R. F. E. Burley	
G-BSRP	Rotorway Executive	R. J. Baker	
G-BSRR	Cessna 182Q	Select Management Services Ltd	
G-BSRT	Denney Kitfox Mk 2	A. J. Lloyd	
G-BSRX	CFM Streak Shadow	P. Williams	
G-BSRZ	Air Command 532 Elite 2-seat	A. S. G. Crabb	
G-BSSA	Luscombe 8E Silvaire	Luscombe Aircraft Ltd/White Waltham	
G-BSSB	Cessna 150L	D. T. A. Rees	
G-BSSC	PA-28-161 Warrior II	Oxford Aviation Services Ltd/Kidlington	
G-BSSE	PA-28 Cherokee 140	Comed Aviation Ltd/Blackpool	
G-BSSF	Denney Kitfox Mk 2	S. G. Moores	
G-BSSI	Rans S.6 Coyote II	R. W. Skelton (G-MWJA)	
G-BSSJ	FRED Srs 2	R. F. Jopling	
G-BSSK	QAC Quickie Q.2	D. G. Greatrex	
G-BSSO	Cameron O-90 balloon	R. R. & J. E. Hatton	
G-BSSP	Robin DR.400/180R	Soaring (Oxford) Ltd	
G-BSSR	PA-28-151 Warrior	Flying Pig Aviation Ltd/Biggin Hill	
G-BSST	Concorde 002 ★	F.A.A. Museum/Yeovilton	
G-BSSV	CFM Streak Shadow	R. W. Payne	
G-BSSW	PA-28-161 Warrior II	R. L. Hayward	
G-BSSX	PA-28-161 Warrior II	Airways Aero Associations Ltd/Booker	
G-BSTC	Aeronca 11AC Chief	B. Bridgman & N. J. Mortimore	
G-BSTE	AS.355F-2 Twin Squirrel	Hygrade Foods Ltd	
G-BSTH	PA-25 Pawnee 235	Scottish Gliding Union Ltd/Portmoak	
G-BSTI	Piper J-3C-65 Cub	I. Fraser & G. L. Nunn	
G-BSTK	Thunder Ax8-90 balloon	M. Williams	
G-BSTL	Rand Robinson KR-2	C. S. Hales	
G-BSTM	Cessna 172L	G-BSTM Group/Cambridge	
G-BSTO	Cessna 152 II	Plymouth School of Flying Ltd	
G-BSTP	Cessna 152 II	FR Aviation Ltd/Bournemouth	
G-BSTR	AA-5 Traveler	James Allan (Aviation & Engineering) Ltd/ Dundee	
G-BSTT	Rans S.6 Coyote II	D. G. Palmer	
G-BSTV	PA-32 Cherokee Six 300	B. C. Hudson	
G-BSTX	Luscombe 8A Silvaire	A. A. Alderdice	
G-BSTY	Thunder Ax8-90 balloon	J. W. Cato	
G-BSTZ	PA-28 Cherokee 140	Air Navigation & Trading Co Ltd/Blackpool	
G-BSUA	Rans S.6 Coyote II	A. J. Todd	
G-BSUB	Colt 77A balloon	R. R. J. Wilson & M. P. Hill	
G-BSUD	Luscombe 8A Silvaire	I. G. Harrison/Egginton	
G-BSUE	Cessna U.206G	R. A. Robinson	
G-BSUF	PA-32RT-300 Lance II	M. J. Parker	
G-BSUJ	Brügger MB.2 Colibri	M. A. Farrelly	
G-BSUK	Colt 77A balloon	A. J. Moore	
G-BSUO	Scheibe SF.25C Falke	British Gliding Association Ltd	
G-BSUR	Rotorway Executive 90	Psion Manufacturing Ltd	
G-BSUT	Rans S.6-ESA Coyote II	J. Bell	
G-BSUU	Colt 180A balloon	British School of Ballooning	
G-BSUV	Cameron O-77 balloon	R. Moss	
G-BSUW	PA-34-200T Seneca II	TG Aviation Ltd/Manston	
G-BSUX	Carlson Sparrow II	J. Stephenson	
G-BSUZ	Denney Kitfox Mk 3	M. J. Clark	
G-BSVB	PA-28-181 Archer II	B. J. Janman & PEPS International Ltd	
G-BSVE	Binder CP.301S Smaragd	Smaragd Flying Group	
G-BSVF	PA-28-161 Warrior II	Airways Aero Associations Ltd/Booker	
G-BSVG	PA-28-161 Warrior II	Airways Aero Associations Ltd/Booker	
G-BSVH	Piper J-3C-65 Cub	A. R. Meakin	
G-BSVI	PA-16 Clipper	I. R. Blakemore	
G-BSVJ	Piper J-3C-65 Cub	V. S. E. Norman/Rendcomb	
G-BSVK	Denney Kitfox Mk 2	C. M. Looney	
G-BSVM	PA-28-161 Warrior II	EFG Flying Services/Biggin Hill	
G-BSVN	Thorp T-18	J. H. Kirkham	
G-BSVP	PA-23 Aztec 250	Time Electronics Ltd/Biggin Hill	

Notes	Reg.	Type	Owner or Operator
	G-BSVR	Schweizer 269C	Martinair Ltd
	G-BSVS	Robin DR.400/100	D. McK. Chalmers
	G-BSVV	PA-38-112 Tomahawk	J. Maffia & H. Merkado/Panshanger
	G-BSVW	PA-38-112 Tomahawk	EFG Flying Services Ltd/Biggin Hill
	G-BSVX	PA-38-112 Tomahawk	D. J. Hockings/Biggin Hill
	G-BSVY	PA-38-112 Tomahawk	Cardiff-Wales Flying Club Ltd
	G-BSVZ	Pietenpol Air Camper	G. F. M. Garner
	G-BSWB	Rans S.10 Sakota	F. A. Hewitt
	G-BSWC	Boeing Stearman E.75 (112)	R. R. White
	G-BSWF	PA-16 Clipper	T. M. Storey
	G-BSWG	PA-17 Vagabond	P. E. J. Sturgeon
	G-BSWH	Cessna 152 II	Airspeed Aviation Ltd
	G-BSWI	Rans S.10 Sakota	J. M. Mooney
	G-BSWJ	Cameron O-77 balloon	G. A. Board
	G-BSWL	Slingsby T.61F Venture T.2	K. Richards
	G-BSWM	Slingsby T.61F Venture T.2	L. J. McKelvie/Bellarena
	G-BSWR	BN-2T-26 Turbine Islander	Police Authority for Northern Ireland
	G-BSWV	Cameron N-77 balloon	Leicester Mercury Ltd
	G-BSWX	Cameron V-90 balloon	B. J. Burrows
	G-BSWY	Cameron N-77 balloon	Nottingham Hot Air Balloon Club
	G-BSWZ	Cameron A-180 balloon	G. C. Ludlow
	G-BSXA	PA-28-161 Warrior II	Falcon Flying Services/Biggin Hill
	G-BSXB	PA-28-161 Warrior II	Aeroshow Ltd
	G-BSXC	PA-28-161 Warrior II	L. T. Halpin/Booker
	G-BSXD	Soko P-2 Kraguj (30146)	L. C. Macknight
	G-BSXI	Mooney M.20E	A. N. Pain
	G-BSXM	Cameron V-77 balloon	C. A. Oxby
	G-BSXN	Robinson R-22B	J. G. Gray
	G-BSXP	Air Command 532 Elite	B. J. West
	G-BSXS	PA-28-181 Archer II	Pipe-Air Ltd/Shoreham
	G-BSXT	Piper J-5A Cub Cruiser	M. G. & K. J. Thompson
	G-BSXX	Whittaker MW.7	H. J. Stanley
	G-BSYA	Jodel D.18	S. Harrison
	G-BSYB	Cameron N-120 balloon	M. Buono/Italy
	G-BSYC	PA-32R-300 Lance	M. N. Pinches
	G-BSYD	Cameron A-180 balloon	A. A. Brown
	G-BSYF	Luscombe 8A Silvaire	Atlantic Aviation
	G-BSYG	PA-12 Super Cruiser	Fat Cub Group
	G-BSYH	Luscombe 8A Silvaire	N. R. Osborne
	G-BSYI	AS.355F-1 Twin Squirrel	Lynton Aviation Ltd/Denham
	G-BSYJ	Cameron N-77 balloon	Chubb Fire Ltd
	G-BSYM	PA-38-112 Tomahawk II	Flychoice Ltd/Coventry
	G-BSYO	Piper J-3C-90 Cub	C. R. Reynolds & J. D. Fuller (G-BSMJ/G-BRHE)
	G-BSYP	Bensen B.8MR	C. R. Gordon/Carlisle
	G-BSYU	Robin DR.400/180	K. J. J. Jarman & P. D. Smoothy
	G-BSYV	Cessna 150M	Fenland Flying School
	G-BSYW	Cessna 150M	J. Cropper
	G-BSYY	PA-28-161 Warrior II	Oxford Aviation Services Ltd/Kidlington
	G-BSYZ	PA-28-161 Warrior II	Piper Air (Glasgow) Ltd
	G-BSZB	Stolp SA.300 Starduster Too	D. T. Gethin/Swansea
	G-BSZC	Beech C-45H (51-11701A)	A. A. Hodgson
	G-BSZD	Robin DR.400/180	R. Hitchman & Son & P. J. Rowland & Sons (Farmers) Ltd
	G-BSZF	Jodel DR.250/160	J. B. Randle
	G-BSZG	Stolp SA.100 Starduster	S. W. Watkins & D. F. Chapman
	G-BSZH	Thunder Ax7-77 balloon	K. E. Viney & L. J. Weston
	G-BSZI	Cessna 152 II	Eglinton Flying Club Ltd
	G-BSZJ	PA-28-181 Archer II	M. L. A. Pudney & R. D. Fuller
	G-BSZL	Colt 77A balloon	Staedtler Mars GmbH/Germany
	G-BSZM	Montgomerie-Bensen B.8MR	A. McCredie
	G-BSZN	Bücker Bü133D-1 Jungmeister	Norman Aeroplane Trust/Rendcomb
	G-BSZO	Cessna 152	Aerohire Ltd/Halfpenny Green
	G-BSZS	Robinson R-22B	Blade Runner Helicopters
	G-BSZT	PA-28-161 Warrior II	Airbase Aircraft Ltd
	G-BSZU	Cessna 150F	M. J. Tarrant
	G-BSZV	Cessna 150F	Kirmington Aviation Ltd
	G-BSZW	Cessna 152	Haimoss Ltd
	G-BSZY	Cameron A-180 balloon	K. H. Benning/Germany
	G-BTAB	BAe 125 Srs 800B	Dean Finance Co Ltd (G-BOOA)
	G-BTAG	Cameron O-77 balloon	R. A. Shapland
	G-BTAH	Bensen B.8M	T. B. Johnson

Reg.	Type	Owner or Operator	Notes
G-BTAK	EAA Acro Sport II	P. G. Harrison	
G-BTAL	Cessna F.152 II	Thanet Flying Club/Manston	
G-BTAM	PA-28-181 Archer II	Tri-Star Films Ltd	
G-BTAN	Thunder Ax7-65Z balloon	A. S. Newham	
G-BTAP	PA-38-112 Tomahawk	Western Air (Thruxton) Ltd	
G-BTAR	PA-38-112 Tomahawk	Aerohire Ltd/Halfpenny Green	
G-BTAS	PA-38-112 Tomahawk	B. Brooks	
G-BTAT	Denney Kitfox Mk 2	O. W. Owen & M. D. Harris	
G-BTAU	Thunder Ax7-77 balloon	S. & G. Gebauer/Germany	
G-BTAV	Colt 105A balloon	D. C. Chipping/Portugal	
G-BTAW	PA-28-161 Warrior II	A. J. Wiggins	
G-BTAZ	Evans VP-2	G. S. Poulter	
G-BTBA	Robinson R-22B	Heliflight (UK) Ltd/Halfpenny Green	
G-BTBB	Thunder Ax8-90 balloon	W. J. Brogan	
G-BTBC	PA-28-161 Warrior II	M. J. L. MacDonald	
G-BTBF	Super Koala	E. A. Taylor (G-MWOZ)	
G-BTBG	Denney Kitfox	J. Catley	
G-BTBH	Ryan ST3KR (854)	Ryan Group	
G-BTBI	WAR P-47 Thunderbolt (replica) (85)	E. C. Murgatroyd	
G-BTBJ	Cessna 195B	J. Griffin	
G-BTBL	Montgomerie-Bensen B.8MR	R. de H. Dobree-Carey	
G-BTBN	Denney Kitfox Mk 2	R. C. Bowley	
G-BTBP	Cameron N-90 balloon	Chianti Balloon Club/Italy	
G-BTBR	Cameron DP-80 airship	Cameron Balloons Ltd	
G-BTBU	PA-18 Super Cub 150	G-BTBU Syndicate	
G-BTBV	Cessna 140	A. Brinkley	
G-BTBW	Cessna 120	M. J. Willies	
G-BTBX	Piper J-3C-65 Cub	Henlow Taildraggers	
G-BTBY	PA-17 Vagabond	G. J. Smith	
G-BTCA	PA-32R-300 Lance	P. Taylor	
G-BTCB	Air Command 582 Sport	G. Scurrah	
G-BTCC	Grumman F6F-5 Hellcat (40467)	Patina Ltd/Duxford	
G-BTCD	P-51D-25-NA Mustang (463221)	Pelham Ltd/Duxford	
G-BTCE	Cessna 152	S. T. Gilbert	
G-BTCH	Luscombe 8E Silvaire	J. Grewcock & R. C. Carroll	
G-BTCI	PA-17 Vagabond	T. R. Whittome	
G-BTCJ	Luscombe 8AE Silvaire	J. M. Lovell	
G-BTCK	Cameron A-210 balloon	H-O-T Air Balloons	
G-BTCM	Cameron N-90 balloon	J. D. & K. Griffiths (G-BMPW)	
G-BTCO	FRED Srs 2	I. P. Manley	
G-BTCR	Rans S.10 Sakota	B. J. Hewitt	
G-BTCS	Colt 90A balloon	R. C. Stone	
G-BTCT	AS.332L Super Puma	Bristow Helicopters Ltd	
G-BTCW	Cameron A-180 balloon	Bristol Balloons	
G-BTCZ	Cameron 84 Chateau SS balloon	Forbes Europe Inc/France	
G-BTDA	Slingsby T.61G Falke	RAFGSA/Bicester	
G-BTDC	Denney Kitfox Mk 2	D. Smith	
G-BTDD	CFM Streak Shadow	R. D. Davidson/Defford	
G-BTDE	Cessna C-165 Airmaster	G. S. Moss	
G-BTDF	Luscombe 8A Silvaire	Delta Foxtrot Group	
G-BTDH	P.56 Provost T.1 (WV666)	Flying Services	
G-BTDI	Robinson R-22B	R. L. Moody/Denham	
G-BTDN	Denney Kitfox Mk 2	Foxy Flyers Group	
G-BTDP	TBM-3R Avenger (53319)	A. Haig-Thomas/North Weald	
G-BTDR	Aero Designs Pulsar	M. Jordan	
G-BTDS	Colt 77A balloon	C. P. Witter Ltd	
G-BTDT	C.A.S.A. 1.131E Jungmann 2000	T. A. Reed	
G-BTDV	PA-28-161 Warrior II	R. E. Thorne	
G-BTDW	Cessna 152 II	J. A. Blenkharn/Carlisle	
G-BTDX	PA-18 Super Cub 150	Hammond Aviation	
G-BTDY	PA-18 Super Cub 150	Rodger Aircraft Ltd	
G-BTDZ	C.A.S.A. 1.131E Jungmann 2000	R. J. Pickin & I. M. White	
G-BTEA	Cameron N-105 balloon	H.O.T. Air Balloons	
G-BTEE	Cameron O-120 balloon	W. H. & J. P. Morgan	
G-BTEF	Pitts S-1 Special	Northwest Aerobatics	
G-BTEI	Everett Srs 3 gyroplane	R. A. Jarvis	
G-BTEK	SOCATA TB.20 Trinidad	D. F. Fagan/Booker	
G-BTEL	CFM Streak Shadow	J. E. Eatwell	
G-BTES	Cessna 150H	R. A. Forward	
G-BTET	Piper J-3C-65 Cub	R. M. Jones	
G-BTEU	SA.365N-2 Dauphin	Bond Helicopters Ltd	
G-BTEV	PA-38-112 Tomahawk	T. R. Blockley/Cardiff	

Notes	Reg.	Type	Owner or Operator
	G-BTEW	Cessna 120	K. F. Mason
	G-BTEX	PA-28 Cherokee 140	McAully Flying Group Ltd/Little Snoring
	G-BTFA	Denney Kitfox Mk 2	K. R. Peek
	G-BTFB	Cameron DG-14 airship	Cameron Balloons Ltd
	G-BTFC	Cessna F.152 II	Tayside Aviation Ltd/Dundee
	G-BTFD	Colt AS-105 airship Mk II	Media Fantasy Aviation UK Ltd
	G-BTFE	Bensen-Parsons 2-seat gyroplane	N. C. White
	G-BTFF	Cessna T.310R II	United Sales Equipment Dealers Ltd
	G-BTFG	Boeing Stearman A.75N1 (441)	D. W. N. Johnson
	G-BTFJ	PA-15 Vagabond	Vagabond FJ Flying Group
	G-BTFK	Taylorcraft BC-12D	J. J. Sheeran
	G-BTFL	Aeronca 11AC Chief	BTFL Group
	G-BTFM	Cameron O-105 balloon	Edinburgh University Hot Air Balloon Club
	G-BTFO	PA-28-161 Warrior II	Flyfar Ltd
	G-BTFP	PA-38-112 Tomahawk	Teesside Flight Centre Ltd
	G-BTFS	Cessna A.150M	K. Ford
	G-BTFT	Beech 58 Baron	Fastwing Air Charter Ltd
	G-BTFU	Ciameron N-90 balloon	J. J. Rudoni & A. C. K. Rawson
	G-BTFV	Whittaker MW.7	S. J. Luck
	G-BTFW	Montgomerie-Bensen B.8MR	A. Mansfield
	G-BTFX	Bell 206B JetRanger 2	J. Selwyn Smith (Shepley) Ltd
	G-BTGA	Boeing Stearman A.751N1	D. J. Morris
	G-BTGD	Rand-Robinson KR-2 (modified)	J. N. Kerr
	G-BTGG	Rans S.10 Sakota	A. R. Cameron
	G-BTGH	Cessna 152 II	C & S Aviation Ltd/Halfpenny Green
	G-BTGI	Rearwin 175 Skyranger	A. H. Hunt/St Just
	G-BTGJ	Smith DSA-1 Miniplane	G. J. Knowles
	G-BTGL	Light Aero Avid Flyer	A. F. Vizoso
	G-BTGM	Aeronca 7AC Champion	J. R. L. White/France
	G-BTGN	Cessna 310R	-
	G-BTGO	PA-28 Cherokee 140	Rankart Ltd
	G-BTGP	Cessna 150M	Billins Air Service Ltd
	G-BTGR	Cessna 152 II	A. J. Gomes/Shoreham
	G-BTGS	Stolp SA.300 Starduster Too	A. E. Bailey & ptnrs (G-AYMA)
	G-BTGT	CFM Streak Shadow	G. Arscott (G-MWPY)
	G-BTGU	PA-34-220T Seneca III	Carill Aviation Ltd
	G-BTGV	PA-34-200T Seneca II	MS 124 Ltd/Shobdon
	G-BTGW	Cessna 152 II	Stapleford Flying Club Ltd
	G-BTGX	Cessna 152 II	Stapleford Flying Club Ltd
	G-BTGY	PA-28-161 Warrior II	Stapleford Flying Club Ltd
	G-BTGZ	PA-28-181 Archer II	Allzones Travel Ltd/Biggin Hill
	G-BTHA	Cessna 182P	Hotel Alpha Flying Group/Liverpool
	G-BTHD	Yakovlev Yak-3U	Patina Ltd/Duxford
	G-BTHE	Cessna 150L	Humberside Police Flying Club
	G-BTHF	Cameron V-90 balloon	N. J. & S. J. Langley
	G-BTHH	Jodel DR.100A	H. R. Leefe
	G-BTHI	Robinson R-22B	G. R. Day
	G-BTHJ	Evans VP-2	C. J. Moseley
	G-BTHK	Thunder Ax7-77 balloon	M. J. Chandler
	G-BTHM	Thunder Ax8-105 balloon	Anglia Balloons
	G-BTHN	Murphy Renegade 912	F. A. Purvis
	G-BTHP	Thorp T.211	M. Gardner
	G-BTHR	SOCATA TB.10 Tobago	M. J. Newton
	G-BTHU	Light Aero Avid Flyer	R. C. Bowley
	G-BTHV	MBB Bo 105DBS/4	Bond Air Services/Aberdeen
	G-BTHW	Beech F33C Bonanza	Robin Lance Aviation Associates Ltd
	G-BTHX	Colt 105A balloon	R. Ollier
	G-BTHY	Bell 206B JetRanger 3	Sterling Helicopters Ltd
	G-BTHZ	Cameron V-56 balloon	C. N. Marshall/Kenya
	G-BTIC	PA-22 Tri-Pacer 150	T. Richards & G. C. Winters
	G-BTID	PA-28-161 Warrior II	Plymouth School of Flying Ltd
	G-BTIE	SOCATA TB.10 Tobago	JGH Computer Services Ltd
	G-BTIF	Denney Kitfox Mk 3	D. A. Murchie
	G-BTIG	Montgomerie-Bensen B.8MR	K. Jarvis
	G-BTII	AA-5B Tiger	B. D. Greenwood
	G-BTIJ	Luscombe 8E Silvaire	S. J. Hornsby
	G-BTIK	Cessna 152 II	P. R. Edwards & E. Alexandert
	G-BTIL	PA-38-112 Tomahawk	B. J. Pearson/Eaglescott
	G-BTIM	PA-28-161 Cadet	Mid-Sussex Timber Co Ltd
	G-BTIN	Cessna 150C	Cormack (Aircraft Services) Ltd/ Cumbernauld
	G-BTIO	SNCAN Stampe SV-4C	M. D. & C. F. Garratt

Reg.	Type	Owner or Operator	Notes
G-BTIR	Denney Kitfox Mk 2	R. B. Wilson	
G-BTIS	AS.355F-1 Twin Squirrel	Walsh Aviation (G-TALI)/Elstree	
G-BTIU	M.S.892A Rallye Commodore 150	W. H. Cole	
G-BTIV	PA-28-161 Warrior II	Warrior Group/Eaglescott	
G-BTIW	Jodel DR.1050/M1 ★	(stored)/Crosland Moor	
G-BTIX	Cameron V-77 balloon	D. J. Cook	
G-BTIZ	Cameron A-105 balloon	Glenn Board Promotions	
G-BTJA	Luscombe 8E Silvaire	M. W. Rudkin	
G-BTJB	Luscombe 8E Silvaire	M. Loxton	
G-BTJC	Luscombe 8F Silvaire	A. M. Noble	
G-BTJD	Thunder Ax8-90 balloon	S. J. Wardle	
G-BTJF	Thunder Ax10-180 balloon	Airborne Adventures Ltd	
G-BTJH	Cameron O-77 balloon	H. Stringer	
G-BTJK	PA-38-112 Tomahawk	Western Air (Thruxton) Ltd	
G-BTJL	PA-38-112 Tomahawk	J. S. Devlin & Z. Islam/Redhill	
G-BTJO	Thunder Ax9-140 balloon	G. P. Lane	
G-BTJS	Montgomerie-Bensen B.8MR	T. C. & P. K. Jackson	
G-BTJU	Cameron V-90 balloon	C. W. Jones (Floorings) Ltd	
G-BTJV	PZL SZD-50-3 Puchacz (GCK)	Kent Gliding Club Ltd/Challock	
G-BTJX	Rans S.10 Sakota	W. C. Dobson	
G-BTKA	Piper J-5A Cub Cruiser	J. M. Lister	
G-BTKB	Renegade Spirit 912	G. S. Blundell	
G-BTKD	Denney Kitfox Mk 4	J. F. White	
G-BTKG	Light Aero Avid Flyer	I. Holt	
G-BTKI	NA T-6G Texan	P. S. & S. M. Warner	
G-BTKL	MBB Bo 105DB-4	Veritair Ltd/Halfpenny Green	
G-BTKP	CFM Streak Shadow	G. D. Martin	
G-BTKS	Rans S.10 Sakota	J. R. I. Rolfe & ptnrs	
G-BTKT	PA-28-161 Warrior II	Eastern Executive Air Charter Ltd	
G-BTKV	PA-22 Tri-Pacer 160	R. A. More	
G-BTKW	Cameron O-105 balloon	P. Spellward	
G-BTKX	PA-28-181 Archer II	R. M. Pannell	
G-BTKZ	Cameron V-77 balloon	S. P. Richards	
G-BTLA	Sikorsky S-76B	Skyhopper Ltd	
G-BTLB	Wassmer WA.52 Europa	M. D. O'Brien/Shoreham	
G-BTLE	PA-31-350 Navajo Chieftain	Boal Air Services (UK) Ltd	
G-BTLG	PA-28R Cherokee Arrow 200	A. P. Reilly	
G-BTLL	Pilatus P3-03 (A-806) ★	(stored)/Headcorn	
G-BTLM	PA-22 Tri-Pacer 160	F & H (Aircraft)	
G-BTLP	AA-1C Lynx	Partlease Ltd	
G-BTMA	Cessna 172N	East of England Flying Group Ltd	
G-BTMH	Colt 90A balloon	European Balloon Corporation	
G-BTMJ	Maule MX-7-180	C. M. McGill/Biggin Hill	
G-BTMK	Cessna R.172K XPII	S. P. & A. C. Barker	
G-BTMN	Thunder Ax9-120 balloon	D. J. Farrer Batman	
G-BTMO	Colt 69A balloon	Thunder & Colt	
G-BTMP	Campbell Cricket	P. W. McLaughlin	
G-BTMR	Cessna 172M	Cumbria Aero Club/Carlisle	
G-BTMS	Light Aero Avid Speedwing	D. L. Docking	
G-BTMT	Denney Kitfox Mk 1	Skulk Flying Group	
G-BTMV	Everett Srs 2 gyroplane	L. Armes	
G-BTMW	Zenair CH.701 STOL	L. Lewis	
G-BTMX	Denney Kitfox Mk 3	P. B. Lowry	
G-BTNA	Robinson R-22B	Heli Charter Ltd	
G-BTNB	Robinson R-22B	G. Kidger	
G-BTNC	AS.365N-2 Dauphin 2	Bond Helicopters Ltd	
G-BTND	PA-38-112 Tomahawk	R. B. Turner	
G-BTNE	PA-28-161 Warrior II	D. Rowe/Wellesbourne	
G-BTNL	Thunder Ax10-180 balloon	M. P. A. Sevrin/Belgium	
G-BTNN	Colt 21A balloon	Cameron Balloons Ltd	
G-BTNO	Aeronca 7AC Champion	November Oscar Group/Netherthorpe	
G-BTNP	Light Aero Avid Flyer Commuter	N. Evans	
G-BTNR	Denney Kitfox Mk 3	D. E. Steade	
G-BTNS	PZL-104 Wilga 80	D. Rowland	
G-BTNT	PA-28-151 Warrior	Britannia Airways Ltd/Luton	
G-BTNV	PA-28-161 Warrior II	D. K. Oakeley & A. M. Dawson	
G-BTNW	Rans S.6-ESA Coyote II	A. F. Stafford	
G-BTOA	Mong Sport MS-2	G. Gilding	
G-BTOC	Robinson R-22B	N. Parkhouse	
G-BTOD	PA-38-112 Tomahawk	GB Training On Demand Ltd	
G-BTOG	D.H.82A Tiger Moth	P. T. Szluha	
G-BTOI	Cameron N-77 balloon	The Nestle Co Ltd	
G-BTOL	Denney Kitfox Mk 3	P. J. Gibbs	

Notes	Reg.	Type	Owner or Operator
	G-BTON	PA-28 Cherokee 140	S. G. Woodsford
	G-BTOO	Pitts S-1C Special	G. H. Matthews
	G-BTOP	Cameron V-77 balloon	J. J. Winter
	G-BTOS	Cessna 140	J. L. Kaiser/France
	G-BTOT	PA-15 Vagabond	P. J. Rutter
	G-BTOU	Cameron O-120 balloon	R. S. Gillespie
	G-BTOW	SOCATA Rallye 180GT	Cambridge University Gliding Trust Ltd/ Gransden Lodge
	G-BTOZ	Thunder Ax9-120 S2 balloon	H. G. Davies
	G-BTPB	Cameron N-105 balloon	Test Valley Balloon Group
	G-BTPT	Cameron N-77 balloon	Derbyshire Building Soc
	G-BTPX	Thunder Ax8-90 balloon	E. Cordall
	G-BTPZ	Isaacs Fury II	M. A. Farrelly
	G-BTRB	Thunder Colt Mickey Mouse SS balloon	Benedikt Haggeney GmbH/Germany
	G-BTRC	Light Aero Avid Speedwing	Grangecote Ltd
	G-BTRE	Cessna F.172H	M. L. J. Warwick
	G-BTRF	Aero Designs Pulsar	C. Smith
	G-BTRG	Aeronca 65C Super Chief	H. J. Cox
	G-BTRH	Aeronca 7AC Champion	M. A. N. Newall
	G-BTRI	Aeronca 11CC Super Chief	P. A. Wensak
	G-BTRK	PA-28-161 Warrior II	Stapleford Flying Club Ltd
	G-BTRL	Cameron N-105 balloon	J. Lippett
	G-BTRN	Thunder Ax9-120 S2 balloon	P. B. D. Bird
	G-BTRO	Thunder Ax8-90 balloon	Capital Balloon Club Ltd
	G-BTRP	Hughes 369E	P. C. Shann
	G-BTRR	Thunder Ax7-77 balloon	S. M. Roberts
	G-BTRS	PA-28-161 Warrior II	Tyberry Aviation/Liverpool
	G-BTRT	PA-28R Cherokee Arrow 200-II	C. E. Yates/Barton
	G-BTRU	Robin DR.400/180	R. & M. Engineering Ltd
	G-BTRW	Slingsby T.61F Venture T.2	B. Kerby & G. Grainger
	G-BTRY	PA-28-161 Warrior II	Oxford Aviation Services Ltd/Kidlington
	G-BTRZ	Jodel D.18	R. M. Johnson & R. Collin
	G-BTSB	Corben Baby Ace D	D. G. Kelly
	G-BTSC	Evans VP-2	G. B. O'Neill
	G-BTSJ	PA-28-161 Warrior II	Plymouth School of Flying Ltd
	G-BTSL	Cameron 70 Glass SS balloon	M. R. Humphrey & J. R .Clifton
	G-BTSM	Cessna 180A	C. Couston
	G-BTSN	Cessna 150G	N. A. Bilton/Norwich
	G-BTSP	Piper J-3C-65 Cub	J. A. Walshe & A. Corcoran
	G-BTSR	Aeronca 11AC Chief	R. D. & E. G. N. Morris
	G-BTST	Bensen B.9	V. Scott
	G-BTSV	Denney Kitfox Mk 3	M. G. Dovey
	G-BTSW	Colt AS-80 Mk II airship	Gefa-Flug GmbH/Germany
	G-BTSX	Thunder Ax7-77 balloon	C. Moris-Gallimore
	G-BTSY	EE Lightning F.6 (XR724)	Lightning Association
	G-BTSZ	Cessna 177A	K. D. Harvey
	G-BTTA	Hawker Sea Fury FB.10 (243)	Classic Aviation Ltd/Duxford
	G-BTTB	Cameron V-90 balloon	Royal Engineers Balloon Club
	G-BTTD	Montgomerie-Bensen B.8MR	K. B. Gutridge
	G-BTTE	Cessna 150L	Premiair Flying Club Ltd/Shoreham
	G-BTTK	Thunder Ax8-105 balloon	Tempowish Ltd
	G-BTTL	Cameron V-90 balloon	A. J. Baird
	G-BTTO	BAe ATP	British Aerospace (G-OEDE)
	G-BTTP	BAe 146-300	K.L.M. uk/Buzz/Stansted
	G-BTTR	Aerotek Pitts S-2A Special	T. W. Cassells
	G-BTTS	Colt 77A balloon	Rutland Balloon Club
	G-BTTW	Thunder Ax7-77 balloon	J. Kenny
	G-BTTY	Denney Kitfox Mk 2	K. J. Fleming
	G-BTTZ	Slingsby T.61F Venture T.2	G. J. Bridgewater
	G-BTUA	Slingsby T.61F Venture T.2	Shenington Gliding Club
	G-BTUB	Yakovlev C.11	M. G. & J. R. Jefferies
	G-BTUG	SOCATA Rallye 180T	Herefordshire Gliding Club Ltd/Shobdon
	G-BTUH	Cameron N-65 balloon	B. J. Godding
	G-BTUJ	Thunder Ax9-120 balloon	ECM Construction Ltd
	G-BTUK	Aerotek Pitts S-2A Special	S. H. Elkington/Wickenby
	G-BTUL	Aerotek Pitts S-2A Special	J. M. Adams
	G-BTUM	Piper J-3C-65 Cub	G-BTUM Syndicate
	G-BTUR	PA-18 Super Cub 95 (modified)	K. E. Wilson
	G-BTUS	Whittaker MW.7	J. D. Webb
	G-BTUU	Cameron O-120 balloon	J. L. Guy
	G-BTUV	Aeronca A65TAC Defender	J. T. Ingrouille
	G-BTUW	PA-28-151 Warrior	T. S. Kemp

Reg.	Type	Owner or Operator	Notes
G-BTUX	AS.365N-2 Dauphin 2	Bond Helicopters Ltd/Aberdeen	
G-BTUZ	American General AG-5B Tiger	Grocontinental Ltd/Tilstock	
G-BTVA	Thunder Ax7-77 balloon	A. H. Symonds	
G-BTVB	Everett Srs 3 gyroplane	J. Pumford	
G-BTVC	Denney Kitfox Mk 2	P. Mitchell	
G-BTVE	Hawker Demon I (K8203)	Demon Displays Ltd	
G-BTVF	Rotorway Executive 90	E. P. Sadler	
G-BTVG	Cessna 140	V. C. Gover	
G-BTVH	Colt 77A balloon	D. N. & L. J. Close (G-ZADT/G-ZBCA)	
G-BTVR	PA-28 Cherokee 140	Full Sutton Flying Centre Ltd	
G-BTVU	Robinson R-22B	B. Enzo/Italy	
G-BTVV	Cessna FA.337G	B. Maddock	
G-BTVW	Cessna 152 II	Rankart Ltd	
G-BTVX	Cessna 152 II	Traffic Management Services	
G-BTWC	Slingsby T.61F Venture T.2	RAFGSA/Bicester	
G-BTWD	Slingsby T.61F Venture T.2	York Gliding Centre/Rufforth	
G-BTWE	Slingsby T.61F Venture T.2	RAFGSA/Bicester	
G-BTWF	D.H.C.1 Chipmunk 22 (WK549)	J. A. & V. G. Sims	
G-BTWI	EAA Acro Sport I	WI Group	
G-BTWJ	Cameron V-77 balloon	S. J. & J. A. Bellaby	
G-BTWL	WAG-Aero Acro Sport Trainer	I. M. Ashpole	
G-BTWM	Cameron V-77 balloon	R. C. Franklin	
G-BTWN	Maule MXT-7-180	C. T. Rolls/Redhill	
G-BTWR	Bell P-63A-7-BE Kingcobra (269097)	Patina Ltd/Duxford	
G-BTWU	PA-22 Tri-Pacer 135	Prestige Air (Engineers) Ltd	
G-BTWV	Cameron O-90 balloon	S. F. Hancke	
G-BTWX	SOCATA TB.9 Tampico	British Car Rentals	
G-BTWY	Aero Designs Pulsar	M. Stevenson	
G-BTWZ	Rans S.10 Sakota	D. G. Hey	
G-BTXB	Colt 77A balloon	Shellgas South-West Area	
G-BTXD	Rans S.6-ESA Coyote II	M. Isterling	
G-BTXF	Cameron V-90 balloon	G. Thompson	
G-BTXH	Colt AS-56 airship	L. Kiefer/Germany	
G-BTXI	Noorduyn AT-16 Harvard IIB (FE695)	Patina Ltd/Duxford	
G-BTXK	Thunder Ax7-65 balloon	T. M. Dawson	
G-BTXM	Colt 21A balloon	Virgin Airship & Balloon Co Ltd	
G-BTXS	Cameron O-120 balloon	Southern Balloon Group	
G-BTXT	Maule MXT-7-180	W. C. Evans	
G-BTXV	Cameron A-210 balloon	The Ballooning Business Ltd	
G-BTXW	Cameron V-77 balloon	P. C. Waterhouse	
G-BTXX	Bellanca 8KCAB Decathlon	Tatenhill Aviation	
G-BTXZ	Zenair CH.250	I. Parris & P. W. J. Bull	
G-BTYC	Cessna 150L	Polestar Aviation Ltd	
G-BTYE	Cameron A-180 balloon	K. J. A. Maxwell & D. S. Messmer	
G-BTYF	Thunder Ax10-180 S2 balloon	P. Glydon	
G-BTYH	Pottier P.80S	R. Pickett	
G-BTYI	PA-28-181 Archer II	C. E. Wright	
G-BTYK	Cessna 310R	Revere Aviation Ltd	
G-BTYT	Cessna 152 II	M. J. Green	
G-BTYW	Cessna 120	G-BTYW Group	
G-BTYX	Cessna 140	G-BTYX Group	
G-BTYY	Curtiss Robin C-2	R. R. L. Windus	
G-BTYZ	Colt 210A balloon	T. M. Donnelly	
G-BTZA	Beech F33A Bonanza	G-BTZA Group/Edinburgh	
G-BTZB	Yakovlev Yak-50 (69)	J. S. Allison	
G-BTZD	Yakovlev Yak-1	Historic Aircraft Collection Ltd/Audley End	
G-BTZE	LET Yakovlev C.11	Bianchi Aviation Film Services Ltd/Booker	
G-BTZG	BAe ATP	Trident Aviation Leasing Ltd	
G-BTZJ	BAe ATP	BAe (Operations) Ltd	
G-BTZL	Oldfield Baby Lakes	J. M. Roach	
G-BTZO	SOCATA TB.20 Trinidad	M. R. Munn	
G-BTZP	SOCATA TB.9 Tampico	M. R. Clark	
G-BTZR	Colt 77B balloon	P. J. Fell	
G-BTZS	Colt 77A balloon	P. T. R. Ollivere	
G-BTZU	Cameron Concept SS balloon	A. C. Rackham	
G-BTZV	Cameron V-77 balloon	A. W. Sumner/Belgium	
G-BTZX	Piper J-3C-65 Cub	D. A. Woodhams & J. T. Coulthard	
G-BTZY	Colt 56A balloon	T. M. Donnelly	
G-BTZZ	CFM Streak Shadow	D. R. Stennett	
G-BUAA	Corben Baby Ace D	J. M. Walsh	

Notes	Reg.	Type	Owner or Operator
	G-BUAB	Aeronca 11AC Chief	J. Reed
	G-BUAC	Slingsby T.31 Motor Cadet III	D. A. Wilson
	G-BUAF	Cameron N-77 balloon	T. H. Wadden
	G-BUAG	Jodel D.18	A. L. Silcox
	G-BUAI	Everett Srs 3 gyroplane	C. J. Sullivan
	G-BUAJ	Cameron N-90 balloon	J. R. & S. J. Huggins
	G-BUAM	Cameron V-77 balloon	N. Florence
	G-BUAN	Cessna 172N	R. J. Cawdell
	G-BUAO	Luscombe 8A Silvaire	D. Gough
	G-BUAR	V.S.358 Seafire LF.IIIc (PP972)	Wizzard Investments Ltd
	G-BUAT	Thunder Ax9-120 balloon	J. Fenton
	G-BUAU	Cameron A-180 balloon	Out Of This World Balloons
	G-BUAW	Pitts S-1C Special	A. J. Seymour
	G-BUAX	Rans S.10 Sakota	S. P. Wakeham
	G-BUAY	Cameron A-210 balloon	Virgin Balloon Flights Ltd
	G-BUBA	PA-18S Super Cub 150 (floatplane)	Sunseeker Sales (UK) Ltd
	G-BUBC	QAC Quickie Tri-Q.200	D. J. Clarke
	G-BUBL	Thunder Ax8-105 balloon ★	British Balloon Museum/Newbury
	G-BUBN	BN-2B-26 Islander	Isles of Scilly Skybus Ltd/St Just
	G-BUBR	Cameron A-250 balloon	Bath Hot-Air Balloon Club
	G-BUBS	Lindstrand LBL-77B balloon	B. J. Bower
	G-BUBT	Stoddard-Hamilton Glasair IIRGS	M. D. Evans
	G-BUBU	PA-34-220T Seneca III	Brinor (Holdings) Ltd
	G-BUBW	Robinson R-22B	Forth Helicopter Services Ltd/Edinburgh
	G-BUBY	Thunder Ax8-105 S2 balloon	T. M. Donnelly
	G-BUCA	Cessna A.150K	T. R. Kingsley
	G-BUCB	Cameron H-34 balloon	A. S. Jones
	G-BUCC	C.A.S.A. 1.131E Jungmann 2000 (BU+CC)	P. L. Gaze (G-BUEM)
	G-BUCG	Schleicher ASW.20L (modified)	W. B. Andrews
	G-BUCH	Stinson V-77 Reliant	Pullmerit Ltd
	G-BUCI	Auster AOP.9 (XP242)	Historic Aircraft Flight Reserve Collection/Middle Wallop
	G-BUCJ	D.H.C.2 Beaver 1 (XP772)	British Aerial Museum/Duxford
	G-BUCK	C.A.S.A. 1.131E Jungmann 1000 (BU+CK)	Jungmann Flying Group/White Waltham
	G-BUCM	Hawker Sea Fury FB.11 (WE724)	Patina Ltd/Duxford
	G-BUCO	Pietenpol Air Camper	A. James
	G-BUCS	Cessna 150F	Atlantic Bridge Aviation Ltd/Lydd
	G-BUCT	Cessna 150L	J. K. Aviation Services Ltd/Biggin Hill
	G-BUDA	Slingsby T.61F Venture T.2	RAFGSA/Bicester
	G-BUDB	Slingsby T.61F Venture T.2	RAFGSA/Bicester
	G-BUDC	Slingsby T.61F Venture T.2	R. A. Boddy
	G-BUDE	PA-22 Tri-Pacer 135 (tailwheel)	B. A. Bower/Thruxton
	G-BUDF	Rand-Robinson KR-2	E. C. King
	G-BUDI	Aero Designs Pulsar	R. W. L. Oliver
	G-BUDK	Thunder Ax7-77 balloon	W. Evans
	G-BUDL	Auster 3 (NX534)	M. Pocock
	G-BUDN	Cameron 90 Shoe SS balloon	L. V. Mastis
	G-BUDO	PZL-110 Koliber 150	A. S. Vine/Goodwood
	G-BUDR	Denney Kitfox Mk 3	N. J. P. Mayled
	G-BUDS	Rand-Robinson KR-2	D. W. Munday
	G-BUDT	Slingsby T.61F Venture T.2	G-BUDT Group
	G-BUDU	Cameron V-77 balloon	T. M. G. Amery
	G-BUDW	Brügger MB.2 Colibri	J. M. Hoblyn (G-GODS)
	G-BUEC	Van's RV-6	R. D. Harper
	G-BUED	Slingsby T.61F Venture T.2	SE Kent Civil Service Flying Club
	G-BUEE	Cameron A-210 balloon	Bristol Balloons
	G-BUEF	Cessna 152 II	Channel Aviation
	G-BUEG	Cessna 152 II	Plymouth School of Flying Ltd
	G-BUEI	Thunder Ax8-105 balloon	Anglia Balloons
	G-BUEK	Slingsby T.61F Venture T.2	Norfolk Gliding Club Ltd/Tibenham
	G-BUEN	VPM M.14 Scout	W. M. Day
	G-BUEO	Maule MX-7-180	K. & S. C. Knight
	G-BUEP	Maule MX-7-180	G. M. Bunn
	G-BUES	Cameron N-77 balloon	R. J. Shortall
	G-BUEV	Cameron O-77 balloon	R. R. McCormack & R. J. Mercer
	G-BUEX	Schweizer 269C	Group 2 Aviation (G-HFLR)
	G-BUEZ	Hawker Hunter F.6A (XF375)	Old Flying Machine Co Ltd/Duxford
	G-BUFA	Cameron R-77 gas balloon	Noble Adventures Ltd
	G-BUFC	Cameron R-77 gas balloon	Noble Adventures Ltd
	G-BUFE	Cameron R-77 gas balloon	Noble Adventures Ltd

Reg.	Type	Owner or Operator	Notes
G-BUFG	Slingsby T.61F Venture T.2	T. W. Eagles/Hinton-in-the-Hedges	
G-BUFH	PA-28-161 Warrior II	The Tiger Leisure Group	
G-BUFJ	Cameron V-90 balloon	S. P. Richards	
G-BUFK	Cassutt Racer IIIM	D. I. H. Johnstone & W. T. Barnard	
G-BUFN	Slingsby T.61F Venture T.2	BUFN Group	
G-BUFO	Cameron 70 UFO SS balloon	Virgin Airship & Balloon Co Ltd	
G-BUFP	Slingsby T.61F Venture T.2 (ZA663)	London Sailplanes Ltd	
G-BUFR	Slingsby T.61F Venture T.2	R. F. Warren & P. A. Hazell	
G-BUFT	Cameron O-120 balloon	N. D. Hicks	
G-BUFV	Light Aero Avid Flyer	S. C. Ord	
G-BUFX	Cameron N-90 balloon	Kerridge Computer Co Ltd	
G-BUFY	PA-28-161 Warrior II	Bickertons Aerodromes Ltd/Denham	
G-BUGB	Stolp SA.750 Acroduster Too	D. Burnham	
G-BUGC	Jurca MJ.5 Sirocco	A. Burani (G-BWDJ)	
G-BUGD	Cameron V-77 balloon	P. Haslett/France	
G-BUGE	Bellanca 7GCAA Cltabria	P. White	
G-BUGG	Cessna 150F	C. P. J. Taylor & D. M. Forshaw/ Panshanger	
G-BUGH	Rans S.10 Sakota	D. T. Smith	
G-BUGI	Evans VP-2	D. G. Gibson	
G-BUGJ	Robin DR.400/180	Alfred Graham Ltd	
G-BUGL	Slingsby T.61F Venture T.2	VMG Group	
G-BUGM	CFM Streak Shadow	The Shadow Group	
G-BUGN	Colt 210A balloon	R. W. Batchelor	
G-BUGO	Colt 56B balloon	Escuela de Aerostacion Mica/Spain	
G-BUGP	Cameron V-77 balloon	R. Churcher	
G-BUGT	Slingsby T.61F Venture T.2	R. W. Hornsey/Rufforth	
G-BUGV	Slingsby T.61F Venture T.2	Oxfordshire Sportflying Ltd/Enstone	
G-BUGW	Slingsby T.61F Venture T.2	Rankart Ltd/Hinton-in-the-Hedges	
G-BUGX	M.S.880B Rallye Club	R. W. H. Watson	
G-BUGY	Cameron V-90 balloon	Dante Balloon Group	
G-BUGZ	Slingsby T.61F Venture T.2	Dishforth Flying Group	
G-BUHA	Slingsby T.61F Venture T.2 (ZA634)	A. W. Swales/Rufforth	
G-BUHC	BAe 146-300	K.L.M. uk (G-BTMI)/Stansted	
G-BUHJ	Boeing 737-4Q8	British Airways/Gatwick	
G-BUHK	Boeing 737-4Q8	British Airways/Gatwick	
G-BUHL	Boeing 737-4S3	GB Airways Ltd/Gatwick	
G-BUHM	Cameron V-77 balloon	L. A. Watts	
G-BUHO	Cessna 140	W. B. Bateson/Blackpool	
G-BUHP	Flyair 1100 balloon	R. White	
G-BUHR	Slingsby T.61F Venture T.2	Denbeigh Falke Group	
G-BUHS	Stoddard-Hamilton Glasair SH-TD-1	E. J. Spalding	
G-BUHU	Cameron N-105 balloon	Unipart Balloon Club	
G-BUHY	Cameron A-210 balloon	Adventure Balloon Co Ltd	
G-BUHZ	Cessna 120	G. L. Brown	
G-BUIB	MBB Bo 105DBS/4	Bond Air Services (G-BDYZ)	
G-BUIC	Denney Kitfox Mk 2	C. R. Northrop & B. M. Chilvers	
G-BUIE	Cameron N-90 balloon	Flying Pictures Ltd	
G-BUIF	PA-28-161 Warrior II	Newcastle-upon-Tyne Aero Club Ltd	
G-BUIG	Campbell Cricket (replica)	T. A. Holmes	
G-BUIH	Slingsby T.61F Venture T.2	Yorkshire Gliding Club (Pty) Ltd/ Sutton Bank	
G-BUIJ	PA-28-161 Warrior II	Ashurst Technologies Ltd	
G-BUIK	PA-28-161 Warrior II	Falcon Flying Services/Biggin Hill	
G-BUIL	CFM Streak Shadow	P. N. Bevan & L. M. Poor	
G-BUIN	Thunder Ax7-77 balloon	Free Flight Aerostat Group	
G-BUIP	Denney Kitfox Mk 2	Avcomm Developments Ltd	
G-BUIR	Light Aero Avid Speedwing Mk 4	K. N. Pollard/Sturgate	
G-BUIU	Cameron V-90 balloon	H. Micketeit/Germany	
G-BUIZ	Cameron N-90 balloon	Virgin Airship & Balloon Co Ltd	
G-BUJA	Slingsby T.61F Venture T.2	RAFGSA/Cosford	
G-BUJB	Slingsby T.61F Venture T.2	Falke Syndicate/Shobdon	
G-BUJE	Cessna 177B	FG93 Group	
G-BUJH	Colt 77B balloon	R. P. Cross & R. Stanley	
G-BUJI	Slingsby T.61F Venture T.2	R. A. Boddy/Rufforth	
G-BUJJ	Light Aero Avid Flyer	P. A. Ellis	
G-BUJK	Montgomerie-Bensen B.8MR	C. Moffat	
G-BUJL	Aero Designs Pulsar	J. J. Lynch	
G-BUJM	Cessna 120	Cessna 120 Flying Group	
G-BUJN	Cessna 172N	De Cadenet Engineering Ltd/Coventry	

Notes	Reg.	Type	Owner or Operator
	G-BUJO	PA-28-161 Warrior II	Channel Islands Aero Holdings Ltd
	G-BUJP	PA-28-161 Warrior II	APB Leasing Ltd/Welshpool
	G-BUJR	Cameron A-180 balloon	W. I. Hooker & C. Parker
	G-BUJU	Cessna 150H	BUJU Flying Group & Associates
	G-BUJV	Light Aero Avid Speedwing Mk 4	C. Thomas
	G-BUJW	Thunder Ax8-90 S2 balloon	R. T. Fagan
	G-BUJX	Slingsby T.61F Venture T.2	R. J. Chichester-Constable
	G-BUJY	D.H.82A Tiger Moth	Aero Vintage Ltd
	G-BUJZ	Rotorway Executive 90	T. W. Aisthorpe & R. J. D. Crick
	G-BUKA	Fairchild SA227AC Metro III	Atlantic Air Transport Ltd/Coventry
	G-BUKB	Rans S.10 Sakota	M. K. Blatch & M. P. Lee
	G-BUKE	Boeing Stearman A.75N1 (243)	R. G. Rance (G-BRIP)/Goodwood
	G-BUKF	Denney Kitfox Mk 4	Kilo Foxtrot Group
	G-BUKH	D.31 Turbulent	P. M. Newman
	G-BUKI	Thunder Ax7-77 balloon	Adventures Aloft
	G-BUKK	Bücker Bü133C Jungmeister (U-80)	E. J. F. McEntee/White Waltham
	G-BUKN	PA-15 Vagabond	M. A. & A. M. Watts
	G-BUKO	Cessna 120	N. G. Abbott
	G-BUKP	Denney Kitfox Mk 2	T. D. Reid/Newtownards
	G-BUKR	M.S.880B Rallye Club 100T	G-BUKR Flying Group
	G-BUKS	Colt 77B balloon	R. & M. Bairstow
	G-BUKT	Luscombe 8A Silvaire	M. G. Talbot & J. N. Willshaw
	G-BUKU	Luscombe 8E Silvaire	F. G. Miskelly
	G-BUKV	Colt AS-105 Mk II Airship	A. Ockelmann/Germany
	G-BUKX	PA-28-161 Warrior II	LNP Ltd
	G-BUKY	CCF Harvard IVM (52-8543)	R. A. Fleming/Breighton
	G-BUKZ	Evans VP-2	P. R. Farnell
	G-BULB	Thunder Ax7-77 balloon	Shiltons of Rothbury
	G-BULC	Light Aero Avid Flyer Mk 4	C. Nice
	G-BULD	Cameron N-105 balloon	S. J. Boxall
	G-BULE	Price TPB.2 balloon	A. G. R. Calder
	G-BULF	Colt 77A balloon	M. V. Farrant
	G-BULG	Van's RV-4	R. I. Warman
	G-BULH	Cessna 172N	Comed Aviation Ltd/Blackpool
	G-BULJ	CFM Steak Shadow	C. C. Brown
	G-BULK	Thunder Ax9-120 S2 balloon	Skybus Ballooning/Austria
	G-BULL	SA Bulldog Srs 120/128	C. D. Weiswall
	G-BULM	Aero Designs Pulsar	J. Webb
	G-BULN	Colt 210A balloon	H. G. Davies
	G-BULO	Luscombe 8A Silvaire	A. F. S. Caldecourt
	G-BULR	PA-28 Cherokee 140	R. & H. Wale (General Woodworks) Ltd
	G-BULT	Campbell Cricket	A. T. Pocklington
	G-BULY	Light Aero Avid Flyer	D. R. Piercy
	G-BULZ	Denney Kitfox Mk 2	T. G. F. Trenchard
	G-BUMP	PA-28-181 Archer II	Marnham Investments Ltd
	G-BUNB	Slingsby T.61F Venture T.2	RAFGSA Cranwell Gliding Club
	G-BUNC	PZL-104 Wilga 35	Paravia Group
	G-BUND	PA-28RT-201T Turbo Arrow IV	Jenrick Ltd & A. Somerville
	G-BUNG	Cameron N-77 balloon	The Bungle Balloon Group
	G-BUNH	PA-28RT-201T Turbo Arrow IV	JB Consultents (Aviation)
	G-BUNI	Cameron 90 Bunny SS balloon	Virgin Airship & Balloon Co Ltd
	G-BUNJ	Squarecraft SA.102-5 Cavalier	J. A. Smith
	G-BUNM	Denney Kitfox Mk 3	P. J. Carter
	G-BUNO	Lancair 320	J. Softley
	G-BUNS	Cessna F.150K	R. W. H. Cole
	G-BUNV	Thunder Ax7-77 balloon	J. A. Lister
	G-BUNZ	Thunder Ax10-180 S2 balloon	T. M. Donnelly
	G-BUOA	Whittaker MW.6-S Fatboy Flyer	D. A. Izod
	G-BUOB	CFM Streak Shadow	A. M. Simmons
	G-BUOC	Cameron A-210 balloon	Bailey Balloons
	G-BUOD	SE-5A (replica) (B595)	M. D. Waldron/Belgium
	G-BUOE	Cameron V-90 balloon	Dusters & Co
	G-BUOF	D.62B Condor	R. P. Loxton
	G-BUOI	PA-20 Pacer	Foley Farm Flying Group
	G-BUOJ	Cessna 172N	EFG Flying Services Ltd/Biggin Hill
	G-BUOK	Rans S.6-ESA Coyote II	M. Morris
	G-BUOL	Denney Kitfox Mk 3	J. G. D. Barbour
	G-BUON	Light Aero Avid Aerobat	I. A. J. Lappin/Newtownards
	G-BUOO	QAC Quickie Tri-Q.200	J. J. Donely & A. D. P. Thompson
	G-BUOP	Skycycle D.2 airship	G. E. Dorrington
	G-BUOR	C.A.S.A. 1.131E Jungmann 2000	M. I. M. S. Voest/Lelystad

Reg.	Type	Owner or Operator	Notes
G-BUOS	V.S.394 Spitfire FR.XVIII (SM845)	Historic Flying Ltd/Audley End	
G-BUOW	Aero Designs Pulsar XP	DRA Bedford Flying Club	
G-BUOX	Cameron V-77 balloon	R. M. Pursey & C. M. Richardson	
G-BUPA	Rutan LongEz	G. J. Banfield	
G-BUPB	Stolp SA.300 Starduster Too	Starduster PB Group	
G-BUPC	Rollason Beta B.2	C. A. Rolph	
G-BUPF	Bensen B.8R	P. W. Hewitt-Dean	
G-BUPG	Cessna 180K	T. P. A. Norman/Rendcomb	
G-BUPI	Cameron V-77 balloon	S. A. Masey (G-BOUC)	
G-BUPJ	Fournier RF-4D	M. R. Shelton	
G-BUPM	VPM M.16 Tandem Trainer	J. G. Erskine	
G-BUPO	Zlin Z.526F Trener Master	P. J. Behr & F. Mendelssohn/France	
G-BUPP	Cameron V-42 balloon	M. W. A. Shemlit	
G-BUPR	Jodel D.18	R. W. Burrows	
G-BUPS	Aérospatiale ATR-42-300	Titan Airways Ltd/Stansted	
G-BUPT	Cameron O-105 balloon	Chiltern Balloons	
G-BUPU	Thunder Ax7-77 balloon	R. C. Barkworth & D. G. Maguire/USA	
G-BUPV	Great Lakes 2T-1A	R. J. Fray	
G-BUPW	Denney Kitfox Mk 3	Kitfox Group	
G-BURD	Cessna F.172N	L. M. Bateman & Co Ltd/Halfpenny Green	
G-BURE	Jodel D.9	L. J. Kingsford	
G-BURF	Rand-Robinson KR-2	P. J. H. Moorhouse & B. L. Hewart	
G-BURG	Colt 77A balloon	S. T. Humphreys	
G-BURH	Cessna 150E	BURH Flying Group	
G-BURI	Enstrom F-28C	India Helicopters Group	
G-BURL	Colt 105A balloon	J. E. Rose	
G-BURM	EE Canberra TT.18 (WJ680)	Mitchell Aircraft Ltd/Kemble	
G-BURN	Cameron O-120 balloon	Innovation Ballooning Ltd	
G-BURP	Rotorway Executive 90	N. K. Newman	
G-BURR	Auster AOP.9 (WZ706)	R. P. D. Folkes/Middle Wallop	
G-BURS	Sikorsky S-76A	Lynton Aviation Ltd (G-OHTL)	
G-BURT	PA-28-161 Warrior II	J. D. F. Fendick	
G-BURZ	Hawker Nimrod II (K3661)	Historic Aircraft Collection Ltd	
G-BUSB	Airbus A.320-111	British Airways	
G-BUSC	Airbus A.320-111	British Airways	
G-BUSD	Airbus A.320-111	British Airways	
G-BUSE	Airbus A.320-111	British Airways	
G-BUSF	Airbus A.320-111	British Airways	
G-BUSG	Airbus A.320-211	British Airways	
G-BUSH	Airbus A.320-211	British Airways	
G-BUSI	Airbus A.320-211	British Airways	
G-BUSJ	Airbus A.320-211	British Airways	
G-BUSK	Airbus A.320-211	British Airways	
G-BUSN	Rotorway Executive 90	J. A. McGinley	
G-BUSR	Aero Designs Pulsar	S. S. Bateman & R. A. Watts	
G-BUSS	Cameron 90 Bus SS balloon	L. V. Mastis/USA	
G-BUST	Lancair IV	C. C. Butt	
G-BUSV	Colt 105A balloon	M. N. J. Kirby	
G-BUSW	R. Commander 114	P. A. Nesbitt/USA	
G-BUSY	Thunder Ax6-56A balloon	M. E. Hooker	
G-BUSZ	Light Aero Avid Speedwing Mk 4	T. J. Allan	
G-BUTA	C.A.S.A. 1.131E Jungmann 2000	A. G. Dunkerley/Breighton	
G-BUTB	CFM Streak Shadow	S. Vestuti	
G-BUTC	Cyclone AX3/582	P. R. Berridge	
G-BUTD	Van's RV-6	N. W. Beadle	
G-BUTE	Anderson EA-1 Kingfisher	T. Crawford (G-BRCK)	
G-BUTF	Aeronca 11AC Chief	N. J. Mortimore	
G-BUTG	Zenair CH.601HD	J. M. Palmer	
G-BUTH	CEA DR.220 2+2	A. A. M. & C. W. N. Huke	
G-BUTJ	Cameron O-77 balloon	A. J. A. Bubb	
G-BUTK	Murphy Rebel	A. Allen	
G-BUTL	PA-24 Comanche 250	D. Heater (G-ARLB)/Blackbushe	
G-BUTM	Rans S.6-116 Coyote II	G-BUTM Group	
G-BUTT	Cessna FA.150K	C. R. Guggenheim (G-AXSJ)/ Bournemouth	
G-BUTX	C.A.S.A. 1.133C Jungmeister	A. J. E. Smith/Breighton	
G-BUTY	Brügger MB.2 Colibri	R. M. Lawday	
G-BUTZ	PA-28 Cherokee 180C	A. J. & J. M. Davis (G-DARL)	
G-BUUA	Slingsby T.67M Mk II	Hunting Aviation Ltd/Newton	
G-BUUB	Slingsby T.67M Mk II	Hunting Aviation Ltd/Newton	
G-BUUC	Slingsby T.67M Mk II	Hunting Aviation Ltd/Newton	
G-BUUD	Slingsby T.67M Mk II	Hunting Aviation Ltd/Newton	

Notes	Reg.	Type	Owner or Operator
	G-BUUE	Slingsby T.67M Mk II	Hunting Aviation Ltd/Newton
	G-BUUF	Slingsby T.67M Mk II	Hunting Aviation Ltd/Newton
	G-BUUG	Slingsby T.67M Mk II	Hunting Aviation Ltd/Newton
	G-BUUI	Slingsby T.67M Mk II	Hunting Aviation Ltd/Newton
	G-BUUJ	Slingsby T.67M Mk II	Hunting Aviation Ltd/Newton
	G-BUUK	Slingsby T.67M Mk II	Hunting Aviation Ltd/Newton
	G-BUUL	Slingsby T.67M Mk II	Hunting Aviation Ltd/Newton
	G-BUUM	PA-28RT-201 Arrow IV	Bluebird Flying Group
	G-BUUN	Lindstrand LBL-105A balloon	Flying Pictures Ltd
	G-BUUO	Cameron N-90 balloon	Bryan Bros Ltd
	G-BUUT	Interavia 70TA balloon	Aero Vintage Ltd
	G-BUUU	Cameron 77 Bottle SS balloon	United Distillers UK Ltd
	G-BUUX	PA-28 Cherokee 180D	Aero Group 78/Netherthorpe
	G-BUVA	PA-22 Tri-Pacer 135	Oaksey VA Group
	G-BUVB	Colt 77A balloon	T. L. Regan
	G-BUVE	Colt 77B balloon	G. D. Philpot
	G-BUVG	Cameron N-56 balloon	Cameron Balloons Ltd
	G-BUVL	Fisher Super Koala	A. D. Malcolm
	G-BUVM	CEA DR.250/160	G. G. Milton
	G-BUVN	C.A.S.A. 1.131E Jungmann 2000 (BI-005)	W. Van Egmond/Netherlands
	G-BUVO	Cessna F.182P	BUVO Group (G-WTFA)/Southend
	G-BUVP	C.A.S.A. 1.131E Jungmann 2000	M. I. M. S. Voest/Netherlands
	G-BUVR	Christen A.1 Husky	A. E. Poulson
	G-BUVS	Colt 77A balloon	Supergas Ltd
	G-BUVT	Colt 77A balloon	Supergas Ltd
	G-BUVW	Cameron N-90 balloon	Bristol Balloon Fiestas Ltd
	G-BUVX	CFM Streak Shadow	G. K. R. Linney
	G-BUVZ	Thunder Ax10-180 S2 balloon	Lakeside Lodge Balloon Rides (Cambridgeshire) Ltd
	G-BUWA	V.S.349 Spitfire F.Vc (AR614)	Alpine Deer Group/New Zealand
	G-BUWE	SE-5A (replica) (C9533)	Taildragger Classics
	G-BUWF	Cameron N-105 balloon	R. E. Jones
	G-BUWH	Parsons 2-seat gyroplane	R. V. Brunskill
	G-BUWI	Lindstrand LBL-77A balloon	Capital Balloon Club Ltd
	G-BUWJ	Pitts S-1C Special	P. A. Willmington
	G-BUWK	Rans S.6-116 Coyote II	R. Warriner
	G-BUWR	CFM Streak Shadow	T. Harvey
	G-BUWS	Denney Kitfox Mk 2	J. E. Brewis
	G-BUWT	Rand-Robinson KR-2	C. M. Coombe
	G-BUWU	Cameron V-77 balloon	G. Thompson
	G-BUWW	Cameron O-105 balloon	M. T. Evans
	G-BUWY	Cameron V-77 balloon	P. A. Sachs
	G-BUWZ	Robin HR.200/120B	A. Cox/Shoreham
	G-BUXA	Colt 210A balloon	Balloon Safaris
	G-BUXB	Sikorsky S-76A	Lynton Aviation Ltd/Denham
	G-BUXC	CFM Streak Shadow	J. P. Mimnagh
	G-BUXD	Maule MXT-7-160	S. Baigent
	G-BUXI	Steen Skybolt	M. Frankland/Liverpool
	G-BUXJ	Slingsby T.61F Venture T.2	XIX Crawley Flying Club/Redhill
	G-BUXK	Pietenpol Air Camper	G. R. G. Smith/Shobdon
	G-BUXL	Taylor JT.1 Monoplane	M. W. Elliott
	G-BUXM	QAC Quickie Q.2	A. J. Ross & D. Ramwell
	G-BUXN	Beech C23 Sundowner	Private Pilots Syndicate
	G-BUXO	Pober P-9 Pixie	P-9 Flying Group
	G-BUXP	Falcon XPS	J. C. & B. E. Greenslade
	G-BUXR	Cameron A-250 balloon	Celebration Balloon Flights
	G-BUXS	MBB Bo 105DBS/4	Bond Air Services (G-PASA/G-BGWP)
	G-BUXT	Dornier Do.228-202K	ScotAirways Ltd/Cambridge
	G-BUXU	Beech D.17S	S. J. Ellis
	G-BUXV	PA-22 Tri-Pacer 160 (tailwheel)	Bogavia Two
	G-BUXW	Thunder Ax8-90 S2 balloon	J. M. Percival
	G-BUXX	PA-17 Vagabond	R. H. Hunt/Old Sarum
	G-BUXY	PA-25 Pawnee 235	Bath, Wilts & North Dorset Gliding Club Ltd
	G-BUYB	Aero Designs Pulsar	A. P. Fenn/Shobdon
	G-BUYC	Cameron 80 Concept balloon	P. J. Dorward
	G-BUYD	Thunder Ax8-90 balloon	Anglia Balloons
	G-BUYE	Aeronca 7AC Champion	R. Mazey
	G-BUYF	Falcon XP	J. C. Greenslade
	G-BUYG	Colt 12 Flying Bottle SS balloon	United Distillers PLC/Spain
	G-BUYH	Cameron A-210 balloon	A. J. Street
	G-BUYI	Thunder Ax7-77 balloon	Chelmsford Management Ltd

Reg.	Type	Owner or Operator	Notes
G-BUYJ	Lindstrand LBL-105A balloon	D. K. Fish	
G-BUYK	Denney Kitfox Mk 4	I. Burrows	
G-BUYL	RAF 2000GT gyroplane	Newtonair Gyroplanes Ltd	
G-BUYM	Thunder Ax8-105 balloon	Scotair Balloons	
G-BUYN	Cameron O-84 balloon	J. T. L. Challenger	
G-BUYO	Colt 77A balloon	S. F. Burden	
G-BUYR	Mooney M.20C	C. R. Weldon/Eire	
G-BUYS	Robin DR.400/180	F. A. Spear	
G-BUYT	Ken Brock KB-2 gyroplane	J. E. Harris	
G-BUYU	Bowers Fly-Baby 1A	J. A. Nugent	
G-BUYY	PA-28 Cherokee 180	G-BUYY Group	
G-BUZA	Denney Kitfox Mk 3	R. Hill	
G-BUZB	Aero Designs Pulsar XP	S. M. Lancashire	
G-BUZC	Everett Srs 3A gyroplane	M. P. L'Hermette	
G-BUZD	AS.332L Super Puma	Brintel Helicopters Ltd	
G-BUZE	Light Aero Avid Speedwing	G. J. Bridgewater	
G-BUZF	Colt 77B balloon	I. J. Jackson	
G-BUZG	Zenair CH.601HD	N. C. White	
G-BUZH	Aero Designs Star-Lite SL-1	C. Moffatt	
G-BUZK	Cameron V-77 balloon	J. T. Wilkinson	
G-BUZL	VPM M.16 Tandem Trainer	Roger Savage (Photography)/Carlisle	
G-BUZM	Light Aero Avid Flyer Mk 3	R. McLuckie & O. G. Jones	
G-BUZN	Cessna 172H	H. Jones/Barton	
G-BUZO	Pietenpol Air Camper	D. A. Jones	
G-BUZR	Lindstrand LBL-77A balloon	Lindstrand Balloons Ltd	
G-BUZS	Colt Flying Pig SS balloon	Banco Bilbao Vizcaya/Spain	
G-BUZT	Kölb Twinstar Mk 3	A. C. Goadby	
G-BUZV	Ken Brock KB-2 gyroplane	K. Hughes	
G-BUZY	Cameron A-250 balloon	P. J. D. Kerr	
G-BUZZ	AB-206B JetRanger 2	Virgin Helicopters Ltd/Booker	
G-BVAA	Light Aero Avid Aerobat Mk 4	D. T. Searchfield	
G-BVAB	Zenair CH.601HDS	A. R. Bender	
G-BVAC	Zenair CH.601HD	A. G. Cozens	
G-BVAF	Piper J-3C-65 Cub	N. M. Hitchman/France	
G-BVAG	Lindstrand LBL-90A balloon	T. Moult & ptnrs	
G-BVAH	Denney Kitfox Mk 3	V. A. Hutchinson	
G-BVAI	PZL-110 Koliber 150	N. J. & R. F. Morgan	
G-BVAJ	Rotorway Executive 90	Rotorbuild Helicopters Ltd	
G-BVAM	Evans VP-1	R. F. Selby	
G-BVAN	M.S.892E Rallye 150	D. R. Stringer/Elstree	
G-BVAO	Colt 25A balloon	J. M. Frazer	
G-BVAW	Staaken Z-1 Flitzer (D-692)	D. J. Evans & L. R. Williams	
G-BVAX	Colt 77A balloon	P. H. Porter	
G-BVAY	Rutan Vari-Eze	D. A. Young	
G-BVBD	Sikorsky S-52-3	J. Windmill	
G-BVBG	PA-32R Cherokee Lance 300	R. K. Spence	
G-BVBL	PA-38-112 Tomahawk	Aerohire Ltd/Halfpenny Green	
G-BVBN	Cameron A-210 balloon	Heart of England Balloons	
G-BVBO	Sikorsky S-52-3	Ilkeston Contractors	
G-BVBP	Avro 683 Lancaster X (KB994) ★	Aces High Ltd/North Weald	
G-BVBR	Light Aero Avid Speedwing	N. M. Robbins & A. A. Jones	
G-BVBS	Cameron N-77 balloon	Marley Building Materials Ltd	
G-BVBT	D.H.C.1 Chipmunk T.10 (WK511)	T. J. Manna/Cranfield	
G-BVBU	Cameron V-77 balloon	J. Manclark	
G-BVBV	Light Aero Avid Flyer	L. W. M. Summers	
G-BVCA	Cameron N-105 balloon	Unipart Balloon Club	
G-BVCB	Rans S.10 Sakota	M. D. T. Barley	
G-BVCC	Monnett Sonerai 2LT	J. Eggleston	
G-BVCG	Van's RV-6	C. A. Simmonds	
G-BVCJ	Agusta A.109A-II	Castle Air Charters Ltd (G-CLRL/G-EJCB)	
G-BVCL	Rans S.6-116 Coyote II	S. R. A. Blackbourn & J. K. McFarlane	
G-BVCM	Cessna 525 CitationJet	Kwik Fit PLC/Edinburgh	
G-BVCN	Colt 56A balloon	N. R. Mason	
G-BVCO	FRED Srs 2	I. W. Bremner	
G-BVCP	Piper CP.1 Metisse	C. W. R. Piper	
G-BVCS	Aeronca 7BCM Champion	P. C. Isbell	
G-BVCT	Denney Kitfox Mk 4	A. F. Reid	
G-BVCY	Cameron H-24 balloon	Bryant Group PLC	
G-BVCZ	Colt 240A balloon	Schemedraw Ltd/USA	
G-BVDB	Thunder Ax7-77 balloon	M. J. Smith & J. Towler (G-ORDY)	
G-BVDC	Van's RV-3	D. Calabritto	

Notes	Reg.	Type	Owner or Operator
	G-BVDD	Colt 69A balloon	R. M. Cambridge & D. Harrison-Morris
	G-BVDE	Taylor JT.1 Monoplane	C. R. J. Norman
	G-BVDF	Cameron 115 Doll SS balloon	Cameron Balloons Ltd/Germany
	G-BVDH	PA-28RT-201 Arrow IV	P. Heffron
	G-BVDI	Van's RV-4	J. P. Leigh
	G-BVDJ	Campbell Cricket (replica)	S. Jennings
	G-BVDM	Cameron C-60 balloon	M. P. Young
	G-BVDN	PA-34-220T Seneca III	Convergence Aviation Ltd (G-IGHA/G-IPUT)
	G-BVDO	Lindstrand LBL-105A balloon	J. Burlinson
	G-BVDP	Sequoia F.8L Falco	T. G. Painter
	G-BVDR	Cameron O-77 balloon	T. Duggan
	G-BVDS	Lindstrand LBL-69A balloon	I. Ollerenshaw
	G-BVDT	CFM Streak Shadow	H. J. Bennet
	G-BVDW	Thunder Ax8-90 balloon	J. G. Wilson
	G-BVDX	Cameron V-90 balloon	R. K. Scott
	G-BVDY	Cameron 60 Concept balloon	K. A. & G. N. Connolly
	G-BVDZ	Taylorcraft BC-12D	P. N. W. England
	G-BVEA	Mosler Motors N.3 Pup	N. Lynch (G-MWEA)/Breighton
	G-BVEB	PA-32R-301 Saratoga HP	Transea Trading Co. Ltd
	G-BVEC	Aérospatiale ATR-42-300	CityFlyer Express Ltd/BA Express
	G-BVED	Aérospatiale ATR-42-300	CityFlyer Express Ltd/BA Express
	G-BVEF	Aérospatiale ATR-42-300	CityFlyer Express Ltd/BA Express
	G-BVEH	Jodel D.112	M. L. Copland
	G-BVEJ	Cameron V-90 balloon	J. D. A. Snields & A. R. Craze
	G-BVEK	Cameron C-80 balloon	S. Andrews
	G-BVEN	Cameron 80 Concept balloon	Aire Valley Balloons
	G-BVEP	Luscombe 8A Master	B. H. Austen
	G-BVER	D.H.C.2 Beaver 1 (XV268)	A. F. Allen (G-BTDM)
	G-BVES	Cessna 340A	Firfax Systems Ltd
	G-BVEU	Cameron O-105 balloon	H. C. Wright
	G-BVEV	PA-34-200 Seneca	R. W. Harris & ptnrs
	G-BVEW	Lindstrand LBL-150A balloon	P. Trumper
	G-BVEY	Denney Kitfox Mk 4-1200	J. H. H. Turner
	G-BVEZ	P.84 Jet Provost T.3A (XM479)	Newcastle Jet Provost Co Ltd
	G-BVFA	Rans S.10 Sakota	M/ W. Hanley
	G-BVFB	Cameron N-31 balloon	Bath City Council
	G-BVFF	Cameron V-77 balloon	R. G. Barry
	G-BVFM	Rans S.6-116 Coyote II	P. G. Walton
	G-BVFN	Pitts S-1E Special	N. W. Parkinson
	G-BVFO	Light Aero Avid Speedwing	P. Chisman
	G-BVFP	Cameron V-90 balloon	C. Duppa-Miller
	G-BVFR	CFM Streak Shadow	R. W. Chatterton
	G-BVFS	Slingsby T.31M Cadet	V. M. Crabb
	G-BVFT	Maule M5-235C	Avon Air Services
	G-BVFU	Cameron 105 Sphere SS balloon	Lascar Investments Ltd/Luxembourg
	G-BVFX	Nanchang CJ-6A (1532008)	B. Brown/Sandtoft
	G-BVFZ	Maule M5-180C Lunar Rocket	C. N. White
	G-BVGA	Bell 206B JetRanger	Findon Air Services/Shoreham
	G-BVGB	Thunder Ax8-105 S2 balloon	Flying Pictures Ltd
	G-BVGE	W.S.55 Whirlwind HAR.10 (XJ729)	J. F. Kelly
	G-BVGF	Shaw Europa	A. Graham & G. G. Beal
	G-BVGG	Lindstrand LBL-69A balloon	Lindstrand Balloons Ltd
	G-BVGH	Hawker Hunter T.7 (XL573)	B. J. Pover
	G-BVGI	Pereira Osprey II	A. A. Knight
	G-BVGJ	Cameron C-80 balloon	D. T. Watkins
	G-BVGO	Denney Kitfox Mk 4-1200	A. Morgan
	G-BVGP	Bücker Bü133C Jungmeister (U-95)	J. P. H. A. Delvaux/France
	G-BVGR	RAF BE-2e (A1325)	Aero Vintage Ltd
	G-BVGS	Robinson R-22B	Bristol & Wessex Helicopters Ltd
	G-BVGT	Auster J/1 (modified)	P. N. Birch
	G-BVGW	Luscombe 8A Silvaire	L. A. Groves
	G-BVGX	Thunder Ax8-90 S2 balloon	G-BVGX Group
	G-BVGY	Luscombe 8E Silvaire	T. Groves
	G-BVGZ	Fokker Dr.1 (replica) (450/17) ★	Taildragger Classics
	G-BVHC	Grob G.115D-2 Heron	Short Bros PLC/Plymouth
	G-BVHD	Grob G.115D-2 Heron	Short Bros PLC/Plymouth
	G-BVHE	Grob G.115D-2 Heron	Short Bros PLC/Plymouth
	G-BVHF	Grob G.115D-2 Heron	Short Bros PLC/Plymouth
	G-BVHG	Grob G.115D-2 Heron	Short Bros PLC/Plymouth
	G-BVHI	Rans S.10 Sakota	P. D. Rowley

Reg.	Type	Owner or Operator	Notes
G-BVHK	Cameron V-77 balloon	A. R. Rich	
G-BVHM	PA-38-112 Tomahawk	A. J. Gomes (G-DCAN)	
G-BVHO	Cameron V-90 balloon	N. W. B. Bews	
G-BVHP	Colt 42A balloon	Danny Bertels Ballooning BVBA/Belgium	
G-BVHR	Cameron V-90 balloon	G. P. Walton	
G-BVHS	Murphy Rebel	J. Brown & ptnrs/Breighton	
G-BVHT	Light Aero Avid Speedwing Mk 4	R. S. Holt	
G-BVHU	Colt 13 Flying Bottle SS balloon	BIAS International Ltd/Brasil	
G-BVHV	Cameron N-105 balloon	Flying Pictures Ltd	
G-BVHX	BN-2T-4R Defender 4000	Britten-Norman Ltd/Bembridge	
G-BVHY	BN-2T-4R Defender 4000	Britten-Norman Ltd/Bembridge	
G-BVIA	Rand-Robinson KR-2	K. Atkinson	
G-BVIC	EE Canberra B.6 (XH568)	Classic Aviation Projects Ltd/ Bruntingthorpe	
G-BVID	Lindstrand Lozenge SS balloon	Respatex International Ltd	
G-BVIE	PA-18 Super Cub 95 (modified)	J. C. Best (G-CLIK/G-BLMB)	
G-BVIF	Montgomerie-Bensen B.8MR	R. M. & D. Mann	
G-BVIG	Cameron A-250 balloon	Balloon Flights International Ltd	
G-BVIH	PA-28-161 Warrior II	Ocean Developments Ltd (G-GFCE/ G-BNJP)	
G-BVIK	Maule MXT-7-180 Star Rocket	R. D. Masters	
G-BVIL	Maule MXT-7-180 Star Rocket	K. & S. C. Knight	
G-BVIM	Cameron V-77 balloon	The Ballooning Business Ltd	
G-BVIN	Rans S.6-ESA Coyote II	K. J. Vincent	
G-BVIO	Colt Flying Drinks Can SS balloon	Virgin Balloon & Airship Co Ltd	
G-BVIR	Lindstrand LBL-69A balloon	Aerial Promotions Ltd	
G-BVIS	Brügger MB.2 Colibri	M. J. Sharp	
G-BVIT	Campbell Cricket	A. N. Nisbet	
G-BVIV	Light Aero Avid Speedwing	J. & V. Hobday	
G-BVIW	PA-18-Super Cub 150	Rodger Aircraft Ltd	
G-BVIX	Lindstrand LBL-180A balloon	European Balloon Display Co Ltd	
G-BVIZ	Shaw Europa	T. J. Punter & P. G. Jeffers	
G-BVJA	Fokker 100	British Midland Airways Ltd/E. Midlands	
G-BVJB	Fokker 100	British Midland Airways Ltd/E. Midlands	
G-BVJC	Fokker 100	British Midland Airways Ltd/E. Midlands	
G-BVJD	Fokker 100	British Midland Airways Ltd/E. Midlands	
G-BVJE	AS.350B-1 Ecureuil	I. S. & G. Steel Stockholders Ltd	
G-BVJF	Montgomerie-Bensen B.8MR	D. M. F. Harvey	
G-BVJG	Cyclone AX3/K	T. D. Reid (G-MYOP)	
G-BVJH	Aero Designs Pulsar	J. A. C. Tweedle	
G-BVJJ	Cameron DP-90 airship	Cameron Balloons Ltd/Brasil	
G-BVJK	Glaser-Dirks DG.400	B. A. Eastwell	
G-BVJN	Shaw Europa	JN Europa Group	
G-BVJO	Cameron R-77 balloon	Bondbaste Ltd/Belgium	
G-BVJP	Aérospatiale ATR-42-300	Gill Airways Ltd/Newcastle	
G-BVJT	Cessna F.406	Nor Leasing	
G-BVJU	Evans VP-1	BVJU Flying Club & Associates	
G-BVJW	Airbus A.320-231	-	
G-BVJX	Marquart MA.5 Charger	M. L. Martin/Redhill	
G-BVJZ	PA-28-161 Warrior II	A. R. Fowkes/Denham	
G-BVKA	Boeing 737-59D	British Midland Airways Ltd/E. Midlands	
G-BVKB	Boeing 737-59D	British Midland Airways Ltd/E. Midlands	
G-BVKC	Boeing 737-59D	British Midland Airways Ltd/E. Midlands	
G-BVKD	Boeing 737-59D	British Midland Airways Ltd/E. Midlands	
G-BVKF	Shaw Europa	T. R. Sinclair	
G-BVKG	Colt Flying Hot Dog SS balloon	Longbreak Ltd/USA	
G-BVKH	Thunder Ax8-90 balloon	R. G. Gruzelier	
G-BVKJ	Bensen B.8	A. G. Foster	
G-BVKK	Slingsby T.61F Venture T.2	K. E. Ballington	
G-BVKL	Cameron A-180 balloon	W. I. & C. Hooker	
G-BVKM	Rutan Vari-Eze	J. P. G. Lindquist/Switzerland	
G-BVKR	Sikorsky S-76A	Bristow Helicopters Ltd	
G-BVKU	Slingsby T.61F Venture T.2	G-BVKU Syndicate	
G-BVKV	Cameron N-90 balloon	Pringle of Scotland Ltd	
G-BVKX	Colt 14A balloon	H. C. J. Williams	
G-BVKZ	Thunder Ax9-120 balloon	D. J. Head	
G-BVLA	Lancair 320	A. R. Welstead	
G-BVLC	Cameron N-42 balloon	Cameron Balloons Ltd	
G-BVLD	Campbell Cricket (replica)	C. Berry	
G-BVLE	McCandless M.4 gyroplane	H. Walls	
G-BVLF	CFM Starstreak Shadow SS-D	B. R. Johnson	
G-BVLG	AS.355F-1 Twin Squirrel	PLM Dollar Group PLC	

Notes	Reg.	Type	Owner or Operator
	G-BVLH	Shaw Europa	D. Barraclough
	G-BVLI	Cameron V-77 balloon	J. Lewis-Richardson
	G-BVLK	Rearwin 8125 Cloudster	M. C. Hiscock
	G-BVLL	Lindstrand LBL-210A balloon	A. G. E. Faulkner
	G-BVLN	Aero Designs Pulsar XP	D. A. Campbell
	G-BVLP	PA-38-112 Tomahawk	D. A. Whitmore
	G-BVLR	Van's RV-4	RV4 Group
	G-BVLS	Thunder Ax8-90 S2 balloon	J. R. Henderson
	G-BVLT	Bellanca 7GCBC Citabria	M. D. Hinge
	G-BVLU	D.31 Turbulent	C. D. Bancroft
	G-BVLV	Shaw Europa	Euro 39 Group
	G-BVLW	Light Aero Avid Flyer Mk 4	D. M. Johnstone/Shobdon
	G-BVLX	Slingsby T.61F Venture T.2	Fulmar Gliding Club/Kinloss
	G-BVLZ	Lindstrand LBL-120A balloon	Balloon Flights Club Ltd
	G-BVMA	Beech 200 Super King Air	Manhattan Air Ltd (G-VPLC)/Blackbushe
	G-BVMB	Hawker Hunter T.7 (XL613)	Hunter Aviation Ltd
	G-BVMC	Robinson R-44 Astro	E. Wooton
	G-BVMD	Luscombe 8E Silvaire	G. M. Scott
	G-BVMF	Cameron V-77 balloon	P. A. Meecham
	G-BVMG	Bensen B.80V	D. Moffat
	G-BVMH	WAG-Aero Sport Trainer (39624)	D. M. Jagger
	G-BVMI	PA-18 Super Cub 150	T. P. & M. M. Spurge
	G-BVMJ	Cameron 95 Eagle SS balloon	R. D. Sargeant
	G-BVML	Lindstrand LBL-210A balloon	Ballooning Adventures Ltd
	G-BVMM	Robin HR.200/100	R. H. Ashforth
	G-BVMN	Ken Brock KB-2 gyroplane	S. McCullagh
	G-BVMR	Cameron V-90 balloon	I. R. Comley
	G-BVMU	Yakovlev Yak-52 (09)	J. E. & A. Ashby
	G-BVMX	Short SD3-60 Variant 100	Aurigny Air Services Ltd (G-BPFS/G-REGN/G-OCIA)/Guernsey
	G-BVMZ	Robin HR.100/210	Chiltern Handbags (London) Ltd)/Booker
	G-BVNG	D.H.60G-III Moth Major	J. A. Pothecary/Shoreham
	G-BVNH	Agusta A.109C	Lochbrae Ltd (G-LAXO)
	G-BVNI	Taylor JT-2 Titch	T. V. Adamson/Rufforth
	G-BVNL	R. Commander 114	W. J. Hemmings & ptnrs
	G-BVNM	Boeing 737-4S3	British Airways (G-BPKA)
	G-BVNN	Boeing 737-4S3	British Airways (G-BPKB)
	G-BVNO	Boeing 737-4S3	British Airways (G-BPKE)
	G-BVNR	Cameron N-105 balloon	Liquigas SPA/Italy
	G-BVNS	PA-28-181 Archer II	Scottish Airways Flyers (Prestwick) Ltd
	G-BVNU	FLS Aerospace Sprint Club	Sunhawk Ltd/North Weald
	G-BVNY	Rans S.7 Courier	Sportair UK Ltd
	G-BVOA	PA-28-181 Archer II	Millen Aviation Services
	G-BVOB	F.27 Friendship Mk 500	BAC Express Airlines Ltd
	G-BVOC	Cameron V-90 balloon	S. A. Masey
	G-BVOD	Montgomerie-Parsons 2-seat gyroplane	J. M. Montgomerie
	G-BVOG	Cameron RN-9 balloon	Cameron Balloons Ltd
	G-BVOH	Campbell Cricket (replica)	G. A. Speich
	G-BVOI	Rans S.6-116 Coyote II	A. P. Bacon
	G-BVOK	Yakovlev Yak-52 (55)	D. J. Gilmour/North Weald
	G-BVON	Lindstrand LBL-105A balloon	P. A. Lindstrand
	G-BVOO	Lindstrand LBL-105A balloon	T. G. Church/USA
	G-BVOP	Cameron N-90 balloon	Cambury Ltd
	G-BVOR	CFM Streak Shadow	J. A. Lord
	G-BVOS	Shaw Europa	Durham Europa Group
	G-BVOU	H.S.748 Srs 2A	Emerald Airways Ltd/Liverpool
	G-BVOV	H.S.748 Srs 2A	Emerald Airways Ltd/Liverpool
	G-BVOW	Shaw Europa	Europa Syndicate
	G-BVOX	Taylorcraft F-22	Cubair Ltd/Redhill
	G-BVOY	Rotorway Executive 90	E. Drinkwater
	G-BVOZ	Colt 56A balloon	British School of Ballooning
	G-BVPA	Thunder Ax8-105 S2 balloon	Firefly Balloon Promotions
	G-BVPD	C.A.S.A. 1.131E Jungmann 2000	D. Bruton
	G-BVPH	Bensen-Parsons 2-seat gyroplane	I. A. Leedham
	G-BVPK	Cameron O-90 balloon	D. V. Fowler
	G-BVPL	Zenair CH.601HD	A. D. Walker
	G-BVPM	Evans VP-2 Coupé	P. Marigold
	G-BVPN	Piper J-3C-65 Cub	J. Esteban (G-TAFY)/Spain
	G-BVPP	Folland Gnat T.1 (XR993)	T. J. Manna/Cranfield
	G-BVPR	Robinson R-22B	E. Bailey (G-KNIT)/Staverton
	G-BVPS	Jodel D.112	P. J. Sharp

Reg.	Type	Owner or Operator	Notes
G-BVPU	Cameron A-140 balloon	Cameron Balloons Ltd/Canada	
G-BVPV	Lindstrand LBL-77B balloon	A. R. Greensides	
G-BVPW	Rans S.6-116 Coyote II	J. G. Beesley	
G-BVPX	Bensen B.8 (modified) Tyro Gyro	A. W. Harvey	
G-BVPY	CFM Streak Shadow	R. J. Mitchell	
G-BVRA	Shaw Europa	E. J. J. & S. W. Pels	
G-BVRD	VPM M.16 Tandem Trainer	Whisky Mike (Aviation) Ltd	
G-BVRE	Van's RV-6A	C. M. Dixon	
G-BVRI	Thunder Ax6-56 balloon	Aivan Wyk	
G-BVRK	Rans S.6-ESA Coyote II	J. Secular (G-MYPK)	
G-BVRL	Lindstrand LBL-21A balloon	Blown Away UK Ltd	
G-BVRM	Cameron A-210 balloon	Virgin Balloon Flights Ltd/Oman	
G-BVRP	Lindstrand LBL-90A balloon	Lindstrand Balloons Ltd/Austria	
G-BVRR	Lindstrand LBL-77A balloon	G. C. Elson/Spain	
G-BVRS	Beech B90 King Air	City Flight Ltd (G-KJET/G-AXFE)	
G-BVRU	Lindstrand LBL-105A balloon	Flying Pictures Ltd	
G-BVRV	Van's RV-4	A. Troughton	
G-BVRY	Cyclone AX3/582	A. N. Bowerman	
G-BVRZ	PA-18 Super Cub 95	R. G. Warwick	
G-BVSB	Team Minimax	D. G. Palmer	
G-BVSD	SE.3130 Alouette II (V-54)	M. J. Cuttell	
G-BVSF	Aero Designs Pulsar	S. N. & R. J. Freestone	
G-BVSJ	BN-2T Turbine Islander	Britten-Norman Ltd/Bembridge	
G-BVSL	BN-2B-26 Islander	Britten-Norman Ltd/Bembridge	
G-BVSM	RAF 2000 gyroplane	K. Quigley	
G-BVSN	Light Aero Avid Speedwing	D. J. & C. Park	
G-BVSO	Cameron A-120 balloon	Up & Away Ballooning Ltd	
G-BVSP	P.84 Jet Provost T.3A (XM370)	Shoal Ltd	
G-BVSR	Colt 210A balloon	Eagle Security Ltd	
G-BVSS	Jodel D.150	A. P. Burns	
G-BVST	Jodel D.150	A. Shipp/Breighton	
G-BVSV	Cameron C-80 balloon	Cameron Balloons Ltd/Beirut, Lebanon	
G-BVSW	Cameron C-80 balloon	Cameron Balloons Ltd/Beirut, Lebanon	
G-BVSX	Team Minimax 91	G. N. Smith	
G-BVSY	Thunder Ax9-120 balloon	G. R. Elson/Spain	
G-BVSZ	Pitts S-1E (S) Special	R. C. F. Bailey	
G-BVTA	Tri-R Kis	P. J. Webb	
G-BVTC	P.84 Jet Provost T.5A (XW333)	Global Aviation Ltd/Binbrook	
G-BVTD	CFM Streak Shadow	M. Walton	
G-BVTE	Fokker 70	British Midland Airways Ltd/E. Midlands	
G-BVTF	Fokker 70	British Midland Airways Ltd/E. Midlands	
G-BVTG	Fokker 70	British Midland Airways Ltd/E. Midlands	
G-BVTJ	Aérospatiale ATR-72-202	CityFlyer Express Ltd/BA Express	
G-BVTK	Aérospatiale ATR-72-202	CityFlyer Express Ltd/BA Express	
G-BVTL	Colt 31A balloon	A. Lindsay	
G-BVTM	Cessna F.152 II	RAF Halton Aeroplane Club (G-WACS)	
G-BVTN	Cameron N-90 balloon	P. Zulehner/Austria	
G-BVTO	PA-28-151 Warrior	Falcon Flying Services (G-SEWL)/ Biggin Hill	
G-BVTV	Rotorway Executive 90	H. G. Orchin	
G-BVTW	Aero Designs Pulsar	J. D. Webb	
G-BVTX	D.H.C.1 Chipmunk 22A (WP809)	TX Flying Group	
G-BVUA	Cameron O-105 balloon	D. C. Eager	
G-BVUC	Colt 56A balloon	Thunder & Colt	
G-BVUD	Cameron A-250 balloon	British School of Ballooning	
G-BVUE	Cameron C-80 balloon	British School of Ballooning	
G-BVUF	Thunder Ax10-180 S2 balloon	A. J. Nunns	
G-BVUG	Betts TB.1 (Stampe SV-4C)	William Tomkins Ltd (G-BEUS)	
G-BVUH	Thunder Ax6-65B balloon	N. C. A. Crawley	
G-BVUI	Lindstrand LBL-25A balloon	Lindstrand Balloons Ltd	
G-BVUJ	Ken Brock KB-2 gyroplane	R. J. Hutchinson	
G-BVUK	Cameron V-77 balloon	H. G. Griffiths & W. A. Steel	
G-BVUM	Rans S.6-116 Coyote II	M. A. Abbott	
G-BVUN	Van's RV-4	I. G. & M. Glenn	
G-BVUO	Cameron R-150 balloon	M. Sevrin/Belgium	
G-BVUP	Schleicher ASW-24E	E. & C. F. Sprecht/Husbands Bosworth	
G-BVUU	Cameron C-80 balloon	T. M. C. McCoy	
G-BVUV	Shaw Europa	R. J. Mills	
G-BVUZ	Cessna 120	N. O. Anderson	
G-BVVA	Yakovlev Yak-52	T. W. Freeman/Little Gransden	
G-BVVB	Carlson Sparrow Mk II	L. M. McCullen	
G-BVVC	Hawker Hunter F.6A (XF516)	Classic Jet Aircraft Co	
G-BVVE	Jodel D.112	G. W. Jarvis	

Notes	Reg.	Type	Owner or Operator
	G-BVVF	Nanchang CJ-6A (2028)	R. A. Fleming & A. J. E. Smith
	G-BVVG	Nanchang CJ-6A	G. Beda/France
	G-BVVH	Shaw Europa	T. G. Hoult
	G-BVVI	Hawker Audax I (K5600)	Aero Vintage Ltd
	G-BVVK	D.H.C.6 Twin Otter 310	Loganair Ltd/BA Express
	G-BVVL	EAA Acro Sport II	G. A. Breen/Portugal
	G-BVVM	Zenair CH.601HD	J. G. Small
	G-BVVN	Brügger MB.2 Colibri	N. F. Andrews
	G-BVVP	Shaw Europa	W. Komm
	G-BVVR	Stits SA-3A Playboy	I. T. James
	G-BVVS	Van's RV-4	E. G. & N. S. C. English
	G-BVVT	Colt 240A balloon	R. W. Keron
	G-BVVW	Yakovlev Yak-52	J. E. Blackman
	G-BVVX	Yakovlev Yak-18A	J. M. & E. M. Wicks
	G-BVVZ	Corby CJ-1 Starlet	A. E. Morris
	G-BVWA	M. S. 880B Rallye Club	G. K. Brunwin
	G-BVWB	Thunder Ax8-90 S2 balloon	S. C. Clayton
	G-BVWC	EE Canberra B.6 (WK163)	Classic Aviation Projects Ltd/ Bruntingthorpe
	G-BVWE	Cameron C-80 balloon	Daicel Polymers Ltd
	G-BVWH	Cameron N-90 Bulb SS balloon	Virgin Airship & Balloon Co Ltd
	G-BVWI	Cameron 65 Bulb SS balloon	Virgin Airship & Balloon Co Ltd
	G-BVWK	Air & Space 18A gyroplane	Whisky Mike (Aviation) Ltd
	G-BVWL	Air & Space 18A gyroplane	Whisky Mike (Aviation) Ltd
	G-BVWM	Shaw Europa	Europa Syndicate
	G-BVWP	D.H.C.1 Chipmunk 22 (WP856)	T. W. M. Beck
	G-BVWW	Lindstrand LBL-90A balloon	R. B. Naylor
	G-BVWX	VPM M.16 Tandem Trainer	M. L. Smith
	G-BVWY	Porterfield CP.65	B. Morris
	G-BVWZ	PA-32-301 Saratoga	J. W. V. Edmonds
	G-BVXA	Cameron N-105 balloon	R. E. Jones
	G-BVXB	Cameron V-77 balloon	J. A. Lawton
	G-BVXC	EE Canberra B.6 (WT333)	Classic Aviation Projects Ltd/ Bruntingthorpe
	G-BVXD	Cameron O-84 balloon	N. J. Langley
	G-BVXE	Steen Skybolt	J. Buglass (G-LISA)
	G-BVXF	Cameron O-120 balloon	Gone With The Wind Ltd/Chile
	G-BVXG	Lindstrand LBL-90A balloon	G. C. Elson/Spain
	G-BVXI	Klemm Kl.35D	J. J. van Egmond/Netherlands
	G-BVXJ	C.A.S.A. 1.133 Jungmeister	J. D. Haslam
	G-BVXK	Yakovlev Yak-52 (26)	E. Gavazzi
	G-BVXM	AS.350B Ecureuil	The Berkeley Leisure Group Ltd
	G-BVXP	Cameron N-105 balloon	P. M. Gaines
	G-BVXR	D.H.104 Devon C.2 (XA880)	M. Whale & M. W. A. Lunn
	G-BVXS	Taylorcraft BC-12D	J. M. Allison
	G-BVXW	SC.7 Skyvan Srs 3A Variant 100	Hunting Aviation Ltd/ Weston-on-the-Green
	G-BVYA	Airbus A.320-231	jmc Airlines Ltd
	G-BVYB	Airbus A.320-231	jmc Airlines Ltd
	G-BVYC	Airbus A.320-231	jmc Airlines Ltd
	G-BVYF	PA-31-350 Navajo Chieftain	Warwickshire Aerocentre Ltd (G-SAVE)/Birmingham
	G-BVYG	CEA DR.300/180	Ulster Gliding Club Ltd
	G-BVYJ	Cameron 90 Fire Extinguisher SS balloon	Chubb Fire Ltd
	G-BVYK	Team Minimax	S. B. Churchill
	G-BVYM	CEA DR. 300/180	London Gliding Club (Pty) Ltd/Dunstable
	G-BVYO	Robin R.2160	The Cotswold Aero Club Ltd/Staverton
	G-BVYP	PA-25 Pawnee 235B ★	Bidford Gliding Centre Ltd
	G-BVYR	Cameron A-250 balloon	Voyager Balloons Ltd
	G-BVYT	QAC Quickie Q.2	Quickie Club
	G-BVYU	Cameron A-120 balloon	B. J. Petteford
	G-BVYX	Light Aero Avid Speedwing Mk 4	G. J. Keen
	G-BVYY	Pietenpol Air Camper	J. R. Orchard
	G-BVYZ	Stemme S.10V	L. Gubbay & S. Sagar
	G-BVZD	Tri Kis	R. T. Clegg
	G-BVZE	Boeing 737-59D	British Midland Airways Ltd/E. Midlands
	G-BVZF	Boeing 737-59D	British Midland Airways Ltd/E. Midlands
	G-BVZG	Boeing 737-5Q8	British Midland Airways Ltd/E. Midlands
	G-BVZH	Boeing 737-5Q8	British Midland Airways Ltd/E. Midlands
	G-BVZI	Boeing 737-5Q8	British Midland Airways Ltd/E. Midlands
	G-BVZJ	Rand-Robinson KR-2	J. P. McConnell-Wood
	G-BVZM	Cessna 210M	R. W. Bonner-Davies

Reg.	Type	Owner or Operator	Notes
G-BVZN	Cameron C-80 balloon	Sky Fly Balloons	
G-BVZO	Rans S.6-116 Coyote II	P. Atkinson	
G-BVZR	Zenair CH.601HD	J. D. White	
G-BVZT	Lindstrand LBL-90A balloon	Pork Farms Bowyers	
G-BVZU	Airbus A.320-231	-	
G-BVZV	Rans S.6-116 Coyote II	A. G. Cameron & W. G. Dunn	
G-BVZX	Cameron H-34 balloon	Chianti Balloon Club/Italy	
G-BVZZ	D.H.C.1 Chipmunk 22 (WP795)	Portsmouth Naval Gliding Club/ Lee-on-Solent	
G-BWAA	Cameron N-133 balloon	Bailey Balloons	
G-BWAB	Jodel D.14	W. A. Braim	
G-BWAC	Waco YKS-7	D. N. Peters	
G-BWAD	RAF 2000GT gyroplane	Newtonair Gyroplanes Ltd	
G-BWAE	RAF 2000GT gyroplane	B. J. Crockett	
G-BWAF	Hawker Hunter F.6A (XG160)	R. V. Aviation Ltd/Bournemouth	
G-BWAG	Cameron O-120 balloon	M. F. Glue	
G-BWAH	Montgomerie-Bensen B.8MR	S. J. O. Tinn	
G-BWAI	CFM Streak Shadow	I. G. Hunt	
G-BWAJ	Cameron V-77 balloon	R. S. & S. H. Ham	
G-BWAK	Robinson R-22B	Caudwell Communications Ltd	
G-BWAN	Cameron N-77 balloon	Virgin Airship & Balloon Co Ltd	
G-BWAO	Cameron C-80 balloon	Virgin Airship & Balloon Co Ltd	
G-BWAP	FRED Srs 3	R. J. Smyth	
G-BWAR	Denney Kitfox Mk 3	B. J. Finch/Defford	
G-BWAT	Pietenpol Air Camper	M. H. James/Tollerton	
G-BWAU	Cameron V-90 balloon	K. M. & A. M. F. Hall	
G-BWAV	Schweizer 269C	Helihire	
G-BWAW	Lindstrand LBL-77A balloon	D. Bareford	
G-BWBA	Cameron V-65 balloon	Dante Balloon Group	
G-BWBB	Lindstrand LBL-14A balloon	Oxford Promotions (UK) Ltd	
G-BWBC	Cameron N-90AS balloon	Kurhessischer Verein Fur Luftfahrt/ Germany	
G-BWBE	Colt Flying Ice Cream Cone SS balloon	Benedikt Haggeney GmbH/Germany	
G-BWBF	Colt Flying Ice Cream Cone SS balloon	Benedikt Haggeney GmbH/Germany	
G-BWBG	Cvjetkovic CA-65 Skyfly	T. White & M. C. Fawkes	
G-BWBH	Colt Fork Lift Truck SS balloon	Jungheinrich AG/Germany	
G-BWBI	Taylorcraft F-22A	P. J. Wallace	
G-BWBJ	Colt 21A balloon	U. Schneider/Germany	
G-BWBO	Lindstrand LBL-77A balloon	R. C. McCarthy/USA	
G-BWBT	Lindstrand LBL-90A balloon	British Telecommunications PLC	
G-BWBY	Schleicher ASH.26E	F. B. Jeynes	
G-BWBZ	ARV Super 2	J. N. C. Shields/Newtownards	
G-BWCA	CFM Streak Shadow	R. Thompson	
G-BWCC	Van Den Bemden Gas balloon	Piccard Balloon Group	
G-BWCE	Campbell Cricket	M. K. Hoban	
G-BWCG	Lindstrand LBL-42A balloon	Oxford Promotions (UK) Ltd	
G-BWCI	Light Aero Avid Hauler Mk 4	Avid Group	
G-BWCK	Everett Srs 2 gyroplane	A. C. S. M. Hart	
G-BWCL	Lindstrand LBL-180A balloon	G. McFarland	
G-BWCO	Dornier Do.28D-2	Wingglider Ltd/Hibaldstow	
G-BWCS	P.84 Jet Provost T.5 (XW293)	R. E. Todd/Sandtoft	
G-BWCT	Tipsy T.66 Nipper 1	J. S. Hemmings & C. R. Steer	
G-BWCU	Bell 206L-1 Long Ranger	Aeromega Ltd	
G-BWCV	Shaw Europa	M. P. Chetwynd-Talbot	
G-BWCW	Barnett J4B rotorcraft	S. H. Kirkby	
G-BWCY	Murphy Rebel	A. Konieczek	
G-BWCZ	Mini-500	D. Nieman	
G-BWDA	Aérospatiale ATR-72-202	Gill Airways Ltd/Newcastle	
G-BWDB	Aérospatiale ATR-72-202	Gill Airways Ltd/Newcastle	
G-BWDE	PA-31P Pressurised Navajo	Tomkat Aviation Ltd (G-HWKN)	
G-BWDF	PZL-104 Wilga 35A	Shivair Ltd	
G-BWDH	Cameron N-105 balloon	Bridges Van Hire Ltd	
G-BWDM	Lindstrand LBL-120A balloon	G. D. & L. Fitzpatrick	
G-BWDO	Sikorsky S-76B	A	
G-BWDP	Shaw Europa	H. Linke/Germany	
G-BWDR	P.84 Jet Provost T.3A (XM376)	W. O. Bayazid/North Weald	
G-BWDS	P.84 Jet Provost T.3A (XM424)	J. Sinclair	
G-BWDT	PA-34-220T Seneca II	A. C. Morgan (G-BKHS)/Biggin Hill	
G-BWDU	Cameron V-90 balloon	Bath & West Security	
G-BWDV	Schweizer 269C	Oxford Aviation Services Ltd/Kidlington	

Notes	Reg.	Type	Owner or Operator
	G-BWDX	Shaw Europa	J. B. Crane
	G-BWDY	Sky 65-24 balloon	Sky Balloons Ltd
	G-BWDZ	Sky 105-24 balloon	Skyride Balloons Ltd
	G-BWEA	Lindstrand LBL-120A balloon	S. R. Seager
	G-BWEB	P.84 Jet Provost T.5A	D. W. N. Johnson
	G-BWEC	Cassutt-Colson Variant	N. R. Thomason & M. P. J. Hill
	G-BWED	Thunder Ax7-77 balloon	J. Tod
	G-BWEE	Cameron V-42 balloon	Aeromantics Ltd
	G-BWEF	SNCAN Stampe SV-4C	Acebell BWEF Syndicate (G-BOVL)
	G-BWEG	Shaw Europa	Wessex Europa Group
	G-BWEH	HOAC Katana DV.20	Diamond Aircraft Industries GmbH/Austria
	G-BWEL	Sky 200-24 balloon	H-O-T Air Balloons
	G-BWEM	V.S.358 Seafire L.IIIC (RX168)	C. J. Warrilow & S. W. Atkins
	G-BWEN	Macair Merlin GT	B. W. Davies
	G-BWEO	Lindstrand AM400 balloon	Lindstrand Balloons Ltd
	G-BWEP	Lindstrand AM2200 balloon	Lindstrand Balloons Ltd
	G-BWER	Lindstrand AM400 balloon	Lindstrand Balloons Ltd
	G-BWEU	Cessna F.152 II	Sky Pro Ltd
	G-BWEV	Cessna 152 II	Haimoss Ltd
	G-BWEW	Cameron N-105 balloon	Unipart Balloon Club
	G-BWEY	Bensen B.8	F. G. Shepherd
	G-BWEZ	Piper J-3C-65 Cub (436021)	J. G. McTaggart/Cumbernauld
	G-BWFD	HOAC Katana DV.20	Diamond Aircraft Industries GmbH/Austria
	G-BWFE	HOAC Katana DV.20	Diamond Aircraft Industries GmbH/Austria
	G-BWFG	Robin HR.200/120B	Air Caernarfon Ltd
	G-BWFH	Shaw Europa	B. L. Wratten
	G-BWFI	HOAC Katana DV.20	Diamond Aircraft Industires GmbH/Austria
	G-BWFJ	Evans VP-1	P. A. West
	G-BWFK	Lindstrand LBL-77A balloon	Virgin Airship & Balloon Co. Ltd
	G-BWFM	Yakovlev Yak-50	Classic Aviation Ltd/Duxford
	G-BWFN	Hapi Cygnet SF-2A	T. Crawford
	G-BWFO	Colomban MC.15 Cri-Cri	O. G. Jones
	G-BWFP	Yakovlev Yak-52	M. C. Lee/Manchester
	G-BWFR	Hawker Hunter F.58 (J-4031)	The Old Flying Machine Co. Ltd/Duxford
	G-BWFS	Hawker Hunter F.58 (J-4058)	The Old Flying Machine Co. Ltd/Duxford
	G-BWFT	Hawker Hunter T.8M (XL602)	T8M Group
	G-BWFV	HOAC Katana DV.20	South Warwickshire Flying Club
	G-BWFX	Shaw Europa	A. D. Stewart
	G-BWFY	AS.350B-1 Ecureuil	PLM Dollar Group Ltd/Inverness
	G-BWFZ	Murphy Rebel	I. E. Spencer (G-SAVS)
	G-BWGF	P.84 Jet Provost T.5A (XW325)	Specialscope Jet Provost Group/ Woodford
	G-BWGG	MH.1521C-1 Broussard	M. J. Burnett & R. B. Maalouf/France
	G-BWGH	Shaw Europa	M. H. B. Heathman
	G-BWGJ	Chilton DW.1A	T. J. Harrison
	G-BWGK	Hawker Hunter GA.11 (XE689)	B. J. Pover/Exeter
	G-BWGL	Hawker Hunter T.8C (XF357)	Mach 2 Enterprises Ltd
	G-BWGM	Hawker Hunter T.8C (XE665)	B. J. Pover/Exeter
	G-BWGN	Hawker Hunter T.8C (WT722)	T8C Group
	G-BWGO	Slingsby T.67M-200	R. Gray
	G-BWGP	Cameron C-80 balloon	P. J. & C. M. Gentle
	G-BWGR	NA TB-25N Mitchell (151632)	Aces High Ltd/North Weald
	G-BWGS	P.84 Jet Provost T.5A	K. K. Gerstorfer
	G-BWGT	P.84 Jet Provost T.4	R. E. Todd/Sandtoft
	G-BWGU	Cessna 150F	W. Davies
	G-BWGX	Cameron N-42 balloon	Newbury Building Soc.
	G-BWGY	HOAC Katana DV.20	HOAC Austria Weiner Neustadt GmbH
	G-BWGZ	HOAC Katana DV.20	HOAC Austria Weiner Neustadt GmbH
	G-BWHA	Hawker Hurricane IIB (Z5252)	Historic Flying Ltd/Audley End
	G-BWHB	Cameron O-65 balloon	G. Aimo/Italy
	G-BWHC	Cameron N-77 balloon	R. B. Craik
	G-BWHD	Lindstrand LBL-31A balloon	Army Air Corps Balloon Club
	G-BWHF	PA-31-325 Navajo	Awyr Cymru Cyf/Welshpool
	G-BWHG	Cameron N-65 balloon	Coffee Nannini SRL/Italy
	G-BWHH	PA-18 Super Cub 135 (44)	J. W. McLeod
	G-BWHI	D.H.C.1 Chipmunk 22A (WK624)	N. E. M. Clare
	G-BWHJ	Starstreak Shadow SA-II	N. Irwin
	G-BWHK	Rans S.6-116 Coyote II	M. Knowles
	G-BWHM	Sky 140-24 balloon	C. J. S. Limon
	G-BWHP	C.A.S.A. 1.131E Jungmann (S4+A07)	J. F. Hopkins
	G-BWHR	Tipsy T.66 Nipper Srs 1	L. R. Marnef/Belgium
	G-BWHS	RAF 2000 gyroplane	V. G. Freke

Reg.	Type	Owner or Operator	Notes
G-BWHU	Westland Scout AH.1 (XR595)	N. J. F. Boston	
G-BWHV	Denney Kitfox Mk 2	A. C. Dove	
G-BWHW	Cameron A-180 balloon	Societe Bombard SARL/France	
G-BWHY	Robinson R-22	Helicentre Ltd/Blackpool	
G-BWIA	Rans S.10 Sakota	P. A. Beck	
G-BWIB	SA Bulldog Srs 120/122	Aerofab Restorations	
G-BWID	D.31 Turbulent	A. M. Turney	
G-BWII	Cessna 150G	J. D. G. Hicks (G-BSKB)	
G-BWIJ	Shaw Europa	R. Lloyd	
G-BWIK	D.H.82A Tiger Moth (NL985)	B. J. Ellis	
G-BWIL	Rans S.10 Sakota	J. C. Longmore (G-WIEN)	
G-BWIP	Cameron N-90 balloon	Noble Adventures Ltd	
G-BWIR	Dornier Do.328-100	ScotAirways Ltd	
G-BWIT	QAC Quickie 1	D. E. Johnson & ptnrs/Coventry	
G-BWIU	Hawker Hunter F.58 (XG232)	Classic Aviation Ltd/Duxford	
G-BWIV	Shaw Europa	T. G. Ledbury	
G-BWIW	Sky 180-24 balloon	G. D. & L. Fitzpatrick	
G-BWIX	Sky 120-24 balloon	J. M. Percival	
G-BWJB	Thunder Ax8-105 balloon	Justerini & Brooks Ltd	
G-BWJC	Cameron N-65 balloon	Cameron Balloons Ltd	
G-BWJE	Sky 105-24 balloon	Sky Balloons Ltd	
G-BWJG	Mooney M.20J	Samic Ltd	
G-BWJH	Shaw Europa	A. R. D. & J. A. S. T. Hood	
G-BWJI	Cameron V-90 balloon	Calarel Developments Ltd	
G-BWJK	Rotorway Executive 152	B. Singh (G-OKIT)	
G-BWJM	Bristol M1C (replica) (C4918)	The Shuttleworth Collection/O. Warden	
G-BWJN	Montgomerie-Bensen B.8	M. G. Mee	
G-BWJO	BN-2T Turbine Islander	Britten-Norman Ltd/Bembridge	
G-BWJP	Cessna 172C	Heron Air Services Ltd/Bournemouth	
G-BWJR	Sky 120-24 balloon	B. Brogan/Austria	
G-BWJT	Yakovlev Yak-50 (01385)	W. R. M. Beesley/Brighton	
G-BWJW	Westland Scout AH.1 (XV130)	C. L. Holdsworth	
G-BWJY	D.H.C.1 Chipmunk 22 (WG469)	K. J. Thompson	
G-BWJZ	D.H.C.1 Chipmunk 22 (WK638)	J. Zemlik/Brighton	
G-BWKB	Hawker Hunter F.58 (J-4081)	Classic Aviation Ltd/Duxford	
G-BWKD	Cameron O-120 balloon	K.E. Viney	
G-BWKE	Cameron AS-105GD airship	Gefa-Flug GmbH/Germany	
G-BWKF	Cameron N-105 balloon	R. M. M. Botti/Italy	
G-BWKG	Shaw Europa	T. C. Jackson	
G-BWKJ	Rans S.7 Courier	J. P. Kovacs	
G-BWKK	Auster A.O.P.9 (XP279)	C. A. Davis & D. R. White	
G-BWKR	Sky 90-24 balloon	B. Drawbridge	
G-BWKT	Stephens Akro Laser	P. D. Begley	
G-BWKU	Cameron A-250 balloon	British School of Ballooning	
G-BWKV	Cameron V-77 balloon	Poppies (UK) Ltd	
G-BWKW	Thunder Ax8-90 balloon	Venice Simplon Orient Express Ltd	
G-BWKX	Cameron A-250 balloon	Hot Airlines/Thailand	
G-BWKZ	Lindstrand LBL-77A balloon	Lambert Smith Hampton Group Ltd	
G-BWLA	Lindstrand LBL-69A balloon	Virgin Airship & Balloon Co Ltd	
G-BWLD	Cameron O-120 balloon	D. Pedri & ptnrs/Italy	
G-BWLE	Bell 212	Bristow Helicopters Ltd/Redhill	
G-BWLF	Cessna 404	Nor Leasing (G-BNXS)	
G-BWLH	Lindstrand LBL HS-110 airship	Ramdon International	
G-BWLJ	Taylorcraft DCO-65	C. Evans	
G-BWLL	Murphy Rebel	F. W. Parker	
G-BWLM	Sky 65-24 balloon	Dachstein Tauern Balloons KG/Austria	
G-BWLN	Cameron O-84 balloon	Reggiana Riduttori SRL/Italy	
G-BWLP	HOAC Katana DV.20	Blackbushe School of Flying Ltd	
G-BWLR	MH.1521M Broussard (185)	Chicory Crops Ltd	
G-BWLS	HOAC Katana DV.20	Blackbushe School of Flying Ltd	
G-BWLT	HOAC Katana DV.20	Blackbushe School of Flying Ltd	
G-BWLV	HOAC Katana DV.20	HOAC Austria Weiner Neustadt GmbH	
G-BWLW	Light Aero Avid Speedwing Mk4	P. C. & S. A. Creswick	
G-BWLX	Westland Scout AH.1 (XV134)	R. E. Dagless	
G-BWLY	Rotorway Executive 90	P. W. & I. P. Bewley	
G-BWMA	Colt 105A balloon	C. C. Duppa-Miller	
G-BWMB	Jodel D.119	C. Hughes	
G-BWMC	Cessna 182P	Eggesford Eagles Flying Group	
G-BWMD	Enstrom 480	Southern Air Ltd/Shoreham	
G-BWMF	Gloster Meteor T.7 (WA591)	Meteor Flight (Yatesbury)	
G-BWMG	AS.332L Super Puma	Bristow Helicopters Ltd	
G-BWMH	Lindstrand LBL-77B balloon	J. W. Hole	
G-BWMI	PA-28RT-201T Turbo Arrow IV	C. H. R. Hewitt & D. H. Saunders	

Notes	Reg.	Type	Owner or Operator
	G-BWMJ	Nieuport 17/2B (replica) (B3459)	R. Gauld-Galliers & L. J. Day
	G-BWMK	D.H.82A Tiger Moth (T8191)	Schneider Trophy Ltd/Welshpool
	G-BWML	Cameron A-275 balloon	A. J. Street
	G-BWMN	Rans S.7 Courier	G. J. Knee & G. Keyser
	G-BWMO	Oldfield Baby Lakes	P. J. Tanulak (G-CIII)
	G-BWMS	D.H.82A Tiger Moth	Foundation Early Birds/Netherlands
	G-BWMU	Cameron 105 Monster Truck SS balloon	Cameron Balloons Ltd
	G-BWMV	Colt AS-105 Mk II airship	D. Stuber/Germany
	G-BWMX	D.H.C.1 Chipmunk 22 (WG407)	W. H. Sanaghan
	G-BWMY	Cameron Bradford & Bingley SS balloon	L. V, Mastis
	G-BWNB	Cessna 152 II	Galair International Ltd
	G-BWNC	Cessna 152 II	Galair International Ltd
	G-BWND	Cessna 152 II	Galair International Ltd
	G-BWNF	BN-2B-20 Islander	Britten-Norman Ltd/Bembridge
	G-BWNG	BN-2B-20 Islander	Britten-Norman Ltd/Bembridge
	G-BWNH	Cameron A-375 balloon	Noble Adventures Ltd
	G-BWNI	PA-24 Comanche 180	T. D. Cooper & D. F. Hurn
	G-BWNJ	Hughes 269C	L. R. Fenwick
	G-BWNK	D,H,C,1 Chipmunk 22 (WD390)	B. Whitworth
	G-BWNL	Shaw Europa	H. Smith
	G-BWNM	PA-28R Cherokee Arrow 180	D. Houghton
	G-BWNN	Rand Robinson KR-2	C. Clark
	G-BWNO	Cameron O-90 balloon	M. A. Pratt & N. I. Cakebread
	G-BWNP	Cameron 90 Club SS balloon	C. J. Davies & P. Spellward
	G-BWNR	PA-38-112 Tomahawk	APB Leasing Ltd/Liverpool
	G-BWNS	Cameron O-90 balloon	Smithair Ltd
	G-BWNT	D.H.C.1 Chipmunk 22 (WP901)	Three Point Aviation
	G-BWNU	PA-38-112 Tomahawk	G-BWNU Group
	G-BWNV	PA-38-112 Tomahawk	CEA Aircraft Leasing
	G-BWNX	Thunder Ax10-180 S2 balloon	MJN Balloon Management Ltd (G-OWBC)
	G-BWNY	Aeromot AMT-200 Super Ximango	H. G. Nicklin
	G-BWNZ	Agusta A.109C	Anglo Beef Processors Ltd
	G-BWOA	Sky 105-24 balloon	Akhter Group Holdings PLC
	G-BWOB	Luscombe 8F Silvaire	P. J. Tanulak & H. T. Law
	G-BWOD	Yakovlev Yak-52 (139)	Insurefast Ltd/Sywell
	G-BWOE	Yakovlev Yak-3U	R. G. Hanna/Duxford
	G-BWOF	P.84 Jet Provost T.5	Techair London Ltd
	G-BWOH	PA-28-161 Cadet	Oxford Aviation Services Ltd/Kidlington
	G-BWOI	PA-28-161 Cadet	Oxford Aviation Services Ltd/Kidlington
	G-BWOJ	PA-28-161 Cadet	Oxford Aviation Services Ltd/Kidlington
	G-BWOK	Lindstrand LBL GB-1000 balloon	Lindstrand Balloons Ltd
	G-BWOL	Hawker Sea Fury FB.11	Old Flying Machine Co Ltd/Duxford
	G-BWOM	Cessna 550 Citation II	Ferron Trading Ltd
	G-BWON	Shaw Europa	G. T. Birks
	G-BWOR	PA-18 Super Cub 135	C. D. Baird
	G-BWOS	Bell 212	RCR Aviation Ltd/Thruxton
	G-BWOT	P.84 Jet Provost T.3A (XN459)	Quasi Mondi Ltd/North Weald
	G-BWOU	Hawker Hunter F.58A (XF303)	Old Flying Machine Co. Ltd/Duxford
	G-BWOV	Enstrom F-28A	Austen Associates
	G-BWOW	Cameron N-105 balloon	S. J. Colin & A. S. Pinder
	G-BWOX	D.H.C.1 Chipmunk 22 (WP844)	J. St. Clair-Quentin
	G-BWOY	Sky 31-24 balloon	Virgin Airship & Balloon Co. Ltd
	G-BWOZ	CFM Streak Shadow SA	N. P. Harding
	G-BWPA	Cameron A-340 balloon	A. A. Brown
	G-BWPB	Cameron V-77 balloon	Fair Weather Friends Ballooning Co
	G-BWPC	Cameron V-77 balloon	H. Vaughan
	G-BWPE	Murphy Renegade Spirit UK	G. Wilson
	G-BWPF	Sky 120-24 balloon	Humbug Balloon Group
	G-BWPH	PA-28-181 Archer II	J. Maffia
	G-BWPI	Sky 120-24 balloon	Sky Balloons Ltd/USA
	G-BWPJ	Steen Skybolt	W. R. Penaluna
	G-BWPL	Airtour AH-56 balloon	A. S. Newham (G-OAFC)
	G-BWPM	BN-2T-4R Defender 4000	Britten-Norman Ltd/Bembridge
	G-BWPP	Sky 105-24 balloon	The Sarnia Balloon Group
	G-BWPR	BN-2T-4S Defender 4000	Britten-Norman Ltd/Bembridge
	G-BWPS	CFM Streak Shadow SA	P. G. A. Sumner
	G-BWPT	Cameron N-90 balloon	Workplace Technologies Ltd
	G-BWPU	BN-2T-4S Defender 4000	Britten-Norman Ltd/Bembridge
	G-BWPV	BN-2T-4S Defender 4000	Britten-Norman Ltd/Bembridge

Reg.	Type	Owner or Operator	Notes
G-BWPW	BN-2T-4S Defender 4000	Britten-Norman Ltd/Bembridge	
G-BWPX	BN-2T-4S Defender 4000	Britten-Norman Ltd/Bembridge	
G-BWPY	Diamond Katana DV.20	Diamond Aircraft Industries GmbH/Austria	
G-BWPZ	Cameron N-105 balloon	Flying Pictures Ltd	
G-BWRA	Sopwith LC-1T Triplane (replica) (N500)	S. M. Truscott & J. M. Hoblyn (G-PENY)	
G-BWRC	Light Aero Avid Speedwing	B. Williams	
G-BWRM	Colt 105A balloon	N. Charbonnier/Italy	
G-BWRO	Shaw Europa	J. G. M. McDiarmid	
G-BWRP	Beech 58 Baron	Astra Aviation Ltd	
G-BWRR	Cessna 182Q	D. O. Halle	
G-BWRS	SNCAN Stampe SV-4C	G. P. J. M. Valvekens/Belgium	
G-BWRT	Cameron Concept 60 balloon	European Balloon Display Co Ltd	
G-BWRV	Lindstrand LBL-90A balloon	Flying Pictures Ltd	
G-BWRW	Sky 220-24 balloon	Sky Trek Ballooning Ltd	
G-BWRY	Cameron N-105 balloon	G. Aimo/Italy	
G-BWRZ	Lindstrand LBL-105A balloon	Flying Pictures Ltd	
G-BWSB	Lindstrand LBL-105A balloon	Flying Pictures Ltd	
G-BWSC	PA-38-112 Tomahawk II	APB Leasing Ltd/Welshpool	
G-BWSD	Campbell Cricket	R. F. G. Moyle	
G-BWSF	Sky 180-24 balloon	A. Bolger	
G-BWSG	P.84 Jet Provost T.5 (XW324)	Den Air Aviation Ltd/Southend	
G-BWSH	P.84 Jet Provost T.3A (XN498)	Global Aviation Ltd/Binbrook	
G-BWSI	K & S SA.102.5 Cavalier	B. W. Shaw	
G-BWSJ	Denney Kitfox Mk 3	J. M. Miller	
G-BWSK	Enstrom 280FX	M. A. & M. Gradwell	
G-BWSL	Sky 77-24 balloon	The Balloon Co Ltd	
G-BWSN	Denney Kitfox Mk 3	W. J. Forrest	
G-BWSO	Cameron 90 Apple SS balloon	Flying Pictures Ltd	
G-BWSP	Cameron 80 Carrots SS balloon	Flying Pictures Ltd	
G-BWST	Sky 200-24 balloon	S. A. Townley	
G-BWSU	Cameron N-105 balloon	A. M. Marten	
G-BWSV	Yakovlev Yak-52	P. Traynor	
G-BWSX	PA-28-236 Dakota	C. & C. Bowie	
G-BWSY	BAe 125 Srs 800B	British Aerospace Airbus Ltd (G-OCCI)/Filton	
G-BWSZ	Montgomerie-Bensen B.8MR	D. Cawkwell	
G-BWTA	Diamond Katana DV.20	Diamond Aircraft Industries GmbH/Austria	
G-BWTB	Lindstrand LBL-105A balloon	Servatruc Ltd	
G-BWTC	Zlin Z.242L	Oxford Aviation Services Ltd/Kidlington	
G-BWTD	Zlin Z.242L	Oxford Aviation Services Ltd/Kidlington	
G-BWTE	Cameron O-140 balloon	R. J. & A. J. Mansfield	
G-BWTF	Lindstrand LBL Bear SS balloon	Free Enterprise Balloons Ltd	
G-BWTG	D.H.C.1 Chipmunk 22	Chipmunk 4 Ever Foundation/Netherlands	
G-BWTH	Robinson R-22B	Heli Air Ltd	
G-BWTJ	Cameron V-77 balloon	A. J. Montgomery	
G-BWTK	RAF 2000 GTX-SE gyroplane	Terrafirma Services Ltd	
G-BWTL	Aérospatiale ATR-72-202	CityFlyer Express Ltd/BA Express	
G-BWTM	Aérospatiale ATR-72-202	CityFlyer Express Ltd/BA Express	
G-BWTN	Lindstrand LBL-90A balloon	Clarks Drainage Ltd	
G-BWTO	D.H.C.1 Chipmunk 22 (WP984)	Skycraft Services Ltd	
G-BWTR	Slingsby T.61F Venture T.2	P. R. Williams	
G-BWTU	Lindstrand LBL-77A balloon	Virgin Airship & Balloon Co Ltd	
G-BWTW	Mooney M.20C	R. C. Volkers	
G-BWUA	Campbell Cricket	R. T. Lancaster	
G-BWUB	PA-18S Super Cub 135	Caledonian Seaplanes Ltd/Cumbernauld	
G-BWUD	Lavochkin LA-9	Classic Aviation Ltd/Duxford	
G-BWUE	Hispano HA.1112M1L	R. A. Fleming(G-AWHK)/Breighton	
G-BWUF	WSK Lim-5 (1211)	Classic Aviation Ltd/Duxford	
G-BWUG	Piper J-5C Cub Cruiser	W. D. Lincoln	
G-BWUH	PA-28-181 Archer III	R. Paston	
G-BWUJ	Rotorway Executive 162F	Southern Helicopters Ltd	
G-BWUK	Sky 160-24 balloon	Blagdon Balloons Ltd	
G-BWUL	Noorduyn AT-16 Harvard IIB	Aereo Servizi Bresciana SRL/Italy	
G-BWUM	Sky 105-24 balloon	P. Stern & F. Kirchberger/Germany	
G-BWUN	D.H.C.1 Chipmunk 22 (WD310)	T. Henderson	
G-BWUP	Shaw Europa	T. J. Harrison	
G-BWUR	Thunder Ax10-210 S2 balloon	T. J. Bucknall	
G-BWUS	Sky 65-24 balloon	N. A. P. Bates	
G-BWUT	D.H.C.1 Chipmunk 22 (WZ879)	Aero Vintage Ltd	
G-BWUU	Cameron N-90 balloon	South Western Electricity PLC	
G-BWUV	D.H.C.1 Chipmunk 22A (WK640)	P. Ray	
G-BWUW	P.84 Jet Provost T.5A (XW423)	Tinton Ltd/Little Snoring	

Notes	Reg.	Type	Owner or Operator
	G-BWUZ	Campbell Cricket	M. A. Concannon
	G-BWVB	Pietenpol Air Camper	M. J. Whatley
	G-BWVC	Jodel D.18	R. W. J. Cripps
	G-BWVE	Bell 206B JetRanger 3	Elialfa SRL (G-BOSX)/Italy
	G-BWVF	Pietenpol Air Camper	R. M. Sharphouse
	G-BWVG	Robin HR.200/120	Air Caernarfon Ltd
	G-BWVH	Robinson R-44 Astro	Twinlite Developments Ltd
	G-BWVI	Stern ST.80	P. E. Barker
	G-BWVL	Cessna 150M	Dualworld Ltd
	G-BWVM	Cameron AA-1050 balloon	D. A. Gleed/Canada
	G-BWVN	Whittaker MW.7	J. W. May
	G-BWVP	Sky 160-24 balloon	Sky Balloons Ltd
	G-BWVR	Yakovlev Yak-52 (52)	Thunderer Ltd/Barton
	G-BWVS	Shaw Europa	D. R. Bishop
	G-BWVT	D.H.A.82A Tiger Moth	R. Jewitt
	G-BWVU	Cameron O-90 balloon	J. Atkinson
	G-BWVV	Jodel D.18	P. Cooper
	G-BWVX	Yakovlev Yak-52	C. J. M. Van Den Broek & R. V. De Vries/Netherlands
	G-BWVY	D.H.C.1 Chipmunk 22A (WP896)	P. W. Portelli
	G-BWVZ	D.H.C.1 Chipmunk 22A (WK590)	D. Campion/Belgium
	G-BWWA	Pelican Club GS	T. J. Franklin & D. S. Simpson
	G-BWWB	Shaw Europa	M. G. Dolphin
	G-BWWC	D.H.104 Dove 7 (XM223)	Cormack (Aircraft Services) Ltd
	G-BWWE	Lindstrand LBL-90A balloon	B. J. Newman
	G-BWWF	Cessna 185A	S. M. Craig Harvey
	G-BWWG	SOCATA Rallye 235E	J. McEleney
	G-BWWH	Yakovlev Yak-50	De Cadenet Motor Racing Ltd
	G-BWWI	AS.332L Super Puma	Bristow Helicopters Ltd
	G-BWWJ	Hughes 269C	Dave Nieman Models Ltd (G-BMYZ)
	G-BWWK	Hawker Nimrod I (S1581)	Historic Aircraft Collection Ltd
	G-BWWL	Colt Flying Egg SS balloon	L. V. Mastis
	G-BWWN	Isaacs Fury II	D. H. Pattison
	G-BWWP	Rans S.6-116 Coyote II	S. A. Beddus
	G-BWWS	RAF 2000 GTX-SE gyroplane	G. R. Williams
	G-BWWT	Dornier Do.328-100	ScotAirways Ltd
	G-BWWU	PA-22 Tri-Pacer 150	Aerocars Ltd
	G-BWWW	BAe Jetstream 3102	British Aerospace PLC/Warton
	G-BWWX	Yakovlev Yak-50	J. L. Pfundt/Netherlands
	G-BWWY	Lindstrand LBL-105A balloon	M. J. Smith
	G-BWWZ	Denney Kitfox Mk 3	K. M. Allan
	G-BWXA	Slingsby T.67M-260	Hunting Aviation Ltd/Barkston Heath
	G-BWXB	Slingsby T.67M-260	Hunting Aviation Ltd/Barkston Heath
	G-BWXC	Slingsby T.67M-260	Hunting Aviation Ltd/Barkston Heath
	G-BWXD	Slingsby T.67M-260	Hunting Aviation Ltd/Barkston Heath
	G-BWXE	Slingsby T.67M-260	Hunting Aviation Ltd/Barkston Heath
	G-BWXF	Slingsby T.67M-260	Hunting Aviation Ltd/Barkston Heath
	G-BWXG	Slingsby T.67M-260	Hunting Aviation Ltd/Barkston Heath
	G-BWXH	Slingsby T.67M-260	Hunting Aviation Ltd/Barkston Heath
	G-BWXI	Slingsby T.67M-260	Hunting Aviation Ltd/Barkston Heath
	G-BWXJ	Slingsby T.67M-260	Hunting Aviation Ltd/Barkston Heath
	G-BWXK	Slingsby T.67M-260	Hunting Aviation Ltd/Barkston Heath
	G-BWXL	Slingsby T.67M-200	Hunting Aviation Ltd/Barkston Heath
	G-BWXM	Slingsby T.67M-260	Hunting Aviation Ltd/Barkston Heath
	G-BWXN	Slingsby T.67M-260	Hunting Aviation Ltd/Barkston Heath
	G-BWXO	Slingsby T.67M-260	Hunting Aviation Ltd/Barkston Heath
	G-BWXP	Slingsby T.67M-260	Hunting Aviation Ltd/Barkston Heath
	G-BWXR	Slingsby T.67M-260	Hunting Aviation Ltd/Barkston Heath
	G-BWXS	Slingsby T.67M-260	Hunting Aviation Ltd/Barkston Heath
	G-BWXT	Slingsby T.67M-260	Hunting Aviation Ltd/Barkston Heath
	G-BWXU	Slingsby T.67M-260	Hunting Aviation Ltd/Barkston Heath
	G-BWXV	Slingsby T.67M-260	Hunting Aviation Ltd/Barkston Heath
	G-BWXW	Slingsby T.67M-260	Hunting Aviation Ltd/Barkston Heath
	G-BWXX	Slingsby T.67M-260	Hunting Aviation Ltd/Barkston Heath
	G-BWXY	Slingsby T.67M-260	Hunting Aviation Ltd/Barkston Heath
	G-BWXZ	Slingsby T.67M-260	Hunting Aviation Ltd/Barkston Heath
	G-BWYB	PA-28 Cherokee 160	I. M. Latiff
	G-BWYC	Cameron N-90 balloon	Cameron Balloons Ltd
	G-BWYD	Shaw Europa	H. J. Bendiksen
	G-BWYE	Cessna 310R II	Edinburgh Air Centre Ltd
	G-BWYG	Cessna 310R II	Kissair Aviation
	G-BWYH	Cessna 310R II	Edinburgh Air Centre Ltd
	G-BWYI	Denney Kitfox Mk3	J. Adamson

Reg.	Type	Owner or Operator	Notes
G-BWYK	Yakovlev Yak-50	Titan Airways Ltd/Stansted	
G-BWYL	Cameron A-200 balloon	Aire Valley Balloons	
G-BWYM	Diamond Katana DV.20	Diamond Aircraft Industries GmbH	
G-BWYN	Cameron O-77 balloon	W. H. Morgan (G-ODER)	
G-BWYO	Sequoia F.8L Falco	N. G. Abbott & J. Copeland	
G-BWYP	Sky 56-24 balloon	Sky High Leisure	
G-BWYR	Rans S.6-116 Coyote II	Stephen Palmer Ltd	
G-BWYS	Cameron O-120 balloon	Aire Valley Balloons	
G-BWYU	Sky 120-24 balloon	Bramley Park Garages	
G-BWYW	BN-2B-20 Islander	Britten-Norman Ltd/Bembridge	
G-BWYX	BN-2B-20 Islander	Britten-Norman Ltd/Bembridge	
G-BWYY	BN-2B-20 Islander	Britten-Norman Ltd/Bembridge	
G-BWYZ	BN-2B-20 Islander	Britten-Norman Ltd/Bembridge	
G-BWZA	Shaw Europa	M. C. Costin	
G-BWZD	Light Aero Avid Flyer Mk 4	B. Moore	
G-BWZE	P.84 Jet Provost T.3A (XM378)	Lorch Airways (UK) Ltd	
G-BWZF	BN-2B-20 Islander	Britten-Norman Ltd/Bembridge	
G-BWZG	Robin R.2160	Sherburn Aero Club Ltd	
G-BWZI	Agusta A. 109A II	Pendley Farm	
G-BWZJ	Cameron A-250 balloon	Balloon Club of Great Britain	
G-BWZK	Cameron A-210 balloon	Balloon Club of Great Britain	
G-BWZP	Cameron 105 Home Special SS balloon	Flying Pictures Ltd	
G-BWZT	Shaw Europa	G-BWZT Group	
G-BWZU	Lindstrand LBL-90B balloon	K. D. Pierce	
G-BWZW	Bell 206B JetRanger 2	R. & M. International Engineering Ltd (G-CTEK)	
G-BWZX	AS.332L Super Puma	Bristow Helicopters Ltd	
G-BWZY	Hughes 269A	K. B. Elliott (G-FSDT)	
G-BWZZ	P.84 Jet Provost T.3A (XM470)	R. G. Schreiber & J. P. Trevor	
G-BXAB	PA-28-161 Warrior II	TG Aviation Ltd (G-BTGK)	
G-BXAC	RAF 2000 GTX-SE gyroplane	D. C. Fairbrass	
G-BXAD	Thunder Ax11-225 S2 balloon	C. E. Wood	
G-BXAF	Pitts S-1D Special	F. Sharples	
G-BXAH	CP.301A Emeraude	G. E. Valler	
G-BXAI	Colt 120A balloon	E. F. & R. F. Casswell	
G-BXAJ	Lindstrand LBL-14A balloon	Oscair Project AB/Sweden	
G-BXAK	Yakovlev Yak-52	S. L. Flannigan	
G-BXAL	Cameron 90 Bertie Bassett SS balloon	Trebor Bassett Ltd	
G-BXAM	Cameron N-90 balloon	Trebor Bassett Ltd	
G-BXAN	Scheibe SF-25C	Falke Syndicate/Winthorpe	
G-BXAO	Jabiru SK	P. J. Thompson	
G-BXAR	Avro RJ100	CityFlyer Express Ltd/BA Express	
G-BXAS	Avro RJ100	CityFlyer Express Ltd/BA Express	
G-BXAU	Pitts S-1 Special	P. Heckles	
G-BXAV	Yakovlev Yak-52 (72)	G. M. Sharp/North Weald	
G-BXAW	Airbus A.321-211	jmc Airlines Ltd	
G-BXAX	Cameron N-77 balloon	Flying Pictures Ltd	
G-BXAY	Bell 206B JetRanger 3	Mainland Car Delivery Services Ltd	
G-BXBA	Cameron A-210 balloon	Reach For The Sky Ltd	
G-BXBB	PA-20 Pacer 150	M. E. R. Coghlan	
G-BXBC	EA.1 Kingfisher amphibian	S. Bichan	
G-BXBD	C.A.S.A. 1.131E Jungmann	B. Childs & B. L. Robinson	
G-BXBG	Cameron A-275 balloon	M. L. Gabb	
G-BXBH	P.84 Jet Provost T.3A (XM365)	G-BXBH Provost Ltd	
G-BXBI	P.84 Jet Provost T.3A	Global Aviation Ltd/Binbrook	
G-BXBK	Avions Mudry CAP-10B	S. Skipworth	
G-BXBL	Lindstrand LBL-240A balloon	Firefly Balloon Promotions	
G-BXBM	Cameron O-105 balloon	Bristol University Hot Air Ballooning Soc	
G-BXBN	Rans S.6-116 Coyote II	W. S. Long	
G-BXBP	Denney Kitfox	G. S. Adams	
G-BXBR	Cameron A-120 balloon	M. G. Barlow	
G-BXBS	Cameron V-90 balloon	D. C. Boxall	
G-BXBT	AS.355F-1 Twin Squirrel	McAlpine Helicopters Ltd (G-TMMC/G-JLCO)/Kidlington	
G-BXBU	Avions Mudry CAP.10B	J. F. Cosgrave & H. R. Pearson	
G-BXBV	Aérospatiale ATR-42-300	Gill Airways Ltd/Newcastle	
G-BXBW	HOAC Katana DV.20	Diamond Aircraft Industries GmbH	
G-BXBY	Cameron A-105 balloon	S. P. Watkins	
G-BXBZ	PZL-104 Wilga 80	RCR Aviation Ltd	
G-BXCA	Hapi Cygnet SF-2A	G. E. Collard	

Notes	Reg.	Type	Owner or Operator
	G-BXCB	Agusta A.109A-II	Vulture Ventures Ltd (G-ISEB/G-IADT/G-HBCA)
	G-BXCC	PA-28-201T Turbo Dakota	Greer Aviation Ltd
	G-BXCD	Team Minimax 91A	R. Davies
	G-BXCG	Jodel DR.250/160	G-BXCG Group
	G-BXCH	Shaw Europa	D. M. Stevens
	G-BXCJ	Campbell Cricket (replica)	J. R. Cooper
	G-BXCK	Cameron 110 Douglas SS balloon	Flying Pictures Ltd
	G-BXCL	Montgomerie-Bensen B.8MR	A. V. Francis
	G-BXCM	Lindstrand LBL-150A balloon	Blown Away (UK) Ltd
	G-BXCN	Sky 105-24 balloon	Capricorn Balloons Ltd
	G-BXCO	Colt 120A balloon	G. C. Ludlow
	G-BXCP	D.H.C.1 Chipmunk 22 (WP859)	S. Conlan
	G-BXCS	Cameron N-90 balloon	Flying Pictures (Balloons) Ltd
	G-BXCT	D.H.C.1 Chipmunk 22 (WB697)	Wickenby Aviation Ltd
	G-BXCU	Rans S.6-116 Coyote II	M. R. McNeil
	G-BXCV	D.H.C.1 Chipmunk 22 (WP929)	Propshop Ltd
	G-BXCW	Denney Kitfox Mk 3	M. J. Blanchard
	G-BXCX	Robinson R-22B	Plane Talking Ltd (G-MFHL)/Elstree
	G-BXCY	AA-5A Cheetah	Plane Talking Ltd/Elstree
	G-BXCZ	AA-5A Cheetah	Plane Talking Ltd/Elstree
	G-BXDA	D.H.C.1 Chipmunk 22 (WP860)	S. R. Cleary
	G-BXDB	Cessna U.206F	Tindon Ltd (G-BMNZ)/Little Snoring
	G-BXDC	Montgomerie-Bensen B.8MR	D. L. Smerdon
	G-BXDD	RAF 2000 GTX-SE gyroplane	Roger Savage (Photography)/Carlisle
	G-BXDE	RAF 2000 GTX-SE gyroplane	A. McRedie
	G-BXDF	Beech 95-B55 Baron	Chesh-Air Ltd
	G-BXDG	D.H.C.1 Chipmunk 22 (WK630)	R. E. Dagless
	G-BXDH	D.H.C.1 Chipmunk 22 (WD331)	Victory Workware Ltd
	G-BXDI	D.H.C.1 Chipmunk 22 (WD373)	J. R. Gore/Perth
	G-BXDL	P.84 Jet Provost T.3A (XM478)	Jet Provost Promotions Ltd
	G-BXDM	D.H.C.1 Chipmunk 22 (WP840)	Halton Aeroplane Club Ltd
	G-BXDN	D.H.C.1 Chipmunk 22 (WK609)	W. D. Lowe & L. A. Edwards
	G-BXDO	Rutan Cozy	C. R. Blackburn
	G-BXDP	D.H.C.1 Chupmunk 22 (WK642)	J. S. J. Valentine & J. P. Conlan
	G-BXDR	Lindstrand LBL-77A balloon	British Telecommunications PLC
	G-BXDT	Robin HR.200/120B	Multiflight Ltd/Leeds-Bradford
	G-BXDU	Aero Designs Pulsar	M. P. Board
	G-BXDV	Sky 105-24 balloon	J. Skinner
	G-BXDW	Sky 105-24 balloon	M. & S. M. Sarti
	G-BXDX	Lindstrand LBL-77M balloon	Lindstrand Balloons Ltd
	G-BXDY	Shaw Europa	D. G. & S. Watts
	G-BXDZ	Lindstrand LBL-105A balloon	M. A. Webb
	G-BXEA	RAF 2000 GTX-SE gyroplane	R. Firth
	G-BXEB	RAF 2000 GTX-SE gyroplane	Penny Hydraulics Ltd
	G-BXEC	D.H.C.1 Chipmunk 22 (WK633)	M.A.D. Flying Group
	G-BXEE	Enstrom 280C	S. T. Rabt
	G-BXEF	Shaw Europa	C. & W. P. Busuttil-Reynaud
	G-BXEG	Aérospatiale ATR-42-300	CityFlyer Express Ltd/BA Express
	G-BXEJ	VPM M.16 Tandem Trainer	AES Radionic Surveillance Systems
	G-BXEM	Campbell Cricket Mk 4	D. M. Bracken
	G-BXEN	Cameron N-105 balloon	G. Aimo/Italy
	G-BXEP	Lindstrand LBL-14M balloon	Lindstrand Balloons Ltd
	G-BXER	PA-46-350P Malibu Mirage	Sunseeker Sales (UK) Ltd
	G-BXES	P.66 Pembroke C.1 (XL954)	Atlantic Air Transport Ltd/Coventry
	G-BXET	PA-38-112 Tomahawk II	APB Leasing Ltd/Welshpool
	G-BXEX	PA-28-181 Archer II	Tunjet Ltd
	G-BXEY	Colt AS-105GD airship	D. Mayer/Germany
	G-BXEZ	Cessna 182P	Ray Thompson Engineering Ltd
	G-BXFB	Pitts S-1 Special	D. Dobson
	G-BXFC	Jodel D.18	B. S. Godbold
	G-BXFD	Enstrom 280C	A. Smithson
	G-BXFE	Avions Mudry CAP.10B	R. W. H. Cole
	G-BXFG	Shaw Europa	A. Rawicz-Szczerbo
	G-BXFI	Hawker Hunter T.7 (WV372)	Fox-One Ltd/Bournemouth
	G-BXFK	CFM Streak Shadow	D. Adcock
	G-BXFN	Colt 77A balloon	Cameron Balloons Ltd
	G-BXFP	BAC.145 Strikemaster 87 (NZ6361)	C. J. & S. M. Thompson/North Weald
	G-BXFS	BAC.145 Strikemaster 87	Gone Flying Ltd/North Weald
	G-BXFU	BAC.167 Strikemaster 83	Global Aviation Ltd/Binbrook
	G-BXFV	BAC.167 Strikemaster 83	Global Aviation Ltd/Binbrook

Reg.	Type	Owner or Operator	Notes
G-BXFX	BAC.167 Strikemaster 83	Global Aviation Ltd/Binbrook	
G-BXFY	Cameron 90 Bierkrug SS balloon	Cameron Balloons Ltd	
G-BXFZ	Sky 65-24 balloon	Aerial Promotions Ltd	
G-BXGA	AS.350B-2 Ecureuil	PLM Dollar Group Ltd/Inverness	
G-BXGC	Cameron N-105 balloon	Cliveden Ltd	
G-BXGD	Sky 90-24 balloon	Servo & Electronic Sales Ltd	
G-BXGE	Cessna 152	APB Leasing Ltd/Welshpool	
G-BXGG	Shaw Europa	B. W. Faulkner	
G-BXGH	HOAC Katana DA.20A-1	Diamond Aircraft Industries GmbH	
G-BXGI	Hoffmann HK-36TTC Super Dimona	Enstone Flying Club	
G-BXGK	Lindstrand LBL-203M balloon	Lindstrand Balloons Ltd	
G-BXGL	D.H.C.1 Chipmunk 22	Airways Aero Associations Ltd/Booker	
G-BXGM	D.H.C.1 Chipmunk 22 (WP928)	M. A. Petrie	
G-BXGO	D.H.C.1 Chipmunk 22 (WB654)	Trees Group/Booker	
G-BXGP	D.H.C.1 Chipmunk 22 (WZ882)	Eaglescott Chipmunk Group	
G-BXGS	RAF 2000 gyroplane	C. R. Gordon	
G-BXGT	Sky Arrow 650T	Sky Arrow (Kits) UK Ltd/Old Sarum	
G-BXGV	Cessna 172R	Grandfort Properties Ltd/Elstree	
G-BXGW	Robin HR.200/120B	Multiflight Ltd/Leeds-Bradford	
G-BXGX	D.H.C.1 Chipmunk 22 (WK586)	Interflight (Air Charter) Ltd	
G-BXGY	Cameron V-65 balloon	Gone With The Wind Ltd	
G-BXGZ	Stemme S.10V	D. B. Smith	
G-BXHA	D.H.C.1 Chipmunk 22 (WP925)	A. J. Keeling	
G-BXHD	Beech 76 Duchess	Liddell Aircraft Ltd	
G-BXHE	Lindstrand LBL-105A balloon	Independent Insurance Co Ltd	
G-BXHF	D.H.C.1 Chipmunk 22 (WP930)	R. Beresford	
G-BXHH	AA-5A Cheetah	Oaklands Flying/Biggin Hill	
G-BXHI	Hughes 269C	Redhill Helicopter Centre (G-GBHH)	
G-BXHJ	Hapi Cygnet SF-2A	I. J. Smith	
G-BXHL	Sky 77-24 balloon	R. A. Messenger	
G-BXHM	Lindstrand LBL-25A balloon	Virgin Balloon & Airship Co Ltd	
G-BXHN	Lindstrand Pop Can SS balloon	Virgin Balloon & Airship Co Ltd	
G-BXHO	Lindstrand Telewest Sphere SS balloon	Flying Pictures Ltd	
G-BXHP	Lindstrand LBL-105A balloon	Flying Pictures Ltd	
G-BXHR	Stemme S.10V	J. H. Rutherford	
G-BXHT	Bushby-Long Midget Mustang	P. P. Chapman	
G-BXHU	Campbell Cricket Mk 6	P. C. Lovegrove	
G-BXHY	Shaw Europa	Jupiter Flying Group	
G-BXHZ	V.S.361 Spitfire HF.IX	A. G. Dunkerley	
G-BXIA	D.H.C.1 Chipmunk 22 (WB615)	Dales Aviation	
G-BXIB	Bell 206L-3 LongRanger	Kelwaiver Ltd	
G-BXIC	Cameron A-275 balloon	A. J. Street	
G-BXID	Yakovlev Yak-52 (74)	L. F. Clayton	
G-BXIE	Colt 77B balloon	The Aerial Display Co Ltd	
G-BXIF	PA-28-161 Warrior II	Piper Flight Ltd	
G-BXIG	Zenair CH.701 STOL	A. J. Perry	
G-BXIH	Sky 200-24 balloon	G. C. Ludlow	
G-BXII	Shaw Europa	D. A. McFadyean	
G-BXIJ	Shaw Europa	D. G. & E. A. Bligh	
G-BXIM	D.H.C.1 Chipmunk 22 (WK512)	A. B. Ashcroft & P. R. Joshua	
G-BXIO	Jodel DR.1050M	D. N. K. & M. A. Symon	
G-BXIT	ZebedeeV-31 balloon	Zebedee Balloon Service	
G-BXIV	Agusta A.109A	Castle Air Charters Ltd	
G-BXIW	Sky 105-24 balloon	L. A. Watts	
G-BXIX	VPM M.16 Tandem Trainer	D. Beevers	
G-BXIY	Blake Bluetit (BAPC37)	The Shuttleworth Collection/O. Warden	
G-BXIZ	Lindstrand LBL-31A balloon	Hyundai Car (UK) Ltd	
G-BXJA	Cessna 402B	Air Ward Ltd	
G-BXJB	Yakovlev Yak-52	Aero Anglia	
G-BXJC	Cameron A-210 balloon	British School of Ballooning	
G-BXJD	PA-28 Cherokee 180C	BCT Aircraft Leasing Ltd	
G-BXJG	Lindstrand LBL-105B balloon	C. E. Wood	
G-BXJH	Cameron N-42 balloon	Flying Pictures Ltd	
G-BXJI	Tri-R Kis	R. M. Wakeford	
G-BXJJ	PA-28-161 Cadet	Walsh Aviation (G-GFCC)	
G-BXJK	SA.341G Gazelle 1	R. A. Kingston	
G-BXJL	Cameron 90 Real Fruit SS balloon	Cameron Balloons Ltd	
G-BXJM	Cessna 152	E. Alexander	
G-BXJO	Cameron O-90 balloon	W. I. & C. Hooker	
G-BXJP	Cameron C-80 balloon	AR. Cobaleno Pasta Fresca SRL/Italy	

Notes	Reg.	Type	Owner or Operator
	G-BXJS	Schempp-Hirth Janus CM	Janus Syndicate
	G-BXJT	Sky 90-24 balloon	Sky Operations Ltd
	G-BXJU	Sky 90-24 balloon	Sky Operations Ltd
	G-BXJV	Diamond Katana DA.20-A1	Tayside Aviation Ltd/Dundee
	G-BXJW	Diamond Katana DA.20-A1	Tayside Aviation Ltd/Dundee
	G-BXJY	Van's RV-6	D. J. Sharland
	G-BXJZ	Cameron C-60 balloon	R. S. Mohr
	G-BXKA	Airbus A.320-214	jmc Airlines Ltd
	G-BXKB	Airbus A.320-214	jmc Airlines Ltd
	G-BXKC	Airbus A.320-214	jmc Airlines Ltd
	G-BXKD	Airbus A.320-214	jmc Airlines Ltd
	G-BXKF	Hawker Hunter T.7(XL577)	R. F. Harvey
	G-BXKH	Colt 90 Sparkasse Box SS balloon	Westfalisch-Lippischer Sparkasse UND/ Germany
	G-BXKI	Robinson R-44 Astro	A. D. Russell
	G-BXKJ	Cameron A-275 balloon	The Balloon Club Ltd
	G-BXKK	Colt 105 Golf Ball SS balloon	Longbreak Ltd
	G-BXKL	Bell 206B JetRanger 3	Swattons Aviation Ltd
	G-BXKM	RAF 2000 GTX-SE gyroplane	J. R. Huggins
	G-BXKO	Sky 65-24 balloon	P. J. Beglan/France
	G-BXKU	Colt AS-120 Mk II airship	D. C. Chipping
	G-BXKW	Slingsby T.67M-200	W. R. Tandy
	G-BXKX	Auster V	A. L. Jubb
	G-BXKY	Cameron DP-90 airship	Cameron Balloons Ltd
	G-BXLA	Robinson R-22B	Fast Helicopters Ltd
	G-BXLC	Sky 120-24 balloon	Sky Balloons Ltd
	G-BXLF	Lindstrand LBL-90A balloon	Variohm Components
	G-BXLG	Cameron C-80 balloon	D. & L. S. Litchfield
	G-BXLI	Bell 206B JetRanger 3	Williams Grand Prix Engineering Ltd (G-JODY)
	G-BXLK	Shaw Europa	R. G. Fairall
	G-BXLN	Fournier RF-4D	E. H. Booker
	G-BXLO	P.84 Jet Provost T.4 (XR673)	HCR Aviation Ltd
	G-BXLP	Sky 90-24 balloon	Sky Balloons Ltd
	G-BXLR	PZL-110 Koliber 160A	PZL International Aviation Marketing & Sales PLC
	G-BXLS	PZL-110 Koliber 160A	P. A. Rickells
	G-BXLT	SOCATA TB.200 Tobago XL	R. M. Shears
	G-BXLV	Enstrom F-28F	Solent Projects Ltd
	G-BXLW	Enstrom F-28F	M. & P. Food Products Ltd
	G-BXLX	Enstrom F-28F	Dixon Development Corporation Ltd
	G-BXLY	PA-28-151 Warrior	Air Nova PLC (G-WATZ)/Liverpool
	G-BXLZ	Shaw Europa	A. R. Round
	G-BXMA	Beech 200 Super King Air	Manhattan Air Ltd
	G-BXMF	Cassutt Racer IIIM	J. F. Bakewell
	G-BXMG	RAF 2000 GTX gyroplane	B. D. Jones
	G-BXMH	Beech 76 Duchess	R. Clarke
	G-BXML	Mooney M.20A	G. Kay
	G-BXMM	Cameron A-180 balloon	Flying Pictures Ltd
	G-BXMU	PZL-104 Wilga 80	RCR Aviation Ltd/Thruxton
	G-BXMV	Scheibe SF.25C Falke 1700	Falcon Flying Group
	G-BXMW	Cameron A-275 balloon	Balloon Flights International Ltd
	G-BXMX	Currie Wot	N. J. Hayman
	G-BXMY	Hughes 269C	P. J. Brown
	G-BXMZ	Diamond Katana DA.20-A1	Tayside Aviation Ltd/Dundee
	G-BXNA	Light Aero Avid Flyer	I. Brooks
	G-BXNC	Shaw Europa	J. K. Cantwell
	G-BXND	Cameron 110 Thomas SS balloon	Flying Pictures Ltd
	G-BXNG	Beech 58 Baron	Bonanza Flying Club Ltd
	G-BXNH	PA-28-161 Warrior II	CC Management Associates Ltd/Redhill
	G-BXNL	Cameron A-120 balloon	R. G. Griffin
	G-BXNM	Cameron A-210 balloon	Horizon Ballooning
	G-BXNN	D.H.C.1 Chipmunk 22 (WP983)	J. N. Robinson
	G-BXNO	Yakovlev Yak-50	N. J. Radford
	G-BXNS	Bell 206B JetRanger 3	Sterling Helicopters Ltd/Norwich
	G-BXNT	Bell 206B JetRanger 3	Sterling Helicopters Ltd/Norwich
	G-BXNU	Jabiru SK	J. Smith
	G-BXNV	Colt AS-105GD airship	The Sleeping Soc./Belgium
	G-BXNX	Lindstrand LBL-210A balloon	J. H. Cuthbert
	G-BXNZ	Hawker Hunter F.58 (J-4066)	Classic Aviation Ltd/Duxford
	G-BXOA	Robinson R-22B	MG Group Ltd
	G-BXOB	Shaw Europa	S. J. Willett
	G-BXOC	Evans VP-2	H. J. & E. M. Cox

Reg.	Type	Owner or Operator	Notes
G-BXOF	Diamond Katana DA.20-A1	Tayside Aviation Ltd/Dundee	
G-BXOI	Cessna 172R	Anglo American Airmotive Ltd/ Bournemouth	
G-BXOJ	PA-28-161 Warrior III	Bournemouth Flying Club Ltd	
G-BXOM	Isaacs Spitfire	J. H. Betton	
G-BXON	Auster AOP.9	C. J. & D. J. Baker	
G-BXOO	AA-5A Cheetah	Blackbushe School of Flying Ltd	
G-BXOR	Robin HR.200/120B	Multiflight Ltd	
G-BXOS	Cameron A-200 balloon	Airbourne Balloon Management	
G-BXOT	Cameron C-70 balloon	Gone With The Wind Ltd	
G-BXOU	CEA DR.360	S. H. & J. A. Williams	
G-BXOV	Colt 105A balloon	The Aerial Display Co Ltd	
G-BXOW	Colt 105A balloon	The Aerial Display Co Ltd	
G-BXOX	AA-5A Cheetah	Plane Talking Ltd/Elstree	
G-BXOY	QAC Quickie Q.200	C. C. Clapham	
G-BXOZ	PA-28-181 Archer II	Spritetone Ltd	
G-BXPB	Diamond Katana DA.20-A1	Tayside Aviation Ltd/Dundee	
G-BXPC	Diamond Katana DA.20-A1	Cubair Flight Training Ltd/Redhill	
G-BXPD	Diamond Katana DA.20-A1	Tayside Aviation Ltd/Dundee	
G-BXPE	Diamond Katana DA.20-A1	Tayside Aviation Ltd/Dundee	
G-BXPF	Thorp T.211	AD Aerospace Ltd	
G-BXPH	Sky 220-24 balloon	J. Nolte/Germany	
G-BXPI	Van's RV-4	Cavendish Aviation Ltd	
G-BXPK	Cameron A-250 balloon	Broadland Balloons Ltd	
G-BXPL	PA-28 Cherokee 140	M. Jones	
G-BXPM	Beech 58 Baron	Foyle Flyers Ltd	
G-BXPO	Thorp T.211	DM Aerospace Ltd	
G-BXPP	Sky 90-24 balloon	Adam Associates Ltd	
G-BXPR	Colt 110 Can SS balloon	FRB Fleischwarenfabrik Rostock-Bramow/ Germany	
G-BXPS	PA-23 Aztec 250C	W. A. Moore (G-AYLY)	
G-BXPT	Ultramagic H-77 balloon	G. D. Bartram	
G-BXPV	PA-34-220T Seneca IV	Oxford Aviation Services Ltd/Kidlington	
G-BXPW	PA-34-220T Seneca IV	Oxford Aviation Services Ltd/Kidlington	
G-BXPY	Robinson R-44 Astro	O. Desmet & B. Mornie/Belgium	
G-BXPZ	D.H.C-8-311 Dash Eight	Brymon Airways Ltd/British Airways	
G-BXRA	Avions Mudry CAP.10B	P. A. Soper	
G-BXRB	Avions Mudry CAP.10B	T. T. Duhig	
G-BXRC	Avions Mudry CAP.10B	Group Alpha/Sibson	
G-BXRD	Enstrom 280FX	G. Firbank	
G-BXRE	F.28 Fellowship 4000	Aero Engine Support Ltd	
G-BXRF	CP.1310-C3 Super Emeraude	D. T. Gethin	
G-BXRG	PA-28-181 Archer II	Alderney Flying Training Ltd	
G-BXRH	Cessna 185A	R. E. M. Holmes	
G-BXRI	Cessna T.303	I. F. Vaughan	
G-BXRK	Robinson R-22B	Moy Motorsport Ltd	
G-BXRL	Westland Scout AH.1	Raffia Enterprises Ltd	
G-BXRM	Cameron A-210 balloon	W. & C. Hooker	
G-BXRN	Cessna F.152	Aerohire Ltd (G-RICH)/Halfpenny Green	
G-BXRO	Cessna U.206G	M. Penny	
G-BXRP	Schweizer 269C	AH Helicopters Services Ltd	
G-BXRR	Westland Scout AH.1	R. P. Coplestone	
G-BXRS	Westland Scout AH.1	R. P. Coplestone	
G-BXRT	Robin DR.400-180	Mistral Aviation Ltd	
G-BXRV	Van's RV-4	B. J. Oke00	
G-BXRY	Bell 206B JetRanger	R & M International Ltd	
G-BXRZ	Rans S.6-116 Coyote II	C. M. White	
G-BXSA	Cameron PM-80 balloon	Flying Pictures Ltd	
G-BXSB	Cameron PM-80 balloon	Flying Pictures Ltd	
G-BXSC	Cameron C-80 balloon	S. J. Coates	
G-BXSD	Cessna 172R	Sierra Delta Group	
G-BXSE	Cessna 172R	MK Aero Support Ltd/Andrewsfield	
G-BXSG	Robinson R-22B	R. M. Goodenough	
G-BXSH	Glaser-Dirks DG.800B	D. S. McKay	
G-BXSI	Jabiru SK	V. R. Leggott	
G-BXSJ	Cameron C-80 balloon	British School of Ballooning	
G-BXSK	Beech 76 Duchess	Aradian Aviation Ltd	
G-BXSL	Westland Scout AH.1	Airpro Engineering	
G-BXSM	Cessna 172R	East Midlands Flying School Ltd	
G-BXSN	Sikorsky S-61N	Bristow Helicopters Ltd	
G-BXSO	Lindstrand LBL-105A balloon	Lindstrand Balloons Ltd	
G-BXSP	Grob G.109B	I. M. Donnelly	
G-BXSR	Cessna F172N	J. A. Havers	

Notes	Reg.	Type	Owner or Operator
	G-BXST	PA-25 Pawnee 235C	P. Channon
	G-BXSU	Team Minimax 91A	A. R. Carr (G-MYGL)
	G-BXSW	Cameron 120 Mountie SS balloon	Cameron Balloons Ltd
	G-BXSX	Cameron V-77 balloon	D. R. Metcalf
	G-BXSY	Robinson R-22B	N. M. G. Pearson
	G-BXTB	Cessna 152	Haimoss Ltd
	G-BXTC	Taylor JT.1 Monoplane	R. Holden-Rushworth
	G-BXTD	Shaw Europa	P. R. Anderson
	G-BXTE	Cameron A-275 balloon	Adventure Balloon Co Ltd
	G-BXTF	Cameron N-105 balloon	Flying Pictures Ltd
	G-BXTG	Cameron N-42 balloon	Flying Pictures Ltd
	G-BXTH	Westland Gazelle HT.1 (XW866)	Flightline Ltd/Southend
	G-BXTI	Pitts S-1S Special	A. B. Treherne-Pollock
	G-BXTJ	Cameron N-77 balloon	Chubb Fire Ltd
	G-BXTK	Dornier Do.28D-2	R. Ebke/Germany
	G-BXTL	Schweizer 269C-1	Oxford Aviation Services Ltd/Kidlington
	G-BXTN	Aérospatiale ATR-72-202	CityFlyer Express Ltd/BA Express
	G-BXTO	Hindustan HAL-6 Pushpak	A. A. Marshall
	G-BXTP	Diamond Katana DA.20-A1	Solent Flight Aircraft Ltd
	G-BXTR	Diamond Katana DA.20-A1	Solent Flight Aircraft Ltd
	G-BXTS	Diamond Katana DA.20-A1	Solent Flight Aircraft Ltd
	G-BXTT	AA-5B Tiger	G-BXTT Group/Gamston
	G-BXTU	Robinson R-22B	TDR Aviation Ltd
	G-BXTV	Bug	B. R. Cope
	G-BXTW	PA-28-181 Archer III	Davison Plant Hire
	G-BXTY	PA-28-161 Cadet	Plane Talking Ltd/Elstree
	G-BXTZ	PA-28-161 Cadet	Plane Talking Ltd/Elstree
	G-BXUA	Campbell Cricket Mk.5	P. C. Lovegrove
	G-BXUB	Lindstrand Syrup Bottle SS balloon	Free Enterprise Balloons Ltd
	G-BXUC	Robinson R-22B	C. W. B. Wrightson
	G-BXUE	Sky 240-24 balloon	Scotair Balloons
	G-BXUF	AB-206B JetRanger 3	SJ Contracting Services Ltd
	G-BXUG	Lindstrand Baby Bel SS balloon	Virgin Airship & Balloon Co Ltd
	G-BXUH	Lindstrand LBL-31A balloon	Virgin Airship & Balloon Co Ltd
	G-BXUI	Glaser-Dirks DG.800B	J. Le Coyte
	G-BXUK	Robinson R-44 Astro	Speed Services PLC
	G-BXUL	Goodyear FG-1D Corsair (NZ5648)	Old Flying Machine (Air Museum) Co Ltd/Duxford
	G-BXUM	Shaw Europa	D. Bosomworth
	G-BXUO	Lindstrand LBL-105A balloon	Lindstrand Balloons Ltd
	G-BXUP	Schweizer 269C	Aviation Bureau
	G-BXUS	Sky 65-24 balloon	Sky Balloons Ltd
	G-BXUT	PA-34-200 Seneca	H. Merkado
	G-BXUU	Cameron V-65 balloon	D. I. Gray-Fisk
	G-BXUW	Colt 90A balloon	Zycomm Electronics Ltd
	G-BXUX	Fountain Cherry BX-2	M. F. Fountain
	G-BXUY	Cessna 310Q	D. A. D. Rowntree
	G-BXUZ	Cessna 152 II	Stapleford Flying Club Ltd
	G-BXVA	SOCATA TB.200 Tobago XL	AMC Ltd
	G-BXVB	Cessna 152 II	PJC (Leasing) Ltd
	G-BXVC	PA-28RT-201T Turbo Arrow IV	J. S. Develin & I. Zahurul
	G-BXVD	CFM Streak Shadow SA	Rotech Fabrication Ltd
	G-BXVE	Lindstrand LBL-330A balloon	Adventure Balloon Co Ltd
	G-BXVF	Thunder Ax11-250 S2 balloon	Anglian Countryside Balloons
	G-BXVG	Sky 77-24 balloon	M. Wolf
	G-BXVH	Sky 25-16 balloon	Flying Pictures Ltd
	G-BXVJ	Cameron O-120 balloon	Gone With The Wind Ltd (G-IMAX)
	G-BXVK	Robin HR.200/120B	Northamptonshire School of Flying Ltd/ Sywell
	G-BXVL	Sky 180-24 balloon	Purple Balloons
	G-BXVM	Van's RV-6A	J. G. Small
	G-BXVN	Sky 105-24 balloon	Skydance
	G-BXVO	Van's RV-6A	P. J. Hynes & M. E. Holden
	G-BXVP	Sky 31-24 balloon	Sky Balloons Ltd
	G-BXVR	Sky 90-24 balloon	P. Hegarty
	G-BXVS	Brügger MB.2 Colibri	G. T. Snoddon
	G-BXVT	Cameron O-77 balloon	R. P. Wade
	G-BXVU	PA-28-161 Warrior II	Atlantic Bridge Aviation Ltd/Lydd
	G-BXVV	Cameron V-90 balloon	Floating Sensations Ltd
	G-BXVW	Colt Piggy Bank SS balloon	G. Binder
	G-BXVX	Rutan Cozy	G. E. Murray
	G-BXVY	Cessna 152	Stapleford Flying Club Ltd

Reg.	Type	Owner or Operator	Notes
G-BXVZ	WSK-PZL Mielec TS-11 Iskra	J.Ziubrzynski	
G-BXWA	Beech 76 Duchess	Plymouth School of Flying Ltd	
G-BXWB	Robin HR.100/200B	W. A. Brunwin	
G-BXWC	Cessna 152	PJC (Leasing) Ltd/Stapleford	
G-BXWD	Agusta A.109A II	Castle Air Charters Ltd	
G-BXWE	Fokker 100	British Midland Airways Ltd	
G-BXWF	Fokker 100	British Midland Airways Ltd	
G-BXWG	Sky 120-24 balloon	Airborne Adventures Ltd	
G-BXWH	Denney Kitfox Mk.4-1200	R. Horton	
G-BXWI	Cameron N-120 balloon	Flying Pictures Ltd	
G-BXWJ	Robinson R-22B	M. Horrell	
G-BXWK	Rans S.6-ESA Coyote II	C. Churchyard	
G-BXWL	Sky 90-24 balloon	The Shropshire Hills Balloon Co	
G-BXWO	PA-28-181 Archer II	J. S. Develin & Z. Islam	
G-BXWP	PA-32 Cherokee Six 300	Alliance Aviation	
G-BXWR	CFM Streak Shadow	M. A. Hayward (G-MZMI)	
G-BXWS	Scheibe SF.25E Super Falke	M. M. Martin	
G-BXWT	Van's RV-6	R. C. Owen	
G-BXWU	FLS Aerospace Sprint 160	Sunhawk Ltd/North Weald	
G-BXWV	FLS Aerospace Sprint 160	Sunhawk Ltd/North Weald	
G-BXWX	Sky 25-16 balloon	Sky Balloons Ltd	
G-BXWY	Cameron A-105 balloon	Richard Nash Cars Ltd	
G-BXWZ	Cameron A-210 balloon	Kent & Canterbury Ballooning	
G-BXXA	Aérospatiale ATR-72-202	Gill Airways Ltd	
G-BXXC	Scheibe SF.25C Falke 1700	K. E. Ballington	
G-BXXD	Cessna 172R	Denston Hall Estate	
G-BXXE	Rand KR-2	N. Rawlinson	
G-BXXF	Cameron A-210 balloon	Gone With The Wind Ltd	
G-BXXG	Cameron N-105 balloon	Allen Owen Ltd	
G-BXXH	Hatz CB-1	R. F. Shingler	
G-BXXI	Grob G.109B	M. N. Martin	
G-BXXJ	Colt Flying Yacht SS balloon	L. V. Mastis	
G-BXXK	Cessna FR.172N	E. Alexander	
G-BXXL	Cameron N-105 balloon	Flying Pictures Ltd	
G-BXXN	Robinson R-22B	Sloane Helicopters Ltd/Sywell	
G-BXXO	Lindstrand LBL-90B balloon	Lindstrand Balloons Ltd	
G-BXXP	Sky 77-24 balloon	L. Van Den Avyle/Belgium	
G-BXXR	Lovegrove AV-8 gyroplane	P. C. Lovegrove	
G-BXXS	Sky 105-24 balloon	Flying Pictures Ltd	
G-BXXT	Beech 76 Duchess	Solent Flight Aircraft Ltd	
G-BXXU	Colt 31A balloon	Sade Balloons Ltd	
G-BXXV	Eurocopter EC.135T-1	Multiflight Ltd	
G-BXXY	PA-34-220T Seneca III	Air Medical Ltd	
G-BXXZ	CFM Starstreak Shadow SA-II	A. V. & B. T. Orchard	
G-BXYC	Schweizer 269C	L. Williamson & A. Hamilton	
G-BXYD	Eurocopter EC.120B	John Finlay (Concrete Pipes) Ltd	
G-BXYE	CP.301-C1 Emeraude	D. T. Gethin	
G-BXYF	Colt AS-105GD airship	J. Schneider/Germany	
G-BXYG	Cessna 310D	Equirus SARL/France	
G-BXYH	Cameron N-105 balloon	Virgin Airship & Balloon Co Ltd	
G-BXYI	Cameron H-34 balloon	Virgin Airship & Balloon Co Ltd	
G-BXYJ	Jodel DR.1050	R. Manning	
G-BXYK	Robinson R-22B	Hields Aviation	
G-BXYL	Cameron A-275 balloon	Bristol Balloons	
G-BXYM	PA-28 Cherokee 235	E. Francis	
G-BXYN	Van's RV-6	J. A. Tooley	
G-BXYO	PA-28RT-201 Arrow IV	Oxford Aviation Services Ltd/Kidlington	
G-BXYP	PA-28RT-201 Arrow IV	Oxford Aviation Services Ltd/Kidlington	
G-BXYR	PA-28RT-201 Arrow IV	Oxford Aviation Services Ltd/Kidlington	
G-BXYS	PA-28RT-201 Arrow IV	Oxford Aviation Services Ltd/Kidlington	
G-BXYT	PA-28RT-201 Arrow IV	Oxford Aviation Services Ltd/Kidlington	
G-BXYV	Aérospatiale ATR-72-202	Gill Airways Ltd/Newcastle	
G-BXYX	Van's RV-6	D. Coles	
G-BXYY	Cessna FR.172E	Haimoss Ltd	
G-BXZA	PA-38-112 Tomahawk	D. A. Whitmore	
G-BXZB	Nanchang CJ-6A (2632016)	Wingglider Ltd	
G-BXZD	Westland Gazelle HT.2 (XW895)	KB Aviation Services	
G-BXZE	Westland Gazelle HT.3 (XW910)	KB Aviation Services	
G-BXZF	Lindstrand LBL-90A balloon	L. Van Den Avyle/Portugal	
G-BXZG	Cameron A-210 balloon	Societe Bombard SARL/France	
G-BXZH	Cameron A-210 balloon	Societe Bombard SARL/France	
G-BXZI	Lindstrand LBL-90A balloon	Purple Balloons	
G-BXZK	McD Douglas MD.900 Explorer	Dorset Police Air Support Unit	

Notes	Reg.	Type	Owner or Operator
	G-BXZM	Cessna 182S	Rankart Ltd
	G-BXZN	CH1 ATI	Intora-Firebird PLC
	G-BXZO	Pietenpol Air Camper	P. J. Cooke
	G-BXZS	Sikorsky S-76A (modified)	Bristow Helicopters Ltd
	G-BXZT	M.S.880B Rallye Club	K. P. Snipe
	G-BXZU	Bantam B.22-S	M. R. M. Welch
	G-BXZV	CFM Streak Shadow Srs SA	CFM Aircraft Ltd
	G-BXZX	Bell 206B JetRanger 3	Titan Airways Ltd/Stansted
	G-BXZY	CFM Streak Shadow Srs DD	CFM Aircraft Ltd
	G-BXZZ	Sky 160-24 balloon	Skybus Ballooning
	G-BYAA	Boeing 767-204ER	Britannia Airways Ltd *Sir Matt Busby CBE*
	G-BYAB	Boeing 767-204ER	Britannia Airways Ltd *Brian Johnston CBE MC*
	G-BYAD	Boeing 757-204	Britannia Airways Ltd
	G-BYAE	Boeing 757-204	Britannia Airways Ltd
	G-BYAF	Boeing 757-204	Britannia Airways Ltd
	G-BYAH	Boeing 757-204	Britannia Airways Ltd
	G-BYAI	Boeing 757-204	Britannia Airways Ltd
	G-BYAJ	Boeing 757-204	Britannia Airways Ltd
	G-BYAK	Boeing 757-28A	Britannia Airways Ltd
	G-BYAL	Boeing 757-28A	Britannia Airways Ltd
	G-BYAN	Boeing 757-204	Britannia Airways Ltd
	G-BYAO	Boeing 757-204	Britannia Airways Ltd
	G-BYAP	Boeing 757-204	Britannia Airways Ltd
	G-BYAR	Boeing 757-204	Britannia Airways Ltd
	G-BYAS	Boeing 757-204	Britannia Airways Ltd
	G-BYAT	Boeing 757-204	Britannia Airways Ltd
	G-BYAU	Boeing 757-204	Britannia Airways Ltd
	G-BYAV	Taylor JT.1 Monoplane	C. D. Pidler
	G-BYAW	Boeing 757-204	Britannia Airways Ltd *Eric Morecambe OBE*
	G-BYAX	Boeing 757-204	Britannia Airways Ltd
	G-BYAY	Boeing 757-204	Britannia Airways Ltd
	G-BYAZ	CFM Streak Shadow	A. G. Wright
	G-BYBA	AB-206B JetRanger 3	R. Forests Ltd (G-BHXV/G-OWJM)
	G-BYBC	AB-206B JetRanger 2	RCR Aviation Ltd (G-BTWW)
	G-BYBD	Cessna F.172H	Skytrax Aviation Ltd (G-OBHX/G-AWMU)
	G-BYBE	Jodel D.120A	R. J. Page
	G-BYBF	Robin R.2160i	D. J. R. Lloyd-Evans
	G-BYBI	Bell 206B JetRanger 3	R. & M. Engineering Ltd
	G-BYBJ	Medway Hybred 44XLR	M. Gardner
	G-BYBK	Murphy Rebel	D. Webb
	G-BYBL	GY-80 Horizon 160D	P. T. Harmsworth
	G-BYBM	Jabiru SK	M. Rudd
	G-BYBN	Cameron N-77 balloon	M. G. & R. D. Howard
	G-BYBO	Medway Hybred 44XLR Eclipser	R. Skene
	G-BYBP	Cessna A.185F	J. M. Thorpe
	G-BYBR	Rans S.6-116 Coyote II	J. B. Robinson
	G-BYBS	Sky 80-16 balloon	G. W. G. Sudlow
	G-BYBU	Renegade Spirit UK	K. R. Anderson
	G-BYBV	Mainair Rapier	M. W. Robson
	G-BYBW	Team Minimax	N. E. Johnson
	G-BYBX	Slingsby T.67M-260	Slingsby Aviation Ltd
	G-BYBY	ThorpT.18-C Tiger	L. J. Joyce
	G-BYBZ	Jabiru SK	A. W. Harris
	G-BYCA	PA-28 Cherokee 140D	R. A. Wakefield
	G-BYCB	Sky 21-16 balloon	Sky Balloons Ltd
	G-BYCC	Jabiru SK	A. R. Sylvester
	G-BYCD	Cessna 140 (modified)	G. P. James
	G-BYCE	Robinson R-44 Astro	Walters Plant Hire Ltd
	G-BYCF	Robinson R-22B	Lisair
	G-BYCJ	CFM Shadow Srs DD	J. W. E. Pearson
	G-BYCL	Raj Hamsa X'Air 582	M. J. Sullivan
	G-BYCM	Rans S.6-ES Coyote II	E. W. McMullan
	G-BYCN	Rans S.6-ES Coyote II	J. K. & R. L. Dunseath
	G-BYCO	Rans S.6-ES Coyote II	T. J. Croskery
	G-BYCP	Beech B200 Super King Air	Comex Services Ltd
	G-BYCS	Jodel DR.1051	R. A. Bragger
	G-BYCT	Aero L-29 Delfin	M. Beesley
	G-BYCU	Robinson R-22B	K. S. & S. A. Faria (G-OCGJ)
	G-BYCV	Meridian Maverick	P. C. Vallence
	G-BYCW	Mainair Blade 912	P. Hacking

Reg.	Type	Owner or Operator	Notes
G-BYCX	Westland Wasp HAS.1	Austen Associates	
G-BYCY	III-Sky Arrow 650T	A. S. Sprigings	
G-BYCZ	Jabiru SK	Business Operational Services Ltd	
G-BYDA	Douglas DC-10-30	Airtours International Airways Ltd	
G-BYDB	Grob G.115B	A. F. Jones	
G-BYDD	Mooney M.20J	J. Akin	
G-BYDE	V.S.361 Spitfire LF.IX (PT879)	A. H. Soper	
G-BYDF	Sikorsky S-76A	Brecqhou Development Ltd	
G-BYDG	Beech C24R Sierra	Liddell Aircraft Ltd	
G-BYDH	Airbus A.300B4-203F	TNT Express Worldwide (UK) Ltd	
G-BYDI	Cameron A-210 balloon	First Flight	
G-BYDJ	Colt 120A balloon	D. K. Hempleman-Adams	
G-BYDK	SNCAN Stampe SV-4C	Bianchi Aviation Film Services Ltd/Booker	
G-BYDL	Hawker Hurricane IIB (Z5207)	R. A. Roberts	
G-BYDM	Pegasus Quantum 15-912	B. J. Fallows	
G-BYDN	Fokker 100	Gill Airways Ltd/Air France (G-FIOZ)	
G-BYDO	Fokker 100	Gill Airways Ltd/Air France (G-FIOT)	
G-BYDP	Fokker 100	Gill Airways Ltd/Air France (G-FIOS)	
G-BYDR	NA B-25D-3-ND Mitchell (KL161)	Patina Ltd/Duxford	
G-BYDT	Cameron N-90 balloon	Virgin Airship & Balloon Co Ltd	
G-BYDU	Cameron Cart SS balloon	Virgin Airship & Balloon Co Ltd	
G-BYDV	Van's RV-6	B. F. Hill	
G-BYDW	RAF 2000 GTX-SE gyroplane	M. T. Byrne	
G-BYDX	American General AG-5B Tiger	Bibit Group	
G-BYDY	Beech 58 Baron	J. F. Britten	
G-BYDZ	Pegasus Quantum 15-912	W.McCormack	
G-BYEA	Cessna 172P	London Aviation Ltd/Elstree	
G-BYEB	Cessna 172P	London Aviation Ltd/Elstree	
G-BYEC	Glaser-Dirks DG.800B	R. L. McLean	
G-BYED	P.84 Jet Provost T.5A	R. E. Todd	
G-BYEE	Mooney M.20K	Double Echo Flying Group	
G-BYEF	L.188CF Electra	Channel Express (Air Services) Ltd/ Bournemouth	
G-BYEG	Cessna 182S	High Flying Aviation Ltd	
G-BYEH	CEA Jodel DR.250	E. J. Horsfall/Blackpool	
G-BYEI	Cameron 90 Chick SS balloon	Virgin Airship & Balloon Co Ltd	
G-BYEJ	Scheibe SF-28A Tandem Falke	Total Support Inc (UK) Ltd	
G-BYEK	Stoddard-Hamilton Glastar	B. M. New	
G-BYEL	Van's RV-6	D. T. Smith	
G-BYEM	Cessna R.182 RG	Swiftair Ltd	
G-BYEN	Cessna 172P	Transcraft Ltd/Elstree	
G-BYEO	Zenair CH.601HDS	Cloudbase Flying Group	
G-BYEP	Lindstrand LBL-90B balloon	R. C. Barkworth & D. G. Maguire	
G-BYER	Cameron C-80 balloon	Cameron Balloons Ltd	
G-BYES	Cessna 172P	London Aviation Ltd/Elstree	
G-BYET	Cessna 172P	London Aviation Ltd/Elstree	
G-BYEU	Pegasus Quantum 15	T. C. Brown	
G-BYEW	Pegasus Quantum 15	D. McCormack	
G-BYEX	Sky 120-24 balloon	Ballongflyg Upp & Ner AB/Sweden	
G-BYEY	Lindstrand LBL-21 Silver Dream balloon	Oscair Project Ltd	
G-BYEZ	Dyn' Aero MCR-01	J. P. Davis	
G-BYFA	Cessna F.152 II	A. J. Gomes (G-WACA)	
G-BYFB	Cameron N-105 balloon	Cameron Balloons Ltd	
G-BYFC	Jabiru SK	A. C. N. Freeman	
G-BYFD	Grob G.115A	Southern Sailplanes (G-BSGE)	
G-BYFE	Pegasus Quantum 15-912	G-BYFE Flying Group	
G-BYFF	Pegasus Quantum 15-912	Kemble Flying Club	
G-BYFG	Shaw Europa XS	P. R. Brodie	
G-BYFH	Bede BD-5B	G. M. J. Monaghan	
G-BYFI	CFM Starstreak Shadow SA	D. G. Cook	
G-BYFJ	Cameron N-105 balloon	R. R. McCormack	
G-BYFK	Cameron Printer SS balloon	Flying Pictures Ltd	
G-BYFL	Diamond HK.36 TTS	Seahawk Gliding Club/Culdrose	
G-BYFM	Jodel DR.1050M-1	P. M. Standen & A. J. Roxburgh	
G-BYFN	Thruster T.600N	Thruster Air Services Ltd	
G-BYFP	PA-28-181 Archer II	B. Badley	
G-BYFR	PA-32R-301 Saratoga II HP	Hatpin Ltd	
G-BYFT	Pietenpol Air Camper	M. W. Elliott	
G-BYFU	Lindstrand LBL-105B balloon	Balloons Lindstrand France	
G-BYFV	Team Minimax 91	W. E. Gillham	
G-BYFX	Colt 77A balloon	Flying Pictures Ltd	
G-BYFY	Avions Mudry CAP.10B	Cole Aviation	

Notes	Reg.	Type	Owner or Operator
	G-BYGA	Boeing 747-436	British Airways
	G-BYGB	Boeing 747-436	British Airways
	G-BYGC	Boeing 747-436	British Airways
	G-BYGD	Boeing 747-436	British Airways
	G-BYGE	Boeing 747-436	British Airways
	G-BYGF	Boeing 747-436	British Airways
	G-BYGG	Boeing 747-436	British Airways
	G-BYHC	Cameron Z-90 balloon	The Balloon Co
	G-BYHD	Robinson R-22B	A. S. Owen
	G-BYHE	Robinson R-22B	Helicopter Services
	G-BYHG	Dornier Do.328-100	ScotAirways Ltd
	G-BYHH	PA-28-161 Warrior III	Stapleford Flying Club Ltd
	G-BYHI	PA-28-161 Warrior II	Haimoss Ltd
	G-BYHK	PA-28-181 Archer III	Southnet Ltd
	G-BYHL	D.H.C.1 Chipmunk 22	W. F. Higgins & ptnrs
	G-BYHM	BAe 125 Srs 800B	Corporate Aircraft Leasing Ltd
	G-BYHN	Mainair Blade 912	R. Stone
	G-BYHO	Mainair Blade 912	P. J. Morton
	G-BYHP	CEA DR.253B	M. A. Recht
	G-BYHR	Pegasus Quantum 15-912	T. Lee
	G-BYHS	Mainair Blade 912	D. A. Bolton
	G-BYHT	Robin DR.400/180R	M. A. Recht
	G-BYHU	Cameron N-105 balloon	Freeup Ltd
	G-BYHV	Raj Hamsa X'Air 582	S. N. J. Huxtable
	G-BYHW	Cameron A-160 balloon	R. H. Etherington/Italy
	G-BYHX	Cameron A-250 balloon	Global Ballooning
	G-BYHY	Cameron V-77 balloon	P. Spellward
	G-BYHZ	Sky 160-24 balloon	Skyride Balloons Ltd
	G-BYIA	Jabiru SK	G. M. Geary
	G-BYIB	Rans S.6-ES Coyote II	G. A. Clayton
	G-BYIC	Cessna U.206G	Wild Geese Parachute Club
	G-BYID	Rans S.6-ES Coyote II	D. J. Brotherhood
	G-BYIE	Robinson R-22B	Moorland Windows
	G-BYIF	Jabiru XL	D. Cassidy
	G-BYIG	Murphy Renegade Spirit	J. Hatswell
	G-BYII	Team Minimax	J. S. R. Moodie
	G-BYIJ	C.A.S.A. 1.131E Jungmann 2000	P. R. Teager & R. N. Crosland
	G-BYIK	Shaw Europa	P. M. Davis
	G-BYIL	Cameron N-105 balloon	Oakfield Farm Products Ltd
	G-BYIM	Jabiru UL	W. J. Dale & R. F. Hinton
	G-BYIN	RAF 2000 gyroplane	J. R. Legge
	G-BYIO	Colt 105A balloon	N. Charbonnier
	G-BYIP	Aerotek Pitts S-2A Special	Hampshire Aeroplane Co Ltd/St Just
	G-BYIR	Aerotek Pitts S-1S Special	Hampshire Aeroplane Co Ltd/St Just
	G-BYIS	Pegasus Quantum 15-912	A. J. Ridell
	G-BYIT	Robin DR.400/500	P. R. Liddle
	G-BYIU	Cameron V-90 balloon	H. Micketeit
	G-BYIV	Cameron PM-80 balloon	Flying Pictures Ltd
	G-BYIW	Cameron PM-80 balloon	Flying Pictures Ltd
	G-BYIX	Cameron PM-80 balloon	Flying Pictures Ltd
	G-BYIY	Lindstrand LBL-105B balloon	Lindstrand Balloons Ltd
	G-BYIZ	Pegasus Quantum 15-912	J. D. Gray
	G-BYJA	RAF 2000 GTX-SE gyroplane	B. Errington-Weddle
	G-BYJB	Mainair Blade 912	J. H. Bradbury
	G-BYJC	Cameron N-90 balloon	D. E. Bentley Ltd
	G-BYJD	Jabiru UL	M. W. Knights
	G-BYJE	Team Minimax 91	A. W. Austin
	G-BYJF	Thorpe T.211	AD Aerospace Ltd
	G-BYJG	Lindstrand LBL-77A balloon	Lindstrand Balloons Ltd
	G-BYJH	Grob G.109B	J. D. Scott
	G-BYJI	Shaw Europa	A. F. D. Kingdon (G-ODTI)
	G-BYJJ	Cameron C-80 balloon	Proximm Franchising SRL/Italy
	G-BYJK	Pegasus Quantum 15-912	K. M. MacRae
	G-BYJL	Aero Designs Pulsar	F. A. H. Ashmead
	G-BYJM	Cyclone AX2000	Caunton AX2000 Syndicate
	G-BYJN	Lindstrand LBL-105A balloon	B. Meeson
	G-BYJO	Rans S.6-ES Coyote II	G. Ferguson
	G-BYJP	Aerotek Pitts S-1S Special	Eaglescott Pitts Group
	G-BYJR	Lindstrand LBL-77B balloon	C. D. Duthy-James
	G-BYJS	SOCATA TB-20 Trinidad	J. K. Sharkey
	G-BYJT	Zenair CH.601HD	J. D. T. Tannock
	G-BYJU	Raj Hamsa X'Air 582	C. W. Payne
	G-BYJV	Cameron A-210 balloon	Societe Bombard SRL/France

Reg.	Type	Owner or Operator	Notes
G-BYJW	Cameron 105 Sphere SS balloon	Forbes Europe Inc	
G-BYJX	Cameron C-70 balloon	B. Perona	
G-BYJY	Lindstrand Pharmacist SS balloon	D. E. Wells	
G-BYJZ	Lindstrand LBL-105A balloon	Virgin Airship & Balloon Co Ltd	
G-BYKA	Lindstrand LBL-69A balloon	Aerial Promotions Ltd	
G-BYKB	R. Commander 114	Gwent Timber Products Ltd	
G-BYKC	Mainair Blade 912	D. Gabott	
G-BYKD	Mainair Blade 912	D. C. Boyle	
G-BYKE	Rans S.6-ESA Coyote II	C. Townsend	
G-BYKF	Enstrom F-28F	S. G. Oliphant-Hope	
G-BYKG	Pietenpol Air Camper	K. B. Hodge	
G-BYKI	Cameron N-105 balloon	Flying Pictures Ltd	
G-BYKJ	Westland Scout AH.1	Austen Associates	
G-BYKK	Robinson R-44 Astro	Transrent PLC	
G-BYKL	PA-28-181 Archer II	Oxford Aviation Services Ltd/Kidlington	
G-BYKM	PA-34-220T Seneca III	Oxford Aviation Services Ltd/Kidlington	
G-BYKN	PA-28-161 Warrior II	Oxford Aviation Services Ltd/Kidlington	
G-BYKO	PA-28-161 Warrior II	Oxford Aviation Services Ltd/Kidlington	
G-BYKP	PA-28R-201T Turbo Arrow IV	Oxford Aviation Services Ltd/Kidlington	
G-BYKR	PA-28-161 Warrior II	Oxford Aviation Services Ltd/Kidlington	
G-BYKS	Leopoldoff L-6 Colibri	I. M. Callier	
G-BYKT	Pegasus Quantum 15-912	A. R. Lloyd	
G-BYKU	BFC Challenger II	K. W. Seedhouse	
G-BYKV	Avro 504K (replica)	Hawker Restorations Ltd	
G-BYKW	Lindstrand LBL-77B balloon	Ballons Lindstrand France	
G-BYKX	Cameron N-90 balloon	G. Davis	
G-BYKY	Jabiru SK	N. J. Bond	
G-BYKZ	Sky 140-24 balloon	D. J. Head	
G-BYLA	FRED Srs 3	R. Holden-Rushworth	
G-BYLB	D.H.82A Tiger Moth	R. Trickett	
G-BYLC	Pegasus Quantum 15-912	T. Marriott	
G-BYLD	Pietenpol Air Camper	S. Bryan	
G-BYLE	PA-38-112 Tomahawk	Surrey & Kent Flying Club Ltd/Biggin Hill	
G-BYLF	Zenair CH.601HDS	M. Thomas	
G-BYLG	Robin HR.200/120B	The Cotswold Aero Club Ltd	
G-BYLH	Robin HR.200/120B	Mistral Aviation Ltd	
G-BYLI	Nova Vertex 22	M. N. Maclean	
G-BYLJ	Letov LK-2M Sluka	N. E. Stokes	
G-BYLK	Mainair Blade	Hummingbird Microlight Flight Training Ltd	
G-BYLL	F.8L Falco	N. J. Langrick/Breighton	
G-BYLM	PA-46-350P Malibu Mirage	Palace Aviation Ltd	
G-BYLN	Raj Hamsa X'Air 582	R. Gillespie & S. P. McGirr	
G-BYLO	T.66 Nipper Srs 1	M. J. A. Trudgill	
G-BYLP	Rand KR-2	C. S. Hales	
G-BYLR	Cessna 404	Edinburgh Air Charter Ltd	
G-BYLS	Bede BD-4	G. H. Bayliss/Shobdon	
G-BYLT	Raj Hamsa X'Air 582	R. J. Turner	
G-BYLU	Cameron A-140 balloon	Cameron Balloons Ltd	
G-BYLV	Thunder Ax8-105 S2 balloon	Wind Line SRL/Italy	
G-BYLW	Lindstrand LBL-77A balloon	Associazione Gran Premio Italiano	
G-BYLX	Lindstrand LBL-105A balloon	Italiana Aeronavi	
G-BYLY	Cameron V-77 balloon	R. Bayly	
G-BYLZ	Rutan Cozy	E. R. Allen	
G-BYMA	BAe Jetstream 3202	Eastern Airways Ltd	
G-BYMB	Diamond Katana DA.20-C1	Diamond Aircraft Industries GmbH/Austria	
G-BYMC	PA-38-112 Tomahawk II	Surrey & Kent Flying Club Ltd/Biggin Hill	
G-BYMD	PA-38-112 Tomahawk II	Surrey & Kent Flying Club Ltd/Biggin Hill	
G-BYME	GY-80 Horizon 180	G. C. J. Glenn	
G-BYMF	Pegasus Quantum 15-912	G. R. Stockdale	
G-BYMG	Cameron A-210 balloon	Cloud Nine Balloon Co	
G-BYMH	Cessna 152	PJC (Leasing) Ltd/Stapleford	
G-BYMI	Pegasus Quantum 15	N. C. Grayson	
G-BYMJ	Cessna 152	PJC (Leasing) Ltd/Stapleford	
G-BYMK	Dornier Do.328-100	ScotAirways Ltd	
G-BYML	Dornier Do.328-100	ScotAirways Ltd	
G-BYMM	Raj Hamsa X'Air	J. Pearce	
G-BYMN	Rans S.6-ESA Coyote II	H. Smith	
G-BYMO	Campbell Cricket	D. G. Hill	
G-BYMP	Campbell Cricket Mk 1	J. J. Fitzgerald	
G-BYMR	Raj Hamsa X'Air 582	W. M. McMinn	
G-BYMT	Pegasus Quantum 15-912	S. A. Owen	
G-BYMU	Rans S.6-ES Coyote II	I. R. Russell & B. Frogley	

Notes	Reg.	Type	Owner or Operator
	G-BYMV	Rans S.6-ES Coyote II	G. A. Squires
	G-BYMW	Boland 52-12 balloon	C. Jones
	G-BYMX	Cameron A-105 balloon	H. Reis/Germany
	G-BYMY	Cameron N-90 balloon	Cameron Balloons Ltd
	G-BYMZ	Robin R.2160	Mistral Aviation Ltd
	G-BYNA	Cessna F.172H	Heliview Ltd
	G-BYNB	Boeing 737-804	Britannia Airways Ltd
	G-BYNC	Boeing 737-804	Britannia Airways Ltd
	G-BYND	Pegasus Quantum 15	Jeff Howarth Ltd
	G-BYNE	Pilatus PC-6/B2-H4 Turbo Porter	D. M. Penny
	G-BYNH	Rotorway Executive 162F	R. C. MacKenzie
	G-BYNI	Rotorway Exec 90	M. Bunn
	G-BYNJ	Cameron N-77 balloon	A. Giovanni
	G-BYNK	Robin HR.200/160	Mistral Aviation Ltd
	G-BYNL	Jabiru SK	R. C. Daykin
	G-BYNM	Mainair Blade 912	M. W. Holmes
	G-BYNN	Cameron V-90 balloon	M. K. Grigson
	G-BYNO	Pegasus Quantum 15-912	R. J. Newsham
	G-BYNP	Rans S.6-ES Coyote II	R. J. Lines
	G-BYNR	Jabiru UL	A. Parker
	G-BYNS	Jabiru SK	D. K. Lawry
	G-BYNT	Raj Hamsa X'Air 582 (1)	G. R. Wallis
	G-BYNU	Cameron Thunder Ax7-77 balloon	Aerial Promotions Ltd
	G-BYNV	Sky 105-24 balloon	Par Rovelli Construzioni SRL/Italy
	G-BYNW	Cameron H-34 balloon	Flying Pictures Ltd
	G-BYNX	Cameron RX-105 balloon	Cameron Balloons Ltd
	G-BYNY	Beech 76 Duchess	Magenta Ltd
	G-BYNZ	Westland Scout AH.1	Military Helicopters Ltd/Thruxton
	G-BYOA	Slingsby T.67M-260	Slingsby Aviation Ltd/Kirkbymoorside
	G-BYOB	Slingsby T.67M-260	Slingsby Aviation Ltd/Kirkbymoorside
	G-BYOF	Robin R.2160I	Mistral Aviation Ltd
	G-BYOG	Pegasus Quantum 15-912	A. Foote & M. Fizelle
	G-BYOH	Raj Hamsa X'Air 582 (1)	G. A. J. Salter
	G-BYOI	Sky 80-16 balloon	I. S. & S. W. Watthews
	G-BYOJ	Raj Hamsa X'Air 582 (1)	R. R. Hadley
	G-BYOK	Cameron V-90 balloon	D. S. Wilson
	G-BYOM	Sikorsky S-76C (modified)	Skyhopper Ltd (G-IJCB)
	G-BYON	Mainair Blade	S. Mills & G. M. Hobman
	G-BYOO	CFM Streak Shadow	C. I. Chegwen
	G-BYOP	Robinson R-22B	Sloane Helicopters Ltd/Sywell
	G-BYOR	Raj Hamsa X'Air 582 (1)	A. R. Walker
	G-BYOS	Mainair Blade 912	Baxby Airsports Club
	G-BYOT	Rans S.6-ES Coyote II	H. F. Blakeman
	G-BYOU	Rans S.6-ES Coyote II	R. Germany
	G-BYOV	Pegasus Quantum 15-912	K. W. A. Ballinger
	G-BYOW	Mainair Blade	N. Forster
	G-BYOZ	Mainair Rapier	M. Morgan
	G-BYPA	AS.355F-2 Twin Squirrel	Aeromega Aviation Ltd (G-NWPI)
	G-BYPB	Pegasus Quantum 15-912	G. J. Slater
	G-BYPC	Lindstrand LBL-AS2 balloon	Lindstrand Balloons Ltd
	G-BYPE	GY-80 Horizon 160D	H. I. Smith & P. R. Hendry-Smith
	G-BYPF	Thruster T.600N	S. Reid
	G-BYPG	Thruster T.600N	Thruster Air Services Ltd
	G-BYPH	Thruster T.600N	Thruster Air Services Ltd
	G-BYPJ	Pegasus Quantum 15-912	P. J. Manders
	G-BYPK	Shaw Europa	N. J. France
	G-BYPL	Pegasus Quantum 15-912	C. I. D. H. Garrison
	G-BYPM	Shaw Europa XS	P. Mileham
	G-BYPN	M.S.880B Rallye Club	R. & T. C. Edwards
	G-BYPO	Raj Hamsa X'Air 582 (1)	N. G. Woodall & A. S. Leach
	G-BYPP	Medway Rebel SS	J. L. Gowens
	G-BYPT	Rans S.6-ES Coyote II	G. R. & J. A. Pritchard
	G-BYPU	PA-32R-301 Saratoga SP	Plane Talking Ltd/Elstree
	G-BYPV	Colt 120A balloon	Cameron Balloons Ltd
	G-BYPW	Raj Hamsa X'Air 582 (3)	P. A. Mercer
	G-BYPY	Ryan ST3KR	P. B. Rice/Brighton
	G-BYPZ	Rans S.6-116 Coyote II	P. G. Hayward
	G-BYRA	BAe Jetstream 3202	Eastern Airways Ltd
	G-BYRC	WS.58 Wessex HC.2 (XT671)	D. Rrem-Wilson
	G-BYRF	Cameron N-77 balloon	AAA Entertainments Ltd
	G-BYRG	Rans S.6-ES Coyote II	Sport Air UK Ltd
	G-BYRH	Medway Hybred 44XLR	D. J. Stock
	G-BYRI	Boeing 737-229	European Aviation Ltd

Reg.	Type	Owner or Operator	Notes
G-BYRJ	Pegasus Quantum 15-912	V. Causey & F. G. Green	
G-BYRK	Cameron V-42 balloon	Gone With The Wind Ltd	
G-BYRL	Diamond HK.36 TTC Super Dimona	Diamond Aircraft UK Ltd	
G-BYRM	BAe Jetstream 3202	Air Kilroe Ltd	
G-BYRO	Mainair Blade	G. P. Jones	
G-BYRP	Mainair Blade 912	B. J. Bowditch	
G-BYRR	Mainair Blade 912	G. R. Sharples	
G-BYRS	Rans S.6-ES Coyote II	R. Beniston	
G-BYRT	Beech F33A Bonanza	ILS Air Ltd	
G-BYRU	Pegasus Quantum 15-912	Sarum QTM 912 Group	
G-BYRV	Raj Hamsa X'Air 582 (1)	A, Hipkin	
G-BYRX	Westland Scout AH.1 (XT634)	Military Helicopters Ltd	
G-BYRY	Slingsby T.67M-200	D. S. Balman & W. R. Tandy	
G-BYRZ	Lindstrand LBL-77M balloon	Lindstrand Balloons Ltd	
G-BYSA	Shaw Europa XS	B. Allsop	
G-BYSE	AB-206B JetRanger 2	Bewise Ltd (G-BFND)	
G-BYSF	Jabiru UL	M. I. M. Smith	
G-BYSG	Robin HR.200/120B	Mistral Aviation Ltd	
G-BYSJ	D.H.C.1 Chipmunk 22 (WB569)	Propshop Ltd/Duxford	
G-BYSL	Cameron O-56 balloon	S. S. M. Askey	
G-BYSN	Rans S.6-ES Coyote II	A. L. & A. R. Roberts	
G-BYSP	PA-28-181 Archer II	Bobbington Air Training School Ltd	
G-BYSS	Medway Rebel SS	C. R. Stevens	
G-BYST	Cameron 105 Home Special SS balloon	Cameron Balloons Ltd	
G-BYSU	Cameron 105 Freddo SS balloon	Cameron Balloons Ltd	
G-BYSV	Cameron N-120 balloon	Cameron Balloons Ltd	
G-BYSX	Pegasus Quantum 15-912	RAF Microlight Flying Association	
G-BYSY	Raj Hamsa X'Air 582 (1)	J. M. Davidson	
G-BYTA	Kölb Twinstar Mk 3	R. E. Gray	
G-BYTC	Pegasus Quantum 15-912	J. Hood	
G-BYTD	Robinson R-22B	Ace Air Flights Ltd	
G-BYTE	Robinson R-22B	J. W. Lanchbury	
G-BYTG	Glaser-Dirks DG.400	P. R. Williams & B. Sebesik	
G-BYTH	Airbus A.320-231	Airtours International Airways Ltd/ Fly FTI (D-AUKT)	
G-BYTI	PA-24 Comanche 250	B. Richardson	
G-BYTJ	Cameron C-80 balloon	M. White	
G-BYTK	Jabiru UL	K. A. Fagan & S. Pike	
G-BYTL	Mainair Blade 912	A. J. Sharp	
G-BYTM	Dyn' Aero MCR-01	I. Lang	
G-BYTN	D.H.82A Tiger Moth	B. D. Hughes	
G-BYTO	Aérospatiale ATR-72-212	CityFlyer Express Ltd (G-OILA)	
G-BYTP	Aérospatiale ATR-72-212	CityFlyer Express Ltd (G-OILB)	
G-BYTR	Raj Hamsa X'Air 582 (1)	A. P. Roberts & R. Dunn	
G-BYTS	Montgomerie-Bensen B.8MR gyroplane	M. G. Mee	
G-BYTT	Raj Hamsa X'Air 582 (1)	R. P. & C. E. Reeves	
G-BYTU	Mainair Blade 912	L. Chesworth	
G-BYTV	Jabiru UK	E. Bentley	
G-BYTX	Whittaker MW.6-S Fatboy Flyer	J. K. Ewing	
G-BYTY	Dornier Do.328-110	ScotAirways Ltd	
G-BYTZ	Raj Hamsa X'Air 582 (1)	A. B. Wilson & K. C. Millar	
G-BYUA	Grob G.115E Tutor	Bombardier Services (UK) Ltd	
G-BYUB	Grob G.115E Tutor	Bombardier Services (UK) Ltd	
G-BYUC	Grob G.115E Tutor	Bombardier Services (UK) Ltd	
G-BYUD	Grob G.115E Tutor	Bombardier Services (UK) Ltd	
G-BYUE	Grob G.115E Tutor	Bombardier Services (UK) Ltd	
G-BYUF	Grob G.115E Tutor	Bombardier Services (UK) Ltd	
G-BYUG	Grob G.115E Tutor	Bombardier Services (UK) Ltd	
G-BYUH	Grob G.115E Tutor	Bombardier Services (UK) Ltd	
G-BYUI	Grob G.115E Tutor	Bombardier Services (UK) Ltd	
G-BYUJ	Grob G.115E Tutor	Bombardier Services (UK) Ltd	
G-BYUK	Grob G.115E Tutor	Bombardier Services (UK) Ltd	
G-BYUL	Grob G.115E Tutor	Bombardier Services (UK) Ltd	
G-BYUM	Grob G.115E Tutor	Bombardier Services (UK) Ltd	
G-BYUN	Grob G.115E Tutor	Bombardier Services (UK) Ltd	
G-BYUO	Grob G.115E Tutor	Bombardier Services (UK) Ltd	
G-BYUP	Grob G.115E Tutor	Bombardier Services (UK) Ltd	
G-BYUR	Grob G.115E Tutor	Bombardier Services (UK) Ltd	
G-BYUS	Grob G.115E Tutor	Bombardier Services (UK) Ltd	
G-BYUT	Grob G.115E Tutor	Bombardier Services (UK) Ltd	

Notes	Reg.	Type	Owner or Operator
	G-BYUU	Grob G.115E Tutor	Bombardier Services (UK) Ltd
	G-BYUV	Grob G.115E Tutor	Bombardier Services (UK) Ltd
	G-BYUW	Grob G.115E Tutor	Bombardier Services (UK) Ltd
	G-BYUX	Grob G.115E Tutor	Bombardier Services (UK) Ltd
	G-BYUY	Grob G.115E Tutor	Bombardier Services (UK) Ltd
	G-BYUZ	Grob G.115E Tutor	Bombardier Services (UK) Ltd
	G-BYXU	PA-28-161 Warrior II	W. T. King (G-BNUP)
	G-BYXV	Medway Eclipser	K, Swann
	G-BYXW	Medway Eclipser	J. Swann
	G-BYYC	Hapi Cygnet SF-2A	C. D. Hughes
	G-BYYE	Lindstrand LBL-77A balloon	D. J. Cook
	G-BYYG	Slingsby T.67C	B. Dixon
	G-BYYJ	Lindstrand LBL-25A balloon	A. M. Barton
	G-BYYL	Jabiru UL	C. Jackson
	G-BYYR	Raj Hamsa X'Air 582 (1)	T. D. Bawden
	G-BYYY	Pegasus Quantum 15-912	Light Flight Ltd
	G-BYYM	Raj Hamsa X'Air 582 (1)	G-BYYM Group
	G-BYYT	Jabiru UL	T. D. Saveker
	G-BYYZ	Staaken Z-21A Flitzer	A. E. Morris
	G-BYZA	AS.355F-2 Twin Squirrel	Aeromega Aviation PLC
	G-BYZD	KIS Cruiser	R. T. Clegg
	G-BYZJ	Boeing 737-3Q8	British Midland Airways (G-COLE)
	G-BYZP	Robinson R-22B	Helicopter Training & Hire Ltd
	G-BYZY	Pietenpol Air Camper	D. N. Hanchet
	G-BYZZ	Robinson R-22B	Sloane Helicopters Ltd/Sywell
	G-BZAA	Mainair Blade	R. Locke
	G-BZAB	Mainair Rapier	S. T. Morris
	G-BZAM	Shaw Europa	D. Corbett
	G-BZAP	Jabiru UL	S. Derwin
	G-BZAT	Avro RJ100	CityFlyer Express Ltd/BA Express
	G-BZAU	Avro RJ100	CityFlyer Express Ltd/BA Express
	G-BZAV	Avro RJ100	CityFlyer Express Ltd/BA Express
	G-BZAW	Avro RJ100	CityFlyer Express Ltd/BA Express
	G-BZAX	Avro RJ100	CityFlyer Express Ltd/BA Express
	G-BZAY	Avro RJ100	CityFlyer Express Ltd/BA Express
	G-BZAZ	Avro RJ100	CityFlyer Express Ltd/BA Express
	G-BZBF	Cessna 172M	F. & H. (Aircraft)
	G-BZBH	Thunder Ax6-65 balloon	R. B. & G. Clarke
	G-BZGC	AS.355F-1 Twin Squirrel	McAlpine Helicopters Ltd (G-CCAO/ G-SETA/G-NEAS/G-CMMM/ G-BNBJ)/Kidlington
	G-BZGE	Medway Eclipser	J. A. McGill
	G-BZGH	Cessna F.172N	Golf Hotel Group
	G-BZHA	Boeing 767-336ER	British Airways
	G-BZHB	Boeing 767-336ER	British Airways
	G-BZHC	Boeing 767-336ER	British Airways
	G-BZHI	Enstrom F-28A-UK	Tindon Ltd (G-BPOZ)/Little Snoring
	G-BZKK	Cameron V-56 balloon	P. J. Green & C. Bosley *Gemini II*
	G-BZZA	Boeing 737-3L9	K.L.M.uk/Buzz/Stansted
	G-BZZB	Boeing 737-3L9	K.L.M.uk/Buzz/Stansted
	G-BZZD	Cessna F.172M	S. & C. Barry (G-BDPF)

Reg.	Type	Owner or Operator	Notes
G-CAHA	PA-34-200T Seneca II	R. Marshall	
G-CAIN	CFM Shadow Srs CD	A, J, Cain (G-MTKU)	
G-CALL	PA-23 Aztec 250F	Woodgate Aviation (IOM) Ltd	
G-CAMB	AS.355F-2 Twin Squirrel	Cambridgeshire & Essex Air Support	
G-CAMM	Hawker Cygnet (replica)	D. M. Cashmore	
G-CAMP	Cameron N-105 balloon	Hong Kong Balloon & Airship Club	
G-CAMR	BFC Challenger II	P. R. A. Walker	
G-CAPI	Mudry/CAARP CAP.10B	I. Valentine (G-BEXR)	
G-CAPX	Avions Mudry CAP.10B	Cole Aviation	
G-CARS†	Pitts S-2A Special (replica) (BAPC134) ★	Toyota Ltd	
G-CBAC	Short SD3-60 Variant 200	BAC Leasing Ltd (G-BLYH)	
G-CBAL	PA-28-161 Warrior II	Britannia Airways Ltd	
G-CBCL	Stoddard-Hamilton Glastar	C. F. M. Norman	
G-CBIL	Cessna 182K	G. H. Parsons (G-BFZZ)	
G-CBKT	Cameron O-77 balloon	Caledonian Airways Ltd	
G-CBNB	Eurocopter EC.120B	Sea & Air Charter Ltd	
G-CBOR	Cessna F.172N	P. Seville	
G-CCAR	Cameron N-77 balloon	D. P. Turner	
G-CCAT	AA-5A Cheetah	Plane Talking Ltd (G-OAJH/G-KILT/ G-BJFA)/Elstree	
G-CCAU	Eurocopter EC.135T-1	West Mercia Constabulary	
G-CCCC	Cessna 172H	K. E. Wilson	
G-CCCP	Yakoviev Yak-52	R. J. N. Howarth	
G-CCLY	Bell 206B JetRanger 3	Ciceley Ltd (G-TILT/G-BRJO)	
G-CCOA	SA Bulldog Srs 120/122	Cranfield University (G-BCUU)	
G-CCOL	AA-5A Cheetah	Lowlog Ltd (G-BIVU)/Elstree	
G-CCOZ	Monnett Sonerai II	P. R. Cozens	
G-CCSC	Cameron N-77 balloon	C. J. Royden	
G-CCUB	Piper J-3C-65 Cub	Cormack (Aircraft Services) Ltd	
G-CDAV	PA-34-220T Seneca V	Neric Ltd	
G-CDBS	MBB Bo 105DBS	Bond Air Services/Aberdeen	
G-CDET	Culver LCA Cadet	H. B. Fox/Booker	
G-CDGA	Taylor JT.1 Monoplane	R. M. Larimore	
G-CDON	PA-28-161 Warrior II	East Midlands Flying Club PLC	
G-CDRU	C.A.S.A. 1.131E Jungmann 2000	P. Cunniff/White Waltham	
G-CEAA	Airbus A.300B2-1C	European Aviation Ltd/Bournemouth	
G-CEAB	Airbus A.300B2-1C	European Aviation Ltd/Bournemouth	
G-CEAC	Boeing 737-229	Palmair European/Bournemouth	
G-CEAD	Boeing 737-229	European Aviation Ltd/Bournemouth	
G-CEAE	Boeing 737-229	European Aviation Ltd/Bournemouth	
G-CEAF	Boeing 737-229	European Aviation Ltd/Bournemouth	
G-CEAL	Short SD3-60 Variant 100	BAC Express Airlines Ltd (G-BPXO)	
G-CEGA	PA-34-200T Seneca II	Oxford Aviation Services Ltd	
G-CEGR	Beech 200 Super King Air	CEGA Aviation Ltd	
G-CEJA	Cameron V-77 balloon	L. & C. Gray (G-BTOF)	
G-CERT	Mooney M.20K	K. A. Hemming/Fowlmere	
G-CEXA	F.27 Friendship Mk 500	Channel Express (Air Services) Ltd	
G-CEXB	F.27 Friendship Mk 500	Channel Express (Air Services) Ltd	
G-CEXC	Airbus A.300B4-103F	Channel Express (Air Services) Ltd	
G-CEXD	F.27 Friendship Mk 600	Channel Express (Air Services) Ltd	
G-CEXE	F.27 Friendship Mk 500	Channel Express (Air Services) Ltd	
G-CEXF	F.27 Friendship Mk 500	Channel Express (Air Services) Ltd	
G-CEXH	Airbus A.300B4-203F	Channel Express (Air Services) Ltd	
G-CEXI	Airbus A.300B4-203F	Channel Express (Air Services) Ltd	
G-CEXP	HPR-7 Herald 209 ★	Spectators' Terrace/Gatwick	
G-CEXS	L.188C Electra	Channel Express (Air Services) Ltd	
G-CFAA	Avro RJ100	CityFlyer Express Ltd/BA Express	
G-CFBI	Colt 56A balloon	G. A. Fisher	
G-CFLY	Cessna 172F	I. Hughes & B. T. Williams	
G-CFME	SOCATA TB.10 Tobago	Charles Funke Associates Ltd	
G-CGCG	Robinson R-22B	J .M. Henderson	
G-CGHM	PA-28 Cherokee 140	C. M. Jones	
G-CGOD	Cameron N-77 balloon	G. P. Lane	
G-CHAA	Cameron O-90 balloon	The Balloon Club Ltd	
G-CHAM	Cameron 90 Pott SS balloon	High Exposure Balloons	
G-CHAP	Robinson R-44 Astro	Brierley Lifting Tackle Co Ltd	
G-CHAR	Grob G.109B	RAFGSA/Bicester	
G-CHAS	PA-28-181 Archer II	C. H. Elliott	
G-CHAV	Shaw Europa	Chavenage Flying Group	
G-CHCC	AS.332L Super Puma	British International Helicopters	
G-CHCD	Sikorsky S-76A (modified)	British International Helicopters (G-CBJB)	

Notes	Reg.	Type	Owner or Operator
	G-CHEB	Shaw Europa	C. H. P. Bell
	G-CHEM	PA-34-200T Seneca II	London Executive Aviation Ltd
	G-CHES	BN-2A-26 Islander	The Cheshire Constabulary (G-PASY/ G-BPCB/G-BEXA/G-MALI/G-DIVE)/ Hawarden
	G-CHET	Shaw Europa	H. P. Chetwynd-Talbot
	G-CHGL	Bell 206B JetRanger 2	Capital Helicopter Group Ltd (G-BPNG/G-ORTC)
	G-CHIK	Cessna F.152	Stapleford Flying Club Ltd (G-BHAZ)
	G-CHIP	PA-28-181 Archer II	C. M. Hough/Fairoaks
	G-CHIS	Robinson R-22B	Bradmore Helicopter Leasing
	G-CHKL	Cameron 120 Kookaburra SS balloon	Eagle Ltd/Australia
	G-CHLT	Stemme S.10	J. Abbess
	G-CHMP	Bellanca 7ACA Champ	I. J. Langley
	G-CHNX	L.188AF Electra	Channel Express (Air Services) Ltd
	G-CHOK	Cameron V-77 balloon	A. J. Moore
	G-CHOP	Westland-Bell 47G-3B1	Dolphin Property (Management) Ltd
	G-CHPY	D.H.C.1 Chipmunk 22 (WB652)	J. G. H. Computer Services Ltd
	G-CHSU	Eurocopter EC.135T-1	Thames Valley Police Authority Chiltern Air Support Unit/Bensen
	G-CHTA	AA-5A Cheetah	Quick Spin Ltd (G-BFRC)
	G-CHTG	Rotorway Executive 90	G. Cooper (G-BVAJ)
	G-CHUB	Colt N-51 balloon	Chubb Fire Security Ltd
	G-CHUG	Shaw Europa	C. M. Washington
	G-CHUK	Cameron O-77 balloon	L. C. Taylor
	G-CHYL	Robinson R-22B	C. M. Gough-Cooper
	G-CHZN	Robinson R-22B	Cloudbase Ltd
	G-CIAO	Sky Arrow 1450-L	J. Hosier
	G-CIAS	BN-2B-21 Islander	Channel Island Air Search Ltd (G-BKJM)
	G-CICI	Cameron R-15 balloon	Ballooning Endeavours Ltd
	G-CIFR	PA-28-181 Archer II	Aeroshow Ltd
	G-CIGY	Westland-Bell 47G-3B-1	R. A. Perrot (G-BGXP)
	G-CIPI	AJEP Wittman W.8 Tailwind	N. R. Hurley (G-AYDU)/France
	G-CITI	Cessna 501 Citation	Euro Executive Jet Ltd
	G-CITY	PA-31-350 Navajo Chieftain	Woodgate Aviation (IOM) Ltd
	G-CITZ	Bell 206B JetRanger 2	Euro Executive Jet Ltd (G-BRTB)
	G-CIVA	Boeing 747-436	British Airways
	G-CIVB	Boeing 747-436	British Airways
	G-CIVC	Boeing 747-436	British Airways
	G-CIVD	Boeing 747-436	British Airways
	G-CIVE	Boeing 747-436	British Airways
	G-CIVF	Boeing 747-436	British Airways
	G-CIVG	Boeing 747-436	British Airways
	G-CIVH	Boeing 747-436	British Airways
	G-CIVI	Boeing 747-436	British Airways
	G-CIVJ	Boeing 747-436	British Airways
	G-CIVK	Boeing 747-436	British Airways
	G-CIVL	Boeing 747-436	British Airways
	G-CIVM	Boeing 747-436	British Airways
	G-CIVN	Boeing 747-436	British Airways
	G-CIVO	Boeing 747-436	British Airways
	G-CIVP	Boeing 747-436	British Airways
	G-CIVR	Boeing 747-436	British Airways
	G-CIVS	Boeing 747-436	British Airways
	G-CIVT	Boeing 747-436	British Airways
	G-CIVU	Boeing 747-436	British Airways
	G-CIVV	Boeing 747-436	British Airways
	G-CIVW	Boeing 747-436	British Airways
	G-CIVX	Boeing 747-436	British Airways
	G-CIVY	Boeing 747-436	British Airways
	G-CIVZ	Boeing 747-436	British Airways
	G-CJBC	PA-28 Cherokee 180	J. B. Cave/Halfpenny Green
	G-CJCI	Pilatus P2-06 (CC+43)	Pilatus P2 Flying Group
	G-CJUD	Denney Kitfox Mk 3	M. D. Hamwee
	G-CKCK	Enstrom 280FX	Farmax Ltd
	G-CKEN	Wombat gyroplane	K. H. Durran
	G-CLAC	PA-28-161 Warrior II	M. A. Steadman
	G-CLAG	Lindstrand LBL-90A balloon	Cargolifter AG/Germany
	G-CLAS	Short SD3-60 Variant 100	BAC Express Ltd (G-BLED)
	G-CLAX	Jurca MJ.5 Sirocco F2/39	G. D. Claxton (G-AWKB)
	G-CLEA	PA-28-161 Warrior II	R. J. Harrison & A. R. Carpenter
	G-CLEM	Bo 208A2 Junior	Bolkow Group (G-ASWE)

Reg.	Type	Owner or Operator	Notes
G-CLEO	Zenair CH.601HD	H. & K. M. Bowen	
G-CLIC	Cameron A-105 balloon	R. S. Mohr	
G-CLIP	AS.355N Twin Squirrel	Quantel Ltd/Biggin Hill	
G-CLKE	Robinson R-44 Astro	Clarke Business (G-HREH)	
G-CLOE	Sky 90-24 balloon	C. J. Sandell	
G-CLOS	PA-34-200 Seneca II	S. H. Kirkby	
G-CLOW	Beech 200 Super King Air	Clowes (Estates) Ltd	
G-CLRK	Sky 77-24 balloon	William Clark & Son (Parkgate) Ltd	
G-CLUB	Cessna FRA.150N	D. C. C. Handley	
G-CLUE	PA-34-200T Seneca II	Bristol Office Machines Ltd	
G-CLUX	Cessna F.172N	J. & K. Aviation	
G-CMGC	PA-25 Pawnee 235	Midland Gliding Club Ltd (G-BFEX)/ Long Mynd	
G-CNDY	Robinson R-22B	Testgate Ltd (G-BXEW)	
G-COAI	Cranfield A.1	Cranfield University (G-BCIT)	
G-COCO	Cessna F.172M	P. C. Sheard & R. C. Larder	
G-CODE	Bell 206B JetRanger 3	Datel Direct Ltd	
G-COEZ	Airbus A.320-231	Airtours International Airways Ltd	
G-COIN	Bell 206B JetRanger 2	C. Sarno	
G-COLA	Beech F33C Bonanza	J. A.Kelman & Cola Aviation Ltd (G-BUAZ)	
G-COLL	Enstrom 280C-UK-2 Shark	SG Aviation Services Ltd	
G-COLR	Colt 69A balloon	British School of Ballooning	
G-COMB	PA-30 Twin Comanche 160B	J. T. Bateson (G-AVBL)/Ronaldsway	
G-COMP	Cameron N-90 balloon	Computacenter Ltd	
G-CONB	Robin DR.400/180	Winchcombe Farm (G-BUPX)	
G-CONC	Cameron N-90 balloon	British Airways	
G-CONL	SOCATA TB.10 Tobago	J. MacGilvray	
G-COOK	Cameron N-77 balloon	IAZ (International) Ltd	
G-COOP	Cameron N-31 balloon	Rango Balloon & Kite Co	
G-COOT	Taylor Coot A	P. M. Napp	
G-COPS	Piper J-3C-65 Cub	R. W. Sproat & C. E. Simpson	
G-COPT	AS.350B Ecureuil	Owenlars Ltd	
G-CORB	SOCATA TB-20 Trinidad	G. D. Corbin	
G-CORC	Bell 206B JetRanger 2	Air Corcoran Ltd (G-CJHI/G-BBFB)	
G-CORD	Slingsby T.66 Nipper 3	B. A. Wright & K. E. Wilson (G-AVTB)	
G-CORN	Bell 206B JetRanger 3	John A.Wells Ltd (G-BHTR)	
G-CORP	BAe ATP	BAe (Operations) Ltd (G-BTNK)	
G-CORT	AB-206B JetRanger 3	Helicopter Training & Hire Ltd	
G-COSY	Lindstrand LBL-56A balloon	D. D. Owen	
G-COTT	Cameron 60 Cottage SS balloon	Nottingham Hot-Air Balloon Club	
G-COUP	Ercoupe 415C	S. M. Gerrard	
G-COVE	Jabiru UL	A. A. Rowson	
G-COWS	ARV Super 2	T. C. Harrold (G-BONB)	
G-COZI	Rutan Cozy III	D. G. Machin	
G-CPCD	CEA DR.221	P. G. Bumpus & R. Thwaites	
G-CPEL	Boeing 757-236	British Airways (G-BRJE)	
G-CPEM	Boeing 757-236	British Airways	
G-CPEN	Boeing 757-236	British Airways	
G-CPEO	Boeing 757-236	British Airways	
G-CPEP	Boeing 757-2Y0	British Airways	
G-CPER	Boeing 757-236	British Airways	
G-CPES	Boeing 757-236	British Airways	
G-CPET	Boeing 757-236	British Airways	
G-CPEU	Boeing 757-236	British Airways	
G-CPEV	Boeing 757-236	British Airways	
G-CPFC	Cessna F.152 II	Falcon Flying Services/Biggin Hill	
G-CPMK	D.H.C.1 Chipmunk 22 (WZ847)	Towerdrive Ltd	
G-CPMS	SOCATA TB.20 Trinidad	Charlotte Park Management Services Ltd	
G-CPOL	AS.355F-1 Twin Squirrel	Thames Valley Police Authority	
G-CPSF	Cameron N-90 balloon	S. A. Simington & J. D. Rigden (G-OISK)	
G-CPTM	PA-28-151 Warrior	T. J. Mackay & C. M. Pollett (G-BTOE)	
G-CPTS	AB-206B JetRanger 2	A. R. B. Aspinall	
G-CRAK	Cameron N-77 balloon	Mobile Windscreens Ltd	
G-CRAY	Robinson R-22B	W. H. Grimshaw	
G-CRES	Denney Kitfox Mk 3	K. M. James	
G-CRIC	Colomban MC.15 Cri-Cri	R. S. Stoddart-Stones	
G-CRIL	R. Commander 112B	Rockwell Aviation Group/Cardiff	
G-CRIS	Taylor JT.1 Monoplane	C. R. Steer	
G-CROL	Maule MXT-7-180	D. C. Croll & ptnrs	
G-CROY	Shaw Europa	A. Croy	
G-CRPH	Airbus A.320-231	Airtours International Airways Ltd	
G-CRPS	Bell 206B JetRanger 2	Helisport Ltd/Biggin Hill	

Notes	Reg.	Type	Owner or Operator
	G-CRUM	Westland Scout AH.1	Crummock Development Ltd
	G-CRUS	Cessna T.303	B. A. Groves
	G-CRUZ	Cessna T.303	Bank Farm Ltd
	G-CRZY	Thunder Ax8-105 balloon	R. Carr (G-BDLP)/France
	G-CSBM	Cessna F.150M	Motorglider Centre Ltd
	G-CSCS	Cessna F.172N	C. Sullivan/Stapleford
	G-CSDJ	Jabiru UL	D. W. Johnston
	G-CSFC	Cessna 150L	Foxtrot Charlie Flying Group
	G-CSFT	PA-23 Aztec 250D ★	Aces High Ltd (G-AYKU)/North Weald
	G-CSJS	Airbus A.330-243	Airtours International Airways Ltd
	G-CSNA	Cessna 421C	Claessens International Ltd
	G-CSPJ	Hughes 369HS	JWL Services (G-BXJF)/Biggin Hill
	G-CSWL	Bell 206L-1 LongRanger	Capital Helicopter Group Ltd (G-SIRI)
	G-CTCL	SOCATA TB.10 Tobago	Merryfield Leasing Ltd (G-BSIV)
	G-CTEC	Stoddard-Hamilton Glastar	A. J. Clarry
	G-CTEL	Cameron N-90 balloon	Cabletel Surrey & Hampshire Ltd
	G-CTGR	Cameron N-77 balloon	T. G. Read (G-CCDI)
	G-CTIX	V.S.509 Spitfire T.IX (PT462)	A. A. Hodgson
	G-CTKL	Noorduyn AT-16 Harvard IIB (54137)	A. P. Williams/North Weald
	G-CTOY	Denney Kitfox Mk 3	B. McNeilly
	G-CTPW	Bell 206B JetRanger 3	C. T. Wheatley
	G-CTWW	PA-34-200T Seneca II	Kensington Aviation Ltd (G-ROYZ/G-GALE)
	G-CUBB	PA-18 Super Cub 180	Bidford Gliding Centre Ltd
	G-CUBJ	PA-18 Super Cub 150 (56-5395)	R. A. Fleming
	G-CUBP	PA-18 Super Cub 150	P. Grenet
	G-CUBY	Piper J-3C-65 Cub	C. A. Bloom (G-BTZW)
	G-CUCU	Colt 180A balloon	G. M. N. & S. Spencer
	G-CUPN	PA-46-350P Malibu Mirage	Airpark
	G-CURR	Cessna 172R II	JS Aviation Ltd (G-BXOH)
	G-CUTE	Dyn' Aero MCR-01	E. G. Shimmin
	G-CUTY	Shaw Europa	D. J. & M. Watson
	G-CVBF	Cameron A-210 balloon	Virgin Balloon Flights Ltd
	G-CVIL	Piper J-3C-65 Cub	H. A. D. Munro
	G-CVIX	D.H.110 Sea Vixen D.3 (XP924)	De Havilland Aviation Ltd/Swansea
	G-CVPM	VPM M.16 Tandem Trainer	C. S. Teuber/Germany
	G-CVYD	Airbus A.320-231	jmc Airlines Ltd
	G-CVYE	Airbus A.320-231	jmc Airlines Ltd
	G-CVYG	Airbus A.320-231	jmc Airlines Ltd
	G-CWAG	Sequoia F. 8L Falco	B. B. Wagner
	G-CWBM	Currie Wot	B. V. Mayo (G-BTVP)
	G-CWCW	Cameron R-900 balloon	Around The World Balloon Ltd
	G-CWFA	PA-38-112 Tomahawk	Cardiff-Wales Flying Club Ltd (G-BTGC)
	G-CWFZ	PA-28-151 Warrior	Cardiff Wales Flying Club Ltd (G-CPCH/G-BRGJ)
	G-CWIZ	AS.350B Ecureuil	HFI Engineering (G-DJEM/G-ZBAC/ G-SEBI/G-BMCU)
	G-CWOT	Currie Wot	J. P. Conlan
	G-CXCX	Cameron N-90 balloon	Cathay Pacific Airways (London) Ltd
	G-CYLS	Cessna T.303	Gledhill Water Storage Ltd (G-BKXI)/Blackpool
	G-CYMA	GA-7 Cougar	Cyma Petroleum Ltd (G-BKOM)/Elstree
	G-CZAG	Sky 90-24 balloon	S. McCarthy
	G-CZAR	Cessna 560 Citation V	Chauffair (CI) Ltd
	G-CZCZ	Avions Mudry CAP.10B	M. F. R. B. Collett & P. R. Moorhead
	G-DAAH	PA-28RT-201T Turbo Arrow IV	R. Peplow/Halfpenny Green
	G-DAAM	Robinson R-22B	Kenley Consultacy Ltd
	G-DACA	P.57 Sea Prince T.1 (WF118) ★	P. G. Vallance Ltd/Charlwood
	G-DACC	Cessna 401B	Niglon Ltd (G-AYOU)/Birmingham
	G-DACF	Cessna 152 II	T. M. & M. L. Jones (G-BURY)/Egginton
	G-DACS	Short SD3-30 Variant 100	Air Cavrel Ltd (G-BKDM)
	G-DADS	Hughes 369HS	Executive Aviation Services Ltd
	G-DAFY	Beech 58 Baron	P. R. Earp
	G-DAIR	Luscombe 8A Silvaire	D. F. Soul (G-BURK)
	G-DAJB	Boeing 757-2T7	Monarch Airlines Ltd/Luton
	G-DAJC	Boeing 767-31KER	Airtours International Airways Ltd
	G-DAKK	Douglas C-47A	South Coast Airways/Bournemouth
	G-DAKO	PA-28-236 Dakota	First European Airways Ltd
	G-DAMY	Shaw Europa	M. J. Ashby-Arnold
	G-DAND	SOCATA TB.10 Tobago	Whitemoor Engineering Co Ltd
	G-DANT	R. Commander 114	D. P. Tierney

Reg.	Type	Owner or Operator	Notes
G-DANZ	AS.355N Twin Squirrel	Frewton Ltd	
G-DAPH	Cessna 180K	M. R. L. Astor	
G-DARA	PA-34-220T Seneca III	SYS (Scaffolding Contractors) Ltd	
G-DASH	R. Commander 112A	Josef D. J. Jons & Co Ltd (G-BDAJ)	
G-DASI	Short SD3-60 Variant 100	Gill Airways Ltd (G-BKKW)/Newcastle	
G-DASU	Cameron V-77 balloon	D. & L. S. Litchfield	
G-DAVD	Cessna FR.172K	D. M. Driver	
G-DAVE	Jodel D.112	D. A. Porter/Sturgate	
G-DAVO	AA-5B Tiger	Kadala Aviation Ltd (G-GAGA/ G-BGPG/G-BGRW)/Elstree	
G-DAVT	Schleicher ASH-26E	D. A. Triplett	
G-DAYI	Shaw Europa	A. F. Day	
G-DAYS	Shaw Europa	D. J. Bowie	
G-DBDB	VPM M.16 Tandem Trainer	D. R. Bolsover	
G-DBHH	AB-206B JetRanger	UK Helicopter Charter Ltd (G-AWVO)	
G-DBMW	Bell 206B JetRanger 4	Lind Ltd	
G-DBYE	Mooney M.20M	A. J. Thomas	
G-DCAV	PA-32R-301Saratoga IIHP	Airsys Communications Technology Ltd	
G-DCCH	MBB Bo 105D	Bond Air Services Ltd/Aberdeen	
G-DCDB	Bell 407	Paycourt Ltd	
G-DCEA	PA-34-200T Seneca II	Chazair Ltd	
G-DCKK	Cessna F.172N	M. Manston	
G-DCPA	MBB BK.117C-1C	Devon & Cornwall Constabulary (G-LFBA)	
G-DCSE	Robinson R-44	DCS Europe PLC	
G-DCXL	Jodel D.140C	X-Ray Lima Group	
G-DDAY	PA-28R-201T Turbo Arrow III	G-DDAY Group (G-BPDO)	
G-DDMV	NA T-6G Texan (493209)	E. A. Morgan	
G-DDOD	Enstrom 280FX	Sunseeker Sales (UK) Ltd	
G-DEAN	Solar Wings Pegasus XL-Q	D. C. P. Cardey & G. D. Tannahill (G-MVJV)	
G-DEBA	BAe 146-200	-	
G-DEBB	Beech 35-B33 Debonair	Spitfire Aviation Ltd/Bournemouth	
G-DEBC	BAe 146-200	-	
G-DEBD	BAe 146-200	-	
G-DEBF	BAe 146-200	-	
G-DEBG	BAe 146-200	-	
G-DEBH	BAe 146-200	-	
G-DEBJ	BAe 146-100	- (G-OJET/G-BRJS/G-OBAF)	
G-DEER	Robinson R-22B	M. Taylor	
G-DEFE	BAe 146-200	Flightline Ltd/Lufthansa City Line	
G-DEFK	BAe 146-200	Flightline Ltd (G-DEBK)	
G-DEFL	BAe 146-200	Flightline Ltd/Swissair (G-DEBL)	
G-DEFM	BAe 146-200	Flightline Ltd (G-DEBM)	
G-DELF	Aero L-29A Delfin	P. A. Greenhalgh & B. R. Green/Manston	
G-DELT	Robinson R-22B	Virgin Helicopters Ltd	
G-DEMH	Cessna F.172M (modified)	M. Hammond (G-BFLO)	
G-DENA	Cessna F.150G	Plane Talking Ltd (G-AVEO)/Elstree	
G-DENB	Cessna F.150G	Plane Talking Ltd (G-ATZZ)/Elstree	
G-DENC	Cessna F.150G	Plane Talking Ltd (G-AVAP)/Elstree	
G-DEND	Cessna F.150M	Plane Talking Ltd (G-WAFC/ G-BDFI)/Elstree	
G-DENE	PA-28 Cherokee 140	Den Air Aviation Ltd (G-ATOS)/Southend	
G-DENH	PA-28-161 Warrior II	Plane Talking Ltd (G-BTNH)/Elstree	
G-DENI	PA-32 Cherokee Six 300	A. Bendkowski (G-BAIA)	
G-DENK	PA-28-181 Archer II	Plane Talking Ltd (G-BXRJ)/Elstree	
G-DENN	Bell 206B JetRanger 3	Abbey Flight Ltd	
G-DENR	Cessna F.172N	Den Air Aviation Ltd (G-BGNR)/Southend	
G-DENS	Binder CP.301S Smaragd	J. K. Davies	
G-DENT	Cameron N-145 balloon	Deproco UK Ltd	
G-DENZ	PA-44-180 Seminole	Den Air Aviation Ltd (G-INDE/G-BHNM)/ Southend	
G-DERB	Robinson R-22B	Derbyshire Helicopters (G-BPYH)	
G-DERV	Cameron Truck SS balloon	J. M. Percival	
G-DESI	Aero Designs Pulsar XP	D. F. Gaughan	
G-DESS	Mooney M.20J	W. E. Newnes	
G-DEST	Mooney M.20J	Allegro Aviation Ltd	
G-DESY	Cessna A.152	General Airline Ltd (G-BNJE)	
G-DEVS	PA-28 Cherokee 180	180 Group (G-BGVJ)	
G-DEXP	ARV Super 2	W. G. McKinnon	
G-DEXY	Beech E90 King Air	Specsavers Aviation Ltd	
G-DEZC	H.S.125 Srs 700B	Frewton Ltd (G-BWCR)	
G-DFLY	PA-38-112 Tomahawk	H. M. Simmonds	

Notes	Reg.	Type	Owner or Operator
	G-DFVA	Cessna R.172K	R. A. Plowright
	G-DGDG	Glaser-Dirks DG.400/17	DG400 Flying Group/Lasham
	G-DGIV	Glaser-Dirks DG.800B	W. R. McNair
	G-DGLM	Glaser-Dirks DG.400	L. C. McKelvie
	G-DGWW	Rand-Robinson KR-2	W. Wilson/Liverpool
	G-DHAV	D.H.115 Vampire T.11 (U-1234)	J. Jones/Swansea
	G-DHCB	D.H.C.2 Beaver 1	Seaflite Ltd (G-BTDL)
	G-DHCC	D.H.C.1 Chipmunk 22	Eureka Aviation NV/Belgium
	G-DHCI	D.H.C.1 Chipmunk 22	Felthorpe Flying Group Ltd (G-BBSE)
	G-DHDV	D.H.104 Dove 8 (VP981)	Air Atlantique Ltd/Coventry
	G-DHGS	Robinson R-22B	Driver Hire Group Services Ltd
	G-DHLB	Cameron N-90 balloon	DHL International (UK) Ltd
	G-DHSS	D.H.112 Venom FB.50	D. J. L. Wood/Bournemouth
	G-DHTM	D.H.82A Tiger Moth (replica)	E. G. Waite-Roberts
	G-DHTT	D.H.112 Venom FB.50 (WR421)	Source Classic Jet Flight (G-BMOC)
	G-DHUU	D.H.112 Venom FB.50 (WR410)	Source Classic Jet Flight (G-BMOD)
	G-DHVV	D.H.115 Vampire T.55 (XE897)	Source Classic Jet Flight
	G-DHWW	D.H.115 Vampire T.55 (XG775)	Source Classic Jet Flight
	G-DHXX	D.H.100 Vampire FB.6 (VT871)	Source Classic Jet Flight
	G-DHYY	D.H.115 Vampire T.11 (WZ553)	Source Classic Jet Flight
	G-DHZF	D.H.82A Tiger Moth (N9192)	M. R. Parker (G-BSTJ)/Sywell
	G-DHZZ	D.H.115 Vampire T.55 (WZ589)	Source Classic Jet Flight
	G-DIAL	Cameron N-90 balloon	A. J. Street
	G-DIAT	PA-28 Cherokee 140	RAF Benevolent Fund's IAT/Bristol & Wessex Aeroplane Club (G-BCGK)/ Lulsgate
	G-DICE	Enstrom F-28F	Dice Aviation Services Ltd
	G-DICK	Thunder Ax6-56Z balloon	R. D. Sargeant
	G-DIGI	PA-32 Cherokee Six 300	D. Stokes
	G-DIKY	Murphy Rebel	R. J. P. Herivel
	G-DIMB	Boeing 767-31KER	Airtours International Airways Ltd
	G-DIME	R. Commander 114	H. B. Richardson
	G-DINA	AA-5B Tiger	Portway Aviation
	G-DING	Colt 77A balloon	G. J. Bell
	G-DINO	Pegasus Quantum 15	G. D. Hall (G-MGMT)
	G-DINT	B.156 Beaufighter IF	T. E. Moore
	G-DIPI	Cameron Tub SS balloon	D. K. Fish
	G-DIRE	Robinson R-22B	Holly Aviation Ltd
	G-DIRK	Glaser-Dirks DG.400	C. J. Lowrie
	G-DISK	PA-24 Comanche 250	A. Johnston (G-APZG)
	G-DISO	Jodel 150	P. F. Craven & J. H. Shearer
	G-DIVA	Cessna R.172K XPII	Bob Crowe Aircraft Sales Ltd
	G-DIWY	PA-32 Cherokee Six 300	IFS Chemicals Ltd
	G-DIXY	PA-28-181 Archer III	Lyons Aviation
	G-DIZO	Jodel D.120A	D. Aldersea (G-EMKM)/Breighton
	G-DIZY	PA-28R-201T Turbo Arrow III	Medway Arrow Group
	G-DIZZ	Hughes 369HE	H. J. Pelham
	G-DJAE	Cessna 500 Citation	Source Ltd (G-JEAN)
	G-DJAR	Airbus A.320-231	Airtours International Airways Ltd
	G-DJCR	Varga 2150A Kachina	D. J. C. Robertson (G-BLWG)
	G-DJEA	Cessna 421C	Source Ltd
	G-DJHB	Beech A23-19 Musketeer	Nayland Aiglet Group (G-AZZE)
	G-DJJA	PA-28-181 Archer II	Choice Aircraft/Fowlmere
	G-DJNH	Denney Kitfox Mk 3	D. J. N. Hall
	G-DKDP	Grob G.109	D. W. & J. E. Page
	G-DKGF	Viking Dragonfly	P. C. Dowbor
	G-DLCB	Shaw Europa	D. J. Lockett
	G-DLDL	Robinson R-22B	A. J. Wagstaff
	G-DLFN	Aero L-29 Delfin	T. W. Freeman & N. Gooderham/ North Weald
	G-DLOM	SOCATA TB.20 Trinidad	J. N. A. Adderley/Guernsey
	G-DLTR	PA-28 Cherokee 180E	BCT Aircraft Leasing Ltd (G-AYAV)
	G-DMAC	Jabiru UL	C. J. Pratt
	G-DMCA	Douglas DC-10-30	Monarch Airlines Ltd/Luton
	G-DMCD	Robinson R-22B	R. W. Pomphrett (G-OOLI)
	G-DMCS	PA-28R Cherokee Arrow 200-II	Arrow Associates (G-CPAC)
	G-DMWW	CFM Shadow Srs DD	CFM Aircraft Ltd
	G-DNCN	AB-206A JetRanger	Heli-Tele Ltd
	G-DNCS	PA-28R-201T Turbo Arrow III	BC Arrow Ltd
	G-DNLB	MBB Bo 105DBS/4	Bond Air Services (G-BCDH/G-BTBD/ G-BUDP)
	G-DNVT	G.1159C Gulfstream IV	Shell Aircraft Ltd/Heathrow
	G-DOBN	Cessna 402B	Fraggle Leasing Ltd/Edinburgh

Reg.	Type	Owner or Operator	Notes
G-DOCA	Boeing 737-436	British Airways	
G-DOCB	Boeing 737-436	British Airways	
G-DOCC	Boeing 737-436	British Airways	
G-DOCD	Boeing 737-436	British Airways	
G-DOCE	Boeing 737-436	British Airways	
G-DOCF	Boeing 737-436	British Airways	
G-DOCG	Boeing 737-436	British Airways	
G-DOCH	Boeing 737-436	British Airways	
G-DOCI	Boeing 737-436	British Airways	
G-DOCJ	Boeing 737-436	British Airways	
G-DOCK	Boeing 737-436	British Airways	
G-DOCL	Boeing 737-436	British Airways	
G-DOCM	Boeing 737-436	British Airways	
G-DOCN	Boeing 737-436	British Airways	
G-DOCO	Boeing 737-436	British Airways	
G-DOCP	Boeing 737-436	British Airways	
G-DOCR	Boeing 737-436	British Airways	
G-DOCS	Boeing 737-436	British Airways	
G-DOCT	Boeing 737-436	British Airways	
G-DOCU	Boeing 737-436	British Airways	
G-DOCV	Boeing 737-436	British Airways	
G-DOCW	Boeing 737-436	British Airways	
G-DOCX	Boeing 737-436	British Airways	
G-DOCY	Boeing 737-436	British Airways (G-BVBY)	
G-DOCZ	Boeing 737-436	British Airways (G-BVBZ)	
G-DODB	Robinson R-22B	Exmoor Helicopters Ltd	
G-DODD	Cessna F.172P-II	K. Watts/Denham	
G-DODI	PA-46-350P Malibu	CAVOK SRL/Italy	
G-DODR	Robinson R-22B	Exmoor Helicopters Ltd	
G-DOEA	AA-5A Cheetah	Plane Talking Ltd (G-RJMI)/Elstree	
G-DOFY	Bell 206B JetRanger 3	Cinnamond Ltd	
G-DOGZ	Horizon 1	J. E. D. Rogerson	
G-DOLY	Cessna T.303	R. M. Jones (G-BJZK)	
G-DONG	Sky 105-24 balloon	G. J. Bell (G-BWKP)	
G-DONI	AA-5B Tiger	D. M. Maclean (G-BLLT)	
G-DONS	PA-28RT-201T Turbo Arrow IV	D. J. Murphy	
G-DONZ	Shaw Europa	D. J. Smith & D. McNicholl	
G-DOOZ	AS.355F-2 Twin Squirrel	Lynton Aviation Ltd (G-BNSX)	
G-DORB	Bell 206B JetRanger 3	Dorb Crest Homes Ltd	
G-DORN	EKW C-3605	R. G. Gray	
G-DOVE	Cessna 182Q	Carel Investments Ltd	
G-DOVE†	D. H. 104 Devon C.2 ★	East Surrey College (G-KOOL)	
G-DOWN	Colt 31A balloon	M. Williams	
G-DPPH	Agusta A.109E	Sloane Helicopters Ltd (G-BYMS)	
G-DPST	Phillips ST.2	S. E. Phillips	
G-DPUK	Mooney M.20K	K. A. Horne (G-BNZS)	
G-DRAC	Cameron Dracula Skull SS balloon	Shiplake Investments Ltd	
G-DRAG	Cessna 152 (tailwheel)	L. A. Maynard & M. E. Scouller (G-REME/G-BRNF)	
G-DRAM	Cessna FR.172F (floatplane)	Off-Water Group	
G-DRAR	Hughes 369E	Readmans Ltd	
G-DRAW	Colt 77A balloon	C. Wolstenholme	
G-DRAY	Taylor JT.1 Monoplane	L. J. Dray	
G-DRBG	Cessna 172M	J. W. Halfpenny (G-MUIL)	
G-DREX	Cameron 110 Saturn SS balloon	LRC Products Ltd	
G-DREY	Cessna 172R	C. J. Wardill	
G-DRGN	Cameron N-105 balloon	W. I. Hooker & C. Parker	
G-DRGS	Cessna 182S	Walter Scott & Partners Ltd	
G-DRHL	AS.350B-2 Ecureuil	Lytonworth Ltd	
G-DRMM	Shaw Europa	M. W. Mason	
G-DRNT	Sikorsky S-76A	Bristow Helicopters Ltd	
G-DROP	Cessna U.206C	Peterborough Parachute Centre Ltd (G-UKNO/G-BAMN)/Sibson	
G-DRSV	CEA DR.315 (modified)	R. S. Voice	
G-DRUM	Thruster TST Mk.1	C. C. Mercer (G-MVBR)	
G-DRYI	Cameron N-77 balloon	J. Barbour & Sons Ltd	
G-DRYS	Cameron N-90 balloon	J. Barbour & Sons Ltd	
G-DRZF	CEA DR.360	M. R. Parker/Sywell	
G-DSGC	PA-25 Pawnee 235C	Devon & Somerset Gliding Club Ltd	
G-DSID	PA-34-220T Seneca III	R. Howton	
G-DSPI	Robinson R-44 Astro	Focal Point Communications Ltd (G-DPSI)	

Notes	Reg.	Type	Owner or Operator
	G-DTCP	PA-32R Cherokee Lance 300	Campbell Aviation Ltd (G-TEEM)
	G-DUDE	Van's RV-8	W. M. Hodgkins
	G-DUDS	C.A.S.A. 1.131E Jungmann 2000	R. D. Loder
	G-DUDZ	Robin DR.400/180	D. H. Pattison (G-BXNK)
	G-DUET	Wood Duet	C. Wood
	G-DUGI	Lindstrand LBL-90A balloon	D. J. Cook
	G-DUNG	Sky 65-24 balloon	G. J. Bell
	G-DUNN	Zenair CH.250	A. Dunn
	G-DURO	Shaw Europa	D. J. Sagar
	G-DURX	Thunder 77A balloon	V. Trimble
	G-DUSK	D.H.115 Vampire T.11 (XE856)	R. M. A. Robinson & R. Horsfield
	G-DUST	Stolp SA.300 Starduster Too	J. V. George
	G-DUVL	Cessna F.172N	A. J. Simpson/Denham
	G-DVBF	Lindstrand LBL-210A balloon	Virgin Balloon Flights Ltd
	G-DVON	D.H.104 Devon C.2 (VP955)	C. L. Thatcher
	G-DWIA	Chilton D.W.1A	D. Elliott
	G-DWIB	Chilton D.W.1B (replica)	J. Jennings
	G-DWPH	Ultramagic M-77	Ultramagic UK
	G-DYAK	Yakovlev C-11	M. Rusche (G-BWFU)/Germany
	G-DYNE	Cessna 414	Commair Aviation Ltd/E. Midlands
	G-DYNG	Colt 105A balloon	G. J. Bell (G-HSHS)
	G-DYOU	PA-38-112 Tomahawk	Airways Aero Associations Ltd/Booker
	G-EAGL	Cessna 421C	Moseley Group (PSV) Ltd & Clowes Estates Ltd/E. Midlands
	G-EBJI	Hawker Cygnet (replica)	C. J. Essex
	G-ECAB	Curtiss JN-4D	V. S. E. Norman/Rendcomb
	G-ECAS	Boeing 737-36N	British Midland Airways Ltd/E. Midlands
	G-ECAW	Bell 206L-4 LongRanger	A. J. Walter Aviation Ltd
	G-ECBH	Cessna F.150K	ECBH Flying Group
	G-ECDX	D.H.71 Tiger Moth (replica)	M. D. Souch
	G-ECGC	Cessna F.172N-II	Euroair Flying Club Ltd/Cranfield
	G-ECGO	Bo 208C1 Junior	A Flight Aviation Ltd
	G-ECHO	Enstrom 280C-UK-2 Shark	ALP Electrical (Maidenhead) Ltd (G-LONS/G-BDIB)/Booker
	G-ECJM	PA-28R-201T Turbo Arrow III	Regishire Ltd (G-FESL/G-BNRN)
	G-ECKE	Avro 504K (replica) (D8781)	N. Wright & C. M. Kettlewell
	G-ECLI	Schweizer 269C	Eclipse (UK) Ltd
	G-ECOS	AS.355F-1 Twin Squirrel	Multiflight Ltd (G-DOLR/G-BPVB)
	G-ECOX	Grega GN.1 Air Camper	H. C. Cox
	G-ECZZ	Eurocopter EC.120B	Faiman Aviation Ltd
	G-EDEN	SOCATA TB.10 Tobago	N. G. Pistol & ptnrs
	G-EDFS	Pietenpol Air Camper	D. F. Slaughter
	G-EDGE	Jodel 150	A. D. Edge
	G-EDGI	PA-28-161 Warrior II	R. A. Forster
	G-EDMC	Pegasus Quantum 15-912	E. McCallum
	G-EDNA	PA-38-112 Tomahawk	D. J. Clucas
	G-EDRV	Van's RV-6A	E. A. Yates
	G-EDRY	Cessna T.303	Pat Eddery Ltd
	G-EDVL	PA-28R Cherokee Arrow 200-II	J. S. Devlin & Z. Islam (G-BXIN)
	G-EEAC	PA-31 Turbo Navajo	Universal Consumer Products (G-SKKA/G-FOAL/G-RMAE/G-BAEG)
	G-EEGL	Christen Eagle II	A. J. Wilson
	G-EELS	Cessna 208B Caravan 1	Glass Eels Ltd
	G-EEMV	Hawker Sea Fury FB.11 (WH588)	P. J. Morgan
	G-EENA	PA-32R-301 Saratoga SP	Gamit Ltd
	G-EENI	Shaw Europa	M. P. Grimshaw
	G-EENY	GA-7 Cougar	Walsh Aviation
	G-EESA	Shaw Europa	C. B. Stirling (G-HIIL)
	G-EEUP	SNCAN Stampe SV-4C	A. M. Wajih
	G-EEZS	Cessna 182P	Small World Aviation
	G-EFIR	PA-28-181 Archer II	Small World Aviation
	G-EFRY	Light Aero Avid Aerobat	F. E. Telling
	G-EFSM	Slingsby T.67M-260	Slingsby Aviation Ltd (G-BPLK)
	G-EFTE	Bolkow Bo 207	L. J. & A. A. Rice
	G-EGAL	Christen Eagle II	P. N. Davis/Coventry
	G-EGEE	Cessna 310Q	P. G. Lawrence (G-AZVY)
	G-EGEL	Christen Eagle II	R. Kirchhofer & ptnrs/Germany
	G-EGGS	Robin DR.400/180	R. Foot
	G-EGHB	Ercoupe 415D	J. H. Spanton
	G-EGHH	Hawker Hunter F.58 (J-4083)	G. R. Lacey/Bournemouth
	G-EGHR	SOCATA TB.20 Trinidad	B. M. Prescott
	G-EGJA	SOCATA TB.20 Trinidad	D. A. Williamson/Alderney

Reg.	Type	Owner or Operator	Notes
G-EGLD	PA-28-161 Cadet	J. Appleton/Denham	
G-EGLE	Christen Eagle II	R. L. Mitcham & ptnrs	
G-EGLT	Cessna 310R	Tilling Associates Ltd (G-BHTV)	
G-EGNR	PA-38-112 Tomahawk	Chester Aero Services Ltd/Hawarden	
G-EGTR	PA-28-161 Cadet	Plane Talking Ltd (G-BRSI)/Elstree	
G-EGUL	Christen Eagle II	G-EGUL Flying Group (G-FRYS)	
G-EGUY	Sky 220-24 balloon	Black Sheep Balloons	
G-EHBJ	C.A.S.A. 1.131E Jungmann 2000	E. P. Howard	
G-EHLX	PA-28-181 Archer II	I. R. Carver	
G-EHMJ	Beech S35 Bonanza	A. L. Burton & A. J. Daley	
G-EHMM	Robin DR.400/180R	Booker Gliding Club Ltd	
G-EHUP	SA.341G Gazelle 1	MW Helicopters Ltd	
G-EIBM	Robinson R-22B	Abbey Quantity Surveyors (G-BUCL)	
G-EIIR	Cameron N-77 balloon	D. V. Howard	
G-EIKY	Shaw Europa	J. D. Milbank	
G-EIWT	Cessna FR.182RG	P. P. D. Howard-Johnston/Edinburgh	
G-EJGO	Z.226HE Trener	Golf Oscar Flying Group	
G-EJMG	Cessna F.150H	Bagby Aviation	
G-EJOC	AS.350B Ecureuil	Elmsdale (UK) Ltd (G-GEDS/G-HMAN/ G-SKIM/G-BIVP)	
G-EKKL	PA-28-161 Warrior II	Fynair Ltd	
G-EKOS	Cessna FR.182 RG	S. Charlton	
G-ELBC	PA-34-200 Seneca II	Stapleford Flying Club Ltd (G-BANS)	
G-ELEN	Robin DR.400/180	N. R. & E. Foster	
G-ELFI	Robinson R-22B	Tiger Helicopters/Shobdon	
G-ELIT	Bell 206L LongRanger	Aeroturbine Ltd	
G-ELIZ	Denney Kitfox Mk 2	A. J. Ellis	
G-ELKA	Christen Eagle II	D. Aitken & Skydance Aviation Ltd	
G-ELKS	Avid Speedwing Mk 4	H. S. Elkins	
G-ELLA	PA-32R-301 Saratoga IIHP	C. C. W. Hart	
G-ELLE	Cameron N-90 balloon	LE Electrical	
G-ELLI	Bell 206B JetRanger 3	R. A. Fleming Ltd	
G-ELMH	NA AT-6D Harvard III (42-84555)	M. Hammond	
G-ELZN	PA-28-161 Warrior II	Northamptonshire School of Flying Ltd/ Sywell	
G-ELZY	PA-28-161 Warrior II	Goodwood Road Racing School Ltd	
G-EMAK	PA-28R-201 Arrow III	D. & G. Rathbone	
G-EMAS	Eurocopter EC.135T-1	East Midlands Air Support Unit	
G-EMAX	PA-31-350 Navajo Chieftain	AM & T Aviation Ltd	
G-EMAZ	PA-28-181 Archer II	E. J. Stanley	
G-EMBA	Embraer RJ145EU	British Regional Airlines Ltd/BA	
G-EMBB	Embraer RJ145EU	British Regional Airlines Ltd/BA	
G-EMBC	Embraer RJ145EU	British Regional Airlines Ltd/BA	
G-EMBD	Embraer RJ145EU	British Regional Airlines Ltd/BA	
G-EMBE	Embraer RJ145EU	British Regional Airlines Ltd/BA	
G-EMBF	Embraer RJ145EU	British Regional Airlines Ltd/BA	
G-EMBG	Embraer RJ145EU	British Regional Airlines Ltd/BA	
G-EMBH	Embraer RJ145EU	British Regional Airlines Ltd/BA	
G-EMBI	Embraer RJ145EU	British Regional Airlines Ltd/BA	
G-EMBJ	Embraer RJ145EU	British Regional Airlines Ltd/BA	
G-EMBK	Embraer RJ145EU	British Regional Airlines Ltd/BA	
G-EMBL	Embraer RJ145EU	British Regional Airlines Ltd/BA	
G-EMBM	Embraer RJ145EU	British Regional Airlines Ltd/BA	
G-EMBN	Embraer RJ145EU	British Regional Airlines Ltd/BA	
G-EMBO	Embraer RJ145EU	British Regional Airlines Ltd/BA	
G-EMER	PA-34-200 Seneca II	Haimoss Ltd & R. P. Thomas/Old Sarum	
G-EMHH	AS.355F-2 Twin Squirrel	Hancocks Holdings Ltd (G-BYKH)	
G-EMIN	Shaw Europa	Gemini Group	
G-EMJA	C.A.S.A. 1.131E Jungmann 2000	P. J. Brand	
G-EMLY	Pegasus Quantum 15	A. R. White	
G-EMMA	Cessna F.182Q	Watkiss Group Aviation	
G-EMMS	PA-38-112 Tomahawk	Ravenair/Liverpool	
G-EMMY	Rutan Vari-Eze	M. J. Tooze	
G-EMNI	Speedtwin Mk 2	A. J. Clarry	
G-EMSI	Shaw Europa	P. W. L. Thomas	
G-EMSY	D.H.82A Tiger Moth	B. E. Micklewright (G-ASPZ)	
G-ENCE	Partenavia P.68B	Bettany Aircraft Holdings Ltd (G-OROY/G-BFSU)	
G-ENIE	Tipsy T.66 Nipper 3	E. J. Clarke	
G-ENII	Cessna F.172M	J. Howley	
G-ENNI	Robin R.3000/180	P. F. Taylor	
G-ENNY	Cameron V-77 balloon	B. G. Jones	
G-ENOA	Cessna F.172F	M. K. Acors (G-ASZW)	

Notes	Reg.	Type	Owner or Operator
	G-ENRI	Lindstrand LBL-105A balloon	P. G. Hall
	G-ENRY	Cameron N-105 balloon	P. G. & G. R. Hall
	G-ENSI	Beech F33A Bonanza	J. M. Eskes
	G-ENTT	Cessna F.152 II	Bournemouth Flying Club Ltd (G-BHHI)
	G-ENTW	Cessna F.152 II	Firecrest Aviation Ltd & G. Bliss (G-BFLK)
	G-ENUS	Cameron N-90 balloon	Wye Valley Aviation Ltd
	G-EOFF	Taylor JT.2 Titch	G. H. Wylde
	G-EOFS	Shaw Europa	G. T. Leedham
	G-EOFW	Pegasus Quantum 15-912	G. C. Weighell
	G-EOHL	Cessna 182L	G. B. Dale & M. C. Terris
	G-EOIN	Zenair CH.701UL	I. M. Donnelly
	G-EOMA	Airbus A.330-243	Monarch Airlines Ltd
	G-EORG	PA-38-112 Tomahawk	Airways Aero Association/Booker
	G-EORJ	Shaw Europa	P. E. George
	G-EPAR	Robinson R-22B	Jepar Rotorcraft
	G-EPDI	Cameron N-77 balloon	R. Moss
	G-EPED	PA-31-350 Navajo Chieftain	Pedley Furniture International Ltd (G-BMCJ)
	G-EPFR	Airbus A.320-231	Airtours International Airways Ltd (G-BVJV)
	G-EPJM	PA-28-181 Archer III	E. J. Moorey
	G-EPOL	AS.355F-1 Twin Squirrel	Cambridge & Essex Air Support Unit (G-SASU/G-BSSM/G-BMTC/G-BKUK)
	G-EPOX	Aero Designs Pulsar XP	K. F. Farey
	G-EPTR	PA-28R Cherokee Arrow 200-II	T. I. Moore
	G-ERBL	Robinson R-22B	G. V. Maloney
	G-ERCO	Ercoupe 415D	A. R. & M. V. Tapp
	G-ERDS	D.H.82A Tiger Moth	W. A. Gerdes
	G-ERIC	R. Commander 112TC	Atomchoice Ltd
	G-ERIK	Cameron N-77 balloon	T. M. Donnelly
	G-ERIS	Hughes 369D	R. J. Howard (G-PJMD/G-BMJV)
	G-ERIX	Boeing Stearman A75N-1	P. P. Stanitzeck/Munich
	G-ERJA	Embraer RJ145EU	Brymon Airways Ltd/BA
	G-ERJB	Embraer RJ145EU	Brymon Airways Ltd/BA
	G-ERJC	Embraer RJ145EU	Brymon Airways Ltd/BA
	G-ERJD	Embraer RJ145EU	Brymon Airways Ltd/BA
	G-ERJE	Embraer RJ145EU	Brymon Airways Ltd/BA
	G-ERJF	Embraer RJ145EU	Brymon Airways Ltd/BA
	G-ERJG	Embraer RJ145EU	Brymon Airways Ltd/BA
	G-ERMO	ARV Super 2	P. R. Booth (G-BMWK)
	G-ERMS	Thunder Ax3 balloon	B. R. & M. Boyle
	G-ERNI	PA-28-181 Archer II	P. C. & M. A. Greenaway (G-OSSY)
	G-EROS	Cameron H-34 balloon	Evening Standard Co Ltd
	G-ERRY	AA-5B Tiger	Gemini Aviation (G-BFMJ)/Shobdon
	G-ESFT	PA-28-161 Warrior II	SFT Europe Ltd (G-ENNA)/ Bournemouth
	G-ESKY	PA-23 Aztec 250D	A. Watson (G-BBNN)/Shoreham
	G-ESSX	PA-28-161 Warrior II	Courtenay Enterprises (G-BHYY)
	G-ESTA	Cessna 550 Citation II	Executive Aviation Services Ltd (G-GAUL)
	G-ESTE	AA-5A Cheetah	Plane Talking Ltd (G-GHNC)/Elstree
	G-ESUS	Rotorway Executive 162F	J. Tickner
	G-ETBY	PA-32 Cherokee Six 260	G-ETBY Group (G-AWCY)
	G-ETDA	PA-28-161 Warrior II	T. Griffiths
	G-ETDC	Cessna 172P	Osprey Air Services Ltd
	G-ETFT	Colt Financial Times SS balloon	Financial Times Ltd (G-BSGZ)
	G-ETHY	Cessna 208	N. A. Moore
	G-ETIN	Robinson R-22B	Forestdale Hotels Ltd
	G-EUOA	Airbus A.320-200	British Airways
	G-EUOB	Airbus A.320-200	British Airways
	G-EUOC	Airbus A.320-200	British Airways
	G-EUOD	Airbus A.320-200	British Airways
	G-EUOE	Airbus A.320-200	British Airways
	G-EUOF	Airbus A.320-200	British Airways
	G-EUPA	Airbus A.319-131	British Airways
	G-EUPB	Airbus A.319-131	British Airways
	G-EUPC	Airbus A.319-131	British Airways
	G-EUPD	Airbus A.319-131	British Airways
	G-EUPE	Airbus A.319-131	British Airways
	G-EUPF	Airbus A.319-131	British Airways
	G-EUPG	Airbus A.319-131	British Airways
	G-EUPH	Airbus A.319-131	British Airways

Reg.	Type	Owner or Operator	Notes
G-EUPI	Airbus A.319-131	British Airways	
G-EUPJ	Airbus A.319-131	British Airways	
G-EUPK	Airbus A.319-131	British Airways	
G-EUPL	Airbus A.319-131	British Airways	
G-EUPM	Airbus A.319-131	British Airways	
G-EUPN	Airbus A.319-131	British Airways	
G-EUPO	Airbus A.319-131	British Airways	
G-EVES	Dassault Falcon 900B	Northern Executive Aviation Ltd	
G-EVET	Cameron 80 Concept balloon	K. J. Foster	
G-EVNT	Lindstrand LBL-180A balloon	Redmalt Ltd	
G-EWAN	Prostar PT-2C	C. G. Shaw	
G-EWFN	SOCATA TB-20 Trinidad	Trinidair Ltd (G-BRTY)	
G-EWIZ	Pitts S-2E Special	S. J. Carver & D. Howdle	
G-EXEA	Extra EA.300/L	Brandish Holdings Ltd	
G-EXEC	PA-34-200 Seneca	Sky Air Travel Ltd	
G-EXEX	Cessna 404	Atlantic Air Transport Ltd/Coventry	
G-EXIT	M.S.893E Rallye 180GT	K. J. Reynolds/Rochester	
G-EXPL	Champion 7GCBC Citabria	J. J. Young	
G-EXPR	Colt 90A balloon	Lakeside Lodge Golf Centre	
G-EXPS	Short SD3-60 Variant 100	BAC Express Airlines Ltd (G-BLRT)	
G-EXTR	Extra EA.260	D. M. Britten	
G-EYAS	Denney Kitfox Mk 2	E. J. Young	
G-EYCO	Robin DR.400/180	L. M. Gould	
G-EYES	Cessna 402C	Atlantic Air Transport Ltd (G-BLCE)/ Coventry	
G-EYET	Robinson R-44 Astro	Eye-T Aviation Ltd (G-JPAD)	
G-EYNL	MBB Bo 105DBS/5	Humberside Police Helicopter Support Project	
G-EYOR	Van's RV-6	S. I. Fraser	
G-EYRE	Bell 206L-1 LongRanger	Hideroute Ltd (G-STVI)	
G-EZOS	Rutan Vari-Eze	O. Smith/Teesside	
G-EZYB	Boeing 737-3M8	easyJet Airline Co Ltd/Luton	
G-EZYC	Boeing 737-3Y0	easyJet Airline Co Ltd (G-BWJA/ G-TEAA)/Luton	
G-EZYD	Boeing 737-3M8	easyJet Airline Co Ltd/Luton	
G-EZYF	Boeing 737-375	easyJet Airline Co Ltd/Luton	
G-EZYG	Boeing 737-33V	easyJet Airline Co Ltd/Luton	
G-EZYH	Boeing 737-33V	easyJet Airline Co Ltd/Luton	
G-EZYI	Boeing 737-33V	easyJet Airline Co Ltd/Luton	
G-EZYJ	Boeing 737-33V	easyJet Airline Co Ltd/Luton	
G-EZYK	Boeing 737-33V	easyJet Airline Co Ltd/Luton	
G-EZYL	Boeing 737-33V	easyJet Airline Co Ltd/Luton	
G-EZYM	Boeing 737-33V	easyJet Airline Co Ltd/Luton	
G-EZYO	Boeing 737-33V	easyJet Airline Co Ltd/Luton	
G-EZYP	Boeing 737-33V	easyJet Airline Co Ltd/Luton	
G-EZYR	Boeing 737-33V	easyJet Airline Co Ltd/Luton	
G-FABB	Cameron V-77 balloon	P. Trumper	
G-FABI	Robinson R-44 Astro	J. Froggatt	
G-FABM	Beech 95-B55 Baron	F. B. Miles (G-JOND/G-BMVC)	
G-FAGN	Robinson R-22B	C. R. Weldon	
G-FALC	Aeromere F.8L Falco	P. W. Hunter (G-AROT)/Elstree	
G-FAME	Starstreak Shadow SA-II	T. J. Palmer	
G-FAMH	Zenair CH.701	A. M. Harrhy	
G-FAMY	Maule M5-180C	R. J. & K. C. Grimstead	
G-FANC	Fairchild 24R-46 Argus III	A. T. Fines	
G-FANL	Cessna FR.172K XP-II	J. A. Rees	
G-FARM	SOCATA Rallye 235GT	Bristol Cars Ltd	
G-FARO	Aero Designs Star-Lite SL.1	M. K. Faro	
G-FARR	Jodel 150	G. H. Farr	
G-FATB	R. Commander 114B	Ferrier Holdings Ltd	
G-FAYE	Cessna F.150M	Cheshire Air Training Services Ltd/ Liverpool	
G-FBIX	D.H.100 Vampire FB.9 (WL505)	D. G. Jones	
G-FBMW	Cameron N-90 balloon	K-J. Schwer/Germany	
G-FBPI	ANEC IV Missel Thrush	R. Trickett	
G-FBRN	PA-28-181 Archer II	Herefordshire Aero Club Ltd/Shobdon	
G-FBWH	PA-28R Cherokee Arrow 180	F. A. Short	
G-FCAL	Cessna 441	Cobham Leasing Ltd/Bournemouth	
G-FCLA	Boeing 757-28A	jmc Airlines Ltd	
G-FCLB	Boeing 757-28A	jmc Airlines Ltd	
G-FCLC	Boeing 757-28A	jmc Airlines Ltd	
G-FCLD	Boeing 757-25F	jmc Airlines Ltd	

Notes	Reg.	Type	Owner or Operator
	G-FCLE	Boeing 757-28A	jmc Airlines Ltd
	G-FCLF	Boeing 757-28A	jmc Airlines Ltd
	G-FCLG	Boeing 757-28A	jmc Airlines Ltd
	G-FCLH	Boeing 757-28A	jmc Airlines Ltd
	G-FCLI	Boeing 757-28A	jmc Airlines Ltd
	G-FCLJ	Boeing 757-2Y0	jmc Airlines Ltd
	G-FCLK	Boeing 757-2Y0	jmc Airlines Ltd
	G-FCSP	Robin DR.400/180	FCS Photochemicals
	G-FDAV	SA.341G Gazelle 1	Federal Aviation Ltd (G-RIFA/G-ORGE/ G-BBHU)
	G-FEBE	Cessna 340A	C. Dugard Ltd & E. C. Dugard
	G-FEFE	Scheibe SF.25B Falke	Aston Down Falke Syndicate
	G-FELL	Shaw Europa	J. A. Fell
	G-FELT	Cameron N-77 balloon	Allan Industries Ltd
	G-FEZZ	AB-206B JetRanger 2	Helicopter Services
	G-FFAB	Cameron N-105 balloon	The Andrew Broadsword Collection
	G-FFEN	Cessna F.150M	Fast Aerospace Ltd
	G-FFOR	Cessna 310R II	ILS Air Ltd(G-BMGF)
	G-FFOX	Hawker Hunter T.7B (WV318)	Delta Engineering Aviation Ltd/Kemble
	G-FFRA	Dassault Falcon 20DC	FR Aviation Ltd/Bournemouth
	G-FFRI	AS.355F-1 Twin Squirrel	Ford Farm Racing (G-GLOW/G-PAPA/ G-CNET/G-MCAH)
	G-FFTI	SOCATA TB.20 Trinidad	Romsure Ltd
	G-FFUN	Pegasus Quantum 15	P. Simpson (G-MYMD)
	G-FFWD	Cessna 310R	Keef & Co Ltd (G-TVKE/G-EURO)
	G-FGID	Vought FG-1D Corsair (KD345)	Patina Ltd/Duxford
	G-FHAS	Scheibe SF.25E Super Falke	Burn Gliding Club Ltd
	G-FIAT	PA-28 Cherokee 140	RAF Benevolent Fund's IAT/ Bristol & Wessex Aeroplane Club (G-BBYW)/Lulsgate
	G-FIBS	AS.350B Ecureuil	Groveair Freight Ltd
	G-FIFE	Cessna FA.152	Tayside Aviation Ltd (G-BFYN)/Dundee
	G-FIFI	SOCATA TB.20 Trinidad	OLM Aviation Ltd (G-BMWS)/Denham
	G-FIGA	Cessna 152	Aerohire Ltd/Halfpenny Green
	G-FIGB	Cessna 152	Aerohire Ltd/Halfpenny Green
	G-FIJJ	Cessna FR.177RG	Middleton Miniature Mouldings Ltd (G-AZFP)
	G-FIJR	L.188PF Electra	Atlantic Airlines Ltd/Coventry
	G-FIJV	L.188CF Electra	Atlantic Airlines Ltd/Coventry
	G-FILE	PA-34-200T Seneca	Barnes Olson Aeroleasing Ltd
	G-FILL	PA-31-310 Navajo	P. V. Naylor-Leyland
	G-FILO	Robin DR.400/180	Baron G. van der Elst/Belgium
	G-FINA	Cessna F.150L	D. Norris (G-BIFT)
	G-FIRS	Robinson R-22B	M. & S. Chantler
	G-FIRZ	Renegade Spirit UK	D. M. Wood
	G-FISH	Cessna 310R-II	Warner Group
	G-FISK	Pazmany PL.4A	K. S. Woodard
	G-FITZ	Cessna 335	D. S. Hodgetts (G-RIND)
	G-FIZU	L.188CF Electra	Atlantic Airlines Ltd/Coventry
	G-FIZY	Shaw Europa XS	G. N. Holland (G-DDSC)
	G-FIZZ	PA-28-161 Warrior II	Tecair Aviation Ltd
	G-FJCE	Thruster T.600T	Thruster Air Services Ltd
	G-FJET	Cessna 550 Citation II	London Executive Aviation Ltd (G-DCFR/G-WYLX/G-JETD)
	G-FJMS	Partenavia P.68B	F. J. M. Sanders (G-SVHA)
	G-FKNH	PA-15 Vagabond	M. J. Mothershaw/Liverpool
	G-FLAG	Colt 77A balloon	B. A. Williams
	G-FLAK	Beech 95-E55 Baron	Thunder Aviation Ltd/Belgium
	G-FLAV	PA-28-161 Warrior II	The Crew Flying Group/Tollerton
	G-FLCA	Fleet Model 80 Canuck	E. C. Taylor
	G-FLCT	Hallam Fleche	R. G. Hallam
	G-FLEA	SOCATA TB-10 Tobago	J. J. Berry
	G-FLEW	Lindstrand LBL-90A balloon	Lindstrand Balloons Ltd
	G-FLII	GA-7 Cougar	Plane Talking Ltd (G-GRAC)/Elstree
	G-FLIK	Pitts S-1S Special	R. P. Millinship/Leicester
	G-FLIP	Cessna FA.152	Walkbury Aviation Ltd (G-BOES)
	G-FLIT	Rotorway Executive 162F	R. F. Rhodes
	G-FLIZ	Staaken Z-21 Flitzer	G. P. Gregg
	G-FLOA	Cameron O-120 balloon	Floating Sensations Ltd
	G-FLOR	Shaw Europa	A. F. C. van Eldik
	G-FLOX	Shaw Europa	DPT Group
	G-FLPI	R. Commander 112A	L. Freeman & Son/Newcastle
	G-FLSI	FLS Aerospace Sprint 160	Sunhawk Ltd/North Weald

Reg.	Type	Owner or Operator	Notes
G-FLTA	BAe 146-200	Flightline Ltd/Swissair Express	
G-FLTI	Beech F90 King Air	Flightline Ltd/Southend	
G-FLTY	EMB-110P1 Bandeirante	Flightline Ltd (G-ZUSS/G-REGA)/ Southend	
G-FLTZ	Beech 58 Baron	Stesco Ltd (G-PSVS)	
G-FLUF	Lindstrand Bunny SS balloon	Lindstrand Balloons Ltd	
G-FLVU	Cessna 501 Citation	Neonopal Ltd	
G-FLYA	Mooney M.20J	BRF Aviation Ltd	
G-FLYE	Cameron A-210 balloon	Bakers World Travel Ltd	
G-FLYP	Beagle B.206 Srs 2	Key Publishing Ltd (G-AVHO)/Cranfield	
G-FLYS	Robinson R-44 Astro	Brilliant PR	
G-FLYT	Shaw Europa	D. W. Adams	
G-FLYZ	Robinson R-44 Astro	Rotaflite Helicopter Sales	
G-FMAM	PA-28-151 Warrior	B. Barr (G-BBXV)	
G-FMSG	Cessna FA.150K	G. Owen (G-POTS/G-AYUY)/Gamston	
G-FNLD	Cessna 172N	Papa Hotel Flying Group	
G-FNLY	Cessna F.172M	P. M. Hopkinson (G-WACX/G-BAEX)	
G-FODI	Robinson R-44 Astro	Sanna Industries Ltd	
G-FOGG	Cameron N-90 balloon	J. P. E. Money-Kyrle	
G-FOGY	Robinson R-22B	P. Turvey	
G-FOLD	Light Aero Avid Speedwing	A. G. Edwards	
G-FOLI	Robinson R-22B	K. Duckworth	
G-FOLY	Aerotek Pitts S-2A Modified	A. A. Laing	
G-FOPP	Lancair 320	Airsport (UK) Ltd	
G-FORC	SNCAN Stampe SV-4C	I. A. Marsh/Elstree	
G-FORD	SNCAN Stampe SV-4C	P. H. Meeson	
G-FORS	Slingsby T.67C	Open Slies Partnership	
G-FORZ	Pitts S-1S Special	N. W. Parkinson	
G-FOTO	PA-E23 Aztec 250F	Aerofilms Ltd (G-BJDH/G-BDXV)	
G-FOWL	Colt 90A balloon	G-FOWL Ballooning Group	
G-FOWS	Cameron N-105 balloon	Fowlers of Bristol Ltd	
G-FOXA	PA-28-161 Cadet	Leicestershire Aero Club Ltd	
G-FOXC	Denney Kitfox Mk 3	W. N. Clark	
G-FOXD	Denney Kitfox	M. Hanley	
G-FOXE	Denney Kitfox Mk 2	K. M. Pinkard	
G-FOXG	Denney Kitfox Mk 2	Kitfox Group	
G-FOXI	Denney Kitfox	B. Johns	
G-FOXM	Bell 206B JetRanger 2	Tyringham Charter & Group Services (G-STAK/G-BNIS)	
G-FOXS	Denney Kitfox Mk 2	S. P. Watkins & C. C. Rea	
G-FOXZ	Denney Kitfox	S. C. Goozee	
G-FPLA	Beech 200 Super King Air	Cobham Leasing Ltd	
G-FPLB	Beech 200 Super King Air	Cobham Leasing Ltd	
G-FPLC	Cessna 441	Cobham Leasing Ltd (G-FRAX/G-BMTZ)	
G-FRAD	Dassault Falcon 20E	FR Aviation Ltd (G-BCYF)/Bournemouth	
G-FRAE	Dassault Falcon 20E	FR Aviation Ltd/Bournemouth	
G-FRAF	Dassault Falcon 20E	FR Aviation Ltd/Bournemouth	
G-FRAG	PA-32 Cherokee Six 300E	G-FRAG Group/Sherburn	
G-FRAH	Dassault Falcon 20DC	FR Aviation Ltd/Bournemouth	
G-FRAI	Dassault Falcon 20E	FR Aviation Ltd/Bournemouth	
G-FRAJ	Dassault Falcon 20E	FR Aviation Ltd/Bournemouth	
G-FRAK	Dassault Falcon 20DC	FR Aviation Ltd/Bournemouth	
G-FRAL	Dassault Falcon 20DC	FR Aviation Ltd/Bournemouth	
G-FRAM	Dassault Falcon 20DC	FR Aviation Ltd/Bournemouth	
G-FRAN	Piper J-3C-90 Cub(480321)	Essex L-4 Group (G-BIXY)	
G-FRAO	Dassault Falcon 20DC	FR Aviation Ltd/Bournemouth	
G-FRAP	Dassault Falcon 20DC	FR Aviation Ltd/Bournemouth	
G-FRAR	Dassault Falcon 20DC	FR Aviation Ltd/Bournemouth	
G-FRAS	Dassault Falcon 20C	FR Aviation Ltd/Bournemouth	
G-FRAT	Dassault Falcon 20C	FR Aviation Ltd/Bournemouth	
G-FRAU	Dassault Falcon 20C	FR Aviation Ltd/Bournemouth	
G-FRAW	Dassault Falcon 20ECM	FR Aviation Ltd/Bournemouth	
G-FRAY	Cassutt IIIM (modified)	C. I. Fray	
G-FRAZ	Cessna 441	FR Aviation Ltd/Bournemouth	
G-FRBA	Dassault Falcon 20C	FR Aviation Ltd/Bournemouth	
G-FRBY	Beech E55 Baron	FR Aviation Ltd/Bournemouth	
G-FRCE	H.S. Gnat T.1	Butane Buzzard Aviation Ltd/Cranfield	
G-FRGN	PA-28-236 Dakota	Fregon Aviation Ltd	
G-FRJB	Britten Sheriff SA-1 ★	Aeropark/E. Midlands	
G-FRST	PA-44-180T Turbo Seminole	TDR Aviation Ltd	
G-FRYI	Beech 200 Super King Air	London Executive Aviation Ltd (G-OAVX/ G-IBCA/G-BMCA)/London City	
G-FSFT	PA-44-180 Seminole	M. J. Love	

Notes	Reg.	Type	Owner or Operator
	G-FSHA	Denney Kitfox Mk 2	S. J. Alston
	G-FTAX	Cessna 421C	CRV Leasing (G-BFFM)
	G-FTIL	Robin DR.400/180R	RAF Wyton Flying Club Ltd
	G-FTIM	Robin DR.400/100	Bird Investment Properties Ltd
	G-FTIN	Robin DR.400/100	G. D. Clark & M. J. D. Theobold/ Blackpool
	G-FTUO	Van's RV-4	Euroclip 2000 Ltd
	G-FTWO	AS.355F-2 Twin Squirrel	McAlpine Helicopters Ltd (G-OJOR/ G-BMUS)/Hayes
	G-FUEL	Robin DR.400/180	R. Darch/Compton Abbas
	G-FULL	PA-28R Cherokee Arrow 200-II	Stapleford Flying Club Ltd (G-HWAY/ G-JULI)
	G-FUND	Thunder Ax7-65Z balloon	Soft Sell Ltd
	G-FUNK	Yakovlev Yak-50	Intrepid Aviation Co/North Weald
	G-FUNN	Plumb BGP-1	J. D. Anson
	G-FUSI	Robinson R-22B	F. M. Usher-Smith
	G-FUZY	Cameron N-77 balloon	Allan Industries Ltd
	G-FUZZ	PA-18 Super Cub 95	G. W. Cline
	G-FVBF	Lindstrand LBL-210A balloon	Virgin Balloon Flights Ltd
	G-FWPW	PA-28-236 Dakota	P. A. & F. C. Winters
	G-FWRP	Cessna 421C	Continental Services PLC
	G-FXII	V.S.366 Spitfire F.XII (EN224)	P. R. Arnold
	G-FZZA	General Avia F.22-A	APB Leasing Ltd/Welshpool
	G-FZZI	Cameron H-34 balloon	L. V. Mastis
	G-GABD	GA-7 Cougar	Scotia Safari Ltd/Prestwick
	G-GACA	P.57 Sea Prince T.1 ★	P. G. Vallance Ltd/Charlwood
	G-GAFA	PA-34-200T Seneca II	SRC Contractors Ltd
	G-GAFX	Boeing 747-245F	Airfreight Express Ltd
	G-GAII	Hawker Hunter GA.11 (XE685)	B. J. Pover/Exeter
	G-GAIW	Cameron A-140 balloon	Cameron Balloons Ltd
	G-GAJB	AA-5B Tiger	G. A. J. Bowles (G-BHZN)
	G-GALA	PA-28 Cherokee 180E	E. Alexander (G-AYAP)
	G-GAME	Cessna T.303	M. C. Choksey
	G-GANE	Sequoia F.8L Falco	S. J. Gane
	G-GANJ	Fournier RF-6B-100	Soaring Equipment Ltd/Coventry
	G-GASC	Hughes 369HS	Crewhall Ltd (G-WELD/G-FROG)
	G-GASP	PA-28-181 Archer II	G-GASP Flying Group
	G-GASS	Thunder Ax7-77 balloon	Servowarm Balloon Syndicate
	G-GAWA	Cessna 140	E. C. Murgatroyd (G-BRSM)
	G-GAZA	SA.341G Gazelle 1	The Auster Aircraft Co Ltd (G-RALE/ G-SFTG)
	G-GAZI	SA.341G Gazelle 1	Stratton Motor Co (Norfolk) Ltd & UCC International Group Ltd (G-BKLU)
	G-GAZZ	SA.341G Gazelle 1	Stratton Motor Co (Norfolk) Ltd & UCC International Group Ltd
	G-GBAO	Robin R.1180TD	J. Kay-Movat
	G-GBFF	Cessna F.172N	J. S. Malcolm
	G-GBHI	SOCATA TB.10 Tobago	A. B. S. Garden
	G-GBLP	Cessna F.172M	Edinburgh Air Centre Ltd (G-GWEN)
	G-GBLR	Cessna F.150L	Blue Max Flying Group
	G-GBSL	Beech 76 Duchess	M. H. Cundsy (G-BGVG)
	G-GBTA	Boeing 737-436	British Airways (G-BVHA)
	G-GBTB	Boeing 737-436	British Airways (G-BVHB)
	G-GBUE	Robin DR.400/120A	G-GBUE Group (G-BPXD)
	G-GBXS	Shaw Europa XS	Europa Aircraft Co Ltd
	G-GCAT	PA-28 Cherokee 140B	H. Skelton (G-BFRH)
	G-GCCL	Beech 76 Duchess	Aerolease Ltd
	G-GCJL	BAe Jetstream 4100	British Aerospace (Operations) Ltd
	G-GCKI	Mooney M.20K	B. Barr
	G-GCUB	PA-18 Super Cub 150	N. J. Morgan
	G-GDAY	Robinson R-22B	G. R. Day
	G-GDER	Robin R.1180TD	Berkshire Aviation Services Ltd
	G-GDEZ	BAe 125-1000B	Frewton Ltd
	G-GDGR	SOCATA TB-20 Trinidad	Willwright Aviation Ltd
	G-GDOG	PA-28R Cherokee Arrow 200-II	R. K. & S. Perry (G-BDXW)
	G-GDTU	Avions Mudry CAP.10B	Sherburn Aero Club Ltd
	G-GDXK	Cameron A-140 balloon	Cameron Balloons Ltd
	G-GEAR	Cessna FR.182Q	Wycombe Air Centre Ltd
	G-GEDI	Dassault Falcon 2000	Victoria Aviation Ltd
	G-GEEE	Hughes 369HS	B. P. Stein (G-BDOY)
	G-GEEP	Robin R.1180T	Organic Concentrates Ltd/Booker
	G-GEES	Cameron N-77 balloon	N. A. Carr

Reg.	Type	Owner or Operator	Notes
G-GEEZ	Cameron N-77 balloon	Charnwood Forest Turf Accountants Ltd	
G-GEGE	Robinson R-22B	S. K. Miles	
G-GEHP	PA-28RT-201 Arrow IV	Aeroshow Ltd	
G-GEMS	Thunder Ax8-90 S2 balloon	B. Sevenich & ptnrs/Germany	
G-GENN	GA-7 Cougar	Chalrey Ltd (G-BNAB/G-BGYP)	
G-GEOF	Pereira Osprey 2	G. Crossley	
G-GEUP	Cameron N-77 balloon	G. Everett	
G-GFAB	Cameron N-105 balloon	The Andrew Brownsword Collection Ltd	
G-GFCA	PA-28-161 Cadet	Aeroshow Ltd	
G-GFCB	PA-28-161 Cadet	AM & T Aviation Ltd	
G-GFCD	PA-34-220T Seneca III	Stonehurst Aviation Ltd (G-KIDS)	
G-GFCF	PA-28-161 Cadet	Aerohire Ltd (G-RHBH)	
G-GFEY	PA-34-200T Seneca II	Topa Panama Inc	
G-GFFA	Boeing 737-59D	British Airways (G-BVZF)	
G-GFFB	Boeing 737-500	British Airways	
G-GFFC	Boeing 737-500	British Airways	
G-GFFD	Boeing 737-500	British Airways	
G-GFFE	Boeing 737-500	British Airways	
G-GFFF	Boeing 737-500	British Airways	
G-GFFG	Boeing 737-500	British Airways	
G-GFFH	Boeing 737-500	British Airways	
G-GFFI	Boeing 737-500	British Airways	
G-GFFJ	Boeing 737-500	British Airways	
G-GFKY	Zenair CH.250	D. M. Edes	
G-GFLY	Cessna F.150L	Tindon Ltd	
G-GFTA	PA-28-161 Warrior III	One Zero Three Ltd	
G-GFTB	PA-28-161 Warrior III	One Zero Three Ltd	
G-GGGG	Thunder Ax7-77A balloon	T. A. Gilmour	
G-GGLE	PA-22 Colt 108 (tailwheel)	S. C. Hobden	
G-GGOW	Colt 77A balloon	G. Everett	
G-GGTT	Agusta-Bell 47G-4A	Thorneygrove Ltd	
G-GHCL	Bell 206B JetRanger 2	Scotia Helicopters Ltd (G-SHVV)	
G-GHIA	Cameron N-120 balloon	J. A. Marshall	
G-GHIN	Thunder Ax7-77 balloon	N. T. Parry	
G-GHKX	PA-28-161 Warrior II	Oxford Aviation Services Ltd/Kidlington	
G-GHRW	PA-28RT-201 Arrow IV	Leavesden Flight Centre Ltd (G-ONAB /G-BHAK)	
G-GHSI	PA-44-180T Turbo Seminole	M. G. Roberts	
G-GHZJ	SOCATA TB.9 Tampico	M. Haller	
G-GIGI	M.S.893A Rallye Commodore	D. J. Moore (G-AYVU)	
G-GILT	Cessna 421C	Air Nova PLC (G-BMZC)/Liverpool	
G-GIRO	Schweizer 269C	D. E. McDowell	
G-GIRY	AG-5B Tiger	M. J. Sparshatt-Worley	
G-GJCD	Robinson R-22B	J. C. Lane	
G-GJET	Learjet 35A	DPS Aviation Ltd (G-CJET/G-SEBE/ G-ZIPS/G-ZONE)	
G-GJKK	Mooney M.20K	Davey & Shaw	
G-GKAT	Enstrom 280C	Cheshire Aviators Ltd	
G-GKFC	RL-5A LW Sherwood Ranger	K. F. Crumplin (G-MYZI)	
G-GLAD	Gloster G.37 Gladiator II (N5903)	Patina Ltd/Duxford	
G-GLAW	Cameron N-90 balloon	George Law Ltd	
G-GLBL	Lindstrand AM-32000 balloon	Lindstrand Balloons Ltd	
G-GLED	Cessna 150M	Firecrest Aviation Ltd/Booker	
G-GLTT	PA-31-350 Navajo Chieftain	J. A. Robson	
G-GLUC	Van's RV-6	K. D. Pearce	
G-GLUE	Cameron N-65 balloon	L. J. M. Muir & G. D. Hallett	
G-GLUG	PA-31-350 Navajo Chieftain	Champagne-Air Ltd (G-BLOE/ G-NITE)/Newcastle	
G-GMAX	SNCAN Stampe SV-4C	Glidegold Ltd (G-BXNW)	
G-GMPA	AS.355F-2 Twin Squirrel	Greater Manchester Police Authority (G-BPOI)	
G-GMSI	SOCATA TB.9 Tampico	M. L. Rhodes	
G-GNAT	H.S. Gnat T.1 (XS101)	Brutus Holdings Ltd/Cranfield	
G-GNTA	SAAB SF.340A	British Midland Commuter	
G-GNTB	SAAB SF.340A	British Midland Commuter	
G-GNTC	SAAB SF.340A	Aurigny Air Services Ltd	
G-GNTD	SAAB SF.340A	British Midland Commuter	
G-GNTE	SAAB SF.340A	British Regional Airlines/BA Express	
G-GNTF	SAAB SF.340A	British Midland Commuter	
G-GNTG	SAAB SF.340A	British Midland Commuter	
G-GNTH	SAAB SF.340B	British Midland Commuter	
G-GNTI	SAAB SF.340B	British Midland Commuter	

Notes	Reg.	Type	Owner or Operator
	G-GNTJ	SAAB SF.340B	British Midland Commuter
	G-GNTZ	BAe 146-200	British Regional Airlines
	G-GOBT	Colt 77A balloon	British Telecom PLC
	G-GOCC	AA-5A Cheetah	Lowlog Ltd (G-BPIX)/Elstree
	G-GOCX	Cameron N-90 balloon	R. D. Parry/Hong Kong
	G-GOGW	Cameron N-90 balloon	Great Western Trains Ltd
	G-GOKT	Douglas DC-10-30	jmc Airlines Ltd
	G-GOLD	Thunder Ax6-56A balloon	Joseph Terry & Sons Ltd
	G-GOLF	SOCATA TB.10 Tobago	E. H. Scamell & ptnrs
	G-GOMM	PA-32R-300 Lance	L. Major
	G-GONE	D.H.112 Venom FB.50	G. R. Lacey/Bournemouth
	G-GOOD	SOCATA TB-20 Trinidad	N. J. Vetch
	G-GORE	CFM Streak Shadow	M. S. Clinton
	G-GOSS	Jodel DR.221	Avon Flying Group
	G-GOTC	GA-7 Cougar	Cambridge Aircraft Ltd
	G-GOTO	PA-32R-301T Turbo Saratoga II	J. A. Varndell
	G-GOZO	Cessna R.182	Transmatic Fyllan Ltd (G-BJZO)/ Cranfield
	G-GPMW	PA-28RT-201T Turbo Arrow IV	M. Worrall & ptnrs
	G-GPST	Phillips ST.1 Speedtwin	S. E. Phillips
	G-GPWH	Dassault Falcon 900EX	Lynton Corporate Jet Ltd
	G-GRAY	Cessna 172N	Truman Aviation Ltd/Tollerton
	G-GREN	Cessna T.310R	J. M. Robinson
	G-GRID	AS.355F-1 Twin Squirrel	National Grid Co PLC
	G-GRIF	R. Commander 112TCA	Nicol Aviation (G-BHXC)
	G-GRIN	Van's RV-6	A. Phillips
	G-GRIP	Colt 110 Bibendum SS balloon	The Aerial Display Co Ltd
	G-GROL	Maule MXT-7-180	D. C. Croll & ptnrs
	G-GROW	Cameron N-77 balloon	Derbyshire Building Soc.
	G-GRRC	PA-28-161 Warrior II	Goodwood Road Racing Co Ltd (G-BXJS)
	G-GRRR	SA Bulldog Srs 120/122	L. Bax (G-BXGU)
	G-GRYZ	Beech F33A Bonanza	V. G. Negre
	G-GSFC	Robinson R-22B	Thurston Helicopters (Engineering) Ltd/ Redhill
	G-GSFT	PA-44-180 Seminole	SFT Europe Ltd/Bournemouth
	G-GTAX	PA-31-350 Navajo Chieftain	Hadagain Investments Ltd (G-OIAS)
	G-GTHM	PA-38-112 Tomahawk	D. A. Whitmore
	G-GTPL	Mooney M.20K	W. R. Emberton/Spain
	G-GUAY	Enstrom 480	Heliway Aviation
	G-GUCK	Beech C23 Sundowner 180	S. Imber (G-BPYG)
	G-GUFO	Cameron 80 Saucer SS balloon	L. V. Mastis (G-BOUB)
	G-GUGI	Eurocopter EC.135T-1	McAlpine Helicopters Ltd/Kidlington
	G-GULF	Lindstrand LBL-105A balloon	Virgin Balloon Flights Ltd/Oman
	G-GULL	Petrel Amphibian	Amphibians UK Ltd
	G-GUNS	Cameron V-77 balloon	Royal School of Artillery Hot Air Balloon Club
	G-GUSS	PA-28-151 Warrior	A. M. B. Dudley (G-BJRY)
	G-GUST	AB-206B JetRanger 2	Gatehouse Estates Ltd (G-CBHH/G-AYBE)
	G-GUYS	PA-34-200T Seneca	R. J. & J. M. Z. Keel (G-BMWT)
	G-GVBF	Lindstrand LBL-180A balloon	Virgin Balloon Flights Ltd
	G-GVIP	Agusta A.109E	Sloane Helicopters Ltd/Sywell
	G-GWIZ	Colt Clown SS balloon	L. V. Mastis
	G-GWYN	Cessna F.172M	Gwyn Aviation
	G-GYAV	Cessna 172N	Southport & Merseyside Aero Club (1979) Ltd/Liverpool
	G-GYBO	GY-80 Horizon 180	M. J. Strother
	G-GYMM	PA-28R Cherokee Arrow 200	GYMM Group (G-AYWW)
	G-GYRO	Campbell Cricket	J. W. Pavitt
	G-GZDO	Cessna 172N	Cambridge Hall Aviation
	G-HACK	PA-18 Super Cub 150	Intrepid Aviation Co/North Weald
	G-HADA	Enstrom 480	W. B. Steele
	G-HAEC	CAC-18 Mustang 23 (472218)	R. W. Davies/Duxford
	G-HAIG	Rutan LongEz	R. Carey & D. W. Parfrey/Coventry
	G-HAJJ	Glaser-Dirks DG.400	P. W. Endean
	G-HALC	PA-28R Cherokee Arrow 200	Halcyon Aviation Ltd
	G-HALE	Robinson R-44 Astro	Barhale Surveying Ltd
	G-HALJ	Cessna 140	H. A. Lloyd-Jennings
	G-HALL	PA-22 Tri-Pacer 160	F. P. Hall (G-ARAH)
	G-HALO	Elisport CH-7 Angel	Taylor Woodhouse Ltd
	G-HALP	SOCATA TB.10 Tobago	D. H. Halpern (G-BITD)/Elstree
	G-HAMA	Beech 200 Super King Air	Gama Aviation Ltd/Fairoaks

Reg.	Type	Owner or Operator	Notes
G-HAMI	Fuji FA.200-180	S. A. R. Rose & K. G. Cameron (G-OISF/G-BAPT)	
G-HAMP	Bellanca 7ACA Champ	K. MacDonald	
G-HAND	Cameron 105 Startac SS balloon	Redmalt Ltd	
G-HANS	Robin DR.400 2+2	Bagby Aviation	
G-HAPR	B.171 Sycamore HR.14 (XG547) ★	IHM/Weston-s-Mare	
G-HAPY	D.H.C.1 Chipmunk 22A (WP803)	G-HAPY Ltd/Booker	
G-HARE	Cameron N-77 balloon	C. E. & J. Falkingham	
G-HARF	G.1159C Gulfstream 4	Fayair (Jersey) 1984 Ltd	
G-HARH	Sikorsky S-76B	Air Harrods Ltd/Stansted	
G-HARI	X'Air	D. Mahajan	
G-HARO	AS.355F-2 Twin Squirrel	Air Harrods Ltd (G-DAFT/G-BNNN)	
G-HART	Cessna 152 (tailwheel)	Atlantic Air Transport Ltd (G-BPBF)/ Coventry	
G-HARY	Alon A-2 Aircoupe	M. R. Clark (G-ATWP)	
G-HASI	Cessna 421B	C. C. Butt (G-BTDK)	
G-HATZ	Hatz CB-1	S. P. Rollason	
G-HAUL	Westland WG.30 Srs 300 ★	IHM/Weston-super-Mare	
G-HAUS	Hughes 369HM	Autohaus Ltd (G-KBOT/G-RAMM)	
G-HAZE	Thunder Ax8-90 balloon	T. G. Church	
G-HBBC	D.H.104 Dove 8	BBC Air Ltd (G-ALFM)	
G-HBMW	Robinson R-22	J. Anderson (G-BOFA)	
G-HBUG	Cameron N-90 balloon	R. T. & H. Revel (G-BRCN)	
G-HCFR	BAe 125 Srs 800B	Chauffair (CI) Ltd (G-SHEA/G-BUWC)	
G-HCSL	PA-34-220T Seneca III	Colony Aviation	
G-HDEW	PA-32R-301 Saratoga SP	Lord Howard de Walden (G-BRGZ)	
G-HDIX	Enstrom 280FX	J. Poupard	
G-HDPP	Eurocopter EC.135T-1	McAlpine Helicopters Ltd (G-HDDP)	
G-HEAD	Colt Flying Head SS balloon	E. K. Nyberg/Sweden	
G-HEBE	Bell 206B JetRanger 3	MGGR (UK) Ltd	
G-HELE	Bell 206B JetRanger 3	B. E. E. Smith (G-OJFR)	
G-HELN	PA-18 Super Cub 95	J. J. Anziani (G-BKDG)/Booker	
G-HELV	D.H.115 Vampire T.55 (215)	Hunter Wing Ltd/Bournemouth	
G-HEMS	SA.365N Dauphin 2	Virgin Executive Aviation Ltd	
G-HENS	Cameron N-65 balloon	Harrells Dairies Ltd	
G-HENY	Cameron V-77 balloon	R. S. D'Alton	
G-HERB	PA-28R-201 Arrow III	Appleton Aviation Ltd	
G-HERO	PA-32RT-300 Lance II	Air Alize Communication (G-BOGN)/ Stapleford	
G-HERS	Cessna750 Citation X	Red Aviation Services Ltd	
G-HEWI	Piper J-3C-90 Cub	Denham Grasshopper Group (G-BLEN)	
G-HEWS	Hughes 369D ★	Spares' use/Sywell	
G-HEYY	Cameron 72 Bear SS balloon	L. V. Mastis	
G-HFBM	Curtiss Robin C-2	D. M. Forshaw	
G-HFCA	Cessna A.150L	Horizon Flying Club Ltd	
G-HFCB	Cessna F.150L	Horizon Flying Club Ltd (G-AZVR)	
G-HFCI	Cessna F.150L	Horizon Flying Club Ltd	
G-HFCL	Cessna F.152	Horizon Flying Club Ltd (G-BGLR)	
G-HFCT	Cessna F.152	Stapleford Flying Club Ltd	
G-HFIX	V.S.361 Spitfire HF.IXe (MJ730)	D. W. Pennell (G-BLAS)	
G-HFLA	Schweizer 269C	Sterling Helicopters Ltd/Norwich	
G-HFTG	PA-23 Aztec 250E	Hawkair (G-BSOB/G-BCJR)	
G-HGAS	Cameron N-77 balloon	N. J. Tovey	
G-HGPI	SOCATA TB.20 Trinidad	M. J. Jackson/Bournemouth	
G-HIBM	Cameron N-145 balloon	Dragonfly Balloons	
G-HIEL	Robinson R-22B	Hields Aviation/Sherburn	
G-HIII	Extra EA.300	Firebird Aerobatics Ltd/Booker	
G-HILO	R. Commander 114	F. H. Parkes	
G-HILS	Cessna F.172H	Lowdon Aviation Group (G-AWCH)	
G-HILT	SOCATA TB.10 Tobago	Insight Marketing & Communications Ltd	
G-HIND	Maule MT-7-235	R. G. Humphries	
G-HIPE	Sorrell SNS-7 Hiperbipe	T. A. S. Rayner/Glenrothes	
G-HIPO	Robinson R-22B	Fleet Street Travel Ltd (G-BTGB)	
G-HIRE	GA-7 Cougar	London Aerial Tours Ltd (G-BGSZ)/ Biggin Hill	
G-HISS	Aerotek Pitts S-2A Special	L. V. Adams & J. Maffia (G-BLVU)/ Panshanger	
G-HIUP	Cameron A-250 balloon	Bridges Van Hire Ltd	
G-HIVA	Cessna 337A	G. J. Banfield (G-BAES)	
G-HIVE	Cessna F.150M	M. P. Lynn (G-BCXT)/Sibson	
G-HJSS	AIA Stampe SV-4C (modified)	H. J. Smith (G-AZNF)	
G-HKHM	Hughes 369B	Heli Air Ltd	

Notes	Reg.	Type	Owner or Operator
	G-HKIT	BAC One-Eleven 521FH	European Aviation Ltd
	G-HLAA	Airbus A.300B4-203F	HeavyLift Cargo Airlines Ltd
	G-HLAB	Airbus A.300B4-203F	HeavyLift Cargo Airlines Ltd
	G-HLAC	Airbus A.300B4-203F	HeavyLift Cargo Airlines Ltd
	G-HLCF	Starstreak Shadow	S. M. E. Solomon
	G-HLEN	AS.350B Ecureuil	N. Edmonds (G-LOLY)
	G-HLFT	SC.5 Belfast 2	HeavyLift Cargo Airlines Ltd/Stansted
	G-HMBJ	R. Commander 114B	B. A. Groves
	G-HMED	PA-28-161 Warrior III	H. Faizal
	G-HMES	PA-28-161 Warrior II	Cleveland Flying School Ltd/Teesside
	G-HMJB	PA-34-220T Seneca III	Cross Atlantic Ventures Ltd
	G-HMPH	Bell 206B JetRanger 2	Mightycraft Ltd (G-BBUY)
	G-HMPT	AB-206B JetRanger 2	S. & M. L. Lee
	G-HNRY	Cessna 650 Citation VI	Quantel Ltd/Biggin Hill
	G-HNTR	Hawker Hunter T.7 (XL572) ★	Yorkshire Air Museum/Elvington
	G-HOBO	Denney Kitfox Mk 4	P. Caton
	G-HOCK	PA-28 Cherokee 180	Arabact Ltd (G-AVSH)
	G-HOFC	Shaw Europa	J. W. Lang
	G-HOFM	Cameron N-56 balloon	L. V. Mastis
	G-HOGS	Cameron 90 Pig SS balloon	Flying Pictures Ltd
	G-HOHO	Colt Santa Claus SS balloon	Oxford Promotions (UK) Ltd/USA
	G-HOLY	ST.10 Diplomate	M. K. Barsham
	G-HOME	Colt 77A balloon	Anglia Balloon School Tardis
	G-HONG	Slingsby T.67M-200	Hunting Aviation Ltd
	G-HONK	Cameron O-105 balloon	T. F. W. Dixon & Son Ltd
	G-HONY	Lilliput Type 1 Srs A balloon	A. E. & D. E. Thomas
	G-HOOV	Cameron N-56 balloon	H. R. Evans
	G-HOPE	Beech F33A Bonanza	Hurn Aviation Ltd
	G-HOPI	Cameron N-42 balloon	Ballonwerbung Hamburg GmbH/ Germany
	G-HOPS	Thunder Ax8-90 balloon	A. C. & B. Munn
	G-HOPY	Van's RV-6A	R. C. Hopkinson
	G-HORN	Cameron V-77 balloon	S. Herd
	G-HOST	Cameron N-77 balloon	D. Grimshaw
	G-HOTI	Colt 77A balloon	R. Ollier
	G-HOTT	Cameron O-120 balloon	D. L. Smith
	G-HOTZ	Colt 77B balloon	C. J. & S. M. Davies
	G-HOUS	Colt 31A balloon	Anglia Balloons Ltd
	G-HOWE	Thunder Ax7-77 balloon	M. F. Howe
	G-HPAA	BN-2B-26 Islander	Hampshire Police Authority (Air Support Unit) (G-BSWP)
	G-HPSE	Commander 114B	Al Nisr Ltd
	G-HPSM	Commander 114TC	Fifth Floor Aviation Services Europe Ltd
	G-HPUX	Hawker Hunter T.7 (XL587)	Classic Aviation Ltd/Duxford
	G-HPWH	Agusta A.109E	Aviation Partnership (G-HWPH)
	G-HRHE	Robinson R-22B	R. H. Everett (G-BTWP)
	G-HRHI	B.206 Srs 1 Basset (XS770)	Lawgra (No.386) Ltd/Cranfield
	G-HRHS	Robinson R-44 Astro	Stratus Aviation Ltd/Hong Kong
	G-HRIO	Robin HR.100/120	T. W. Evans
	G-HRLK	SAAB 91D/2 Safir	Sylmar Aviation & Services Ltd (G-BRZY)
	G-HRLM	Brügger MB.2 Colibri	S. J. Perkins & D. Dobson
	G-HRNT	Cessna 182S	Dingle Star Ltd
	G-HROI	R. Commander 112A	Intereuropean Aviation Ltd
	G-HRON	D.H.114 Heron 2 (XR442)	M. E. R. Coghlan (G-AORH)
	G-HRVD	CCF Harvard IV	J. K. Avis (G-BSBC)
	G-HRZN	Colt 77A balloon	A. J. Spindler
	G-HSDW	Bell 206B JetRanger	Winfield Shoe Co Ltd
	G-HSFT	PA-44-180 Seminole	Magenta Ltd
	G-HSOO	Hughes 369HE	Edwards Aviation (G-BFYJ)
	G-HSTH	Lindstrand LBL HS-110 balloon	Ballonsport Helmut Seitz/Germany
	G-HTAX	PA-31-350 Navajo Chieftain	Hadagain Investments Ltd
	G-HTPS	SA. 341G Gazelle 1	J. Malcolm (G-BRNI)
	G-HTVI	Cameron N-90 balloon	HTV Group PLC (G-PRIT)
	G-HUBB	Partenavia P.68B	G-HUBB Ltd
	G-HUCH	Cameron 80 Carrots SS balloon	L. V. Mastis (G-BYPS)
	G-HUEY	Bell UH-1H	Butane Buzzard Aviation Corporation Ltd
	G-HUFF	Cessna 182P	A. E. G. Cousins
	G-HUGG	Learjet 35A	1427 Ltd
	G-HUGO	Colt 240A balloon	P. G. Hall
	G-HULL	Cessna F.150M	A. D. McLeod
	G-HUMF	Robinson R-22B	Plane Talking Ltd/Elstree
	G-HUNI	Bellanca 7GCBC Scout	T. I. M. Paul

Reg.	Type	Owner or Operator	Notes
G-HUNK	Lindstrand LBL-77A balloon	Lindstrand Balloons Ltd	
G-HUNY	Cessna F.150G	M. P. Lynn (G-AVGL)	
G-HURI	CCF Hawker Hurricane XIIA (Z7381)	Patina Ltd/Duxford	
G-HURN	Robinson R-22B	Coventry Helicopter Centre Ltd	
G-HURR	Hawker Hurricane XIIB (BE417)	R. A. Fleming/Brighton	
G-HURY	Hawker Hurricane IV (KZ321)	Patina Ltd/Duxford	
G-HUTT	Denney Kitfox Mk 2	D. Watt	
G-HVAN	RL-5A LW Sherwood Ranger	H. T. H. van Neck	
G-HVBF	Lindstrand LBL-210A balloon	Virgin Balloon Flights Ltd	
G-HVDM	V.S.361 Spitfire F.IX (MK732)	Nostalgic Flying/Netherlands	
G-HVIP	Hawker Hunter T.68	Golden Europe Jet De Luxe Club Ltd/Bournemouth	
G-HVRD	PA-31-350 Navajo Chieftain	London Flight Centre (Stansted) Ltd (G-BEZU)	
G-HWKR	Colt 90A balloon	P. A. Henderson	
G-HYHY	PA-46-350P Malibu Mirage	Longslow Dairy Ltd	
G-HYLT	PA-32R-301 Saratoga SP	H. Young Transport Ltd	
G-HYST	Enstrom 280FX	Ocean Shields Ltd	
G-IAFT	Cessna 152 II	Marnham Investments Ltd	
G-IAGD	Robinson R-22B	Ramsgill Aviation Ltd	
G-IAMP	Cameron H-34 balloon	Virgin Airship & Balloon Co Ltd	
G-IANG	Bell 206L LongRanger	Lothian Helicopters Ltd	
G-IANJ	Cessna F.150K	B. Murelli (G-AXVW)	
G-IARC	Stoddard-Hamilton Glastar	A. A. Craig	
G-IASL	Beech 60 Duke	Applied Sweepers Ltd (G-SING)	
G-IBBC	Cameron 105 Sphere SS balloon	Virgin Airship & Balloon Co Ltd	
G-IBBO	PA-28-181 Archer II	M. Gibbon	
G-IBBS	Shaw Europa	R. H. Gibbs	
G-IBED	Robinson R-22A	Brian Seedle Helicopters (G-BMHN)	
G-IBET	Cameron 70 Can SS balloon	M. R. Humphrey & J. R. Clifton	
G-IBFC	BFC Challenger II	K. N. Dickinson	
G-IBFW	PA-28R-201 Arrow III	A. W. Collett	
G-IBHH	Hughes 269C	Biggin Hill Helicopters (G-BSCD)	
G-IBRO	Cessna F.152 II	Leicestershire Aero Club Ltd	
G-IBZS	Cessna 185S	Oxford Aviation Services Ltd/Kidlington	
G-ICAB	Robinson R-44 Astro	J. R. Clark Ltd	
G-ICAS	Pitts S-2B Special	J. C. Smith	
G-ICCL	Robinson R-22B	G. Kidger (G-ORZZ)	
G-ICES	Thunder Ax6-56 balloon	British Balloon Museum & Library Ltd	
G-ICEY	Lindstrand LBL-77A balloon	G. C. Elson/Spain	
G-ICFR	BAe 125 Srs 800A	Chauffair (CI) Ltd (G-BUCR)/ Farnborough	
G-ICKY	Lindstrand LBL-77A balloon	Blown Away UK Ltd	
G-ICOI	Lindstrand LBL-105A balloon	Virgin Airship & Balloon Co Ltd	
G-ICOM	Cessna F.172M	T. J. & P. S. Nicholson (G-BFXI)	
G-ICOZ	Lindstrand LBL-105A balloon	Virgin Airship & Balloon Co Ltd	
G-ICSG	AS.355F-1 Twin Squirrel	MW Helicopters Ltd (G-PAMI/G-BUSA)	
G-IDAY	Skyfox CA-25N Gazelle	The Anglo-Pacific Aircraft Co & G. Horne	
G-IDDI	Cameron N-77 balloon	Allen & Harris Ltd	
G-IDEA	AA-5A Cheetah	Lowlog Ltd (G-BGNO)	
G-IDII	DR.107 One Design	C. Darlow	
G-IDUP	Enstrom 280C Shark	Antique Buildings Ltd (G-BRZF)	
G-IDWR	Hughes 369HS	Copley Electrical Contractors (G-AXEJ)	
G-IEJH	Jodel 150A	E. J. Horsfall (G-BPAM)/Blackpool	
G-IEYE	Robin DR. 400/180	E. Hopper	
G-IFAB	Cessna F.182Q	Chatham Glyn Fabrics Ltd	
G-IFFR	PA-32 Cherokee Six 300	D. J. D. Ritchie & ptnrs (G-BWVO)	
G-IFIT	PA-31-350 Navajo Chieftain	Dart Group PLC (G-NABI/ G-MARG)/Bournemouth	
G-IFLI	AA-5A Cheetah	ABC Aviation Ltd	
G-IFLP	PA-34-200T Seneca II	AD Aviation Ltd	
G-IFTC	H.S.125 Srs F3B/RA	Albion Aviation Management Ltd (G-OPOL/G-BXPU/G-IBIS/G-AXPU)	
G-IFTE	H.S.125 Srs 700B	Albion Aviation Management Ltd (G-BFVI)	
G-IFTS	Robinson R-44 Astro	Colony Aviation	
G-IGEL	Cameron N-90 balloon	Computacenter Ltd	
G-IGGL	SOCATA TB-10 Tobago	M. P. & J. S. Perkin (G-BYDC)/ White Waltham	
G-IGHH	Enstrom 480	G. H. Harding	
G-IGLA	Colt 240A balloon	Heart of England Balloons	

Notes	Reg.	Type	Owner or Operator
	G-IGLE	Cameron V-90 balloon	A. A. Laing
	G-IGOA	Boeing 737-3Y0	Go-Fly Ltd/Stansted
	G-IGOC	Boeing 737-3Y0	Go-Fly Ltd/Stansted
	G-IGOE	Boeing 737-3Y0	Go-Fly Ltd/Stansted
	G-IGOF	Boeing 737-3Q8	Go-Fly Ltd/Stansted
	G-IGOG	Boeing 737-3Y0	Go-Fly Ltd/Stansted
	G-IGOH	Boeing 737-3Y0	Go-Fly Ltd/Stansted
	G-IGOI	Boeing 737-33A	Go-Fly Ltd (G-OBMD)/Stansted
	G-IGOJ	Boeing 737-36N	Go-Fly Ltd/Stansted
	G-IGOK	Boeing 737-36N	Go-Fly Ltd/Stansted
	G-IGOL	Boeing 737-36N	Go-Fly Ltd/Stansted
	G-IGOM	Boeing 737-36N	Go-Fly Ltd/Stansted
	G-IGOP	Boeing 737-36N	Go-Fly Ltd/Stansted
	G-IGOR	Boeing 737-36N	Go-Fly Ltd/Stansted
	G-IGPW	Eurocopter EC.120B	Helihopper Ltd (G-CBRI)
	G-IHSB	Robinson R-22B	M. Walker
	G-IIAC	Aeronca 11AC Chief	P. K. Sheppard & ptnrs (G-BTPY)
	G-IIAN	Aero Designs Pulsar	I. G. Harrison
	G-IICM	Extra EA.300/L	Phonetiques Ltd
	G-IIFR	Robinson R-22B	Sloane Helicopters Ltd/Sywell
	G-IIIG	Boeing Stearman A.75N1	Aerosuperbatics Ltd (4) (G-BSDR)/Rendcomb
	G-IIIH	BAC One-Eleven 518FG	European Aviation Ltd (G-AXMF)
	G-IIII	Aerotek Pitts S-2B Special	B. K. Lecomber
	G-IIIL	Pitts S-1T Special	I. T. Dall
	G-IIIR	Pitts S-1S Special	R. O. Rogers
	G-IIIT	Aerotek Pitts S-2A Special	Aerobatic Displays Ltd
	G-IIIV	Pitts Super Stinker 11-260	A. N. R. Houghton
	G-IIIX	Pitts S-1S Special	G. C. J. Cooper (G-LBAT/G-UCCI/G-BIYN)
	G-IIPM	AS.350B Ecureuil	Fly West Aviation Ltd (G-GWIL)
	G-IIRG	Stoddard-Hamilton Glasair IIRGS	D. S. Watson
	G-IITI	Extra EA.300	Aerobatic Displays Ltd/Booker
	G-IIXX	Parsons 2-seat gyroplane	J. M. Montgomerie
	G-IIZI	Extra EA.300	11-21 Flying Group
	G-IJAC	Light Aero Avid Speedwing Mk 4	I. J. A. Charlton
	G-IJBB	Enstrom 480	Southern Air Ltd (G-LIVA/G-PBTT)
	G-IJJB	Beech B200 Super King Air	JJB Sports Ltd (G-BMVY)
	G-IJMC	VPM M.16 Tandem Trainer	I. J. McTear (G-POSA/G-BVJM)
	G-IJOE	PA-28RT-201T Turbo Arrow IV	R. P. Wilson
	G-IJYS	BAe Jetstream 3102	Air Kilroe Ltd (G-BTZT)
	G-IKAP	Cessna T.303	T. M. Beresford
	G-IKBP	PA-28-161 Warrior II	K. B. Page
	G-IKIS	Cessna 210M	A. C. Davison
	G-IKPS	PA-31-310 Navajo C	Channel Aviation Ltd
	G-ILEA	PA-31-310 Navajo C	K. Payne
	G-ILEE	Colt 56A balloon	G. I. Lindsay
	G-ILES	Cameron O-90 balloon	G. N. Lantos
	G-ILLE	Boeing Stearman A.75L3 (379)	J. Griffin
	G-ILLY	PA-28-181 Archer II	A. G. & K. M. Spiers
	G-ILSE	Corby CJ-1 Starlet	S. Stride
	G-ILTS	PA-32 Cherokee Six 300	P. G. Teasdale (G-CVOK)
	G-ILYS	Robinson R-22B	Thurston Helicopters (Engineering) Ltd
	G-IMAG	Colt 77A balloon	Flying Pictures Ltd
	G-IMAN	Colt 31A balloon	Benedikt Haggeney GmbH/Germany
	G-IMBY	Pietenpol Air Camper	P. F. Bockh
	G-IMGL	Beech B200 Super King Air	IM Aviation Ltd
	G-IMLI	Cessna 310Q	M. V. Rijkse & N. M. R. Richards (G-AZYK)
	G-IMOK	Hoffmann HK-36R Super Dimona	A. L. Garfield
	G-IMPX	R. Commander 112B	T. L. & S. Hull
	G-IMPY	Light Aero Avid Flyer C	T. R. C. Griffin
	G-IMVA	PA-28-181 Archer III	IMVA Holdings Ltd
	G-INAV	Aviation Composites Mercury	I. Shaw
	G-INCA	Glaser-Dirks DG.400	J. S. Wand
	G-INCH	Montgomerie-Bensen B.8MR	I. H. C. Branson (G-BRES)
	G-INDC	Cessna T.303	Godolphin Management Co Ltd
	G-INDY	Robinson R-44 Astro	Reynard Racing Cars Ltd
	G-INGA	Thunder Ax8-84 balloon	M. L. J. Ritchie
	G-INGE	Thruster T.600N	Thruster Air Services Ltd
	G-INGR	Cessna F.150J	R. M. Hughes & A. M. Duffill (G-AWXU)
	G-INKS	Robinson R-22B	The Ink Shop Printing & Colour Copy Ltd
	G-INNI	Jodel D.112	R. G. Andrews

Reg.	Type	Owner or Operator	Notes
G-INNY	SE-5A (replica) (F5459)	K. S. Matcham	
G-INOW	Monnett Moni	W. C. Brown	
G-INSR	Cameron N-90 balloon	M. J. Betts & The Smith & Pinching Group	
G-INVU	AB-206B JetRanger 2	Burman Aviation Ltd (G-XXII/G-GGCC/G-BEHG)	
G-IOCO	Beech 58 Baron	Sea & Air Charter Ltd	
G-IOIO	Bell 206B JetRanger 3	Lynton Air Ltd/Denham	
G-IOOI	Robin DR.400/160	N. B. Mason & S. J. O'Rourke	
G-IOPT	Cessna 182P	M. J. Valentine & P. R. Davis	
G-IOSI	Jodel DR.1051	Sicile Flying Group	
G-IOWE	Shaw Europa XS	P. A. Lowe	
G-IPSI	Grob G.109B	G-IPSI Ltd (G-BMLO)	
G-IPSY	Rutan Vari-Eze	R. A. Fairclough/Biggin Hill	
G-IPUP	B.121 Pup 2	M. Sowerby/Elstree	
G-IRAF	RAF 2000 GTX-SE gyroplane	M. S. R. Allen	
G-IRAN	Cessna 152	E. Alexander	
G-IRIS	AA-5B Tiger	Carlisle Flight Centre (G-BIXU)	
G-IRLY	Colt 90A balloon	S. A. Burnett & L. P. Purfield	
G-IROY	Rotorway Executive RW-152	R. R. Orr	
G-IRPC	Cessna 182Q	Barmoor Aviation (G-BSKM)	
G-ISCA	PA-28RT-201 Arrow IV	D. J. & P. Pay	
G-ISDB	PA-28-161 Warrior II	Action Air Services Ltd (G-BWET)	
G-ISDN	Boeing Stearman A.75N1	D. R. L. Jones	
G-ISEH	Cessna 182R	Hadsley Ltd (G-BIWS)	
G-ISFC	PA-31-310 Turbo Navajo B	SFC (Air Taxis) Ltd (G-BNEF)	
G-ISIS	D.H.82A Tiger Moth	D. R. & M. Wood (G-AODR)	
G-ISKY	Bell 206B JetRanger 3	Kwik-Fit (GB) Ltd (G-PSCI/G-BOKD)	
G-ISLA	BN-2A-26 Islander	Hoe Leasing Ltd (G-BNEA)	
G-ISMO	Robinson R-22B	Hields Aviation	
G-ISTT	Thunder Ax8-84 balloon	RAF Halton Hot Air Balloon Club	
G-ITII	Aerotech Pitts S-2A Special	Aerobatic Displays Ltd	
G-ITON	Maule MX-7-235	J. R. S. Heaton	
G-IUAN	Cessna 525 CitationJet	R. F. Celada SPA/Italy	
G-IVAC	Airtour AH-77B balloon	T. D. Gibbs	
G-IVAN	Shaw TwinEze	A. M. Aldridge	
G-IVAR	Yakovlev Yak-50	Foley Farm Flying Group	
G-IVEL	Fournier RF-4D	V. S. E. Norman (G-AVNY)/Rendcomb	
G-IVET	Shaw Europa	K. J. Fraser	
G-IVIV	Robinson R-44 Astro	Rahtol Ltd	
G-IVOR	Aeronca 11AC Chief	South Western Aeronca Group/Plymouth	
G-IWON	Cameron V-90 balloon	D. P. P. Jenkinson (G-BTCV)	
G-IYAK	Yakovlev C-11	E. K. Coventry/Earls Colne	
G-IZIT	Rans S.6-ESD Coyote II	C. Wren	
G-IZZS	Cessna 172S	Rankart Ltd	
G-IZZY	Cesna 172R	T. J. & P. S. Nicholson (G-BXSF)	
G-JABA	Jabiru SK	A. P. Gornall	
G-JACK	Cessna 421C	JCT 600 Ltd	
G-JACO	Jabiru UL	S. Jackson	
G-JACS	PA-28-181 Archer III	Vector Air Ltd	
G-JADJ	PA-28-181 Archer III	D. J. Cooke	
G-JAHL	Bell 206B JetRanger 3	Jet Air Helicopters	
G-JAJK	PA-31-350 Navajo Chieftain	Keen Leasing (IOM) Ltd (G-OLDB/G-DIXI)	
G-JAKE	D.H.C.1 Chipmunk 22	K. Ritter (G-BBMY)	
G-JAKI	Mooney M.20R	A. Pound	
G-JAKS	PA-28 Cherokee 160	M. & K. Harper (G-ARVS)	
G-JALC	Boeing 757-225	Airtours International Airways Ltd	
G-JAMP	PA-28-151 Warrior	ANP Ltd (G-BRJU)/White Waltham	
G-JANA	PA-28-181 Archer II	Croaker Aviation/Stapleford	
G-JANB	Colt Flying Bottle SS balloon	Justerini & Brooks Ltd	
G-JANI	Robinson R-44 Astro	Myraluck Transport Ltd	
G-JANK	PA-E23 Aztec 250C	Liverpool Flying School Ltd (G-ATCY)	
G-JANN	PA-34-220T Seneca III	MBC Aviation Ltd/Headcorn	
G-JANO	PA-28RT-201 Arrow IV	Abertawe Aviation Ltd	
G-JANS	Cessna FR.172J	I. G. Aizlewood/Luton	
G-JANT	PA-28-181 Archer II	Janair Aviation Ltd	
G-JARA	Robinson R-22B	J. A. R. Allwright	
G-JASE	PA-28-161 Warrior II	Mid-Anglia School of Flying	
G-JAVO	PA-28-161 Warrior II	I. N. T. Thornhill (G-BSXW)	
G-JAWZ	Pitts S-1S Special	A. R. Harding	
G-JAXS	Jabiru UL	C. A. Palmer	

Notes	Reg.	Type	Owner or Operator
	G-JAYI	J/1 Autocrat	Bravo Aviation Ltd/Coventry
	G-JAZZ	AA-5A Cheetah	Jazz Club
	G-JBDB	AB-206B JetRanger	Brad Helicopters Ltd (G-OOPS/G-BNRD)
	G-JBDH	Robin DR.400/180	W. A. Clark
	G-JBJB	Colt 69A balloon	Justerini & Brooks Ltd
	G-JBPR	Wittman W.10 Tailwind	P. A. Rose & J. P. Broadhurst
	G-JBRN	Cessna 182S	J. Byrne (G-RITZ)
	G-JBSP	Jabiru SP	C. R. James
	G-JCAR	PA-46-350P Malibu Mirage	Anglo American Airmotive Ltd
	G-JCAS	PA-28-181 Archer II	Charlie Alpha Ltd
	G-JCBA	Sikorsky S-76B	J. C. Bamford Excavators Ltd/ E. Midlands
	G-JCBG	Dassault Falcon 900EX	J. C. Bamford Excavators Ltd/ E. Midlands
	G-JCBI	Dassault Falcon 2000	J. C. Bamford Excavators Ltd/ E. Midlands
	G-JCBJ	Sikorsky S-76C	J. C. Bamford Excavators Ltd/ E. Midlands
	G-JCFR	Cessna 550 Citation II	Chauffair Ltd (G-JETC)/Gatwick
	G-JCKT	Stemme S.10VT	J. C. Taylor
	G-JCMW	Rand KR-2	M. Wildish & J. Cook
	G-JCUB	PA-18 Super Cub 135	Piper Cub Consortium Ltd/Jersey
	G-JDEE	SOCATA TB.20 Trinidad	JDEE Group (G-BKLA)
	G-JDEL	Jodel 150	K. F. & R. Richardson (G-JDLI)
	G-JDIX	Mooney M.20B	ADH Ltd (G-ARTB)
	G-JDTI	Cessna 421C	MCP Aviation (Charter) Ltd
	G-JEAD	F.27 Friendship Mk 500	BAC Leasing Ltd
	G-JEAE	F.27 Friendship Mk 500	BAC Leasing Ltd
	G-JEAH	F.27 Friendship Mk 500	Jersey European Airways Ltd
	G-JEAI	F.27 Friendship Mk 500	Jersey European Airways Ltd
	G-JEAJ	BAe 146-200	Jersey European Airways (UK) Ltd (G-OLCA) Pride of Guernsey
	G-JEAK	BAe 146-200	Jersey European Airways (UK) Ltd (G-OLCB)
	G-JEAM	BAe 146-300	Jersey European Airways (UK) Ltd/ Air France (G-BTJT)
	G-JEAO	BAe 146-100	Jersey European Airways Ltd/Air France (G-UKPC/G-BKXZ)
	G-JEAP	F.27 Friendship Mk 500	Channel Express (Air Services) Ltd
	G-JEAR	BAe 146-200	Jersey European Airways (UK) Ltd (G-HWPB/G-BSRU/G-OSKI)
	G-JEAS	BAe 146-200	Jersey European Airways (UK) Ltd/Air France (G-OLHB/G-BSRV/G-OSUN)
	G-JEAT	BAe 146-100	Jersey European Airways Ltd/Air France (G-BVUY)
	G-JEAU	BAe 146-100	Jersey European Airways Ltd/Air France (G-BVUW)
	G-JEAV	BAe 146-200	Jersey European Airways (UK) Ltd
	G-JEAW	BAe 146-200	Jersey European Airways (UK) Ltd
	G-JEAX	BAe 146-200	Jersey European Airways (UK) Ltd
	G-JEBA	BAe 146-300	Jersey European Airways (UK) Ltd (G-BSYR)
	G-JEBB	BAe 146-300	Jersey European Airways (UK) Ltd/ Air France
	G-JEBC	BAe 146-300	Jersey European Airways (UK) Ltd
	G-JEBD	BAe 146-300	Jersey European Airways (UK) Ltd
	G-JEBE	BAe 146-300	Jersey European Airways (UK) Ltd
	G-JECA	Canadair CL.600-2B19 RJ	Jersey European Airways (UK) Ltd/ Air France
	G-JECB	Canadair CL.600-2B19 RJ	Jersey European Airways (UK) Ltd
	G-JECC	Canadair CL.600-2B19 RJ	Jersey European Airways (UK) Ltd
	G-JEDA	D.H.C.8-314 Dash Eight	Jersey European Airways (UK) Ltd
	G-JEDB	D.H.C.8-314 Dash Eight	Jersey European Airways (UK) Ltd
	G-JEDC	D.H.C.8Q-311 Dash Eight	Jersey European Airways (UK) Ltd
	G-JEDD	D.H.C.8Q-311 Dash Eight	Jersey European Airways (UK) Ltd
	G-JEDE	D.H.C.8Q-311 Dash Eight	Jersey European Airways (UK) Ltd
	G-JEDF	D.H.C.8Q-311 Dash Eight	Jersey European Airways (UK) Ltd
	G-JEDG	D.H.C.8Q-400 Dash Eight	Jersey European Airways (UK) Ltd
	G-JEDH	Robin DR.400/180	J. B. Hoolahan/Biggin Hill
	G-JEDI	D.H.C.8Q-400 Dash Eight	Jersey European Airways (UK) Ltd
	G-JEDJ	D.H.C.8Q-400 Dash Eight	Jersey European Airways (UK) Ltd
	G-JEDX	D.H.C.8Q-200 Dash Eight	Jersey European Airways (UK) Ltd
	G-JEDY	D.H.C.8Q-200 Dash Eight	Jersey European Airways (UK) Ltd

Reg.	Type	Owner or Operator	Notes
G-JEDZ	D.H.C.8Q-200 Dash Eight	Jersey European Airways (UK) Ltd	
G-JEET	Cessna FA.152	Luton Flight Training (G-BHMF)	
G-JEFF	PA-38-112 Tomahawk	R. J. Alford	
G-JEFS	PA-28R-201T Turbo Arrow III	Barneyline Ltd (G-BFDG)	
G-JEKP	AB-206B JetRanger 3	K. Payne (G-ESAL/G-BHXW)	
G-JENA	Mooney M.20K	P. Leverkuehn/Biggin Hill	
G-JENI	Cessna R.182	R. A. Bentley	
G-JENN	AA-5B Tiger	Shadow Aviation	
G-JERS	Robinson R-22B	Preveda Ltd	
G-JESS	PA-28R-201T Turbo Arrow III	N. E. & M. A. Bedggood (G-REIS)	
G-JETG	Learjet 35A	Gama Aviation Ltd (G-JETN/G-JJSG)	
G-JETH	Hawker Sea Hawk FGA.6 (XE489) ★	P. G. Vallance Ltd/Charlwood	
G-JETI	BAe 125 Srs 800B	Ford Motor Co Ltd/Stansted	
G-JETJ	Cessna 550 Citation II	Widehawk Aviation Ltd (G-EJET/ G-DJBE)	
G-JETM	Gloster Meteor T.7 (VZ638) ★	P. G. Vallance Ltd/Charlwood	
G-JETU	AS.355F-2 Twin Squirrel	Helimand Ltd	
G-JETX	Bell 206B JetRanger 3	Tripgate Ltd	
G-JETZ	Hughes 369E	John Matchett Ltd	
G-JFWI	Cessna F.172N	Staryear Ltd	
G-JGMN	C.A.S.A. 1.131E Jungmann 2000	P. D. Scandrett/Staverton	
G-JGSI	Pegasus Quantum 15-912	J. G. Spinks	
G-JHAS	Schweizer 269C	Barton & Co (Farmers) Ltd	
G-JHEW	Robinson R-22B	Burbage Farms Ltd	
G-JIII	Stolp SA.300 Starduster Too	VTIO Co/Cumbernauld	
G-JILL	R. Commander 112TCA	Westcroft American Motorhomes Ltd	
G-JIMB	B.121 Pup 1	K. D. H. Gray & P. G. Fowler (G-AWWF)	
G-JIMW	AB-206B JetRanger 2	R. J. Watt (G-UNIK/G-TPPH/G-BCYP)	
G-JJAN	PA-28-181 Archer II	Redhill Flying Club	
G-JLCA	PA-34-200T Seneca II	C. A. S. Atha (G-BOKE)	
G-JLEE	AB-206B JetRanger 3	Lee Aviation Ltd (G-JOKE/G-CSKY/ G-TALY)	
G-JLHS	Beech A36 Bonanza	I. G. Meredith	
G-JLMW	Cameron V-77 balloon	J. L. McK. Watkins	
G-JLRW	Beech 76 Duchess	Moorfield Developments Ltd/Elstree	
G-JMAC	BAe Jetstream 4100	BAe (Operations) Ltd (G-JAMD/G-JXLI)	
G-JMDI	Schweizer 269C	J. J. Potter (G-FLAT)	
G-JMTS	Robin DR.400/180	J. R. Whiting	
G-JMTT	PA-28R-201T Turbo Arrow III	C. E. Passmore (G-BMHM)	
G-JNEE	Cameron R-420 balloon	Bondbaste Ltd	
G-JNNB	Colt 90A balloon	Justerini & Brooks Ltd	
G-JODL	Jodel DR.1050/M	P. A. Marsh	
G-JOEL	Bensen B.8M	G. C. Young	
G-JOEM	Boeing 757-236	Airtours International Airways Ltd	
G-JOEY	BN-2A Mk III-2 Trislander	Aurigny Air Services (G-BDGG)/ Guernsey	
G-JOIN	Cameron V-65 balloon	Derbyshire Building Society	
G-JOJO	Cameron A-210 balloon	Worcester Balloons	
G-JOLY	Cessna 120	B. V. Meade	
G-JONB	Robinson R-22B	J. Bignall	
G-JONE	Cessna 172M	A. Pierce	
G-JONH	Robinson R-22B	Scotia Helicopters Ltd	
G-JONI	Cessna FA.152	Euroair Flying Club (G-BFTU)/Cranfield	
G-JONO	Colt 77A balloon	The Sandcliffe Motor Group	
G-JONY	Cyclone AX2000 HKS	A. Parker	
G-JONZ	Cessna 172P	Truman Aviation Ltd/Tollerton	
G-JOON	Cessna 182D	G. Jackson	
G-JOSS	AS.350B Ecureuil	M. Burby (G-WILX/G-RAHM/G-UNIC/ G-COLN/G-BHIV)	
G-JOST	Shaw Europa	J. A. Austin	
G-JOYT	PA-28-181 Archer II	John K. Cathcart Ltd (G-BOVO)	
G-JOYZ	PA-28-181 Archer III	S. W. & J. E. Taylor	
G-JPMA	Jabiru UL	J. P. Metcalfe	
G-JPOT	PA-32R-301 Saratoga SP	S. W. Turley (G-BIYM)	
G-JPRO	P.84 Jet Provost T.5A (XW433)	Ruddington Aviation Ltd	
G-JPTV	P.84 Jet Provost T.5A	M. P. Grimshaw	
G-JPVA	P.84 Jet Provost T.5A (XW289)	T. J. Manna (G-BVXT)/Cranfield	
G-JRBH	Robinson R-22B	B. C. Hunter & ptnrs	
G-JRSL	Agusta A.109E	Perment Ltd	
G-JSAK	Robinson R-22B	Tukair Aircraft Charter	
G-JSAT	BN-2T Turbine Islander	Rhine Army Parachute Centre (G-BVFK)/ Germany	

Notes	Reg.	Type	Owner or Operator
	G-JSJX	Airbus A.321-211	Airtours International Airways Ltd
	G-JSON	Cameron N-105 balloon	Up and Away Ballooning Ltd
	G-JSPC BUBG)/	BN-2T Turbine Islander	Rhine Army Parachute Centre (G-
			Germany
	G-JSSD	H.P.137 Jetstream 3001 ★	Museum of Flight/E. Fortune
	G-JTCA	PA-23 Aztec 250E	J. D. Tighe (G-BBCU)/Sturgate
	G-JTPC	Aeromot AMT.200 Super Ximango	G-JTPC Falcon 3 Group
	G-JTWO	Piper J-2 Cub	A. T. Hooper & C. C. Silk (G-BPZR)
	G-JTYE	Aeronca 7AC Champion	G. D. Horn
	G-JUDE	CEA DR.400/180	R. G. Carrell
	G-JUDI	AT-6D Harvard III (FX301)	A. A. Hodgson
	G-JUDY	AA-5A Cheetah	Plane Talking Ltd/Elstree
	G-JUIN	Cessna 303	M. J. Newman/Denham
	G-JULS	Stemme S.10V	J. P. C. Fuchs
	G-JULU	Cameron V-90 balloon	Datacentre Ltd
	G-JULZ	Shaw Europa	M. Parkin
	G-JUNG	C.A.S.A. 1.131E Jungmann 1000 (E3B-143)	K. H. Wilson/White Waltham
	G-JURE	SOCATA TB.10 Tobago	P. M. Ireland
	G-JURG	R. Commander 114A	Blue Line Trailers
	G-JVBF	Lindstrand LBL-210A balloon	Virgin Balloon Flights Ltd
	G-JVMD	Cessna 172N	C. A. Morris (G-BNTV)
	G-JWBB	Jodel DR.1050	B. F. Baldock (G-LAKI)
	G-JWBI	AB-206B JetRanger 2	J. W. Bonser (Walsall) Ltd (G-RODS/ G-NOEL/G-BCWN)
	G-JWCM	SA Bulldog Srs 120/408	M. L. J. Goff (G-BHXB)
	G-JWDG	AA-5A Cheetah	Lowlog Ltd (G-OCML/G-JAVA)
	G-JWDS	Cessna F.150G	C. R. & S. A. Hardiman (G-AVNB)
	G-JWFT	Robinson R-22B	Giles Bros
	G-JWIV	Jodel DR.1051	C. M. Fitton
	G-JWLS	Bell 206B JetRanger 2	JWL Services (G-BSXE)
	G-KAFE	Cameron N-65 balloon	M. Sarti
	G-KAIR	PA-28-181 Archer II	Belfast Flying Club Ltd
	G-KAMM	Hawker Hurricane XIIA (BW881)	Alpine Deer Group Ltd/New Zealand
	G-KAMP	PA-18 Super Cub 135	E. Alexander & P. R. Edwards
	G-KAOM	Scheibe SF.25C Falke	E. Baker
	G-KAPW	P.56 Provost T.1 (XF603)	T. J. Manna/Cranfield
	G-KARA	Brügger MB.2 Colibri	C. L. Hill (G-BMUI)
	G-KARI	Fuji FA.200-160	I. Mansfield & F. M. Fiore (G-BBRE)
	G-KART	PA-28-161 Warrior II	Newcastle-upon-Tyne Aero Club Ltd
	G-KARY	Fuji FA.200-180AO	Kary-On Flying Group (G-BEYP)
	G-KATA	HOAC Katana DV.20	Total Support Inc (UK) Ltd
	G-KATE	Westland WG.30 Srs 100 ★	(stored)/Yeovil
	G-KATI	Rans S.7 Courier	S. M. & K. E. Hall
	G-KATS	PA-28 Cherokee 140	Airlaunch/Old Buckenham (G-BIRC)
	G-KATT	Cessna 152 II	Aerohire Ltd (G-BMTK)/Halfpenny Green
	G-KAUR	Colt 315A balloon	Balloon Safaris
	G-KAWA	Denney Kitfox Mk 2	T. W. Maton
	G-KAWW	Westland Wasp HAS.1	T. J. Manna/Cranfield
	G-KAXF	Hawker Hunter F.6A (XF515)	T. J. Manna/Cranfield
	G-KAXL	Westland Scout AH.1 (XV140)	T. J. Manna/Cranfield
	G-KBAC	Short SD3-60 Variant 100	Gill Airways Ltd (G-BPXL)
	G-KBKB	Thunder Ax8-90 S2 balloon	G. Boulden
	G-KBPI	PA-28-161 Warrior II	Goodwood Aerodrome & Motor Circuit Ltd (G-BFSZ)
	G-KCIG	Sportavia RF-5B	Deeside Fournier Group
	G-KDET	PA-28-161 Cadet	Rapidspin Ltd/Biggin Hill
	G-KDEY	Scheibe SF.25E Super Falke	Falke Syndicate Wickham House
	G-KDFF	Scheibe SF.25E Super Falke	K. & S. C. A. Dudley
	G-KDIX	Jodel D.9 Bebe	D. J. Wells
	G-KDLN	Zlin Z.37A-2 Cmelak	J. Richards
	G-KEAB	Beech 65-B80 Queen Air ★	Instructional airframe (G-BSSL/ G-BFEP)/Shoreham
	G-KEAC	Beech 65-A80 Queen Air	G-KEAC Flying Group (G-REXY/ G-AVNG)/ Elstree
	G-KEEN	Stolp SA.300 Starduster Too	Sharp Aerobatics Ltd/Lelystad
	G-KEES	PA-28 Cherokee 180	C. N. Ellerbrook
	G-KELC	PA-28 Cherokee 140	P. J. Kelsey (G-AVLT)
	G-KELL	Van's RV-6	J. D. Kelsall
	G-KEMC	Grob G.109	Eye-Fly

Reg.	Type	Owner or Operator	Notes
G-KEMI	PA-28-181 Archer III	K. B. Kempster	
G-KENB	Air Command 503 Commander	K. Brogden	
G-KENI	Rotorway Executive	A. J. Wheatley	
G-KENM	Luscombe 8EF Silvaire	M. G. Waters	
G-KERY	PA-28 Cherokee 180	Seawing Flying Club Ltd (G-ATWO)/ Southend	
G-KEST	Steen Skybolt	G-KEST Syndicate	
G-KEVB	PA-28-181 Archer III	Palmair Ltd	
G-KEVN	Robinson R-22B	Helicopter Training & Hire Ltd (G-BONX)	
G-KEYS	PA-23 Aztec 250F	T. M. Tuke & W. T. McCarter/Eglinton	
G-KEYY	Cameron N-77 balloon	B. N. Trowbridge (G-BORZ)	
G-KFAN	Scheibe SF.25B Falke	R. G. & J. A. Boyes	
G-KFOX	Denney Kitfox	I. R. Lawrence	
G-KFRA	PA-32 Cherokee Six 300	West India Flying Group (G-BGII)	
G-KFZI	KFZ-1 Tigerfalck	L. R. Williams	
G-KGAO	Scheibe SF.25C Falke 1700	Falke 2000 Group	
G-KGMT	AS.355F-1 Twin Squirrel	Police Aviation Services Ltd (G-PASE)	
G-KHRE	M.S.893E Rallye 150SV	D. M. Gale & K. F. Crumplin	
G-KHOM	Aeromot AMT-200 Super Ximango	O. C. Masters & K. M. Haslett	
G-KIMB	Robin DR.340/140	R. M. Kimbell	
G-KIMM	Shaw Europa XS	P. A. D. Clarke	
G-KINE	AA-5A Cheetah	Walsh Aviation	
G-KIRK	Piper J-3C-65 Cub	M. J. Kirk	
G-KISS	Rand KR-2	E. A. Rooney	
G-KITE	PA-28-181 Archer II	L. G. Kennedy	
G-KITF	Denney Kitfox	R. Burgun	
G-KITI	Pitts S-2E Special	B. R. Cornes	
G-KITS	Shaw Europa	Europa Aviation Ltd	
G-KITT	Curtiss P-40M Kittyhawk (43-5802)	Patina Ltd/Duxford	
G-KITY	Denney Kitfox Mk 2	Kitfox KFM Group	
G-KIWI	Cessna 404	Aviation Beauport Ltd (G-BHNI)	
G-KKDL	SOCATA TB.20 Trinidad	M. S. Thompson (G-BSHU)	
G-KKER	Jabiru UL	K. Kerr	
G-KKES	SOCATA TB.20 Trinidad	Polestar Holdings Ltd (G-BTLH)	
G-KLEE	Bell 206B JetRanger 3	Taylor-Ryan Aviation (G-SIZL/G-BOSW)	
G-KNAP	PA-28-161 Warrior II	Newland Aeroleasing Ltd (G-BIUX)	
G-KNOB	Lindstrand LBL-180A balloon	Wye Valley Aviation Ltd	
G-KNOT	P.84 Jet Provost T.3A (XN629)	R. S. Partridge-Hicks (G-BVEG)	
G-KNOW	PA-32 Cherokee Six 300	Hi Fly Ltd	
G-KODA	Cameron O-77 balloon	N. J. Milton	
G-KOFM	Glaser-Dirks DG.600/18M	A. Mossman	
G-KOKL	Hoffmann H-36 Dimona	R. Smith & R. Stembrowicz	
G-KOLB	Kölb Twinstar Mk 3	T. R. Sinclair	
G-KOLI	PZL-110 Koliber 150	D. Sadler	
G-KONE	Rotorway Executive 162F	G. Kresfelder	
G-KONG	Slingsby T.67M-200	Hunting Aviation Ltd	
G-KOOL	D.H.104 Devon C.2 ★	E. Surrey Technical College at Gatton Point, Redhill	
G-KORN	Cameron 70 Berentzen SS balloon	Balloon Preservation Flying Group	
G-KOTA	PA-28-236 Dakota	JF Packaging	
G-KPAO	Robinson R-44 Astro	Avonline Group Ltd (G-SSSS)	
G-KRAY	Robinson R-22HP	Direct Helicopters (Southend) Ltd (G-BOBO)	
G-KRES	Stoddard-Hamilton Glasair IISRG	G. Kresfelder	
G-KRII	Rand KR-2	M. R. Cleveley	
G-KRIS	Maule M5-235C Lunar Rocket	M. Penny	
G-KSFT	PA-23 Aztec 250F	SFT Europe Ltd (G-BLXX/G-PIED)	
G-KSIR	Stoddard-Hamilton Glasair IISRG	R. Cayzer	
G-KSKY	Sky 77-24 balloon	C. R. Kirby	
G-KSVB	PA-24 Comanche 260	J. R. Pettit (G-ENIU/G-AVJU)	
G-KTEE	Cameron V-77 balloon	D. C. & N. P. Bull	
G-KTKT	Sky 260-24 balloon	T. M. Donnelly	
G-KUTU	Quickie Q.2	R. Nash & J. Parkinson	
G-KVBF	Cameron A-340HL balloon	Virgin Balloon Flights Ltd	
G-KWAX	Cessna 182E Skylane	J. E. & V. T. Brewis	
G-KWIK	Partenavia P.68B	ACD Cidra BV/Belgium	
G-KWIP	Shaw Europa	D. Elliott	
G-KWKI	QAC Quickie Q.200	B. M. Jackson	
G-KWLI	Cessna 421C	Golden Eagle Haulage Ltd (G-DARR/ G-BNEZ)	

Notes	Reg.	Type	Owner or Operator
	G-KYAK	Yakovlev Yak C-11	M. Gainza
	G-KYDD	Robinson R-44 Astro	EK Aviation Ltd
	G-KYNG	Aviamilano F.8L Falco Srs 1	A. E. Hutton/North Weald
	G-LABS	Shaw Europa	C. T. H. Pattinson
	G-LACA	PA-28-161 Warrior II	LAC (Enterprises) Ltd/Barton
	G-LACB	PA-28-161 Warrior II	LAC (Enterprises) Ltd/Barton
	G-LACD	PA-28-181 Archer III	Cavok Aviation (G-BYBG)
	G-LACE	Shaw Europa	J. H. Phillingham
	G-LACR	Denney Kitfox	C. M. Rose
	G-LADD	Enstrom 480	Lantway Properties Ltd
	G-LADE	PA-32 Cherokee Six 300E	Telefax 2000 Ltd
	G-LADI	PA-30 Twin Comanche 160	S. H. Eastwood (G-ASOO)
	G-LADS	R. Commander 114	D. F. Soul
	G-LAGR	Cameron N-90 balloon	J. R. Clifton
	G-LAIN	Robinson R-22B	Quay Contracts Ltd
	G-LAIR	Stoddard-Hamilton Glasair IIS	D. L. Swallow
	G-LAKE	Lake LA-250 Renegade	Stanford Ltd
	G-LAMA	SA.315B Lama	PLM Dollar Group Ltd
	G-LAMM	Shaw Europa	S. A Lamb
	G-LAMS	Cessna F.152 II	Rentair Ltd
	G-LANC	Avro 683 Lancaster X (KB889) ★	Imperial War Museum/Duxford
	G-LAND	Robinson R-22B	Helicopter Training & Hire Ltd/Belfast
	G-LANE	Cessna F.172N	G. C. Bantin
	G-LAOL	PA-28RT-201 Arrow IV	Phoenix House Developments Ltd
	G-LAPN	Light Aero Avid Aerobat	R. M. & A. P. Shorter
	G-LARA	Robin DR.400/180	K. D. & C. A. Brackwell
	G-LARE	PA-39 Twin Comanche 160 C/R	Glareways (Neasden) Ltd
	G-LARK	Helton Lark 95	J. Fox
	G-LASR	Stoddard-Hamilton Glasair II	G. Lewis
	G-LASS	Rutan Vari-Eze	S. Roberts/Liverpool
	G-LAST	Cessna 340 II	Last Engineering Ltd (G-UNDY/G-BBNR)
	G-LATK	Robinson R-44 Astro	Holly Aviation Ltd (G-BVMK)
	G-LAVE	Cessna 172R	R. W. & A. M. Glaves (G-BYEV)
	G-LAWS	Sikorsky S-61N Mk.II	Laws Helicopter Ltd (G-BHOF)
	G-LAXY	Everett Srs 3 gyroplane	G. D. Western
	G-LAZA	Lazer Z.200	M. Hammond
	G-LAZL	PA-28-161 Warrior II	Hawk Aero Leasing/Cranfield
	G-LAZR	Cameron O-77 balloon	Laser Civil Engineering Ltd
	G-LAZY	Lindstrand Armchair SS balloon	The Air Chair Co. Ltd/USA
	G-LAZZ	Stoddard-Hamilton Glastar	A. P. Hinchcliffe
	G-LBCS	Colt 31A balloon	Virgin Airship & Balloon Co Ltd
	G-LBLI	Lindstrand LBL-105A balloon	Lindstrand Balloons Ltd
	G-LBMM	PA-28-161 Warrior II	Flexi-Soft Ltd
	G-LBNK	Cameron N-105 balloon	Virgin Airship & Balloon Co. Ltd
	G-LBRC	PA-28RT-201 Arrow IV	D. J. V. Morgan
	G-LCGL	CLA.7 Swift (replica)	J. M. Greenland
	G-LCOK	Colt 69A balloon	Hot-Air Balloon Co Ltd (G-BLWI)
	G-LCON	AS.355N Twin Squirrel	Lancashire Constabulary/Warton
	G-LCRC	Boeing 757-23A	Airtours International Airways Ltd (G-IEAB)
	G-LDYS	Colt 56A balloon	P. Glydon & J. Coote
	G-LEAF	Cessna F.406	Atlantic Air Transport Ltd/Coventry
	G-LEAM	PA-28-236 Dakota	C. S. Doherty (G-BHLS)
	G-LEAP	BN-2T Turbine Islander	Army Parachute Association (G-BLND)/ Netheravon
	G-LEAR	Learjet 35A	Northern Executive Aviation Ltd/ Manchester
	G-LEAS	Sky 90-24 balloon	Leasing Group PLC
	G-LEAU	Cameron N-31 balloon	P. L. Mossman
	G-LECA	AS.355F-1 Twin Squirrel	S. W. Electricity Board (G-BNBK)/Bristol
	G-LEDA	Robinson R-22B	E. D. Obeng (G-IFOX)
	G-LEDN	Short SD3-30 Variant 100	Streamline Aviation (SW) Ltd (G-BIOF)/Exeter
	G-LEED	Denney Kitfox Mk 2	G. T. Leedham
	G-LEES	Glaser-Dirks DG.400 (800)	J. Bradley
	G-LEEZ	Bell 206L-1 LongRanger 2	Pennine Helicopters Ltd (G-BPCT)
	G-LEGG	Cessna F.182Q	P. J. Clegg (G-GOOS)/Barton
	G-LEGO	Cameron O-77 balloon	C. H. Pearce Construction PLC
	G-LEGS	Short SD3-60 Variant 100	Loganair Ltd/BA Express (G-BLEF)
	G-LEIC	Cessna FA.152	Leicestershire Aero Club Ltd
	G-LEMJ	Hughes 269C	L. J. J. Leeman (G-BMYW)/Belgium

168

Reg.	Type	Owner or Operator	Notes
G-LEND	Cameron N-77 balloon	Southern Flight Co Ltd	
G-LENI	AS.355F-1 Twin Squirrel	Grid Aviation Ltd (G-ZFDB/G-BLEV)	
G-LENN	Cameron V-56 balloon	M. D. H. Jenkins	
G-LENS	Thunder Ax7-77Z balloon	Big Yellow Balloon Group	
G-LEOS	Robin DR.400/120	P. G. Newens	
G-LEPF	Fairchild 24R-46A Argus III	J. M. Greenland	
G-LESJ	Denney Kitfox Mk 3	G-LESJ Flying Group/Kirkbride	
G-LEVI	Aeronca 7AC Champion	G-LEVI Group	
G-LEXI	Cameron N-77 balloon	Sedgemoor 500 Balloon Group	
G-LEZE	Rutan LongEz	K. G. M. Loyal & ptnrs	
G-LEZJ	Denney Kitfox Mk 4-1200 Speedster	C. E. Brookes	
G-LEZZ	Glastar	L. A. James (G-BYCR)	
G-LFIX	V.S.509 Spitfire T.IX (ML407)	C. S. Grace	
G-LFJB	Boeing 737-81Q	Sabre Airways	
G-LFSA	PA-38-112 Tomahawk	Liverpool Flying School Ltd (G-BSFC)	
G-LFSB	PA-38-112 Tomahawk	Liverpool Flying School Ltd (G-BLYC)	
G-LFSC	PA-28 Cherokee 140	Liverpool Flying School Ltd (G-BGTR)	
G-LFSD	PA-38-112 Tomahawk II	Liverpool Flying School Ltd (G-BNPT)	
G-LFSE	PA-28R Cherokee Arrow 200-II	Liverpool Flying School Ltd (G-BAXT)	
G-LFSF	Cessna 150M	Liverpool Flying School Ltd (G-BSRC)	
G-LFSI	PA-28 Cherokee 140	J. Vickers (G-AYKV)/Liverpool	
G-LFVB	V.S.349 Spitfire LF.Vb (EP120)	Patina Ltd/Duxford	
G-LFVC	V.S.349 Spitfire LF.Vc (JG891)	Historic Flying Ltd	
G-LGNA	SAAB SF.340B	Loganair Ltd	
G-LGNB	SAAB SF.340B	Loganair Ltd	
G-LGNC	SAAB SF.340B	Loganair Ltd	
G-LGRM	Bell 206B JetRanger 2	Aeromega Ltd (G-OBRU)	
G-LHPL	AS.350B Ecureuil	Thruston Helicopters (Engineering) Ltd	
G-LIBB	Cameron V-77 balloon	R. R. McCormick & R. J. Mercer	
G-LIBS	Hughes 369HS	A. Harvey & R. White	
G-LIDA	Hoffmann HK-36R Super Dimona	W. D. Inglis	
G-LIDE	PA-31-350 Navajo Chieftain	Keen Leasing Ltd	
G-LIDR	Hoffmann H-36 Dimona	J. MacGilvray (G-BMSK)	
G-LIDS	Robinson R-22B	A. Wall	
G-LIFE	Thunder Ax6-56Z balloon	Lakeside Lodge Golf Centre	
G-LILY	Bell 206B JetRanger 3	T. S. Brown (G-NTBI)	
G-LIMA	R. Commander 114	Tricolore Aeroclub Ltd	
G-LINA	Stemme S.10	J. D. Bally	
G-LINC	Hughes 369HS	Sleekform Ltd	
G-LINE	AS.355N Twin Squirrel	National Grid PLC	
G-LIOA	Lockheed 10A Electra ★ (NC5171N)	Science Museum/S. Kensington	
G-LION	PA-18 Super Cub 135 (R-167)	C. Moore	
G-LIOT	Cameron O-77 balloon	D. Eliot	
G-LIPE	Robinson R-22B	F. C. Owen (G-BTXJ)	
G-LISE	Robin DR.400/500	J. Marks	
G-LITE	R. Commander 112A	J. E. Dixon	
G-LITZ	Pitts S-1E Special	J. A. Hughes/Leicester	
G-LIVH	Piper J-3C-65 Cub (330238)	M. D. Cowburn/Barton	
G-LIVR	Enstrom 480	Southern Air Ltd/Shoreham	
G-LIZA	Cessna 340A II	J. H. Fry & J. C. Merkens (G-BMDM)	
G-LIZI	PA-28 Cherokee 160	R. J. Walker & J. R. Lawson (G-ARRP)	
G-LIZY	Westland Lysander III (V9673) ★	G. A. Warner/Duxford	
G-LIZZ	PA-E23 Aztec 250E	T. D. Nathan & ptnrs (G-BBWM)	
G-LJCC	Murphy Rebel	J. H. A. Clarke	
G-LJET	Learjet 35A	Gama Aviation Ltd	
G-LLTT	PA-32R-301 Saratoga IIHP	M. J. Start	
G-LLYD	Cameron N-31 balloon	Virgin Airship & Balloon Co Ltd	
G-LMLV	Dyn'Aero MCR-01	L. & M. La Vecchia	
G-LNYS	Cessna F.177RG	J. W. Clarke (G-BDCM)	
G-LOAN	Cameron N-77 balloon	P. Lawman	
G-LOAT	Rutan Cozy	P. S. & N. G. Pritchard	
G-LOBO	Cameron O-120 balloon	Solo Aerostatics	
G-LOCH	Piper J-3C-90 Cub	J. M. Greenland	
G-LOFB	L.188CF Electra	Air Atlantique Ltd/Coventry	
G-LOFC	L.188CF Electra	Air Atlantique Ltd/Coventry	
G-LOFD	L.188CF Electra	Air Atlantique Ltd/Coventry	
G-LOFE	L.188CF Electra	Air Atlantique Ltd/Coventry	
G-LOFM	Maule MX-7-180A	Atlantic Air Transport Ltd/Coventry	
G-LOFT	Cessna 500 Citation I	Atlantic Air Transport Ltd/Coventry	
G-LOGO	Hughes 369E	R. M. Briggs (G-BWLC)	

Notes	Reg.	Type	Owner or Operator
	G-LOKM	WSK PZL Koliber 160A	PZL International Aviation Marketing & Sales PLC (G-BYSH)/North Weald
	G-LOLL	Cameron V-77 balloon	Test Valley Balloon Group
	G-LOOP	Pitts S-1C Special	G-LOOP Flying Group
	G-LOOT	EMB-110P1 Bandeirante	(stored) (G-BNOC)/Southend
	G-LORA	Cameron A-250 balloon	Global Ballooning Ltd
	G-LORC	PA-28-161 Cadet	Tindon Ltd/Little Snoring
	G-LORD	PA-34-200T Seneca II	Aerohire Ltd/Halfpenny Green
	G-LORI	H.S.125 Srs 403B	Re-Enforce Trading Co Ltd (G-AYOJ)
	G-LORN	Avions Mudry CAP.10B	AWB Aeronautics Ltd
	G-LORR	PA-28-181 Archer III	B. Galt
	G-LORT	Light Aero Avid Speedwing 4	G. E. Laucht
	G-LORY	Thunder Ax4-31Z balloon	A. J. Moore
	G-LOSM	Gloster Meteor NF.11 (WM167)	Hunter Wing Ltd/Bournemouth
	G-LOSS	Cameron N-77 balloon	D. K. Fish
	G-LOST	Denney Kitfox Mk 3	P. N. & S. E. Akass
	G-LOTI	Bleriot XI (replica) ★	Brooklands Museum Trust Ltd
	G-LOTO	BN-2A-26 Islander	Scottish Parachute Club (Islander) Ltd (G-BDWG)
	G-LOUN	AS.355N Twin Squirrel	Loune Ltd/Kidlington
	G-LOVB	BAe Jetstream 3102	London Flight Centre (Stansted) Ltd (G-BLCB)
	G-LOWA	Colt 77A balloon	K. D. Pierce
	G-LOWE	Monnett Sonerai I	R. M. Kinch
	G-LOWS	Sky 77-24 balloon	A. J. Byrne & D. J. Bellinger
	G-LOYA	Cessna FR.172J	T. R. Scorer (G-BLVT)
	G-LOYD	SA.341G Gazelle 1	Apollo Manufacturing (Derby) Ltd (G-SFTC)
	G-LPAD	Lindstrand LBL-105A balloon	Line Packaging & Display Ltd
	G-LPGI	Cameron A-210 balloon	A. Derbyshire
	G-LSFI	AA-5A Cheetah	T. G. Dughan (G-BGSK)
	G-LSFT	PA-28-161 Warrior II	SFT Europe Ltd (G-BXTX)
	G-LSHI	Colt 77A balloon	Lambert Smith Hampton Group Ltd
	G-LSMI	Cessna F.152	Falcon Flying Services/Biggin Hill
	G-LSTR	Kendai Glastar	R. Y. Kendal
	G-LTFB	PA-28 Cherokee 140	London Transport Flying Club Ltd (G-AVLU)/Fairoaks
	G-LTFC	PA-28 Cherokee 140B	London Transport Flying Club Ltd (G-AXTI)/Fairoaks
	G-LTRF	Sportavia Fournier RF-7	L. J. Trute (G-EHAP)
	G-LTSB	Cameron LTSB-90 balloon	Virgin Airship & Balloon Co Ltd
	G-LUBE	Cameron N-77 balloon	A. C. K. Rawson
	G-LUCK	Cessna F.150M	Taylor Aviation Ltd/Elstree
	G-LUED	Aero Designs Pulsar	J. C. Anderson
	G-LUFF	Rotorway Executive 90	D. C. Luffingham
	G-LUFT	Pützer Elster C	Bath Stone Co Ltd (G-BOPY)
	G-LUKE	Rutan LongEz	S. G. Busby
	G-LUKY	Robinson R-44 Astro	English Braids Ltd
	G-LULU	Grob G.109	A. P. Bowden
	G-LUMA	Jabiru SK	B. Luyckx
	G-LUNA	PA-32RT-300T Turbo Lance II	R. J. H. Creese
	G-LUSC	Luscombe 8E Silvaire	M. Fowler
	G-LUSI	Luscombe 8F Silvaire	J. P. Hunt & D. M. Robinson
	G-LUST	Luscombe 8E Silvaire	M. Griffiths
	G-LUXE	BAe 146-300	British Aerospace PLC (G-SSSH)
	G-LYDA	Hoffmann H-36 Dimona	G-LYDA Flying Group/Booker
	G-LYND	PA-25 Pawnee 235	Glyndwr Soaring Group (G-BSFZ/ G-ASFZ)/Lleweni Parc
	G-LYNE	P-51D-20-NA Mustang (44-72028)	E. N. Robinson & M. C. B. Anderson
	G-LYNK	CFM Shadow Srs DD	G. Linskey
	G-LYNX	Westland WG.13 Lynx (ZB500) ★	IHM/Weston-s-Mare
	G-LYON	Douglas DC-10-30	jmc Airlines Ltd
	G-LYPG	Jabiru UL	P. G. Gale
	G-LYTE	Thunder Ax7-77 balloon	G. M. Bulmer
	G-MAAC	Advanced Airship Corporation ANR-1	Advanced Airship Corporation Ltd
	G-MABE	Cessna F.150L	Herefordshire Aero Club Ltd (G-BLJP)/ Shobdon
	G-MABR	BAe 146-100	Manx Airlines Ltd (G-DEBN)
	G-MACH	SIAI-Marchetti SF.260	Cheyne Motors Ltd/Popham
	G-MACK	PA-28R Cherokee Arrow 200-II	Haimoss Ltd

Reg.	Type	Owner or Operator	Notes
G-MAFA	Cessna F.406	Directflight Ltd (G-DFLT)	
G-MAFB	Cessna F.406	Directflight Ltd	
G-MAFE	Dornier Do.228-202K	FR Aviation Ltd (G-OALF/G-MLDO)/ Bournemouth	
G-MAFF	BN-2T Turbine Islander	FR Aviation Ltd (G-BJEO)/Bournemouth	
G-MAFI	Dornier Do.228-200	FR Aviation Ltd/Bournemouth	
G-MAGC	Cameron Grand Illusion SS balloon	L. V. Mastis	
G-MAGG	Pitts S-1SE Special	C. A. Boardman	
G-MAGL	Sky 77-24 balloon	RCM SRL/Luxembourg	
G-MAIK	PA-34-220T Seneca V	TEL (IoM) Ltd	
G-MAIN	Mainair Blade 912	Mainair Sports Ltd	
G-MAIR	PA-34-200T Seneca II	Barnes Olson Aeroleasing Ltd	
G-MAJA	BAe Jetstream 4102	Manx Airlines Ltd	
G-MAJB	BAe Jetstream 4102	British Regional Airlines/BA (G-BVKT)	
G-MAJC	BAe Jetstream 4102	British Regional Airlines/BA (G-LOGJ)	
G-MAJD	BAe Jetstream 4102	British Regional Airlines/BA (G-WAWR)	
G-MAJE	BAe Jetstream 4102	British Regional Airlines/BA (G-LOGK)	
G-MAJF	BAe Jetstream 4102	British Regional Airlines/BA (G-WAWL)	
G-MAJG	BAe Jetstream 4102	British Regional Airlines/BA (G-LOGL)	
G-MAJH	BAe Jetstream 4102	British Regional Airlines/BA (G-WAYR)	
G-MAJI	BAe Jetstream 4102	British Regional Airlines/BA (G-WAND)	
G-MAJJ	BAe Jetstream 4102	British Regional Airlines/BA (G-WAFT)	
G-MAJK	BAe Jetstream 4102	British Regional Airlines/BA	
G-MAJL	BAe Jetstream 4102	British Regional Airlines/BA	
G-MAJM	BAe Jetstream 4102	British Regional Airlines/BA	
G-MAJR	D.H.C.1 Chipmunk 22 (WP805)	Chipmunk Shareholders	
G-MAJS	Airbus A.300-605R	Monarch Airlines Ltd/Luton	
G-MALA	PA-28-181 Archer II	M. & D. Aviation (G-BIIU)	
G-MALC	AA-5 Traveler	B. P. Hogan (G-BCPM)	
G-MALS	Mooney M.20K-231	G-MALS Group	
G-MALT	Colt Flying Hop SS balloon	P. J. Stapley	
G-MAMC	Rotorway Executive 90	J. R. Carmichael	
G-MAMD	Beech B200 Super King Air	Gamston Aviation Ltd	
G-MAMO	Cameron V-77 balloon	The Marble Mosaic Co Ltd	
G-MANA	BAe ATP	Manx Airlines Ltd (G-LOGH)	
G-MANB	BAe ATP	Manx Airlines Ltd (G-LOGG/G-JATP)	
G-MANC	BAe ATP	Manx Airlines Ltd (G-LOGF)	
G-MAND	PA-28-161 Warrior II	Halfpenny Green Flight Centre Ltd (G-BRKT)	
G-MANE	BAe ATP	British Regional Airlines/BA (G-LOGB)	
G-MANF	BAe ATP	British Regional Airlines/BA (G-LOGA)	
G-MANG	BAe ATP	British Regional Airlines/BA (G-LOGD/G-OLCD)	
G-MANH	BAe ATP	British Regional Airlines/BA (G-LOGC/G-OLCC)	
G-MANI	Cameron V-90 balloon	M. P. G. Papworth	
G-MANJ	BAe ATP	British Regional Airlines/BA (G-LOGE/G-BMYL)	
G-MANL	BAe ATP	Manx Airlines Ltd (G-ERIN/G-BMYK)	
G-MANM	BAe ATP	British Regional Airlines/BA (G-OATP/G-BZWW)	
G-MANN	SA.341G Gazelle 1	First City Air PLC (G-BKLW)	
G-MANO	BAe ATP	Manx Airlines Ltd (G-UIET)	
G-MANP	BAe ATP	British Regional Airlines/BA (G-PEEL)	
G-MANS	BAe 146-200	British Regional Airlines/BA (G-CHSR)	
G-MANU	BAe ATP	Manx Airlines Ltd (G-BUUP)	
G-MANW	Tri-R Kis	M. T. Manwaring	
G-MANX	FRED Srs 2	S. Styles	
G-MAPP	Cessna 402B	Simmons Mapping (UK) Ltd	
G-MAPR	Beech A36 Bonanza	Openair Ltd	
G-MAPS	Sky Flying Map SS balloon	Virgin Airship & Balloon Co Ltd	
G-MARA	Airbus A.321-231	Monarch Airlines Ltd/Luton	
G-MARE	Schweizer 269C	The Earl of Caledon	
G-MASC	Jodel 150A	K. F. & R. Richardson	
G-MASF	PA-28-181 Archer II	Mid-Anglia School of Flying	
G-MASH	Westland-Bell 47G-4A	Defence Products Ltd (G-AXKU)	
G-MASS	Cessna 152 II	MK Aero Support Ltd (G-BSHN)	
G-MASX	Masquito M.80	Masquito Aircraft NV/Belgium	
G-MASY	Masquito M.80	Masquito Aircraft NV/Belgium	
G-MASZ	Masquito M.58	Masquito Aircraft NV/Belgium	
G-MATE	Moravan Zlin Z.50LX	J. H. Askew	
G-MATT	Robin R.2160	D. J. Nicholson (G-BKRC)	

Notes	Reg.	Type	Owner or Operator
	G-MATZ	PA-28 Cherokee 140	Midland Air Training School (G-BASI)/Coventry
	G-MAUD	BAe ATP	British Regional Airlines/BA (G-BMYM)
	G-MAUK	Colt 77A balloon	B. Meeson
	G-MAVI	Robinson R-22B	R. M. Weyman
	G-MAWL	Maule M4-210C Rocket	D. Wallace
	G-MAXI	PA-34-200T Seneca II	Draycott Seneca Syndicate Ltd
	G-MAXX	Lindstrand LBL Battery SS balloon	M. E. White
	G-MAYA	Aero L-29A Delfin	Red 64 Ltd
	G-MAYO	PA-28-161 Warrior II	Jermyk Engineering/Fairoaks
	G-MAZY†	D.H.82A Tiger Moth ★	Newark Air Museum
	G-MCAR	PA-32 Cherokee Six 300D	Erintech Ltd (G-LADA/G-AYWK)
	G-MCEA	Boeing 757-225	Airtours International Airways Ltd
	G-MCJL	Pegasus Quantum 15-912	M. C. J. Ludlow
	G-MCMS	Aero Designs Pulsar	M. C. Manning
	G-MCOX	Fuji FA.200-180AO	W. Surrey Engineering (Shepperton) Ltd
	G-MCPI	Bell 206B JetRanger 3	D. A. C. Pipe (G-ONTB)
	G-MDAC	PA-28-181 Archer II	Alpha Charlie Flying Group
	G-MDBD	Airbus A.330-243	Airtours International Airways Ltd
	G-MDKD	Robinson R-22B	Brian Seedle Helicopters
	G-MEAH	PA-28R Cherokee Arrow 200-II	Stapleford Flying Club Ltd (G-BSNM)
	G-MEDA	Airbus A.320-231	British Mediterranean Airways Ltd/BA
	G-MEDB	Airbus A.320-231	British Mediterranean Airways Ltd/BA
	G-MEDD	Airbus A.320-231	British Mediterranean Airways Ltd/BA
	G-MEGA	PA-28R-201T Turbo Arrow III	Multi Ltd
	G-MELD	AA-5A Cheetah	Plane Talking Ltd (G-BHCB)/Elstree
	G-MELT	Cessna F.172H	Vectair Aviation 1995 Ltd (G-AWTI)
	G-MELV	SOCATA Rallye 235E	Wallis & Sons Ltd (G-BIND)
	G-MEME	PA-28R-201 Arrow III	Henry J. Clare Ltd
	G-MEOW	CFM Streak Shadow	S. D. Hicks
	G-MERC	Colt 56A balloon	A. F. & C. D. Selby
	G-MERE	Lindstrand LBL-77A balloon	G. T. Restell
	G-MERF	Grob G.115A	G-MERF Group
	G-MERI	PA-28-181 Archer II	Scotia Safari Ltd/Glasgow
	G-MERL	PA-28RT-201 Arrow IV	M. Giles
	G-METE	Gloster Meteor F.8 (VZ467)	Classic Jets Ltd (stored)/Biggin Hill
	G-MEUP	Cameron A-120 balloon	Innovation Ballooning Ltd
	G-MEYO	Enstrom 280FX	L. G. King
	G-MFHI	Shaw Europa	M. F. Howe
	G-MFHT	Robinson R-22B	MFH Ltd
	G-MFLI	Cameron V-90 balloon	J. M. Percival
	G-MFMF	Bell 206B JetRanger 3	S.W. Electricity Board (G-BJNJ)/Bristol
	G-MFMM	Scheibe SF.25C Falke	J. A. Rees
	G-MGAN	Robinson R-44 Astro	Meegan Motors Ltd
	G-MHCA	Enstrom F-28C-UK	A. G. Forshaw (G-SHWW/G-SMUJ/ G-BHTF)
	G-MHCB	Enstrom 280C	J. W. Beswick
	G-MHCD	Enstrom 280C-UK	S. J. Ellis (G-SHGG)
	G-MHCE	Enstrom F-28A	K. Bickley (G-BBHD)/Barton
	G-MHCF	Enstrom 280C-UK	HKC Helicopter Services (G-GSML/ G-BNNV)
	G-MHCG	Enstrom 280C-UK	D & E Motor Factors Ltd (G-HAYN/ G-BPOX)
	G-MHCH	Enstrom 280C	J. & S. Lewis Ltd
	G-MHCI	Enstrom 280C	Charlie India Helicopters Ltd/Barton
	G-MHCJ (CTRN)	Enstrom F-28C-UK	Manchester Helicopter Centre (G-
	G-MHCK	Enstrom 280FX	Manchester Helicopter Centre (G-BXXB)
	G-MHCL	Enstrom 280C	Altolink Ltd
	G-MICH	Robinson R-22B	A. P. Codling (G-BNKY)/Shobdon
	G-MICK	Cessna F.172N	G-MICK Flying Group
	G-MICY	Everett Srs 1 gyroplane	D. M. Hughes
	G-MICZ	PA-46-310P Malibu	Mitchell Instruments Ltd
	G-MIDA	Airbus A.321-231	British Midland Airways Ltd
	G-MIDC	Airbus A.321-231	British Midland Airways Ltd
	G-MIDD	PA-28 Cherokee 140	Midland Air Training School (G-BBDD)/ Coventry
	G-MIDE	Airbus A.321-231	British Midland Airways Ltd
	G-MIDF	Airbus A.321-231	British Midland Airways Ltd
	G-MIDG	Midget Mustang	C. E. Bellhouse
	G-MIDH	Airbus A.321-231	British Midland Airways Ltd
	G-MIDI	Airbus A.321-231	British Midland Airways Ltd
	G-MIDJ	Airbus A.321-231	British Midland Airways Ltd

Reg.	Type	Owner or Operator	Notes
G-MIDK	Airbus A.321-231	British Midland Airways Ltd	
G-MIDL	Airbus A.321-231	British Midland Airways Ltd	
G-MIDM	Airbus A.321-231	British Midland Airways Ltd	
G-MIDN	Airbus A.321-231	British Midland Airways Ltd	
G-MIDO	Airbus A.321-231	British Midland Airways Ltd	
G-MIDP	Airbus A.320-232	British Midland Airways Ltd	
G-MIDR	Airbus A.320-232	British Midland Airways Ltd	
G-MIDS	Airbus A.320-232	British Midland Airways Ltd	
G-MIDT	Airbus A.320-232	British Midland Airways Ltd	
G-MIDU	Airbus A.320-232	British Midland Airways Ltd	
G-MIDV	Airbus A.320-232	British Midland Airways Ltd	
G-MIDW	Airbus A.320-232	British Midland Airways Ltd	
G-MIDX	Airbus A.320-232	British Midland Airways Ltd	
G-MIDY	Airbus A.320-232	British Midland Airways Ltd	
G-MIDZ	Airbus A.320-232	British Midland Airways Ltd	
G-MIFF	Robin DR.400/180	G. E. Snushall	
G-MIII	Extra EA.300/L	Firebird Aerobatics Ltd	
G-MIKE	Brookland Hornet	M. H. J. Goldring	
G-MIKI	Rans S.6-ESA Coyote II	S. P. Slade	
G-MILA	Cessna F.172N	P. J. Miller	
G-MILE	Cameron N-77 balloon	Miles Air Ltd	
G-MILI	Bell 206B JetRanger 3	CK's Supermarket	
G-MILN	Cessna 182Q	Meon Hill Farms (Stockbridge) Ltd	
G-MILY	AA-5A Cheetah	Plane Talking Ltd (G-BFXY)/Elstree	
G-MIMA	BAe 146-200	Manx Airlines Ltd (G-CNMF)	
G-MIME	Shaw Europa	N. W. Charles	
G-MIND	Cessna 404	Atlantic Air Transport Ltd (G-SKKC/G-OHUB)/Coventry	
G-MINS	Nicollier HN.700 Menestrel II	R. Fenion	
G-MINT	Pitts S-1S Special	T. G. Sanderson/Tollerton	
G-MINX	Bell 47G-4A	R. F. Warner (G-FOOR)	
G-MIOO	M.100 Student ★	Museum of Berkshire Aviation (G-APLK)/ Woodley	
G-MISH	Cessna 182R	M. Konstantinovic (G-RFAB/G-BIXT)	
G-MISS	Taylor JT.2 Titch	P. L. A. Brenen	
G-MIST	Cessna T.210K	J. Summers (G-AYGM)	
G-MITS	Cameron N-77 balloon	Colt Car Co Ltd	
G-MITZ	Cameron N-77 balloon	Colt Car Co Ltd	
G-MIWS	Cessna 310R II	Bob Warner Aviation (G-ODNP)	
G-MKAK	Colt 77A balloon	Virgin Airship & Balloon Co Ltd	
G-MKAS	PA-28 Cherokee 140	MK Aero Support Ltd (G-BKVR)	
G-MKPU	Shaw Europa	M. K. Papworth (G-DZEL)	
G-MKVB	V.S.349 Spitfire LF.VB (BM597)	Historic Aircraft Collection/Duxford	
G-MKVI	D.H. Vampire FB.6 (WL505)	De Havilland Aviation Ltd/Swansea	
G-MKXI	V.S.365 Spitfire PR.XI (PL965)	R. A. Fleming & A. J. E. Smith/Duxford	
G-MLAS	Cessna 182E ★	Parachute jump trainer/St Merryn	
G-MLFF	PA-23 Aztec 250E	Channel Islands Aero Services Ltd (G-WEBB/G-BJBU)	
G-MLJL	Airbus A.330-243	Airtours International Airways Ltd	
G-MLTI	Dassault Falcon 900B	Mulitflight Ltd/Leeds-Bradford	
G-MLTY	AS.365N-2 Dauphin 2	Mulitflight Ltd/Leeds-Bradford	
G-MLWI	Thunder Ax7-77 balloon	M. L. & L. P. Willoughby	
G-MOAC	Beech F33A Bonanza	R. M. Camrass	
G-MOAK	Schempp-Hirth Nimbus 3DM (929)	P. W. Lever/Portmoak	
G-MOBI	AS.355F-1 Twin Squirrel	M. J. O'Brien (G-MUFF/G-CORR)	
G-MOFB	Cameron O-120 balloon	D. M. Moffat	
G-MOFF	Cameron O-77 balloon	D. M. Moffat	
G-MOFZ	Cameron O-90 balloon	D. M. Moffat	
G-MOGI	AA-5A Cheetah	TL Aviation Ltd (G-BFMU)	
G-MOGY	Robinson R-22B	Dragonfly Aviation	
G-MOHS	PA-31-350 Navajo Chieftain	Sky Air Travel Ltd (G-BWOC)	
G-MOJO	Airbus A.330-243	Airtours International Airways Ltd	
G-MOKE	Cameron V-77 balloon	D. D. Owen/Luxembourg	
G-MOLE	Taylor JT.2 Titch	S. R. Mowle	
G-MOLI	Cameron A-250 balloon	J. J. Rudoni	
G-MOLL	PA-32-301T Turbo Saratoga	M. S. Bennett	
G-MOLY	PA-23 Apache 160	R. R. & M. T. Thorogood (G-APFV)/ St Just	
G-MONB	Boeing 757-2T7	Monarch Airlines Ltd/Luton	
G-MONC	Boeing 757-2T7	Monarch Airlines Ltd/Luton	
G-MOND	Boeing 757-2T7	Monarch Airlines Ltd/Luton	
G-MONE	Boeing 757-2T7	Monarch Airlines Ltd/Luton	
G-MONI	Monnett Moni	B. S. Carpenter/Brize Norton	

G-MONJ – G-MUFY

UK OUT OF SEQUENCE

Notes	Reg.	Type	Owner or Operator
	G-MONJ	Boeing 757-2T7	Monarch Airlines Ltd/Luton
	G-MONK	Boeing 757-2T7	Monarch Airlines Ltd/Luton
	G-MONR	Airbus A.300-605R	Monarch Airlines Ltd/Luton
	G-MONS	Airbus A.300-605R	Monarch Airlines Ltd/Luton
	G-MONW	Airbus A.320-212	Monarch Airlines Ltd/Luton
	G-MONX	Airbus A.320-212	Monarch Airlines Ltd/Luton
	G-MONY	Airbus A.320-212	Monarch Airlines Ltd/Skyservice (C-FLSF)/Luton
	G-MONZ	Airbus A.320-212	Monarch Airlines Ltd/ Skyservice (C-FTDI)/Luton
	G-MOON	Mooney M.20K	M. A. Eccles
	G-MOOR	SOCATA TB.10 Tobago	WG & R Communications Ltd (G-MILK)
	G-MOOS	P.56 Provost T.1 (XF690)	T. J. Manna (G-BGKA)/Cranfield
	G-MOSS	Beech 95-D55 Baron	S. C. Tysoe (G-AWAD)
	G-MOSY	Cameron O-84 balloon	P. L. Mossman
	G-MOTA	Bell 206B JetRanger 3	J. W. Sandle
	G-MOTH	D.H.82A Tiger Moth (K2567)	M. C. Russell
	G-MOTI	Robin DR.400/500	Tango India Flying Group
	G-MOTO	PA-24 Comanche 180	L. T. & S. Evans (G-EDHE/G-ASFH)/ Sandown
	G-MOTT	Light Aero Avid Speedwing	J. B. Ott
	G-MOUL	Maule M6-235	M. Klinge
	G-MOUR	H.S. Gnat T.1 (XR991)	D. J. Gilmour/North Weald
	G-MOVE	PA-60-601P Aerostar	A. Cazaz & A1 Hydraulics Ltd
	G-MOVI	PA-32R-301 Saratoga SP	G-BOON Ltd (G-MARI)
	G-MOZZ	Avions Mudry CAP.10B	N. Skipworth & M. B. Smith
	G-MPBH	Cessna FA.152	Metropolitan Police Flying Club (G-FLIC/ G-BILV)/Biggin Hill
	G-MPBI	Cessna 310R	M. P. Bolshaw & Co Ltd
	G-MPCD	Airbus A.320-212	Monarch Airlines Ltd/Skyservice (C-FTDU)
	G-MPWH	Rotorway Executive	Neric Ltd
	G-MPWI	Robin HR.100/210	Propwash Investments Ltd/Cardiff
	G-MPWT	PA-34-220T Seneca III	Modern Air (UK) Ltd
	G-MRAJ	Hughes 369E	A. Jardine
	G-MRAM	Mignet HM.1000 Balerit	R. A. Marven
	G-MRED	Christavia Mk 1	E. Hewett
	G-MRKT	Lindstrand LBL-90A balloon	Marketplace Public Relations (London) Ltd
	G-MRLN	Sky 240-24 balloon	Merlin Balloons
	G-MRMR	PA-31-350 Navajo Chieftain	MRMR (Flight Services) (G-WROX/ G-BNZI)
	G-MROC	Pegasus Quantum 15-912	M. Convine
	G-MRSN	Robinson R-22B	Leeds Lighting Ltd
	G-MRST	PA-28 RT-201 Arrow IV	C. P. Scamp
	G-MRTN	SOCATA TB.10 Tobago	Underwood Kitchens Ltd (G-BHET)
	G-MRTY	Cameron N-77 balloon	R. A. & P. G. Vale
	G-MSAL	MS.733 Alcyon (143)	North Weald Flying Services Ltd
	G-MSDJ	AS.350B-1 Ecureuil	Denis Ferranti Hoverknights Ltd (G-BPOH)
	G-MSFC	PA-38-112 Tomahawk	Sherwood Flying Club Ltd/Tollerton
	G-MSFT	PA-28-161 Warrior II	M. J. Love (G-MUMS)
	G-MSIX	Glaser Dirks DG.800B	G-MSIX Group
	G-MSKA	Boeing 737-5L9	Maersk Air Ltd/BA/Birmingham
	G-MSKB	Boeing 737-5L9	Maersk Air Ltd/BA/Birmingham
	G-MSKC	Boeing 737-5L9	Maersk Air Ltd/BA/Birmingham
	G-MSKD	Boeing 737-5L9	Maersk Air Ltd/BA/Birmingham
	G-MSKE	Boeing 737-5L9	Maersk Air Ltd/BA/Birmingham
	G-MSKK	Canadair CL.600-2B19 RJ	Maersk Air Ltd/BA/Birmingham
	G-MSKL	Canadair CL.600-2B19 RJ	Maersk Air Ltd/BA/Birmingham
	G-MSKM	Canadair CL.600-2B19 RJ	Maersk Air Ltd/BA/Birmingham
	G-MSKN	Canadair CL.600-2B19 RJ	Maersk Air Ltd/BA/Birmingham
	G-MSKO	Canadair CL.600-2B19 RJ	Maersk Air Ltd/BA/Birmingham
	G-MSKP	Canadair CL.600-2B19 RJ	Maersk Air Ltd/BA/Birmingham
	G-MSKR	Canadair CL.600-2B19 RJ	Maersk Air Ltd/BA/Birmingham
	G-MSKS	Canadair CL.600-2B19 RJ	Maersk Air Ltd/BA/Birmingham
	G-NSOF	Robin HR.200/120B	Northamptonshire School of Flying Ltd/ Sywell
	G-MSOO	Mini-500	R. H. Ryan
	G-MSTC	AA-5A Cheetah	Mid-Sussex Timber Co Ltd (G-BIJT)
	G-MSTG	NA P-51D Mustang	M. Hammond
	G-MUFY	Robinson R-22B	Rotormurf Ltd

174

Reg.	Type	Owner or Operator	Notes
G-MUIR	Cameron V-65 balloon	L. C. M. Muir	
G-MUNI	Mooney M.20J	M. W. Fane	
G-MURI	Learjet 35A	G-MURI Ltd	
G-MURR	Whittaker MW.6 Merlin	D. Murray	
G-MURY	Robinson R-44 Astro	Simlot Ltd	
G-MUSO	Rutan LongEz	C. J. Tadjeran/Sweden	
G-MUTE	Colt 31A balloon	Redmalt Ltd	
G-MUVG	Cessna 421C	Air Montgomery Ltd	
G-MUZO	Shaw Europa	J. T. Grant	
G-MXVI	V.S.361 Spitfire LF.XVIe (TE184)	De Cadenet Motor Racing Ltd	
G-NAAA AZTI)/Aberdeen	MBB Bo.105DBS/4	Bond Air Services (G-BUTN/G-	
G-NAAB	MBB Bo.105DBS/4	Bond Air Services/Aberdeen	
G-NAAS	AS.355F-1 Twin Squirrel	Northumbria Ambulance Service NHS Trust (G-BPRG/G-NWPA)	
G-NACA	Norman NAC.2 Freelance 180	NDN Aircraft Ltd/Sandown	
G-NACI	Norman NAC.1 Srs 100	L. J. Martin (G-AXFB)	
G-NACL	Norman NAC.6 Fieldmaster	EPA Aircraft Co Ltd (G-BNEG)	
G-NACO	Norman NAC-6 Fieldmaster	EPA Aircraft Co Ltd	
G-NACP	Norman NAC-6 Fieldmaster	EPA Aircraft Co Ltd	
G-NADS	Team Minimax 91	P. M. Spencer	
G-NANA	VPM M.16 Tandem Trainer	J. W. P. Lewis	
G-NARO	Cassutt Racer	D. A. Wirdnam (G-BTXR)	
G-NASA	Lockheed T-33A-5-LO (91007)	De Havilland Aviation Ltd (G-TJET)/ Swansea	
G-NASH	AA-5A Cheetah	Flying Services	
G-NATT	R. Commander 114A	Northgleam Ltd	
G-NATX	Cameron O-65 balloon	A. G. E. Faulkner	
G-NATY	H. S. Gnat T.1 (XR537)	F. C. Hackett-Jones/Bournemouth	
G-NBDD	Robin DR.400/180	J. N. Binks	
G-NBSI	Cameron N-77 balloon	Nottingham Hot-Air Balloon Club	
G-NCFC	PA-38-112 Tomahawk II	Light Aircraft Leasing (UK) Ltd (G-BNOA)	
G-NCFE	PA-38-112 Tomahawk	APB Leasing Ltd (G-BKMK)/Welshpool	
G-NCFR	H.S.125 Srs 700B	Chauffair (CI) Ltd (G-BVJY)	
G-NCUB	Piper J-3C-65 Cub	N. Thomson (G-BGXV)/Norwich	
G-NDGC	Grob G.109	M. Newton	
G-NDNI	NDN.1 Firecracker	N. W. G. Marsh	
G-NDOL	Shaw Europa	S. Longstaff	
G-NDRW	Colt AS-80 Mk II airship	Huntair Ltd/Germany	
G-NEAL	PA-32 Cherokee Six 260	VSD Group (G-BFPY)	
G-NEAT	Shaw Europa	M. Burton	
G-NEEL	Rotorway Executive 90	M. B. Sims	
G-NEGS	Thunder Ax7-77 balloon	M. Rowlands	
G-NEIL	Thunder Ax3 balloon	N. A. Robertson	
G-NEPB	Cameron N-77 balloon	The Post Office	
G-NERC	PA-31-350 Navajo Chieftain	Natural Environment Research Council (G-BBXX)/Coventry	
G-NESI	Van's RV-6	G. Ness	
G-NESU	BN-2B-20 Islander	Northumbria Police Authority (G-BTVN)/ Teesside	
G-NESV	Eurocopter EC.135T-1	Northumbria Police Authority	
G-NETY	PA-18 Super Cub 150	N. B. Mason	
G-NEUF	Bell 206L-1 LongRanger 2	Yendle Roberts Ltd (G-BVVV)	
G-NEVS	Aero Designs Pulsar XP	N. Warrener	
G-NEWR	PA-31-350 Navajo Chieftain	Eastern Air Executive Ltd/Sturgate	
G-NEWS	Bell 206B JetRanger 3	Abington Aviation Ltd	
G-NEWT	Beech 35 Bonanza	J. A. West (G-APVW)	
G-NEWZ	Bell 206B JetRanger 3	Peter Press Ltd	
G-NFLC	H.P.137 Jetstream 1	Cranfield University (G-AXUI)	
G-NGRM	Spezio DAL.1 Tuholer	S. H. Crook	
G-NHRH	PA-28 Cherokee 140	J. E. & I. Parkinson	
G-NHRJ	Shaw Europa XS	D. A. Lowe	
G-NHVH	Maule M5-235C Lunar Rocket	Commercial Go-Karts Ltd/Exeter	
G-NICH	Robinson R-22B	Skyhopper Ltd & D. J. Pearce	
G-NIGE	Luscombe 8E Silvaire	Garden Party Ltd (G-BSHG)	
G-NIGL	Shaw Europa	N. M. Graham	
G-NIGS	Thunder Ax7-65 balloon	A. N. F. Pertwee	
G-NIKE	PA-28-181 Archer II	Key Properties Ltd/White Waltham	
G-NINA	PA-28-161 Warrior II	P. A. Layzell (G-BEUC)	
G-NINB	PA-28 Cherolee 180G	P. A. Layzell	
G-NINE	Murphy Renegade 912	R. F. Bond	
G-NIOS	PA-32R-301 Saratoga SP	Plant Aviation	

Notes	Reg.	Type	Owner or Operator
	G-NIPA	Slingsby T.66 Nipper 3	R. J. O. Walker (G-AWDD)
	G-NIPY	Hughes 369HS	Jet Aviation (Northwest) Ltd
	G-NISR	R. Commander 690A	Z. I. Bilbeisi
	G-NITA	PA-28 Cherokee 180	T. Clifford (G-AVVG)
	G-NJAG	Cessna 207	G. H. Nolan Ltd
	G-NJIA	BAe 146-300	National Jet Italia/BA
	G-NJIB	BAe 146-300	National Jet Italia/BA
	G-NJIC	BAe 146-300	National Jet italia/BA
	G-NJID	BAe 146-300	National Jet Italia/BA
	G-NJIE	BAe 146-300	National Jet Italia/BA
	G-NJSH	Robinson R-22B	A. J. Hawes
	G-NLEE	Cessna 182Q	J. S. Lee (G-TLTD)
	G-NMHS	AS.355N Twin Squirrel	North Midlands Helicopter Support Unit (G-DPPS)
	G-NNAC	PA-18 Super Cub 135	P. A. Wilde
	G-NOBI	Spezio HES-1 Tuholer Sport	A. D. Pearce
	G-NOCK	Cessna FR.182RG II	R. D. Masters (G-BGTK)
	G-NODE	AA-5B Tiger	Strategic Telecom Networks Ltd
	G-NODY	American General AG-5B Tiger	Curd & Green Ltd/Elstree
	G-NOIR	Bell 222	Arlington Securities PLC (G-OJLC/ G-OSEB/G-BNDA)
	G-NONI	AA-5 Traveler	November India Flying Group(G-BBDA)
	G-NOOR	Commander 114B	As-Al Ltd
	G-NORD	SNCAN NC.854	W. J. McCollum
	G-NOSE	Cessna 402B	Atlantic Air Transport Ltd (G-MPCU)/ Coventry
	G-NOTE	PA-28-181 Archer III	General Aeroplane Trading Co Ltd
	G-NOTR	McD Douglas MD-520N Notar	Air Hanson Ltd/Blackbushe
	G-NOTT	Nott ULD-2 balloon	J. R. P. Nott
	G-NOTY	Westland Scout AH.1	R. P. Coplestone
	G-NOVO	Colt AS-56 airship	Astec Communications Ltd
	G-NOWW	Mainair Blade 912	C. Bodill
	G-NPKJ	Van's RV-4	K. Jones
	G-NPNP	Cameron N-105 balloon	Virgin Airship & Balloon Co Ltd (G-BURX)
	G-NRDC	NDN-6 Fieldmaster	EPA Aircraft Co Ltd
	G-NROY	PA-32RT-300 Lance II	Roys Motor Co (G-LYNN/G-BGNY)
	G-NSEW	Robinson R-44 Astro	Pebblestar Ltd
	G-NSHR	Robinson R-22B	F. J. Sytner
	G-NSTG	Cessna F.150F	N. S. T. Griffin (G-ATNI)/Blackpool
	G-NTEE	Robinson R-44 Astro	Central Aviation (Helicopters) Ltd
	G-NUTY	AS.350B Ecureuil	Arena Aviation Ltd (G-BXKT)
	G-NVBF	Lindstrand LBL-210A balloon	Virgin Balloon Flights Ltd
	G-NVSA	D.H.C.8-311 Dash Eight	Brymon Airways Ltd/British Airways
	G-NVSB	D.H.C.8-311 Dash Eight	Brymon Airways Ltd/British Airways
	G-NVSC	D.H.C.8-311 Dash Eight	Brymon Airways Ltd/British Airways
	G-NVSD	D.H.C.8-311 Dash Eight	Brymon Airways Ltd/British Airways
	G-NWAC	PA-31-310 Turbo Navajo	North West Air Charters Ltd (G-BDUJ)/ Liverpool
	G-NWPS	Eurocopter EC.135T-1	Northwest Police Authority
	G-NYTE	Cessna F.337G	I. M. Latiff (G-BATH)
	G-NZGL	Cameron O-105 balloon	P. G. & P. M. Vale
	G-NZSS	Boeing Stearman N2S-5 (343251)	Ace Aviation Ltd
	G-OAAA	PA-28-161 Warrior II	Halfpenny Green Flight Centre Ltd
	G-OAAC	Airtour AH-77B balloon	Army Air Corps
	G-OAAL	PA-38-112 Tomahawk	Cardiff-Wales Aviation Services Ltd
	G-OABB	Jodel D.150	A. B. Bailey
	G-OABC	Colt 69A balloon	P. A. C. Stuart-Kregor
	G-OABO	Enstrom F-28A	ABO Ltd (G-BAIB)
	G-OABR	AG-5B Tiger	Abraxas Aviation Ltd
	G-OACE	Valentin Taifun 17E	J. E. Dallison
	G-OACG	PA-34-200T Seneca II	ACG Building Contractors Ltd (G-BUNR)
	G-OACI	M.S.893E Rallye 180GT	A. M. Quayle (G-DOOR)
	G-OACP	OGMA D.H.C.1 Chipmunk 20	Aeroclub de Portugal
	G-OADY	Beech 76 Duchess	Multiflight Ltd
	G-OAER	Lindstrand LBL-105A balloon	T. M. Donnelly
	G-OAFT	Cessna 152 II	Bobbington Air Training School Ltd (G-BNKM)/Halfpenny Green
	G-OAHC	Beech F33C Bonanza	V. D. Speck (G-BTTF)/Clacton
	G-OAJB	Cyclone AX2000	A. J. Blackwell (G-MZFJ)
	G-OAJS	PA-39 Twin Comanche 160 C/R	Go-AJS Ltd (G-BCIO)

UK OUT OF SEQUENCE

Reg.	Type	Owner or Operator	Notes
G-OAKJ	BAe Jetstream 3202	Eastern Airways Ltd (G-BOTJ)	
G-OALD	SOCATA TB.20 Trinidad	Gold Aviation/Biggin Hill	
G-OAMG	Bell 206B JetRanger 3	Alan Mann Helicopters Ltd/Fairoaks	
G-OAML	Cameron AML-105 balloon	Cheqair Ltd	
G-OAMP	Cessna F.177R	Vale Aero Group (G-AYPF)	
G-OAMS	Boeing 737-37Q	British Airways/Manchester	
G-OAMT	PA-31-350 Navajo Chieftain	AM & T Solutions Ltd (G-BXKS)	
G-OAMY	Cessna 152 II	Cardiff-Wales Aviation Services Ltd	
G-OANI	PA-28-161 Warrior II	J. F. Mitchell	
G-OANN	Zenair CH.601HDS	P. Noden	
G-OAPB	Colt 14 Bottle SS balloon	Airborne Images Ltd	
G-OAPE	Cessna T.303	C. Twiston-Davies & P. L. Drew	
G-OAPR	Brantly B.2B	Helicopter International Magazine	
G-OAPW	Glaser-Dirks DG.400	D. T. S. Walsh	
G-OARA	PA-28R-201 Arrow III	London School of Flying Ltd/Elstree	
G-OARC	PA-28RT-201 Arrow IV	ARC Precision Engineering Ltd (G-	
BMVE)			
G-OARG	Cameron C-80 balloon	G. & R. Madelin	
G-OART	PA-23 Aztec 250D	Levenmere Ltd (G-AXKD)	
G-OARV	ARV Super 2	N. R. Beale	
G-OASH	Robinson R-22B	J. C. Lane	
G-OASP	AS.355F-2 Twin Squirrel	Avon & Somerset Constabulary & Gloucestershire Constabulary	
G-OATS	PA-38-112 Tomahawk	Truman Aviation Ltd/Tollerton	
G-OATV	Cameron V-77 balloon	W. G. Andrews	
G-OAUS	Sikorsky S-76A	Darley Stud Management Co Ltd	
G-OAWS	Colt 77A balloon	Auto Windscreens Ltd	
G-OAXA	Cameron 90 Cup SS balloon	Cameron Balloons Ltd	
G-OBAL	Mooney M.20J	Britannia Airways Ltd/Luton	
G-OBAM	Bell 206B JetRanger 3	Shawford Park Helicopters Ltd	
G-OBAN	Jodel D.140B	S. R. Cameron (G-ATSU)/North Connel	
G-OBAY	Bell 206B JetRanger	Helixair Ltd (G-BVWR)	
G-OBBC	Colt 90A balloon	R. A. & M. A. Riley	
G-OBBO	Cessna 182S	F. Friedenberg	
G-OBDA	Diamond Katana DA.20-A1	Diamond Aircraft Industries GmbH	
G-OBEN	Cessna 152 II	Airbase Aircraft Ltd (G-NALI/G-BHVM)	
G-OBEV	Shaw Europa	M. B. Hill & N. I. Wingfield	
G-OBEY	PA-23 Aztec 250C	Creaton Aircraft Services (G-BAAJ)	
G-OBFC	PA-28-161 Warrior II	Bournemouth Flying Club Ltd	
G-OBFS	PA-28-161 Warrior III	Bournemouth Flying Club Ltd	
G-OBGC	SOCATA TB-20 Trinidad	Bidford Airfield Ltd	
G-OBHD	Short SD3-60 Variant 100	Jersey European Airways Ltd (G-BNDK)	
G-OBIB	Colt 120A balloon	The Aerial Display Co Ltd	
G-OBIG	AS.355F-1 Twin Squirrel	Plane Talking Ltd (G-SVJM/G-BOPS)/ Elstree	
G-OBIL	Robinson R-22B	C. A. Rosenberg	
G-OBIO	Robinson R-22B	A. E. Churchill	
G-OBJB	Lindstrand LBL-90A balloon	2B Designs Ltd	
G-OBJH	Colt 77A balloon	Eurogas & Corralgas	
G-OBLC	Beech 76 Duchess	Pridenote Ltd	
G-OBLK	Short SD3-60 Variant 100	Jersey European Airways Ltd (G-BNDI)	
G-OBLN	D.H.115 Vampire T.11 (XE956)	De Havilland Aviation Ltd/Swansea	
G-OBMF	Boeing 737-4Y0	British Midland Airways Ltd/E. Midlands	
G-OBMH	Boeing 737-33A	British Midland Airways Ltd/E. Midlands	
G-OBMJ	Boeing 737-33A	British Midland Airways Ltd/E. Midlands	
G-OBMM	Boeing 737-4Y0	British Midland Airways Ltd/E. Midlands	
G-OBMO	Boeing 737-4Q8	British Midland Airways Ltd/E. Midlands	
G-OBMP	Boeing 737-3Q8	British Midland Airways Ltd/E. Midlands	
G-OBMR	Boeing 737-5Y0	British Midland Airways Ltd/E. Midlands	
G-OBMS	Cessna F.172N	D. Beverley & W. F. van Schoten	
G-OBMW	AA-5 Traveler	Fretcourt Ltd (G-BDFV)	
G-OBMX	Boeing 737-59D	British Midland Airways Ltd/E. Midlands	
G-OBMZ	Boeing 737-53A	British Midland Airways Ltd/E. Midlands	
G-OBNF	Cessna 310K	Fadmoor Flying Group	
G-OBPL	EMB-110P2 Bandeirante	Comed Aviation Ltd (G-OEAB/G-BKWB/ G-CHEV)	
G-OBRY	Cameron N-180 balloon	Bryant Group PLC	
G-OBTS	Cameron C-80 balloon	Bedford Tyre Service (Chichester) Ltd	
G-OBUY	Colt 69A balloon	Virgin Airship & Balloon Co Ltd	
G-OBWA	BAC One-Eleven 518FG	British World Airlines PLC (G-BDAT/ G-AYOR)	
G-OBWB	BAC One-Eleven 518FG	British World Airlines PLC (G-BDAS/ G-AXMH)	

Notes	Reg.	Type	Owner or Operator
	G-OBWC	BAC One-Eleven 520FN	British World Airlines PLC (G-BEKA)
	G-OBWD	BAC One-Eleven 518FG	British World Airlines PLC (G-BDAE/ G-AXMI)
	G-OBWE	BAC One-Eleven 531FS	British World Airlines PLC (G-BJYM)
	G-OBWL	BAe ATP	British World Airlines PLC
	G-OBWM	BAe ATP	British World Airlines PLC
	G-OBWN	BAe ATP	British World Airlines PLC (G-BVEO)
	G-OBWO	BAe ATP	British World Airlines PLC
	G-OBWP	BAe ATP	British World Airways PLC (G-BTPO)
	G-OBWR	BAe ATP	British World Airways PLC (G-BUWP)
	G-OBWZ	Boeing 737-3Q8	British World Airways PLC
	G-OBYA	Boeing 767-304ER	Britannia Airways Ltd/Britannia Deutsche (D-AGYA)
	G-OBYB	Boeing 767-304ER	Britannia Airways Ltd
	G-OBYC	Boeing 767-304ER	Britannia Airways Ltd
	G-OBYD	Boeing 767-304ER	Britannia Airways Ltd
	G-OBYE	Boeing 767-304ER	Britannia Airways Ltd/Britannia Deutsche (D-AGYE)
	G-OBYF	Boeing 767-304ER	Britannia Airways Ltd/Britannia Deutsche (D-AGYF)
	G-OBYG	Boeing 767-3Q8ER	Britannia Airways Ltd
	G-OBYH	Boeing 767-3Q8ER	Britannia Airways Ltd/Britannia Deutsche (D-AGYH)
	G-OBYI	Boeing 767-304ER	Britannia Airways Ltd
	G-OBYJ	Boeing 767-304ER	Britannia Airways Ltd
	G-OBYT	AB-206A JetRanger	Sloane Helicopters Ltd (G-BNRC)
	G-OCAA	H.S.125 Srs 700B	MAGEC Aviation Ltd (G-BHLF)/Luton
	G-OCAD	Sequoia F.8L Falco	Falco Flying Group
	G-OCAM	AA-5A Cheetah	Plane Talking Ltd (G-BLHO)/Elstree
	G-OCAR	Colt 77A balloon	S. C. J. Derham
	G-OCAT	Eiri PIK-20E	D. Bonucchi
	G-OCAW	Lindstrand LBL Bananas SS balloon	Flying Pictures Ltd
	G-OCBB	Bell 206B JetRanger 2	Corby Motor Group Ltd (G-BASE)
	G-OCBS	Lindstrand LBL-210A balloon	G. Binder
	G-OCDB	Cessna 550 Citation II	Paycourt Ltd (G-ELOT)
	G-OCDS	Aviamilano F.8L Falco II	C. O. P. Barth (G-VEGL)
	G-OCEA	Short SD3-60 Variant 100	BAC Express Airlines Ltd (G-BRMX)
	G-OCFR	Learjet 35A	Chauffair (CI) Ltd (G-VIPS/G-SOVN/ G-PJET)
	G-OCIN	Cessna 150K	F. McGovern (G-BSXG)
	G-OCJK	Schweizer 269C	P. Crawley
	G-OCJS	Cameron V-90 balloon	C. J. Sandell
	G-OCJW	Cessna 182R	C. J. Ward (G-SJGM)
	G-OCND	Cameron O-77 balloon	D. P. H. Smith & Dalby
	G-OCPC	Cessna FA.152	Westward Airways (Lands End) Ltd/ St Just
	G-OCPF	PA-32 Cherokee Six 300	Syndicate Clerical Services Ltd (G-BOCH)
	G-OCPS	Colt 120A balloon	CPS Fuels Ltd
	G-OCRI	Colomban MC.15 Cri-Cri	M. J. J. Dunning
	G-OCSB	Cessna 525 Citationjet	Kestrel Aviation Ltd
	G-OCSI	EMB-110P2 Bandeirante	Air Tabernacle Ltd(G-BHJZ)
	G-OCST	AB-206B JetRanger 3	Fieldgrove Trading (G-BMKM)
	G-OCSZ	EMB-110P1 Bandeirante	Air Tabernacle (G-DORK)
	G-OCTA	BN-2A Mk III-2 Trislander	Aurigny Air Services Ltd (G-BCXW)
	G-OCTI	PA-32 Cherokee Six 260	D. G. Williams (G-BGZX)
	G-OCTU	PA-28-161 Cadet	Plane Talking Ltd/Elstree
	G-OCUB	Piper J-3C-90 Cub	C. A. Foss & P. A. Brook/Shoreham
	G-ODAC	Cessna F.152 II	T. M. Jones (G-BITG)/Egginton
	G-ODAD	Colt 77A balloon	K. Meehan
	G-ODAM	AA-5A Cheetah	Stop & Go Ltd (G-FOUX)
	G-ODAT	Aero L-29 Delfin	DAT Enterprises Ltd
	G-ODBN	Lindstrand LBL Flowers SS balloon	Flying Pictures Ltd
	G-ODCS	Robinson R-22B	Gibb Helicopters
	G-ODDY	Lindstrand LBL-105A balloon	P. & T. Huckle
	G-ODEB	Cameron A-250 balloon	A. Derbyshire
	G-ODEL	Falconar F-11-3	G. F. Brummell
	G-ODEN	PA-28-161 Cadet	J. Appleton/Denham
	G-ODGS	Jabiru UL	D. G. Salt
	G-ODHL	Cameron N-77 balloon	DHL International (UK) Ltd
	G-ODIG	Bell 206B JetRanger 2	Valley Engineering Ltd (G-NEEP)

Reg.	Type	Owner or Operator	Notes
G-ODIN	Avions Mudry CAP.10B	T. W. Harris	
G-ODIS	Cameron Cabin SS balloon	Cameron Balloons Ltd	
G-ODIY	Colt 69A balloon	P. Glydon	
G-ODJG	Shaw Europa	D. J. Goldsmith	
G-ODJH	Mooney M.20C	R. M. Schweitzer (G-BMLH)/Netherlands	
G-ODLY	Cessna 310J	R. J. Huband (G-TUBY/G-ASZZ)	
G-ODMC	AS.350B-1 Ecureuil	D. M. Coombs (G-BPVF)/Denham	
G-ODOC	Robinson R-44 Astro	Gas & Air Ltd	
G-ODOG	PA-28R Cherokee Arrow 200-II	Advanced Investments Ltd (G-BAAR)	
G-ODOT	Robinson R-22B	Farm Aviation Ltd	
G-ODSK	Boeing 737-37Q	British Midland Airways Ltd/E. Midlands	
G-ODTW	Shaw Europa	D. T. Walters	
G-ODUS	Boeing 737-36Q	British Airways Regional	
G-ODVB	CFM Shadow Srs DD	D. V. Brunt (G-MGDB)	
G-OEAC	Mooney M.20J	Welding Alloys Group Ltd/Fowlmere	
G-OEAT	Robinson R-22B	C. Y. O. Seeds Ltd (G-RACH)	
G-OECH	AA-5A Cheetah	Plane Talking Ltd (G-BKBE)/Elstree	
G-OEDB	PA-38-112 Tomahawk	Air Delta Bravo Ltd (G-BGGJ)/Elstree	
G-OEDP	Cameron N-77 balloon	M. J. Betts	
G-OEGG	Cameron 65 Egg SS balloon	Virgin Airship & Balloon Co Ltd	
G-OEGL	Christen Eagle II	D. I. Cooke & J. Penfold	
G-OEJA	Cessna 500 Citation	Eurojet Aviation Ltd (G-BWFL)	
G-OERR	Lindstrand LBL-60A balloon	Lindstrand Balloons Ltd	
G-OERS	Cessna 172N	E. R. Stevens (G-SSRS)	
G-OERX	Cameron O-65 balloon	R. Roehsler/Austria	
G-OEST	BAe Jetstream 3202	Air Kilroe Ltd/Manchester	
G-OEWA	D.H.104 Dove 8	D. C. Hunter (G-DDCD/G-ARUM)	
G-OEYE	Rans S.10 Sakota	P. Thompson	
G-OEZY	Shaw Europa	A. W. Wakefield	
G-OFAS	Robinson R-22B	Findon Air Services/Shoreham	
G-OFBJ	Thunder Ax7-77 balloon	N. D. Hicks	
G-OFCM	Cessna F.172L	F. C. M. Aviation Ltd (G-AZUN)/Guernsey	
G-OFER	PA-18 Super Cub 150	M. S. W. Meagher/Edgehill	
G-OFFA	Pietenpol Air Camper	OFFA Group	
G-OFHL	AS.350B Ecureuil	Ford Helicopters Ltd (G-BLSP)	
G-OFIL	Robinson R-44 Astro	P. & J. Twigg	
G-OFIN	AS.355F-2 Twin Squirrel	Salehurst Aviation Ltd (G-DANS/G-BTNM)	
G-OFIT	SOCATA TB.10 Tobago	GFI Aviation Group (G-BRIU)	
G-OFIZ	Cameron 80 Can SS balloon	Virgin Airship & Balloon Co Ltd	
G-OFJC	Eiri PIK-20E	M. J. Aldridge	
G-OFJS	Robinson R-22B	Burman Aviation Ltd (G-BNXJ)/Cranfield	
G-OFLG	SOCATA TB.10 Tobago	R. Noble Ltd (G-JMWT)	
G-OFLI	Colt 105A balloon	Virgin Airship & Balloon Co Ltd	
G-OFLT	EMB-110P1 Bandeirante	Flightline Ltd (G-MOBL/G-BGCS)/ Southend	
G-OFLY	Cessna 210M	A. P. Mothew/Stapleford	
G-OFMB	Rand-Robinson KR-2	F. M. & S. I. Burden	
G-OFOA	BAe 146-100	Formula One Administration Ltd (G-BKMN/G-ODAN)	
G-OFOR	Thunder Ax3 balloon	T. J. Ellenreider & ptnrs	
G-OFOX	Denney Kitfox	P. R. Skeels	
G-OFRA	Boeing 737-36Q	British Airways Regional	
G-OFRT	L.188C Electra	Channel Express (Air Services) Ltd/ Bournemouth	
G-OFRY	Cessna 152 II	Devon School of Flying Ltd (G-BPHS)/Dunkeswell	
G-OFTI	PA-28 Cherokee 140	P. E. Richardson (G-BRKU)	
G-OGAN	Shaw Europa	G-OGAN Group	
G-OGAR	PZL SZD-45A Ogar	N. C. Grayson	
G-OGAS	Westland WG.30 Srs 100	(stored) (G-BKNW)/Yeovil	
G-OGAV	Lindstrand LBL-240A balloon	Out Of This World	
G-OGAZ	SA.341G Gazelle 1	Killochries Fold (G-OCJR/G-BRGS)	
G-OGBA	Boeing 737-4S3	GB Airways Ltd (G-OBMK)/Gatwick	
G-OGBB	Boeing 737-34S	GB Airways Ltd/Gatwick	
G-OGBC	Boeing 737-34S	GB Airways Ltd/Gatwick	
G-OGBD	Boeing 737-3L9	GB Airways Ltd/Gatwick	
G-OGBE	Boeing 737-3L9	GB Airways Ltd/Gatwick	
G-OGCA	PA-28-161 Warrior II	Aerohire Ltd/Halfpenny Green	
G-OGEE	Pitts S-2B Special	Management Consultancy Services Inc Ltd	
G-OGEM	PA-28-181 Archer II	GEM Rewinds Ltd	

Notes	Reg.	Type	Owner or Operator
	G-OGET	PA-39 Twin Comanche 160 C/R	P. G. Kitchingman (G-AYXY)
	G-OGGS	Thunder Ax8-84 balloon	G. Gamble & Sons (Quorn) Ltd
	G-OGHH	Enstrom 480	Silver Lining Finance SA
	G-OGHL	AS.355F-1 Twin Squirrel	Grampian Helicopter Charter Ltd
	G-OGIL	Short SD3-30 Variant 100 ★	N.E. Aircraft Museum (G-BITV)/Usworth
	G-OGJS	Puffer Cozy	G. J. Stamper
	G-OGOA (NIAL)	AS.350B Ecureuil	Lomas Helicopters Ltd (G-PLMD/G-
	G-OGOB	Schweizer 269C	Kingfisher Helicopters Ltd (G-GLEE/ G-BRUW)
	G-OGOG	Robinson R-22B	Lake Services (G-TILL)
	G-OGRK	AS.355F-1 Twin Squirrel	Kelwaiver Ltd (G-BWZC)
	G-OGTS	Air Command 532 Elite	GTS Engineering (Coventry) Ltd
	G-OHAJ	Boeing 737-36Q	British Airways Regional
	G-OHAL	Pietenpol Air Camper	H. C. Danby
	G-OHCP	AS.355F-1 Twin Squirrel	Cabair Helicopters Ltd (G-BTVS/ G-STVE/G-TOFF/G-BKJX)
	G-OHDC	Colt Agfa Film Cassette SS balloon	Flying Pictures Ltd
	G-OHEA	H.S.125 Srs 3B/RA	B. L. Schroder (G-AVRG)
	G-OHHI	Bell 206L-1 LongRanger	Bradmore Helicopters (G-BWYJ)
	G-OHIG	EMB-110P1 Bandeirante ★	Valley Nurseries (G-OPPP)/Alton
	G-OHKS	Pegasus Quantum 15-912	Pegasus Aviation
	G-OHLL	Robinson R-22B	Plane Talking Ltd (G-CHAL)/Elstree
	G-OHMS	AS.355F-1 Twin Squirrel	S.W. Electricity PLC
	G-OHNA	Mainair Blade 912	P. A. Lee
	G-OHSA	Cameron N-77 balloon	D. N. & L. J. Close
	G-OHWV	Raj Hamsa X'Air 582 (5)	H. W. Vasey
	G-OIBM	R. Commander 114	I. Rosewell (G-BLVZ)
	G-OIBO	PA-28 Cherokee 180	Britannia Airways Ltd (G-AVAZ)/Luton
	G-OICE	Cessna 525 Citationjet	Airshare Holdings Ltd
	G-OICO	Lindstrand LBL-42A balloon	Virgin Airship & Balloon Co Ltd
	G-OIDW	Cessna F.150G	I. D. Wakeling
	G-OIEA	PA-31P Pressurised Navajo	Skyrock Aviation Ltd (G-BBTW)/Cyprus
	G-OIFM	Cameron 90 Dude SS balloon	L. V. Masti
	G-OIMC	Cessna 152 II	E. Midlands Flying School Ltd
	G-OING	AA-5A Cheetah ★	Abraxas Aviation Ltd (G-BFPD)/Denham
	G-OINK	Piper J-3C-65 Cub	A. R. Harding (G-BILD/G-KERK)
	G-OINV	BAe 146-300	British Regional Airlines/BA
	G-OIOZ	Thunder Ax9-120 S2 balloon	The Flying Doctors Hot Air Balloon Co Ltd
	G-OISO	Cessna FRA.150L	Les Oiseaux (G-BBJW)
	G-OITN	AS.355F-1 Twin Squirrel	Lynton Aviation Ltd/Denham
	G-OITV	Enstrom 280C-UK-2	M. A. Crook & A.Wright (G-HRVY/ G-DUGY/G-BEEL)
	G-OJAB	Jabiru SK	ST Aviation Ltd
	G-OJAC	Mooney M.20J	Hornet Engineering Ltd
	G-OJAE	Hughes 269C	J. A. & C. M. Wilson
	G-OJAV	BN-2A Mk III-2 Trislander	Air Tabernacle Ltd (G-BDOS)
	G-OJBB	Enstrom 280FX	Adenstar Developments Ltd
	G-OJBW	Lindstrand LBL J & B Bottle SS balloon	P. Spinlove Justerini & Brooks Ltd
	G-OJCB	AB-206B JetRanger 2	R. & M. International Engineering Ltd
	G-OJCW	PA-32RT-300 Lance II	CW Group
	G-OJDA	EAA Acrosport II	D. B. Almey
	G-OJDC	Thunder Ax7-77 balloon	J. Crosby
	G-OJEG	Airbus A.321-231	Monarch Airlines Ltd/Luton
	G-OJEN	Cameron V-77 balloon	Jensport Ltd
	G-OJGT	Maule M.5-235C	J. G. Townsend
	G-OJHB	Colt Flying Ice Cream Cone SS balloon	Benedikt Haggeney GmbH/Germany
	G-OJHL	Shaw Europa	J. H. Lace
	G-OJIL	PA-31-350 Navajo Chieftain	Redhill Aviation Ltd
	G-OJIM	PA-28R-201T Turbo Arrow III	Piper Arrow Group
	G-OJJB	Mooney M.20K	Fly Over Ltd
	G-OJJF	D.31 Turbulent	J. J. Ferguson
	G-OJMR	Airbus A.300-605R	Monarch Airlines Ltd/Luton
	G-OJNB	Linsdstrand LBL-21A balloon	Justerini & Brooks Ltd
	G-OJON	Taylor JT.2 Titch	J. H. Fell
	G-OJPB	H.S.125 Srs F600B	Widehawk Aviation Ltd (G-BFAN/ G-AZHS)
	G-OJRH	Robinson R-44 Astro	Holgate Construction Ltd

UK OUT OF SEQUENCE

Reg.	Type	Owner or Operator
G-OJSW	Boeing 737-8Q8	Sabre Airways Ltd
G-OJSY	Short SD3-60 Variant 100	BAC Express Ltd (G-BKKT)
G-OJTA	Stemme S.10V	OJT Associates
G-OJTW	Boeing 737-36N	British Midland Airways Ltd (G-JTWF)/ E. Midlands
G-OJVA	Van's RV-6	J. A. Village
G-OJVH	Cessna F.150H	Yorkshire Light Aircraft Ltd (G-AWJZ)/ Leeds
G-OJWS	PA-28-161 Warrior II	L. E. Guernieri
G-OKAG	PA-28R Cherokee Arrow 180	N. F. & B. R. Green/Stapleford
G-OKAY	Pitts S-1E Special	J. S. Mortimore & R. J. Allan
G-OKBT	Colt 25A Mk II balloon	British Telecommunications PLC
G-OKCC	Cameron N-90 balloon	D. J. Head
G-OKDN	Boeing 737-8Q8	Sabre Airways Ltd
G-OKED	Cessna 150L	Haimoss Ltd/Old Sarum
G-OKEN	PA-28R-201T Turbo Arrow III	W. B. Bateson/Blackpool
G-OKES	Robinson R-44 Astro	Direct Helicopters (Southend) Ltd
G-OKEV	Shaw Europa	K. R. Pilcher
G-OKEY	Robinson R-22B	Key Properties Ltd/Booker
G-OKIS	Tri-R Kis	B. W. Davies
G-OKJN	Boeing 727-225	Sabre Airways Ltd
G-OKMA	Tri-R Kis	K. Miller
G-OKPW	Tri-R Kis	K. P. Wordsworth
G-OKYA	Cameron V-77 balloon	Army Balloon Club
G-OKYM	PA-28 Cherokee 140	B. Marshall (G-AVLS)
G-OLAH	Short SD3-60 Variant 100	Gill Airways Ltd (G-BPCO/G-RMSS/ G-BKKU)/Newcastle
G-OLAU	Robinson R-22B	MPW Aviation Ltd
G-OLAW	Lindstrand LBL-25A balloon	George Law Plant
G-OLBL	Lindstrand LBL-90A balloon	Alois Geudon Balloons/Germany
G-OLDD	BAe 125 Srs 800B	Gold Air International Ltd
G-OLDM	Pegasus Quantum 15-912	P. A. M. Morgan
G-OLDN	Bell 206L LongRanger	Gulfstream Air Services (UK) Ltd (G-TBCA/G-BFAL)
G-OLDY	Luton LA-5 Major	M. P. & A. P. Sargent
G-OLEE	Cessna F.152	Aerohire Ltd/Halfpenny Green
G-OLEO	Thunder Ax10-210 S2 balloon	P. J. Waller
G-OLFC	PA-38-112 Tomahawk	M. W. Glencross (G-BGZG)
G-OLFT	R. Commander 114	B. C. Richens & B. N. Woodward (G-WJMN)
G-OLGA	CFM Starstreak Shadow SA-II	N. F. Smith
G-OLIZ	Robinson R-22B	Randall Photographic
G-OLJT	Mainair Gemini Flash IIA	L. J. Taylor (G-MTKY)
G-OLLE	Cameron O-84 balloon	N. A. Robertson
G-OLLI	Cameron O-31 SS balloon	N. A. Robertson
G-OLLY	PA-31-350 Navajo Chieftain	Barnes Olsen Aeroleasing Ltd (G-BCES)
G-OLMA	Partenavia P.68B	C. M. Evans (G-BGBT)
G-OLOW	Robinson R-44 Astro	Healds Aviation
G-OLPG	Colt 77A balloon	Eurogas & Corralgas
G-OLRT	Robinson R-22B	Morhire
G-OLSF	PA-28-161 Cadet	Plane Talking Ltd (G-OTYJ)/Elstree
G-OLVR	FRED Srs 2	C. P. Whitwell
G-OLYD	Beech 58 Baron	I. G. Lloyd
G-OLYN	Sky 260-24 balloon	C. J. Sandell
G-OMAC	Cessna FR.172E	RK Consultants
G-OMAF	Dornier Do.228-200	FR Aviation Ltd/Bournemouth
G-OMAK	Airbus A.319-132	Alkharafi Aviation 2000 Ltd
G-OMAP	R. Commander 685	Cooper Aerial Surveys Ltd/Sandtoft
G-OMAR	PA-34-220T Seneca III	Redhill Flying Club
G-OMAT	PA-28 Cherokee 140	Midland Air Training School (G-JIMY/ G-AYUG)/Coventry
G-OMAX	Brantly B.2B	P. D. Benmax (G-AVJN)
G-OMDD	Thunder Ax8-90 S2 balloon	M. D. Dickinson
G-OMDG	Hoffmann H-36 Dimona	P. Turner
G-OMDH	Hughes 369E	Stilgate Ltd/Booker
G-OMDR	AB-206B JetRanger 3	Aeromega Ltd (G-HRAY/G-VANG/ G-BIZA)
G-OMEC	AB-206B JetRanger 3	Kallas Ltd (G-OBLD)/Monaco
G-OMEL	Robinson R-44 Astro	Nedair Ltd (G-BVPB)
G-OMGD	H.S.125 Srs 700B	MAGEC Aviation Ltd/Luton
G-OMGE	BAe 125 Srs 800B	Marconda Services Ltd (G-BTMG)/Luton
G-OMGG	BAe 125 Srs 800B	MAGEC Aviation Ltd/Luton
G-OMHC	PA-28RT-201 Arrow IV	Tatenhill Aviation

Notes	Reg.	Type	Owner or Operator
	G-OMHI	Mills MH-1	J. P. Mills
	G-OMIA	M.S.893A Rallye Commodore 180	P. W. Portelli
	G-OMIG	Aero-Vodochody MiG-15UTI (6247)	Classic Aviation Ltd/Duxford
	G-OMIK	Shaw Europa	
	G-OMJB	Bell 206B JetRanger 2	M. J. Clews
	G-OMJT	Rutan LongEz	Coventry Helicopter Centre Ltd
	G-OMKF	Aero Designs Pulsar	M. J. Timmons
	G-OMMG	Robinson R-22B	M. K. Faro
	G-OMMM	Colt 90A balloon	Abraxas Aviation Ltd(G-BPYX)
	G-OMNH	Beech 200 Super King Air	3M Health Care Ltd
	G-OMNI	PA-28R Cherokee Arrow 200D	Maynard & Harris Holdings Ltd
	G-OMOG	AA-5A Cheetah	Excel Automation Ltd (G-BAWA)
	G-OMRB	Cameron V-77 balloon	Solent Flight Aircraft Ltd (G-BHWR)
	G-OMRG	Hoffmann H-36 Dimona	M. R. Bayne
	G-OMSG	Robinson R-22B	M. R. Grimwood (G-BLHG)
	G-OMUC	Boeing 737-36Q	S. Freedman
	G-OMUM	R. Commander 114	British Airways Regional
	G-OMWE	Zenair CH.601HD	Armadafleet Ltd
			Mid-West Engines Ltd (G-BVXU)/ Staverton
	G-OMXS	Lindstrand LBL-105A balloon	Virgin Airship & Balloon Co Ltd
	G-ONAF	Naval Aircraft Factory N3N-3	R. P. W. Steel & J. E. Hutchinson
	G-ONAV	PA-31-310 Turbo Navajo C	Panther Aviation Ltd (G-IGAR)
	G-ONCB	Lindstrand LBL-31A balloon	Flying Pictures Ltd
	G-ONCL	Colt 77A balloon	D. R. Pearce
	G-ONEB	Westland Scout AH.1	N. E. Bailey (G-BXOE)
	G-ONET	PA-28 Cherokee 180E	J. Blackburn & J. J. Feeney (G-AYAU)
	G-ONFL	Meridian Maverick	K. M. Dando (G-MYUJ)
	G-ONGC	Robin DR.400/180R	Norfolk Gliding Club Ltd/Tibenham
	G-ONHH	Forney F-1A Aircoupe	R. D. I. Tarry (G-ARHA)
	G-ONIX	Cameron C-80 balloon	Hillwalk Ltd
	G-ONKA	Aeronca K	N. J. R. Minchin
	G-ONMT	Robinson R-22B	Redcourt Enterprises Ltd
	G-ONON	RAF 2000 GTX-SE gyroplane	M. S. R. Allen
	G-ONOW	Bell 206A JetRanger 2	J. Luckett (G-AYMX)
	G-ONPA	PA-31-350 Navajo Chieftain	Anglo American Airmotive Ltd/ Bournemouth
	G-ONTV	AB-206B JetRanger 3	Castle Air Charters Ltd
	G-ONUN	Van's RV-6A	R. E. Nunn
	G-ONYX	Bell 206B JetRanger 3	Burgoyne Group (G-BXPN)
	G-ONZO	Cameron N-77 balloon	K. Temple
	G-OOAA	Airbus A.320-231	Air 2000 Ltd
	G-OOAB	Airbus A.320-231	Air 2000 Ltd
	G-OOAC	Airbus A.320-231	Air 2000 Ltd
	G-OOAD	Airbus A.320-231	Air 2000 Ltd
	G-OOAE	Airbus A.321-211	Air 2000 Ltd (G-UNIF)
	G-OOAF	Airbus A.321-211	Air 2000 Ltd (G-UNID/G-UKLO)
	G-OOAG	Airbus A.321-211	Air 2000 Ltd
	G-OOAH	Airbus A.321-211	Air 2000 Ltd (G-UNIE)
	G-OOAI	Airbus A.321-211	Air 2000 Ltd
	G-OOAJ	Airbus A.321-211	Air 2000 Ltd
	G-OOAL	Boeing 767-38AER	Air 2000 Ltd
	G-OOAN	Boeing 767-39HER	Air 2000 Ltd (G-UKLH)
	G-OOAO	Boeing 767-39HER	Air 2000 Ltd (G-UKLI)
	G-OODE	SNCAN Stampe SV-4C (G)	A. R. Radford (G-AZNN)
	G-OODI	Pitts S-1D Special	M. J. Walden (G-BBBU)
	G-OODW	PA-28-181 Archer II	Goodwood Terrena Ltd
	G-OOER	Lindstrand LBL-25A balloon	Airborne Adventures Ltd
	G-OOGA	GA-7 Cougar	Plane Talking Ltd/Elstree
	G-OOGI	GA-7 Cougar	Plane Talking Ltd (G-PLAS/G-BGHL)
	G-OOGO	GA-7 Cougar	Leonard F. Jollye (Brookmans Park) Ltd /Elstree
	G-OOGS	GA-7 Cougar	Bournemouth Flying Club Ltd (G-BGJW)
	G-OOJB	Cessna 421C	Melman Investments Ltd (G-BKSO)
	G-OOJC	Bensen B.8MR	J. R. Cooper
	G-OOJP	Commander 114B	Plato Management Ltd
	G-OOLE	Cessna 172M	P. S. Eccersley (G-BOSI)
	G-OONE	Mooney M.20J	J. H. Donald & K. B. Moore
	G-OONI	Thunder Ax7-77 balloon	Fivedata Ltd
	G-OONY	PA-28-161 Warrior II	D. A. Field & P. B. Jenkins
	G-OOOA	Boeing 757-28A	Air 2000 Ltd
	G-OOOB	Boeing 757-28A	Air 2000 Ltd/Royal Airlines (C-FRYH)
	G-OOOC	Boeing 757-28A	Air 2000 Ltd/Royal Airlines (C-FRYL)

Reg.	Type	Owner or Operator
G-OOOD	Boeing 757-28A	Air 2000 Ltd/Royal Airlines (C-GRYU)
G-OOOG	Boeing 757-23A	Air 2000 Ltd/Royal Airlines (C-GRYY)
G-OOOI	Boeing 757-23A	Air 2000 Ltd
G-OOOJ	Boeing 757-23A	Air 2000 Ltd
G-OOOM	Boeing 757-225	Air 2000 Ltd
G-OOOO	Mooney M.20J	Pergola Ltd
G-OOOS	Boeing 757-236	Air 2000 Ltd (G-BRJD)
G-OOOU	Boeing 757-2Y0	Air 2000 Ltd
G-OOOV	Boeing 757-225	Air 2000 Ltd
G-OOOW	Boeing 757-225	Air 2000 Ltd
G-OOOX	Boeing 757-2Y0	Air 2000 Ltd
G-OOOY	Boeing 757-2Q8	B. O. Smith & J. A. Towers
G-OOSE	Rutan Vari-Eze	M. Goosey
G-OOSY	D.H.82A Tiger Moth	H. Daines Electronics Ltd (G-CLIV)
G-OOTC	PA-28R-201T Turbo Arrow III	Shiplake Investments Ltd
G-OOUT	Colt Flying Shuttlecock SS balloon	
G-OOXP	Aero Designs Pulsar XP	T. D. Baker
G-OPAG	PA-34-200 Seneca II	A. H. Lavender (G-BNGB)/Biggin Hill
G-OPAL	Robinson R-22B	Hell Air Ltd/Wellesbourne
G-OPAM	Cessna F.152 II (tailwheel)	PJC Leasing Ltd (G-BFZS)
G-OPAT	Beech 76 Duchess	R. D. J. Axford (G-BHAO)
G-OPAZ	Pazmany PL.2	K. Morris
G-OPBH	Aero Designs Pulsar	P. B. Hutchinson
G-OPDM	Enstrom 280FX	Lancroft Air Ltd
G-OPDS	Denney Kitfox Mk 4	P. D. Sparling
G-OPEP	PA-28RT-201T Turbo Arrow IV	A. J. Keen
G-OPFT	Cessna 172R	Rankart Ltd
G-OPFW	H.S.748 Srs 2A	Emerald Airways Ltd (G-BMFT)/Liverpool
G-OPHT	Schleicher ASH-26E (T1)	Scheibler Filters Ltd
G-OPIC	Cessna FRA.150L	Air Survey (G-BGNZ)
G-OPIK	Eiri PIK-20E	A. J. McWilliam/Newtownards
G-OPIT	CFM Streak Shadow Srs SA	W. M. Kilner
G-OPJC	Cessna 152 II	PJC Leasing Ltd/Stapleford
G-OPJD	PA-28RT-201T Turbo Arrow IV	M. J. S. Worley
G-OPJH	D.62B Condor	P. J. Hall (G-AVDW)
G-OPJK	Shaw Europa	P. J. Kember
G-OPLB	Cessna 340A II	Ridgewood Ltd (G-FCHJ/G-BJLS)
G-OPLC	D.H.104 Dove 8	W. G. T. Pritchard & I. Darcy-Bean (G-BLRB)
G-OPME	PA-23 Aztec 250D	Oxspeed Ltd (G-ODIR/G-AZGB)
G-OPMN	Boeing 727-225	Sabre Airways Ltd
G-OPMT	Lindstrand LBL-105A balloon	Pace Micro Technology Ltd
G-OPNH	Stoddard-Hamilton Glasair IIRG	P. N. Haigh (G-CINY)
G-OPNI	Bell 206B JetRanger	P & I Data Services Ltd (G-BXAA/ G-BHMV)
G-OPPL	AA-5A Cheetah	London School of Flying Ltd (G-BGNN)/ Elstree
G-OPSF	PA-38-112 Tomahawk	Panshanger School of Flying (G-BGZI)
G-OPSL	PA-32R-301 Saratoga SP	Photonic Science Ltd (G-IMPW)
G-OPST	Cessna 182R	Lota Ltd/Shoreham
G-OPTS	Robinson R-22B	ZB Ltd
G-OPUB	Slingsby T.67M Firefly 160	P. M. Barker (G-DLTA/G-SFTX)
G-OPUP	B.121 Pup 2	Brinkley Light Aircraft Services (G-AXEU)
G-OPUS	Jabiru SK	Opus Software Ltd
G-OPWK	AA-5A Cheetah	A. H. McVicar (G-OAEL)/Prestwick
G-OPWS	Mooney M.20K	A. R. Mills
G-OPYE	Cessna 172S	Pye Consulting Group Ltd
G-ORAC	Cameron 110 RAC Van SS balloon	Virgin Airship & Balloon Co Ltd
G-ORAF	CFM Streak Shadow	A. P. Hunn
G-ORAL	H.S.748 Srs 2A	Emerald Airways Ltd (G-BPDA/G-GLAS) /Liverpool
G-ORAR	PA-28-181 Archer III	P. N. & S. M. Thornton
G-ORAY	Cessna F.182Q II	G. A. Barrett (G-BHDN)
G-ORDO	PA-30 Twin Comanche B	C. A. Ringrose
G-ORED	BN-2T Turbine Islander	The Red Devils Aviation Ltd (G-BJYW)
G-OREV	Mini -500	R. H. Everett
G-ORFC	Jurca MJ.5 Sirocco	D. J. Phillips
G-ORFH	Aérospatiale ATR-42-300	Gill Airways Ltd/Air France Express
G-ORHE	Cessna 500 Citation	R. H. Everett (G-OBEL/G-BOGA)
G-ORIG	Glaser-Dirks DG.800A	I. Godfrey
G-ORIX	ARV K1 Super 2	Burel Air Ltd (G-BUXH/G-BNVK)

Notes	Reg.	Type	Owner or Operator
	G-ORJB	Cessna 500 Citation	L'Equipe Air Ltd (G-OKSP)
	G-ORJW	Laverda F.8L Falco Srs 4	W. R. M. Sutton
	G-ORMA	AS.355F-1 Twin Squirrel	Autopilot Ltd (G-SITE/G-BPHC)
	G-ORMB	Robinson R-22B	R. M. Bailey
	G-ORMG	Cessna 172R II	J. R. T. Royle
	G-OROB	Robinson R-22B	Corniche Helicopters (G-TBFC)
	G-OROD	PA-18 Super Cub 150	R. J. O. Walker
	G-ORON	Cameron 77A balloon	Orion Hot Air Balloon Group
	G-OROZ	AS.350B-2 Ecureuil	Fisher Engineering Ltd
	G-ORPR	Cameron O-77 balloon	T. Strauss & A. Sheehan
	G-ORSP	Beech A36 Bonanza	Makins
	G-ORTM	Glaser-Dirks DG.400	D. P. Holdcroft
	G-ORTW	Lindstrand AM-25000 balloon	Lindstrand Balloons Ltd
	G-ORVB	McCulloch J-2	R. V. Bowles (G-BLGI/G-BKKL)
	G-ORVR	Partenavia P.68B	Ravenair (G-BFBD)/Liverpool
	G-OSAL	Cessna 421C	Yorkshire Helicopters/Leeds
	G-OSCA	Cessna 500 Citation	Oscar Aviation Ltd (G-SWET)
	G-OSCC	PA-32 Cherokee Six 300	BG & G Airlines Ltd (G-BGFD)
	G-OSCH	Cessna 421C	Sureflight Aviation Ltd (G-SALI)
	G-OSCO	Team Minimax	P. J. Schofield
	G-OSDI	Beech 95-58 Baron	D. Darling (G-BHFY)
	G-OSEA	BN-2B-26 Islander	W. T. Johnson & Sons (Huddersfield) Ltd (G-BKOL)
	G-OSEE	Robinson R-22B	Burman Aviation Ltd/Cranfield
	G-OSFA	Diamond HK.36TC Super Dimona	Diamond Aircraft Industries GmbH/ Austria
	G-OSFC	Cessna F.152	Stapleford Flying Club Ltd (G-BIVJ)
	G-OSGB	PA-31-350 Navajo Chieftain	Gold Air International Ltd (G-YSKY)
	G-OSHL	Robinson R-22B	Sloane Helicopters Ltd/Sywell
	G-OSII	Cessna 172N	K. J. Abrams (G-BIVY)
	G-OSIP	Robinson R-22B	Heli Air Ltd
	G-OSIS	Pitts S-1S Special	M. C. Boddington & I. M. Castle
	G-OSIX	PA-32 Cherokee Six 260	A. E. Whittle (G-AZMO)
	G-OSKP	Enstrom 480	Eastern Atlantic Helicopters
	G-OSKY	Cessna 172M	Skyhawk Leasing Ltd/Wellesbourne
	G-OSLO	Schweizer 269C	A. H. Helicopter Services Ltd
	G-OSMD	Bell 206B JetRanger 2	Stuart Aviation Ltd (G-LTEK/G-BMIB)
	G-OSMR	Lake LA-4-200 Buccaneer	J. P. Billingham
	G-OSMS	Robinson R-22B	Heli Air Ltd (G-BXYW)/Wellesbourne
	G-OSMT	Shaw Europa	S. M. Thomas
	G-OSND	Cessna FRA.150M	Wilkins & Wilkins Special Auctions Ltd (G-BDOU)
	G-OSNI	PA-23 Aztec 250C	Marham Investments Ltd (G-AWER)
	G-OSOE	H.S.748 Srs 2A	Emerald Airways Ltd (G-AYYG)/Liverpool
	G-OSOO	Hughes 369E	Methan Aviation Ltd
	G-OSPS	PA-18 Super Cub 95	J. W. Macleod
	G-OSST	Colt 77A balloon	British Airways PLC
	G-OSTA	J/1 Autocrat	D. & M. Nelson (G-AXUJ)
	G-OSTC	AA-5A Cheetah	5th Generation Designs Ltd
	G-OSTU	AA-5A Cheetah	Airhouse Corporation Ltd (G-BGCL)/ Elstree
	G-OSTY	Cessna F.150G	C. R. Guggenheim (G-AVCU)
	G-OSUP	Lindstrand LBL-90A balloon	British Airways Balloon Club
	G-OSUS	Mooney M.20K	J. B. King/Goodwood
	G-OSVO	Cameron 30 Hopper Servo SS balloon	Servo & Electronic Sales Ltd
	G-OSVY	Sky 31-24 balloon	Virgin Airship & Balloon Co Ltd
	G-OTAC	Robinson R-22B	Aviation Corporation PLC
	G-OTAF	Aero L-39ZO Albatros (28-02)	C. P. B. Horsley/Duxford
	G-OTAL	ARV Super 2	N. R. Beale (G-BNGZ)
	G-OTAM	Cessna 172M	G. V. White
	G-OTAN	PA-18 Super Cub 135	S. D. Turner
	G-OTBY	PA-32 Cherokee Six 300	GOTBY Ltd
	G-OTCH	CFM Streak Shadow	H. E. Gotch
	G-OTDB	MDH Hughes 369E	D. E. McDowell(G-BXUR)
	G-OTED	Robinson R-22HP	Andrews Heli-Lease Ltd (G-BMYR)
	G-OTEL	Thunder Ax8-90 balloon	D. N. Belton
	G-OTFT	PA-38-112 Tomahawk	N. Papadroushotis (G-BNKW)
	G-OTGT	Cessna 560 Citation V	Ferron Trading Ltd
	G-OTHE	Enstrom 280C-UK Shark	GTS Engineering (Coventry) Ltd (G-OPJT/G-BKCO)
	G-OTHL	Robinson R-22B	Thurston Helicopters (Engineering) Ltd (G-DSGN)

Reg.	Type	Owner or Operator	Notes
G-OTIM	Bensen B.8MV	T. J. Deane	
G-OTNT	Cameron Cider Bottle SS balloon	A. J. Round	
G-OTOE	Aeronca 7AC Champion	J. M. Gale (G-BRWW)	
G-OTOO	Stolp SA.300 Starduster Too	I. M. Castle	
G-OTOY	Robinson R-22B	Tickstop Ltd (G-BPEW)	
G-OTRG	Cessna TR.182RG	Thermodata Components	
G-OTRV	Van's RV-6	W. R. C. Williams-Wynne	
G-OTSP	AS.355F-1 Twin Squirrel	Aeromega Ltd (G-XPOL/G-BPRF)	
G-OTTI	Cameron 34 Otti SS balloon	Ballonwerbung Hamburg GmbH/ Germany	
G-OTTO	Cameron 82 Katalog SS balloon	Ballonwerbung Hamburg GmbH/ Germany	
G-OTUG	PA-18 Super Cub 150	B. F. Walker	
G-OTUP	Lindstrand LBL-180A balloon	Airborne Adventures Ltd	
G-OTVS	BN-2T Turbine Islander	Headcorn Parachute Club Ltd (G-BPBN/ G-BCMY) (stored)	
G-OTWO	Rutan Defiant	A. J. Baggerley	
G-OURO	Shaw Europa	D. Pitt	
G-OURS	Sky 120-24 balloon	M. P. A. Sevrin	
G-OUVI	Cameron O-105 balloon	Bristol University Hot Air Ballooning Soc	
G-OUZO	Airbus A.320-231	Virgin Atlantic Airways Ltd Spirit of Melina	
G-OVAA	Colt Jumbo SS balloon	Virgin Airship & Balloon Co Ltd	
G-OVAX	Colt AS-80 Mk II airship	H. Dahlhoff/Germany	
G-OVBF	Cameron A-250 balloon	Virgin Balloon Flights Ltd	
G-OVBJ	Bell 206B JetRanger 3	Aeromega Ltd (G-BXDS)	
G-OVET	Cameron O-56 balloon	E. J. A. Macholc	
G-OVFM	Cessna 120	Commair Group	
G-OVFR	Cessna F.172N	Western Air (Thruxton) Ltd	
G-OVID	Light Aero Avid Flyer	J. M. Walsh & D. F. Chamberlain	
G-OVMC	Cessna F.152 II	Staverton Flying School	
G-OVNR	Robinson R-22B	Rally Repaints/Breighton	
G-OWAC	Cessna F.152	Barnes Olson Aeroleasing Ltd (G-BHEB)	
G-OWAK	Cessna F.152	Falcon Flying Services (G-BHEA)/ Biggin Hill	
G-OWAL	PA-34-220T Seneca III	Parkers Properties Ltd	
G-OWAR	PA-28-161 Warrior II	Bickertons Aerodromes Ltd	
G-OWAZ	Pitts S-1C Special	P. E. S. Latham (G-BRPI)	
G-OWCG	Bell 222	Phoenix Helicopter Charters Ltd (G-VERT/G-JLBZ/G-BNDB)	
G-OWDB	H.S.125 Srs 700B	Bizair Ltd (G-BXFO/G-OWEB)	
G-OWEL	Colt 105A balloon	S. R. Seager	
G-OWEN	K & S Jungster	R. C. Owen	
G-OWET	Thurston TSC-1A2 Teal	D. Nieman	
G-OWGC	Slingsby T.61F Venture T.2	Wolds Gliding Club Ltd/Pocklington	
G-OWIN	BN-2A-8 Islander	North London Parachute Centre (G-AYXE)	
G-OWIZ	Luscombe 8A Silvaire	R. J. Pearson/France	
G-OWLC	PA-31 Turbo Navajo	Top Nosh Ltd (G-AYFZ)	
G-OWND	Robinson R-44 Astro	W. N. Dore	
G-OWOW	Cessna 152 II	Falcon Flying Services (G-BMSZ)/ Biggin Hill	
G-OWWW	Shaw Europa	J. F. & W. R. C. Williams-Wynne	
G-OWYN	Aviamilano F.14 Nibbio	D. Kynaston	
G-OXBY	Cameron N-90 balloon	C. A. Oxby	
G-OXKB	Cameron 110 Sports Car SS balloon	Flying Pictures Ltd	
G-OXTC	PA-23 Aztec 250D	Falcon Flying Services (G-AZOD)/ Biggin Hill	
G-OXVI	V.S.361 Spitfire LF.XVIe (TD248)	Silver Victory BVBA/Belgium	
G-OYAK	Yakovlev C-11 (27)	A. H. Soper/Earls Colne	
G-OYES	Mainair Blade 912	M. Irving	
G-OZAR	Enstrom 480	Lancroft Air Ltd (G-BWFF)	
G-OZBA	Airbus A.320-212	Monarch Airlines Ltd (G-MALE)/Luton	
G-OZBB	Airbus A.320-212	Monarch Airlines Ltd/Skyservice (C-FTDW)/Luton	
G-OZBD	Airbus A.321-231	Monarch Airlines Ltd/Luton	
G-OZEE	Light Aero Avid Speedwing Mk 4	S. C. Goozee	
G-OZLN	Zlin Z.242L	R. L. McDonald	
G-OZOI	Cessna R.182	J. R. G. & F. L. G. Fleming (G-ROBK)	
G-OZOO	Cessna 172N	Atlantic Bridge Aviation Ltd (G-BWEI)/ Lydd	
G-OZRH	BAe 146-200	Flightline Ltd/Stansted	

Notes	Reg.	Type	Owner or Operator
	G-OZZI	Jabiru SK	A. H. Godfrey & E. J. Stradling
	G-PACE	Robin R.1180T	Millicron Instruments Ltd/Coventry
	G-PACL	Robinson R-22B	R. Wharam
	G-PADI	Cameron V-77 balloon	R. F. Penney
	G-PADS	R. Commander 114B	J. D'Arcy Mounter
	G-PAGS	SA.341G Gazelle 1	P. A. G. Seers (G-OAFY/G-SFTH/ G-BLAP)
	G-PAIZ	PA-12 Super Cruiser	B. R. Pearson/Eaglescott
	G-PALL	PA-46-250P Malibu Mirage	Pressurised Aircraft Leasing Ltd (G-RMST)
	G-PALS	Enstrom 280C-UK-2 Shark	G. Firbank
	G-PAMS	PA-60 Aerostar 601P	P. A. Brook (G-GAIR)
	G-PAPS	PA-32R-301T Turbo Saratoga SP	Pump & Plant Services Ltd
	G-PARI	Cessna 172RG Cutlass	Applied Signs Ltd
	G-PARR	Cameron 90 Bottle SS balloon	Virgin Airship & Balloon Co Ltd
	G-PASC	MBB Bo 105DBS/4	Lincolnshire Ambulance Service (G-BNPS)/Waddington
	G-PASD	MBB Bo 105DBS/4	Police Aviation Services Ltd (G-BNRS)
	G-PASF	AS.355F-1 Twin Squirrel	Police Aviation Services Ltd (G-SCHU)
	G-PASG	MBB Bo 105DBS/4	Police Aviation Services Ltd (G-MHSL)
	G-PASH	AS.355F-1 Twin Squirrel	Police Aviation Services Ltd
	G-PASS	McD Douglas MD.900/902	Police Aviation Services Ltd
	G-PASU	BN-2T Turbine Islander	Police Aviation Services Ltd (G-BJYY)
	G-PASV	BN-2B-21 Islander	Police Aviation Services Ltd (G-BKJH)
	G-PASX	MBB Bo 105DBS/4	Police Aviation Services Ltd
	G-PATF	Shaw Europa	E. P. Farrell
	G-PATG	Cameron O-90 balloon	P. A. & A. J. A. Bubb
	G-PATN	SOCATA TB.10 Tobago	A. T. Paton (G-LUAR)
	G-PATP	Lindstrand LBL-77A balloon	P. Pruchnickyj
	G-PATS	Shaw Europa	D. J. D. Kesterton
	G-PATZ	Shaw Europa	H. P. H. Griffin
	G-PAVL	Robin R.3000/120	Newcharter (UK) Ltd
	G-PAWL	PA-28 Cherokee 140	G-PAWL Group (G-AWEU)
	G-PAWS	AA-5A Cheetah	Plane Talking Ltd/Elstree
	G-PAXX	PA-20 Pacer 135	D. W. & M. R. Grace
	G-PAZY	Pazmany PL.4A	C. R. Nash (G-BLAJ)
	G-PBBT	Cameron N-56 balloon	E. C. Moore
	G-PBEL	CFM Shadow Srs DD	P. C. Bell
	G-PBES	Robinson R-22B	Brian Seedle Helicopters (G-EXOR/ G-CMCM)
	G-PBUS	Jabiru SK	G. R. Pybus
	G-PBYY	Enstrom 280FX	Southern Air Ltd (G-BXKV)
	G-PCAF	Pietenpol Air Camper	C. C. & F. M. Barley
	G-PCDP	Zlin Z.526F Trener Master	Zlin Group
	G-PCOM	PA-30 Twin Comanche 160B	P. & H. Robinson
	G-PDGG	Aeromere F.8L Falco Srs 3	P. D. G. Grist
	G-PDHJ	Cessna T.182R	P. G. Vallance Ltd
	G-PDMH	Cessna 340A II	D. R. C. Knight (G-RITA)
	G-PDOC	PA-44-180 Seminole	Medicare (G-PVAF)/Newcastle
	G-PDOG	Cessna 305C Bird Dog	N. D. Needham
	G-PDON	WMB.2 Windtracker balloon	P. J. Donnellan
	G-PDSI	Cessna 172N	DA Flying Group
	G-PDWI	Mini-500	P. Waterhouse
	G-PEAK	AB-206B JetRanger 2	Leisure Park Management Ltd (G-BLJE)
	G-PEAL	Aerotek Pitts S-2A	Plymouth Executive Aviation Ltd
	G-PEAT	Cessna 421B	Golden Airways Ltd (G-BBIJ)
	G-PEGG	Colt 90A balloon	Ballon Vole Association/France
	G-PEGI	PA-34-200T Seneca II	Tayflite Ltd
	G-PEKT	SOCATA TB.20 Trinidad	A. J. Dales
	G-PELG	Avions Mudry CAP.231	J. P. M. Groot (G-OPPS)/Netherlands
	G-PENN	AA-5B Tiger	L. F. Banks
	G-PENT	Bell 206B JetRanger 3	Flying Tonight Ltd (G-IIRB)
	G-PERR	Cameron 60 Bottle SS balloon ★	British Balloon Museum/Newbury
	G-PERS	Colt Soapbox SS balloon	G. V. Beckwith
	G-PERZ	Bell 206B JetRanger 3	Intrepid Aviation Co/North Weald
	G-PEST	Hawker Tempest II	Tempest Two Ltd/Sandtoft
	G-PETR	PA-28 Cherokee 140	Marnham Investments Ltd (G-BCJL)
	G-PFAA	EAA Biplane Model P	E. W. B. Comber
	G-PFAF	FRED Srs 2	M. S. Perkins
	G-PFAG	Evans VP-1	J. A. Hatch
	G-PFAH	Evans VP-1	J. A. Scott
	G-PFAL	FRED Srs 2	J. McD. Robinson/Bann Foot

UK OUT OF SEQUENCE

Reg.	Type	Owner or Operator	Notes
G-PFAO	Evans VP-1	P. W. Price	
G-PFAP	Currie Wot/SE-5A (C1904)	J. H. Seed	
G-PFAR	Isaacs Fury II (K2059)	K. M. Potts	
G-PFAT	Monnett Sonerai II	H. B. Carter	
G-PFAW	Evans VP-1	R. F. Shingler	
G-PFML	Robinson R-44 Astro	Helicopter Training & Hire Ltd	
G-PGAC	Dyn Aero MCR-01	G. A. Coatesworth	
G-PGUY	Sky 70-16 balloon	Black Sheep Balloons (G-BXZJ)	
G-PHAA	Cessna F.150M	PHA Aviation Ltd (G-BCPE)	
G-PHEL	Robinson R-22B	Focal Point Communications Ltd (G-RUMP)	
G-PHIL	Brookland Hornet	A. J. Philpotts	
G-PHON	Cameron Phone SS balloon	Redmalt Ltd (G-BTEY)	
G-PHOT	Thunder Film Cassette SS balloon	Flying Pictures Ltd	
G-PHSI	Colt 90A balloon	P. H. Strickland & Simpson (Piccadilly) Ltd	
G-PHTG	SOCATA TB.10 Tobago	A. J. Baggarley	
G-PHYL	Denney Kitfox Mk 4	J. Dunn	
G-PIAF	Thunder Ax7-65 balloon	L. Battersley	
G-PICT	Colt 180A balloon	J. L. Guy	
G-PIDG	Robinson R-44 Astro	T. Pidgley	
G-PIDS	Boeing 757-225	Airtours International Airways Ltd	
G-PIEL	CP.301A Emeraude	P. R. Thorne (G-BARY)	
G-PIES	Thunder Ax7-77Z balloon	Pork Farms Ltd	
G-PIET	Pietenpol Air Camper	N. D. Marshall	
G-PIGG	Lindstrand LBL Pig SS balloon	I. Heidenreich	
G-PIGS	SOCATA Rallye 150ST	Boonhill Flying Group (G-BDWB)	
G-PIGY	SC.7 Skyvan Srs 3A Variant 100	Hunting Aviation Ltd/ Weston-on-the-Green	
G-PIIX	Cessna P.210N	J. R. Colthurst (G-KATH)	
G-PIKE	Robinson R-22 Mariner	Sloane Helicopters Ltd/Sywell	
G-PIKK	PA-28 Cherokee 140	L. P. & I. Keegan (G-AVLA)	
G-PILE	Rotorway Executive 90	J. B. Russell	
G-PILL	Light Aero Avid Flyer Mk 4	D. R. Meston	
G-PINE	Thunder Ax8-90 balloon	J. A. Pine	
G-PING	AA-5A Cheetah	Plane Talking Ltd (G-OCWC/G-WULL)/ Elstree	
G-PINT	Cameron 65 Barrel SS balloon	D. K. Fish	
G-PINX	Lindstrand Pink Panther SS balloon	L. V. Mastis	
G-PIPR	PA-18 Super Cub 95	R. G. Trute (G-BCDC)	
G-PIPS	Van's RV-4	C. J. Marsh	
G-PIPY	Cameron 105 Pipe SS balloon	Cameron Balloons Ltd	
G-PITS	Pitts S-2AE Special	The Eitlean Group	
G-PITZ	Pitts S-2A Special	A. K. Halvorsen	
G-PIXI	Pegasus Quantum 15-912	D. L. Goode	
G-PIXS	Cessna 336	Atlantic Bridge Aviation Ltd/Biggin Hill	
G-PIZZ	Lindstrand LBL-105A balloon	HD Bargain SRL/Italy	
G-PJMT	Lancair 320	M. T. Holland	
G-PJTM	Cessna FR.172K II	Jane Air (G-BFIF)	
G-PKPK	Schweizer 269C	C. H. Dobson	
G-PLAC	PA-31-350 Navajo Chieftain	Vale Aviation Ltd (G-OLDA/G-BNDS)	
G-PLAH	BAe Jetstream 3102	Osprey Aviation Ltd (G-LOVA/ G-OAKA/G-BUFM/G-LAKH)	
G-PLAN	Cessna F.150L	G-PLAN Flying Group	
G-PLAT	Beech 200 Super King Air	Bevair Services Ltd	
G-PLAY	Robin R.2100A	D. R. Austin	
G-PLEE	Cessna 182Q	Peterlee Parachute Centre	
G-PLIV	Pazmany PL.4	B. P. North	
G-PLMB	AS.350B Ecureuil	PLM Dollar Group Ltd (G-BMMB)	
G-PLMC	AS.350B Ecureuil	PLM Dollar Group Ltd (G-BKUM)	
G-PLMH	AS.350B-2 Ecureuil	PLM Dollar Group Ltd	
G-PLMI	SA.365C-1 Dauphin	PLM Dollar Group Ltd	
G-PLOW	Hughes 269B	Sulby Aerial Surveys Ltd (G-AVUM)	
G-PLPC	Schweizer Hughes 269C	Power Lines, Pipes & Cables Ltd (G-JMAT)	
G-PLUS	PA-34-200T Seneca II	C. G. Strasser/Jersey	
G-PLXI	BAe ATP/Jetstream 61	BAe (Operations) Ltd (G-MATP)/ Woodford	
G-PMAM	Cameron V-65 balloon	P. A. Meecham	
G-PMAX	PA-31-350 Navajo Chieftain	AM & T Aviation Ltd (G-GRAM/G-BRHF)	
G-PMNF	V.S.361 Spitfire HF.IX (TA805)	P. R. Monk	
G-PNEU	Colt 110 Bibendum SS balloon	The Aerial Display Co Ltd	

Notes	Reg.	Type	Owner or Operator
	G-PNNI	PA-28-181 Archer III	Dorset Aircraft Leasing Ltd
	G-POAH	Sikorsky S-76B	P&O Aviation Ltd
	G-POLT	Robinson R-44 Astro	Lyntonworth Ltd
	G-POLY	Cameron N-77 balloon	Empty Wallets Balloon Group
	G-POND	Oldfield Baby Lakes	H. Hillenbrand/Germany
	G-POOH	Piper J-3C-65 Cub	P. & H. Robinson
	G-POOL	ARV Super 2	P. A. Dawson (G-BNHA)
	G-POOP	Dyn Aero MCR-01	P. Bondar
	G-POPA	Beech A36 Bonanza	C. J. O'Sullivan
	G-POPE	Eiri PIK-20E-1	C. J. Hadley
	G-POPI	SOCATA TB.10 Tobago	I. S. Hacon & C. J. Earle (G-BKEN)
	G-POPS	PA-34-220T Seneca III	Alpine Ltd
	G-POPW	Cessna 182S	D. L. Price
	G-PORK	AA-5B Tiger	J. W. & B. A. Flint (G-BFHS)
	G-PORT	Bell 206B JetRanger 3	Image Computer System Ltd
	G-POSH	Colt 56A balloon	B. K. Rippon (G-BMPT)
	G-POTT	Robinson R-44 Astro	Ranc Care Homes Ltd
	G-POWL	Cessna 182R	Hillhouse Estates Ltd
	G-POWR	Agusta A.109E	Powersense Ltd (G-BXUD)
	G-PPAH	Enstrom 480	Cumbrian Seafoods Ltd
	G-PPLH	Robinson R-22B	Status Investments Ltd
	G-PPPP	Denney Kitfox Mk 3	S. P. Woodhouse & S. A. Tuff
	G-PPTS	Robinson R-44 Astro	Superstore Ltd
	G-PRAG	Brügger MB.2 Colibri	Colibri Flying Group
	G-PRET	Robinson R-44 Astro	First Degree Air Ltd
	G-PREY	Pereira Osprey II	D. W. Gibson (G-BEPB)
	G-PRII	Hawker Hunter PR.11	Stick & Rudder Aviation Ltd/Belgium
	G-PRIM	PA-38-112 Tomahawk	Braddock Ltd
	G-PRNT	Cameron V-90 balloon	E. K. Gray
	G-PROD	AS.350B-2 Ecureuil	Prodrive Ltd
	G-PROM	AS.350B Ecureuil	JPM Ltd (G-MAGY/G-BIYC)
	G-PROP	AA-5A Cheetah	Fortune Technology Ltd (G-BHKU)
	G-PROV	P.84 Jet Provost T.52A (T.4)	D. S. Milne
	G-PRSI	Pegasus Quantum 15-912	P. R. Stevens
	G-PRTT	Cameron N-31 balloon	J. M. Albury
	G-PRXI	V.S.365 Spitfire PR.XI (PL983)	Wizzard Investments Ltd/North Weald
	G-PSFT	PA-28-161 Warrior II	SFT Europe Ltd (G-BPDS)/ Bournemouth
	G-PSIC	NA P-51C Mustang (2106449)	Patina Ltd/Duxford
	G-PSON	Colt Cylinder One SS balloon	M. E. White
	G-PSRT	PA-28-151 Warrior	P. A. S. Dyke
	G-PSST	Hunter F.58A	Heritage Aviation Developments Ltd/ Bournemouth
	G-PSUE	CFM Shadow Srs CD	P. F. Lorroman (G-MYAA)
	G-PTAG	Shaw Europa	R. C. Harrison
	G-PTRE	SOCATA TB.20 Trinidad	Trantshore Ltd (G-BNKU)
	G-PTWO	Pilatus P2-05 (U-110)	Rentair Ltd
	G-PTYE	Shaw Europa	J. Tye
	G-PUDL	PA-18 Super Cub 150	R. A. Roberts
	G-PUDS	Shaw Europa	I. Milner
	G-PUFF	Thunder Ax7-77A balloon	Intervarsity Balloon Club
	G-PUFN	Cessna 340A	The Puffin Club
	G-PUMA	AS.332L Super Puma	Bond Helicopters Ltd
	G-PUMB	AS.332L Super Puma	Bond Helicopters Ltd
	G-PUMD	AS.332L Super Puma	Bond Helicopters Ltd
	G-PUME	AS.332L Super Puma	Bond Helicopters Ltd
	G-PUMG	AS.332L Super Puma	Bond Helicopters Ltd
	G-PUMH	AS.332L Super Puma	Bristow Helicopters Ltd
	G-PUMI	AS.332L Super Puma	Bristow Helicopters Ltd
	G-PUMK	AS.332L Super Puma	Bond Helicopters Ltd
	G-PUML	AS.332L Super Puma	Bond Helicopters Ltd
	G-PUMM	AS.332L-2 Super Puma	Bond Helicopters Ltd
	G-PUMN	AS.332L Super Puma	Bond Helicopters Ltd
	G-PUMO	AS.332L-2 Super Puma	Bond Helicopters Ltd
	G-PUNK	Thunder Ax8-105 balloon	D. J. Farrar
	G-PUPP	B.121 Pup 2	P. A. Teichman (G-BASD)/Elstree
	G-PURR	AA-5A Cheetah	Nabco Retail Display (G-BJDN)
	G-PURS	Rotorway Executive	J. E. Houseman
	G-PUSH	Rutan LongEz	E. G. Peterson
	G-PUSI	Cessna T.303	W. R. Swinburn Ltd
	G-PUSS	Cameron N-77 balloon	Bristol Balloons
	G-PUSY	RL-5A LW Sherwood Ranger	B. J. Chester-Master (G-MZNF)
	G-PUTT	Cameron 76 Golf SS balloon	Lakeside Lodge Golf Centre

Reg.	Type	Owner or Operator
G-PVBF	Lindstrand LBL-260S balloon	Virgin Balloon Flights Ltd
G-PVCU	Cameron N-77 balloon	R. G. March
G-PVET	D.H.C.1 Chipmunk 22 (WB565)	Connect Properties Ltd
G-PWBE	D.H.82A Tiger Moth	P. W. Beales
G-PWEL	Robinson R-22B	DJP Ltd
G-PYCO	Dassault Falcon 2000	Charyo Corporation Ltd
G-PYLN	Cameron Pylon SS balloon	Virgin Airship & Balloon Co Ltd (G-BUSO)
G-PYOB	SA.341G Gazelle 1	MW Helicopters Ltd (G-WELA/G-SFTD/G-RIFC)
G-PYRO	Cameron N-65 balloon	A. C. Booth
G-PZAZ	PA-31-350 Navajo Chieftain	Air Medical Ltd (G-VTAX/G-UTAX)
G-PZIZ	PA-31-350 Navajo Chieftain	Air Medical Ltd (G-CAFZ/G-BPPT)
G-RACO	PA-28R Cherokee Arrow 200-II	Graco Group Ltd
G-RACY	Cessna 182S	N. J. Fuller
G-RADA	Soko P-2 Kraguj (30140)	Steerworld Ltd
G-RADI	PA-28-181 Archer II	G. S. & D. V. Foster
G-RAEM	Rutan LongEz	G. F. H. Singleton
G-RAES	Boeing 777-236	British Airways
G-RAFA	Grob G.115	RAF College Flying Club Ltd/Cranwell
G-RAFB	Grob G.115	RAF College Flying Club Ltd/Cranwell
G-RAFC	Robin R.2112	RAF Charlie Group
G-RAFE	Thunder Ax7-77 balloon	Giraffe Balloon Syndicate
G-RAFF	Learjet 35A	Graff Aviation Ltd/Heathrow
G-RAFG	Slingsby T.67C	Arrow Flying Ltd
G-RAFI	P.84 Jet Provost T.4 (XP672)	G. R. Lacey/Bournemouth
G-RAFT	Rutan LongEz	H. C. Mackinnon
G-RAFW	Mooney M.20E	Vinola (Knitwear) Manufacturing Co. Ltd (G-ATHW)
G-RAGG	Maule M5-235C Lunar Rocket	P. Ragg
G-RAGS	Pietenpol Air Camper	R. F. Billington
G-RAID	AD-4NA Skyraider (126922)	Patina Ltd/Duxford
G-RAIL	Colt 105A balloon	Ballooning World Ltd
G-RAIN	Maule M5-235C Lunar Rocket	D. S. McKay & J. A. Rayment/ Hinton-in-the-Hedges
G-RAIX	CCF AT-16 Harvard 4 (KF584)	M. R. Paul & P. A. Shaw (G-BIWX)
G-RAJA	Raj Hamsa X'Air 582 (2)	Priory Flyers
G-RAJS	General Avia F-22C	R. A. J. Spurrell
G-RALD	Robinson R-22HP	Heli Air Ltd (G-CHIL)
G-RAMI	Bell 206B JetRanger 3	Yorkshire Helicopters/Leeds
G-RAMP	Piper J-3C-65 Cub	J. Whittall
G-RAMS	PA-32R-301 Saratoga SP	Air Tobago Ltd/Netherthorpe
G-RAMY	Bell 206B JetRanger 2	A. Drewry
G-RANA	Cameron 82 Cheese SS balloon	Consorizio per la Tutela del Formaggio/ Italy
G-RANS	Rans S.10 Sakota	J. D. Weller
G-RANZ	Rans S.10 Sakota	R. J. Humphries
G-RAPA	BN-2T-4R Defender 4000	Brittan-Norman Ltd (G-BJBH)/Bembridge
G-RAPH	Cameron O-77 balloon	P. B. D. Bird & M. E. Mason
G-RAPP	Cameron H-34 balloon	Cameron Balloons Ltd
G-RARB	Cessna 172N	Richlyn Aviation Ltd (G-BOII)
G-RARE	Thunder Ax5-42 SS balloon	Justerini & Brooks Ltd
G-RASC	Evans VP-2	K. A. Stewart & G. Oldfield
G-RATE	AA-5A Cheetah	Holmes Rentals (G-BIFF)
G-RATZ	Shaw Europa	W. Goldsmith
G-RAVE	Southdown Raven X	M. J. Robbins (G-MNZV)
G-RAVL	H.P.137 Jetstream Srs 200	Cranfield University (G-AWVK)
G-RAYA	Denney Kitfox Mk 4	A. K. Ray
G-RAYE	PA-32 Cherokee Six 260	F. J. Wadia (G-ATTY)
G-RAYS	Zenair CH.250	B. O. & F. A. Smith
G-RAZA	AS.365N-2 Dauphin 2	Blanco Real SA/Cayman Islands
G-RBBB	Shaw Europa	T. J. Hartwell
G-RBMV	Cameron O-31 balloon	P. D. Griffiths
G-RBOS	Colt AS-105 airship ★	Science Museum/Wroughton
G-RBOW	Thunder Ax-7-65 balloon	A. C. Hall
G-RCED	R. Commander 114	Echo Delta Ltd
G-RCEJ	BAe 125 Srs 800B	Aravco Ltd (G-GEIL)/Farnborough
G-RCHA	PA-28-181 Archer III	R. Day
G-RCMC	Murphy Renegade 912	R. C. M. Collisson
G-RCMF	Cameron V-77 balloon	Mouldform Ltd
G-RCML	Sky 77-24 balloon	R. C. M. Sarl/Luxembourg
G-RDBS	Cessna 550 Citation II	Redbus Charter Aviation Ltd (G-JETA)

Notes	Reg.	Type	Owner or Operator
	G-RDCI	R. Commander 112A	P. Turner (G-BFWG)
	G-RDON	WMB.2 Windtracker balloon	P. J. Donnellan (G-BICH)
	G-RDVE	Airbus A.320-231	Airtours International Airways Ltd
	G-READ	Colt 77A balloon	J. Keena
	G-REAH	PA-32R-301 Saratoga SP	M. Q. Tolbod & S. J. Rogers (G-CELL)
	G-REAP	Pitts S-1S Special	R. Dixon
	G-REAS	Van's RV-6A	E. J. D. Proctor
	G-REAT	GA-7 Cougar	Goodtechnique Ltd
	G-REBK	Beech B200 Super King Air	Gold Air International Ltd
	G-REBL	Hughes 269B	GTS Engineering (Coventry) Ltd
	G-RECK	PA-28 Cherokee 140B	R. J. Grantham & D. Boatswain (G-AXJW)
	G-RECO	Jurca MJ-5L Sirocco	J. D. Tseliki
	G-REDB	Cessna 310Q	Leisure Park Management Ltd (G-BBIC)
	G-REDC	Pegasus Quantum 15-912	Red Communications Ltd
	G-REDD	Cessna 310R II	G. Wightman (G-BMGT)
	G-REDX	Experimental Aviation Berkut	G. V. Waters
	G-REEC	Sequoia F.8L Falco	J. D. Tseliki
	G-REEK	AA-5A Cheetah	J. & A. Pearson
	G-REEM	AS.355F-1 Twin Squirrel	Heliking Ltd (G-EMAN/G-WEKR/ G-CHLA)
	G-REEN	Cessna 340	E. & M. Green (G-AZYR)/Guernsey
	G-REES	Jodel D.140C	W. H. Greenwood
	G-RENE	Murphy Renegade 912	P. M. Whitaker
	G-RENO	SOCATA TB.10 Tobago	Lamond Ltd
	G-RENT	Robinson R-22B	Rentatruck Self Drive Ltd
	G-REPM	PA-38-112 Tomahawk	Nultree Ltd
	G-REST	Beech P35 Bonanza	C. R. Taylor (G-ASFJ)
	G-RETA	C.A.S.A. 1.131 Jungmann 2000	N. S. C. & G. English (G-BGZC)
	G-REXS	PA-28-181 Archer II	Tatenhill Aviation
	G-REZE	Rutan Vari-Eze	S. D. Brown & S. P. Evans
	G-RFDS	Agusta A.109A II	Castle Air Charters Ltd (G-BOLA)
	G-RFIL	Thunder Colt 77A balloon	G. Davis
	G-RFIO	Aeromot AMT-200 Super Ximango	G. McLean & R. B. Beck/Rufforth
	G-RFSB	Sportavia RF-5B	S. W. Brown
	G-RGEN	Cessna T.337D	R. J. Willies (G-EDOT/G-BJIY)
	G-RGUS	Fairchild 24A-46A Argus III	Fenlands Ltd
	G-RHCB	Schweizer 269C-1	Oxford Aviation Services Ltd
	G-RHHT	PA-32RT-300 Lance II	R. W. & M. Struth
	G-RHYS	Rotorway Executive 90	A. K. Voase & K. Matthews
	G-RIAN	AB-206A JetRanger	Thorneygrove Ltd (G-SOOR/G-FMAL/ G-BHSG)
	G-RIAT	Robinson R-22B	Pinetree Car Centre
	G-RIBS	Diamond Katana DA.20-A1	West London Models (G-BWWM)
	G-RIBV Ltd	Cessna 560 Citation Ultra	Rothmans International Tobacco (UK)
	G-RICA	AG-5B Tiger	Plane Talking Ltd/Elstree
	G-RICC	AS.350B-2 Ecureuil	Specialist Helicopters Ltd (G-BTXA)
	G-RICE	Robinson R-22B	Warwickshire Flying Training Centre Ltd
	G-RICK	Beech 95-B55 Baron	James Jack (Invergordon) Ltd (G-BAAG)
	G-RICO	AG.5B Tiger	Dynasty Trading Ltd
	G-RICS	Shaw Europa	The Flying Property Doctor
	G-RIDE	Stephens Akro	R. Mitchell/Coventry
	G-RIFB	Hughes 269C	J. McHugh & Son (Civil Engineering Contractors) Ltd
	G-RIFN	Avion Mudry CAP.10B	S. A. W. Becker
	G-RIGB	Thunder Ax7-77 balloon	Antrum & Andrews Ltd
	G-RIGH	PA-32R-301 Saratoga IIHP	Rentair
	G-RIGS	PA-60 Aerostar 601P	Techno Engineering
	G-RIMM	Westland Wasp HAS.1	P. A. Shaw & M. P. Grimshaw
	G-RINO	Thunder Ax7-77 balloon	D. J. Head
	G-RINS	Rans S.6-ESD Coyote II	D. Watt
	G-RINT	CFM Streak Shadow	D. Grint
	G-RIPS	Cameron 110 Parachutist SS balloon	Virgin Airship & Balloon Co Ltd
	G-RISE	Cameron V-77 balloon	D. L. Smith
	G-RIST	Cessna 310R II	J. M. Jackson (G-DATS)
	G-RIVR	Thruster T.600N	Thruster Air Services Ltd
	G-RIVT	Van's RV-6	N. Reddish
	G-RIZE	Cameron O-90 balloon	S. F. Burden/Netherlands
	G-RIZI	Cameron N-90 balloon	R. Wiles

Reg.	Type	Owner or Operator	Notes
G-RIZZ	PA-28-161 Warrior II	Northamptonshire School of Flying Ltd/ Sywell	
G-RJAH	Boeing Stearman A.75N1	R. J. Horne	
G-RJCP	R. Commander 114B	W. P. J. Davison	
G-RJGR	Boeing 757-225	Airtours International Airways Ltd	
G-RJMS	PA-28R-201 Arrow III	M. G. Hill	
G-RJWW	Maule M5-235C Lunar Rocket	Paw Flying Services Ltd (G-BRWG)	
G-RJXA	Embraer RJ145EU	British Midland Commuter Ltd	
G-RJXB	Embraer RJ145EU	British Midland Commuter Ltd	
G-RJXC	Embraer RJ145EU	British Midland Commuter Ltd	
G-RKET	Taylor JY.2 Titch	P. A. Dunkley (G-BIBK)	
G-RLFI	Cessna FA.152	Tayside Aviation Ltd (G-DFTS)/Aberdeen	
G-RLMC	Cessna 421C	R. D. Lygo	
G-RMAC	Shaw Europa	P. J. Lawless	
G-RMAN	Aero Designs Pulsar	M. B. Redman	
G-RMAX	Cameron C-80 balloon	M. Quinn	
G-RMCT	Short SD3-60 Variant 100	Gill Airways Ltd (G-BLPU)/Newcastle	
G-RMIT	Van's RV-4	J. P. Kloos	
G-RMUG	Cameron 90 Mug SS balloon	Nestle UK Ltd	
G-RNBW	Bell 206B JetRanger 2	Rainbow Helicopters Ltd	
G-RNEE	Cameron R-420 balloon	Bondbaste Ltd	
G-RNIE	Cameron 70 Ball SS balloon	Virgin Airship & Balloon Co Ltd	
G-RNLD	Agusta A.109C	Irvine Aviation Ltd	
G-RNLI	V.S.236 Walrus I (W2718) ★	R. E. Melton	
G-RNRM	Cessna A.185F	RN & R. Marines Sport Parachute Association/Dunkeswell	
G-ROAM	Schempp-Hirth Nimbus 4DM	B. A. Eastwell	
G-ROAR	Cessna 401	Special Scope Ltd (G-BZFL/G-AWSF)	
G-ROBD	Shaw Europa	R. D. Davies	
G-ROBN	Robin R.1180T	Bustard Flying Club Ltd	
G-ROBT	Hawker Hurricane I	R. A. Roberts	
G-ROBY	Colt 17A balloon	Virgin Airship & Balloon Co Ltd	
G-ROCH	Cessna T.303	R. S. Bentley	
G-ROCK	Thunder Ax7-77 balloon	M. A. Green	
G-ROCR	Schweizer 269C	Oxford Aviation Services Ltd/Kidlington	
G-RODD	Cessna 310R II	R. J. Herbert Engineering Ltd (G-TEDD/ G-MADI)	
G-RODG	Jabiru UL	I. M. Donnelly	
G-RODI	Isaacs Fury (K3731)	M. R. Baker/Shoreham	
G-ROGG	Robinson R-22B	Burman Aviation Ltd/Cranfield	
G-ROGY	Cameron 60 Concept balloon	A. A. Laing	
G-ROIN	AS.350BA Ecureuil	C. C. Blakey	
G-ROLA	PA-34-200T Seneca	Deer Hill Aviation Ltd & Goss Challenges Ltd	
G-ROLF	PA-32R-301 Saratoga SP	P. F. Larkins	
G-ROLL	Pitts S-2A Special	Aerial & Aerobatic Services	
G-ROLO	Robinson R-22B	Plane Talking Ltd/Elstree	
G-ROMA	Hughes 369HS	Helicopters (Northern) Ltd (G-ROPI/ G-ONPP)/Blackpool	
G-ROME	I.I.I. Sky Arrow 650TC	C. J. Farrell	
G-ROMS	Lindstrand LBL-105G balloon	International Balloons Ltd	
G-ROMW	Cyclone AX2000	Financial Planning (Wells) Ltd	
G-RONA	Shaw Europa	C. M. Noakes	
G-RONG	PA-28R Cherokee Arrow 200-II	E. Tang	
G-RONI	Cameron V-77 balloon	R. E. Simpson	
G-RONN	Robinson R-44 Astro	R. Hallam & S. E. Watts	
G-RONS	Robin DR.400/180	R. & K. Baker	
G-RONW	FRED Srs 2	K. Atkinson	
G-ROOK	Cessna F.172P	Rolim Ltd	
G-ROOV	Shaw Europa XS	D. K. Richardson	
G-RORI	Folland Gnat T.1 (XR538)	D, S, Milne	
G-RORO	Cessna 337B	H. D. Hezlett (G-AVIX)	
G-RORY	Piaggio FWP.149D	Bushfire Investments Ltd (G-TOWN)/ North Weald	
G-ROSE	Evans VP-1	A. P. M. Long	
G-ROSI	Thunder Ax7-77 balloon	J. E. Rose	
G-ROSS	Practavia Pilot Sprite	A. D. Janaway	
G-ROTI	Luscombe 8A Silvaire	A. L. Chapman & R. Ludgate	
G-ROTR	Brantly B.2B	GP Services	
G-ROTS	CFM Streak Shadow Srs SA	P. White	
G-ROUP	Cessna F.172M	Stapleford Flying Club Ltd (G-BDPH)	
G-ROUS	PA-34-200T Seneca II	Oxford Aviation Services Ltd/Kidlington	
G-ROUT	Robinson R-22B	Ramsgill Aviation Ltd	

Notes	Reg.	Type	Owner or Operator
	G-ROVE	PA-18 Super Cub 135	S. J. Gaveston
	G-ROVY	Robinson R-22B	R. Rice
	G-ROWE	Cessna F.182P	D. Rowe/Liverpool
	G-ROWI	Shaw Europa XS	R. M. Carson
	G-ROWL	AA-5B Tiger	Plane Talking Ltd/Elstree
	G-ROWN	Beech 200 Super King Air	Valentia Air Ltd (G-BHLC)
	G-ROWS	PA-28-151 Warrior	Mustarrow Ltd/Woodford
	G-ROZI	Robinson R-44 Astro	Vitapage Ltd
	G-ROZY	Cameron R.36 balloon	Jacques W. Soukup Enterprises Ltd/USA
	G-RPEZ	Rutan LongEz	B. A. Fairston & D. Richardson
	G-RRCU	CEA DR.221B Dauphin	Merlin Flying Club Ltd
	G-RRGN	V.S.390 Spitfire PR.XIX (PS853)	Rolls-Royce PLC (G-MXIX)/Filton
	G-RSCJ	Cessna 525 CitationJet	SMD Investments Ltd
	G-RSFT	PA-28-161 Warrior II	SFT Europe Ltd (G-WARI)/Bournemouth
	G-RSKR	PA-28-161 Warrior II	P. M. Forte & ptnrs (G-BOJY)/Shoreham
	G-RSSF	Denney Kitfox Mk 2	R. W. Somerville
	G-RSVP	Robinson R-22B	Pearce Enterprise Ltd
	G-RSWO	Cessna 172R	Printcentre
	G-RSWW	Robinson R-22B	Woodstock Enterprises
	G-RTBI	Thunder Ax6-56 balloon	P. J. Waller
	G-RTWI	Cameron R-550 balloon	Spirit of Peace Ltd
	G-RTWW	Robinson R-44 Astro	Rotorvation
	G-RUBB	AA-5B Tiger	D. E. Gee
	G-RUBI	Thunder Ax7-77 balloon	Warren & Johnson
	G-RUBY	PA-28RT-201T Turbo Arrow IV	Arrow Aircraft Group (G-BROU)
	G-RUDD	Cameron V-65 balloon	N. A. Apsey
	G-RUFF	Mainair Blade 912	C. G. P. Holden
	G-RUFS	Jabiru UL	J. W. Holland
	G-RUGS	Campbell Cricket Mk 4 gyroplane	J. L. G. McLane
	G-RUIA	Cessna F.172N	Knockin Flying Club Ltd
	G-RUMM	Grumman F8F-2P Bearcat (21714)	Patina Ltd/Duxford
	G-RUMN	AA-1A Trainer	D. W. Reast
	G-RUMT	Grumman F7F-3P Tigercat (80425)	Patina Ltd/Duxford
	G-RUMW	Grumman FM-2 Wildcat (JV579)	Patina Ltd/Duxford
	G-RUNG	SAAB SF.340A	Aurigny Air Services Ltd
	G-RUNT	Cassutt Racer IIIM	Coulson Flying Services Ltd
	G-RUSA	Pegasus Quantum 15-912	Euroflight Microlight Club Ltd
	G-RUSO	Robinson R-22B	R. M. Barnes-Gorell
	G-RUSS	Cessna 172N ★	Leisure Lease (stored)/Southend
	G-RVAN	Van's RV-6	J. R. Heaps & D. Broom
	G-RVAW	Van's RV-6	A. A. Wordsworth
	G-RVBA	Van's RV-8A	S. Hawksworth
	G-RVCL	Van's RV-6	C. T. Lamb
	G-RVDJ	Van's RV-6	J. D. Jewitt
	G-RVEE	Van's RV-6	J. C. A. Wheeler
	G-RVET	Van's RV-6	D. R. Coleman
	G-RVGA	Van's RV-6A	D. P. Dawson
	G-RVHT	Cessna 550 Citation 2	Ravenheat Manufacturing Ltd
	G-RVIA	Van's RV-6A	A. J. Rose
	G-RVIB	Van's RV-6	I. M. Belmore
	G-RVIN	Van's RV-6	N. Reddish
	G-RVIT	Van's RV-6	P. J. Shotbolt
	G-RVIV	Van's RV-4	G. S. Scott
	G-RVMJ	Van's RV-4	M. J. de Ruiter
	G-RVMZ	Van's RV-8	M. W. Zipfell
	G-RVRA	PA-28 Cherokee 140	Ravenair (G-OWVA)/Liverpool
	G-RVRB	PA-34-200T Seneca II	Ravenair (G-BTAJ)/Liverpool
	G-RVRC	PA-23 Aztec 250E	Ravenair (G-BNPD)/Liverpool
	G-RVRD	PA-23 Aztec 250E	Ravenair (G-BRAV/G-BBCM)/Liverpool
	G-RVRF	PA-38-112 Tomahawk	Ravenair (G-BGEL)/Liverpool
	G-RVRG	PA-38-112 Tomahawk	Ravenair (G-BHAF)/Liverpool
	G-RVRV	Van's RV-4	P. Jenkins
	G-RVSA	Van's RV-6A	W. H. Knott
	G-RVSX	Van's RV-6	R. L. & V. A. West
	G-RVVI	Van's RV-6	J. E. Alsford & J. N. Parr
	G-RWHC	Cameron A-180 balloon	Wickers World Hot Air Balloon Co
	G-RWIN	Rearwin 175	G. Kay
	G-RWSS	Denney Kitfox Mk 2	R. W. Somerville
	G-RWWW	W.S.55 Whirlwind HCC.12 (XR486)	Whirlwind Helicopters Ltd/Redhill
	G-RXUK	Lindstrand LBL-105A balloon	P. A. Hames

Reg.	Type	Owner or Operator
G-RYAL	Jabiru UL	A. C. Ryall
G-SAAB	R. Commander 112TC	SAAB Group (G-BEFS)
G-SAAM	Cessna T.182R	H. C. Danby & M. D. Harvey (G-TAGL)
G-SABA	PA-28R-201T Turbo Arrow III	R. J. Howard (G-BFEN)
G-SABR	NA F-86A Sabre (8178)	Golden Apple Operations Ltd/Bournemouth
G-SACB	Cessna F.152 II	Sky Pro Ltd (G-BFRB)
G-SACD	Cessna F.172H	Northbrook College of Design & Technology (G-AVCD)/Shoreham
G-SACH	Glaster	R. S. Holt
G-SACI	PA-28-161 Warrior II	PJC (Leasing) Ltd
G-SACK	Robin R.2160	Sherburn Aero Club Ltd
G-SACO	PA-28-161 Warrior II	The Barn Gallery
G-SACR	PA-28-161 Cadet	Sherburn Aero Club Ltd
G-SACS	PA-28-161 Cadet	Sherburn Aero Club Ltd
G-SACT	PA-28-161 Cadet	Sherburn Aero Club Ltd
G-SACU	PA-28-161 Cadet	Sherburn Aero Club Ltd
G-SACZ	PA-28-161 Warrior II	Lima Delta Aviation Ltd
G-SADE	Cessna F.150L	N. E. Sams (G-AZJW)
G-SAEW	AS.355F-2 Twin Squirrel	Veritair Ltd
G-SAFE	Cameron N-77 balloon	P. J. Waller
G-SAFR	SAAB 91D Safir	B. Johansson
G-SAGA	Grob G.109B	G-GROB Ltd/Booker
G-SAGE	Luscombe 8A Silvaire	R. J. P. Herivel (G-AKTL)
G-SAHI	Trago Mills SAH-1	Sunhawk Ltd/North Weald
G-SAIR	Cessna 421C	Air Support Aviation Services Ltd (G-OBCA)
G-SAIX	Cameron N-77 balloon	C. Walther & ptnrs
G-SALA	PA-32 Cherokee Six 300E	Stonebold Ltd
G-SALL	Cessna F.150L (Tailwheel)	D. & P. A. Hailey
G-SAMG	Grob G.109B	RAFGSA/Bicester
G-SAMI	Cameron N-90 balloon	Flying Pictures Ltd (G-BWSE)
G-SAMM	Cessna 340A	M. R. Cross
G-SAMY	Shaw Europa	K. R. Tallent
G-SAMZ	Cessna 150D	N. E. Sams (G-ASSO)/Cranfield
G-SAND	Schweizer 269C	Aerocroft Ltd
G-SANS	Robinson R-22B	The Type Marketing Co (G-BUHX)
G-SARA	PA-28-181 Archer II	R. P. Lewis
G-SARH	PA-28-161 Warrior II	Sussex Flying Club Ltd/Shoreham
G-SARK	BAC.167 Strikemaster Mk 84 (311)	Sark International Airways Ltd
G-SARO	Saro Skeeter Mk 12 (XL812)	Skeeter Heritage Trust
G-SASK	PA-31P Pressurised Navajo	Middle East Business Club Ltd (G-BFAM)
G-SATL	Cameron 105 Sphere SS balloon	Ballonwerbung Hamburg GmbH/ Germany
G-SAUF	Colt 90A balloon	K. H. Medau
G-SAWI	PA-32RT-300T Turbo Lance II	S. A. & K. J. Williams
G-SAXO	Cameron N-105 balloon	Flying Pictures Ltd
G-SBAE	Cessna F.172P	BAe (Operations) Ltd
G-SBAS	Beech B200 Super King Air	Gama Aviation Ltd (G-BJJV)
G-SBLT	Steen Skybolt	Skybolt Group
G-SBMO	Robin 2160I	D. Henderson & ptnrs
G-SBUS	BN-2A-26 Islander	Isles of Scilly Skybus Ltd (G-BMMH)/ St Just
G-SBUT	Robinson R-22B	Princepro Ltd (G-BXMT)
G-SCAH	Cameron V-77 balloon	D. P. Busby
G-SCAN	Vinten-Wallis WA-116/100	K. H. Wallis
G-SCAT	Cessna F.150F (tailwheel)	G. D. Cooper (G-ATRN)
G-SCBI	SOCATA TB.20 Trinidad	Ace Services
G-SCFO	Cameron O-77 balloon	M. K. Grigson
G-SCLX	FLS Aerospace Sprint 160	Sunhawk Ltd (G-PLYM)/North Weald
G-SCOW	AS.355F-2 Twin Squirrel	B. K. Scowcroft (G-POON/G-MCAL)
G-SCOX	Enstrom F-28F	S. Cox (G-BXXW)
G-SCPL	PA-28 Cherokee 140	Aeroshow Ltd (G-BPVL)/Staverton
G-SCRU	Cameron A-250 balloon	Societe Bombard SARL (G-BWWO)/ France
G-SCTA	Westland Scout AH.1 (XV126)	Austen Associates
G-SCUB	PA-18 Super Cub 135 (542447)	N. D. Needham Farms
G-SCUD	Montgomerie-Bensen B.8MR	D. Taylor
G-SCUL	Rutan Cozy	K. R. W. Scull
G-SDEV	D.H.104 Sea Devon C.20	Wyndeham Press Group PLC (XK895)/ Shoreham
G-SDLW	Cameron O-105 balloon	P. J. Smart

Notes	Reg.	Type	Owner or Operator
	G-SEAB	Republic RC-3 Seabee	B. A. Farries
	G-SEAI	Cessna U.206G (amphibian)	Aerofloat Ltd
	G-SEAT	Colt 42 balloon	Virgin Airship & Balloon Co Ltd
	G-SEED	Piper J-3C-65 Cub	J. H. Seed
	G-SEEK	Cessna T.210N	A. Hopper
	G-SEGA	Cameron 90 Sonic SS balloon	Virgin Airship & Balloon Co Ltd
	G-SEGO	Robinson R-22B	Burman Aviation Ltd/Cranfield
	G-SEJW	PA-28-161 Warrior II	Keen Leasing Ltd
	G-SELL	Robin DR.400/180	G-SELL Regent Group
	G-SELY	AB-206B JetRanger 3	Petrochem Aviation Services Ltd
	G-SEMI	PA-44-180 Seminole	T. Hiscox (G-DENW)
	G-SENA	Rutan LongEz	G. Bennett
	G-SEND	Colt 90A balloon	Redmalt Ltd
	G-SENV	PA-34-220T Seneca V	Technical Flight Services Ltd
	G-SENX	PA-34-200T Seneca II	JGH Computer Services Ltd & Maze Computers Ltd (G-DARE/G-WOTS/G-SEVL)
	G-SEPA	AS.355N Twin Squirrel	Receiver for the Metropolitan Police (G-METD/G-BUJF)
	G-SEPB	AS.355N Twin Squirrel	Metropolitan Police (G-BVSE)
	G-SEPC	AS.355N Twin Squirrel	Receiver for the Metropolitan Police (G-BWGV)
	G-SEPT	Cameron N-105 balloon	P. Gooch
	G-SERA	Enstrom F-28A-UK	W. R. Pitcher (G-BAHU)
	G-SERL	SOCATA TB.10 Tobago	R. J. & G. Searle (G-LANA)/Rochester
	G-SEUK	Cameron 80 TV SS balloon	Flying Pictures Ltd
	G-SEVA	SE-5A (replica) (F141)	I. D. Gregory
	G-SEVE	Cessna 172N	MK Aero Support Ltd
	G-SEXI	Cessna 172M	European Flyers
	G-SEXY	AA-1 Yankee ★	(stored)/Liverpool (G-AYLM)
	G-SFBH	Boeing 737-46N	British Midland Airways Ltd/E. Midlands
	G-SFHR	PA-23 Aztec 250F	Comed Aviation Ltd (G-BHSO)
	G-SFOX	Rotorway Executive 90	Magpie Computer Services Ltd (G-BUAH)
	G-SFPA	Cessna F.406	Scottish Fisheries Protection Agency
	G-SFPB	Cessna F.406	Scottish Fisheries Protection Agency
	G-SFRY	Thunder Ax7-77 balloon	K. J. Baxter & P. Szczepanski
	G-SFTZ	Slingsby T.67M Firefly 160	Airborne Services Ltd
	G-SGAS	Colt 77A balloon	Avongas Ltd
	G-SGSE	PA-28-181 Archer II	Mountune Racing Ltd (G-BOJX)
	G-SHAA	Enstrom 280-UK	ELT Radio Telephones
	G-SHAH	Cessna F.152	E. Alexander
	G-SHAM	Beech C90 King Air (modified)	Aerospeed Ltd
	G-SHAW	PA-30 Twin Comanche 160B	E. R. Meredith & M. D. Faiers
	G-SHCB	Schweizer 269C-1	Oxford Aviation Services Ltd/Kidlington
	G-SHCC	AB-206B JetRanger 2	R. & M. International Engineering Ltd
	G-SHED	PA-28-181 Archer II	P. T. Crouch & R. M. Gingell (G-BRAU)
	G-SHIM	CFM Streak Shadow	E. S. Shimmin/Shobdon
	G-SHIP	PA-23 Aztec 250F ★	Midland Air Museum/Coventry
	G-SHIV	GA-7 Cougar	Westley Aircraft Lts/Cranfield
	G-SHNN	Enstrom 280C	CJ Services
	G-SHOG	Colomban MC.15 Cri-Cri	V. S. E. Norman (G-PFAB)/Rendcomb
	G-SHOT	Cameron V-77 balloon	E. C. Moore
	G-SHOW	M.S.733 Alycon	Vintage Aircraft Team/Cranfield
	G-SHPP	Hughes TH-55A	R. P. Bateman
	G-SHRK	Enstrom 280C-UK	Aviation Bureau (G-BGMX)
	G-SHRL	Jodel D.18	M. W. Kilvert & G. Trevor
	G-SHSH	Shaw Europa	D. G. Hillam
	G-SHSP	Cessna 172S	Shropshire Aero Club Ltd/Sleap
	G-SHSS	Enstrom 280C-UK	St. Angelo Helicopters (G-BENO)
	G-SHUG	PA-28R-201T Turbo Arrow III	N. E. Rennie
	G-SHUU	Enstrom 280C-UK-2	D. Ellis (G-OMCP/G-KENY/G-BJFG)
	G-SIAL	Hawker Hunter F.58 (J-4090)	Classic Aviation Ltd/Duxford
	G-SIGN	PA-39 Twin Comanche 160 C/R	D. Buttle
	G-SIIB	Pitts S-2B Special	G. Ferriman (G-BUVY)
	G-SIII	Extra EA.300	Firebird Aerobatics Ltd/Booker
	G-SILS	Pietenpol Skyscout	D. Silsbury
	G-SIMI	Cameron A-315 balloon	Balloon Safaris
	G-SIMN	Robinson R-22B	Simlot Ltd
	G-SION	PA-38-112 Tomahawk II	Naiad Air Services
	G-SIPA	SIPA 903	Mersey SIPA Group (G-BGBM)
	G-SIRR	NA P-51D Mustang (474008)	Intrepid Aviation Co/North Weald
	G-SIVA	MDH Hughes 369E	Davron Aviation (G-TBIX)

Reg.	Type	Owner or Operator
G-SIXC	Douglas DC-6A	Atlantic Air Transport Ltd/Coventry
G-SIXD	PA-32 Cherokee Six 300D	G-SIXD Ltd
G-SIXX	Colt 77A balloon	P. B. D. Bird & R. J. Maud
G-SIXY	Van's RV-6	C. J. Hall & C. R. P. Hamlett
G-SIZE	Lindstrand LBL-310A balloon	Adventure Balloon Co Ltd
G-SJAB	PA-39 Twin Comanche 160 C/R	Foyle Flyers Ltd
G-SJCH	BN-2T-4S Defender 4000	Britten-Norman Ltd (G-BWPK)/ Bembridge
G-SJDI	Robinson R-44 Astro	Total Asset Ltd
G-SJMC	Boeing 767-31KER	Airtours International Airways Ltd
G-SKAN	Cessna F.172M	Bustard Flying Club Ltd (G-BFKT)
G-SKID	Lake LA-4-200 Buccaneer	D. J. L. Wood (G-BMGY/G-BWKS/ G-BDDI)
G-SKIE	Steen Skybolt	S. Gray
G-SKIL	Cameron N-77 balloon	Sky Trek Ballooning Ltd
G-SKIP	Cameron N-77 balloon	Skipton Building Soc
G-SKIS	Tri-R Kis	S. D. Barnard
G-SKYC	Slingsby T.67M Firefly	T. W. Cassells (G-BLDP)
G-SKYD	Pitts S-2B Special	SHYD Syndicate
G-SKYE	Cessna TU.206G	RAF Sport Parachute Association
G-SKYG	I.I.I. Sky Arrow 650TC	G. F. Smith
G-SKYH	Cessna 172N	Elgor Hire Purchase & Credit Ltd/ Southend
G-SKYI	Air Command 532 Elite	P. J. Troy-Davies
G-SKYL	Cessna 182S	Skylane Aviation Ltd/Sherburn
G-SKYM	Cessna F.337E	Bencray Ltd (G-AYHW) (stored)/Blackpool
G-SKYR	Cameron A-180 balloon	PSH Skypower Ltd
G-SKYT	I.I.I. Sky Arrow 650TC	I. R. Malby
G-SKYX	Cameron A-210 balloon	PSH Skypower Ltd
G-SKYY	Cameron A-250 balloon	PSH Skypower Ltd
G-SKYZ	PA-34-200T Seneca II	Park Aeroleasing Ltd
G-SLAC	Cameron N-77 balloon	The Scottish Life Assurance Co
G-SLCE	Cameron C-80 balloon	SLC Europe Ltd
G-SLEA	Mudry/CAARP CAP.10B	P. D. Southerington/Sturgate
G-SLII	Cameron O-90 balloon	R. B. & A. M. Harris
G-SLNE	Agusta A.109A-II	Sloane Helicopters Ltd (G-EEVS/ G-OTSL)/Sywell
G-SLOW	Pietenpol Air Camper	C. Newton
G-SLTN	SOCATA TB.20 Trinidad	S. N. Adamson
G-SLYN	PA-28-161 Warrior II	G. E. Layton
G-SMAF	Sikorsky S-76A	Air Harrods Ltd/Stansted
G-SMAN	Airbus A.330-243	Monarch Airlines Ltd
G-SMAX	Cameron O-105 balloon	Cameron Balloons Ltd
G-SMDB	Boeing 737-36N	British Midland Airways Ltd/E. Midlands
G-SMDH	Shaw Europa XS	S. W. Pitt
G-SMDJ	AS350B-2 Ecureuil	Denis Ferranti Hoverknights Ltd
G-SMIG	Cameron O-65 balloon	Hong Kong Balloon & Airship Club
G-SMJJ	Cessna 414A	Gull Air Ltd/Guernsey
G-SMTC	Colt Flying Hut SS balloon	Shiplake Investments Ltd/Switzerland
G-SMTH	PA-28 Cherokee 140	T. I. Mason & C. J. Mewis (G-AYJS)
G-SNAK	Lindstrand LBL-105A balloon	Ballooning Adventures Ltd
G-SNAP	Cameron V-77 balloon	C. J. S. Limon
G-SNAX	Colt 69A balloon	United Biscuits (UK) Ltd
G-SNAZ	Enstrom F-28F	Thornhill Aviation Ltd (G-BRCP)
G-SNDY	Piper J-3C-65 Cub	R. R. K. Mayall
G-SNEV	CFM Streak Shadow SA	N. G. Smart
G-SNOW	Cameron V-77 balloon	M. J. Ball
G-SOAR	Eiri PIK-20E	F. W. Fay
G-SOEI	H.S.748 Srs 2A	Emerald Airways Ltd/Liverpool
G-SOFA	Cameron N-65 balloon	M. J. Axtell
G-SOFT	Thunder Ax7-77 balloon	A. J. Bowen
G-SOHI	Agusta A.109E	Tri-Ventures Group Ltd
G-SOKO	Soko P-2 Kraguj (30149)	M. R. Keen (G-BRXK)
G-SOLA	Aero Designs Star-Lite SL.1	J. P. Lethaby
G-SOLD	Robinson R-22A	J. F. H. James
G-SOLH	Bell 47G-5	SOL Helicopters Ltd (G-AZMB)
G-SOLO	Pitts S-2S Special	Landitfast Ltd
G-SONA	SOCATA TB.10 Tobago	C. D. Brack (G-BIBI)/Breighton
G-SONY	Aero Commander 200D	General Airline Ltd (G-BGPS)
G-SOOC	Hughes 369HS	Repetek Ltd (G-BRRX)
G-SOOE	Hughes 369E	R. W. Nash
G-SOOK	Sukhoi Su-26M	V. Rahmani

Notes	Reg.	Type	Owner or Operator
	G-SOOM	Glaser-Dirks DG.500M	Glaser-Dirks UK/Rufforth
	G-SOOS	Colt 21A balloon	P. J. Stapley
	G-SOOT	PA-28 Cherokee 180	J. A. Bridger (G-AVNM)/Exeter
	G-SOPP	Enstrom 280FX	F. J. Sopp (G-OSAB)
	G-SORT	Cameron N-90 balloon	A. Brown
	G-SOUL	Cessna 310R	Atlantic Air Transport Ltd/Coventry
	G-SOUP	Cameron C-80 balloon	M. G. Barlow
	G-SPAM	Light Aero Avid Aerobat	R. W. Fair
	G-SPEE	Robinson R-22B	Speed Helicopters Ltd (G-BPJC)/Redhill
	G-SPEL	Sky 220-24 balloon	Pendle Balloon Co
	G-SPEY	AB-206B JetRanger 3	Castle Air Charters Ltd (G-BIGO)
	G-SPFX	Rutan Cozy	B. D. Tutty
	G-SPIN	Pitts S-2A Special	R. P. Grace & P. L. Goldberg
	G-SPIT	V.S.379 Spitfire FR.XIV (MV293)	Patina Ltd (G-BGHB)/Duxford
	G-SPOG	Jodel DR.1050	A. C. Frost (G-AXVS)
	G-SPOL	MBB Bo 105CBS/4	Bond Air Services/Aberdeen
	G-SPUR	Cessna 550 Citation II	Amsail Ltd
	G-SPYI	Bell 206B JetRanger 3	A. J. Sinclair (G-BVRC/G-BSJC)
	G-SROE	Westland Scout AH.1 (XP907)	Bolenda Engineering Ltd
	G-SRVO	Cameron N-90 balloon	Servo & Electronic Sales Ltd
	G-SSCL	MDH Hughes 369E	Shaun Stevens Contractors Ltd
	G-SSFC	PA-34-200 Seneca II	SFC (Air Taxis) Ltd (G-BBXG)/ Stapleford
	G-SSFT	PA-28-161 Warrior II	SFT Europe Ltd (G-BHIL)/Bournemouth
	G-SSGS	Shaw Europa	SGS Partnership
	G-SSIX	Rans S.6-116 Coyote II	T. J. Bax
	G-SSKY	BN-2B-26 Islander	Isles of Scilly Skybus Ltd (G-BSWT)
	G-SSSC	Sikorsky S-76C	Bond Helicopters Ltd/Aberdeen
	G-SSSD	Sikorsky S-76C	Bond Helicopters Ltd/Aberdeen
	G-SSSE	Sikorsky S-76C	Bond Helicopters Ltd/Aberdeen
	G-SSTI	Cameron N-105 balloon	British Airways
	G-SSWA	Short SD3-30 Variant 100	Streamline Aviation (SW) Ltd (G-BHHU)
	G-SSWT	Short SD3-30 Variant 100	Freshleave Ltd (G-BNYA/G-BKSU)
	G-SSWU	Short SD3-30 Variant 100	Streamline Aviation (SW) Ltd (G-BIYH)
	G-SSWV	Sportavia Fournier RF-5B	Skylark Flying Group
	G-SSWX	Short SD3-60 Variant 200	Streamline Aviation (SW) Ltd (G-BNDL)
	G-STAG	Cameron O-65 balloon	The New Holker Estates Co Ltd
	G-STAT	Cessna U.206F	Wingglider Ltd
	G-STAV	Cameron O-84 balloon	F. Horsfall
	G-STEF	Hughes 369HS	Source Ltd (G-BKTK)/Thruxton
	G-STEM	Stemme S.10V	Warwickshire Aerocentre Ltd
	G-STEN	Stemme S.10 (4)	W. A. H. Kahn
	G-STEP	Schweizer 269C	M. Johnson
	G-STER	Bell 206B JetRanger 3	P. J. Brown
	G-STEV	Jodel DR.221	S. W. Talbot/Long Marston
	G-STMP	SNCAN Stampe SV-4A	A. C. Thorne
	G-STOW	Cameron 90 Wine Box SS balloon	Flying Enterprise Partnership
	G-STOX	Bell 206B JetRanger 2	Burman Aviation Ltd (G-BNIR)/Cranfield
	G-STOY	Robinson R-22B	Burman Aviation Ltd/Cranfield
	G-STPI	Cameron A-210 balloon	A. D. Pinner
	G-STRK	CFM Streak Shadow Srs SA	E. J. Hadley/Switzerland
	G-STRM	Cameron N-90 balloon	High Profile Balloons
	G-STUA	Aerotek Pitts S-2A Special (modified)	Rollquick Ltd/Stapleford
	G-STUB	Christen Pitts S-2B Special	R. N. Goode & T. L. P. Delaney/ White Waltham
	G-STWO	ARV Super 2	G. E. Morris
	G-STYL	Pitts S-1S Special	C. A. Wills
	G-SUEE	Airbus A.320-231	Airtours International Airways Ltd (G-IEAG)
	G-SUEZ	AB-206B JetRanger 2	Aerospeed Ltd
	G-SUIT	Cessna 210N	Edinburgh Air Centre Ltd
	G-SUKI	PA-38-112 Tomahawk	Western Air (Thruxton) Ltd (G-BPNV)
	G-SUMT	Robinson R-22B	Frankham Bros Ltd (G-BUKD)
	G-SUPA	PA-18 Super Cub 150	Supa Group
	G-SURG	PA-30 Twin Comanche 160B	A. R. Taylor (G-VIST/G-AVHZ)/Kidlington
	G-SURV	BN-2T-4R Defender 4000	Britten-Norman Ltd (G-BVHZ)/Bembridge
	G-SUSI	Cameron V-77 balloon	J. H. Dryden
	G-SUSY	P-51D-25-NA Mustang (472773)	P. J. Morgan
	G-SUTN	I.I.I. Sky Arrow 650TC	G. C. Sutton
	G-SUZI	Beech 95-B55 Baron	Bebecar (UK) Ltd (G-BAXR)
	G-SUZN	PA-28-161 Warrior II	The St. George Flying Club/Teesside

Reg.	Type	Owner or Operator	Notes
		D. I. Law	
G-SUZY	Taylor JT.1 Monoplane	Virgin Balloon Flights Ltd	
G-SVBF	Cameron A-180 balloon	Avion Aviation	
G-SVEA	PA-28-161 Warrior II	Stephenson Marine Co Ltd (G-BNYJ)	
G-SVIP	Cessna 421B	A. J. Clarry & S. F. Bancroft	
G-SVIV	SNCAN Stampe SV-4C	South Western Electricity PLC	
G-SWEB	Cameron N-90 balloon	I. C. & L. E. Stigwell (G-RBUT)	
G-SWEL	Hughes 369HS	Heritage Aviation Developments Ltd	
G-SWIF	V.S.541 Swift F.7 (XF114)	Jet Heritage Museum/Bournemouth	
G-SWIS	D.H.100 Vampire FB.6 (J-1149) ★	OY Air Scandic International Aviation AB	
G-SWJW	Airbus A.300B4-203	D. Watt	
G-SWOT	Currie Super Wot (C3011)	A. Brown	
G-SWPR	Cameron N-56 balloon	Aerial Enterprises Ltd	
G-SWSH	Mini-500	T. G. Lloyd (G-BSXH)	
G-SWUN	Pitts S-1M Special (modified)	J. T. Fillingham	
G-SYCO	Shaw Europa	M. R. Parr	
G-SYFW	Focke-Wulf Fw.190 replica (2+1)	South Yorkshire Police Authority	
G-SYPA	AS.355F-2 Twin Squirrel	(G-BPRE)	
G-TAAL	Cessna 172R	Eagle Cruise Aviation Ltd	
G-TABS	EMB-110P1 Bandeirante	Thornhill Aviation Ltd (G-PBAC)	
G-TACK	Grob G.109B	A. P. Mayne	
G-TAFF	C.A.S.A. 1.131E Jungmann 1000	A. Horsfall (G-BFNE)/Breighton	
G-TAFI	Bücker Bü133 Jungmeister	R. J. Lamplough	
G-TAGS	PA-28-161 Warrior II	Oxford Aviation Services Ltd/Kidlington	
G-TAIL	Cessna 150J	Aviators Flight Centre/Southend	
G-TAIR	PA-34-200T Seneca II	Branksome Dene Garage/Bournemouth	
G-TAMY	Cessna 421B	Malcolm Enamellers (Midlands) Ltd	
G-TAND	Robinson R-44 Astro	Southwest Helicharter Ltd	
G-TANI	GA-7 Cougar	S. Spier (G-VJAI/G-OCAB/G-BICF)/	
		Elstree	
G-TANK	Cameron N-90 balloon	Hoyers (UK) Ltd	
G-TANS	SOCATA TB-20 Trinidad	Tettenhall Leisure	
G-TAPE	PA-23 Aztec 250D	D. J. Hare (G-AWVW)	
G-TARN	Pietenpol Air Camper	P. J. Heilbron	
G-TART	PA-28-236 Dakota	Dateworld Ltd	
G-TARV	ARV Super 2	M. F. Filer	
G-TASH	Cessna 172N (modified)	A. Ashpitel	
G-TASK	Cessna 404	Bravo Aviation Ltd	
G-TATT	GY-20 Minicab	Tatt's Group	
G-TATY	Robinson R-44 Astro	W. R. Walker	
G-TAXI	PA-23 Aztec 250E	SWL Leasing/Leeds	
G-TAYI	Grob G.115	K. P. Widdowson (G-DODO)	
G-TAYS	Cessna F.152 II	Tayside Aviation Ltd (G-LFCA)/Aberdeen	
G-TBAG	Murphy Renegade II	M. R. Tetley	
G-TBBC	Pagasus Quantum 15-912	Big Bamboo Co Ltd	
G-TBEE	Dyn'Aero MCR-01	A. D. S. Baker	
G-TBGL	Agusta A.109A II	Thomas Bolton Group Ltd (G-VJCB/	
		G-BOUA)	
G-TBIC	BAe 146-200	Flightline Ltd/Stansted	
G-TBIO	SOCATA TB.10 Tobago	D. Hayes/Lydd	
G-TBMW	Renegade Spirit	S. J. Spavins (G-MYIG)	
G-TBRD	Lockheed T-33A (54-21261)	Golden Apple Operations Ltd (G-JETT/	
		G-OAHB)/Duxford	
G-TBXX	SOCATA TB.20 Trinidad	D. A. Phillips & Co	
G-TBZI	SOCATA TB.21 Trinidad TC	W. R. M. Beesley	
G-TBZO	SOCATA TB.20 Trinidad	D. L. Clarke & M. J. M. Hopper/	
		Shoreham	
G-TCAN	Colt 69A balloon	H. C. J. Williams	
G-TCAP	BAe 125 Srs 800B	British Aerospace PLC	
G-TCDI	H.S.125 Srs 403B	Aravco Ltd (G-SHOP/G-BTUF)	
G-TCMP	Robinson R-22B	Thornhill Aviation Ltd	
G-TCOM	PA-30 Twin Comanche 160B	C. A. C. Burrough	
G-TCTC	PA-28RT-201 Arrow IV	STMS	
G-TCUB	Piper J-3C-65 Cub	C. Kirk	
G-TDFS	IMCO Callair A.9	Dollarhigh Ltd (G-AVZA)	
G-TDTW	Hawker Hurricane XIIB (5450)	Hawker Restorations Ltd	
G-TEAL	Thurston TSC-1A1 Teal	K. Heeley/Crosland Moor	
G-TECC	Aeronca 7AC Champion	T. E. C. Cushing/Little Snoring	
G-TECH	R. Commander 114	P. A. Reed (G-BEDH)/Denham	
G-TECK	Cameron V-77 balloon	G. M. N. Spencer	
G-TEDF	Cameron N-90 balloon	Fort Vale Engineering Ltd	
G-TEDS	SOCATA TB.10 Tobago	E. W. Lyon (G-BHCO)	

Notes	Reg.	Type	Owner or Operator
	G-TEDY	Evans VP-1	N. K. Marston (G-BHGN)
	G-TEDZ	Tipsy T.66 Nipper Srs 3	C. J. D. Edwards
	G-TEEZ	Cameron N-90 balloon	Fresh Air Ltd
	G-TEFC	PA-28 Cherokee 140	A. R. Knight
	G-TEHL	CFM Streak Shadow Srs M	A. K. Paterson (G-MYJE)
	G-TELY	Agusta A.109A-II	Castle Air Charters Ltd
	G-TEMP	PA-28 Cherokee 180	BEV Piper Group (G-AYBK)/Andrewsfield
	G-TEMT	Hawker Tempest II (MW763)	Tempest Two Ltd/Sandtoft
	G-TENT	J/1N Alpha	R. Callaway-Lewis (G-AKJU)
	G-TERN	Shaw Europa	J. E. G Lundesjo
	G-TERY	PA-28-181 Archer II	T. Barlow (G-BOXZ)/Barton
	G-TEST	PA-34-200 Seneca	Stapleford Flying Club Ltd (G-BLCD)
	G-TEWS	PA-28 Cherokee 140	G-TEWS Flying Group (G-KEAN/ G-AWTM)/Liverpool
	G-TFCI	Cessna FA.152	Tayside Aviation Ltd/Dundee
	G-TFOX	Denney Kitfox Mk 2	F. A. Bakir
	G-TFRB	Air Command 532 Elite	F. R. Blennerhassett
	G-TFUN	Valentin Taifun 17E	NW Taifun Group
	G-TGAS	Cameron O-160 balloon	Zebedee Balloon Service
	G-TGER Hill	AA-5B Tiger	Photonic Science Ltd(G-BFZP)/Biggin
	G-TGRS	Robinson R-22B	Tiger Helicopters Ltd (G-DELL)/Shobdon
	G-THCL	Cessna 550 Citation II	Tower House Consultants Ltd
	G-THEL	Robinson R-44 Astro	Thurston Helicopters (Engineering) Ltd (G-OCCB/G-STMM)
	G-THEO	Team Minimax 91	T. Willford
	G-THLS	MBB Bo 105DBS/4	Bond Air Services (G-BCXO)/Aberdeen
	G-THOM	Thunder Ax6-56 balloon	T. H. Wilson
	G-THOS	Thunder Ax7-77 balloon	C. E. A. Breton
	G-THOT	Jabiru SK	N. V. Cook
	G-THRE	Cessna 182S	S. J. G. Mole
	G-THSL	PA-28R-201 Arrow III	D. M. Markscheffe
	G-THUN	Republic P-47D Thunderbolt (226671)	Patina Ltd/Duxford
	G-THZL	SOCATA TB.20 Trinidad	Ewan Ltd
	G-TICL	Airbus A.320-231	Airtours International Airways Ltd
	G-TIDS	Jodel 150	J. B. Dovey
	G-TIGA	D.H.82A Tiger Moth	D. E. Leatherland (G-AOEG)
	G-TIGB	AS.332L Super Puma	Bristow Helicopters Ltd (G-BJXC)
	G-TIGC	AS.332L Super Puma	Bristow Helicopters Ltd (G-BJYH)
	G-TIGE	AS.332L Super Puma	Bristow Heliocpters Ltd (G-BJYJ)
	G-TIGF	AS.332L Super Puma	Bristow Helicopters Ltd
	G-TIGG	AS.332L Super Puma	Bristow Helicopters Ltd
	G-TIGI	AS.332L Super Puma	Bristow Helicopters Ltd
	G-TIGJ	AS.332L Super Puma	Bristow Helicopters Ltd
	G-TIGL	AS.332L Super Puma	Bristow Helicopters Ltd
	G-TIGM	AS.332L Super Puma	Bristow Helicopters Ltd
	G-TIGO	AS.332L Super Puma	Bristow Helicopters Ltd
	G-TIGP	AS.332L Super Puma	Bristow Helicopters Ltd
	G-TIGR	AS.332L Super Puma	Bristow Helicopters Ltd
	G-TIGS	AS.332L Super Puma	Bristow Helicopters Ltd
	G-TIGT	AS.332L Super Puma	Bristow Helicopters Ltd
	G-TIGV	AS.332L Super Puma	Bristow Helicopters Ltd
	G-TIGZ	AS.332L Super Puma	British International Helicopters
	G-TIII	Aerotek Pitts S-2A	D. G. Cowden (G-BGSE)
	G-TIKO	Hatz CB-1	Tiko Architecture
	G-TILE	Robinson R-22B	M. J. Webb & C. R. Woodwise
	G-TILI	Bell 206B JetRanger 2	CIM Helicopters
	G-TIMB	Rutan Vari-Eze	T. M. Bailey (G-BKXJ)
	G-TIME	Ted Smith Aerostar 601P	T. & G. Engineering Co Ltd
	G-TIMK	PA-28-181 Archer II	T. Baker
	G-TIMM	Folland Gnat T.1 (XM693)	T. J. Manna/Cranfield
	G-TIMP	Aeronca 7BCM Champion	T. E. Phillips
	G-TIMS	Falconar F-12A	T. Sheridan
	G-TIMW	PA-28 Cherokee 140C	W. H. Sanders (G-AXSH)
	G-TINA	SOCATA TB.10 Tobago	A. Lister
	G-TING	Cameron O-120 balloon	Floating Sensations Ltd
	G-TINS	Cameron N-90 balloon	J. R. Clifton
	G-TINY	Z.526F Trener Master	Air V8 Ltd
	G-TIPS	Tipsy T.66 Nipper Srs 5	R. F. L. Cuypers/Belgium
	G-TJAY	PA-22 Tri-Pacer 135	D. D. Saint
	G-TJHI	Cessna 500 Citation	Trustair Ltd (G-CCCL/G-BEIZ)/Blackpool

Reg.	Type	Owner or Operator	Notes
G-TJPM	BAe 146-300QT	TNT Express Worldwide (UK) Ltd (G-BRGK)	
G-TKAY	Shaw Europa	A. M. Kay	
G-TKGR	Lindstrand LBL Racing Car SS balloon	Brown & Williams Tobacco Corporation (Export) Ltd/USA	
G-TKIS	Tri-R Kis	T. J. Bone	
G-TKPZ	Cessna 310R	Fraggle Leasing Ltd (G-BRAH)	
G-TLDK	PA-22 Tri-Pacer 150	A. M. Thomson	
G-TLME	Robinson R-44 Astro	TJB Associates Ltd	
G-TMCC	Cameron N-90 balloon	Prudential Assurance Co Ltd	
G-TMDP	Airbus A.320-231	Airtours International Airways Ltd	
G-TMKI	P.56 Provost T.1	B. L. Robinson (WW453)	
G-TNTB	BAe 146-200QT	TNT Express Worldwide Ltd	
G-TNTD	BAe 146-200QT	GD Express Worldwide NV (G-BOMJ)	
G-TNTE	BAe 146-300QT	TNT Express Worldwide Ltd (G-BRPW)	
G-TNTG	BAe 146-300QT	TNT European Airlines Ltd (G-BSUY)	
G-TNTI	Airbus A,300B4-203F	TNT Worldwide (UK) Ltd	
G-TNTK	BAe 146-300QT	TNT European Airlines Ltd (G-BSXL)	
G-TNTL	BAe 146-300QT	TNT European Airlines Ltd (G-BSGI)	
G-TNTM	BAe 146-300QT	TNT European Airlines Ltd (G-BSLZ)	
G-TNTN	Thunder Ax6-56 balloon	D. P. & A. Dickinson	
G-TOAD	Jodel D.140B	J. H. Stevens	
G-TOAK	SOCATA TB.20 Trinidad	R. Chown/Newcastle	
G-TOBA	SOCATA TB.10 Tobago	E. Downing	
G-TOBI	Cessna F.172K	G. Hall (G-AYVB)	
G-TODD	ICA IS-28M2A	C. I. Roberts & C. D. King/Shobdon	
G-TODE	Ruschmeyer R.90-230RG	Tode Ltd	
G-TOFT	Colt 90A balloon	C. S. Perceval	
G-TOGO	Van's RV-6	G. Schwetz	
G-TOMS	PA-38-112 Tomahawk	R. J. Alford	
G-TOOL	Thunder Ax8-105 balloon	W. J. Honey	
G-TOPC	AS.355F-1 Twin Squirrel	Bridge Street Nominees Ltd	
G-TOPS	AS.355F-1 Twin Squirrel	Sterling Helicopters (G-BPRH)	
G-TORE	P.84 Jet Provost T.3A (XM405)	Butane Buzzard Aviation Ltd/Cranfield	
G-TOSH	Robinson R-22B	Heli-Air Ltd	
G-TOTO	Cessna F.177RG	W. G. Walton (G-OADE/G-AZKH)	
G-TOUR	Robin R.2112	Mardenair Ltd	
G-TOWS	PA-25 Pawnee 260	Lasham Gliding Soc Ltd	
G-TOYS	Enstrom 280C-UK-2 Shark	Stephenson Aviation Ltd (G-BISE)	
G-TOYZ	Bell 206B JetRanger 3	P. B. Ellis (G-RGER)	
G-TPSL	Cessna 182S	A. N. Purslow	
G-TPTS	Robinson R-44 Astro	Superstore Ltd	
G-TRAC	Robinson R-44 Astro	C. J. Sharples	
G-TRAM	Pegasus Quantum 15-912	T. F. J. Roach	
G-TRAN	Beech 76 Duchess	G. T. Peck (G-NIFR)	
G-TRCY	Robinson R-44 Astro	T. Fletcher	
G-TREC	Cessna 421C	C. P. Lockyer (G-TLOL)	
G-TRED	Colt 110 Bibendum balloon	The Aerial Display Co. Ltd	
G-TREE	Bell 206B JetRanger 3	LGH Aviation Ltd	
G-TREK	Jodel D.18	R. H. Mole/Leicester	
G-TREN	Boeing 737-4S3	GB Airways Ltd (G-BRKG)/Gatwick	
G-TRIB	Lindstrand HS-110 airship		
G-TRIC	D.H.C.1 Chipmunk 22A (18013)	D. M. Barnett (G-AOSZ)	
G-TRIM	Monnett Moni	J. E. Bennell	
G-TRIN	SOCATA TB.20 Trinidad	Isnet Ltd	
G-TRIO	Cessna 172M	C. M. B. Reid (G-BNXY)	
G-TRIX	V.S.509 Spitfire T.IX (PV202)	R. A. Roberts/Goodwood	
G-TROP	Cessna 310R II	Southern Aircharter Ltd/Shoreham	
G-TROY	NA T-28A Fennec (51-7692)	S. G. Howell & S. Tilling	
G-TRUE	MDH Hughes 369E	Horizon Helicopter Hire	
G-TRUK	Stoddard-Hamilton Glasair RG	M. P. Jackson	
G-TRUX	Colt 77A balloon	Highway Truck Rental Ltd	
G-TSAM	BAe 125 Srs 800B	British Aerospace PLC/Warton	
G-TSAR	Beech 58 Baron	Thornfield Enterprises Ltd	
G-TSFT	PA-28-161 Warrior II	SFT Europe Ltd (G-BLDJ)/Bournemouth	
G-TSGJ	PA-28-181 Archer II	Gold Juliet Flying Club	
G-TSIX	AT-6C Harvard IIA (111836)	J. Zemlik/Breighton	
G-TSKY	B.121 Pup 2	R. G. Hayes (G-AWDY)	
G-TSMI	R. Commander 114	J. J. J. C. Herbaux/Belgium	
G-TTDD	Zenair CH.701 STOL	D. B. Dainton & V. D. Asque	
G-TTFN	Cessna 560 Citation V	Corporate Administration Management Ltd	
G-TTHC	Robinson R-22B	North West Auto Engineering	

G-TTIM – G-UKRB

Notes	Reg.	Type	Owner or Operator
	G-TTIM	Cassutt Racer IIIM	J. D. Llewellyn
	G-TTMC	Airbus A.300B4-203	OY Air Scandic International Aviation AB
	G-TTOY	CFM Streak Shadow	S. Marriott
	G-TUBB	Jabiru UL	A. H. Bower
	G-TUDR	Cameron V-77 balloon	Jacques W. Soukup Enterprises Ltd
	G-TUGG	PA-18 Super Cub 150	Ulster Gliding Club Ltd/Bellarena
	G-TUGY	Robin DR.400/180	Buckminster Gliding Club/Saltby
	G-TUKE	Robin DR.400/160	Tukair/Headcorn
	G-TULL	Jabiru UL	W. R. Tull
	G-TUNE	Robinson R-22B	Ecurie Ecosse (Scotland) Ltd (G-OJVI)
	G-TURF	Cessna F.406	Atlantic Air Transport Ltd/Coventry
	G-TURK	Cameron 80 Sultan SS balloon	Forbes Europe Inc/France
	G-TURN	Steen Skybolt	R. C. Berger
	G-TUSK	Bell 206B JetRanger 3	Zeuros Ltd (G-BWZH)
	G-TVAA	Agusta A.109E	Thames Valley Air Ambulance
	G-TVBF	Lindstrand LBL-310A balloon	Virgin Balloons Flights Ltd
	G-TVII	Hawker Hunter T.7 (XX467)	G. R. Montgomery/Perth
	G-TVIJ	CCF Harvard IV (T-6J) (28521)	R. W. Davies (G-BSBE)
	G-TVMM	Cessna 310Q II	Carroll Aviation (Hurn) Ltd (G-CETA/G-BBIM)
	G-TVSI	Campbell Cricket	C. Smith (G-AYHH)
	G-TVTV	Cameron 90 TV SS balloon	J. Krebs/Germany
	G-TWEL	PA-28-181 Archer II	International Aerospace Engineering Ltd
	G-TWEY	Colt 69A balloon	N. Bland
	G-TWIG	Cessna F.406	Highland Airways Ltd/Inverness
	G-TWIN	PA-44-180 Seminole	Bonus Aviation Ltd/Cranfield
	G-TWIZ	R. Commander 114	B. C. & P. M. Cox
	G-TWTD	Hawker Sea Hurricane X (AE977)	Hawker Restorations Ltd
	G-TXSE	RAF 2000 gyroplane	Software Development International Ltd
	G-TYGA	AA-5B Tiger	G. J. Wilshurst (G-BHNZ)
	G-TYNE	SOCATA TB.20 Trinidad	D. T. Watkins
	G-TYPO	Robinson R-22B	The Type Marketing Co (G-JBWI)
	G-TYRE	Cessna F.172M	Staverton Flying School
	G-TZII	Thorp T.211B	AD Aerospace Ltd
	G-UAPA	Robin DR.400/140B	Aeromarine Ltd
	G-UAPO	Ruschmeyer R.90-230RG	S. J. Green/Portugal
	G-UCCC	Cameron 90 Sign SS balloon	Flying Pictures Ltd
	G-UDAY	Robinson R-22B	Newmarket Plant Hire Ltd
	G-UDGE	Thruster T.600N	L. J. Appleby (G-BYPI)
	G-UEST	Bell 206B JetRanger 2	E. & S. Vandyk (G-RYOB/G-BLWU)
	G-UESY	Robinson R-22B	E. W. Guess (Holdings) Ltd
	G-UFLY	Cessna F.150H	Westair Flying Services Ltd (G-AVVY)/Blackpool
	G-UIDE	Jodel D.120	S. T. Gilbert
	G-UILD	Grob G.109B	Runnymede Consultants Ltd
	G-UILE	Lancair 320	R. J. Martin
	G-UINN	Stolp SA.300 Starduster Too	J. D. H. Gordon
	G-UJAB	Jabiru UL	C. A. Thomas
	G-UKAC	BAe 146-300	K.L.M. uk/Buzz/Stansted
	G-UKAG	BAe 146-300	K.L.M. uk/Buzz/Stansted
	G-UKFA	Fokker 100	K.L.M. uk/Stansted
	G-UKFB	Fokker 100	K.L.M. uk/Stansted
	G-UKFC	Fokker 100	K.L.M. uk/Stansted
	G-UKFD	Fokker 100	K.L.M. uk/Stansted
	G-UKFE	Fokker 100	K.L.M. uk/Stansted
	G-UKFF	Fokker 100	K.L.M. uk/Stansted
	G-UKFG	Fokker 100	K.L.M. uk/Stansted
	G-UKFH	Fokker 100	K.L.M. uk/Stansted
	G-UKFI	Fokker 100	K.L.M. uk/Stansted
	G-UKFJ	Fokker 100	K.L.M. uk/Stansted
	G-UKFK	Fokker 100	K.L.M. uk/Stansted
	G-UKFL	Fokker 100	K.L.M. uk/Stansted
	G-UKFM	Fokker 100	K.L.M. uk/Stansted
	G-UKFN	Fokker 100	K.L.M. uk/Stansted
	G-UKFO	Fokker 100	K.L.M. uk/Stansted
	G-UKFP	Fokker 100	K.L.M. uk/Stansted
	G-UKFR	Fokker 100	K.L.M. uk/Stansted
	G-UKHP	BAe 146-300	K.L.M. uk/Buzz/Stansted
	G-UKID	BAe 146-300	K.L.M. uk/Buzz/Stansted
	G-UKOZ	Jabiru SK	D. J. Burnett
	G-UKRB	Colt 105A balloon	Virgin Airship & Balloon Co Ltd

Reg.	Type	Owner or Operator	Notes
G-UKRC	BAe 146-300	K.L.M. uk/Buzz/Stansted	
G-UKSC	BAe 146-300	K.L.M. uk/Buzz/Stansted	
G-UKTA	Fokker 50	K.L.M. uk/Stansted	
G-UKTB	Fokker 50	K.L.M. uk/Stansted	
G-UKTC	Fokker 50	K.L.M. uk/Stansted	
G-UKTD	Fokker 50	K.L.M. uk/Stansted	
G-UKTE	Fokker 50	K.L.M. uk/Stansted	
G-UKTF	Fokker 50	K.L.M. uk/Stansted	
G-UKTG	Fokker 50	K.L.M. uk/Stansted	
G-UKTH	Fokker 50	K.L.M. uk/Stansted	
G-UKTI	Fokker 50	K.L.M. uk/Stansted	
G-UKTJ	Aérospatiale ATR-72-202	Gill Airways Ltd	
G-UKTK	Aérospatiale ATR-72-202	-	
G-UKTL	Aérospatiale ATR-72-202	Gill Airways Ltd	
G-UKTM	Aérospatiale ATR-72-202	-	
G-UKTN	Aérospatiale ATR-72-202	-	
G-UKUK	Head Ax8-105 balloon	P. A. George	
G-ULAB	Robinson R-22B	Bradmore Helicopter Leasing	
G-ULAS	D.H.C.1 Chipmunk 22 (WK517)	Search & Management Services Ltd	
G-ULIA	Cameron V-77 balloon	J. M. Dean	
G-ULLS	Lindstrand LBL-90A balloon	Tanswell of Towcester Ltd	
G-ULPS	Everett Srs 1 gyroplane	The Aziz Corporation Ltd (G-BMNY)	
G-ULTR	Cameron A-105 balloon	P. Glydon	
G-UMBO	Thunder Ax7-77A balloon	Virgin Airship & Balloon Co Ltd	
G-UMMI	PA-31-310 Turbo Navajo	Messrs Rees of Poynston West (G-BGSO)	
G-UNGE	Lindstrand LBL-90A balloon	Silver Ghost Balloon Club (G-BVPJ)	
G-UNIP	Cameron Oil Container SS balloon	Flying Pictures Ltd	
G-UNIT	Partenavia P.68B	Phlight Aviation Ltd (G-BCNT)/Coventry	
G-UNIV	Montgomerie-Parsons 2-seat gyroplane	University of Glasgow (G-BWTP)	
G-UNNY	BAC.167 Strikemaster 87	Gone Flying Ltd (G-AYHR)	
G-UNRL	Lindstrand LBL-21A balloon	Virgin Balloon & Airship Co. Ltd	
G-UNYT	Robinson R-22B	Cambridge Helicopters Ltd (G-BWZV/ G-LIAN)	
G-UORO	Shaw Europa	D. Dufton	
G-UPHL	Cameron 80 Concept SS balloon	Uphill Motor Co Ltd	
G-UPMW	Robinson R-22B	Burman Aviation Ltd/Cranfield	
G-UPPP	Colt 77A balloon	M. Williams	
G-UPPY	Cameron DP-80 airship	Jacques W. Soukup Enterprises Ltd/USA	
G-UPUP	Cameron V-77 balloon	S. F. Burden/Netherlands	
G-URCH	Rotorway Executive 162F	D. L. Urch	
G-UROP	Beech 95-B55 Baron	Pooler International Ltd/Sleap	
G-URRR	Air Command 582 Sport	L. Armes	
G-URUH	Robinson R-44 Astro	Heli Air Ltd	
G-USAM	Cameron Uncle Sam SS balloon	Jacques W. Soukup Enterprises Ltd/USA	
G-USFT	PA-23 Aztec 250F	SFT Europe Ltd (G-BEGV)/ Bournemouth	
G-USGB	Colt 105A balloon	Virgin Airship & Balloon Co. Ltd	
G-USIL	Thunder Ax7-77 balloon	Window On The World Ltd	
G-USMC	Cameron 90 Chestie SS balloon	Jacques W. Soukup Enterprises Ltd/USA	
G-USSR	Cameron 90 Doll SS balloon	Jacques W. Soukup Enterprises Ltd/USA	
G-USSY	PA-28-181 Archer II	Western Air (Thruxton) Ltd	
G-USTB	Agusta A.109A	Newton Aviation Ltd	
G-USTE	Robinson R-44 Astro	Westleigh Construction Ltd	
G-USTY	FRED Srs 2	Gusty Group	
G-UTSI	Rand KR-2	K. B. Gutridge/Thruxton	
G-UTSY	PA-28R-201 Arrow III	Arrow Aviation Ltd	
G-UTZY	SA.341G Gazelle 1	Goldcalm Ltd (G-BKLV)	
G-UVIP	Cessna 421C	Capital Trading Aviation Ltd (G-BSKH)	
G-UZEL	SA.341G Gazelle 1	S. E. Hobbs (UK) Ltd (G-BRNH)	
G-UZLE	Colt 77A balloon	Flying Pictures Ltd	
G-VAEL	Airbus A.340-311	Virgin Atlantic Airways Ltd *Maiden Toulouse*	
G-VAGA	PA-15 Vagabond	I. M. Callier/White Waltham	
G-VAIR	Airbus A.340-313	Virgin Atlantic Airways Ltd *Maiden Tokyo*	
G-VAJT	M.S.894E Rallye 220GT	W. M. Patterson	
G-VALS	Pietenpol Air Camper	I. G. & V. A. Brice	
G-VANS	Van's RV-4	T. R. Grief	
G-VANZ	Van's RV-6A	S. J. Baxter	
G-VARG	Varga 2150A Kachina	A. C. Fletcher	

Notes	Reg.	Type	Owner or Operator
	G-VASA	PA-34-200 Seneca	V. Babic (G-BNNB)
	G-VAST	Boeing 747-41R	Virgin Atlantic Airways Ltd *Ladybird*
	G-VAUN	Cessna 340	K. L. Burnett
	G-VBAC	Short SD3-60 Variant 100	BAC Leasing Ltd (G-BOEJ)
	G-VBEE	Boeing 747-219B	Virgin Atlantic Airways Ltd *Honeypie*
	G-VBIG	Boeing 747-4Q8	Virgin Atlantic Airways Ltd *Tinker Belle*
	G-VBUS	Airbus A.340-311	Virgin Atlantic Airways Ltd *Lady in Red*
	G-VCAT	Boeing 747-267B	Virgin Atlantic Airways Ltd
	G-VCED	Airbus A.320-211	Airtours International Airways Ltd
	G-VCIO	EAA Acro Sport II	R. F. Bond
	G-VCJH	Robinson R-22B	Great Northern Helicopters Ltd
	G-VCML	Beech 58 Baron	St Angelo Aviation Ltd
	G-VDIR	Cessna T.310R	Thornhill Aviation Ltd
	G-VEGA	Slingsby T.65A Vega (BGA2729)	C. H. Griffiths
	G-VELA	SIAI-Marchetti S.205-22R	G-VELA Partnership
	G-VELD	Airbus A.340-313	Virgin Atlantic Airways Ltd *African Queen*
	G-VENI	D.H.112 Venom FB.50 (WE402)	Lindsay Wood Promotions Ltd/ Bournemouth
	G-VENM	D.H.112 Venom FB.1	T. J. Manna (G-BLIE)/Cranfield
	G-VERA	GY-201 Minicab	D. K. Shipton
	G-VETA	Hawker Hunter T.7	Jet Heritage Ltd (G-BVWN)/ Bournemouth
	G-VETS	Enstrom 280C-UK Shark	C. Upton (G-FSDC/G-BKTG)
	G-VEZE	Rutan Vari-Eze	S. D. Brown & ptnrs
	G-VFAB	Boeing 747-4Q8	Virgin Atlantic Airways Ltd Lady Penelope
	G-VFAR	Airbus A.340-313	Virgin Atlantic Airways Ltd *Diana*
	G-VFLY	Airbus A.340-311	Virgin Atlantic Airways Ltd *Dragon Lady*
	G-VFSI	Robinson R-22B	Survey & Construction (Roofing) Ltd
	G-VGIN	Boeing 747-243B	Virgin Atlantic Airways Ltd *Scarlet Lady*
	G-VHOL	Airbus A.340-311	Virgin Atlantic Airways Ltd *Jetstreamer*
	G-VHOT	Boeing 747-4Q8	Virgin Atlantic Airways Ltd *Tubalar Belle*
	G-VIBA	Cameron DP-80 airship	Jacques W. Soukup Enterprises Ltd/USA
	G-VIBE	Boeing 747-219B	Virgin Atlantic Airways Ltd
	G-VICC	PA-28-161 Warrior II	A. W. Collett (G-JFHL)
	G-VICE	MDH Hughes 369E	Controlled Demolition Group Ltd
	G-VICI	D.H.112 Venom FB.50 (J-1573)	Lindsay Wood Promotions Ltd/ Bournemouth
	G-VICM	Beech F33C Bonanza	Velocity Engineering Ltd
	G-VICS	Commander 114B	Millennium Aviation Ltd
	G-VICT	PA-31-310 Turbo Navajo	Victoria Wharf Ltd (G-BBZI)
	G-VICW	Beech 200 Super King Air	Victoria Wharf Ltd (G-ECAV)
	G-VIEW	Vinten-Wallis WA-116/100	K. H. Wallis
	G-VIIA	Boeing 777-236	British Airways
	G-VIIB	Boeing 777-236	British Airways
	G-VIIC	Boeing 777-236	British Airways
	G-VIID	Boeing 777-236	British Airways
	G-VIIE	Boeing 777-236	British Airways
	G-VIIF	Boeing 777-236	British Airways
	G-VIIG	Boeing 777-236	British Airways
	G-VIIH	Boeing 777-236	British Airways
	G-VIIJ	Boeing 777-236	British Airways
	G-VIIK	Boeing 777-236	British Airways
	G-VIIL	Boeing 777-236	British Airways
	G-VIIM	Boeing 777-236	British Airways
	G-VIIN	Boeing 777-236	British Airways
	G-VIIO	Boeing 777-236	British Airways
	G-VIIP	Boeing 777-236	British Airways
	G-VIIR	Boeing 777-236	British Airways
	G-VIIS	Boeing 777-236	British Airways
	G-VIIT	Boeing 777-236	British Airways
	G-VIIU	Boeing 777-236	British Airways
	G-VIIV	Boeing 777-236	British Airways
	G-VIIW	Boeing 777-236	British Airways
	G-VIIX	Boeing 777-236	British Airways
	G-VIIY	Boeing 777-236	British Airways
	G-VIKE	Bellanca 1730A Viking	W. G. Prout
	G-VIKY	Cameron A-120 balloon	D. W. Pennell
	G-VILL	Lazer Z.200 (modified)	M. G. Jefferies (G-BOYZ) /Little Gransden
	G-VINO	Sky 90-24 balloon	Fivedata Ltd
	G-VIPI	BAe 125 Srs 800B	Yeates of Leicester Ltd

Reg.	Type	Owner or Operator	Notes
G-VIPP	PA-31-350 Navajo Chieftain	Capital Trading Aviation Ltd (G-OGRV/ G-BMPX)	
G-VIPY	PA-31-350 Navajo Chieftain	Capital Trading Aviation Ltd (G-POLO)	
G-VIRG	Boeing 747-287B	Virgin Atlantic Airways Ltd Maiden Voyager	
G-VITE	Robin R.1180T	G-VITE Flying Group	
G-VIVA	Thunder Ax7-65 balloon	R. J. Mitchener	
G-VIVI	Taylor JT.2 Titch	D. G. Tucker	
G-VIVM	P.84 Jet Provost T.5	Flight Test Associates Ltd (G-BVWF)	
G-VIXN	D.H.110 Sea Vixen FAW.2 (XS587) ★	P. G. Vallance Ltd/Charlwood	
G-VIZZ	Sportavia RS.180 Sportsman	Exeter Fournier Group	
G-VJAB	Jabiru UL	ST Aviation Ltd	
G-VJET	Avro 698 Vulcan B.2 (XL426) ★	Vulcan Restoration Trust/Southend	
G-VJFK	Boeing 747-238B	Virgin Atlantic Airways Ltd Boston Belle	
G-VJIM	Colt 77 Jumbo Jim SS balloon	L. V. Mastis	
G-VKID	Airbus A.320-214	Virgin Atlantic/Sun	
G-VKIS	Airbus A.320-211	Virgin Atlantic/Sun	
G-VLAD	Yakovlev Yak-50	M. B. Smith/Booker	
G-VLAX	Boeing 747-238B	Virgin Atlantic Airways Ltd California Girl	
G-VMAX	Mooney M.20K	Aerokits GmbH/Germany	
G-VMDE	Cessna P.210N	Royton Express Deliveries (Welwyn) Ltd	
G-VMED	Airbus A.320-214	Virgin Sun	
G-VMIA	Boeing 747-123	Virgin Atlantic Airways Ltd (G-HIHO) Spirit of Sir Freddie	
G-VMJM	SOCATA TB.10 Tobago	J. H. Michaels (G-BTOK)/Denham	
G-VMPR	D.H.115 Vampire T.11 (XE920)	J. N. Kerr & J. Jones/Swansea	
G-VMSL	Robinson R-22A	L. L. F. Smith (G-KILY)	
G-VNOM	D.H.112 Venom FB.50 (J-1632)	T. J. Manna/Cranfield	
G-VOAR	PA-28-181 Archer III	JSE Systems	
G-VODA	Cameron N-77 balloon	Racal Telecom PLC	
G-VOID	PA-28RT-201 Arrow IV	Newbus Aviation Ltd	
G-VOLH	Airbus A.321-211	Airtours International Airways Ltd	
G-VOLT	Cameron N-77 balloon	National Power	
G-VOTE	Ultramagic M-77 balloon	Window On The World Ltd	
G-VPII	Evans VP-2	V. D. J. Hitchings (G-EDIF)	
G-VPSJ	Shaw Europa	J. D. Bean	
G-VPUF	Boeing 747-219B	Virgin Atlantic Airways Ltd	
G-VROE	Avro 652A Anson T.21 (WD413)	Air Atlantique Ltd (G-BFIR)/Coventry	
G-VRST	PA-46-350P Malibu Mirage	Winchfield Enterprises Ltd	
G-VRUM	Boeing 747-267B	Virgin Atlantic Airways Ltd	
G-VRVI	Cameron O-90 balloon	Cooling Services Ltd	
G-VSBC	Beech B200 Super King Air	Vickers Shipbuilding & Engineering Ltd/Walney Island	
G-VSEA	Airbus A.340-311	Virgin Atlantic Airways Ltd Plane Sailing	
G-VSFT	PA-23 Aztec 250F	SFT Europe Ltd (G-TOMK/G-BFEC)/ Bournemouth	
G-VSKY	Airbus A.340-311	Virgin Atlantic Airways Ltd China Girl	
G-VSSS	Boeing 747-219B	Virgin Atlantic Airways Ltd	
G-VSUN	Airbus A.340-313	Virgin Atlantic Airways Ltd First Lady	
G-VTAN	Airbus A.320-214	Virgin Sun (G-BXTA)	
G-VTII	D.H.115 Vampire T.11 (WZ507)	De Havilland Aviation Ltd/Swansea	
G-VTOL	H.S. Harrier T.52 (ZA250) ★	Brooklands Museum of Aviation/ Weybridge	
G-VTOP	Boeing 747-4Q8	Virgin Atlantic Airways Ltd Virginia Plain	
G-VULC	Avro 698 Vulcan B.2A (XM655) ★	Radarmoor Ltd/Wellesbourne	
G-VVBF	Colt 315A balloon	Virgin Balloon Flights Ltd	
G-VVBK	PA-34-200T Seneca II	Magyar Construction Ltd (G-BSBS/ G-BDRI)	
G-VVIP	Cessna 421C	Capital Trading Aviation Ltd (G-BMWB)	
G-VXLG	Boeing 747-41R	Virgin Atlantic Airways Ltd Ruby Tuesday	
G-VYGR	Colt 120A balloon	A. van Wyk	
G-VZZZ	Boeing 747-219B	Virgin Atlantic Airways Ltd	
G-WAAC	Cameron N-56 balloon	N. P. Hemsley	
G-WACB	Cessna F.152 II	Wycombe Air Centre Ltd	
G-WACE	Cessna F.152 II	Wycombe Air Centre Ltd	
G-WACF	Cessna 152 II	Wycombe Air Centre Ltd	
G-WACG	Cessna 152 II	Wycombe Air Centre Ltd	
G-WACH	Cessna FA.152 II	Wycombe Air Centre Ltd	
G-WACI	Beech 76 Duchess	Wycombe Air Centre Ltd	
G-WACJ	Beech 76 Duchess	Wycombe Air Centre Ltd	
G-WACL	Cessna F.172N	Wycombe Air Centre Ltd (G-BHGG)	

Notes	Reg.	Type	Owner or Operator
	G-WACO	Waco UPF-7	RGV (Aircraft Services) & Co/Staverton
	G-WACP	PA-28 Cherokee 180	Wycombe Air Centre Ltd (G-BBPP)
	G-WACR	PA-28 Cherokee 180	Wycombe Air Centre Ltd (G-BCZF)
	G-WACT	Cessna F.152 II	Wycombe Air Centre Ltd (G-BKFT)
	G-WACU	Cessna FA.152	Wycombe Air Centre Ltd (G-BJZU)
	G-WACW	Cessna 172P	Wycombe Air Centre Ltd
	G-WACY	Cessna F.172P	Wycombe Air Centre Ltd
	G-WACZ	Cessna F.172M	Professional Air Training Ltd (G-BCUK)
	G-WADI	PA-46-350P Malibu Mirage	Albatross Air Ltd
	G-WADS	Robinson R-22B	Pyramid Precision Engineering Ltd (G-NICO)
	G-WAGG	Robinson R-22B	N. J. Wagstaff Leasing
	G-WAIR	PA-32-301 Saratoga	Thorne Aviation
	G-WAIT	Cameron V-77 balloon	C. P. Brown
	G-WALS	Cessna A.152	Redhill Flying Club
	G-WARA	PA-28-161 Warrior III	Solent Flight Aircraft Ltd
	G-WARB	PA-28-161 Warrior III	London School of Flying Ltd/Elstree
	G-WARC	PA-28-161 Warrior III	London School of Flying Ltd/Elstree
	G-WARD	Taylor JT.1 Monoplane	R. P. J. Hunter
	G-WARE	PA-28-161 Warrior II	W. J. Ware
	G-WARF	Cessna 182S	Victoria Wharf Ltd
	G-WARK	Schweizer 269C	K. Sutcliffe
	G-WARO	PA-28-161 Warrior III	London School of Flying Ltd/Elstree
	G-WARP	Cessna 182F	Army Parachute Association (G-ASHB)
	G-WARR	PA-28-161 Warrior II	T. J. & G. M. Laundy
	G-WARS	PA-28-161 Warrior III	London School of Flying Ltd/Elstree
	G-WARU	PA-28-161 Warrior III	Solent Flight Aircraft Ltd/Southampton
	G-WARV	PA-28-161 Warrior III	London Aviation Ltd/Biggin Hill
	G-WARW	PA-28-161 Warrior III	London School of Flying Ltd/Elstree
	G-WARX	PA-28-161 Warrior III	C. M. A. Clark
	G-WARY	PA-28-161 Warrior III	London School of Flying Ltd/Elstree
	G-WARZ	PA-28-161 Warrior III	London Aviation Ltd/Elstree
	G-WASH	Noble 1250 balloon	Noble Adventures Ltd
	G-WASP	Brantly B.2B	N. J. R. Minchin (G-ASXE)
	G-WATH	Colt 77A balloon	Ballooning Adventures Ltd
	G-WATS	PA-34-220T Seneca III	Oxford Aviation Services Ltd (G-BOYJ)/Kidlington
	G-WATT	Cameron Cooling Tower SS balloon	National Power
	G-WAVE	Grob G.109B	M. L. Murdoch/Cranfield
	G-WAZZ	Pitts S-1S Special	D. T. Knight (G-BRRP)
	G-WBMG	Cameron N Ele-90 SS balloon	P. H. E. van Overwalle (G-BUYV) Belgium
	G-WBPR	BAe 125 Srs 800B	Granada Group PLC
	G-WBTS	Falconar F-11	W. C. Brown (G-BDPL)
	G-WCAT	Colt Flying Mitt SS balloon	Balloon Preservation Flying Group
	G-WCEI	M.S.894E Rallye 220GT	R. A. L. Lucas (G-BAOC)
	G-WDEB	Thunder Ax-7-77 balloon	W. de Bock
	G-WDEV	SA.341G Gazelle 1	MW Helicopters Ltd (G-IZEL/G-BBHW)
	G-WEAC	BN-2A Mk III-2 Trislander	Keen Leasing Ltd (G-BEFP)
	G-WELI	Cameron N-77 balloon	M. A. Shannon
	G-WELL	Beech E90 King Air	Colt Transport Ltd
	G-WELS	Cameron N-65 balloon	K. J. Vickery
	G-WEND	PA-28RT-201 Arrow IV	G-WEND Group
	G-WERY	SOCATA TB.20 Trinidad	WERY Flying Group/Sherburn
	G-WEST	Agusta A.109A	Westland Helicopters Ltd/Yeovil
	G-WESX	CFM Streak Shadow	D. J. Sagar
	G-WETI	Cameron N-31 balloon	C. A. Butter & J. J. T. Cooke
	G-WFEP	Aérospatiale ATR-42-300	Gill Airways Ltd
	G-WFFW	PA-28-161 Warrior II	N. F. Duke
	G-WFOX	Robinson R-22B	Heli Air Ltd
	G-WGAL	Bell 206B JetRanger 3	Watkiss Group Aviation Ltd (G-OICS)
	G-WGCL	Aero Commander 685	Cooper Aerial Surveys Ltd/Sandtoft
	G-WGCS	PA-18 Super Cub 95	S. C. Thompson
	G-WGHB	Canadair T-33AN Silver Star 3	R. H. & G. C. Cooper
	G-WGSC	Pilatus PC-6/B2-H4 Turbo Porter	D. M. Penny
	G-WHAT	Colt 77A balloon	M. A. Scholes
	G-WHAZ	AB-206A JetRanger 2	J. E. Mills
	G-WHDP	Cessna 182S	Heatherford Ltd
	G-WHEE	Pegasus Quantum 15-912	N. & R. Harwood
	G-WHIM	Colt 77A balloon	D. L. Morgan
	G-WHOG	CFM Streak Shadow	B. R. Cannell
	G-WHRL	Schweizer 269C	Graham Wood Decorators

Reg.	Type	Owner or Operator	Notes
G-WHST	AS.350B2 Ecureuil	Hawkrise Ltd (G-BWYA)	
G-WHZZ	Aero L-39C Albatros (84)	B. J. Berry	
G-WIBB	Jodel D.18	J. & D. Wibberley	
G-WIBS	C.A.S.A. 1-131E Jungmann 2000	C. Willoughby	
G-WILD	Pitts S-1T Special	The Aerobatics Co Ltd	
G-WILG	PZL-104 Wilga 35	M. H. Bletsoe-Brown (G-AZYJ)	
G-WILS	PA-28RT-201T Turbo Arrow IV	T. W. Stanley & V. F. A. Dimock	
G-WILY	Rutan LongEz	B. Wronski & W. S. Allen	
G-WIMP	Colt 56A balloon	T. & B. Chamberlain	
G-WINE	Thunder Ax7-77Z balloon	S. M. Miles	
G-WINK	AA-5B Tiger	B. St J. Cooke	
G-WINS	PA-32 Cherokee Six 300	Cheyenne Ltd	
G-WIRE	AS.355F-1 Twin Squirrel	National Grid Co PLC (G-CEGB/G-BLJL)	
G-WIRL	Robinson R-22B	C. A. Rosenberg	
G-WISH	Lindstrand LBL Cake SS balloon	Oxford Promotions (UK) Ltd/USA	
G-WIXI	Avions Mudry CAP.10B	J. M. & E. M. Wicks	
G-WIZA	Robinson R-22B	Burman Aviation Ltd (G-PERL)/Cranfield	
G-WIZB	Grob G.115A	A. G. Wisbey	
G-WIZD	Lindstrand LBL-180A balloon	Bignell Surgical Instruments Ltd	
G-WIZO	PA-34-220T Seneca III	B. J. Booty	
G-WIZR	Robinson R-22B	Clifton Helicopter Hire	
G-WIZY	Robinson R-22B	Central Aviation (Helicopters) Ltd (G-BMWX)	
G-WIZZ	AB-206B JetRanger 2	Rivermead Aviation Ltd	
G-WJAN	Boeing 757-21K	Airtours International Airways Ltd	
G-WKRD	AS.350B-2 Ecureuil	Wickford Development Co (G-BUJG/G-HEAR)	
G-WLAC	PA-18 Super Cub 150	White Waltham Airfield Ltd (G-HAHA/G-BSWE)	
G-WLGA	PZL-104 Wilga 80	A. J. Renham	
G-WLLY	Bell 206B JetRanger	Blue Five Aviation Ltd (G-OBHH/ G-RODY/G-ROGR/G-AXMM)	
G-WLMS	Mainair Blade 912	J. R. North	
G-WMAA	MBB Bo 105DBS/4	W. Midlands Air Ambulance (G-PASB/ G-BDMC)	
G-WMAN	SA.341G Gazelle 1	J. Wightman	
G-WMID	McD Douglas MD-900	W. Midlands Police Authority	
G-WMPA	AS.355F-2 Twin Squirrel	W. Midlands Police Authority	
G-WMTM	AA-5B Tiger	S. A. Westhorp	
G-WNGS	Cameron N-105 balloon	Redmalt Ltd	
G-WOLF	PA-28 Cherokee 140	Werewolf Aviation Ltd	
G-WOOD	Beech 95-B55A Baron	T. D. Broadhurst (G-AYID)/Sleap	
G-WOOF	Enstrom 480	Westover Park Ltd	
G-WOOL	Colt 77A balloon	Whacko Balloon Group	
G-WORM	Thruster T.600N	Thruster Air Services Ltd	
G-WOTG	BN-2T Turbine Islander	RAF Sport Parachute Association (G-BJYT)	
G-WPAS	MD-900 Explorer	Police Aviation Services Ltd	
G-WREN	Pitts S-2A Special	Northamptonshire School of Flying Ltd/ Sywell	
G-WRFM	Enstrom 280C-UK Shark	Skywalker Enterprises (G-CTSI/ G-BKIO)/Shoreham	
G-WRIT	Thunder Ax7-77A balloon	G. Pusey	
G-WRWR	Robinson R-22B	Choppertech Ltd	
G-WSEC	Enstrom F-28C	M. J. Easey (G-BONF)	
G-WSFT	PA-23 Aztec 250F	SFT Europe Ltd (G-BTHS)/ Bournemouth	
G-WSKY	Enstrom 280C-UK-2 Shark	M. I. Edwards Engineers (G-BEEK)	
G-WUFF	Shaw Europa	M. A. Barker	
G-WULF	WAR Focke-Wulf Fw.190 (8)	S. N. Lester	
G-WURL	Robinson R-22B	Heli Air Ltd (G-BXMS)/Wellesbourne	
G-WVBF	Lindstrand LBL-210A balloon	Virgin Balloon Flights Ltd	
G-WWAL	PA-28R Cherokee Arrow 180	White Waltham Airfield Ltd (G-AZSH)	
G-WWAS	PA-34-220T Seneca III	D. Intzevidis (G-BPPB)/Greece	
G-WWIZ	Beech 95-58 Baron	Chase Aviation Ltd (G-GAMA/G-BBSD)	
G-WWWG	Shaw Europa	C. F. Williams-Wynne	
G-WYAT	CFM Streak Shadow Srs SA	M. G. Whyatt	
G-WYCH	Cameron 90 Witch SS balloon	Jacques W. Soukup Enterprises Ltd/ USA	
G-WYMP	Cessna F.150J	R. Hall (G-BAGW)	
G-WYMR	Robinson R-44 Astro	Heli Air Ltd	
G-WYND	Wittman W.8 Tailwind	Forge Group	

Notes	Reg.	Type	Owner or Operator
	G-WYNN	Rand KR-2	W. Thomas
	G-WYNS	Aero Designs Pulsar XP	S. L. Bauza/Majorca
	G-WYNT	Cameron N-56 balloon	Jacques W. Soukup Enterprises Ltd/ USA
	G-WYPA	MBB Bo 105DBS/4	W. Yorkshire Police Authority
	G-WYSP	Robinson R-44 Astro	Heli Air Ltd
	G-WZOL	RL.5B LWS Sherwood Ranger	G. W. F. Webb (G-MZOL)
	G-WZZZ	Colt AS-56 airship	Lindstrand Balloons Ltd
	G-XALP	Schweizer 269C	Teknowledge Ltd
	G-XANT	Cameron N-105 balloon	Flying Pictures Ltd
	G-XARV	ARV Super 2	N. R. Beale (G-OPIG/G-BMSJ)
	G-XBHX	Boeing 737-36N	British Airways Regional
	G-XCEL	AS.355F-1 Twin Squirrel	Tri-Ventures Group Ltd (G-HBAC/G-HJET)
	G-XCUB	PA-18 Super Cub 150	M. C. Barraclough
	G-XENA	PA-28-161 Warrior II	Braddock Ltd
	G-XLTG	Cessna 182S	GX Aviation Ltd
	G-XLXL	Robin DR.400/160	40-40 Aero Group (G-BAUD)/Biggin Hill
	G-XMAN	Boeing 737-36N	British Airways Regional
	G-XPBI	Letov LK-2M Sluka	P. Bishop
	G-XPTS	Robinson R-44 Astro	Heli Air Ltd
	G-XPXP	Aero Designs Pulsar XP	B. J. Edwards
	G-XRAY	Rand KR-2	R. S. Smith
	G-XRMC	BAe 125 Srs 800B	RMC Group Services Ltd
	G-XRXR	Raj Hamsa X'Air 582 (1)	I. S. Walsh
	G-XSDJ	Shaw Europa XS	D. N. Joyce
	G-XSFT	PA-23 Aztec 250F	SFT Europe Ltd (G-CPPC/G-BGBH)/ Bournemouth
	G-XSKY	Cameron N-77 balloon	T. D. Gibbs
	G-XTEC	Robinson R-22B	Simax Services Ltd (G-BYCK)
	G-XTEK	Robinson R-44 Astro	Xitec Software PLC
	G-XTOR	BN-2A Mk III-2 Trislander	Aurigny Air Services Ltd (G-BAXD)
	G-XTRA	Extra EA.230	I. A. Scott/Sweden
	G-XTRS	Extra EA.300/L	D. J. & L. F. Daly
	G-XTUN	Westland-Bell 47G-3B-1	Zonki Aviation Ltd (G-BGZK)
	G-XVIE	V.S.361 Spitfire LF.XVIe (TB252)	Historic Flying Ltd
	G-XWWF	Lindstrand LBL-56A balloon	D. D. Maimone
	G-XXEA	Sikorsky S-76C	Director of Royal Travel/Blackbushe
	G-XXIV	AB-206B JetRanger 3	Hampton Printing (Bristol) Ltd
	G-XXVI	Sukhoi Su-26M	A. N. Onn & T. R. G. Barnaby
	G-YAKA	Yakovlev Yak-50	J. Griffin
	G-YAKI	Yakovlev Yak-52 (100)	Yak One Ltd/White Waltham
	G-YAKO	Yakovlev Yak-52	M. K. Shaw
	G-YAKS	Yakovlev Yak-52 (2)	Two Bees Associates Ltd
	G-YAKX	Yakovlev Yak-52 (27)	The X Flyers Ltd
	G-YAKY	Yakovlev Yak-52	Kilo Yankee Group
	G-YANK	PA-28-181 Archer II	G-YANK Flying Group
	G-YAWW	PA-28RT-201T Turbo Arrow IV	Barton Aviation Ltd
	G-YBAA	Cessna FR.172J	H. Norman
	G-YCUB	PA-18 Super Cub 150	F. W. Rogers Garage (Saltash) Ltd
	G-YEAR	Mini-500	D. J. Waddington
	G-YELL	Murphy Rebel	A. D. Keen
	G-YEOM	PA-31-350 Navajo Chieftain	Foster Yeoman Ltd/Exeter
	G-YFLY	VPM M.16 Tandem Trainer	A. J. Unwin (G-BWGI)
	G-YIII	Cessna F.150L	Sherburn Aero Club Ltd
	G-YIIK	Robinson R-44 Astro	The Websiteshop (UK) Ltd
	G-YJBM	Airbus A.320-231	Airtours International Airways Ltd (G-IEAF)
	G-YJET	Montgomerie-Bensen B.8MR	A. Shuttleworth (G-BMUH)
	G-YKEN	Robinson R-22B	S. M. & Y. J. Kenmore
	G-YKSZ	Yakovlev Yak-52	J. N. & C. J. Carter
	G-YLYB	Cameron N-105 balloon	Virgin Airship & Balloon Co Ltd
	G-YMBO	Robinson R-22M Mariner	J. Robinson
	G-YMMA	Boeing 777-236ER	British Airways
	G-YMMB	Boeing 777-236ER	British Airways
	G-YMMC	Boeing 777-236ER	British Airways
	G-YMMD	Boeing 777-236ER	British Airways
	G-YMME	Boeing 777-236ER	British Airways
	G-YMMF	Boeing 777-236ER	British Airways
	G-YMYM	Lindstrand LBL Ice Cream Cone SS balloon	Lindstrand Balloons Ltd

Reg.	Type	Owner or Operator	Notes
G-YNOT	D.62B Condor	T. Littlefair (G-AYFH)	
G-YOGI	Robin DR.400/140B	R. M. & A. M. Gosling (G-BDME)	
G-YORK	Cessna F.172M	B. Berry	
G-YOYO	Pitts S-1E Special	J. D. L. Richardson (G-OTSW/G-BLHE)	
G-YPSY	Andreasson BA-4B	C. W. N. Huke & A-L. N. M. Cox	
G-YRIL	Luscombe 8E Silvaire	C. Potter	
G-YROI	Air Command 532 Elite	W. B. Lumb	
G-YROS	Montgomerie-Bensen B.8M	N. B. Gray	
G-YROY	Montgomerie-Bensen B.8MR	R. D. Armishaw	
G-YSFT	PA-23 Aztec 250F	SFT Europe Ltd (G-BEJT)/Bournemouth	
G-YSTT	PA-32R-301 Saratoga II HP	A. W. Kendrick	
G-YTUK	Cameron A-210 balloon	Societe Bombard SRL	
G-YUGO	H.S.125 Srs 1B/R-522 H	Fire Section (G-ATWH)/Dunsfold	
G-YULL	PA-28 Cherokee 180E	Fortescue Investments Ltd (G-BEAJ)	
G-YUMM	Cameron N-90 balloon	Wunderbar Ltd	
G-YUPI	Cameron N-90 balloon	MCVH SA/Belgium	
G-YURO	Shaw Europa ★	Yorkshire Air Museum/Elvington	
G-YVBF	Lindstrand LBL-317S balloon	Virgin Balloon Flights Ltd	
G-YVET	Cameron V-90 balloon	K. J. Foster	
G-ZABC	Sky 90-24 balloon	Rishtons (Chichester) Ltd	
G-ZACH	Robin DR.400/100	A. P. Wellings (G-FTIO)/Sandown	
G-ZAIR	Zenair CH 601HD	Speedfreak Ltd	
G-ZAPD	Short SD3-60 Variant 100	Titan Airways Ltd (G-OLGW/ G-BOFK)	
G-ZAPJ	Aérospatiale ATR-42-300	Titan Airways Ltd	
G-ZAPK	BAe 146-200QC	Titan Airways Ltd (G-BTIA/G-PRIN)	
G-ZAPL	BAe 146-200	Titan Airways Ltd/CityJet	
G-ZAPM	Boeing 737-33A	Titan Airways Ltd	
G-ZAPN	BAe 146-200QC	Titan Airways Ltd (G-BPBT)	
G-ZAPS	Hughes 269C	Aviation Bureau (G-AYLX)	
G-ZAPY	Robinson R-22B	Heli Air Ltd (G-INGB)	
G-ZARI	AA-5B Tiger	ZARI Aviation Ltd (G-BHVY)	
G-ZARV	ARV Super 2	P. R. Snowden	
G-ZAZA	PA-18 Super Cub 95	Airborne Taxi Services Ltd	
G-ZBED	Robinson R-22B	A. Harrison (Bedding) Ltd	
G-ZBHH	Hughes 269C	Biggin Hill Helicopters (G-GINZ)	
G-ZBRA	Thunder Ax10-160 balloon	Zebra Ballooning Ltd	
G-ZEBO	Thunder Ax8-105 S2 balloon	S. M. Waterton	
G-ZEBR	Colt 210A balloon	Zebra Ballooning Ltd	
G-ZEIN	Slingsby T.67M-260	R.V. Aviation Ltd/Bournemouth	
G-ZENO	Learjet 35A	Northern Executive Aviation Ltd (G-GAYL/G-ZING)/Manchester	
G-ZEPI	Colt GA-42 gas airship	Lindstrand Balloons Ltd (G-ISPY/ G-BPRB)	
G-ZEPY	Colt GA-42 gas airship	Keelex 195 Ltd (G-BSCU)	
G-ZERO	AA-5B Tiger	G-ZERO Syndicate	
G-ZIGG	Robinson R-22B	Uriah Woodhead & Son Ltd	
G-ZIGI	Robin DR.400/180	R. J. Dix	
G-ZIPA	R. Commander 114A	M. F. Luke (G-BHRA)	
G-ZIPI	Robin DR.400/180	H. U. & D. C. Stahlberg/Headcorn	
G-ZIPY	Wittman W.8 Tailwind	M. J. Butler	
G-ZIZI	Cessna 525 CitationJet	Ortac Air Ltd	
G-ZLIN	Z.526 Trener Master	N. J. Arthur	
G-ZLOJ	Beech A36 Bonanza	C. J. Parker	
G-ZLYN	Z.526F Trener	Air V8 Ltd	
G-ZONK	Robinson R-44 Astro	Zonk Aviation Ltd (G-EDIE)	
G-ZOOI	Lindstrand LBL-105A balloon	Flying Pictures Ltd	
G-ZOOL	Cessna FA.152	Falcon Flying Services (G-BGXZ)/ Biggin Hill	
G-ZORO	Shaw Europa	N. T. Read	
G-ZSFT	PA-23 Aztec 250F	SFT Europe Ltd (G-SALT/G-BGTH)/ Bournemouth	
G-ZTED	Shaw Europa	J. J. Kennedy & E. W. Gladstone	
G-ZULU	PA-28-161 Warrior II	S. F. Tebby & Son	
G-ZVBF	Cameron A-400 balloon	Virgin Balloon Flights Ltd	
G-ZZAG	Cameron Z-77 balloon	T. Charlwood	
G-ZZIP	Mooney M.20J	D. A. H. Dixon	

G-BDOG — SA Bulldog Srs 2000.

G-BWGG— MH.1521C-1 Broussard.

G-IGGL — SOCATA TB-10 Tobago. *M. P. & J. S. Perkin*

Serial carried	Civil identity	Serial carried	Civil identity
2 (USAAC)	G-AZLE	1211(N. Korean AF)	G-BWUF
2 (CIS)	G-YAKS	1377 (Portuguese AF)	G-BARS
5 (USAAC)	G-BEEW	1420 (Korean AF)	G-BMZF
09 (DOSAAF)	G-BVMU	1747 (Portuguese AF)	G-BGPB
19 (USN)	G-BTCC	2028 (69 China AF)	G-BVVF
23 (USAAC)	N49272	2345	G-ATVP
26 (US)	G-BAVO	2807 (V-103 USN)	G-BHTH
26 (DOSAAF)	G-BVXK	3066	G-AETA
27 (CIS)	G-YAKX	5450 (RCAF)	G-TDTW
27 (USN)	G-BRVG	5894	G-BFVH
27 (CIS)	G-OYAK	6136 (205 USN)	G-BRUJ
27 (USAAC)	G-AGYY	6232	BAPC41
28 (USAAC)	N8162G	6247 (Polish AF)	G-OMIG
31 (DOSAAF)	RA-02209	7198/18	G-AANJ
40 (DOSAAF)	G-YAKM	7797 (USAAF)	G-BFAF
41/BA (USN)	G-DDMV	8178 (FU-178 USAF)	G-SABR
42 (DOSAAF)	LY-AMU	8449M	G-ASWJ
43 (SC USAF)	G-AZSC	01385 (CIS)	G-BWJT
44 (USAAF)	G-BWHH	02538 (USAAF)	N33870
44 (K-33 USAAF)	G-BJLH	07539 (143 USN)	N63590
52 (DOSAAF)	LY-AMP	1/4513 (Fr AF)	G-BFYO
52	G-BWVR	14863 (USAAF)	G-BGOR
55 (DOSAAF)	G-BVOK	16693 (693 RCAF)	G-BLPG
64	G-MAYA	18013 (013 RCAF)	G-TRIC
69 (DOSAAF)	G-BTZB	18263 (822 USAAF)	N38940
72 (DOSAAF)	G-BXAV	18393 (RCAF)	G-BCYK
74 (DOSAAF)	G-BXID	18671 (671 RCAF)	G-BNZC
84 (Russian AF)	G-WHZZ	20310 (310 RCAF)	G-BSBG
85 (DOSAAF)	G-BTBI	21714 (201-B USN)	G-RUMM
100 (DOSAAF)	G-YAKI	28521 (TA-521 USAF)	G-TVIJ
112 (DOSAAF)	LY-AFB	30140 (Yugoslav Army)	G-RADA
112 (USAAC)	G-BSWC	30146 (Yugoslav Army)	G-BSXD
115 (DOSAAF)	RA-02293	30149 (Yugoslav Army)	G-SOKO
118 (USAAC)	G-BSDS	30861 (USAAF)	N9089Z
120 (Fr AF)	G-AZGC	31145 (G-26 USAAF)	G-BBLH
124 (Fr AF)	G-BOSJ	31171 (USMarines)	N7614C
139 (DOSAAF)	G-BWOD	31923 (USAAC)	G-BRHP
143 (Fr AF)	G-MSAL	31952 (USAAC)	G-BRPR
152/17	G-ATJM	34037 (USAAF)	N9115Z
168	G-BFDE	39624 (D-39 USAAF)	G-BVMH
177 (Irish AC)	G-BLIW	40467 (19 USN)	G-BTCC
185 (Fr AF)	G-BWLR	43578 (578 USN)	N1364V
208 (USN)	N75664	46867 (USN)	N909WJ
210/16	BAPC56	53319 (319/RB USN)	G-BTDP
215	G-HELV	54137 (69 USN)	G-CTKL
243 (Iraq A F)	G-BTTA	56321 (U-AB RNorAF)	G-BKPY
243 (USAAC)	G-BUKE	79863 (00 USN)	N79863
304	BAPC62	80242 (USAF)	N196B
311 (SingaporeAF)	G-SARK	80425 (WT-14 USN)	G-RUMT
379 (USAAC)	G-ILLE	86711 (USN)	G-RUMW
422-15	G-AVJO	91007 (USAF)	G-NASA
427 (RNorAF)	G-AMRK	93542 (LTA-542 USAF)	G-BRLV
441 (USN)	G-BTFG	111836 (JZ-6 USN)	G-TSIX
450/17	G-BVGZ	111989 (US Army)	N33600
503 (Hungarian AF)	G-BRAM	115042 (TA-042 USAF)	G-BGHU
540 (USAAF)	G-BCNX	115302 (TP USAAF)	G-BJTP
626/8	N6268	115684 (D-C USAAF)	G-BKVM
669 (USAAC)	N75TL	122179 (NP-9 USN)	N179PT
781-25 (Span AF)	G-BRSH	124485 (DF-A USAAF)	G-BEDF
781-32 (Span AF)	G-BPDM	126922 (402/AK USN)	G-RAID
796 (USAAC)	N43SV	146289 (2W USAF)	N99153
854 (USAAC)	G-BTBH	150225 (123 USAF)	G-AWOX
855 (USAAC)	N56421	15-1585	BAPC58
897 (E USN)	G-BJEV	151632 (USAAF)	G-BWGR
1164 (USAAC)	G-BKGL	1532008 (08 China AAF)	G-BVFX
1180 (USN)	G-BRSK	18-2001 (USAAF)	G-BIZV
1197	G-BPVE	211672 (USAAF)	N50755

Serial carried	Civil identity	Serial carried	Civil identity
217786 (25 USAAF)	CF-EQS	B6401	G-AWYY
219993 (USAAF)	N139DP	B7270	G-BFCZ
2106449 (HO-W USAAF)	G-PSIC	C1904 (Z)	G-PFAP
226413 (UN-Z USAAF)	N47DD	C3011 (S)	G-SWOT
226671 (MX-X USAAF)	G-THUN	C4918	G-BWJM
231983 (IY-G USAAF)	F-BDRS	C4994	G-BLWM
236800 (A-44 USAAF)	G-BHPK	C9533 (M)	G-BUWE
269097 (USAF)	G-BTWR	D-692	G-BVAW
2632016 (China AF)	G-BXZB	D3419	BAPC59
314887 (USAAF)	G-AJPI	D5397/17	G-BFXL
315211 (J8-Z USAAF)	N1944A	D7889	G-AANM
315509 (W7-S USAAF)	G-BHUB	D8084	G-ACAA
329405 (A-23 USAAF)	G-BCOB	D8096 (D)	G-AEPH
329417 (USAAF)	G-BDHK	D8781	G-ECKE
329471 (F-44 USAAF)	G-BGXA	E-15 (RNethAF)	G-BIYU
329601 (D-44 USAAF)	G-AXHR	E3B-143 (Span AF)	G-JUNG
329854 (R-44 USAAF)	G-BMKC	E3B-153 (781-75 Span AF)	G-BPTS
329934 (B-72 USAAF)	G-BCPH	E3B-350 (05-97 Span AF)	G-BHPL
330238 (A-24 USAAF)	G-LIVH	E449	G-EBJE
330485 (C-44 USAAF)	G-AJES	F141 (G)	G-SEVA
343251 (27 USAAC)	G-NZSS	F235 (B)	G-BMDB
413573 (B6-V USAAF)	N6526D	F904	G-EBIA
414151 (HO-M USAF)	NL314BG	F938	G-EBIC
436021 (USAAF)	G-BWEZ	F943	G-BIHF
454467 (J-44 USAAF)	G-BILI	F943	G-BKDT
454537 (J-04 USAAF)	G-BFDL	F5447 (N)	G-BKER
461748 (Y USAF)	G-BHDK	F5459 (Y)	G-INNY
463221 (G4-S USAAF)	G-BTCD	F8010 (Z)	G-BDWJ
472216 (AJ-L USAAF)	G-BIXL	F8614	G-AWAU
472218 (WZ-I USAAF)	G-HAEC	G-48-1 (Class B)	G-ALSX
472773 (QP-M USAAF)	G-SUSY	H1968	BAPC42
474008 (VF-R USAAF)	G-SIRR	H5199	G-ADEV
479744 (M-49 USAAF)	G-BGPD	J-1149 (Swiss AF)	G-SWIS
479766 (D-63 USAAF)	G-BKHG	J-1573 (Swiss AF)	G-VICI
480015 (M-44 USAAF)	G-AKIB	J-1605 (Swiss AF)	G-BLID
480133 (B-44 USAAF)	G-BDCD	J-1614 (Swiss AF)	G-VENM
480321 (H-44 USAAF)	G-FRAN	J-1632 (Swiss AF)	G-VNOM
480480 (E-44 USAAF)	G-BECN	J-1758 (Swiss AF)	G-BLSD
480636 (A-58 USAAF)	G-AXHP	J-4031 (Swiss AF)	G-BWFR
480752 (E-39 USAAF)	G-BCXJ	J-4058 (Swiss AF)	G-BWFS
483868 (A-N USAAF)	N5237V	J-4066 (Swiss AF)	G-BXNZ
493209 (US ANG)	G-DDMV	J-4081 (Swiss AF)	G-BWKB
41-33275 (CE USAAC)	G-BICE	J-4083 (Swiss AF)	G-EGHH
42-58678 (IY USAAC)	G-BRIY	J-4090 (Swiss AF)	G-SIAL
42-78044 (USAAC)	G-BRXL	J7326	G-EBQP
42-84555 (EP-H)	G-ELMH	J9941 (57)	G-ABMR
43-5802 (49 USAAC)	G-KITT	K-682 (RDanAF)	OY-BPB
44-72028	G-LYNE	K1786	G-AFTA
44-79609 (PR USAAF)	G-BHXY	K2050	G-ASCM
44-63507 (USAAF)	N51EA	K2059	G-PFAR
44-80594 (USAAF)	G-BEDJ	K2060	G-BKZM
542447	G-SCUB	K2075	G-BEER
542474 (R-184)	G-PCUB	K2227	G-ABBB
51-7545 (113 USAF)	N14113	K2567	G-MOTH
51-11701A (AF258 USAF)	G-BSZC	K2572	G-AOZH
51-14526 (USAF)	G-BRWB	K2587	G-BJAP
51-15227 (10 USN)	G-BKRA	K3215	G-AHSA
52-8543 (66 USAF)	G-BUKY	K3661	G-BURZ
54-21261 (USAF)	G-TBRD	K3731	G-RODI
56-5395 (CDG Fr AF)	G-CUBJ	K4259 (71)	G-ANMO
607327 (09-L USAAF)	G-ARAO	K5054	G-BRDV
A-10 (Swiss AF)	G-BECW	K5414 (XV)	G-AENP
A16-199 (SF-R RAAF)	G-BEOX	K5600	G-BVVI
A17-48 (RAAF)	G-BPHR	K8203	G-BTVE
A-57 (Swiss AF)	G-BECT	K9853 (QV-H)	G-AIST
A-806 (Swiss AF)	G-BTLL	L1592	BAPC63
A1325	G-BVGR	L2301	G-AIZG
A1742	BAPC38	L8841	G-BPIV
A8226	G-BIDW	N500	G-BWRA
B595 (W)	G-BUOD	N1854	G-AIBE
B1807	G-EAVX	N4877 (VX-F)	G-AMDA
B2458	G-BPOB	N5182	G-APUP
B3459	G-BWMJ	N5195	G-ABOX

Serial carried	Civil identity	Serial carried	Civil identity
N5903 (H)	G-GLAD	BI-005 (RNethAF)	G-BUVN
N6181	G-EBKY	BM597 (JH-C)	G-MKVB
N6290	G-BOCK	DE208	G-AGYU
N6452	G-BIAU	DE470	G-ANMY
N6466	G-ANKZ	DE623	G-ANFI
N6532	G-ANTS	DE673	G-ADNZ
N6797	G-ANEH	DE992	G-AXXV
N6847	G-APAL	DF128 (RCO-U)	G-AOJJ
N6965 (FL-J)	G-AJTW	DF155	G-ANFV
N6985	G-AHMN	DF198	G-BBRB
N9191	G-ALND	DG590	G-ADMW
N9192 (RCO-N)	G-DHZF	DR613	G-AFJB
N9389	G-ANJA	DR628	N18V
P3059	BAPC64	EJ693 (SA-J)	N7027E
P6382	G-AJRS	EM720	G-AXAN
R-151 (RNethAF)	G-BIYR	EN224	G-FXII
R-163 (RNethAF)	G-BIRH	EP120 (AE-A)	G-LFVB
R-167 (RNethAF)	G-LION	FB226 (MT-A)	G-BDWM
R1914	G-AHUJ	FE695	G-BTXI
R5250	G-AODT	FE992 (K-T)	G-BDAM
S1287	G-BEYB	FH153	G-BBHK
S1579 (571)	G-BBVO	FJ777 (RCAF)	G-BRTK
S1581	G-BWWK	FJ992 (442)	G-BPTB
T5424	G-AJOA	FR886	G-BDMS
T5672	G-ALRI	FT391	G-AZBN
T5854	G-ANKK	FX301 (FD-NQ)	G-JUDI
T5879	G-AXBW	HB275	G-BKGM
T6313	G-AHVU	HB751	G-BCBL
T6562	G-ANTE	HD-75 (RBelAF)	G-AFDX
T6818 (91)	G-ANKT	HM580	G-ACUU
T6991	G-ANOR	JV579 (F)	G-RUMW
T7230	G-AFVE	KB889 (NA-I)	G-LANC
T7281	G-ARTL	KB994	G-BVBP
T7404 (04)	G-ANMV	KD345 (130)	G-FGID
T7471	G-AJHU	KF584 (RAI-X)	G-RAIX
T7793	G-ANKV	KL161 (VO-B)	G-BYDR
T7842	G-AMTF	KZ321	G-HURY
T7909	G-ANON	LB294	G-AHWJ
T7997	G-AHUF	LB312	G-AHXE
T8191	G-BWMK	LB375	G-AHGW
T9707	G-AKKR	LF858	G-BLUZ
T9738	G-AKAT	LZ766	G-ALCK
U-0247 (Class B identity)	G-AGOY	MD497	G-ANLW
U-80 (Swiss AF)	G-BUKK	MH434 (PK-K)	G-ASJV
U-95 (Swiss AF)	G-BVGP	MJ627 (9G-P)	G-BMSB
U-99 (Swiss AF)	G-AXMT	MJ730 (GZ-?)	G-HFIX
U-108 (Swiss AF)	G-BJAX	MK732 (OU-U)	G-HVDM
U-110 (Swiss AF)	G-PTWO	MK912 (MN-P)	G-BRRA
U-142 (Swiss AF)	G-BONE	ML407 (OU-V)	G-LFIX
U-1234 (Swiss AF)	G-DHAV	ML417 (2I-T)	G-BJSG
V-54 (Swiss AF)	G-BVSD	MP425	G-AITB
V1075	G-AKPF	MS824 (Fr AF)	G-AWBU
V3388	G-AHTW	MT438	G-AREI
V9441 (AR-A)	G-AZWT	MT928 (ZX-M)	G-BKMI
V9673 (MA-J)	G-LIZY	MV293 (OI-C)	G-SPIT
W7 (Italian AF)	G-AGFT	MW763 (HF-A)	G-TEMT
W2718	G-RNLI	MW800 (HF-V)	G-BSHW
W5856 (A2A)	G-BMGC	NJ673	G-AOCR
W9385 (YG-L)	G-ADND	NJ695	G-AJXV
Z2033 (N/275)	G-ASTL	NJ703	G-AKPI
Z5207	G-BYDL	NJ719	G-ANFU
Z5252 (GO-B)	G-BWHA	NL750	G-AOBH
Z7015 (7-L)	G-BKTH	NL985	G-BWIK
Z7197	G-AKZN	NM181	G-AZGZ
Z7381 (XR-T)	G-HURI	NP303	G-ANZJ
AE977 (LE-D)	G-TWTD	NX534	G-BUDL
AP506	G-ACWM	NX611 (LE-C/DX-C)	G-ASXX
AP507 (KX-P)	G-ACWP	NZ5648 (648 RNZAF)	G-BXUL
AR213 (PR-D)	G-AIST	NZ6361 (RNZAF)	G-BXFP
AR501 (NN-A)	G-AWII	PL965 (R)	G-MKXI
AR614 (DU-Z)	G-BUWA	PL983	G-PRXI
BB807	G-ADWO	PP972 (6M-D)	G-BUAR
BE417 (LK-A)	G-HURR	PS853 (C)	G-RRGN

Serial carried	Civil identity	Serial carried	Civil identity
PT462 (SW-A)	G-CTIX	WB703	G-ARMC
PT879	G-BYDE	WB711	G-APPM
PV202 (5R-Q)	G-TRIX	WB726 (E)	G-AOSK
RG333	G-AIEK	WB763 (14)	G-BBMR
RG333	G-AKEZ	WD286 (J)	G-BBND
RH377	G-ALAH	WD288	G-AOSO
RL962	G-AHED	WD292	G-BCRX
RM221	G-ANXR	WD305	G-ARGG
RN218 (N)	G-BBJI	WD310 (B)	G-BWUN
RT486 (PF-A)	G-AJGJ	WD331 (J)	G-BXDH
RT520	G-ALYB	WD363 (5)	G-BCIH
RX168	G-BWEM	WD373 (12)	G-BXDI
SG-3 (RBelAF)	G-BSKP	WD379 (K)	G-APLO
SM845	G-BUOS	WD390 (68)	G-BWNK
SM969 (D-A)	G-BRAF	WD413	G-VROE
SX336	G-BRMG	WE402	G-VENI
TA634 (8K-K)	G-AWJV	WE569	G-ASAJ
TA719 (6T)	G-ASKC	WE724 (062)	G-BUCM
TA805	G-PMNF	WF118	G-DACA
TB252 (GW-H)	G-XVIE	WF877	G-BPOA
TD248 (D)	G-OXVI	WG307	G-BCYJ
TE184	G-MXVI	WG316	G-BCAH
TJ324	G-APAH	WG348	G-BBMV
TJ569	G-AKOW	WG350	G-BPAL
TJ672	G-ANIJ	WG407	G-BWMX
TJ704 (JA)	G-ASCD	WG422 (16)	G-BFAX
TS423	N147DC	WG465	G-BCEY
TS798	G-AGNV	WG469 (72)	G-BWJY
TW439	G-ANRP	WG472	G-AOTY
TW467 (ROD-F)	G-ANIE	WG719	G-BRMA
TW511	G-APAF	WH588 (114/NW RAusN)	G-EEMV
TW517	G-BDFX	WJ358	G-ARYD
TW536 (TS-V)	G-BNGE	WJ680 (C-T)	G-BURM
TW591 (N)	G-ARIH	WJ945 (21)	G-BEDV
TW641	G-ATDN	WK163	G-BVWC
TX183	G-BSMF	WK511 (905 RN)	G-BVBT
VF512 (PF-M)	G-ARRX	WK512 (A)	G-BXIM
VF516	G-ASMZ	WK517 (84)	G-ULAS
VF526 (T)	G-ARXU	WK522	G-BCOU
VF548	G-ASEG	WK549 (Y)	G-BTWF
VL348	G-AVVO	WK586	G-BXGX
VL349	G-AWSA	WK590 (69)	G-BWVZ
VM360	G-APHV	WK609 (93)	G-BXDN
VP955	G-DVON	WK611	G-ARWB
VP981	G-DHDV	WK622	G-BCZH
VR192	G-APIT	WK624 (M)	G-BWHI
VR249 (FA-EL)	G-APIY	WK628	G-BBMW
VR259 (M)	G-APJB	WK630 (11)	G-BXDG
VS356	G-AOLU	WK633 (A)	G-BXEC
VS610 (K-L)	G-AOKL	WK638 (83)	G-BWJZ
VS623	G-AOKZ	WK640 (C)	G-BWUV
VT871	G-DHXX	WK642 (94)	G-BXDP
VX118	G-ASNB	WL505	G-FBIX
VX147	G-AVIL	WL505	G-MKVI
VX926	G-ASKJ	WL626	G-BHDD
VZ467 (A)	G-METE	WM167	G-LOSM
VZ638 (HF)	G-JETM	WP788	G-BCHL
VZ728	G-AGOS	WP790 (T)	G-BBNC
WA576	G-ALSS	WP795 (901)	G-BVZZ
WA577	G-ALST	WP800 (2)	G-BCXN
WA591 (W)	G-BWMF	WP803	G-HAPY
WB531	G-BLRN	WP805 (D)	G-MAJR
WB565 (X)	G-PVET	WP808	G-BDEU
WB569	G-BYSJ	WP809 (78 RN)	G-BVTX
WB571 (34)	G-AOSF	WP840 (9)	G-BXDM
WB585 (RCU-X)	G-AOSY	WP843 (F)	G-BDBP
WB588 (D)	G-AOTD	WP844 (85)	G-BWOX
WB615	G-BXIA	WP851	G-BDET
WB652	G-CHPY	WP856 (904 RN)	G-BVWP
WB654	G-BXGO	WP857 (24)	G-BDRJ
WB660	G-ARMB	WP859 (E)	G-BXCP
WB697 (95)	G-BXCT	WP860 (6)	G-BXDA
WB702	G-AOFE	WP896 (M)	G-BWVY

Serial carried	Civil identity	Serial carried	Civil identity
WP901 (B)	G-BWNT	XL573	G-BVGH
WP903	G-BCGC	XL577	G-BXKF
WP925 (C)	G-BXHA	XL587	G-HPUX
WP928	G-BXGM	XL602	G-BWFT
WP929 (F)	G-BXCV	XL613	G-BVMB
WP930	G-BXHF	XL621	G-BNCX
WP971	G-ATHD	XL714	G-AOGR
WP983	G-BXNN	XL809	G-BLIX
WP984 (H)	G-BWTO	XL812	G-SARO
WR410 (N)	G-BLKA	XL929	G-BNPU
WR421	G-DHUU	XL954	G-BXES
WR421	G-DHTT	XM223 (J)	G-BWWC
WT333	G-BVXC	XM365 (37)	G-BXBH
WT722 (878/VL)	G-BWGN	XM370 (10)	G-BVSP
WT933	G-ALSW	XM376 (27)	G-BWDR
WV198 (K)	G-BJWY	XM378 (34)	G-BWZE
WV318 (A)	G-FFOX	XM405 (42)	G-TORE
WV372 (R)	G-BXFI	XM424	G-BWDS
WV493 (29)	G-BDYG	XM470 (12)	G-BWZZ
WV666 (O-D)	G-BTDH	XM478 (33)	G-BXDL
WV740	G-BNPH	XM479 (54)	G-BVEZ
WV783	G-ALSP	XM553	G-AWSV
WW453 (W-S)	G-TMKI	XM575	G-BLMC
WZ507	G-VTII	XM655	G-VULC
WZ553 (40)	G-DHYY	XM685 (513/PO)	G-AYZJ
WZ589	G-DHZZ	XM693	G-TIMM
WZ662	G-BKVK	XM819	G-APXW
WZ706	G-BURR	XN351	G-BKSC
WZ711	G-AVHT	XN435	G-BGBU
WZ847 (F)	G-CPMK	XN437	G-AXWA
WZ868 (H CUAS)	G-ARMF	XN441	G-BGKT
WZ879 (73)	G-BWUT	XN459 (N)	G-BWOT
WZ882 (K)	G-BXGP	XN498 (16)	G-BWSH
XA880	G-BVXR	XN629	G-KNOT
XD693 (Z-Q)	G-AOBU	XN637 (03)	G-BKOU
XE489	G-JETH	XP242	G-BUCI
XE665 (876/VL)	G-BWGM	XP254	G-ASCC
XE685 (861/VL)	G-GAII	XP279	G-BWKK
XE689 (864/VL)	G-BWGK	XP282	G-BGTC
XE856	G-DUSK	XP355	G-BEBC
XE897	G-DHVV	XP672 (27)	G-RAFI
XE920 (A)	G-VMPR	XP772	G-BUCJ
XE956	G-OBLN	XP907	G-SROE
XF114	G-SWIF	XP924	G-CVIX
XF303 (105-A)	G-BWOU	XR240	G-BDFH
XF357 (871/VL)	G-BWGL	XR241	G-AXRR
XF375 (05)	G-BUEZ	XR246	G-AZBU
XF515 (R)	G-KAXF	XR442	G-HRON
XF516 (66.F)	G-BVVC	XR486	G-RWWW
XF597 (AH)	G-BKFW	XR537 (T)	G-NATY
XF603	G-KAPW	XR538 (69)	G-RORI
XF690	G-MOOS	XR595 (M)	G-BWHU
XF785	G-ALBN	XR673 (L)	G-BXLO
XF836 (J-G)	G-AWRY	XR724	G-BTSY
XF877 (JX)	G-AWVF	XR944	G-ATTB
XG169 (U)	G-BWAF	XR991	G-MOUR
XG232	G-BWIU	XR993	G-BVPP
XG452	G-BRMB	XS101	G-GNAT
XG547	G-HAPR	XS165 (37)	G-ASAZ
XG588	VP-BEP	XS587 (252/V)	G-VIXN
XG775	G-DHWW	XS765	G-BSET
XH568	G-BVIC	XS770	G-HRHI
XJ389	G-AJJP	XT634	G-BYRX
XJ729	G-BVGE	XT671	G-BYRC
XJ763 (P)	G-BKHA	XT788 (316)	G-BMIR
XK416	G-AYUA	XV126 (X)	G-SCTA
XK417	G-AVXY	XV130 (R)	G-BWJW
XK482	G-BJWC	XV134 (P)	G-BWLX
XK895 (19/CU)	G-SDEV	XV140 (K)	G-KAXL
XK940	G-AYXT	XV268	G-BVER
XL426	G-VJET	XW289 (73)	G-JPVA
XL502	G-BMYP	XW293	G-BWCS
XL572	G-HNTR	XW324 (U)	G-BWSG

Serial carried	Civil identity	Serial carried	Civil identity
XW325 (E)	G-BWGF	8+ (Luftwaffe)	G-WULF
XW333 (79)	G-BVTC	14+ (Luftwaffe)	G-BBII
XW423 (14)	G-BWUW	28-02	G-OTAF
XW433 (63)	G-JPRO	F+IS (Luftwaffe)	G-BIRW
XW635	G-AWSW	BU+CC (Luftwaffe)	G-BUCC
XW784	G-BBRN	BU+CK (Luftwaffe)	G-BUCK
XW866 (E)	G-BVTH	CC+43 (Luftwaffe)	G-CJCI
XW895 (51/CU)	G-BXZD	CF+HF (Luftwaffe)	EI-AUY
XW910 (K)	G-BXZE	LG+01 (Luftwaffe)	G-AYSJ
XX467	G-TVII	LG+03 (Luftwaffe)	G-AEZX
XX469	G-BNCL	NJ+C11 (Luftwaffe)	G-ATBG
ZA250	G-VTOL	S4+A07 (Luftwaffe)	G-BWHP
ZA634 (C)	G-BUHA	S5-B06 (Luftwaffe)	G-BSFB
ZA663	G-BUFP	TA+RC (Luftwaffe)	G-BPHZ
ZB500	G-LYNX	6J+PR (Luftwaffe)	G-AWHB
ZH647	G-EHIL	57-H (USAAC)	G-AKAZ
2+1 (7334 Luftwaffe)	G-SYFW	97+04 (Luftwaffe)	G-APVF
3+ (Luftwaffe)	G-BAYV	+114 (Luftwaffe)	G-BSMD
4+ (Luftwaffe)	G-BSLX	146-11042 (7)	G-BMZX
07 (Russian AF)	G-BMJY	146-11083 (5)	G-BNAI

Toy Balloons

Notes	Reg.	Type	Owner or Operator
	G-FYAN	Williams	M. D. Williams
	G-FYAO	Williams	M. D. Williams
	G-FYAU	Williams MK 2	M. D. Williams
	G-FYAV	Osprey Mk 4E2	C. D. Egan & C. Stiles
	G-FYBP	European E.84PW	D. Eaves
	G-FYBR	Osprey Mk 4G2	A. J. Pugh
	G-FYBX	Portswood Mk XVI	I. Chadwick
	G-FYCL	Osprey Mk 4G	P. J. Rogers
	G-FYCV	Osprey Mk 4D	M. Thomson
	G-FYCZ	Osprey Mk 4D2	P. Middleton
	G-FYDC	European EDH-1	D. Eaves & H. Goddard
	G-FYDF	Osprey Mk 4D	K. A. Jones
	G-FYDI	Williams Westwind Two	M. D. Williams
	G-FYDN	European 8C	P. D. Ridout
	G-FYDO	Osprey Mk 4D	N. L. Scallan
	G-FYDP	Williams Westwind Three	M. D. Williams
	G-FYDS	Osprey Mk 4D	N. L. Scallan
	G-FYDW	Osprey Mk 4B	R. A. Balfre
	G-FYEB	Rango Rega	N. H. Ponsford
	G-FYEJ	Rango NA.24	N. H. Ponsford
	G-FYEK	Unicorn UE.1C	D. & D. Eaves
	G-FYEL	European E.84Z	D. Eaves
	G-FYEO	Eagle Mk 1	M. E. Scallan
	G-FYEV	Osprey Mk 1C	M. E. Scallan
	G-FYEZ	Firefly Mk 1	M. E. & N. L. Scallan
	G-FYFA	European E.84LD	D. Goddard & D. Eaves
	G-FYFG	European E.84DE	D. Eaves
	G-FYFH	European E.84DS	D. Eaves
	G-FYFI	European E.84DS	M. Stelling
	G-FYFJ	Williams Westland 2	M. D. Williams
	G-FYFN	Osprey Saturn 2	J. & M. Woods
	G-FYFT	Rango NA-32BC	Rango Kite & Balloon Co
	G-FYFW	Rango NA-55	Rango Kite & Balloon Co
	G-FYFY	Rango NA-55RC	A. M. Lindsay
	G-FYGA	Rango NA-50RC	Rango Kite & Balloon Co
	G-FYGB	Rango NA-105RC	Rango Kite & Balloon Co
	G-FYGC	Rango NA-42B	L. J. Wardle
	G-FYGI	Rango NA-55RC	Advertair Ltd
	G-FYGJ	Airspeed 300	N. Wells
	G-FYGK	Rango NA-42POC	Rango Balloon & Kite Co
	G-FYGM	Saffrey/Smith Princess	A. Smith

G-DAJC — Boeing 767-31KER of Airtours International Airways.

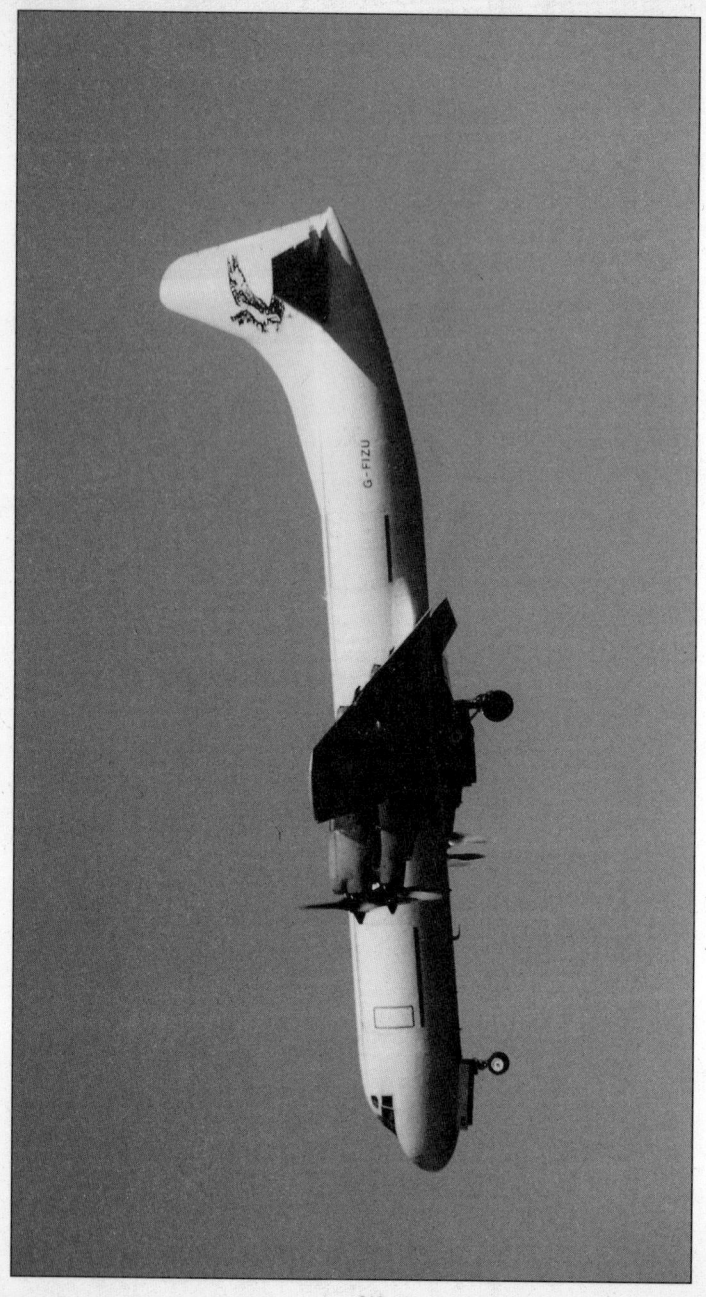

G-FIZU — L.188C Electra of Atlantic Airways.

G-RUNG — SAAB SF.340A of Aurigny Air Services.

G-CRUS — Cessna T.303.

Microlights

Reg.	Type	Notes	Reg.	Type	Notes
G-MBAA	Hiway Skytrike Mk 2		G-MBIA	Flexiform Sealander	
G-MBAB	Hovey Whing-Ding II			Skytrike	
G-MBAD	Weedhopper JC-24A		G-MBIO	American Aerolights Eagle	
G-MBAF	R. J. Swift 3			Z Drive	
G-MBAL	Hiway Demon		G-MBIT	Hiway Demon Skytrike	
G-MBAN	American Aerolights Eagle		G-MBIV	Flexiform Skytrike	
G-MBAR	Skycraft Scout		G-MBIW	Hiway Demon Tri-Flyer	
G-MBAS	Typhoon Tripacer 250			Skytrike	
G-MBAU	Hiway Skytrike		G-MBIY	Ultrasports Tripacer	
G-MBAW	Pterodactyl Ptraveller		G-MBIZ	Mainair Tri-Flyer	
G-MBAZ	Rotec Rally 2B		G-MBJA	Eurowing Goldwing	
G-MBBB	Skycraft Scout 2		G-MBJD	American Aerolights Eagle	
G-MBBG	Weedhopper JC-24B		G-MBJE	Airwave Nimrod	
G-MBBM	Eipper Quicksilver MX		G-MBJF	Hiway Skytrike Mk II	
G-MBBT	Ultrasports Tripacer 330		G-MBJG	Airwave Nimrod	
G-MBBY	Flexiform Sealander		G-MBJI	Southern Aerosports	
G-MBCA	Chargus Cyclone T.250			Scorpion	
G-MBCI	Hiway Skytrike		G-MBJK	American Aerolights Eagle	
G-MBCJ	Mainair Sports Tri-Flyer		G-MBJL	Airwave Nimrod	
G-MBCK	Eipper Quicksilver MX		G-MBJM	Striplin Lone Ranger	
G-MBCL	Hiway Demon Triflyer		G-MBJN	Electraflyer Eagle	
G-MBCM	Hiway Demon 175		G-MBJP	Hiway Skytrike	
G-MBCO	Flexiform Sealander		G-MBJR	American Aerolights Eagle	
	Buggy		G-MBJT	Hiway Skytrike II	
G-MBCU	American Aerolights Eagle		G-MBJU	American Eagle 215B	
G-MBCX	Airwave Nimrod 165		G-MBJZ	Eurowing Catto CP.16	
G-MBCZ	Chargus Skytrike 160		G-MBKS	Hiway Skytrike 160	
G-MBDE	Flexiform Skytrike		G-MBKT	Mitchell Wing B.10	
G-MBDF	Rotec Rally 2B		G-MBKU	Hiway Demon Skytrike	
G-MBDG	Eurowing Goldwing		G-MBKY	American Aerolight Eagle	
G-MBDJ	Flexiform Sealander		G-MBKZ	Hiway Skytrike	
	Triflyer		G-MBLB	Eipper Quicksilver MX	
G-MBDM	Southdown Sigma Trike		G-MBLF	Hiway Demon 195 Tri	
G-MBDZ	Eipper Quicksilver MX			Pacer	
G-MBEA	Hornet Nimrod		G-MBLJ	Eipper Quicksilver MX	
G-MBED	Chargus Titan 38		G-MBLM	Hiway Skytrike	
G-MBEG	Eipper Quicksilver MX		G-MBLN	Pterodactyl Ptraveller	
G-MBEJ	Electraflyer Eagle		G-MBLU	Southdown Lightning	
G-MBEN	Eipper Quicksilver MX			L.195	
G-MBEP	American Aerolights Eagle		G-MBLV	Ultrasports Hybrid	
G-MBES	Skyhook Cutlass		G-MBLY	Flexiform Sealander Trike	
G-MBET	MEA Mistral Trainer		G-MBLZ	Southern Aerosports	
G-MBEU	Hiway Demon T.250			Scorpion	
G-MBEV	Chargus Titan 38		G-MBME	American Aerolights	
G-MBFA	Hiway Skytrike 250			Eagle Z Drive	
G-MBFE	American Aerolights Eagle		G-MBMG	Rotec Rally 2B	
G-MBFF	Southern Aerosports		G-MBMJ	Mainair Tri-Flyer	
	Scorpion		G-MBMO	Hiway Skytrike 160	
G-MBFK	Hiway Demon		G-MBMR	Ultrasports Tripacer	
G-MBFM	Hiway Hang Glider			Typhoon	
G-MBFU	Ultrasports Tripacer		G-MBMS	Hornet	
G-MBFY	Mirage II		G-MBMT	Southdown Lightning 195	
G-MBFZ	M. S. S. Goldwing		G-MBMU	Eurowing Goldwing	
G-MBGA	Solar Wings Typhoon		G-MBNA	American Aerolights Eagle	
G-MBGF	Twamley Trike		G-MBNH	Southern Airsports	
G-MBGJ	Hiway Skytrike Mk 2			Scorpion	
G-MBGK	Electra Flyer Eagle		G-MBNJ	Eipper Quicksilver MX	
G-MBGP	Solar Wings Typhoon		G-MBNK	American Aerolights Eagle	
G-MBGS	Rotec Rally 2B		G-MBNN	Southern Microlight	
G-MBGX	Southdown Lightning			Gazelle P.160N	
G-MBGY	Hiway Demon Skytrike		G-MBNT	American Aerolights Eagle	
G-MBHA	Trident Trike		G-MBOA	Flexiform Hilander	
G-MBHE	American Aerolights Eagle		G-MBOE	Solar Wing Typhoon Trike	
G-MBHK	Flexiform Skytrike		G-MBOF	Pakes Jackdaw	
G-MBHP	American Aerolights		G-MBOH	Microlight Engineering	
	Eagle II			Mistral	
G-MBHT	Chargus T.250		G-MBOK	Dunstable Microlight	
G-MBHZ	Pterodactyl Ptraveller		G-MBOM	Hiway Hilander	

Reg.	Type	Notes	Reg.	Type	Notes
G-MBON	Eurowing Goldwing Canard		G-MBYM	Eipper Quicksilver MX	
G-MBOR	Chotia 460B Weedhopper		G-MBYY	Southern Aerosports Scorpion	
G-MBOT	Hiway 250 Skytrike		G-MBZB	Hiway Skytrike	
G-MBOX	American Aerolights Eagle		G-MBZF	American Aerolights Eagle	
G-MBPA	Weedhopper Srs 2		G-MBZG	Twinflight Scorpion 2 seat	
G-MBPD	American Aerolights Eagle		G-MBZH	Eurowing Goldwing	
G-MBPG	Hunt Skytrike		G-MBZJ	Southdown Puma	
G-MBPJ	Moto-Delta		G-MBZK	Tri-Pacer 250	
G-MBPM	Eurowing Goldwing		G-MBZM	UAS Storm Buggy	
G-MBPN	American Aerolights Eagle		G-MBZN	Ultrasports Puma	
G-MBPO	Volnik Arrow		G-MBZO	Tri-Pacer 330	
G-MBPX	Eurowing Goldwing		G-MBZP	Skyhook TR2	
G-MBPY	Ultrasports Tripacer 330		G-MBZV	American Aerolights Eagle	
G-MBRB	Electraflyer Eagle 1		G-MBZZ	Southern Aerosports Scorpion	
G-MBRD	American Aerolights Eagle				
G-MBRE	Wheeler Scout		G-MGAA	BFC Challenger II	
G-MBRH	Ultraflight Mirage Mk II		G-MGAG	Aviasud Mistral	
G-MBRM	Hiway Demon		G-MGCA	Jabiru UL	
G-MBRS	American Aerolights Eagle		G-MGCB	Pegasus XL-Q	
G-MBRV	Eurowing Goldwing		G-MGDL	Pegasus Quantum 15	
G-MBSD	Southdown Puma DS		G-MGDM	Pegasus Quantum 15	
G-MBSN	American Aerolights Eagle		G-MGEC	Rans S.6-ESD Coyote IIXL	
G-MBSS	Ultrasports Puma 2		G-MGEF	Pegasus Quantum 15	
G-MBST	Mainair Gemini Sprint		G-MGFK	Pegasus Quantum 15	
G-MBSX	Ultraflight Mirage II		G-MGGG	Pegasus Quantum 15	
G-MBTA	UAS Storm Buggy 5 Mk 2		G-MGGT	CFM Streak Shadow SAM	
G-MBTC	Weedhopper JC-24B		G-MGGV	Pegasus Quantum 15-912	
G-MBTE	Hiway Demon		G-MGMC	Pegasus Quantum 15	
G-MBTF	Mainair Tri-Flyer Skytrike		G-MGND	Rans S.6-ESD Coyote IIXL	
G-MBTG	Mainair Gemini		G-MGOD	Medway Raven	
G-MBTH	Whittaker MW.4		G-MGOM	Medway Hybred 44XLR	
G-MBTI	Hovey Whing Ding		G-MGOO	Renegade Spirit UK Ltd	
G-MBTJ	Solar Wings Microlight		G-MGPD	Pegasus XL-R	
G-MBTO	Mainair Tri-Flyer 250		G-MGPH	CFM Streak Shadow (G-RSPH)	
G-MBTW	Raven Vector 600				
G-MBUA	Hiway Demon		G-MGRW	Cyclone AX3/503	
G-MBUB	Horne Sigma Skytrike		G-MGTG	Pegasus Quantum 15 (G-MZIO)	
G-MBUC	Huntair Pathfinder				
G-MBUH	Hiway Skytrike		G-MGTR	Hunt Wing	
G-MBUI	Wheeler Scout Mk I		G-MGTW	CFM Shadow Srs DD	
G-MBUO	Southern Aerosports Scorpion		G-MGUN	Cyclone AX2000	
G-MBUP	Hiway Skytrike		G-MGUX	Hunt Wing	
G-MBUZ	Wheeler Scout Mk II		G-MGUY	CFM Shadow Srs BD	
G-MBVA	Volmer Jensen VJ-23E		G-MGWH	Thruster T.300	
G-MBVC	American Aerolights Eagle				
G-MBVK	Ultraflight Mirage II		G-MJAB	Ultrasports Skytrike	
G-MBVL	Southern Aerosports Scorpion		G-MJAD	Eipper Quicksilver MX	
G-MBVV	Hiway Skytrike		G-MJAE	American Aerolights Eagle	
G-MBVW	Skyhook TR.2		G-MJAG	Skyhook TR1	
G-MBWA	American Aerolights Eagle		G-MJAH	American Aerolights Eagle	
G-MBWB	Hiway Skytrike		G-MJAI	American Aerolights Eagle	
G-MBWF	Mainair Triflyer Striker		G-MJAJ	Eurowing Goldwing	
G-MBWG	Huntair Pathfinder		G-MJAL	Wheeler Scout 3	
G-MBWH	Designability Duet I		G-MJAM	Eipper Quicklsilver MX	
G-MBWL	Huntair Pathfinder		G-MJAN	Hiway Skytrike	
G-MBWP	Ultrasports Trike		G-MJAP	Hiway 160	
G-MBWT	Huntair Pathfinder		G-MJAY	Eurowing Goldwing	
G-MBWW	Southern Aerosports Scorpion		G-MJAZ	Aerodyne Vector 610	
G-MBWX	Southern Aerosports Scorpion		G-MJBI	Eipper Quicksilver MX	
			G-MJBL	American Aerolights Eagle	
G-MBXK	Ultrasports Puma		G-MJBS	Ultralight Stormbuggy	
G-MBXO	Sheffield Trident		G-MJBV	American Aerolights Eagle	
G-MBXR	Hiway Skytrike 150		G-MJBZ	Huntair Pathfinder	
G-MBXT	Eipper Quicksilver MX2		G-MJCB	Hornet 330	
G-MBXX	Ultraflight Mirage II		G-MJCD	Sigma Tetley Skytrike	
G-MBYD	American Aerolights Eagle		G-MJCE	Ultrasports Tripacer	
G-MBYI	Ultraflight Lazair		G-MJCI	Kruchek Firefly 440	
G-MBYK	Huntair Pathfinder Mk 1		G-MJCJ	Hiway Spectrum	
G-MBYL	Huntair Pathfinder 330		G-MJCK	Southern Aerosports Scorpion	
			G-MJCL	Eipper Quicksilver MX	

Reg.	Type	Notes	Reg.	Type	Notes
G-MJCN	S.M.C. Flyer Mk 1		G-MJKE	Mainair Triflyer 330	
G-MJCU	Tarjani		G-MJKF	Hiway Demon	
G-MJCW	Hiway Super Scorpion		G-MJKG	John Ivor Skytrike	
G-MJCX	American Aerolights Eagle		G-MJKH	Eipper Quicksilver MX II	
G-MJCZ	Southern Aerosports Scorpion 2		G-MJKJ	Eipper Quicksilver MX	
			G-MJKO	Goldmarque 250 Skytrike	
G-MJDE	Huntair Pathfinder		G-MJKS	Mainair Triflyer	
G-MJDG	Hornet Supertrike		G-MJKV	Hornet	
G-MJDH	Huntair Pathfinder		G-MJKX	Ultralight Skyrider Phantom	
G-MJDJ	Hiway Skytrike Demon		G-MJLB	Ultrasports Puma 2	
G-MJDK	American Aerolights Eagle		G-MJLH	American Aerolights Eagle 2	
G-MJDO	Southdown Puma 440				
G-MJDP	Eurowing Goldwing		G-MJLI	Hiway Demon Skytrike	
G-MJDR	Hiway Demon Skytrike		G-MJLL	Hiway Demon Skytrike	
G-MJDU	Eipper Quicksilver àMX2		G-MJLR	Skyhook SK-1	
G-MJDW	Eipper Quicksilver MX		G-MJLS	Rotec Rally 2B	
G-MJEE	Mainair Triflyer Trike		G-MJLT	American Aerolights Eagle	
G-MJEF	Gryphon 180		G-MJMA	Hiway Demon	
G-MJEG	Eurowing Goldwing		G-MJME	Ultrasports Tripacer Mega II	
G-MJEJ	American Aerolights Eagle				
G-MJEL	GMD-01 Trike		G-MJMM	Chargus Vortex	
G-MJEO	American Aerolights Eagle		G-MJMP	Eipper Quicksilver MX	
G-MJER	Flexiform Striker		G-MJMR	Solar Wings Typhoon	
G-MJET	Stratos Prototype 3 Axis 1		G-MJMS	Hiway Skytrike	
G-MJEX	Eipper Quicksilver MX		G-MJMT	Hiway Demon Skytrike	
G-MJEY	Southdown Lightning		G-MJMU	Hiway Demon	
G-MJFB	Flexiform Striker		G-MJMW	Eipper Quicksilver MX2	
G-MJFD	Ultrasports Tripacer		G-MJMX	Ultrasports Tripacer	
G-MJFJ	Hiway Skytrike 250		G-MJNB	Hiway Skytrike	
G-MJFK	Flexiform Skytrike Dual		G-MJNE	Hornet Supreme Dual Trike	
G-MJFM	Huntair Pathfinder				
G-MJFO	Eipper Quicksilver MX		G-MJNK	Hiway Skytrike	
G-MJFP	American Aerolights Eagle		G-MJNL	American Aerolights Eagle	
G-MJFV	Ultrasports Tripacer		G-MJNM	American Aerolights Double Eagle	
G-MJFX	Skyhook TR-1				
G-MJGI	Eipper Quicksilver MX		G-MJNN	Ultraflight Mirage II	
G-MJGN	Greenslade Monotrike		G-MJNO	American Aerolights Double Eagle	
G-MJGO	Barnes Avon Skytrike				
G-MJGT	Skyhook Cutlass Trike		G-MJNR	Ultralight Solar Buggy	
G-MJGV	Eipper Quicksilver MX2		G-MJNS	Swallow AeroPlane Swallow B	
G-MJGW	Solar Wings TrikeB				
G-MJHC	Ultrasports Tripacer 330		G-MJNT	Hiway Skytrike	
G-MJHF	Skyhook Sailwing Trike		G-MJNU	Skyhook Cutlass	
G-MJHK	Hiway Demon 195		G-MJNY	Skyhook Sabre Trike	
G-MJHM	Ultrasports Trike		G-MJOC	Huntair Pathfinder	
G-MJHN	American Aerolights Eagle		G-MJOE	Eurowing Goldwing	
G-MJHR	Southdown Lightning		G-MJOG	American Aerolights Eagle	
G-MJHU	Eipper Quicksilver MX		G-MJOI	Hiway Demon	
G-MJHV	Hiway Demon 250		G-MJOJ	Flexiform Skytrike	
G-MJHW	Ultrasports Puma 1		G-MJOL	Skyhook Cutlass	
G-MJHX	Eipper Quicksilver MX		G-MJOM	Southdown Puma 40F	
G-MJHZ	Southdown Sailwings		G-MJOU	Hiway Demon 175	
G-MJIA	Flexiform Striker		G-MJOW	Eipper Quicksilver MX	
G-MJIC	Ultrasports Puma 330		G-MJPA	Rotec Rally 2B	
G-MJIF	Mainair Triflyer		G-MJPE	Hiway Demon Skytrike	
G-MJIJ	Ultrasports Tripacer 250		G-MJPG	American Aerolights Eagle 430R	
G-MJIK	Southdown Sailwings Lightning				
			G-MJPI	Flexiform Striker	
G-MJIN	Hiway Skytrike		G-MJPK	Hiway Vulcan	
G-MJIR	Eipper Quicksilver MX		G-MJPO	Eurowing Goldwing	
G-MJIY	Striker/Panther		G-MJPT	Dragon	
G-MJIZ	Southdown Lightning		G-MJPU	Solar Wings Typhoon	
G-MJJA	Huntair Pathfinder		G-MJPV	Eipper Quicksilver MX	
G-MJJB	Eipper Quicksilver MX		G-MJRE	Hiway Demon	
G-MJJF	Solar Wings Typhoon		G-MJRI	American Aerolights Eagle	
G-MJJJ	Moyes Knight		G-MJRK	Flexiform Striker	
G-MJJK	Eipper Quicksilver MX2		G-MJRL	Eurowing Goldwing	
G-MJJM	Birdman Cherokee Mk 1		G-MJRN	Flexiform Striker	
G-MJJO	Flexiform Skytrike Dual		G-MJRO	Eurowing Goldwing	
G-MJJV	Wheeler Scoutá		G-MJRP	Mainair Triflyer 330	
G-MJJX	Hiway Skytrike		G-MJRR	Striplin Skyranger Srs 1	
G-MJJY	Tirith Firefly		G-MJRS	Eurowing Goldwing	
G-MJKB	Striplin Skyranger		G-MJRT	Southdown Lightning DS	

Reg.	Type	Notes	Reg.	Type	Notes
G-MJRU	MBA Tiger Cub 440		G-MJXY	Hiway Demon Skytrike	
G-MJRV	Eurowing Goldwing		G-MJYA	Huntair Pathfinder	
G-MJRX	Ultrasports Puma II		G-MJYC	Ultrasports Panther XL	
G-MJSA	Mainair 2-Seat Trike			Dual 440	
G-MJSE	Skyrider Airsports		G-MJYD	MBA Tiger Cub 440	
	Phantom		G-MJYF	Mainair Gemini Flash	
G-MJSF	Skyrider Airsports		G-MJYG	Skyhook Orion Canard	
	Phantom		G-MJYM	Southdown Puma Sprint	
G-MJSL	Dragon 200		G-‹MJYP	Mainair Triflyer 440	
G-MJSO	Hiway Skytrike		G-MJYR	Catto CP.16	
G-MJSP	Romain Tiger Cub 440		G-MJYS	Southdown Puma Sprint	
G-MJSS	American Aerolights Eagle		G-MJYT	Southdown Puma Sprint	
G-MJST	Pterodactyl Ptraveler		G-MJYV	Mainair Triflyer 2 Seat	
G-MJSV	MBA Tiger Cub		G-MJYW	Wasp Gryphon III	
G-MJSY	Eurowing Goldwing		G-MJYX	Mainair Triflyer	
G-MJSZ	DH Wasp		G-MJYY	Hiway Demon	
G-MJTD	Gardner T-M Scout		G-MJZA	MBA Tiger Cub	
G-MJTE	Skyrider Airsports Phantom		G-MJZC	MBA Tiger Cub 440	
G-MJTF	Gryphon Wing		G-MJZD	Mainair Gemini Flash	
G-MJTM	Aerostructure Pipistrelle 2B		G-MJZE	MBA Tiger Cub 440	
G-MJTN	Eipper Quicksilver MX		G-MJZH	Southdown Lightning 195	
G-MJTO	Jordan Duet Srs 1		G-MJZJ	Hiway Cutlass Skytrike	
G-MJTP	Flexiform Striker		G-MJZK	Southdown Puma Sprint	
G-MJTR	Southdown Puma DS Mk 1			440	
G-MJTW	Eurowing Trike		G-MJZL	Eipper Quicksilver MX II	
G-MJTX	Skyrider Phantom		G-MJZO	Flexiform Striker	
G-MJTZ	Skyrider Airsports Phantom		G-MJZT	Flexiform Striker	
G-MJUC	MBA Tiger Cub 440		G-MJZU	Flexiform Striker	
G-MJUE	Southdown Lightning II		G-MJZW	Eipper Quicksilver MX II	
G-MJUI	Flexiform Striker		G-MJZX	Hummer TX	
G-MJUJ	Eipper Quicksilver Mk II				
G-MJUM	Flexiform Striker		G-MMAC	Dragon Srs 150	
G-MJUR	Skyrider Airsports Phantom		G-MMAE	Dragon Srs 150	
G-MJUS	MBA Tiger Cub 440		G-MMAG	MBA Tiger Cub 440	
G-MJUT	Eurowing Goldwing		G-MMAH	Eipper Quicksilver MX II	
G-MJUU	Eurowing Goldwing		G-MMAI	Dragon Srs 150	
G-MJUV	Huntair Pathfinder 1		G-MMAJ	Mainair Tri-Flyer 440	
G-MJUW	MBA Tiger Cub 440		G-MMAK	MBA Tiger Cub 440	
G-MJUX	Skyrider Airsports Phantom		G-MMAL	Flexiform Striker Dual	
G-MJUZ	Dragon Srs 150		G-MMAM	MBA Tiger Cub 440	
G-MJVA	Skyrider Airsports Phantom		G-MMAN	Flexiform Striker	
G-MJVE	Hybred Skytrike		G-MMAO	Southdown Puma Sprint	
G-MJVF	CFM Shadow		G-MMAP	Hummer TX	
G-MJVG	Hiway Skytrike		G-MMAR	Southdown Puma Sprint	
G-MJVJ	Flexiform Striker Dual		G-MMAT	Southdown Puma Sprint	
G-MJVM	Dragon 150		G-MMAW	Mainair Rapier	
G-MJVN	Ultrasports Puma 440		G-MMAX	Dual Striker	
G-MJVP	Eipper Quicksilver MX II		G-MMAZ	Southdown Puma Sprint	
G-MJVR	Flexiform Striker		G-MMBD	Spectrum 330	
G-MJVT	Eipper Quicksilver MX		G-MMBE	MBA Tiger Cub 440	
G-MJVU	Eipper Quicksilver MX II		G-MMBH	MBA Super Tiger Cub 440	
G-MJVW	Airwave Nimrod		G-MMBJ	Solar Wings Typhoon	
G-MJVX	Skyrider Phantom		G-MMBL	Southdown Puma	
G-MJVY	Dragon Srs 150		G-MMBN	Eurowing Goldwing	
G-MJVZ	Hiway Demon Tripacer		G-MMBS	Flexiform Striker	
G-MJWB	Eurowing Goldwing		G-MMBT	MBA Tiger Cub 440	
G-MJWF	Tiger Cub 440		G-MMBU	Eipper Quicksilver MX II	
G-MJWG	MBA Tiger Cub		G-MMBV	Huntair Pathfinder	
G-MJWJ	MBA Tiger Cub 440		G-MMBX	MBA Tiger Cub 440	
G-MJWK	Huntair Pathfinder		G-MMBY	Solar Wings Panther XL	
G-MJWN	Flexiform Striker		G-MMBZ	Solar Wings Typhoon P	
G-MJWR	MBA Tiger Cub 440		G-MMCD	Southdown Lightning DS	
G-MJWU	Maxair Hummer TX		G-MMCE	MBA Tiger Cub 440	
G-MJWW	MBA Super Tiger Cub 440		G-MMCF	Solar Wings Panther 330	
G-MJWZ	Ultrasports Panther XL		G-MMCI	Southdown Puma Sprint	
G-MJXD	MBA Tiger Cub 440		G-MMCJ	Flexiform Striker	
G-MJXE	Hiway Demon		G-MMCM	Southdown Puma Sprint	
G-MJXF	MBA Tiger Cub 440		G-MMCS	Southdown Puma Sprint	
G-MJXM	Hiway Skytrike		G-MMCV	Solar Wings Typhoon III	
G-MJXR	Huntair Pathfinder II		G-MMCW	Southdown Puma Sprint	
G-MJXS	Huntair Pathfinder II		G-MMCX	MBA Super Tiger Cub 440	
G-MJXV	Flexiform Striker		G-MMCY	Flexiform Striker	
G-MJXX	Flexiform Striker Dual		G-MMCZ	Flexiform Striker	

Reg.	Type	Notes	Reg.	Type	Notes
G-MMDC	Eipper Quicksilver MXII		G-MMJD	Southdown Puma Sprint	
G-MMDE	Solar Wings Typhoon		G-MMJE	Southdown Puma Sprint	
G-MMDF	Southdown Lightning II		G-MMJF	Ultrasports Panther Dual	
G-MMDK	Flexiform Striker			440	
G-MMDN	Flexiform Striker		G-MMJG	Mainair Tri-Flyer 440	
G-MMDO	Southdown Sprint		G-MMJJ	Solar Wings Typhoon	
G-MMDP	Southdown Sprint		G-MMJM	Southdown Puma Sprint	
G-MMDR	Huntair Pathfinder II		G-MMJN	Eipper Quicksilver MX II	
G-MMDS	Ultrasports Panther XLS		G-MMJT	Southdown Puma Sprint	
G-MMDV	Ultrasports Panther		G-MMJU	Hiway Demon	
G-MMDW	Pterodactyl Pfledgling		G-MMJV	MBA Tiger Cub 440	
G-MMDX	Solar Wings Typhoon		G-MMJX	Teman Mono-Fly	
G-MMDY	Puma Sprint X		G-MMJY	MBA Tiger Cub 440	
G-MMDZ	Flexiform Dual Strike		G-MMKA	Ultrasports Panther Dual	
G-MMEE	American Aerolights Eagle		G-MMKD	Southdown Puma Sprint	
G-MMEF	Hiway Super Scorpion		G-MMKE	Birdman Chinook WT-11	
G-MMEI	Hiway Demon		G-MMKG	Solar Wings Typhoon XL	
G-MMEJ	Flexiform Striker		G-MMKH	Solar Wings Typhoon XL	
G-MMEK	Medway Hybred 44XL		G-MMKI	Ultrasports Panther 330	
G-MMEN	Solar Wings Typhoon XL2		G-MMKK	Mainair Flash	
G-MMEP	MBA Tiger Cub 440		G-MMKL	Mainair Flash	
G-MMET	Skyhook Sabre TR-1 Mk II		G-MMKM	Flexiform Dual Striker	
G-MMEW	MBA Tiger Cub 440		G-MMKP	MBA Tiger Cub 440	
G-MMFD	Flexiform Striker		G-MMKR	Southdown Lightning DS	
G-MMFE	Flexiform Striker		G-MMKU	Southdown Puma Sprint	
G-MMFG	Flexiform Striker		G-MMKV	Southdown Puma Sprint	
G-MMFI	Flexiform Striker		G-MMKW	Solar Wings Storm	
G-MMFK	Flexiform Striker		G-MMKX	Skyrider Phantom 330	
G-MMFL	Flexiform Striker		G-MMKZ	Ultrasports Puma 440	
G-MMFN	MBA Tiger Cub 440		G-MMLB	MBA Tiger Cub 440	
G-MMFS	MBA Tiger Cub 440		G-MMLE	Eurowing Goldwing SP	
G-MMFT	MBA Tiger Cub 440		G-MMLH	Hiway Demon	
G-MMFV	Tri-Flyer 440		G-MMLM	MBA Tiger Cub 440	
G-MMFZ	AES Sky Ranger		G-MMLO	Skyhook Pixie	
G-MMGA	Bass Gosling		G-MMLP	Southdown Sprint	
G-MMGB	Southdown Puma Sprint		G-MMLV	Southdown Puma 330	
G-MMGC	Southdown Puma Sprint		G-MMLX	Solar Wings Panther XL-S	
G-MMGD	Southdown Puma Sprint		G-MMMB	Mainair Tri-Flyer	
G-MMGE	Hiway Super Scorpion		G-MMMD	Flexiform Dual Striker	
G-MMGF	MBA Tiger Cub 440		G-MMMG	Eipper Quicksilver MXL	
G-MMGL	MBA Tiger Cub 440		G-MMMH	Hadland Willow	
G-MMGN	Southdown Puma Sprint		G-MMMI	Southdown Lightning	
G-MMGP	Southdown Puma Sprint		G-MMMJ	Southdown Sprint	
G-MMGS	Solar Wings Panther XL		G-MMMK	Hornet Invader	
G-MMGT	Solar Wings Typhoon		G-MMML	Dragon 150	
G-MMGU	Flexiform Sealander		G-MMMN	Ultrasports Panther Dual	
G-MMGV	Whittaker MW-5 Sorcerer			440	
G-MMGX	Southdown Puma		G-MMMP	Flexiform Dual Striker	
G-MMHE	Southdown Puma Sprint		G-MMMR	Flexiform Striker	
G-MMHF	Southdown Puma Sprint		G-MMMW	Flexiform Striker	
G-MMHK	Hiway Super Scorpion		G-MMNB	Eipper Quicksilver MX	
G-MMHL	Hiway Super Scorpion		G-MMNC	Eipper Quicksilver MX	
G-MMHM	Goldmarque Gyr		G-MMND	Eipper Quicksilver MX	
G-MMHN	MBA Tiger Cub 440			II-Q2	
G-MMHP	Hiway Demon		G-MMNF	Hornet	
G-MMHR	Southdown Puma Sprint		G-MMNG	Solar Wings Typhoon XL	
G-MMHS	SMD Viper		G-MMNH	Dragon 150	
G-MMHX	Hornet Invader 440		G-MMNM	Skyhook Sabre	
G-MMHY	Hornet Invader 440		G-MMNN	Buzzard	
G-MMHZ	Solar Wings Typhoon XL		G-MMNS	Mitchell U-2 Super Wing	
G-MMIC	Luscombe Vitality		G-MMNT	Flexiform Striker	
G-MMIE	MBA Tiger Cub 440		G-MMNW	Mainair Tri-Flyer 330	
G-MMIF	Wasp Gryphon		G-MMNX	Solar Wings Panther XL	
G-MMIH	MBA Tiger Cub 440		G-MMOB	Southdown Sprint	
G-MMII	Southdown Puma Sprint		G-MMOF	MBA Tiger Cub 440	
	440		G-MMOH	Solar Wings Typhoon XL	
G-MMIJ	Ultrasports Tripacer		G-MMOI	MBA Tiger Cub 440	
G-MMIL	Eipper Quicksilver MX II		G-MMOK	Solar Wings Panther XL	
G-MMIM	MBA Tiger Cub 440		G-MMOL	Skycraft Scout R3	
G-MMIR	Mainair Tri-Flyer 440		G-MMOW	Mainair Gemini Flash	
G-MMIW	Southdown Puma Sprint		G-MMOY	Mainair Gemini Sprint	
G-MMIX	MBA Tiger Cub 440		G-MMPG	Southdown Puma	
G-MMIY	Eurowing Goldwing		G-MMPH	Southdown Puma Sprint	

Reg.	Type	Notes	Reg.	Type	Notes
G-MMPI	Pterodactyl Ptraveller		G-MMUW	Mainair Gemini Flash	
G-MMPJ	Mainair Tri-Flyer 440		G-MMUX	Mainair Gemini	
G-MMPL	Flexiform Dual Striker		G-MMVA	Southdown Puma Sprint	
G-MMPN	Chargus T250		G-MMVC	Ultrasports Panther XL	
G-MMPO	Mainair Gemini Flash		G-MMVH	Southdown Raven	
G-MMPT	SMD Gazelle		G-MMVI	Southdown Puma Sprint	
G-MMPU	Ultrasports Tripacer 250		G-MMVL	Ultrasports Panther XL-S	
G-MMPW	Airwave Nimrod		G-MMVM	Whiteley Orion 1	
G-MMPX	Ultrasports Panther Dual 440		G-MMVO	Southdown Puma Sprint	
			G-MMVP	Mainair Gemini Flash	
G-MMPZ	Teman Mono-Fly		G-MMVR	Hiway Skytrike 1	
G-MMRA	Mainair Tri-Flyer 250		G-MMVS	Skyhook Pixie	
G-MMRF	MBA Tiger Cub 440		G-MMVX	Southdown Puma Sprint	
G-MMRH	Hiway Demon		G-MMVZ	Southdown Puma Sprint	
G-MMRJ	Solar Wings Panther XL		G-MMWA	Mainair Gemini Flash	
G-MMRK	Ultrasports Panther XL		G-MMWC	Eipper Quicksilver MXII	
G-MMRL	Solar Wings Panther XL		G-MMWF	Hiway Skytrike 250	
G-MMRN	Southdown Puma Sprint		G-MMWG	Greenslade Mono-Trike	
G-MMRO	Mainair Gemini 440		G-MMWH	Southdown Puma Sprint 440	
G-MMRP	Mainair Gemini				
G-MMRT	Southdown Puma Sprint		G-MMWI	Southdown Lightning	
G-MMRU	Tirith Firebird FB-2		G-MMWJ	Pterodactyl Ptraveler	
G-MMRW	Flexiform Dual Striker		G-MMWL	Eurowing Goldwing	
G-MMRY	Chargus T.250		G-MMWN	Ultrasports Tripacer	
G-MMRZ	Ultrasports Panther Dual 440		G-MMWO	Ultrasports Panther XL	
			G-MMWS	Mainair Tri-Flyer	
G-MMSA	Ultrasports Panther XL		G-MMWT	CFM Shadow	
G-MMSC	Mainair Gemini		G-MMWX	Southdown Puma Sprint	
G-MMSE	Eipper Quicksilver MX		G-MMWZ	Southdown Puma Sprint	
G-MMSG	Solar Wings Panther XL-S		G-MMXC	Mainair Gemini Flash	
G-MMSH	Solar Wings Panther XL		G-MMXD	Mainair Gemini Flash	
G-MMSO	Mainair Tri-Flyer 440		G-MMXE	Mainair Gemini Flash	
G-MMSP	Mainair Gemini Flash		G-MMXG	Mainair Gemini Flash	
G-MMSR	MBA Tiger Cub 440		G-MMXH	Mainair Gemini Flash	
G-MMSS	Southdown Lightning		G-MMXI	Horizon Prototype	
G-MMST	Southdown Puma Sprint		G-MMXJ	Mainair Gemini Flash	
G-MMSV	Southdown Puma Sprint		G-MMXK	Mainair Gemini Flash	
G-MMSW	MBA Tiger Cub 440		G-MMXL	Mainair Gemini Flash	
G-MMSZ	Medway Half Pint		G-MMXM	Mainair Gemini Flash	
G-MMTA	Ultrasports Panther XL		G-MMXN	Southdown Puma Sprint	
G-MMTC	Ultrasports Panther Dual		G-MMXO	Southdown Puma Sprint	
G-MMTD	Mainair Tri-Flyer 330		G-MMXP	Southdown Puma Sprint	
G-MMTG	Mainair Gemini		G-MMXU	Mainair Gemini Flash	
G-MMTH	Southdown Puma Sprint		G-MMXV	Mainair Gemini Flash	
G-MMTI	Southdown Puma Sprint		G-MMXW	Mainair Gemini	
G-MMTJ	Southdown Puma Sprint		G-MMXX	Mainair Gemini	
G-MMTK	Medway Hybred		G-MMYA	Solar Wings Pegasus XL	
G-MMTL	Mainair Gemini		G-MMYB	Solar Wings Pegasus XL	
G-MMTM	Mainair Tri-Flyer 440		G-MMYD	CFM Shadow Srs B	
G-MMTO	Mainair Tri-Flyer		G-MMYF	Southdown Puma Sprint	
G-MMTR	Ultrasports Panther		G-MMYI	Southdown Puma Sprint	
G-MMTS	Solar Wings Panther XL		G-MMYJ	Southdown Puma Sprint	
G-MMTT	Solar Wings Panther XL		G-MMYL	Cyclone 70	
G-MMTV	American Aerolights Eagle		G-MMYN	Ultrasports Panther XL	
G-MMTX	Mainair Gemini 440		G-MMYO	Southdown Puma Sprint	
G-MMTY	Fisher FP.202U		G-MMYR	Eipper Quicksilver MXII	
G-MMTZ	Eurowing Goldwing		G-MMYS	Southdown Puma Sprint	
G-MMUA	Southdown Puma Sprint		G-MMYT	Southdown Puma Sprint	
G-MMUC	Mainair Gemini 440		G-MMYU	Southdown Puma Sprint	
G-MMUE	Mainair Gemini Flash		G-MMYV	Webb Trike	
G-MMUG	Mainair Tri-Flyer		G-MMYY	Southdown Puma Sprint	
G-MMUH	Mainair Tri-Flyer		G-MMYZ	Southdown Puma Sprint	
G-MMUK	Mainair Tri-Flyer		G-MMZA	Mainair Gemini Flash	
G-MMUL	Ward Elf E.47		G-MMZB	Mainair Gemini Flash	
G-MMUM	MBA Tiger Cub 440		G-MMZE	Mainair Gemini Flash	
G-MMUN	Ultrasports Panther Dual XL		G-MMZF	Mainair Gemini Flash	
			G-MMZG	Ultrasports Panther XL-S	
G-MMUO	Mainair Gemini Flash		G-MMZI	Medway 130SX	
G-MMUP	Airwave Nimrod 140		G-MMZJ	Mainair Gemini Flash	
G-MMUS	Mainair Gemini		G-MMZK	Mainair Gemini Flash	
G-MMUT	Mainair Gemini Flash		G-MMZL	Mainair Gemini Flash	
G-MMUU	ParaPlane PM-1		G-MMZM	Mainair Gemini Flash	
G-MMUV	Southdown Puma Sprint		G-MMZN	Mainair Gemini Flash	

Reg.	Type	Notes
G-MMZO	Microflight Spectrum	
G-MMZP	Ultrasports Panther XL	
G-MMZR	Southdown Puma Sprint	
G-MMZS	Eipper Quicksilver MX1	
G-MMZV	Mainair Gemini Flash	
G-MMZW	Southdown Puma Sprint	
G-MMZX	Southdown Puma Sprint	
G-MMZY	Ultrasports Tripacer 330	
G-MMZZ	Maxair Hummer	
G-MNAA	Striplin Sky Ranger	
G-MNAC	Mainair Gemini Flash	
G-MNAE	Mainair Gemini Flash	
G-MNAF	Solar Wings Panther XL-S	
G-MNAH	Solar Wings Panther XL	
G-MNAI	Ultrasports Panther XL-S	
G-MNAJ	Solar Wings Panther XL-S	
G-MNAK	Solar Wings Panther XL-S	
G-MNAM	Solar Wings Panther XL-S	
G-MNAN	Solar Wings Panther XL-S	
G-MNAO	Solar Wings Panther XL-S	
G-MNAT	Solar Wings Pegasus XL-R	
G-MNAU	Solar Wings Pegasus XL-R	
G-MNAV	Southdown Puma Sprint	
G-MNAW	Solar Wings Pegasus XL-R	
G-MNAX	Solar Wings Pegasus XL-R	
G-MNAY	Ultrasports Panther XL-S	
G-MNAZ	Solar Wings Pegasus XL-R	
G-MNBA	Solar Wings Pegasus XL-R	
G-MNBB	Solar Wings Pegasus XL-R	
G-MNBC	Solar Wings Pegasus XL-R	
G-MNBD	Mainair Gemini Flash	
G-MNBE	Southdown Puma Sprint	
G-MNBF	Mainair Gemini Flash	
G-MNBG	Mainair Gemini Flash	
G-MNBH	Southdown Puma Sprint	
G-MNBI	Ultrasports Panther XL	
G-MNBJ	Skyhook Pixie	
G-MNBM	Southdown Puma Sprint	
G-MNBN	Mainair Gemini Flash	
G-MNBP	Mainair Gemini Flash	
G-MNBR	Mainair Gemini Flash	
G-MNBS	Mainair Gemini Flash	
G-MNBT	Mainair Gemini Flash	
G-MNBU	Mainair Gemini Flash	
G-MNBV	Mainair Gemini Flash	
G-MNBW	Mainair Gemini Flash	
G-MNCA	Hiway Demon 175	
G-MNCF	Mainair Gemini Flash	
G-MNCG	Mainair Gemini Flash	
G-MNCI	Southdown Puma Sprint	
G-MNCJ	Mainair Gemini Flash	
G-MNCK	Southdown Puma Sprint	
G-MNCL	Southdown Puma Sprint	
G-MNCM	CFM Shadow Srs B	
G-MNCO	Eipper Quicksilver MXII	
G-MNCP	Southdown Puma Sprint	
G-MNCR	Flexiform Striker	
G-MNCS	Skyrider Airsports Phantom	
G-MNCU	Medway Hybred	
G-MNCV	Medway Hybred 44XL	
G-MNCZ	Solar Wings Pegasus XL	
G-MNDA	Thruster TST	
G-MNDC	Mainair Gemini Flash	
G-MNDD	Mainair Scorcher Solo	
G-MNDE	Medway Half Pint	
G-MNDF	Mainair Gemini Flash	
G-MNDG	Southdown Puma Sprint	
G-MNDH	Hiway Skytrike	
G-MNDI	MBA Tiger Cub 440	
G-MNDM	Mainair Gemini Flash	
G-MNDO	Mainair Flash	
G-MNDP	Southdown Puma Sprint	
G-MNDU	Midland Sirocco 377GB	
G-MNDV	Midland Sirocco 377GB	
G-MNDW	Midland Sirocco 377GB	
G-MNDY	Southdown Puma Sprint	
G-MNDZ	Southdown Puma Sprint	
G-MNEF	Mainair Gemini Flash	
G-MNEH	Mainair Gemini Flash	
G-MNEI	Medway Hybred 440	
G-MNEK	Medway Half Pint	
G-MNEL	Medway Half Pint	
G-MNEM	Solar Wings Pegasus Dual	
G-MNEP	Aerostructure Pipstrelle P.2B	
G-MNER	CFM Shadow Srs B	
G-MNET	Mainair Gemini Flash	
G-MNEV	Mainair Gemini Flash	
G-MNEY	Mainair Gemini Flash	
G-MNEZ	Skyhook TR1 Mk 2	
G-MNFA	Solar Wings Typhoon	
G-MNFB	Southdown Puma Sprint	
G-MNFE	Mainair Gemini Flash	
G-MNFF	Mainair Gemini Flash	
G-MNFG	Southdown Puma Sprint	
G-MNFH	Mainair Gemini Flash	
G-MNFJ	Mainair Gemini Flash	
G-MNFK	Mainair Gemini Flash	
G-MNFL	AMF Chevvron	
G-MNFM	Mainair Gemini Flash	
G-MNFN	Mainair Gemini Flash	
G-MNFP	Mainair Gemini Flash	
G-MNFW	Medway Hybred 44XL	
G-MNFX	Southdown Puma Sprint	
G-MNFY	Hornet 250	
G-MNFZ	Southdown Puma Sprint	
G-MNGA	Aerial Arts Chaser 110SX	
G-MNGB	Mainair Gemini Flash	
G-MNGD	Quest Air Services	
G-MNGF	Solar Wings Pegasus	
G-MNGG	Solar Wings Pegasus XL-R	
G-MNGH	Skyhook Pixie	
G-MNGJ	Skyhook Zipper	
G-MNGK	Mainair Gemini Flash	
G-MNGL	Mainair Gemini Flash	
G-MNGM	Mainair Gemini Flash	
G-MNGN	Mainair Gemini Flash	
G-MNGO	Solar Wings Storm	
G-MNGR	Southdown Puma Sprint	
G-MNGS	Southdown Puma 330	
G-MNGT	Mainair Gemini Flash	
G-MNGU	Mainair Gemini Flash	
G-MNGW	Mainair Gemini Flash	
G-MNGX	Southdown Puma Sprint	
G-MNGZ	Mainair Gemini Flash	
G-MNHB	Solar Wings Pegasus XL-R	
G-MNHC	Solar Wings Pegasus XL-R	
G-MNHD	Solar Wings Pegasus XL-R	
G-MNHE	Solar Wings Pegasus XL-R	
G-MNHF	Solar Wings Pegasus XL-R	
G-MNHH	Solar Wings Panther XL-S	
G-MNHI	Solar Wings Pegasus XL-R	
G-MNHJ	Solar Wings Pegasus XL-R	
G-MNHK	Solar Wings Pegasus XL-R	
G-MNHL	Solar Wings Pegasus XL-R	
G-MNHM	Solar Wings Pegasus XL-R	
G-MNHN	Solar Wings Pegasus XL-R	
G-MNHP	Solar Wings Pegasus XL-R	
G-MNHR	Solar Wings Pegasus XL-R	
G-MNHS	Solar Wings Pegasus XL-R	
G-MNHT	Solar Wings Pegasus XL-R	
G-MNHU	Solar Wings Pegasus XL-R	
G-MNHV	Solar Wings Pegasus XL-R	
G-MNHX	Solar Wings Typhoon S4	
G-MNHZ	Mainair Gemini Flash	

Reg.	Type	Notes	Reg.	Type	Notes
G-MNIA	Mainair Gemini Flash		G-MNLV	Southdown Raven	
G-MNID	Mainair Gemini Flash		G-MNLW	Medway Half Pint	
G-MNIE	Mainair Gemini Flash		G-MNLX	Mainair Gemini Flash	
G-MNIF	Mainair Gemini Flash		G-MNLY	Mainair Gemini Flash	
G-MNIG	Mainair Gemini Flash		G-MNLZ	Southdown Raven	
G-MNIH	Mainair Gemini Flash		G-MNMC	Southdown Puma MS	
G-MNII	Mainair Gemini Flash		G-MNMD	Southdown Raven	
G-MNIK	Pegasus Photon		G-MNME	Hiway Skytrike	
G-MNIL	Southdown Puma Sprint		G-MNMG	Mainair Gemini Flash	
G-MNIM	Maxair Hummer		G-MNMH	Mainair Gemini Flash	
G-MNIO	Mainair Gemini Flash		G-MNMI	Mainair Gemini Flash	
G-MNIP	Mainair Gemini Flash		G-MNMJ	Mainair Gemini Flash	
G-MNIS	CFM Shadow Srs B		G-MNMK	Solar Wings Pegasus XL-R	
G-MNIT	Aerial Arts 130SX		G-MNML	Southdown Puma Sprint	
G-MNIU	Solar Wings Pegasus Photon		G-MNMM	Aerotech MW.5 Sorcerer	
			G-MNMN	Medway Hybred 44XLR	
G-MNIV	Solar Wings Typhoon		G-MNMO	Mainair Gemini Flash	
G-MNIW	Airwave Nimrod 165		G-MNMR	Solar Wings Typhoon 180	
G-MNIX	Mainair Gemini Flash		G-MNMT	Southdown Raven	
G-MNIY	Skyhook Pixie Zipper		G-MNMU	Southdown Raven	
G-MNIZ	Mainair Gemini Flash		G-MNMV	Mainair Gemini Flash	
G-MNJB	Southdown Raven		G-MNMW	Aerotech MW.6 Merlin	
G-MNJC	MBA Tiger Cub 440		G-MNMY	Cyclone 70	
G-MNJD	Southdown Puma Sprint		G-MNNA	Southdown Raven	
G-MNJF	Dragon 150		G-MNNB	Southdown Raven	
G-MNJG	Mainair Tri-Flyer		G-MNNC	Southdown Raven	
G-MNJH	SW Pegasus Flash		G-MNND	SW Pegasus Flash	
G-MNJI	SW Pegasus Flash		G-MNNE	Mainair Gemini Flash	
G-MNJJ	SW Pegasus Flash		G-MNNF	Mainair Gemini Flash	
G-MNJK	SW Pegasus Flash		G-MNNG	Solar Wings Photon	
G-MNJL	SW Pegasus Flash		G-MNNI	Mainair Gemini Flash	
G-MNJM	SW Pegasus Flash		G-MNNK	Mainair Gemini Flash	
G-MNJN	SW Pegasus Flash		G-MNNL	Mainair Gemini Flash	
G-MNJO	SW Pegasus Flash		G-MNNM	Mainair Scorcher Solo	
G-MNJR	SW Pegasus Flash		G-MNNN	Southdown Raven	
G-MNJS	Southdown Puma Sprint		G-MNNO	Southdown Raven	
G-MNJT	Southdown Raven		G-MNNP	Mainair Gemini Flash	
G-MNJU	Mainair Gemini Flash		G-MNNR	Mainair Gemini Flash	
G-MNJV	Medway Half Pint		G-MNNS	Eurowing Goldwing	
G-MNJW	Mitchell Wing B10		G-MNNU	Mainair Gemini Flash	
G-MNJX	Medway Hybred 44XL		G-MNNV	Mainair Gemini Flash	
G-MNKB	SW Pegasus Photon		G-MNNY	SW Pegasus Flash	
G-MNKC	SW Pegasus Photon		G-MNNZ	SW Pegasus Flash	
G-MNKD	SW Pegasus Photon		G-MNPA	SW Pegasus Flash	
G-MNKE	SW Pegasus Photon		G-MNPB	SW Pegasus Flash	
G-MNKG	SW Pegasus Photon		G-MNPC	Mainair Gemini Flash	
G-MNKH	SW Pegasus Photon		G-MNPF	Mainair Gemini Flash	
G-MNKI	SW Pegasus Photon		G-MNPG	Mainair Gemini Flash	
G-MNKK	SW Pegasus Photon		G-MNPH	Flexiform Dual Striker	
G-MNKL	Mainair Gemini Flash		G-MNPI	Southdown Pipistrelle 2C	
G-MNKM	MBA Tiger Cub 440		G-MNPL	Ultrasports Panther 330	
G-MNKO	SW Pegasus Flash		G-MNPV	Mainair Scorcher Solo	
G-MNKP	SW Pegasus Flash		G-MNPW	AMF Chevvron	
G-MNKR	SW Pegasus Flash		G-MNPY	Mainair Scorcher Solo	
G-MNKS	SW Pegasus Flash		G-MNPZ	Mainair Scorcher Solo	
G-MNKT	Solar Wings Typhoon S4		G-MNRA	CFM Shadow Srs B	
G-MNKU	Southdown Puma Sprint		G-MNRD	Ultraflight Lazair	
G-MNKV	SW Pegasus Flash		G-MNRE	Mainair Scorcher Solo	
G-MNKW	SW Pegasus Flash		G-MNRF	Mainair Scorcher Solo	
G-MNKX	SW Pegasus Flash		G-MNRG	Mainair Scorcher Solo	
G-MNKZ	Southdown Raven		G-MNRI	Hornet Dual Trainer	
G-MNLB	Southdown Raven X		G-MNRJ	Hornet Dual Trainer	
G-MNLE	Southdown Raven X		G-MNRK	Hornet Dual Trainer	
G-MNLH	Romain Cobra Biplane		G-MNRL	Hornet Dual Trainer	
G-MNLI	Mainair Gemini Flash		G-MNRM	Hornet Dual Trainer	
G-MNLK	Southdown Raven		G-MNRN	Hornet Dual Trainer	
G-MNLL	Southdown Raven		G-MNRP	Southdown Raven	
G-MNLM	Southdown Raven		G-MNRS	Southdown Raven	
G-MNLN	Southdown Raven		G-MNRT	Midland Ultralights Sirocco	
G-MNLO	Southdown Raven		G-MNRW	Mainair Gemini Flash II	
G-MNLP	Southdown Raven		G-MNRX	Mainair Gemini Flash II	
G-MNLT	Southdown Raven		G-MNRY	Mainair Gemini Flash	
G-MNLU	Southdown Raven		G-MNRZ	Mainair Scorcher Solo	

Reg.	Type	Notes	Reg.	Type	Notes
G-MNSA	Mainair Gemini Flash		G-MNWA	Southdown Raven X	
G-MNSB	Southdown Puma Sprint		G-MNWB	Thruster TST	
G-MNSD	Solar Wings Typhoon S4		G-MNWD	Mainair Gemini Flash	
G-MNSE	Mainair Gemini Flash		G-MNWF	Southdown Raven X	
G-MNSF	Hornet Dual Trainer		G-MNWG	Southdown Raven X	
G-MNSH	SW Pegasus Flash II		G-MNWI	Mainair Gemini Flash II	
G-MNSI	Mainair Gemini Flash		G-MNWJ	Mainair Gemini Flash II	
G-MNSJ	Mainair Gemini Flash		G-MNWK	CFM Shadow Srs B	
G-MNSL	Southdown Raven X		G-MNWL	Aerial Arts 130SX	
G-MNSM	Hornet Demon		G-MNWN	Mainair Gemini Flash II	
G-MNSN	SW Pegasus Flash II		G-MNWO	Mainair Gemini Flash II	
G-MNSP	Aerial Arts 130SX		G-MNWP	SW Pegasus Flash II	
G-MNSR	Mainair Gemini Flash		G-MNWR	Medway Hybred 44LR	
G-MNSS	American Aerolights Eagle		G-MNWU	SW Pegasus Flash II	
G-MNSV	CFM Shadown Srs B		G-MNWV	SW Pegasus Flash II	
G-MNSW	Southdown Raven X		G-MNWW	Solar Wings Pegasus XL-R	
G-MNSX	Southdown Raven X		G-MNWX	Solar Wings Pegasus XL-R	
G-MNSY	Southdown Raven X		G-MNWY	CFM Shadown Srs B	
G-MNTC	Southdown Raven X		G-MNWZ	Mainair Gemini Flash II	
G-MNTD	Aerial Arts Chaser 110SX		G-MNXA	Southdown Raven X	
G-MNTE	Southdown Raven X		G-MNXB	Solar Wings Photon	
G-MNTF	Southdown Raven X		G-MNXC	Aerial Arts 110SX	
G-MNTG	Southdown Raven X		G-MNXD	Southdown Raven	
G-MNTH	Mainair Gemini Flash		G-MNXE	Southdown Raven X	
G-MNTI	Mainair Gemini Flash		G-MNXF	Southdown Raven	
G-MNTK	CFM Shadow Srs B		G-MNXG	Southdown Raven X	
G-MNTM	Southdown Raven X		G-MNXI	Southdown Raven X	
G-MNTN	Southdown Raven X		G-MNXM	Medway Hybred 44XLR	
G-MNTO	Southdown Raven X		G-MNXN	Medway Hybred 44XLR	
G-MNTP	CFM Shadow Srs B		G-MNXO	Medway Hybred 44XLR	
G-MNTS	Mainair Gemini Flash II		G-MNXR	Mainair Gemini Flash II	
G-MNTT	Medway Half Pint		G-MNXS	Mainair Gemini Flash II	
G-MNTU	Mainair Gemini Flash II		G-MNXT	Mainair Gemini Flash II	
G-MNTV	Mainair Gemini Flash II		G-MNXU	Mainair Gemini Flash II	
G-MNTW	Mainair Gemini Flash II		G-MNXX	CFM Shadow Srs BD	
G-MNTX	Mainair Gemini Flash II		G-MNXZ	Whittaker MW.5 Sorcerer	
G-MNTY	Southdown Raven X		G-MNYA	SW Pegasus Flash II	
G-MNTZ	Mainair Gemini Flash II		G-MNYB	Solar Wings Pegasus XL-R	
G-MNUA	Mainair Gemini Flash II		G-MNYC	Solar Wings Pegasus XL-R	
G-MNUB	Mainair Gemini Flash II		G-MNYD	Aerial Arts 110SX Chaser	
G-MNUD	SW Pegasus Flash II		G-MNYE	Aerial Arts 110SX Chaser	
G-MNUE	SW Pegasus Flash II		G-MNYF	Aerial Arts 110SX Chaser	
G-MNUF	Mainair Gemini Flash II		G-MNYG	Southdown Raven	
G-MNUG	Mainair Gemini Flash II		G-MNYH	Southdown Puma Sprint	
G-MNUH	Southdown Raven X		G-MNYI	Southdown Raven X	
G-MNUI	Skyhook Cutlass Dual		G-MNYJ	Mainair Gemini Flash II	
G-MNUM	Southdown Puma Sprint		G-MNYK	Mainair Gemini Flash II	
G-MNUO	Mainair Gemini Flash II		G-MNYL	Southdown Raven X	
G-MNUR	Mainair Gemini Flash II		G-MNYM	Southdown Raven X	
G-MNUT	Southdown Raven X		G-MNYO	Southdown Raven X	
G-MNUU	Southdown Raven X		G-MNYP	Southdown Raven X	
G-MNUW	Southdown Raven X		G-MNYS	Southdown Raven X	
G-MNUX	Solar Wings Pegasus XL-R		G-MNYT	Solar Wings Pegasus XL-R	
G-MNUY	Mainair Gemini Flash II		G-MNYU	Solar Wings Pegasus XL-R	
G-MNVA	Solar Wings Pegasus XL-R		G-MNYV	Solar Wings Pegasus XL-R	
G-MNVB	Solar Wings Pegasus XL-R		G-MNYW	Solar Wings Pegasus XL-R	
G-MNVC	Solar Wings Pegasus XL-R		G-MNYX	Solar Wings Pegasus XL-R	
G-MNVE	Solar Wings Pegasus XL-R		G-MNYZ	SW Pegasus Flash	
G-MNVG	SW Pegasus Flash II		G-MNZA	SW Pegasus Flash	
G-MNVH	SW Pegasus Flash II		G-MNZB	Mainair Gemini Flash II	
G-MNVI	CFM Shadow Srs B		G-MNZC	Mainair Gemini Flash II	
G-MNVJ	CFM Shadow Srs CD		G-MNZD	Mainair Gemini Flash II	
G-MNVK	CFM Shadow Srs B		G-MNZE	Mainair Gemini Flash II	
G-MNVN	Southdown Raven X		G-MNZF	Mainair Gemini Flash II	
G-MNVO	Hovey Whing-Ding II		G-MNZI	Solar Wings Typhoon	
G-MNVP	Southdown Raven X		G-MNZJ	CFM Shadow Srs BD	
G-MNVR	Mainair Gemini Flash II		G-MNZK	Solar Wings Pegasus XL-R	
G-MNVS	Mainair Gemini Flash II		G-MNZL	Solar Wings Pegasus XL-R	
G-MNVT	Mainair Gemini Flash II		G-MNZM	Solar Wings Pegasus XL-R	
G-MNVU	Mainair Gemini Flash II		G-MNZN	SW Pegasus Flash II	
G-MNVV	Mainair Gemini Flash II		G-MNZO	SW Pegasus Flash II	
G-MNVW	Mainair Gemini Flash II		G-MNZP	CFM Shadow Srs B	
G-MNVZ	SW Pegasus Photon		G-MNZR	CFM Shadown Srs BD	

G-MNZS– G-MTGW

Reg.	Type	Notes	Reg.	Type	Notes
G-MNZS	Aerial Arts 130SX		G-MTDI	Solar Wings Pegasus XL-R	
G-MNZU	Eurowing Goldwing		G-MTDJ	Medway Hybred 44XL	
G-MNZY	Striker Tri-Flyer 330		G-MTDK	Aerotech MW.5 Sorcerer	
G-MNZZ	CFM Shadow Srs B		G-MTDM	Mainair Gemini Flash II	
			G-MTDN	Ultraflight Lazair IIIE	
G-MTAA	Solar Wings Pegasus XL-R		G-MTDO	Eipper Quicksilver MXII	
G-MTAB	Mainair Gemini Flash II		G-MTDP	Solar Wings Pegasus XL-R	
G-MTAC	Mainair Gemini Flash II		G-MTDR	Mainair Gemini Flash II	
G-MTAE	Mainair Gemini Flash II		G-MTDS	Solar Wings Photon	
G-MTAF	Mainair Gemini Flash II		G-MTDT	Solar Wings Pegasus XL-R	
G-MTAG	Mainair Gemini Flash II		G-MTDU	CFM Shadow Srs BD	
G-MTAH	Mainair Gemini Flash II		G-MTDV	Solar Wings Pegasus XL-R	
G-MTAI	Solar Wings Pegasus XL-R		G-MTDW	Mainair Gemini Flash II	
G-MTAJ	Solar Wings Pegasus XL-R		G-MTDX	CFM Shadow Srs BD	
G-MTAK	Solar Wings Pegasus XL-R		G-MTDY	Mainair Gemini Flash II	
G-MTAL	Solar Wings Photon		G-MTDZ	Eipper Quicksilver MXII	
G-MTAM	SW Pegasus Flash		G-MTEA	Solar Wings Pegasus XL-R	
G-MTAO	Solar Wings Pegasus XL-R		G-MTEB	Solar Wings Pegasus XL-R	
G-MTAP	Southdown Raven X		G-MTEC	Solar Wings Pegasus XL-R	
G-MTAR	Mainair Gemini Flash II		G-MTED	Solar Wings Pegasus XL-R	
G-MTAS	Whittaker MW.5 Sorcerer		G-MTEE	Solar Wings Pegasus XL-R	
G-MTAT	Solar Wings Pegasus XL-R		G-MTEG	Mainair Gemini Flash II	
G-MTAV	Solar Wings Pegasus XL-R		G-MTEH	Mainair Gemini Flash II	
G-MTAW	Solar Wings Pegasus XL-R		G-MTEJ	Mainair Gemini Flash II	
G-MTAX	Solar Wings Pegasus XL-R		G-MTEK	Mainair Gemini Flash II	
G-MTAY	Solar Wings Pegasus XL-R		G-MTEN	Mainair Gemini Flash II	
G-MTAZ	Solar Wings Pegasus XL-R		G-MTEO	Midland Ultralight Sirocco 337	
G-MTBA	Solar Wings Pegasus XL-R				
G-MTBB	Southdown Raven X		G-MTER	Solar Wings Pegasus XL-R	
G-MTBD	Mainair Gemini Flash II		G-MTES	Solar Wings Pegasus XL-R	
G-MTBE	CFM Shadow Srs BD		G-MTET	Solar Wings Pegasus XL-R	
G-MTBF	Mirage Mk II		G-MTEU	Solar Wings Pegasus XL-R	
G-MTBG	Mainair Gemini Flash II		G-MTEW	Solar Wings Pegasus XL-R	
G-MTBH	Mainair Gemini Flash II		G-MTEX	Solar Wings Pegasus XL-R	
G-MTBI	Mainair Gemini Flash II		G-MTEY	Mainair Gemini Flash II	
G-MTBJ	Mainair Gemini Flash II		G-MTFA	Solar Wings Pegasus XL-R	
G-MTBK	Southdown Raven X		G-MTFB	Solar Wings Pegasus XL-R	
G-MTBL	Solar Wings Pegasus XL-R		G-MTFC	Medway Hybred 44XLR	
G-MTBN	Southdown Raven X		G-MTFE	Solar Wings Pegasus XL-R	
G-MTBO	Southdown Raven X		G-MTFF	Mainair Gemini Flash II	
G-MTBP	Aerotech MW.5 Sorcerer		G-MTFG	AMF Chevvron 232	
G-MTBR	Aerotech MW.5 Sorcerer		G-MTFI	Mainair Gemini Flash II	
G-MTBS	Aerotech MW.5 Sorcerer		G-MTFJ	Mainair Gemini Flash II	
G-MTBU	Solar Wings Pegasus XL-R		G-MTFL	AMF Lazair IIIE	
G-MTBV	Solar Wings Pegasus XL-R		G-MTFM	Solar Wings Pegasus XL-R	
G-MTBX	Mainair Gemini Flash II		G-MTFN	Aerotech MW.5 Sorcerer	
G-MTBY	Mainair Gemini Flash II		G-MTFO	Solar Wings Pegasus XL-R	
G-MTBZ	Southdown Raven X		G-MTFP	Solar Wings Pegasus XL-R	
G-MTCA	CFM Shadow Srs B		G-MTFR	Solar Wings Pegasus XL-R	
G-MTCB	Snowbird Mk III		G-MTFS	Solar Wings Pegasus XL-R	
G-MTCC	Mainair Gemini Flash II		G-MTFT	Solar Wings Pegasus XL-R	
G-MTCE	Mainair Gemini Flash II		G-MTFU	CFM Shadow Series BD	
G-MTCG	Solar Wings Pegasus XL-R		G-MTFX	Mainair Gemini Flash	
G-MTCH	Solar Wings Pegasus XL-R		G-MTFZ	CFM Shadow Srs BD	
G-MTCK	SW Pegasus Flash		G-MTGA	Mainair Gemini Flash	
G-MTCL	Southdown Raven X		G-MTGB	Thruster TST Mk 1	
G-MTCM	Southdown Raven X		G-MTGC	Thruster TST Mk 1	
G-MTCN	Solar Wings Pegasus XL-R		G-MTGD	Thruster TST Mk 1	
G-MTCO	Solar Wings Pegasus XL-R		G-MTGE	Thruster TST Mk 1	
G-MTCP	Aerial Arts Chaser 110SX		G-MTGF	Thruster TST Mk 1	
G-MTCR	Solar Wings Pegasus XL-R		G-MTGH	Mainair Gemini Flash IIA	
G-MTCT	CFM Shadow Srs BD		G-MTGJ	Solar Wings Pegasus XL-R	
G-MTCU	Mainair Gemini Flash II		G-MTGK	Solar Wings Pegasus XL-R	
G-MTCV	Microflight Spectrum		G-MTGL	Solar Wings Pegasus XL-R	
G-MTCW	Mainair Gemini Flash II		G-MTGM	Solar Wings Pegasus XL-R	
G-MTCX	Solar Wings Pegasus XL-R		G-MTGO	Mainair Gemini Flash	
G-MTCZ	Ultrasports Tripacer 250		G-MTGP	Thruster TST Mk 1	
G-MTDA	Hornet Dual Trainer		G-MTGR	Thruster TST Mk 1	
G-MTDD	Aerial Arts Chaser 110SX		G-MTGS	Thruster TST Mk 1	
G-MTDE	American Aerolights 110SX		G-MTGT	Thruster TST Mk 1	
G-MTDF	Mainair Gemini Flash II		G-MTGU	Thruster TST Mk 1	
G-MTDG	Solar Wings Pegasus XL-R		G-MTGV	CFM Shadow Srs BD	
G-MTDH	Solar Wings Pegasus XL-R		G-MTGW	CFM Shadow Srs BD	

Reg.	Type	Notes	Reg.	Type	Notes
G-MTGX	Hornet Dual Trainer		G-MTKO	Mainair Gemini Flash IIA	
G-MTGY	Southdown Lightning		G-MTKP	Solar Wings Pegasus XL-R	
G-MTHB	Aerotech MW.5B Sorcerer		G-MTKR	CFM Shadow Srs BD	
G-MTHC	Raven X		G-MTKS	CFM Shadow Srs BD	
G-MTHD	Hiway Demon 195		G-MTKW	Mainair Gemini Flash IIA	
G-MTHG	Solar Wings Pegasus XL-R		G-MTKX	Mainair Gemini Flash IIA	
G-MTHH	Solar Wings Pegasus XL-R		G-MTKZ	Mainair Gemini Flash IIA	
G-MTHI	Solar Wings Pegasus XL-R		G-MTLB	Mainair Gemini Flash IIA	
G-MTHJ	Solar Wings Pegasus XL-R		G-MTLC	Mainair Gemini Flash IIA	
G-MTHK	Solar Wings Pegasus XL-R		G-MTLD	Mainair Gemini Flash IIA	
G-MTHN	Solar Wings Pegasus XL-R		G-MTLE	See main Register	
G-MTHO	Solar Wings Pegasus XL-R		G-MTLG	Solar Wings Pegasus XL-R	
G-MTHT	CFM Shadow Srs BD		G-MTLH	Solar Wings Pegasus XL-R	
G-MTHU	Hornet Dual Trainer		G-MTLI	Solar Wings Pegasus XL-R	
G-MTHV	CFM Shadow Srs BD		G-MTLJ	Solar Wings Pegasus XL-R	
G-MTHW	Mainair Gemini Flash II		G-MTLK	Raven X	
G-MTHY	Mainair Gemini Flash IIA		G-MTLL	Mainair Gemini Flash IIA	
G-MTHZ	Mainair Gemini Flash IIA		G-MTLM	Thruster TST Mk 1	
G-MTIA	Mainair Gemini Flash IIA		G-MTLN	Thruster TST Mk 1	
G-MTIB	Mainair Gemini Flash IIA		G-MTLO	Thruster TST Mk 1	
G-MTIC	Mainair Gemini Flash IIA		G-MTLR	Thruster TST Mk 1	
G-MTID	Southdown Raven X		G-MTLS	Solar Wings Pegasus XL-R	
G-MTIE	Solar Wings Pegasus XL-R		G-MTLT	Solar Wings Pegasus XL-R	
G-MTIH	Solar Wings Pegasus XL-R		G-MTLU	Solar Wings Pegasus XL-R	
G-MTII	Solar Wings Pegasus XL-R		G-MTLV	Solar Wings Pegasus XL-R	
G-MTIJ	Solar Wings Pegasus XL-R		G-MTLW	Solar Wings Pegasus XL-R	
G-MTIK	Southdown Raven X		G-MTLX	Medway Hybred 44XLR	
G-MTIL	Mainair Gemini Flash IIA		G-MTLY	Solar Wings Pegasus XL-R	
G-MTIM	Mainair Gemini Flash IIA		G-MTLZ	Whittaker MW.5 Sorceror	
G-MTIN	Mainair Gemini Flash IIA		G-MTMA	Mainair Gemini Flash IIA	
G-MTIO	Solar Wings Pegasus XL-R		G-MTMB	Mainair Gemini Flash IIA	
G-MTIP	Solar Wings Pegasus XL-R		G-MTMC	Mainair Gemini Flash IIA	
G-MTIR	Solar Wings Pegasus XL-R		G-MTMD	Whittaker MW.6 Merlin	
G-MTIS	Solar Wings Pegasus XL-R		G-MTME	Solar Wings Pegasus XL-R	
G-MTIT	Solar Wings Pegasus XL-R		G-MTMF	Solar Wings Pegasus XL-R	
G-MTIU	Solar Wings Pegasus XL-R		G-MTMG	Solar Wings Pegasus XL-R	
G-MTIV	Solar Wings Pegasus XL-R		G-MTMH	Solar Wings Pegasus XL-R	
G-MTIW	Solar Wings Pegasus XL-R		G-MTMI	Solar Wings Pegasus XL-R	
G-MTIX	Solar Wings Pegasus XL-R		G-MTMK	Raven X	
G-MTIY	Solar Wings Pegasus XL-R		G-MTML	Mainair Gemini Flash IIA	
G-MTIZ	Solar Wings Pegasus XL-R		G-MTMO	Raven X	
G-MTJA	Mainair Gemini Flash IIA		G-MTMP	Hornet Dual Trainer/Raven	
G-MTJB	Mainair Gemini Flash IIA		G-MTMR	Hornet Dual Trainer/Raven	
G-MTJC	Mainair Gemini Flash IIA		G-MTMT	Mainair Gemini Flash IIA	
G-MTJD	Mainair Gemini Flash IIA		G-MTMV	Mainair Gemini Flash IIA	
G-MTJE	Mainair Gemini Flash IIA		G-MTMW	Mainair Gemini Flash IIA	
G-MTJG	Medway Hybred 44XLR		G-MTMX	CFM Shadow Srs BD	
G-MTJH	SW Pegasus Flash		G-MTMY	CFM Shadow Srs BD	
G-MTJI	Raven X		G-MTMZ	CFM Shadow Srs BD	
G-MTJK	Mainair Gemini Flash IIA		G-MTNB	Raven X	
G-MTJL	Mainair Gemini Flash IIA		G-MTNC	Mainair Gemini Flash IIA	
G-MTJM	Mainair Gemini Flash IIA		G-MTND	Medway Hybred 44XLR	
G-MTJN	Midland Ultralights Sirocco 377GB		G-MTNE	Medway Hybred 44XLR	
			G-MTNF	Medway Hybred 44XLR	
G-MTJP	Medway Hybred 44XLR		G-MTNG	Mainair Gemini Flash IIA	
G-MTJR	Solar Wings Pegasus XL-R		G-MTNH	Mainair Gemini Flash IIA	
G-MTJS	Solar Wings Pegasus XL-Q		G-MTNI	Mainair Gemini Flash IIA	
G-MTJT	Mainair Gemini Flash IIA		G-MTNJ	Mainair Gemini Flash IIA	
G-MTJV	Mainair Gemini Flash IIA		G-MTNK	Weedhopper JC-24B	
G-MTJW	Mainair Gemini Flash IIA		G-MTNL	Mainair Gemini Flash IIA	
G-MTJX	Hornet Dual Trainer		G-MTNM	Mainair Gemini Flash IIA	
G-MTJY	Mainair Gemini Flash IIA		G-MTNO	Solar Wings Pegasus XL-Q	
G-MTJZ	Mainair Gemini Flash IIA		G-MTNP	Solar Wings Pegasus XL-Q	
G-MTKA	Thruster TST Mk 1		G-MTNR	Thruster TST Mk 1	
G-MTKB	Thruster TST Mk 1		G-MTNS	Thruster TST Mk 1	
G-MTKD	Thruster TST Mk 1		G-MTNT	Thruster TST Mk 1	
G-MTKE	Thruster TST Mk 1		G-MTNU	Thruster TST Mk 1	
G-MTKG	Solar Wings Pegasus XL-R		G-MTNV	Thruster TST Mk 1	
G-MTKH	Solar Wings Pegasus XL-R		G-MTNW	Thruster TST Mk 1	
G-MTKI	Solar Wings Pegasus XL-R		G-MTNX	Mainair Gemini Flash II	
G-MTKJ	Solar Wings Pegasus XL-R		G-MTNY	Mainair Gemini Flash IIA	
G-MTKM	Gardner T-M Scout S.2		G-MTOA	Solar Wings Pegasus XL-R	
G-MTKN	Mainair Gemini Flash IIA		G-MTOB	Solar Wings Pegasus XL-R	

Reg.	Type	Notes	Reg.	Type	Notes
G-MTOC	Solar Wings Pegasus XL-R		G-MTSG	CFM Shadow Srs BD	
G-MTOD	Solar Wings Pegasus XL-R		G-MTSH	Thruster TST Mk 1	
G-MTOE	Solar Wings Pegasus XL-R		G-MTSI	Thruster TST Mk 1	
G-MTOF	Solar Wings Pegasus XL-R		G-MTSJ	Thruster TST Mk 1	
G-MTOG	Solar Wings Pegasus XL-R		G-MTSK	Thruster TST Mk 1	
G-MTOH	Solar Wings Pegasus XL-R		G-MTSL	Thruster TST Mk 1	
G-MTOI	Solar Wings Pegasus XL-R		G-MTSM	Thruster TST Mk 1	
G-MTOJ	Solar Wings Pegasus XL-R		G-MTSN	Solar Wings Pegasus XL-R	
G-MTOK	Solar Wings Pegasus XL-R		G-MTSO	Solar Wings Pegasus XL-R	
G-MTOL	Solar Wings Pegasus XL-R		G-MTSP	Solar Wings Pegasus XL-R	
G-MTOM	Solar Wings Pegasus XL-R		G-MTSR	Solar Wings Pegasus XL-R	
G-MTON	Solar Wings Pegasus XL-R		G-MTSS	Solar Wings Pegasus XL-R	
G-MTOO	Solar Wings Pegasus XL-R		G-MTST	Thruster TST Mk 1	
G-MTOP	Solar Wings Pegasus XL-R		G-MTSU	Solar Wings Pegasus XL-R	
G-MTOR	Solar Wings Pegasus XL-R		G-MTSV	Solar Wings Pegasus XL-R	
G-MTOS	Solar Wings Pegasus XL-R		G-MTSX	Solar Wings Pegasus XL-R	
G-MTOT	Solar Wings Pegasus XL-R		G-MTSY	Solar Wings Pegasus XL-R	
G-MTOU	Solar Wings Pegasus XL-R		G-MTSZ	Solar Wings Pegasus XL-R	
G-MTOV	Solar Wings Pegasus XL-R		G-MTTA	Solar Wings Pegasus XL-R	
G-MTOW	Solar Wings Pegasus XL-R		G-MTTB	Solar Wings Pegasus XL-R	
G-MTOX	Solar Wings Pegasus XL-R		G-MTTD	Solar Wings Pegasus XL-R	
G-MTOY	Solar Wings Pegasus XL-R		G-MTTE	Solar Wings Pegasus XL-R	
G-MTOZ	Solar Wings Pegasus XL-R		G-MTTF	Aerotech MW.6 Merlin	
G-MTPA	Mainair Gemini Flash IIA		G-MTTH	CFM Shadow Srs BD	
G-MTPB	Mainair Gemini Flash IIA		G-MTTI	Mainair Gemini Flash IIA	
G-MTPC	Raven X		G-MTTK	Southdown Lightning DS	
G-MTPE	Solar Wings Pegasus XL-R		G-MTTL	Hiway Sky-Trike	
G-MTPF	Solar Wings Pegasus XL-R		G-MTTM	Mainair Gemini Flash IIA	
G-MTPG	Solar Wings Pegasus XL-R		G-MTTN	Ultralight Flight Phantom	
G-MTPH	Solar Wings Pegasus XL-R		G-MTTO	Mainair Gemini Flash IIA	
G-MTPI	Solar Wings Pegasus XL-R		G-MTTP	Mainair Gemini Flash IIA	
G-MTPJ	Solar Wings Pegasus XL-R		G-MTTR	Mainair Gemini Flash IIA	
G-MTPK	Solar Wings Pegasus XL-R		G-MTTS	Mainair Gemini Flash IIA	
G-MTPL	Solar Wings Pegasus XL-R		G-MTTU	Solar Wings Pegasus XL-R	
G-MTPM	Solar Wings Pegasus XL-R		G-MTTW	Mainair Gemini Flash IIA	
G-MTPN	Solar Wings Pegasus XL-Q		G-MTTX	Solar Wings Pegasus XL-Q	
G-MTPO	Solar Wings Pegasus XL-Q		G-MTTZ	Solar Wings Pegasus XL-Q	
G-MTPP	Solar Wings Pegasus XL-R		G-MTUA	Solar Wings Pegasus XL-R	
G-MTPR	Solar Wings Pegasus XL-R		G-MTUB	Thruster TST Mk 1	
G-MTPS	Solar Wings Pegasus XL-Q		G-MTUC	Thruster TST Mk 1	
G-MTPT	Thruster TST Mk 1		G-MTUD	Thruster TST Mk 1	
G-MTPU	Thruster TST Mk 1		G-MTUE	Thruster TST Mk 1	
G-MTPV	Thruster TST Mk 1		G-MTUF	Thruster TST Mk 1	
G-MTPW	Thruster TST Mk 1		G-MTUG	Thruster TST Mk 1	
G-MTPX	Thruster TST Mk 1		G-MTUH	Solar Wings Pegasus XL-R	
G-MTPY	Thruster TST Mk 1		G-MTUI	Solar Wings Pegasus XL-R	
G-MTRA	Mainair Gemini Flash IIA		G-MTUJ	Solar Wings Pegasus XL-R	
G-MTRB	Mainair Gemini Flash IIA		G-MTUK	Solar Wings Pegasus XL-R	
G-MTRC	Midlands Ultralights Sirocco 377GB		G-MTUL	Solar Wings Pegasus XL-R	
			G-MTUN	Solar Wings Pegasus XL-Q	
G-MTRD	Midlands Ultralights Sirocco 377GB		G-MTUP	Solar Wings Pegasus XL-Q	
			G-MTUR	Solar Wings Pegasus XL-Q	
G-MTRE	Whittaker MW.6 Merlin		G-MTUS	Solar Wings Pegasus XL-Q	
G-MTRF	Mainair Gemini Flash IIA		G-MTUT	Solar Wings Pegasus XL-Q	
G-MTRJ	AMF Chevvron 232		G-MTUU	Mainair Gemini Flash IIA	
G-MTRK	Hornet Dual Trainer		G-MTUV	Mainair Gemini Flash IIA	
G-MTRL	Hornet Dual Trainer		G-MTUX	Medway Hybred 44XLR	
G-MTRM	Solar Wings Pegasus XL-R		G-MTUY	Solar Wings Pegasus XL-Q	
G-MTRN	Solar Wings Pegasus XL-R		G-MTVA	Solar Wings Pegasus XL-R	
G-MTRO	Solar Wings Pegasus XL-R		G-MTVB	Solar Wings Pegasus XL-R	
G-MTRP	Solar Wings Pegasus XL-R		G-MTVC	Solar Wings Pegasus XL-R	
G-MTRR	Solar Wings Pegasus XL-R		G-MTVE	Solar Wings Pegasus XL-R	
G-MTRS	Solar Wings Pegasus XL-R		G-MTVF	Solar Wings Pegasus XL-R	
G-MTRT	Raven X		G-MTVG	Mainair Gemini Flash IIA	
G-MTRU	Solar Wings Pegasus XL-Q		G-MTVH	Mainair Gemini Flash IIA	
G-MTRV	Solar Wings Pegasus XL-Q		G-MTVI	Mainair Gemini Flash IIA	
G-MTRW	Raven X		G-MTVJ	Mainair Gemini Flash IIA	
G-MTRX	Whittaker MW.5 Sorceror		G-MTVK	Solar Wings Pegasus XL-R	
G-MTRY	Snowbird Mk 4		G-MTVL	Solar Wings Pegasus XL-R	
G-MTRZ	Mainair Gemini Flash IIA		G-MTVM	Solar Wings Pegasus XL-R	
G-MTSB	Mainair Gemini Flash IIA		G-MTVN	Solar Wings Pegasus XL-R	
G-MTSC	Mainair Gemini Flash IIA		G-MTVO	Solar Wings Pegasus XL-R	
G-MTSD	Raven X		G-MTVP	Thruster TST Mk 1	

Reg.	Type	Notes	Reg.	Type	Notes
G-MTVR	Thruster TST Mk 1		G-MTZJ	Solar Wings Pegasus XL-R	
G-MTVS	Thruster TST Mk 1		G-MTZK	Solar Wings Pegasus XL-R	
G-MTVT	Thruster TST Mk 1		G-MTZL	Mainair Gemini Flash IIA	
G-MTVV	Thruster TST Mk 1		G-MTZK	Solar Wings Pegasus XL-R	
G-MTVX	Solar Wings Pegasus XL-Q		G-MTZM	Mainair Gemini Flash IIA	
G-MTVZ	Powerchute Raider		G-MTZN	Mainair Gemini Flash IIA	
G-MTWA	Solar Wings Pegasus XL-R		G-MTZO	Mainair Gemini Flash IIA	
G-MTWB	Solar Wings Pegasus XL-R		G-MTZP	Solar Wings Pegasus XL-Q	
G-MTWD	Solar Wings Pegasus XL-R		G-MTZR	Solar Wings Pegasus XL-Q	
G-MTWE	Solar Wings Pegasus XL-R		G-MTZS	Solar Wings Pegasus XL-Q	
G-MTWF	Mainair Gemini Flash IIA		G-MTZT	Solar Wings Pegasus XL-Q	
G-MTWG	Mainair Gemini Flash IIA		G-MTZV	Mainair Gemini Flash IIA	
G-MTWH	CFM Shadow Srs BD		G-MTZW	Mainair Gemini Flash IIA	
G-MTWK	CFM Shadow Srs BD		G-MTZX	Mainair Gemini Flash IIA	
G-MTWL	CFM Shadow Srs BD		G-MTZY	Mainair Gemini Flash IIA	
G-MTWM	CFM Shadow Srs BD		G-MTZZ	Mainair Gemini Flash IIA	
G-MTWN	CFM Shadow Srs BD		G-MVAA	Mainair Gemini Flash IIA	
G-MTWP	CFM Shadow Srs BD		G-MVAB	Mainair Gemini Flash IIA	
G-MTWR	Mainair Gemini Flash IIA		G-MVAC	CFM Shadow Srs BD	
G-MTWS	Mainair Gemini Flash IIA		G-MVAD	Mainair Gemini Flash IIA	
G-MTWX	Mainair Gemini Flash IIA		G-MVAF	Southdown Puma Sprint	
G-MTWY	Thruster TST Mk 1		G-MVAG	Thruster TST Mk 1	
G-MTWZ	Thruster TST Mk 1		G-MVAH	Thruster TST Mk 1	
G-MTXA	Thruster TST Mk 1		G-MVAI	Thruster TST Mk 1	
G-MTXB	Thruster TST Mk 1		G-MVAJ	Thruster TST Mk 1	
G-MTXC	Thruster TST Mk 1		G-MVAK	Thruster TST Mk 1	
G-MTXD	Thruster TST Mk 1		G-MVAL	Thruster TST Mk 1	
G-MTXE	Hornet Dual Trainer		G-MVAM	CFM Shadow Srs BD	
G-MTXH	Solar Wings Pegasus XL-Q		G-MVAN	CFM Shadow Srs BD	
G-MTXI	Solar Wings Pegasus XL-Q		G-MVAO	Mainair Gemini Flash IIA	
G-MTXJ	Solar Wings Pegasus XL-Q		G-MVAP	Mainair Gemini Flash IIA	
G-MTXK	Solar Wings Pegasus XL-Q		G-MVAR	Solar Wings Pegasus XL-R	
G-MTXL	Noble Hardman Snowbird Mk IV		G-MVAS	Solar Wings Pegasus XL-R	
			G-MVAT	Solar Wings Pegasus XL-R	
G-MTXM	Mainair Gemini Flash IIA		G-MVAU	Solar Wings Pegasus XL-R	
G-MTXO	Whittaker MW.6		G-MVAV	Solar Wings Pegasus XL-R	
G-MTXP	Mainair Gemini Flash IIA		G-MVAW	Solar Wings Pegasus XL-Q	
G-MTXR	CFM Shadow Srs BD		G-MVAX	Solar Wings Pegasus XL-Q	
G-MTXS	Mainair Gemini Flash IIA		G-MVAY	Solar Wings Pegasus XL-Q	
G-MTXT	MBA Tiger Cub 440		G-MVAZ	Solar Wings Pegasus XL-Q	
G-MTXW	Noble Hardman Snowbird Mk IV		G-MVBA	Solar Wings Pegasus XL-Q	
			G-MVBB	CFM Shadow Srs BD	
G-MTXY	Hornet Dual Trainer		G-MVBC	Aerial Arts Tri-Flyer 130SX	
G-MTXZ	Mainair Gemini Flash IIA		G-MVBD	Mainair Gemini Flash IIA	
G-MTYA	Solar Wings Pegasus XL-Q		G-MVBE	Mainair Scorcher	
G-MTYC	Solar Wings Pegasus XL-Q		G-MVBF	Mainair Gemini Flash IIA	
G-MTYD	Solar Wings Pegasus XL-Q		G-MVBG	Mainair Gemini Flash IIA	
G-MTYE	Solar Wings Pegasus XL-Q		G-MVBH	Mainair Gemini Flash IIA	
G-MTYF	Solar Wings Pegasus XL-Q		G-MVBI	Mainair Gemini Flash IIA	
G-MTYG	Solar Wings Pegasus XL-Q		G-MVBJ	Solar Wings Pegasus XL-R	
G-MTYH	Solar Wings Pegasus XL-Q		G-MVBK	Mainair Gemini Flash IIA	
G-MTYI	Solar Wings Pegasus XL-Q		G-MVBL	Mainair Gemini Flash IIA	
G-MTYL	Solar Wings Pegasus XL-Q		G-MVBM	Mainair Gemini Flash IIA	
G-MTYM	Solar Wings Pegasus XL-Q		G-MVBN	Mainair Gemini Flash IIA	
G-MTYN	Solar Wings Pegasus XL-Q		G-MVBO	Mainair Gemini Flash IIA	
G-MTYP	Solar Wings Pegasus XL-Q		G-MVBP	Thruster TST Mk 1	
G-MTYR	Solar Wings Pegasus XL-Q		G-MVBS	Thruster TST Mk 1	
G-MTYS	Solar Wings Pegasus XL-Q		G-MVBT	Thruster TST Mk 1	
G-MTYT	Solar Wings Pegasus XL-Q		G-MVBU	Thruster TST Mk 1	
G-MTYU	Solar Wings Pegasus XL-Q		G-MVBY	Solar Wings Pegasus XL-R	
G-MTYV	Raven X		G-MVBZ	Solar Wings Pegasus XL-R	
G-MTYW	Ravan X		G-MVCA	Solar Wings Pegasus XL-R	
G-MTYX	Raven X		G-MVCB	Solar Wings Pegasus XL-R	
G-MTYY	Solar Wings Pegasus XL-R		G-MVCC	CFM Shadow Srs BD	
G-MTZA	Thruster TST Mk 1		G-MVCD	Medway Hybred 44XLR	
G-MTZB	Thruster TST Mk 1		G-MVCE	Mainair Gemini Flash IIA	
G-MTZC	Thruster TST Mk 1		G-MVCF	Mainair Gemini Flash IIA	
G-MTZD	Thruster TST Mk 1		G-MVCH	Noble Hardman Snowbird Mk IV	
G-MTZE	Thruster TST Mk 1				
G-MTZF	Thruster TST Mk 1		G-MVCI	Noble Hardman Snowbird Mk IV	
G-MTZG	Mainair Gemini Flash IIA				
G-MTZH	Mainair Gemini Flash IIA		G-MVCJ	Noble Hardman Snowbird Mk IV	
G-MTZI	Solar Wings Pegasus XL-R				

Reg.	Type	Notes	Reg.	Type	Notes
G-MVCL	Solar Wings Pegasus XL-Q		G-MVFX	Solar Wings Pegasus XL-R	
G-MVCM	Solar Wings Pegasus XL-Q		G-MVFY	Solar Wings Pegasus XL-R	
G-MVCN	Solar Wings Pegasus XL-Q		G-MVFZ	Solar Wings Pegasus XL-R	
G-MVCO	Solar Wings Pegasus XL-Q		G-MVGA	Aerial Arts Chaser S	
G-MVCP	Solar Wings Pegasus XL-Q		G-MVGB	Medway Hybred 44XLR	
G-MVCR	Solar Wings Pegasus XL-Q		G-MVGC	AMF Chevvron 2-32	
G-MVCS	Solar Wings Pegasus XL-Q		G-MVGD	AMF Chevvron 2-32	
G-MVCT	Solar Wings Pegasus XL-Q		G-MVGE	AMF Chevvron 2-32	
G-MVCV	Solar Wings Pegasus XL-Q		G-MVGF	Aerial Arts Chaser S	
G-MVCW	CFM Shadow Srs BD		G-MVGG	Aerial Arts Chaser S	
G-MVCY	Mainair Gemini Flash IIA		G-MVGH	Aerial Arts Chaser S	
G-MVDA	Mainair Gemini Flash IIA		G-MVGI	Aerial Arts Chaser S	
G-MVDB	Medway Hybred 44XLR		G-MVGJ	Aerial Arts Chaser S	
G-MVDC	Medway Hybred 44XLR		G-MVGK	Aerial Arts Chaser S	
G-MVDD	Thruster TST Mk 1		G-MVGL	Medway Hybred 44XLR	
G-MVDE	Thruster TST Mk 1		G-MVGM	Mainair Gemini Flash IIA	
G-MVDF	Thruster TST Mk 1		G-MVGN	Solar Wings Pegasus XL-R	
G-MVDG	Thruster TST Mk 1		G-MVGO	Solar Wings Pegasus XL-R	
G-MVDH	Thruster TST Mk 1		G-MVGR	Solar Wings Pegasus XL-R	
G-MVDJ	Medway Hybred 44XLR		G-MVGS	Solar Wings Pegasus XL-R	
G-MVDK	Aerial Arts Chaser S		G-MVGT	Solar Wings Pegasus XL-Q	
G-MVDL	Aerial Arts Chaser S		G-MVGU	Solar Wings Pegasus XL-Q	
G-MVDN	Aerial Arts Chaser S		G-MVGV	Solar Wings Pegasus XL-Q	
G-MVDO	Aerial Arts Chaser S		G-MVGW	Solar Wings Pegasus XL-Q	
G-MVDP	Aerial Arts Chaser S		G-MVGX	Solar Wings Pegasus XL-Q	
G-MVDR	Aerial Arts Chaser S		G-MVGY	Medway Hybred 44XL	
G-MVDT	Mainair Gemini Flash IIA		G-MVGZ	Ultraflight Lazair IIIE	
G-MVDU	Solar Wings Pegasus XL-R		G-MVHA	Aerial Arts Chaser S	
G-MVDV	Solar Wings Pegasus XL-R		G-MVHB	Powerchute Raider	
G-MVDW	Solar Wings Pegasus XL-R		G-MVHC	Powerchute Raider	
G-MVDX	Solar Wings Pegasus XL-R		G-MVHD	CFM Shadow Srs BD	
G-MVDY	Solar Wings Pegasus XL-R		G-MVHE	Mainair Gemini Flash IIA	
G-MVDZ	Solar Wings Pegasus XL-R		G-MVHF	Mainair Gemini Flash IIA	
G-MVEA	Solar Wings Pegasus XL-R		G-MVHG	Mainair Gemini Flash IIA	
G-MVEC	Solar Wings Pegasus XL-R		G-MVHH	Mainair Gemini Flash IIA	
G-MVED	Solar Wings Pegasus XL-R		G-MVHI	Thruster TST Mk 1	
G-MVEE	Medway Hybred 44XLR		G-MVHJ	Thruster TST Mk 1	
G-MVEF	Solar Wings Pegasus XL-R		G-MVHK	Thruster TST Mk 1	
G-MVEG	Solar Wings Pegasus XL-R		G-MVHL	Thruster TST Mk 1	
G-MVEH	Mainair Gemini Flash IIA		G-MVHM	Whittaker MW.5 Sorcerer	
G-MVEI	CFM Shadow Srs BD		G-MVHN	Aerial Arts Chaser S	
G-MVEJ	Mainair Gemini Flash IIA		G-MVHO	Solar Wings Pegasus XL-Q	
G-MVEK	Mainair Gemini Flash IIA		G-MVHP	Solar Wings Pegasus XL-Q	
G-MVEL	Mainair Gemini Flash IIA		G-MVHR	Solar Wings Pegasus XL-Q	
G-MVEN	CFM Shadow Srs BD		G-MVHS	Solar Wings Pegasus XL-Q	
G-MVEO	Mainair Gemini Flash IIA		G-MVHT	Solar Wings Pegasus XL-Q	
G-MVER	Mainair Gemini Flash IIA		G-MVHU	Solar Wings Pegasus XL-Q	
G-MVES	Mainair Gemini Flash IIA		G-MVHV	Solar Wings Pegasus XL-Q	
G-MVET	Mainair Gemini Flash IIA		G-MVHW	Solar Wings Pegasus XL-Q	
G-MVEV	Mainair Gemini Flash IIA		G-MVHX	Solar Wings Pegasus XL-Q	
G-MVEW	Mainair Gemini Flash IIA		G-MVHY	Solar Wings Pegasus XL-Q	
G-MVEX	Solar Wings Pegasus XL-Q		G-MVHZ	Hornet Dual Trainer	
G-MVEZ	Solar Wings Pegasus XL-Q		G-MVIA	Solar Wings Pegasus XL-R	
G-MVFA	Solar Wings Pegasus XL-Q		G-MVIB	Mainair Gemini Flash IIA	
G-MVFB	Solar Wings Pegasus XL-Q		G-MVIC	Mainair Gemini Flash IIA	
G-MVFC	Solar Wings Pegasus XL-Q		G-MVID	Aerial Arts Chaser 5	
G-MVFD	Solar Wings Pegasus XL-Q		G-MVIE	Aerial Arts Chaser S	
G-MVFE	Solar Wings Pegasus XL-Q		G-MVIF	Medway Hybred 44XLR	
G-MVFF	Solar Wings Pegasus XL-Q		G-MVIG	CFM Shadow Srs B	
G-MVFG	Solar Wings Pegasus XL-Q		G-MVIH	Mainair Gemini Flash IIA	
G-MVFH	CFM Shadow Srs BD		G-MVIL	Noble Hardman Snowbird Mk IV	
G-MVFJ	Thruster TST Mk 1				
G-MVFK	Thruster TST Mk 1		G-MVIM	Noble Hardman Snowbird Mk IV	
G-MVFL	Thruster TST Mk 1				
G-MVFM	Thruster TST Mk 1		G-MVIN	Noble Hardman Snowbird Mk IV	
G-MVFN	Thruster TST Mk 1				
G-MVFO	Thruster TST Mk 1		G-MVIO	Noble Hardman Snowbird Mk IV	
G-MVFP	Solar Wings Pegasus XL-R				
G-MVFR	Solar Wings Pegasus XL-R		G-MVIP	AMF Chevvron 232	
G-MVFS	Solar Wings Pegasus XL-R		G-MVIR	Thruster TST Mk 1	
G-MVFT	Solar Wings Pegasus XL-R		G-MVIS	Thruster TST Mk 1	
G-MVFV	Solar Wings Pegasus XL-R		G-MVIU	Thruster TST Mk 1	
G-MVFW	Solar Wings Pegasus XL-R				

Reg.	Type	Notes	Reg.	Type	Notes
G-MVIV	Thruster TST Mk 1		G-MVMK	Medway Hybred 44XLR	
G-MVIX	Mainair Gemini Flash IIA		G-MVML	Aerial Arts Chaser S	
G-MVIY	Mainair Gemini Flash IIA		G-MVMM	Aerial Arts Chaser S	
G-MVIZ	Mainair Gemini Flash IIA		G-MVMO	Mainair Gemini Flash IIA	
G-MVJA	Mainair Gemini Flash IIA		G-MVMR	Mainair Gemini Flash IIA	
G-MVJB	Mainair Gemini Flash IIA		G-MVMT	Mainair Gemini Flash IIA	
G-MVJC	Mainair Gemini Flash IIA		G-MVMU	Mainair Gemini Flash IIA	
G-MVJD	Solar Wings Pegasus XL-R		G-MVMV	Aerotech MW.5 (K)	
G-MVJE	Mainair Gemini Flash IIA			Sorcerer	
G-MVJF	Aerial Arts Chaser S		G-MVMW	Mainair Gemini Flash IIA	
G-MVJG	Aerial Arts Chaser S		G-MVMX	Mainair Gemini Flash IIA	
G-MVJH	Aerial Arts Chaser S		G-MVMY	Mainair Gemini Flash IIA	
G-MVJI	Aerial Arts Chaser S		G-MVMZ	Mainair Gemini Flash IIA	
G-MVJJ	Aerial Arts Chaser S		G-MVNA	Powerchute Raider	
G-MVJK	Aerial Arts Chaser S		G-MVNB	Powerchute Raider	
G-MVJL	Mainair Gemini Flash IIA		G-MVNC	Powerchute Raider	
G-MVJM	Microflight Spectrum		G-MVNF	Powerchute Raider	
G-MVJN	Solar Wings Pegasus XL-Q		G-MVNI	Powerchute Raider	
G-MVJO	Solar Wings Pegasus XL-Q		G-MVNK	Powerchute Raider	
G-MVJP	Solar Wings Pegasus XL-Q		G-MVNL	Powerchute Raider	
G-MVJR	Solar Wings Pegasus XL-Q		G-MVNM	Mainair Gemini Flash IIA	
G-MVJS	Solar Wings Pegasus XL-Q		G-MVNN	Whittaker MW.5 (K)	
G-MVJT	Solar Wings Pegasus XL-Q			Sorcerer	
G-MVJU	Solar Wings Pegasus XL-Q		G-MVNO	Aerotech MW.5 (K)	
G-MVJW	Solar Wings Pegasus XL-Q			Sorcerer	
G-MVJZ	Birdman Cherokee		G-MVNP	Aerotech MW.5 (K)	
G-MVKB	Medway Hybred 44XLR			Sorcerer	
G-MVKC	Mainair Gemini Flash IIA		G-MVNR	Aerotech MW.5 (K)	
G-MVKE	Solar Wings Pegasus XL-R			Sorcerer	
G-MVKF	Solar Wings Pegasus XL-R		G-MVNS	Aerotech MW.5 (K)	
G-MVKG	Solar Wings Pegasus XL-R			Sorcerer	
G-M˜VKH	Solar Wings Pegasus XL-R		G-MVNT	Whittaker MW.5 (K)	
G-MVKJ	Solar Wings Pegasus XL-R			Sorcerer	
G-MVKK	Solar Wings Pegasus XL-R		G-MVNU	Aerotech MW.5 Sorcerer	
G-MVKL	Solar Wings Pegasus XL-R		G-MVNV	Aerotech MW.5 Sorcerer	
G-MVKM	Solar Wings Pegasus XL-R		G-MVNW	Mainair Gemini Flash IIA	
G-MVKN	Solar Wings Pegasus XL-Q		G-MVNX	Mainair Gemini Flash IIA	
G-MVKO	Solar Wings Pegasus XL-Q		G-MVNY	Mainair Gemini Flash IIA	
G-MVKP	Solar Wings Pegasus XL-Q		G-MVNZ	Mainair Gemini Flash IIA	
G-MVKR	Solar Wings Pegasus XL-Q		G-MVOA	Aerial Arts Alligator	
G-MVKS	Solar Wings Pegasus XL-Q		G-MVOB	Mainair Gemini Flash IIA	
G-MVKT	Solar Wings Pegasus XL-Q		G-MVOD	Aerial Arts Chaser 110SX	
G-MVKU	Solar Wings Pegasus XL-Q		G-MVOE	Solar Wings Pegasus XL-R	
G-MVKV	Solar Wings Pegasus XL-Q		G-MVOF	Mainair Gemini Flash IIA	
G-MVKW	Solar Wings Pegasus XL-Q		G-MVOH	CFM Shadow Srs B	
G-MVKX	Solar Wings Pegasus XL-Q		G-MVOI	Noble Hardman Snowbird	
G-MVKY	Aerial Arts Chaser S			Mk IV	
G-MVKZ	Aerial Arts Chaser S		G-MVOJ	Noble Hardman Snowbird	
G-MVLA	Aerial Arts Chaser S			Mk IV	
G-MVLB	Aerial Arts Chaser S		G-MVOK	Noble Hardman Snowbird	
G-MVLC	Aerial Arts Chaser S			Mk IV	
G-MVLD	Aerial Arts Chaser S		G-MVOL	Noble Hardman Snowbird	
G-MVLE	Aerial Arts Chaser S			Mk IV	
G-MVLF	Aerial Arts Chaser S		G-MVON	Mainair Gemini Flash IIA	
G-MVLG	Aerial Arts Chaser S		G-MVOO	AMF Chevvron 2-32	
G-MVLH	Aerial Arts Chaser S		G-MVOP	Aerial Arts Chaser S	
G-MVLJ	CFM Shadow Srs B		G-MVOR	Mainair Gemini Flash IIA	
G-MVLL	Mainair Gemini Flash IIA		G-MVOS	Southdown Raven	
G-MVLP	CFM Shadow Srs BD		G-MVOT	Thruster TST Mk 1	
G-MVLR	Mainair Gemini Flash IIA		G-MVOU	Thruster TST Mk 1	
G-MVLS	Aerial Arts Chaser S		G-MVOV	Thruster TST Mk 1	
G-MVLT	Aerial Arts Chaser S		G-MVOW	Thruster TST Mk 1	
G-MVLU	Aerial Arts Chaser S		G-MVOX	Thruster TST Mk 1	
G-MVLW	Aerial Arts Chaser S		G-MVOY	Thruster TST Mk 1	
G-MVLX	Solar Wings Pegasus XL-Q		G-MVPA	Mainair Gemini Flash IIA	
G-MVLY	Solar Wings Pegasus XL-Q		G-MVPB	Mainair Gemini Flash IIA	
G-MVMA	Solar Wings Pegasus XL-Q		G-MVPC	Mainair Gemini Flash IIA	
G-MVMB	Solar Wings Pegasus XL-Q		G-MVPD	Mainair Gemini Flash IIA	
G-MVMC	Solar Wings Pegasus XL-Q		G-MVPE	Mainair Gemini Flash IIA	
G-MVMD	Powerchute Raider		G-MVPF	Medway Hybred 44XLR	
G-MVME	Thruster TST Mk 1		G-MVPG	Medway Hybred 44XLR	
G-MVMG	Thruster TST Mk 1		G-MVPH	Whittaker MW.6 Merlin	
G-MVMI	Thruster TST Mk 1		G-MVPI	Mainair Gemini Flash IIA	

Reg.	Type	Notes	Reg.	Type	Notes
G-MVPJ	Rans S.5		G-MVUE	Solar Wings Pegasus XL-Q	
G-MVPK	CFM Shadow Srs B		G-MVUF	Solar Wings Pegasus XL-Q	
G-MVPL	Medway Hybred 44XLR		G-MVUG	Solar Wings Pegasus XL-Q	
G-MVPM	Whittaker MW.6 Merlin		G-MVUH	Solar Wings Pegasus XL-Q	
G-MVPN	Whittaker MW.6 Merlin		G-MVUI	Solar Wings Pegasus XL-Q	
G-MVPO	Mainair Gemini Flash IIA		G-MVUJ	Solar Wings Pegasus XL-Q	
G-MVPR	Solar Wings Pegasus XL-Q		G-MVUL	Solar Wings Pegasus XL-Q	
G-MVPS	Solar Wings Pegasus XL-Q		G-MVUM	Solar Wings Pegasus XL-Q	
G-MVPT	Solar Wings Pegasus XL-Q		G-MVUN	Solar Wings Pegasus XL-Q	
G-MVPU	Solar Wings Pegasus XL-Q		G-MVUO	AMF Chevvron 2-32	
G-MVPW	Solar Wings Pegasus XL-R		G-MVUP	Aviasud Mistral	
G-MVPX	Solar Wings Pegasus XL-Q		G-MVUR	Hornet ZA	
G-MVPY	Solar Wings Pegasus XL-Q		G-MVUS	Aerial Arts Chaser S	
G-MVRA	Mainair Gemini Flash IIA		G-MVUT	Aerial Arts Chaser S	
G-MVRB	Mainair Gemini Flash IIA		G-MVUU	Hornet R-ZA	
G-MVRC	Mainair Gemini Flash IIA		G-MVVF	Medway Hybred 44XLR	
G-MVRD	Mainair Gemini Flash IIA		G-MVVG	Medway Hybred 44XLR	
G-MVRE	CFM Shadow Srs BD		G-MVVH	Medway Hybred 44XLR	
G-MVRF	Rotec Rally 2B		G-MVVI	Medway Hybred 44XLR	
G-MVRG	Aerial Arts Chaser S		G-MVVK	Solar Wings Pegasus XL-R	
G-MVRH	Solar Wings Pegasus XL-Q		G-MVVM	Solar Wings Pegasus XL-R	
G-MVRI	Solar Wings Pegasus XL-Q		G-MVVN	Solar Wings Pegasus XL-Q	
G-MVRJ	Solar Wings Pegasus XL-Q		G-MVVP	Solar Wings Pegasus XL-Q	
G-MVRL	Aerial Arts Chaser S		G-MVVR	Medway Hybred 44XLR	
G-MVRM	Mainair Gemini Flash IIA		G-MVVT	CFM Shadow Srs BD	
G-MVRN	Rans S.4 Coyote		G-MVVU	Aerial Arts Chaser S	
G-MVRO	CFM Shadow Srs BD		G-MVVV	AMF Chevvron 2-32	
G-MVRP	CFM Shadow Srs BD		G-MVVW	Aerial Arts Chaser S	
G-MVRR	CFM Shadow Srs BD		G-MVVZ	Powerchute Raider	
G-MVRT	CFM Shadow Srs BD		G-MVWB	Powerchute Raider	
G-MVRU	Solar Wings Pegasus XL-Q		G-MVWD	Powerchute Raider	
G-MVRV	Powerchute Kestrel		G-MVWE	Powerchute Raider	
G-MVRW	Solar Wings Pegasus XL-Q		G-MVWF	Powerchute Raider	
G-MVRX	Solar Wings Pegasus XL-Q		G-MVWH	Powerchute Raider	
G-MVRY	Medway Hybred 44XLR		G-MVWN	Thruster T.300	
G-MVRZ	Medway Hybred 44XLR		G-MVWO	Thruster T.300	
G-MVSA	Solar Wings Pegasus XL-Q		G-MVWP	Thruster T.300	
G-MVSB	Solar Wings Pegasus XL-Q		G-MVWR	Thruster T.300	
G-MVSD	Solar Wings Pegasus XL-Q		G-MVWS	Thruster T.300	
G-MVSE	Solar Wings Pegasus XL-Q		G-MVWV	Medway Hybred 44XLR	
G-MVSG	Aerial Arts Chaser S		G-MVWW	Aviasud Mistral	
G-MVSI	Medway Hybred 44XLR		G-MVWX	Microflight Spectrum	
G-MVSJ	Aviasud Mistral 532		G-MVWZ	Aviasud Mistral	
G-MVSK	Aerial Arts Chaser S		G-MVXA	Whittaker MW.6 Merlin	
G-MVSL	Aerial Arts Chaser S		G-MVXB	Mainair Gemini Flash IIA	
G-MVSM	Midland Ultralights Sirocco		G-MVXC	Mainair Gemini Flash IIA	
G-MVSN	Mainair Gemini Flash IIA		G-MVXD	Medway Hybred 44XLR	
G-MVSO	Mainair Gemini Flash IIA		G-MVXE	Medway Hybred 44XLR	
G-MVSP	Mainair Gemini Flash IIA		G-MVXG	Aerial Arts Chaser S	
G-MVSR	Medway Hybred 44XLR		G-MVXH	Spectrum	
G-MVSS	Hornet RS-ZA		G-MVXI	Medway Hybred 44XLR	
G-MVST	Mainair Gemini Flash IIA		G-MVXJ	Medway Hybred 44XLR	
G-MVSU	Microflight Spectrum		G-MVXL	Thruster TST Mk 1	
G-MVSV	Mainair Gemini Flash IIA		G-MVXM	Medway Hybred 44XLR	
G-MVSW	Solar Wings Pegasus XL-Q		G-MVXN	Aviasud Mistral	
G-MVSX	Solar Wings Pegasus XL-Q		G-MVXP	Aerial Arts Chaser S	
G-MVSY	Solar Wings Pegasus XL-Q		G-MVXR	Mainair Gemini Flash IIA	
G-MVSZ	Solar Wings Pegasus XL-Q		G-MVXS	Mainair Gemini Flash IIA	
G-MVTA	Solar Wings Pegasus XL-Q		G-MVXT	Mainair Gemini Flash IIA	
G-MVTC	Mainair Gemini Flash IIA		G-MVXV	Aviasud Mistral	
G-MVTD	Whittaker MW.6 Merlin		G-MVXW	Rans S.4 Coyote	
G-MVTE	Whittaker MW.6 Merlin		G-MVXX	AMF Chevvron 232	
G-MVTF	Aerial Arts Chaser S		G-MVXZ	Minimax	
G-MVTG	Solar Wings Pegasus XL-Q		G-MVYA	Aerial Arts Chaser S	
G-MVTI	Solar Wings Pegasus XL-Q		G-MVYB	Solar Wings Pegasus XL-Q	
G-MVTJ	Solar Wings Pegasus XL-Q		G-MVYC	Solar Wings Pegasus XL-Q	
G-MVTK	Solar Wings Pegasus XL-Q		G-MVYD	Solar Wings Pegasus XL-Q	
G-MVTL	Aerial Arts Chaser S		G-MVYE	Thruster TST Mk 1	
G-MVTM	Aerial Arts Chaser S		G-MVYG	Hornet R-ZA	
G-MVUA	Mainair Gemini Flash IIA		G-MVYH	Hornet R-ZA	
G-MVUB	Thruster T.300		G-MVYI	Hornet R-ZA	
G-MVUC	Medway Hybred 44XLR		G-MVYJ	Hornet R-ZA	
G-MVUD	Medway Hybred 44XLR		G-MVYK	Hornet R-ZA	

Reg.	Type	Notes	Reg.	Type	Notes
G-MVYL	Hornet R-ZA		G-MWBW	Hornet RS-ZA	
G-MVYM	Hornet R-ZA		G-MWBX	Hornet RS-ZA	
G-MVYN	Hornet R-ZA		G-MWBY	Hornet RS-ZA	
G-MVYO	Hornet R-ZA		G-MWBZ	Hornet RS-ZA	
G-MVYP	Medway Hybred 44XLR		G-MWCA	Hornet RS-ZA	
G-MVYR	Medway Hybred 44XLR		G-MWCB	Solar Wings Pegasus XL-Q	
G-MVYS	Mainair Gemini Flash IIA		G-MWCE	Mainair Gemini Flash IIA	
G-MVYT	Noble Hardman Snowbird Mk IV		G-MWCF	Solar Wings Pegasus XL-R	
G-MVYU	Noble Hardman Snowbird Mk IV		G-MWCG	Microflight Spectrum	
			G-MWCH	Rans S.6 Coyote	
G-MVYV	Noble Hardman Snowbird Mk IV		G-MWCI	Powerchute Kestrel	
			G-MWCJ	Powerchute Kestrel	
G-MVYW	Noble Hardman Snowbird Mk IV		G-MWCK	Powerchute Kestrel	
			G-MWCM	Powerchute Kestrel	
G-MVYX	Noble Hardman Snowbird Mk IV		G-MWCN	Powerchute Kestrel	
			G-MWCO	Powerchute Kestrel	
G-MVYY	Aerial Arts Chaser S508		G-MWCP	Powerchute Kestrel	
G-MVYZ	CFM Shadow Srs BD		G-MWCR	Southdown Puma Sprint	
G-MVZA	Thruster T.300		G-MWCS	Powerchute Kestrel	
G-MVZB	Thruster T.300		G-MWCU	Solar Wings Pegasus XL-R	
G-MVZC	Thruster T.300		G-MWCV	Solar Wings Pegasus XL-Q	
G-MVZD	Thruster T.300		G-MWCW	Mainair Gemini Flash IIA	
G-MVZE	Thruster T.300		G-MWCX	Medway Hybred 44XLR	
G-MVZG	Thruster T.300		G-MWCY	Medway Hybred 44XLR	
G-MVZH	Thruster T.300		G-MWCZ	Medway Hybred 44XLR	
G-MVZI	Thruster T.300		G-MWDB	CFM Shadow Srs BD	
G-MVZJ	Solar Wings Pegasus XL-Q		G-MWDC	Solar Wings Pegasus XL-R	
G-MVZK	Challenger II		G-MWDD	Solar Wings Pegasus XL-Q	
G-MVZL	Solar Wings Pegasus XL-Q		G-MWDE	Hornet RS-ZA	
G-MVZM	Aerial Arts Chaser S		G-MWDF	Hornet RS-ZA	
G-MVZN	Aerial Arts Chaser S		G-MWDG	Hornet RS-ZA	
G-MVZO	Medway Hybred 44XLR		G-MWDH	Hornet RS-ZA	
G-MVZP	Renegade Spirit UK		G-MWDI	Hornet RS-ZA	
G-MVZR	Aviasud Mistral		G-MWDJ	Mainair Gemini Flash IIA	
G-MVZS	Mainair Gemini Flash IIA		G-MWDK	Solar Wings Pegasus XL-R	
G-MVZT	Solar Wings Pegasus XL-Q		G-MWDL	Solar Wings Pegasus XL-R	
G-MVZU	Solar Wings Pegasus XL-Q		G-MWDM	Renegade Spirit UK	
G-MVZV	Solar Wings Pegasus XL-Q		G-MWDN	CFM Shadow Srs BD	
G-MVZW	Hornet R-ZA		G-MWDP	Thruster TST Mk 1	
G-MVZX	Renegade Spirit UK		G-MWDS	Thruster T.300	
G-MVZY	Aerial Arts Chaser S		G-MWDZ	Eipper Quicksilver MXL II	
G-MVZZ	AMF Chevvron 232		G-MWEE	Solar Wings Pegasus XL-Q	
			G-MWEF	Solar Wings Pegasus XL-Q	
G-MWAB	Mainair Gemini Flash IIA		G-MWEG	Solar Wings Pegasus XL-Q	
G-MWAC	Solar Wings Pegasus XL-Q		G-MWEH	Solar Wings Pegasus XL-Q	
G-MWAD	Solar Wings Pegasus XL-Q		G-MWEK	Whittaker MW.5 Sorcerer	
G-MWAE	CFM Shadow Srs BD		G-MWEL	Mainair Gemini Flash IIA	
G-MWAF	Solar Wings Pegasus XL-R		G-MWEN	CFM Shadow Srs BD	
G-MWAG	Solar Wings Pegasus XL-R		G-MWEO	Whittaker MW.5 Sorcerer	
G-MWAI	Solar Wings Pegasus XL-R		G-MWEP	Rans S.4 Coyote	
G-MWAJ	Renegade Spirit UK		G-MWER	Solar Wings Pegasus XL-Q	
G-MWAL	Solar Wings Pegasus XL-Q		G-MWES	Rans S.4 Coyote	
G-MWAN	Thruster T.300		G-MWEU	Hornet RS-ZA	
G-MWAP	Thruster T.300		G-MWEV	Hornet RS-ZA	
G-MWAR	Thruster T.300		G-MWEY	Hornet RS-ZA	
G-MWAS	Thruster T.300		G-MWEZ	CFM Shadow Srs CD	
G-MWAT	Solar Wings Pegasus XL-Q		G-MWFA	Solar Wings Pegasus XL-R	
G-MWAU	Mainair Gemini Flash IIA		G-MWFB	CFM Shadow Srs BD	
G-MWAV	Solar Wings Pegasus XL-R		G-MWFC	Team Minimax (G-BTXC)	
G-MWAW	Whittaker MW.6 Merlin		G-MWFD	Team Minimax	
G-MWBH	Hornet RS-ZA		G-MWFE	Robin 330/Lightning 195	
G-MWBI	Medway Hybred 44XLR		G-MWFF	Rans S.4 Coyote	
G-MWBJ	Medway Sprint		G-MWFG	Powerchute Kestrel	
G-MWBK	Solar Wings Pegasus XL-Q		G-MWFH	Powerchute Kestrel	
G-MWBL	Solar Wings Pegasus XL-Q		G-MWFI	Powerchute Kestrel	
G-MWBM	Hornet RS-ZA		G-MWFL	Powerchute Kestrel	
G-MWBN	Hornet RS-ZA		G-MWFN	Powerchute Kestrel	
G-MWBO	Rans S.4 Coyote		G-MWFP	Solar Wings Pegasus XL-R	
G-MWBP	Hornet RS-ZA		G-MWFS	Solar Wings Pegasus XL-Q	
G-MWBR	Hornet RS-ZA		G-MWFT	MBA Tiger Cub 440	
G-MWBS	Hornet RS-ZA		G-MWFU	Quad City Challenger II UK	
G-MWBU	Hornet RS-ZA		G-MWFV	Quad City Challenger II UK	
			G-MWFW	Rans S.4 Coyote	

Reg.	Type	Notes	Reg.	Type	Notes
G-MWFX	Quad City Challenger II UK		G-MWJK	SW Pegasus Quasar	
G-MWFY	Quad City Challenger II UK		G-MWJL	AMF Chevvron 232	
G-MWFZ	Quad City Challenger II UK		G-MWJM	AMF Chevvron 232	
G-MWGA	Rans S.5 Coyote		G-MWJN	Solar Wings Pegasus XL-Q	
G-MWGC	Medway Hybred 44XLR		G-MWJO	Solar Wings Pegasus XL-Q	
G-MWGD	Medway Hybred 44XLR		G-MWJP	Medway Hybred 44XLR	
G-MWGF	Renegade Spirit UK		G-MWJR	Medway Hybred 44XLR	
G-MWGG	Mainair Gemini Flash IIA		G-MWJS	SW Pegasus Quasar	
G-MWGI	Whittaker MW.5 (K) Sorcerer		G-MWJT	SW Pegasus Quasar	
			G-MWJU	SW Pegasus Quasar	
G-MWGJ	Whittaker MW.5 (K) Sorcerer		G-MWJV	SW Pegasus Quasar	
			G-MWJW	Whittaker MW.5 Sorcerer	
G-MWGK	Whittaker MW.5 (K) Sorcerer		G-MWJX	Medway Puma Sprint	
			G-MWJY	Mainair Gemini Flash IIA	
G-MWGL	Solar Wings Pegasus XL-Q		G-MWJZ	CFM Shadow Srs CD	
G-MWGM	Solar Wings Pegasus XL-Q		G-MWKA	Renegade Spirit UK	
G-MWGN	Rans S.4 Coyote		G-MWKE	Hornet R-ZA	
G-MWGO	Aerial Arts Chaser 110SX		G-MWKO	Solar Wings Pegasus XL-Q	
G-MWGR	Solar Wings Pegasus XL-Q		G-MWKP	Solar Wings Pegasus XL-Q	
G-MWGT	Powerchute Kestrel		G-MWKW	Microflight Spectrum	
G-MWGU	Powerchute Kestrel		G-MWKX	Microflight Spectrum	
G-MWGV	Powerchute Kestrel		G-MWKY	Solar Wings Pegasus XL-Q	
G-MWGW	Powerchute Kestrel		G-MWKZ	Solar Wings Pegasus XL-Q	
G-MWGY	Powerchute Kestrel		G-MWLA	Rans S.4 Coyote	
G-MWGZ	Powerchute Kestrel		G-MWLB	Medway Hybred 44XLR	
G-MWHC	Solar Wings Pegasus XL-Q		G-MWLC	Medway Hybred 44XLR	
G-MWHD	Microflight Spectrum		G-MWLD	CFM Shadow Srs BD	
G-MWHE	Microflight Spectrum		G-MWLE	Solar Wings Pegasus XL-R	
G-MWHF	Solar Wings Pegasus XL-Q		G-MWLF	Solar Wings Pegasus XL-R	
G-MWHG	Solar Wings Pegasus XL-Q		G-MWLG	Solar Wings Pegasus XL-R	
G-MWHH	Team Minimax		G-MWLH	Solar Wings Pegasus XL-R	
G-MWHI	Mainair Gemini Flash IIA		G-MWLI	SW Pegasus Quasar	
G-MWHJ	Solar Wings Pegasus XL-Q		G-MWLJ	SW Pegasus Quasar	
G-MWHL	Solar Wings Pegasus XL-Q		G-MWLK	SW Pegasus Quasar	
G-MWHM	Whittaker MW.6 Merlin		G-MWLL	Solar Wings Pegasus XL-Q	
G-MWHO	Mainair Gemini Flash IIA		G-MWLM	Solar Wings Pegasus XL-Q	
G-MWHP	Rans S.6-ESD Coyote		G-MWLN	Whittaker MW.6-S Fatboy Flyer	
G-MWHR	Mainair Gemini Flash IIA				
G-MWHT	SW Pegasus Quasar		G-MWLO	Whittaker MW.6 Merlin	
G-MWHU	SW Pegasus Quasar		G-MWLP	Mainair Gemini Flash IIA	
G-MWHV	SW Pegasus Quasar		G-MWLR	Mainair Gemini Flash IIA	
G-MWHW	Solar Wings Pegasus XL-Q		G-MWLS	Medway Hybred 44XLR	
G-MWHX	Solar Wings Pegasus XL-Q		G-MWLT	Mainair Gemini Flash IIA	
G-MWHZ	Trion J-1		G-MWLU	Solar Wings Pegasus XL-R	
G-MWIA	Mainair Gemini Flash IIA		G-MWLW	Team Minimax	
G-MWIB	Aviasud Mistral		G-MWLX	Mainair Gemini Flash IIA	
G-MWIC	Whittaker MW.5 Sorcerer		G-MWLY	Rans S.4 Coyote	
G-MWID	Solar Wings Pegasus XL-Q		G-MWLZ	Rans S.4 Coyote	
G-MWIE	Solar Wings Pegasus XL-Q		G-MWMA	Powerchute Kestrel	
G-MWIF	Rans S.6-ESD Coyote II		G-MWMB	Powerchute Kestrel	
G-MWIG	Mainair Gemini Flash IIA		G-MWMC	Powerchute Kestrel	
G-MWIH	Mainair Gemini Flash IIA		G-MWMD	Powerchute Kestrel	
G-MWIK	Medway Hybred 44XLR		G-MWMF	Powerchute Kestrel	
G-MWIL	Medway Hybred 44XLR		G-MWMG	Powerchute Kestrel	
G-MWIM	SW Pegasus Quasar		G-MWMH	Powerchute Kestrel	
G-MWIN	Mainair Gemini Flash IIA		G-MWMI	SW Pegasus Quasar	
G-MWIO	Rans S.4 Coyote		G-MWMJ	SW Pegasus Quasar	
G-MWIP	Whittaker MW.6 Merlin		G-MWMK	SW Pegasus Quasar	
G-MWIR	Solar Wings Pegasus XL-Q		G-MWML	SW Pegasus Quasar	
G-MWIS	Solar Wings Pegasus XL-Q		G-MWMM	Mainair Gemini Flash IIA	
G-MWIT	Solar Wings Pegasus XL-Q		G-MWMN	Solar Wings Pegasus XL-Q	
G-MWIU	Solar Wings Pegasus XL-Q		G-MWMO	Solar Wings Pegasus XL-Q	
G-MWIV	Mainair Gemini Flash IIA		G-MWMP	Solar Wings Pegasus XL-Q	
G-MWIW	SW Pegasus Quasar		G-MWMR	Solar Wings Pegasus XL-R	
G-MWIX	SW Pegasus Quasar		G-MWMS	Mainair Gemini Flash	
G-MWIY	SW Pegasus Quasar		G-MWMT	Mainair Gemini Flash IIA	
G-MWIZ	CFM Shadow Srs BD		G-MWMU	CFM Shadow Srs CD	
G-MWJD	SW Pegasus Quasar		G-MWMV	Solar Wings Pegasus XL-R	
G-MWJF	CFM Shadow Srs BD		G-MWMW	Renegade Spirit UK	
G-MWJG	Solar Wings Pegasus XL-R		G-MWMX	Mainair Gemini Flash IIA	
G-MWJH	SW Pegasus Quasar		G-MWMY	Mainair Gemini Flash IIA	
G-MWJI	SW Pegasus Quasar		G-MWMZ	Solar Wings Pegasus XL-Q	
G-MWJJ	SW Pegasus Quasar		G-MWNA	Solar Wings Pegasus XL-Q	

Reg.	Type	Notes	Reg.	Type	Notes
G-MWNB	Solar Wings Pegasus XL-Q		G-MWRM	Medway Hybred 44XLR	
G-MWNC	Solar Wings Pegasus XL-Q		G-MWRN	Solar Wings Pegasus XL-R	
G-MWND	Tiger Cub Developments RL.5A		G-MWRO	Solar Wings Pegasus XL-R	
			G-MWRP	Solar Wings Pegasus XL-R	
G-MWNE	Mainair Gemini Flash IIA		G-MWRR	Mainair Gemini Flash IIA	
G-MWNF	Renegade Spirit UK		G-MWRS	Ultravia Super Pelican	
G-MWNG	Solar Wings Pegasus XL-Q		G-MWRT	Solar Wings Pegasus XL-R	
G-MWNK	SW Pegasus Quasar		G-MWRU	Solar Wings Pegasus XL-R	
G-MWNL	SW Pegasus Quasar		G-MWRV	Solar Wings Pegasus XL-R	
G-MWNM	SW Pegasus Quasar		G-MWRW	Solar Wings Pegasus XL-Q	
G-MWNN	SW Pegasus Quasar		G-MWRX	Solar Wings Pegasus XL-Q	
G-MWNO	AMF Chevvron 232		G-MWRY	CFM Shadow Srs CD	
G-MWNP	AMF Chevvron 232		G-MWRZ	AMF Chevvron 232	
G-MWNR	Renegade Spirit UK		G-MWSA	Team Minimax	
G-MWNS	Mainair Gemini Flash IIA		G-MWSB	Mainair Gemini Flash IIA	
G-MWNT	Mainair Gemini Flash IIA		G-MWSC	Rans S.6-ESD Coyote II	
G-MWNU	Mainair Gemini Flash IIA		G-MWSD	Solar Wings Pegasus XL-Q	
G-MWNV	Powerchute Kestrel		G-MWSE	Solar Wings Pegasus XL-R	
G-MWNX	Powerchute Kestrel		G-MWSF	Solar Wings Pegasus XL-R	
G-MWNY	Powerchute Kestrel		G-MWSG	Solar Wings Pegasus XL-R	
G-MWNZ	Powerchute Kestrel		G-MWSH	SW Pegasus Quasar TC	
G-MWOB	Powerchute Kestrel		G-MWSI	SW Pegasus Quasar TC	
G-MWOC	Powerchute Kestrel		G-MWSJ	Solar Wings Pegasus XL-Q	
G-MWOD	Powerchute Kestrel		G-MWSK	Solar Wings Pegasus XL-Q	
G-MWOE	Powerchute Kestrel		G-MWSL	Mainair Gemini Flash IIA	
G-MWOH	Solar Wings Pegasus XL-R		G-MWSM	Mainair Gemini Flash IIA	
G-MWOI	Solar Wings Pegasus XL-R		G-MWSN	SW Pegasus Quasar TC	
G-MWOJ	Mainair Gemini Flash IIA		G-MWSO	Solar Wings Pegasus XL-R	
G-MWOK	Mainair Gemini Flash IIA		G-MWSP	Solar Wings Pegasus XL-R	
G-MWOL	Mainair Gemini Flash IIA		G-MWSR	Solar Wings Pegasus XL-R	
G-MWOM	SW Pegasus Quasar TC		G-MWSS	Medway Hybred 44XLR	
G-MWON	CFM Shadow Srs CD		G-MWST	Medway Hybred 44XLR	
G-MWOO	Renegade Spirit UK		G-MWSU	Medway Hybred 44XLR	
G-MWOP	SW Pegasus Quasar		G-MWSV	SW Pegasus Quasar TC	
G-MWOR	Solar Wings Pegasus XL-Q		G-MWSW	Whittaker MW.6 Merlin	
G-MWOS	Cosmos Chronos		G-MWSX	Whittaker MW.5 Sorcerer	
G-MWOV	Whittaker MW.6 Merlin		G-MWSY	Whittaker MW.5 Sorcerer	
G-MWOW	CFM Shadow Srs B		G-MWSZ	CFM Shadow Srs CD	
G-MWOX	Solar Wings Pegasus XL-Q		G-MWTA	Solar Wings Pegasus XL-Q	
G-MWOY	Solar Wings Pegasus XL-Q		G-MWTB	Solar Wings Pegasus XL-Q	
G-MWPA	Mainair Gemini Flash IIA		G-MWTC	Solar Wings Pegasus XL-Q	
G-MWPB	Mainair Gemini Flash IIA		G-MWTD	Microflight Spectrum	
G-MWPC	Mainair Gemini Flash IIA		G-MWTE	Microflight Spectrum	
G-MWPD	Mainair Gemini Flash IIA		G-MWTF	Mainair Gemini	
G-MWPE	Solar Wings Pegasus XL-Q		G-MWTG	Mainair Gemini Flash IIA	
G-MWPF	Mainair Gemini Flash IIA		G-MWTH	Mainair Gemini Flash IIA	
G-MWPG	Microflight Spectrum		G-MWTI	Solar Wings Pegasus XL-Q	
G-MWPH	Microflight Spectrum		G-MWTJ	CFM Shadow Srs CD	
G-MWPI	Microflight Spectrum		G-MWTK	Solar Wings Pegasus XL-R	
G-MWPJ	Solar Wings Pegasus XL-Q		G-MWTL	Solar Wings Pegasus XL-R	
G-MWPK	Solar Wings Pegasus XL-Q		G-MWTM	Solar Wings Pegasus XL-R	
G-MWPL	MBA Tiger Cub 440		G-MWTN	CFM Shadow Srs CD	
G-MWPN	CFM Shadow Srs CD		G-MWTO	Mainair Gemini Flash IIA	
G-MWPO	Mainair Gemini Flash IIA		G-MWTP	CFM Shadow Srs CD	
G-MWPP	CFM Streak Shadow (G-BTEM)		G-MWTR	Mainair Gemini Flash IIA	
			G-MWTS	Whittaker MW.6-S Fatboy Flyer	
G-MWPR	Whittaker MW.6 Merlin				
G-MWPS	Renegade Spirit UK		G-MWTT	Rans S.6-ESD Coyote II	
G-MWPT	Hunt Wing		G-MWTU	Solar Wings Pegasus XL-R	
G-MWPU	SW Pegasus Quasar TC		G-MWTY	Mainair Gemini Flash IIA	
G-MWPX	Solar Wings Pegasus XL-R		G-MWTZ	Mainair Gemini Flash IIA	
G-MWPZ	Renegade Spirit UK		G-MWUA	CFM Shadow Srs CD	
G-MWRB	Mainair Gemini Flash IIA		G-MWUB	Solar Wings Pegasus XL-R	
G-MWRC	Mainair Gemini Flash IIA		G-MWUC	Solar Wings Pegasus XL-R	
G-MWRD	Mainair Gemini Flash IIA		G-MWUD	Solar Wings Pegasus XL-R	
G-MWRE	Mainair Gemini Flash IIA		G-MWUF	Solar Wings Pegasus XL-R	
G-MWRF	Mainair Gemini Flash IIA		G-MWUG	Solar Wings Pegasus XL-R	
G-MWRG	Mainair Gemini Flash IIA		G-MWUH	Renegade Spirit UK	
G-MWRH	Mainair Gemini Flash IIA		G-MWUI	AMF Chevvron 2-32C	
G-MWRI	Mainair Gemini Flash IIA		G-MWUJ	Medway Hybred 44XLR	
G-MWRJ	Mainair Gemini Flash IIA		G-MWUK	Rans S.6-ESD Coyote II	
G-MWRK	Rans S.6 Coyote II		G-MWUL	Rans S.6-ESD Coyote II	
G-MWRL	CFM Shadow Srs CD		G-MWUO	Solar Wings Pegasus XL-Q	

Reg.	Type	Notes	Reg.	Type	Notes
G-MWUP	Solar Wings Pegasus XL-R		G-MWXZ	Cyclone Chaser S 508	
G-MWUR	Solar Wings Pegasus XL-R		G-MWYA	Mainair Gemini Flash IIA	
G-MWUS	Solar Wings Pegasus XL-R		G-MWYB	Solar Wings Pegasus XL-Q	
G-MWUU	Solar Wings Pegasus XL-R		G-MWYC	Solar Wings Pegasus XL-Q	
G-MWUV	Solar Wings Pegasus XL-R		G-MWYD	CFM Shadow Srs C	
G-MWUW	Solar Wings Pegasus XL-R		G-MWYE	Rans S.6-ESD Coyote II	
G-MWUX	Solar Wings Pegasus XL-Q		G-MWYF	Rans S.6 Coyote II	
G-MWUY	Solar Wings Pegasus XL-Q		G-MWYG	Mainair Gemini Flash IIA	
G-MWUZ	Solar Wings Pegasus XL-Q		G-MWYH	Mainair Gemini Flash IIA	
G-MWVA	Solar Wings Pegasus XL-Q		G-MWYI	SW Pegasus Quasar II	
G-MWVB	Solar Wings Pegasus XL-R		G-MWYJ	SW Pegasus Quasar IITC	
G-MWVE	Solar Wings Pegasus XL-R		G-MWYL	Mainair Gemini Flash IIA	
G-MWVF	Solar Wings Pegasus XL-R		G-MWYM	Cyclone Chaser S 1000	
G-MWVG	CFM Shadow Srs CD		G-MWYN	Rans S.6-ESD Coyote II	
G-MWVH	CFM Shadow Srs CD		G-MWYS	CGS Hawk 1 Arrow	
G-MWVK	Mainair Mercury		G-MWYT	Mainair Gemini Flash IIA	
G-MWVL	Rans S.6-ESD Coyote II		G-MWYU	Solar Wings Pegasus XL-Q	
G-MWVM	SW Pegasus Quasar II		G-MWYV	Mainair Gemini Flash IIA	
G-MWVN	Mainair Gemini Flash IIA		G-MWYX	Mainair Gemini Flash IIA	
G-MWVO	Mainair Gemini Flash IIA		G-MWYY	Mainair Gemini Flash IIA	
G-MWVP	Renegade Spirit UK		G-MWYZ	Solar Wings Pegasus XL-Q	
G-MWVS	Mainair Gemini Flash IIA		G-MWZA	Mainair Mercury	
G-MWVT	Mainair Gemini Flash IIA		G-MWZB	AMF Chevvron 2-32C	
G-MWVU	Medway Hybred 44XLR		G-MWZC	Mainair Gemini Flash IIA	
G-MWVW	Mainair Gemini Flash IIA		G-MWZD	SW Pegasus Quasar IITC	
G-MWVY	Mainair Gemini Flash IIA		G-MWZE	SW Pegasus Quasar IITC	
G-MWVZ	Mainair Gemini Flash IIA		G-MWZF	SW Pegasus Quasar IITC	
G-MWWA	SW Pegasus Quasar II		G-MWZG	Mainair Gemini Flash IIA	
G-MWWB	Mainair Gemini Flash IIA		G-MWZH	Solar Wings Pegasus XL-R	
G-MWWC	Mainair Gemini Flash IIA		G-MWZI	Solar Wings Pegasus XL-R	
G-MWWD	Renegade Spirit		G-MWZJ	Solar Wings Pegasus XL-R	
G-MWWE	Team Minimax		G-MWZK	Solar Wings Pegasus XL-R	
G-MWWF	Kolb Twinstar Mk 3		G-MWZL	Mainair Gemini Flash IIA	
G-MWWG	Solar Wings Pegasus XL-Q		G-MWZM	Team Minimax 91	
G-MWWH	Solar Wings Pegasus XL-Q		G-MWZN	Mainair Gemini Flash IIA	
G-MWWI	Mainair Gemini Flash IIA		G-MWZO	SW Pegasus Quasar IITC	
G-MWWJ	Mainair Gemini Flash IIA		G-MWZP	SW Pegasus Quasar IITC	
G-MWWK	Mainair Gemini Flash IIA		G-MWZR	SW Pegasus Quasar IITC	
G-MWWL	Rans S.6-ESD Coyote II		G-MWZS	SW Pegasus Quasar IITC	
G-MWWM	Kolb Twinstar Mk 2		G-MWZT	Solar Wings Pegasus XL-R	
G-MWWN	Mainair Gemini Flash IIA		G-MWZU	Solar Wings Pegasus XL-R	
G-MWWO	Solar Wings Pegasus XL-R		G-MWZV	Solar Wings Pegasus XL-R	
G-MWWP	Rans S.4 Coyote		G-MWZX	Solar Wings Pegasus XL-R	
G-MWVR	Mainair Gemini Flash IIA		G-MWZY	Solar Wings Pegasus XL-R	
G-MWWR	Microflight Spectrum		G-MWZZ	Solar Wings Pegasus XL-R	
G-MWWS	Thruster T.300				
G-MWWT	Thruster Super T.300		G-MYAB	Solar Wings Pegasus XL-R	
G-MWWU	Air Creation Fun 18 GTBI		G-MYAC	Solar Wings Pegasus XL-Q	
G-MWWV	Solar Wings Pegasus XL-Q		G-MYAD	Solar Wings Pegasus XL-Q	
G-MWWW	Whittaker MW.6-S Fatboy Flyer		G-MYAE	Solar Wings Pegasus XL-Q	
			G-MYAF	Solar Wings Pegasus XL-Q	
G-MWWZ	Cyclone Chaser S		G-MYAG	Quad City Challenger II	
G-MWXA	Mainair Gemini Flash IIA		G-MYAH	Whittaker MW.5 Sorcerer	
G-MWXB	Mainair Gemini Flash IIA		G-MYAI	Mainair Mercury	
G-MWXC	Mainair Gemini Flash IIA		G-MYAJ	Rans S.6-ESD Coyote II	
G-MWXE	Flexiform Skytrike		G-MYAK	SW Pegasus Quasar IITC	
G-MWXF	Mainair Mercury		G-MYAM	Renegade Spirit UK	
G-MWXG	SW Pegasus Quasar IITC		G-MYAN	Whittaker MW.5 (K) Sorcerer	
G-MWXH	SW Pegasus Quasar IITC				
G-MWXI	SW Pegasus Quasar IITC		G-MYAO	Mainair Gemini Flash IIA	
G-MWXJ	Mainair Mercury		G-MYAP	Thruster T.300	
G-MWXK	Mainair Mercury		G-MYAR	Thruster T.300	
G-MWXL	Mainair Gemini Flash IIA		G-MYAS	Mainair Gemini Flash IIA	
G-MWXN	Mainair Gemini Flash IIA		G-MYAT	Team Minimax	
G-MWXO	Mainair Gemini Flash IIA		G-MYAU	Mainair Gemini Flash IIA	
G-MWXP	Solar Wings Pegasus XL-Q		G-MYAV	Mainair Mercury	
G-MWXR	Solar Wings Pegasus XL-Q		G-MYAW	Team Minimax	
G-MWXS	Mainair Gemini Flash IIA		G-MYAY	Microflight Spectrum	
G-MWXU	Mainair Gemini Flash IIA		G-MYAZ	Renegade Spirit UK	
G-MWXV	Mainair Gemini Flash IIA		G-MYBA	Rans S.6-ESD Coyote II	
G-MWXW	Cyclone Chaser S		G-MYBB	Maxair Drifter	
G-MWXX	Cyclone Chaser S 447		G-MYBC	CFM Shadow Srs CD	
G-MWXY	Cyclone Chaser S 447		G-MYBD	SW Pegasus Quaser IITC	

Reg.	Type	Notes	Reg.	Type	Notes
G-MYBE	SW Pegasus Quaser IITC		G-MYEM	SW Pegasus Quasar IITC	
G-MYBF	Solar Wings Pegasus XL-Q		G-MYEN	SW Pegasus Quasar IITC	
G-MYBG	Solar Wings Pegasus XL-Q		G-MYEO	SW Pegasus Quasar IITC	
G-MYBI	Rans S.6-ESD Coyote II		G-MYEP	CFM Shadow Srs CD	
G-MYBJ	Mainair Gemini Flash IIA		G-MYER	Cyclone AX3/503	
G-MYBK	SW Pegasus Quasar IITC		G-MYES	Rans S.6-ESD Coyote II	
G-MYBL	CFM Shadow Srs C		G-MYET	Whittaker MW.6 Merlin	
G-MYBM	Team Minimax		G-MYEU	Mainair Gemini Flash IIA	
G-MYBN	Hiway Demon 175		G-MYEV	Whittaker MW.6 Merlin	
G-MYBO	Solar Wings Pegasus XL-R		G-MYEX	Powerchute Kestrel	
G-MYBP	Solar Wings Pegasus XL-R		G-MYFA	Powerchute Kestrel	
G-MYBR	Solar Wings Pegasus XL-Q		G-MYFE	Rans S.6-ESD Coyote II	
G-MYBS	Solar Wings Pegasus XL-Q		G-MYFG	Hunt Avon Skytrike	
G-MYBT	SW Pegasus Quasar IITC		G-MYFH	Quad City Challenger II	
G-MYBU	Cyclone Chaser S447		G-MYFI	Cyclone AX3/503	
G-MYBV	Solar Wings Pegasus XL-Q		G-MYFJ	SW Pegasus Quasar IITC	
G-MYBW	Solar Wings Pegasus XL-Q		G-MYFK	SW Pegasus Quasar IITC	
G-MYBX	Solar Wings Pegasus XL-Q		G-MYFL	SW Pegasus Quasar IITC	
G-MYBY	Solar Wings Pegasus XL-Q		G-MYFM	Renegade Spirit UK	
G-MYBZ	Solar Wings Pegasus XL-Q		G-MYFN	Rans S.5 Coyote	
G-MYCA	Whittaker MW.6 Merlin		G-MYFO	Cyclone Chaser S	
G-MYCB	Cyclone Chaser S 447		G-MYFP	Mainair Gemini Flash IIA	
G-MYCE	SW Pegasus Quasar IITC		G-MYFR	Mainair Gemini Flash IIA	
G-MYCF	SW Pegasus Quasar IITC		G-MYFS	Solar Wings Pegasus XL-R	
G-MYCJ	Mainair Mercury		G-MYFT	Mainair Scorcher	
G-MYCK	Mainair Gemini Flash IIA		G-MYFU	Mainair Gemini Flash IIA	
G-MYCL	Mainair Mercury		G-MYFV	Cyclone AX3/503	
G-MYCM	CFM Shadow Srs CD		G-MYFW	Cyclone AX3/503	
G-MYCN	Mainair Mercury		G-MYFX	Solar Wings Pegasus XL-Q	
G-MYCO	Renegade Spirit UK		G-MYFY	Cyclone AX3/503	
G-MYCP	Whittaker MW.6 Merlin		G-MYFZ	Cyclone AX3/503	
G-MYCR	Mainair Gemini Flash IIA		G-MYGD	Cyclone AX3/503	
G-MYCS	Mainair Gemini Flash IIA		G-MYGE	Whittaker MW.6 Merlin	
G-MYCT	Team Minimax		G-MYGF	Team Minimax	
G-MYCV	Mainair Mercury		G-MYGG	Mainair Mercury	
G-MYCW	Powerchute Kestrel		G-MYGH	Rans S.6-ESD Coyote II	
G-MYCX	Powerchute Kestrel		G-MYGI	Cyclone Chaser S 447	
G-MYCY	Powerchute Kestrel		G-MYGJ	Mainair Mercury	
G-MYCZ	Powerchute Kestrel		G-MYGK	Cyclone Chaser S 508	
G-MYDA	Powerchute Kestrel		G-MYGL	Team Minimax	
G-MYDB	Powerchute Kestrel		G-MYGM	Quad City Challenger II	
G-MYDC	Mainair Mercury		G-MYGN	AMF Chevvron 2-32C	
G-MYDD	CFM Shadow Srs CD		G-MYGO	CFM Shadow Srs CD	
G-MYDE	CFM Shadow Srs CD		G-MYGP	Rans S.6-ESD Coyote II	
G-MYDF	Team Minimax		G-MYGR	Rans S.6-ESD Coyote II	
G-MYDG	Solar Wings Pegasus XL-R		G-MYGS	Whittaker MW.5 (K) Sorcerer	
G-MYDI	Solar Wings Pegasus XL-R				
G-MYDJ	Solar Wings Pegasus XL-R		G-MYGT	Solar Wings Pegasus XL-R	
G-MYDK	Rans S.6-ESD Coyote II		G-MYGU	Solar Wings Pegasus XL-R	
G-MYDL	Whittaker MW.5 (K) Sorcerer		G-MYGV	Solar Wings Pegasus XL-R	
			G-MYGZ	Mainair Gemini Flash IIA	
G-MYDM	Whittaker MW.6-S Fatboy Flyer		G-MYHF	Mainair Gemini Flash IIA	
			G-MYHG	Cyclone AX/503	
G-MYDN	Quad City Challenger II		G-MYHH	Cyclone AX/503	
G-MYDO	Rans S.5 Coyote		G-MYHI	Rans S.6-ESD Coyote II	
G-MYDP	Kolb Twinstar Mk 3		G-MYHJ	Cyclone AX3/503	
G-MYDR	Thruster Tn.300		G-MYHK	Rans S.6-ESD Coyote II	
G-MYDS	Quad City Challenger II		G-MYHL	Mainair Gemini Flash IIA	
G-MYDT	Thruster T.300		G-MYHM	Cyclone AX3/503	
G-MYDU	Thruster T.300		G-MYHN	Mainair Gemini Flash IIA	
G-MYDV	Thruster T.300		G-MYHP	Rans S.6-ESD Coyote II	
G-MYDW	Whittaker MW.6 Merlin		G-MYHR	Cyclone AX3/503	
G-MYDX	Rans S.6-ESD Coyote II		G-MYHS	Powerchute Kestrel	
G-MYDZ	Mignet HM.1000 Balerit		G-MYHX	Mainair Gemini Flash IIA	
G-MYEA	Solar Wings Pegasus XL-Q		G-MYIA	Quad City Challenger II	
G-MYEC	Solar Wings Pegasus XL-Q		G-MYIE	Whittaker MW.6 Merlin	
G-MYED	Solar Wings Pegasus XL-R		G-MYIF	CFM Shadow Srs CD	
G-MYEG	Solar Wings Pegasus XL-R		G-MYIH	Mainair Gemini Flash IIA	
G-MYEH	Solar Wings Pegasus XL-R		G-MYII	Team Minimax	
G-MYEI	Cyclone Chaser S447		G-MYIJ	Cyclone AX3/503	
G-MYEJ	Cyclone Chaser S447		G-MYIK	Kolb Twinstar Mk 3	
G-MYEK	SW Pegasus Quasar IITC		G-MYIL	Cyclone Chaser S 508	
G-MYEL	SW Pegasus Quasar IITC		G-MYIN	SW Pegasus Quasar IITC	

MICROLIGHTS

Reg.	Type	Notes	Reg.	Type	Notes
G-MYIO	SW Pegasus Quasar IITC		G-MYLP	Kölb Twinstar Mk 3	
G-MYIP	CFM Shadow Srs CD			(G-BVCR)	
G-MYIR	Rans S.6-ESD Coyote II		G-MYLR	Mainair Gemini Flash IIA	
G-MYIS	Rans S.6-ESD Coyote II		G-MYLS	Mainair Mercury	
G-MYIT	Cyclone Chaser S 508		G-MYLT	Mainair Blade	
G-MYIU	Cyclone AX3/503		G-MYLU	Experience/Hunt Wing	
G-MYIV	Mainair Gemini Flash IIA		G-MYLV	CFM Shadow Srs CD	
G-MYIW	Mainair Mercury		G-MYLW	Rans S.6-ESD Coyote II	
G-MYIX	Quad City Challenger II		G-MYLX	Medway Raven	
G-MYIY	Mainair Gemini Flash IIA		G-MYLY	Medway Raven	
G-MYIZ	Team Minimax 2		G-MYLZ	SW Pegasus Quantum 15	
G-MYJA	—		G-MYMB	SW Pegasus Quantum 15	
G-MYJB	Mainair Gemini Flash IIA		G-MYMC	SW Pegasus Quantum 15	
G-MYJC	Mainair Gemini Flash IIA		G-MYME	Cyclone AX3/503	
G-MYJD	Rans S.6-ESD Coyote II		G-MYMF	Cyclone AX3/503	
G-MYJF	Thruster T.300		G-MYMH	Rans S.6-ESD Coyote II	
G-MYJG	Thruster Super T.300		G-MYMI	Kölb Twinstar Mk 3	
G-MYJH	Thruster Super T.300		G-MYMJ	Medway Raven	
G-MYJJ	SW Pegasus Quasar IITC		G-MYMK	Mainair Gemini Flash IIA	
G-MYJK	SW Pegasus Quasar IITC		G-MYML	Mainair Mercury	
G-MYJL	Rans S.6-ESD Coyote II		G-MYMM	Ultraflight Fun 18S	
G-MYJM	Mainair Gemini Flash IIA		G-MYMN	Whittaker MW.6 Merlin	
G-MYJN	Mainair Mercury		G-MYMO	Mainair Gemini Flash IIA	
G-MYJO	Cyclone Chaser S 508		G-MYMP	Rans S.6-ESD Coyote II	
G-MYJP	Renegade Spirit UK			(G-CHAZ)	
G-MYJR	Mainair Mercury		G-MYMR	Rans S.6-ESD Coyote II	
G-MYJS	SW Pegasus Quasar IITC		G-MYMS	Rans S.6-ESD Coyote II	
G-MYJT	SW Pegasus Quasar IITC		G-MYMT	Mainair Mercury	
G-MYJU	SW Pegasus Quasar IITC		G-MYMV	Mainair Gemini Flash IIA	
G-MYJW	Cyclone Chaser S 508		G-MYMW	Cyclone AX3/503	
G-MYJX	Whittaker MW.8		G-MYMX	SW Pegasus Quantum 15	
G-MYJY	Rans S.6-ESD Coyote II		G-MYMY	Cyclone Chaser S 508	
G-MYJZ	Whittaker MW.5D Sorcerer		G-MYMZ	Cyclone AX3/503	
G-MYKA	Cyclone AX3/503		G-MYNA	CFM Shadow Srs BD	
G-MYKB	Kölb Twinstar Mk 3		G-MYNB	SW Pegasus Quantum 15	
G-MYKC	Mainair Gemini Flash IIA		G-MYNC	Mainair Mercury	
G-MYKD	Cyclone Chaser S 447		G-MYND	Mainair Gemini Flash IIA	
G-MYKE	CFM Shadow Srs BD		G-MYNE	Rans S.6-ESD Coyote II	
G-MYKF	Cyclone AX3/503		G-MYNF	Mainair Mercury	
G-MYKG	Mainair Gemini Flash IIA		G-MYNH	Rans S.6-ESD Coyote II	
G-MYKH	Mainair Gemini Flash IIA		G-MYNI	Team Minimax	
G-MYKI	Mainair Mercury		G-MYNJ	Mainair Mercury	
G-MYKJ	Team Minimax		G-MYNK	SW Pegasus Quantum 15	
G-MYKK	—		G-MYNL	SW Pegasus Quantum 15	
G-MYKL	Medway Raven		G-MYNN	SW Pegasus Quantum 15	
G-MYKM	Medway Raven		G-MYNO	SW Pegasus Quantum 15	
G-MYKN	Rans S.6-ESD Coyote II		G-MYNP	SW Pegasus Quantum 15	
G-MYKO	Whittaker MW.6-S Fat Boy		G-MYNR	SW Pegasus Quantum 15	
	Flyer		G-MYNS	SW Pegasus Quantum 15	
G-MYKP	SW Pegasus Quasar IITC		G-MYNT	SW Pegasus Quantum 15	
G-MYKR	SW Pegasus Quasar IITC		G-MYNU	SW Pegasus Quantum 15	
G-MYKS	SW Pegasus Quasar IITC		G-MYNV	SW Pegasus Quantum 15	
G-MYKT	Cyclone AX3/503		G-MYNW	Cyclone Chaser S 447	
G-MYKU	Medway Raven		G-MYNX	CFM Streak Shadow	
G-MYKV	Mainair Gemini Flash IIA			Srs S-A1	
G-MYKW	Mainair Mercury		G-MYNY	Kölb Twinstar Mk 3	
G-MYKY	Mainair Mercury		G-MYNZ	SW Pegasus Quantum 15	
G-MYKZ	Team Minimax (G-BVAV)		G-MYOA	Rans S.6-ESD Coyote II	
G-MYLA	Rans S.6-ESD Coyote II		G-MYOB	Mainair Mercury	
G-MYLB	Team Minimax		G-MYOE	SW Pegasus Quantum 15	
G-MYLC	SW Pegasus Quantum 15		G-MYOF	Mainair Mercury	
G-MYLD	Rans S.6-ESD Coyote II		G-MYOG	Kölb Twinstar Mk 3	
G-MYLE	SW Pegasus Quantum 15		G-MYOH	CFM Shadow Srs CD	
G-MYLF	Rans S.6-ESD Coyote II		G-MYOI	Rans S.6-ESD Coyote II	
G-MYLG	Mainair Gemini Flash IIA		G-MYOL	Air Creation Fun 18S	
G-MYLH	SW Pegasus Quantum 15			GTBIS	
G-MYLI	SW Pegasus Quantum 15		G-MYOM	Mainair Gemini Flash IIA	
G-MYLJ	Cyclone Chaser S 447		G-MYON	CFM Shadow Srs CD	
G-MYLK	SW Pegasus Quantum 15		G-MYOO	Kölb Twinstar Mk 3	
G-MYLL	SW Pegasus Quantum 15		G-MYOR	Kölb Twinstar Mk 3	
G-MYLM	SW Pegasus Quantum 15		G-MYOT	Rans S.6-ESD Coyote II	
G-MYLN	Kölb Twinstar Mk 3		G-MYOU	SW Pegasus Quantum 15	
G-MYLO	Rans S.6-ESD Coyote II		G-MYOV	Mainair Mercury	

Reg.	Type	Notes	Reg.	Type	Notes
G-MYOW	Mainair Gemini Flash IIA		G-MYSX	SW Pegasus Quantum 15	
G-MYOX	Mainair Mercury		G-MYSY	SW Pegasus Quantum 15	
G-MYOY	Cyclone AX3/503		G-MYSZ	Mainair Mercury	
G-MYOZ	Quad City Challenger II UK		G-MYTA	Team Minimax	
G-MYPA	Rans S.6-ESD Coyote II		G-MYTB	Mainair Mercury	
G-MYPB	Cyclone Chaser S 447		G-MYTC	SW Pegasus XL-Q	
G-MYPC	Kölb Twinstar Mk 3		G-MYTD	Mainair Blade	
G-MYPD	Mainair Mercury		G-MYTE	Rans S.6-ESD Coyote II	
G-MYPE	Mainair Gemini Flash IIA		G-MYTG	Mainair Blade	
G-MYPF	SW Pegasus Quasar IITC		G-MYTH	CFM Shadow Srs CD	
G-MYPG	SW Pegasus XL-Q		G-MYTI	Pegasus Quantum 15	
G-MYPH	SW Pegasus Quantum 15		G-MYTJ	SW Pegasus Quantum 15	
G-MYPI	SW Pegasus Quantum 15		G-MYTK	Mainair Mercury	
G-MYPJ	Rans S.6-ESD Coyote II		G-MYTL	Mainair Blade	
G-MYPK	Rans S.6-ESD Coyote II		G-MYTM	Cyclone AX3/503	
G-MYPL	CFM Shadow Srs CD		G-MYTN	SW Pegasus Quantum 15	
G-MYPM	Cyclone AX3/503		G-MYTO	Quad City Challenger II	
G-MYPN	SW Pegasus Quantum 15		G-MYTP	Arrowflight Hawk II	
G-MYPO	Hunt Wing/Experience		G-MYTR	Pegasus Quantum 15	
G-MYPP	Whittaker MW.6-S Fatboy Flyer		G-MYTT	Quad City Challenger II	
			G-MYTU	Mainair Blade	
G-MYPR	Cyclone AX3/503		G-MYTV	Hunt Avon Skytrike	
G-MYPS	Whittaker MW.6 Merlin		G-MYTW	Mainair Blade	
G-MYPT	CFM Shadow Srs CD		G-MYTX	Mainair Mercury	
G-MYPV	Mainair Mercury		G-MYTY	CFM Streak Shadow Srs M	
G-MYPW	Mainair Gemini Flash IIA		G-MYTZ	Air Creation Fun 18S GTBIS	
G-MYPX	SW Pegasus Quantum 15				
G-MYPY	SW Pegasus Quantum 15		G-MYUA	Air Creation Fun 18S GTBIS	
G-MYPZ	Quad City Challenger II				
G-MYRA	Kölb Twinstar Mk 3		G-MYUB	Mainair Mercury	
G-MYRB	Whittaker MW.5 Sorcerer		G-MYUC	Mainair Blade	
G-MYRC	Mainair Blade		G-MYUD	Mainair Mercury	
G-MYRD	Mainair Blade		G-MYUE	Mainair Mercury	
G-MYRE	Cyclone Chaser S		G-MYUF	Renegade Spirit	
G-MYRF	SW Pegasus Quantum 15		G-MYUH	SW Pegasus XL-Q	
G-MYRG	Team Minimax		G-MYUK	Mainair Mercury	
G-MYRH	Quad City Challenger II		G-MYUL	Quad City Challenger II	
G-MYRI	Medway 44XLR		G-MYUM	Mainair Blade	
G-MYRJ	Quad City Challenger II		G-MYUN	Mainair Blade	
G-MYRK	Renegade Spirit UK		G-MYUO	Pegasus Quantum 15	
G-MYRL	Team Minimax		G-MYUP	Letov LK-2M Sluka	
G-MYRM	SW Pegasus Quantum 15		G-MYUR	Hunt Wing	
G-MYRN	SW Pegasus Quantum 15		G-MYUS	CFM Shadow Srs CD	
G-MYRO	Cyclone AX3/503		G-MYUT	Hunt Wing	
G-MYRP	Letov LK-2M Sluka		G-MYUU	Pegasus Quantum 15	
G-MYRR	Letov LK-2M Sluka		G-MYUV	Pegasus Quantum 15	
G-MYRS	SW Pegasus Quantum 15		G-MYUW	Mainair Mercury	
G-MYRT	SW Pegasus Quantum 15		G-MYUY	Microchute UQ	
G-MYRU	Cyclone AX3/503		G-MYUZ	Rans S.6-ESD Coyote II	
G-MYRV	Cyclone AX3/503		G-MYVA	Kolb Twinstar Mk 3	
G-MYRW	Mainair Mercury		G-MYVB	Mainair Blade	
G-MYRX	Mainair Gemini Flash IIA		G-MYVC	Pegasus Quantum 15	
G-MYRY	SW Pegasus Quantum 15		G-MYVE	Mainair Blade	
G-MYRZ	SW Pegasus Quantum 15		G-MYVF	Pegasus Quantum 15	
G-MYSA	Cyclone Chaser S 508		G-MYVG	Letov LK-2M Sluka	
G-MYSB	SW Pegasus Quantum 15		G-MYVH	Mainair Mercury	
G-MYSC	SW Pegasus Quantum 15		G-MYVI	Air Creation Fun 18S GTBIS	
G-MYSD	Quad City Challlenger II				
G-MYSG	Mainair Mercury		G-MYVJ	Pegasus Quantum 15	
G-MYSH	Mainair Blade		G-MYVK	Pegasus Quantum 15	
G-MYSI	HM14/93		G-MYVL	Mainair Mercury	
G-MYSJ	Mainair Gemini Flash IIA		G-MYVM	Pegasus Quantum 15	
G-MYSK	Team Minimax		G-MYVN	Cyclone AX3/503	
G-MYSL	Aviasud Mistral		G-MYVO	Mainair Blade	
G-MYSM	CFM Shadow Srs CD		G-MYVP	Rans S.6-ESD Coyote II	
G-MYSN	Whittaker MW.6 Merlin		G-MYVR	Pegasus Quantum 15	
G-MYSO	Cyclone AX3/503		G-MYVS	Mainair Mercury	
G-MYSP	Rans S.6-ESD Coyote II		G-MYVT	Letov LK-2M Sluka	
G-MYSR	SW Pegasus Quatum 15		G-MYVU	Medway Raven	
G-MYST	Aviasud Mistral		G-MYVV	Medway Hybred 44XLR	
G-MYSU	Rans S.6-ESD Coyote II		G-MYVW	Medway Raven	
G-MYSV	Aerial Arts Chaser		G-MYVX	Medway Hybred 44XLR	
G-MYSW	SW Pegasus Quantum 15		G-MYVY	Mainair Blade	

Reg.	Type	Notes	Reg.	Type	Notes
G-MYVZ	Mainair Blade		G-MYYY	Mainair Blade	
G-MYWA	Mainair Mercury		G-MYYZ	Medway Raven X	
G-MYWC	Hunt Wing		G-MYZA	Whittaker MW.6 Merlin	
G-MYWD	Thruster T.600		G-MYZB	Pegasus Quantum 15	
G-MYWE	Thruster T.600		G-MYZC	Cyclone AX3/503	
G-MYWF	CFM Shadow Srs CD		G-MYZD	Pegasus Quantum 15	
G-MYWG	Pegasus Quantum 15		G-MYZE	Team Minimax	
G-MYWH	Hunt Wing/Experience		G-MYZF	Cyclone AX3/503	
G-MYWI	Pegasus Quantum 15		G-MYZG	Cyclone AX3/503	
G-MYWJ	Pegasus Quantum 15		G-MYZH	Chargus Titan 38	
G-MYWK	Pegasus Quantum 15		G-MYZJ	Pegasus Quantum 15	
G-MYWL	Pegasus Quantum 15		G-MYZK	Pegasus Quantum 15	
G-MYWM	CFM Shadow Srs CD		G-MYZL	Pegasus Quantum 15	
G-MYWN	Cyclone Chaser S 508		G-MYZM	Pegasus Quantum 15	
G-MYWO	Pegasus Quantum 15		G-MYZN	Whittaker MW.6-S Fatboy Flyer	
G-MYWP	Kolb Twinstar Mk 3				
G-MYWR	Pegasus Quantum 15		G-MYZO	Medway Raven X	
G-MYWS	Cyclone Chaser S 447		G-MYZP	CFM Shadow Srs DD	
G-MYWT	Pegasus Quantum 15		G-MYZR	Rans S.6-ESD Coyote II	
G-MYWU	Pegasus Quantum 15		G-MYZS	Airwave Rave	
G-MYWV	Rans S.4 Coyote		G-MYZT	Airwave Rave	
G-MYWW	Pegasus Quantum 15		G-MYZU	Airwave Rave	
G-MYWX	Pegasus Quantum 15		G-MYZV	Rans S.6-ESD Coyote II	
G-MYWY	Pegasus Quantum 15		G-MYZW	Cyclone Chaser S 508	
G-MYWZ	Thruster TST Mk 1		G-MYZX	Cyclone Chaser S 508	
G-MYXA	Team Minimax 91		G-MYZY	Pegasus Quantum 15	
G-MYXB	Rans S.6-ESD Coyote II		G-MYZZ	Pegasus Quantum 15	
G-MYXC	Quad City Challenger II				
G-MYXD	Pegasus Quasar IITC		G-MZAA	Mainair Blade	
G-MYXE	Rans S.6-ESD Coyote II		G-MZAC	Quad City Challenger II	
G-MYXF	Air Creation Fun GT503		G-MZAD	Mainair Blade 912	
G-MYXG	Rans S.6-ESD Coyote II		G-MZAE	Mainair Blade	
G-MYXH	Cyclone AX3/503		G-MZAF	Mainair Blade	
G-MYXI	Aries 1		G-MZAG	Mainair Blade	
G-MYXJ	Mainair Blade		G-MZAH	Rans S.6-ESD Coyote II	
G-MYXK	Quad City Challenger II		G-MZAI	Mainair Blade	
G-MYXL	Mignet HM.1000 Balerit		G-MZAJ	Mainair Blade	
G-MYXM	Mainair Blade		G-MZAK	Mainair Mercury	
G-MYXN	Mainair Blade		G-MZAL	Mainair Blade	
G-MYXO	Letov LK-2M Sluka		G-MZAM	Mainair Blade	
G-MYXP	Rans S.6-ESD Coyote II		G-MZAN	Pegasus Quantum 15	
G-MYXR	Renegade Spirit UK		G-MZAO	Mainair Blade 912	
G-MYXS	Kolb Twinstar Mk 3		G-MZAP	Mainair Blade	
G-MYXT	Pegasus Quantum 15		G-MZAR	Mainair Blade	
G-MYXU	Thruster T.300		G-MZAS	Mainair Blade	
G-MYXV	Quad City Challenger II		G-MZAT	Mainair Blade	
G-MYXW	Pegasus Quantum 15		G-MZAV	Mainair Blade	
G-MYXX	Pegasus Quantum 15		G-MZAW	Pegasus Quantum 15	
G-MYXY	CFM Shadow Srs CD		G-MZAX	Pegasus Quantum 15	
G-MYXZ	Pegasus Quantum 15		G-MZAY	Mainair Blade	
G-MYYA	Mainair Blade		G-MZAZ	Mainair Blade	
G-MYYB	Pegasus Quantum 15		G-MZBA	Mainair Blade 912	
G-MYYC	Pegasus Quantum 15		G-MZBB	Pegasus Quantum 15	
G-MYYD	Cyclone Chaser S 447		G-MZBC	Pegasus Quantum 15	
G-MYYE	Hunt Wing		G-MZBD	Rans S.6-ESD Coyote II	
G-MYYF	Quad City Challenger II		G-MZBE	CFM Streak Shadow Srs SA-M	
G-MYYG	Mainair Blade				
G-MYYH	Mainair Blade		G-MZBF	Letov LK-2M Sluka	
G-MYYI	Pegasus Quantum 15		G-MZBG	Whittaker MW.6-S Fatboy Flyer	
G-MYYJ	Hunt Wing				
G-MYYK	Pegasus Quantum 15		G-MZBH	Rans S.6-ESD Coyote II	
G-MYYL	Cyclone AX3/503		G-MZBI	Pegasus Quantum 15	
G-MYYM	Microchute Motor 27		G-MZBK	Letov LK-2M Sluka	
G-MYYN	Pegasus Quantum 15		G-MZBL	Mainair Blade	
G-MYYO	Medway Raven X		G-MZBM	Pegasus Quantum 15	
G-MYYP	AMF Chevvron 2-45CS		G-MZBN	CFM Shadow Srs BD	
G-MYYR	Team Minimax 91		G-MZBO	Pegasus Quantum 15	
G-MYYS	Team Minimax		G-MZBP	Microchute UQ/Motor 27	
G-MYYT	Hunt Wing		G-MZBR	Southdown Raven	
G-MYYU	Mainair Mercury		G-MZBS	CFM Shadow Srs D	
G-MYYV	Rans S.6-ESD Coyote IIXL		G-MZBT	Pegasus Quantum 15	
G-MYYW	Mainair Blade		G-MZBU	Rans S.6-ESD Coyote II	
G-MYYX	Pegasus Quantum 15		G-MZBV	Rans S.6-ESD Coyote II	

Reg.	Type	Notes	Reg.	Type	Notes
G-MZBW	Quad City Challenger II UK		G-MZER	Cyclone AX2000	
G-MZBX	Whittaker MW.6-S Fatboy Flyer		G-MZES	Letov LK-2N Sluka	
			G-MZET	Pegasus Quantum 15	
G-MZBY	Pegasus Quantum 15		G-MZEU	Rans S.6-ESD Coyote IIXL	
G-MZBZ	Quad City Challenger II UK		G-MZEV	Mainair Rapier	
G-MZCA	Rans S.6-ESD Coyote II		G-MZEW	Mainair Blade	
G-MZCB	Cyclone Chaser S 447		G-MZEX	Pegasus Quantum 15	
G-MZCC	Mainair Blade 912		G-MZEY	Micro Bantam B.22	
G-MZCD	Mainair Blade		G-MZEZ	Pegasus Quantum 15	
G-MZCE	Mainair Blade		G-MZFA	Cyclone AX2000	
G-MZCF	Mainair Blade		G-MZFB	Mainair Blade	
G-MZCG	Mainair Blade		G-MZFC	Letov LK-2M Sluka	
G-MZCH	Whittaker MW.6-S Fatboy Flyer		G-MZFD	Mainair Rapier	
			G-MZFE	Hunt Wing	
G-MZCI	Pegasus Quantum 15		G-MZFF	Hunt Wing	
G-MZCJ	Pegasus Quantum 15		G-MZFG	Pegasus Quantum 15	
G-MZCK	AMF Chevvron 2-32C		G-MZFH	AMF Chevvron 2-32C	
G-MZCL	Ultrasports Tri-Pacer		G-MZFI	Iolaire	
G-MZCM	Pegasus Quantum 15		G-MZFK	Whittaker MW.6 Merlin	
G-MZCN	Mainair Blade		G-MZFL	Rans S.6-ESD Coyote IIXL	
G-MZCO	Mainair Mercury		G-MZFM	Pegasus Quantum 15	
G-MZCP	SW Pegasus XL-Q		G-MZFN	Rans S.6.ESD Coyote IIXL	
G-MZCR	Pegasus Quantum 15		G-MZFO	Thruster T.600N	
G-MZCS	Team Minimax		G-MZFP	Thruster T.600N	
G-MZCT	CFM Shadow Srs CD		G-MZFR	Thruster T.600N	
G-MZCU	Mainair Blade		G-MZFS	Mainair Blade	
G-MZCV	Pegasus Quantum 15		G-MZFT	Pegasus Quantum 15	
G-MZCW	Pegasus Quantum 15		G-MZFU	Thruster T.600N	
G-MZCX	Hunt Wing		G-MZFV	Pegasus Quantum 15	
G-MZCY	Pegasus Quantum 15		G-MZFW	Mainair Rapier	
G-MZCZ	Hunt Wing		G-MZFX	Cyclone AX2000	
G-MZDA	Rans S.6-ESD Coyote IIXL		G-MZFY	Rans S.6-ESD Coyote IIXL	
G-MZDB	Pegasus Quantum 15		G-MZFZ	Mainair Blade	
G-MZDC	Pegasus Quantum 15		G-MZGA	Cyclone AX2000	
G-MZDD	Pegasus Quantum 15		G-MZGB	Cyclone AX2000	
G-MZDE	Pegasus Quantum 15		G-MZGC	Cyclone AX2000	
G-MZDF	Mainair Blade		G-MZGD	Rans S.6 Coyote II	
G-MZDG	Rans S.6-ESD Coyote IIXL		G-MZGE	Medway Hybred 44XLR	
G-MZDH	Pegasus Quantum 15		G-MZGF	Letov LK-2M Sluka	
G-MZDI	Whittaker MW.6-S Fatboy Flyer (G-BUNN)		G-MZGG	Pegasus Quantum 15	
			G-MZGH	Hunt Wing	
G-MZDJ	Medway Raven X		G-MZGI	Mainair Blade 912	
G-MZDK	Mainair Blade		G-MZGJ	Kolb Twinstar Mk 1	
G-MZDL	Whittaker MW.6-S Fatboy Flyer		G-MZGK	Pegasus Quantum 15	
			G-MZGL	Mainair Rapier	
G-MZDM	Rans S.6-ESD Coyote II		G-MZGM	Cyclone AX2000	
G-MZDN	Pegasus Quantum 15		G-MZGN	Pegasus Quantum 15	
G-MZDO	Cyclone AX3/503		G-MZGO	Pegasus Quantum 15	
G-MZDP	AMF Chevvron 2-32		G-MZGP	Cyclone AX2000	
G-MZDR	Rans S.6-ESD Coyote IIXL		G-MZGR	Team Minimax	
G-MZDS	Cyclone AX3/503		G-MZGS	CFM Shadow Srs BD	
G-MZDT	Mainair Blade		G-MZGT	RH78 Tiger Light	
G-MZDU	Pegasus Quantum 15		G-MZGU	Arrowflight Hawk II (UK)	
G-MZDV	Pegasus Quantum 15		G-MZGV	Pegasus Quantum 15	
G-MZDW	Microchute UQ		G-MZGW	Mainair Blade	
G-MZDX	Letov LK-2M Sluka		G-MZGX	Thruster T.600N	
G-MZDY	Pegasus Quantum 15		G-MZGY	Thruster T.600N	
G-MZDZ	Hunt Wing		G-MZGZ	Thruster T.600N	
G-MZEA	Quad City Challenger II UK		G-MZHA	Thruster T.600N	
G-MZEB	Mainair Blade		G-MZHB	Mainair Blade	
G-MZEC	Pegasus Quantum 15		G-MZHC	Thruster T.600N	
G-MZED	Mainair Blade		G-MZHD	Thruster T.600N	
G-MZEE	Pegasus Quantum 15		G-MZHE	Thruster T.600N	
G-MZEG	Mainair Blade		G-MZHF	Thruster T.600N	
G-MZEH	Pegasus Quantum 15		G-MZHG	Whittaker MW.6-T	
G-MZEI	Whittaker MW.5-D Sorcerer		G-MZHI	Pegasus Quantum 15	
G-MZEJ	Mainair Blade		G-MZHJ	Mainair Rapier	
G-MZEK	Mainair Mercury		G-MZHK	Pegasus Quantum 15	
G-MZEL	Cyclone AX3/503		G-MZHL	Mainair Rapier	
G-MZEM	Pegasus Quantum 15		G-MZHM	Team Himax 1700R	
G-MZEN	Rans S.6-ESD Coyote II		G-MZHN	Pegasus Quantum 15	
G-MZEO	Rans S.6-ESD Coyote IIXL		G-MZHO	Quad City Challenger II	
G-MZEP	Mainair Rapier		G-MZHP	Pegasus Quantum 15	

Reg.	Type	Notes	Reg.	Type	Notes
G-MZHR	Cyclone AX2000		G-MZKP	Thruster T.600N	
G-MZHS	Thruster T.600T		G-MZKR	Thruster T.600N	
G-MZHT	Whittaker MW.6 Merlin		G-MZKS	Thruster T.600N	
G-MZHU	Thruster T.600T		G-MZKT	Thruster T.600N	
G-MZHV	Thruster T.600T		G-MZKU	Thruster T.600N	
G-MZHW	Thruster T.600N		G-MZKV	Mainair Blade 912	
G-MZHX	Thruster T.600N		G-MZKW	Quad City Challenger II	
G-MZHY	Thruster T.600N		G-MZKX	Pegasus Quantum 15	
G-MZHZ	Thruster T.600N		G-MZKY	Pegasus Quantum 15	
G-MZIA	Team Himax 1700R		G-MZKZ	Mainair Blade	
G-MZIB	Pegasus Quantum 15		G-MZLA	Pegasus Quantum 15	
G-MZIC	Pegasus Quantum 15		G-MZLB	Hunt Wing	
G-MZID	Whittaker MW.6 Merlin		G-MZLC	Mainair Blade 912	
G-MZIE	Pegasus Quantum 15		G-MZLD	Pegasus Quantum 15	
G-MZIF	Pegasus Quantum 15		G-MZLE	Maverick (G-BXSZ)	
G-MZIH	Mainair Blade		G-MZLF	Pegasus Quantum 15	
G-MZII	Team Minimax		G-MZLG	Rans S.6-ESD Coyote IIXL	
G-MZIJ	Pegasus Quantum 15		G-MZLH	Pegasus Quantum 15	
G-MZIK	Pegasus Quantum 15		G-MZLI	Mignet HM.1000 Balerit	
G-MZIL	Mainair Rapier		G-MZLJ	Pegasus Quantum 15	
G-MZIM	Mainair Rapier		G-MZLL	Rans S.6-ESD Coyote II	
G-MZIN	Whittaker MW-6 Merlin		G-MZLM	Cyclone AX2000	
G-MZIP	Renegade Spirit UK		G-MZLN	Pegasus Quantum 15	
G-MZIR	Mainair Blade		G-MZLO	CFM Shadow Srs O	
G-MZIS	Mainair Blade		G-MZLP	CFM Shadow Srs O	
G-MZIT	Mainair Blade 912		G-MZLR	SW Pegasus XL-Q	
G-MZIU	Pegasus Quantum 15		G-MZLS	Cyclone AX2000	
G-MZIV	Cyclone AX2000		G-MZLT	Pegasus Quantum 15	
G-MZIW	Mainair Blade		G-MZLU	Cyclone AX2000	
G-MZIX	Mignet HM.1000 Balerit		G-MZLV	Pegasus Quantum 15	
G-MZIY	Rans S.6-ESD Coyote II		G-MZLW	Pegasus Quantum 15	
G-MZIZ	Renegade Spirit UK		G-MZLX	Micro Bantam B.22-5	
	(G-MWGP)		G-MZLY	Letov LK-2M Sluka	
G-MZJA	Mainair Blade		G-MZLZ	Mainair Blade 912	
G-MZJB	Aviasud Mistral		G-MZMA	SW Pegasus Quasar IITC	
G-MZJC	Micro Bantam B22-S		G-MZMB	Mainair Blade	
G-MZJD	Mainair Blade		G-MZMC	Pegasus Quantum 15	
G-MZJE	Mainair Rapier		G-MZMD	Mainair Blade 912	
G-MZJF	Cyclone AX2000		G-MZMG	Pegasus Quantum 15	
G-MZJG	Pegasus Quantum 15		G-MZMH	Pegasus Quantum 15	
G-MZJH	Pegasus Quantum 15		G-MZMJ	Mainair Blade	
G-MZJI	Rans S.6-ESD Coyote II		G-MZMK	Chevvron 2-32C	
G-MZJJ	Maverick		G-MZML	Mainair Blade 912	
G-MZJK	Mainair Blade		G-MZMM	Mainair Blade 912	
G-MZJL	Cyclone AX2000		G-MZMN	Pegasus Quantum 912	
G-MZJM	Rans S.6-ESD Coyote IIXL		G-MZMO	Team Minimax 91	
G-MZJN	Pegasus Quantum 15		G-MZMP	Mainair Blade	
G-MZJO	Pegasus Quantum 15		G-MZMR	Rans S.6-ESA Coyote II	
G-MZJP	Whittaker MW.6-S Fatboy		G-MZMS	Rans S.6-ESD Coyote II	
	Flyer		G-MZMT	Pegasus Quantum 15	
G-MZJR	Cyclone AX2000		G-MZMU	Rans S.6-ESD Coyote II	
G-MZJS	Meridian Maverick		G-MZMV	Mainair Blade	
G-MZJT	Pegasus Quantum 15		G-MZMW	Mignet HM.1000 Balerit	
G-MZJU	Pegasus Quantum 15		G-MZMX	Cyclone AX2000	
G-MZJV	Mainair Blade 912		G-MZMY	Mainair Blade	
G-MZJW	Pegasus Quantum 15		G-MZMZ	Mainair Blade	
G-MZJX	Mainair Blade		G-MZNA	Quad City Challenger II UK	
G-MZJY	Pegasus Quantum 15		G-MZNB	Pegasus Quantum 15	
G-MZJZ	Mainair Blade		G-MZNC	Mainair Blade 912	
G-MZKA	Pegasus Quantum 15		G-MZND	Mainair Rapier	
G-MZKC	Cyclone AX2000		G-MZNE	Whittaker MW.6-S Fatboy	
G-MZKD	Pegasus Quantum 15			Flyer	
G-MZKE	Rans S.6-ESD Coyote IIXL		G-MZNG	Pegasus Quantum 15	
G-MZKF	Pegasus Quantum 15		G-MZNH	CFM Shadow Srs DD	
G-MZKG	Mainair Blade		G-MZNI	Mainair Blade 912	
G-MZKH	CFM Shadow Srs DD		G-MZNJ	Mainair Blade	
G-MZKI	Mainair Blade		G-MZNK	Mainair Blade 912	
G-MZKJ	Mainair Blade		G-MZNL	Mainair Blade 912	
G-MZKK	Mainair Blade 912		G-MZNM	Team Minimax	
G-MZKL	Pegasus Quantum 15		G-MZNN	Team Minimax	
G-MZKM	Mainair Blade 912		G-MZNO	Mainair Blade	
G-MZKN	Mainair Rapier		G-MZNP	Pegasus Quantum 15	
G-MZKO	Mainair Blade		G-MZNR	Pegasus Quantum 15	

Reg.	Type	Notes	Reg.	Type	Notes
G-MZNS	Pegasus Quantum 15		G-MZOT	Letov LK-2M Sluka	
G-MZNT	Pegasus Quantum 15-912		G-MZOV	Pegasus Quantum 15	
G-MZNU	Mainair Rapier		G-MZOW	Pegasus Quantum 15-912	
G-MZNV	Rans S.6-ESD Coyote II		G-MZOX	Letov LK-2M Sluka	
G-MZNW	Thruster T.600N HKS		G-MZOZ	Rans S.6-ESD Coyote IIXL	
G-MZNX	Thruster T.600N		G-MZPB	Mignet HM.1000 Balerit	
G-MZNY	Thruster T.600N		G-MZPD	Pegasus Quantum 15	
G-MZOA	Thruster T.600T		G-MZPH	Mainair Blade	
G-MZOB	Thruster T.600T		G-MZPJ	Team Minimax	
G-MZOC	Mainair Blade		G-MZPW	Pegasus Quantum 15	
G-MZOD	Pegasus Quantum 15		G-MZRC	Pegasus Quantum 15	
G-MZOE	Cyclone AX2000		G-MZRH	Pegasus Quantum 15	
G-MZOF	Mainair Blade		G-MZRM	Pegasus Quantum 15	
G-MZOG	Pegasus Quantum 15-912		G-MZRS	CFM Shadow Srs CD	
G-MZOH	Whittaker MW.5D Sorcerer		G-MZSC	Pegasus Quantum 15	
G-MZOI	Letov LK-2M Sluka		G-MZSD	Mainair Blade 912	
G-MZOJ	Pegasus Quantum 15		G-MZSM	Mainair Blade	
G-MZOK	Whittaker MW.6 Merlin		G-MZTA	Mignet HM.1000 Balerit	
G-MZOM	CFM Shadow Srs DD		G-MZTS	Aerial Arts Chaser S	
G-MZON	Mainair Rapier			(G-MVDM)	
G-MZOP	Mainair Blade 912		G-MZUB	Rans S.6-ESD Coyote IIXL	
G-MZOR	Mainair Blade 912		G-MZZT	Kolb Twinstar Mk 3	
G-MZOS	Pegasus Quantum 15-912		G-MZZY	Mainair Blade 912	

EC-FXP — Boeing 737-4Q8 of Air Europa.

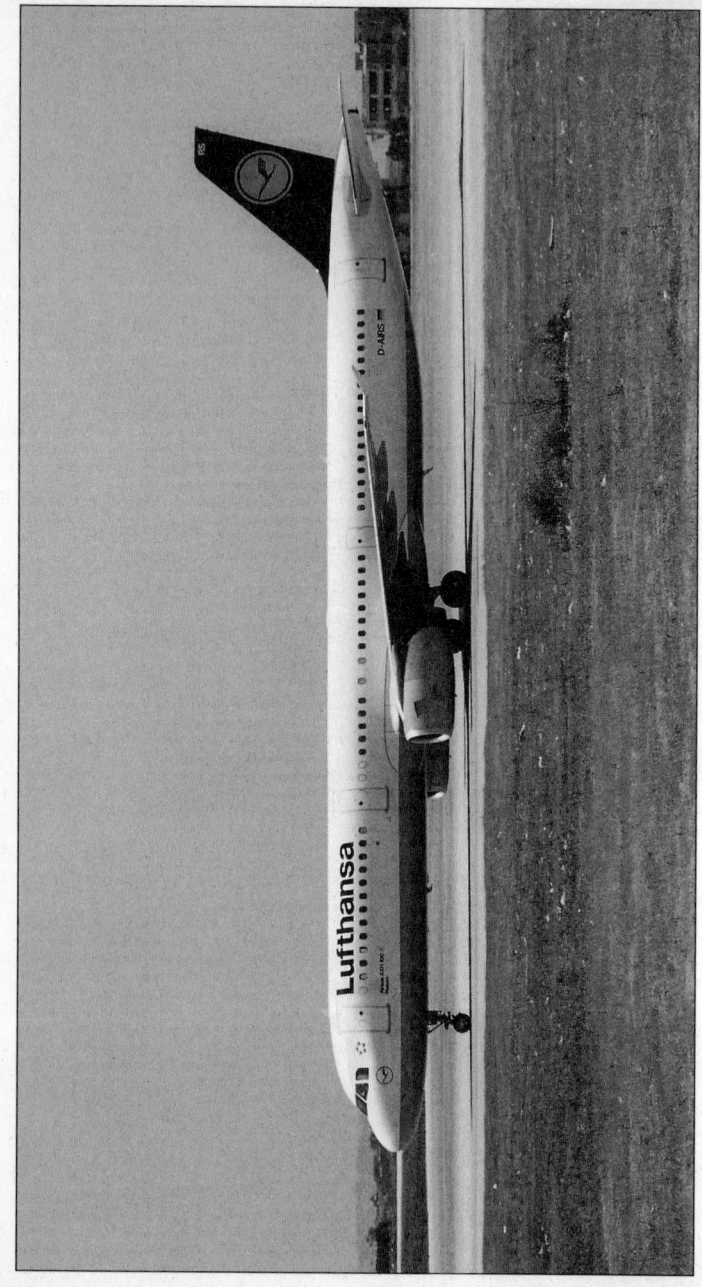

D-AIRS — Airbus A.321-131 of Lufthansa.

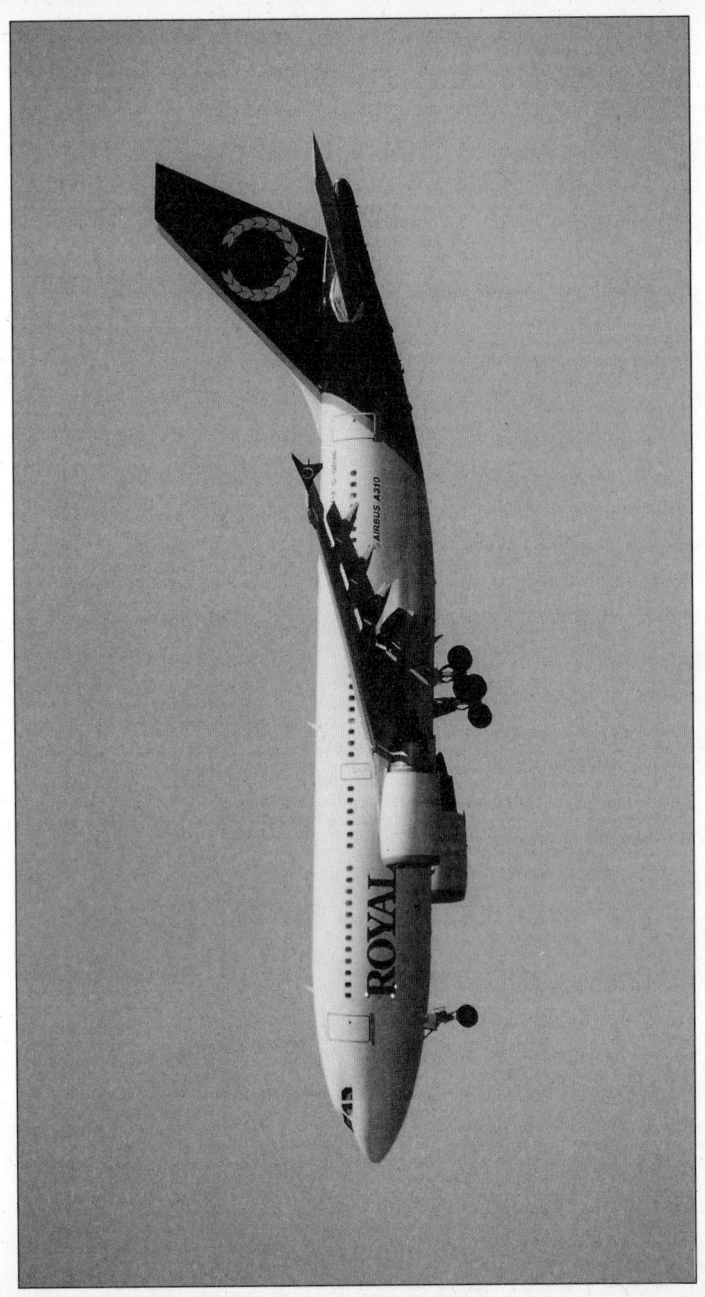

C-GRYA — Airbus A.310-304 of Royal Airlines.

EI-CSA — Boeing 737-8AS of Ryanair.

Overseas Airliner Registrations

(Aircraft included in this section are those most likely to be seen at UK and major European airports on scheduled or charter services.)

Reg.	Type	Owner or Operator	Notes

A4O (Oman)

Reg.	Type	Owner or Operator	Notes
A4O-GH	Boeing 767-3P6ER (603)	Gulf Air	
A4O-GI	Boeing 767-3P6ER (604)	Gulf Air	
A4O-GJ	Boeing 767-3P6ER (605)	Gulf Air *Al Muharraq*	
A4O-GK	Boeing 767-3P6ER (606)	Gulf Air *Al Burami*	
A4O-GS	Boeing 767-3P6ER (613)	Gulf Air	
A4O-GT	Boeing 767-3P6ER (614)	Gulf Air *Auwakrah*	
A4O-GU	Boeing 767-3P6ER (615)	Gulf Air	
A4O-GV	Boeing 767-3P6ER (616)	Gulf Air *Dohat*	
A4O-GY	Boeing 767-3P6ER (619)	Gulf Air	
A4O-GZ	Boeing 767-3P6ER (620)	Gulf Air	
A4O-KA	Airbus A.330-243 (501)	Gulf Air	
A4O-KB	Airbus A.330-243 (502)	Gulf Air	
A4O-KC	Airbus A.330-243 (503)	Gulf Air	
A4O-KD	Airbus A.330-243 (504)	Gulf Air	
A4O-KE	Airbus A.330-243 (505)	Gulf Air	
A4O-KF	Airbus A.330-243 (506)	Gulf Air	
A4O-LB	Airbus A.340-312 (402)	Gulf Air *Al Fateh*	
A4O-LC	Airbus A.340-312 (403)	Gulf Air *Doha*	
A4O-LD	Airbus A.340-312 (404)	Gulf Air *Abu Dhabi*	
A4O-LE	Airbus A.340-312 (405)	Gulf Air	
A4O-LF	Airbus A.340-312 (406)	Gulf Air	
A4O-SO	Boeing 747SP-27	Oman Royal Flight	
A4O-SP	Boeing 747SP-27	Oman Government	

A6 (United Arab Emirates)

Reg.	Type	Owner or Operator	Notes
A6-EKB	Airbus A.310-304	Emirate Airlines	
A6-EKD	Airbus A.300-605R	Emirate Airlines	
A6-EKE	Airbus A.300-605R	Emirate Airlines	
A6-EKF	Airbus A.300-605R	Emirate Airlines	
A6-EKG	Airbus A.310-308	Emirate Airlines	
A6-EKH	Airbus A.310-308	Emirate Airlines	
A6-EKI	Airbus A.310-308	Emirate Airlines	
A6-EKJ	Airbus A.310-308	Emirate Airlines	
A6-EKK	Airbus A.310-308	Emirate Airlines	
A6-EKL	Airbus A.310-308	Emirate Airlines	
A6-EKM	Airbus A.300-605R	Emirate Airlines	
A6-EKO	Airbus A.300-605R	Emirate Airlines	
A6-EKP	Airbus A.310-308	Emirate Airlines	
A6-EKQ	Airbus A.330-243	Emirate Airlines	
A6-EKR	Airbus A.330-243	Emirate Airlines	
A6-EKS	Airbus A.330-243	Emirate Airlines	
A6-EKT	Airbus A.330-243	Emirate Airlines	
A6-EKU	Airbus A.330-243	Emirate Airlines	
A6-EKV	Airbus A.330-243	Emirate Airlines	
A6-EKW	Airbus A.330-243	Emirate Airlines	
A6-EKX	Airbus A.330-243	Emirate Airlines	
A6-EKY	Airbus A.330-243	Emirate Airlines	
A6-EKZ	Airbus A.330-243	Emirate Airlines	
A6-EMD	Boeing 777-21H	Emirate Airlines	
A6-EME	Boeing 777-21H	Emirate Airlines	
A6-EMF	Boeing 777-21H	Emirate Airlines	
A6-EMG	Boeing 777-21HER	Emirate Airlines	
A6-EMH	Boeing 777-21HER	Emirate Airlines	
A6-EMI	Boeing 777-21HER	Emirate Airlines	
A6-EMJ	Boeing 777-21HER	Emirate Airlines	
A6-EMK	Boeing 777-21HER	Emirate Airlines	
A6-EML	Boeing 777-21HER	Emirate Airlines	
A6-EMM	Boeing 777-31HER	Emirate Airlines	
A6-SMM	Boeing 747SP-31	United Arab Emirates	
A6-SMR	Boeing 747SP-31	United Arab Emirates	

Notes	Reg.	Type	Owner or Operator

A7 (Qatar)

A7-AAF	Airbus A.310-304	Qatar Government
A7-AAG	Airbus A.320-232	Qatar Government
A7-ABN	Airbus A.300-622R	Qatar Airways
A7-ABO	Airbus A.300-622R	Qatar Airways
A7-ABP	Airbus A.300-622R	Qatar Airways
A7-AHM	Boeing 747SP-27	Qatar Airways
A7-HHK	Airbus A.340-211	Qatar Government

AP (Pakistan)

AP-AXG	Boeing 707-340C	Pakistan International Airlines
AP-AYV	Boeing 747-282B	Pakistan International Airlines
AP-AYW	Boeing 747-282B	Pakistan International Airlines
AP-BAK	Boeing 747-240B (SCD)	Pakistan International Airlines
AP-BAT	Boeing 747-240B (SCD)	Pakistan International Airlines
AP-BBK	Boeing 707-323C	Pakistan International Airlines
AP-BCL	Boeing 747-217B	Pakistan International Airlines
AP-BCM	Boeing 747-217B	Pakistan International Airlines
AP-BCN	Boeing 747-217B	Pakistan International Airlines
AP-BCO	Boeing 747-217B	Pakistan International Airlines
AP-BDZ	Airbus A.310-308	Pakistan International Airlines
AP-BEB	Airbus A.310-308	Pakistan International Airlines
AP-BEC	Airbus A.310-308	Pakistan International Airlines
AP-BEG	Airbus A.310-308	Pakistan International Airlines
AP-BEQ	Airbus A.310-308	Pakistan International Airlines
AP-BEU	Airbus A.310-308	Pakistan International Airlines
AP-BFU	Boeing 747-367	Pakistan International Airlines
AP-BFV	Boeing 747-367	Pakistan International Airlines
AP-BFW	Boeing 747-367	Pakistan International Airlines
AP-BFX	Boeing 747-367	Pakistan International Airlines
AP-BFY	Boeing 747-367	Pakistan International Airlines

B (China/Taiwan/Hong Kong)

B-HIA	Boeing 747-267B	Cathay Pacific Airways
B-HIB	Boeing 747-267B	Cathay Pacific Airways
B-HIH	Boeing 747-267F (SCD)	Cathay Pacific Airways
B-HMD	Boeing 747-2L5F (SCD)	Air Hong Kong
B-HME	Boeing 747-2L5F (SCD)	Air Hong Kong
B-HMF	Boeing 747-2L5F (SCD)	Air Hong Kong
B-HOO	Boeing 747-467	Cathay Pacific Airways
B-HOP	Boeing 747-467	Cathay Pacific Airways
B-HOR	Boeing 747-467	Cathay Pacific Airways
B-HOS	Boeing 747-467	Cathay Pacific Airways
B-HOT	Boeing 747-467	Cathay Pacific Airways
B-HOU	Boeing 747-467	Cathay Pacific Airways
B-HOV	Boeing 747-467	Cathay Pacific Airways
B-HOW	Boeing 747-467	Cathay Pacific Airways
B-HOX	Boeing 747-467	Cathay Pacific Airways
B-HOY	Boeing 747-467	Cathay Pacific Airways
B-HOZ	Boeing 747-467	Cathay Pacific Airways
B-HUA	Boeing 747-467	Cathay Pacific Airways
B-HUB	Boeing 747-467	Cathay Pacific Airways
B-HUD	Boeing 747-467	Cathay Pacific Airways
B-HUE	Boeing 747-467	Cathay Pacific Airways
B-HUF	Boeing 747-467	Cathay Pacific Airways
B-HUG	Boeing 747-467	Cathay Pacific Airways
B-HUH	Boeing 747-467F	Cathay Pacific Airways
B-HUI	Boeing 747-467	Cathay Pacific Airways
B-HUJ	Boeing 747-467	Cathay Pacific Airways
B-HUK	Boeing 747-467F	Cathay Pacific Airways
B-HVX	Boeing 747-267F (SCD)	Cathay Pacific Airways
B-HVY	Boeing 747-236F (SCD)	Cathay Pacific Airways
B-HVZ	Boeing 747-267F (SCD)	Cathay Pacific Airways
B-HXH	Airbus A.340-313X	Cathay Pacific Airways
B-HXI	Airbus A.340-313X	Cathay Pacific Airways
B-105EV	McD Douglas MD-11F	EVA Airways
B-151	McD Douglas MD-11	China Airlines
B-152	McD Douglas MD-11	China Airlines

Reg.	Type	Owner or Operator	Notes
B-153	McD Douglas MD-11	China Airlines	
B-160	Boeing 747-209F (SCD)	China Airlines	
B-161	Boeing 747-409	China Airlines	
B-162	Boeing 747-409	China Airlines	
B-163	Boeing 747-409	China Airlines	
B-164	Boeing 747-409	China Airlines	
B-1862	Boeing 747SP-09	China Airlines	
B-2438	Boeing 747SP-J6	Air China	
B-2442	Boeing 747SP-J6	Air China	
B-2443	Boeing 747-4J6	Air China	
B-2445	Boeing 747-4J6	Air China	
B-2446	Boeing 747-2J6B (SCD)	Air China	
B-2447	Boeing 747-4J6	Air China	
B-2448	Boeing 747-2J6B (SCD)	Air China	
B-2450	Boeing 747-2J6B (SCD)	Air China	
B-2454	Boeing 747SP-27	Air China	
B-2456	Boeing 747-4J6 (SCD)	Air China	
B-2458	Boeing 747-4J6 (SCD)	Air China	
B-2460	Boeing 747-4J6 (SCD)	Air China	
B-2462	Boeing 747-2J6F (SCD)	Air China	
B-2464	Boeing 747-4J6	Air China	
B-2466	Boeing 747-4J6	Air China	
B-2467	Boeing 747-4J6	Air China	
B-2468	Boeing 747-4J6	Air China	
B-2469	Boeing 747-4J6	Air China	
B-2470	Boeing 747-4J6	Air China	
B-2471	Boeing 747-4J6	Air China	
B-2472	Boeing 747-4J6	Air China	
B-16101	McD Douglas MD-11	EVA Airways	
B-16102	McD Douglas MD-11	EVA Airways	
B-16103	McD Douglas MD-11	EVA Airways	
B-16106	McD Douglas MD-11F	EVA Airways	
B-16107	McD Douglas MD-11F	EVA Airways	
B-16108	McD Douglas MD-11F	EVA Airways	
B-16109	McD Douglas MD-11F	EVA Airways	
B-16110	McD Douglas MD-11F	EVA Airways	
B-16111	McD Douglas MD-11F	EVA Airways	
B-16112	McD Douglas MD-11F	EVA Airways	
B-16113	McD Douglas MD-11F	EVA Airways	
B-16401	Boeing 747-45E	EVA Airways	
B-16402	Boeing 747-45E	EVA Airways	
B-16406	Boeing 747-45E	EVA Airways	
B-16407	Boeing 747-45E	EVA Airways	
B-16410	Boeing 747-45E	EVA Airways	
B-16411	Boeing 747-45E	EVA Airways	
B-16412	Boeing 747-45E	EVA Airways	
B-16461	Boeing 747-45E (SCD)	EVA Airways	
B-16462	Boeing 747-45E (SCD)	EVA Airways	
B-16463	Boeing 747-45E (SCD)	EVA Airways	
B-16465	Boeing 747-45E (SCD)	EVA Airways	
B-16481	Boeing 747-45E	EVA Airways	
B-18202	Boeing 747-409	China Airlines	
B-18203	Boeing 747-409	China Airlines	
B-18205	Boeing 747-409	China Airlines	
B-18206	Boeing 747-409	China Airlines	
B-18207	Boeing 747-409	China Airlines	
B-18208	Boeing 747-409	China Airlines	
B-18209	Boeing 747-409	China Airlines	
B-18253	Boeing 747SP-09	China Airlines	
B-18255	Boeing 747-209B	China Airlines	
B-18751	Boeing 747-209F	China Airlines	
B-18752	Boeing 747-209F (SCD)	China Airlines	
B-18753	Boeing 747-209B	China Airlines	
B-18755	Boeing 747-209B	China Airlines	

Note: China Airlines also operates N4508H and N4522V, both Boeing 747SP-09s. EVA Airways operates Boeing 747-45Es which retain the US registrations N403EV, N405EV, N408EV and N409EV. The airline also operates the MD-11 N103EV and the MD-11F N105EV together with Boeing 767-3T7ERs N601EV and N602EV.

Notes	Reg.	Type	Owner or Operator

C-F and C-G (Canada)

C-FBCA	Boeing 747-475 (884)	Canadian Airlines *Grant McConachie*
C-FBEF	Boeing 767-233ER (617)	Air Canada
C-FBEG	Boeing 767-233ER (618)	Air Canada
C-FBEM	Boeing 767-233ER (619)	Air Canada
C-FBUS	Airbus A.330-322	Skyservice
C-FCAB	Boeing 767-375ER (631)	Canadian Airlines
C-FCAE	Boeing 767-375ER (632)	Canadian Airlines
C-FCAF	Boeing 767-375ER (633)	Canadian Airlines
C-FCAG	Boeing 767-375ER (634)	Canadian Airlines
C-FCRA	Boeing 747-475 (882)	Canadian Airlines *T. Russ Baker*
C-FCRD	Douglas DC-10-30 (912)	Canadian Airlines *Pride of Canadian*
C-FGHZ	Boeing 747-4F6 (885)	Canadian Airlines *Rhys T. Eyton*
C-FICA	Airbus A.300B4-203	ICC Air Cargo
C-FICB	Airbus A.300B4-203	ICC Air Cargo
C-FICR	Airbus A.300B4-203	ICC Air Cargo
C-FMWP	Boeing 767-333ER (631)	Air Canada
C-FMWQ	Boeing 767-333ER (632)	Air Canada
C-FMWU	Boeing 767-333ER (633)	Air Canada
C-FMWV	Boeing 767-333ER (634)	Air Canada
C-FMWY	Boeing 767-333ER (635)	Air Canada
C-FMXC	Boeing 767-333ER (636)	Air Canada
C-FOCA	Boeing 767-375ER (640)	Canadian Airlines
C-FOOE	Boeing 757-28A	Canada 3000 Airlines
C-FOOH	Boeing 757-23A	Canada 3000 Airlines
C-FOON	Boeing 757-28A	Canada 3000 Airlines
C-FPCA	Boeing 767-375ER (637)	Canadian Airlines
C-FRYH	Boeing 757-28A	Royal Airlines/Air 2000 (G-OOOB)
C-FRYL	Boeing 757-28A	Royal Airlines/Air 2000 (G-OOOC)
C-FTCA	Boeing 767-375ER (638)	Canadian Airlines
C-FTDI	Airbus A.320-212	Skyservice/Monarch Airlines (G-MONZ)
C-FTDU	Airbus A.320-212	Skyservice/Monarch Airlines (G-MPCD)
C-FTDW	Airbus A.320-212	Skyservice/Monarch Airlines (G-OZBB)
C-FTNA	L.1011-385 TriStar 150 (501)	Air Transat
C-FTNB	L.1011-385 TriStar 150 (549)	Air Transat
C-FTNC	L.1011-385 TriStar 150 (503)	Air Transat
C-FTNG	L.1011-385 TriStar 150 (507)	Air Transat
C-FTNH	L.1011-385 TriStar 150 (508)	Air Transat
C-FTNL	L.1011-385 TriStar 100 (512)	Air Transat
C-FTNP	Airbus A.340-313 (982)	Air Canada
C-FTNQ	Airbus A.340-313 (981)	Air Canada
C-FTSI	L.1011-385 TriStar 1	Air Transat
C-FTSW	L.1011-385 TriStar 500	Air Transat
C-FUCL	Boeing 767-209ER (622)	Air Canada
C-FVNM	Boeing 767-209ER (621)	Air Canada
C-FXCA	Boeing 767-375ER (639)	Canadian Airlines
C-FXOF	Boeing 757-28A	Canada 3000 Airlines
C-FXOK	Boeing 757-23A	Canada 3000 Airlines
C-FXOO	Boeing 757-2Q8	Canada 3000 Airlines
C-FYKX	Airbus A.340-313 (901)	Air Canada
C-FYKZ	Airbus A.340-313 (902)	Air Canada
C-FYLC	Airbus A.340-313 (903)	Air Canada
C-FYLD	Airbus A.340-313 (904)	Air Canada
C-FYLG	Airbus A.340-313 (905)	Air Canada
C-FYLU	Airbus A.340-313 (906)	Air Canada
C-FYXI	L.100-385 TriStar 50	Royal Airlines
C-GAGA	Boeing 747-233B (SCD) (306)	Air Canada
C-GAGB	Boeing 747-233B (SCD) (307)	Air Canada
C-GAGC	Boeing 747-238B (SCD) (308)	Air Canada
C-GAGL	Boeing 747-433 (SCD) (341)	Air Canada
C-GAGM	Boeing 747-433 (SCD) (342)	Air Canada
C-GAGN	Boeing 747-433 (SCD) (343)	Air Canada
C-GAUW	Boeing 767-233ER (608)	Air Canada
C-GAUY	Boeing 767-233ER (609)	Air Canada
C-GAVA	Boeing 767-233ER (610)	Air Canada
C-GAVC	Boeing 767-233ER (611)	Air Canada
C-GAVF	Boeing 767-233ER (612)	Air Canada
C-GBBS	L.1011-385 TriStar 100	Air Transat
C-GBQM	Airbus A.340-313 (907)	Air Canada
C-GBQQ	Douglas DC-10-30	Canadian Airlines
C-GBWB	Airbus A.330-202	Canada 3000 Airlines

Reg.	Type	Owner or Operator	Notes
C-GBZR	Boeing 767-38EER	Canadian Airlines	
C-GCPC	Douglas DC-10-30 (901)	Canadian Airlines	
C-GCPD	Douglas DC-10-30 (902)	Canadian Airlines	
C-GCPE	Douglas DC-10-30ER (903)	Canadian Airlines	
C-GCPF	Douglas DC-10-30ER (904)	Canadian Airlines	
C-GCPG	Douglas DC-10-30ER (905)	Canadian Airlines	
C-GCPH	Douglas DC-10-30ER (906)	Canadian Airlines	
C-GCPI	Douglas DC-10-30ER (907)	Canadian Airlines	
C-GDSP	Boeing 767-233ER (613)	Air Canada	
C-GDSS	Boeing 767-233ER (614)	Air Canada	
C-GDSU	Boeing 767-233ER (615)	Air Canada	
C-GDSY	Boeing 767-233ER (616)	Air Canada	
C-GDUZ	Boeing 767-38EER	Canadian Airlines	
C-GDVV	Airbus A.340-313X (908)	Air Canada	
C-GDVW	Airbus A.340-313X (909)	Air Canada	
C-GDVZ	Airbus A.340-313X (910)	Air Canada	
C-GEOQ	Boeing 767-375ER (647)	Canadian Airlines	
C-GEOU	Boeing 767-375ER (648)	Canadian Airlines	
C-GFAF	Airbus A.330-343	Air Canada	
C-GFAH	Airbus A.330-343X	Air Canada	
C-GFAJ	Airbus A.330-343X	Air Canada	
C-GGTS	Airbus A.330-243	Air Transat	
C-GGWA	Airbus A.330-202	Canada 3000 Airlines	
C-GGWB	Airbus A.330-202	Canada 3000 Airlines	
C-GGWC	Airbus A.330-202	Canada 3000 Airlines	
C-GGWD	Airbus A.330-202	Canada 3000 Airlines	
C-GITS	Airbus A.330-243	Air Transat	
C-GKTS	Airbus A.330-243	Air transat	
C-GLCA	Boeing 767-375ER (641)	Canadian Airlines	
C-GMPG	Airbus A.320-231	Transmeridean/TransAer International	
C-GMWW	Boeing 747-475 (881)	Canadian Airlines *Maxwell W. Ward*	
C-GRYA	Airbus A.310-304	Royal Airlines	
C-GRYD	Airbus A.310-304	Royal Airlines	
C-GRYI	Airbus A.310-304	Royal Airlines	
C-GRYK	Boeing 757-236	Royal Airlines	
C-GRYO	Boeing 757-236	Royal Airlines	
C-GRYU	Boeing 757-28A	Royal Airlines/Air 2000 (G-OOOD)	
C-GRYV	Airbus A.310-304	Royal Airlines	
C-GRYY	Boeing 757-23A	Royal Airlines/Air 2000 (G-OOOG)	
C-GRYZ	Boeing 757-236	Royal Airlines	
C-GSCA	Boeing 767-375ER (642)	Canadian Airlines	
C-GTSB	L.1011-385 TriStar 100 (122)	Air Transat	
C-GTSE	Boeing 757-23A	Air Transat	
C-GTSF	Boeing 757-23A	Air Transat	
C-GTSJ	Boeing 757-236	Air Transat	
C-GTSK	L.1011-385 TriStar 1 (502)	Air Transat	
C-GTSN	Boeing 757-28A	Air Transat	
C-GTSP	L.1011-385 TriStar 500 (242)	Air Transat	
C-GTSQ	L.1011-385 TriStar 500 (243)	Air Transat	
C-GTSR	L.1011-385 TriStar 500 (239)	Air Transat	
C-GTSV	Boeing 757-28A	Air Transat	
C-GTSX	L.1011-385 TriStar 1 (547)	Air Transat	
C-GTSZ	L.1011-385 TriStar 100 (548)	Air Transat	
C-G	Airbus A.330-242	Air Transat	
C-G	Airbus A.330-242	Air Transat	
C-GVNY	Airbus A.320-212	Skyservice/Monarch Airlines (G-MONY)	

Note: Airline fleet number carried on aircraft is shown in parenthesis.

CN (Morocco)

CN-RGA	Boeing 747-428	Royal Air Maroc	
CN-RME	Boeing 747-2B6B (SCD)	Royal Air Maroc	
CN-RMF	Boeing 737-4B6	Royal Air Maroc	
CN-RMG	Boeing 737-4B6	Royal Air Maroc	
CN-RMI	Boeing 737-2B6	Royal Air Maroc *El Ayounne*	
CN-RMJ	Boeing 737-2B6	Royal Air Maroc *Oujda*	
CN-RMK	Boeing 737-2B6	Royal Air Maroc *Smara*	
CN-RML	Boeing 737-2B6	Royal Air Maroc	
CN-RMM	Boeing 737-2B6C	Royal Air Maroc	
CN-RMN	Boeing 737-2B6C	Royal Air Maroc	
CN-RMT	Boeing 757-2B6	Royal Air Maroc	
CN-RMV	Boeing 737-5B6	Royal Air Maroc	

Notes	Reg.	Type	Owner or Operator
	CN-RMW	Boeing 737-5B6	Royal Air Maroc
	CN-RMX	Boeing 737-4B6	Royal Air Maroc
	CN-RMY	Boeing 737-5B6	Royal Air Maroc
	CN-RMZ	Boeing 757-2B6	Royal Air Maroc
	CN-RNA	Boeing 737-4B6	Royal Air Maroc
	CN-RNB	Boeing 737-5B6	Royal Air Maroc
	CN-RNC	Boeing 737-4B6	Royal Air Maroc
	CN-RND	Boeing 737-4B6	Royal Air Maroc
	CN-RNF	Boeing 737-4B6	Royal Air Maroc
	CN-RNG	Boeing 737-5B6	Royal Air Maroc
	CN-RNH	Boeing 737-5B6	Royal Air Maroc
	CN-RNJ	Boeing 737-8B6	Royal Air Maroc
	CN-RNK	Boeing 737-8B6	Royal Air Maroc
	CN-RNL	Boeing 737-7B6	Royal Air Maroc
	CN-RNM	Boeing 737-7B6	Royal Air Maroc
	CN-RNN	Boeing 737-86N	Royal Air Maroc
	CN-RNO	Boeing 737-86N	Royal Air Maroc

CS (Portugal)

	Reg.	Type	Owner or Operator
	CS-DBY	Short SD3.30 Variant 100	Air Luxor
	CS-TEB	L.1011-385 TriStar 500	Air Zarco
	CS-TEH	Airbus A.310-304	TAP - Air Portugal *Bartolomeu Dias*
	CS-TEI	Airbus A.310-304	TAP - Air Portugal *Fernao de Magalhaes*
	CS-TEJ	Airbus A.310-304	TAP - Air Portugal *Pedro Nunes*
	CS-TEW	Airbus A.310-304	TAP - Air Portugal *Vasco da Gama*
	CS-TEX	Airbus A.310-304	TAP - Air Portugal *Joao XXI*
	CS-TGP	Boeing 737-3Q8	SATA International
	CS-TGQ	Boeing 737-36N	SATA International
	CS-TGR	Boeing 737-300	SATA Air Acores *Pico*
	CS-TGU	Airbus A.310-304	SATA Air Acores
	CS-TIB	Boeing 737-382	TAP - Air Portugal *Acores*
	CS-TIF	Boeing 737-3K9	TAP - Air Portugal *Costa Verde*
	CS-TIG	Boeing 737-3K9	TAP - Air Portugal
	CS-TIH	Boeing 737-3K9	TAP - Air Portugal
	CS-TIK	Boeing 737-382	TAP - Air Portugal *Costa do Estoril*
	CS-TML	Convair Cv.440	Atlantic Cargo
	CS-TNA	Airbus A.320-211	TAP - Air Portugal *Grao Vasco*
	CS-TNB	Airbus A.320-211	TAP - Air Portugal *Gil Vicente*
	CS-TNC	Airbus A.320-211	TAP - Air Portugal *Pero da Covilha*
	CS-TND	Airbus A.320-211	TAP - Air Portugal *Garcia de Orta*
	CS-TNE	Airbus A.320-211	TAP - Air Portugal *Sa de Miranda*
	CS-TNF	Airbus A.320-211	TAP - Air Portugal *Fernao Lopes*
	CS-TNG	Airbus A.320-214	TAP - Air Portugal *Mouzinhp de Silveria*
	CS-TNH	Airbus A.320-214	TAP - Air Portugal *Almada Negreiros*
	CS-TNI	Airbus A.320-214	TAP - Air Portugal
	CS-TNJ	Airbus A.320-214	TAP - Air Portugal
	CS-TNK	Airbus A.320-214	TAP - Air Portugal
	CS-TNL	Airbus A.320-214	TAP - Air Portugal
	CS-TNM	Airbus A.320-214	TAP - Air Portugal
	CS-TOA	Airbus A.340-312	TAP - Air Portugal *Ferrei Mendes Pinto*
	CS-TOB	Airbus A.340-312	TAP - Air Portugal *D. Joao de Castro*
	CS-TOC	Airbus A.340-312	TAP - Air Portugal *Wenceslau de Moraes*
	CS-TOD	Airbus A.340-312	TAP - Air Portugal *D. Francisco de Almeida*
	CS-TPA	Fokker 100	Portugalia *Albatroz*
	CS-TPB	Fokker 100	Portugalia *Pelican*
	CS-TPC	Fokker 100	Portugalia *Flamingo*
	CS-TPD	Fokker 100	Portugalia *Condor*
	CS-TPE	Fokker 100	Portugalia *Gaviao*
	CS-TPF	Fokker 100	Portugalia *Grifo*
	CS-TPG	Embraer RJ145	Portugalia *Melro*
	CS-TPH	Embraer RJ145	Portugalia *Pardal*
	CS-TPI	Embraer RJ145	Portugalia *Cuca*
	CS-TPJ	Embraer RJ145	Portugalia
	CS-TPK	Embraer RJ145	Portugalia *Gaio*
	CS-TPL	Embraer RJ145	Portugalia *Pisco*
	CS-TTA	Airbus A.319-111	TAP - Air Portugal *Vieira da Silva*
	CS-TTB	Airbus A.319-111	TAP - Air Portugal *Gago Coutinho*
	CS-TTC	Airbus A.319-111	TAP - Air Portugal *Fernando Pessoa*
	CS-TTD	Airbus A.319-111	TAP - Air Portugal *Amadeo de Souza Cardoso*

Reg.	Type	Owner or Operator	Notes
CS-TTE	Airbus A.319-111	TAP - Air Portugal *Francisco d'Ollanda*	
CS-TTF	Airbus A.319-111	TAP - Air Portugal *Calouste Gulbenkian*	
CS-TTG	Airbus A.319-111	TAP - Air Portugal *Humberto Delgado*	
CS-TTH	Airbus A.319-111	TAP - Air Portugal *Antonio Sergio*	
CS-TTI	Airbus A.319-111	TAP - Air Portugal *Eca de Queiros*	
CS-TTJ	Airbus A.319-111	TAP - Air Portugal *Viana da Mota*	
CS-TTK	Airbus A.319-111	TAP - Air Portugal *Miguel Torga*	
CS-TTL	Airbus A.319-111	TAP - Air Portuagl *Almeida Garrett*	
CS-TTM	Airbus A.319-111	TAP - Air Portugal *Alexandre Herculano*	
CS-TTN	Airbus A.319-111	TAP - Air Portugal *Camilo Castelo Branco*	
CS-TTO	Airbus A.319-111	TAP - Air Portugal *Antero de Quental*	
CS-TTP	Airbus A.319-111	TAP - Air Portugal	

CU (Cuba)

CU-T1208	Ilyushin IL-62M	Cubana *Capt Wifredo Perez*	
CU-T1209	Ilyushin IL-62M	Cubana	
CU-T1215	Ilyushin IL-62M	Cubana	
CU-T1216	Ilyushin IL-62M	Cubana	
CU-T1217	Ilyushin IL-62M	Cubana	
CU-T1218	Ilyushin IL-62M	Cubana	
CU-T1225	Ilyushin IL-62M	Cubana	
CU-T1259	Ilyushin IL-62M	Cubana	
CU-T1280	Ilyushin IL-62M	Cubana	
CU-T1282	Ilyushin IL-62M	Cubana	
CU-T1283	Ilyushin IL-62M	Cubana	
CU-T1284	Iluushin IL-62M	Cubana	

Note: AOM French Airlines operate European flights for Cubana using DC-10-30s.

D2 (Angola)

D2-TOK	Boeing 707-324C	Angola Air Charter	
D2-TOL	Boeing 707-347C	Angola Air Charter	
D2-TON	Boeing 707-324C	Angola Air Charter	
D2-TOP	Boeing 707-382B	TAAG Angola Airlines	
D2-	Boeing 707-312 (SCD)	TAAG Angola Airlines	

D (Germany)

D-AAAC	F.27 Friendship Mk 500	Express Airways	
D-AAMS	Airbus A.320-231	Fly FTI (G-EPFR)	
D-ABAB	Boeing 737-4K5	Air Berlin	
D-ABAC	Boeing 737-86J	Air Berlin	
D-ABAH	Boeing 737-46J	Air Berlin	
D-ABAI	Boeing 737-46J	Air Berlin	
D-ABAK	Boeing 737-46J	Air Berlin	
D-ABAL	Boeing 737-46J	Air Berlin	
D-ABAM	Boeing 737-46J	Air Berlin	
D-ABAN	Boeing 737-86J	Air Berlin	
D-ABAO	Boeing 737-86J	Air Berlin	
D-ABAP	Boeing 737-86J	Air Berlin	
D-ABAQ	Boeing 737-86J	Air Berlin	
D-ABAR	Boeing 737-86J	Air Berlin	
D-ABAS	Boeing 737-86J	Air Berlin	
D-ABAT	Boeing 737-86J	Air Berlin	
D-ABAU	Boeing 737-86J	Air Berlin	
D-ABAV	Boeing 737-86J	Air Berlin	
D-ABAW	Boeing 737-86J	Air Berlin	
D-ABAX	Boeing 737-86J	Air Berlin	
D-ABAY	Boeing 737-86J	Air Berlin	
D-ABAZ	Boeing 737-86J	Air Berlin	
D-ABEA	Boeing 737-330	Lufthansa *Saarbrücken*	
D-ABEB	Boeing 737-330	Lufthansa *Xanten*	
D-ABEC	Boeing 737-330	Lufthansa *Karlsrühe*	
D-ABED	Boeing 737-330	Lufthansa *Hagen*	
D-ABEE	Boeing 737-330	Lufthansa *Ulm*	
D-ABEF	Boeing 737-330	Lufthansa *Eeiden i.d Opf*	
D-ABEH	Boeing 737-330	Lufthansa *Bad Kissingen*	
D-ABEI	Boeing 737-330	Lufthansa *Bamberg*	
D-ABEK	Boeing 737-330	Lufthansa *Wuppertal*	

Notes	Reg.	Type	Owner or Operator
	D-ABEL	Boeing 737-330	Lufthansa *Pforzheim*
	D-ABEM	Boeing 737-330	Lufthansa *Eberswalde*
	D-ABEN	Boeing 737-330	Lufthansa *Neubrandenburg*
	D-ABEO	Boeing 737-330	Lufthansa *Plauen*
	D-ABEP	Boeing 737-330	Lufthansa *Naumburg (Saale)*
	D-ABER	Boeing 737-330	Lufthansa *Merseburg*
	D-ABES	Boeing 737-330	Lufthansa *Koethen/Anhalt*
	D-ABET	Boeing 737-330	Lufthansa *Gelsenkirchen*
	D-ABEU	Boeing 737-330	Lufthansa *Goslar*
	D-ABEW	Boeing 737-330	Lufthansa *Detmold*
	D-ABIA	Boeing 737-530	Lufthansa *Greifswald*
	D-ABIB	Boeing 737-530	Lufthansa *Esslingen*
	D-ABIC	Boeing 737-530	Lufthansa *Krefeld*
	D-ABID	Boeing 737-530	Lufthansa *Aachen*
	D-ABIE	Boeing 737-530	Lufthansa *Hildesheim*
	D-ABIF	Boeing 737-530	Lufthansa *Landau*
	D-ABIH	Boeing 737-530	Lufthansa *Bruchsal*
	D-ABII	Boeing 737-530	Lufthansa *Lörrach*
	D-ABIK	Boeing 737-530	Lufthansa *Rastatt*
	D-ABIL	Boeing 737-530	Lufthansa *Memmingen*
	D-ABIM	Boeing 737-530	Lufthansa *Salzgitter*
	D-ABIN	Boeing 737-530	Lufthansa *Langenhagen*
	D-ABIO	Boeing 737-530	Lufthansa *Wesel*
	D-ABIP	Boeing 737-530	Lufthansa *Oberhausen*
	D-ABIR	Boeing 737-530	Lufthansa *Anklam*
	D-ABIS	Boeing 737-530	Lufthansa *Rendsburg*
	D-ABIT	Boeing 737-530	Lufthansa *Neumünster*
	D-ABIU	Boeing 737-530	Lufthansa *Limburg a.d. Lahn*
	D-ABIW	Boeing 737-530	Lufthansa *Bad Nauheim*
	D-ABIX	Boeing 737-530	Lufthansa *Iserlohn*
	D-ABIY	Boeing 737-530	Lufthansa *Lingen*
	D-ABIZ	Boeing 737-530	Lufthansa *Kirchheim unter Teck*
	D-ABJA	Boeing 737-530	Lufthansa *Bad Segeberg*
	D-ABJB	Boeing 737-530	Lufthansa *Rheine*
	D-ABJC	Boeing 737-530	Lufthansa *Erding*
	D-ABJD	Boeing 737-530	Lufthansa *Freising*
	D-ABJE	Boeing 737-530	Lufthansa *Ingelheim am Rhein*
	D-ABJF	Boeing 737-530	Lufthansa *Aalen*
	D-ABJH	Boeing 737-530	Lufthansa *Heppenheim/Bergstrasse*
	D-ABJI	Boeing 737-530	Lufthansa *Siegburg*
	D-ABNA	Boeing 757-230	Condor Flugdienst
	D-ABNB	Boeing 757-230	Condor Flugdienst
	D-ABNC	Boeing 757-230	Condor Flugdienst
	D-ABND	Boeing 757-230	Condor Flugdienst
	D-ABNE	Boeing 757-230	Condor Flugdienst
	D-ABNF	Boeing 757-230	Condor Flugdienst
	D-ABNH	Boeing 757-230	Condor Flugdienst
	D-ABNI	Boeing 757-230	Condor Flugdienst
	D-ABNK	Boeing 757-230	Condor Flugdienst
	D-ABNL	Boeing 757-230	Condor Flugdienst
	D-ABNM	Boeing 757-230	Condor Flugdienst
	D-ABNN	Boeing 757-230	Condor Flugdienst
	D-ABNO	Boeing 757-230	Condor Flugdienst
	D-ABNP	Boeing 757-230	Condor Flugdienst
	D-ABNR	Boeing 757-230	Condor Flugdienst
	D-ABNS	Boeing 757-230	Condor Flugdienst
	D-ABNT	Boeing 757-230	Condor Flugdienst
	D-ABNX	Boeing 757-230	Condor Flugdienst
	D-ABOA	Boeing 757-330	Condor Flugdienst
	D-ABOB	Boeing 757-330	Condor Flugdienst
	D-ABOC	Boeing 757-330	Condor Flugdienst
	D-ABOE	Boeing 757-330	Condor Flugdienst
	D-ABOF	Boeing 757-330	Condor Flugdienst
	D-ABOG	Boeing 757-330	Condor Flugdienst
	D-ABOH	Boeing 757-330	Condor Flugdienst
	D-ABOI	Boeing 757-330	Condor Flugdienst
	D-ABOJ	Boeing 757-330	Condor Flugdienst
	D-ABOK	Boeing 757-330	Condor Flugdienst
	D-ABOL	Boeing 757-330	Condor Flugdienst
	D-ABOM	Boeing 757-330	Condor Flugdienst
	D-ABON	Boeing 757-330	Condor Flugdienst
	D-ABTA	Boeing 747-430 (SCD)	Lufthansa *Sachsen*
	D-ABTB	Boeing 747-430 (SCD)	Lufthansa *Brandenburg*

Reg.	Type	Owner or Operator	Notes
D-ABTC	Boeing 747-430 (SCD)	Lufthansa *Mecklenburg-Verpommern*	
D-ABTD	Boeing 747-430 (SCD)	Lufthansa/Condor Flugdienst *Hamburg*	
D-ABTE	Boeing 747-430 (SCD)	Lufthansa *Sachsen-Anhalt*	
D-ABTF	Boeing 747-430 (SCD)	Lufthansa *Thüringen*	
D-ABTH	Boeing 747-430 (SCD)	Lufthansa *Duisburg*	
D-ABUA	Boeing 767-330ER	Condor Flugdienst	
D-ABUB	Boeing 767-330ER	Condor Flugdienst	
D-ABUC	Boeing 767-330ER	Condor Flugdienst/Lufthansa	
D-ABUD	Boeing 767-330ER	Condor Flugdienst	
D-ABUE	Boeing 767-330ER	Condor Flugdienst	
D-ABUF	Boeing 767-330ER	Condor Flugdienst	
D-ABUH	Boeing 767-330ER	Condor Flugdienst	
D-ABUI	Boeing 767-330ER	Condor Flugdienst	
D-ABUZ	Boeing 767-330ER	Condor Flugdienst	
D-ABVA	Boeing 747-430	Lufthansa *Berlin*	
D-ABVB	Boeing 747-430	Lufthansa *Bonn*	
D-ABVC	Boeing 747-430	Lufthansa *Baden-Württemberg*	
D-ABVD	Boeing 747-430	Lufthansa *Bochum*	
D-ABVE	Boeing 747-430	Lufthansa *Potsdam*	
D-ABVF	Boeing 747-430	Lufthansa *Frankfurt am Main*	
D-ABVG	Boeing 747-430	Lufthansa	
D-ABVH	Boeing 747-430	Lufthansa *Düsseldorf*	
D-ABVK	Boeing 747-430	Lufthansa *Hannover*	
D-ABVL	Boeing 747-430	Lufthansa *Muenchen*	
D-ABVM	Boeing 747-430	Lufthansa	
D-ABVN	Boeing 747-430	Lufthansa *Dortmund*	
D-ABVO	Boeing 747-430	Lufthansa *Mülheim a.d.Ruhr*	
D-ABVP	Boeing 747-430	Lufthansa	
D-ABVR	Boeing 747-430	Lufthansa	
D-ABVS	Boeing 747-430	Lufthansa	
D-ABVT	Boeing 747-430	Lufthansa	
D-ABVU	Boeing 747-430	Lufthansa	
D-ABVW	Boeing 747-430	Lufthansa *Wolfsburg*	
D-ABVX	Boeing 747-430	Lufthansa	
D-ABVY	Boeing 747-430	Lufthansa	
D-ABVZ	Boeing 747-430	Lufthansa	
D-ABWC	Boeing 737-330QC	Lufthansa	
D-ABWD	Boeing 737-330QC	Lufthansa *Westerland/Sylt*	
D-ABWE	Boeing 737-330QC	Lufthansa *Goerlitz*	
D-ABWF	Boeing 737-330F	Lufthansa *Rüdesheim am Rhein*	
D-ABWH	Boeing 737-330	Lufthansa *Rothenburg*	
D-ABXA	Boeing 737-330QC	Lufthansa *Giessen*	
D-ABXB	Boeing 737-330QC	Lufthansa *Passau*	
D-ABXC	Boeing 737-330QC	Lufthansa *Delmenhorst*	
D-ABXD	Boeing 737-330	Lufthansa	
D-ABXE	Boeing 737-330	Lufthansa *Hamm*	
D-ABXF	Boeing 737-330	Lufthansa *Minden*	
D-ABXH	Boeing 737-330	Lufthansa *Cuxhaven*	
D-ABXI	Boeing 737-330	Lufthansa *Berchtesgaden*	
D-ABXK	Boeing 737-330	Lufthansa *Ludwigsburg*	
D-ABXL	Boeing 737-330	Lufthansa *Neuss*	
D-ABXM	Boeing 737-330	Lufthansa *Herford*	
D-ABXN	Boeing 737-330	Lufthansa *Böblingen*	
D-ABXO	Boeing 737-330	Lufthansa *Schwäbisch-Gmünd*	
D-ABXP	Boeing 737-330	Lufthansa *Fulda*	
D-ABXR	Boeing 737-330	Lufthansa *Celle*	
D-ABXS	Boeing 737-330	Lufthansa *Sindelfingen*	
D-ABXT	Boeing 737-330	Lufthansa *Reutlingen*	
D-ABXU	Boeing 737-330	Lufthansa *Seeheim-Jugenheim*	
D-ABXW	Boeing 737-330	Lufthansa *Hanau*	
D-ABXX	Boeing 737-330	Lufthansa *Bad Homburg v.d. Höhe*	
D-ABXY	Boeing 737-330	Lufthansa *Hof*	
D-ABXZ	Boeing 737-330	Lufthansa *Bad Mergentheim*	
D-ABYM	Boeing 747-230B (SCD)	Lufthansa *Schleswig-Holstein*	
D-ABYO	Boeing 747-230F (SCD)	Lufthansa Cargo *America*	
D-ABYP	Boeing 747-230B	Lufthansa *Niedersachen*	
D-ABYQ	Boeing 747-230B	Lufthansa *Bremen*	
D-ABYR	Boeing 747-230B (SCD)	Lufthansa *Nordrhein-Westfalen*	
D-ABYT	Boeing 747-230F (SCD)	Lufthansa Cargo	
D-ABYU	Boeing 747-230F (SCD)	Lufthansa Cargo *Asia*	
D-ABYX	Boeing 747-230B (SCD)	Lufthansa *Köln*	
D-ABYY	Boeing 747-230F (SCD)	Lufthansa Cargo	
D-ABYZ	Boeing 747-230F (SCD)	Lufthansa Cargo	

Notes	Reg.	Type	Owner or Operator
	D-ABZA	Boeing 747-230F (SCD)	Lufthansa Cargo *Düsseldorf*
	D-ABZB	Boeing 747-230F (SCD)	Lufthansa Cargo *New York*
	D-ABZC	Boeing 747-230F (SCD)	Lufthansa Cargo
	D-ABZD	Boeing 747-230B	Lufthansa *Kiel*
	D-ABZE	Boeing 747-230B (SCD)	Lufthansa *Stuttgart*
	D-ABZF	Boeing 747-230F (SCD)	Lufthansa Cargo *Africa*
	D-ABZH	Boeing 747-230B	Lufthansa *Bonn*
	D-ABZI	Boeing 747-230F (SCD)	Lufthansa Cargo *Australia*
	D-ACAF	Airbus A.320-231	Fly FTI
	D-ACCS	F.27 Friendship Mk 500	ECCS Air Cargo Service
	D-ACCT	F.27 Friendship Mk 500	Skyteam
	D-ACFA	BAe 146-200	Eurowings
	D-ACJA	Canadair CL.600-2B19 RJ	Lufthansa CityLine
	D-ACJB	Canadair CL.600-2B19 RJ	Lufthansa CityLine
	D-ACJC	Canadair CL.600-2B19 RJ	Lufthansa CityLine
	D-ACJD	Canadair CL.600-2B19 RJ	Lufthansa CityLine
	D-ACJE	Canadair CL.600-2B19 RJ	Lufthansa CityLine
	D-ACJF	Canadair CL.600-2B19 RJ	Lufthansa CityLine
	D-ACJG	Canadair CL.600-2B19 RJ	Lufthansa CityLine
	D-ACJH	Canadair CL.600-2B19 RJ	Lufthansa CityLine
	D-ACJI	Canadair CL.600-2B19 RJ	Lufthansa CityLine
	D-ACJJ	Canadair CL.600-2B19 RJ	Lufthansa CityLine
	D-ACJK	Canadair CL.600-2B19 RJ	Lufthansa CityLine
	D-ACJL	Canadair CL.600-2B19 RJ	Lufthansa CityLine
	D-ACJM	Canadair CL.600-2B19 RJ	Lufthansa CityLine
	D-ACJN	Canadair CL.600-2B19 RJ	Lufthansa CityLine
	D-ACJO	Canadair CL.600-2B19 RJ	Luthansa City Line
	D-ACJP	Canadair CL.600-2B19 RJ	Lufthansa CityLine
	D-ACJQ	Canadair CL.600-2B19 RJ	Lufthansa CityLine
	D-ACJR	Canadair CL.600-2B19 RJ	Lufthansa CityLine
	D-ACJS	Canadair CL.600-2B19 RJ	Lufthansa CityLine
	D-ACJT	Canadair CL.600-2B19 RJ	Lufthansa CityLine
	D-ACLA	Canadair CL.600-2B19 RJ	Lufthansa CityLine
	D-ACLB	Canadair CL.600-2B19 RJ	Lufthansa CityLine
	D-ACLC	Canadair CL.600-2B19 RJ	Lufthansa CityLine
	D-ACLD	Canadair CL.600-2B19 RJ	Lufthansa CityLine
	D-ACLE	Canadair CL.600-2B19 RJ	Lufthansa CityLine
	D-ACLF	Canadair CL.600-2B19 RJ	Lufthansa CityLine
	D-ACLG	Canadair CL.600-2B19 RJ	Lufthansa CityLine
	D-ACLH	Canadair CL.600-2B19 RJ	Lufthansa CityLine
	D-ACLI	Canadair CL.600-2B19 RJ	Lufthansa CityLine
	D-ACLJ	Canadair CL.600-2B19 RJ	Lufthansa CityLine
	D-ACLK	Canadair CL.600-2B19 RJ	Lufthansa CityLine
	D-ACLL	Canadair CL.600-2B19 RJ	Lufthansa CityLine
	D-ACLM	Canadair CL.600-2B19 RJ	Lufthansa CityLine
	D-ACLN	Canadiar CL.600-2B19 RJ	Lufthansa CityLine
	D-ACLO	Canadair CL.600-2B19 RJ	Lufthansa CityLine
	D-ACLP	Canadair CL.600-2B19 RJ	Lufthansa CityLine
	D-ACLQ	Canadair CL.600-2B19 RJ	Lufthansa CityLine
	D-ACLR	Canadair CL.600-2B19 RJ	Lufthansa CityLine
	D-ACLS	Canadair CL.600-2B19 RJ	Lufthansa CityLine
	D-ACLT	Canadiar CL.600-2B19 RJ	Lufthansa CityLine
	D-ACLU	Canadiar CL.600-2B19 RJ	Lufthansa CityLine
	D-ACLV	Canadair CL.600-2B19 RJ	Lufthansa CityLine
	D-ACLW	Canadair CL.600-2B19 RJ	Lufthansa CityLine
	D-ACLX	Canadiar CL.600-2B19 RJ	Lufthansa CityLine
	D-ACLY	Canadair CL.600-2B19 RJ	Lufthansa CityLine
	D-ACLZ	Canadiar CL.600-2B19 RJ	Lufthansa CityLine
	D-ADBH	Boeing 737-3L9	Deutsche BA
	D-ADBI	Boeing 737-3L9	Deutsche BA
	D-ADBK	Boeing 737-31S	Deutsche BA
	D-ADBL	Boeing 737-31S	Deutsche BA
	D-ADBM	Boeing 737-31S	Deutsche BA
	D-ADBN	Boeing 737-31S	Deutsche BA
	D-ADBO	Boeing 737-31S	Deutsche BA
	D-ADBP	Boeing 737-31S	Deutsche BA
	D-ADBQ	Boeing 737-31S	Deutsche BA
	D-ADBR	Boeing 737-31S	Deutsche BA
	D-ADBS	Boeing 737-31S	Deutsche BA
	D-ADBT	Boeing 737-31S	Deutsche BA
	D-ADBU	Boeing 737-31S	Deutsche BA
	D-ADBV	Boeing 737-31S	Deutsche BA
	D-ADBW	Boeing 737-31S	Deutsche BA

Reg.	Type	Owner or Operator	Notes
D-ADEP	F.27 Friendship Mk 600	WDL	
D-ADIA	Boeing 737-36Q	Deutsche BA	
D-ADIB	Boeing 737-36Q	Deutsche BA *Enzian*	
D-ADIC	Boeing 737-36Q	Deutsche BA	
D-ADOP	F.27 Friendship Mk 600	WDL	
D-ADUP	F.27 Friendship Mk 500	Sky Team	
D-AELC	F.27 Friendship Mk 600	WDL	
D-AELD	F.27 Friendship Mk 600	WDL	
D-AELE	F.27 Friendship Mk 600	WDL	
D-AELF	F.27 Friendship Mk 600	WDL	
D-AELG	F.27 Friendship Mk 600	WDL	
D-AELH	F.27 Friendship Mk 600	WDL	
D-AELI	F.27 Friendship Mk 600	WDL	
D-AELJ	F.27 Friendship Mk 600	WDL	
D-AELK	F.27 Friendship Mk 600	WDL	
D-AELM	F.27 Friendship Mk 600	WDL	
D-AERD	Airbus A.330-322	LTU	
D-AERF	Airbus A.330-322	LTU	
D-AERG	Airbus A.330-322	LTU	
D-AERH	Airbus A.330-322	LTU	
D-AERK	Airbus A.330-322	LTU	
D-AERQ	Airbus A.330-322	LTU	
D-AERS	Airbus A.330-322	LTU	
D-AEWA	BAe 146-300	Eurowings	
D-AEWB	BAe 146-300	Eurowings	
D-AEWD	BAe 146-200	Eurowings/Air France Express	
D-AEWE	BAe 146-200	Eurowings/Air France Express	
D-AEWG	Aérospatiale ATR-72-212	Eurowings	
D-AEWH	Aérospatiale ATR-72-212	Eurowings	
D-AEWI	Aérospatiale ATR-72-212	Eurowings	
D-AEWK	Aérospatiale ATR-72-212	Eurowings	
D-AEWL	Aérospatiale ATR-72-212	Eurowings	
D-AFFI	Fokker 50	Contactair/Team Lufthansa	
D-AFFX	Fokker 50	Contactair/Team Lufthansa	
D-AFFY	Fokker 50	Contactair/Team Lufthansa	
D-AFFZ	Fokker 50	Contactair/Team Lufthansa	
D-AFKK	Fokker 50	Contactair/Team Lufthansa	
D-AFKL	Fokker 50	Contactair/Team Lufthansa	
D-AFKM	Fokker 50	Contactair/Team Lufthansa	
D-AFKN	Fokker 50	Contactair/Team Lufthansa	
D-AFKO	Fokker 50	Contactair/Team Lufthansa	
D-AFKP	Fokker 50	Contactair/Team Lufthansa	
D-AFKU	Fokker 50	Contactair/Team Lufthansa	
D-AFRO	Airbus A.320-231	Fly FTI	
D-AFTI	Airbus A.320-231	Fly FTI	
D-AGEJ	Boeing 737-3L9	Germania	
D-AGEK	Boeing 737-3M8	Germania	
D-AGEL	Boeing 737-75B	Germania	
D-AGEM	Boeing 737-75B	Germania	
D-AGEN	Boeing 737-75B	Germania	
D-AGEO	Boeing 737-75B	Germania	
D-AGEP	Boeing 737-75B	Germania	
D-AGEQ	Boeing 737-75B	Germania	
D-AGER	Boeing 737-75B	Germania	
D-AGES	Boeing 737-75B	Germania	
D-AGET	Boeing 737-75B	Germania	
D-AGEU	Boeing 737-75B	Germania	
G-AGEV	Boeing 737-75B	Germania	
D-AGEW	Boeing 737-75B	Germania	
D-AGEY	Boeing 737-73S	Germania	
D-AGEZ	Boeing 737-73S	Germania§	
D-AGWB	McD Douglas MD-83	Aero Lloyd	
D-AGYA	Boeing 767-304ER	Britannia Airways Deutsche/Britannia Airways (G-OBYA)	
D-AGYE	Boeing 767-304ER	Britannia Airways Deutsche/Britannia Airways (G-OBYE)	
D-AGYF	Boeing 767-304ER	Britannia Airways Deutsche/Britannia Airways (G-OBYF)	
D-AGYH	Boeing 767-304ER	Britannia Airways Deutsche/Britannia Airways (G-OBYH)	
D-AHFA	Boeing 737-8K5	Hapag-Lloyd	
D-AHFB	Boeing 737-8K5	Hapag-Lloyd	
D-AHFC	Boeing 737-8K5	Hapag-Lloyd	

Notes	Reg.	Type	Owner or Operator
	D-AHFD	Boeing 737-8K5	Hapag-Lloyd
	D-AHFE	Boeing 737-8K5	Hapag-Lloyd
	D-AHFF	Boeing 737-8K5	Hapag-Lloyd
	D-AHFG	Boeing 737-8K5	Hapag-Lloyd
	D-AHFH	Boeing 737-8K5	Hapag-Lloyd
	D-AHFI	Boeing 737-8K5	Hapag-Lloyd
	D-AHFJ	Boeing 737-8K5	Hapag-Lloyd
	D-AHFK	Boeing 737-8K5	Hapag-Lloyd
	D-AHFL	Boeing 737-8K5	Hapag-Lloyd
	D-AHFM	Boeing 737-8K5	Hapag-Lloyd
	D-AHFN	Boeing 737-8K5	Hapag-Lloyd
	D-AHFO	Boeing 737-8K5	Hapag-Lloyd
	D-AHFP	Boeing 737-8K5	Hapag-Lloyd
	D-AHFQ	Boeing 737-8K5	Hapag-Lloyd
	D-AHLA	Airbus A.310-304	Hapag-Lloyd
	D-AHLB	Airbus A.310-304	Hapag-Lloyd
	D-AHLC	Airbus A.310-308	Hapag-Lloyd
	D-AHLF	Boeing 737-5K5	Hapag-Lloyd
	D-AHLG	Boeing 737-4K5	Hapag-Lloyd
	D-AHLI	Boeing 737-5K5	Hapag-Lloyd
	D-AHLJ	Boeing 737-4K5	Hapag-Lloyd
	D-AHLK	Boeing 737-4K5	Hapag-Lloyd
	D-AHLL	Boeing 737-4K5	Hapag-Lloyd
	D-AHLM	Boeing 737-4K5	Hapag-Lloyd
	D-AHLN	Boeing 737-5K5	Hapag-Lloyd
	D-AHLO	Boeing 737-4K5	Hapag-Lloyd
	D-AHLS	Boeing 737-4K5	Hapag-Lloyd
	D-AHLT	Boeing 737-4K5	Hapag-Lloyd
	D-AHLU	Boeing 737-4K5	Hapag-Lloyd
	D-AHLV	Airbus A.310-204	Hapag-Lloyd
	D-AHLW	Airbus A.310-204	Hapag-Lloyd
	D-AHLX	Airbus A.310-204	Hapag-Lloyd
	D-AHLZ	Airbus A.310-204	Hapag-Lloyd
	D-AHOI	BAe 146-300	Eurowings
	D-AIAH	Airbus A.300-603	Lufthansa *Lindau/Bodensee*
	D-AIAI	Airbus A.300-603	Lufthansa *Erbach/Odenwald*
	D-AIAK	Airbus A.300-603	Lufthansa *Kronberg/Taunus*
	D-AIAL	Airbus A.300-603	Lufthansa *Stade*
	D-AIAM	Airbus A.300-603	Lufthansa *Rosenheim*
	D-AIAN	Airbus A.300-603	Lufthansa *Nördlingen*
	D-AIAP	Airbus A.300-603	Lufthansa *Donauwörth*
	D-AIAR	Airbus A.300-603	Lufthansa *Bingen am Rhein*
	D-AIAS	Airbus A.300-603	Lufthansa *Mönchengladbach*
	D-AIAT	Airbus A.300-603	Lufthansa *Bottrop*
	D-AIAU	Airbus A.300-603	Lufthansa *Bocholt*
	D-AIAW	Airbus A.300-605R	Lufthansa *Witten*
	D-AIAX	Airbus A.300-605R	Lufthansa *Fürth*
	D-AIBA	Airbus A.340-211	Lufthansa *Neurnberg*
	D-AIBC	Airbus A.340-211	Lufthansa *Leverkusen*
	D-AIBD	Airbus A.340-211	Lufthansa *Essen*
	D-AIBE	Airbus A.340-211	Lufthansa *Stuttgart*
	D-AIBF	Airbus A.340-211	Lufthansa *Luebeck*
	D-AIBH	Airbus A.340-211	Lufthansa *Bremerhaven*
	D-AICA	Airbus A.320-212	Condor Berlin
	D-AICB	Airbus A.320-212	Condor Berlin
	D-AICC	Airbus A.320-212	Condor Berlin
	D-AICD	Airbus A.320-212	Condor Berlin
	D-AICE	Airbus A.320-212	Condor Berlin
	D-AICF	Airbus A.320-212	Condor Berlin
	D-AICG	Airbus A.320-212	Condor Berlin
	D-AICH	Airbus A.320-212	Condor Berlin
	D-AICI	Airbus A.320-212	Condor Berlin
	D-AICJ	Airbus A.320-212	Condor Berlin
	D-AIDD	Airbus A.310-304	Lufthansa *Emden*
	D-AIDF	Airbus A.310-304	Lufthansa *Aschaffenburg*
	D-AIDH	Airbus A.310-304	Lufthansa *Wetzlar*
	D-AIDL	Airbus A.310-304	Lufthansa *Obersdorf*
	D-AIGA	Airbus A.340-311	Lufthansa *Oldenburg*
	D-AIGB	Airbus A.340-311	Lufthansa *Recklinghausen*
	D-AIGC	Airbus A.340-311	Lufthansa *Wilhelmshaven*
	D-AIGD	Airbus A.340-311	Lufthansa *Remscheid*
	D-AIGE	Airbus A.340-313	Lufthansa
	D-AIGF	Airbus A.340-311	Lufthansa *Gottingen*

Reg.	Type	Owner or Operator	Notes
D-AIGG	Airbus A.340-313	Lufthansa	
D-AIGH	Airbus A.340-311	Lufthansa *Koblenz*	
D-AIGI	Airbus A.340-311	Lufthansa *Worms*	
D-AIGK	Airbus A.340-311	Lufthansa *Bayreuth*	
D-AIGL	Airbus A.340-313	Lufthansa *Herne*	
D-AIGM	Airbus A.340-313	Lufthansa *Wolfsburg*	
D-AIGN	Airbus A.340-313	Lufthansa	
D-AIGO	Airbus A.340-313	Lufthansa	
D-AIGP	Airbus A.340-313	Lufthansa	
D-AIGR	Airbus A.340-313	Lufthansa	
D-AIGS	Airbus A.340-313	Lufthansa	
D-AIGT	Airbus A.340-313	Lufthansa	
D-AIGU	Airbus A.340-313	Lufthansa	
D-AIGV	Airbus A.340-313	Lufthansa	
D-AIGW	Airbus A.340-313	Lufthansa	
D-AIGX	Airbus A.340-313	Lufthansa	
D-AIGY	Airbus A.340-313	Lufthansa	
D-AIGZ	Airbus A.340-313	Lufthansa	
D-AILA	Airbus A.319-114	Lufthansa *Frankfurt (Oder)*	
D-AILB	Airbus A.319-114	Lufthansa *Lutherstadt Wittenburg*	
D-AILC	Airbus A.319-114	Lufthansa *Russelsheim*	
D-AILD	Airbus A.319-114	Lufthansa *Dinkelsbühl*	
D-AILE	Airbus A.319-114	Lufthansa *Kelsterbach*	
D-AILF	Airbus A.319-114	Lufthansa *Trier*	
D-AILH	Airbus A.319-114	Lufthansa *Norderstedt*	
D-AILI	Airbus A.319-114	Lufthansa *Ingolstadt*	
D-AILK	Airbus A.319-114	Lufthansa *Landshut*	
D-AILL	Airbus A.319-114	Lufthansa *Marburg*	
D-AILM	Airbus A.319-114	Lufthansa *Friedrichshafen*	
D-AILN	Airbus A.319-114	Lufthansa *Idar-Oberstein*	
D-AILP	Airbus A.319-114	Lufthansa *Tubingen*	
D-AILR	Airbus A.319-114	Lufthansa *Tegernsee*	
D-AILS	Airbus A.319-114	Lufthansa *Heide*	
D-AILT	Airbus A.319-114	Lufthansa *Straubing*	
D-AILU	Airbus A.319-114	Lufthansa *Verden*	
D-AILW	Airbus A.319-114	Lufthansa *Donaueschingen*	
D-AILX	Airbus A.319-114	Lufthansa *Fellbach*	
D-AILY	Airbus A.319-114	Lufthansa *Schweinfurt*	
D-AIPA	Airbus A.320-211	Lufthansa *Buxtehude*	
D-AIPB	Airbus A.320-211	Lufthansa *Heidelberg*	
D-AIPC	Airbus A.320-211	Lufthansa *Braunschweig*	
D-AIPD	Airbus A.320-211	Lufthansa *Freiburg*	
D-AIPE	Airbus A.320-211	Lufthansa *Kassel*	
D-AIPF	Airbus A.320-211	Lufthansa *Leipzig*	
D-AIPH	Airbus A.320-211	Lufthansa *Münster*	
D-AIPK	Airbus A.320-211	Lufthansa *Wiesbaden*	
D-AIPL	Airbus A.320-211	Lufthansa *Ludwigshafen am Rhein*	
D-AIPM	Airbus A.320-211	Lufthansa *Troisdorf*	
D-AIPP	Airbus A.320-211	Lufthansa *Starnberg*	
D-AIPR	Airbus A.320-211	Lufthansa *Kaufbeuren*	
D-AIPS	Airbus A.320-211	Lufthansa *Augsburg*	
D-AIPT	Airbus A.320-211	Lufthansa *Cottbus*	
D-AIPU	Airbus A.320-211	Lufthansa *Dresden*	
D-AIPW	Airbus A.320-211	Lufthansa *Schwerin*	
D-AIPX	Airbus A.320-211	Lufthansa *Mannheim*	
D-AIPY	Airbus A.320-211	Lufthansa *Magdeburg*	
D-AIPZ	Airbus A.320-211	Lufthansa *Erfurt*	
D-AIQA	Airbus A.320-211	Lufthansa *Mainz*	
D-AIQB	Airbus A.320-211	Lufthansa *Bielefeld*	
D-AIQC	Airbus A.320-211	Lufthansa *Zwickau*	
D-AIQD	Airbus A.320-211	Lufthansa *Jena*	
D-AIQE	Airbus A.320-211	Lufthansa *Gera*	
D-AIQF	Airbus A.320-211	Lufthansa *Halle a.d. Saale*	
D-AIQH	Airbus A.320-211	Lufthansa *Dessau*	
D-AIQK	Airbus A.320-211	Lufthansa *Rostock*	
D-AIQL	Airbus A.320-211	Lufthansa *Stralsund*	
D-AIQM	Airbus A.320-211	Lufthansa *Nordenham*	
D-AIQN	Airbus A.320-211	Lufthansa *Laupheim*	
D-AIQP	Airbus A.320-211	Lufthansa *Suhl*	
D-AIQR	Airbus A.320-211	Lufthansa *Lahr/Schwarzwald*	
D-AIQS	Airbus A.320-211	Lufthansa *Eisenach*	
D-AIRA	Airbus A.321-131	Lufthansa *Finkenwerder*	
D-AIRB	Airbus A.321-131	Lufthansa *Baden-Baden*	

Notes	Reg.	Type	Owner or Operator
	D-AIRC	Airbus A.321-131	Lufthansa *Erlangen*
	D-AIRD	Airbus A.321-131	Lufthansa *Coburg*
	D-AIRE	Airbus A.321-131	Lufthansa *Osnabrueck*
	D-AIRF	Airbus A.321-131	Lufthansa *Kempten*
	D-AIRH	Airbus A.321-131	Lufthansa *Garmisch-Partenkirchen*
	D-AIRK	Airbus A.321-131	Lufthansa *Freudenstadt/Schwarzwald*
	D-AIRL	Airbus A.321-131	Lufthansa *Kulmbach*
	D-AIRM	Airbus A.321-131	Lufthansa *Darmstadt*
	D-AIRN	Airbus A.321-131	Lufthansa *Kaiserslautern*
	D-AIRO	Airbus A.321-131	Lufthansa *Konstanz*
	D-AIRP	Airbus A.321-131	Lufthansa *Lüneburg*
	D-AIRR	Airbus A.321-131	Lufthansa *Wismar*
	D-AIRS	Airbus A.321-131	Lufthansa *Husum*
	D-AIRT	Airbus A.321-131	Lufthansa *Regensburg*
	D-AIRU	Airbus A.321-131	Lufthansa *Würzburg*
	D-AIRW	Airbus A.321-131	Lufthansa *Heilbronn*
	D-AIRX	Airbus A.321-131	Lufthansa *Weimar*
	D-AIRY	Airbus A.321-131	Lufthansa *Flensburg*
	D-AISB	Airbus A.321-231	Lufthansa *Hameln*
	D-AISC	Airbus A.321-231	Lufthansa
	D-AISD	Airbus A.321-231	Lufthansa
	D-AISE	Airbus A.321-231	Lufthansa
	D-AISF	Airbus A.321-231	Lufthansa
	D-AISG	Airbus A.321-231	Lufthansa
	D-AISY	F.27 Friendship Mk 600	WDL
	D-AJET	BAe 146-200	Eurowings
	D-AKNF	Airbus A.319-112	Eurowings *Albrecht Durer*
	D-AKNG	Airbus A.319-112	Eurowings *Johan Wolfgang von Goethe*
	D-AKNH	Airbus A.319-112	Eurowings *Heinrich Heine*
	D-AKNI	Airbus A.319-112	Eurowings *Johannes Gutenburg*
	D-AKNJ	Airbus A.319-112	Eurowings
	D-AKNK	Airbus A.319-112	Eurowings
	D-ALAA	Airbus A.320-232	Aero Lloyd
	D-ALAB	Airbus A.320-232	Aero Lloyd
	D-ALAD	Airbus A.320-232	Aero Lloyd
	D-ALAE	Airbus A.320-232	Aero Lloyd
	D-ALAF	Airbus A.320-232	Aero Lloyd
	D-ALAG	Airbus A.321-231	Aero Lloyd *Stadt Linz*
	D-ALAH	Airbus A.321-231	Aero Lloyd
	D-ALAI	Airbus A.321-231	Aero Lloyd
	D-ALAJ	Airbus A.320-232	Aero Lloyd
	D-ALAK	Airbus A.321-231	Aero Lloyd
	D-A	Airbus A.321-231	Aero Lloyd
	D-A	Airbus A.321-231	Aero Lloyd
	D-A	Airbus A.321-231	Aero Lloyd
	D-ALCA	McD Douglas MD-11F	Lufthansa Cargo
	D-ALCB	McD Douglas MD-11F	Lufthansa Cargo
	D-ALCC	McD Douglas MD-11F	Lufthansa Cargo
	D-ALCD	McD Douglas MD-11F	Lufthansa Cargo
	D-ALCE	McD Douglas MD-11F	Lufthansa Cargo
	D-ALCF	McD Douglas MD-11F	Lufthansa Cargo
	D-ALCG	McD Douglas MD-11F	Lufthansa Cargo
	D-ALCH	McD Douglas MD-11F	Lufthansa Cargo
	D-ALCI	McD Douglas MD-11F	Lufthansa Cargo
	D-ALCJ	McD Douglas MD-11F	Lufthansa Cargo
	D-ALCK	McD Douglas MD-11F	Lufthansa Cargo
	D-ALCL	McD Douglas MD-11F	Lufthansa Cargo
	D-ALCM	McD Douglas MD-11F	Lufthansa Cargo
	D-ALCN	McD Douglas MD-11F	Lufthansa Cargo
	D-ALLE	McD Douglas MD-83	Aero Lloyd
	D-ALLF	McD Douglas MD-83	Aero Lloyd
	D-ALLO	McD Douglas MD-83	Aero Lloyd
	D-ALLQ	McD Douglas MD-83	Aero Lloyd
	D-ALLR	McD Douglas MD-83	Aero Lloyd
	D-ALLV	McD Douglas MD-83	Aero Lloyd
	D-ALOA	BAe 146-200	Eurowings
	D-ALTA	Airbus A.320-232	LTU
	D-AMUA	Boeing 757-2G5	LTU
	D-AMUB	Boeing 757-2G5	LTU
	D=AMUC	Boeing 757-2G5	LTU
	D-AMUG	Boeing 757-2G5	LTU
	D-AMUH	Boeing 757-2G5	LTU
	D-AMUI	Boeing 757-2G5	LTU

Reg.	Type	Owner or Operator	Notes
D-AMUJ	Boeing 767-3G5ER	LTU	
D-AMUK	Boeing 757-225	LTU	
D-AMUM	Boeing 757-2G5	LTU	
D-AMUN	Boeing 767-3G5ER	LTU	
D-AMUO	Boeing 767-3G5ER	LTU	
D-AMUP	Boeing 767-33AER	LTU	
D-AMUQ	Boeing 757-2G5	LTU	
D-AMUR	Boeing 767-3G5ER	LTU	
D-AMUS	Boeing 767-3G5ER	LTU	
D-AMUU	Boeing 757-225	LTU	
D-AMUV	Boeing 757-2G5	LTU	
D-AMUW	Boeing 757-2G5	LTU	
D-AMUX	Boeing 757-2G5	LTU	
D-AMUY	Boeing 757-2G5	LTU	
D-AMUZ	Boeing 757-2G5	LTU	
D-ANFA	Aérospatiale ATR-72-202	Eurowings	
D-ANFB	Aérospatiale ATR-72-202	Eurowings/Lufthansa	
D-ANFC	Aérospatiale ATR-72-202	Eurowings	
D-ANFD	Aérospatiale ATR-72-202	Eurowings/Lufthansa	
D-ANFE	Aérospatiale ATR-72-202	Eurowings	
D-ANFF	Aérospatiale ATR-72-202	Eurowings	
D-AOFM	Airbus A.320-212	Condor Flugdienst	
D-AOFN	Airbus A.320-212	Condor Flugdienst	
D-AOFP	Airbus A.320-212	Condor Flugdienst	
D-AOFQ	Airbus A.320-212	Condor Flugdienst	
D-AOFR	Airbus A.320-212	Condor Flugdienst	
D-AOFS	Airbus A.320-212	Condor Flugdienst	
D-AQUA	BAe 146-300	Eurowings	
D-AQUI	Junkers Ju.52/3m	Lufthansa Traditionsflug	
D-ASKH	Boeing 737-73S	Hamburg International	
D-ASRA	Airbus A.310-322	Hapag-Lloyd	
D-ASRB	Airbus A.310-322	Hapag-Lloyd/Air Kazakstan	
D-ASSR	Airbus A.320-231	Fly FTI	
D-AUKT	Airbus A.320-231	Fly FTI (G-BYTH)	
D-AVRA	Avro RJ85	Lufthansa CityLine	
D-AVRB	Avro RJ85	Lufthansa CityLine	
D-AVRC	Avro RJ85	Lufthansa CityLine	
D-AVRD	Avro RJ85	Lufthansa CityLine	
D-AVRE	Avro RJ85	Lufthansa CityLine	
D-AVRF	Avro RJ85	Lufthansa CityLine	
D-AVRG	Avro RJ85	Lufthansa CityLine	
D-AVRH	Avro RJ85	Lufthansa CityLine	
D-AVRI	Avro RJ85	Lufthansa CityLine	
D-AVRJ	Avro RJ85	Lufthansa CityLine	
D-AVRK	Avro RJ85	Lufthansa CityLine	
D-AVRL	Avro RJ85	Lufthansa CityLine	
D-AVRM	Avro RJ85	Lufthansa CityLine	
D-AVRN	Avro RJ85	Lufthansa CityLine	
D-AVRO	Avro RJ85	Lufthansa CityLine	
D-AVRP	Avro RJ85	Lufthansa CityLine	
D-AVRQ	Avro RJ85	Lufthansa CityLine	
D-AVRR	Avro RJ85	Lufthansa CityLine	
D-AWDL	BAe 146-100	WDL	
D-AWUE	BAe 146-200	WDL	
D-AZUR	BAe 146-200	Eurowings	
D-BAAA	Aérospatiale ATR-42-310	Filder Air Service	
D-BACH	D.H.C.8-311 Dash Eight	Augsburg Airways/Team Lufthansa	
D-BAGB	D.H.C.8-103 Dash Eight	Augsburg Airways/Team Lufthansa	
D-BAHL	D.H.C.8-202B Dash Eight	Augsburg Airways/Team Lufthansa	
D-BAKB	F.27 Friendship Mk 600	WDL	
D-BAKC	F.27 Friendship Mk 600	WDL	
D-BBBB	Aérospatiale ATR-42-310	Filder Air Service	
D-BCRO	Aérospatiale ATR-42-300QC	Eurowings	
D-BCRP	Aérospatiale ATR-42-300QC	Eurowings	
D-BCRQ	Aérospatiale ATR-42-300	Eurowings	
D-BCRR	Aérospatiale ATR-42-300	Eurowings	
D-BCRS	Aérospatiale ATR-42-300	Eurowings	
D-BCRT	Aérospatiale ATR-42-300	Eurowings	
D-BDUS	D.H.C.8-106 Dash Eight	Augsburg Airways/Team Lufthansa	
D-BHAL	D.H.C.8Q-202 Dash Eight	Augsburg Airways/Team Lufthansa	
D-BHAM	D.H.C.8-311 Dash Eight	Augsburg Airways/Team Lufthansa	
D-BHAS	D.H.C.8Q-311 Dash Eight	Augsburg Airways/Team Lufthansa	
D-BHAT	D.H.C.8Q-311 Dash Eight	Augsburg Airways/Team Lufthansa	

Notes	Reg.	Type	Owner or Operator
	D-BIER	D.H.C.8-102 Dash Eight	Augsburg Airways/Team Lufthansa
	D-BIRT	D.H.C.8-103 Dash Eight	Augsburg Airways
	D-BJJJ	Aérospatiale ATR-42-300	Eurowings
	D-BKIM	D.H.C.8-311 Dash Eight	Augsburg Airways/Team Lufthansa
	D-BKKK	Aérospatiale ATR-42-512	Eurowings
	D-BLEJ	D.H.C.8Q-314 Dash Eight	Augsburg Airways/Team Lufthansa
	D-BLLL	Aérospatiale ATR-42-512	Eurowings
	D-BMMM	Aérospatiale ATR-42-512	Eurowings
	D-BMUC	D.H.C.8-314 Dash Eight	Augsburg Airways
	D-BNNN	Aérospatiale ATR-42-512	Eurowings
	D-BOBL	D.H.C.8-102A Dash Eight	Cirrus Air
	D-BOBO	D.H.C.8-102 Dash Eight	Baden-Air
	D-BOBY	D.H.C.8-102 Dash Eight	Cirrus Air
	D-BOOO	Aérospatiale ATR-42-512	Eurowings
	D-BPAD	D.H.C.8Q-314 Dash Eight	Augsburg Airways/Team Lufthansa
	D-BPPP	Aérospatiale ATR-42-512	Eurowings
	D-BQQQ	Aérospatiale ATR-42-512	Eurowings
	D-BRRR	Aérospatiale ATR-42-512	Eurowings
	D-BSSS	Aérospatiale ATR-42-512	Eurowings
	D-BTHF	D.H.C.8-202 Dash Eight	Augsburg Airways/Team Lufthansa
	D-BTTT	Aérospatiale ATR-42-512	Eurowings
	D-CFAO	Short SD3-60 Variant 100	Farnair Europe/Federal Express
	D-CFDX	Short SD3-60 Variant 100	Farnair Europe/Federal Express
	D-CFXA	Short SD3-60 Variant 100	Farnair Europe/Federal Express
	D-CFXB	Short SD3-60 Variant 100	Farnair Europe/Federal Express
	D-CFXC	Short SD3-60 Variant 100	Farnair Europe/Federal Express
	D-CFXD	Short SD3-60 Variant 100	Farnair Europe/Federal Express
	D-CFXE	Short SD3-60 Variant 100	Farnair Europe/Federal Express
	D-CFXF	Short SD3-60 Variant 100	Farnair Europe/Federal Express
	D-CGAN	Dornier Do.328-100	Gandalf Airlines
	D-CGAO	Dornier Do.328-100	Gandalf Airlines
	D-CGAP	Dornier Do.328-100	Gandalf Airlines
	D-CNAF	Swearingen SA227AC Metro III	Northern Air Freight
	D-COLB	Swearingen SA227AC Metro III	OLT/Roland Air
	D-COLC	Swearingen SA227AC Metro III	OLT/Roland Air
	D-COLD	Swearingen SA227AC Metro III	OLT/Roland Air
	D-COLE	SAAB SF.340A	OLT/Roland Air
	D-COLT	Swearingen SA226AC Metro III	OLT/Roland Air
	D-COSA	Dornier Do.328-110	Cosmos Air
	D-CUTT	Dornier Do.228-212	Arcus Air
	D-IHCW	Swearingen SA226TC Metro II	OLT/Roland Air

EC (Spain)

	EC-BIH	Douglas DC-9-32	Iberia *Roncesvalles*
	EC-BIM	Douglas DC-9-32	Iberia *Ciudad de Santander*
	EC-BIP	Douglas DC-9-32	Iberia *Castillo de Monteagudo*
	EC-BIR	Douglas DC-9-32	Iberia *Ciudad de Valencia*
	EC-BQY	Douglas DC-9-32	Iberia *Mar Menor*
	EC-BQZ	Douglas DC-9-32	Iberia *Ciudad de sta Cruz de la Palma*
	EC-BYE	Douglas DC-9-32	Iberia *Cala Galdana*
	EC-BYF	Douglas DC-9-32	Iberia *Hernan Cortes*
	EC-BYI	Douglas DC-9-32	Iberia *Pedro de Valdivia*
	EC-BYJ	Douglas DC-9-32	Iberia
	EC-CBA	Boeing 727-256	Iberia *Vascongadas*
	EC-CBF	Boeing 727-256	Iberia *Gran Canaria*
	EC-CBG	Boeing 727-256	Iberia *Extremadura*
	EC-CBO	Douglas DC-10-30	Iberia *Costa del Sol*
	EC-CBP	Douglas DC-10-30	Iberia *Costa Dorada*
	EC-CEZ	Douglas DC-10-30	Iberia *Costa del Azahar*
	EC-CFA	Boeing 727-256	Iberia *Jerez Xeres Sherry*
	EC-CFB	Boeing 727-256	Iberia *Rioja*
	EC-CFD	Boeing 727-256	Iberia *Montilla-Moriles*
	EC-CFE	Boeing 727-256	Iberia *Penedes*
	EC-CFF	Boeing 727-256	Iberia *Valdepenas*
	EC-CFG	Boeing 727-256	Iberia *La Mancha*
	EC-CFH	Boeing 727-256	Iberia *Priorato*
	EC-CFI	Boeing 727-256	Iberia *Carinena*
	EC-CFK	Boeing 727-256	Iberia *Rivero*
	EC-CGN	Douglas DC-9-32	Iberia *Martin Alonso Pinzon*
	EC-CGO	Douglas DC-9-32	Iberia *Pedro Alonso Nino*
	EC-CGP	Douglas DC-9-32	Iberia *Juan Sebastian Elcano*

Reg.	Type	Owner or Operator	Notes
EC-CGQ	Douglas DC-9-32	Iberia *Alonso de Ojeda*	
EC-CGR	Douglas DC-9-32	Iberia *Francisco de Orellana*	
EC-CID	Boeing 727-256	Iberia *Malaga*	
EC-CIE	Boeing 727-256	Iberia *Esparragosa*	
EC-CLD	Douglas DC-9-32	Iberia *Hernando de Soto*	
EC-CTS	Douglas DC-9-34CF	Iberia *Francisco de Pizarro*	
EC-CTU	Douglas DC-9-34CF	Iberia *Pedro de Alvarado*	
EC-DCC	Boeing 727-256	Iberia *Albarino*	
EC-DCD	Boeing 727-256	Iberia *Chacoli*	
EC-DCE	Boeing 727-256	Iberia *Mentrida*	
EC-DDZ	Boeing 727-256	Iberia *Murallas de Avila*	
EC-DEA	Douglas DC-10-30	Iberia *Rias Gallegas*	
EC-DGC	Douglas DC-9-34	Iberia *Castillo de Sotomayor*	
EC-DGD	Douglas DC-9-34	Iberia *Castillo de Arcos*	
EC-DGE	Douglas DC-9-34	Iberia *Castillo de Bellver*	
EC-DHZ	Douglas DC-10-30	Iberia *Costas Canarias*	
EC-DIA	Boeing 747-256B	Iberia *Tirso de Molina*	
EC-DIB	Boeing 747-256B	Iberia *Cervantes*	
EC-DLC	Boeing 747-256B (SCD)	Iberia *Francisco de Quevedo*	
EC-DLD	Boeing 747-256B (SCD)	Iberia *Lupe de Vega*	
EC-DLF	Airbus A.300B4-120	Iberia *Canadas del Teide*	
EC-DLG	Airbus A.300B4-120	Iberia *Las Tablas de Daimiel*	
EC-DLH	Airbus A.300B4-120	Iberia *Aigues Tortes*	
EC-DNP	Boeing 747-256B	Iberia *Juan Ramon Jimenez*	
EC-DNQ	Airbus A.300B4-120	Iberia *Islas Cies*	
EC-DNR	Airbus A.300B4-120	Iberia *Ordesa*	
EC-EEK	Boeing 747-256B (SCD)	Iberia *Garcia Lorca*	
EC-ELT	BAe 146-200QT	Pan Air Lineas Aéreas/TNT	
EC-ELY	Boeing 737-3K9	Leisure Air/Seven Air	
EC-EMD	Douglas DC-8-62F	Cygnus Air	
EC-EMX	Douglas DC-8-62F	Cygnus Air	
EC-EON	Airbus A.300B4-203	Iberia Penalara	
EC-EPA	BAe 146-200QT	Pan Air Lineas Aéreas/TNT	
EC-EXF	McD Douglas MD-87	Iberia *Ciudad de Pamplona*	
EC-EXG	McD Douglas MD-87	Iberia *Ciudad de Almeria*	
EC-EXM	McD Douglas MD-87	Iberia *Ciudad de Zaragoza*	
EC-EXN	McD Douglas MD-87	Iberia *Ciudad de Badajoz*	
EC-EXR	McD Douglas MD-87	Iberia *Ciudad de Oviedo*	
EC-EXT	McD Douglas MD-87	Iberia *Ciudad de Albacete*	
EC-EYB	McD Douglas MD-87	Iberia *Cangas de Onis*	
EC-EYX	McD Douglas MD-87	Iberia *Ciudad de Caceres*	
EC-EYY	McD Douglas MD-87	Iberia *Ciudad de Barcelona*	
EC-EYZ	McD Douglas MD-87	Iberia *Ciudad de Las Palmas*	
EC-EZA	McD Douglas MD-87	Iberia *Ciudad de Segovia*	
EC-EZS	McD Douglas MD-87	Iberia *Ciudad de Mahon*	
EC-FCB	Airbus A.320-211	Iberia *Montana de Covadonga*	
EC-FCU	Boeing 767-3Y0ER	Spanair *Baleares*	
EC-FDA	Airbus A.320-211	Iberia *Lagunas de Ruidera*	
EC-FDB	Airbus A.320-211	Iberia *Lago de Sanabria*	
EC-FEE	Boeing 757-236	Iberia *Catalunya*	
EC-FEY	McD Douglas MD-87	Iberia *Ciudad de Jaen*	
EC-FEZ	McD Douglas MD-87	Iberia *Ciudad de Malaga*	
EC-FFA	McD Douglas MD-87	Iberia *Ciudad de Avila*	
EC-FFH	McD Douglas MD-87	Iberia *Ciudad de Logrono*	
EC-FFI	McD Douglas MD-87	Iberia *Ciudad de Cuenca*	
EC-FFK	Boeing 757-236	Air Europa *Galicia*	
EC-FFN	Boeing 737-36E	Iberia	
EC-FFY	BAe 146-300QT	Pan Air Lineas Aéreas/TNT	
EC-FGH	Airbus A.320-211	Iberia *Caldera de Taburiente*	
EC-FGM	McD Douglas MD-88	Iberia *Torre de Hercules*	
EC-FGR	Airbus A.320-211	Iberia *Dehesa de Moncayo*	
EC-FGU	Airbus A.320-211	Iberia *Sierra Espuna*	
EC-FGV	Airbus A.320-211	Iberia *Monfrague*	
EC-FHA	Boeing 767-3Y0ER	Spanair *Canarias*	
EC-FHD	McD Douglas MD-87	Iberia *Ciudad de Leon*	
EC-FHG	McD Douglas MD-88	Iberia *La Almudiana*	
EC-FHK	McD Douglas MD-87	Iberia *Ciudad de Tarragona*	
EC-FHR	Boeing 737-36E	Iberia	
EC-FIA	Airbus A.320-211	Iberia *Isla de la Cartuja*	
EC-FIC	Airbus A.320-211	Iberia *Sierra de Grazalema*	
EC-FIG	McD Douglas MD-88	Iberia *Penon de Ifach*	
EC-FIH	McD Douglas MD-88	Iberia *Albaicin*	
EC-FJE	McD Douglas MD-88	Iberia *Gibralfaro*	

Notes	Reg.	Type	Owner or Operator
	EC-FJZ	Boeing 737-3Y0	Air Europa
	EC-FKD	Airbus A.320-211	Iberia *Monte Alhoya*
	EC-FKJ	Boeing 737-3Y0	Air Europa
	EC-FLF	Boeing 737-36E	Iberia
	EC-FLG	Boeing 737-36E	Iberia
	EC-FLK	McD Douglas MD-88	Iberia *Palacio de la Magdalena*
	EC-FLN	McD Douglas MD-88	Iberia *Puerta de Tierra*
	EC-FLP	Airbus A.320-211	Iberia *Torcal de Antequera*
	EC-FLQ	Airbus A.320-211	Iberia *Dunas de Liencres*
	EC-FML	Airbus A.320-211	Iberia *Hayedo de Tejera Negra*
	EC-FMN	Airbus A.320-211	Iberia *Cadi Moixero*
	EC-FND	McD Douglas MD-88	Iberia *Playa de la Concha*
	EC-FNR	Airbus A.320-211	Iberia *Monte el Valle*
	EC-FOF	McD Douglas MD-88	Iberia *Cesar Manrique Lanzarote*
	EC-FOG	McD Douglas MD-88	Iberia *La Giralda*
	EC-FOZ	McD Douglas MD-88	Iberia *Montjuic*
	EC-FPD	McD Douglas MD-88	Iberia *Lagos de Coradonga*
	EC-FPJ	McD Douglas MD-88	Iberia *Ria de Vigo*
	EC-FQY	Airbus A.320-211	Iberia *Joan Miro*
	EC-FTR	Boeing 757-256	Iberia *Sierra de Guadarrama*
	EC-FTS	McD Douglas MD-83	Spanair *Sunbird*
	EC-FVY	BAe 146-200QT	Pan Air Lineas Aéreas/TNT
	EC-FXA	McD Douglas MD-83	Spanair *Sunstar*
	EC-FXI	McD Douglas MD-83	Spanair *Sunseeker*
	EC-FXP	Boeing 737-4Q8	Air Europa *Villanueva del Conde*
	EC-FXQ	Boeing 737-4Q8	Air Europa *Salamanca*
	EC-FXU	Boeing 757-256	Iberia *Xacobeo 93*
	EC-FXV	Boeing 757-256	Iberia *Argentina*
	EC-FXY	McD Douglas MD-83	Spanair *Sunbeam*
	EC-FYJ	Boeing 757-256	Iberia *Venezuela*
	EC-FYK	Boeing 757-256	Iberia *Chile*
	EC-FYM	Boeing 757-256	Iberia *Mexico*
	EC-FYN	Boeing 757-256	Iberia *Costa Rica*
	EC-FZC	McD Douglas MD-83	Spanair *Sunflower*
	EC-FZE	BAe 146-200QT	Pan Air Lineas Aéreas/TNT
	EC-FZZ	Boeing 737-4Y0	Air Europa *Baleares*
	EC-GAG	Boeing 747-256B	Iberia *Calderon de la Barca*
	EC-GAT	McD Douglas MD-83	Spanair *Sunmyth*
	EC-GAZ	Boeing 737-4Y0	Air Europa/Iberia
	EC-GBA	McD Douglas MD-83	Spanair *Sungod*
	EC-GBG	Fokker 50	Air Nostrum
	EC-GBH	Fokker 50	Air Nostrum
	EC-GBN	Boeing 737-4Y0	Air Europa/Iberia
	EC-GBX	Boeing 757-236	Air Europa
	EC-GCA	Boeing 757-236	Air Europa/Iberia
	EC-GCB	Boeing 757-236	Air Europa/Iberia
	EC-GCI	Boeing 727-256	Iberia *Murcia*
	EC-GCJ	Boeing 727-256	Iberia *Galicia*
	EC-GCK	Boeing 727-256	Iberia *Asturias*
	EC-GCL	Boeing 727-256	Iberia *Andalucia*
	EC-GCM	Boeing 727-256	Iberia *Tenerife*
	EC-GCV	McD Douglas MD-82	Spanair *Sunburst*
	EC-GDD	Fokker 50	Air Nostrum
	EC-GEQ	Boeing 737-3Y0	Air Europa
	EC-GEU	Boeing 737-375	Air Europa *Lugo*
	EC-GFP	Fokker 50	Air Nostrum
	EC-GFU	Boeing 737-3Y0	Air Europa
	EC-GGO	Boeing 737-3M8	Air Europa
	EC-GGS	Airbus A.340-313	Iberia *Concha Espina*
	EC-GGV	McD Douglas MD-83	Spanair *Sunbow*
	EC-GHB	Fokker 50	Air Nostrum
	EC-GHC	Fokker 50	Air Nostrum
	EC-GHD	Boeing 737-3M8	Air Europa
	EC-GHE	McD Douglas MD-83	Spanair *Sunset*
	EC-GHH	McD Douglas MD-83	Spanair *Sundance*
	EC-GHM	Boeing 767-204ER	Air Europa
	EC-GHX	Airbus A.340-313	Iberia *Rosalia de Castro*
	EC-GJI	Fokker 50	Air Nostrum
	EC-GJT	Airbus A.340-313	Iberia *Rosa Chacel*
	EC-GJY	Fokker 50	Air Nostrum
	EC-GKE	Fokker 50	Air Nostrum
	EC-GKF	McD Douglas MD-87	Spanair *Sundream*
	EC-GKG	McD Douglas MD-83	Spanair *Sunshine*

Reg.	Type	Owner or Operator	Notes
EC-GKU	Fokker 50	Air Nostrum	
EC-GKV	Fokker 50	Air Nostrum	
EC-GKX	Fokker 50	Air Nostrum	
EC-GLE	Airbus A.340-313	Iberia *Concepcion Arenal*	
EC-GLT	Airbus A.320-231	Iberworld	
EC-GMU	Airbus A.310-324	Air Plus Comet	
EC-GMY	Boeing 737-36Q	Air Europa *Camnini de Santiago*	
EC-GNC	Boeing 737-4Y0	Futura International Airways	
EC-GNG	Douglas DC-10-30	Iberia *Conisa Cantabrica*	
EC-GNU	Boeing 737-36Q	Air Europa	
EC-GNY	McD Douglas MD-83	Spanair *Sunflash*	
EC-GNZ	Boeing 737-4Y0	Futura International Airways	
EC-GOJ	Boeing 767-204ER	Air Europa	
EC-GOM	McD Douglas MD-83	Spanair *Sunlight*	
EC-GOT	Airbus A.310-324	Air Plus Comet	
EC-GOU	McD Douglas MD-83	Spanair *Sunlover*	
EC-GPB	Airbus A.340-313	Iberia	
EC-GPI	Boeing 737-46Q	Air Europa/Iberia	
EC-GPS	Swearingen SA227AC Metro III	Euro Continental Air	
EC-GQG	McD Douglas MD-83	Spanair *Sunrise*	
EC-GQI	Fokker 50	Air Nostrum	
EC-GQK	Airbus A.340-313	Iberia	
EC-GQO	BAe 146-200QT	Pan Air/TNT Express	
EC-GQP	BAe 146-200QT	Pan Air/TNT Express	
EC-GQT	Fokker 50	Air Nostrum	
EC-GQU	Aérospatiale ATR-72-201	Air Nostrum/Iberia Regional	
EC-GQV	Aérospatiale ATR-72-201	Air Nostrum/Iberia Regional	
EC-GQZ	McD Douglas MD-82	Spanair *Sunbear*	
EC-GRE	Airbus A.320-211	Iberia *Sierra de Cazorla*	
EC-GRF	Airbus A.320-211	Iberia *Montseny*	
EC-GRG	Airbus A.320-211	Iberia *Timanfaya*	
EC-GRH	Airbus A.320-211	Iberia *Sierra de Segura*	
EC-GRI	Airbus A.320-211	Iberia *Delta del Ebro*	
EC-GRJ	Airbus A.320-211	Iberia *Canon del Rio Lobos*	
EC-GRK	McD Douglas MD-87	Iberia *Ciudad de Savilla*	
EC-GRL	McD Douglas MD-87	Iberia *Ciudad de Toledo*	
EC-GRM	McD Douglas MD-87	Iberia *Ciudad de Burgos*	
EC-GRN	McD Douglas MD-87	Iberia *Ciudad de Cadiz*	
EC-GRO	McD Douglas MD-87	Iberia *Arrecife de Lanzarote*	
EC-GRX	Boeing 737-46B	Futura International Airways	
EC-GRY	Fokker 50	Air Nostrum	
EC-GRZ	Fokker 50	Air Nostrum	
EC-GSJ	Convair 580	Swiftair	
EC-GSU	Boeing 767-3Y0ER	Air Europa/Iberia	
EC-GTB	Douglas DC-10-30	Iberia	
EC-GTC	Douglas DC-10-30	Iberia	
EC-GTD	Douglas DC-10-30	Iberia	
EC-GTE	Fokker 50	Air Nostrum	
EC-GTG	Canadair CL.600-2B19 RJ	Air Nostrum/Iberia Regional	
EC-GTI	Boeing 767-3Y0ER	Air Europa/Iberia	
EC-GTO	McD Douglas MD-82	Spanair *Sunjet*	
EC-GUG	Boeing 737-4S3	Futura International Airways	
EC-GUI	Boeing 737-4Y0	Futura International Airways	
EC-GUO	Boeing 737-4Q8	Air Europa	
EC-GUP	Airbus A.340-313	Iberia *Agustina De Aragon*	
EC-GUQ	Airbus A.340-313	Iberia *Beatriz Galindo*	
EC-GUR	Airbus A.320-231	Iberworld	
EC-GVB	Boeing 737-4Y0	Futura International Airways	
EC-GVI	McD Douglas MD-83	Spanair *Sunup*	
EC-GVO	McD Douglas MD-83	Spanair *Sunspot*	
EC-GXR	Boeing 737-4Y0	Futura International Airways	
EC-GXU	McD Douglas MD-83	Spanair *Sunray*	
EC-GYI	Canadair CL.600-2B19 RJ	Air Nostrum/Iberia Regional	
EC-GYK	Boeing 737-4Y0	Futura International Airways	
EC-GZA	Canadair CL.600-2B19 RJ	Air Nostrum/Iberia Regional	
EC-GZD	Airbus A.320-214	Iberworld	
EC-GZE	Airbus A.320-214	Iberworld	
EC-GZI	Embraer RJ145EU	European Regions Airlines	
EC-GZU	Embraer RJ145EU	European Regions Airlines	
EC-GZY	Boeing 757-256	Iberia	
EC-GZZ	Boeing 757-256	Iberia	
EC-HAA	Boeing 757-256	Iberia	
EC-HAB	Airbus A.320-214	Iberia *Cabaneros*	

Notes	Reg.	Type	Owner or Operator
	EC-HAC	Airbus A.321-211	Iberia *Benidorm*
	EC-HAD	Airbus A.320-214	Iberia *Garajonay*
	EC-HAE	Airbus A.321-211	Iberia *Comunidad de La Rioja*
	EC-HAF	Airbus A.320-214	Iberia
	EC-HAG	Airbus A.320-214	Iberia *Senorio de Bertiz*
	EC-HAH	Boeing 727-223F	DHL
	EC-HAL	Airbus A.310-324	Iberworld
	EC-HBL	Boeing 737-85P	Air Europa
	EC-HBM	Boeing 737-85P	Air Europa
	EC-HBN	Boeing 737-85P	Air Europa *Lluchmajor*
	EC-HBP	McD Douglas MD-83	Spanair
	EC-HBT	Boeing 737-4Y0	Futura International Airways
	EC-HBY	Aérospatiale ATR-72-212A	Air Nostrum/Iberia Regional
	EC-HBZ	Boeing 737-4Y0	Futura International Airways
	EC-HCG	Aérospatiale ATR-72-212A	Air Nostrum/Iberia Regional
	EC-HCN	Boeing 737-4Y0	Futura International Airways
	EC-HCP	Boeing 737-46B	Futura International Airways
	EC-HCR	Airbus A.320-231	Iberworld
	EC-HDG	Boeing 757-236	Air Europa/Iberia
	EC-HDH	BAe 146-200QT	Pan Air Lineas Aéreas/TNT
	EC-HDK	Airbus A.320-214	Iberia *Mar Ortigola*
	EC-HDL	Airbus A.320-214	Iberia *Corredor del Duero*
	EC-HDM	Boeing 757-256	Iberia *Brasil*
	EC-HDN	Airbus A.320-214	Iberia *Parque National de Omiedo*
	EC-HDO	Airbus A.320-214	Iberia *Formentera*
	EC-HDP	Airbus A.320-214	Iberia *Parque de Cabarceno*
	EC-HDQ	Airbus A.340-313X	Iberia
	EC-HDR	Boeing 757-256	Iberia
	EC-HDS	Boeing 757-256	Iberia
	EC-HDT	Airbus A.320-214	Iberia *Museo Guggenheim Bilbao*
	EC-HDU	Boeing 757-256	Iberia
	EC-HDV	Boeing 757-256	Iberia
	EC-HEI	Aérospatiale ATR-72-212A	Air Nostrum/Iberia Regional
	EC-HEJ	Aérospatiale ATR-72-212A	Air Nostrum/Iberia Regional
	EC-HEK	Canadair CL.600-2B19 RJ	Air Nostrum/Iberia Regional
	EC-HFB	Airbus A.310-324	Air Plus Comet
	EC-HFP	McD Douglas MD-83	Spanair *Sunbreeze*
	EC-HFQ	Airbus A.310-324	Air Plus Comet
	EC-HFS	McD Douglas MD-82	Spanair *Sunbeach*
	EC-HFT	McD Douglas MD-82	Spanair *Sunspirit*
	EC-HFZ	EMB-120RT Brasilia	Regional Airlines
	EC-HGA	McD Douglas MD-83	Spanair *Sunisland*
	EC-HGJ	McD Douglas MD-82	Spanair *Sunworld*
	EC-HGO	Boeing 737-85P	Air Europa
	EC-HGP	Boeing 737-85P	Air Europa
	EC-HGQ	Boeing 737-85P	Air Europa
	EC-HGR	Airbus A.319-112	Iberia
	EC-HHF	McD Douglas MD-82	Spanair
	EC-HHG	Boeing 737-86N	Futura International Airways
	EC-HHH	Boeing 737-86N	Futura International Airways
	EC-HHI	Canadair CL.600-2B19 RJ	Air Nostrum/Iberia
	EC-HHP	McD Douglas MD-82	Spanair
	EC-HHV	Canadair CL.600-2B19 RJ	Air Nostrum/Iberia

Note: Iberia also employs Boeing 747s TF-ABA and TF-ABP on lease from Air Atlanta

EI (Republic of Ireland)

Including complete current Irish Civil Register.

EI-ABI	D.H.84 Dragon	Aer Lingus Teo *Iolar* (EI-AFK)
EI-ADV	PA-12 Super Cruiser	R. E. Levis
EI-AFE	Piper J3C-65 Cub	J. Conlon
EI-AFF	B.A. Swallow 2	J. J. Sullivan & ptnrs
EI-AFN	B.A. Swallow 2 ★	J. McCarthy
EI-AGB	Miles M.38 Messenger 4 ★	J. McLoughlin
EI-AGD	Taylorcraft Plus D	B. & K. O'Sullivan
EI-AGJ	J/1 Autocrat	W. G. Rafter
EI-AHA	D.H.82A Tiger Moth ★	J. H. Maher
EI-AHI	D.H.82A Tiger Moth	High Fidelity Flyers
EI-AHR	D.H.C.1 Chipmunk 22 ★	C. Lane
EI-AKM	Piper J-3C-65 Cub	Setanta Flying Group
EI-ALH	Taylorcraft Plus D	N. Reilly
EI-ALP	Avro 643 Cadet	J. C. O'Loughlin

Reg.	Type	Owner or Operator	Notes
EI-ALU	Avro 631 Cadet	M. P. Cahill *(stored)*	
EI-AMK	J/1 Autocrat	Irish Aero Club	
EI-ANT	Champion 7ECA Citabria	S. Donohoe	
EI-ANY	PA-18 Super Cub 95	Bogavia Group	
EI-AOB	PA-28 Cherokee 140	J. Surdival & ptnrs	
EI-AOK	Cessna F.172G	O. Bruton	
EI-AOP	D.H.82A Tiger Moth ★	Institute of Technology/Dublin	
EI-AOS	Cessna 310B	Joyce Aviation Ltd	
EI-APF	Cessna F.150F	Sligo Aero Club	
EI-APS	Schleicher ASK.14	SLG Group	
EI-ARH	Currie Wot/S.E.5 Replica	L. Garrison	
EI-ARM	Currie Wot/S.E.5 Replica	L. Garrison	
EI-ARW	Jodel D.R.1050	P. Walsh & P. Ryan	
EI-AST	Cessna F.150H	P. McKenna	
EI-ATJ	B.121 Pup 1	L. O'Leary	
EI-ATK	PA-28 Cherokee 140	Mayo Flying Club Ltd	
EI-ATS	M.S.880B Rallye Club	ATS Group	
EI-AUC	Cessna FA.150K	O. Bruton	
EI-AUE	M.S.880B Rallye Club	Kilkenny Flying Club Ltd	
EI-AUG	M.S.894 Rallye Minerva 220	K. O'Leary	
EI-AUJ	M.S.880B Rallye Club	Ormond Flying Club Ltd	
EI-AUM	J/1 Autocrat	J. G. Rafter	
EI-AUO	Cessna FA.150K Aerobat	Kerry Aero Club	
EI-AUS	J/5F Aiglet Trainer	T. Stephens & T. Lennon	
EI-AUT	Forney F-1A Aircoupe	*(stored)*	
EI-AUV	PA-23 Aztec 250C	Shannon Executive Aviation	
EI-AUY	Morane-Saulnier M.S.502 (CF+HF)	G. Warner/Duxford	
EI-AVB	Aeronca 7AC Champion	T. Brett	
EI-AVC	Cessna F.337F	Christy Keane (Saggart) Ltd	
EI-AVM	Cessna F.150L	J. Cowell	
EI-AWE	Cessna F.150M	D. Bruton	
EI-AWH	Cessna 210J	Rathcode Flying Club Ltd	
EI-AWP	D.H.82A Tiger Moth	A. P. Bruton	
EI-AWR	Malmö MFI-9 Junior	M. Bevan & P. Byrne	
EI-AWU	M.S.880B Rallye Club	Longford Aviation Ltd	
EI-AYA	M.S.880B Rallye Club	Limerick Flying Club Ltd	
EI-AYB	GY-80 Horizon 180	J. B. Smith	
EI-AYD	AA-5 Traveler	P. Howick & ptnrs	
EI-AYF	Cessna FRA.150L	K. A. O'Connor	
EI-AYI	M.S.880B Rallye Club	J. McNamara	
EI-AYK	Cessna F.172M	D. Gallagher	
EI-AYN	BN-2A-8 Islander	Galway Aviation Services Ltd	
EI-AYO	Douglas DC-3A ★	Science Museum, Wroughton	
EI-AYR	Schleicher ASK-16	Kilkenny Airport Ltd	
EI-AYS	PA-22 Colt 108	M. F. Skelly	
EI-AYV	M.S.892A Rallye Commodore 150	P. Murtagh	
EI-AYY	Evans VP-1	M. Donoghue	
EI-BAF	Thunder Ax6-56 balloon ★	British Balloon Museum	
EI-BAO	Cessna F.172G	D. Bruton	
EI-BAR	Thunder Ax8-105 balloon	J. Burke & V. Hourihane	
EI-BAS	Cessna F.172M	Falcon Aviation Ltd	
EI-BAT	Cessna F.150M	K. A. O'Connor	
EI-BAV	PA-22 Colt 108	J. Davy	
EI-BBC	PA-28 Cherokee 180C	Piper Aero Club Ltd	
EI-BBD	Evans VP-1	Volksplane Group	
EI-BBE	Champion 7FC Tri-Traveler (tailwheel)	P. Forde & D. Connaire	
EI-BBG	M.S.880B Rallye Club ★	Weston Ltd *(stored)*	
EI-BBI	M.S.892 Rallye Commodore	Kilkenny Airport Ltd	
EI-BBJ	M.S.880B Rallye Club	Weston Ltd	
EI-BBM	Cameron O-65 balloon	Dublin Ballooning Club	
EI-BBO	M.S.893E Rallye 180GT	G. P. Moorhead	
EI-BBV	Piper J-3C-65 Cub	F. Cronin	
EI-BCE	BN-2A-26 Islander	Galway Aviation Services Ltd	
EI-BCF	Bensen B.8M	P. Flanagan	
EI-BCH	M.S.892A Rallye Commodore 150	B. Foley	
EI-BCJ	F.8L Falco 1 Srs 3	D. Kelly	
EI-BCK	Cessna F.172N II	K. A. O'Connor	
EI-BCL	Cessna 182P	L. Burke	
EI-BCM	Piper J-3C-65 Cub	Kilmoon Flying Group	

Notes	Reg.	Type	Owner or Operator
	EI-BCN	Piper J-3C-65 Cub	Snowflake Flying Group
	EI-BCO	Piper J-3C-65 Cub	J. Molloy
	EI-BCP	D.628 Condor	A. Delaney
	EI-BCS	M.S.880B Rallye Club	Organic Fruit & Vegetables of Ireland Ltd
	EI-BCU	M.S.880B Rallye Club	Weston Ltd
	EI-BCW	M.S.880B Rallye Club	Kilkenny Flying Club
	EI-BDH	M.S.880B Rallye Club	Munster Wings Ltd
	EI-BDK	M.S.880B Rallye Club	Limerick Flying Club Ltd
	EI-BDL	Evans VP-2	P. Buggle
	EI-BDM	PA-23 Aztec 250D ★	Industrial Training School
	EI-BDR	PA-28 Cherokee 180	Cherokee Group
	EI-BEA	M.S.880B Rallye 100ST ★	Weston Ltd (stored)
	EI-BEN	Piper J-3C-65 Cub	J. J. Sullivan
	EI-BEO	Cessna 310Q	C. Keane
	EI-BEP	M.S.892A Rallye Commodore 150	H. Lynch & J. O'Leary
	EI-BEY	Naval N3N-3 ★	Huntley & Huntley Ltd
	EI-BFF	Beech A.23 Musketeer	P. Furlong
	EI-BFI	M.S.880B Rallye 100ST	J. O'Neill
	EI-BFM	M.S.893E Rallye 235GT	Limerick Flying Group
	EI-BFO	Piper J-3C-90 Cub	D. Gordon
	EI-BFP	M.S.800B Rallye 100ST	Weston Ltd
	EI-BFR	M.S.880B Rallye 100ST	J. Power
	EI-BFV	M.S.880B Rallye 100T	Ormond Flying Club
	EI-BGA	SOCATA Rallye 100ST	J. J. Frew
	EI-BGB	M.S.880B Rallye Club	Limerick Flying Club Ltd
	EI-BGD	M.S.880B Rallye Club	N. Kavanagh
	EI-BGG	M.S.880B Rallye Club	J. Dowling & M. Martin
	EI-BGJ	Cessna F.152	Sligo Aero Club Ltd
	EI-BGT	Colt 77A balloon	K. Haugh
	EI-BGU	M.S.880B Rallye Club	M. F. Neary
	EI-BHC	Cessna F.177RG	B. Palfrey & ptnrs
	EI-BHF	M.S.892A Rallye Commodore 150	B. Mullen
	EI-BHI	Bell 206B JetRanger 2	J. Mansfield
	EI-BHK	M.S.880B Rallye Club	D. Bruton
	EI-BHL	Beech E90 King Air	Stewart Singlam Fabrics Ltd
	EI-BHM	Cessna F.337E ★	Dublin Institute of Technology
	EI-BHN	M.S.893A Rallye Commodore 180T	T. Garvan
	EI-BHP	M.S.893A Rallye Commodore 180T	Spanish Point Flying Club
	EI-BHT	Beech 77 Skipper	Waterford Aero Club
	EI-BHV	Champion 7EC Traveler	E. P. O'Donnell
	EI-BHW	Cessna F.150F	R. Sharpe
	EI-BHY	SOCATA Rallye 150ST	Liberty Flying Group
	EI-BIB	Cessna F.152	Galway Flying Club
	EI-BIC	Cessna F.172N	Oriel Flying Group Ltd
	EI-BID	PA-18 Super Cub 95	D. MacCarthy
	EI-BIG	Zlin 526	P. von Lonkhuyzen
	EI-BIJ	AB-206B JetRanger 2	Medavia Properties Ltd
	EI-BIK	PA-18 Super Cub 180	Dublin Gliding Club
	EI-BIM	M.S.880B Rallye Club	D. Millar
	EI-BIO	Piper J-3C-65 Cub	Monasterevin Flying Club
	EI-BIR	Cessna F.172M	B. Harrison & ptnrs
	EI-BIS	Robin R.1180TD	Robin Aiglon Group
	EI-BIT	M.S.887 Rallye 125	Spanish Point Flying Club
	EI-BIU	Robin R.2112A	Wicklow Flying Group
	EI-BIV	Bellanca 8KCAB Citabria	Aerocrats Flying Group
	EI-BIW	M.S.880B Rallye Club	E. J. Barr
	EI-BJA	Cessna FRA.150L	Blackwater Flying Group
	EI-BJB	Aeronca 7DC Champion	W. Kennedy
	EI-BJC	Aeronca 7AC Champion	E. Griffin
	EI-BJG	Robin R.1180	N. Hanley
	EI-BJJ	Aeronca 15AC Sedan	O. Bruton
	EI-BJK	M.S.880B Rallye 110ST	Jordan Larkin Flying Group
	EI-BJM	Cessna A.152	Leinster Aero Club
	EI-BJO	Cessna R.172K	P. Hogan & G. Ryder
	EI-BJS	AA-5B Tiger	P. Morrisey
	EI-BJT	PA-38-112 Tomahawk	S. Corrigan & W. Lennon
	EI-BKC	Aeronca 15AC Sedan	J. Lynch
	EI-BKF	Cessna F.172H	E. McEllim
	EI-BKK	Taylor JT.1 Monoplane	Waterford Aero Club

Reg.	Type	Owner or Operator	Notes
EI-BKN	M.S.880B Rallye 100ST	Weston Ltd	
EI-BKS	Eipper Quicksilver	Irish Microlight Ltd	
EI-BKT	AB-206B JetRanger 3	Irish Helicopters Ltd	
EI-BKU	M.S.892A Rallye Commodore 150	Limerick Flying Club Ltd	
EI-BLB	SNCAN Stampe SV-4C	J. E. Hutchinson & R. A. Stafford	
EI-BLD	Bolkow Bo 105C	Irish Helicopters Ltd	
EI-BLE	Eipper Microlight	R. P. St George-Smith	
EI-BLN	Eipper Quicksilver MX	O. J. Conway & B. Daffy	
EI-BLO	Catto CP.16	R. W. Hall	
EI-BLU	Evans VP-1	S. Pallister	
EI-BLW	PA-23 Aztec 250C	— (stored)	
EI-BMA	M.S.880B Rallye Club	W. Rankin & M. Kelleher	
EI-BMB	M.S.880B Rallye 100T	Clyde Court Development Ltd	
EI-BMC	Hiway Demon Skytrike	S. Pallister	
EI-BMF	Laverda F.8L Falco	M. Slazenger & H. McCann	
EI-BMH	M.S.880B Rallye Club	N. J. Bracken	
EI-BMI	SOCATA TB.9 Tampico	Ashford Flying Group	
EI-BMJ	M.S.880B Rallye 100T	Weston Ltd	
EI-BML	PA-23 Aztec 250	Bruton Aircraft Engineering Ltd	
EI-BMM	Cessna F.152 II	P. Redmond	
EI-BMN	Cessna F.152 II	Iona National Airways Ltd	
EI-BMU	Monnet Sonerai IIL	A. Fenton	
EI-BMV	AA-5 Traveler	E. Tierney & K. Harold	
EI-BMW	Vulcan Air Trike	L. Maddock	
EI-BNF	Goldwing Canard	T. Morelli	
EI-BNG	M.S.892A Rallye Commodore 150	Shannon Executive Aviation	
EI-BNH	Hiway Skytrike	M. Martin	
EI-BNJ	Evans VP-2	G. A. Cashman	
EI-BNK	Cessna U.206F	Irish Parachute Club Ltd	
EI-BNL	Rand KR-2	K. Hayes	
EI-BNP	Rotorway 133	R. L. Renfroe	
EI-BNT	Cvjetkovic CA-65	B. Tobin & P. G. Ryan	
EI-BNU	M.S.880B Rallye Club	P. A. Doyle	
EI-BOA	Pterodactyl Ptraveller	A. Murphy	
EI-BOE	SOCATA TB.10 Tobago	P. Byron & ptnrs	
EI-BOH	Eipper Quicksilver	J. Leech	
EI-BOR	Bell 222	Westair Ltd	
EI-BOV	Rand KR-2	G. O'Hara & G. Callan	
EI-BOX	Duet	K. Riccius	
EI-BPE	Viking Dragonfly	G. Bracken	
EI-BPJ	Cessna 182A	Falcon Parachute Club Ltd	
EI-BPL	Cessna F.172K	Phoenix Flying	
EI-BPO	Southdown Sailwings	A. Channing	
EI-BPP	Quicksilver MX	J. A. Smith	
EI-BPT	Skyhook Sabre	T. McGrath	
EI-BPU	Hiway Demon	A. Channing	
EI-BRH	Mainair Gemini Flash	J. Deeney	
EI-BRK	Flexiform Trike	L. Maddock	
EI-BRS	Cessna P.172D	D. & M. Hillery	
EI-BRU	Evans VP-1	R. Smith & T. Coughlan	
EI-BRV	Hiway Demon	M. Garvey & C. Tully	
EI-BRW	Ultralight Deltabird	A. & E. Aerosports	
EI-BRX	Cessna FRA.150L	Trim Flying Club Ltd	
EI-BSB	Jodel D.112	J. M. Finnan & M. O'Reilly	
EI-BSC	Cessna F.172N	S. Phelan	
EI-BSD	Enstrom F-28A	Clark Aviation	
EI-BSF	Avro 748 Srs 1 ★	Ryanair cabin trainer/Dublin	
EI-BSG	Bensen B.80	J. Todd	
EI-BSK	SOCATA TB.9 Tampico	Weston Ltd	
EI-BSL	PA-34-220T Seneca	E. L. Symmons	
EI-BSN	Cameron O-65 balloon	W. Woollett	
EI-BSO	PA-28 Cherokee 140B	H. M. Hanley	
EI-BST	Bell 206B JetRanger	Celtic Helicopters Ltd	
EI-BSU	Champion 7KCAB	R. Bentley	
EI-BSV	SOCATA TB.20 Trinidad	J. Condron	
EI-BSW	Solar Wings Pegasus XL-R	E. Fitzgerald	
EI-BSX	Piper J-3C-65 Cub	J. & T. O'Dwyer	
EI-BTX	McD Douglas MD-82	Air Tara Ltd (leased to AeroMexico)	
EI-BTY	McD Douglas MD-82	Air Tara Ltd	
EI-BUA	Cessna 172M	Skyhawks Flying Club	
EI-BUC	Jodel D.9 Bebe	D. Lyons	

Notes	Reg.	Type	Owner or Operator
	EI-BUF	Cessna 210N	210 Group
	EI-BUG	SOCATA ST.10 Diplomate	J. Cooke
	EI-BUH	Lake LA.4-200 Buccaneer	T. Henderson
	EI-BUJ	M.S.892A Rallye Commodore 150	T. Cunniffe
	EI-BUL	MW-5 Sorcerer	J. Conlon
	EI-BUN	Beech 76 Duchess	K. A. O'Connor & ptnrs
	EI-BUO	Quickkit Glass S.005E	C. J. Lavery & A. C. Donaldson
	EI-BUR	PA-38-112 Tomahawk	Westair Aviation Ltd
	EI-BUS	PA-38-112 Tomahawk	Westair Aviation Ltd
	EI-BUT	M.S.893A Commodore 180	T. Keating
	EI-BUU	Solar Wings Pegasus XL-R	R. L. T. Hudson
	EI-BUV	Cessna 172RG	J. J. Spollen
	EI-BUW	Noble Hardman Snowbird IIIA	T.I.F.C. & I.S. Ltd
	EI-BUX	Agusta A.109A	Orring Ltd
	EI-BVB	Whittaker MW.6 Merlin	R. England
	EI-BVF	Cessna F.172N	First Phantom Group
	EI-BVJ	AMF Chevvron 232	S. J. Dunn
	EI-BVK	PA-38-112 Tomahawk	Pegasus Flying Group Ltd
	EI-BVN	Bell 206B Jet Ranger 3	Helicopter Hire (Ireland) Ltd
	EI-BVT	Evans VP-2	P. Morrison
	EI-BVY	Zenith 200AA-RW	J. Matthews & ptnrs
	EI-BWD	McD Douglas MD-83	Airplanes IAL Ltd (leased to TWA)
	EI-BWH	Partenavia P.68C	K. Buckley
	EI-BXA	Boeing 737-448	Aer Lingus Teo St Conleth
	EI-BXB	Boeing 737-448	Aer Lingus Teo St Gall
	EI-BXC	Boeing 737-448	Aer Lingus Teo St Brendan
	EI-BXD	Boeing 737-448	Aer Lingus Teo St Colman
	EI-BXI	Boeing 737-448	Aer Lingus Teo St Finnian
	EI-BXK	Boeing 737-448	Aer Lingus Teo St Caimin
	EI-BXL	Polaris F1B-OK350	M. McKeon
	EI-BXM	Boeing 737-2T4	Air Tara Ltd
	EI-BXO	Fouga CM.170 Magister	G. W. Connolly
	EI-BXT	D.62B Condor	S. Bruton
	EI-BXX	AB-206B JetRanger 3	Westair Aviation Ltd
	EI-BYA	Thruster TST Mk 1	E. Fagan
	EI-BYD	Cessna 150J	Kestrel Flying Group
	EI-BYF	Cessna 150M	Twentieth Air Training Group
	EI-BYG	SOCATA TB.9 Tampico	Weston Ltd
	EI-BYJ	Bell 206B JetRanger	Celtic Helicopters Ltd
	EI-BYL	Zenith CH.250	M. Guckian
	EI-BYR	Bell 206L-3 LongRanger 3	Donloe Management Services Ltd
	EI-BYV	Hughes 369D	Irish Helicopters Ltd
	EI-BYX	Champion 7GCAA	P. J. Gallagher
	EI-BYY	Piper J-3C-85 Cub	V. Murphy
	EI-BZE	Boeing 737-3Y0	GPA Group Ltd
	EI-BZF	Boeing 737-3Y0	Pergola Ltd
	EI-BZJ	Boeing 737-3Y0	Pergola Ltd
	EI-BZL	Boeing 737-3Y0	GECAS Ltd
	EI-BZM	Boeing 737-3Y0	GECAS Ltd
	EI-BZN	Boeing 737-3Y0	Airplanes Finance Ltd
	EI-CAC	Grob G.115A	G. Muller
	EI-CAE	Grob G.115A	D. Kehoe
	EI-CAN	Aerotech MW.5 Sorcerer	V. Vaughan
	EI-CAP	Cessna R.182RG	M. J. Hanlon
	EI-CAU	AMF Chevvron 232	J. Farrant
	EI-CAW	Bell 206B JetRanger	Celtic Helicopters Ltd
	EI-CAX	Cessna P.210N	J. Rafter
	EI-CAY	Mooney M.20C	Ranger Flights Ltd
	EI-CBB	Douglas DC-9-15	GPA Finance Ltd (stored)
	EI-CBJ	D.H.C. 8-102 Dash Eight	Aerfi Jetprop Ltd (leased to US Air)
	EI-CBK	Aérospatiale ATR-42-310	GPA-ATR Ltd (leased to Italair)
	EI-CBO	McD Douglas MD-83	Irish Aerospace Ltd (leased to Nouvelair Tunisie)
	EI-CBR	McD Douglas MD-83	Airplanes 111 Ltd (leased to Avianca)
	EI-CBS	McD Douglas MD-83	GECAS Ltd (leased to Avianca)
	EI-CBY	McD Douglas MD-83	GECAS Ltd (leased to Avianca)
	EI-CBZ	McD Douglas MD-83	GECAS Ltd (leased to Avianca)
	EI-CCA	Beech 19A Musketeer	P. F. McCooke
	EI-CCC	McD Douglas MD-83	Airplanes 111 Ltd (leased to Avianca)
	EI-CCD	Grob G.115A	M.O.D. Aviation Ltd
	EI-CCE	McD Douglas MD-83	GECAS Ltd (leased to Avianca)
	EI-CCF	Aeronca 11AC Chief	L. Murray & ptnrs

Reg.	Type	Owner or Operator	Notes
EI-CCH	Piper J-3C-65 Cub	J. Matthews & ptnrs	
EI-CCJ	Cessna 152 II	Irish Aero Club	
EI-CCK	Cessna 152 II	Irish Aero Club	
EI-CCM	Cessna 152 II	E. Hopkins	
EI-CCV	Cessna R.172K-XP	Kerry Aero Club	
EI-CCY	AA-1B Trainer	N. & C. Whisler	
EI-CDB	Boeing 737-548	Aer Lingus Teo *St Albert*	
EI-CDC	Boeing 737-548	Aer Lingus Teo *St Munchin*	
EI-CDD	Boeing 737-548	Aer Lingus Teo *St Macartan*	
EI-CDE	Boeing 737-548	Aer Lingus Teo *St Jarlath*	
EI-CDF	Boeing 737-548	Aer Lingus Teo *St Cronan*	
EI-CDG	Boeing 737-548	Aer Lingus Teo *St Moling*	
EI-CDH	Boeing 737-548	Aer Lingus Teo *St Ronan*	
EI-CDP	Cessna 182L	Irish Parachute Club Ltd	
EI-CDV	Cessna 150G	K. A. O'Connor	
EI-CDX	Cessna 210K	Falcon Aviation Ltd	
EI-CDY	McD Douglas MD-83	GECAS Ltd *(leased to Avianca)*	
EI-CEG	M.S.893A Rallye 180GT	M. Farrelly	
EI-CEK	McD Douglas MD-83	Airplanes IAL Ltd *(leased to Eurofly)*	
EI-CEL	Rans S.6 Coyote	D. J. O'Gorman	
EI-CEN	Thruster T.300	P. J. Murphy	
EI-CEP	McD Douglas MD-83	GECAS Ltd *(leased to Avianca)*	
EI-CEQ	McD Douglas MD-83	GECAS Ltd *(leased to Avianca)*	
EI-CER	McD Douglas MD-83	Airplanes 111 Ltd *(leased to Avianca)*	
EI-CES	Taylorcraft BC-65	N. O'Brien	
EI-CEX	Lake LA-4-200	Derg Developments Ltd	
EI-CEY	Boeing 757-2Y0	Pergola Ltd *(leased to Avianca)*	
EI-CEZ	Boeing 757-2Y0	GPA 11 Ltd *(leased to Avianca)*	
EI-CFE	Robinson R-22B	Toriamos Ltd	
EI-CFF	PA-12 Super Cruiser	J. O'Dwyer & J. Molloy	
EI-CFG	CP.301B Emeraude	Southlink Ltd	
EI-CFH	PA-12 Super Cruiser	G. Treacy	
EI-CFL	Airbus A.300B4	Air Tara Ltd	
EI-CFM	Cessna 172P	Hibernian Flying Club	
EI-CFN	Cessna 172P	B. Fitzmaurice & G. G. O'Connell	
EI-CFO	Piper J-3C-65 Cub	J. Mathews & ptnrs	
EI-CFP	Cessna 172P (floatplane)	K. A. O'Connor	
EI-CFV	M.S.880B Rallye Club	Kilkenny Flying Club	
EI-CFX	Robinson R-22B	Glenwood Transport	
EI-CFY	Cessna 172N	K. A. O'Connor	
EI-CFZ	McD Douglas MD-83	Airplanes 111 Ltd *(leased to Avianca)*	
EI-CGB	Team Minimax	M. Garvey	
EI-CGC	Stinson 108-3	A. P. Bruton	
EI-CGD	Cessna 172M	W. Phelan & M. Casey	
EI-CGE	Hiway Demon	T. E. Carr	
EI-CGF	Luton LA-5 Major	F. Doyle & J. Duggan	
EI-CGG	Ercoupe 415C	Irish Ercoupe Group	
EI-CGH	Cessna 210N	J. J. Spollen	
EI-CGI	McD Douglas MD-83	Irish Aerospace Ltd *(leased to Air Liberte Tunisia)*	
EI-CGJ	Solar Wings Pegasus XL-R	P. Heraty	
EI-CGK	Robinson R-22B	Skyfare Ltd	
EI-CGM	Solar Wings Pegasus XL-R	Microflight Ltd	
EI-CGN	Solar Wings Pegasus XL-R	V. Power	
EI-CGO	Douglas DC-8-63AF	Aer Turas Teo	
EI-CGP	PA-28 Cherokee 140C	G. Cashman	
EI-CGQ	AS.350B Ecureuil	Caulstown Air Ltd	
EI-CGT	Cessna 152 II	J. Rafter	
EI-CGV	Piper J-5A Cub Cruiser	J5 Group	
EI-CGW	Powerchute Kestrel	C. Kiernan	
EI-CHF	PA-44-180 Seminole	A. Barlow	
EI-CHK	Piper J-3C-65 Cub	N. Higgins	
EI-CHM	Cessna 150M	K. A. O'Connor	
EI-CHN	M.S.880B Rallye Club	Limerick Flying Club (Coonagh) Ltd	
EI-CHP	D.H.C.8-103 Dash Eight	Airplanes Jetprop Finance Ltd *(leased to US Airways Express)*	
EI-CHR	CFM Shadow Srs BD	J. Smith	
EI-CHS	Cessna 172M	Kerry Aero Club Ltd	
EI-CHT	Solar Wings Pegasus XL-R	G. W. Maher	
EI-CHV	Agusta A.109A	Celtic Helicopters Ltd	
EI-CIA	M.S.880B Rallye Club	G. Hackett & C. Mason	
EI-CIF	PA-28 Cherokee 180C	AA Flying Group	
EI-CIG	PA-18 Super Cub 150	K. A. O'Connor	

Notes	Reg.	Type	Owner or Operator
	EI-CIH	Ercoupe 415CD	J. T. Haycock
	EI-CIJ	Cessna 340	Airlink Airways Ltd
	EI-CIK	Mooney M.20C	A. & P. Aviation Ltd
	EI-CIM	Light Aero Avid Speedwing Mk IV	P. Swan
	EI-CIO	Bell 206L-3 LongRanger	Sean Quinn Properties Ltd
	EI-CIR	Cessna 551 Citation II	Air Group Finance Ltd
	EI-CIV	PA-28 Cherokee 140	G. Cashman & E. Callanan
	EI-CIW	McD Douglas MD-83	Carotene Ltd *(leased to Meridiana)*
	EI-CIZ	Steen Skybolt	J. Keane
	EI-CJC	Boeing 737-204ADV	Ryanair Ltd
	EI-CJD	Boeing 737-204ADV	Ryanair Ltd *(Ercell)*
	EI-CJE	Boeing 737-204ADV	Ryanair Ltd *(Jaguar)*
	EI-CJF	Boeing 737-204ADV	Ryanair Ltd
	EI-CJG	Boeing 737-204ADV	Ryanair Ltd
	EI-CJH	Boeing 737-204ADV	Ryanair Ltd
	EI-CJI	Boeing 737-2E7ADV	Ryanair Ltd
	EI-CJK	Airbus A.300B4-103	Airplane Holdings Ltd
	EI-CJR	SNCAN Stampe SV-4A	C. Scully & P. Ryan
	EI-CJS	Jodel D.120A	K. Houlihan
	EI-CJT	Slingsby Motor Cadet III	J. Tarrant
	EI-CJV	Moskito 2	M. Peril & ptnrs
	EI-CJZ	Whittaker MW.6 Merlin	M. McCarthy
	EI-CKD	Boeing 767-3Y0ER	GECAS Ltd *(leased to Delta A/L)*
	EI-CKE	Boeing 767-3Y0ER	GECAS Ltd *(leased to Delta A/L)*
	EI-CKG	Avon Hunt Weightlift	B. Kelly
	EI-CKH	PA-18 Super Cub 95	G. Brady & C. Keenan
	EI-CKI	Thruster TST Mk 1	S. Pallister
	EI-CKJ	Cameron N-77 balloon	F. Meldon
	EI-CKM	McD Douglas MD-83	Airplanes IAL Finance Ltd *(leased to Meridiana)*
	EI-CKN	Whittaker MW.6-S Fatboy Flyer	F. Byrne & M. D.'Carroll
	EI-CKP	Boeing 737-2K2	Ryanair Ltd
	EI-CKQ	Boeing 737-2K2	Ryanair Ltd
	EI-CKR	Boeing 737-2K2	Ryanair Ltd
	EI-CKS	Boeing 737-2T5	Ryanair Ltd
	EI-CKT	Mainair Gemini Flash	C. Burke
	EI-CKU	Solar Wings Pegasus SLR	M. O'Regan
	EI-CKX	Jodel D.112	J. Greene
	EI-CKZ	Jodel D.18	J. O'Brien
	EI-CLA	HOAC Katana DV.20	Weston Ltd
	EI-CLB	Aérospatiale ATR-72-212	Tarquin Ltd *(leased to Alitalia)*
	EI-CLC	Aérospatiale ATR-72-212	Tarquin Ltd *(leased to Alitalia)*
	EI-CLD	Aérospatiale ATR-72-212	Tarquin Ltd *(leased to Alitalia)*
	EI-CLF	FH.227E Friendship	Westair Cargo
	EI-CLG	BAe 146-300	Aer Lingus Commuter *St Finbarr*
	EI-CLH	BAe 146-300	Aer Lingus Commuter *St Aoife*
	EI-CLI	BAe 146-300	Aer Lingus Commuter *St Eithne*
	EI-CLJ	BAe 146-300	Aer Lingus Commuter *St Senan*
	EI-CLL	Whittaker MW.6-S Fat Boy Flyer	M. McCarthy
	EI-CLQ	Cessna F.172N	K. Dardis & ptnrs
	EI-CLR	Boeing 767-3Y0ER	Airplanes Funding 1 Ltd
	EI-CLS	Boeing 767-352ER	ILFC Ireland *(leased to Air Europe SpA)*
	EI-CLT	Bell 206B JetRanger	Mistwood Ltd
	EI-CLW	Boeing 737-3Y0	Airplanes Finance Ltd *(leased to Air One)*
	EI-CLY	BAe 146-300	Aer Lingus Commuter *St Eugene*
	EI-CLZ	Boeing 737-3Y0	Airplanes Finance Ltd *(leased to Air One)*
	EI-CMB	PA-28 Cherokee 140	Kestrel Flying Group Ltd
	EI-CMF	CFM Streak Shadow	O. Williams
	EI-CMI	Robinson R-22B	Toriamos Ltd
	EI-CMJ	Aérospatiale ATR-72-212	Tarquin Ltd *(leased to Alitalia)*
	EI-CMK	Goldwing ST	M. Gavigan
	EI-CML	Cessna 150M	K. A. O'Connor
	EI-CMM	McD Douglas MD-83	Irish Aerospace Ltd *(leased to Eurofly)*
	EI-CMN	PA-12 Super Cruiser	D. Graham & ptnrs
	EI-CMR	Rutan LongEz	F. & C. O'Caoimh
	EI-CMS	BAe 146-200	CityJet Ltd
	EI-CMT	PA-34-200T Seneca II	Atlantic Air Ltd
	EI-CMU	Mainair Mercury	J. Deeney
	EI-CMV	Cessna 150L	K. A. O'Connor
	EI-CMW	Rotorway Executive	B. McNamee
	EI-CMY	BAe 146-200	CityJet Ltd
	EI-CMZ	McD Douglas MD-83	Airplane Finances Ltd *(leased to Eurofly)*
	EI-CNA	Letov LK-2M Sluka	G. H. Doody

Reg.	Type	Owner or Operator	Notes
EI-CNB	BAe 146-200	CityJet Ltd	
EI-CNC	Team Minimax	A. M. S. Allen	
EI-CNG	Air & Space 18A gyroplane	P. Joyce	
EI-CNH	—	—	
EI-CNI	Avro RJ85	Azzurra Air	
EI-CNJ	Avro RJ85	Azzurra Air	
EI-CNK	Avro RJ85	Azzurra Air	
EI-CNL	Sikorsky S-61N	Bond Helicopters (Ireland) Ltd	
EI-CNM	PA-31-350 Navajo Chieftain	M. Goss	
EI-CNN	L.1011-385 TriStar 1	Aer Turas Teo	
EI-CNO	McD Douglas MD-83	Airplanes Finance Ltd *(leased to Nouvelair Tunisie)*	
EI-CNQ	BAe 146-200	CityJet Ltd/Air France Express	
EI-CNR	McD Douglas MD-83	Aircraft Finance Trust Ltd *(leased to Eurofly)*	
EI-CNS	Boeing 767-3Q8ER	ILFC (Ireland) Ltd *(leased to Air Europe SpA)*	
EI-CNT	Boeing 737-230ADV	Ryanair Ltd *(The Sun/News of the World)*	
EI-CNU	Pegasus Quantum 15-912	M. Ffrench	
EI-CNV	Boeing 737-230ADV	Ryanair Ltd	
EI-CNW	Boeing 737-230ADV	Ryanair Ltd	
EI-CNX	Boeing 737-230ADV	Ryanair Ltd *(Tipperary Crystal)*	
EI-CNY	Boeing 737-230ADV	Ryanair Ltd *(Kilkenny)*	
EI-CNZ	Boeing 737-230ADV	Ryanair Ltd	
EI-COA	Boeing 737-230ADV	Ryanair Ltd	
EI-COB	Boeing 737-230ADV	Ryanair Ltd	
EI-COD	Aérospatiale ATR-42-310	Duntington Ltd *(leased to Italair)*	
EI-COE	Shaw Europa	F. Flynn	
EI-COG	Gyroscopic Rotorcraft gyroplane	R. C. Fidler & D. Bracken	
EI-COH	Boeing 737-430	Maike Ltd *(leased to Air One)*	
EI-COI	Boeing 737-430	Challey Ltd *(leased to Air One)*	
EI-COJ	Boeing 737-430	Challey Ltd *(leased to Air One)*	
EI-COK	Boeing 737-430	Challey Ltd *(leased to Air One)*	
EI-COM	Whittaker MW.6-S Fatboy Flyer	M. Watson	
EI-CON	Boeing 737-2T5	Ryanair Ltd	
EI-COO	Carlson Sparrow II	D. Logue	
EI-COP	Cessna F.150L	High Kings Flying Group Ltd	
EI-COQ	Avro RJ70	Azzurra Air	
EI-COT	Cessna F.172N	Kawasaki Distributors (Ireland) Ltd	
EI-COV	H.S.125 Srs 700B	Wilton Bridge Ltd	
EI-COX	Boeing 737-230	Ryanair Ltd	
EI-COY	Piper J-3C-65 Cub	P. McWade	
EI-COZ	PA-28 Cherokee 140C	G. Cashman	
EI-CPB	McD Douglas MD-83	Irish Aerospace Ltd *(leased to Eurofly)*	
EI-CPC	Airbus A.321-211	Aer Lingus Teo *St Fergus*	
EI-CPD	Airbus A.321-211	Aer Lingus Teo *St Davnet*	
EI-CPE	Airbus A.321-211	Aer Lingus Teo *St Enda*	
EI-CPF	Airbus A.321-211	Aer Lingus Teo *St Ide*	
EI-CPG	Airbus A.321-211	Aer Lingus Teo	
EI-CPH	Airbus A.321-211	Aer Lingus Teo *St Dervilla*	
EI-CPI	Rutan LongEz	D. J. Ryan	
EI-CPJ	Avro RJ70	Azzurra Air	
EI-CPK	Avro RJ70	Azzurra Air	
EI-CPL	Avro RJ70	Azzurra Air	
EI-CPM	SAAB 2000	CityJet Ltd	
EI-CPN	Auster J/4	E. Fagan	
EI-CPO	Robinson R-22B	Santail Ltd	
EI-CPP	Piper J-3C-65 Cub	E. Fitzgerald	
EI-CPR	Short SD3-60 Variant 100	Aer Arann	
EI-CPS	Beech 95-58 Baron	F. Doherty	
EI-CPT	Aérospatiale ATR-42-320	GPA-ATR Ltd *(leased to Italair)*	
EI-CPW	SAAB 2000	CityJet Ltd	
EI-CPX	Sky Arrow 650T	N. Irwin	
EI-CPY	BAe 146-100	CityJet Ltd	
EI-CRB	Lindstrand LBL-90A balloon	J. & C. Concannon	
EI-CRD	Boeing 767-31BER	ILFC Ireland *(leased to Alitalia)*	
EI-CRE	McD Douglas MD-83	Crane Aircraft Ltd *(leased to Meridiana)*	
EI-CRF	Boeing 767-31BER	ILFC Ireland Ltd *(leased to Eurofly)*	
EI-CRG	Robin DR.400/180R	D. & B. Lodge	
EI-CRH	McD Douglas MD-83	*(leased to Meridiana)*	
EI-CRJ	McD Douglas MD-83	C. A. Aviation Ltd *(leased to Meridiana)*	
EI-CRK	Airbus A.330-301	Aer Lingus Teo *St Brigid*	
EI-CRL	Boeing 767-343ER	GECAS Ltd *(leased to Alitalia)*	

Notes	Reg.	Type	Owner or Operator
	EI-CRM	Boeing 767-343ER	GECAS Ltd *(leased to Alitalia)*
	EI-CRN	Boeing 737-228	Air Sicilia
	EI-CRO	Boeing 767-3Q8ER	ILFC Ireland *(leased to Alitalia)*
	EI-CRP	Boeing 737-73S	Pembroke Capital *(leased to Azzura Air)*
	EI-CRQ	Boeing 737-73S	Pembroke Capital *(leased to Azzura Air)*
	EI-CRR	Aeronca 11AC Chief	L. Maddock & ptnrs
	EI-CRS	Boeing 777-2Q8	ILFC Ireland Ltd *(leased to Air Europe SpA)*
	EI-CRT	Boeing 777-2Q8	ILFC Ireland Ltd *(leased to Air Europe SpA)*
	EI-CRU	Cessna 152	W. Reilly
	EI-CRV	Hoffmann H-36 Dimona	Falcon Aviation Ltd
	EI-CRW	McD Douglas MD-83	Airplanes IAL Ltd *(leased to Meridiana)*
	EI-CRX	SOCATA TB-9 Tampico	Hotel Bravo Flying Club Ltd
	EI-CRY	Medway Eclipse	G. A. Murphy
	EI-CRZ	Boeing 737-36E	ILFC Ireland Ltd *(leased to Air One)*
	EI-CSA	Boeing 737-8AS	Ryanair Ltd
	EI-CSB	Boeing 737-8AS	Ryanair Ltd
	EI-CSC	Boeing 737-8AS	Ryanair Ltd
	EI-CSD	Boeing 737-8AS	Ryanair Ltd
	EI-CSE	Boeing 737-8AS	Ryanair Ltd
	EI-CSF	Boeing 737-8AS	Ryanair Ltd
	EI-CSG	Boeing 737-8AS	Ryanair Ltd
	EI-CSH	Boeing 737-8AS	Ryanair Ltd
	EI-CSI	Boeing 737-8AS	Ryanair Ltd
	EI-CSJ	Boeing 737-8AS	Ryanair Ltd
	EI-CSK	BAe 146-200	Aer Lingus Commuter *St Ciara*
	EI-CSL	BAe 146-200	Aer Lingus Commuter *St Cormac*
	EI-CSM	Boeing 737-8AS	Ryanair Ltd
	EI-CSN	Boeing 737-8AS	Ryanair Ltd
	EI-CSO	Boeing 737-8AS	Ryanair Ltd
	EI-CSU	Boeing 737-36E	ILFC Ireland Ltd *(leased to Air One)*
	EI-CTC	Medway Eclipse	C. Brogan
	EI-CTD	Airbus A.320-211	Aerco Ireland Ltd *(leased to Air Europe SpA)*
	EI-CTG	Stoddard-Hamilton Glasair RG	K. Higgins
	EI-CTH	SE.313 Alouette	-
	EI-CTI	Cessna FRA.150L	O. Bruton
	EI-CTJ	McD Douglas MD-82	GECAS Ltd *(leased to Nouvelair)*
	EI-CTK	Sikorsky S-61N	Irish Helicopters Ltd
	EI-CTL	Aerotech MW-5B Sorcerer	M. Wade
	EI-CTM	BAe 146-300	Aer Lingus Commuter *St Fiacre*
	EI-CTT	PA-28-161 Warrior II	M. Farrell
	EI-CTW	Boeing 767-341ER	*(leased to Alitalia/Eurofly)*
	EI-CTX	Boeing 737-228	Rancemont Ltd *(leased to Air Sicilia)*
	EI-CUA	Boeing 737-4K5	Blue Panorama
	EI-CUB	Piper J-3C-65 Cub	J. Conneely & ptnrs
	EI-CUC	Airbus A.320-214	GECAS Ltd *(leased to Volare Airlines)*
	EI-CUE	Cameron balloon	Bord Telecom Eireann
	EI-CUF	Douglas DC-9-82	GECAS Ltd
	EI-CUG	Bell 206B Jet Ranger	J. O'Reilly & B. McNamara
	EI-CUU	Cessna 172N	M. Casey
	EI-CUK	Airbus A.320-214	GECAS Ltd *(leased to Volare Airlines)*
	EI-CVA	Airbus A.320-214	Aer Lingus Teo
	EI-CVB	Airbus A.320-214	Aer Lingus Teo
	EI-CVC	Airbus A.320-214	Aer Lingys Teo
	EI-DLA	Douglas DC-10-30	GECAS Ltd *(leased to Continental)*
	EI-DUB	Airbus A.330-301	Aer Lingus Teo *St Patrick*
	EI-DWN	Cessna 421C	Dawn Meats (Waterford) Ltd
	EI-EAA	Airbus A.300B4-203F	Air Contractors (Ireland) Ltd/DHL
	EI-EAB	Airbus A.300B4-203F	Air Contractors (Ireland) Ltd/DHL
	EI-EAC	Airbus A.300B4-203F	Air Contractors (Ireland) Ltd/DHL
	EI-EAD	Airbus A.300B4-203F	Air Contractors (Ireland) Ltd/DHL
	EI-EAT	Airbus A.300B4-203F	Air Contractors (Ireland) Ltd/DHL
	EI-ECA	Agusta A.109A	Backdrive Ltd
	EI-EDR	PA-28R Cherokee Arrow 200	Victor Mike Flying Group Ltd
	EI-EEC	PA-23 Aztec 250	Westair Ltd
	EI-EIO	PA-34-200T Seneca II	K. A. O'Connor
	EI-ELL	Medway Eclipse	Microflex Ltd
	EI-EWR	Airbus A.330-202	Aer Lingus Teo
	EI-EXP	Short SD3-30 Variant 100 ★	Valley Nurseries/Alton
	EI-FKC	Fokker 50	Aer Lingus Commuter *St Fidelma*
	EI-FKD	Fokker 50	Aer Lingus Commuter *St Flannan*

Reg.	Type	Owner or Operator	Notes
EI-FKE	Fokker 50	Aer Lingus Commuter *St Pappin*	
EI-FKF	Fokker 50	Aer Lingus Commuter *St Ultan*	
EI-GER	Maule MX7-180A	P. J. Lanigan Ryan	
EI-GFC	SOCATA TB.9 Tampico	B. McGrath & ptnrs	
EI-GHL	Bell 206B JetRanger 3	Marwing Trading Ltd	
EI-GSM	Cessna 182S	Westpoint Flying Group Ltd	
EI-GWY	Cessna 172R	Galway Flying Club Ltd	
EI-HAM	Light Aero Avid Flyer	H. Goulding	
EI-HCA	Boeing 727-225F	Air Contractors (Ireland) Ltd	
EI-HCB	Boeing 727-223F	Air Contractors (Ireland) Ltd	
EI-HCC	Boeing 727-223F	Air Contractors (Ireland) Ltd	
EI-HCD	Boeing 727-223F	Air Contractors (Ireland) Ltd	
EI-HCI	Boeing 727-225F	Air Contractors (Ireland) Ltd	
EI-HCS	Grob G.109B	H. Sydner	
EI-HER	Bell 206B JetRanger 3	SELC Ireland Ltd & ptnrs	
EI-IRV	AS.350B Ecureuil	Rathalope Ltd	
EI-JAK	Jabiru UL	S. Walshe	
EI-JBC	Agusta A.109A	Medeva Properties Ltd	
EI-JFK	Airbus A.330-301	Aer Lingus Teo *Colmcille*	
EI-JWM	Robinson R-22B	C. Shiel	
EI-LAX	Airbus A.330-202	Aer Lingus Teo	
EI-LCH	Boeing 727-281F	Air Contractors (Ireland) Ltd	
EI-LIT	MBB Bo 105S	Irish Helicopters Ltd	
EI-LJR	Dassault Falcon 2000	EAT Executive Air Transport (Management) Ltd	
EI-LRS	Hughes 269C	Lynch Roofing Systems Ltd	
EI-MER	Bell 206B JetRanger	Mercury Engineering Ltd	
EI-MES	Sikorsky S-61N	Bond Helicopters (Ireland) Ltd	
EI-MIP	SA.365N Dauphin 2	Bond Helicopters (Ireland) Ltd	
EI-MLA	F.27 Friendship Mk 600	-	
EI-ONE	Bell 206B JetRanger	TCI Aircraft Ltd	
EI-ORD	Airbus A.330-301	Aer Lingus Teo	
EI-PAT	BAe 146-200	CityJet Ltd	
EI-PMI	AB-206B JetRanger 3	Ping Golf Equipment Ltd	
EI-POD	Cessna 177B	Trim Flying Club Ltd	
EI-RRR	H.S.125 Srs 700A	Starair Inc	
EI-RYR	Boeing Stearman N2S-5	Ryanair Ltd	
EI-SAR	Sikorsky S-61N	Bond Helicopters (Ireland) Ltd	
EI-SAT	Steen Skybolt	B. O'Sullivan	
EI-SHN	Airbus A.330-301	Aer Lingus Teo *St Flannan*	
EI-SPA	Airbus A.320-200	Sun Premier Airlines	
EI-SPB	Airbus A.320-200	Sun Premier Airlines	
EI-SPC	Boeing 757-200	Sun Premier Airlines	
EI-SPD	Boeing 757-200	Sun Premier Airlines	
EI-SXT	Canadair CL.600 Challenger	Sextant Ireland Ltd	
EI-TAR	Bell 222A	Westair Aviation Ltd	
EI-TKI	Robinson R-22B	J. McDaid	
EI-TLB	Airbus A.300B4-203	Airplanes Holdings Ltd	
EI-TLG	Airbus A.320-231	TransAer International Airlines/Libyan Arab	
EI-TLH	Airbus A.320-231	TransAer International Airlines	
EI-TLI	Airbus A.320-231	TransAer International Airlines	
EI-TLJ	Airbus A.320-231	TransAer International Airlines	
EI-TLK	Airbus A.300B4-203	GECAS Ltd *(leased to TransAer)*	
EI-TLL	Airbus A.300B4-203	GECAS Ltd *(leased to TransAer)*	
EI-TLM	Airbus A.300B4-103	TransAer International Airlines	
EI-TLO	Airbus A.320-232	TransAer International Airlines	
EI-TLP	Airbus A.320-232	TransAer International Airlines	
EI-TLQ	Airbus A.300B4-203	TransAer International Airlines	
EI-TLR	Airbus A.320-231	TransAer International Airlines	
EI-TLS	Airbus A.320-231	TransAer International Airlines	
EI-TLT	Airbus A.320-231	TransAer International Airways/Libyan Arab	
EI-TVA	Boeing 737-43Q	Virgin Express (Ireland)	
EI-TVB	Boeing 737-43Q	Virgin Express (Ireland)	
EI-TVC	Boeing 737-43Q	Virgin Express (Ireland)	
EI-TVN	Boeing 737-36N	Virgin Express (Ireland)	
EI-TVO	Boeing 737-36M	Virgin Express (Ireland)	
EI-TVP	Boeing 737-3M8	Virgin Express (Ireland)	
EI-TWO	-	P. A. Wynne	
EI-UFO	PA-22 Tri-Pacer 150 (tailwheel)	W. Treacy	
EI-VIP	Hughes 269C	Cloghran Helicopter Club Ltd	
EI-WAC	PA-23 Aztec 250E	Westair Aviation Ltd	
EI-WAV	Bell 430	Westair Aviation Ltd	
EI-WCC	Robinson R-22B	Westair Aviation Ltd	

Notes	Reg.	Type	Owner or Operator
	EI-WDC	H.S.125 Srs 3B	Westair Aviation Ltd
	EI-WGV	G.1159 Gulfstream 5	Westair Aviation Ltd
	EI-WHE	Beech B200 Super King Air	Westair Aviation Ltd
	EI-WRN	PA-28-151 Warrior	Westair Aviation Ltd
	EI-XMA	Robinson R-22B	Westair Aviation Ltd

EK (Armenia)

The following are operated by Armenian Airlines with the registrations prefixed by EK.

Notes	Reg.	Type	Notes	Reg.	Type
	65044	Tu-134A-3		85210	Tu-154B
	65072	Tu-134A		85279	Tu-154B-1
	65650	Tu-134A		85403	Tu-154B-2
	65822	Tu-134A		85442	Tu-154B-2
	65831	Tu-134A		85536	Tu-154B-2
	65848	Tu-134A		85566	Tu-154B-2
	85166	Tu-154B		86117	IL-86
	85200	Tu-154B		86118	IL-86

Note: Armenian Airlines also operates the A310-222 registered F-OGYW.

Notes	Reg.	Type	Owner or Operator

EL (Liberia)

	EL-AJB	Boeing 707-351C	Scibe Airlift Zaïre
	EL-AJO	Douglas DC-8-55F	Liberia World Airlines
	EL-AJQ	Douglas DC-8-54F	Liberia World Airlines
	EL-AJS	Boeing 707-320C	Sky Air Cargo
	EL-AKF	Boeing 707-321B	SlovTrans
	EL-AKJ	Boeing 707-321C	Omega Air
	EL-AKL	Boeing 707-351C	Liberia World Airlines
	EL-ALG	Boeing 707-369C	Shuttle Air Cargo
	EL-JNS	Boeing 707-323C	Sky Air Cargo
	EL-WXA	B.175 Britannia 253F ★	Britannia Aircraft Preservation Trust/Kemble

EP (Iran)

	EP-IAA	Boeing 747SP-86	Iran Air *Kurdistan*
	EP-IAB	Boeing 747SP-86	Iran Air
	EP-IAC	Boeing 747SP-86	Iran Air *Fars*
	EP-IAD	Boeing 747SP-86	Iran Air
	EP-IAG	Boeing 747-286B (SCD)	Iran Air *Azarabadegan*
	EP-IAH	Boeing 747-286B (SCD)	Iran Air *Khuzestan*
	EP-IAM	Boeing 747-186B	Iran Air
	EP-IBA	Airbus A.300-605R	Iran Air
	EP-IBB	Airbus A.300-605R	Iran Air
	EP-ICC	Boeing 747-2J9F	Iran Air
	EP-SHA	Boeing 747-2J9F	Saha Air Cargo
	EP-SHB	Boeing 747-2J9F	Saha Air Cargo

ER (Moldova)

The following are operated by Air Moldova (MLD) and Moldavian Airlines (MDV) with the registrations prefixed by ER.

Notes	Reg.	Type	Notes	Reg.	Type
	SGA	SAAB SF.340A (MLD)		65741	Tu-134A-3 (MLD)
	TCF	Tu-134A (MDV)		65791	Tu-134A-3 (MLD)
	65036	Tu-134A-3 (MLD)		65897	Tu-134A-3 (MLD)
	65050	Tu-134A-3 (MLD)		85285	Tu-154B-1 (MLD)
	65051	Tu-134A-3 (MLD)		85324	Tu-154B-2 (MLD)
	65071	Tu-134A-3 (MLD)		85332	Tu-154B-2 (MLD)
	65094	Tu-134A-3 (MLD)		85384	Tu-154B-2 (MLD)
	65140	Tu-134A-3 (MLD)		85405	Tu-154B-2 (MLD)
	65707	Tu-134A-3 (MLD)		85565	Tu-154B-2 (MLD)
	65736	Tu-134A-3 (MLD)			

ES (Estonia)

Reg.	Type	Owner or Operator
ES-ABC	Boeing 737-5Q8	Estonian Air *Koit*
ES-ABD	Boeing 737-5Q8	Estonian Air *Hamarik*
ES-ABE	Boeing 737-5L9	Estonian Air
ES-AFK	Fokker 50	Estonian Air
ES-AFL	Fokker 50	Estonian Air
ES-LTP	Tupolev Tu-154M	ELK Airways
ES-LTR	Tupolev Tu-154M	ELK Airways

ET (Ethiopia)

Reg.	Type	Owner or Operator
ET-AIE	Boeing 767-260ER	Ethiopian Airlines
ET-AIF	Boeing 767-260ER	Ethiopian Airlines
ET-AJS	Boeing 757-260PF	Ethiopian Airlines
ET-AJX	Boeing 757-260	Ethiopian Airlines
ET-AKC	Boeing 757-260	Ethiopian Airlines
ET-AKE	Boeing 757-260	Ethiopian Airlines
ET-AKF	Boeing 757-260	Ethiopian Airlines
ET-AKW	Boeing 767-33AER	Ethiopian Airlines
ET-ALC	Boeing 767-33AER	Ethiopian Airlines

EW (Belarus)

The following are operated by Belavia with the registrations prefixed by EW.

Reg.	Type	Notes	Reg.	Type	Notes
65082	Tu-134A		85509	Tu-154B-2	
65085	Tu-134A		85538	Tu-154B-2	
65106	Tu-134A		85545	Tu-154B-2	
65108	Tu-134A		85580	Tu-154B-2	
65133	Tu-134A-3		85581	Tu-154B-2	
65145	Tu-134A		85582	Tu-154B-2	
65149	Tu-134A		85591	Tu-154B-2	
65754	Tu-134A		85593	Tu-154B-2	
65772	Tu-134A		85703	Tu-154M	
65803	Tu-134A		85706	Tu-154M	
65821	Tu-134A		85741	Tu-154M	
65832	Tu-134A		85748	Tu-154M	
85260	Tu-154B-1		85815	Tu-154M	
85339	Tu-154B-2				
85352	Tu-154B-2		The following are operated by		
85411	Tu-154B-2		Belair		
85419	Tu-154B-2		65565	Tu-134A	
85465	Tu-154B-2		76837	IL-76TD	

EX (Kyrgyzstan)

The following are operated by Kyrgyzstan Airlines with the registrations prefixed by EX.

Reg.	Type	Reg.	Type
65111	Tu-134A-3	85294	Tu-154B-1
65119	Tu-134A-3	85313	Tu-154B-2
65125	Tu-134A-3	85369	Tu-154B-2
65778	Tu-134A-3	85444	Tu-154B-2
65779	Tu-134A-3	85491	Tu-154B-2
65789	Tu-134A-3	85497	Tu-154B-2
76815	IL-76TD	85519	Tu-154B-2
85021	Tu-154B-1	85590	Tu-154B-2
85252	Tu-154B-1	85718	Tu-154M
85257	Tu-154B-1	85762	Tu-154M
85259	Tu-154B-1		

Note: Kyrgyzstan Airlines also operates the A.320 registered F-OHGA

EY (Tajikistan)

The following are operated by Tajikistan Airlines with the registrations prefixd by EY.

Reg.	Type	Reg.	Type
65003	Tu-134A-3	65814	Tu-134A-3
65763	Tu-134A-3	65820	Tu-134A-3
65788	Tu-134A-3	65835	Tu-134A-3

Notes	Reg.	Type	Notes	Reg.	Type
	65876	Tu-134A-3		85475	Tu-154B-2
	85247	Tu-154B-1		85487	Tu-154B-2
	85251	Tu-154B-1		85511	Tu-154B-2
	85406	Tu-154B-2		85691	Tu-154M
	85440	Tu-154B-2		85692	Tu-154M
	85466	Tu-154B-2		85717	Tu-154M
	85469	Tu-154B-2			

EZ (Turkmenistan)

Turkmenistan Airlines operates the following with the registrations prefixed by EZ.

Reg.	Type	Reg.	Type
A001	Boeing 737-341	F428	IL-76TD
A002	Boeing 737-332	85241	Tu-154B-1
A003	Boeing 737-332	85246	Tu-154B-1
A010	Boeing 757-23A	85345	Tu-154B-2
A011	Boeing 757-22K	85383	Tu-154B-2
A012	Boeing 757-22K	85394	Tu-154B-2
F421	IL-76TD	85410	Tu-154B-2
F422	IL-76TD	85492	Tu-154B-2
F423	IL-76TD	85507	Tu-154B-2
F424	IL-76TD	85532	Tu-154B-2
F425	IL-76TD	85549	Tu-154B-2
F426	IL-76TD	85560	Tu-154B-2
F427	IL-76TD		

Notes	Reg.	Type	Owner or Operator

F (France)

Reg.	Type	Owner or Operator
F-BPUA	F.27 Friendship Mk 500	Air France
F-BPUC	F.27 Friendship Mk 500	Air France
F-BPUD	F.27 Friendship Mk 500	Air France
F-BPUE	F.27 Friendship Mk 500	Air France
F-BPUF	F.27 Friendship Mk 500	Air France
F-BPUG	F.27 Friendship Mk 500	Air France
F-BPUH	F.27 Friendship Mk 500	Air France
F-BPUJ	F.27 Friendship Mk 500	Air France
F-BPVJ	Boeing 747-128	Air France
F-BPVM	Boeing 747-128	Air France
F-BPVR	Boeing 747-228F (SCD)	Air France
F-BPVS	Boeing 747-228B (SCD)	Air France
F-BPVT	Boeing 747-228B (SCD)	Air France
F-BPVU	Boeing 747-228B (SCD)	Air France
F-BPVX	Boeing 747-228B (SCD)	Air France
F-BPVY	Boeing 747-228B	Air France
F-BPVZ	Boeing 747-228F (SCD)	Air France
F-BSUO	F.27 Friendship Mk 500	Air France
F-BTDD	Douglas DC-10-30	AOM French Airlines
F-BTDE	Douglas DC-10-30	AOM French Airlines
F-BTDG	Boeing 747-2B3B (SCD)	Air France
F-BTDH	Boeing 747-2B3B (SCD)	Air France
F-BTSC	Concorde 101	Air France
F-BTSD	Concorde 101	Air France
F-BVFA	Concorde 101	Air France
F-BVFB	Concorde 101	Air France
F-BVFC	Concorde 101	Air France
F-BVFF	Concorde 101	Air France
F-BVJL	Beech 99A	Air Liberte
F-GBLE	EMB-110P2 Bandeirante	Air Atlantique
F-GBME	EMB-110P2 Bandeirante	Air Atlantique
F-GBOX	Boeing 747-2B3F (SCD)	Air France Cargo
F-GBRU	F.27J Friendship	Air Liberte
F-GBYA	Boeing 737-228	Air France
F-GBYB	Boeing 737-228	Air France
F-GBYC	Boeing 737-228	Air France
F-GBYD	Boeing 737-228	Air France
F-GBYF	Boeing 737-228	Air France
F-GBYI	Boeing 737-228	Air France
F-GBYJ	Boeing 737-228	Air France
F-GBYK	Boeing 737-228	Air France
F-GBYL	Boeing 737-228	Air France

Reg.	Type	Owner or Operator	Notes
F-GBYM	Boeing 737-228	Air France	
F-GBYN	Boeing 737-228	Air France	
F-GBYO	Boeing 737-228	Air France	
F-GBYP	Boeing 737-228	Air France	
F-GBYQ	Boeing 737-228	Air France	
F-GCBA	Boeing 747-228B	Air France	
F-GCBB	Boeing 747-228B (SCD)	Air France	
F-GCBD	Boeing 747-228B (SCD)	Air France Asie	
F-GCBE	Boeing 747-228F (SCD)	Air France	
F-GCBF	Boeing 747-228B (SCD)	Air France	
F-GCBG	Boeing 747-228F (SCD)	Air France Cargo	
F-GCBH	Boeing 747-228F (SCD)	Air France Asia Cargo	
F-GCBI	Boeing 747-228B (SCD)	Air France	
F-GCBJ	Boeing 747-228B (SCD)	Air France	
F-GCBK	Boeing 747-228F (SCD)	Air France Cargo	
F-GCBL	Boeing 747-228F (SCD)	Air France Cargo	
F-GCBM	Boeing 747-228F	Air France Asia Cargo	
F-GCGQ	Boeing 727-227	Belair *Ile de France*	
F-GCJL	Boeing 737-222	Air Mediterranee	
F-GCSL	Boeing 737-222	Air Mediterranee	
F-GDFD	F.28 Fellowship 4000	Air Liberte	
F-GDPP	Douglas DC-3C	SA Publi-Air (France)	
F-GDUS	F.28 Fellowship 2000	Air Liberte	
F-GDUT	F.28 Fellowship 2000	Air Liberte	
F-GDUU	F.28 Fellowship 2000	Air Liberte/British Airways	
F-GDUV	F.28 Fellowship 2000	Air Liberte/British Airways	
F-GDUZ	F.28 Fellowship 4000	Air Liberte	
F-GDXL	Aérospatiale ATR-42-300	Brit Air/Air France	
F-GEGD	Aérospatiale ATR-42-300	Air Littoral	
F-GEGE	Aérospatiale ATR-42-300	Air Littoral	
F-GEMA	Airbus A.310-203	Air France	
F-GEMB	Airbus A.310-203	Air France	
F-GEMC	Airbus A.310-203	Air France	
F-GEMD	Airbus A.310-203	Air France	
F-GEME	Airbus A.310-203	Air France	
F-GEMG	Airbus A.310-203	Air France	
F-GEMN	Airbus A.310-304	Air France	
F-GEMO	Airbus A.310-304	Air France	
F-GEMP	Airbus A.310-304	Air France	
F-GEMQ	Airbus A.310-304	Air France	
F-GEQJ	Aérospatiale ATR-42-300	Regional Airlines	
F-GETA	Boeing 747-3B3 (SCD)	Air France	
F-GETB	Boeing 747-3B3 (SCD)	Air France	
F-GEXA	Boeing 747-4B3	Air France	
F-GEXB	Boeing 747-4B3	Air France	
F-GEXI	Boeing 737-2L9	Aeris International	
F-GFEO	EMB-120RT Brasilia	Regional Airlines	
F-GFEQ	EMB-120RT Brasilia	Regional Airlines	
F-GFKA	Airbus A.320-111	Air France *Ville de Paris*	
F-GFKB	Airbus A.320-111	Air France *Ville de Rome*	
F-GFKD	Airbus A.320-111	Air France *Ville de Londres*	
F-GFKE	Airbus A.320-111	Air France *Ville de Bonn*	
F-GFKF	Airbus A.320-111	Air France *Ville de Madrid*	
F-GFKG	Airbus A.320-111	Air France *Ville d'Amsterdam*	
F-GFKH	Airbus A.320-211	Air France *Ville de Bruxelles*	
F-GFKI	Airbus A.320-211	Air France *Ville de Lisbonne*	
F-GFKJ	Airbus A.320-211	Air France *Ville de Copenhague*	
F-GFKK	Airbus A.320-211	Air France *Ville d'Athenes*	
F-GFKL	Airbus A.320-211	Air France/Air Charter *Ville de Dublin*	
F-GFKM	Airbus A.320-211	Air France *Ville de Luxembourg*	
F-GFKN	Airbus A.320-211	Air France *Ville de Strasbourg*	
F-GFKO	Airbus A.320-211	Air France	
F-GFKP	Airbus A.320-211	Air France *Ville de Nice*	
F-GFKQ	Airbus A.320-111	Air France *Ville de Berlin*	
F-GFKR	Airbus A.320-211	Air France *Ville de Barcelona*	
F-GFKS	Airbus A.320-211	Air France	
F-GFKT	Airbus A.320-211	Air France *Ville de Lyon*	
F-GFKU	Airbus A.320-211	Air France *Ville de Manchester*	
F-GFKV	Airbus A.320-211	Air France *Ville de Bordeaux*	
F-GFKX	Airbus A.320-211	Air France/Air Charter *Ville de Francfurt*	
F-GFKY	Airbus A.320-211	Air France *Ville de Toulouse*	
F-GFKZ	Airbus A.320-211	Air France *Ville de Turin*	
F-GFLV	Boeing 737-2K5	Air France	

Notes	Reg.	Type	Owner or Operator
	F-GFLX	Boeing 737-2K5	Air France
	F-GFPR	Swearingen SA226AT Merlin IVA	Regional Airlines
	F-GFUA	Boeing 737-33A	Air France
	F-GFUD	Boeing 737-33A	Air France
	F-GFUE	Boeing 737-3B3QC	L'Aéropostale
	F-GFUF	Boeing 737-3B3QC	L'Aéropostale
	F-GFUG	Boeing 737-4B3	Corsair
	F-GFUH	Boeing 737-4B3	Corsair
	F-GFUI	Boeing 737-3M8	Corsair
	F-GFUJ	Boeing 737-33A	Air France
	F-GFVI	Boeing 737-230C	L'Aéropostale
	F-GFYL	Boeing 737-2A9C	Euralair International
	F-GFZB	McD Douglas MD-83	Air Liberte
	F-GGEA	Airbus A.320-111	Air France
	F-GGEB	Airbus A.320-111	Air France
	F-GGEC	Airbus A.320-111	Air France
	F-GGEE	Airbus A.320-111	Air France
	F-GGEF	Airbus A.320-111	Air France
	F-GGEG	Airbus A.320-111	Air France
	F-GGGR	Boeing 727-2H3	Belair *Villa Squeville*
	F-GGLK	Aérospatiale ATR-42-300	T.A.T. European
	F-GGLR	Aérospatiale ATR-42-300	Brit Air/Air France
	F-GGMA	McD Douglas MD-83	AOM French Airlines
	F-GGMB	McD Douglas MD-83	AOM French Airlines
	F-GGMD	McD Douglas MD-83	AOM French Airlines
	F-GGME	McD Douglas MD-83	AOM French Airlines
	F-GGMF	McD Douglas MD-83	AOM French Airlines
	F-GGTD	EMB-120ER Brasilia	Flandre Air/Air Liberte
	F-GGVP	Boeing 737-2K2C	L'Aéropostale
	F-GGVQ	Boeing 737-2K2C	L'Aéropostale
	F-GHEB	McD Douglas MD-83	Air Liberte
	F-GHEC	McD Douglas MD-83	Air Liberte
	F-GHED	McD Douglas MD-83	Air Liberte
	F-GHEI	McD Douglas MD-83	Air Liberte
	F-GHEK	McD Douglas MD-83	Air Liberte
	F-GHEX	EMB-120ER Brasilia	Flandre Air
	F-GHEY	EMB-120ER Brasilia	Flandre Air
	F-GHGF	Boeing 767-3Q8ER	Air France
	F-GHGG	Boeing 767-3Q8ER	Air France
	F-GHGH	Boeing 767-37EER	Air France
	F-GHGI	Boeing 767-328ER	Air France
	F-GHGJ	Boeing 767-328ER	Air France
	F-GHHO	McD Douglas MD-83	Air Liberte
	F-GHHP	McD Douglas MD-83	Air Liberte
	F-GHIA	EMB-120ER Brasilia	Flandre Air
	F-GHIB	EMB-120ER Brasilia	Flandre Air
	F-GHJE	Aérospatiale ATR-42-300	Brit Air/Air France Express
	F-GHMJ	SAAB SF.340A	Brit Air/Air France Express
	F-GHOI	Douglas DC-10-30	AOM French Airlines
	F-GHOL	Boeing 737-53C	AOM French Airlines
	F-GHPI	Aérospatiale ATR-42-300	Brit Air/Air France Express
	F-GHPK	Aérospatiale ATR-42-300	Brit Air/Air France Express
	F-GHPS	Aérospatiale ATR-42-300	Brit Air/Air France Express
	F-GHPU	Aérospatiale ATR-72-101	Brit Air/Air France Express
	F-GHPV	Aérospatiale ATR-72-101	Brit Air/Air France Express
	F-GHPY	Aérospatiale ATR-42-300	Brit Air/Air France
	F-GHPZ	Aérospatiale ATR-42-300	Brit Air/Air France
	F-GHQA	Airbus A.320-211	Air France
	F-GHQB	Airbus A.320-211	Air France
	F-GHQC	Airbus A.320-211	Air France
	F-GHQD	Airbus A.320-211	Air France
	F-GHQE	Airbus A.320-211	Air France
	F-GHQF	Airbus A.320-211	Air France
	F-GHQG	Airbus A.320-211	Air France
	F-GHQH	Airbus A.320-211	Air France
	F-GHQI	Airbus A.320-211	Air France
	F-GHQJ	Airbus A.320-211	Air France
	F-GHQK	Airbus A.320-211	Air France
	F-GHQL	Airbus A.320-211	Air France
	F-GHQM	Airbus A.320-211	Air France
	F-GHQO	Airbus A.320-211	Air France
	F-GHQP	Airbus A.320-211	Air France
	F-GHQQ	Airbus A.320-211	Air France

Reg.	Type	Owner or Operator	Notes
F-GHQR	Airbus A.320-211	Air France	
F-GHSE	Beech 1900C-1	Flandre Air	
F-GHSI	Beech 1900C-1	Flandre Air	
F-GHUL	Boeing 737-53C	AOM French Airlines	
F-GHVA	Swearingen SA227AC Metro III	Regional Airlines	
F-GHVG	Swearingen SA227AC Metro III	Regional Airlines	
F-GHVM	Boeing 737-33A	Air France	
F-GHVN	Boeing 737-33A	Air France	
F-GHVO	Boeing 737-33A	Air France	
F-GHVT	SAAB SF.340B	Regional Airlines	
F-GHXK	Boeing 737-2A1	Corsair/Aeris International	
F-GHXL	Boeing 737-2S3	Aeris International	
F-GHXM	Boeing 737-53A	Air France	
F-GIAH	F.28 Fellowship 1000	Air Liberte	
F-GIAI	F.28 Fellowship 1000	Air Liberte	
F-GIDK	Douglas DC-3C	Dakota Air	
F-GIIA	Aérospatiale ATR-42-300	Air Atlantique	
F-GIJS	Airbus A.300B4-203	Air France	
F-GILN	Swearingen SA227AC Metro III	Regional Airlines	
F-GIMJ	Boeing 747-121	Corsair	
F-GINL	Boeing 737-53C	AOM French Airlines	
F-GIOA	Fokker 100	Air Liberte	
F-GIOG	Fokker 100	Air Liberte	
F-GIOH	Fokker 100	Air Liberte	
F-GIOI	Fokker 100	Air Liberte/British Airways	
F-GIOJ	Fokker 100	Air Liberte	
F-GIOK	Fokker 100	Air Liberte	
F-GIRC	Aérospatiale ATR-42-300	Air Liberte	
F-GISA	Boeing 747-428 (SCD)	Air France	
F-GISB	Boeing 747-428 (SCD)	Air France	
F-GISC	Boeing 747-428 (SCD)	Air France	
F-GISD	Boeing 747-428 (SCD)	Air France	
F-GISE	Boeing 747-428 (SCD)	Air France	
F-GITA	Boeing 747-428	Air France	
F-GITB	Boeing 747-428	Air France	
F-GITC	Boeing 747-428	Air France	
F-GITD	Boeing 747-428	Air France	
F-GITE	Boeing 747-428	Air France	
F-GITF	Boeing 747-428	Air France	
F-GIVG	Aérospatiale ATR-42-300	Regional Airlines	
F-GIVK	EMB-120ER Brasilia	Flandre Air	
F-GIXA	Boeing 737-2K2C	L'Aéropostale	
F-GIXB	Boeing 737-33AQC	L'Aéropostale	
F-GIXC	Boeing 737-38BQC	L'Aéropostale	
F-GIXD	Boeing 737-33AQC	L'Aéropostale	
F-GIXE	Boeing 737-3B3QC	L'Aéropostale	
F-GIXF	Boeing 737-3B3QC	L'Aéropostale	
F-GIXG	Boeing 737-382QC	L'Aéropostale	
F-GIXH	Boeing 737-3S3QC	L'Aéropostale	
F-GIXI	Boeing 737-348QC	L'Aéropostale	
F-GIXJ	Boeing 737-3Y0QC	L'Aéropostale	
F-GIXK	Boeing 737-33AQC	L'Aéropostale	
F-GIXL	Boeing 737-348QC	L'Aéropostale	
F-GIXO	Boeing 737-3Q8QC	L'Aéropostale	
F-GIXP	Boeing 737-3M8F	L'Aéropostale	
F-GIYH	EMB-120ER Brasilia	Flandre Air	
F-GIYI	EMB-120RT Brasilia	Flandre Air	
F-GJAK	EMB-120ER Brasilia	Flandre Air	
F-GJEG	Beech 1900-1	Air Liberte	
F-GJHQ	McD Douglas MD-83	Air Liberte	
F-GJNA	Boeing 737-528	Air France	
F-GJNB	Boeing 737-528	Air France	
F-GJNC	Boeing 737-528	Air France	
F-GJND	Boeing 737-528	Air France	
F-GJNE	Boeing 737-528	Air France	
F-GJNF	Boeing 737-528	Air France	
F-GJNG	Boeing 737-528	Air France	
F-GJNH	Boeing 737-528	Air France	
F-GJNI	Boeing 737-528	Air France	
F-GJNJ	Boeing 737-528	Air France	
F-GJNK	Boeing 737-528	Air France	
F-GJNM	Boeing 737-528	Air France	
F-GJNN	Boeing 737-528	Air France	

Notes	Reg.	Type	Owner or Operator
	F-GJNO	Boeing 737-528	Air France
	F-GJNQ	Boeing 737-5H6	Air France
	F-GJNR	Boeing 737-5H6	Air France
	F-GJNS	Boeing 737-53S	Air France
	F-GJNT	Boeing 737-53S	Air France
	F-GJNU	Boeing 737-53S	Air France
	F-GJNV	Boeing 737-548	Air France
	F-GJVA	Airbus A.320-211	Air France
	F-GJVB	Airbus A.320-211	Air France
	F-GJVC	Airbus A.320-211	Air France
	F-GJVD	Airbus A.320-211	Air France
	F-GJVE	Airbus A.320-211	Air France
	F-GJVF	Airbus A.320-211	Air France
	F-GJVG	Airbus A.320-211	Air France
	F-GJVU	Airbus A.320-211	Air France
	F-GJVV	Airbus A.320-211	Air France
	F-GJVW	Airbus A.320-211	Air France
	F-GJVX	Airbus A.320-211	Air France
	F-GKHD	Fokker 100	Air Liberte
	F-GKHE	Fokker 100	Air Liberte
	F-GKLJ	Boeing 747-121	Corsair
	F-GKMY	Douglas DC-10-30	AOM French Airlines
	F-GKNB	Aérospatiale ATR-42-300	Air Liberte
	F-GKNC	Aérospatiale ATR-42-300	Air Liberte
	F-GKND	Aérospatiale ATR-42-300	Air Liberte
	F-GKOA	Aérospatiale ATR-72-202	Air Liberte
	F-GKOB	Aérospatiale ATR-72-202	Air Liberte/Airlinair
	F-GKOC	Aérospatiale ATR-72-202	Air Liberte/Airlinair
	F-GKPC	Aérospatiale ATR-72-102	Compagnie Corse Mediterranée
	F-GKPD	Aéropsatiale ATR-72-102	Compagnie Corse Mediterranée
	F-GKPE	Aérospatiale ATR-72-102	Compagnie Corse Mediterranée
	F-GKPF	Aérospatiale ATR-72-102	Compagnie Corse Mediterranée
	F-GKPH	Aérospatiale ATR-72-202	Compagnie Corse Mediterranée
	F-GKST	Beech 1900-1	Proteus Airlines
	F-GKTA	Boeing 737-3M8	TEA Europe/Air One
	F-GKTB	Boeing 737-3M8	TEA Europe/Air One
	F-GKXA	Airbus A.320-211	Air France *Ville de Nantes*
	F-GKZL	McD Douglas MD-83	Belair
	F-GLGG	Airbus A.320-212	Air France/Air Charter
	F-GLGH	Airbus A.320-212	Air France/Air Charter
	F-GLIA	Aérospatiale ATR-42-300	Brit Air/Air France
	F-GLIB	Aérospatiale ATR-42-300	Brit Air/Air France
	F-GLIJ	Canadair CL.600-2B19 RJ	Air Littoral/Team Lufthansa
	F-GLIK	Canadair CL.600-2B19 RJ	Air Littoral/Team Lufthansa
	F-GLIR	Fokker 100	Air Littoral/Air France
	F-GLIS	Fokker 70	Air Littoral/Air France
	F-GLIT	Fokker 70	Air Littoral/Air France
	F-GLIU	Fokker 70	Air Littoral/Air France
	F-GLIV	Fokker 70	Air Littoral/Air France
	F-GLIX	Fokker 70	Air Littoral/Air France
	F-GLIY	Canadair CL.600-2B19 RJ	Air Littoral/Air France
	F-GLIZ	Canadair CL.600-2B19 RJ	Air Littoral/Air France
	F-GLMX	Douglas DC-10-30	AOM French Airlines
	F-GLNA	Boeing 747-206B	Corsair
	F-GLND	Beech 1900D	Flandre Air
	F-GLNE	Beech 1900D	Flandre Air
	F-GLNF	Beech 1900D	Flandre Air/Air Liberte
	F-GLNH	Beech 1900D	Flandre Air
	F-GLNI	BAe 146-200QC	Air Jet
	F-GLNK	Beech 1900D	Flandre Air
	F-GLPJ	Beech 1900C-1	Flandre Air
	F-GLPL	Beech 1900C-1	Flandre Air
	F-GLRG	EMB-120RT Brasilia	Flandre Air
	F-GLXF	Boeing 737-219	Aeris International
	F-GLXH	Boeing 737-2D6	Aeris International
	F-GLZA	Airbus A.340-311	Air France
	F-GLZB	Airbus A.340-311	Air France
	F-GLZC	Airbus A.340-311	Air France
	F-GLZE	Airbus A.340-211	AOM French Airlines
	F-GLZF	Airbus A.340-211	AOM French Airlines
	F-GLZG	Airbus A.340-311	Air France
	F-GLZH	Airbus A.340-311	Air France
	F-GLZI	Airbus A.340-311	Air France

Reg.	Type	Owner or Operator	Notes
F-GLZJ	Airbus A.340-313X	Air France	
F-GLZK	Airbus A.340-313X	Air France	
F-GLZL	Airbus A.340-313X	Air France	
F-GLZM	Airbus A.340-313X	Air France	
F-GLZN	Airbus A.340-313X	Air France	
F-GLZO	Airbus A.340-313X	Air France	
F-BLZP	Airbus A.340-313X	Air France	
F-GLZQ	Airbus A.340-313X	Air France	
F-GLZR	Airbus A.340-313X	Air France	
F-GLZS	Airbus A.340-313X	Air France	
F-GLZT	Airbus A.340-313X	Air France	
F-GMAD	Beech 1900D	Proteus Airlines *Ville de Rodez*	
F-GMJD	Boeing 737-2K5	Corsair	
F-GMMP	BAe 146-200QC	Air Jet	
F-GMPG	Fokker 100	Compagnie Corse Mediterranée	
F-GMVB	SAAB 2000	Regional Airlines	
F-GMVC	SAAB 2000	Regional Airlines	
F-GMVD	SAAB 2000	Regional Airlines/Air France Express	
F-GMVE	SAAB 2000	Regional Airlines	
F-GMVF	SAAB 2000	Regional Airlines	
F-GMVG	SAAB 2000	Regional Airlines	
F-GMVH	BAe Jetstream 3206	Regional Airlines/Air Normandie	
F-GMVI	BAe Jetstream 3206	Regional Airlines	
F-GMVJ	BAe Jetstream 3206	Regional Airlines	
F-GMVK	BAe Jetstream 3206	Regional Airlines	
F-GMVL	BAe Jetstream 3206	Regional Airlines	
F-GMVM	BAe Jetstream 3206	Regional Airlines	
F-GMVN	BAe Jetstream 3206	Regional Airlines	
F-GMVO	BAe Jetstream 3206	Regional Airlines	
F-GMVP	BAe Jetstream 3206	Regional Airlines	
F-GMVQ	SAAB SF.340B	Regional Airlines	
F-GMVY	SAAB SF.340B	Regional Airlines	
F-GMZA	Airbus A.321-111	Air France	
F-GMZB	Airbus A.321-111	Air France	
F-GMZC	Airbus A.321-111	Air France	
F-GMZD	Airbus A.321-111	Air France	
F-GMZE	Airbus A.321-111	Air France	
F-GNAD	Beech 1900C-1	Proteus Airlines	
F-GNAH	Beech 1900C-1	Proteus Airlines	
F-GNBS	Dornier Do.328-110	Proteus Airlines	
F-GNDC	Douglas DC-10-30	AOM French Airlines	
F-GNEM	Douglas DC-10-30	AOM French Airlines	
F-GNFC	Boeing 737-36E	Aeris SA	
F-GNFD	Boeing 737-36E	Aeris SA	
F-GNFE	Boeing 737-36E	Aeris SA	
F-GNIF	Airbus A.340-313X	Air France	
F-GNIG	Airbus A.340-313X	Air France	
F-GNIH	Airbus A.340-313X	Air France	
F-GNLG	Fokker 100	Air Liberte	
F-GNLH	Fokker 100	Air Liberte	
F-GNLI	Fokker 100	Air Liberte	
F-GNLJ	Fokker 100	Air Liberte	
F-GNLK	Fokker 100	Air Liberte	
F-GNMN	Canadair CL.600-2B19	Air Littoral/Air France Express	
F-GNPA	Dornier Do.328-110	Proteus Airlines	
F-GNPL	Aérospatiale ATR-42-310	Chalair	
F-GNPM	Beech 1900C-1	Proteus Airlines	
F-GNPR	Dornier Do.328-110	Proteus Airlines	
F-GNYL	Beech 1900C-1	Proteus Airlines	
F-GNZB	F.28 Fellowship 1000	Air Liberte/Delta Air Transport	
F-GOAC	Dornier Do.328-110	Proteus Airlines	
F-GOAF	Boeing 737-242C	Air Mediterranee	
F-GOFB	Dornier Do.328-110	Proteus Airlines	
F-GOMA	BAe 146-200QC	Air Jet	
F-GOPK	Beech 1900D	Prest'Affair/UPS	
F-GOZA	Airbus A.300B4-103F	Aéropostale	
F-GOZB	Airbus A.300B4-103F	Aéropostale	
F-GPAN	Boeing 747-2B3F (SCD)	Air France Cargo	
F-GPBM	Beech 1900D	Proteus Airlines	
F-GPJM	Boeing 747-206B	Corsair	
F-GPKD	SAAB SF.340B	Crossair Europe	
F-GPKG	SAAB SF.340B	Crossair Europe	
F-GPMA	Airbus A.319-113	Air France	

Notes	Reg.	Type	Owner or Operator
	F-GPMB	Airbus A.319-113	Air France
	F-GPMC	Airbus A.319-113	Air France
	F-GPMD	Airbus A.319-113	Air France
	F-GPME	Airbus A.319-113	Air France
	F-GPMF	Airbus A.319-113	Air France
	F-GPMG	Airbus A.319-113	Air France
	F-GPMH	Airbus A.319-113	Air France
	F-GPMI	Airbus A.319-113	Air France
	F-GPOC	Aérospatiale ATR-72-212	L'Aeropostale
	F-GPOD	Aérospatiale ATR-72-212	L'Aeropostale
	F-GPSD	Beech 1900D	Proteus Airlines *Ville de Dijon*
	F-GPTB	Canadair CL.600-2B19 RJ	Air Littoral
	F-GPTC	Canadair CL.600-2B19 RJ	Air Littoral
	F-GPTD	Canadair CL.600-2B19 RJ	Air Littoral
	F-GPTE	Canadair CL.600-2B19 RJ	Air Littoral
	F-GPTF	Canadair CL.600-2B19 RJ	Air Littoral/Team Lufthansa
	F-GPTG	Canadair CL.600-2B19 RJ	Air Littoral
	F-GPTH	Canadair CL.600-2B19 RJ	Air Littoral
	F-GPTI	Canadair CL.600-2B19 RJ	Air Littoral
	F-GPTJ	Canadair CL.600-2B19 RJ	Air Littoral
	F-GPTK	Canadair CL.600-2B19 RJ	Air Littoral
	F-GPVA	Douglas DC-10-30	Air Liberte
	F-GPVC	Douglas DC-10-30	Air Liberte
	F-GPVD	Douglas DC-10-30	Air Liberte
	F-GPVV	Boeing 747-228F (SCD)	Air France
	F-GPXA	Fokker 100	Brit Air/Air France
	F-GPXB	Fokker 100	Brit Air/Air France
	F-GPXC	Fokker 100	Brit Air/Air France
	F-GPXD	Fokker 100	Brit Air/Air France
	F-GPXE	Fokker 100	Brit Air/Air France
	F-GPYA	Aérospatiale ATR-42-512	Air Littoral
	F-GPYB	Aérospatiale ATR-42-512	Air Littoral
	F-GPYC	Aérospatiale ATR-42-512	Air Littoral
	F-GPYD	Aérospatiale ATR-42-512	Air Littoral
	F-GPYF	Aérospatiale ATR 42-512	Air Littoral *Marie Sara*
	F-GPYG	Aérospatiale ATR-42-512	Air Littoral
	F-GPYH	Aérospatiale ATR-42-512	Air Littoral
	F-GPYI	Aérospatiale ATR-42-512	Air Littoral
	F-GPYJ	Aérospatiale ATR-42-512	Air Littoral
	F-GPYK	Aérospatiale ATR-42-512	Air Littoral
	F-GPYL	Aérospatiale ATR-42-512	Air Littoral
	F-GPYM	Aérospatiale ATR-42-512	Air Littoral
	F-GPYN	Aérospatiale ATR-42-512	Air Littoral
	F-GPYO	Aérospatiale ATR-42-512	Air Littoral
	F-GPYP	Canadair CL.600-2B19 RJ	Air Littoral/Team Lufthansa
	F-GPYQ	Canadair CL.600-2B19 RJ	Air Littoral
	F-GPYR	Canadair CL.600-2B19 RJ	Air Littoral
	F-GPYS	Beech 1900C-1	Air Littoral/UPS
	F-GPYT	Beech 1900C-1	Air Littoral/UPS
	F-GPYU	Beech 1900C-1	Air Littoral/UPS
	F-GPYV	Beech 1900C-1	Air Littoral/UPS
	F-GPYX	Beech 1900C-1	Air Littoral/UPS
	F-GPYY	Beech 1900C-1	Air Littoral/UPS
	F-GPZA	McD Douglas MD-83	Air Liberte/British Airways
	F-GRCD	Beech 1900D	Proteus Airlines
	F-GREA	Beech 1900D	Proteus Airlines
	F-GRFA	Boeing 737-36N	Air France
	F-GRFB	Boeing 737-36N	Air France
	F-GRFC	Boeing 737-36N	Air France
	F-GRGA	Embraer RJ145EU	Regional Airlines
	F-GRGB	Embraer RJ145EU	Regional Airlines
	F-GRGC	Embraer RJ145EU	Regional Airlines
	F-GRGD	Embraer RJ145EU	Regional Airlines
	F-GRGE	Embraer RJ145EU	Regional Airlines
	F-GRGF	Embraer RJ145EU	Regional Airlines
	F-GRGG	Embraer RJ145EU	Regional Airlines
	F-GRGH	Embraer RJ145EU	Regional Airlines
	F-GRGI	Embraer RJ145EU	Regional Airlines
	F-GRGP	Embraer RJ135ER	Regional Airlines
	F-GRHA	Airbus A.319-111	Air France
	F-GRHB	Airbus A.319-111	Air France
	F-GRHC	Airbus A.319-111	Air France
	F-GRHD	Airbus A.319-111	Air France

Reg.	Type	Owner or Operator	Notes
F-GRHE	Airbus A.319-111	Air France	
F-GRHF	Airbus A.319-111	Air France	
F-GRHG	Airbus A.319-111	Air France	
F-GRHH	Airbus A.319-111	Air France	
F-GRHI	Airbus A.319-111	Air France	
F-GRJA	Canadair CL.600-2B19 RJ	Brit Air/Air France Express	
F-GRJB	Canadair CL.600-2B19 RJ	Brit Air/Air France Express	
F-GRJC	Canadair CL.600-2B19 RJ	Brit Air/Air France Express	
F-GRJD	Canadair CL.600-2B19 RJ	Brit Air/Air France Express	
F-GRJE	Canadair CL.600-2B19 RJ	Brit Air/Air France Express	
F-GRJF	Canadair CL.600-2B19 RJ	Brit Air/Air France Express	
F-GRJG	Canadair CL.600-2B19 RJ	Brit Air/Air France Express	
F-GRJH	Canadair CL.600-2B19 RJ	Brit Air/Air France Express	
F-GRJI	Canadair CL.600-2B19 RJ	Brit Air/Air France Express	
F-GRJJ	Canadair CL.600-2B19 RJ	Brit Air/Air France Express	
F-GRJK	Canadair CL.600-2B19 RJ	Brit Air/Air France Express	
F-GRJL	Canadair CL.600-2B19 RJ	Brit Air/Air France Express	
F-GRJM	Canadair CL.600-2B19 RJ	Brit Air/Air France Express	
F-GRJN	Canadair CL.600-2B19 RJ	Brit Air/Air France Express	
F-GRJO	Canadair CL.600-2B19 RJ	Brit Air/Air France Express	
F-GRJP	Canadair CL.600-2B19 RJ	Brit Air/Air France Express	
F-GRJQ	Canadair CL.600-2B19 RJ	Brit Air/Air France Express	
F-GRJR	Canadair CL.600-2B19 RJ	Brit Air/Air France Express	
F-GRJS	Canadair CL.600-2B19 RJ	Brit Air/Air France Express	
F-GRJT	Canadair CL.600-2B19 RJ	Brit Air/Air France Express	
F-GRMC	McD Douglas MD-83	AOM French Airlines	
F-GRMD	Beech 1900D	Proteus Airlines	
F-GRMG	McD Douglas MD-83	AOM French Airlines	
F-GRMH	McD Douglas MD-83	AOM French Airlines	
F-GRMI	McD Douglas MD-83	AOM French Airlines	
F-GRMJ	McD Douglas MD-83	AOM French Airlines	
F-GRML	McD Douglas MD-83	Air Liberte	
F-GRNA	Boeing 737-85F	Euralair	
F-GRNC	Boeing 737-85F	Euralair	
F-GRPM	Beech 1900D	Proteus Airlines	
F-GRSD	Airbus A.320-214	Star Airlines	
F-GRSE	Airbus A.320-214	Star Airlines	
F-GRSF	Airbus A.320-214	Star Airlines	
F-GRSG	Airbus A.320-214	Star Airlines	
F-GRSH	Airbus A.320-214	Star Airlines	
F-GRSI	Airbus A.320-214	Star Airlines	
F-GRYL	Beech 1900D	Proteus Airlines	
F-GSEA	Boeing 747-312	Corsair	
F-GSPA	Boeing 777-228ER	Air France	
F-GSPB	Boeing 777-228ER	Air France	
F-GSPC	Boeing 777-228ER	Air France	
F-GSPD	Boeing 777-228ER	Air France	
F-GSPE	Boeing 777-228ER	Air France	
F-GSPF	Boeing 777-228ER	Air France	
F-GSPG	Boeing 777-228ER	Air France	
F-GSPH	Boeing 777-228ER	Air France	
F-GSPI	Boeing 777-228ER	Air France	
F-GSPJ	Boeing 777-228ER	Air France	
F-GSPK	Boeing 777-228ER	Air France	
F-GSTA	Airbus A.300-608ST Beluga (1)	Airbus Inter Transport	
F-GSTB	Airbus A.300-608ST Beluga (2)	Airbus Inter Transport	
F-GSTC	Airbus A.300-608ST Beluga (3)	Airbus Inter Transport	
F-GSTD	Airbus A.300-608ST Beluga (4)	Airbus Inter Transport	
F-GSUN	Boeing 747-312	Corsair	
F-GTAA	Airbus A.321-211	Air France	
F-GTAB	Airbus A.321-211	Air France	
F-GTAC	Airbus A.321-211	Air France	
F-GTAD	Airbus A.321-211	Air France	
F-GTAE	Airbus A.321-211	Air France	
F-GTAF	Airbus A.321-211	Air France	
F-GTAG	Airbus A.321-211	Air France	
F-GTAH	Airbus A.321-211	Air France	
F-GTAI	Airbus A.321-211	Air France	
F-GTAJ	Airbus A.321-211	Air France	
F-GTAK	Airbus A.321-211	Air France	
F-GTDF	Douglas DC-10-30	AOM French Airlines	
F-GTDG	Douglas DC-10-30	AOM French Airlines	
F-GTDH	Douglas DC-10-30	AOM French Airlines	

Notes	Reg.	Type	Owner or Operator
	F-GTOM	Boeing 747SP-44	Corsair
	F-GTSB	SAAB 2000	Regional Airlines
	F-GTSG	EMB-120ER Brasilia	Regional Airlines
	F-GTSH	EMB-120ER Brasilia	Regional Airlines
	F-GTSI	EMB-120ER Brasilia	Regional Airlines
	F-GTSJ	EMB-120ER Brasilia	Regional Airlines
	F-GTSK	EMB-120ER Brasilia	Regional Airlines
	F-GTSL	SAAB 2000	Regional Airlines
	F-GTSU	EMB-120ER Brasilia	Regional Airlines
	F-GUCB	Beech 1900D	Proteus Airlines/Air France
	F-GVAC	Boeing 737-229	Aigle Azur Transports Aeriens
	F-GVHD	Embraer RJ145EU	Proteus Airlines
	F-GYAB	Beech 1900D	Air Bretagne
	F-ODJG	Boeing 747-2Q2B	Air Gabon *President Leon Mba*
	F-ODLX	Douglas DC-10-30	AOM French Airlines *Diamant*
	F-ODLY	Douglas DC-10-30	AOM French Airlines *Turquoise*
	F-ODLZ	Douglas DC-10-30	AOM French Airlines *Saphir*
	F-ODTK	Airbus A.300-622R	Sudan Airways
	F-ODVF	Airbus A.310-304	Royal Jordanian
	F-ODVG	Airbus A.310-304	Royal Jordanian *Prince Faisal*
	F-ODVH	Airbus A.310-304	Royal Jordanian *Prince Hamzeh*
	F-ODVI	Airbus A.310-304	Royal Jordanian *Princess Haya*
	F-OGQQ	Airbus A.310-308	Aeroflot *Tchaikovsky*
	F-OGQR	Airbus A.310-308	Aeroflot *Rachmaninov*
	F-OGQT	Airbus A.310-308	Aeroflot *Moussorgski*
	F-OGQU	Airbus A.310-308	Aeroflot *Skriabin*
	F-OGYA	Airbus A.320-211	Royal Jordanian *Cairo*
	F-OGYB	Airbus A.320-211	Royal Jordanian *Baghdad*
	F-OGYC	Airbus A.320-212	Royal Jordanian
	F-OGYP	Airbus A.310-324	Aeroflot *Rymsky Korsakov*
	F-OGYQ	Airbus A.310-324	Aeroflot
	F-OGYT	Airbus A.310-324	Aeroflot
	F-OGYU	Airbus A.310-324	Aeroflot *Alyabiev*
	F-OGYV	Airbus A.310-324	Aeroflot *Igor Stravinsky*
	F-OGYW	Airbus A.310-222	Armenian Airlines
	F-OHFR	Airbus A.320-212	Volare Airlines
	F-OHFT	Airbus A.320-212	Volare Airlines
	F-OHFU	Airbus A.320-212	Volare Airlines
	F-OHGB	Airbus A.320-211	Royal Jordanian
	F-OHGC	Airbus A.320-211	Royal Jordanian
	F-OHLH	Airbus A.310-304	Middle East Airlines
	F-OHLI	Airbus A.310-304	Middle East Airlines
	F-OHMO	Airbus A.320-232	Middle East Airlines
	F-OHMP	Airbus A.321-231	Middle East Airlines
	F-OHMQ	Airbus A.321-231	Middle East Airlines
	F-OHMR	Airbus A.320-232	Middle East Airlines
	F-OHPP	Airbus A.310-222	Air Maldives
	F-OHPQ	Airbus A.310-222	Libyan Arab Airlines
	F-OHPR	Airbus A.310-325	Yemenia
	F-OHPS	Airbus A.310-325	Yemenia
	F-OIHA	Airbus A.300-622R	Sudan Airways
	F-OIHB	Airbus A.300-622R	Sudan Airways
	F-OIHS	Airbus A.310-324	Air Maldives

HA (Hungary)

	HA-FAB	F.27 Friendship Mk 500	Farnair Air Transport Hungary
	HA-LCO	Tupolev Tu-154B-2	Malev
	HA-LCP	Tupolev Tu-154B-2	Malev
	HA-LCR	Tupolev Tu-154B-2	Malev
	HA-LCU	Tupolev Tu-154B-2	Malev
	HA-LCV	Tupolev Tu-154B-2	Malev
	HA-LED	Boeing 737-3Y0	Malev
	HA-LEF	Boeing 737-3Y0	Malev
	HA-LEG	Boeing 737-3Y0	Malev *Szent Istvan-Sanctus Stephanus*
	HA-LEI	Boeing 737-2T4	Malev
	HA-LEJ	Boeing 737-3Q8	Malev
	HA-LEK	Boeing 737-2K9	Malev
	HA-LEM	Boeing 737-2T4	Malev
	HA-LEN	Boeing 737-4Y0	Malev
	HA-LEO	Boeing 737-4Y0	Malev
	HA-LEP	Boeing 737-5K5	Malev

Reg.	Type	Owner or Operator	Notes
HA-LER	Boeing 737-5K5	Malev	
HA-LHA	Boeing 767-27GER	Malev	
HA-LHB	Boeing 767-27GER	Malev	
HA-LMA	Fokker 70	Malev	
HA-LMB	Fokker 70	Malev	
HA-LMC	Fokker 70	Malev	
HA-LMD	Fokker 70	Malev	
HA-LME	Fokker 70	Malev	
HA-LMF	Fokker 70	Malev	
HA-LMG	Fokker 70	Malev	

HB (Switzerland)

Reg.	Type	Owner or Operator	Notes
HB-AEE	Dornier Do.328-110	Air Engiadina/KLM alps	
HB-AEF	Dornier Do.328-110	Air Engiadina/KLM alps	
HB-AEG	Dornier Do.328-110	Air Engiadina/KLM alps	
HB-AEH	Dornier Do.328-110	Air Engiadina/KLM alps	
HB-AKA	SAAB SF.340B	Crossair	
HB-AKB	SAAB SF.340B	Crossair	
HB-AKC	SAAB SF.340B	Crossair	
HB-AKE	SAAB SF.340B	Crossair	
HB-AKF	SAAB SF.340B	Crossair	
HB-AKH	SAAB SF.340B	Crossair	
HB-AKI	SAAB SF.340B	Crossair	
HB-AKL	SAAB SF.340B	Crossair	
HB-AKM	SAAB SF.340B	Crossair	
HB-AKN	SAAB SF.340B	Crossair	
HB-AKO	SAAB SF.340B	Crossair	
HB-IEE	Boeing 757-23A	PrivatAir	
HB-IHT	Boeing 767-35HER	Balair CTA Leisure	
HB-IHU	Boeing 767-35HER	Balair CTA Leisure	
HB-IHX	Airbus A.320-214	Edelweiss Air *Calvaro*	
HB-IHY	Airbus A.320-214	Edelweiss Air *Upali*	
HB-IHZ	Airbus A.320-214	Edelweiss Air *Viktoria*	
HB-IIB	Boeing 737-3M8	easyJet Switzerland	
HB-IIE	Boeing 737-3Q8	easyJet Switzerland	
HB-III	Boeing 737-33V	easyJet Switzerland	
HB-IIJ	Boeing 737-33V	easyJet Switzerland	
HB-IIN	Boeing 737-3L9	PrivatAir	
HB-IIO	Boeing 737-7AK	PrivatAir	
HB-IIP	Boeing 737-7AK	PrivatAir	
HB-IJA	Airbus A.320-214	Swissair *Opfikon*	
HB-IJB	Airbus A.320-214	Swissair *Embrach*	
HB-IJC	Airbus A.320-214	Swissair *Winkle*	
HB-IJD	Airbus A.320-214	Swissair *Regensdorf*	
HB-IJE	Airbus A.320-214	Swissair *Dubendorf*	
HB-IJF	Airbus A.320-214	Swissair *Bellevue*	
HB-IJG	Airbus A.320-214	Swissair *Illnau-Effretikon*	
HB-IJH	Airbus A.320-214	Swissair *Wangen-Bruttisellen*	
HB-IJI	Airbus A.320-214	Swissair *Binningen*	
HB-IJJ	Airbus A.320-214	Swissair *Dietlikon*	
HB-IJK	Airbus A.320-214	Swissair *Genthod*	
HB-IJL	Airbus A.320-214	Swissair *Bassersdorf*	
HB-IJM	Airbus A.320-214	Swissair *Wallisellen*	
HB-IJN	Airbus A.320-214	Swissair *Meyrin*	
HB-IJO	Airbus A.320-214	Swissair *Grand-Saconnex*	
HB-IJP	Airbus A.320-214	Swissair *Vernier*	
HB-IJQ	Airbus A.320-214	Swissair *Niederhasli*	
HB-IJR	Airbus A.320-214	Swissair	
HB-IJS	Airbus A.320-214	Swissair	
HB-IJT	Airbus A.320-214	Swissair	
HB-IJU	Airbus A.320-214	Swissair	
HB-ILJ	F.27 Friendship Mk 500	Farner Air Transport	
HB-ILQ	F.27 Friendship Mk 500	Farner Air Transport	
HB-INR	McD Douglas MD-82	Crossair	
HB-INV	McD Douglas MD-83	Crossair	
HB-INW	McD Douglas MD-83	Crossair	
HB-INZ	McD Douglas MD-83	Crossair	
HB-IOA	Airbus A.321-111	Swissair *Neuchâtel*	
HB-IOB	Airbus A.321-111	Swissair *Aargau*	
HB-IOC	Airbus A.321-111	Swissair *Lausanne*	
HB-IOD	Airbus A.321-111	Swissair *Kloten*	

Notes	Reg.	Type	Owner or Operator
	HB-IOE	Airbus A.321-111	Swissair *Solothurn*
	HB-IOF	Airbus A.321-111	Swissair *Winterthur*
	HB-IOG	Airbus A.321-111	Swissair *Bülach*
	HB-IOH	Airbus A.321-111	Swissair *Würenlos*
	HB-IOI	Airbus A.321-111	Swissair
	HB-IOJ	Airbus A.321-111	Swissair
	HB-IOK	Airbus A.321-111	Swissair
	HB-IOL	Airbus A.321-111	Swissair
	HB-IPR	Airbus A.319-111	Swissair
	HB-IPS	Airbus A.319-112	Swissair *Weiach*
	HB-IPT	Airbus A.319-112	Swissair *Stadel*
	HB-IPU	Airbus A.319-112	Swissair *Hochfelden*
	HB-IPV	Airbus A.319-112	Swissair *Rumlang*
	HB-IPW	Airbus A.319-112	Swissair *Bachenbulach*
	HB-IPX	Airbus A.319-112	Swissair *Steinmaur*
	HB-IPY	Airbus A.319-112	Swissair *Hori*
	HB-IPZ	Airbus A.319-112	Swissair *Oberglatt*
	HB-IQA	Airbus A.330-223	Swissair
	HB-IQB	Airbus A.330-223	Swissair
	HB-IQC	Airbus A.330-223	Swissair
	HB-IQD	Airbus A.330-223	Swissair
	HB-IQE	Airbus A.330-222	Swissair
	HB-IQF	Airbus A.330-223	Swissair
	HB-IQG	Airbus A.330-223	Swissair
	HB-IQH	Airbus A.330-223	Swissair
	HB-IQI	Airbus A.330-223	Swissair
	HB-IQJ	Airbus A.330-223	Swissair
	HB-IQK	Airbus A.330-223	Swissair
	HB-IQL	Airbus A.330-223	Swissair/Novair Airlines
	HB-IQM	Airbus A.330-223	Swissair
	HB-IQN	Airbus A.330-223	Swissair
	HB-IQO	Airbus A.330-223	Swissair/Novair Airlines
	HB-IQP	Airbus A.330-223	Swissair
	HB-IQQ	Airbus A.330-223	Swissair/Novair Airlines
	HB-IQR	Airbus A.330-223	Swissair
	HB-ISB	Douglas DC-3C	Classic Air
	HB-ISC	Douglas DC-3C	Classic Air
	HB-ISQ	F.27 Friendship Mk 500	Farnair Europe
	HB-ISX	McD Douglas MD-83	Crossair
	HB-ISZ	McD Douglas MD-83	Crossair
	HB-ITQ	F.27 Friendship Mk 400	Farnair Europe
	HB-IUG	McD Douglas MD-83	Crossair
	HB-IUH	McD Douglas MD-83	Crossair/McDonald's
	HB-IUM	McD Douglas MD-83	Crossair
	HB-IUN	McD Douglas MD-83	Crossair
	HB-IUO	McD Douglas MD-83	Crossair
	HB-IUP	McD Douglas MD-83	Crossair
	HB-IWA	McD Douglas MD-11	Swissair *Obwalden*
	HB-IWB	McD Douglas MD-11	Swissair *Graubünden*
	HB-IWC	McD Douglas MD-11	Swissair *Schaffhausen*
	HB-IWD	McD Douglas MD-11	Swissair *Thurgau*
	HB-IWE	McD Douglas MD-11	Swissair *Nidwalden*
	HB-IWG	McD Douglas MD-11	Swissair *Asia Valais/Wallis*
	HB-IWH	McD Douglas MD-11	Swissair *St Gallen*
	HB-IWI	McD Douglas MD-11	Swissair *Uri*
	HB-IWK	McD Douglas MD-11	Swissair *Fribourg*
	HB-IWL	McD Douglas MD-11	Swissair *Appenzell* a.Rh
	HB-IWM	McD Douglas MD-11	Swissair *Jura*
	HB-IWN	McD Douglas MD-11	Swissair *Basel-Land*
	HB-IWO	McD Douglas MD-11	Swissair *Schwyz*
	HB-IWP	McD Douglas MD-11	Swissair
	HB-IWQ	McD Douglas MD-11	Swissair
	HB-IWR	McD Douglas MD-11	Swissair
	HB-IWS	McD Douglas MD-11	Swissair
	HB-IWT	McD Douglas MD-11	Swissair
	HB-IWU	McD Douglas MD-11	Swissair
	HB-IXF	Avro RJ85	Crossair
	HB-IXG	Avro RJ85	Crossair
	HB-IXH	Avro RJ85	Crossair
	HB-IXK	Avro RJ85	Crossair
	HB-IXM	Avro RJ100	Crossair
	HB-IXN	Avro RJ100	Crossair
	HB-IXO	Avro RJ100	Crossair

Reg.	Type	Owner or Operator	Notes
HB-IXP	Avro RJ100	Crossair	
HB-IXQ	Avro RJ100	Crossair	
HB-IXR	Avro RJ100	Crossair	
HB-IXS	Avro RJ100	Crossair	
HB-IXT	Avro RJ100	Crossair	
HB-IXU	Avro RJ100	Crossair	
HB-IXV	Avro RJ100	Crossair	
HB-IXW	Avro RJ100	Crossair	
HB-IXX	Avro RJ100	Crossair	
HB-IYA	SAAB 2000	Crossair	
HB-IYB	SAAB 2000	Crossair	
HB-IYC	SAAB 2000	Crossair	
HB-IYD	SAAB 2000	Crossair	
HB-IYE	SAAB 2000	Crossair	
HB-IYF	SAAB 2000	Crossair	
HB-IYG	SAAB 2000	Crossair	
HB-IYH	SAAB 2000	Crossair	
HB-IYW	Avro RJ100	Crossair	
HB-IYX	Avro RJ100	Crossair	
HB-IYY	Avro RJ100	Crossair/Eurocross	
HB-IYZ	Avro RJ100	Crossair	
HB-IZA	SAAB 2000	Crossair	
HB-IZB	SAAB 2000	Crossair	
HB-IZC	SAAB 2000	Crossair	
HB-IZD	SAAB 2000	Crossair	
HB-IZE	SAAB 2000	Crossair	
HB-IZF	SAAB 2000	Crossair	
HB-IZG	SAAB 2000	Crossair	
HB-IZH	SAAB 2000	Crossair	
HB-IZI	SAAB 2000	Crossair	
HB-IZJ	SAAB 2000	Crossair	
HB-IZK	SAAB 2000	Crossair	
HB-IZL	SAAB 2000	Crossair	
HB-IZM	SAAB 2000	Crossair	
HB-IZN	SAAB 2000	Crossair	
HB-IZO	SAAB 2000	Crossair	
HB-IZP	SAAB 2000	Crossair	
HB-IZQ	SAAB 2000	Crossair	
HB-IZR	SAAB 2000	Crossair	
HB-IZS	SAAB 2000	Crossair	
HB-IZT	SAAB 2000	Crossair	
HB-IZU	SAAB 2000	Crossair	
HB-IZV	SAAB 2000	Crossair	
HB-IZW	SAAB 2000	Crossair	
HB-IZX	SAAB 2000	Crossair	
HB-IZY	SAAB 2000	Crossair	
HB-IZZ	SAAB 2000	Crossair	
HB-JAA	Embraer RJ145	Crossair	
HB-JAB	Embraer RJ145	Crossair	
HB-JAC	Embraer RJ145	Crossair	
HB-JAD	Embraer RJ145	Crossair	
HB-JAE	Embraer RJ145	Crossair	
HB-JAF	Embraer RJ145	Crossair	
HB-JAG	Embraer RJ145	Crossair	
HB-JAH	Embraer RJ145	Crossair	
HB-JAI	Embraer RJ145	Crossair	
HB-JAJ	Embraer RJ145	Crossair	
HB-JAK	Embraer RJ145	Crossair	
HB-JAL	Embraer RJ145	Crossair	
HB-JAM	Embraer RJ145	Crossair	
HB-JAN	Embraer RJ145	Crossair	
HB-JAO	Embraer RJ145	Crossair	

HK (Colombia)

Note: Avianca operates Boeing 767s registered N984AN, N985AN, N986AN and N988AN.

Notes	Reg.	Type	Owner or Operator

HL (Korea)

HL7371	McD Douglas MD-11F	Korean Air Cargo
HL7372	McD Douglas MD-11F	Korean Air Cargo
HL7374	McD Douglas MD-11F	Korean Air Cargo
HL7375	McD Douglas MD-11F	Korean Air Cargo
HL7402	Boeing 747-4B5	Korean Air
HL7403	Boeing 747-4B5F	Korean Air Cargo
HL7404	Boeing 747-4B5	Korean Air
HL7405	Boeing 747-2B5F (SCD)	Korean Air Cargo
HL7407	Boeing 747-4B5	Korean Air
HL7408	Boeing 747-2B5F (SCD)	Korean Air Cargo
HL7409	Boeing 747-4B5	Korean Air
HL7412	Boeing 747-4B5	Korean Air
HL7419	Boeing 747-48EF (SCD)	Asiana Airlines
HL7420	Boeing 747-48EF (SCD)	Asiana Airlines
HL7422	Boeing 747-48EF (SCD)	Asiana Airlines
HL7424	Boeing 747-2S4F (SCD)	Korean Air Cargo
HL7428	Boeing 747-48EF (SCD)	Asiana Airlines
HL7441	Boeing 747-230F	Korean Air Cargo
HL7443	Boeing 747-2B5B	Korean Air
HL7448	Boeing 747-4B5F	Korean Air Cargo
HL7449	Boeing 747-4B5F	Korean Air Cargo
HL7452	Boeing 747-2B5F (SCD)	Korean Air Cargo
HL7454	Boeing 747-2B5F (SCD)	Korean Air Cargo
HL7458	Boeing 747-2B5F (SCD)	Korean Air Cargo
HL7459	Boeing 747-2B5F (SCD)	Korean Air Cargo
HL7460	Boeing 747-4B5	Korean Air
HL7461	Boeing 747-4B5	Korean Air
HL7462	Boeing 747-4B5F	Korean Air Cargo
HL7463	Boeing 747-2B5B	Korean Air
HL7464	Boeing 747-2B5B	Korean Air
HL7469	Boeing 747-3B5	Korean Air
HL7470	Boeing 747-3B5 (SCD)	Korean Air
HL7471	Boeing 747-273C	Korean Air Cargo
HL7472	Boeing 747-4B5	Korean Air
HL7473	Boeing 747-4B5	Korean Air
HL7480	Boeing 747-4B5 (SCD)	Korean Air
HL7481	Boeing 747-4B5	Korean Air
HL7482	Boeing 747-4B5	Korean Air
HL7483	Boeing 747-4B5	Korean Air
HL7484	Boeing 747-4B5	Korean Air
HL7485	Boeing 747-4B5	Korean Air
HL7486	Boeing 747-4B5	Korean Air
HL7487	Boeing 747-4B5	Korean Air
HL7488	Boeing 747-4B5	Korean Air
HL7489	Boeing 747-4B5	Korean Air
HL7490	Boeing 747-4B5	Korean Air
HL7491	Boeing 747-4B5	Korean Air
HL7492	Boeing 747-4B5	Korean Air
HL7493	Boeing 747-4B5	Korean Air
HL7494	Boeing 747-4B5	Korean Air
HL7495	Boeing 747-4B5	Korean Air
HL7496	Boeing 747-4B5	Korean Air
HL7497	Boeing 747-4B5	Korean Air
HL7498	Boeing 747-4B5	Korean Air

HS (Thailand)

HS-TGD	Boeing 747-3D7	Thai Airways International *Suchada*
HS-TGE	Boeing 747-3D7	Thai Airways International *Chutamat*
HS-TGH	Boeing 747-4D7	Thai Airways International *Chaiprakarn*
HS-TGJ	Boeing 747-4D7	Thai Airways International *Hariphunchai*
HS-TGK	Boeing 747-4D7	Thai Airways International *Alongkorn*
HS-TGL	Boeing 747-4D7	Thai Airways International *Theparat*
HS-TGM	Boeing 747-4D7	Thai Airways International *Chao Phraya*
HS-TGN	Boeing 747-4D7	Thai Airways International *Simongkhon*
HS-TGO	Boeing 747-4D7	Thai Airways International *Bowonrangsi*
HS-TGP	Boeing 747-4D7	Thai Airways International *Thepprasit*
HS-TGR	Boeing 747-4D7	Thai Airways International *Siriwatthana*
HS-TGT	Boeing 747-4D7	Thai Airways International *Watthanothai*

Reg.	Type	Owner or Operator	Notes
HS-TGW	Boeing 747-4D7	Thai Airways International *Visuthakasatriya*	
HS-TGX	Boeing 747-4D7	Thai Airways International *Sirisobhakya*	
HS-TGY	Boeing 747-4D7	Thai Airways International *Dararasmi*	
HS-TGZ	Boeing 747-4D7	Thai Airways International	
HS-TJA	Boeing 777-2D7	Thai Airways International	
HS-TJB	Boeing 777-2D7	Thai Airways International	
HS-TJC	Boeing 777-2D7	Thai Airways International	
HS-TJD	Boeing 777-2D7	Thai Airways International	
HS-TJE	Boeing 777-2D7	Thai Airways International	
HS-TJF	Boeing 777-2D7	Thai Airways International	
HS-TJG	Boeing 777-2D7	Thai Airways International	
HS-TJH	Boeing 777-2D7	Thai Airways International	
HS-TKA	Boeing 777-3D7	Thai Airways International	
HS-TKB	Boeing 777-3D7	Thai Airways International	
HS-TKC	Boeing 777-3D7	Thai Airways International	
HS-TKD	Boeing 777-3D7	Thai Airways International	
HS-TKE	Boeing 777-3D7	Thai Airways International	
HS-TKF	Boeing 777-3D7	Thai Airways International	
HS-TMD	McD Douglas MD-11	Thai Airways International *Phra Nakhon*	
HS-TME	McD Douglas MD-11	Thai Airways International *Pathumwan*	
HS-TMF	McD Douglas MD-11	Thai Airways International *Phichit*	
HS-TMG	McD Douglas MD-11	Thai Airways International *Nakhon Sawan*	

HZ (Saudi Arabia)

HZ-AIA	Boeing 747-168B	Saudia — Saudi Arabian Airlines	
HZ-AIB	Boeing 747-168B	Saudia — Saudi Arabian Airlines	
HZ-AIC	Boeing 747-168B	Saudia — Saudi Arabian Airlines	
HZ-AID	Boeing 747-168B	Saudia — Saudi Arabian Airlines	
HZ-AIE	Boeing 747-168B	Saudia — Saudi Arabian Airlines	
HZ-AIF	Boeing 747SP-68	Saudia — Saudi Arabian Airlines	
HZ-AIG	Boeing 747-168B	Saudia — Saudi Arabian Airlines	
HZ-AII	Boeing 747-168B	Saudia — Saudi Arabian Airlines	
HZ-AIJ	Boeing 747SP-68	Saudi Royal Flight	
HZ-AIK	Boeing 747-368	Saudia - Saudi Arabian Airlines	
HZ-AIL	Boeing 747-368	Saudia - Saudi Arabian Airlines	
HZ-AIM	Boeing 747-368	Saudia - Saudi Arabian Airlines	
HZ-AIN	Boeing 747-368	Saudia - Saudi Arabian Airlines	
HZ-AIO	Boeing 747-368	Saudia - Saudi Arabian Airlines	
HZ-AIP	Boeing 747-368	Saudia - Saudi Arabian Airlines	
HZ-AIQ	Boeing 747-368	Saudia - Saudi Arabian Airlines	
HZ-AIR	Boeing 747-368	Saudia - Saudi Arabian Airlines	
HZ-AIS	Boeing 747-368	Saudia - Saudi Arabian Airlines	
HZ-AIT	Boeing 747-368	Saudia - Saudi Arabian Airlines	
HZ-AIU	Boeing 747-268F (SCD)	Saudia -Saudi Arabian Airlines	
HZ-AIV	Boeing 747-468	Saudia - Saudi Arabian Airlines	
HZ-AIW	Boeing 747-468	Saudia - Saudi Arabian Airlines	
HZ-AIX	Boeing 747-468	Saudia - Saudi Arabian Airlines	
HZ-AIY	Boeing 747-468	Saudia - Saudi Arabian Airlines	
HZ-AIZ	Boeing 747-468	Saudia - Saudi Arabian Airlines	
HZ-AKA	Boeing 777-268ER	Saudia - Saudi Arabian Airlines	
HZ-AKB	Boeing 777-268ER	Saudia - Saudi Arabian Airlines	
HZ-AKC	Boeing 777-268ER	Saudia - Saudi Arabian Airlines	
HZ-AKD	Boeing 777-268ER	Saudia - Saudi Arabian Airlines	
HZ-AKE	Boeing 777-268ER	Saudia - Saudi Arabian Airlines	
HZ-AKF	Boeing 777-268ER	Saudia - Saudi Arabian Airlines	
HZ-AKG	Boeing 777-268ER	Saudia - Saudi Arabian Airlines	
HZ-AKH	Boeing 777-268ER	Saudia - Saudi Arabian Airlines	
HZ-AKI	Boeing 777-268ER	Saudia - Saudi Arabian Airlines	
HZ-AKJ	Boeing 777-268ER	Saudia - Saudi Arabian Airlines	
HZ-AKK	Boeing 777-268ER	Saudia - Saudi Arabian Airlines	
HZ-AKL	Boeing 777-268ER	Saudia - Saudi Arabian Airlines	
HZ-AKM	Boeing 777-268ER	Saudia - Saudi Arabian Airlines	
HZ-AKN	Boeing 777-268ER	Saudia - Saudi Arabian Airlines	
HZ-AKO	Boeing 777-268ER	Saudia - Saudi Arabian Airlines	
HZ-AKP	Boeing 777-268ER	Saudia - Saudi Arabian Airlines	
HZ-AKQ	Boeing 777-268ER	Saudia - Saudi Arabian Airlines	
HZ-AKR	Boeing 777-268ER	Saudia - Saudi Arabian Airlines	
HZ-AKS	Boeing 777-268ER	Saudia - Saudi Arabian Airlines	
HZ-ANA	McD Douglas MD-11F	Saudia - Saudi Arabian Airlines	
HZ-ANB	McD Douglas MD-11F	Saudia - Saudi Arabian Airlines	

Notes	Reg.	Type	Owner or Operator
	HZ-ANC	McD Douglas MD-11F	Saudia - Saudi Arabian Airlines
	HZ-AND	McD Douglas MD-11F	Saudia - Saudi Arabian Airlines
	HZ-HM5	L.1011-385 TriStar 500	Saudia VIP
	HZ-HM6	L.1011-385 TriStar 500	Saudia VIP

I (Italy)

Notes	Reg.	Type	Owner or Operator
	I-AEIY	Boeing 767-330ER	Air Europe SpA
	I-AIMQ	Boeing 767-3Q8ER	Air Europe SpA
	I-ALPK	Fokker 100	Alpi Eagles *San Antonio*
	I-ALPL	Fokker 100	Alpi Eagles *San Marco*
	I-ALPQ	Fokker 100	Alpi Eagles
	I-ALPS	Fokker 100	Alpi Eagles *San Zeno*
	I-ALPX	Fokker 100	Alpi Eagles
	I-ALPZ	Fokker 100	Alpi Eagles *San Pietro*
	I-ATMC	Aérospatiale ATR-72-212A	Alitalia Express *Fiume Arno*
	I-ATSL	Aérospatiale ATR-72-212A	Alitalia Express *Lago di Garda*
	I-BIKA	Airbus A.320-214	Alitalia
	I-BIKB	Airbus A.320-214	Alitalia
	I-BIKC	Airbus A.320-214	Alitalia
	I-BIKD	Airbus A.320-214	Alitalia
	I-BIKE	Airbus A.320-214	Alitalia *Franz Liszt*
	I-BIKF	Airbus A.320-214	Alitalia
	I-BIKG	Airbus A.320-214	Alitalia
	I-BIKI	Airbus A.320-214	Alitalia
	I-BIKO	Airbus A.320-214	Alitalia
	I-BIXA	Airbus A.321-112	Alitalia Team *Piazza del Duomo Milano*
	I-BIXB	Airbus A.321-112	Alitalia Team *Piazza Castello Torino*
	I-BIXC	Airbus A.321-112	Alitalia Team *Piazza del Campo Siena*
	I-BIXD	Airbus A.321-112	Alitalia Team *Piazza Pretoria Palermo*
	I-BIXE	Airbus A.321-112	Alitalia Team *Piazza di Spagna Roma*
	I-BIXF	Airbus A.321-112	Alitalia Team *Piazza Maggiore Bologna*
	I-BIXG	Airbus A.321-112	Alitalia Team *Piazza dei Miracoli Pisa*
	I-BIXH	Airbus A.321-112	Alitalia Team
	I-BIXI	Airbus A.321-112	Alitalia Team *Piazza San Marco-Venezia*
	I-BIXJ	Airbus A.321-112	Alitalia Team
	I-BIXK	Airbus A.321-112	Alitalia Team
	I-BIXL	Airbus A.321-112	Alitalia Team *Piazza del Duomo Lecce*
	I-BIXM	Airbus A.321-112	Alitalia Team *Piazza di San Franceso Assisi*
	I-BIXN	Airbus A.321-112	Alitalia Team *Piazza del Duomo Catania*
	I-BIXO	Airbus A.321-112	Alitalia Team *Piazza Plebiscito Napoli*
	I-BIXP	Airbus A.321-112	Alitalia Team *Carlo Morelli*
	I-BIXQ	Airbus A.321-112	Alitalia Team *Domenico Colapietro*
	I-BIXR	Airbus A.321-112	Alitalia Team *Piazza dell Campidoglio-Roma*
	I-BIXS	Airbus A.321-112	Alitalia Team *Piazza San Martino-Lucca*
	I-BIXT	Airbus A.321-112	Alitalia *Piazza dei Miracoli Pisa*
	I-BIXU	Airbus A.321-112	Alitalia *Piazza dell Signori Firenze*
	I-BIXV	Airbus A.321-112	Alitalia *Piazza dell Rinaccimento-Urbino*
	I-BIXZ	Airbus A.321-112	Alitalia *Piazza dell Duomo Orvieto*
	I-DACM	McD Douglas MD-82	Alitalia *La Spezia*
	I-DACN	McD Douglas MD-82	Alitalia *Rieti*
	I-DACP	McD Douglas MD-82	Alitalia *Padova*
	I-DACQ	McD Douglas MD-82	Alitalia *Taranto*
	I-DACR	McD Douglas MD-82	Alitalia *Carrara*
	I-DACS	McD Douglas MD-82	Alitalia *Maratea*
	I-DACT	McD Douglas MD-82	Alitalia *Valtellina*
	I-DACU	McD Douglas MD-82	Alitalia *Fabriano*
	I-DACV	McD Douglas MD-82	Alitalia *Riccione*
	I-DACW	McD Douglas MD-82	Alitalia *Vieste*
	I-DACX	McD Douglas MD-82	Alitalia *Piacenza*
	I-DACY	McD Douglas MD-82	Alitalia Team *Novara*
	I-DACZ	McD Douglas MD-82	Alitalia *Castelfidardo*
	I-DAND	McD Douglas MD-82	Alitalia *Bolzano*
	I-DANF	McD Douglas MD-82	Alitalia *Vicenza*
	I-DANG	McD Douglas MD-82	Alitalia *Benevento*
	I-DANH	McD Douglas MD-82	Alitalia *Messina*
	I-DANL	McD Douglas MD-82	Alitalia *Cosenza*
	I-DANM	McD Douglas MD-82	Alitalia *Vicenza*

Reg.	Type	Owner or Operator	Notes
I-DANP	McD Douglas MD-82	Alitalia *Fabriano*	
I-DANQ	McD Douglas MD-82	Alitalia *Lecce*	
I-DANR	McD Douglas MD-82	Alitalia *Matera*	
I-DANU	McD Douglas MD-82	Alitalia *Trapani*	
I-DANV	McD Douglas MD-82	Alitalia *Forte dei Marmi*	
I-DANW	McD Douglas MD-82	Alitalia *Siena*	
I-DATA	McD Douglas MD-82	Alitalia *Gubbio*	
I-DATB	McD Douglas MD-82	Alitalia *Bergamo*	
I-DATC	McD Douglas MD-82	Alitalia *Foggia*	
I-DATD	McD Douglas MD-82	Alitalia *Savona*	
I-DATE	McD Douglas MD-82	Alitalia *Grosseto*	
I-DATF	McD Douglas MD-82	Alitalia *Vittorio Veneto*	
I-DATG	McD Douglas MD-82	Alitalia *Arezzo*	
I-DATH	McD Douglas MD-82	Alitalia *Pescara*	
I-DATI	McD Douglas MD-82	Alitalia *Siracusa*	
I-DATJ	McD Douglas MD-82	Alitalia *Lunigiana*	
I-DATK	McD Douglas MD-82	Alitalia *Ravenna*	
I-DATL	McD Douglas MD-82	Alitalia *Alghero*	
I-DATM	McD Douglas MD-82	Alitalia Team *Cividale del Friuli*	
I-DATN	McD Douglas MD-82	Alitalia *Sondrio*	
I-DATO	McD Douglas MD-82	Alitalia Team *Reggio Emilia*	
I-DATP	McD Douglas MD-82	Alitalia Team *Latina*	
I-DATQ	McD Douglas MD-82	Alitalia Team *Modena*	
I-DATR	McD Douglas MD-82	Alitalia Team *Livorno*	
I-DATS	McD Douglas MD-82	Alitalia *Foligno*	
I-DATU	McD Douglas MD-82	Alitalia *Verona*	
I-DAVA	McD Douglas MD-82	Alitalia *Cuneo*	
I-DAVB	McD Douglas MD-82	Alitalia *Ferrara*	
I-DAVC	McD Douglas MD-82	Alitalia *Lucca*	
I-DAVD	McD Douglas MD-82	Alitalia *Mantova*	
I-DAVF	McD Douglas MD-82	Alitalia *Oristano*	
I-DAVG	McD Douglas MD-82	Alitalia *Pesaro*	
I-DAVH	McD Douglas MD-82	Alitalia *Salerno*	
I-DAVI	McD Douglas MD-82	Alitalia *Assisi*	
I-DAVJ	McD Douglas MD-82	Alitalia *Parma*	
I-DAVK	McD Douglas MD-82	Alitalia *Pompei*	
I-DAVL	McD Douglas MD-82	Alitalia *Reggio Calabria*	
I-DAVM	McD Douglas MD-82	Alitalia *Caserta*	
I-DAVN	McD Douglas MD-82	Alitalia *Volterra*	
I-DAVP	McD Douglas MD-82	Alitalia *Gorizia*	
I-DAVR	McD Douglas MD-82	Alitalia *Pisa*	
I-DAVS	McD Douglas MD-82	Alitalia *Catania*	
I-DAVT	McD Douglas MD-82	Alitalia *Como*	
I-DAVU	McD Douglas MD-82	Alitalia *Udine*	
I-DAVV	McD Douglas MD-82	Alitalia *Pavia*	
I-DAVW	McD Douglas MD-82	Alitalia *Camerino*	
I-DAVX	McD Douglas MD-82	Alitalia *Asti*	
I-DAVZ	McD Douglas MD-82	Alitalia *Brescia*	
I-DAWA	McD Douglas MD-82	Alitalia *Roma*	
I-DAWB	McD Douglas MD-82	Alitalia *Cagliari*	
I-DAWC	McD Douglas MD-82	Alitalia *Campobasso*	
I-DAWD	McD Douglas MD-82	Alitalia *Catanzaro*	
I-DAWE	McD Douglas MD-82	Alitalia *Milano*	
I-DAWF	McD Douglas MD-82	Alitalia *Firenze*	
I-DAWG	McD Douglas MD-82	Alitalia *L'Aquila*	
I-DAWH	McD Douglas MD-82	Alitalia *Palermo*	
I-DAWI	McD Douglas MD-82	Alitalia *Ancona*	
I-DAWJ	McD Douglas MD-82	Alitalia *Genova*	
I-DAWL	McD Douglas MD-82	Alitalia *Perugia*	
I-DAWM	McD Douglas MD-82	Alitalia *Potenza*	
I-DAWO	McD Douglas MD-82	Alitalia *Bari*	
I-DAWP	McD Douglas MD-82	Alitalia *Torino*	
I-DAWQ	McD Douglas MD-82	Alitalia *Trieste*	
I-DAWR	McD Douglas MD-82	Alitalia *Venezia*	
I-DAWS	McD Douglas MD-82	Alitalia *Aosta*	
I-DAWT	McD Douglas MD-82	Alitalia *Napoli*	
I-DAWU	McD Douglas MD-82	Alitalia *Bologna*	
I-DAWV	McD Douglas MD-82	Alitalia *Trento*	
I-DAWW	McD Douglas MD-82	Alitalia *Riace*	
I-DAWY	McD Douglas MD-82	Alitalia *Agrigento*	
I-DAWZ	McD Douglas MD-82	Alitalia *Avellino*	
I-DEIB	Boeing 767-33AER	Alitalia Team *Pier Paolo Racchetti*	
I-DEIC	Boeing 767-33AER	Alitalia Team *Alberto Nassetti*	

I

Notes	Reg.	Type	Owner or Operator
	I-DEID	Boeing 767-33AER	Alitalia Team *Marco Polo*
	I-DEIF	Boeing 767-33AER	Alitalia Team *Cristoforo Colombo*
	I-DEIG	Boeing 767-33AER	Alitalia Team *Francesco Agello*
	I-DEIL	Boeing 767-33AER	Alitalia Team *Arturo Ferrarin*
	I-DEMC	Boeing 747-243B (SCD)	Alitalia *Taormina*
	I-DEMF	Boeing 747-243B (SCD)	Alitalia *Portofino*
	I-DEMG	Boeing 747-243B	Alitalia *Cervinia*
	I-DEML	Boeing 747-243B	Alitalia *Sorrento*
	I-DEMN	Boeing 747-243B	Alitalia *Portocervo*
	I-DEMP	Boeing 747-243B	Alitalia *Capri*
	I-DEMR	Boeing 747-243F (SCD)	Alitalia *Titano*
	I-DEMS	Boeing 747-243B	Alitalia *Monte Argentario*
	I-DEMV	Boeing 747-243B	Alitalia *Sestriere*
	I-DEMY	Boeing 747-230B	Alitalia *Asolo*
	I-DIKR	Douglas DC-9-32	Alitalia *Piemonte*
	I-DIZE	Douglas DC-9-32	Alitalia *Isola della Meloria*
	I-DUPA	McD Douglas MD-11C	Alitalia *Gioacchino Rossini*
	I-DUPB	McD Douglas MD-11	Alitalia *Pietro Mascagni*
	I-DUPC	McD Douglas MD-11	Alitalia *V. Bellini*
	I-DUPD	McD Douglas MD-11	Alitalia *G. Donizetti*
	I-DUPE	McD Douglas MD-11C	Alitalia *Giuseppe Verdi*
	I-DUPI	McD Douglas MD-11C	Alitalia *Gioacomo Puccini*
	I-DUPO	McD Douglas MD-11C	Alitalia *Nicolo Paganini*
	I-DUPU	McD Douglas MD-11C	Alitalia *Antonio Vivaldi*
	I-FLRE	BAe 146-200	Meridiana
	I-FLRI	BAe 146-200	Meridiana
	I-FLRO	BAe 146-200	Meridiana
	I-FLRU	BAe 146-200	Meridiana
	I-FLYY	Douglas DC-9-51	Eurofly
	I-FLYZ	Douglas DC-9-51	Eurofly
	I-GANL	Dornier Do.328-300	Gandalf Airlines
	I-	Dornier Do.328-300	Gandalf Airlines
	I-	Dornier Do.328-300	Gandalf Airlines
	I-	Dornier Do.328-300	Gandalf Airlines
	I-JETA	Boeing 737-229	Air Sicilia
	I-JETC	Boeing 737-230	Air One
	I-JETD	Boeing 737-230	Air One
	I-RIML	Aérospatiale ATR-42-300	Italy First
	I-RIMS	Aérospatiale ATR-42-300	Italy First
	I-SMEB	McD Douglas MD-82	Meridiana
	I-SMEC	McD Douglas MD-83	Meridiana
	I-SMED	McD Douglas MD-83	Meridiana
	I-SMEE	Douglas DC-9-51	Meridiana
	I-SMEL	McD Douglas MD-82	Meridiana
	I-SMEM	McD Douglas MD-82	Meridiana
	I-SMEP	McD Douglas MD-82	Meridiana
	I-SMER	McD Douglas MD-82	Meridiana
	I-SMES	McD Douglas MD-82	Meridiana
	I-SMET	McD Douglas MD-82	Meridiana
	I-SMEV	McD Douglas MD-82	Meridiana
	I-SMEZ	McD Douglas MD-83	Meridiana
	I-TNTC	BAe 146-200QT	Mistral Air/TNT
	I-VLEO	Airbus A.320-214	Volare Airlines

Note: Meridiana also operates MD-83s which retain the registrations EI-CIW, EI-CKM, EI-CRE, EI-CRH, EI-CRJ and EI-CRW. Air Europe SpA also operates Boeing 767s registered EI-CJA, EI-CJB, EI-CLS and EI-CNS, plus Boeing 777s EI-CRS and EI-CRT. Air One also operates Boeing 737s EI-CLW, EI-CLZ, EI-COH, EI-COI, EI-COJ, EI-COK, F-GKTA and F-GKTB, while Eurofly leases the MD-83s EI-CEK, EI-CMM, EI-CMZ and EI-CNR. Azzurra Air employs Avro RJs which retain the Irish marks EI-CNI, EI-CNJ, EI-CNK and EI-COQ. The Boeing 767s EI-CRL EI-CRM, EI-CRO and EI-CTW are operated by Alitalia. The A.320s F-OHFR, F-OHFT, F-OHFU, EI-CUC and EI-CUK are operated by Volare Airlines. Gandalf Airlines employs the Dornier Do.328-110s D-CGAN, D-CGAO and D-CGAP.

Reg.	Type	Owner or Operator	Notes

JA (Japan)

Reg.	Type	Owner or Operator	Notes
JA401A	Boeing 747-481	All Nippon Airways	
JA402A	Boeing 747-481	All Nippon Airways	
JA403A	Boeing 747-481	All Nippon Airways	
JA404A	Boeing 747-481	All Nippon Airways	
JA811J	Boeing 747-246F	Japan Airlines	
JA812J	Boeing 747-346	Japan Airlines	
JA813J	Boeing 747-346	Japan Airlines	
JA8071	Boeing 747-446	Japan Airlines	
JA8072	Boeing 747-446	Japan Airlines	
JA8073	Boeing 747-446	Japan Airlines	
JA8074	Boeing 747-446	Japan Airlines	
JA8075	Boeing 747-446	Japan Airlines	
JA8076	Boeing 747-446	Japan Airlines	
JA8077	Boeing 747-446	Japan Airlines	
JA8078	Boeing 747-446	Japan Airlines	
JA8079	Boeing 747-446	Japan Airlines	
JA8080	Boeing 747-446	Japan Airlines	
JA8081	Boeing 747-446	Japan Airlines	
JA8082	Boeing 747-446	Japan Airlines	
JA8085	Boeing 747-446	Japan Airlines	
JA8086	Boeing 747-446	Japan Airlines	
JA8087	Boeing 747-446	Japan Airlines	
JA8088	Boeing 747-446	Japan Airlines	
JA8089	Boeing 747-446	Japan Airlines	
JA8094	Boeing 747-481	All Nippon Airways	
JA8095	Boeing 747-481	All Nippon Airways	
JA8096	Boeing 747-481	All Nippon Airways	
JA8097	Boeing 747-481	All Nippon Airways	
JA8098	Boeing 747-481	All Nippon Airways	
JA8104	Boeing 747-246B	Japan Airlines	
JA8108	Boeing 747-246B	Japan Airlines	
JA8122	Boeing 747-246B	Japan Airlines	
JA8123	Boeing 747-246F (SCD)	Japan Airlines	
JA8130	Boeing 747-246B	Japan Airlines	
JA8131	Boeing 747-246B	Japan Airlines	
JA8132	Boeing 747-246F	Japan Airlines	
JA8140	Boeing 747-246B	Japan Airlines	
JA8141	Boeing 747-246B	Japan Airlines	
JA8151	Boeing 747-246F	Japan Airlines	
JA8154	Boeing 747-246B	Japan Airlines	
JA8160	Boeing 747-221F (SCD)	Japan Airlines	
JA8161	Boeing 747-246B	Japan Airlines	
JA8162	Boeing 747-246B	Japan Airlines	
JA8163	Boeing 747-346	Japan Airlines	
JA8165	Boeing 747-221F (SCD)	Japan Airlines	
JA8166	Boeing 747-346	Japan Airlines	
JA8167	Boeing 747-281F (SCD)	Nippon Cargo Airlines	
JA8168	Boeing 747-281F (SCD)	Nippon Cargo Airlines	
JA8169	Boeing 747-246B	Japan Airlines	
JA8171	Boeing 747-246F (SCD)	Japan Airlines	
JA8172	Boeing 747-281F (SCD)	Nippon Cargo Airlines	
JA8173	Boeing 747-346	Japan Airlines	
JA8174	Boeing 747-281B	All Nippon Airways	
JA8175	Boeing 747-281B	All Nippon Airways	
JA8177	Boeing 747-346	Japan Airlines	
JA8178	Boeing 747-346	Japan Airlines	
JA8179	Boeing 747-346	Japan Airlines	
JA8180	Boeing 747-246F (SCD)	Japan Airlines	
JA8181	Boeing 747-281F	All Nippon Airways	
JA8182	Boeing 747-281B	All Nippon Airways	
JA8184	Boeing 747-346	Japan Airlines	
JA8185	Boeing 747-346	Japan Airlines	
JA8186	Boeing 747-346	Japan Airlines	
JA8188	Boeing 747-281F (SCD)	Nippon Cargo Airlines	
JA8190	Boeing 747-281B	All Nippon Airways	
JA8191	Boeing 747-281F (SCD)	Nippon Cargo Airlines	
JA8192	Boeing 747-2D3F(SCD)	Nippon Cargo Airlines	
JA8193	Boeing 747-212F (SCD)	Japan Airlines	
JA8194	Boeing 747-281F (SCD)	Nippon Cargo Airlines	
JA8580	McD Douglas MD-11	Japan Airlines	

Notes	Reg.	Type	Owner or Operator
	JA8581	McD Douglas MD-11	Japan Airlines
	JA8582	McD Douglas MD-11	Japan Airlines
	JA8583	McD Douglas MD-11	Japan Airlines
	JA8584	McD Douglas MD-11	Japan Airlines
	JA8586	McD Douglas MD-11	Japan Airlines
	JA8587	McD Douglas MD-11	Japan Airlines
	JA8588	McD Douglas MD-11	Japan Airlines
	JA8589	McD Douglas MD-11	Japan Airlines
	JA8901	Boeing 747-446	Japan Airlines
	JA8902	Boeing 747-446	Japan Airlines
	JA8906	Boeing 747-446	Japan Airlines
	JA8909	Boeing 747-446	Japan Airlines
	JA8910	Boeing 747-446	Japan Airlines
	JA8911	Boeing 747-446	Japan Airlines
	JA8912	Boeing 747-446	Japan Airlines
	JA8913	Boeing 747-446	Japan Airlines
	JA8914	Boeing 747-446	Japan Airlines
	JA8915	Boeing 747-446	Japan Airlines
	JA8916	Boeing 747-446	Japan Airlines
	JA8917	Boeing 747-446	Japan Airlines
	JA8918	Boeing 747-446	Japan Airlines
	JA8937	Boeing 747-246F	Japan Airlines
	JA8957	Boeing 747-481F	All Nippon Airways
	JA8958	Boeing 747-481	All Nippon Airways
	JA8962	Boeing 747-481	All Nippon Airways

JY (Jordan)

	JY-AGK	Airbus A.310-308	Royal Jordanian
	JY-AGL	Airbus A.310-304	Royal Jordanian
	JY-AGS	Airbus A.310-304	Royal Jordanian
	JY-AGT	Airbus A.310-308	Royal Jordanian
	JY-AGU	Airbus A.310-203	Royal Jordanian
	JY-AGV	Airbus A.310-	Royal Jordanian
	JY-AJN	Boeing 707-3J6C	Royal Jordanian Cargo
	JY-AJO	Boeing 707-3J6C	Royal Jordanian Cargo

Note: Royal Jordanian also operates four A.310-304s registered F-ODVF, F-ODVG, F-ODVH and F-ODVI. Similarly A.320s retain the registrations F-OGYA, F-OGYB, F-OGYC, F-OHGB and F-OHGC.

LN (Norway)

	LN-BBA	Fokker 50	Norwegian Air Shuttle
	LN-BBB	Fokker 50	Norwegian Air Shuttle
	LN-BBC	Fokker 50	Norwegian Air Shuttle
	LN-BRC	Boeing 737-505	Braathens *Haakon IV Haakonsson*
	LN-BRD	Boeing 737-505	Braathens *Harald Gille*
	LN-BRE	Boeing 737-405	Braathens *Haakon V Magnusson*
	LN-BRF	Boeing 737-505	Braathens *Magnus Lagaboeter*
	LN-BRG	Boeing 737-505	Braathens *Oystein Magnusson*
	LN-BRH	Boeing 737-505	Braathens *Haakon den Gode*
	LN-BRI	Boeing 737-405	Braathens *Harald Haarfagre*
	LN-BRJ	Boeing 737-505	Braathens *Magnus Barfot*
	LN-BRK	Boeing 737-505	Braathens *Olav Tryggvason*
	LN-BRM	Boeing 737-505	Braathens *Olav den Hellige*
	LN-BRN	Boeing 737-505	Braathens *Haakon Herdebrei*
	LN-BRO	Boeing 737-505	Braathens *Magnus Haraldsson*
	LN-BRP	Boeing 737-405	Braathens *Harald Hardraade*
	LN-BRQ	Boeing 737-505	Braathens *Harald Graafell*
	LN-BRR	Boeing 737-505	Braathens *Halvdan Svarte*
	LN-BRS	Boeing 737-505	Braathens *Olav Kyrre*
	LN-BRT	Boeing 737-505	Braathens *Sigurd Jorsalfar*
	LN-BRU	Boeing 737-505	Braathens *Eirik Magnusson*
	LN-BRV	Boeing 737-505	Braathens *Haakon Sverresson*
	LN-BRX	Boeing 737-505	Braathens *Sigurd Munn*
	LN-BUB	Boeing 737-505	Braathens *Magnus den Gode*
	LN-BUC	Boeing 737-505	Braathens *Magnus Erlingsson*
	LN-BUD	Boeing 737-505	Braathens *Inge Krokrygg*
	LN-BUE	Boeing 737-505	Braathens *Erling Skjalgsson*
	LN-BUF	Boeing 737-405	Braathens
	LN-BUG	Boeing 737-505	Braathens *Oystein Haraldsson*

Reg.	Type	Owner or Operator	Notes
LN-BUH	Boeing 737-505	Braathens	
LN-BUI	Boeing 737-505	Braathens	
LN-FAJ	BAe Jetstream 3100	Coast Air	
LN-FAL	BAe Jetstream 3100	Coast Air	
LN-FAM	BAe Jetstream 3100	Coast Air	
LN-FAV	BAe Jetstream 3100	Coast Air	
LN-FAZ	BAe Jetstream 3100	Coast Air	
LN-KKA	Fokker 50	Norwegian Air Shuttle	
LN-KKD	Fokker 50	Norwegian Air Shuttle	
LN-KKE	Fokker 50	Norwegian Air Shuttle	
LN-RCD	Boeing 767-383ER	Scandinavian Airlines System (S.A.S.) Gyda Viking	
LN-RCE	Boeing 767-383ER	S.A.S. *Aase Viking*	
LN-RCG	Boeing 767-383ER	S.A.S. *Yrsa Viking*	
LN-RCH	Boeing 767-383ER	S.A.S. *Ingegerd Viking*	
LN-RCI	Boeing 767-383ER	S.A.S. *Helga Viking*	
LN-RCK	Boeing 767-383ER	S.A.S. *Tor Viking*	
LN-RCL	Boeing 767-383ER	S.A.S. *Sven Viking*	
LN-RCM	Boeing 767-383ER	S.A.S. *Gudrun Viking*	
LN-RDA	D.H.C.8Q-401 Dash Eight	S.A.S. Commuter *Fret Viking*	
LN-RDB	D.H.C.8Q-401 Dash Eight	S.A.S. Commuter *Kari Viking*	
LN-RDC	D.H.C.8Q-401 Dash Eight	S.A.S. Commuter	
LN-RDD	D.H.C.8Q-401 Dash Eight	S.A.S. Commuter	
LN-RLE	McD Douglas MD-82	S.A.S. *Ketiil Viking*	
LN-RLF	McD Douglas MD-82	S.A.S. *Finn Viking*	
LN-RLG	McD Douglas MD-82	S.A.S. *Trond Viking*	
LN-RLR	McD Douglas MD-82	S.A.S. *Vegard Viking*	
LN-RMA	McD Douglas MD-82	S.A.S. *Hasting Viking*	
LN-RMD	McD Douglas MD-82	S.A.S. *Fenge Viking*	
LN-RMF	McD Douglas MD-83	S.A.S. *Torgny Viking*	
LN-RMG	McD Douglas MD-87	S.A.S. *Snorre Viking*	
LN-RMH	McD Douglas MD-87	S.A.S. *Solmund Viking*	
LN-RMJ	McD Douglas MD-82	S.A.S. *Rand Viking*	
LN-RMK	McD Douglas MD-87	S.A.S. *Ragnhild Viking*	
LN-RML	McD Douglas MD-82	S.A.S. *Aud Viking*	
LN-RMM	McD Douglas MD-81	S.A.S. *Blenda Viking*	
LN-RMN	McD Douglas MD-82	S.A.S. *Ivar Viking*	
LN-RMO	McD Douglas MD-81	S.A.S. *Bergljot Viking*	
LN-RMP	McD Douglas MD-87	S.A.S. *Reidun Viking*	
LN-RMR	McD Douglas MD-81	S.A.S. *Olav Viking*	
LN-RMS	McD Douglas MD-81	S.A.S. *Nial Viking*	
LN-RMT	McD Douglas MD-81	S.A.S. *Jarl Viking*	
LN-RMU	McD Douglas MD-87	S.A.S. *Grim Viking*	
LN-RMX	McD Douglas MD-87	S.A.S. *Vidar Viking*	
LN-RMY	McD Douglas MD-87	S.A.S. *Ingolf Viking*	
LN-RNB	Fokker 50	S.A.S. Commuter *Brae Viking*	
LN-RNC	Fokker 50	S.A.S. Commuter *Elvink Viking*	
LN-RND	Fokker 50	S.A.S. Commuter *Inge Viking*	
LN-RNE	Fokker 50	S.A.S. Commuter *Ebbe Viking*	
LN-RNF	Fokker 50	S.A.S. Commuter *Leif Viking*	
LN-RNG	Fokker 50	S.A.S. Commuter *Gudrid Viking*	
LN-RNH	Fokker 50	S.A.S. Commuter *Harald Viking*	
LN-ROA	McD Douglas MD-90-30	S.A.S. *Sigurd Viking*	
LN-ROB	McD Douglas MD-90-30	S.A.S. *Isrid Viking*	
LN-ROM	McD Douglas MD-81	S.A.S. *Albin Viking*	
LN-RON	McD Douglas MD-81	S.A.S. *Holmfrid Viking*	
LN-ROO	McD Douglas MD-81	S.A.S. *Kristin Viking*	
LN-ROP	McD Douglas MD-82	S.A.S. *Bjoern Viking*	
LN-ROR	McD Douglas MD-82	S.A.S. *Assur Viking*	
LN-ROS	McD Douglas MD-82	S.A.S. *Isulv Viking*	
LN-ROT	McD Douglas MD-82	S.A.S. *Ingjaid Viking*	
LN-ROU	McD Douglas MD-82	S.A.S. *Ring Viking*	
LN-ROW	McD Douglas MD-82	S.A.S. *Ottar Viking*	
LN-ROX	McD Douglas MD-82	S.A.S. *Ulvrik Viking*	
LN-ROY	McD Douglas MD-82	S.A.S. *Spjute Viking*	
LN-ROZ	McD Douglas MD-87	S.A.S. *Slagfinn Viking*	
LN-RPA	Boeing 737-683	S.A.S. *Arnljot Viking*	
LN-RPB	Boeing 737-683	S.A.S. *Bure Viking*	
LN-RPC	Boeing 737-683	S.A.S.	
LN-RPD	Boeing 737-683	S.A.S.	
LN-RPE	Boeing 737-683	S.A.S. *Edla Viking*	
LN-RPF	Boeing 737-683	S.A.S. *Freda Viking*	
LN-RPG	Boeing 737-683	S.A.S *Geinnund Viking*	

Notes	Reg.	Type	Owner or Operator
	LN-RPH	Boeing 737-683	S.A.S. *Hamder Viking.*
	LN-RPJ	Boeing 737-783	S.A.S. *Grimhild Viking*
	LN-RPK	Boeing 737-683	S.A.S.
	LN-RPL	Boeing 737-683	S.A.S.
	LN-RPM	Boeing 737-683	S.A.S.
	LN-RPN	Boeing 737-883	S.A.S.
	LN-RPO	Boeing 737-683	S.A.S.
	LN-RPW	Boeing 737-683	S.A.S. *Alvid Viking*
	LN-RPX	Boeing 737-683	S.A.S. *Nanna Viking*
	LN-RPY	Boeing 737-683	S.A.S. *Olov Viking*
	LN-RPZ	Boeing 737-683	S.A.S. *Bera Viking*
	LN-TUA	Boeing 737-705	Braathens *Ingeborg Eriksdatter*
	LN-TUB	Boeing 737-705	Braathens
	LN-TUC	Boeing 737-705	Braathens
	LN-TUD	Boeing 737-705	Braathens
	LN-TUE	Boeing 737-705	Braathens
	LN-TUF	Boeing 737-705	Braathens
	LN-TUG	Boeing 737-705	Braathens
	LN-TUH	Boeing 737-705	Braathens
	LN-TUI	Boeing 737-705	Braathens
	LN-TUK	Boeing 737-705	Braathens
	LN-WND	Douglas DC-3C	Dakota Norway

LV (Argentina)

	Reg.	Type	Owner or Operator
	LV-MLO	Boeing 747-287B	Aerolineas Argentinas
	LV-MLP	Boeing 747-287B	Aerolineas Argentinas
	LV-MLR	Boeing 747-287B	Aerolineas Argentinas
	LV-OEP	Boeing 747-287B	Aerolineas Argentinas
	LV-OOZ	Boeing 747-287B	Aerolineas Argentinas
	LV-OPA	Boeing 747-287B	Aerolineas Argentinas
	LV-WYT	Boeing 747-238B	Aerolineas Argentinas
	LV-YPC	Boeing 747-212B	Aerolineas Argentinas
	LV-YSB	Boejng 747-257B	Aerolineas Argentinas
	LV-ZPJ	Airbus A.340-211	Aerolineas Argentinas
	LV-ZRA	Airbus A.340-211	Aerolineas Argentinas

LX (Luxembourg)

	Reg.	Type	Owner or Operator
	LX-EAC	EMB-120RT Brasilia	Europe Air Charter
	LX-FCV	Boeing 747-4R7F (SCD)	Cargolux *City of Luxembourg*
	LX-GCV	Boeing 747-4R7F (SCD)	Cargolux *City of Esch/Alzette*
	LX-ICV	Boeing 747-428F (SCD)	Cargolux *City of Ettelbruck*
	LX-KCV	Boeing 747-4R7F (SCD)	Cargolux *City of Dudelange*
	LX-LCV	Boeing 747-4R7F (SCD)	Cargolux *City of Grevenmacher*
	LX-LGB	Fokker 50	Luxair
	LX-LGC	Fokker 50	Luxair *Prince Guillaume*
	LX-LGD	Fokker 50	Luxair *Prince Felix*
	LX-LGE	Fokker 50	Luxair *Prince Louis*
	LX-LGF	Boeing 737-4C9	Sobelair
	LX-LGG	Boeing 737-4C9	Luxair *Château de Bourscheid*
	LX-LGO	Boeing 737-5C9	Luxair *Château de Clervaux*
	LX-LGP	Boeing 737-5C9	Luxair *Château de Bourglinster*
	LX-LGR	Boeing 737-528	Luxair *Chateau de Beaufort*
	LX-LGS	Boeing 737-528	Luxair *Château de Schengen*
	LX-LGT	Embraer RJ145LR	Luxair *Princess Alexandra*
	LX-LGU	Embraer RJ145LR	Luxair *Prince Sebastien*
	LX-LGV	Embraer RJ145LR	Luxair
	LX-LGW	Embraer RJ145LR	Luxair
	LX-LGX	Embraer RJ145LR	Luxair
	LX-LGY	Embraer RJ145LR	Luxair
	LX-MCV	Boeing 747-4R7F (SCD)	Cargolux *City of Echternach*
	LX-NCV	Boeing 747-4R7F (SCD)	Cargolux *City of Vianden*
	LX-OCV	Boeing 747-4R7F (SCD)	Cargolux *Differdange*
	LX-PCV	Boeing 747-4R7F (SCD)	Cargolux *City of Diekirch*
	LX-PTU	EMB-120RT Brasilia	Europe Air Charter
	LX-RCV	Boeing 747-4R7F (SCD)	Cargolux *Spirit of Schengen*
	LX-RGI	EMB-120RT Brasilia	Regional Airlines
	LX-SKS	EMB-110P1 Bandeirante	Sky Service
	LX-TLA	Douglas DC-8-62F	Cargo Lion
	LX-TLB	Douglas DC-8-62F	Cargo Lion

Reg.	Type	Owner or Operator
LX-TLC	Douglas DC-8-62F	Cargo Lion
LX-TLD	Douglas DC-10-30F	Cargo Lion
LX-TLE	Douglas DC-10-30F	Cargo Lion

Note: Cargolux also operates the Boeing 747-271Cs N537MC and N538MC.

LY (Lithuania)

Reg.	Type	Owner or Operator
LY-AAO	Yakovlev Yak-42	Lithuanian Airlines
LY-AAQ	Yakovlev Yak-42	Lithuanian Airlines
LY-AAR	Yakovlev Yak-42	Lithuanian Airlines
LY-AAT	Yakovlev Yak-42	Lithuanian Airlines
LY-AAU	Yakovlev Yak-42D	Lithuanian Airlines
LY-AAV	Yakovlev Yak-42D	Lithuanian Airlines
LY-AAW	Yakovlev Yak-42D	Lithuanian Airlines
LY-AAX	Yakovlev Yak-42D	Lithuanian Airlines
LY-BFV	Boeing 737-59D	Lithuanian Airlines
LY-BSD	Boeing 737-2T4	Lithuanian Airlines *Steponas Darius*
LY-BSG	Boeing 737-2T2	Lithuanian Airlines
LY-SBC	SAAB 2000	Lithuanian Airlines
LY-SBD	SAAB 2000	Lithuanian Airlines

LZ (Bulgaria)

Reg.	Type	Owner or Operator
LZ-AZO	Ilyushin IL-18V	Air Zory
LZ-BAC	Antonov An-12	Balkan Bulgarian Airlines/HeavyLift
LZ-BAE	Antonov An-12	Balkan Bulgarian Airlines
LZ-BAF	Antonov An-12	Balkan Bulgarian Airlines
LZ-BEH	Ilyushin IL-18V	Balkan Bulgarian Airlines
LZ-BEU	Ilyushin IL-18V	Balkan Bulgarian Airlines
LZ-BOA	Boeing 737-53A	Balkan Bulgarian Airlines *City of Sofia*
LZ-BOB	Boeing 737-53A	Balkan Bulgarian Airlines *City of Plovdiv*
LZ-BOC	Boeing 737-53A	Balkan Bulgarian Airlines *City of Varna*
LZ-BTG	Tupolev Tu-154B	Balkan Bulgarian Airlines
LZ-BTH	Tupolev Tu-154M	Balkan Bulgarian Airlines
LZ-BTI	Tupolev Tu-154M	Balkan Bulgarian Airlines
LZ-BTJ	Tupolev Tu-154B-1	Balkan Bulgarian Airlines
LZ-BTK	Tupolev Tu-154B	Balkan Bulgarian Airlines
LZ-BTL	Tupolev Tu-154B	Balkan Bulgarian Airlines
LZ-BTN	Tupolev Tu-154M	Balkan Bulgarian Airlines
LZ-BTO	Tupolev Tu-154B-1	Balkan Bulgarian Airlines
LZ-BTP	Tupolev Tu-154B-1	Balkan Bulgarian Airlines
LZ-BTQ	Tupolev Tu-154M	Balkan Bulgarian Airlines
LZ-BTS	Tupolev Tu-154B-2	Balkan Bulgarian Airlines
LZ-BTT	Tupolev Tu-154B-2	Balkan Bulgarian Airlines
LZ-BTV	Tupolev Tu-154B-2	Balkan Bulgarian Airlines
LZ-BTW	Tupolev Tu-154M	Balkan Bulgarian Airlines
LZ-BTX	Tupolev Tu-154M	Balkan Bulgarian Airlines
LZ-BTY	Tupolev Tu-154M	Balkan Bulgarian Airlines
LZ-BTZ	Tupolev Tu-154M	Balkan Bulgarian Airlines
LZ-ITA	Antonov An-12	Inter Trans Air
LZ-LTA	Tupolev Tu-154M	Balkan Bulgarian Airlines
LZ-LTB	Tupolev Tu-154B-2	Balkan Bulgarian Airlines
LZ-LTC	Tupolev Tu-154M	Balkan Bulgarian Airlines
LZ-LTE	Tupolev Tu-154M	Balkan Bulgarian Airlines
LZ-LTF	Tupolev Tu-154M	Balkan Bulgarian Airlines
LZ-LTG	Tupolev Tu-154M	Balkan Bulgarian Airlines
LZ-MIG	Tupolev Tu-154M	Air VIA Bulgarian Airways
LZ-MIK	Tupolev Tu-154M	Air VIA Bulgarian Airways
LZ-MIL	Tupolev Tu-154M	Air VIA Bulgarian Airways
LZ-MIR	Tupolev Tu-154M	Air VIA Bulgarian Airways
LZ-MIS	Tupolev Tu-154M	Air VIA Bulgarian Airways
LZ-MIV	Tupolev Tu-154M	Air VIA Bulgarian Airways
LZ-SFA	Antonov An-12BP	Air Sofia
LZ-SFL	Antonov An-12BP	Air Sofia
LZ-SFM	Antonov An-12BP	Air Sofia
LZ-SFS	Antonov An-12BP	Air Sofia
LZ-TUH	Tupolev Tu-134A-3	Hemus Air/Albanian Airlines
LZ-TUJ	Tupolev Tu-134A-3	Hemus Air/Albanian Airlines
LZ-TUL	Tupolev Tu-134A-3	Hemus Air

Notes	Reg.	Type	Owner or Operator
	LZ-TUN	Tupolev Tu-134A-3	Hemus Air/Albanian Airlines
	LZ-TUP	Tupolev Tu-134A	Hemus Air
	LZ-TUT	Tupolev Tu-134B-3	Hemus Air

N (USA)

	Reg.	Type	Owner or Operator
	N24UA	Douglas DC-8-61F	Kitty Hawk International
	N75AA	L.1011-385 TriStar 200	Tradewinds Airlines
	N100UN	Boeing 737-7K9	Transaero
	N101UN	Boeing 737-7K9	Transaero
	N102CK	L.1011-385 TriStar 200	Kitty Hawk International
	N102UN	Boeing 737-7K9	Transaero
	N103CK	L.1011-385 TriStar 200	Kitty Hawk International
	N103UN	Boeing 737-7K9	Transaero
	N104CK	L.1011-385 TriStar 200F	Kitty Hawk International
	N104TR	Boeing 747-237BF	Tower Air
	N104UA	Boeing 747-422	United Airlines
	N105CK	L.1011-385 TriStar 200	Kitty Hawk International
	N105EV	McD Douglas MD-11F	EVA Airways
	N105UA	Boeing 747-451	United Airlines
	N105TR	Boeing 747-2U3BF	Polar Air Cargo
	N106CK	L.1011-385 TriStar 200	Kitty Hawk International
	N106TR	Boeing 747-2U3BF	Polar Air Cargo
	N106UA	Boeing 747-451	United Airlines
	N107CK	L.1011-385 TriStar200F	Kitty Hawk International
	N107UA	Boeing 747-422	United Airlines
	N107WA	Douglas DC-10-30CF	World Airways/Federal Express
	N108CK	L.1011-385 TriStar 200	Kitty Hawk International
	N108UA	Boeing 747-422	United Airlines
	N109CK	L.1011-385 TriStar 200	Kitty Hawk International
	N109UA	Boeing 747-422	United Airlines
	N116UA	Boeing 747-422	United Airlines
	N117UA	Boeing 747-422	United Airlines
	N117WA	Douglas DC-10-30	World Airways
	N118UA	Boeing 747-422	United Airlines
	N119UA	Boeing 747-422	United Airlines
	N120UA	Boeing 747-422	United Airlines
	N121UA	Boeing 747-422	United Airlines
	N122UA	Boeing 747-422	United Airlines
	N127UA	Boeing 747-422	United Airlines
	N128UA	Boeing 747-422	United Airlines
	N129UA	Boeing 747-422	United Airlines
	N130UA	Boeing 747-422	United Airlines
	N131UA	Boeing 747-422	United Airlines
	N132UA	Boeing 747-422	United Airlines
	N133JC	Douglas DC-10-40	Northwest Airlines
	N133UA	Boeing 747-422	United Airlines
	N134UA	Boeing 747-422	United Airlines
	N135UA	Boeing 747-422	United Airlines
	N141US	Douglas DC-10-40	Northwest Airlines
	N144JC	Douglas DC-10-40	Northwest Airlines
	N145US	Douglas DC-10-40	Northwest Airlines
	N146US	Douglas DC-10-40	Northwest Airlines
	N147US	Douglas DC-10-40	Northwest Airlines
	N148US	Douglas DC-10-40	Northwest Airlines
	N149US	Douglas DC-10-40	Northwest Airlines
	N150US	Douglas DC-10-40	Northwest Airlines
	N151UA	Boeing 747-222B	United Airlines
	N151US	Douglas DC-10-40	Northwest Airlines
	N152UA	Boeing 747-222B	United Airlines
	N152US	Douglas DC-10-40	Northwest Airlines
	N153UA	Boeing 747-123	United Airlines
	N153US	Douglas DC-10-40	Northwest Airlines
	N154DL	Boeing 767-3P6ER	Delta Air Lines
	N154US	Douglas DC-10-40	Northwest Airlines
	N155DL	Boeing 767-3P6ER	Delta Air Lines
	N155UA	Boeing 747-123	United Airlines
	N155US	Douglas DC-10-40	Northwest Airlines
	N156DL	Boeing 767-3P6ER	Delta Air Lines
	N156UA	Boeing 747-123	United Airlines
	N156US	Douglas DC-10-40	Northwest Airlines
	N157UA	Boeing 747-123	United Airlines

Reg.	Type	Owner or Operator	Notes
N157US	Douglas DC-10-40	Northwest Airlines	
N158UA	Boeing 747-238B	United Airlines	
N158US	Douglas DC-10-40	Northwest Airlines	
N159UA	Boeing 747-238B	United Airlines	
N159US	Douglas DC-10-40	Northwest Airlines	
N160AT	L.1011-385 TriStar 500	American Trans Air	
N160UA	Boeing 747-238B	United Airlines	
N160US	Douglas DC-10-40	Northwest Airlines	
N161AT	L.1011-385 TriStar 500	American Trans Air	
N161UA	Boeing 747-238B	United Airlines	
N161US	Douglas DC-10-40	Northwest Airlines	
N162AT	L.1011-385 TriStar 500	American Trans Air	
N162US	Douglas DC-10-40	Northwest Airlines	
N163AA	Douglas DC-10-30	American Airlines	
N163AT	L.1011-385 TriStar 500	American Trans Air	
N163UA	Boeing 747-238B	United Airlines	
N164AA	Douglas DC-10-30	American Airlines	
N164AT	L.1011-385 TriStar 500	American Trans Air	
N164UA	Boeing 747-238B	United Airlines	
N165UA	Boeing 747-238B	United Airlines	
N166AA	Douglas DC-10-10ER	American Airlines	
N169DZ	Boeing 767-332ER	Delta Air Lines	
N171DN	Boeing 767-332ER	Delta Air Lines	
N171DZ	Boeing 767-332ER	Delta Air Lines	
N171UA	Boeing 747-422	United Airlines *Spirit of Seattle II*	
N172DN	Boeing 767-332ER	Delta Air Lines	
N172DZ	Boeing 767-332ER	Delta Air Lines	
N172UA	Boeing 747-422	United Airlines	
N173DN	Boeing 767-332ER	Delta Air Lines	
N173DZ	Boeing 767-332ER	Delta Air Lines	
N173UA	Boeing 747-422	United Airlines	
N174DN	Boeing 767-332ER	Delta Air Lines	
N174DZ	Boeing 767-332ER	Delta Air Lines	
N174UA	Boeing 747-422	United Airlines	
N175DN	Boeing 767-332ER	Delta Air Lines	
N175DZ	Boeing 767-332ER	Delta Air Lines	
N175UA	Boeing 747-422	United Airlines	
N176DN	Boeing 767-332ER	Delta Air Lines	
N176DZ	Boeing 767-332ER	Delta Air Lines	
N176UA	Boeing 747-422	United Airlines	
N177DN	Boeing 767-332ER	Delta Air Lines	
N177DZ	Boeing 767-332ER	Delta Air Lines	
N177UA	Boeing 747-422	United Airlines	
N178DN	Boeing 767-332ER	Delta Air Lines	
N178DZ	Boeing 767-332ER	Delta Air Lines	
N178UA	Boeing 747-422	United Airlines	
N179DN	Boeing 767-332ER	Delta Air Lines	
N179DZ	Boeing 767-332ER	Delta Air Lines	
N179UA	Boeing 747-422	United Airlines	
N180DN	Boeing 767-332ER	Delta Air Lines	
N180UA	Boeing 747-422	United Airlines	
N181DN	Boeing 767-332ER	Delta Air Lines	
N181SK	Douglas DC-8-62F	Trans Continental Airlines	
N181UA	Boeing 747-422	United Airlines	
N182DN	Boeing 767-332ER	Delta Air Lines	
N182SK	Douglas DC-8-55F	Trans Continental Airlines	
N182UA	Boeing 747-422	United Airlines	
N183DN	Boeing 767-332ER	Delta Air Lines	
N183UA	Boeing 747-422	United Airlines	
N184DN	Boeing 767-332ER	Delta Air Lines	
N184SK	Douglas DC-8-61F	Trans Continental Airlines	
N184UA	Boeing 747-422	United Airlines	
N185AT	L.1011-385 TriStar 50	American Trans Air	
N185DN	Boeing 767-332ER	Delta Air Lines	
N185UA	Boeing 747-422	United Airlines	
N186AT	L.1011-385 TriStar 50	American Trans Air	
N186DN	Boeing 767-332ER	Delta Air Lines	
N186UA	Boeing 747-422	United Airlines	
N187AT	L.1011-385 TriStar 50	American Trans Air	
N187DN	Boeing 767-332ER	Delta Air Lines	
N187UA	Boeing 747-422	United Airlines	
N188AT	L.1011-385 TriStar 50	American Trans Air	
N188DN	Boeing 767-332ER	Delta Air Lines	

Notes	Reg.	Type	Owner or Operator
	N188UA	Boeing 747-422	United Airlines
	N189AT	L.1011-385 TriStar 50	American Trans Air
	N189DN	Boeing 767-332ER	Delta Air Lines
	N189UA	Boeing 747-422	United Airlines
	N190AT	L.1011-385 TriStar 50	American Trans Air
	N190DN	Boeing 767-332ER	Delta Air Lines
	N190UA	Boeing 747-422	United Airlines
	N191AT	L.1011-385 TriStar 50	American Trans Air
	N191DN	Boeing 767-332ER	Delta Air Lines
	N191UA	Boeing 747-422	United Airlines
	N192AT	L.1011-385 TriStar 50	American Trans Air
	N192DN	Boeing 767-332ER	Delta Air Lines
	N192UA	Boeing 747-422	United Airlines
	N193AT	L.1011-385 TriStar 50	American Trans Air
	N193DN	Boeing 767-332ER	Delta Air Lines
	N193UA	Boeing 747-422	United Airlines
	N194AT	L.1011-385 TriStar 100	American Trans Air
	N194DN	Boeing 767-332ER	Delta Air Lines
	N194UA	Boeing 747-422	United Airlines
	N195AT	L.1011-385 TriStar 150	American Trans Air
	N195DN	Boeing 767-332ER	Delta Air Lines
	N195UA	Boeing 747-422	United Airlines
	N196AT	L.1011-385 TriStar 50	American Trans Air
	N196DN	Boeing 767-332ER	Delta Air Lines
	N196UA	Boeing 747-422	United Airlines
	N197AT	L.1011-385 TriStar 50	American Trans Air
	N197DN	Boeing 767-332ER	Delta Air Lines
	N197UA	Boeing 747-422	United Airlines
	N198AT	L.1011-385 TriStar 100	American Trans Air
	N198DN	Boeing 767-332ER	Delta Air Lines
	N198UA	Boeing 747-422	United Airlines
	N199DN	Boeing 767-332ER	Delta Air Lines
	N199UA	Boeing 747-422	United Airlines
	N202PH	Boeing 747-121	Tower Air
	N204UA	Boeing 777-222ER	United Airlines
	N205UA	Boeing 777-222ER	United Airlines
	N206UA	Boeing 777-222ER	United Airlines
	N207UA	Boeing 777-222ER	United Airlines
	N208UA	Boeing 777-222ER	United Airlines
	N209UA	Boeing 777-222ER	United Airlines
	N210UA	Boeing 777-222ER	United Airlines
	N211UA	Boeing 777-222ER	United Airlines
	N212UA	Boeing 777-222ER	United Airlines
	N211NW	Douglas DC-10-30	Northwest Airlines
	N220AU	Douglas DC-10-10	Orbis
	N220NW	Douglas DC-10-30	Northwest Airlines
	N221NW	Douglas DC-10-30	Northwest Airlines
	N223NW	Douglas DC-10-30	Northwest Airlines
	N224NW	Douglas DC-10-30	Northwest Airlines
	N225NW	Douglas DC-10-30	Northwest Airlines
	N226NW	Douglas DC-10-30	Northwest Airlines
	N227NW	Douglas DC-10-30	Northwest Airlines
	N228NW	Douglas DC-10-30	Northwest Airlines
	N229NW	Douglas DC-10-30	Northwest Airlines
	N230NW	Douglas DC-10-30	Northwest Airlines
	N232NW	Douglas DC-10-30	Northwest Airlines
	N234NW	Douglas DC-10-30	Northwest Airlines
	N235NW	Douglas DC-10-30	Northwest Airlines
	N236NW	Douglas DC-10-30	Northwest Airlines
	N237NW	Douglas DC-10-30	Northwest Airlines
	N238NW	Douglas DC-10-30	Northwest Airlines
	N239NW	Douglas DC-10-30	Northwest Airlines
	N240NW	Douglas DC-10-30	Northwest Airlines
	N241NW	Douglas DC-10-30	Northwest Airlines
	N242NW	Douglas DC-10-30	Northwest Airlines
	N271WA	McD Douglas MD-11	World Airways
	N272WA	McD Douglas MD-11	World Airways
	N273WA	McD Douglas MD-11	World Airways
	N274WA	McD Douglas MD-11F	World Airways
	N275WA	McD Douglas MD-11CF	World Airways
	N276WA	McD Douglas MD-11CF	World Airways
	N277WA	McD Douglas MD-11	World Airways
	N278WA	McD Douglas MD-11	World Airways

Reg.	Type	Owner or Operator	Notes
N301FE	Douglas DC-10-30AF	Federal Express	
N301UP	Boeing 767-34AFER	United Parcel Service	
N302FE	Douglas DC-10-30AF	Federal Express	
N302UP	Boeing 767-34AFER	United Parcel Service	
N303EA	L.1011 TriStar 1	Rich International Airways	
N303FE	Douglas DC-10-30AF	Federal Express	
N303UP	Boeing 767-34AFER	United Parcel Service	
N304FE	Douglas DC-10-30AF	Federal Express	
N304UP	Boeing 767-34AFER	United Parcel Service	
N305FE	Douglas DC-10-30AF	Federal Express *John David*	
N305UP	Boeing 767-34AFER	United Parcel Service	
N306FE	Douglas DC-10-30AF	Federal Express *John Peter Jr*	
N306GB	L.1011-385 TriStar 200F	Arrow Air	
N306UP	Boeing 767-34AFER	United Parcel Service	
N307FE	Douglas DC-10-30AF	Federal Express *Erin Lee*	
N307GB	L.1011-385 TriStar 200F	Arrow Air *San Juan*	
N307UP	Boeing 767-34AFER	United Parcel Service	
N308AS	Boeing 727-227F	Express One International/DHL	
N308FE	Douglas DC-10-30AF	Federal Express *Ann*	
N308GB	L.1011-385 TriStar 200F	Arrow Air	
N308UP	Boeing 767-34AFER	United Parcel Service	
N309FE	Douglas DC-10-30AF	Federal Express *Stacey*	
N309UP	Boeing 767-34AFER	United Parcel Service	
N310FE	Douglas DC-10-30AF	Federal Express *John Shelby*	
N310SS	L.1011-385 TriStar 1	Tradewinds Airlines	
N310UP	Boeing 767-34AFER	United Parcel Service	
N311FE	Douglas DC-10-30AF	Federal Express *Abe*	
N311UP	Boeing 767-34AFER	United Parcel Service	
N312AA	Boeing 767-223ER	American Airlines	
N312FE	Douglas DC-10-30AF	Federal Express *Angela*	
N312UP	Boeing 767-34AFER	United Parcel Service	
N313AA	Boeing 767-223ER	American Airlines	
N313FE	Douglas DC-10-30AF	Federal Express *Brandon Parks*	
N313UP	Boeing 767-34AFER	United Parcel Service	
N314FE	Douglas DC-10-30AF	Federal Express *Caitlin-Ann*	
N314UP	Boeing 767-34AFER	United Parcel Service	
N315AA	Boeing 767-223ER	American Airlines	
N315FE	Douglas DC-10-30AF	Federal Express *Kevin*	
N315UP	Boeing 767-34AFER	United Parcel Service	
N316AA	Boeing 767-223ER	American Airlines	
N316FE	Douglas DC-10-30AF	Federal Express *Brandon*	
N317AA	Boeing 767-223ER	American Airlines	
N317FE	Douglas DC-10-30CF	Federal Express	
N317UP	Boeing 767-34AFER	United Parcel Service	
N318FE	Douglas DC-10-30CF	Federal Express	
N318UP	Boeing 767-34AFER	United Parcel Service	
N319AA	Boeing 767-223ER	American Airlines	
N319FE	Douglas DC-10-30CF	Federal Express	
N319UP	Boeing 767-34AFER	United Parcel Service	
N320AA	Boeing 767-223ER	American Airlines	
N320FE	Douglas DC-10-30CF	Federal Express	
N320UP	Boeing 767-34AFER	United Parcel Service	
N321AA	Boeing 767-223ER	American Airlines	
N321FE	Douglas DC-10-30CF	Federal Express	
N321UP	Boeing 767-34AFER	United Parcel Service	
N322AA	Boeing 767-223ER	American Airlines	
N322FE	Douglas DC-10-30CF	Federal Express *King Frank*	
N322UP	Boeing 767-34AFER	United Parcel Service	
N323AA	Boeing 767-223ER	American Airlines	
N323MC	Boeing 747-2D7B	Atlas Air	
N323UP	Boeing 767-34AFER	United Parcel Service	
N324AA	Boeing 767-223ER	American Airlines	
N324UP	Boeing 767-34AFER	United Parcel Service	
N325AA	Boeing 767-223ER	American Airlines	
N325UP	Boeing 767-34AFER	United Parcel Service	
N326UP	Boeing 767-34AFER	United Parcel Service	
N327AA	Boeing 767-223ER	American Airlines	
N327UP	Boeing 767-34AFER	United Parcel Service	
N328AA	Boeing 767-223ER	American Airlines	
N328UP	Boeing 767-34AFER	United Parcel Service	
N329AA	Boeing 767-223ER	American Airlines	
N329UP	Boeing 767-34AER	United Parcel Service	
N330AA	Boeing 767-223ER	American Airlines	

Notes	Reg.	Type	Owner or Operator
	N330UP	Boeing 767-34AER	United Parcel Service
	N331UP	Boeing 767-34AER	United Parcel Service
	N332AA	Boeing 767-223ER	American Airlines
	N334AA	Boeing 767-223ER	American Airlines
	N335AA	Boeing 767-223ER	American Airlines
	N336AA	Boeing 767-223ER	American Airlines
	N338AA	Boeing 767-223ER	American Airlines
	N339AA	Boeing 767-223ER	American Airlines
	N341HA	L.188AF Electra	Channel Express (Air Services) Ltd
	N343HA	L.188AF Electra	Channel Express (Air Services) Ltd
	N344HA	L.188AF Electra	Channel Express (Air Services) Ltd
	N345JW	Douglas DC-8-63AF	CLA Air Transport
	N351AA	Boeing 767-323ER	American Airlines
	N352AA	Boeing 767-323ER	American Airlines
	N352PA	Boeing 727-225F	Express One
	N353AA	Boeing 767-323ER	American Airlines
	N354AA	Boeing 767-323ER	American Airlines
	N355AA	Boeing 767-323ER	American Airlines
	N357AA	Boeing 767-323ER	American Airlines
	N358AA	Boeing 767-323ER	American Airlines
	N359AA	Boeing 767-323ER	American Airlines
	N360AA	Boeing 767-323ER	American Airlines
	N360Q	L.188F Electra	Channel Express (Air Services) Ltd
	N361AA	Boeing 767-323ER	American Airlines
	N361DH	Airbus A.300-103F	DHL Airways
	N362AA	Boeing 767-323ER	American Airlines
	N363AA	Boeing 767-323ER	American Airlines
	N364DH	Airbus A.300B4-203F	DHL Airways
	N365DH	Airbus A.300B4-203F	DHL Airways
	N366AA	Boeing 767-323ER	American Airlines
	N366DH	Airbus A.300B4-203F	DHL Airways
	N367DH	Airbus A.300B4-203F	DHL Airways
	N368AA	Boeing 767-323ER	American Airlines
	N369AA	Boeing 767-323ER	American Airlines
	N370AA	Boeing 767-323ER	American Airlines
	N371AA	Boeing 767-323ER	American Airlines
	N372AA	Boeing 767-323ER	American Airlines
	N373AA	Boeing 767-323ER	American Airlines
	N374AA	Boeing 767-323ER	American Airlines
	N376AN	Boeing 767-323ER	American Airlines
	N377AN	Boeing 767-323ER	American Airlines
	N378AN	Boeing 767-323ER	American Airlines
	N379AA	Boeing 767-323ER	American Airlines
	N380AN	Boeing 767-323ER	American Airlines
	N381AN	Boeing 767-323ER	American Airlines
	N382AN	Boeing 767-323ER	American Airlines
	N383AN	Boeing 767-323ER	American Airlines
	N384AA	Boeing 767-323ER	American Airlines
	N385AM	Boeing 767-323ER	American Airlines
	N386AA	Boeing 767-323ER	American Airlines
	N387AM	Boeing 767-323ER	American Airlines
	N388AA	Boeing 767-323ER	American Airlines
	N389AA	Boeing 767-323ER	American Airlines
	N390AA	Boeing 767-323ER	American Airlines
	N391AA	Boeing 767-323ER	American Airlines
	N392AN	Boeing 767-323ER	American Airlines
	N393AN	Boeing 767-323ER	American Airlines
	N394AN	Boeing 767-323ER	American Airlines
	N394DL	Boeing 767-324ER	Delta Air Lines
	N395AN	Boeing 767-323ER	American Airlines
	N396AN	Boeing 767-323ER	American Airlines
	N397AN	Boeing 767-323ER	American Airlines
	N398AN	Boeing 767-323ER	American Airlines
	N399AN	Boeing 767-323ER	American Airlines
	N408MC	Boeing 747-47UF	Atlas Air
	N441J	Douglas DC-8-63CF	Arrow Air
	N470EV	Boeing 747-273C	Evergreen International Airlines
	N471EV	Boeing 747-273C	Evergreen International Airlines
	N472EV	Boeing 747-131	Evergreen International Airlines
	N474EV	Boeing 747-121	Evergreen International Airlines
	N479EV	Boeing 747-132 (SCD)	Evergreen International Airlines
	N480EV	Boeing 747-121F	Evergreen International Airlines
	N481EV	Boeing 747-132 (SCD)	Evergreen International Airlines

Reg.	Type	Owner or Operator	Notes
N482EV	Boeing 747-212B (SCD)	Evergreen International Airlines	
N483EV	Boeing 747-121	Evergreen International Airlines	
N484EV	Boeing 747-121	Evergreen International Airlines	
N485EV	Boeing 747-212B (SCD)	Evergreen International Airlines	
N491MC	Boeing 747-47UF	Atlas Air	
N492MC	Boeing 747-47UF	Atlas Air *Spirit of Panalpina*	
N493MC	Boeing 747-47UF	Atlas Air	
N494MC	Boeing 747-47UF	Atlas Air	
N495MC	Boeing 747-47UF	Atlas Air/BA World Cargo	
N496MC	Boeing 747-47UF	Arlas Air	
N497MC	Boeing 747-47UF	Atlas Air	
N498MC	Boeing 747-47UF	Atlas Air	
N499MC	Boeing 747-47UF	Atlas Air	
N505MC	Boeing 747-2D3B (SCD)	Atlas Air	
N506MC	Boeing 747-2D3B (SCD)	Atlas Air	
N507MC	Boeing 747-230B (SCD)	Atlas Air	
N508MC	Boeing 747-230B (SCD)	Atlas Air	
N509MC	Boeing 747-230B (SCD)	Atlas Air	
N512MC	Boeing 747-230B (SCD)	Atlas Air	
N514AT	Boeing 757-23N	American Trans Air	
N515AT	Boeing 757-23N	American Trans Air	
N516AT	Boeing 757-23N	American Trans Air	
N516MC	Boeing 747-243F (SCD)	Atlas Air	
N517AT	Boeing 757-23N	American Trans Air	
N517MC	Boeing 747-243F (SCD)	Atlas Air	
N518MC	Boeing 747-243F (SCD)	Atlas Air	
N519AT	Boeing 757-23N	American Trans Air	
N520AT	Boeing 757-23N	American Trans Air	
N520UP	Boeing 747-212BF	United Parcel Service	
N521AT	Boeing 757-28A	American Trans Air	
N521UP	Boeing 747-212BF	United Parcel Service	
N522AT	Boeing 757-23N	American Trans Air	
N522MC	Boeing 747-2D7B (SCD)	Atlas Air	
N522SJ	L.100-20 Hercules	Southern Air Transport	
N522UP	Boeing 747-212F	United Parcel Service	
N523AT	Boeing 757-23N	American Trans Air	
N523MC	Boeing 747-2D7BF	Atlas Air	
N523UP	Boeing 747-283F	United Parcel Service	
N524AT	Boeing 757-23N	American Trans Air	
N524MC	Boeing 747-2D7BF	Atlas Air	
N524MD	Douglas DC-10-30	Aeroflot	
N525AT	Boeing 757-23N	American Trans Air	
N526MC	Boeing 747-2D7BF	Atlas Air	
N527MC	Boeing 747-2D7BF	Atlas Air	
N528MC	Boeing 747-2D7B	Atlas Air	
N534MC	Boeing 747-2F6B	Atlas Air	
N535MC	Boeing 747-2F6B	Atlas Air	
N537MC	Boeing 747-271C (SCD)	Atlas Air	
N538MC	Boeing 747-271C (SCD)	Atlas Air	
N539MC	Boeing 747-271C (SCD)	Atlas Air	
N582FE	McD Douglas MD-11F	Federal Express *Jamie*	
N583FE	McD Douglas MD-11F	Federal Express *Nancy*	
N584FE	McD Douglas MD-11F	Federal Express *Jeffrey Wellington*	
N585FE	McD Douglas MD-11F	Federal Express	
N586FE	McD Douglas MD-11F	Federal Express *Dylan*	
N587FE	McD Douglas MD-11F	Federal Express *Jeanna*	
N590FE	McD Douglas MD-11F	Federal Express	
N600GC	Douglas DC-10-30F	Gemini Air Cargo	
N601EV	Boeing 767-3T7ER	EVA Airways	
N601FE	McD Douglas MD-11F	Federal Express *Jim Riedmeyer*	
N601GC	Douglas DC-10-30F	Gemini Air Cargo	
N601TW	Boeing 767-231ER	Trans World Airlines	
N602AA	Boeing 747SP-31	American Airlines	
N602EV	Boeing 767-3T7ER	EVA Airways	
N602FE	McDouglas MD-11F	Federal Express *Malcolm Baldrige 1990*	
N602FF	Boeing 747-124	Tower Air	
N602GC	Douglas DC-10-30F	Gemini Air Cargo	
N602TW	Boeing 767-231ER	Trans World Airlines	
N602UA	Boeing 767-222ER	United Airlines	
N603FE	McD Douglas MD-11F	Federal Express *Elizabeth*	
N603FF	Boeing 747-130	Tower Air	
N603GC	Douglas DC-10-30F	Gemini Air Cargo	
N603TW	Boeing 767-231ER	Trans World Airlines	

Notes	Reg.	Type	Owner or Operator
	N604FE	McD Douglas MD-11F	Federal Express *Hollis*
	N604FF	Boeing 747-121	Tower Air
	N604GC	Douglas DC-10-30F	Gemini Air Cargo
	N605FE	McD Douglas MD-11F	Federal Express *April Star*
	N605GC	Douglas DC-10-30F	Gemini Air Cargo
	N605TW	Boeing 767-231ER	Trans World Airlines
	N605UA	Boeing 767-222ER	United Airlines
	N606FE	McD Douglas MD-11F	Federal Express *Charles & Theresa*
	N606FF	Boeing 747-136	Tower Air
	N606GC	Douglas DC-10-30F	Gemini Air Cargo
	N606TW	Boeing 767-231ER	Trans World Airlines
	N606UA	Boeing 767-222ER	United Airlines *City of Chicago*
	N607FE	McD Douglas MD-11F	Federal Express *Christina*
	N607GC	Douglas DC-10-30F	Gemini Air Cargo
	N607FF	Boeing 747-238B	Tower Air
	N607TW	Boeing 767-231ER	Trans World Airlines
	N607UA	Boeing 767-222ER	United Airlines *City of Denver*
	N608FE	McD Douglas MD-11F	Federal Express *Dana Elena*
	N608FF	Boeing 747-131	Tower Air
	N608GC	Douglas DC-10-30F	Gemini Air Cargo
	N608TW	Boeing 767-231ER	Trans World Airlines
	N608UA	Boeing 767-222ER	United Airlines
	N609FE	McD Douglas MD-11F	Federal Express *Scott*
	N609FF	Boeing 747-121	Tower Air
	N609GC	Douglas DC-10-30	Gemini Air Cargo
	N609UA	Boeing 767-222ER	United Airlines
	N610FE	McD Douglas MD-11F	Federal Express *Marisa*
	N610FF	Boeing 747-282B	Tower Air
	N610TW	Boeing 767-231ER	Trans World Airlines
	N610UA	Boeing 767-222ER	United Airlines
	N611FF	Boeing 747-282B	Tower Air
	N611UA	Boeing 767-222ER	United Airlines
	N612FE	McD Douglas MD-11F	Federal Express *Alyssa*
	N612US	Boeing 747-251B	Northwest Airlines
	N613FE	McD Douglas MD-11F	Federal Express *Krista*
	N613FF	Boeing 747-121F (SCD)	Tower Air
	N613US	Boeing 747-251B	Northwest Airlines
	N614FE	McD Douglas MD-11F	Federal Express *Christy Allison*
	N614US	Boeing 747-251B	Northwest Airlines
	N615FE	McD Douglas MD-11F	Federal Express *Max*
	N615US	Boeing 747-251B	Northwest Airlines
	N616FE	McD Douglas MD-11F	Federal Express *Shanita*
	N616FF	Boeing 747-212B	Tower Air
	N616US	Boeing 747-251F (SCD)	Northwest Airlines
	N617FE	McD Douglas MD-11F	Federal Express *Travis*
	N617FF	Boeing 747-121F (SCD)	Tower Air
	N617US	Boeing 747-251F (SCD)	Northwest Airlines
	N618FE	McD Douglas MD-11F	Federal Express *Justin*
	N618FF	Boeing 747-212B	Tower Air
	N618US	Boeing 747-251F (SCD)	Northwest Airlines
	N619FE	McD Douglas MD-11F	Federal Express *Tara Lynn*
	N619FF	Boeing 747-212B	Tower Air
	N619US	Boeing 747-251F (SCD)	Northwest Airlines
	N620FE	McD Douglas MD-11F	Federal Express
	N620FF	Boeing 747-212B	Tower Air
	N621FE	McD Douglas MD-11F	Federal Express
	N621FF	Boeing 747-259B (SCD)	Tower Air
	N622FF	Boeing 747-283B	Tower Air
	N622US	Boeing 747-251B	Northwest Airlines
	N623FE	McD Douglas MD-11F	Federal Express
	N623FF	Boeing 747-2F6B	Tower Air
	N624FF	Boeing 747-212B	Tower Air
	N623US	Boeing 747-251B	Northwest Airlines
	N624US	Boeing 747-251B	Northwest Airlines
	N625US	Boeing 747-251B	Northwest Airlines
	N626US	Boeing 747-251B	Northwest Airlines
	N627US	Boeing 747-251B	Northwest Airlines
	N628US	Boeing 747-251B	Northwest Airlines
	N629US	Boeing 747-251F (SCD)	Northwest Airlines
	N630US	Boeing 747-2J9F	Northwest Airlines
	N631US	Boeing 747-251B	Northwest Airlines
	N632TW	Boeing 767-3Y0ER	Trans World Airlines
	N632US	Boeing 747-251B	Northwest Airlines

Reg.	Type	Owner or Operator	Notes
N633US	Boeing 747-227B	Northwest Airlines	
N634TW	Boeing 767-3Q8ER	Trans World Airlines	
N634US	Boeing 747-227B	Northwest Airlines	
N635TW	Boeing 767-3Q8ER	Trans World Airlines	
N635US	Boeing 747-227B	Northwest Airlines	
N636FE	Boeing 747-245F (SCD)	Federal Express	
N636TW	Boeing 767-3Q8ER	Trans World Airlines	
N636US	Boeing 747-251B	Northwest Airlines	
N637TW	Boeing 767-33AER	Trans World Airlines	
N637US	Boeing 747-251B	Northwest Airlines	
N638FE	Boeing 747-245F (SCD)	Federal Express	
N638US	Boeing 747-251B	Northwest Airlines	
N639FE	Boeing 747-2R7F (SCD)	Federal Express	
N639US	Boeing 747-251F (SCD)	Northwest Airlines	
N640FE	Boeing 747-245F (SCD)	Federal Express	
N640US	Boeing 747-251F (SCD)	Northwest Airlines	
N641NW	Boeing 747-212B	Northwest Airlines	
N641UA	Boeing 767-322ER	United Airlines	
N642NW	Boeing 747-212B	Northwest Airlines	
N642UA	Boeing 767-322ER	United Airlines	
N643NW	Boeing 747-249F	Northwest Airlines	
N643UA	Boeing 767-322ER	United Airlines	
N644NW	Boeing 747-212F	Northwest Airlines	
N644UA	Boeing 767-322ER	United Airlines	
N645UA	Boeing 767-322ER	United Airlines	
N645US	Boeing 767-201ER	US Airways	
N646UA	Boeing 767-322ER	United Airlines	
N646US	Boeing 767-201ER	US Airways	
N647UA	Boeing 767-322ER	United Airlines	
N647US	Boeing 767-201ER	US Airways	
N648UA	Boeing 767-322ER	United Airlines	
N648US	Boeing 767-201ER	US Airways	
N649UA	Boeing 767-322ER	United Airlines	
N649US	Boeing 767-201ER	US Airways	
N650TW	Boeing 767-205ER	Trans World Airlines	
N650UA	Boeing 767-322ER	United Airlines	
N650US	Boeing 767-201ER	US Airways	
N651TW	Boeing 767-205ER	Trans World Airlines	
N651UA	Boeing 767-322ER	United Airlines	
N651US	Boeing 767-2B7ER	US Airways	
N652UA	Boeing 767-322ER	United Airlines	
N652US	Boeing 767-2B7ER	US Airways	
N653UA	Boeing 767-322ER	United Airlines	
N653US	Boeing 767-2B7ER	US Airways	
N654UA	Boeing 767-322ER	United Airlines	
N654US	Boeing 767-2B7ER	US Airways	
N655UA	Boeing 767-322ER	United Airlines	
N655US	Boeing 767-2B7ER	US Airways	
N656UA	Boeing 767-322ER	United Airlines	
N656US	Boeing 767-2B7ER	US Airways	
N657UA	Boeing 767-322ER	United Airlines	
N658UA	Boeing 767-322ER	United Airlines	
N659UA	Boeing 767-322ER	United Airlines	
N660UA	Boeing 767-322ER	United Airlines	
N661AV	Douglas DC-8-63AF	Arrow Air	
N661UA	Boeing 767-322ER	United Airlines	
N661US	Boeing 747-451	Northwest Airlines	
N662UA	Boeing 767-322ER	United Airlines	
N662US	Boeing 747-451	Northwest Airlines	
N663UA	Boeing 767-322ER	United Airlines	
N663US	Boeing 747-451	Northwest Airlines	
N664UA	Boeing 767-322ER	United Airlines	
N664US	Boeing 747-451	Northwest Airlines	
N665US	Boeing 747-451	Northwest Airlines	
N666UA	Boeing 767-322ER	United Airlines	
N666US	Boeing 747-451	Northwest Airlines	
N667UA	Boeing 767-322ER	United Airlines	
N667US	Boeing 747-451	Northwest Airlines	
N668UA	Boeing 767-322ER	United Airlines	
N668US	Boeing 747-451	Northwest Airlines	
N669UA	Boeing 767-322ER	United Airlines	
N669US	Boeing 747-451	Northwest Airlines	
N670UA	Boeing 767-322ER	United Airlines	

Notes	Reg.	Type	Owner or Operator
	N670US	Boeing 747-451	Northwest Airlines
	N671UA	Boeing 767-322ER	United Airlines
	N671US	Boeing 747-451	Northwest Airlines
	N672UA	Boeing 767-322ER	United Airlines
	N672UP	Boeing 747-123F (SCD)	United Parcel Service
	N672US	Boeing 747-451	Northwest Airlines
	N673UA	Boeing 767-322ER	United Airlines
	N673UP	Boeing 747-123F (SCD)	United Parcel Service
	N673US	Boeing 747-451	Northwest Airlines
	N674UA	Boeing 767-322ER	United Airlines
	N674UP	Boeing 747-123F (SCD)	United Parcel Service
	N674US	Boeing 747-451	Northwest Airlines
	N675UA	Boeing 767-322ER	United Airlines
	N675UP	Boeing 747-123F (SCD)	United Parcel Service
	N676UA	Boeing 767-322ER	United Airlines
	N676UP	Boeing 747-123F (SCD)	United Parcel Service
	N677UA	Boeing 767-322ER	United Airlines
	N677UP	Boeing 747-123F (SCD)	United Parcel Service
	N681UP	Boeing 747-121F (SCD)	United Parcel Service
	N682UP	Boeing 747-121F (SCD)	United Parcel Service
	N683UP	Boeing 747-121F (SCD)	United Parcel Service
	N687AA	Boeing 757-223ET	American Airlines
	N688AA	Boeing 757-223ET	American Airlines
	N689AA	Boeing 757-223ET	American Airlines
	N690AA	Boeing 757-223ET	American Airlines
	N691AA	Boeing 757-223ET	American Airlines
	N692AA	Boeing 757-223ET	American Airlines
	N701CK	Boeing 747-146F (SCD)	Kitty Hawk International
	N701TW	Boeing 757-2Q8	Trans World Airlines
	N702CK	Boeing 747-146F (SCD)	Kitty Hawk International
	N703CK	Boeing 747-146F (SCD)	Kitty Hawk International
	N704CK	Boeing 747-146F (SCD)	Kitty Hawk international
	N706CK	Boeing 747-238B	Kitty Hawk International
	N707CK	Boeing 747-269B (SCD)	Kitty Hawk International
	N707TW	Boeing 757-2Q8	Trans World Airlines
	N708CK	Boeing 747-269B (SCD)	Kitty Hawk International
	N708TW	Boeing 757-231	Trans World Airlines
	N709CK	Boeing 747-132F	Kitty Hawk International
	N709TW	Boeing 757-2Q8	Trans World Airlines
	N710CK	Boeing 747-2B4BF	Kitty Hawk International
	N712CK	Boeing 747-2B4BF	Kitty Hawk International
	N713CK	Boeing 747-2B4BF	Kitty Hawk International
	N718TW	Boeing 757-231	Trans World Airlines
	N719TW	Boeing 757-231	Trans World Airlines
	N720TW	Boeing 757-231	Trans World Airlines
	N721RW	Boeing 727-2M7F	Express One
	N721TW	Boeing 757-231	Trans World Airlines
	N722TW	Boeing 757-231	Trans World Airlines
	N723TW	Boeing 757-231	Trans World Airlines
	N724TW	Boeing 757-231	Trans World Airlines
	N725TW	Boeing 757-231	Trans World Airlines
	N726TW	Boeing 757-231	Trans World Airlines
	N727TW	Boeing 757-231	Trans World Airlines
	N735SJ	Boeing 747-121F (SCD)	Polar Air Cargo
	N736DY	L.1011-385 TriStar 250	Delta Air Lines
	N737D	L.1011-385 TriStar 250	Delta Air Lines
	N740DA	L.1011-385 TriStar 250	Delta Air Lines
	N741DA	L.1011-385 TriStar 250	Delta Air Lines
	N742RW	Boeing 727-2M7F	Express One
	N742SA	Boeing 747-230F (SCD)	Southern Air
	N753DA	L.1011-385 TriStar 500	Delta Air Lines
	N754DL	L.1011-385 TriStar 500	Delta Air Lines
	N755AT	Boeing 757-2Q8	American Trans Air
	N755DL	L.1011-385 TriStar 500	Delta Air Lines
	N756DR	L.1011-385 TriStar 500	Delta Air Lines
	N759DA	L.1011-385 TriStar 500	Delta Air Lines
	N760DH	L.1011-385 TriStar 500	Delta Air Lines
	N761DA	L.1011-385 TriStar 500	Delta Air Lines
	N762DA	L.1011-385 TriStar 500	Delta Air Lines
	N763DL	L.1011-385 TriStar 500	Delta Air Lines
	N764DA	L.1011-385 TriStar 500	Delta Air Lines
	N765DA	L.1011-385 TriStar 500	Delta Air Lines
	N766DA	L.1011-385 TriStar 500	Delta Air Lines

Reg.	Type	Owner or Operator	Notes
N766UA	Boeing 777-222	United Airlines	
N767DA	L.1011-385 TriStar 500	Delta Air Lines	
N767UA	Boeing 777-222	United Airlines	
N768DL	L.1011-385 TriStar 500	Delta Air Lines	
N768UA	Boeing 777-222	United Airlines	
N769DL	L.1011-385 TriStar 500	Delta Air Lines	
N769UA	Boeing 777-222	United Airlines	
N770AN	Boeing 777-223ER	American Airlines	
N770UA	Boeing 777-222	United Airlines	
N771AN	Boeing 777-223ER	American Airlines	
N771UA	Boeing 777-222	United Airlines	
N772AN	Boeing 777-223ER	American Airlines	
N772UA	Boeing 777-222	United Airlines	
N773AN	Boeing 777-223ER	American Airlines	
N773UA	Boeing 777-222	United Airlines	
N774AN	Boeing 777-223ER	American Airlines	
N774UA	Boeing 777-222	United Airlines	
N775AN	Boeing 777-223ER	American Airlines	
N775UA	Boeing 777-222	United Airlines	
N776AN	Boeing 777-223ER	American Airlines	
N776UA	Boeing 777-222	United Airlines	
N777AN	Boeing 777-223ER	American Airlines	
N777UA	Boeing 777-222	United Airlines	
N778AN	Boeing 777-223ER	American Airlines	
N778UA	Boeing 777-222	United Airlines	
N779AN	Boeing 777-223ER	American Airlines	
N779UA	Boeing 777-222ER	United Airlines	
N780AN	Boeing 777-223ER	American Airlines	
N780UA	Boeing 777-222ER	United Airlines	
N781AN	Boeing 777-223ER	American Airlines	
N781UA	Boeing 777-222	United Airlines	
N782AN	Boeing 777-223ER	American Airlines	
N782UA	Boeing 777-222B	United Airlines	
N783AN	Boeing 777-223ER	American Airlines	
N783UA	Boeing 777-222B	United Airlines	
N784AL	Douglas DC-8-63CF	Air Transport International	
N784AN	Boeing 777-223ER	American Airlines	
N784UA	Boeing 777-222B	United Airlines	
N785AN	Boeing 777-223ER	American Airlines	
N785UA	Boeing 777-222B	United Airlines	
N786AN	Boeing 777-223ER	American Airlines	
N786UA	Boeing 777-222B	United Airlines	
N787AL	Boeing 777-223ER	American Airlines	
N787M	L.1011-385 TriStar 100	Operation Blessing International Relief	
N787UA	Boeing 777-222B	United Airlines	
N788AN	Boeing 777-223ER	American Airlines	
N788UA	Boeing 777-222B	United Airlines	
N789AN	Boeing 777-223ER	American Airlines	
N789UA	Boeing 777-222B	United Airlines	
N790AN	Boeing 777-223ER	American Airlines	
N790UA	Boeing 777-222B	United Airlines	
N791AL	Douglas DC-8-62AF	Arrow Air	
N791AN	Boeing 777-223ER	American Airlines	
N791FT	Douglas DC-8-73AF	Emery Worldwide	
N791UA	Boeing 777-222B	United Airlines	
N792AN	Boeing 777-223ER	American Airlines	
N792FT	Douglas DC-8-73AF	Emery Worldwide	
N792UA	Boeing 777-222B	United Airlines	
N793AN	Boeing 777-223ER	American Airlines	
N793UA	Boeing 777-222B	United Airlines	
N794AN	Boeing 777-223ER	American Airlines	
N794UA	Boeing 777-222B	United Airlines	
N795FT	Douglas DC-8-73AF	Emery Worldwide	
N795UA	Boeing 777-222B	United Airlines	
N796AL	Douglas DC-8-63AF	Emery Worldwide	
N796FT	Douglas DC-8-73AF	Emery Worldwide	
N796UA	Boeing 777-222ER	United Airlines	
N797AL	Douglas DC-8-63AF	Emery Worldwide	
N797UA	Boeing 777-222ER	United Airlines	
N798UA	Boeing 777-222ER	United Airlines	
N799UA	Boeing 777-222ER	United Airlines	
N801CK	Douglas DC-8-55F	Kitty Hawk International	
N801DE	McD Douglas MD-11	Delta Air Lines	

Notes	Reg.	Type	Owner or Operator
	N801DH	Douglas DC-8-73AF	DHL Worldwide
	N801GP	Douglas DC-8-71AF	Emery Worldwide
	N801UP	Douglas DC-8-73AF	United Parcel Service
	N802BN	Douglas DC-8-62AF	Arrow Air
	N802CK	Douglas DC-8-54F	Kitty Hawk International
	N802DE	McD Douglas MD-11	Delta Air Lines
	N802DH	Douglas DC-8-73AF	DHL Worldwide
	N802UP	Douglas DC-8-73AF	United Parcel Service
	N803DE	McD Douglas MD-11	Delta Air Lines
	N803DH	Douglas DC-8-73AF	DHL Worldwide
	N803UP	Douglas DC-8-63AF	United Parcel Service
	N804CK	Douglas DC-8-51F	Kitty Hawk International
	N804DE	McD Douglas MD-11	Delta Air Lines
	N804DH	Douglas DC-8-73AF	DHL Worldwide
	N804UP	Douglas DC-8-51	United Parcel Service
	N805CK	Douglas DC-8-51F	Kitty Hawk International
	N805DE	McD Douglas MD-11	Delta Air Lines
	N805DH	Douglas DC-8-73AF	DHL Worldwide
	N805UP	Douglas DC-8-73CF	United Parcel Service
	N806CK	Douglas DC-8-54F	Kitty Hawk International
	N806DE	McD Douglas MD-11	Delta Air Lines
	N806DH	Douglas DC-8-73CF	DHL Worldwide
	N806FT	Boeing 747-249F (SCD)	Polar Air Cargo
	N806UP	Douglas DC-8-73AF	United Parcel Service
	N807CK	Douglas DC-8-55F	Kitty Hawk International
	N807DE	McD Douglas MD-11	Delta Air Lines
	N807DH	Douglas DC-8-73CF	DHL Worldwide
	N807UP	Douglas DC-8-73AF	United Parcel Service
	N808DE	McD Douglas MD-11	Delta Air Lines
	N808MC	Boeing 747-212B (SCD)	Atlas Air
	N808UP	Douglas DC-8-73AF	United Parcel Service
	N809CK	Douglas DC-8-55F	Kitty Hawk International
	N809DE	McD Douglas MD-11	Delta Air Lines
	N809MC	Boeing 747-228F (SCD)	Atlas Air/Cargolux
	N809UP	Douglas DC-8-73AF	United Parcel Service
	N810CK	Douglas DC-8-52F	Kitty Hawk International
	N810DE	McD Douglas MD-11	Delta Air Lines
	N810UP	Douglas DC-8-71AF	United Parcel Service
	N811CK	Douglas DC-8-63AF	Kitty Hawk International
	N811DE	McD Douglas MD-11	Delta Air Lines
	N811UP	Douglas DC-8-73AF	United Parcel Service
	N812CK	Douglas DC-8-61AF	Kitty Hawk International
	N812DE	McD Douglas MD-11	Delta Air Lines
	N812UP	Douglas DC-8-73AF	United Parcel Service
	N813CK	Douglas DC-8-61AF	Kitty Hawk International
	N813DE	McD Douglas MD-11	Delta Air Lines
	N813UP	Douglas DC-8-73AF	United Parcel Service
	N814DE	McD Douglas MD-11	Delta Air Lines
	N814UP	Douglas DC-8-73AF	United Parcel Service
	N815CK	Douglas DC-8-63F	Kitty Hawk International
	N815DE	McD Douglas MD-11	Delta Air Lines
	N815EV	Douglas DC-8-73CF	Evergreen International Airlines
	N816CK	Douglas DC-8-61F	Kitty Hawk International
	N817CK	Douglas DC-8-61F	Kitty Hawk International
	N818CK	Douglas DC-8-62F	Kitty Hawk International
	N818UP	Douglas DC-8-73AF	United Parcel Service
	N819UP	Douglas DC-8-73AF	United Parcel Service
	N820BX	Douglas DC-8-71AF	BAX Global
	N821BX	Douglas DC-8-71AF	BAX Global
	N822BX	Douglas DC-8-71AF	BAX Global
	N823BX	Douglas DC-8-71AF	BAX Global
	N824BX	Douglas DC-8-71AF	BAX Global
	N826CR	L.1011-385 TriStar 1	Tradewinds Airlines
	N830FT	Boeing 747-121F	Polar Air Cargo
	N831AL	Douglas DC-8-73CF	Emery Worldwide Airlines
	N831LA	Douglas DC-10-30	Laker Airways
	N832AL	Douglas DC-8-73F	Emery Worldwide Airlines
	N832FT	Boeing 747-121F (SCD)	Polar Air Cargo
	N832LA	Douglas DC-10-30	Laker Airways
	N835AB	Airbus A.310-324	Air Jamaica *Spirit of May Pen*
	N836UP	Douglas DC-8-73AF	United Parcel Service
	N838AB	Airbus A.310-324	Air Jamaica *Spirit of Spanish Town*
	N839AD	Airbus A.310-324	Air Jamaica *Spirit of Negril*

Reg.	Type	Owner or Operator	Notes
N840AB	Airbus A.310-324	Air Jamaica *Spirit of Mandeville*	
N840UP	Douglas DC-8-73AF	United Parcel Service	
N841AB	Airbus A.310-324	Air Jamaica	
N845FT	Boeing 747-122F	Polar Air Cargo	
N850FT	Boeing 747-122F	Polar Air Cargo	
N851FT	Boeing 747-122F	Polar Air Cargo *Sandy Moore*	
N851UP	Douglas DC-8-73AF	United Parcel Service	
N852FT	Boeing 747-122	Polar Air Cargo *Martin Moore*	
N852UP	Douglas DC-8-73AF	United Parcel Service	
N853FT	Boeing 747-122F	Polar Air, Cargo	
N854FT	Boeing 747-122F	Polar Air Cargo *Sunny Lam*	
N855FT	Boeing 747-124F	Polar Air Cargo *Thomas J. Fowler*	
N856FT	Boeing 747-132F (SCD)	Polar Air Cargo *Paul Zinca*	
N857FT	Boeing 747-132F	Polar Air Cargo	
N858FT	Boeing 747-123F	Polar Air Cargo	
N859FT	Boeing 747-123F	Polar Air Cargo	
N860DA	Boeing 777-232ER	Delta Air Lines	
N861DA	Boeing 777-232ER	Delta Air Lines	
N862DA	Boeing 777-232ER	Delta Air Lines	
N863BX	Boeing 707-321C	BAX Global	
N863DA	Boeing 777-232ER	Delta Air Lines	
N864DA	Boeing 777-232ER	Delta Air Lines	
N865DA	Boeing 777-232ER	Delta Air Lines	
N865F	Douglas DC-8-63AF	Emery Worldwide	
N866DA	Boeing 777-232ER	Delta Air Lines	
N866UP	Douglas DC-8-73AF	United Parcel Service	
N867BX	Douglas DC-8-63AF	BAX Global	
N867DA	Boeing 777-232ER	Delta Air Lines	
N867UP	Douglas DC-8-73AF	United Parcel Service	
N868BX	Douglas DC-8-63AF	BAX Global	
N868DA	Boeing 777-232ER	Delta Air Lines	
N868UP	Douglas DC-8-73AF	United Parcel Service	
N869BX	Douglas DC-8-63AF	BAX Global	
N869DA	Boeing 777-232ER	Delta Air Lines	
N870BX	Douglas DC-8-63AF	BAX Global	
N870DA	Boeing 777-232ER	Delta Air Lines	
N870TV	Douglas DC-8-73AF	Emery Worldwide	
N871DA	Boeing 777-232ER	Delta Air Lines	
N872DA	Boeing 777-232ER	Delta Air Lines	
N873DA	Boeing 777-232ER	Delta Air Lines	
N874UP	Douglas DC-8-73AF	United Parcel Service	
N880UP	Douglas DC-8-73AF	United Parcel Service	
N894UP	Douglas DC-8-73AF	United Parcel Service	
N906R	Douglas DC-8-63CF	Air Transport International	
N920FT	Boeing 747-249F (SCD)	Polar Air Cargo	
N921FT	Boeing 747-283F	Polar Air Cargo	
N921R	Douglas DC-8-63AF	Emery Worldwide	
N923FT	Boeing 747-2U3BF	Polar Air Cargo	
N950R	Douglas DC-8-63AF	Emery Worldwide	
N951R	Douglas DC-8-63AF	Emery Worldwide	
N952R	Douglas DC-8-63AF	Emery Worldwide	
N957R	Douglas DC-8-63AF	Emery Worldwide	
N959R	Douglas DC-8-63AF	Emery Worldwide	
N961R	Douglas DC-8-73AF	Emery Worldwide	
N964R	Douglas DC-8-63AF	Emery Worldwide	
N984AN	Boeing 767-383ER	Avianca	
N985AN	Boeing 767-259ER	Avianca *Cristobal Colon*	
N986AN	Boeing 767-259ER	Avianca	
N988AN	Boeing 767-284ER	Avianca	
N990CF	Douglas DC-8-62AF	Emery Worldwide	
N993CF	Douglas DC-8-62AF	Emery Worldwide	
N994CF	Douglas DC-8-62AF	Emery Worldwide	
N995CF	Douglas DC-8-62AF	Emery Worldwide	
N996CF	Douglas DC-8-62AF	Emery Worldwide	
N997CF	Douglas DC-8-62AF	Emery Worldwide	
N998CF	Douglas DC-8-62AF	Emery Worldwide	
N1200K	Boeing 767-332ER	Delta Air Lines	
N1201P	Boeing 767-332ER	Delta Air Lines	
N1501P	Boeing 767-3P6ER	Delta Air Lines	
N1602	Boeing 767-332ER	Delta Air Lines	
N1603	Boeing 767-332ER	Delta Air Lines	
N1604R	Boeing 767-332ER	Delta Air Lines	
N1605	Boeing 767-332ER	Delta Air Lines	

Notes	Reg.	Type	Owner or Operator
	N1606P	Boeing 767-332ER	Delta Air Lines
	N1607	Boeing 767-332ER	Delta Air Lines
	N1738D	L.1011-385 TriStar 250	Delta Air Lines
	N1739D	L.1011-385 TriStar 250	Delta Air Lines
	N1755	McD Douglas MD-11 (1AF)	American Airlines
	N1756	McD Douglas MD-11 (1AG)	American Airlines
	N1758B	McD Douglas MD-11 (1AJ)	American Airlines
	N1760A	McD Douglas MD-11 (1AM)	American Airlines
	N1761R	McD Douglas MD-11 (1AN)	American Airlines
	N1762B	McD Douglas MD-11 (1AP)	American Airlines
	N1763	McD Douglas MD-11 (1AR)	American Airlines
	N1764B	McD Douglas MD-11 (1AS)	American Airlines
	N1765B	McD Douglas MD-11 (1AT)	American Airlines
	N1766A	McD Douglas MD-11 (1AU)	American Airlines
	N1767A	McD Douglas MD-11 (1AV)	American Airlines
	N1808E	Douglas DC-8-62AF	Arrow Air
	N2674U	Douglas DC-8-73AF	Emery Worldwide
	N3140D	L.1011-385 TriStar 500 (598)	B.W.I.A. *Sunjet St. Lucia*
	N4508H	Boeing 747SP-09	China Airlines
	N4522V	Boeing 747SP-09	China Airlines
	N6813	Boeing 727-223F	Express One/DHL
	N6815	Boeing 727-223F	Express One
	N6819	Boeing 727-223F	Express One/DHL
	N6826	Boeing 727-223F	Express One/DHL
	N6839	Boeing 727-223F	Express One
	N7036T	L.1011-385 TriStar 100	Trans World Airlines
	N7375A	Boeing 767-323ER	American Airlines
	N8067A	Airbus A.300-605R	American Airlines
	N8076U	Douglas DC-8-71AF	Emery Worldwide
	N8079U	Douglas DC-8-71AF	Emery Worldwide
	N8084U	Douglas DC-8-71AF	Emery Worldwide
	N8085U	Douglas DC-8-71AF	Emery Worldwide
	N8087U	Douglas DC-8-71AF	Emery Worldwide
	N8177U	Douglas DC-8-71AF	Emery Worldwide
	N8968U	Douglas DC-8-62AF	Arrow Air
	N12061	Douglas DC-10-30	Continental Airlines *Richard M. Adams*
	N12064	Douglas DC-10-30	Continental Airlines
	N12080	Douglas DC-10-30	Continental Airlines
	N12089	Douglas DC-10-30	Continental Airlines
	N12090	Douglas DC-10-30	Continental Airlines
	N12109	Boeing 757-224	Continental Airlines
	N12114	Boeing 757-224	Continental Airlines
	N12116	Boeing 757-224	Continental Airlines
	N12125	Boeing 757-224	Continental Airlines
	N13066	Douglas DC-10-30	Continental Airlines
	N13067	Douglas DC-10-30	Continental Airlines
	N13086	Douglas DC-10-30	Continental Airlines
	N13088	Douglas DC-10-30	Continental Airlines
	N13110	Boeing 757-224	Continental Airlines
	N13113	Boeing 757-224	Continental Airlines
	N13138	Boeing 757-224	Continental Airlines
	N14062	Douglas DC-10-30	Continental Airlines
	N14063	Douglas DC-10-30	Continental Airlines
	N14065	Airbus A.300-605R	American Airlines
	N14068	Airbus A.300-605R	American Airlines
	N14074	Douglas DC-10-30	Continental Airlines
	N14075	Douglas DC-10-30	Continental Airlines
	N14090	Douglas DC-10-30	Continental Airlines
	N14102	Boeing 757-224	Continental Airlines
	N14106	Boeing 757-224	Continental Airlines
	N14107	Boeing 757-224	Continental Airlines
	N14115	Boeing 757-224	Continental Airlines
	N14118	Boeing 757-224	Continental Airlines
	N14120	Boeing 757-224	Continental Airlines
	N14121	Boeing 757-224	Continental Airlines
	N15069	Douglas DC-10-30	Continental Airlines
	N16065	Boeing 767-332ER	Delta Air Lines
	N16078	Boeing 767-332ER	Delta Air Lines
	N17011	Boeing 747-143	Continental Airlines
	N17025	Boeing 747-238B	Continental Airlines
	N17085	Douglas DC-10-30	Continental Airlines
	N17087	Douglas DC-10-30	Continental Airlines
	N17104	Boeing 757-224	Continental Airlines

Reg.	Type	Owner or Operator	Notes
N17105	Boeing 757-224	Continental Airlines	
N17122	Boeing 757-224	Continental Airlines	
N17133	Boeing 757-224	Continental Airlines	
N17139	Boeing 757-224	Continental Airlines	
N18066	Airbus A.300-605R	American Airlines	
N18112	Boeing 757-224	Continental Airlines	
N18119	Boeing 757-224	Continental Airlines	
N19072	Douglas DC-10-30	Continental Airlines	
N19117	Boeing 757-224	Continental Airlines	
N19141	Boeing 757-224	Continental Airlines	
N21108	Boeing 757-224	Continental Airlines	
N25071	Airbus A.300-605R	American Airlines	
N26123	Boeing 757-224	Continental Airlines	
N29124	Boeing 757-224	Continental Airlines	
N33021	Boeing 747-243B	Continental Airlines	
N33069	Airbus A.300-605R	American Airlines	
N33103	Boeing 757-224	Continental Airlines	
N34131	Boeing 757-224	Continental Airlines	
N34137	Boeing 757-224	Continental Airlines	
N35084	Douglas DC-10-30	Continental Airlines	
N37077	Douglas DC-10-30	Continental Airlines	
N37078	Douglas DC-10-30	Continental Airlines	
N39081	Douglas DC-10-30	Continental Airlines	
N39356	Boeing 767-323ER	American Airlines	
N39364	Boeing 767-323ER	American Airlines	
N39365	Boeing 767-323ER	American Airlines	
N39367	Boeing 767-323ER	American Airlines	
N41068	Douglas DC-10-30	Continental Airlines	
N41140	Boeing 757-224	Continental Airlines	
N42086	Douglas DC-8-62AF	Arrow Air	
N49082	Douglas DC-10-30	Continental Airlines	
N57111	Boeing 757-224	Continental Airlines	
N58101	Boeing 757-224	Continental Airlines	
N59083	Douglas DC-10-30	Continental Airlines	
N68044	Douglas DC-10-30	Continental Airlines	
N68060	Douglas DC-10-30	Continental Airlines	
N68065	Douglas DC-10-30	Continental Airlines *Robert P. Gallaway*	
N70072	Airbus A.300-605R	American Airlines	
N70073	Airbus A.300-605R	American Airlines	
N70074	Airbus A.300-605R	American Airlines	
N74007	Boeing 777-224ER	Continental Airlines	
N74014	Boeing 777-224ER	Continental Airlines	
N76010	Boeing 777-224ER	Continental Airlines	
N76073	Douglas DC-10-30	Continental Airlines	
N77006	Boeing 777-224ER	Continental Airlines	
N77012	Boeing 777-224ER	Continental Airlines	
N77014	Boeing 777-224ER	Continental Airlines	
N78001	Boeing 777-224ER	Continental Airlines	
N78002	Boeing 777-224ER	Continental Airlines	
N78003	Boeing 777-224ER	Continental Airlines	
N78004	Boeing 777-224ER	Continental Airlines	
N78005	Boeing 777-224ER	Continental Airlines	
N78008	Boeing 777-224ER	Continental Airlines	
N78009	Boeing 777-224ER	Continental Airlines	
N78013	Boeing 777-224ER	Continental Airlines	
N79011	Boeing 777-224ER	Continental Airlines	
N83071	Douglas DC-10-30ER	Continental Airlines	
N87070	Douglas DC-10-30ER	Continental Airlines	
N90070	Airbus A.300-605R	American Airlines	

OD (Lebanon)

OD-AGD	Boeing 707-323C	TMA of Lebanon	
OD-AGO	Boeing 707-321C	TMA of Lebanon	
OD-AGP	Boeing 707-321C	TMA of Lebanon	
OD-AGS	Boeing 707-331C	TMA of Lebanon	
OD-AGV	Boeing 707-347C	Middle East Airlines	
OD-AGX	Boeing 707-327C	TMA of Lebanon	
OD-AGY	Boeing 707-327C	TMA of Lebanon	
OD-AHC	Boeing 707-323C	Middle East Airlines	

Notes	Reg.	Type	Owner or Operator
	OD-AHD	Boeing 707-323C	Middle East Airlines
	OD-AHF	Boeing 707-323B	Middle East Airlines

Note: MEA also operates A.310s registered F-OHLH, F-OHLI, F-OHPQ, 3B-STI, 3B-STJ and 3B-STK, two A.320s registered F-OHMO and F-OHMR and a pair of A.321s which carry the identities F-OHMP and F-OHMQ.

OE (Austria)

	OE-ILA	L.188AF Electra	Amerer Air
	OE-ILB	L.188AF Electra	Amerer Air
	OE-ILF	Boeing 737-3Z9	Lauda Air *Bob Marley*
	OE-ILG	Boeing 737-3Z9	Lauda Air *John Lennon*
	OE-ILW	F.27 Friendship Mk.500	Amerer Air
	OE-LAA	Airbus A.310-324	Austrian Airlines *New York*
	OE-LAC	Airbus A.310-324	Austrian Airlines *Paris*
	OE-LAD	Airbus A.310-325	Austrian Airlines *Chicago*
	OE-LAG	Airbus A.340-212	Austrian Airlines *Europe*
	OE-LAH	Airbus A.340-212	Austrian Airlines *Asia*
	OE-LAK	Airbus A.340-313	Austrian Airlines *Afrika*
	OE-LAL	Airbus A.340-313	Austrian Airlines *America*
	OE-LAM	Airbus A.330-223	Austrian Airlines *Daschstein*
	OE-LAN	Airbus A.330-223	Austrian Airlines *Grossglockner*
	OE-LAO	Airbus A.330-223	Austrian Airlines
	OE-LAP	Airbus A.330-223	Austrian Airlines
	OE-LAS	Boeing 767-33AER	Lauda Air Spa *Ayrton Senna*
	OE-LAT	Boeing 767-31AER	Lauda Air *Enzo Ferrari*
	OE-LAU	Boeing 767-3Z9ER	Lauda Air *Marilyn Munroe*
	OE-LAW	Boeing 767-3Z9ER	Lauda Air *Franz Schubert*
	OE-LAX	Boeing 767-3Z9ER	Lauda Air *James Dean*
	OE-LAY	Boeing 767-3Z9ER	Lauda Air
	OE-LAZ	Boeing 767-3Z9ER	Lauda Air
	OE-LBA	Airbus A.321-111	Austrian Airlines *Salzkammergut*
	OE-LBB	Airbus A.321-111	Austrian Airlines *Pinzgau*
	OE-LBC	Airbus A.321-111	Austrian Airlines *Sudtirol*
	OE-LBD	Airbus A.321-111	Austrian Airlines
	OE-LBE	Airbus A.321-111	Austrian Airlines
	OE-LBF	Airbus A.321-111	Austrian Airlines
	OE-LBN	Airbus A.320-214	Austrian Airlines
	OE-LBO	Airbus A.320-214	Austrian Airlines
	OE-LBP	Airbus A.320-214	Austrian Airlines
	OE-LBQ	Airbus A.320-214	Austrian Airlines
	OE-LCF	Canadair CL.600-2B19 RJ	Tyrolean Airways *Stadt Dusseldorf*
	OE-LCG	Canadair CL.600-2B19 RJ	Tyrolean Airways *Stadt Köln*
	OE-LCH	Canadair CL.600-2B19 RJ	Tyrolean Airways *Stadt Amsterdam*
	OE-LCI	Canadair CL.600-2B19 RJ	Tyrolean Airways *Stadt Zürich*
	OE-LCJ	Canadair CL.600-2B19 RJ	Tyrolean Airways *Stadt Hannover*
	OE-LCK	Canadair CL.600-2B19 RJ	Tyrolean Airways *Stadt Brussel*
	OE-LCL	Canadair CL.600-2B19 RJ	Tyrolean Airways *Stadt Oslo*
	OE-LCM	Canadair CL.600-2B19 RJ	Tyrolean Airways *Stadt Bologna*
	OE-LDX	McD Douglas MD-82	Austrian Airlines *Tirol*
	OE-LDY	McD Douglas MD-82	Austrian Airlines *Vorarlberg*
	OE-LDZ	McD Douglas MD-82	Austrian Airlines *Graz*
	OE-LFG	Fokker 70	Tyrolean Airways *Stadt Innsbruck*
	OE-LFH	Fokker 70	Tyrolean Airways *Stadt Salzburg*
	OE-LFJ	Fokker 70	Tyrolean Airways *Stadt Graz*
	OE-LFK	Fokker 70	Tyrolean Airways *Stadt Wien*
	OE-LFL	Fokker 70	Tyrolean Airways *Stadt Linz*
	OE-LFO	Fokker 70	Austrian Airlines *Wiener Neustadt*
	OE-LFP	Fokker 70	Austrian Airlines *Wels*
	OE-LFQ	Fokker 70	Austrian Airlines *Dornbirn*
	OE-LFR	Fokker 70	Austrian Airlines *Steyr*
	OE-LFS	Fokker 70	Austrian Airlines *Schwechat*
	OE-LFT	Fokker 70	Austrian Airlines *Tulin*
	OE-LKA	Dornier Do.328-100	K.L.M. alps
	OE-LKB	Dornier Do.328-100	K.L.M. alps
	OE-LKC	Dornier Do.328-100	K.L.M. alps
	OE-LLE	D.H.C.8-106 Dash Eight	Tyrolean Airways *Zillertal*
	OE-LLF	D.H.C.8-106 Dash Eight	Tyrolean Airways *Seefeld*
	OE-LLG	D.H.C.8-106 Dash Eight	Tyrolean Airways *Kufstein*
	OE-LLH	D.H.C.8-106 Dash Eight	Tyrolean Airways *Stadt Kitzbühel*
	OE-LLJ	D.H.C.8-106 Dash Eight	Tyrolean Airways *Arlburg*
	OE-LLU	D.H.C.7-102 Dash Seven	Tyrolean Airways

Reg.	Type	Owner or Operator	Notes
OE-LLY	D.H.C.8-314 Dash Eight	Tyrolean Airways *Land Vorariberg*	
OE-LLZ	D.H.C.8-314 Dash Eight	Tyrolean Airways *Land Burgenland*	
OE-LMA	McD Douglas MD-82	Austrian Airlines *Linz*	
OE-LMB	McD Douglas MD-82	Austrian Airlines *Eisenstadt*	
OE-LMC	McD Douglas MD-82	Austrian Airlines *Baden*	
OE-LMD	McD Douglas MD-83	Austrian Airlines *Villach*	
OE-LME	McD Douglas MD-83	Austrian Airlines *Krems*	
OE-LMK	McD Douglas MD-87	Austrian Airlines *St Pölten*	
OE-LML	McD Douglas MD-87	Austrian Airlines *Salzburg*	
OE-LMM	McD Douglas MD-87	Austrian Airlines *Innsbruck*	
OE-LMN	McD Douglas MD-87	Austrian Airlines *Klagenfurt*	
OE-LMO	McD Douglas MD-87	Austrian Airlines *Bregenz*	
OE-LNH	Boeing 737-4Z9	Lauda Air *Elvis Presley*	
OE-LNI	Boeing 737-4Z9	Lauda Air *Janise Joplin*	
OE-LNJ	Boeing 737-8Z9	Lauda Air *Falco*	
OE-LNK	Boeing 737-8Z9	Lauda Air	
OE-LPA	Boeing 777-2Z9	Lauda Air	
OE-LPB	Boeing 777-2Z9	Lauda Air	
OE-LRA	Canadair CL.600-2B19 RJ	Lauda Air	
OE-LRB	Canadair CL.600-2B19 RJ	Lauda Air	
OE-LRC	Canadair CL.600-2B19 RJ	Lauda Air	
OE-LRD	Canadair CL.600-2B19 RJ	Lauda Air	
OE-LRE	Canadair CL.600-2B19 RJ	Lauda Air	
OE-LRF	Canadair CL.600-2B19 RJ	Lauda Air	
OE-LRG	Canadair CL.600-2B19 RJ	Lauda Air	
OE-LRH	Canadair CL.600-2B19 RJ	Lauda Air *Jochen Rindt*	
OE-LSA	D.H.C.8Q-314 Dash Eight	Rheintalflug/Team Lufthansa	
OE-LSB	D.H.C.8Q-314 Dash Eight	Rheintalflug/Yeam Lufthansa	
OE-	D.H.C.8Q-314 Dash Eight	Rheintalflug/Team Lufthansa	
OE-	D.H.C.8Q-401 Dash Eight	Rheintalflug	
OE-LTD	D.H.C.8-314 Dash Eight	Tyrolean Airways *Land Oberösterreich*	
OE-LTF	D.H.C.8-314 Dash Eight	Tyrolean Airways *Land Niederösterreich*	
OE-LTG	D.H.C.8-314 Dash Eight	Tyrolean Airways *Land Tirol*	
OE-LTH	D.H.C.8-314 Dash Eight	Tyrolean Airways	
OE-LTI	D.H.C.8-314 Dash Eight	Tyrolean Airways	
OE-LTJ	D.H.C.8-314 Dash Eight	Tyrolean Airways	
OE-LTK	D.H.C.8-314 Dash Eight	Tyrolean Airways	
OE-LTL	D.H.C.8-314 Dash Eight	Tyrolean Airways	
OE-LTM	D.H.C.8-314 Dash Eight	Tyrolean Airways	
OE-TLN	D.H.C.8-314 Dash Eight	Tyrolean Airways	

OH (Finland)

OH-LBO	Boeing 757-2Q8	Finnair	
OH-LBR	Boeing 757-2Q8	Finnair	
OH-LBS	Boeing 757-2Q8	Finnair	
OH-LBT	Boeing 757-2Q8	Finnair	
OH-LBU	Boeing 757-2Q8	Finnair	
OH-LGA	McD Douglas MD-11	Finnair	
OH-LGB	McD Douglas MD-11	Finnair	
OH-LGC	McD Douglas MD-11	Finnair	
OH-LGD	McD Douglas MD-11	Finnair	
OH-LMA	McD Douglas MD-87	Finnair	
OH-LMB	McD Douglas MD-87	Finnair	
OH-LMC	McD Douglas MD-87	Finnair	
OH-LMG	McD Douglas MD-83	Finnair	
OH-LMH	McD Douglas MD-82	Finnair	
OH-LMN	McD Douglas MD-82	Finnair	
OH-LMO	McD Douglas MD-82	Finnair	
OH-LMP	McD Douglas MD-82	Finnair	
OH-LMR	McD Douglas MD-83	Finnair	
OH-LMS	McD Douglas MD-83	Finnair	
OH-LMT	McD Douglas MD-82	Finnair	
OH-LMU	McD Douglas MD-83	Finnair	
OH-LMV	McD Douglas MD-83	Finnair	
OH-LMW	McD Douglas MD-82	Finnair	
OH-LMX	McD Douglas MD-82	Finnair	
OH-LMY	McD Douglas MD-82	Finnair	
OH-LMZ	McD Douglas MD-82	Finnair	
OH-LPA	McD Douglas MD-82	Finnair	
OH-LPB	McD Douglas MD-83	Finnair	
OH-LPC	McD Douglas MD-83	Finnair	

Notes	Reg.	Type	Owner or Operator
	OH-LPD	McD Douglas MD-83	Finnair
	OH-LPE	McD Douglas MD-83	Finnair
	OH-LPF	McD Douglas MD-83	Finnair
	OH-LPG	McD Douglas MD-83	Finnair
	OH-LPH	McD Douglas MD-83	Finnair
	OH-LVA	Airbus A.319-112	Finnair
	OH-LVB	Airbus A.319-112	Finnair
	OH-LYP	Douglas DC-9-51	Finnair
	OH-LYR	Douglas DC-9-51	Finnair
	OH-LYS	Douglas DC-9-51	Finnair
	OH-LYT	Douglas DC-9-51	Finnair
	OH-LYU	Douglas DC-9-51	Finnair
	OH-LYV	Douglas DC-9-51	Finnair
	OH-LYW	Douglas DC-9-51	Finnair
	OH-LYX	Douglas DC-9-51	Finnair
	OH-LYY	Douglas DC-9-51	Finnair
	OH-LYZ	Douglas DC-9-51	Finnair
	OH-LZA	Airbus A,321-112	Finnair
	OH-LZB	Airbus A.321-112	Finnair
	OH-LZC	Airbus A.321-112	Finnair
	OH-LZD	Airbus A.321-112	Finnair

OK (Czech Republic)

	OK-ABA	F.27 Friendship Mk 500	ABA Air
	OK-ABB	F.27 Friendship Mk 500	ABA Air
	OK-BFG	Aérospatiale ATR-42-320	CSA Czech Airlines
	OK-BFH	Aérospatiale ATR-42-320	CSA Czech Airlines
	OK-CGH	Boeing 737-55S	CSA Czech Airlines Usti n. Labem
	OK-CGJ	Boeing 737-55S	CSA Czech Airlines Hradec Kralove
	OK-CGK	Boeing 737-55S	CSA Czech Airlines Pardubice
	OK-DGL	Boeing 737-55S	CSA Czech Airlines Tabor
	OK-DGM	Boeing 737-45S	CSA Czech Airlines
	OK-DGN	Boeing 737-45S	CSA Czech Airlines Trebic
	OK-EGO	Boeing 737-55S	CSA Czech Airlines
	OK-EGP	Boeing 737-45S	CSA Czech Airlines
	OK-FAN	Boeing 737-33A	Fischer Air
	OK-FGR	Boeing 737-45S	CSA Czech Airlines
	OK-FGS	Boeing 737-45S	CSA Czexh Airlines
	OK-FIT	Boeing 737-36N	Fischer Air
	OK-FUN	Boeing 737-33A	Fischer Air
	OK-PEP	SAAB SF.340A	Air Ostrava
	OK-REK	SAAB SF.340A	Air Ostrava
	OK-TVR	Boeing 737-4Y0	Travel Service Airlines
	OK-TVS	Boeing 737-4Y0	Travel Service Airlines
	OK-UFO	SAAB SF.340A	Air Ostrava
	OK-VCG	Tupolev Tu-154M	CSA Czech Airlines Luhacovice
	OK-VCP	Tupolev Tu-154M	Travel Service Airlines
	OK-WAA	Airbus A.310-304	CSA Czech Airlines Praha
	OK-WAB	Airbus A.310-304	CSA Czech Airlines Bratislava
	OK-WGF	Boeing 737-4Y0	CSA Czech Airlines Jihlava
	OK-WGG	Boeing 737-4Y0	CSA Czech Airlines Liberec
	OK-XGA	Boeing 737-55S	CSA Czech Airlines Pizen
	OK-XGB	Boeing 737-55S	CSA Czech Airlines Olomouc
	OK-XGC	Boeing 737-55S	CSA Czech Airlines Ceske Budejovice
	OK-XGD	Boeing 737-55S	CSA Czech Airlines Poprad
	OK-XGE	Boeing 737-55S	CSA Czech Airlines Kosice
	OK-	Boeing 737-45S	CSA Czech Airlines
	OK-	Boeing 737-45S	CSA Czech Airlines

OM (Slovakia)

	OM-AAA	Tupolev Tu-154M	Slovak Airlines
	OM-AAB	Tupolev Tu-154M	Slovak Airlines
	OM-AAC	Tupolev Tu-154M	Slovak Airlines
	OM-BAA	SAAB SF.340A	Slovak Airlines
	OM-BWJ	Boeing 737-230	Air Slovakia Bradlo
	OM-BYO	Tupolev Tu-154M	Slovak Government.
	OM-BYR	Tupolev Tu-154M	Slovak Government
	OM-CHD	Boeing 727-230	Air Slovakia
	OM-DGA	SAAB 2000	Tatra Air

Reg.	Type	Owner or Operator	Notes
OM-GAT	Tupolev Tu-134A-3	Air Transport Europe *David*	
OM-NKD	BAe Jetstream 3102	SK Air	

OO (Belgium)

OO-AEY	Airbus A.320-212	Airtours/Air Belgium (G-TPTT)	
OO-AEZ	Airbus A.320-212	Airtours/Air Belgium	
OO-CPS	Airbus A.321-131	Brussels International	
OO-CTB	McD Douglas MD-11	City Bird	
OO-CTC	McD Douglas MD-11	City Bird/SABENA	
OO-CTQ	Boeing 767-33AER	City Bird	
OO-CTR	Boeing 767-33AER	City Bird	
OO-CTS	McD Douglas MD-11	City Bird/SABENA	
OO-CTT	Airbus A.300C4-605R	City Bird *Pelican*	
OO-CTU	Airbus A.300C4-605R	City Bird *Toucan*	
OO-CTV	Boeing 737-46Q	City Bird	
OO-CTW	Boeing 737-46Q	City Bird	
OO-DHC	Convair Cv.580	European Air Transport (DHL)	
OO-DHE	Convair Cv.580	European Air Transport (DHL)	
OO-DHF	Convair Cv.580	European Air Transport (DHL)	
OO-DHJ	Convair Cv.580	European Air Transport (DHL)	
OO-DHK	Boeing 727-277F	European Air Transport (DHL)	
OO-DHL	Convair Cv.580	European Air Transport (DHL)	
OO-DHM	Boeing 727-31F	European Air Transport (DHL)	
OO-DHN	Boeing 727-31F	European Air Transport (DHL)	
OO-DHO	Boeing 727-31F	European Air Transport (DHL)	
OO-DHR	Boeing 727-35F	European Air Transport (DHL)	
OO-DHS	Boeing 727-223F	European Air Transport (DHL)	
OO-DHT	Boeing 727-223F	European Air Transport (DHL)	
OO-DHU	Boeing 727-223F	European Air Transport (DHL)	
OO-DHW	Boeing 727-223F	European Air Transport (DHL)	
OO-DHX	Boeing 727-223F	European Air Transport (DHL)	
OO-DHY	Boeing 727-230F	European Air Transport (DHL)	
OO-DHZ	Boeing 727-2Q4F	European Air Transport (DHL)	
OO-DJE	BAe 146-200	Delta Air Transport/SABENA	
OO-DJF	BAe 146-200	Delta Air Transport/SABENA	
OO-DJG	BAe 146-200	Delta Air Transport/SABENA	
OO-DJH	BAe 146-200	Delta Air Transport/SABENA	
OO-DJJ	BAe 146-200	Delta Air Transport/SABENA	
OO-DJK	Avro RJ85	Delta Air Transport/SABENA	
OO-DJL	Avro RJ85	Delta Air Transport/SABENA	
OO-DJN	Avro RJ85	Delta Air Transport/SABENA	
OO-DJO	Avro RJ85	Delta Air Transport/SABENA	
OO-DJP	Avro RJ85	Delta Air Transport/SABENA	
OO-DJQ	Avro RJ85	Delta Air Transport/SABENA	
OO-DJR	Avro RJ85	Delta Air Transport/SABENA	
OO-DJS	Avro RJ85	Delta Air Transport/SABENA	
OO-DJT	Avro RJ85	Delta Air Transport/SABENA	
OO-DJV	Avro RJ85	Delta Air Transport/SABENA	
OO-DJW	Avro RJ85	Delta Air Transport/SABENA	
OO-DJX	Avro RJ85	Delta Air Transport/SABENA	
OO-DJY	Avro RJ85	Delta Air Transport/SABENA	
OO-DJZ	Avro RJ85	Delta Air Transport/SABENA	
OO-DLB	Boeing 727-277F	European Air Transport (DHL)	
OO-DLC	Airbus A.300B4-203F	European Air Transport (DHL)	
OO-DLD	Airbus A.300B4-203F	European Air Transport (DHL)	
OO-DLE	Airbus A.300B4-203F	European Air Transport (DHL)	
OO-DLG	Airbus A.300B4-203F	European Air Transport (DHL)	
OO-DLI	Airbus A.300B4-203F	European Air Transport (DHL)	
OO-DLJ	Boeing 757APF	DHL Airways	
OO-DWA	Avro RJ100	Delta Air Transport/SABENA	
OO-DWB	Avro RJ100	Delta Air Transport/SABENA	
OO-DWC	Avro RJ100	Delta Air Transport/SABENA	
OO-DWD	Avro RJ100	Delta Air Transport/SABENA	
OO-DWE	Avro RJ100	Delta Air Transport/SABENA	
OO-DWF	Avro RJ100	Delta Air Transport/SABENA	
OO-DWG	Avro RJ100	Delta Air Transport/SABENA	
OO-DWH	Avro RJ100	Delta Air Transport/SABENA	
OO-DWI	Avro RJ100	Delta Air Transport/SABENA	
OO-DWJ	Avro RJ100	Delta Air Transport/SABENA	
OO-DWK	Avro RJ100	Delta Air Transport/SABENA	
OO-DWL	Avro RJ100	Delta Air Transport/SABENA	

Notes	Reg.	Type	Owner or Operator
	OO-ILJ	Boeing 737-46B	Airtours/Air Belgium International
	OO-LTM	Boeing 737-3M8	Virgin Express
	OO-LTP	Boeing 737-33A	Virgin Express
	OO-LTU	Boeing 737-33A	Virgin Express
	OO-LTV	Boeing 737-3Y0	Virgin Express
	OO-LTW	Boeing 737-33A	Virgin Express
	OO-LTY	Boeing 737-3Q8	Virgin Express
	OO-MJE	BAe 146-200	Delta Air Transport/SABENA
	OO-SBJ	Boeing 737-46B	Sobelair Juliette
	OO-SBM	Boeing 737-429	Sobelair
	OO-SBX	Boeing 737-3M8	Sobelair
	OO-SBY	Boeing 767-33AER	Sobelair
	OO-SBZ	Boeing 737-329	Sobelair
	OO-SCU	Airbus A.340-312	SABENA
	OO-SCW	Airbus A.340-211	SABENA
	OO-SCX	Airbus A.340-211	SABENA
	OO-SCY	Airbus A.340-311	SABENA
	OO-SCZ	Airbus A.340-311	SABENA
	OO-SDF	Boeing 737-229	SABENA
	OO-SDG	Boeing 737-229	SABENA
	OO-SDJ	Boeing 737-229C	SABENA
	OO-SDL	Boeing 737-229	SABENA
	OO-SDN	Boeing 737-229	SABENA
	OO-SDO	Boeing 737-229	SABENA
	OO-SDP	Boeing 737-229C	SABENA
	OO-SDV	Boeing 737-329	SABENA
	OO-SDW	Boeing 737-329	SABENA
	OO-SDX	Boeing 737-329	SABENA
	OO-SDY	Boeing 737-329	SABENA
	OO-SFM	Airbus A.330-301	SABENA
	OO-SFN	Airbus A.330-301	SABENA
	OO-SFO	Airbus A.330-301	SABENA
	OO-SFP	Airbus A.330-223	SABENA
	OO-SFQ	Airbus A.330-223	SABENA
	OO-SFR	Airbus A.330-223	SABENA
	OO-SFS	Airbus A.330-223	SABENA
	OO-SFT	Airbus A.330-223	SABENA
	OO-SFU	Airbus A.330-223	SABENA
	OO-SFX	Airbus A.330-322	SABENA
	OO-SLK	Boeing 737-33S	Sobelair
	OO-SNE	Airbus A.320-214	SABENA
	OO-SNF	Airbus A.320-214	SABENA
	OO-SNG	Airbus A.320-214	SABENA
	OO-SNH	Airbus A.320-214	SABENA
	OO-SNI	Airbus A.320-214	SABENA
	OO-SSA	Airbus A.319-112	SABENA
	OO-SSB	Airbus A.319-112	SABENA
	OO-SSC	Airbus A.319-112	SABENA
	OO-SSD	Airbus A.319-112	SABENA
	OO-SSE	Airbus A.319-112	SABENA
	OO-SSF	Airbus A.319-112	SABENA
	OO-SSG	Airbus A.319-112	SABENA
	OO-SSH	Airbus A.319-112	SABENA
	OO-STF	Boeing 767-328ER	Sobelair *Spirit of Brussels*
	OO-SUA	Airbus A.321-211	SABENA
	OO-SUB	Airbus A.321-211	SABENA
	OO-SUC	Airbus A.321-211	SABENA
	OO-SYA	Boeing 737-329	SABENA
	OO-SYB	Boeing 737-329	SABENA
	OO-SYC	Boeing 737-429	SABENA
	OO-SYD	Boeing 737-429	SABENA
	OO-SYE	Boeing 737-529	SABENA
	OO-SYF	Boeing 737-429	SABENA
	OO-SYG	Boeing 737-529	SABENA
	OO-SYH	Boeing 737-529	SABENA
	OO-SYI	Boeing 737-529	SABENA
	OO-SYJ	Boeing 737-529	SABENA
	OO-SYK	Boeing 737-529	SABENA
	OO-TAA	BAe 145-300QT	TNT Airways (G-TNTR)
	OO-VBR	Boeing 737-4Y0	Virgin Express
	OO-VEC	Boeing 737-46M	Virgin Express
	OO-VED	Boeing 737-46M	Virgin Express
	OO-VEE	Boeing 737-3Y0	Virgin Express

Reg.	Type	Owner or Operator	Notes
OO-VEF	Boeing 737-430	Virgin Express	
OO-VEG	Boeing 737-36N	Virgin Express	
OO-VEH	Boeing 737-36N	Virgin Express	
OO-VEJ	Boeing 737-405	Virgin Express/Sobelair	
OO-VEK	Boeing 737-405	Virgin Express	
OO-VEX	Boeing 737-36N	Virgin Express	
OO-VJO	Boeing 737-4Y0	Virgin Express	
OO-VLE	Fokker 50	V.L.M. *City of Düsseldorf*	
OO-VLG	Fokker 50	V.L.M. *Royal Jersey*	
OO-VLJ	Fokker 50	V.L.M. *Diana Princess of Wales*	
OO-VLK	Fokker 50	V.L.M. *City of Mönchengladbach*	
OO-VLR	Fokker 50	V.L.M. *City of Luxembourg*	

Note: SABENA also operates Dash Eights, PH-SDM, PH-SDP, PH-SDR, PH-SDT and PH-SDU on lease from Schreiner Airways, while Skyjet employs the DC-10s V2-LER and V2-SKY. Two Fokker 50s are operated by V.L.M. as PH-VLM and PH-VLN.

OY (Denmark)

OY-APC	Boeing 737-5L9	Maersk Air	
OY-APD	Boeing 737-5L9	Maersk Air	
OY-APG	Boeing 737-5L9	Maersk Air	
OY-APH	Boeing 737-5L9	Maersk Air	
OY-API	Boeing 737-5L9	Maersk Air	
OY-APK	Boeing 737-5L9	Maersk Air	
OY-APL	Boeing 737-5L9	Maersk Air	
OY-APN	Boeing 737-5L9	Maersk Air	
OY-APP	Boeing 737-5L9	Maersk Air	
OY-APR	Boeing 737-5L9	Maersk Air	
OY-ASY	EMB-110P1 Bandeirante	Muk Air	
OY-BHT	EMB-110P2 Bandeirante	Muk Air	
OY-BNM	EMB-110P2 Bandeirante	Muk Air	
OY-BPB	Douglas DC-3C (K-682)	Flyvende Museumsfly	
OY-CCL	F.27 Friendship Mk 600	Alkair	
OY-CHA	Swearingen SA226AT Merlin IV	Jetair	
OY-CIB	Aérospatiale ATR-42-300	Cimber Air	
OY-CID	Aérospatiale ATR-42-300	Cimber Air	
OY-CIE	Aérospatiale ATR-42-300	Cimber Air/Team Lufthansa	
OY-CIG	Aérospatiale ATR-42-300	Cimber Air	
OY-CIH	Aérospatiale ATR-42-300	Cimber Air	
OY-CIJ	Aérospatiale ATR-42-512	Cimber Air	
OY-CIK	Aérospatiale ATR-42-512	Cimber Air	
OY-CIL	Aérospatiale ATR-42-512	Cimber Air	
OY-CIM	Aérospatiale ATR-72-212A	Cimber Air	
OY-CIN	Aérospatiale ATR-72-212A	Cimber Air	
OY-CIO	Aérospatiale ATR-72-212A	Cimber Air/Team Lufthansa	
OY-CIR	Aérospatiale ATR-42-310	Cimber Air/Team Lufthansa	
OY-CIS	Aérospatiale ATR-42-300	Cimber Air	
OY-CIT	Aérospatiale ATR-42-300	Cimber Air	
OY-CIU	Aérospatiale ATR-42-310	Cimber Air/Team Lufthansa	
OY-CNA	Airbus A.300B4-120	Premiair	
OY-CNB	Airbus A.320-212	Premiair	
OY-CNC	Airbus A.320-212	Premiair	
OY-CNK	Airbus A.300B4-120	Premiair	
OY-CNL	Airbus A.300B4-120	Premiair	
OY-CNM	Airbus A.320-212	Premiair	
OY-CNP	Airbus A.320-212	Premiair	
OY-CNR	Airbus A.320-212	Premiair	
OY-CNS	Douglas DC-10-10	Premiair *Baloo*	
OY-CNT	Douglas DC-10-10	Premiair *Dumbo*	
OY-CNU	Douglas DC-10-10	Premiair *Bamse*	
OY-CNW	Airbus A.320-212	Premiair	
OY-CNY	Douglas DC-10-10	Premiair *Snoopy*	
OY-EBB	Fokker 50	Newair Airservice	
OY-EBD	Fokker 50	Newair Airservice	
0T-GEP	Beech 1900D	Trans Travel Airline	
OY-GRL	Boeing 757-236	Greenlandair	
OY-JEO	Swearingen SA226TC Metro II	Jetair	
OY-JRF	Beech 1900C	Danish Air Transport	
OY-JRJ	Aérospatiale ATR-42-320	Danish Air Transport	
OY-JRK	SC.7 Skyvan	Danish Air Transport	
OY-JRL	SC.7 Skyvan	Danish Air Transport	
OY-JRV	Beech 1900D	Danish Air Transport	

Notes	Reg.	Type	Owner or Operator
	OY-KAG	Fokker 50	S.A.S. Commuter *Odensis Viking*
	OY-KAH	Fokker 50	S.A.S. Commuter *Bjorn Viking*
	OY-KAI	Fokker 50	S.A.S. Commuter *Skjold Viking*
	OY-KAK	Fokker 50	S.A.S. Commuter *Turid Viking*
	OY-KCA	D.H.C.8Q-401 Dash Eight	S.A.S. Commuter *Huge Viking*
	OY-KCB	D.H.C.8Q-401 Dash Eight	S.A.S. Commuter *Herta Viking*
	OY-KCC	D.H.C.8Q-401 Dash Eight	S.A.S. Commuter
	OY-KCD	D.H.C.8Q-401 Dash Eight	S.A.S. Commuter
	OY-KCE	D.H.C.8Q-401 Dash Eight	S.A.S. Commuter
	OY-KDH	Boeing 767-383ER	S.A.S. *Tyra Viking*
	OY-KDL	Boeing 767-383ER	S.A.S. *Tjodhild Viking*
	OY-KDM	Boeing 767-383ER	S.A.S. *Ingvar Viking*
	OY-KDN	Boeing 767-383ER	S.A.S. *Ulf Viking*
	OY-KDO	Boeing 767-383ER	S.A.S. *Svea Viking*
	OY-KGF	Douglas DC-9-21	S.A.S. *Rolf Viking*
	OY-KGL	Douglas DC-9-41	S.A.S. *Angantyr Viking*
	OY-KGM	Douglas DC-9-41	S.A.S. *Arnfinn Viking*
	OY-KGO	Douglas DC-9-41	S.A.S. *Holte Viking*
	OY-KGP	Douglas DC-9-41	S.A.S. *Torbern Viking*
	OY-KGR	Douglas DC-9-41	S.A.S. *Holger Viking*
	OY-KGS	Douglas DC-9-41	S.A.S. *Hall Viking*
	OY-KGT	McD Douglas MD-81	S.A.S. *Hake Viking*
	OY-KGY	McD Douglas MD-81	S.A.S. *Rollo Viking*
	OY-KGZ	McD Douglas MD-81	S.A.S. *Hagbard Viking*
	OY-KHC	McD Douglas MD-82	S.A.S. *Faste Viking*
	OY-KHE	McD Douglas MD-82	S.A.S.
	OY-KHF	McD Douglas MD-87	S.A.S. *Ragnar Viking*
	OY-KHG	McD Douglas MD-82	S.A.S. *Alle Viking*
	OY-KHI	McD Douglas MD-87	S.A.S. *Torkel Viking*
	OY-KHK	McD Douglas MD-81	S.A.S. *Roald Viking*
	OY-KHL	McD Douglas MD-81	S.A.S. *Knud Viking*
	OY-KHM	McD Douglas MD-81	S.A.S. *Mette Viking*
	OY-KHN	McD Douglas MD-81	S.A.S. *Dan Viking*
	OY-KHP	McD Douglas MD-81	S.A.S. *Arild Viking*
	OY-KHR	McD Douglas MD-81	S.A.S. *Torkild Viking*
	OY-KHT	McD Douglas MD-82	S.A.S. *Gorm Viking*
	OY-KHU	McD Douglas MD-87	S.A.S. *Ravn Viking*
	OY-KHW	McD Douglas MD-87	S.A.S. *Ingemund Viking*
	OY-KIA	Douglas DC-9-21	S.A.S. *Guttorm Viking*
	OY-KID	Douglas DC-9-21	S.A.S. *Rane Viking*
	OY-KIE	Douglas DC-9-21	S.A.S. *Skate Viking*
	OY-KIG	McD Douglas MD-81	S.A.S. *Igor Viking*
	OY-KIH	McD Douglas MD-81	S.A.S. *Oleg Viking*
	OY-KII	McD Douglas MD-81	S.A.S. *Ellisiv Viking*
	OY-KIK	McD Douglas MD-81	S.A.S. *Ole Viking*
	OY-KIL	McD Douglas MD-90-30	S.A.S. *Kaare Viking*
	OY-KIM	McD Douglas MD-90-30	S.A.S. *Jon Viking*
	OY-KIN	McD Douglas MD-90-30	S.A.S. *Tormod Viking*
	OY-KKC	Boeing 737-683	S.A.S. *Gautrek Viking*
	OY-KKD	Boeing 737-683	S.A.S.
	OY-KKE	Boeing 737-683	S.A.S. *Elisabeth Viking*
	OY-KKF	Boeing 737-683	S.A.S. *Fridlev Viking*
	OY-KKG	Boeing 737-683	S.A.S.
	OY-KKH	Boeing 737-683	S.A.S.
	OY-KKI	Boeing 737-683	S.A.S.
	OY-KKK	Boeing 737-683	S.A.S. *Borgny Viking*
	OY-KKL	Boeing 737-683	S.A.S.
	OY-KKM	Boeing 737-683	S.A.S.
	OY-KKN	Boeing 737-683	S.A.S.
	OY-KKP	Boeing 737-683	S.A.S. *Ragne Viking*
	OY-KKR	Boeing 737-683	S.A.S. *Gjuke Viking*
	OY-MAF	Boeing 737-5L9	Maersk Air
	OY-MMG	Fokker 50	Maersk Air
	OY-MMH	Fokker 50	Maersk Air
	OY-MMS	Fokker 50	Maersk Air
	OY-MMU	Fokker 50	Maersk Air/Estonian Air
	OY-MMV	Fokker 50	Maersk Air/Estonian Air
	OY-MRB	Boeing 737-7L9	Maersk Air
	OY-MRC	Boeing 737-7L9	Maersk Air
	OY-MRD	Boeing 737-7L9	Maersk Air
	OY-MRE	Boeing 737-7L9	Maersk Air
	OY-MRF	Boeing 737-7L9	Maersk Air
	OY-MUA	EMB-110P1 Bandeirante	Muk Air

Reg.	Type	Owner or Operator	Notes
OY-MUB	Short SD3-30 Variant 200	Muk Air	
OY-MUD	Short SD3-30 Variant 200	Muk Air	
OY-MUE	BAe Jetstream 3100	Muk Air	
OY-MUF	F.27 Friendship	Newair Airservice	
OY-MUG	Short SD3-60 Variant 100	Muk Air	
OY-MUH	Aérospatiale ATR-42-300	Muk Air	
OY-MUK	Aérospatiale ATR-42-310	Muk Air	
OY-SEA	Boeing 737-8Q8	Sterling European Airlines	
OY-SEB	Boeing 737-8Q8	Sterling European Airlines	
OY-SEC	Boeing 737-8Q8	Sterling European Airways	
OY-SEE	Boeing 737-3Y0	Sterling European Airlines	
OY-SEF	Boeing 737-382	Sterling European Airlines	
OY-SEH	Boeing 737-85H	Sterling European Airlines	
OY-SEI	Boeing 737-85H	Sterling European Airlines	
OY-SER	Boeing 727-232F	Sterling European Airlines/TNT	
OY-SES	Boeing 727-251F	Sterling European Airlines/TNT	
OY-SET	Boeing 727-227F	Sterling European Airlines/TNT	
OY-SEU	Boeing 727-243F	Sterling European Airlines/TNT	
OY-SEV	Boeing 727-281F	Sterling European Airlines/Sky Pak	
OY-SEW	Boeing 727-287F	Sterling European Airlines/TNT	
OY-SEY	Boeing 727-224F	Sterling European Airlines/TNT	
OY-SVF	BAe Jetstream 3102	Sun-Air/British Airways	
OY-SVI	BAe ATP	Sun-Air/British Airways	
OY-SVJ	BAe Jetstream 3102	Sun-Air/British Airways	
OY-SVR	BAe Jetstream 3103	Sun-Air/British Airways	
OY-SVS	BAe Jetstream 4102	Sun-Air/British Airways	
OY-SVT	BAe ATP	Sun-Air/British Airways	
OY-SVU	BAe ATP	Sun-Air/British Airways	
OY-SVW	BAe Jetstream 4102	Sun-Air/British Airways	
OY-SVZ	BAe Jetstream 3102	Sun-Air/British Airways	
OY-TNT	Boeing 727-281F	Sterling European Ailrines/TNT	
OY-UPA	Boeing 727-31C	Starair/UPS	
OY-UPB	Boeing 727-180C	Starair/UPS	
OY-UPD	Boeing 727-22C	Starair/UPS	
OY-UPJ	Boeing 727-22C	Starair/UPS	
OY-UPM	Boeing 727-31C	Starair/UPS	
OY-UPS	Boeing 727-31C	Starair/UPS	
OY-UPT	Boeing 727-22C	Starair/UPS	

Note: Atlas Air operates Boeing 747-243F (SCD) N517MC on behalf of S.A.S.

PH (Netherlands)

PH-ACY	Beech 1900D	Ace Air Charters	
PH-AHE	Boeing 757-27B	Air Holland	
PH-AHI	Boeing 757-27B	Air Holland	
PH-AHP	Boeing 757-23A	Air Holland	
PH-AJU	Douglas DC-2	Dutch Dakota Association	
PH-BDA	Boeing 737-306	Koninklijke Luchtvaart Maatschappij (K.L.M.) Willem Barentsz	
PH-BDB	Boeing 737-306	K.L.M. Olivier van Noort	
PH-BDC	Boeing 737-306	K.L.M. Cornelis De Houteman	
PH-BDD	Boeing 737-306	K.L.M. Anthony van Diemen	
PH-BDE	Boeing 737-306	K.L.M. Abel J. Tasman	
PH-BDG	Boeing 737-306	K.L.M. Michiel A. de Ruyter	
PH-BDH	Boeing 737-306	K.L.M. Petrus Plancius	
PH-BDI	Boeing 737-306	K.L.M. Maarten H. Tromp	
PH-BDK	Boeing 737-306	K.L.M. Jan H. van Linschoten	
PH-BDL	Boeing 737-306	K.L.M. Piet Heyn	
PH-BDN	Boeing 737-306	K.L.M. Willem van Ruysbroeck	
PH-BDO	Boeing 737-306	K.L.M. Jacob van Heemskerck	
PH-BDP	Boeing 737-306	K.L.M. Jacob Roggeveen	
PH-BDR	Boeing 737-406	K.L.M. Willem C. Schouten	
PH-BDS	Boeing 737-406	K.L.M. Jorris van Spilbergen	
PH-BDT	Boeing 737-406	K.L.M. Gerrit de Veer	
PH-BDU	Boeing 737-406	K.L.M. Marco Polo	
PH-BDW	Boeing 737-406	K.L.M. Leifur Eiriksson	
PH-BDY	Boeing 737-406	K.L.M. Vasco da Gama	
PH-BDZ	Boeing 737-406	K.L.M. Christophorus Columbus	
PH-BFA	Boeing 747-406	K.L.M. City of Atlanta	
PH-BFB	Boeing 747-406	K.L.M. City of Bangkok	
PH-BFC	Boeing 747-406 (SCD)	K.L.M. Asia City of Calgary	
PH-BFD	Boeing 747-406 (SCD)	K.L.M. Asia City of Dubai	

Notes	Reg.	Type	Owner or Operator
	PH-BFE	Boeing 747-406 (SCD)	K.L.M. City of Melbourne
	PH-BFF	Boeing 747-406 (SCD)	K.L.M. City of Freetown
	PH-BFG	Boeing 747-406	K.L.M. City of Guayaquil
	PH-BFH	Boeing 747-406 (SCD)	K.L.M. Asia City of Hong Kong
	PH-BFI	Boeing 747-406 (SCD)	K.L.M. City of Jakarta
	PH-BFK	Boeing 747-406 (SCD)	K.L.M. City of Karachi
	PH-BFL	Boeing 747-406	K.L.M. City of Lima
	PH-BFM	Boeing 747-406 (SCD)	K.L.M. Asia City of Mexico
	PH-BFN	Boeing 747-406	K.L.M. City of Nairobi
	PH-BFO	Boeing 747-406 (SCD)	K.L.M. City of Orlando
	PH-BFP	Boeing 747-406 (SCD)	K.L.M. City of Paramaribo
	PH-BFR	Boeing 747-406 (SCD)	K.L.M. City of Rio de Janiero
	PH-BFS	Boeing 747-406 (SCD)	K.L.M. City of Seoul
	PH-BFT	Boeing 747-406 (SCD)	K.L.M. City of Tokyo
	PH-BFU	Boeing 747-406 (SCD)	K.L.M. City of Beijing
	PH-BFV	Boeing 747-406	K.L.M.
	PH-BPA	Boeing 737-4Y0	K.L.M. Albert Einstein
	PH-BPB	Boeing 737-4Y0	K.L.M.
	PH-BPC	Boeing 737-4Y0	K.L.M.
	PH-BPE	Boeing 737-42C	K.L.M. Henri Dunant
	PH-BPF	Boeing 737-42C	K.L.M. Wilhelm Rontgen
	PH-BPG	Boeing 737-42C	K.L.M. Max Planck
	PH-BRI	EMB-120RT Brasilia	BASE Airlines/BA Express
	PH-BRK	EMB-120RT Brasilia	BASE Airlines/BA Express
	PH-BRL	EMB-120RT Brasilia	BASE Airlines/BA Express
	PH-BRM	EMB-120RT Brasilia	BASE Airlines/BA Express
	PH-BRP	EMB-120RT Brasilia	BASE Airlines/BA Express
	PH-BTA	Boeing 737-406	K.L.M. Fernao Magalhaes
	PH-BTB	Boeing 737-406	K.L.M. Henry Hudson
	PH-BTC	Boeing 737-406	K.L.M. David Livingstone
	PH-BTD	Boeing 737-306	K.L.M. James Cook
	PH-BTE	Boeing 737-306	K.L.M. Roald Amundsen
	PH-BTF	Boeing 737-406	K.L.M. Alexander von Humboldt
	PH-BTG	Boeing 737-406	K.L.M. Henry Morton Stanley
	PH-BTH	Boeing 737-306	K.L.M.
	PH-BTI	Boeing 737-306	K.L.M.
	PH-BUH	Boeing 747-206F (SCD)	K.L.M. Dr Albert Plesman
	PH-BUI	Boeing 747-206F (SCD)	K.L.M. Wilbur Wright
	PH-BUK	Boeing 747-306 (SCD)	K.L.M. Louis Blériot
	PH-BUL	Boeing 747-306 (SCD)	K.L.M. Charles A. Lindbergh
	PH-BUM	Boeing 747-306 (SCD)	K.L.M. Charles E. Kingsford-Smith
	PH-BUN	Boeing 747-306 (SCD)	K.L.M. Anthony H. G. Fokker
	PH-BUO	Boeing 747-306	K.L.M. Missouri
	PH-BUP	Boeing 747-306	K.L.M. The Ganges
	PH-BUR	Boeing 747-306	K.L.M. The Indus
	PH-BUT	Boeing 747-306	K.L.M. Admiral Richard E. Byrd
	PH-BUU	Boeing 747-306 (SCD)	K.L.M. Sir Frank Whittle
	PH-BUV	Boeing 747-306 (SCD)	K.L.M. Sir Geoffrey de Havilland
	PH-BUW	Boeing 747-306 (SCD)	K.L.M. Leonardo da Vinci
	PH-BXA	Boeing 737-8K2	K.L.M.
	PH-BXB	Boeing 737-8K2	K.L.M.
	PH-BXC	Boeing 737-8K2	K.L.M.
	PH-BXD	Boeing 737-8K2	K.L.M.
	PH-BXE	Boeing 737-8K2	K.L.M.
	PH-BXF	Boeing 737-8K2	K.L.M.
	PH-BXG	Boeing 737-8K2	K.L.M.
	PH-BXH	Boeing 737-8K2	K.L.M.
	PH-BXI	Boeing 737-8K2	K.L.M.
	PH-BXK	Boeing 737-8K2	K.L.M.
	PH-BXL	Boeing 737-8K2	K.L.M.
	PH-BXM	Boeing 737-8K2	K.L.M.
	PH-BXN	Boeing 737-8K2	K.L.M..
	PH-BZA	Boeing 767-306ER	K.L.M. Blue Bridge
	PH-BZB	Boeing 767-306ER	K.L.M. Pont Neuf
	PH-BZC	Boeing 767-306ER	K.L.M. Brooklyn Bridge
	PH-BZD	Boeing 767-306ER	K.L.M. King Hussain Bridge
	PH-BZE	Boeing 767-306ER	K.L.M. Ponte Rialto
	PH-BZF	Boeing 767-306ER	K.L.M. Golden Gate Bridge
	PH-BZG	Boeing 767-306ER	K.L.M. Erasmus Bridge
	PH-BZH	Boeing 767-306ER	K.L.M. Tower Bridge
	PH-BZI	Boeing 767-306ER	K.L.M. Bosporus Bridge
	PH-BZK	Boeing 767-306ER	K.L.M. Zeeland Bridge
	PH-BZM	Boeing 767-306ER	K.L.M. Garibaldi Bridge

Reg.	Type	Owner or Operator	Notes
PH-BZN	Boeing 767-306ER	K.L.M.	
PH-BZO	Boeing 767-306ER	K.L.M.	
PH-CLA	Airbus A.300B4-203F	Farnair Europe/DHL	
PH-DDY	Douglas DC-4	Dutch Dakota Association	
PH-DDZ	Douglas DC-3	Dutch Dakota Association	
PH-DMB	Fokker 50	Denim Air	
PH-DMC	Fokker 50	Denim Air	
PH-DMD	Fokker 50	Denim Air	
PH-DMG	Fokker 50	Denim Air	
PH-DMK	Fokker 50	Denim Air	
PH-DMO	Fokker 50	Denim Air	
PH-EAD	Airbus A.300B4-203F	Farnair Europe/DHL	
PH-EAN	Airbus A.300B4-103F	Farnair Europe/DHL	
PH-FHL	F.27 Friendship Mk.500	Tulip Air/Farnair Europe	
PH-FNV	F.27 Friendship Mk 500	Tulip Air/Farnair Europe	
PH-FNW	F.27 Friendship Mk 500	Tulip Air/Farnair Europe	
PH-FVA	EMB-110P1 Bandeirante	Sky Service	
PH-FVC	EMB-110P1 Bandeirante	Sky Service	
PH-FYC	F.27 Friendship Mk.500	Tulip Air/Farnair Europe	
PH-GIR	Airbus A.300B4-103F	Farnair Europe/DHL	
PH-HVM	Boeing 737-3K2	Transavia/K.L.M.	
PH-HVN	Boeing 737-3K2	Transavia/K.L.M	
PH-HVT	Boeing 737-3K2	Transavia	
PH-HVV	Boeing 737-3K2	Transavia	
PH-HZA	Boeing 737-8K2	Transavia	
PH-HZB	Boeing 737-8K2	Transavia	
PH-HZC	Boeing 737-8K2	Transavia	
PH-HZD	Boeing 737-8K2	Transavia	
PH-HZE	Boeing 737-8K2	Transavia *City of Rhodos*	
PH-HZF	Boeing 737-8K2	Transavia	
PH-HZG	Boeing 737-8K2	Transavia	
PH-HZI	Boeing 737-8K2	Transavia	
PH-JLH	Airbus A.300B4-203F	Jet Link Holland	
PH-JLI	Airbus A.300B4-203F	Jet Link Holland	
PH-JXJ	Fokker 50	K.L.M. CityHopper	
PH-JXK	Fokker 50	K.L.M. CityHopper	
PH-KCA	McD Douglas MD-11	K.L.M. *Amy Johnson*	
PH-KCB	McD Douglas MD-11	K.L.M. *Maria Montessori*	
PH-KCC	McD Douglas MD-11	K.L.M. *Marie Curie*	
PH-KCD	McD Douglas MD-11	K.L.M. *Florence Nightingale*	
PH-KCE	McD Douglas MD-11	K.L.M. *Audrey Hepburn*	
PH-KCF	McD Douglas MD-11	K.L.M. *Annie Romein*	
PH-KCG	McD Douglas MD-11	K.L.M. *Maria Callas*	
PH-KCH	McD Douglas MD-11	K.L.M. *Anna Pavlova*	
PH-KCI	McD Douglas MD-11	K.L.M. *Ingrid Bergman*	
PH-KCK	McD Douglas MD-11	K.L.M. *Marie Servaes*	
PH-KJB	BAe Jetstream 3108	BASE Airlines/BA Express	
PH-KJG	BAe Jetstream 3108	BASE Airlines/BA Express	
PH-KVA	Fokker 50	K.L.M. CityHopper *Bremen*	
PH-KVB	Fokker 50	K.L.M. CityHopper *Brussels*	
PH-KVC	Fokker 50	K.L.M. CityHopper *Stavanger*	
PH-KVD	Fokker 50	K.L.M. CityHopper *Dusseldorf*	
PH-KVE	Fokker 50	K.L.M. CityHopper *Amsterdam*	
PH-KVF	Fokker 50	K.L.M. CityHopper *Paris/Paris*	
PH-KVG	Fokker 50	K.L.M. CityHopper *Stuttgart*	
PH-KVH	Fokker 50	K.L.M. CityHopper *Hannover*	
PH-KVI	Fokker 50	K.L.M. CityHopper *Bordeaux*	
PH-KVK	Fokker 50	K.L.M. CityHopper *London*	
PH-KXL	Fokker 50	K.L.M. CityHopper	
PH-KXM	Fokker 50	K.L.M. CityHopper	
PH-KZA	Fokker 70	K.L.M. CityHopper	
PH-KZB	Fokker 70	K.L.M. CityHopper	
PH-KZC	Fokker 70	K.L.M. CityHopper	
PH-KZD	Fokker 70	K.L.M. CityHopper	
PH-KZE	Fokker 70	K.L.M. CityHopper	
PH-KZF	Fokker 70	K.L.M. CityHopper	
PH-KZG	Fokker 70	K.L.M. CityHopper	
PH-KZH	Fokker 70	K.L.M. CityHopper	
PH-KZI	Fokker 70	K.L.M. CityHopper	
PH-KZK	Fokker 70	K.L.M. CityHopper	
PH-MCE	Boeing 747-21AC (SCD)	Martinair *Prins van Oranje*	
PH-MCF	Boeing 747-21AC (SCD)	Martinair *Prins Claus*	
PH-MCG	Boeing 767-31AER	Martinair *Prins Johan Friso*	

Notes	Reg.	Type	Owner or Operator
	PH-MCH	Boeing 767-31AER	Martinair *Prins Constantijn*
	PH-MCI	Boeing 767-31AER	Martinair *Prins Pieter-Christiaan*
	PH-MCL	Boeing 767-31AER	Martinair *Koningin Beatrix*
	PH-MCM	Boeing 767-31AER	Martinair *Prins Floris*
	PH-MCN	Boeing 747-228F	Martinair *Prins Bernhard*
	PH-MCP	McD Douglas MD-11CF	Martinair
	PH-MCR	McD Douglas MD-11CF	Martinair
	PH-MCS	McD Douglas MD-11CF	Martinair
	PH-MCT	McD Douglas MD-11CF	Martinair
	PH-MCU	McD Douglas MD-11F	Martinair
	PH-MCV	Boeing 767-31AER	Martinair
	PH-MCW	McD Douglas MD-11CF	Martinair
	PH-OZA	Boeing 737-3L9	Air Holland
	PH-OZB	Boeing 737-3Y0	Air Holland
	PH-PBA	Douglas DC-3C	Dutch Dakota Association
	PH-RAZ	Swearingen SA226TC Metro II	Rijnmond Air Services
	PH-SCY	Aérospatiale ATR-72-201	Schreiner Airways/SABENA
	PH-SCZ	Aérospatiale ATR-72-201	Schreiner Airways/SABENA
	PH-SDK	D.H.C.8-311 Dash Eight	Schreiner Airways
	PH-SDM	D.H.C.8-311 Dash Eight	Schreiner Airways/SABENA
	PH-SDP	D.H.C.8-311 Dash Eight	Schreiner Airways/SABENA
	PH-SDR	D.H.C.8-311 Dash Eight	Schreiner Airways/SABENA
	PH-SDT	D.H.C.8-311 Dash Eight	Schreiner Airways/SABENA
	PH-SDU	D.H.C.8-311 Dash Eight	Schreiner Airways/SABENA
	PH-SEZ	McD Douglas MD-82	Meridiana
	PH-SFL	Airbus A.300B4-203F	Schreiner Airways Cargo
	PH-SFM	Airbus A.300B4-203F	Schreiner Airways Cargo
	PH-TKA	Boeing 757-2K2	Transavia
	PH-TKB	Boeing 757-2K2	Transavia
	PH-TKC	Boeing 757-2K2	Transavia
	PH-TKD	Boeing 757-2K2	Transavia
	PH-TSW	Boeing 737-3L9	Transavia
	PH-TSX	Boeing 737-3K2	Transavia
	PH-TSY	Boeing 737-3K2	Transavia
	PH-TSZ	Boeing 737-3K2	Transavia
	PH-TTA	D.H.C. 8-102 Dash Eight	Trans Travel Airlines
	PH-TTB	D.H. C.8-102 Dash Eight	Trans Travel Airlines
	PH-VLM	Fokker 50	V.L.M. City of Rotterdam
	PH-VLN	Fokker 50	V.L.M. City of Antwerp
	PH-WXA	Fokker 70	K.L.M. CityHopper
	PH-WXC	Fokker 70	K.L.M. CityHopper
	PH-XLA	EMB-120RT Brasilia	K.L.M. exel
	PH-XLB	EMB-120RT Brasilia	K.L.M. exel
	PH-XLC	Aérospatiale ATR-42-320	K.L.M. exel
	PH-XLD	Aérospatiale ATR-42-320	K.L.M. exel
	PH-XLE	Aérospatiale ATR-42-320	K.L.M. exel
	PH-XLF	EMB-120RT Brasilia	K.L M. exel
	PH-XLG	EMB-120RT Brasilia	K.L.M. exel
	PH-XLH	Aérospatiale ATR-72-200	K.L.M. exel
	PH-XLI	Aérospatiale ATR-42-320	K.L.M. exel
	PH-XLK	Aérospatiale ATR-42-320	K.L.M. exel

PK Indonesia)

	PK-GSA	Boeing 747-2U3B	Garuda Indonesian Airways
	PK-GSB	Boeing 747-2U3B	Garuda Indonesian Airways
	PK-GSC	Boeing 747-2U3B	Garuda Indonesian Airways
	PK-GSD	Boeing 747-2U3B	Garuda Indonesian Airways
	PK-GSE	Boeing 747-2U3B	Garuda Indonesian Airways
	PK-GSG	Boeing 747-4U3	Garuda Indonesian Airways
	PK-GSH	Boeing 747-4U3	Garuda Indonesian Airways
	PK-GSI	Boeing 747-441	Daruda Indonesian Airways

PP (Brazil)

	PP-VMA	Douglas DC-10-30	Viacao Aerea Rio Grandense (VARIG)
	PP-VMB	Douglas DC-10-30	VARIG
	PP-VMQ	Douglas DC-10-30	VARIG
	PP-VMT	Douglas DC-10-30F	VARIG Cargo
	PP-VMU	Douglas DC-10-30F	VARIG Cargo
	PP-VOC	Boeing 747-341	VARIG

Reg.	Type	Owner or Operator	Notes
PP-VOI	Boeing 767-341ER	VARIG	
PP-VOJ	Boeing 767-341ER	VARIG	
PP-VOK	Boeing 767-341ER	VARIG	
PP-VOL	Boeing 767-341ER	VARIG	
PP-VOP	McD Douglas MD-11	VARIG	
PP-VOQ	McD Douglas MD-11	VARIG	
PP-VPJ	McD Douglas MD-11	VARIG	
PP-VPK	McD Douglas MD-11	VARIG	
PP-VPL	McD Douglas MD-11	VARIG	
PP-VPM	McD Douglas MD-11	VARIG	
PP-VPN	McD Douglas MD-11	VARIG	
PP-VPO	McD Douglas MD-11	VARIG	
PP-VPP	McD Douglas MD-11	VARIG	
PP-VPV	Boeing 767-375ER	VARIG	
PP-VPW	Boeing 767-375ER	VARIG	
PP-VQF	McD Douglas MD-11	VARIG	
PP-VQG	McD Douglas MD-11	VARIG	
PP-VQH	McD Douglas MD-11	VARIG	
PP-VQI	McD Douglas MD-11	VARIG	
PP-VQJ	McD Douglas MD-11	VARIG	
PP-VQK	McD Douglas MD-11	VARIG	

RA (Russia)

Although many of the aircraft used previously by Aeroflot have been transferred to one of the numerous airlines that have been created in recent years, a large proportion still retain the familiar livery. The following registrations are prefixed by RA and are shown with the operators' code in parenthesis after the type. Those used are AFL (Russia International/Aeroflot), AIS (AIS Airlines), DCA (Dacono Air), EFR (Elf Air), HLA (HeavyLift), IKT (Sakhaavia), JSC (Airstan), LSV (Alak Airlines), MSC (Moscow Airlines) PAR (Spair), PLK (Pulkovo Aviation), PVV (Continental Airways), SDM (Russia State Transport), SVR (Ural Airlines), TEP (Transeuropean), TRJ (AJT Air), TSO (Transaero), TUP (Tupolev Aerotrans), TYM (Tyumen Airlines), UPA (Air Foyle), VDA (Volga Dnepr) and VKO (Vnukovo Airlines).

Reg.	Type	Notes	Reg.	Type	Notes
11003	An-12B (PAR)		65862	Tu-134A-3 (PLK)	
11049	An-12 (PAR)		65872	Tu-134A-3 (PLK)	
11356	An-12 (PAR)				
11415	An-12 (PAR)		76355	IL-76TD (MSC)	
			76369	IL-76TD (JSC)	
65004	Tu-134A-3 (PLK)		76421	IL-76TD (DCA)	
65020	Tu-134A-3 (PLK)		76467	IL-76TD (AFL)	
65042	Tu-134A-3 (PLK)		76468	IL-76TD (AFL)	
65068	Tu-134A-3 (PLK)		76469	IL-76TD (AFL)	
65088	Tu-134A-3 (PLK)		76470	IL-76TD (AFL)	
65093	Tu-134A-3 (PLK)		76476	IL-76TD (AFL)	
65097	Tu-134A (EFR)		76478	IL-76TD (AFL)	
65099	Tu-134A (EFR)		76479	IL-76TD (AFL)	
65109	Tu-134A (PLK)		76482	IL-76TD (AFL)	
65112	Tu-134A (AFL)		76485	IL-76TD (IKT)	
65113	Tu-134A (PLK)		76486	IL-76TD (IKT)	
65128	Tu-134A (PLK)		76487	IL-76TD (IKT)	
65559	Tu-134A (AFL)		76488	IL-76TD (AFL)	
65566	Tu-134A (AFL)		76498	IL-76TD (MSC)	
65567	Tu-134A-3 (AFL)		76527	IL-76T (PAR)	
65568	Tu-134A (AFL)		76750	IL-76TD (AFL)	
65604	Tu-134A (EFR)		76785	IL-76TD (AFL)	
65623	Tu-134A (AFL)		76790	IL-76TD (PAR)	
65626	Tu-134A (AIS)		76795	IL-76TD (AFL)	
65697	Tu-134A-3 (AFL)		76797	IL-76TD (IKT)	
65717	Tu-134A-3 (AFL)		76814	IL-76TD (LSV)	
65759	Tu-134A (PLK)		76842	IL-76TD (JSC)	
65769	Tu-134A-3 (AFL)				
65770	Tu-134A-3 (AFL)		82042	An-124 (VDA/HLA)	
65781	Tu-134A-3 (AFL)		82043	An-124 (VDA/HLA)	
65783	Tu-134A-3 (AFL)		82044	An-124 (VDA/HLA)	
65784	Tu-134A-3 (AFL)		82045	An-124 (VDA/HLA)	
65785	Tu-134A-3 (AFL)		82046	An-124 (VDA/HLA)	
65830	Tu-134A-3 (TSO)		82047	An-124 (VDA/HLA)	
65837	Tu-134A-3 (PLK)		82070	An-124 (AFL)	
65855	Tu-134A-3 (AIS)		82072	An-124 (SDM)	

Notes	Reg.	Type	Notes	Reg.	Type
	82073	An-124 (SDM)		85631	Tu-154M (SDM)
	82078	An-124 (VDA)		85632	Tu-154M (VKO)
				85633	Tu-154M (VKO)
	85075	Tu-154B (AIS)		85634	Tu-154M (AFL)
	85084	Tu-154S (VKO)		85635	Tu-154M (VKO)
	85099	Tu-154B (VKO)		85637	Tu-154M (AFL)
	85107	Tu-154B-1 (PLK)		85638	Tu-154M (AFL)
	85141	Tu-154B-1 (SVR)		85639	Tu-154M (AFL)
	85153	Tu-154B-1 (PLK)		85640	Tu-154M (AFL)
	85156	Tu-154B-1 (VKO)		85641	Tu-154M (AFL)
	85182	Tu-154B-1 (VKO)		85642	Tu-154M (AFL)
	85193	Tu-154B (SVR)		85643	Tu-154M (AFL)
	85215	Tu-154B-1 (VKO)		85644	Tu-154M (AFL)
	85217	Tu-154B-2 (IKT)		85645	Tu-154M (SDM)
	85219	Tu-154B-1 (SVR)		85646	Tu-154M (AFL)
	85229	Tu-154B-1 (PLK)		85647	Tu-154M (AFL)
	85242	Tu-154B-1 (PLK)		85648	Tu-154M (AFL)
	85293	Tu-154B-1 (PLK)		85649	Tu-154M (AFL)
	85299	Tu-154B-2 (VKO)		85650	Tu-154M (AFL)
	85301	Tu-154B-2 (VKO)		85651	Tu-154M (SDM)
	85310	Tu-154B-2 (SVR)		85653	Tu-154M (SDM)
	85319	Tu-154B-2 (SVR)		85658	Tu-154M (SDM)
	85323	Tu-154B-2 (IKT)		85659	Tu-154M (SDM)
	85328	Tu-154B-2 (SVR)		85661	Tu-154M (AFL)
	85334	Tu-154B-2 (PLK)		85662	Tu-154M (AFL)
	85337	Tu-154B-2 (SVR)		85663	Tu-154M (AFL)
	85343	Tu-154B-2 (PLK)		85665	Tu-154M (AFL)
	85346	Tu-154B-2 (PLK)		85666	Tu-154M (SDM)
	85348	Tu-154B-2 (IKT)		85668	Tu-154M (AFL)
	85354	Tu-154B-2 (IKT)		85669	Tu-154M (AFL)
	85357	Tu-154B-2 (SVR)		85670	Tu-154M (AFL)
	85363	Tu-154B-2 (AFL)		85673	Tu-145M (VKO)
	85367	Tu-154B-2 (IKT)		85674	Tu-154M (VKO)
	85374	Tu-154B-2 (SVR)		85675	Tu-154M (SDM)
	85375	Tu-154B-2 (SVR)		85686	Tu-154M (SDM)
	85376	Tu-154B-2 (IKT)		85712	Tu-154M (LSV)
	85377	Tu-154B-2 (PLK)		85713	Tu-154M (LSV)
	85381	Tu-154B-2 (PLK)		85736	Tu-154M (VKO)
	85390	Tu-154B-2 (PLK)		85743	Tu-154M (VKO)
	85432	Tu-154B-2 (SVR)		85754	Tu-154M (AFL)
	85439	Tu-154B-2 (SVR)		85767	Tu-154M (PLK)
	85441	Tu-154B-2 (PLK)		85769	Tu-154M (PLK)
	85459	Tu-154B-2 (SVR)		85770	Tu-154M (PLK)
	85486	Tu-154B-2 (IKT)		85771	Tu-154M (PLK)
	85508	Tu-154B-2 (SVR)		85779	Tu-154M (PLK)
	85520	Tu-154B-2 (IKT)		85785	Tu-154M (PLK)
	85530	Tu-154B-2 (PLK)		85791	Tu-154M (IKT)
	85542	Tu-154B-2 (PLK)		85793	Tu-154M (IKT)
	85552	Tu-154B-2 (PLK)		85794	Tu-154M (IKT)
	85553	Tu-154B-2 (PLK)		85799	Tu-154M (TEP)
	85564	Tu-154B-2 (AFL)		85800	Tu-154M (PLK)
	85568	Tu-154B-2 (IKT)		85807	Tu-154M (SVR)
	85570	Tu-154B-2 (AFL)		85810	Tu-154M (AFL)
	85577	Tu-154B-2 (IKT)		85811	Tu-154M (AFL)
	85579	Tu-154B-2 (PLK)		85812	Tu-154M (IKT)
	85592	Tu-154B-2 (AFL)		85814	Tu-154M (SVR)
	85597	Tu-154B-2 (IKT)			
	85610	Tu-154M (VKO)		86002	IL-86 (AFL)
	85611	Tu-154M (VKO)		86004	IL-86 (VKO)
	85612	Tu-154M (VKO)		86005	IL-86 (VKO)
	85615	Tu-154M (VKO)		86006	IL-86 (VKO)
	85618	Tu-154M (VKO)		86007	IL-86 (VKO)
	85619	Tu-154M (VKO)		86008	IL-86 (VKO)
	85620	Tu-154M (VKO)		86009	IL-86 (VKO)
	85622	Tu-154M (VKO)		86010	IL-86 (VKO)
	85623	Tu-154M (VKO)		86011	IL-86 (VKO)
	85624	Tu-154M (VKO)		86013	IL-86 (VKO)
	85625	Tu-154M (AFL)		86014	IL-18 (VKO)
	85626	Tu-154M (AFL)		86015	IL-86 (AFL)
	85628	Tu-154M (VKO)		86017	IL-86 (VKO)
	85629	Tu-154M (SDM)		86018	IL-86 (VKO)
	85630	Tu-154M (SDM)		86050	IL-86 (PLK)

Reg.	Type	Notes	Reg.	Type	Notes
86051	IL-86 (SVR)		86141	IL-86 (TRJ)	
86054	IL-86 (AFL)				
86055	IL-86 (VKO)		86466	IL-62M (SDM)	
86058	IL-86 (AFL)		86467	IL-62M (SDM)	
86059	IL-86 (AFL)		86468	IL-62M (SDM)	
86060	IL-86 (PLK)		86489	IL-62M (AFL)	
86061	IL-86 (PLK)		86497	IL-62M (AFL)	
86063	IL-86 (PLK)		86502	IL-62M (AFL)	
86065	IL-86 (AFL)		86506	IL-62M (AFL)	
86066	IL-86 (AFL)		86510	IL-62M (AFL)	
86067	IL-86 (AFL)		86512	IL-62M (AFL)	
86070	IL-86 (PLK)		86514	IL-62M (AFL)	
86073	IL-86 (PLK)		86515	IL-62M (MSC)	
86074	IL-86 (AFL)		86517	IL-62M (AFL)	
86075	IL-86 (AFL)		86518	IL-62M (AFL)	
86078	IL-86 (SVR)		86520	IL-62M (AFL)	
86079	IL-86 (AFL)		86522	IL-62M (AFL)	
86080	IL-86 (AFL)		86523	IL-62M (AFL)	
86081	IL-86 (VKO)		86524	IL-62M (AFL)	
86082	IL-86 (VKO)		86531	IL-62M (AFL)	
86084	IL-86 (VKO)		86532	IL-62M (AFL)	
86085	IL-86 (VKO)		86533	IL-62M (AFL)	
86087	IL-86 (AFL)		86534	IL-62M (AFL)	
86088	IL-86 (AFL)		86536	IL-62M (SDM)	
86089	IL-86 (VKO)		86537	IL-62M (SDM)	
86091	IL-86 (VKO)		86540	IL-62M (SDM)	
86092	IL-86 (PLK)		86553	IL-62M (SDM)	
86093	IL-86 (SVR)		86554	IL-62M (SDM)	
86094	IL-86 (PLK)		86558	IL-62M (AFL)	
86095	IL-86 (AFL)		86559	IL-62M (SDM)	
86096	IL-86 (AFL)		86561	IL-62M (SDM)	
86097	IL-86 (VKO)		86562	IL-62M (AFL)	
86103	IL-86 (AFL)		86564	IL-62M (AFL)	
86104	IL-86 (VKO)		86565	IL-62M (AFL)	
86106	IL-86 (PLK)		86566	IL-62M (AFL)	
86108	IL-86 (AFL)		86710	IL-62M (SDM)	
86110	IL-86 (AFL)		86711	IL-62M (SDM)	
86111	IL-86 (VKO)		86712	IL-62M (SDM)	
86113	IL-86 (AFL)				
86114	IL-86 (SVR		96005	IL-96 (AFL)	
86115	IL-86 (TRJ)		96007	IL-96 (AFL)	
86123	IL-86 (TSO)		96008	IL-96 (AFL)	
86124	IL-86 (AFL)		96010	IL-96 (AFL)	
86136	IL-86 (PVV)		96011	IL-96 (AFL)	
86138	IL-86 (PVV)		96015	IL-96 (AFL)	
86140	IL-86 (TRJ)				

Note: Aeroflot also operates the DC-10-30 N524MD, Airbus A.310s F-OGQQ, F-OGQR, F-OGQT, F-OGQU, F-OGYP, F-OGYT, F-OGYU, F-OGYV, VP-BAF and VP-BAG. The airline also employs Boeing 737-4M0s registered VP-BAH, VP-BAI, VP-BAJ, VP-BAL, VP-BAM, VP-BAN, VP-BAO, VP-BAP, VP-BAQ and VP-BAR., Boeing 767-300s EI-CKD, EI-CKE, VP-BAV, VP-BAX, VP-BAY and VP-BAZ, plus Boeing 777s VP-BAS and VP-BAU. Transaero employs Boeing 737-200s VP-BTA, VP-BTB, YL-BAA, YL-BAB and YL-BAC, Boeing 737-700s N100UN, N101UN, N102UN and N103UN.

RP (Philippines)

Note: Financial problems caused Philippine Airlines to suspend operations in late 1998, although a limited number of services were later restored.

S2 (Bangladesh)

S2-ACO	Douglas DC-10-30	Bangladesh Biman *The City of Hazrat-Shah Makhdoom (R.A.)*
S2-ACP	Douglas DC-10-30	Bangladesh Biman *The City of Dhaka*
S2-ACQ	Douglas DC-10-30	Bangladesh Biman *The City of Hazrat-Shah Jalal (R.A.)*
S2-ACR	Douglas DC-10-30	Bangladesh Biman *The New Era*
S2-ADE	Airbus A.310-325	Bangladesh Biman
S2-ADF	Airbus A.310-325	Bangladesh Biman *City of Cittagong*

Notes	Reg.	Type	Owner or Operator

S5 (Slovenia)

S5-AAA	Airbus A.320-231	Adria Airways
S5-AAB	Airbus A.320-231	Adria Airways
S5-AAC	Airbus A.320-231	Adria Airways
S5-AAD	Canadair CL.600-2B19 RJ	Adria Airways
S5-AAE	Canadair CL.600-2B19 RJ	Adria Airways
S5-AAF	Canadair CL.600-2B19 RJ	Adria Airways

S7 (Seychelles)

S7-AAS	Boeing 767-2Q8ER	Air Seychelles *Aldabra*
S7-AHM	Boeing 767-37DER	Air Seychelles *Vailee de Mai*

SE (Sweden)

SE-CFP	Douglas DC-3	Flygande Veteraner *Fridtjof Viking*
SE-DAS	Douglas DC-9-41	S.A.S. *Garder Viking*
SE-DAU	Douglas DC-9-41	S.A.S. *Hadding Viking*
SE-DAW	Douglas DC-9-41	S.A.S. *Gotrik Viking*
SE-DBM	Douglas DC-9-41	S.A.S. *Ossur Viking*
SE-DDP	Douglas DC-9-41	S.A.S. *Brun Viking*
SE-DDR	Douglas DC-9-41	S.A.S. *Atle Viking*
SE-DDS	Douglas DC-9-41	S.A.S. *Alrik Viking*
SE-DDT	Douglas DC-9-41	S.A.S. *Amund Viking*
SE-DGG	F.28 Fellowship 4000	S.A.S. *Gunnhild Viking*
SE-DGI	F.28 Fellowship 4000	S.A.S. *Ingeborg Viking*
SE-DGL	F.28 Fellowship 4000	S.A.S. *Loke Viking*
SE-DGM	F.28 Fellowship 4000	S.A.S. *Hild Viking*
SE-DGN	F.28 Fellowship 4000	S.A.S. *Gunnar Viking*
SE-DGP	F.28 Fellowship 4000	S.A.S. *Steinar Viking*
SE-DGR	F.28 Fellowship 4000	S.A.S. *Randver Viking*
SE-DGS	F.28 Fellowship 4000	S.A.S. *Sigrun Viking*
SE-DGT	F.28 Fellowship 4000	S.A.S. *Tola Viking*
SE-DGU	F.28 Fellowship 4000	S.A.S. *Ulfljot Viking*
SE-DGX	F.28 Fellowship 4000	S.A.S. *Vemund Viking*
SE-DIB	McD Douglas MD-87	S.A.S. *Varin Viking*
SE-DIC	McD Douglas MD-87	S.A.S. *Grane Viking*
SE-DIF	McD Douglas MD-87	S.A.S. *Hjorulv Viking*
SE-DII	McD Douglas MD-82	S.A.S. *Sigtrygg Viking*
SE-DIK	McD Douglas MD-82	S.A.S. *Stenkil Viking*
SE-DIL	McD Douglas MD-82	S.A.S. *Tord Viking*
SE-DIN	McD Douglas MD-82	S.A.S. *Eskil Viking*
SE-DIP	McD Douglas MD-87	S.A.S. *Jarl Viking*
SE-DIR	McD Douglas MD-81	S.A.S. *Nora Viking*
SE-DIS	McD Douglas MD-81	S.A.S. *Sigmund Viking*
SE-DIU	McD Douglas MD-87	S.A.S. *Torsten Viking*
SE-DIX	McD Douglas MD-82	S.A.S. *Adils Viking*
SE-DIZ	McD Douglas MD-82	S.A.S. *Sigyn Viking*
SE-DMA	McD Douglas MD-87	S.A.S. *Lage Viking*
SE-DMB	McD Douglas MD-81	S.A.S. *Bjarne Viking*
SE-DMF	McD Douglas MD-90-30	S.A.S. *Heidrek Viking*
SE-DMG	McD Douglas MD-90-30	S.A.S. *Hervor Viking*
SE-DMH	McD Douglas MD-90-30	S.A.S. *Torolf Viking*
SE-DMT	McD Douglas MD-81	S.A.S.
SE-DMU	McD Douglas MD-81	S.A.S. *Siv Viking*
SE-DMX	McD Douglas MD-81	S.A.S. *Sigvard Viking*
SE-DMZ	McD Douglas MD-81	S.A.S. *Maria Viking*
SE-DNM	Boeing 737-683	S.A.S. *Bernt Viking*
SE-DNP	Boeing 737-683	S.A.S. *Gisla Viking*
SE-DNR	Boeing 737-683	S.A.S. *Ragnfast Viking*
SE-DNS	Boeing 737-683	S.A.S. *Signe Viking*
SE-DNT	Boeing 737-683	S.A.S. *Sneifrid Viking*
SE-DNU	Boeing 737-683	S.A.S. *Unn Viking*
SE-DNX	Boeing 737-683	S.A.S.
SE-DNY	Boeing 737-683	S.A.S. *Yngvar Viking*
SE-DNZ	Boeing 737-683	S.A.S. *Sigfrid Viking*
SE-DOI	Douglas DC-9-41	S.A.S. *Are Viking*
SE-DOK	Douglas DC-9-41	S.A.S. *Audun Viking*
SE-DOL	Douglas DC-9-41	S.A.S. *Halldor Viking*

Reg.	Type	Owner or Operator	Notes
SE-DOM	Douglas DC-9-41	S.A.S. *Bodvar Viking*	
SE-DON	Douglas DC-9-41	S.A.S. *Einar Viking*	
SE-DOO	Douglas DC-9-41	S.A.S. *Froste Viking*	
SE-DPA	Boeing 737-33AQC	Falcon Aviation *Aftonfalken*	
SE-DPB	Boeing 737-33AQC	Falcon Aviation *Pilgrimsfalken*	
SE-DPC	Boeing 737-33AQC	Falcon Aviation *Tornfalken*	
SE-DPI	McD Douglas MD-83	S.A.S. *Erik Viking*	
SE-DRA	BAe 146-200	Braathens Malmö Aviation	
SE-DRB	BAe 146-200	Braathens Malmö Aviation	
SE-DRC	BAe 146-200	Braathens Malmö Aviation	
SE-DRD	BAe 146-200	Braathens Malmö Aviation	
SE-DRE	BAe 146-200	Braathens Malmö Aviation	
SE-DRF	BAe 146-200	Braathens Malmö Aviation	
SE-DRG	BAe 146-200	Braathens Malmö Aviation	
SE-DRI	BAe 146-200	Braathens Malmö Aviation	
SE-DRK	BAe 146-200	Braathens Malmö Aviation	
SE-DRL	BAe 146-200	Braathens Malmö Aviation	
SE-DTC	L.1011-385 TriStar 1	Novair Airlines	
SE-DTF	Boeing 737-683	S.A.S *Torbjorn Viking*	
SE-DTG	Boeing 737-783	S.A.S. *Solveig Viking*	
SE-DTH	Boeing 737-683	S.A.S. *V ile Viking*	
SE-DTI	Boeing 737-783	S.A.S. *Erland Viking*	
SE-DTK	Boeing 737-683	S.A.S.	
SE-DTL	Boeing 737-683	S.A.S	
SE-DTM	Boeing 737-683	S.A.S	
SE-DTN	Boeing 737-883	S.A.S	
SE-DTO	Boeing 737-883	S.A.S..	
SE-DTP	Boeing 737-883	S.A.S.	
SE-DTR	Boeing 737-683	S.A.S..	
SE-DTS	Boeing 737-683	S.A.S.	
SE-DTT	Boeing 737-683	S.A.S.	
SE-DTU	Boeing 737-683	S.A.S.	
SE-DUC	Fokker 100	Braathens Malmö Aviation	
SE-DUD	Fokker 100	Braathens Malmö Aviation	
SE-DUE	Fokker 100	Braathens Malmö Aviation	
SE-DUK	Boeing 757-236	Britannia AB	
SE-DUL	Boeing 757-2Y0	Britannia AB	
SE-DUO	Boeing 757-236	Britannia AB	
SE-DUP	Boeing 757-236	Britannia AB	
SE-DUR	Fokker 100	Braathens Malmö Aviation	
SE-DUT	Boeing 737-548	Braathens Malmö Aviation	
SE-DVC	Boeing 737-85F	Novair Airlines	
SE-DVF	L.1011-385 TriStar 500	Novair Airlines	
SE-DVI	L.1011-385 TriStar 500	Novair Airlines	
SE-DVR	Boeing 737-85F	Novair Airlines	
SE-DVU	Boeing 737-85F	Novair Airlines	
SE-DVX	L.1011-385 TriStar 500	Novair Airlines	
SE-DZA	Embraer RJ145EP	Skyways	
SE-DZB	Embraer RJ145EP	Skyways	
SE-DZC	Embraer RJ145EP	Skyways	
SE-DZD	Embraer RJ145EP	Skyways	
SE-DZH	Boeing 737-804	Britannia AB	
SE-DZI	Boeing 737-804	Britannia AB	
SE-DZK	Boeing 737-804	Britannia AB	
SE-LEA	Fokker 50	Skyways	
SE-LEB	Fokker 50	Skyways	
SE-LEC	Fokker 50	Skyways	
SE-LED	Fokker 50	Skyways	
SE-LEH	Fokker 50	Skyways	
SE-LEL	Fokker 50	Skyways	
SE-LEU	Fokker 50	Skyways	
SE-LEZ	Fokker 50	Skyways	
SE-LFA	Fokker 50	S.A.S. Commuter *Jorund Viking*	
SE-LFB	Fokker 50	S.A.S. Commuter *Sture Viking*	
SE-LFC	Fokker 50	S.A.S. Commuter *Ylva Viking*	
SE-LFK	Fokker 50	S.A.S. Commuter *Alvar Viking*	
SE-LFN	Fokker 50	S.A.S. Commuter *Edmund Viking*	
SE-LFO	Fokker 50	S.A.S. Commuter *Folke Viking*	
SE-LFP	Fokker 50	S.A.S. Commuter *Ingemar Viking*	
SE-LFR	Fokker 50	S.A.S. Commuter *Vagn Viking*	
SE-LFS	Fokker 50	S.A.S. Commuter *Vigge Viking*	
SE-LGC	BAe Jetstream 31	European Executive Express	
SE-LIN	Fokker 50	Skyways	

Notes	Reg.	Type	Owner or Operator
	SE-LIO	Fokker 50	Skyways
	SE-LIP	Fokker 50	Skyways
	SE-LRA	D.H.C.8Q-401 Dash Eight	S.A.S. Commuter *Toke Viking*
	SE-LRB	D.H.C.8Q-401 Dash Eight	S.A.S. Commuter *Ulv Viking*
	SE-LRC	D.H.C.8Q-401 Dash Eight	S.A.S. Commuter *Ingrid Viking*
	SE-LRD	D.H.C.8Q-401 Dash Eight	S.A.S. Commuter
	SE-LRE	D.H.C.8Q-401 Dash Eight	S.A.S. Commuter
	SE-LRF	D.H.C.8Q-401 Dash Eight	S.A.S. Commuter
	SE-LRG	D.H.C.8Q-401 Dash Eight	S.A.S. Commuter
	SE-LRH	D.H.C.8Q-401 Dash Eight	S.A.S. Commuter
	SE-LSA	SAAB 2000	S.A.S. Commuter *Tore Viking*
	SE-LSB	SAAB 2000	S.A.S. Commuter *Rut Viking*
	SE-LSC	SAAB 2000	S.A.S. Commuter *Karl Viking*
	SE-LSE	SAAB 2000	S.A.S. Commuter
	SE-LSF	SAAB 2000	S.A.S. Commuter *Eir Viking*
	SE-LSG	SAAB 2000	S.A.S. Commuter *Ake Viking*

SP (Poland)

	SP-EEA	Aérospatiale ATR-42-310	Eurolot
	SP-EEB	Aérospatiale ATR-42-310	Eurolot
	SP-EEC	Aérospatiale ATR-42-310	Eurolot
	SP-EED	Aérospatiale ATR-42-310	Eurolot
	SP-EEE	Aérospatiale ATR-42-310	Eurolot
	SP-FNF	F.27 Friendship Mk 600	White Eagle/UPS *Blue Eyes*
	SP-LGA	Embraer RJ145EP	Polskie Linie Lotnicze (LOT)
	SP-LGB	Embraer RJ145EP	LOT
	SP-LGC	Embraer RJ145EP	LOT
	SP-LGD	Embraer RJ145EP	LOT
	SP-LGE	Embraer RJ145EP	LOT
	SP-LGF	Embraer RJ145EP	LOT
	SP-LKA	Boeing 737-55D	LOT
	SP-LKB	Boeing 737-55D	LOT
	SP-LKC	Boeing 737-55D	LOT
	SP-LKD	Boeing 737-55D	LOT
	SP-LKE	Boeing 737-55D	LOT
	SP-LKF	Boeing 737-55D	LOT
	SP-LLA	Boeing 737-45D	LOT
	SP-LLB	Boeing 737-45D	LOT
	SP-LLC	Boeing 737-45D	LOT
	SP-LLD	Boeing 737-45D	LOT
	SP-LLE	Boeing 737-45D	LOT
	SP-LLF	Boeing 737-45D	LOT
	SP-LLG	Boeing 737-45D	LOT
	SP-LMC	Boeing 737-36N	LOT
	SP-LMD	Boeing 737-36N	LOT
	SP-LOA	Boeing 767-25DER	LOT *Gneizao*
	SP-LOB	Boeing 767-25DER	LOT *Kracow*
	SP-LPA	Boeing 767-35DER	LOT *Warszawa*
	SP-LPB	Boeing 767-35DER	LOT *Gdansk*
	SP-LPC	Boeing 767-35DER	LOT

ST (Sudan)

	ST-AFA	Boeing 707-3J8C	Sudan Airways
	ST-AFB	Boeing 707-3J8C	Sudan Cargo
	ST-AIX	Boeing 707-369C	Sudan Airways
	ST-AMF	Boeing 707-321C	Trans Arabian Air Transport
	ST-APY	Boeing 707-351C	Trans Arabian Air Transport

Note: Sudan Airways also operates the A.300-622Rs F-ODTK, F-OIHA and F-OIHB.

SU (Egypt)

	SU-AVZ	Boeing 707-366C	Air Memphis
	SU-BDG	Airbus A.300B4-203F	EgyptAir Cargo *Toshki*
	SU-BMM	Airbus A.300B4-203	AMC Aviation
	SU-BMR	McD Douglas MD-90-30	AMC Aviation
	SU-BMS	McD Douglas MD-90-30	AMC Aviation
	SU-BMV	Boeing 707-3B4C	Luxor Air
	SU-EAF	Tupolev Tu-204-120	Air Cairo Cargo

Reg.	Type	Owner or Operator	Notes
SU-EAG	Tupolev Tu-204-120	Air Cairo	
SU-EAH	Tupolev Tu-204-120	Air Cairo	
SU-GAC	Airbus A.300B4-203F	EgyptAir Cargo *New Valley*	
SU-GAJ	Boeing 767-266ER	EgyptAir *Tiye*	
SU-GAL	Boeing 747-366 (SCD)	EgyptAir *Hatshepsut*	
SU-GAM	Boeing 747-366 (SCD)	EgyptAir *Cleopatra*	
SU-GAO	Boeing 767-366ER	EgyptAir *Ramses II*	
SU-GAR	Airbus A.300-622R	EgyptAir *Zoser*	
SU-GAS	Airbus A.300-622R	EgyptAir *Cheops*	
SU-GAT	Airbus A.300-622R	EgyptAir *Chephren*	
SU-GAU	Airbus A.300-622R	EgyptAir *Mycerinus*	
SU-GAV	Airbus A.300-622R	EgyptAir *Menes*	
SU-GAW	Airbus A.300-622R	EgyptAir *Ahmuse*	
SU-GAX	Airbus A.300-622R	EgyptAir *Tut-Ankh-Amun*	
SU-GAY	Airbus A.300-622R	EgyptAir *Seti I*	
SU-GAZ	Airbus A.300-622R	EgyptAir	
SU-GBA	Airbus A.320-231	EgyptAir *Aswan*	
SU-GBB	Airbus A.320-231	EgyptAir *Luxor*	
SU-GBC	Airbus A.320-231	EgyptAir *Hurghada*	
SU-GBD	Airbus A.320-231	EgyptAir *Taba*	
SU-GBE	Airbus A.320-231	EgyptAir *El Alamein*	
SU-GBF	Airbus A.320-231	EgyptAir *Sharm El Sheikh*	
SU-GBG	Airbus A.320-231	EgyptAir *Saint Catherine*	
SU-GBM	Airbus A.340-212	EygptAir *Osirus Express*	
SU-GBN	Airbus A.340-212	EygptAir *Cleo Express*	
SU-GBO	Airbus A.340-212	EygptAir *Hathor Express*	
SU-GBP	Boeing 777-266	EgyptAir *Nefertiti*	
SU-GBR	Boeing 777-266	EgyptAir *Nefertari*	
SU-GBS	Boeing 777-266	EgyptAir *Tyie*	
SU-GBT	Airbus A.321-231	EgyptAir *Red Sea*	
SU-GBU	Airbus A.321-231	EgyptAir *Sinai*	
SU-GBV	Airbus A.321-231	EgyptAir *Mediterranean*	
SU-GBW	Airbus A.321-231	EgyptAir *The Nile*	
SU-LBA	Airbus A.320-211	Lotus Air *The Spirit of Egypt*	
SU-LBB	Airbus A.320-212	Lotus Air	
SU-LBC	Airbus A.320-212	Lotus Air	
SU-MWA	Airbus A.310-304	Midwest Airlines *Almahrousa*	
SU-MWB	Airbus A.310-304	Midwest Airlines *Oasis of Heliopolis*	
SU-PBB	Boeing 707-328C	Air Memphis	
SU-PMA	Boeing 737-222	Pharaoh Airlines *Akhnaton*	
SU-PTA	Boeing 737-4Q8	Pharaoh Airlines	
SU-RAA	Airbus A.320-231	Shorouk Air	
SU-RAB	Airbus A.320-231	Shorouk Air	
SU-RAC	Airbus A.320-231	Shorouk Air	
SU-YAK	Boeing 727-230	Palestinian Airlines	
SU-ZCC	Airbus A.310-222	Heliopolis Airline	
SU-	McD Douglas MD-90-30	Heliopolis Airline	

SX (Greece)

SX-BBT	Boeing 737-33A	Cronus Airlines *Kastalia*	
SX-BBU	Boeing 737-33A	Cronus Airlines	
SX-BCA	Boeing 737-284	Olympic Airways *Apollo*	
SX-BCB	Boeing 737-284	Olympic Airways *Hermes*	
SX-BCC	Boeing 737-284	Olympic Airways *Hercules*	
SX-BCD	Boeing 737-284	Olympic Airways *Hephaestus*	
SX-BCE	Boeing 737-284	Olympic Airways *Dionysus*	
SX-BCF	Boeing 737-284	Olympic Airways *Poseidon*	
SX-BCG	Boeing 737-284	Olympic Airways *Phoebus*	
SX-BCH	Boeing 737-284	Olympic Airways *Triton*	
SX-BCI	Boeing 737-284	Olympic Airways *Proteus*	
SX-BCK	Boeing 737-284	Olympic Airways *Nereus*	
SX-BCL	Boeing 737-284	Olympic Airways *Isle of Thassos*	
SX-BEK	Airbus A.300-605R	Olympic Airways *Macedonia*	
SX-BEL	Airbus A.300-605R	Olympic Airways *Athena*	
SX-BFV	Boeing 737-430	Galaxy Airways *City of Kavala*	
SX-BFT	Boeing 737-3Q8	Princess Air	
SX-BGH	Boeing 737-4Y0	Cronus Airlines *Iniochos*	
SX-BGI	Boeing 737-3L9	Cronus Airlines	
SX-BGJ	Boeing 737-4S3	Cronus Airlines	
SX-BGK	Boeing 737-3Y0	Cronus Airlines	

Notes	Reg.	Type	Owner or Operator
	SX-BKA	Boeing 737-484	Olympic Airways *Vergina*
	SX-BKB	Boeing 737-484	Olympic Airways *Olynthos*
	SX-BKC	Boeing 737-484	Olympic Airways *Philipoli*
	SX-BKD	Boeing 737-484	Olympic Airways *Amphipoli*
	SX-BKE	Boeing 737-484	Olympic Airways *Stagira*
	SX-BKF	Boeing 737-484	Olympic Airways *Dion*
	SX-BKG	Boeing 737-484	Olympic Airways
	SX-BKH	Boeing 737-4Q8	Olympic Airways
	SX-BKI	Boeing 737-4Q8	Olympic Airways
	SX-BKK	Boeing 737-4Q8	Olympic Airways
	SX-BKL	Boeing 737-4Y0	Olympic Airways
	SX-BKM	Boeing 737-4Q8	Olympic Airways
	SX-BKN	Boeing 737-4Q8	Olympic Airways
	SX-BLA	Boeing 737-33R	Olympic Airways
	SX-BLT	Boeing 737-7K9	Axon Airlines
	SX-BLU	Boeing 737-7K9	Axon Airlines
	SX-BMA	Boeing 737-46J	Macedonian Airlines
	SX-BMB	Boeing 737-46J	Macedonian Airlines
	SX-BOA	Boeing 717-200	Olympic Aviation
	SX-BOB	Boeing 717-200	Olympic Aviation
	SX-CBG	Boeing 727-230	Macedonian Airlines
	SX-CBH	Boeing 727-230	Macedonian Airlines
	SX-DFA	Airbus A.340-313X	Olympic Airways *Olympia*
	SX-DFB	Airbus A.340-313X	Olympic Airways *Delphi*
	SX-DFC	Airbus A.340-313X	Olympic Airways *Marathon*
	SX-DFD	Airbus A.340-313X	Olympic Airways
	SX-OAB	Boeing 747-284B	Olympic Airways *Olympic Eagle*
	SX-OAC	Boeing 747-212B	Olympic Airways *Olympic Spirit*
	SX-OAD	Boeing 747-212B	Olympic Airways *Olympic Flame*
	SX-OAE	Boeing 747-212B	Olympic Airways *Olympic Peace*

TC (Turkey)

	TC-ABB	Airbus A.321-131	Air Alfa
	TC-ACA	Boeing 737-4Y0	Istanbul Airlines
	TC-AFA	Boeing 737-4Q8	Pegasus Airlines
	TC-AFJ	Boeing 737-4Y0	Pegasus Airlines
	TC-AFK	Boeing 737-4Y0	Pegasus Airlines
	TC-AFM	Boeing 737-4Q8	Pegasus Airlines
	TC-AFU	Boeing 737-4Y0	Pegasus Airlines
	TC-AFV	Boeing 727-230F	Istanbul Cargo
	TC-AFZ	Boeing 737-4Y0	Pegasus Airlines
	TC-AGA	Boeing 737-4Y0	Istanbul Airlines
	TC-ALL	Airbus A.321-131	Air Alfa
	TC-ALN	Airbus A.300B4-103	Air Alfa *Umay-Ural*
	TC-ALO	Airbus A.321-131	Air Alfa
	TC-ALS	Airbus A.300B4-103	Air Alfa
	TC-ALU	Airbus A.300B4-203	Air Alfa
	TC-APD	Boeing 737-42R	Pegasus Airlines/Khalifa
	TC-APG	Boeing 737-82R	Pegasus Airlines
	TC-APP	Boeing 737-4Q8	Pegasus Airlines
	TC-AVA	Boeing 737-4S3	Istanbul Airlines
	TC-AYA	Boeing 737-4Y0	Istanbul Airlines
	TC-AZA	Boeing 737-4Y0	Istanbul Airlines
	TC-GHB	Boeing 737-33A	Rose Air
	TC-GHC	Boeing 737-7L9	Rose Air
	TC-GTA	Airbus A.300B4-103	Air Anatolia *Dila*
	TC-GTB	Airbus A.300B4-203	Air Anatolia *Ferit Torosluoglu*
	TC-GTC	Airbus A.300B4-203	Air Anatolia *Umay & Ural*
	TC-IAC	Boeing 737-382	Istanbul Airlines
	TC-IAE	Boeing 737-3L9	Istanbul Airlines
	TC-IAF	Boeing 737-43Q	Istanbul Airlines
	TC-IAG	Boeing 737-43Q	Istanbul Airlines
	TC-IAH	Boeing 737-86N	Istanbul Airlines
	TC-IYA	Boeing 727-2F2	Top Air *Hezarfen*
	TC-IYB	Boeing 727-243	Top Air
	TC-IYC	Boeing 727-2F2	Top Air *Merve*
	TC-JBF	Boeing 727-2F2	Turkish Airlines *Adana*
	TC-JBG	Boeing 727-2F2	Kibris Turkish Airlines *Besparmak*
	TC-JBJ	Boeing 727-2F2	Kibris Turkish Airlines
	TC-JCA	Boeing 727-2F2F	Turkish Airlines Cargo *Edirne*
	TC-JCB	Boeing 727-2F2F	Turkish Airlines Cargo *Kars*

Reg.	Type	Owner or Operator	Notes
TC-JCD	Boeing 727-2F2F	Turkish Airlines Cargo *Sinop*	
TC-JCL	Airbus A.310-203	Turkish Airlines *Seyhan*	
TC-JCM	Airbus A.310-203	Turkish Airlines *Ceyhan*	
TC-JCN	Airbus A.310-203	Turkish Airlines *Dicle*	
TC-JCO	Airbus A.310-203	Turkish Airlines *Firat*	
TC-JCR	Airbus A.310-203	Turkish Airlines *Kizilirmak*	
TC-JCS	Airbus A.310-203	Turkish Airlines *Yesilirmak*	
TC-JCU	Airbus A.310-203	Turkish Airlines *Sakarya*	
TC-JCV	Airbus A.310-304	Turkish Airlines *Aras*	
TC-JCY	Airbus A.310-304	Turkish Airlines *Coruh*	
TC-JCZ	Airbus A.310-304	Turkish Airlines *Ergene*	
TC-JDA	Airbus A.310-304	Turkish Airlines *Aksu*	
TC-JDB	Airbus A.310-304ET	Turkish Airlines *Göksu*	
TC-JDC	Airbus A.310-304ET	Turkish Airlines *Meric*	
TC-JDD	Airbus A.310-304ET	Turkish Airlines *Dalaman*	
TC-JDE	Boeing 737-4Y0	Turkish Airlines *Kemer*	
TC-JDF	Boeing 737-4Y0	Turkish Airlines *Ayvalik*	
TC-JDG	Boeing 737-4Y0	Turkish Airlines *Marmaris*	
TC-JDH	Boeing 737-4Y0	Turkish Airlines *Amasra*	
TC-JDI	Boeing 737-4Q8	Turkish Airlines *Urgup*	
TC-JDJ	Airbus A.340-311	Turkish Airlines *Istanbul*	
TC-JDK	Airbus A.340-311	Turkish Airlines *Isparta*	
TC-JDL	Airbus A.340-311	Turkish Airlines *Ankara*	
TC-JDM	Airbus A.340-311	Turkish Airlines *Izmir*	
TC-JDN	Airbus A.340-313	Turkish Airlines *Adana*	
TC-JDO	Airbus A.340-313	Turkish Airlines	
TC-JDP	Airbus A.340-313	Turkish Airlines	
TC-JDT	Boeing 737-4Y0	Turkish Airlines *Alanya*	
TC-JDU	Boeing 737-5Y0	Turkish Airlines *Trabzon*	
TC-JDV	Boeing 737-5Y0	Turkish Airlines *Bursa*	
TC-JDY	Boeing 737-4Y0	Turkish Airlines *Antalya*	
TC-JDZ	Boeing 737-4Y0	Turkish Airlines *Fethiye*	
TC-JEC	Boeing 727-228	Kibris Turkish Airlines *Yesilada*	
TC-JEE	Boeing 737-4Q8	Turkish Airlines *Cesme*	
TC-JEG	Boeing 737-4Q8	Turkish Airlines *Silifke*	
TC-JEH	Boeing 737-4Q8	Turkish Airlines *Tekirdag*	
TC-JEI	Boeing 737-4Q8	Turkish Airlines *Artvin*	
TC-JEJ	Boeing 737-4Q8	Turkish Airlines *Balikesir*	
TC-JEK	Boeing 737-4Q8	Turkish Airlines *Bolu*	
TC-JEL	Boeing 737-4Q8	Turkish Airlines *Eskisehir*	
TC-JEM	Boeing 737-4Q8	Turkish Airlines *Malatya*	
TC-JEN	Boeing 737-4Q8	Turkish Airlines *Gelibolu*	
TC-JEO	Boeing 737-4Q8	Turkish Airlines *Anadolu*	
TC-JER	Boeing 737-4Y0	Turkish Airlines *Mugla*	
TC-JET	Boeing 737-4Y0	Turkish Airlines *Canakkale*	
TC-JEU	Boeing 737-4Y0	Turkish Airlines *Kayseri*	
TC-JEV	Boeing 737-4Y0	Turkish Airlines *Efes*	
TC-JEY	Boeing 737-4Y0	Turkish Airlines *Side*	
TC-JEZ	Boeing 737-4Y0	Turkish Airlines *Bergama*	
TC-JFC	Boeing 737-8F2	Turkish Airlines *Diyarbakir*	
TC-JFD	Boeing 737-8F2	Turkish Airlines *Rize*	
TC-JFE	Boeing 737-8F2	Turkish Airlines *Hatay*	
TC-JFF	Boeing 737-8F2	Turkish Airlines *Afyon*	
TC-JFG	Boeing 737-8F2	Turkish Airlines *Sivas*	
TC-JFH	Boeing 737-8F2	Turkish Airlines *Igdir*	
TC-JFI	Boeing 737-8F2	Turkish Airlines	
TC-JFJ	Boeing 737-8F2	Turkish Airlines	
TC=JFK	Boeing 737-8F2	Turkish Airlines	
TC-JFL	Boeing 737-8F2	Turkish Airlines	
TC-JFM	Boeing 737-8F2	Turkish Airlines	
TC-JFN	Boeing 737-8F2	Turkish Airlines *Bitlis*	
TC-JFO	Boeing 737-8F2	Turkish Airlines *Batman*	
TC-JFP	Boeing 737-8F2	Turkish Airlines	
TC-JFR	Boeing 737-8F2	Turkish Airlines	
TC-JFS	Boeing 737-8F2	Turkish Airlines	
TC-JFT	Boeing 737-8F2	Turkish Airlines	
TC-JFU	Boeing 737-8F2	Turkish Airlines	
TC-JFV	Boeing 737-8F2	Turkish Airlines	
TC-JFW	Boeing 737-8F2	Turkish Airlines	
TC-JFX	Boeing 737-8F2	Turkish Airlines	
TC-JFY	Boeing 737-8F2	Turkish Airlines	
TC-JFZ	Boeing 737-8F2	Turkish Airlines	
TC-JYK	Airbus A.310-203	Kibris Turkish Airlines *Erenkoy*	

Notes	Reg.	Type	Owner or Operator
	TC-JHA	McD Douglas MD-90-30	Turkish Airlines
	TC-JHB	McD Douglas MD-90-30	Turkish Airlines
	TC-MNA	Airbus A.300B4-203F	MNG Cargo Airlines
	TC-MNG	Airbus A. 300C4-203	MNG Cargo Airlines *Hayal*
	TC-ONH	Airbus A.321-131	Onur Air *Nazar*
	TC-ONI	Airbus A.321-131	Onur Air *Icli*
	TC-ONJ	Airbus A.321-131	Onur Air *Kaptan Soray Sahin*
	TC-ONK	Airbus A.300B4-103	Onur Air *Pinar*
	TC-ONL	Airbus A.300B4-103	Onur Air *Selin*
	TC-ONM	McD Douglas MD-88	Onur Air *Yasemin*
	TC-ONN	McD Douglas MD-88	Onur Air *Ece*
	TC-ONO	McD Douglas MD-88	Onur Air *Yonca*
	TC-ONP	McD Douglas MD-88	Onur Air *Esra*
	TC-ONR	McD Douglas MD-88	Onur Air *Evren*
	TC-ONS	Airbus A.321-131	Onur Air *Funda*
	TC-ONV	Airbus A.300B4-2C	Air Anatolia *Urgas-Ugar*
	TC-SUA	Boeing 737-86N	Sun Express
	TC-SUN	Boeing 737-3Y0	Sun Express
	TC-SUP	Boeing 737-3Y0	Sun Express
	TC-SUR	Boeing 737-3Y0	Sun Express
	TC-SUS	Boeing 737-430	Sun Express
	TC-SUT	Boeing 737-4Y0	Sun Express

TF (Iceland)

	Reg.	Type	Owner or Operator
	TF-ABA	Boeing 747-267B	Air Atlanta Iceland/Iberia
	TF-ABD	L.1011-385 TriStar 1	Air Atlanta Iceland
	TF-ABE	L.1011-385 TriStar 1	Air Atlanta Iceland
	TF-ABF	Boeing 737-230C	Air Atlanta Iceland
	TF-ABM	L.1011-385 TriStar 50	Air Atlanta Iceland
	TF-ABO	Boeing 747-1D1	Air Atlanta Iceland
	TF-ABP	L.1011-385 TriStar 1 ★	British Aviation Heritage/Bruntingthorpe
	TF-ABP	Boeing 747-267B	Air Atlanta Iceland/Iberia
	TF-ABQ	Boeing 747-246B	Air Atlanta iceland
	TF-ABT	L.1011-385 TriStar 100	Air Atlanta Iceland
	TF-ABU	L.1011-385 TriStar 1	Air Atlanta Iceland
	TF-ABX	Boeing 737-230C	Air Atlanta Iceland
	TF-ABY	Boeing 747-246B	Air Atlanta Iceland
	TF-ATA	Boeing 747-230B	Air Atlanta Iceland
	TF-ATB	Boeing 747-246B	Air Atlanta Iceland
	TF-ATC	Boeing 747-267B	Air Atlanta Iceland
	TF-ATD	Boeing 747-267B	Air Atlanta Iceland
	TF-ATE	Boeing 747-246B	Air Atlanta Iceland
	TF-BBG	Swearingen SA.227AC Metro III	Islandsflug
	TF-ELJ	Aérospatiale ATR-42-310	Islandsflug
	TF-ELK	Aérospatiale ATR-42-310	Islandsflug
	TF-ELL	Boeing 737-210C	Islandsflug
	TF-ELM	Boeing 737-2M8	Islandsflug
	TF-ELN	Boeing 737-3Q8QC	Islandsflug/DHL
	TF-FIA	Boeing 737-408	Icelandair *Aldis*
	TF-FIB	Boeing 737-408	Icelandair *Eydis*
	TF-FID	Boeing 737-408	Icelandair *Heiddis*
	TF-FIG	Boeing 757-23APF	Icelandair
	TF-FIH	Boeing 757-208	Icelandair *Hafdis*
	TF-FII	Boeing 757-208	Icelandair *Fanndis*
	TF-FIJ	Boeing 757-208	Icelandair *Svandis*
	TF-FIK	Boeing 757-28A	Icelandair *Soldis*
	TF-FIN	Boeing 757-208	Icelandair *Bryndis*
	TF-FIO	Boeing 757-208	Icelandair *Valdis*
	TF-FIR	Fokker 50	Air Iceland *Asdis*
	TF-FIS	Fokker 50	Air Iceland *Sigdis*
	TF-FIT	Fokker 50	Air Iceland *Freydis*
	TF-MKG	Douglas DC-8-62F	MK Airlines

TJ (Cameroon)

	Reg.	Type	Owner or Operator
	TJ-CAB	Boeing 747-2H7B (SCD)	Cameroon Airlines *Mont Cameroun*

TR (Gabon)

Note: Air Gabon operates Boeing 747-2Q2B F-ODJG *President Leon Mba.*

TS (Tunisia)

Reg.	Type	Owner or Operator
TS-IMA	Airbus A.300B4-203	Tunis-Air *Arnilcar*
TS-IMB	Airbus A.320-211	Tunis-Air *Fahrat Hached*
TS-IMC	Airbus A.320-211	Tunis-Air *7 Novembre*
TS-IMD	Airbus A.320-211	Tunis-Air *Khereddine*
TS-IME	Airbus A.320-211	Tunis-Air *Tabarka*
TS-IMF	Airbus A.320-211	Tunis-Air *Jerba*
TS-IMG	Airbus A.320-211	Tunis-Air *Abou el Kacem Chebbi*
TS-IMH	Airbus A.320-211	Tunis-Air *Ali Belhaouane*
TS-IMI	Airbus A.320-211	Tunis-Air *Jughurta*
TS-IMJ	Airbus A.319-114	Tunis-Air *El Kantaoui*
TS-IMK	Airbus A.320.211	Tunis-Air *Kerkenah*
TS-IML	Airbus A.319-114	Tunis-Air *Gafsa del Ksar*
TS-IMM	Airbus A.320-211	Tunis Air
TS-	Airbus A.320-211	Tunis Air
TS-	Airbus A.320-211	Tunis Air
TS-INA	Airbus A.320-214	Nouvelair
TS-INB	Airbus A.320-214	Nouvelair
TS-IOC	Boeing 737-2H3	Tunis-Air *Salammbo*
TS-IOD	Boeing 737-2H3C	Mediterannean Air Service
TS-IOE	Boeing 737-2H3	Tunis-Air *Zarzis*
TS-IOF	Boeing 737-2H3	Tunis-Air *Sousse*
TS-IOG	Boeing 737-5H3	Tunis-Air *Sfax*
TS-IOH	Boeing 737-5H3	Tunis-Air *Hammamet*
TS-IOI	Boeing 737-5H3	Tunis-Air *Mahida*
TS-IOJ	Boeing 737-5H3	Tunis-Air *Monastir*
TS-IOK	Boeing 737-6H3	Tunis Air
TS-IOL	Boeing 737-6H3	Tunis Air
TS-IOM	Boeing 737-6H3	Tunis Air
TS-ION	Boeing 737-6H3	Tunis Air
TS-IOP	Boeing 737-6H3	Tunis Air
TS-IOQ	Boeing 737-6H3	Tunis Air
TS-JHR	Boeing 727-2H3	Tunis-Air *Bizerte*
TS-JHT	Boeing 727-2H3	Tunis-Air *Sidi Bousaid*
TS-JHU	Boeing 727-2H3	Tunis-Air *Hannibal*
TS-JHW	Boeing 727-2H3	Tunis-Air *Ibn Khaldoun*

TU (Ivory Coast)

Reg.	Type	Owner or Operator
TU-TAH	Airbus A.300-605R	Air Afrique
TU-TAI	Airbus A.300-605R	Air Afrique
TU-TAJ	Boeing 737-3Q8	Air Afrique
TU-TAK	Boeing 737-3Q8	Air Afrique
TU-TAO	Airbus A.300B4-203	Air Afrique *Nouackchott*
TU-TAS	Airbus A.300B4-203	Air Afrique *Bangui*
TU-TAT	Airbus A.300B4-203	Air Afrique
TU-TAZ	Airbus A.310-304	Air Afrique

UK (Uzbekistan)

The following are operated by Uzbekistan Airways with registrations prefixed by UK.

Reg.	Type	Notes	Reg.	Type	Notes
31001	Airbus A.310-324		76448	IL-76TD	
31002	Airbus A.310-324		76449	IL-76TD	
31003	Airbus A.310-324		76782	IL-76TD	
75700	Boeing 757-23P		76793	IL-76TD	
75702	Boeing 757-23P		76794	IL-76TD	
76351	IL-76TD		76805	IL-76TD	
76353	IL-76TD		76811	IL-76TD	
76358	IL-76TD		76813	IL-76TD	
76359	IL-76TD		76824	IL-76TD	
76426	IL-76TD		85189	Tu-154B	
76428	IL-76TD		85272	Tu-154B-1	

Notes	Reg.	Type	Notes	Reg.	Type
	85286	Tu-154B-1		86052	IL-86
	85344	Tu-154B-2		86053	IL-86
	85356	Tu-154B-2		86056	IL-86
	85370	Tu-154B-2		86057	IL-86
	85397	Tu-154B-2		86064	IL-86
	85398	Tu-154B-2		86072	IL-86
	85401	Tu-154B-2		86083	IL-86
	85416	Tu-154B-2		86090	IL-86
	85438	Tu-154B-2		86569	IL-62M
	85449	Tu-154B-2		86573	IL-62M
	85575	Tu-154B-2		86574	IL-62M
	85578	Tu-154B-2		86575	IL-62M
	85711	Tu-154M		86576	IL-62M
	85764	Tu-154M		86577	IL-62M
	85776	Tu-154M		86578	IL-62M
	86012	IL-86		86579	IL-62M
	86016	IL-86			

Note: Uzbekistan Airways also operates Boeing 767-33PERs VP-BUA and VP-BUZ plus the Boeing 757-23P VP-BUB and VP-BUD.

UN (Kazakstan)

The following are operated by Air Kazakstan with the registrations prefixed by UN

Notes	Reg.	Type		Owner or Operator
	UN-A3101	Airbus A.310-322		Air Kazakstan
	UN-A3102	Airbus A.310-322		Air Kazakstan
	UN-B3706	Boeing 737-2M8		Air Kazakstan

Notes	Reg.	Type	Notes	Reg.	Type
	65115	Tu-134A-3		85271	Tu-154B-1
	65121	Tu-134A-3		85276	Tu-154B-1
	65130	Tu-134A-3		85290	Tu-154B-1
	65138	Tu-134A		85387	Tu-154B-2
	65147	Tu-134A-3		85396	Tu-154B-2
	65551	Tu-134A-3		85431	Tu-154B-2
	65683	Tu-134A		85455	Tu-154B-2
	65767	Tu-134A-3		85464	Tu-154B-2
	65776	Tu-134A-3		85478	Tu-154B-2
	65787	Tu-134A		85521	Tu-154B-2
	65900	Tu-134A-3		85537	Tu-154B-2
	76371	IL-76TD		85589	Tu-154B-2
	76374	IL-76TD		85719	Tu-154M
	76810	IL-76TD		85775	Tu-154M
	85076	Tu-154B-1		85780	Tu-154M
	85111	Tu-154B-1		85781	Tu-154M
	85113	Tu-154B		86068	IL-86
	85151	Tu-154B-1		86069	IL-86
	85173	Tu-154B		86071	IL-86
	85194	Tu-154B		86077	IL-86
	85221	Tu-154B-1		86086	IL-86
	85230	Tu-154B-1		86101	IL-86
	85231	Tu-154B-1		86116	IL-86
	85240	Tu-154B-1			

UR (Ukraine)

Notes	Reg.	Type		Owner or Operator
	UR-BFA	Boeing 737-2L9		Aerosweet Airlines
	UR-BVY	Boeing 737-2Q8		Aerosweet Airlines
	UR-BVZ	Boeing 737-2Q8		Aerosweet Airlines
	UR-BYC	Boeing 737-2Q8		Aerosweet Airlines
	UR-GAC	Boeing 737-247		Ukraine International
	UR-GAD	Boeing 737-2T4		Ukraine International
	UR-GAF	Boeing 737-35B		Ukraine International
	UR-GAG	Boeing 737-35B		Ukraine International
	UR-GAH	Boeing 737-32Q		Ukraine International
	UR-PAS	Antonov An-12		Veteran Airlines
	UR-UCC	Iluyshin IL-76MD		Khors Air

Reg.	Type	Owner or Operator	Notes
UR-UCE	Ilyushin IL-76MD	Khors Air	
UR-UCF	Ilyushin IL-76MD	Ukraine Cargo Airways	
UR-UCH	Ilyushin IL-76MD	Ukraine Cargo Airways	
UR-UCI	Ilyushin IL-76MD	Ukraine Cargo Airways	
UR-UCJ	Ilyushin IL-76MD	Khors Air	
UR-UCR	Ilyushin IL-76MD	Ukraine Cargo Airways	

Note: The following registrations are prefixed by UR. Airline codes AKO - Transago, BSL - BSL Airlines, KHO - Khors Air, UKC - Air Ukraine Cargo, UKR - Air Ukraine, UPA - Air Foyle, VPB - Veteran Airlines.

Reg.	Type	Notes	Reg.	Type	Notes
65037	Tu-134A-3 (UKR)		76697	IL-76MD (VPB)	
65073	Tu-134A (UKR)		76698	IL-76MD (VPB)	
65076	Tu-134A-3 (UKR)		76705	IL-76MD (UKR)	
65077	Tu-134A-3 (AKO)		76707	IL-76MD (VPB)	
65081	Tu-134A-3 (AKO)		76717	IL-76MD (VPB)	
65089	Tu-134A (UKR)		76728	IL-76MD (VPB)	
65107	Tu-134A (UKR)		76729	IL-76MD (VPB)	
65114	Tu-134A-3 (UKR)		76748	IL-76MD (UKR)	
65123	Tu-134A-3 (UKR)		76749	IL-76MD (UKR)	
65135	Tu-134A-3 (UKR)		76778	IL-76MD (UKR)	
65746	Tu-134A-3 (UKR)		78758	IL-76MD (UKC)	
65752	Tu-134A-3 (UKR)		78772	IL-76MD (UKC)	
65757	Tu-134A (UKR)		78775	IL-76MD (KHO)	
65761	Tu-134A (UKR)		82007	An-124 (UPA)	
65764	Tu-134A-3 (UKR)		82008	An-124 (UPA)	
65765	Tu-134A (UKR)		82009	An-124 (UPA)	
65773	Tu-134A-3 (UKR)		82027	An-124 (UPA)	
65790	Tu-134A-3 (UKR)		82029	An-124 (UPA)	
65877	Tu-134A-3 (UKR)		85316	Tu-154B-2 (UKR)	
76395	IL-76MD (KHO)		85362	Tu-154B-2 (UKR)	
76396	IL-76MD (KHO)		85368	Tu-154B-2 (UKR)	
76397	IL-76MD (KHO)		85379	Tu-154B-2 (UKR)	
76399	IL-76MD (KHO)		85395	Tu-154B-2 (UKR)	
76561	IL-76MD (UKC)		85445	Tu-154B-2 (BSL)	
76581	IL-76MD (UKR)		85460	Tu-154B-2 (UKR)	
76583	IL-76MD (KHO)		85482	Tu-154B-2 (UKR)	
76628	IL-76MD (UKC)		85490	Tu-154B-2 (UKR)	
76647	IL-76MD (VPB)		85526	Tu-154B-2 (UKR)	
76651	IL-76MD (KHO)		85535	Tu-154B-2 (UKR)	
76664	IL-76MD (KHO)		85561	Tu-154B-2 (BSL)	
76667	IL-76MD (VPB)		85707	Tu-154M (UKR)	
76671	IL-76MD (VPB)		86132	IL-62M (UKR)	
76676	IL-76MD (VPB)		86133	IL-62M (UKR)	
76677	IL-76MD (VPB)		86134	IL-62M (UKR)	
76683	IL-76MD (VPB)		86135	IL-62M (UKR)	
76684	IL-76MD (VPB)		86580	IL-62M (UKR)	
76691	IL-76MD (VPB)		86581	IL-62M (UKR)	
76694	IL-76MD (VPB)		86582	IL-62M (UKR)	

Reg.	Type	Owner or Operator	Notes

V2 (Antigua)

V2-LER	Douglas DC-10-15	Skyjet	
V2-SKY	Douglas DC-10-15	Skyjet	

Note: Skyjet also operates a DC-10-30 registered 9G-PHN

V5 (Namibia)

V5-NMA	Boeing 747-48E	Air Namibia	

Note: Air Namibia also leases the Boeing 747SP ZS-SPC from South African Airways.

V8 (Brunei)

V8-AM1	Airbus A.340-211	Brunei Government	
V8-BKH	Airbus A.340-212	Brunei Government	
V8-DPD	Airbus A.310-304	Brunei Royal Flight (Government/VIP)	
V8-JBB	Airbus A.340-213	Brunei Government	
V8-MJB	Boeing 767-27GER	Royal Brunei Airlines (Government/VIP)	
V8-RBA	Boeing 757-2M6	Royal Brunei Airlines	

Notes	Reg.	Type	Owner or Operator
	V8-RBB	Boeing 757-2M6	Royal Brunei Airlines
	V8-RBF	Boeing 767-33AER	Royal Brunei Airlines
	V8-RBG	Boeing 767-33AER	Royal Brunei Airlines
	V8-RBH	Boeing 767-33AER	Royal Brunei Airlines
	V8-RBJ	Boeing 767-33AER	Royal Brunei Airlines
	V8-RBK	Boeing 767-33AER	Royal Brunei Airlines
	V8-RBL	Boeing 767-33AER	Royal Brunei Airlines
	V8-RBM	Boeing 767-328ER	Royal Brunei Airlines

VH (Australia)

	VH-OEB	Boeing 747-48E	Queensland and Northern Territory Aerial Service (QANTAS)
	VH-OED	Boeing 747-4H6	QANTAS
	VH-OJA	Boeing 747-438	QANTAS *City of Canberra*
	VH-OJB	Boeing 747-438	QANTAS *City of Sydney*
	VH-OJC	Boeing 747-438	QANTAS *City of Melbourne*
	VH-OJD	Boeing 747-438	QANTAS *City of Brisbane*
	VH-OJE	Boeing 747-438	QANTAS *City of Adelaide*
	VH-OJF	Boeing 747-438	QANTAS *City of Perth*
	VH-OJG	Boeing 747-438	QANTAS *City of Hobart*
	VH-OJH	Boeing 747-438	QANTAS *City of Darwin*
	VH-OJI	Boeing 747-438	QANTAS *Longreach*
	VH-OJJ	Boeing 747-438	QANTAS *Winton*
	VH-OJK	Boeing 747-438	QANTAS *City of Newcastle*
	VH-OJL	Boeing 747-438	QANTAS *City of Ballaarat*
	VH-OJM	Boeing 747-438	QANTAS *City of Gosford*
	VH-OJN	Boeing 747-438	QANTAS *City of Dubbo*
	VH-OJO	Boeing 747-438	QANTAS *City of Toowoomba*
	VH-OJP	Boeing 747-438	QANTAS *City of Albury*
	VH-OJQ	Boeing 747-438	QANTAS *City of Mandurah*
	VH-OJR	Boeing 747-438	QANTAS *City of Bathurst*
	VH-OJS	Boeing 747-438	QANTAS
	VH-OJT	Boeing 747-438	QANTAS

VP-B (Bermuda)

	VP-BAF	Airbus A.310-304	Aeroflot Russian International
	VP-BAG	Airbus A.310-304	Aeroflot Russian International
	VP-BAH	Boeing 737-4M0	Aeroflot Russian International
	VP-BAI	Boeing 737-4M0	Aeroflot Russian International
	VP-BAJ	Boeing 737-4M0	Aeroflot Russian International
	VP-BAL	Boeing 737-4M0	Aeroflot Russian International
	VP-BAM	Boeing 737-4M0	Aeroflot Russian International
	VP-BAN	Boeing 737-4M0	Aeroflot Russian International
	VP-BAO	Boeing 737-4M0	Aeroflot Russian International
	VP-BAP	Boeing 737-4M0	Aeroflot Russian International
	VP-BAQ	Boeing 737-4M0	Aeroflot Russian International
	VP-BAR	Boeing 737-4M0	Aeroflot Russian International
	VP-BAS	Boeing 777-2Q8ER	Aeroflot Russian International
	VP-BAU	Boeing 777-2Q8ER	Aeroflot Russian International
	VP-BAV	Boeing 767-36NER	Aeroflot Russian International
	VP-BAX	Boeing 767-36NER	Aeroflot Russian International
	VP-BAY	Boeing 767-36NER	Aeroflot Russian International
	VP-BAZ	Boeing 767-36NER	Aeroflot Russian International
	VP-BEA	BAC One-Eleven 524FF	European Aviation *(stored)*
	VP-BEB	BAC One-Eleven 527FK	European Aviation *(stored)*
	VP-BKS	Boeing 767-3P6ER	Kalair
	VP-BTA	Boeing 737-2C9	Transaero Airlines
	VP-BTB	Boeing 737-2C9	Transaero Airlines
	VP-BUA	Boeing 767-33PER	Uzbekistan Airlines *Samarkand*
	VP-BUB	Boeing 757-23P	Uzbekistan Airlines
	VP-BUD	Boeing 757-23P	Uzbekistan Airlines
	VP-BUZ	Boeing 767-33PER	Uzbekistan Airlines *Khiva*

VT (India)

	VT-EBE	Boeing 747-237B	Air-India *Shahjehan*
	VT-EBN	Boeing 747-237B	Air-India *Rajendra Chola*
	VT-EDU	Boeing 747-237B	Air-India *Akbar*

Reg.	Type	Owner or Operator	Notes
VT-EFU	Boeing 747-237B	Air-India *Krishna Deva Raya*	
VT-EGA	Boeing 747-237B	Air-India *Samudra Gupta*	
VT-EGB	Boeing 747-237B	Air-India *Mahendra Varman*	
VT-EGC	Boeing 747-237B	Air-India *Harsha Vardhana*	
VT-EJG	Airbus A.310-304	Air-India *Vamuna*	
VT-EJH	Airbus A.310-304	Air-India *Tista*	
VT-EJI	Airbus A.310-304	Air-India *Saraswati*	
VT-EJJ	Airbus A.310-304	Air-India *Beas*	
VT-EJK	Airbus A.310-304	Air-India *Gomti*	
VT-EJL	Airbus A.310-304	Air-India *Sabarmati*	
VT-EPW	Boeing 747-337 (SCD)	Air-India *Shivaji*	
VT-EPX	Boeing 747-337 (SCD)	Air-India *Narasimha Varman*	
VT-EQS	Airbus A.310-304	Air-India *Krishna*	
VT-EQT	Airbus A.310-304	Air-India *Narmada*	
VT-ESM	Boeing 747-437	Air-India *Konark*	
VT-ESN	Boeing 747-437	Air-India *Tanjore*	
VT-ESO	Boeing 747-437	Air-India *Khajuraho*	
VT-ESP	Boeing 747-437	Air-India *Ajanta*	
VT-EVA	Boeing 747-437	Air-India *Agra*	
VT-EVB	Boeing 747-437	Air-India *Velha Goa*	

YA (Afghanistan)

YA-FAY	Boeing 727-228	Ariana Afghan Airlines	
YA-GAA	Boeing 727-51	Balkh Air	

YI (Iraq)

All aircraft have remained inactive since the Gulf conflict in the early 1990s. Commercial flights have therefore been suspended as a result of UN sanctions, with little prospect of an early resumption.

YK (Syria)

YK-AGA	Boeing 727-294	Syrianair *October 6*	
YK-AGB	Boeing 727-294	Syrianair *Damascus*	
YK-AGC	Boeing 727-294	Syrianair *Palmyra*	
YK-AGD	Boeing 727-269	Syrianair	
YK-AGE	Boeing 727-269	Syrianair	
YK-AGF	Boeing 727-269	Syrianair	
YK-AHA	Boeing 747SP-94	Syrianair *November 16*	
YK-AHB	Boeing 747SP-94	Syrianair *Arab Solidarity*	
YK-AIA	Tupolev Tu-154M	Syrianair	
YK-AIB	Tupolev Tu-154M	Syrianair	
YK-AIC	Tupolev Tu-154M	Syrianair	
YK-AKA	Airbus A.320-232	Syrianair *Ugarit*	
YK-AKB	Airbus A.320-232	Syrianair *Ebla*	
YK-AKC	Airbus A.320-232	Syrianair	
YK-AKD	Airbus A.320-232	Syrianair *Mari*	
YK-AKE	Airbus A.320-232	Syrianair *Bosra*	
YK-AKF	Airbus A.320-232	Syrianair	
YK-ATA	Ilyushin IL-76M	Syrianair	
YK-ATB	Ilyushin IL-76M	Syrianair	
YK-ATC	Ilyushin IL-76M	Syrianair	
YK-ATD	Ilyushin IL-76M	Syrianair	
YK-AYA	Tupolev Tu-134B-3	Syrianair	
YK-AYB	Tupolev Tu-134B-3	Syrianair	
YK-AYC	Tupolev Tu-134B-3	Syrianair	
YK-AYD	Tupolev Tu-134B-3	Syrianair	
YK-AYE	Tupolev Tu-134B-3	Syrianair	
YK-AYF	Tupolev Tu-134B-3	Syrianair	

YL (Latvia)

YL-BAA	Boeing 737-236	Transaero	
YL-BAB	Boeing 737-236	Transaero	
YL-BAC	Boeing 737-236	Transaero	
YL-BAG	SAAB SF.340A	Air Baltic	
YL-BAL	Avro RJ70	Air Baltic	

Notes	Reg.	Type	Owner or Operator
	YL-BAN	Avro RJ70	Air Baltic
	YL-BAP	SAAB SF.340A	Air Baltic
	YL-BAR	Fokker 50	Air Baltic
	YL-LAB	Tupolev Tu-154B-2	Latpass Airlines
	YL-LAJ	Ilyushin IL-76T	Inversia
	YL-LAK	Ilyushin IL-76T	Inversia
	YL-LAL	Ilyushin IL-76T	Inversia
	YL-LBA	Tupolev Tu-134A	Latavio
	YL-LBE	Tupolev Tu-134B-3	LAT Charter
	YL-LBG	Tupolev Tu-134B-3	LAT Charter
	YL-LBI	Tupolev Tu-134B-3	Baltic Express Line
	YL-RAA	Antonov An-26	RAF-Avia
	YL-RAB	Antonov An-26	RAF-Avia
	YL-RAC	Antonov An-26	RAF-Avia

YR (Romania)

	YR-ABC	Boeing 707-3K1C	TAROM
	YR-BGA	Boeing 737-38J	TAROM *Alba Lulia*
	YR-BGB	Boeing 737-38J	TAROM *Bucuresti*
	YR-BGC	Boeing 737-38J	TAROM *Constanta*
	YR-BGD	Boeing 737-38J	TAROM *Deva*
	YR-BGE	Boeing 737-38J	TAROM *Timisoara*
	YR-BGX	Boeing 737-36Q	TAROM *Galati*
	YR-BGY	Boeing 737-36M	TAROM
	YR-BGZ	Boeing 737-548	TAROM
	YR-BRC	RomBac One-Eleven 561RC	TAROM
	YR-JBA	BAC One-Eleven 528FL	Jaro International
	YR-JBB	BAC One-Eleven 528FL	Jaro International
	YR-JCB	Boeing 707-321B	Jaro International
	YR-LCA	Airbus A.310-325	TAROM *Transilvania*
	YR-LCB	Airbus A.310-325	TAROM *Moldova*
	YR-TPB	Tupolev Tu-154B-1	TAROM
	YR-TPG	Tupolev Tu-154B-1	TAROM

YU (Yugoslavia)

	YU-AHN	Douglas DC-9-32	Jugoslovenski Aerotransport (JAT)
	YU-AHU	Douglas DC-9-32	JAT
	YU-AHV	Douglas DC-9-32	JAT
	YU-AJH	Douglas DC-9-32	JAT
	YU-AJI	Douglas DC-9-32	JAT
	YU-AJL	Douglas DC-9-32	JAT
	YU-AJM	Douglas DC-9-32	JAT
	YU-AKB	Boeing 727-2H9	JAT
	YU-AKD	Boeing 727-2L8	Aviogenex *Split*
	YU-AKE	Boeing 727-2H9	JAT
	YU-AKF	Boeing 727-2H9	JAT
	YU-AKG	Boeing 727-2H9	JAT
	YU-AKH	Boeing 727-2L8	Aviogenex *Dubrovnik*
	YU-AKI	Boeing 727-2H9	JAT
	YU-AKJ	Boeing 727-2H9	JAT
	YU-AKK	Boeing 727-2H9	JAT
	YU-AKL	Boeing 727-2H9	JAT
	YU-AKM	Boeing 727-243	Aviogenex *Pula*
	YU-ALO	Aérospatiale ATR-72-201	JAT
	YU-ALP	Aérospatiale ATR-72-201	JAT
	YU-AMB	Douglas DC-10-30	JAT *Edvard Rusijan*
	YU-AND	Boeing 737-3H9	JAT
	YU-ANF	Boeing 737-3H9	JAT
	YU-ANH	Boeing 737-3H9	JAT
	YU-ANI	Boeing 737-3H9	JAT
	YU-ANK	Boeing 737-3H9	JAT
	YU-ANP	Boeing 737-2K3	Aviogenex *Zadar*
	YU-ANV	Boeing 737-3H9	JAT
	YU-ANW	Boeing 737-3H9	JAT
	YU-AOH	F.28 Fellowship 4000	Montenegro Airlines
	YU-AOI	F.28 Fellowship 4000	Montenegro Airlines

Reg.	Type	Owner or Operator	Notes

Z (Zimbabwe)

Z-WPE	Boeing 767-2N0ER	Air Zimbabwe *Victoria Falls*	
Z-WPF	Boeing 767-2N0ER	Air Zimbabwe *Chimanimani*	

Z3 (Macedonia)

Z3-AAA	Boeing 737-300	Macedonian Airlines	
Z3-ARD	Douglas DC-9-32	Macedonian Airlines	
Z3-ARE	Douglas DC-9-32	Macedonian Airlines	
Z3-ARF	Boeing 737-3H9	Macedonian Airlines	

ZK (New Zealand)

ZK-NBS	Boeing 747-419	Air New Zealand	
ZK-NBT	Boeing 747-419	Air New Zealand	
ZK-NBU	Boeing 747-419	Air New Zealand	
ZK-NBV	Boeing 747-419	Air New Zealand	
ZK-NBW	Boeing 747-419	Air New Zealand	
ZK-SUH	Boeing 747-475	Air New Zealand	
ZK-SUI	Boeing 747-441	Air New Zealand	
ZK-SUJ	Boeing 747-4F6	Air New Zealand	

ZS (South Africa)

ZS-JIV	L.100-30 Hercules	Safair	
ZS-JIX	L.100-30 Hercules	Safair	
ZS-JIY	L.100-30 Hercules	Safair	
ZS-JIZ	L.100-30 Hercules	Safair	
ZS-JVL	L.100-30 Hercules	Safair	
ZS-OKK	Boeing 747-312 (SCD)	African Star Airways	
ZS-RSC	L.100-30 Hercules	Safair	
ZS-RSI	L.100-30 Hercules	Safair	
ZS-SAC	Boeing 747-312	South African Airways *Shosholoza*	
ZS-SAJ	Boeing 747-312	South African Airways	
ZS-SAK	Boeing 747-444	South African Airways *Ebhayi*	
ZS-SAL	Boeing 747-244B	South African Airways *Tafelberg*	
ZS-SAM	Boeing 747-244B	South African Airways *Drakensberg*	
ZS-SAN	Boeing 747-244B	South African Airways *Lebombo*	
ZS-SAO	Boeing 747-244B	South African Airways *Magaliesberg*	
ZS-SAP	Boeing 747-244B	South African Airways *Swartberg*	
ZS-SAR	Boeing 747-244F (SCD)	South African Airways *Waterberg*	
ZS-SAT	Boeing 747-344	South African Airways	
ZS-SAU	Boeing 747-344	South African Airways *Cape Town*	
ZS-SAV	Boeing 747-444	South African Airways *Durban*	
ZS-SAW	Boeing 747-444	South African Airways *Bloemfontein*	
ZS-SAX	Boeing 747-444	South African Airways	
ZS-SAY	Boeing 747-444	South African Airways *Vulindlela*	
ZS-SAZ	Boeing 747-444	South African Airways	
ZS-SBK	Boeing 747-4F6	South African Airways	
ZS-SBS	Boeing 747-4F6	South African Airways	
ZS-SPA	Boeing 747SP-44	South African Airways	
ZS-SPC	Boeing 747SP-44	South African Airways	
ZS-SPE	Boeing 747SP-44	South African Airways *Hantarn*	
ZS-SRA	Boeing 767-266ER	South African Airways	
ZS-SRB	Boeing 767-266ER	South African Airways	
ZS-SRC	Boeing 767-266ER	South African Airways	

3B (Mauritius)

3B-NAK	Boeing 767-23BER	Air Mauritius *City of Curepipe*	
3B-NAL	Boeing 767-23BER	Air Mauritius *City of Port Louis*	
3B-NAU	Airbus A.340-312	Air Mauritius *Pink Pigeon*	
3B-NAV	Airbus A.340-312	Air Mauritius *Kestrel*	
3B-NAY	Airbus A.340-313	Air Mauritius *Cardinal*	
3B-NBD	Airbus A.340-313X	Air Mauritius	
3B-NBE	Airbus A.340-313X	Air Mauritius	
3B-STI	Airbus A.310-222	Middle East Airlines	

Notes	Reg.	Type	Owner or Operator
	3B-STJ	Airbus A.310-222	Middle East Airlines
	3B-STK	Airbus A.310-222	Middle East Airlines

3D (Swaziland)

	Reg.	Type	Owner or Operator
	3D-ADV	Douglas DC-8-54F	African International Airways
	3D-AFR	Douglas DC-8-54F	African International Airways
	3D-CSB	Boeing 707-373C	Tradewinds Cargo

Notes	Reg.	Type	Notes	Reg.	Type

4K (Azerbaijan)

The following are operated by Azerbaijan Airlines with the registrations prefixed by 4K.

Reg.	Type	Reg.	Type
AZ1	Boeing 727-235	85177	Tu-154B-1
AZ8	Boeing 727-230	85192	Tu-154B-1
AZ10	Tu-154M	85199	Tu-154B-1
AZ12	Boeing 757-22L	85211	Tu-154B-1
65702	Tu-134B-3	85214	Tu-154B-1
65705	Tu-134B-3	85250	Tu-154B-1
65708	Tu-134B-3	85274	Tu-154B-1
65709	Tu-134B-3	85329	Tu-154B-2
65710	Tu-134B-3	85364	Tu-154B-2
65711	Tu-134B-3	85391	Tu-154B-2
65712	Tu-134B-3	85538	Tu-154B-2
65713	Tu-134B-3	85548	Tu-154B-2
65714	Tu-134B-3	85698	Tu-154M
85147	Tu-154B-1	85729	Tu-154M
85158	Tu-154B-1	85734	Tu-154M

4L (Georgia)

The following registrations are prefixed by 4L with the aircraft operated by Adjarian Airlines (ADJ), Air Georgia (GEO), Air Zena (TGZ) or Orbi Georgia (DVU).

Reg.	Type	Reg.	Type
AAB	Tu-134B-3 (ADJ)	65857	Tu-134A-3 (DVU)
AAD	Tu-134B-3 (ADJ)	85168	Tu-154B (TGZ)
AAF	Tu-154M (DVU)	85430	Tu-154B-2 (DVU)
AAG	Tu-154B-2 (GEO)	85496	Tu-154B-2 (DVU)
AAH	Tu-154B-2 (GEO)	85518	Tu-154B-2 (DVU)
65750	Tu-134A-3 (DVU)	85547	Tu-154B-2 (GEO)
65774	Tu-134A-3 (DVU)	85558	Tu-154B-2 (GEO)
65798	Tu-134A-3 (DVU)		

Notes	Reg.	Type	Owner or Operator

4R (Sri Lanka)

	Reg.	Type	Owner or Operator
	4R-ADA	Airbus A.340-311	SriLankan Airlines
	4R-ADB	Airbus A.340-311	SriLankan Airlines
	4R-ADC	Airbus A.340-311	SriLankan Airlines
	4R-ADD	Airbus A.340-312	SriLankan Airlines
	4R-ALA	Airbus A.330-243	SriLankan Airlines
	4R-ALB	Airbus A.330-243	SriLankan Airlines
	4R-ALC	Airbus A.330-243	SriLankan Airlines
	4R-ALD	Airbus A.330-243	SriLankan Airlines
	4R-ALE	Airbus A.330-243	SriLankan Airlines

4X (Israel)

	Reg.	Type	Owner or Operator
	4X-ABJ	Boeing 737-73S	Israir Airlines
	4X-ABN	Boeing 737-258	El Al/Arkia
	4X-ABO	Boeing 737-258	El Al/Arkia
	4X-ABR	Boeing 737-73S	Israir Airlines
	4X-AXA	Boeing 747-258B	El Al
	4X-AXB	Boeing 747-258B	El Al
	4X-AXC	Boeing 747-258B	El Al

Reg.	Type	Owner or Operator	Notes
4X-AXD	Boeing 747-258C	El Al	
4X-AXF	Boeing 747-258C	El Al	
4X-AXH	Boeing 747-258B (SCD)	El Al	
4X-AXK	Boeing 747-245F (SCD)	El Al	
4X-AXL	Boeing 747-245F (SCD)	El Al	
4X-AXQ	Boeing 747-238B	El Al	
4X-BAF	Boeing 737-281	Arkia	
4X-BAG	Boeing 737-281	Arkia	
4X-BAU	Boeing 757-3E7	Arkia	
4X-BAW	Boeing 757-3E7	Arkia	
4X-BAZ	Boeing 757-236	Arkia	
4X-EAA	Boeing 767-258	El Al	
4X-EAB	Boeing 767-258	El Al	
4X-EAC	Boeing 767-258ER	El Al	
4X-EAD	Boeing 767-258ER	El Al	
4X-EAE	Boeing 767-27EER	El Al	
4X-EAF	Boeing 767-27EER	El Al	
4X-EBF	Boeing 757-27B	El Al	
4X-EBI	Boeing 757-258	El Al	
4X-EBL	Boeing 757-258	El Al/Arkia	
4X-EBM	Boeing 757-258	El Al/Arkia	
4X-EBR	Boeing 757-258	El Al/Arkia	
4X-EBS	Boeing 757-258	El Al	
4X-EBT	Boeing 757-258	El Al	
4X-EBU	Boeing 757-258	El Al	
4X-EBV	Boeing 757-258	El Al	
4X-EKA	Boeing 737-858	El Al	
4X-EKB	Boeing 737-858	El Al	
4X-EKC	Boeing 737-858	El Al	
4X-EKD	Boeing 737-758	El Al	
4X-EKE	Boeing 737-758	El Al	
4X-ELA	Boeing 747-458	El Al	
4X-ELB	Boeing 747-458	El Al	
4X-ELC	Boeing 747-458	El Al	
4X-ELD	Boeing 747-458	El Al	

5A (Libya)

5A-DIB	Boeing 727-2L5	Libyan Arab Airlines	
5A-DIC	Boeing 727-2L5	Libyan Arab Airlines	
5A-DID	Boeing 727-2L5	Libyan Arab Airlines	
5A-DIE	Boeing 727-2L5	Libyan Arab Airlines	
5A-DIF	Boeing 727-2L5	Libyan Arab Airlines	
5A-DIG	Boeing 727-2L5	Libyan Aran Airlines	
5A-DIH	Boeing 727-2L5	Libyan Arab Airlines	
5A-DII	Boeing 727-2L5	Libyan Arab Airlines	
5A-	Airbus A.320-	Libyan Arab Airlines	
5A-DTG	F.28 Fellowship 4000	Libyan Arab Airlines	

Note: The lifting of sanctions in late 1999 is expected to result in Libyan Arab replacing its elderly 727s with Airbus products during 2000. Two A.320s registered EI-TLG and EI-TLT entered service in early 2000. Airbus A.310 F-OHPQ is also operated.

5B (Cyprus)

5B-DAQ	Airbus A.310-203	Cyprus Airways *Soli*	
5B-DAR	Airbus A.310-203	Cyprus Airways *Aepia*	
5B-DAS	Airbus A.310-203	Cyprus Airways *Salamis*	
5B-DAT	Airbus A.320-231	Cyprus Airways *Praxandros*	
5B-DAU	Airbus A.320-231	Cyprus Airways *Evelthon*	
5B-DAV	Airbus A.320-231	Cyprus Airways *Kinyras*	
5B-DAW	Airbus A.320-231	Cyprus Airways *Agapinor*	
5B-DAX	Airbus A.310-204	Cyprus Airways *Engomi*	
5B-DAZ	Boeing 707-328C	Avistar	
5B-DBA	Airbus A.320-231	Cyprus Airways *Evagoras*	
5B-DBB	Airbus A.320-231	Eurocypria Airways *Akamas*	
5B-DBC	Airbus A.320-231	Eurocypria Airways *Tefkros*	
5B-DBD	Airbus A.320-231	Eurocypria Airways *Onosilos*	
5B-DBG	Boeing 737-4YO	Helios Airways	
5B-DBH	Boeing 737-86N	Helios Airways	
5B-DBI	Boeing 737-86N	Helios Airways	

Notes	Reg.	Type	Owner or Operator

5H (Tanzania)

5H-TCA	Boeing 737-33A	Air Tanzania

5N (Nigeria)

5N-AAA	Boeing 747-148	Kabo Air
5N-ANN	Douglas DC-10-30	Nigeria Airways *Yunkari*
5N-AOO	Boeing 707-351C	Air Atlantic Cargo
5N-ARQ	Boeing 707-338C	DAS Air Cargo
5N-BBF	Boeing 727-231	ADC Airlines
5N-BBH	Boeing 727-231	ADC Airlines
5N-BVU	Airbus A.300-600R	Bellview Airlines
5N-EDO	Boeing 747-146	Okada Air *Lady Cherry*
5N-EEO	Boeing 707-321C	Air Atlantic Cargo
5N-MXX	Boeing 707-323C	Merchant Express
5N-TKE	Boeing 727-82	Triax Airlines *Eze-Ukpo*
5N-TKT	Boeing 727-22	Triax Airlines
5N-TNO	Boeing 707-369C	Air Atlantic Cargo
5N-TTK	Boeing 727-264	Triax Airlines *Chinweze*

5R (Madagascar)

5R-MFC	Boeing 767-33AER	Air Madagascar
5R-MFD	Boeing 767-33AER	Air Madagascar
5R-MFT	Boeing 747-2B2B (SCD)	Air Madagascar *Ankoay*

5X (Uganda)

5X-AMM	Boeing 727-76	Skyline International
5X-JEF	Boeing 707-379C	DAS Air Cargo
5X-JET	Boeing 707-351C	DAS Air Cargo
5X-JOE	Douglas DC-10-30	DAS Air Cargo
5X-	Douglas DC-10-30	DAS Air Cargo

5Y (Kenya)

5Y-AXI	Boeing 707-330B	African Airlines International
5Y-BEL	Airbus A.310-304	Kenya Airways *Nyayo Star*
5Y-BEN	Airbus A.310-304	Kenya Airways *Harambee Star*
5Y-BFT	Airbus A.310-304	Kenya Airways *Uhuru Star*
5Y-KQL	Airbus A.310-304	Kenya Airways
5Y-MBA	Douglas DC-10-30	African Safari Airways
5Y-SIM	Boeing 707-336C	Simba Air Cargo

6Y (Jamaica)

6Y-JMC	Airbus A.340-212	Air Jamaica

Note: Air Jamaica also operates Airbus A.310-300s N835AB, N837AB, N838AB, N839AD, N840AB and N841AB.

7O (Yemen)

7O-ACV	Boeing 727-2N8	Yemenia
7O-ACW	Boeing 727-2N8	Yemenia
7O-ACX	Boeing 727-2N8	Yemenia
7O-ACY	Boeing 727-2N8	Yemenia
7O-ADA	Boeing 727-2N8	Yemenia
7O-ADG	Iluyshin IL-76TD	Yemenia
7O-ADJ	Airbus A.310-324	Yemenia

Note: Yemenia also operates a pair of Airbus A.310-325s registered F-OHPR and F-OHPS.

Reg.	Type	Owner or Operator	Notes

7T (Algeria)

7T-VEA	Boeing 727-2D6	Air Algerie *Tassili*
7T-VEB	Boeing 727-2D6	Air Algerie *Hoggar*
7T-VED	Boeing 737-2D6C	Air Algerie *Atlas Saharien*
7T-VEF	Boeing 737-2D6	Air Algerie *Saoura*
7T-VEG	Boeing 737-2D6	Air Algerie *Monts des Ouleds Neils*
7T-VEH	Boeing 727-2D6	Air Algerie *Lalla Khadidja*
7T-VEI	Boeing 727-2D6	Air Algerie *Djebel Amour*
7T-VEJ	Boeing 737-2D6	Air Algerie *Chrea*
7T-VEK	Boeing 737-2D6	Air Algerie *Edough*
7T-VEL	Boeing 737-2D6	Air Algerie *Akfadou*
7T-VEM	Boeing 727-2D6	Air Algerie *Mont du Ksall*
7T-VEN	Boeing 737-2D6	Air Algerie *La Soummam*
7T-VEO	Boeing 737-2D6	Air Algerie *La Titteri*
7T-VEP	Boeing 727-2D6	Air Algerie *Mont du Tessala*
7T-VEQ	Boeing 737-2D6	Air Algerie *Le Zaccar*
7T-VER	Boeing 737-2D6	Air Algerie *Le Souf*
7T-VES	Boeing 737-2D6C	Air Algerie *Le Tadmaït*
7T-VET	Boeing 727-2D6	Air Algerie *Georges du Rhumel*
7T-VEU	Boeing 727-2D6	Air Algerie *Djurdjura*
7T-VEV	Boeing 727-2D6	Air Algerie
7T-VEW	Boeing 727-2D6	Air Algerie *Monts de Tlemcen*
7T-VEX	Boeing 737-2D6	Air Algerie *Djemila*
7T-VEY	Boeing 737-2D6	Air Algerie *Rhoufi*
7T-VEZ	Boeing 737-2T4	Air Algerie *Monts du Daia*
7T-VHG	L.100-30 Hercules	Air Algerie
7T-VHL	L.100-30 Hercules	Air Algerie
7T-VJB	Boeing 737-2T4	Air Algerie *Monts des Bibans*
7T-VJC	Airbus A.310-203	Air Algerie
7T-VJD	Airbus A.310-203	Air Algerie
7T-VJG	Boeing 767-3D6	Air Algerie
7T-VJH	Boeing 767-3D6	Air Algerie
7T-VJI	Boeing 767-3D6	Air Algerie
7T-VVA	Boeing 737-200	Antinea Airlines

8Q (Maldives)

8Q-	Airbus A.310-300	Air Maldives
8Q-	Airbus A.310-300	Air Maldives
8Q	Airbus A.310-300	Air Maldives

Note: Air Maldives also operates Airbus A310-222 F-OHPP and A.310-324 F-OIHS.

9A (Croatia)

9A-CTF	Airbus A.320-211	Croatia Airlines *Rijeka*
9A-CTG	Airbus A.319-112	Croatia Airlines *Zadar*
9A-CTH	Airbus A.319-112	Croatia Airlines
9A-CTI	Airbus A.319-112	Croatia Airlines *Vukovar*
9A-CTJ	Airbus A.320-214	Croatia Airlines
9A-	Airbus A.319-112	Croatia Airlines
9A-	Airbus A.319-112	Croatia Airlines

9G (Ghana)

9G-ADM	Boeing 707-321C	Continental Cargo Airlines
9G-ADS	Boeing 707-323C	Continental Cargo Airlines
9G-ANA	Douglas DC-10-30	Ghana Airways
9G-ANB	Douglas DC-10-30	Ghana Airways
9G-AYO	Boeing 707-323C	Air Ghana
9G-BAN	Douglas DC-8-62CF	Trans Continental Airlines
9G-CDG	Douglas DC-8-55F	Analinde Airlines
9G-FIA	Boeing 707-331C	First International Airways
9G-JNR	Boeing 707-324C	Jason Air
9G-LCA	Canadair CL-44-0	First International Airways
9G-MKA	Douglas DC-8-55F	MK Airlines
9G-MKC	Douglas DC-8-55F	MK Airlines
9G-MKE	Douglas DC-8-55F	MK Airlines
9G-MKF	Douglas DC-8-55F	MK Airlines

Notes	Reg.	Type	Owner or Operator
	9G-MKH	Douglas DC-8-62AF	MK Airlines
	9G-MKI	Boeing 747-246F	MK Airlines
	9G-OLD	Boeing 707-324C	First International Airways
	9G-PHN	Douglas DC-10-30	Ghana Airways

Note: MK Airlines also operates the DC-8-62F registered TF-MKG.

9H (Malta)

	9H-ABE	Boeing 737-2Y5	Air Malta *Alof de Wignacourt*
	9H-ABF	Boeing 737-2Y5	Air Malta *Manuel Pinto*
	9H-ABP	Airbus A.320-211	Air Malta *Nicholas de Cotoner*
	9H-ABQ	Airbus A.320-211	Air Malta *Hughes Loubenx de Verdelle*
	9H-ABR	Boeing 737-3Y5	Air Malta *Juan de Homedes*
	9H-ABS	Boeing 737-3Y5	Air Malta *Antoines de Paule*
	9H-ABT	Boeing 737-3Y5	Air Malta *Ferdinand von Hompesch*
	9H-ADH	Boeing 737-33A	Air Malta
	9H-ADI	Boeing 737-33A	Air Malta

Note: Air Malta usually leases-in one or two aircraft for the summer season.

9K (Kuwait)

	9K-ADB	Boeing 747-269B (SCD)	Kuwait Airways
	9K-ADD	Boeing 747-269B (SCD)	Kuwait Airways *Al-Salmiya*
	9K-ADE	Boeing 747-469 (SCD)	Kuwait Airways *Al-Jabariya*
	9K-AGC	McD Douglas MD-83	Kuwait Government
	9K-ALA	Airbus A.310-308	Kuwait Airways *Al-Jahra*
	9K-ALB	Airbus A.310-308	Kuwait Airways *Gharnada*
	9K-ALD	Airbus A.310-308	Kuwait Government *Al-Salmiya*
	9K-AMA	Airbus A.300-605R	Kuwait Airways *Failaka*
	9K-AMB	Airbus A.300-605R	Kuwait Airways *Burghan*
	9K-AMC	Airbus A.300-605R	Kuwait Airways *Wafra*
	9K-AMD	Airbus A.300-605R	Kuwait Airways *Wara*
	9K-AME	Airbus A.300-605R	Kuwait Airways *Al-Rawdhatain*
	9K-ANA	Airbus A.340-313	Kuwait Airways *Warba*
	9K-ANB	Airbus A.340-313	Kuwait Airways *Al-Sabahiya*
	9K-ANC	Airbus A.340-313	Kuwait Airways *Al-Mobarakiya*
	9K-AND	Airbus A.340-313	Kuwait Airways *Al-Riggah*
	9K-AOA	Boeing 777-269ER	Kuwait Airways
	9K-AOB	Boeing 777-269ER	Kuwait Airways

9M (Malaysia)

	9M-MHI	Boeing 747-236F (SCD)	Malaysian Airlines Cargo *Kuching*
	9M-MHJ	Boeing 747-236F (SCD)	Malaysian Airlines Cargo *Johor Bahru*
	9M-MHL	Boeing 747-4H6 (SCD)	Malaysian Airlines *Kuala Lumpur*
	9M-MHM	Boeing 747-4H6 (SCD)	Malaysian Airlines *Penang*
	9M-MHN	Boeing 747-4H6	Malaysian Airlines *Malacca*
	9M-MPA	Boeing 747-4H6	Malaysian Airlines *Ipoh*
	9M-MPB	Boeing 747-4H6	Malaysian Airlines *Shah Alam*
	9M-MPC	Boeing 747-4H6	Malaysian Airlines *Kuantan*
	9M-MPD	Boeing 747-4H6	Malaysian Airlines *Serembam*
	9M-MPE	Boeing 747-4H6	Malaysian Airlines *Kangar*
	9M-MPF	Boeing 747-4H6	Malaysian Airlines *Kota Bharu*
	9M-MPG	Boeing 747-4H6	Malaysian Airlines *Kuala Terengganu*
	9M-MPH	Boeing 747-4H6	Malaysian Airlines *Langkawi*
	9M-MPI	Boeing 747-4H6	Malaysian Airlines
	9M-MPJ	Boeing 747-4H6	Malaysian Airlines
	9M-MPK	Boeing 747-4H6	Malaysian Airlines
	9M-MPL	Boeing 747-4H6	Malaysian Airlines
	9M-MPM	Boeing 747-4H6	Malaysian Airlines
	9M-MPN	Boeing 747-4H6	Malaysian Airlines
	9M-MPO	Boeing 747-4H6	Malaysian Airlines
	9M-MPP	Boeing 747-4H6	Malaysian Airlines.

9N (Nepal)

	9N-ACA	Boeing 757-2F8	Royal Nepal Airlines
	9N-ACB	Boeing 757-2F8C	Royal Nepal Airlines

Reg.	Type	Owner or Operator	Notes

9Q (Congo)

9Q-BAN	Douglas DC-8-62CF	Air Cargo Chartering	
9Q-CLK	Boeing 707-138B	Government of Congo	
9Q-CQC	Boeing 707-323C	Government of Congo	

9V (Singapore)

9V-SFA	Boeing 747-412F (SCD)	Singapore Airlines	
9V-SFB	Boeing 747-412F (SCD)	Singapore Airlines	
9V-SFC	Boeing 747-412F (SCD)	Singapore Airlines	
9V-SFD	Boeing 747-412F (SCD)	Singapore Airlines	
9V-SFE	Boeing 747-412F (SCD)	Singapore Airlines	
9V-SFF	Boeing 747-412F (SCD)	Singapore Airlines	
9V-SFG	Boeing 747-412F (SCD)	Singapore Airlines	
9V-SFH	Boeing 747-412F (SCD)	Singapore Airlines	
9V-SKA	Boeing 747-312 (SCD)	Singapore Airlines	
9V-SKH	Boeing 747-312 (SCD)	Singapore Airlines	
9V-SKJ	Boeing 747-312 (SCD)	Singapore Airlines	
9V-SMA	Boeing 747-412	Singapore Airlines	
9V-SMB	Boeing 747-412	Singapore Airlines	
9V-SMC	Boeing 747-412	Singapore Airlines	
9V-SME	Boeing 747-412	Singapore Airlines	
9V-SMF	Boeing 747-412	Singapore Airlines	
9V-SMG	Boeing 747-412	Singapore Airlines	
9V-SMH	Boeing 747-412	Singapore Airlines	
9V-SMI	Boeing 747-412	Singapore Airlines	
9V-SMJ	Boeing 747-412	Singapore Airlines	
9V-SMK	Boeing 747-412	Singapore Airlines	
9V-SML	Boeing 747-412	Singapore Airlines	
9V-SMM	Boeing 747-412	Singapore Airlines	
9V-SMN	Boeing 747-412	Singapore Airlines	
9V-SMO	Boeing 747-412	Singapore Airlines	
9V-SMP	Boeing 747-412	Singapore Airlines	
9V-SMQ	Boeing 747-412	Singapore Airlines	
9V-SMR	Boeing 747-412	Singapore Airlines	
9V-SMS	Boeing 747-412	Singapore Airlines	
9V-SMT	Boeing 747-412	Singapore Airlines	
9V-SMU	Boeing 747-412	Singapore Airlines	
9V-SMV	Boeing 747-412	Singapore Airlines	
9V-SMW	Boeing 747-412	Singapore Airlines	
9V-SMY	Boeing 747-412	Singapore Airlines	
9V-SMZ	Boeing 747-412	Singapore Airlines	
9V-SPA	Boeing 747-412	Singapore Airlines	
9V-SPB	Boeing 747-412	Singapore Airlines	
9V-SPC	Boeing 747-412	Singapore Airlines	
9V-SPD	Boeing 747-412	Singapore Airlines	
9V-SPE	Boeing 747-412	Singapore Airlines	
9V-SPF	Boeing 747-412	Singapore Airlines	
9V-SPG	Boeing 747-412	Singapore Airlines	
9V-SPH	Boeing 747-412	Singapore Airlines	
9V-SPI	Boeing 747-412	Singapore Airlines	
9V-SPJ	Boeing 747-412	Singapore Airlines	
9V-SPK	Boeing 747-412	Singapore Airlines	
9V-SPL	Boeing 747-412	Singapore Airlines	
9V-SPM	Boeing 747-412	Singapore Airlines	
9V-SPN	Boeing 747-412	Singapore Airlines	
9V-SPO	Boeing 747-412	Singapore Airlines	
9V-SPP	Boeing 747-412	Singapore Airlines	

9Y (Trinidad and Tobago)

9Y-TGJ	L.1011-385 TriStar 500 (595)	B.W.I.A. West Indies Airways	
9Y-TGN	L.1011-385 TriStar 500 (596)	B.W.I.A. West Indies Airways	
9Y-THA	L.1011-385 TriStar 500 (597)	B.W.I.A. West Indies Airways	

Note: B.W.I.A. West Indies Airways also operates a TriStar 500 which retains the registration N3140D (598).

Overseas Registrations

Aircraft included in this section are those based in the UK but which retain their non-British identities.

Reg.	Type	Owner or Operator
A4O-AB	V.1103 VC10 ★	Brooklands Museum of Aviation (G-ASIX)
CF-EQS	Boeing-Stearman PT-17 (217786) ★	Imperial War Museum/Duxford
CF-KCG	Grumman TBM-3E Avenger AS.3 ★	Imperial War Museum/Duxford
D-HMQV	Bolkow Bo 102 ★	IHM/Weston-s-Mare
D-IFSB	D.H.104 Dove 6 ★	Mosquito Aircraft Museum
ES-YLG	Aero L.29 Delphin	The Jet Centre/North Weald
F-AZFV	NA T-28 Fennec	Old Flying Machin Co/Duxford
F-BDRS	Boeing B-17G (231983) ★	Imperial War Museum/Duxford
F-BGNR	V.708 Viscount ★	Skysport Engineering Ltd
F-BGNX	D.H.106 Comet 1 (G-AOJT) ★	Mosquito Aircraft Museum (fuselage only)
F-BMCY	Potez 840 ★	Sumburgh Fire Service
F-BTGV	Aero Spacelines Super Guppy 201 (1) ★	British Aviation Heritage/Bruntingthorpe
HA-ACL	Dornier Do.28D Turbo	Target Skysports Parachute Centre/Hibaldstow
HA-MEP	Antonov An-2R	AeroSuperBatics Ltd/Rendcomb
HA-MKE	Antonov An-2R	Air Foyle/White Waltham
HA-MKF	Antonov An-2TP	Transair Pilot Shop/White Waltham
HZ-DG1	Boeing 727-51	Dallah Avco/Stansted
HZ-SM3	Dassault Falcon 50	M. M. A. Edrees/Stansted
LN-AMY	AT-6D Harvard	Old Flying Machine Co/Duxford
LY-ABQ	Yakovlev Yak-52 (15)	A. Hyatt
LY-ABW	Antonov An-2	-
LY-AFA	Yakovlev Yak-52	Termikas Co Ltd/Barton
LY-AFB	Yakovlev Yak-52 (112)	Termikas Co Ltd/Little Gransden
LY-AFH	Yakovlev Yak-52	-
LY-AFV	Yakovlev Yak-52	A. Fraser
LY-AFX	Yakovlev Yak-52	D. Hawkins
LY-AKW	Yakovlev Yak-52 (56)	A. Harris
LY-ALJ	Yakovlev Yak-52 (132)	D. Hawkins
LY-ALN	Yakovlev Yak-52 (52)	D. Lewendon
LY-ALO	Yakovlev Yak-52 (135)	Sky Associates (UK) Ltd/Little Gransden
LY-ALS	Yakovlev Yak-52 (69)	M. Jefferies/Little Gransden
LY-ALT	Yakovlev Yak-52 (121)	Titan Airways Ltd/Stansted
LY-ALU	Yakovlev Yak-52 (124)	S. Goodridge
LY-AMI	Yakovlev Yak-18T	M. Webb/White Waltham
LY-AMJ	Yakovlev Yak-18T	-/Earls Colne
LY-AMP	Yakovlev Yak-52 (52)	B. Brown/Breighton
LY-AMS	Yakovlev Yak-52 (51)	Willow Air Ltd/Southend
LY-AMU	Yakovlev Yak-52 (42)	G. Sharpe/North Weald
LY-ANI	Yakovlev Yak-52	-/Little Gransden
LY-AOB	Yakovlev Yak-52	M. Schwarz
LY-AOC	Yakovlev Yak-52 (30)	T. Boxhall
LY-AOK	Yakovlev Yak-52	I. Vaughan
LY-AOX	Yakovlev Yak-52 (122)	-/Biggin Hill
LY-AOZ	Yakovlev Yak-52	-
LY-ASA	Antonov An-2	-
LY-ASD	Yakovlev Yak-50 (82)	-/Breighton
N2FU	Learjet 31A	Motor Racing Development Corpn
N14TV	Cessna 525 Citation	Helios Ltd
N18E	Boeing 247D ★	Science Museum/Wroughton
N18V	Beech D.17S Traveler (DR628)	R. Lamplough
N27TS	Cessna 501 Citation	Eagle SP 147 Inc
N30XX	Cessna 550 Citation II	Freshair Inc
N36SF	Hawker Sea Fury FB.10 (361)	J. Bradshaw/Kemble
N43SV	Boeing Stearman E.75N-1 (796)	V. S. E. Norman/Rendcomb
N46EA	P.66 Pembroke C.1 ★	P. G. Vallance Ltd/Charlwood
N47DD	Republic P-47D Thunderbolt (45-49192) ★	Imperial War Museum/Duxford
N47DG	Republic P-47D Thunderbolt	Flying A Services/Earls Colne
N47FK	Douglas C-47A	European Flyers/North Weald
N47FL	Douglas C-47A	MLP Aviation Ltd
N49AG	Douglas DC-3 (OT-CWG)	Dakota Air/Brussels

Reg.	Type	Owner or Operator	Notes
N75TL	Boeing-Stearman N2S-4 Kaydet (669)	-/Headcorn	
N93GS	Grumman G.21C Goose	T. Friedrich/Elstree	
N111LM	Beech 95-58 Baron	Swift Air Ltd/Cranfield	
N112WG	Westland WG-30-100 ★	IHM/Weston-s-Mare	
N139DP	Bell P-39Q-5-BE Airacobra (219993)	The Fighter Collection/Duxford	
N147DC	Douglas C-47A (TS423)	Aces High USA Inc/North Weald	
N179PT	Vought F4U-5N Corsair (122179)	Wizzard Investments Ltd	
N196B	NA F-86A Sabre (80242) ★	American Air Museum/Duxford	
N260QB	Pitts S-2S Special	D. Baker	
N500LN	Howard 500	D. Baker	
N600KC	BAe 125 Srs 800A	Kimberley Clark Co Inc	
N707KS	Boeing 707-321B	Kalair Corpn/Stansted	
N707TJ	Boeing Stearman A.75N1	V. S. E. Norman/Rendcomb	
N747SY	Mitsubishi Mu.2B-6	Smith Young Partnership/Liverpool	
N909WJ	Grumman FM-2 Wildcat (46867)	Wizzard Investments Ltd	
N999PJ	M.S.760 Paris 2	R. J. Lamplough/North Weald	
N1024L	Beech 60 Duke	R. Ogden/Barton	
N1344	Ryan PT-22	H. Mitchell	
N1364V	Boeing Stearman N2S-5 (43578)	D. Milne	
N1994A	Douglas C-47A (315211)	Wings Venture	
N2929W	PA-28-151 Warrior	R. Lobell	
N3922B	Boeing Stearman E.75N1	Eastern Stearman Ltd/Swanton Morley	
N3929B	Boeing Stearman E.75N1	Eastern Stearman Ltd/Swanton Morley	
N4565L	Douglas DC-3 ★	USAF Museum/Framlingham	
N4596N	Boeing Stearman PT-13D	Intrepid Aviation Co/North Weald	
N4647J	PA-28R Cherokee Arrow 180	R. Breckell/Barton	
N4712V	Boeing Stearman PT-13D	Wessex Aviation & Transport Ltd	
N4806E	Douglas A-26C Invader ★	R. & R. Cadman (stored)/Manston	
N5057V	Boeing Stearman PT-13D	V. S. E. Norman/Rendcomb	
N5237V	Boeing B-17G (483868) ★	RAF Museum/Hendon	
N5345N	Boeing Stearman PT-13D	Eastern Stearman Ltd/Swanton Morley	
N5419	Bristol Scout D (replica) ★	Bristol Aero Collection	
N5824H	PA-38-112 Tomahawk	Lakenheath Aero Club	
N6268	Travel Air Model 2000 (626/8) ★	Personal Plane Services Ltd/Booker	
N6526D	NA P-51D Mustang (413573) ★	RAF Museum/Hendon	
N7027E	Hawker Tempest V (EJ693)	K Weeks/Andover.	
N7374A	Cessna A.150M (tailwheel)	J. Thomas	
N7564J	PA-28R Cherokee Arrow 180	-/Barton	
N7614C	NA B-25J Mitchell (31171) ★	Imperial War Museum/Duxford	
N7777G	L.749A Constellation ★	Science Museum (G-CONI)/Wroughton	
N8162G	Boeing Stearman PT-17 (28)	Eastern Stearman Ltd/Swanton Morley	
N9050T	Douglas C-47A (parts only) ★	Dakota's American Bistro/Fleet	
N9089Z	NA TB-25J Mitchell (44-30861) ★	Aces High Ltd (G-BKXW)/North Weald	
N9115Z	NA TB-25N Mitchell (34037) ★	RAF Museum/Hendon	
N9606H	Fairchild M.62A Cornell ★	Rebel Air Museum/Earls Colne	
N14113	NA T-28A Trojan (51-7545)	Radial Revelations/Duxford	
N23840	Beech C24R Sierra 200	A. Hall/Liverpool	
N26634	PA-24 Comanche 250	P. Biggs (G-BFKR)	
N33600	Cessna L-19A Bird Dog (111989) ★	Museum of Army Flying/Middle Wallop	
N33870	Fairchild M.62A Cornell (02538)	D. Arnold/Tibenham	
N38940	Boeing Stearman PT-17 (18263)	R. W. Sage	
N43069	PA-28-161 Warrior II	D. Wards	
N49272	Fairchild PT-23 (23)	PT Flight/Cosford	
N50755	Boeing Stearman PT-27 (211672)	Eastern Stearman Ltd/Swanton Morley	
N53091	Boeing Stearman PT-17	Eastern Stearman Ltd/Swanton Morley	
N54922	Boeing Stearman N2S-4	V. S. E. Norman (3)/Rendcomb	
N56421	Ryan PT-22 (855)	PT Flight/Cosford	
N56643	Maule M.5-180C	-/Langar	
N58566	BT-13 Valiant	PT Flight/Cosford	
N63590	Boeing Stearman N2S-3 (07539)	R. W. Sage/Tibenham	
N65200	Boeing Stearman D75N1	Eastern Stearman Ltd/Swanton Morley	
N68427	Boeing Stearman N2S-4 ★	Black Barn Aviation/Tibenham	
N73410	Boeing Stearman N2S-3 ★	Blackbarn Aviation/Tibenham	
N75664	Boeing Stearman E.75N1 (208)	—	
N79863	Grumman F6F-5K Hellcat (79863)	Wizzard Investments Ltd	
N91342	PA-28-112 Tomahawk	Lakenheath Aero Club	
N91384	R. Commander 690A	Cooper Aerial Surveys Ltd/Sandtoft	
N91457	PA-38-112 Tomahawk	Lakenheath Aero Club	
N91590	PA-38-112 Tomahawk	Lakenheath Aero Club	

Notes	Reg.	Type	Owner or Operator
	N96240	Beech D.18S	Edward Bros Aviation (G-AYAH)/ North Weald
	N99153	NA T-28C Trojan (146289) ★	Norfolk & Suffolk Aviation Museum/Flixton
	NC5171N	Lockheed 10A Electra ★	Science Museum (G-LIOA)/Wroughton
	NC16403	Cessna C.34 Airmaster	Sylmar Aviation (G-BSEB)
	NC18028	Beech D.17S	P. H. McConnell/Popham
	NL51EA	NA P-51D Mustang (44-63507)	Old Flying Machine Co Ltd/Duxford
	NL314BG	NA P-51D Mustang (414151)	Flying A Services
	NX71MY	Vickers Vimy (replica)(G-EAOU)	Greenco (UK) Ltd
	OY-JRL	Short SC.7 Skyvan 3-100	-/Langar
	OY-JRR	DHC.2 Turbo Beaver III	Ipswich Parachute Centre/Windrush
	P4-SKI	Boeing 727-212	ARAVCO
	RA-01277	Sukhoi Su-29	-/White Waltham
	RA-01278	Sukhoi Su-29	-/White Waltham
	RA-01378	Yakovlev Yak-52	T. Evans
	RA-01480	Sukhoi Su-31	L. Perry
	RA-01496	Sukhoi Su-29	R. N. Goode/White Waltham
	RA-01607	Sukhoi Su-29	-
	RA-01608	Sukhoi Su-31	R. N. Goode/White Waltham
	RA-01609	Sukhoi Su-29	R. N. Goode/White Waltham
	RA-01610	Sukhoi Su-29	P. Williams/White Waltham
	RA-02209	Yakovlev Yak-52 (31)	P. Scandrett
	RA-02293	Yakovlev Yak-52 (115)	A. Tyler
	RA-7803	Sukhoi Su-29	R. N. Goode/White Waltham
	RA-22521	Yakovlev Yak-52 (04)	D. Squires/Wellesbourne
	RA-44467	Yakovlev Yak-18T	-/Little Gransden
	RA-44470	Yakovlev Yak-18T	B. Austen
	RA-44480	Yakovlev Yak-18T	R. N. Goode/White Waltham
	RA-44483	Yakovlev Yak-18T	R. N. Goode/White Waltham
	RA-44500	Yakovlev Yak-55M	B. MacMillan
	UR-67199	LET L-410UVP	-/Langar
	UR-67477	LET L-410UVP	-/Sibson
	UR-67519	LET L-410UVP	East West Aviation Ltd/Wymeswold
	VH-BRC	S.24 Sandringham ★	Southampton Hall of Aviation
	VH-SNB	D.H.84 Dragon ★	Museum of Flight/E. Fortune
	VH-UQB	D.H.80A Puss Moth ★	Museum of Flight (G-ABDW)/E. Fortune
	VH-UTH	GAL Monospar ST-12 ★	Newark Air Museum (stored)
	VP-BAT	Boeing 747SP-21	Worldwide Aircraft Holding Co
	VP-BET	WS.55 Whirlwind 3 ★	IHM (G-ANJV)/Weston-s-Mare
	VP-BEU	WS.55 Whirlwind 3 ★	IHM (G-ATKV)/Weston-s-Mare
	VP-BIF	Boeing 727-1H2RE	SP Transport Ltd
	VP-BKG	Dassault Falcon 50	Sioux Co Ltd/Luton
	VP-BKQ	Bell 430	USAL Inc
	VP-BKY	H.S.125 Srs F.3B	Corporate Jet Services Inc
	VP-BLK	Gulfstream Commander 840	Control Techniques (Bermuda) Ltd/ Welshpool
	VP-BMF	Dassault Falcon 50	Glaxo (Bermuda) Ltd/Heathrow
	VP-BMZ	Gulfstream Commander 690D	Marlborough Fine Art (London) Ltd
	VP-BOO	McD Douglas MD-87	Ford Motor Co Ltd/Stansted
	VP-BOP	McD Douglas MD-87	Ford Motor Co Ltd/Stansted
	VP-BPS	Consolidated PBY-5A Catalina	- (G-BLSC)
	VP-BUL	Cessna 560 Citation V	Fegotila Ltd/Staverton
	VP-CBW	G.1159C Gulfstream 4	Rolls-Royce PLC
	VP-CCK	Agusta A.109A-II	Tarmac PLC/E. Midlands
	VP-CCT	Beech C90-1 King Air	Corgi Investments Ltd
	VP-CEZ	Dassault Falcon 50	IIR Aviation/Biggin Hill
	VP-CGP	Dassault Falcon 50	Frank Williams Motor Racing Ltd/ Kidlington
	VP-CIC	Canadair CL.601 Challenger	TGC Aviation Ltd/Stansted
	VP-CIT	Cessna 550 Citation II	TAG Aviation/Kidlington
	VP-CJB	Cessna 501 Citation	Brown Prestell Ltd/Biggin Hill
	VP-CJR	Cessna 550 Citation II	Broome & Wellington Aviation Ltd
	VP-CLA	Agusta A.109A II	Laura Ashley Holdings Ltd
	VP-CLL	Cessna 421C	Channel Aviation Ltd
	VP-CMF	G.1159C Gulfstream 4	Aravco Ltd/Heathrow
	VP-CMM	Boeing 727-30	MME Farms Maintenance
	VP-COM	Cessna 500 Citation	Robinson Publications Ltd/Leeds
	VP-CPR	Cessna 421C	Fifty North Ltd
	VP-CPT	BAe 125-1000B	Reno Investments Inc/Biggin Hill
	VP-CSP	Cessna 500 Citation	SP Metal Ltd/Biggin Hill
	VP-CYM	G.1159C Gulfstream 4	Jet Fly Aviation Ltd
	VP-FAZ	D.H.C.6-310 Twin Otter	British Antarctic Survey/Fairoaks
	VP-FBB	D.H.C.6-310 Twin Otter	British Antarctic Survey/Fairoaks

Reg.	Type	Owner or Operator	Notes
VP-FBC	D.H.C.6-310 Twin Otter	British Antarctic Survey/Fairoaks	
VP-FBL	D.H.C.6-310 Twin Otter	British Antarctic Survey/Fairoaks	
YL-CBI	Yakovlev Yak-52 (09)	Computaplane Ltd	
YL-CBJ	Yakovlev Yak-52 (20)	Computaplane Ltd	
5N-ABW	Westland Widgeon 2 ★	IHM (G-AOZE)/Weston-s-Mare	
5N-AOK	BAC One-Eleven 320AZ ★	Fuselage stored/Chorley	

EZ-A012 — Boeing 757-22K of Turkmenistan Airlines.

F-GSEA — Boeing 747-312 of Corsair.

HB-IUO — Douglas DC-10-10 of Crossair.

Radio Frequencies

The frequencies used by the larger airfields/airports are listed below. Abbreviations used: TWR — Tower,

Airfield	TWR	APP	A/G	Airfield	TWR	APP	A/G
Aberdeen	118.1	120.4		Inverness	122.6		
Alderney	125.35			Jersey	119.45	120.3	
Andrewsfield			130.55	Kidlington	118.875	125.325	
Audley End			122.35	Land's End	130.7		
Barton			122.7	Leeds Bradford	120.3	123.75	
Barrow			123.2	Leicester	122.125		
Belfast Intl	118.3	120.0		Liverpool	118.1	119.85	
Belfast City	130.75	130.85		London City	118.075	132.7	
Bembridge			123.25	Luton	132.55	129.55	
Biggin Hill	134.8	129.4		Lydd	120.7	129.4	
Birmingham	118.3	118.05		Manchester	118.625	119.4	
Blackbushe			122.3	Manston	119.27	126.35	
Blackpool	118.4	119.95		Netherthorpe			123.275
Bodmin			122.7	Newcastle	119.7	124.375	
Booker			126.55	Newquay	123.4	125.55	
Bourn			129.8	North Denes	123.4		
Bournemouth	125.6	119.625		North Weald			123.525
Bristol/Filton	132.35	122.72		Norwich	124.25	119.35	
Bristol/Lulsgate	133.85	128.55		Old Warden			123.05
Cambridge	122.2	123.6		Perth	119.8	122.3	
Cardiff	125.0	125.85		Plymouth	122.6	133.55	
Carlisle		123.6		Popham			129.8
Compton Abbas			122.7	Prestwick	118.15	120.55	
Conington			129.725	Redhill	120.275		
Coventry	124.8	119.25		Rochester			122.25
Cranfield	134.925	122.85		Ronaldsway	118.9	120.85	
Denham			130.725	Sandown			123.5
Dundee	122.9			Sandtoft			130.425
Dunkeswell			123.475	Scilly Isles			123.15
Dunsfold	124.325	135.17		Seething			122.6
Duxford			122.075	Sheffield			128.525
Earls Colne			122.425	Sherburn			122.6
East Midlands	124.0	119.65		Shipdham			119.55
Edinburgh	118.7	121.2		Shobdon			123.5
Elstree			122.4	Shoreham	125.4	123.15	
Exeter	119.8	128.15		Sibson			122.3
Fairoaks			123.425	Sleap			122.45
Fenland			122.925	Southampton	118.2	120.22	
Fowlmere			120.925	Southend	127.725	128.95	
Gamston			130.475	Stansted	123.8	120.625	
Gatwick	124.225	126.825		Stapleford			122.8
Glasgow	118.8	119.1		Sumburgh	118.25	123.15	
Gloucester/				Swansea	119.7		
Staverton	122.9	125.65		Swanton Morley			123.5
Goodwood	122.45			Sywell			122.7
Guernsey	119.95	128.65		Teesside	119.8	118.85	
Halfpenny Green			123.0	Thruxton			130.45
Haverfordwest			122.2	Tollerton			122.8
Hawarden	124.95	123.35		Wellesbourne			124.02
Headcorn			122.0	White Waltham			122.6
Heathrow	118.7	119.725		Wick	119.7		
	118.5	134.975		Wickenby			122.45
Hethel			122.35	Woodford	120.7	130.75	
Hucknall			130.8	Woodvale	119.75	121.0	
Humberside	118.55	124.675		Yeovil	125.4	130.8	

Those listed below identify both UK and overseas carriers appearing in the book.

Code	Airline	Prefix	Code	Airline	Prefix	Code	Airline	Prefix
AAF	Aigle Azur	F	CIM	Cimber Air	OY	KLM	KLM	PH
AAG	Atlantic A/L	G	CLH	Lufthansa CityLine	D	KQA	Kenya A/W	5Y
AAL	American A/L	N	CLX	Cargolux	LX	KYV	Kibris Turkish	TC
AAR	Asiana A/L	HL	CMM	Canada 3000 A/L	C	LAJ	British Meditrn	G
ABB	Air Belgium	OO	COA	Continental A/L	N	LAZ	Bulgarian A/L	LZ
ABD	Air Atlanta Iceland	TF	CPA	Cathay Pacific	B	LDA	Lauda Air	OE
ABR	Air Contractors	G	CRL	Corsair	F	LFA	Air Alfa	TC
ACA	Air Canada	C	CRX	Crossair	HB	LGL	Luxair	LX
ACF	Air Charter Intl	F	CSA	Czech A/L	OK	LIB	Air Liberte	F
ADR	Adria A/W	S5	CTN	Croatia A/L	9A	LIT	Air Littoral	F
AEA	Air Europa	EC	CUB	Cubana	CU	LKA	Alkair	OY
AEF	Aero Lloyd	D	CYP	Cyprus A/W	5B	LOG	Loganair	G
AEL	Air Europe Spa	I	DAH	Air Algerie	7T	LOT	Polish A/L (LOT)	SP
AFG	Ariana	YA	DAL	Delta A/L	N	LTE	LTE	EC
AFL	Aeroflot	RA	DAN	Maersk Air	OY	LTU	LTU	D
AFM	Affretair	Z	DAT	Delta Air Transport	OO	MAH	Malev	HA
AFR	Air France	F	DBY	Britannia Deutsch	D	MAS	Malaysian A/L	9M
AGX	Aviogenex	YU	DHL	DHL Express	N/OO	MAU	Air Mauritius	3B
AHK	Air Hong Kong	B	DLH	Lufthansa	D	MEA	Middle East A/L	OD
AHR	Air Holland	PH	DNM	Denim Air	PH	MNX	Manx A/L	G
AIC	Air-India	VT	DSR	DAS Air Cargo	5X	MON	Monarch A/L	G
AIH	Airtours (European)	G	EAE	European Air Xp	D	MPH	Martinair	PH
AIJ	Air Jet	F	EAF	European A/Ch	F	MSK	Maersk Air Ltd	G
AJM	Air Jamaica	6Y	EDW	Edelweiss Air	HB	MSR	Egyptair	SU
AKL	Air Kilroe	G	EIA	Evergreen Intl	N	NAW	Newair	OY
ALK	SriLankan A/L	4R	EIN	Aer Lingus	EI	NCA	Nippon Cargo	JA
AMC	Air Malta	9H	ELY	El Al	4X	NEX	Northern Executive	G
AMM	Air 2000	G	ETH	Ethiopian A/L	ET	NGA	Nigeria A/W	5N
AMT	American Trans Air	N	EUL	Euralair	F	NTR	TNT	G
ANA	All Nippon A/W	JA	EWW	Emery	N	NWA	Northwest A/L	N
ANZ	Air New Zealand	ZK	EXS	Channel Express	G	OAL	Olympic A/L	SX
AOM	AOM French A/L	F	EZS	easyJet Switz	HB	OHY	Onur Air	TC
APW	Arrow Air	N	EZY	easyJet	G	PAL	Philippine A/L	RP
ARG	Argentine A/W	LV	FDX	Federal Express	N	PGA	Portugalia	CS
ATT	Aer Turas	EI	FIN	Finnair	OH	PGT	Pegasus	TC
AUA	Austrian A/L	OE	FLT	Flightline	G	PIA	Pakistan Intl	AP
AUB	Augsburg A/W	D	FOB	Ford	G	QFA	Qantas	VH
AUI	Ukraine Intl	UR	FUA	Futura	EC	QSC	African Safaris	5Y
AUR	Aurigny A/S	G	GBL	GB Airways	G	RAM	Royal Air Maroc	CN
AVA	Avianca	HK	GFA	Gulf Air	A40	RBA	Royal Brunei	V8
AWC	Titan A/W	G	GHA	Ghana A/W	9G	RJA	Royal Jordanian	JY
AXL	KLM exel	PH	GIA	Garuda	PK	RNA	Royal Nepal A/L	9N
AZA	Alitalia	I	GIL	Gill A/W	G	ROT	Tarom	YR
AZW	Air Zimbabwe	Z	GMI	Germania	D	RPX	BAC Express A/L	G
BAG	Deutsche BA	D	GNT	British Midland Commuter	G	RWD	Air Rwanda	9XR
BAL	Britannia A/L	G	GOE	Go-Fly	G	RYR	Ryanair	EI
BAW	British Airways	G	HLA	HeavyLift	G	SAA	South African A/W	ZS
BBC	Bangladesh Biman	S2	HLF	Hapag-Lloyd	D	SAB	Sabena	OO
BCS	European A/T	OO	IBE	Iberia	EC	SAS	SAS	SE OY LN
BCY	CityJet	EI	ICE	Icelandair	TF	SAT	ScotAir	G
BER	Air Berlin	D	INS	Instone A/L	G	SBE	Sabre A/W	G
BIH	British Intl Heli	G	IRA	Iran Air	EP	SEU	Star Europe	F
BLX	Britannia AB	SE	IOS	Skybus	G	SEY	Air Seychelles	S7
BMA	British Midland	G	ISS	Meridiana	I	SIA	Singapore A/L	9V
BRA	Braathens	LN	IST	Istanbul A/L	TC	SLR	Sobelair	OO
BRT	British Regional	G	JAL	Japan A/L	JA	SNB	Sterling European	OY
BRU	Belavia	EW	JAT	JAT	YU	SSW	Streamline Avn	G
BTI	Air Baltic	YL	JEA	Jersey European A/W	G	SUD	Sudan A/W	ST
BWA	BWIA	9Y	JEM	Emerald A/W	G	SVA	Saudia	HZ
BWL	British World	G	JKK	Spanair	EC	SWE	Swedair	SE
BZH	Brit Air	F	JMC	jmc A/L	G	SWR	Swissair	HB
CCA	Air China	B	KAC	Kuwait A/W	9K	SXS	Sun Express	TC
CDN	Canadian A/L Intl	C	KAL	Korean Air	HL	SYR	Syrian Arab	YK
CFE	CityFlyer	EI	KIS	Contactair	D	TAP	Air Portugal	CS
CFG	Condor	D				TAR	Tunis Air	TS

AIRLINE FLIGHT CODES

THA	Thai A/W Intl	HS
THY	Turkish A/L	TC
TIH	Airtours (US)	G
TLA	TransAer	EI
TLE	AERIS	F
TOW	Tower Air	N
TQA	Braathens Sweden	SE
TRA	Transavia	PH
TSC	Air Transat	C
TWA	TWA	N
TYR	Tyrolean	OE
UAE	Emirates A/L	A6
UAL	United A/L	N
UGA	Uganda A/L	5X
UKA	KLM uk	G
UKR	Air Ukraine	UR
UPA	Air Foyle	G
UPS	United Parcels	N
UYC	Cameroon A/L	TJ
UZB	Uzbekistan A/W	UK
VEX	Virgin Express	OO
VEI	Virgin Express (Irel)	EI
VIR	Virgin Atlantic	G
VKG	Premiair	OY
VLM	VLM	OO
VRG	Varig	PP
WDL	WDL	D
WOA	World A/W	N

OO-VLG — Fokker 50 of V. L. M..

RA-76369 — Illyushin IL-76TD of Airstan.

British Aircraft Preservation Council Register

The British Aircraft Preservation Council was formed in 1967 to co-ordinate the works of all bodies involved in the preservation, restoration and display of historical aircraft. Membership covers the whole spectrum of national, Service, commercial and voluntary groups, and meetings are held regularly at the bases of member organisations. The Council is able to provide a means of communication, helping to resolve any misunderstandings or duplication of effort. Every effort is taken to encourage the raising of standards of both organisation and technical capacity amongst the member groups to the benefit of everyone interested in aviation. To assist historians, the B.A.P.C. register has been set up and provides an identity for those aircraft which do not qualify for a Service serial or inclusion in the UK Civil Register.

Aircraft on the current B.A.P.C. Register are as follows:

Notes	Reg.	Type	Owner or Operator
	6	Roe Triplane Type IV (replica)	Manchester Museum of Science & Industry
	7	Southampton University MPA	Southampton Hall of Aviation
	8	Dixon ornithopter	The Shuttleworth Collection
	9	Humber Monoplane (replica)	Midland Air Museum/Coventry
	10	Hafner R.II Revoplane	Museum of Army Flying/Middle Wallop
	12	Mignet HM.14	Museum of Flight/E. Fortune
	13	Mignet HM.14	Brimpex Metal Treatments
	14	Addyman standard training glider	N. H. Ponsford
	15	Addyman standard training glider	The Aeroplane Collection
	16	Addyman ultra-light aircraft	N. H. Ponsford
	17	Woodhams Sprite	The Aeroplane Collection
	18	Killick MP Gyroplane	N. H. Ponsford
	20	Lee-Richards annular biplane (replica)	Newark Air Musem
	21	Thruxton Jackaroo	M. J. Brett
	22	Mignet HM.14 (G-AEOF)	Aviodome/Schiphol
	25	Nyborg TGN-III glider	Midland Air Museum
	27	Mignet HM.14	M. J. Abbey
	28	Wright Flyer (replica)	Corn Exchange/Leeds
	29	Mignet HM.14 (replica) (G-ADRY)	Brooklands Museum of Aviation/ Weybridge
	32	Crossley Tom Thumb	Midland Air Museum
	33	DFS.108-49 Grunau Baby IIb	Russavia Collection
	34	DFS.108-49 Grunau Baby IIb	D. Elsdon
	35	EoN primary glider	Russavia Collection
	36	Fieseler Fi.103 (V-1) (replica)	Kent Battle of Britain Museum/Hawkinge
	37	Blake Bluetit (G-BXIY)	The Shuttleworth Collection/O. Warden
	38	Bristol Scout replica (A1742)	K. Williams
	40	Bristol Boxkite (replica)	Bristol City Museum
	41	B.E.2C (replica) (6232)	Historical Aircraft Museum/RAF St Athan
	42	Avro 504 (replica) (H1968)	Yorkshire Air Museum/Elvington
	43	Mignet HM.14	Lincolnshire Aviation Museum
	44	Miles Magister (L6906)	Museum of Berkshire Aviation (G-AKKY)/ Woodley
	45	Pilcher Hawk (replica)	Stanford Hall Museum
	46	Mignet HM.14	Alan McKechnie Racing Ltd
	47	Watkins Monoplane	Historical Aircraft Museum/RAF St Athan
	48	Pilcher Hawk (replica)	Glasgow Museum of Transport
	49	Pilcher Hawk	Royal Scottish Museum/Edinburgh
	50	Roe Triplane Type 1	Science Museum/S. Kensington
	51	Vickers Vimy IV	Science Museum/S. Kensington
	52	Lilienthal glider	Science Museum Store/Hayes
	53	Wright Flyer (replica)	Science Museum/S. Kensington
	54	JAP-Harding monoplane	Science Museum/S. Kensington
	55	Levavasseur Antoinette VII	Science Museum/S. Kensington
	56	Fokker E.III (210/16)	Science Museum/S. Kensington
	57	Pilcher Hawk (replica)	Science Museum/S. Kensington
	58	Yokosuka MXY7 Ohka II (15-1585)	F.A.A. Museum/Yeovilton
	59	Sopwith Camel (replica) (D3419)	Historical Aircraft Museum/RAF St Athan
	60	Murray M.1 helicopter	The Aeroplane Collection Ltd
	61	Stewart man-powered ornithopter	Lincolnshire Aviation Museum
	62	Cody Biplane (304)	Science Museum/S. Kensington
	63	Hurricane (replica) (P3208)	Kent Battle of Britain Museum/Hawkinge
	64	Hurricane (replica) (P3059)	Kent Battle of Britain Museum/Hawkinge
	65	Spitfire (replica) (N3208)	Kent Battle of Britain Museum/Hawkinge

Reg.	Type	Owner or Operator	Notes
66	Bf 109 (replica) (1480)	Kent Battle of Britain Museum/Hawkinge	
67	Bf 109 (replica) (14)	Kent Battle of Britain Museum/Hawkinge	
68	Hurricane (replica) (H3426)	Midland Air Museum	
69	Spitfire (replica) (N3313)	Kent Battle of Britain Museum/Hawkinge	
70	Auster AOP.5 (TJ398)	Museum of Flight/E. Fortune	
71	Spitfire (replica) (P8140)	Norfolk & Suffolk Aviation Museum	
72	Hurricane (replica) (V7767)	N. Weald Aircraft Restoration Flight	
73	Hurricane (replica)	—	
74	Bf 109 (replica) (6357)	Kent Battle of Britain Museum/Hawkinge	
75	Mignet HM.14 (G-AEFG)	N. H. Ponsford	
76	Mignet HM.14 (G-AFFI)	Yorkshire Air Museum/Elvington	
77	Mignet HM.14 (replica) (G-ADRG)	G. Lewis	
78	Hawker Hind (K5414) (G-AENP)	Yhe Shuttleworth Collection/O. Warden	
79	Fiat G.46-4 (MM53211)	British Air Reserve/Lympne	
80	Airspeed Horsa (KJ351)	Museum of Army Flying/Middle Wallop	
81	Hawkridge Dagling	Russavia Collection	
82	Hawker Hind (Afghan)	RAF Museum/Hendon	
83	Kawasaki Ki-100-1b (24)	Aerospace Museum/Cosford	
84	Nakajima Ki-46 (Dinah III)(5439)	Historical Aircraft Museum/RAF St Athan	
85	Weir W-2 autogyro	Museum of Flight/E. Fortune	
86	de Havilland Tiger Moth (replica)	Yorkshire Aircraft Preservation Soc	
87	Bristol Babe (replica) (G-EASQ)	Bristol Aero Collection/Kemble	
88	Fokker Dr 1 (replica) (102/17)	F.A.A. Museum/Yeovilton	
89	Cayley glider (replica)	Manchester Museum of Science & Industry	
90	Colditz Cock (replica)	Imperial War Museum/Duxford	
91	Fieseler Fi 103 (V.1)	Lashenden Air Warfare Museum	
92	Fieseler Fi 103 (V.1)	Historical Aircraft Museum/RAF St Athan	
93	Fieseler Fi 103 (V.1)	Imperial War Museum/Duxford	
94	Fieseler Fi 103 (V.1)	Aerospace Museum/Cosford	
95	Gizmer autogyro	F. Fewsdale	
96	Brown helicopter	N.E. Aircraft Museum/Usworth	
97	Luton L.A.4A Minor	N.E. Aircraft Museum/Usworth	
98	Yokosuka MXY7 Ohka II (997)	Manchester Museum of Science & Industry	
99	Yokosuka MXY7 Ohka II (8486M)	Aerospace Museum/Cosford	
100	Clarke glider	RAF Museum/Hendon	
101	Mignet HM.14	Lincolnshire Aviation Museum	
103	Pilcher glider (replica)	Personal Plane Services Ltd	
105	Blériot XI (replica)	Aviodome/Schiphol	
106	Blériot XI (164)	RAF Museum/Hendon	
107	Blériot XXVII	RAF Museum/Hendon	
108	Fairey Swordfish IV (HS503)	Cosford Aerospace Museum	
109	Slingsby Kirby Cadet TX.1	RAF Museum/Henlow store	
110	Fokker D.VII replica (static) (5125)	—	
111	Sopwith Triplane replica (static) (N5492)	F.A.A. Museum/Yeovilton	
112	D.H.2 replica (static) (5964)	Museum of Army Flying/Middle Wallop	
113	S.E.5A replica (static) (B4863)	—	
114	Vickers Type 60 Viking (static) (G-EBED)	Brooklands Museum of Aviation/ Weybridge	
115	Mignet HM.14	Essex Aviation Group/Andrewsfield	
116	Santos-Dumont Demoiselle (replica)	Cornwall Aero Park/Helston	
117	B.E.2C (replica)(1701)	N. Weald Aircraft Restoration Flight	
118	Albatros D.V (replica) (C19/18)	S. Yorks Aviation Soc/Firbeck	
119	Bensen B.7	N.E. Aircraft Museum/Usworth	
120	Mignet HM.14 (G-AEJZ)	Bomber County Museum/Hemswell	
121	Mignet HM.14 (G-AEKR)	S. Yorks Aviation Soc	
122	Avro 504 (replica)	British Broadcasting Corp	
123	Vickers FB.5 Gunbus (replica)	A. Topen (stored)/Cranfield	
124	Lilienthal Glider Type XI (replica)	Science Museum/S. Kensington	
125	Clay Cherub (G-BDGP)	B. R. Clay	
126	D.31 Turbulent (static)	Midland Air Museum store	
127	Halton Jupiter MPA	The Shuttleworth Collection	
128	Watkinson Cyclogyroplane Mk IV	IHM/Weston-s-Mare	
129	Blackburn 1911 Monoplane (replica)	Cornwall Aero Park/Helston store	
130	Blackburn 1912 Monoplane (replica)	Cornwall Aero Park/Helston store	
131	Pilcher Hawk (replica)	C. Paton	
132	Blériot XI (G-BLXI)	Musée De L'Automobile/France	
133	Fokker Dr 1 (replica) (425/17)	Newark Air Museum	

Notes	Reg.	Type	Owner or Operator
	134	Pitts S-2A static (G-CARS)	Toyota Ltd/Sywell
	135	Bristol M.1C (replica) (C4912)	—
	136	Deperdussin Seaplane (replica)	Reno/Nevada
	137	Sopwith Baby Floatplane (replica) (8151)	—
	138	Hansa Brandenburg W.29 Floatplane (replica) (2292)	—
	139	Fokker Dr 1 (replica) 150/17	—
	142	SE-5A (replica) (F5459)	Cornwall Aero Park/Helston
	143	Paxton MPA	R. A. Paxton/Staverton
	144	Weybridge Mercury MPA	Cranwell Gliding Club
	145	Oliver MPA	D. Oliver (stored)/Warton
	146	Pedal Aeronauts Toucan MPA	The Shuttleworth Collection
	147	Bensen B.7	Norfolk & Suffolk Aviation Museum
	148	Hawker Fury II (replica) (K7271)	Aerospace Museum/Cosford
	149	Short S.27 (replica)	F.A.A. Museum (stored)/Yeovilton
	150	SEPECAT Jaguar GR.1 (replica) (XX725)	RAF Exhibition Flight
	151	SEPECAT Jaguar GR.1 (replica) (XZ363)	RAF Exhibition Flight
	152	BAe Hawk T.1 (replica) (XX226)	RAF Exhibition Flight
	153	Westland WG.33	IHM/Weston-s-Mare
	154	D.31 Turbulent	Lincolnshire Aviation Museum
	155	Panavia Tornado GR.1 (replica) (ZA556)	RAF Exhibition Flight
	157	Waco CG-4A(237123)	Yorkshire Air Museum/Elvington
	158	Fieseler Fi 103 (V.1)	Defence Ordnance Disposal School/ Chattenden
	159	Yokosuka MXY7 Ohka II	Defence Ordnance Disposal School/ Chattenden
	160	Chargus 108 hang glider	Museum of Flight/E. Fortune
	161	Stewart Ornithopter Coppelia	Bomber County Museum
	162	Goodhart Newbury Manflier MPA	Science Museum/Wroughton
	163	AFEE 10/42 Rotabuggy (replica)	Museum of Army Flying/Middle Wallop
	164	Wight Quadruplane Type 1 (replica)	Wessex Aviation Soc/Wimborne
	165	Bristol F.2b (E2466)	RAF Museum/Hendon
	167	S.E.5A replica	Newark Air Museum
	168	D.H.60G Moth (static replica) (G-AAAH)	Hilton Hotel/Gatwick
	169	SEPECAT Jaguar GR.1 (static replica) (XX110)	No 1 S. of T.T. RAF Halton
	170	Pilcher Hawk (replica)	A. Gourlay/Strathallan
	171	BAe Hawk T.1 (replica) (XX253)	RAF Exhibition Flight/Abingdon
	172	Chargus Midas Super 8 hang glider	Science Museum/Wroughton
	173	Birdman Promotions Grasshopper	Science Museum/Wroughton
	174	Bensen B.7	Science Museum/Wroughton
	175	Volmer VJ-23 Swingwing	Manchester Museum of Science & Industry
	176	SE-5A (replica) (A4850)	S. Yorks Aviation Soc/Firbeck
	177	Avro 504K (replica) (G-AACA)	Brooklands Museum of Aviation/ Weybridge
	178	Avro 504K (replica) (E373)	Bygone Times Antique Warehouse/ Eccleston, Lancs
	179	Sopwith Pup (replica) (A7317)	Midland Air Museum/Coventry
	181	RAF B.E.2b (replica) (687)	RAF Museum/Hendon
	182	Wood Ornithopter	Manchester Museum of Science & Industry
	183	Zurowski ZP.1	Newark Air Museum
	184	Spitfire IX (replica) (EN398)	Aces High Ltd/North Weald
	185	Waco CG-4A (243809)	Museum of Army Flying/Middle Wallop
	186	D.H.82B Queen Bee (LF789)	Mosquito Aircraft Museum
	187	Roe Type 1 biplane (replica)	Brooklands Museum of Aviation/ Weybridge
	188	McBroom Cobra 88	Science Museum/Wroughton
	189	Blériot XI (replica)	—
	190	Spitfire (replica) (K5054)	Macclesfield Historical Aviation Soc
	191	BAe Harrier GR.5 (replica) (ZH139)	RAF Exhibition Flight
	192	Weedhopper JC-24	The Aeroplane Collection
	193	Hovey WD-11 Whing Ding	The Aeroplane Collection
	194	Santos Dumont Demoiselle (replica)	Brooklands Museum of Aviation/ Weybridge

Reg.	Type	Owner or Operator	Notes
195	Moonraker 77 hang glider	Museum of Flight/E. Fortune	
196	Sigma 2M hang glider	Museum of Flight/E. Fortune	
197	Cirrus III hang glider	Museum of Flight/E. Fortune	
198	Fieseler Fi.103 (V-1)	Imperial War Museum/Lambeth	
199	Fieseler Fi.103 (V-1)	Science Museum/S. Kensington	
200	Bensen B.7	K. Fern Collection/Stoke	
201	Mignet HM.14	Caernarfon Air Museum	
202	Spitfire V (replica) (MAV467)	Maes Artro Craft Centre	
203	Chrislea LC.1 Airguard (G-AFIN)	The Aeroplane Collection	
204	McBroom hang glider	The Aeroplane Collection	
205	Hurricane (replica) (BE421)	RAF Museum/Hendon	
206	Spitfire (replica) (MH486)	RAF Museum/Hendon	
207	Austin Whippet (replica) (K.158)	N.E. Aircraft Museum/Usworth	
208	SE-5A (replica) (D276)	Prince's Mead Shopping Precinct/ Farnborough	
209	Spitfire IX (replica) (MJ751)	Museum of D-Day Aviation/Shoreham	
210	Avro 504J (replica) (C4451)	Southampton Hall of Aviation	
211	Mignet HM.14 (replica) (G-ADVU)	N.E. Aircraft Museum/Usworth	
212	Bensen B.8	IHM/Weston-s-Mare	
213	Vertigo MPA	IHM/Weston-s-Mare	
214	Spitfire prototype (replica) (K5054)	The Spitfire Soc	
215	Airwave hang-glider	Southampton Hall of Aviation	
216	D.H.88 Comet (replica) (G-ACSS)	The Galleria/Hatfield	
217	Spitfire (replica) (K9926)	RAF Museum/Bentley Priory	
218	Hurricane (replica) (P3386)	RAF Museum/Bentley Priory	
219	Hurricane (replica) (L1710)	RAF Memorial Chapel/Biggin Hill	
220	Spitfire 1 (replica) (N3194)	RAF Memorial Chapel/Biggin Hill	
221	Spitfire LF.IX (replica) (MH777)	RAF Museum/Northolt	
222	Spitfire IX (replica) (BR600)	RAF Museum/Uxbridge	
223	Hurricane 1 (replica) (V7467)	RAF Museum/Coltishall	
224	Spitfire V (replica) (BR600)	Ambassador Hotel/Norwich	
225	Spitfire IX (replica) (P8448)	RAF Museum/Swanton Morley	
226	Spitfire XI (replica) (EN343)	RAF Museum/Benson	
227	Spitfire 1A (replica) (L1070)	RAF Museum/Turnhouse	
228	Olympus hang-glider	N.E. Aircraft Museum/Usworth	
229	Spitfire IX (replica) (MJ832)	RAF Museum/Digby	
230	Spitfire (replica) (AA550)	Eden Camp/Malton	
231	Mignet HM.14	South Copeland Aviation Group	
232	AS.58 Horsa I/II	Mosquito Aircraft Museum	
233	Broburn Wanderlust sailplane	Museum of Berkshire Aviation/Woodley	
234	Vickers FB.5 Gunbus (replica) (2882)	Macclesfield Historical Aviation Soc	
235	Fieseler Fi.103 (V-1) (replica)	Eden Camp Wartime Museum	
236	Hurricane (replica) (P2793)	Eden Camp Wartime Museum	
237	Fieseler Fi.103 (V-1)	RAF Museum/Cardington	
238	Waxflatter ornithopter	Personal Plane Services Ltd	
239	Fokker D.VIII 5/8 scale replica	Norfolk & Suffolk Aviation Museum	
240	Messerschmitt Bf.109G (replica)	Yorkshire Air Museum/Elvington	
241	Hurricane 1 (replica) (L1679)	Tangmere Military Aviation Museum	
242	Spitfire Vb (replica) (BL924)	Tangmere Military Aviation Museum	
243	Mignet HM.14 (replica) (G-ADYV)	P. Ward	
244	Solar Wings Typhoon	Museum of Flight/E. Fortune	
245	Electraflyer Floater	Museum of Flight/E. Fortune	
246	Hiway Cloudbase	Museum of Flight/E. Fortune	
247	Albatross ASG.21 hang glider	Museum of Flight/E. Fortune	
248	McBroom hang glider	Museum of Berkshire Aviation/Woodley	
249	Hawker Fury 1 (replica) (K5673)	Brooklands Museum of Aviation/Weybridge	
250	RAF SE-5A (replica) (F5475)	Brooklands Museum of Aviation/Weybridge	
251	Hiway Spectrum	Manchester Museum of Science & Industry	
252	Flexiform Wing	Manchester Museum of Science & Industry	
253	Mignet HM.14 (G-ADZW)	H. Shore/Sandown	
254	V.S.300 Spitfire I (R6690)	Yorkshire Air Museum/Elvington	
255	NA P-51D Mustang (replica)	American Air Museum/Duxford	
256	Santos Dumont Type 20 (replica)	Brooklands Museum of Aviation/ Weybridge	
257	D.H.88 Comet model	Galleria/Hatfield	
258	Adams balloon	British Balloon Museum	

Note: Registrations/Serials carried are mostly false identities.
MPA = Man Powered Aircraft, IHM = International Helicopter Museum.

Future Allocations Log (In-Sequence)

The grid provides the facility to record future in-sequence registrations as they are issued or seen. To trace a particular code, refer to the left hand column which contains the three letters following the G prefix. The final letter can be found by reading across the columns headed A to Z. For example, the box for G-BZED is located five rows down (BXE) and then four across to the D column.

G-	A	B	C	D	E	F	G	H	I	J	K	L	M	N	O	P	R	S	T	U	V	W	X	Y	Z
BZA																									
BZB																									
BZC																									
BZD																									
BZE																									
BZF																									
BZG																									
BZH																									
BZI																									
BZJ																									
BZK																									
BZL																									
BZM																									
BZN																									
BZO																									
BZP																									
BZR																									
BZS																									
BZT																									
BZU																									
BZV																									
BZW																									
BZX																									
BZY																									
BZZ																									
CAA																									
CAB																									
CAC																									
CAD																									
CAE																									
CAF																									
CAG																									
CAH																									
CAI																									
	A	B	C	D	E	F	G	H	I	J	K	L	M	N	O	P	R	S	T	U	V	W	X	Y	Z

Credit: *Wal Gandy*

Future Allocations Log
(Out-of-Sequence)

This grid can be used to record out-of-sequence registrations as they are issued or seen. The first column is provided for the ranges prefixed with G-B, ie from G-BYxx to G-BZxx. The remaining columns cover the sequences from G-Cxxx to G-Zxxx and in this case it is necessary to insert the last three letters in the appropriate section.

G-C	G-D	G-F	G-H	G-J	G-L	G-N	G-O	G-P	G-S	G-U
											G-V
	G-E	G-G			G-M	G-O				
				G-K						
										G-W
			G-I							
								G-R		
									G-T	
										G-X
G-D	G-F			G-L	G-N					
										G-Y
										G-Z

Overseas Airliners Registration Log

This grid may be used to record airliner registrations not included in the main section.

Reg.	Type	Operator

*For all your transport require-
ments, visit the Ian Allan
Bookshops in Birmingham,
Manchester or London.*

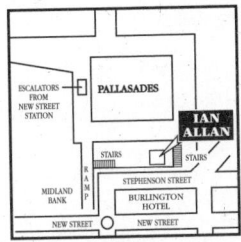

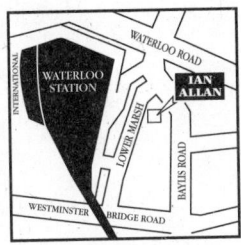

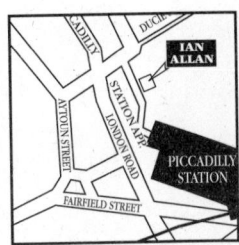

BIRMINGHAM

47 Stephenson Street
Birmingham B2 4DH
Tel: 0121 643 2496
Fax: 0121 643 6855

LONDON

45/46 Lower Marsh
Waterloo
London SE1 7SG
Tel: 0171 401 2100
Fax: 0171 401 2887

MANCHESTER

5 Piccadilly Station
Approach
Manchester M1 2GH
Tel: 0161 237 9840
Fax: 0161 237 9921

*Each shop stocks a comprehensive range of books,
magazines, videos, models, badges, postcards, cal-
endars and much more!*

*For the full range of Ian Allan Publishing Ltd
products plus books and videos from specialist
publishers large and small - call into an Ian
Allan Bookshop TODAY!*

The Ian Allan Bookshops also offer a mail order service -
please call for details.

To find out if an Ian Allan Bookshop is
opening near you —
please telephone: **0161 237 9840.**

ADDENDA

Notes	Reg.	Type	Owner or Operator
	G-AVCN	BN-2A-8 Islander	Airstream International Group Ltd
	G-AVGU	Cessna F.150G	Coulson Flying Services Ltd
	G-BCFU	Thunder Ax6-56 balloon	Zebedee Balloon Service Ltd
	G-BFGX	Cessna FRA.150M	A. D. Hay
	G-BGMG	Bell 212	Bristow Helicopters Ltd
	G-BGSN	Enstrom F-28C	Trindon Ltd (G-OIGS/G-BGSN)/ Little Snoring
	G-BLGS	SOCATA Rallye 180T	A. Waters
	G-BMAF	Cessna 180F	N. H. W. pether
	G-BOSN	AS.355F-1 Twin Squirrel	Helicopter Support Ltd
	G-BRLU	Cameron H-24 balloon	G. J. Bell
	G-BVKP	Sikorsky S-76A (modified)	Eligestone Spa/Italy
	G-BYNF	North American NA-64 Yale	R. S. van Dijk
	G-BYPD	Cameron A-105 balloon	Headland Hotel Co Ltd
	G-BYSI	WSK PZL Koliber 160A	PZL International Aviation Marketing & Sales PLC
	G-BYSO	PA-46-350P Malibu Mirage	Anglo American Airmotive Ltd
	G-BYTH	Airbus A.320-231	Airtours International Airways Ltd (EI-TLE)
	G-BYVA	Grob G.115E Tutor	Bombardier Services (UK) Ltd
	G-BYVB	Grob G.115E Tutor	Bombardier Services (UK) Ltd
	G-BYVC	Grob G.115E Tutor	Bombardier Services (UK) Ltd
	G-BYYF	Boeing 737-229C	European Aviation Air Charter Ltd
	G-BYYK	Boeing 737-229C	European Aviation Air Charter Ltd
	G-BYYN	Pegasus quantum 15-912	E. Clarke
	G0BYYS	Airbus A.300B4-103	SARL Hamloc/France
	G-BYYX	Team Minimax 91	P. L. Turner
	G-BYZB	Mainair Blade	O. Grati
	G-BYZF	Raj Hamsa X'Air 582 (1)	S. W. Grainger
	G-BYZJ	Boeing 737-3Q8	British Midland Airways Ltd (G-COLE)
	G-BYZO	Rans S.6-ES Coyote II	S. C. Jackson
	G-BYZR	III Sky Arrow 650TC	G. F. Jackson
	G-BYZS	Jabiru UL	N. Fielding
	G-BYZT	Nova Vertex 26	M. N. MacLean
	G-BYZW	Raj Hamsa X'Air 582 (2)	P. A. Gilford
	G-BZAF	Raj Hamsa X'Air 582 (1)	P. Hassett
	G-BZAK	Raj Hamsa X'Air 582 (1)	B. W. Austin
	G-BZAL	Mainair Blade 912	K. Worthington
	G-BZBA	BAe 146-200	BAe (Operations) Ltd (G-DEBA)
	G-BZBB	BAe 146-200	BAe (Operations) Ltd (G-DEBA)
	G-BZBG	Thruster T.600N	Thruster Air Services Ltd
	G-BZBX	Rans S.6-ES Coyote II	R. Johnstone
	G-BZDD	Mainair Blade 912	Barton Blade Group
	G-BZEB	Cessna 152	Leisure Aviation (Charters) Ltd
	G-BZEC	Cessna 152	Leisure Aviation (Charters) Ltd

The following in-sequence registrations in the main section have been cancelled.
G-AMSN, G-APRJ, G-AVKJ, G-AWMK, G-AWNP, G-BCPX, G-BCTU, G-BDTW, G-BGTP, G-BITR, G-BKMD, G-BOMK, G-BOSP, G-BUJU, G-BUWA, G-BVBP, G-BVKP, G-BVZF, G-BWGR, G-BWVG, G-BXIZ, G-BYRI.

	G-CEAE	Boeing 737-229	European Aviation Air Charter Ltd
	G-CEAF	Boeing 737-229	European Aviation Air Charter Ltd
	G-CFAA	Avro RJ100	CityFlyer Express Ltd/BA Express
	G-CWFB	PA-38-112 Tomahawk	Cardiff Wales Aviation Services Ltd (G-OAAL)
	GCWFY	Cessna 152	Cardiff Wales Aviation Services Ltd (G-OAMY)
	G-DOME	PA-28-161 Warrior III	Plane Talking Ltd/Elstree
	G-EHXP	R. Commander 112A	R. C. Howe
	G-GAND	AB-206B Jet Ranger	M. D. Souster (G-AWMK)
	G-GORF	Robin HR. 200/120B	J. A. Ingram
	G-HEPY	Robinson R-44 Astro	T. Everett
	G-HONI	Robinson R-22B	Burman Aviation Ltd (G-SEGO)/Cranfield

Reg.	Type	Owner or Operator	Notes
G-IFDM	Robinson R-44 Astro	Bedgbury Aviation Ltd	
G-IORG	Robinson R-22B	G. M. Richardson (G-ZAND)	
G-ITOI	Cameron N-90 balloon	Cameron Balloons Ltd	
G-IVYS	Parsons 2-seat gyroplane	R. M. Harris	
G-LEEE	Jabiru UL	L. E. G. Fekete	
G-LLYY	PA-32R-301T Turbo Saratoga SP	M. J. Start	
G-MABR	BAe 146-100	British Regional Airlines Ltd	
G-MAXV	Vans RV-4	T. P. Jenkinson	
G-NIPP	Slingsby T.66 Nipper 3	T. Dale (G-AVKJ)	
G-ODAK	PA-28-236 Dakota	R. E. Harvey (G-MHCA/G-SHWW/ G-SMUJ/G-BHTF)	
G-OWAX	Beech 200 Super King Air	Dawcroft Ltd	
G-RNGO	Robinson R-22B	MC Air Ltd	
G-SMBM	Pegasus Quantum 15-912B	J. Mould	
G-SUSX	McD Douglas MD.900 Explorer	Sussex Police Authority	
G-TEBZ	PA-28R-201 Arrow III	R. W. Tebby	
G-TIMY	GY-80 Horizon 160	R. G. Whyte	
G-TORS	Robinson R-22B	GT Investigations (International) Ltd	
G-TOSH	Robinson R-22B	Heli Air Ltd/Wellesbourne	
G-TTOA	Airbus A.320-231	GB Airways Ltd	
G-UFCA	Cessna 172S	Oxford Aviation Services Ltd/Kidlington	
G-UFCB	Cessna 172S	Oxford Aviation Services Ltd/Kidlington	
G-URUH	Robinson R-44 Astro	Heli Air Ltd/Wellesbourne	
G-VINS	Cameron N-90 balloon	PSH Skypower Ltd	
G-WHIS	Beech 58 Baron	GKL Management Services	
G-WYMR	Robinson R-44 Astro	Heli Air Ltd/Wellesbourne	
G-XAYR	Raj Hamsa X'Air 582 (6)	M. J. Kaye	
G-XPTS	Robinson R-44	Heli Air Ltd/Wellesbourne	
G-YCII	LET Yakolev-C11	R. W. Davies	
G-YSON	Eurocopter EC.120B	McAlpine Helicopters Ltd/Kidlington	

OVERSEAS AIRLINERS

OO-COF, OO-COH and OO-COL cancelled with the demise of Constellation Airlines, Boeing 737-229s OO-SDD, OO-SDF, OO-SDK and OO-SDR cancelled on sale to European Aviation and F-GCGQ, F-GGGR and F-GKZL cancelled with the failure of Belair Ile de France. Airbus A.321-131 registered OO-CPS with Brussels International Airlines (ex TC-ABC with Air Alfa), while Airbus A.310 5Y-BEN of Kenya Airlines was destroyed. SAS reregistrations include OY-KKA, OY-KKB, SE-DNN and SE-DNO. Royal Air Maroc is adding Boeing 737-8B6 CN-RNP, CN-RNQ and CN-RNR while Sun Express will receive Boeing 737-86N TC-SUA, TC-SUB, TC-SUC and TC-SUD.

John W. R. Taylor

The well-known author who was responsible for *Civil Aircraft Markings* from the early 1960s until 1978 sadly died on 12 December 1999 aged 77. From the very beginning the March publishing date for the pocket-sized annual was eagerly awaited by enthusiasts at the start of another season. John Taylor ensured that they were not disappointed and the popular book always maintained the same standard through the years. His efforts helped to generate an interest in civil aviation at a time when there were few facilities and even fewer books on the subject. John Taylor will be much missed by his friends and associates but he will not be forgotten.

PH-SDM — D.H.C.8-311 of Scheiner Airways/SABENA.

JA8191 — Boeing 747-281F of Nippon Cargo Airlines.

D-AERH — Airbus A.330-322 of LTU.